# HAYTON AND MITCHELL: TEXT, CASES AND MATERIALS ON THE LAW OF TRUSTS AND EQUITABLE REMEDIES

## FOURTEENTH EDITION

By

**BEN MCFARLANE**
Professor of Law, University College London

**CHARLES MITCHELL**
Professor of Law, University College London

**SWEET & MAXWELL**

THOMSON REUTERS

First Edition 1939 by J A Nathan
Second Edition 1951 by O.R. Marshall
Third Edition 1955 by O.R. Marshall
Fourth Edition 1961 by O.R. Marshall
Second Impression 1966 by O.R. Marshall
Fifth Edition 1967 by O.R. Marshall
Second Impression 1971 by O.R. Marshall
Sixth Edition 1975 by D.J. Hayton
Seventh Edition 1980 by DJ. Hayton
Eighth Edition 1986 by D.J. Hayton
Second Impression 1988 by D.J. Hayton
Third Impression 1989 by DJ. Hayton
Ninth Edition 1991 by DJ. Hayton
Second Impression 1994 by D.J. Hayton
Tenth Edition 1996 by DJ. Hayton
Second Impression 1997 by DJ. Hayton
Third Impression 1999 by DJ. Hayton
Fourth Impression 2000 by D.J. Hayton
Eleventh Edition 2001 by D.J. Hayton
Second Impression 2001 by DJ. Hayton
Third Impression 2003 by D.J. Hayton
Twelfth Edition 2005 by D.J. Hayton and C.C.J. Mitchell
Thirteenth Edition 2010 by C.C.J Mitchell

Published in 2015 by Thomson Reuters (Professional) UK Limited
trading as Sweet & Maxwell,
Friars House, 160 Blackfriars Road, London, SE1 8EZ
(Registered in England & Wales, Company No 1679046.
Registered Office and address for service:
2nd floor, 1 Mark Square, Leonard Street, London EC2A 4EG)

*For further information on our products and services, visit www.sweetandmaxwell.co.uk*

*Typeset by Servis Filmsetting Ltd, Stockport, Cheshire*
*Printed in Great Britain by CPI Group (UK) Ltd, Croydon CR0 4YY*

*No natural forests were destroyed to make this product; only farmed timber was used and re-planted.*

A CIP catalogue record for this book is available from the British Library.
ISBN 978-0-414-02747-3

# ACKNOWLEDGMENTS

Grateful acknowledgment is made to the following authors and publishers for permission to quote from their works:

A. Burrows, "We Do This at Common Law But That in Equity" (2002) 22 Oxford Journal of Legal Studies 1, reproduced by permission of Oxford University Press.

C. Daly and C. Mitchell, "*Paragon Finance plc v D.B. Thakerar & Co. (a firm)* (1999)" in C. Mitchell and P. Mitchell (eds), *Landmark Cases in Equity* © Editors and Contributors, 2012, Hart Publishing, an imprint of Bloomsbury Publishing Plc.

J. Edelman, "Two Fundamental Questions for the Law of Trusts" (2013) 129 Law Quarterly Review 66 © 2012 Thomson Reuters (Professional) UK Limited and contributors, reproduced by permission of Thomson Reuters (Professional) UK Limited.

P.W. Edge and J.M. Loughey, "Religious Charities and the Juridification of the Charity Commission" Legal Studies Volume 21, Issue 1, pages 36–64. Copyright © 2001 The Society of Legal Scholars. Published by Wiley on behalf of Society of Legal Scholars.

S. Elliott and C. Mitchell, "Remedies for Dishonest Assistance" The Modern Law Review Volume 67, Issue 1, pages 16–47. Copyright © 2004 The Modern Law Review Limited. Published by Wiley on behalf of Modern Law Review Ltd.

J. Garton, "Charitable Purposes and Activities" (2014) 67 Current Legal Problems 373 © The Author 2013. Published by Oxford University Press.

J. Garton, "*National Anti-Vivisection Society v Inland Revenue Commissioners* (1948)" in C. Mitchell and P. Mitchell (eds), *Landmark Cases in Equity* © Editors and Contributors, 2012, Hart Publishing, an imprint of Bloomsbury Publishing Plc.

J. Kessler, *Drafting Trusts and Will Trusts* (12th ed., Sweet & Maxwell, 2014) © Menikins 2015, reproduced by permission of Thomson Reuters (Professional) UK Limited and James Kessler QC.

B. McFarlane "The Trust and its Civilian Analogues" in L. Smith (ed.), *The Worlds of the Trust* © Cambridge University Press 2013. Reprinted with permission.

B. McFarlane and R. Stevens, "The Nature of Equitable Property" (2010) 4 Journal of Equity 1. Published by LexisNexis, reproduced with permission.

F. Maitland, *Equity: A Course of Lectures* © Cambridge University Press, 1909, 1936. Reprinted with permission.

P. Matthews, "Burgess v Wheate (1759)" in C. Mitchell and P. Mitchell (eds), *Landmark Cases in Equity* © Editors and Contributors, 2012, Hart Publishing, an imprint of Bloomsbury Publishing Plc.

P. Matthews, "The Comparative Importance of the Rule in *Saunders v Vautier*" (2006) 122 Law Quarterly Review 266 © Sweet & Maxwell Limited and contributors 2006, reproduced by permission of Thomson Reuters (Professional) UK Limited.

J. Mee, "'Automatic' Resulting Trusts: Retention, Restitution, or Reposing Trust?" in C. Mitchell (ed.), *Constructive and Resulting Trusts* © Editor and Contributors, 2010, Hart Publishing, used by permission of Bloomsbury Publishing Plc.

Lord Millett, "Pension Schemes and the Law of Trusts" (2000) 14 Trust Law International 66 © Lord Millett, 2000, Bloomsbury Professional, an imprint of Bloomsbury Publishing Plc.

P.J. Millett, "Equity's Place in the Law of Commerce" (1998) 114 Law Quarterly Review 214 © Sweet & Maxwell Limited and contributors 1998, reproduced by permission of Thomson Reuters (Professional) UK Limited.

C. Mitchell, "Equitable Compensation for Breach of Fiduciary Duty" (2013) 66 Current Legal Problems 307 © The Author 2013. Published by Oxford University Press.

C. Mitchell, "Stewardship of Property and Liability to Account" [2014] The Conveyancer and Property Lawyer 215 © 2014 Thomson Reuters (Professional) UK Limited and Contributors, reproduced by permission of Thomson Reuters (Professional) UK Limited.

C. Mitchell and S. Watterson, "Remedies for Knowing Receipt" in C. Mitchell (ed.), *Constructive and Resulting Trusts* © Editor and Contributors, 2010, Hart Publishing, used by permission of Bloomsbury Publishing Plc.

Lord Nicholls, "Trustees and Their Broader Community: Where Duty, Morality and Ethics Converge" (1995) 9 Trust Law International 71 © Lord Nicholls, 1995, Bloomsbury Professional, an imprint of Bloomsbury Publishing Plc.

R. Nolan, "Equitable Property" (2006) 122 Law Quarterly Review 232 © Sweet & Maxwell Limited and contributors 2006, reproduced by permission of Thomson Reuters (Professional) UK Limited.

J. Penner, "Distinguishing Fiduciary, Trust, and Accounting Relationships" (2014) 8 Journal of Equity 201. Published by LexisNexis, reproduced with permission.

J. Penner, "The (True) Nature of a Beneficiary's Equitable Proprietary Interest under a Trust" (2014) 27 Canadian Journal of Law & Jurisprudence 473 © J. Penner. Published by The University of Western Ontario.

H. Smith, "Property, Equity, and the Rule of Law" in L. Austin and D. Klimchuk (eds) *Private Law and the Rule of Law* (2014) © The several contributors 2014. Published by Oxford University Press.

M. Synge, "Poverty: An Essential Element in Charity after All?" [2011] Cambridge Law Journal 649 © Mary Synge, published by Cambridge University Press, reproduced with permission.

P. Turner, "Understanding the Constructive Trust between Vendor and Purchaser" (2012) 128 Law Quarterly Review 582 © 2012 Thomson Reuters (Professional) UK Limited and contributors, reproduced by permission of Thomson Reuters (Professional) UK Limited.

S. Worthington, "Fiduciary Duties and Proprietary Remedies: Addressing the Failure of Equitable Formulae" [2013] Cambridge Law Journal 720 © Sarah Worthington, published by Cambridge University Press, reproduced with permission.

Hague Convention on the Law Applicable to Trusts and on their Recognition (1985) © HCCH, 1951–2015.

Contains public sector information licensed under the Open Government Licence v3.0.

*Whilst every care has been taken to establish and acknowledge copyright, and contact the copyright owners, the publishers tender their apologies for any accidental infringement. They would be pleased to come to a suitable arrangement with the rightful owners in each case.*

# PREFACE

For this 14th edition, Ben McFarlane has joined Charles Mitchell as co-author. Together we have made many significant changes to the text. Ben McFarlane took primary responsibility for Chapters 1–5 and 14–17 and Charles Mitchell took primary responsibility for Chapters 6–13 and 18. Chapters 13 and 17 are new, and many other chapters have been extensively revised. In a move signalled by a change of title to "Text, Cases and Materials" we have also added excerpts from secondary works of academic commentary, to complement the excerpts from legislation and cases and the accompanying text that readers will also find here.

Since the last edition of this work, many significant developments have taken place in the law of trusts and equitable remedies and we have sought to incorporate as much new material as we can to reflect these developments. New legislation includes the Charities Act 2011 and the Trusts (Capital and Income) Act 2013, as well as the EU Regulation on Jurisdiction and the Recognition and Enforcement of Judgments in Civil and Commercial Matters, referred to in Chapter 16 as the Recast Brussels Regulation.

Cases decided since 2010 for which we have also found space are: *Re Lehman Brothers International (Europe) Ltd* [2010] EWHC 2914 (Ch), affirmed [2012] 2 B.C.L.C. 151 (on the use of trusts in commercial dealings and on certainty of subject matter); *Shell UK Ltd v Total UK Ltd* [2011] Q.B. 86 (on the rights of a beneficiary where a stranger interferes with trust property); *Curtis v Pulbrook* [2011] 1 B.C.L.C. 638 (on the circumstances in which equity may perfect an imperfect gift); *Byrnes v Kendle* (2011) 243 C.L.R. 253 (on certainty of intention to create a trust); *Crossco No.4 Unlimited v Jolan Ltd* [2012] 2 All E.R. 754 (on the *Pallant v Morgan* equity); *R (on the application of the Independent Schools Council) v Charity Commission* [2012] Ch. 214 (on charitable purposes); *Attorney General v Charity Commission* [2012] W.T.L.R. 977 (on charitable purposes); *Sutton v England* [2012] 1 W.L.R. 326 (on the courts' power to sanction trustees' administrative acts under the Trustee Act 1925, s. 57); *Jones v Kernott* [2012] 1 A.C. 776 (on constructive trusts of shared homes); *Re St Andrew's (Cheam) Lawn Tennis Club Trust* [2012] 1 W.L.R. 3487 (on resulting trusts arising on the dissolution of an unincorporated body); *Rea v Russell* [2012] NZCA 536 (on tracing); *Wright v Gater* [2012] 1 W.L.R. 802 (on the courts' power to vary the terms of a trust under the Variation of Trusts Act 1958); *Grimaldi v Chameleon Mining NL (No.2)* (2012) 200 F.C.R. 296 (on accounts of profits made through breach of fiduciary duty—and many other matters); *Independent Trustee Services Ltd v GP Noble Trustees Ltd* [2013] Ch. 91 (on personal and proprietary claims against the recipients of misdirected trust funds and the defence of bona fide purchase); *Pitt v Holt; Futter v Futter* [2013] 2 A.C. 108 (on the rule in *Hastings-Bass* and rescission of voluntary settlements made by mistake); *Prest v Petrodel Resources Ltd* [2013] 2 A.C. 415 (on resulting trusts); *Chaudhary v Yavuz* [2013] Ch. 249 (on the circumstances in which a purchaser of land may be subject to a constructive trust); *Libertarian Investments Ltd v Hall* (2013) 16 H.K.C.F.A.R. 681 (on trustee accounting duties); *Lawrence v Fen Tigers Ltd* [2014] A.C. 822 (on equitable damages awarded in lieu of an injunction); *Day v Day* [2014] Ch. 114 (on the rectification of unilateral settlements); *Williams v*

*Central Bank of Nigeria* [2014] A.C. 1189 (on the definition of a trustee for the purposes of s.21 of the Limitation Act 1980 and the nature of third party liability arising on a breach of trust); *Santander U.K. Plc v R.A. Legal Solicitors* [2014] P.N.L.R. 20 (on the courts' power to relieve defaulting trustees under the Trustee Act 1925, s.61); *A.I.B. Group (UK) Plc v Mark Redler & Co (a firm)* [2014] 3 W.L.R. 1367 (on claims for the reconstitution of trust funds following unauthorized misapplications of trust property); *Re Freud (Deceased)* [2014] W.T.L.R. 1453 (on secret trusts); *Sheffield v Sheffield* [2014] W.T.L.R. 1039 (on the rights of a beneficiary of a sub-trust); *Scott v Southern Pacific Mortgages Ltd* [2015] A.C. 385 (on the vendor-purchaser constructive trust); *Graham-York v York* [2015] EWCA Civ 72 (on the quantification of an interest under a common intention constructive trust); *FHR European Ventures LLP v Cedar Capital Partners LLC* [2015] A.C. 250 (on constructive trusts of bribe money paid to fiduciaries); *Les Laboratoires Servier v Apotex Inc* [2015] A.C. 430 and *Bilta (UK) Ltd v Nazir (No.2)* [2015] 2 W.L.R. 1168 (both on the effect of illegality and thus relevant to resulting trusts); and *Novoship (UK) Ltd v Mikhaylyuk* [2015] 2 W.L.R. 526 (on gain-based remedies for dishonest assistance in a breach of fiduciary duty).

We thank David Hayton for his continued support for the book as whole, and Birke Häcker, Sarah Haren and John Mee for their very helpful comments on specific chapters. We also owe general thanks to our students at Oxford and UCL, and to our academic colleagues whose energy, creativity and insights into equity and trusts are a continuing source of inspiration.

Ben is particularly grateful to Michael and Elspeth, and to Sarah, Iris, and Mary, for affording him the time required to finish the book.

Charles thanks Janice, Charlotte, Gwen, Albert, and Reggie, without whom none of it would have been possible.

*Ben McFarlane*
*Charles Mitchell*
*University College London*
*May 2015*

# CONTENTS

## PART V REMEDIES FOR BREACH OF TRUST AND BREACH OF FIDUCIARY DUTY



## PART VI TRUSTS IMPOSED BY LAW

# TABLE OF CASES

References to paragraphs in **BOLD** indicate that the text is reproduced in part or in full

# TABLE OF STATUTES

References to paragraphs in **BOLD** indicate that the text is reproduced in part or in full

# TABLE OF STATUTORY INSTRUMENTS

References to paragraphs in **BOLD** indicate that the text is reproduced in part or in full

# TABLE OF EU, INTERNATIONAL AND FOREIGN LEGISLATION

References to paragraphs in **BOLD** indicate that the text is reproduced in part or in full

# PART I

# INTRODUCTION

# 1

# INTRODUCTION

## 1. The Role of Equity

This is a book on the law of trusts and of equitable remedies. It is clear that rules and principles first developed by courts of Equity have had a profound influence on the law of England and of other common law jurisdictions, and that equity, in the sense of that body of equitable rules and principles, continues to affect the operation and development of the law. Two of the most practically significant parts of equity are its rules and principles as to trusts and as to equitable remedies. 1-001

### *A. Equity and the Court of Chancery*

It is helpful first to explain what we mean by equity. In this context, it refers not to a general concept of fairness or justice but rather, specifically, to the body of rules and principles, forming part of the current law, which have evolved from rules and principles applied and administered by the Court of Chancery. 1-002

The Court of Chancery grew out of the residuum of justice left in the King where his common law courts for some special reason brought about an unjust result, e.g. because they provided no remedy, or only an inadequate remedy.[1] The source of the injustice might, for example, have been the rigidity of the writ system, which meant that a deserving claim could not be formulated in such a way as to be accepted by a common law court; or strict evidential rules which meant that relevant facts could not be put before the court[2]; or the refusal of the common law courts to grant a remedy ordering the defendant to do something other than deliver up land or pay a sum of money. An aggrieved person would petition the King who would refer the complaint to his Chancellor as his right-hand man. The Chancellor, who was an ecclesiastic, with some knowledge of Roman law and canon law, first advised the King and his Council, but towards the end of the fifteenth century began making decrees on his own authority. He was concerned with affording relief in individual cases and made personal orders against parties who were imprisoned for contempt if they did not observe his decrees. Equity did not consist of rules and principles, but rather depended on the particular Chancellor's views of the merits of a particular case, and thus varied according to the Chancellor's conception of justice: or, as Selden remarked, according to the size of the Chancellor's foot.[3] 1-003

---

1 For a short but illuminating account of the history and development of equity, see J. Hackney, *Understanding Equity and Trusts* (Fontana Press, 1987), Ch.1.

2 For fuller accounts see W.S. Holdsworth, *History of English Law*, Vol.1 (Methuen & Co., 1903), pp.395ff.; A. Kiralfy (ed.), *Potter's Historical Introduction to English Law*, 4th edn (Sweet & Maxwell, 1958), pp.152ff.; S.F.C. Milsom, *Historical Foundations of the Common Law*, 2nd edn (Oxford University Press, 1981), pp.82ff.; J. H. Baker, *Introduction to English Legal History*, 4th edn (Oxford University Press, 2002), Chs 6, 14, 15, 16. On the role of equity in overcoming common law limitations on procedure and evidence, see, e.g. M. McNair, "Equity and Conscience" (2007) 27 O.J.L.S. 659.

3 *Table Talk of John Selden*, F. Pollock (ed.) (Selden Society, 1927), p.43.

1–004 The work of hearing petitions led to increasing judicial activity of the Chancellor in what came to be known as the Court of Chancery. Lawyers, like Lord Nottingham at the end of the seventeenth century, instead of ecclesiastics, became Chancellors and began systematically developing a body of rules of equity. The Chancellor was also assisted in his work by other judges appointed to the Court of Chancery. As Jeffrey Hackney has put it, making a distinction between equity in the general sense of fairness and justice and Equity in the specific sense of rules and principles applied by the Court of Chancery[4]:

> a combination of repeated circumstances and a desire to treat like cases alike was ultimately to drive the Chancellor into developing a system of rules. . . In the course of the mid seventeenth to early nineteenth centuries, Equity was turned into a systematic body of principles as refined, rigorous and ultimately unyielding as anything produced by the common law.

## *B. Equity as a Supplement to Common Law*

1–005 It is crucial to appreciate that equity is only a gloss on, or supplement to,[5] the common law. It has never shared common law's aim of being a self-sufficient system that deals with all possible claims that might be made by a party. It would be a mistake to think, for example, that there is a common law of contract, and an opposing law of contract in equity. There is, rather, a set of common law rules and principles covering the whole domain of contract law, which is supplemented by equitable rules and principles which may, for example, regulate the ways and circumstances in which a party can assert the contractual rights she has acquired under those common law rules and principles. For example, in a case where a contract has been entered between A and B as a result of A's innocent misrepresentation to B, equity does not deny that the contract exists, but it limits the circumstances in which A can exercise her rights under the contract by giving B a power, in certain circumtances, to rescind the contract and thus unwind its effects.[6]

1–006 This supplemental aspect of equity is particularly important in relation to both the law of equitable remedies and the law of trusts. As to equitable remedies, such as an order of specific performance and an injunction,[7] when their application is considered, for example, to a breach of contract, it is important to remember that the claimant will, in any case, have access to a common law remedy for that breach. As the remedies of specific performance and of an injunction are thus supplemental, a court is likely to be reluctant to order such remedies as of right,[8] but will consider a range of factors (such as, for example, the potential impact on third parties) in deciding whether to award such a remedy. In relation to a breach of contract, for example, the remedies of specific performance and of an injunction can thus be seen as falling within the "concurrent jurisdiction" of equity, as the claimant has a legal right but seeks to enforce or protect it by means of an equitable remedy.

1–007 Secondly, as to trusts, consider a case in which S (the settlor) transfers property to T (the trustee) to hold for the benefit of B (the beneficiary). B's rights as a beneficiary of the trust are a creation of the courts of Equity, as the view of common law was that T's agreement with S to hold the property for the benefit of B did not give B any rights against T, or in relation to the trust property. In many cases, T's agreement to act as trustee was not binding at all at common law, as no consideration was provided

---

4 J. Hackney, *Understanding Equity and Trusts* (1987), pp.18–19.
5 F.W. Maitland, Equity – *A Course of Lectures*, 2nd edn (Cambridge University Press, 1936), pp.18–19.
6 See further paras 18–244ff. Another example is provided by the equitable rules as to rectification: see paras 18–286ff.
7 See paras 18–083ff and 18–006ff.
8 See, e.g. L. Smith, "Common Law and Equity in the *Restatement (Third) of Restitution and Unjust Enrichment*" (2011) 68 Wash. & Lee L. Rev. 1185, 1195.

and the agreement was not made in a deed; and even if the agreement was binding as a contract with S, for example, then the doctrine of privity meant that S, and not B, had the right to enforce that contract.[9] Equity was, in contrast, prepared to give some effect to T's agreement to hold the property for the benefit of B: as T had received the property on the basis of that agreement, it could be said to be unconscionable for T then to keep the property and renege on the agreement by using it for T's own benefit.[10] The rights of B can thus be seen as falling within the "exclusive jurisdiction" of the equity, as the claimant's right is recognised only at equity, and not at common law.[11] In such a case, in contrast to the "concurrent jurisdiction", there is no common law right for the claimant to fall back on if appeal to equity is denied, and so the equitable claim tends to be recognised as of right, rather than as matter of discretion.[12]

The crucial point for present purposes, however, is that courts of Equity did not dispute the fact **1-008**
that T had title to the property at common law. Rather, those courts accepted that T had that right to the property, but impressed T's holding of that legal right with a duty owed to B. Recognising B's equitable rights did not, therefore, necessarily involve equity's setting up a rival law of property which identified B rather than T as owner of the property. After all, it is in B's interests for T to have extensive rights to the trust property, as long as equity then ensures that T must exercise those rights for B's benefit. As Maitland memorably put it[13]:

> Let me take an instance or two in which something that may for one moment look like a conflict [between common law and equity] becomes no conflict at all when it is examined. Take the case of a trust. An examiner will sometimes be told that whereas the common law said that the trustee was the owner of the land, equity said that the cestui que trust[14] was the owner. Well here in all conscience there seems to be conflict enough. Think what this would mean were it really true. There are two courts of co-ordinate jurisdiction: one says that A is the owner, the other says that B is the owner of Blackacre. That means civil war and utter anarchy. Of course, the statement is an extremely crude one, it is a misleading and dangerous statement . . . Equity did not say that the cestui que trust was the owner of the land, it said that the trustee was the owner of the land, but added that he was bound to hold the land for the benefit of the cestui que trust. There was no conflict here.

Maitland's point cannot be that there is no difference between the rules and principles of common **1-009**
law on the one hand and those of equity on the other. There clearly is a conflict in that sense[15]: in the case of a trust, equity says that B has a right that is enforceable against T (and, as we will see below,[16] against certain third parties too), whereas common law did not recognise any such right of B. Similarly, in a case where the equitable remedy of specific performance of a contract is ordered, equity imposes a duty on the defendant to perform her contract or be in contempt of court, whereas the common law would simply have ordered the defendant to pay a sum of money to the claimant. This is why it was necessary to adopt a general rule that, in the event of a conflict between common law and

---

9 The Contract (Rights of Third Parties) Act 1999 now provides means by which a third party who would benefit from the performance may have a claim against the promisor.

10 For further discussion of this particular form of unconscionable conduct, see paras 15-030ff.

11 See, e.g. L. Smith, "Common Law and Equity in the *Restatement (Third) of Restitution and Unjust Enrichment*" (2011) 68 Wash. & Lee L. Rev. 1185, 1194–1195. In addition to the "concurrent" and "exclusive" jurisdictions, equity has also been said to have an "auxiliary jurisdiction", applicable chiefly to pre-trial procedure: see Smith, ibid., 1195.

12 See, e.g. Smith, ibid., 1195: "There is no whiff of judicial discretion anywhere in the basic principles of the law of express trusts; it is all a matter of rights."

13 F.W. Maitland, Equity – *A Course of Lectures*, 2nd edn (Cambridge University Press, 1936), pp.17–18.

14 [Cestui que trust is an old-fashioned (Law French) term for the beneficiary of a trust.]

15 As noted by, e.g. W. Hohfeld, "The Relations Between Equity and Law" (1913) 11 Michigan Law Rev. 537.

16 See paras 1-048—1-050.

equitable rules, equitable rules were to prevail.[17] The existence of differences between common law and equity necessitated such a general rule; the function of equity as a gloss on common law meant that the rule had to favour equity.

**1-010** Maitland's point is, therefore, perhaps better seen as concerning the nature of the difference between common law and equity: in the case where S transfers her property to T to hold on trust for B, court of Equity did not deny that, as a result of the transfer from S, T now has title to the property, and so has rights to the property that are good against third parties. Equity does, however, contradict the common law by finding that T has a duty to use his rights to the property for the benefit of B, and so is not free to exercise those rights purely for his own benefit. This means, for example, that if X, a stranger were to carelessly damage property held by T on trust for B, equity recognises that T's title to the property gives T a good claim against X, and so there are no equitable rules preventing T from suing X. Equity also insists, however, that, as T is under a duty to use the property for the benefit of B, then: (i) if T does sue X and recover damages representing the value of the property, those damages will be held by T for B's benefit and so, depending on the precise terms of the trust, T may well be required to pay those damages to B; and (ii) if T for some reason chooses not to sue X, B may be able to force T to do so. B can thus use her equitable right against T to force T to use his common law right against X.

## *C. The Judicature Acts 1873–75*

**1-011** The development of the Court of Chancery, and the systematisation of its rules and principles, necessarily posed a problem for the administration of justice: in a single, non-federal legal unit such as England and Wales, how can it make sense to have two sets of courts where there is no clear divide between the jurisdiction of each? As Hackney has put it:

> At the beginning of the nineteenth century, the court structure in England and Wales was in a mess. The population was subject to the jurisdiction of a dual system of superior courts. On the one side were the three 'common law' courts—the Common Pleas, the Queen's Bench and the Exchequer of Pleas – and on the other was the Court of Chancery . . . From any managerial viewpoint, this arrangement was ludicrous.

**1-012** The Judicature Acts 1873–75 dealt with this procedural and managerial problem by allowing the procedural "fusion" which means that rules and principles of common law and equity are now administered in all courts concurrently.[18] Similar legislation has been enacted, at different times, in other common law jurisdictions.[19] The Judicature Act 1873 s.25 set out ten cases in which the equitable and common law rules conflicted, stating that in each case the equitable rules were to prevail. In s.25(11), it then gave statutory force to the general rule that, in the case of conflict, a court should follow the equitable rules:

> Generally in all matters not hereinbefore particularly mentioned, in which there is any conflict or variance between the Rules of Equity and the Rules of Common Law with reference to the same matter, the Rules of Equity shall prevail.

**1-013** The 1873 Act is no longer in force. The relevant legislation now is the Senior Courts Act 1981, s.49 of which states that:

---

17 See, e.g. *Earl of Oxford's Case* (1615) Chan. Rep. 1, examined by D. Ibbetson, "*The Earl of Oxford's Case* (1615)" in *Landmark Cases in Equity*, C. Mitchell and P. Mitchell (eds) (Hart Publishing, 2012). See now Judicature Act 1873 s.25(11).

18 The governing legislation is now contained in the Senior Courts Act 1981.

19 New South Wales held out, retaining a dual court system, until 1972: see Law Reform (Law and Equity) Act 1972 (NSW).

> Every Court exercising jurisdiction in England or Wales in any civil cause or matter shall continue to administer law and equity on the basis that, wherever there is any conflict or variance between the rules of equity and the rules of common law with reference to the same matter, the rules of equity shall prevail.

Maitland relied on this rule as to the resolution of conflicts between common law and equity to support his analysis of the trust.[20] His point was that, if a trust had indeed involved a conflict between common law and equity as to the ownership of the trust property, this conflict would have been resolved by s.25(11) of the 1873 Act in favour of the beneficiary. This would, however, have "abolished the whole law of trusts" as if it were simply the case that the beneficiary were owner of the property, and the trustee had no rights in it at common law, no trust would exist. **1–014**

## *D. The Fusion of Common Law and Equity?*

There is a long-standing and very contentious debate as to the extent to which rules and principles of common law on the one hand, and of equity on the other, are now, or should be, "fused". The debate is notable for the colour of the metaphors used and the strength of the language employed. To engage with this "fusion debate" it is necessary to separate out the questions of: (i) the current position, as determined by the Judicature Acts 1873–75 and later developments; and (ii) the approach that should be taken to the relationship between common law and equity. **1–015**

### i. The Descriptive Question: The Current Position

In *United Scientific Holdings Ltd v Burnley BC*, for example, Lord Diplock stated that[21]: **1–016**

> My Lords, if by 'rules of equity' is meant that body of substantive and adjectival law that, prior to 1875, was administered by the Court of Chancery but not by courts of common law, to speak of the rules of equity as being part of the law of England in 1977 is about as meaningful as to speak similarly of the Statute of Uses or of Quia Emptores. Historically all three have in their time played an important part in the development of the corpus juris into what it is today: but to perpetuate a dichotomy between rules of equity and rules of common law which it was a major purpose of the Supreme Court of Judicature Act 1873 to do away with, Is, In my view, conducive to erroneous conclusions as to the ways in which the law of England has developed in the last hundred years.
>
> Your Lordships have been referred to the vivid phrase traceable to the first edition of *Ashburner's Principles of Equity* where, in speaking in 1902 of the effect of the Supreme Court of Judicature Act, he says:[22] 'the two stream of jurisdiction [law and equity] though they run in the same channel, run side by side and do not mingle their waters.' My Lords, by 1977 this metaphor has in my view become both mischievous and deceptive. The innate conservatism of English lawyers may have made them slow to recognise that by the Supreme Court of Judicature Act 1873 the two systems of substantive and adjectival law formerly administered by the courts of law and Courts of Chancery (as well as those administered by courts of admiralty, probate and matrimonial causes) were fused. At the confluence of the Rhône and Saône, it may be possible for a short distance to discern the source from which each part of the combined stream came, but there comes a point at which this ceases to be possible. If Professor Ashburner's fluvial metaphor is to be retained at all, the waters of the confluent streams of law and equity have surely mingled now. **1–017**

---

20 As set out in para.1–008.

21 [1978] A.C. 904 at 924–925.

22 W. Ashburner, *Principles of Equity* (1902) p.23.

1-018 Lord Diplock's analysis was soon echoed by Lord Denning MR,[23] but in contemplating a substantive as well as a procedural fusion, it gives the Judicature Acts an impact far greater than they were seemingly intended to have,[24] and far greater than they were perceived to have had at the time. In *Salt v Cooper*, a case from 1880, for example, Jessel MR described the reform as "not any fusion, or anything of the kind; it was the one tribunal [of] the administration of Law and Equity in every cause, action or dispute which should come before that tribunal".[25]

1-019 Lord Diplock's analysis has, indeed, been powerfully criticised as involving a "fusion fallacy"[26]: the fact that rules of common law and of equity can be applied by all courts does not mean that there is no longer any substantive difference between those rules, or that the distinction between common law and equity is no longer of significance. The position of B, a beneficiary of a trust, demonstrates this point. If T, the trustee, acts in breach of the terms of the trust and transfers the trust property to C, it may be possible for B to make a claim against C, based on B's initial right under the trust. B, in that sense, has an interest in the trust property. B's equitable interest, however, has a substantive effect that is quite different from the common law property right of a person, O, who simply owns property outright. If, for example, O's property is stolen and then sold by the thief to C, who buys in good faith and with no notice of O's initial property right, O will be able to assert that property right against C.[27] Where the property is goods, O's claim will arise in the tort of conversion. In contrast, if T, the trustee, sells the trust property in breach of the terms of the trust to C, who buys in good faith and with no notice of the trust in B's favour, B can bring no claim against C: in such a case, C is protected by a defence of bona fide purchase that is not available to him in reply to the claim by O.[28]

1-020 It is therefore clear that each of O's common law property right as outright owner, and B's equitable interest under a trust, is subject to different substantive rules. This distinction between legal estates and interests on the one hand, and equitable interests on the other, is, for example, fundamental to the scheme of the Law of Property Act 1925.[29] It is also necessary to make sense of the fact that the rules relating to the *acquisition* of an equitable interest differ from those applying to a legal property right. For example, a purchaser of land can acquire a legal estate in registered land only by registering as the holder of such a right; in contrast, such a purchaser can acquire an equitable interest as soon as the contract for the sale of the land is concluded.[30] If there were no substantive difference in the effect of the legal estate obtained on registration and this equitable interest, it would make no sense to permit the equitable interest to be acquired at that earlier stage, without registration.

1-021 As a result, and to continue with the maritime metaphors, Lord Diplock's view in the *United Scientific*

---

23 *Federal Commerce & Navigation Co Ltd v Molena Alpha Inc (The Nanfri)* [1978] 1 Q.B. 927 at 974 per Lord Denning MR: "Over 100 years have passed since the Judicature Act 1873. During that time the streams of common law and equity have flown together and combined so as to be indistinguishable the one from the other. We have no longer to ask ourselves: what would the courts of common law or the courts of equity have done before the Judicature Act? We have to ask ourselves: what should we do now do as to ensure fair dealing between the parties?"

24 See M. Leeming, "Equity, the Judicature Acts and Restitution" (2011) 5 J. Eq. 45, for a contextual account of the aims of the legislation.

25 (1880) 16 Ch.D. 544 at 549.

26 The term coined by the editors of *Equity: Doctrines and Remedies*. In, for example, the 3rd edn of that work (*Equity: Doctrines and Remedies*, R. Meagher et al (eds) (Butterworths Law, 1992), para.221), it was said that: "Those who commit the fusion fallacy announce or assume the creation by the Judicature system of a new body of law containing elements of law and equity but in character quite different from its components. The fallacy is committed explicitly, covertly, and on occasion with apparent inadvertence. But the state of mind of the culprit cannot lessen the evil of the offence." See now the 5th edn J.D. Heydon et al (eds), 2014), paras 2.130–2.320.

27 See, e.g. *Farquarhson Bros and Co v King and Co* [1902] A.C. 325. Where the property consists of goods, O's claim against C will arise in the tort of conversion.

28 See, e.g. *MCC Proceeds Inc v Lehman Bros International (Europe)* [1998] 4 All E.R. 675.

29 See Law of Property Act 1925 s.1.

30 See paras 15–011ff.

case may be taken as the high watermark of the substantive fusion approach: since then, the tide has turned and there now "seems to be little doubt that the Judicature Acts did not effect a substantive merger of law and equity".[31] The broader fusion debate continues, however, as to what approach *should* be taken to the relationship between common law and equity.

### ii. The Prescriptive Question: What Approach Should be Taken?

In a very important contribution to the "fusion debate", Andrew Burrows has argued that a difference **1–022**
between two particular rules or principles cannot be justifed *merely* by the fact that one of those rules or principles is part of common law, and the other part of equity. Rather, in such a case, care must be taken to ensure that there is a substantive justification for the different outcomes; if not, the law will be inconsistent and will fail in its aim of treating like cases alike.

#### A. Burrows, "We Do This At Common Law But That In Equity" (2002) 22 O.J.L.S. 1, 4

[T]he fusion school of thought argues that the fusion of the administration of the courts brought about **1–023**
by the 1873–5 Acts, whilst not dictating the fusion of the substantive law, rendered this, for the first time, a realistic possibility. While there are areas where common law and equity can happily sit alongside one another, there are many examples of inconsistencies between them. It is important to remove the inconsistencies thereby producing a coherent or harmonized law. In developing the law it is legitimate for the courts to reason from common law to equity and vice versa. A harmonized rule or principle that has features of both common law and equity is at the very least acceptable and, depending on the rule or principle in question, may represent the best way for the law to develop.

[The fusion school of thought] is to be strongly preferred. There are numerous instances of inconsisten- **1–024**
cies between common law and equity; and to support fusion seems self-evident, resting, as it does, on not being slaves to history and on recognizing the importance of coherence in the law and of 'like cases being treated alike'.

Burrows then divides English private law into four categories. The first is where "the law has **1–025**
already reached the advanced position that common law and equity cannot be distinguished at all". Putting those relatively rare cases to one side, he then focusses on the remaining three categories:

The first category is where common law and equity co-exist coherently and where the historical labels of **1–026**
common law and equity remain the best or, at least, useful terminology. I particularly have in mind here that greatest invention of equity, the trust. It is very hard—albeit not impossible as is shown by the approach in some other jurisdictions—to describe the trust without at some stage relying on, and referring to, the split between legal and equitable title. . .

The second category is where common law and equity co-exist coherently but, in contrast to the first **1–027**
category, there is nothing to be gained by adherence to those historical labels. If we are to taken fusion seriously, the labels common law and equity in the areas of law covered by this category should be abandoned at a stroke. . .

The third category is more complex. It comprises probably most of our civil law. In this category, in contrast **1–028**
to both of the first two categories, common law and equity do not co-exist coherently. If we are to take fusion seriously, what is needed is a change in the law, albeit often only a small change, so as to produce a principled product which may combine elements of law and equity.

---

[31] J. Maxton, "Intermingling of Common Law and Equity" in M. Cope (ed.), *Equity: Issues and Trends* (Federation Press, 1995), p.25. See too Lord Evershed, "Reflections on the Fusion of Law and Equity after 75 Years" (1954) 70 L.Q.R. 326, 327.

1-029 The argument made by Burrows has not won universal acceptance.[32] It does however make a very important central point that any apparent differences between common law and equitable rules need to be carefully justified. For example, shortly after Burrows wrote, the Court of Appeal rejected the conventional view that there was a separate equitable doctrine of common mistake which could lead to the rescission of a contract, finding that such a doctrine would be inconsistent with the clear limits to the doctrine of common mistake as applied at common law.[33]

1-030 Burrows' argument is significant when considering equitable remedies and, in fact, his analysis includes a detailed treatment of monetary remedies for civil wrongs, in which it is argued that such cases fall into the third category where "common law and equity do not co-exist coherently". It may be the case, for example, that a remedy recognised in equity in fact closely resembles one available at common law, so that any differences in the rules applying to each remedy must be carefully examined.[34]

1-031 In relation to trusts, it is notable that even a committed fusionist such as Burrows regards the trust as falling into that first category of case, where common law and equity co-exist coherently, and it is helpful to continue to refer to particular rules by reference to their jurisdictional origin either in equity or at common law.[35] It may therefore be that the trust demonstrates how the somewhat illogical dual court system in place in England and Wales until the end of the nineteenth century in fact enriched English private law by producing some very useful concepts.

### iii. Common Law and Equity: A Productive Paradox?

1-032 The argument has often been made that if one were creating a legal system from scratch, one would certainly not design a set of rules (common law), and then design a second set of rules (equity) which overlays the first set, making it necessary to have a third set of rules to determine whether the first or the second set governs cases where the two sets produce different outcomes.[36] It can nonetheless be claimed that this dual system allowed English law to produce a more nuanced, yet also more efficient, form of justice than might be achieved by a simpler, single set of rules. In the article from which the following extract is taken, for example, Henry Smith explores the idea that, by providing a "safety valve" to deal with cases where the application of common law rules lead to a clear injustice, equity plays a vital role in allowing the common law to adopt rules of general application (which are thus clearer and easier to understand)[37] whilst ensuring that an individual party is not permittted to exploit the generality of those rules to act in a way which would "shock the consience of the court".[38]

---

32 For a different view, see, e.g. M. Leeming, "Equity, the Judicature Acts and Restitution" (2011) 5 J. Eq. 45.

33 *Great Peace Shipping Ltd v Tsavlisis Salvage (International) Ltd* [2003] Q.B. 679, disapproving *Solle v Butcher* [1950] 1 K.B. 671. See too, e.g. *Halpern v Halpern (Nos 1 and 2)* [2008] Q.B. 195 at [70]–[77], where Carnwath LJ suggested that the "counter-restitution impossible" bar to rescission should operate in substantially the same way whether the claim rests on duress (at common law) or undue influence (in equity).

34 See paras 18-001–18-005.

35 A. Burrows, "We Do This at Common Law But That in Equity" (2002) 22 O.J.L.S. 1, 5 (extracted at para.1-023).

36 See, e.g. S. Worthington, *Equity*, 2nd edn (Oxford University Press, 2006), Ch.2.

37 See too D. Klimchuk, "Equity and the Rule of Law" in L. Austin and D. Klimchuk (eds), *Private Law and the Rule of Law* (Oxford University Press, 2014), pp.252–255, drawing on Aristotle's observation that: "The nature of the equitable is a correction of law where it is defective owing to its universality."

38 That phrase is used to state a threshold for equitable intervention, through the doctrine of proprietary estoppel (see paras 2-090ff and 3-017ff) by Lord Walker in *Cobbe v Yeoman's Row Management Ltd* [2008] 1 W.L.R. 1752 at [92].

### H. Smith, "Property, Equity, and the Rule of Law"

in L. Austin and D. Klimchuk (eds), *Private Law and the Rule of Law* (Oxford University Press, 2014), pp.232–233

The simple structures of the law are open to exploitation by opportunists . . . Traditionally equity concerned itself with 'near fraud', which is behaviour that is close to the line of fraud or may well be fraud but cannot be proved as such. . . **1–033**

. . . [A] major theme of traditional equity was to counteract opportunism. To do so equity needs to go beyond the *ex ante* bright line rules, because it is difficult to anticipate all the avenues of evasion. Plugging nine out of ten loopholes is hopeless if all the evaders can rush through the tenth. Equity employs *ex post* moral standards, emphasizes good faith and notice, couches its reasoning in terms of morals, and is sometimes vague rather than bright line. To cabin such a powerful tool, equity courts were only supposed to act in personam and not in rem,[39] and the substantive doctrines of equity counselled caution in undermining the law. Equity was not designed to root out every last bit of opportunism and courts recognized that equitable doctrines and remedies, not least injunctions, themselves could be exploited by opportunistic litigants unless courts were on their guard and were willing to stay the hand of equity. **1–034**

As Smith goes on to note, this does not mean that equity is wholly discretionary: over time, of course, particular patterns of unconscionable conduct, or of exploitation of common law rules, can be recognised and specific rules can identify and prevent such conduct. The case in which a settlor (S) transfers property to T (a trustee) to hold for the benefit of a beneficiary (B) provides an example. As noted above,[40] the general rules applied at common law permit T to be free to use the property for T's own benefit. This could be said, however, to amount to a form of fraud, given that, in this particular case, T received the property on the basis of an agreement to hold the property for the benefit of B. This initial insight of equity has hardened into specific rules, and the modern analysis of such a case is simply that S has exercised her power to set up a trust for B, and so B necessarily gains a certain set of rights. Nonetheless, even in modern times, in cases where that simple analysis cannot be used,[41] the courts have resorted to the notion of fraud to justify imposing a duty on T, owed to B, to hold the property for B's benefit.[42] **1–035**

Equity's functioning in this way as a supplemental system, providing a gloss to the common law, may thus have been vital to the development of the trust: it can then be seen as based on "the productive paradox of [English law's] two rival court systems".[43] Certainly, as we will examine later in this chapter,[44] the trust has proved to be of enormous practical value. Indeed, some civil law jurisdictions,[45] which have always been more rationally organised than English law and so have never enjoyed the benefits of separate equitable rules, have made attempts to incorporate structures **1–036**

---

39 [This point will be explored further at para.7–029.]

40 See para.1–007.

41 It may be excluded, for example, as a result of S's failure to comply with a formality rule regulating the creation or proof of the trust: see, e.g. paras 3–032—3–049 and 15–030—15–045.

42 See, e.g. *McCormick v Grogan* (1869–70) L.R. 4 H.L. 82 at 88–89 and 97–98; *Rochefoucauld v Boustead* [1897] 1 Ch. 196 at 205–206; *Bannister v Bannister* [1948] 2 All E.R. 133 at 136; *Lyus v Prowsa Developments Ltd* [1982] 1 W.L.R. 1044 at 1054–1055.

43 B. McFarlane and R. Stevens, "The Nature of Equitable Property" (2010) 4 J. Eq. 1, 9.

44 See paras 1–040—1–052.

45 Forms of the trust have been long-standing parts of the law of mixed jurisdictions such as Scotland, South Africa and Sri Lanka.

based on the trust into their own law.[46] We will now consider the essential features of the English trust.

## 2. Fundamentals of the Trust

### A. The Diversity of Trusts

#### i. Trusts Beyond English Law

**1-037** Our focus on this book is on the English law of trusts. It is important to note, however, that the English law of trusts should not be confused with the law of trusts more generally. First, other common law jurisdictions may take different views on aspects of the operation of the trust, even if those aspects might be seen as a fundamental part of the English law of trusts. For example, the *Saunders v Vautier* principle,[47] discussed in detail in Chapter 7,[48] allows all of the beneficiaries of a trust, acting together, to call for the trust property to be transferred to them by the trustees: if that power is exercised by the beneficiaries, they then have the trust property itself, and the trust comes to an end. This principle may be seen to be a fundamental aspect of the rights of the beneficiaries, recognising their ultimate right to control of the trust property. It is not, however, part of the law of trusts in jurisdictions in the US.[49] Similarly, as we will discuss in detail in Chapter 5, the "beneficiary principle" forms a key part of the English law of trusts, and prevents S establishing a trust for a non-charitable purpose,[50] rather than for the benefit of individuals. However, many offshore common law jurisdictions have legislated to reject, or make wide-ranging exceptions to, that principle,[51] and so accommodate within their law of trusts the situation where T holds property subject to a duty, enforced by a party appointed by S, to hold that property for a particular, non-charitable purpose.

**1-038** Secondly, many civil law jurisdictions allow parties to set up legal structures that share some important features with the English trust. Such structures may fall within definitions of a trust that are intended to have a supra-jurisdictional application. For example, as we will discuss in Chapter 16,[52] the Hague Convention on the Law Applicable to Trusts and on their Recognition[53] sets out general rules, agreed to by the jurisdictions that have ratified or acceded to the Convention,[54] as to when an arrangement governed by foreign law must be recognised and enforced as a trust. The definition of a trust under the Convention is influenecd by, but clearly different from, the English concept of the trust: it includes, for example, a trust for a non-charitable purpose. It is nonetheless useful to consider, as

---

46 See, e.g. D. Hayton, "'Trusts' in Private International Law" (2014) 366 Recueil des Cours 17, 38, noting that legislation has been enacted in, for example, Quebec, Uruguay and France to allow assets to be devoted to an independent patrimony. See too, e.g. China's Trust Law of 2001, Japan's of 1922, and Taiwan's of 1995.

47 (1841) 4 Beav. 115.

48 See paras 7-004—7-029. See too paras 5-031—5-032.

49 See para.7-014 and note the discussion by P. Matthews, "The Comparative Importance of the Rule in *Saunders v Vautier*" (2006) 122 L.Q.R. 266.

50 Trusts for exclusively charitable purposes are permitted under English law: see Ch.6.

51 See, e.g. Bermuda Trusts (Special Provisions) Act 1989 ss.12A and 12B (extracted at paras 5-103—5-104). Other offshore jurisdictions permitting non-charitable purpose trusts include the Cayman Islands; the British Virgin Islands; Jersey; Guernsey; and the Isle of Man. See *The International Trust*, D. Hayton (ed.), 3rd edn (Jordans, 2011), Ch.5.

52 See paras 16-032—16-049.

53 Signed on 1 July 1985, it came into force on 1 January 1992.

54 These jurisdictions include England (as part of the UK), Australia and Canada. For a full list, see para.16-032.

an attempt to produce a definition of the trust capable of applying across both common law and civil law jurisdictions.[55]

**Hague Convention on the Law Applicable to Trusts and on their Recognition (1985) art.2**

For the purposes of this Convention, the term "trust" refers to the legal relationships created—inter vivos or on death—by a person, the settlor, when assets have been placed under the control of a trustee for the benefit of a beneficiary or for a specified purpose. **1-039**

A trust has the following characteristics—

(a) the assets constitute a separate fund and are not a part of the trustee's own estate;
(b) title to the trust assets stands in the name of the trustee or in the name of another person on behalf of the trustee;
(c) the trustee has the power and the duty, in respect of which he is accountable, to manage, employ or dispose of the assets in accordance with the terms of the trust and the special duties imposed upon him by law.

The reservation by the settlor of certain rights and powers, and the fact that the trustee may himself have rights as a beneficiary, are not necessarily inconsistent with the existence of a trust.

## ii. Diversity Within English Trusts Law

We have seen that English law has no monopoly on the trust concept. There is also diversity as to the nature of a trust even within English law. Certainly, judges and commentators have generally been reluctant to provide a comprehensive definition of the trust.[56] As David Hayton has stated[57]: **1-040**

> It is universally acknowledged that, due to the inductive development of the trust, there is no true or conclusive definition of a trust that can enable one to determine whether or not certain legal relationships in particular circumstances give rise to a trust rather than some other legal concept. Instead, one can only look at certain core characteristics that reflect the rules that distinguish trusts from other legal concepts.

### (1) The Modern Express Trust

The impossibility of producing a neat definition of a trust should not be seen as a weakness in the trust concept, but rather as a product of its great practical utility and the diverse range of its applications. Indeed, it is worth noting the exact words used by Maitland when praising the trust[58]: **1-041**

> If we were asked what is the greatest and most distinctive achievement performed by Englishmen in the field of jurisprudence I cannot think that we should have any better answer to give than this, namely, the development from century to century of the trust idea.

---

55 Note however that the definition adopted has been criticised as "shapeless" owing to its being divorced from the principles of any specific legal system: see, e.g. M. Lupoi, "The Shapeless Trust" (1995) T. & T. 15, 15: "Before the Hague Convention you would know a trust when you met one. That is no longer so."

56 Even when attempts have been made to provide a definition, they have generally been prefaced with a disclaimer: see, e.g. *Re Scott* [1948] S.A.S.R. 193 at 196: "No definition of a 'trust' seems to have been accepted as comprehensive and exact"; A. Scott and W. Fratcher, *The Law of Trusts*, 4th edn (Little, Brown and Company, 1989), para.2.3: "All that one can properly attempt to do is to give such a description of a legal concept that others will know in a general way what one is talking about."

57 D. Hayton, " 'Trusts' in Private International Law" (2014) 366 Recueil des Cours 17, 17.

58 F. Maitland, *Selected Historical Essays* (Cambridge University Press, 1936), p.129.

Maitland's praise is thus not for the invention of the trust, but rather for its *development*. This development means that, even within English law itself, there is diversity over time as the trust concept has been adapted, often to suit the changing desires of parties wishing to set up a trust.

**1–042** At the end of this chapter, for example, we will set out a contemporary precedent provided for lawyers instructed to draft a trust settlement. It sets up a form of *discretionary trust*. The key feature of such a trust is that, rather than being instructed simply to hold the property for the benefit of specific, named beneficiaries, the trustees are given a choice either as to the extent of the benefit to be received by each beneficiary or, more usually, as to who amongst a class of possible beneficiaries will receive any of the trust property. Whilst such trusts are far from being a purely modern creation, their current popularity depends on the fact that, from the 1970s onwards, the courts have accepted that S can create a valid trust which confers powers on T to choose who, amongst a potentially very wide class of possible people, might benefit from distributions of the property held on trust.

**1–043** In such a modern trust S may, for example, transfer property to T[59] to hold on trust for a named charity, such as the Red Cross, but subject to a power held by T to distribute any or all of the trust property to anyone other than certain named individuals. As we will see in Chapter 4,[60] it is possible for S to confer such a wide power on T. Usually, in such a case, S's intention is that T will, within the period permitted by the trust, distribute all the trust property, so that the Red Cross will, in the end, receive nothing. Hence the parties benefitting from the trust in practice will be those people chosen by T to receive distributions of the trust property in the exercise of T's discretionary powers. S can also retain some control over T's exercise of those powers: first, of course, in the choice of the particular trustees; secondly by making any exercise of the power by T subject to the consent of another party; and third, by providing T with a document, often referred to as a "letter of wishes" which sets out how S would like T to exercise the power of distrubution.[61] Even if, as is likely, the letter does not form part of the terms of the trust,[62] so that T has no legal duty to comply with it, T has a duty to take the wishes of S into account when exercising the discretionary power.[63]

**1–044** Such a modern trust clearly differs in important respects from the simple example introduced above, where S transfers property to T to hold for the benefit of B. Indeed, S may have no real intention to benefit the party fulfilling the role of beneficiary in the modern trust: the Red Cross in our example. The differences between the possible types of trust, caused by the development of the trust concept over time, mean that, in Hackney's words[64]:

---

59 In practice, there will often be more than one trustee, but we will refer to "T" in the singular for ease of exposition.

60 See paras 4–095ff, discussing *Re Hay's S.T.* [1982] 1 W.L.R. 202.

61 For analysis of the role of a letter of wishes, see, e.g. *Breakspear v Ackland* [2009] Ch. 32; D. Hayton, "English Fiduciary Standards and Trusts Law" (1999) 32 Vanderbilt Journal of Transnational Law 555, 573–577. And note the discussion at paras 9–094—9–110.

62 There are three main reasons why S would choose to express her intentions in a letter of wishes rather than through the terms of the trust. First, S's wishes may be of a general and somewhat vague nature and therefore lack the certainty required of a binding trust duty: see para.4–003. Secondly, if the wishes were to be made part of the trust, it might then seem that S is the true beneficiary of the trust, which would make the trust assets potentially available to creditors of S, or S's spouse in ancillary relief proceedings, and could also allow the value of those assets to be taken into account when S's tax liability is assessed. Thirdly, whilst a court, on application by a beneficiary of a trust, or even by a party likely to receive a benefit through the exercise of a power by T, is likely to order disclosure to that party of a document setting out the terms of the trust, it is more likely to find that a letter of wishes was intended by S to be, and should remain, confidential (see *Breakspear v Ackland* [2009] Ch. 32 at [66]) and so S can thus express preferences in a wish letter without allowing, for example, other family members to discover those wishes.

63 See *Pitt v Holt* [2013] 2 A.C. 108 at [66] per Lord Walker: "[S's] wishes are always a material consideration in the exercise of fiduciary discretions."

64 J. Hackney, *Understanding Equity and Trusts* (1987), p.28.

> One of the greatest errors in creative thinking in trust law is to begin unguardedly, 'This is a trust therefore. . .' and to proceed to attribute to it the characteristics of the express private institutional trust. There are many different kinds of trust, the only common feature of which may be that they involve, or once involved, identifiable property and are subject to a legal regime originating solely in Equity. Perhaps it would better reflect the origin of the jurisdiction to say that there are many different kinds of trustee, ranging from the willing manager to the entrapped villain.

Two observations may be made to support Hackney's point in this passage. First, judges have suggested that, even when dealing simply with what Hackney calls the "express private institutional trust", where S transfers property to T to hold on trust for beneficiaries, different rules may have to be applied in different contexts. On this view, for example, a "traditional trust" which operates to "govern the ownership-management of property for a group of potential beneficiaries over a lengthy number of years"[65] may be distinguished from a "commercial trust" where "the trustee's duties are likely to be closely defined and may be of limited duration".[66] So, even if the basic equitable principles applicable, for example, to a breach by the trustee, extend to each of those cases, the different context of the trusteeship may have a bearing on the relief provided by the court in the event of such a breach.[67] Moreover, whilst employers' pension schemes operate through the mechanism of a trust, it would be surprising if the rights of employees who are the beneficairies of such a trusts and have made contributions to the pension scheme were to be treated in exactly the same way as those of beneficiaries who have given no value in return for their rights under the trust and are simply recipients of the bounty of S.[68] **1–045**

### (2) Constructive and Resulting Trusts

The second observation on Hackney's point relates to his reference to the "many different kinds of trustee, ranging from the willing manager to the entrapped villain". The former may, for example, be a trust corporation, paid remuneration from the trust funds in return for exercising its investment and management skills in relation to those trust frunds.[69] The trust in such a case, as in the examples already seen,[70] is an *express trust*: it arises because S successfully exercised her power to set up a trust. There are also other forms of trust. These non-express trusts arise for some reason other than S's successful exercise of a power to set up a trust. They are instead imposed by operation of law, and are generally split into two groups: *constructive trusts* and *resulting trusts*.[71] **1–046**

The exact dividing line between a constructive trust and a resulting trust is unclear,[72] but also relatively unimportant. The important divide is between express trusts on the one hand and constructive and resulting trusts on the other. This is because, whenever a trust is non-express and thus imposed by law, we need to examine carefully why the trust has arisen. Such trusts are imposed to protect **1–047**

---

65 *A.I.B. Group (UK) Plc v Mark Redler & Co (a firm)* [2014] 3 W.L.R. 1367 at [67] per Lord Toulson.

66 ibid., at [70]. This case is discussed in detail at paras 10–070—10–101.

67 ibid., at [70].

68 See, e.g. paras 9–202—9–204.

69 As noted by Lord Walker in *Pitt v Holt* [2013] 2 A.C. 108 at [66], offshore trusts are "usually run by corporate trustees whose officers and staff (especially if they change with any frequency) may know relatively little about the settlor, and even less about the settlor's family". S trusts such a trustee to be professional in carrying out its role; she does not trust it in the same way one might trust a friend.

70 See paras 1–041—1–045.

71 Note that "statutory trusts" may comprise a further group of trusts imposed by law, where the trust is imposed by operation of statute: see, e.g. Administration of Estates Act 1925 s.33. The term "implied trusts" is often seen in legislative provisions which also apply to constructive and resulting trusts (see, e.g. Law of Property Act 1925 s.53(2): see para.3–026) but its meaning is unclear (it is often used to refer to both resulting and constructive trusts: see, e.g. *Cowcher v Cowcher* [1972] 1 W.L.R. 425 at 430) and such trusts are therefore of little independent significance.

72 See paras 4–017—14–020 and 15–196—15–212.

a claimant (the beneficiary of the constructive or resulting trust) but it is also necessary to ask why that protection takes the form of a trust, rather than of, for example, a simple personal right for the claimant to be paid money by the defendant.

1-048 For example, in *Attorney General for Hong Kong v Reid*,[73] when the defendant agent received a bribe to act contrary to his duty to the claimant principal, he did not merely owe a duty to pay the value of that bribe to the principal, but rather held it on trust for the principal. Clearly, no-one had exercised a power to set up a trust of that bribe, nor had anyone given the bribe to the agent intending that he should hold it on trust. The defendant was, in Hackney's terms, an "entrapped villain", not a "willing manager". The recognition of a trust was of vital importance to the claimant,[74] as the defendant was insolvent and so any personal claim that the defendant simply pay a sum of money would have been of little practical value to the claimant. As a constructive trust had arisen in the claimant's favour when the bribe was received, the claimant was instead able to assert an equitable interest that prevented creditors of the defendant from having access to the bribe, or of assets obtained with the bribe. Moreover, the claimant was able to assert that equitable interest against certain third parties who had received assets obtained with the bribe from the defendant. The crucial question in such a case is whether those far-reaching consequences of finding a trust can be justified, given that no-one exercised a power to set up a trust.[75]

1-049 For the purposes of exposition, we will examine resulting trusts in detail in Chapter 14, and do the same for constructive trusts in Chapter 15. This does not mean, however, that such trusts can be neatly parcelled off from express trusts. On the contrary, we will encounter both resulting and constructive trusts during our examination, in Chapters 2–13, of express trusts. For example, if S transfers property to T intending that T hold it on a particular trust, but the trust fails as S has not properly exercised her power to set up an express trust, the basic position is that T will then hold that property on a resulting trust for S. Similarly, if S has made a promise to B that, if and when she receives particular property, she will set up a trust of that property for B, and B has provided value for that promise, a constructive trust may arise as soon as S receives that property, providing B with protection even if S does not comply with the promise to set up an express trust.

1-050 Moreover, where an express trust has been set up, a key feature of B's right under that trust is that it is capable of binding C, a third party who acquires the trust property as a result of an unauthorised transfer by T. In such a case, it has been said that the trust that binds C is a constructive trust.[76] So, even if B's right arises under an express trust, B may need to rely on a constructive trust to assert that right against C.

1-051 It has therefore been argued that understanding constructive and resulting trusts is crucial to understanding the practical operation of rules relating to express trusts, and, indeed, to understanding the conceptual foundations of the trust in English law.[77] At the least, it is important not to overlook trusts imposed by law when attempting to make general statements about the English law of trusts.

1-052 For example, it is easy to regard the creation of a trust by a settlor as similar, for example, to the creation of a lease by a party with a freehold of land: in each case, a party holding property allocates

---

73 [1994] 1 A.C. 324; approved in *FHR European Ventures LLP v Cedar Capital Partners LLC* [2015] A.C. 250.

74 This point is explained further at para.15–003.

75 That question is examined at 3–126—3–187.

76 See *Independent Trustee Services Ltd v GP Noble Trustees Ltd* [2013] Ch. 91 at [77]–[79] per Lloyd LJ: see further para.15–203. It has similarly been said that, where T uses the trust property in an unauthorised way and acquires a new asset, that asset will be held by T on constructive trust for B: *Re EVTR* [1987] B.C.L.C. 646 at 651 per Dillon LJ: see further paras 12–051—12–056.

77 See, e.g. S. Dix (trans.), M. Lupoi, *Trusts: A Comparative Study* (Cambridge University Press, 2000), Ch.2, arguing that constructive and resulting trusts are at "the heart of the trust"; B. McFarlane, "The Centrality of Constructive and Resulting Trusts" in *Constructive and Resulting Trusts*, C. Mitchell (ed.) (Hart Publishing, 2010).

the benefit of that property in particular ways. On such a model, it might then seem that a trust involves fragmentation of the property initially held outright by the settlor. Certainly, that view of the trust seems to have informed the doubts held in some civil law jurisdictions as to the acceptability of the trust, as such systems often have a clear antipathy to the fragmentation of property.[78] Moreover, on that model, trusts imposed by law may seem inherently dubious, as involving the courts exercising a power to redistribute the defendant's property[79]: after all, there is no concept, for example, of constructive leases. It is, however, possible to accept that a settlor can use a trust to allocate the benefit of property without also accepting that the initial right held by the settlor is thereby fragmented. If, for example, S transfers property to T to hold on trust for B, it is the underlying property right that is transferred[80] and held on trust, and that right remains intact. It is not split up, but is rather encumbered by the terms of the trust, and the duties they impose on T.[81] The same occurs when a constructive or resulting trust is recognised: the court does not deny that the defendant has the particular property right in question; it simply finds that, as a result of her conduct, the defendant came under a duty to hold that right for the benefit of the claimant.

## *B. The Parties to a Trust*

With the warnings given above as to the diversity of trusts firmly in mind, it is possible to describe some of the basic features of the English trust, by examining the positions of the parties generally involved in the creation or operation of a trust. We will set out the basic roles played by each party and also consider the influence of each on the operation of a trust. **1–053**

### i. The Settlor

#### (1) Basic Role

It should first be noted that a trust can arise without a settlor: this is the case where a trust arises by operation of law.[82] An express trust does however require a settlor, as such a trust arises as a result of the settlor's successful exercise of a power to set up a trust. In Chapters 2–6 we will consider the rules that determine whether such a power has been successfully exercised. A settlor's power to set up a trust generally stems from the fact that the settlor (S) holds property outright. In such a case, she can then create a trust in one of two ways. The first entails a transfer to the trustee (T): S transfers the property to T, but subject to the terms of a trust in favour of the beneficiary (B).[83] The second method, recognised by the courts long after the first method,[84] consists of a self-declaration of trust: **1–054**

---

78 As discussed by P. Matthews, "The Compatibility of the Trust with the Civil Law Notion of Property" in *The Worlds of the Trust*, L. Smith (ed.) (Cambridge University Press, 2013), pp.313–340.

79 There is certainly a general view in English law that the courts can redistribute property rights only if given a statutory power to do so: it is seen, for example, in the antipathy of the English courts to the "remedial constructive trust": see paras 15–006—15–008.

80 See further paras 1–057—1–058.

81 This point is made by, e.g. P Matthews, "The Compatibility of the Trust with the Civil Law Notion of Property" in *The Worlds of the Trust* (2013). See too *DKLR Holding Co (No.2) Ltd v Commissioner of Stamp Duties* (1982) 149 C.L.R. 431 at 474 per Brennan J and *Re Transphere Pty Ltd* (1986) 5 N.S.W.L.R. 309 at 311 per McLelland J.

82 See para.1–046.

83 See, e.g. the example discussed at paras para.1–007. As we discuss in Ch.6, it is also possible for S to create a charitable trust by transferring property to T to hold for a particular charitable purpose, but for ease of exposition we will focus here on the creation of a private trust.

84 The validity of a gratuitous self-declaration of trust was not recognised until 1811: *Ex p. Pye* (1811) 18 Ves. Jun. 140.

S becomes a trustee herself, retaining her legal right to the property, but declaring that she now holds that right on trust for B. It is however also possible for a party to have the power to set up a trust of property even if she is not herself free to use that property for her own benefit. For example, there are many trusts in which the trustees are given, by the terms of the initial trust, a power to create new trusts over the trust property: if such a power is exercised, an express trust is created, even though the trustees exercising that power did not hold the property outright, but rather held it on the terms of the initial trust.

**1-055** S's power to set up a trust can be successfully exercised even if she does not invoke it by expressly stating that the arrangement she wishes to set up is a trust. A crucial question, therefore, to be examined in Chapter 2 and 4,[85] is whether an arrangement entered into by S can amount to a trust although she herself does not express it in these terms. In this connection, it is worth noting a general formulation of an express trust given by Aikens LJ in *Williams v Central Bank of Nigeria*[86]:

> Put very generally, in English law an express trust is created when a person (the settlor) directs that certain identified property (the trust property) will be held either by him or others (as trustees) under a legal obligation which binds the trustees to deal with that property, which is owned by them as a separate fund, for the benefit of another (the beneficiary) who has an equitable proprietary interest in the trust property and its fruits from the moment that the trust is created.[87] Thus, if it is intended that a document is to create an express trust, it is sufficient that it demonstrates with reasonable certainty: (a) that there is an intent to create a trust; (b) that the trust property is intended to be kept separately from other property of the trustee; (c) the identity of the trust property; (d) the person(s) intended to be beneficiary(ies); and (e) the purpose of the trust and that it is administratively workable.[88]

**1-056** Some care must be taken with the requirement for trust property. First, it is very clear that, where S has a personal right against X, such as the personal right against a bank constituted by S's bank account, S can set up a trust of the personal right. The trust need not relate to any physical thing. As once stated by Lord Shaw[89]:

> The scope of the trusts recognised in equity is unlimited. There can be a trust of a chattel or of a chose in action, or of a right or obligation[90] under an ordinary legal contract, just as much as a trust of land.

Indeed, in many trusts, the initial trust property consists simply of a bank account in the name of the trustees. As Briggs J noted in *Re Lehman Brothers (International) Europe*[91]:

> [N]o-one doubts the beneficial interest of clients in a solicitor's client account. Yet the subject matter of that fund consists entirely of the solicitor's purely personal rights as a customer of the client account bank or banks.

**1-057** Secondly, it has also been accepted that S can set up a trust of even a non-assignable personal right. In *Don King Productions Inc v Warren*,[92] for example, the Court of Appeal recognised that a trust

---

85 See paras 2-005 and 4-014ff.

86 [2013] Q.B. 499 at [37]. The court was considering a procedural aspect of the substantive dispute eventually determined by the Supreme Court: [2014] A.C. 1189.

87 See *Underhill & Hayton: Law of Trusts and Trustees* (18th edn, 2010) paras 1.1 and 3.1. There are of course other ways of creating express trusts with which we are not concerned.

88 See *Underhill & Hayton: Law of Trusts and Trustees* (18th edn, 2010) para 7.1.

89 *Lord Strathcona Steamship Co Ltd v Dominion Coal Co Ltd* [1926] A.C. 108 at 124.

90 [It is however difficult to see how an obligation can be held on trust: see para.1-090.

91 [2010] EWHC 2914 at [241]. The decision of Briggs J was affirmed on appeal: [2011] EWCA Civ 1544.

92 [2000] Ch. 291.

could arise in relation to S's contractual rights under contracts for the promotion and management of boxers. Those contracts involved the conferral of personal services and many of them in any case contained a term preventing S from assigning the benefit of the contract.[93] The key point seems to be that if S declares that she holds such a right on trust for B, no transfer of that right occurs: S retains the right, but comes under a duty to B to deal with that right for B's benefit.[94] The declaration of trust does not, therefore, allow B to bring any direct claim against the other party to S's contract and, to that extent, is not inconsistent with the purpose behind the non-assignment clause.

If the term "property" is not limited to physical things, and instead extends to any valuable, assignable right, the possibility of the declaration of trust of a non-assignable right shows that the subject matter of a trust need not fall within even that extended defintion of property. For this reason, it has been suggested that it is more accurate to think of the subject matter of the trust as a right, rather than as property.[95] After all, even in a case where the property held on trust is a physical thing, such as land, it is the trustees' right to the land that is held on trust, and not the land itself.[96] We will in this book follow the courts by continuing to use the language of "trust property", but this should not disguise the fact that personal rights, even if non-assignable, may also be the subject matter of a trust. **1-058**

### (2) Influence on the Operation of the Trust

The basic position in English law is that, after having set up a trust, S "drops out of the picture".[97] So, if S transfers property to T to hold on trust for B then, simply in her capacity as settlor, S has no rights against T, and no duties to B. If S wishes to have any such rights, S must reserve them expressly under the terms of the trust: for example, where the trust assets include shares in a family company, S might stipulate that T is not to sell those shares unless S has consented to such a sale. As we have said already,[98] there are also means by which S may assert some practical influence in the operation of the trust, even without reserving any rights under the terms of the trust itself. **1-059**

Matters are obviously different where S sets up a trust by means of a self-declaration of trust. In this case, S becomes the trustee and will have a very significant influence on the operation of the trust *in her capacity as trustee*.[99] Note, too, that it is possible for S to set up a trust, either by transfer or self-declaration, in which S is herself one of the beneficiaries of the trust[100]: in that case, S will acquire rights *in her capacity as a beneficiary*.[101] **1-060**

The basic principle that S drops out of the picture is important for two reasons. First, it shows that, even in the case where the trust is set up by a transfer to T, rather than by a self-declaration by S, **1-061**

---

93 See too *Barbados Trust Co Ltd v Bank of Zambia* [2007] 2 All E.R. (Comm) 445.

94 It is important to note that, on one view (e.g. B. McFarlane and R. Stevens, "The Nature of Equitable Property" (2010) 4 J. Eq. 1, 6–8; J. Edelman and S. Elliott, "Two Conceptions of Equitable Assignment" (2015) 131 L.Q.R. 228) an equitable assignment of a non-contractual right equally does not involve a transfer of S's right. On that view, further differences between an equitable assignment and a declaration of trust must be identified, if it is to make sense for the law to allow the latter but not the former. Such differences are canvassed by Lightman J at first instance in *Don King v Warren* [2000] Ch. 291 at 320–321 and by Waller LJ in *Barbados Trust Co Ltd v Bank of Zambia* [2007] 2 All E.R. (Comm) 445 at [43].

95 See, e.g. B. McFarlane and R. Stevens, "The Nature of Equitable Property" (2010) 4 J. Eq. 1; R. Chambers, *An Introduction to Property Law in Australia*, 3rd edn (Thomson Reuters, 2013), para.13.90.

96 See, e.g. W. Swadling, "Property" in *English Private Law*, edited by A. Burrows, 3rd edn (Oxford University Press, 2013), paras 4.141–4.153.

97 See, e.g. D. Hayton, "'Trusts' in Private International Law" (2014) 366 Recueil des Cours 17, 20–21.

98 See para.1–043.

99 See paras 1–091—1–092.

100 Note there can be no self-declaration of trust where S is the sole beneficiary, as such an arrangement is no difference in substance from S's retaining her initial outright ownership of the trust property.

101 See paras 1–093—1–098.

a trust is quite different from a contract between S and T.[102] If T and S sought to achieve a trust-like arrangement by contract, T's duties in relation to the trust property would give rise to rights enforceable by S, as the other contracting party.[103] In contrast, in English trusts law, the duties of T correlate to rights held by B, the beneficiary of the trust. For the same reason, the relationship of S and T differs from the relationship of principal and agent: the principal may terminate such a relationship, thereby ending the actual authority of the agent to act on the principal's behalf, whereas, unless S expressly reserved such a power when setting up the trust,[104] it is not possible for S to revoke a trust.

**1–062** Secondly, it will often be the case that S has decided to set up a trust precisely because she wishes to dispose immediately of her initial rights in the trust property. In the context of estate planning, for example, S may wish to make an immediate settlement of property, in the hope that S's death will occur more than seven years after that disposition, so that the property disposed of will not count towards the calculation of estate duties (such as inheritance tax) on S's death. The point is that the estate planning advantages of such a transaction depend on the fact that, by making the transfer into a trust, S no longer has rights to the trust property. Indeed, if S is regarded as having reserved a benefit to herself under the terms of the trust, the trust property is still treated as part of her estate on death, and so the estate planning advantages of the transaction are lost.

**1–063** Similarly, part of S's motive in setting up a trust may be to place particular assets beyond the reach of her actual or potential creditors by disposing of her rights in those assets.[105] The trust can have this effect only because S is regarded as dropping out of the picture after having set up the trust. So if, for example, S retains rights under the trust, a court may order that creditors of S (or, for example, S's spouse in ancillary relief proceedings) should be able to have access to those rights.[106] Such an order, indeed, can be made even if T merely has a power, rather than a duty, to make distributions of the trust property to S: in such a case, the making of the order amounts to a "judicious encouragement"[107] of T to exercise that power in favour of S.[108]

**1–064** Where S acts, at least in part, for such reasons, it is worth asking why S would set up a trust in favour of B, rather than simply making an outright gift of the property to B. Consider, for example, a case in which S wishes to make a lifetime disposition, in the hope of limiting tax liability on her death, and has three grandchildren who are all at university. S could make an immediate gift of the property, perhaps dividing it equally between the grandchildren. There is, however, no flexibility in such a gift: it may turn out, for example, that, shortly after the gift is made, one of the grandchildren wins the lottery, whereas another is involved in an accident and requires expensive medical care. By setting up a discretionary trust, in which T has a power to choose when and how to make distributions of the trust property, S can both: (i) dispose of her property; and (ii) ensure that there is some flexibility as to how that property will be distributed between the grandchildren. A further advantage of a discretionary trust, as opposed

---

102 See further *Underhill & Hayton: Law of Trusts and Trustees* (2010), para.1.23.

103 Even in a case where the Contract (Rights of Third Parties) Act 1999 applies to give a third party the right to enforce a contract, the promisor retains rights under the contract and (subject to the conditions imposed by s.2 of the Act) the promisor and promisee may be able to vary or rescind the contract.

104 See para.7–02.

105 Note that s.423 of the Insolvency Act 1986 (which deals with transactions defrauding creditors, whether those transactions take the form of a trust or not) can apply where S acts with a substantial purpose of putting assets beyond the reach of actual or future creditors, allowing a court to make an order restoring the property to S for the benefit of S's creditors. Note too that s.37 of the Matrimonial Causes Act 1973 gives the court a jurisdiction to set aside dispositions made with the intention of defeating a spouse's claim to ancillary relief.

106 See, e.g. *Tasarruf Mevduati Sigorta Fonu v Merrill Lynch Bank and Trust Co (Cayman) Ltd* [2012] 1 W.L.R. 1721 (equitable execution could be ordered in relation to a power held by S to revoke a trust).

107 See *Thomas v Thomas* [1996] 2 F.C.R. 544.

108 See, e.g. *Whaley v Whaley* [2012] 1 F.L.R. 735 (if a discretionary trustee is likely to advance capital to a spouse in the foreseeable future, this can be taken into account in an order for ancillary relief).

to an outright gift, is that creditors of each grandchild will not generally have access to the trust fund, as each grandchild acquires a definite asset only if and when a distribution is made.[109]

It might also be thought that the advantage to S of a discretionary trust, as compared to an outright gift, is that the tax liability of each grandchild (at least prior to a distribution in his or her favour) will be limited. Certainly, it has been held that the interest of a beneficiary under a discretionary trust, as it is not a right to receive any specific distribution of property may lack "the necessary quality of definable extent which must exist before it can be taxed".[110] Parliament, however, does not simply sit back and allow assets to be put beyond the reach of taxation so easily. Indeed, the general rule[111] for any lifetime trust established after 22 March 2006 is that inheritance tax (IHT) is payable as an "entry charge" of 20 per cent of the value of the property (to the extent that the value exceeds the tax-free IHT allowance),[112] a periodic charge to IHT of a maximum of 6 per cent on the value of the assets every 10 years, and as an "exit charge" calculated as a proportion of the most recent periodic charge (if any).[113] Further, if the trust is a discretionary trust and the income received by the trustees from the trust property is not distributed to beneficiaries, the trustees are liable to pay income tax on that income at the trust rate, which at present matches the highest rate of income tax and is therefore 45 per cent. **1–065**

The basic point that S, on setting up a trust, drops out of the picture might be seen as a counter-balance to the fact that S, in choosing the terms of the trust, has a wide initial power to dictate the operation of the trust. It is certainly true that S's intentions, as objectively expressed in the terms of the trust,[114] are critical when defining the content of T's duties, and those duties in turn shape the rights of B. Nonetheless, it is possible to exaggerate S's influence. First, as we have noted,[115] the *Saunders v Vautier* principle[116] allows all of the beneficiaries of a trust, acting together, to call for the trust property to be transferred to them by the trustees, even if such a transfer is inconsistent with the terms of the trust. So, for example, if T holds on trust for B alone, and S has stipulated that B is to receive the trust capital (rather than just the income) only on reaching the age of 25, B, on reaching the age of 18 and thus becoming an adult, can terminate the trust and call for the transfer of the trust capital. The point is that although T has an initial duty not to transfer the capital to B until B is 25, that duty is owed to B alone once the trust is up and running and S drops out of the picture, and so B, if an adult and of sound mind, is free to waive the duty.[117] **1–066**

Secondly, consider a case in which S stipulates that T is to hold family shares on trust for B, and is not permitted to sell those shares without the consent of X. In breach of the terms of the trust, T sells the shares. In such a case, B has the power to "adopt the investment"[118] and treat it as trust property, so that T now holds the proceeds of sale of the shares on trust for B.[119] S clearly did not intend that such a situation **1–067**

109 Although, as noted at para.1–063, the spouse of one of the grandchildren, in ancillary relief proceedings, may claim that the likelihood of that grandchild receiving a distribution under the discretionary trust should be taken into account in assessing the relief.

110 *Gartside v IRC* [1968] A.C. 553 at 617 per Lord Wilberforce. See too *Sainsbury v IRC* [1970] Ch. 712.

111 There are exceptions for particular types of trust, such as trusts for the benefit of a bereaved minor or a disabled person: note that the failure to set up such a special trust, with its attendant tax advantages, was the initial cause of the difficulties in *Pitt v Holt* [2013] 2 A.C. 108.

112 That allowance is often referred to as the "nil rate band": in 2015/16 it is £325,000. A surviving spouse can take advantage of any of the allowance unused by the deceased spouse.

113 The exit charge is calculated on a similar basis if the exit occurs within 10 years of the settlement.

114 See paras 4–006ff.

115 See para.1–037.

116 (1841) 4 Beav. 115. See paras 7–004—7–029.

117 Note that it is not difficult for S to avoid the operation of the *Saunders v Vautier* power: S can, for example, set up a trust under which B's right to the trust capital is conditional on B's reaching the age of 25.

118 See *Wright v Morgan* [1926] A.C. 788 at 798 per Viscount Dunedin.

119 See further paras 12–051ff.

could arise, but, again, as the duties imposed by the trust are owed to B and not to S, it is B who has the power to adopt the investment. In effect, then, the terms of the trusts have been informally varied. There is also a formal, statutory mechanism[120] by which trusts can be varied, which we will examine in Chapter 7[121]: its existence shows again that the terms of the trust as chosen by S are not necessarily definitive.

1-068 Further, whilst it is certainly the case, as we will see in Chapter 4, that the courts are generally keen, where possible, to give effect to the expressed, objective intention of S as to the terms of a trust, some limits are placed on S not only by the rights of B, but also by the general rules of the English law of trusts. For example, as we have already noted,[122] those general rules prohibit the creation of a private purpose trust, whereby T holds trust property not for the benefit of individuals but rather subject to a duty to apply it to a particular, non-charitable purpose. We will also see in Chapter 7 that the rule against perpetuities, one effect of which is to limit the duration of trusts, limits the ways in which S can use a trust to allocate the benefits of property.

1-069 One way of explaining such limits is to note that the interests of settlor, trustee, and beneficiary are not the only ones that must be considered when shaping the law of trusts. It can be argued, for example, that there is a general public interest in preventing property from being insulated from the claims of the creditors of *any* person, as would occur, for example, if a private purpose trust was permitted, and in preventing property from becoming effectively inalienable, as might occur in the absence of the rule against perpetuities. The fact that some jurisdictions permit private purpose trusts,[123] and have greatly extended, or even abolished perpetuity periods[124] does not undermine this point; it simply demonstrates that the public interest of one jurisdiction may differ from that of another.[125]

## ii. The Trustee

### (1) First Basic Role: Holding the Trust Property

1-070 The trust property is vested in the trustee (T). As noted above,[126] that trust property need not consist of ownership of any physical thing, but may instead be a personal right against another party held by T, even a non-assignable personal right. The trust property may also be an equitable interest held by T. This will be the case, for example, where nominees, acting for T, hold the trust property on trust for T. In such a case, the trust between T and B may be seen as a sub-trust, as the right held by T on trust for B is itself an equitable interest under a trust.

1-071 We will consider the operation of such sub-trusts in Chapter 3.[127] They are important conceptually as they show that a trust need not involve a split between legal and equitable title, with legal title in the trustee and equitable title in the beneficiary: it may instead be the case that the trust property held by the trustee is itself an equitable right. Sub-trusts are also important in practice: for example, securities such as shares are today almost always held through a series of intermediaries.[128] The

---

120 Under the Variation of Trusts Act 1958.

121 See paras 7-047ff.

122 See paras 1-037—1-038.

123 See para.1-038.

124 For a survey of the position in the US, see M. Schanzenbach and R. Sitkoff, "Perpetuities or Taxes? Explaining the Rise of the Perpetual Trust" (2006) 27 Cardozo Law Review 2465.

125 Even within a single jurisdiction, there is a distinction between the policies given effect to, perhaps in the name of the public interest, in domestic law and those still more important policies that must be given effect to by the courts of that jurisdiction even when applying foreign law: see arts 15, 16 and 18 of the Hague Convention on the Law Applicable to Trusts and on their Recognition, discussed at paras 16-045—16-049.

126 See para.1-057.

127 See paras 3-080ff.

128 For discussion of the role of the trust in intermediated securitization, see, e.g. *Re Lehman Brothers International (Europe)*

investor, B, may regard herself as "owning" particular shares, but she is very unlikely to have a direct right against the issuer of the shares. It is much more likely that a depositary,[129] specialising in the clearing and settlement of securities, holds the legal title to the shares and hence the direct rights against a company. The depositary then holds that title on trust for intermediaries, and trading in the shares occurs through dealings in the equitable interests held by the intermediaries. Those dealings can therefore take place quickly and easily, without the need for the completion of any formalities (such as registration) that might be required for a transfer of legal title to the shares.[130]

It might be thought that, at least where the trust property does not consist of an equitable interest, the creation of a trust involves S transferring legal title in the trust property to T, and equitable title in that property to B. There are, however, at least two problems with such an analysis. First, the assumption it rests on, that S's initial property consists of both a legal and an equitable title, has been rejected by the House of Lords. In Lord Browne-Wilkinson's words in *Westdeutsche Landesbank Girozentrale v Islington LBC*[131]: **1–072**

> A person solely entitled to the full beneficial ownership of money or property, both at law and in equity, does not enjoy an equitable interest in that property. The legal title carries with it all rights. Unless and until there is a separation of legal and equitable estates, there is no separate equitable title. Therefore to talk about [A] 'retaining' its equitable interest is meaningless. The only question is whether the circumstances under which the money was paid were such as, in equity, to impose a trust on [B]. If so, an equitable interest arose for the first time under that trust.

Secondly, as noted above,[132] the creation of a trust need not involve any fragmentation of the property initially held by S. Rather, T acquires the very same property as held by S, but subject to a duty, owed to B, to comply with the terms of the trust. As James LJ put it in *Smith v Anderson*[133]: **1–073**

> A trustee is a man who is the owner of the property and deals with it as principal, as owner and as master, subject only to an equitable obligation to account to some persons to whom he stands in the relation of trustee.

This analysis is supported, for example, by the approach adopted in the old and factually complex case of *Burgess v Wheate*[134]: in the absence of any legislative provision dealing with the situation, if T holds property subject to a trust, and (perhaps because of the death of B and an absence of any party who can succeed to B's rights under the trust) there is no longer any person to whom T owes her "equitable obligation to account", then T is free to use the property for her own benefit. In the absence of anyone who can enforce the duty imposed by the trust, there is no reason for equity to intervene, and T is free to enjoy her ownership of the trust property. As Paul Matthews has observed[135]: **1–074**

> The decision in *Burgess v Wheate* is like a salutary shock to the system. We are brought up to think that the last thing a trustee can do is to keep the property for himself. What that case shows is that, indeed, *as a last resort*, and only when there is no one else to affect his conscience, it really *is* the last thing he can do.

---

[2010] EWHC 2914 (Ch) at [225]. The decision of Briggs J was affirmed by the Court of Appeal: [2012] 2 B.C.L.C. 151; and B. McFarlane and R. Stevens, "Interests in Securities: Practical Problems and Conceptual Solutions" in *Intermediated Securities*, L. Gullifer and J. Payne (eds) (Hart, 2010).

129 Such as, e.g. Euroclear.

130 The standard formal requirement applying to the disposition of an existing equitable interest has been disapplied in relation to dealings in such intermediated securities: see para.3–104.

131 [1996] A.C. 669 at 706.

132 See para.1–052.

133 (1880) 15 Ch.D. 247 at 275.

134 (1759) 1 Eden 177.

135 P. Matthews, "*Burgess v Wheate* (1759)" in *Landmark Cases in Equity*, C. Mitchell and P. Mitchell (eds) (2012).

> The trustee is a true owner, and has the owner's rights, subject only to the effect on his conscience. If and when that effect runs out, he nevertheless remains the owner, untrammelled by any equity. Of course the law has moved on since *Burgess v Wheate*, and the range of persons who may affect the conscience of the trustee is—quite rightly—larger than it was then. So the chances of a trustee finding himself able lawfully to enjoy the property by virtue of the disappearance of all those who might affect his conscience are correspondingly smaller. But the true principle is there, and in analysing the nature of the trust, and in explaining it to those from outside the common law tradition,[136] we ignore it at our peril.

**1–075** The point that T has more than a mere legal title is also apparent when considering the impact of T's ownership of the trust property on third parties. If, for example, the trust property consists of a contractual right held by T against X, then T is free to enforce that right against X. Where appropriate, T may be awarded an equitable remedy, such as specific performance; T can otherwise receive damages in the usual measure from X. There is no suggestion that any discount should be made because T has "only" legal title to the trust property.[137] Similarly, if the trust property consists of ownership of tangible property, and X wrongfully interferes with that property, T can again get full damages against X, without any discount being made.[138] Indeed, the fact that T is treated, as against strangers such as X, as having a full entitlement to the trust property is actually an advantage to B, since the benefits acquired by T in asserting the right against X will also be held by T on trust for B.

**1–076** We noted when considering the basic role of a settlor[139] that a trust imposed by law (such as a constructive or resulting trust) can arise even if no-one has successfully exercised a power to set up a trust. Is it similarly possible to have a constructive or resulting trust without a trustee? The obvious answer is No: if such a trust exists then the defendant necessarily holds property vested in her subject to a duty to B. In that sense, it is clear that such a trust involves a trustee. In *Williams v Central Bank of Nigeria*,[140] however, the Supreme Court had to consider the meaning to be given to the term "trustee" in the specific context of the Limitation Act 1980. The point arose as no statutory limitation period applies if a claim is made against a trustee by a beneficiary seeking to recover trust property or alleging a fraudulent breach of trust by the trustee.[141] The question to be determined was whether a claim brought by a beneficiary against a third party, alleging that the third party had dishonestly assisted in T's breach of trust, was such a claim.[142] A majority of the Supreme Court held that it was not, as such a third party was not a trustee. That conclusion must be right, because a third party can dishonestly assist a breach of trust without ever having any property vested in her.

**1–077** In *Williams v Central Bank of Nigeria*, however, the majority of the Supreme Court went further than this, and adopted a limited definition of the term "trustee", which can also exclude a third party who has acquired and held trust property. Lord Sumption (with whom Lord Hughes agreed) stated that[143]:

> The problem is that in this all-embracing sense the phrase 'constructive trust' refers to two different things to which very different legal considerations apply. The first comprises persons who have lawfully

---

[136] This is a reference to the point discussed at para.1–052: the hostility of civil lawyers to the trust is sometimes based on the assumption, falsified by, e.g. *Burgess v Wheate*, that a trust necessarily involves a fragmentation of S's right into distinct legal and equitable titles.

[137] Indeed, it is T who is the appropriate party to bring any claim against X: see, e.g. *Vandepitte v Preferred Accident Insurance Corporation of New York* [1933] A.C. 70 at 79.

[138] See, e.g. *Leigh and Sillavan Ltd v Aliakmon Shipping Co Ltd* [1986] A.C. 785 at 812–813 and 819.

[139] See paras 1–054—1–058.

[140] [2014] A.C. 1189.

[141] Limitation Act 1980 s.21(1)(a) and (b).

[142] The nature of a claim based on dishonest assistance in a breach of trust is examined at paras 11–097ff.

[143] [2014] A.C. 1189 at [9].

> assumed fiduciary obligations in relation to trust property, but without a formal appointment. They may be trustees de son tort,[144] who without having been properly appointed, assume to act in the administration of the trusts as if they had been; or trustees under trusts implied from the common intention to be inferred from the conduct of the parties, but never formally created as such. These people can conveniently be called de facto trustees. They intended to act as trustees, if only as a matter of objective construction of their acts. They are true trustees and if the assets are not applied in accordance with the trust, equity will enforce the obligations that they have assumed by virtue of their status exactly as if they had been appointed by deed . . . In its second meaning, the phrase 'constructive trustee' refers to something else. It comprises persons who never assumed and never intended to assume the status of a trustee, whether formally or informally, but have exposed themselves to equitable remedies by virtue of their participation in the unlawful misapplication of trust assets. Either they have dishonestly assisted in a misapplication of the funds by the trustee, or they have received trust assets knowing that the transfer to them was a breach of trust. In either case, they may be required by equity to account as if they were trustees or fiduciaries, although they are not. These can conveniently be called cases of ancillary liability. The intervention of equity in such cases does not reflect any pre-existing obligation but comes about solely because of the misapplication of the assets. It is purely remedial. The distinction between these two categories is not just a matter of the chronology of events leading to liability. It is fundamental.

Lord Neuberger (with whom Lord Hughes also agreed) focused more closely on the particular meaning of the term "trustee" within the context of s.21(1)(a) of the Limitation Act 1980 and, as a result, on the legislative history of the provision,[145] but, in the course of doing so, he also made some more general observations on what it means to be a trustee[146]: **1–078**

> It is unreal to refer to a person who receives property dishonestly as a 'trustee', i.e. a person in whom trust is reposed, given that the trust is said to arise simply as a result of dishonest receipt. Nobody involved, whether the dishonest receiver, the person who passed the property to him, or the claimant, has ever placed any relevant trust and confidence in the recipient.

The definition of "trustee" adopted by the majority of the Supreme Court in the *Williams* case makes good sense in the particular context of limitation rules[147]: if the defendant has received property having agreed to hold it as trustee then, whether or not an express trust has arisen, the defendant's agreement provides a reason to treat her in the same way as a trustee of an express trust, and to limit her ability to rely on a statutory limitation period. Care must be taken, however, in adopting too narrow a meaning of the term "trustee" in other contexts. Certainly, even if the defendant did not agree to hold on trust, it is possible that she may receive property and, because of the circumstances surrounding its receipt, also come under a duty to B. In such a case, even if no trust has been reposed in the defendant, it could well still be argued that, contrary to the language employed by Lord Sumption, a "true trust" has arisen, as property is held by a party subject to a duty, imposed by law and owed to B, to hold that property for the benefit of B.[148] **1–079**

---

144 [The concept of a trustee de son tort is examined at paras 11–014ff.]

145 See [2014] AC 1189 at [49] and [51].

146 [2014] A.C. 1189 at [64].

147 Although note that Lord Mance, in his dissent, argued that a different interpretation of the term was more "historically accurate": see [2014] A.C. 1189 at [120].

148 For example, as we will see at paras 11–074—11–086 the remedies available to B where the defendant is liable in knowing receipt are consistent with the view that the defendant was a true trustee.

### (2) Second Basic Role: Duties of the Trustee

1-080 A trustee, T, is subject to three main duties, each of which will be examined in detail in Chapter 9. It is important to note that those duties are owed to the beneficiary B[149] and not to S, the settlor.[150] First, T has a duty to comply with the terms of the trust; secondly, T has a fiduciary duty to act exclusively in the interests of B; thirdly, T has a duty to take reasonable care in exercising her powers under the trust when, for example, managing or investing the trust property.[151]

1-081 The first of those duties may seem self-evident but, notwithstanding the language generally employed by the courts,[152] it is perhaps more accurate to say that T lacks the power, as against B, to enter into a transaction that is authorised neither by the terms of the trust nor by the general law. We will examine this point further in Chapters 9 and 10,[153] but it may be useful here to refer back to the example given above,[154] where the terms of the trust stipulate that T can sell shares held on trust only with the consent of X, but T then sells those shares to C without that consent of X. The restriction in the trust does not rob T of the power, under the general law, to make the transfer: as against parties other than B, T has the full entitlement to the shares, and this includes the power to transfer the shares to third parties. So C does then acquire that same full entitlement to the shares: the question for C is whether, like T, C is also subject to a duty to use those shares for the benefit of B, and not for C's own benefit. As noted above,[155] if C acquired the shares for value, acting in good faith and without notice of the restriction imposed by the trust, C will be under no duty to B: as a bona fide purchaser for value of the trust property with no notice of the trust, C is protected from any claim of B. That does not mean, however, that T had a power *as against B* to make the transfer of the shares. If B then exercises her power to ask T to account for what has happened to the trust property, T will not be able to rely on the transfer to C to support an argument that she has ceased to be accountable to B for the shares.

1-082 As we will see in Chapter 10,[156] T's inability, as against B, to rely on the unauthorised transfer of the trust property, enables B to bring what can be thought of as a claim for "substitutive performance":[157] B can ask the court for an order that T must dip into T's own pocket to reconstitute the trust fund, either by purchasing equivalent shares, or by paying into the trust fund the current monetary value of the missing property. It is important to note that such a claim does not depend on B showing that T's unauthorised act caused B any loss: it is not a claim for the recovery of loss flowing from a breach of duty committed by T: it is a claim to enforce T's primary duty as trustee "properly to preserve the trust fund".[158] The existence of such a claim is a very important part of the protection available to B, as it is available to B without B needing to prove that T's unauthorised act caused B any loss.[159]

---

149 Obviously a trust may have more than one beneficiary but for ease of exposition we will refer here to a singular "B".

150 See paras 1-059ff.

151 See now Trustee Act 2000 s.1 (extracted at para.9-080).

152 See, e.g. *Youyang Pty Ltd v Minter Ellison Morris Fletcher* (2003) 212 C.L.R. 484 at [32]: "perhaps the most important duty of a trustee is to obey the terms of the trust.

153 See paras 9-005–9-017 and 10-001—10-004.

154 See para.1-067.

155 See para.1-019.

156 See paras 10-020ff.

157 This term is an academic coinage, rather than a judicial one (see, e.g. S. Elliott, "Remoteness Criteria in Equity" (2002) 65 M.L.R. 588) but is nonetheless apt and was discussed by Lord Toulson in *A.I.B. Group (UK) Plc v Mark Redler & Co (a firm)* [2014] 3 W.L.R. 1367 at [50]–[54].

158 See, e.g. *Low v Bouverie* [1891] 3 Ch. 82 at 99 per Lindley LJ: "The duty of a trustee is properly to preserve the trust fund, to pay the income and the corpus to those who are entitled to them respectively, and to give all his [beneficiaries] on demand information with respect to the mode in which the trust fund has been dealt with, and where it is."

159 It is for this reason that such "substitutive performance" claims must be carefully distinguished from "reparation" claims which are instead focussed on the recovery of money to make good loss caused to B by a breach of trust. As we will see at

The second fiduciary duty of T is also of great practical importance. In practical terms, it means that, for example, T must not allow her personal interest to conflict with the interests of B by, for example, using for her own benefit an opportunity offered to T in her capacity as a trustee.[160] Whilst there is some controversy as to the precise nature and purpose of fiduciary duties, this "no conficts" rule clearly has the effect, at least, of buttressing the first duty of T, to abide by the terms of the trust, as complying with the no conflicts rules reduces the temptations that T might otherwise be under to act contrary to the terms of the trust.[161] The existence of the fiduciary duty, and the strictness with which it is enforced,[162] thus provides valuable protection to B. After all, since, as against everyone other than B, T holds a full entitlement to the trust property, the existence of a strict prophylactic duty assists in limiting the potential for T to abuse that entitlement by acting contrary to B's interests. **1–083**

The default fiduciary duty imposed on T is so rigorous, however, that properly drawn trust instruments often permit T to abide by more relaxed standards. For example, the default rule is that T cannot charge for her services, but if the trust contains a charging clause then T can receive remuneration under the express terms of the trust.[163] Exemption clauses in the trust can also give protection to T; but, as Millett LJ stated in *Armitage v Nurse*[164]: **1–084**

> there is an irreducible core of obligations owed by the trustees to the beneficiaries and enforceable by them which is fundamental to the concept of a trust. If the beneficiaries have no rights enforceable against the trustees there are no trusts. But I do not accept [that] these core obligations include the duties of skill and care, prudence and diligence. The duty of the trustees to perform the trusts honestly and in good faith for the benefit of the beneficiaries is the minimum necessary to give substance to the trusts, but in my opinion it is sufficient.

Millett LJ's statement makes clear that, whilst T cannot be given the freedom to depart recklessly or dishonestly from the terms of the trust, the third of the three duties of T that we have identified, the duty of care, may be excluded by the express terms of a trust, and therefore cannot be seen as a fundamental part of what it means to be a trustee. Where it does apply, the duty is no different in its operation from the standard duty of care that arises, for example, when a defendant carries out a service for a claimant. The basic rules applicable to a claim by B in relation to a breach of a duty of care by T are therefore no different to those applying to a standard negligence claim arising in contract or tort.[165] **1–085**

### (3) Third Basic Role: Trusteeship as an Office

We have seen, when considering the role of S, the settlor of a trust, that a trust differs from a contract. This is underlined by the fact that trusteeship is conceived not merely as a set of duties that bind T, the party who, in an express trust, has initially agreed to act as trustee, but also as an office. For **1–086**

---

paras 10–032ff, when examining *Target Holdings Ltd v Redferns* [1996] A.C. 421 and *A.I.B. Group (U.K.) Plc v Mark Redler & Co (a firm)* [2014] 3 W.L.R. 1367, it seems, however, that the courts have not always kept this distinction in mind.

160 See para.9–018. Indeed, the default rule is that T cannot charge for her services, although of course if the trust contains a charging clause then T can receive remuneration under the express terms of the trust: see para.8–061.

161 See, e.g. M. Conaglen, *Fiduciary Loyalty: Protecting the Due Performance of Non-Fiduciary Duties* (Hart Publishing, 2010), pp.61–76.

162 See paras 9–027ff.

163 See paras 8–059ff.

164 [1998] Ch. 241 at 253.

165 See *Bristol and West Building Society v Mothew* [1998] Ch. 1 at 16–18; although note that a different approach is advocated by, e.g. J. Getzler, "Am I My Beneficiary's Keeper? Fusion and Loss-Based Fiduciary Remedies" in *Equity in Commercial Law*, S. Degeling and J. Edelman (eds) (Law Book Co, 2005).

example, if T is not properly performing her duties as trustee, B can apply to court to have T replaced by a new trustee, in whom the trust property will then be vested. If T, a sole trustee, dies, then the trust continues, with T's personal representative becoming trustee and having the power to appoint a new trustee, in whom the trust property will again be vested. If, in a will, S stipulates that property is to be transferred to T to hold on trust for B, but T refuses to act as trustee, B's equitable interest does not lapse; rather, again, a new party will be found to act as trustee, and the trust property will be vested in that party. These points lie behind the maxim that "a trust will not fail for want of a trustee".[166]

**1–087** Further evidence of the clear differences between the position of T and that of a party to a simple contract is provided by the powers of the courts to supervise the proper operation of a trust. As Lord Walker observed in *Schmidt v Rosewood Trust Ltd*[167]:

> It is fundamental to the law of trusts that the court has jurisdiction to supervise and if appropriate intervene in the administration of a trust, including a discretionary trust.

As we will see in Chapter 4,[168] even if S has set up a discretionary trust, and has thus given to T the power to make decisions as to the distribution of the trust property, a court may still have a role to play in executing and enforcing the trust, not only by replacing T with new trustees if necessary but also, potentially, by agreeing to a scheme of distribution proposed by the beneficiaries of the trust, or even by devising its own scheme of distribution.[169]

**1–088** In considering the duties of T, we saw that a trust necessarily involves a relationship between T and B. The notion of trusteeship as involving an office can be seen as involving the depersonalisation of that relationship. As the trust can continue if T dies or is replaced, its existence does not depend on the precise identity of the trustee at any time; what matters is that the trust property is vested in someone. This point can also be seen in a fundamental aspect of the trust: the protection given to B in the event of T's insolvency. As we have seen,[170] as long as the trust property is preserved, B is protected from the risk of T's insolvency, as any assets held on trust cannot be used to meet the claims of T's creditors.[171] This result flows, at least in part, from the fact that as it would have been a breach of the terms of the trust for T to use the trust property to pay her own creditors, those creditors cannot benefit from the fact of T's insolvency. It also shows that the personality, or creditworthiness, of T is not critical to the core duty of the trust: the duty of T not to use the trust property for T's own benefit.

**1–089** One way of explaining both the nature of trusteeship as an office, and the fact that T's creditors cannot have access to the trust assets, is to treat the trust as depending on T's simultaneous holding of two separate patrimonies. The concept of a patrimony is more familiar to civil lawyers, and this explanation of the trust is most prominent outside purely common law systems, as its attraction, in part, lies in its ability to explain some important features of the trust without relying on the divide between common law and equity.[172] Roughly speaking, a patrimony consists of the total assets and liabilities of any legal person. The general rule, in English law as in civilian systems, is that *all* of a defendant's assets are available to meet *any* of the defendant's liabilities. That is not true, however, if

---

166 See para.2–004.
167 [2003] 2 A.C. 709 at [36].
168 See para.4–138.
169 See *Re Baden's Deed Trusts (No.1)* [1971] A.C. 424 at 457 (extracted at paras 4–119ff).
170 See para.1–048.
171 See, e.g. Insolvency Act 1986 s.283(3)(a): in the case of an individual becoming bankrupt, "property held by the bankrupt on trust for any other person" is excluded from the bankrupt's estate and so is not available to the trustee in bankruptcy to use to meet the claims of the bankrupt's creditors.
172 See, e.g. K. Reid, "Patrimony not Equity: The Trust in Scotland" (2000) 8 European Review of Private Law 427; G. Gretton, "Trusts Without Equity" (2000) 49 I.C.L.Q. 599.

the defendant is a trustee: whilst T is fully entitled, as against parties other than B, to the trust property, those assets are not available to meet T's liabilities to T's creditors. One way to explain this result is to see the trust as forming an exception to the general rule that each legal person has only one patrimony. On this view it can said that, a trustee, exceptionally, has two patrimonies[173]: her general patrimony and a special trust patrimony, which is not available to meet T's general liabilities. Or it could be said that the trust assets are outside T's patrimony, and form part of a separate, independent patrimony held by no-one.[174]

There are, however, difficulties with applying this patrimonial explanation of the trust in English law.[175] First, the civilian concept of a patrimony consists of both assets and liabilities, whereas the property held on trust by T consists only of assets: it is not possible for T to hold a liability on trust for B.[176] Secondly, consider a case in which the trust property includes land, and T, acting responsibly and consistently with the terms of the trust, enters into a contract with X under which X is to make repairs to a building on that land.[177] If T fails to pay X, and X makes a claim against T under the contract, X's position is essentially the same as any other creditor of T, and thus the same as if the contract had been to repair T's own home. This means, first, that X has no direct access to the trust assets to satisfy X's claim and secondly, that *all* of T's non-trust assets are available to meet X's claim.[178] The general position, then, is that English law does not make a distinction between debts incurred by T in her capacity as trustee and any other debts of T.[179] This underlines another important point: the trust itself does not have legal personality,[180] and so it does not make sense to speak of a party such as X as a creditor "of the trust": X is a creditor of T and so does not have direct access to the trust property to satisfy the claim, but can only have access to assets at the free disposition of T. 1–090

### (4) Influence on the Operation of the Trust

We have seen that, particularly in a modern discretionary trust, significant powers may be given to T to choose how to distribute the trust property[181]; it is also common for T to be given, for example, powers to set up new trusts that will bind all or part of the original trust property.[182] In such a case, T clearly has a significant influence on the operation of the trust and, whilst T's purported exercise of a power conferred by the trust may be subject to challenge if T does not take into account the expressed wishes of S,[183] there is no duty on T to comply with any such wishes which do not form part of the terms of the trust. 1–091

---

173 This has been suggested as the basis of the Scottish trust: see, e.g. *Ted Jacob Engineering Group Inc v Robert Matthew Johnston-Marshall and Partners* [2014] CSIH 18 at [90] per Lord Drummond Young; Scottish Law Commission, *Report on Trust Law* (Scots Law Com. No.239, 2014) para.3.4, accepting the analyses of Reid and Gretton in the articles cited in the previous footnote.

174 That seems to be the basis, for example, of the "*patrimoine d'affectation*" model adopted in Quebec, Uruguay and France.

175 The discussion in this paragraph is based on the analysis of L. Smith, "Trust and Patrimony" (2008–09) 28 E.T. & P.J. 332.

176 The statement of Lord Shaw in *Lord Strathcona Steamship Co Ltd v Dominion Coal Co Ltd* [1926] A.C. 108 at 124 (set out at para.1–056) therefore seems over-broad, as it suggests that a liability may be held on trust.

177 This example is taken from L. Smith, "Trust and Patrimony" (2008–09) 28 E.T. & P.J. 332, 338.

178 See, e.g. *Fraser v Murdoch* (1881) 6 App. Cas. 855 at 874; *Staniar v Evans* (1886) 34 Ch.D. 470 at 477. It is of course for possible for T, when contracting with X, to specify that certain assets of T will not be available to meet any claim of X; but it is equally open to any contracting party thus to limit the assets available to meet a particular claim.

179 Where the debt to X is properly incurred, T will have a right of indemnity against the trust fund (although only after discharging any liability T has for any other breach of trust), and X may be subrogated to that right of indemnity so as to have access to the trust property to meet T's debt: see, e.g. *Re Frith* [1902] 1 Ch. 342. See further paras 8–083ff.

180 See further L. Smith, "Mistaking the Trust" (2011) H.K.L.J. 747.

181 See para.1–042.

182 For a case concerning a challenge to the exercise of such a power, see *Re Hay's S.T.* [1982] 1 W.L.R. 202 (extracted at paras 4–097ff).

183 See para.1–043.

1-092 In general, when exercising powers under the trust, T must do her best to hold the balance fairly between different beneficiaries or classes of beneficiaries. If T exercises a power with the intention of achieving a result that is not permitted by the terms of the trust, or of favouring one group of beneficiaries over another without justification, then that exercise may be regarded as unauthorised, so that T has a duty to reconstitute the trust fund by replacing any property disposed of by the exercise of the power.[184] T may also play a paternalistic role in the operation of the trust. Even if all of the beneficiaries interested in a particular trust agree that T should exercise her powers under the trust in a particular way, T can refuse to do so if she considers that such an action would not be in the best objective interests of some of the beneficiaries.[185] In such a case, then, the beneficiaries cannot force T to act in a particular way. As we have seen,[186] however, the beneficiaries, acting together, could exercise their *Saunders v Vautier*[187] power to call for the trust property to be vested in them by T, thus terminating the trust.

## iii. The Beneficiary

### (1) Basic Role

1-093 We have seen that, in English law, a trust without a beneficiary can exist only if it is a charitable trust.[188] It is not possible for S to set up a trust where T's duty is simply to apply the trust property for a non-charitable purpose. This principle of English law—as we have seen,[189] it is not a part of the trusts law of many offshore jurisdictions, nor is it a requirement of the defintion of a trust adopted by the Hague Convention on the Law Applicable to Trusts and on their Recognition—is often referred to as "the beneficiary principle" and will be discussed in detail in Chapter 5. It shows that, outside the context of charitable trusts, the existence of a beneficiary is a necessary part of the English trust.[190] Such a beneficiary is required in order to enforce the duties imposed on T: if there were no means of enforcing such duties, there would be no restriction on T's use of the trust property which is, as we have seen,[191] fully vested in T.

1-094 Indeed, it could even be said that the need for a beneficiary is such that, in some cases, the law itself identifies a beneficiary. In Chapter 14,[192] we will examine the type of resulting trust that arises where S transfers property to T to hold subject to a particular trust, but, for some reason,[193] S does not succesfully exercise her power to set up a trust, and so the intended express trust fails. In such a case, given S's clear intention that T should not be free to use the trust property for T's own benefit, and S's equally clear intention to establish a trust, the result is that T holds the intended trust property on trust for S. Whilst there is a debate as to the reason for which such a resulting trust arises,[194] John Mee has suggested that[195]:

---

184 See paras 9-205ff, discussing the doctrine of a "fraud on a power".
185 *Re Brockbank* [1949] Ch. 206: subject to the beneficiaries' power to direct the trustees to retire and appoint other designated persons to become trustees in their place, under the Trusts of Land and Appointment of Trustees Act 1996 s.19.
186 See para.1-037.
187 *Saunders v Vautier* (1841) 4 Beav. 115.
188 See para.1-037. Charitable trusts are discussed in Ch.6.
189 See para.1-038.
190 See too *Armitage v Nurse* [1998] Ch. 241 at 253 (extracted at para.1-084).
191 See paras 1-073—1-075.
192 See paras 14-102ff.
193 The reason may, for example, be a failure to identify the beneficiaries of the trust with sufficient certainty (see paras 4-085ff), or a failure to identify a complete set of beneficial entitlements, as occurs, for example, if S conveys to T to hold on trust for B for B's life, without specifying for whom T should hold on trust after B's death.
194 See paras 14-160ff for discussion of the different views.
195 J Mee, "'Automatic' Resulting Trusts: Retention, Restitution, or Reposing Trust?" in *Constructive and Resulting Trusts*, C. Mitchell (ed.) (2010), p.235.

The rule chosen by equity in this situation, that there should be a resulting trust for the settlor, is difficult to fault as a matter of justice. It has been argued that it proceeds on the basis of a logically prior decision by equity that, once property has been conveyed to a trustee in whom the settlor has reposed trust to hold it according to the settlor's instructions, the trust will not 'fail', even where there is a failure in the particular trusts declared or a failure to declare any such trusts. Once one is willing to accept that a trust has been brought into existence by the conveyance to the trustee, so that someone must become entitled to the beneficial interest under the trust, it is difficult to justify anyone besides the settlor taking any unallocated beneficial interest.

The right acquired by B under a trust is often referred to as a "beneficial interest". The holding of such an interest gives B a great advantage as compared to, say, having a purely personal right to compel T to honour a promise, made to S, to use the trust property for B's benefit. First, as we have seen,[196] B is protected in T's insolvency: as T's duty to B relates to the specific trust property, and is a duty not to use that property other than in compliance with the terms of the trust, the trust property is not available to T's creditors. Secondly, as we have also seen,[197] if T transfers the trust property to C, and has no power under the terms of the trust to do so, it may be possible for B to make a claim against C, and to show that C has also come under a duty to B not to use that trust property for C's own benefit.[198] The possibility of making such a claim against C may be vital if T is insolvent and so cannot in practice perform her duty to dip into her own pocket and reconstitute the trust fund. Thirdly, as we have seen,[199] if T uses the trust property to acquire new property then, whether or not T had a power under the terms of the trust to do so, B can choose to impose a duty on T to hold that new property subject to the terms of the initial trust.[200] **1–095**

It is important to note that a beneficiary of a discretionary trust is also protected in each of these three ways. Even though such a party has no entitlement to any specific part of the trust property, as T owes a duty to B in relation to the trust property, B is protected in T's insolvency; and B may be able to ensure that C does not use the property for C's own benefit but instead transfers the property to a new T to hold on the terms of the original discretionary trust[201]; and B can also, if acting with the consent of the other beneficiaries of the discretionary trust, impose a duty on T in relation to the new property acquired by T by the use of the initial trust property. It therefore seems that, whether the trust is discretionary or not, the three key advantages to B are based not on B's having a current entitlement to the full enjoyment or benefit of any specific property, but rather on B's holding a right that correlates to T's duty not to use particular property other than in compliance with the terms of the trust. **1–096**

There is a long-standing and continuing controversy over the nature of B's interest under a trust: is B best seen as having a purely personal right against the trustee for the time being of the trust; or as having a property right in the trust property; or as having some other type of right, such as a right in relation to the rights held by the trustee? Different views are possible, and different practical consequences flow from an acceptance of each view, so the debate is not of merely academic interest. We will examine it in detail in Chapter 17. **1–097**

---

196 See para.1–048.
197 See para.1–048.
198 See further paras 12–0057ff.
199 See para.1–067.
200 See further para.2–057.
201 See, e.g. *Commissioner for Stamp Duties v Livingston* [1965] A.C. 694 at 714, where it was accepted that a residuary beneficiary under an unadministered estate can assert "the estate's right of property": the same must be true of a beneficiary of a discretionary trust.

### (2) Influence on the Operation of the Trust

1-098 It might be thought that where an express trust has been set up by S, B is merely a passive recipient of S's bounty, and so has little influence on the operation of the trust. We have seen, however, that this is not the case. First, in English law at least, the *Saunders v Vautier* principle[202] allows all of the beneficiaries of a trust, acting together, to call for the trust property to be transferred to them by the trustees, even if such a transfer would be inconsistent with the conditions that S sought to impose on particular beneficiaries' access to the trust property.[203] Secondly, even if T acts in a way which is inconsistent with the terms of the trust, B can adopt that transaction and thus compel T to hold any rights acquired as a result of T's action on the terms of the initial trust.[204] Thirdly, and more generally, the duties imposed on T by the terms of the trust correlate to rights held by B, and so it is B who has the ultimate power to police the trust: even though a court may intervene to execute a trust,[205] it will only do so at B's invitation.

## 3. Trusts in Practice

1-099 We have seen in this chapter that the trust is used in a very wide range of contexts, and for a very wide range of purposes. There is a conception of the "traditional" trust[206] as a vehicle for allocating rights to the benefit of land amongst members and generations of a settlor's family, and trusts are still used for that purpose today. Yet the trust is also vital in modern commercial practice: we have seen, for example, that it provides the basis of the system of intermediated securitisation which is used, for example, for trading in shares[207]; a trust can also arise, often for a very short time, as part of a larger commercial transaction, as when a solicitor holds money advanced by a lender for the specific purpose of acquiring land.[208] It would be impossible to begin to describe all the many contexts in which the trust is used; indeed, one of the great strengths of the trust is its ability to develop over time and adapt to new demands,[209] and so such a list would very quickly be out of date.

1-100 Whilst not forgetting the importance of constructive and resulting trusts, it seems helpful to conclude this introduction by providing a precedent used by lawyers in assisting a settlor to create the type of modern express trust that we have discussed at various points in this chapter.[210]

### A Modern Discretionary Trust Precedent from J. Kessler, *Drafting Trusts and Will Trusts*, 12th edn (Sweet & Maxwell, 2014)

1-101 This Trust is made [date] between:

1 [Name of settlor] of [address] ("the Settlor") of the one part and

2 2.1 [Name of first trustee] of [address] and
2.2 [Name of second trustee] of [address]

("the Original Trustees") of the other part.

---

[202] (1841) 4 Beav. 115. See paras 7-004—7-029.

[203] Note too that a variation of the terms of the trust may be possible, where sought by B, under the Variation of Trusts Act 1958: see paras 7-047ff.

[204] See para.1-067.

[205] See para.4-138.

[206] See para.1-045 and, e.g. *A.I.B. Group (U.K.) Plc v Mark Redler & Co (a firm)* [2014] 3 W.L.R. 1367 at [67] per Lord Toulson.

[207] See para.1-071 and, e.g. *Re Lehman Brothers International (Europe)* [2010] EWHC 2914 at [225].

[208] See, e.g. *Twinsectra v Yardley* [2002] 2 A.C. 164 (extracted at paras 5-036ff) and *A.I.B. Group (U.K.) Plc v Mark Redler & Co (a firm)* [2014] 3 W.L.R. 1367.

[209] See para.1-041.

[210] See paras 1-041—1-045 and 1-091—1-092.

Whereas:

1 The Settlor has [two] children:

1.1 [Adam Smith] ("[Adam]") who was born on [date] and
1.2 [Mary Smith] ("[Mary]") who was born on [date].

2 This Trust shall be known as the [Name-of-settlor Trust 2014].

Now this deed witnesses as follows:

**1 Definitions**

In this Trust: 1–102

1.1 **"The Beneficiaries"** means:

1.1.1 The descendants of the Settlor.
1.1.2 The Spouses of the descendants of the Settlor.
1.1.3 The Surviving Spouses of the descendants of the Settlor.
1.1.4 The Surviving Spouse of the Settlor.
1.1.5 Any Person or class of Persons added to the class of Beneficiaries by the Trustees by deed with the consent in writing of:

1.1.5.1 the Settlor or
1.1.5.2 two Beneficiaries (if the Settlor has died or has no capacity to consent).

1.2 **"Spouse"** includes a civil partner within the meaning of section 1 Civil Partnership Act 2004 and a person is a "**Surviving Spouse**" whether or not they have remarried or entered into another civil partnership.
1.3 **"Person"** Includes a person anywhere in the world and includes a Trustee.
1.4 **"The Trustees"** means the Original Trustees or the trustees of this Trust for the time being.
1.5 **"The Trust Fund"** means:

1.5.1 property transferred to the Trustees to hold on the terms of this Trust; and
1.5.2 all property from time to time representing the above.

1.6 **"The Trust Period"** means the period of 125 years beginning with the date of this Trust.
1.7 **"Trust Property"** means any part of the Trust Fund.

**2 Trust Income**

During the Trust Period and subject to the Overriding Powers below: 1–103

2.1 The Trustees may accumulate the whole or part of the income of the Trust Fund. That income shall be added to the Trust Fund.
2.2 The Trustees shall pay or apply the remainder of the income to or for the benefit of any Beneficiaries, as the Trustees think fit.

**3 Overriding Powers**

The Trustees shall have the following powers ("Overriding Powers"): 1–104

3.1 *Power of appointment*

3.1.1 The Trustees may appoint that they shall hold any Trust Property for the benefit of any Beneficiaries, on such terms as the Trustees think fit.
3.1.2 An appointment may create any provisions and in particular:

3.1.2.1 discretionary trusts;
3.1.2.2 dispositive or administrative powers;

exercisable by any Person.

3.1.3 An appointment shall be made by deed and may be revocable or irrevocable.

3.2 *Transfer of Trust Property to another trust*

3.2.1 The Trustees may by deed declare that they hold any Trust Property on trust to transfer it to trustees of another trust, wherever established, to hold on the terms of that trust, freed and released from the terms of this Trust.

3.2.2 The Trustees shall only exercise this power if:

3.2.2.1 every Person who may benefit is (or would if living be) a Beneficiary; or

3.2.2.2 with the consent in writing of

(a) the Settlor, or

(b) two Beneficiaries (after the death of the Settlor).

3.3 *Power of advancement*

The Trustees may pay or apply any Trust Property for the advancement or benefit of any Beneficiary.

3.4 The Overriding Powers shall be exercisable only:

3.4.1 during the Trust Period; and

3.4.2 at a time when there are at least two Trustees, or the Trustee is a company carrying on a business which consists of or includes the management of trusts.

**4 Default Clause**

**1–105** Subject to that, the Trust Fund shall be held on trust for [Adam and Mary in equal shares - or specify default trusts as appropriate] absolutely.

**5 Appointment of Trustees**

**1–106** The power of appointing trustees is exercisable by the Settlor during [his] life and by will.

**6 Further Provisions**

**1–107** The provisions set out in the schedule below shall have effect.
[For a shorter form, say instead:
"The standard provisions and all of the special provisions of the Society of Trust and Estate Practitioners (2nd Edition) shall apply."
And omit the schedule.]

**7 Exclusion of Settlor and Spouse**

**1–108** Notwithstanding anything else in this Trust, no power conferred by this Trust shall be exercisable, and no provision shall operate so as to allow Trust Property or its income to become payable to or applicable for the benefit of the Settlor or the Spouse of the Settlor in any circumstances whatsoever.

**8 Irrevocability**

**1–109** This Trust is irrevocable.
In witness, [etc.]

THE SCHEDULE: FURTHER PROVISIONS

**1 Additional powers**

**1–110** The Trustees have the following additional powers:

1.1 *Investment*

1.1.1 The Trustees may make any kind of investment that they could make if they were absolutely entitled to the Trust Fund. In particular the Trustees may invest in land in any part of the world and unsecured loans.

1.1.2 The Trustees may invest in speculative or hazardous investments but this power may only be exercised at the time when there are at least two Trustees, or the Trustee is a company carrying on a business which consists of or includes the management of trusts.

1.2 *Joint property*

The Trustees may acquire property jointly with any Person and may blend Trust Property with other property.

1.3 *General power of management and disposition*

The Trustees may effect any transaction relating to the management or disposition of Trust Property as if they were absolutely entitled to it.

1.4 *Improvement*

The Trustees may develop or improve Trust Property in any way. Capital expenses need not be repaid out of income under section 84(2) of the Settled Land Act 1925, if the Trustees think fit.

1.5 *Income and capital*

1.5.1 The Trustees may acquire:

1.5.1.1 wasting assets and
1.5.1.2 assets which yield little or no income

for investment or any other purpose.

1.5.2 The Trustees are under no duty to procure distributions from a company in which they are interested.

1.5.3 The Trustees may pay taxes and other expenses out of capital or income whether or not they would otherwise be so payable.

1.5.4 Generally, the Trustees are under no duty to hold a balance between conflicting interests of Beneficiaries.

1.5.5 Income may be set aside and invested to answer any liabilities which in the opinion of the Trustees ought to be borne out of income or to meet depreciation of the capital value of any Trust Property. In particular, income may be applied for a leasehold sinking fund policy.

1.6 *Application of trust capital as income*

The Trustees may apply Trust Property as if it were income arising in the current year. In particular, the Trustees may pay such income to an Income Beneficiary as his income, for the purpose of augmenting his income.

"**Income Beneficiary**" here means a Person to whom income of the Property is payable (as of right or at the discretion of the Trustees).

1.7 *Use of trust property*

1.7.1 The Trustees may acquire any interest in property anywhere in the world for occupation or use by an Income Beneficiary.

1.7.2 The Trustees may permit an Income Beneficiary to occupy or enjoy the use of Trust Property on such terms as they think fit.

1.7.3 The Trustees may lend trust money to an Income Beneficiary. The loan may be interest free and unsecured, or on such terms as the Trustees think fit. The Trustees may charge Trust Property as security for any debts or obligations of an Income Beneficiary.

1.7.4 "**Income Beneficiary**" here means a Person to whom income of the Property is payable (as of right or at the discretion of the Trustees).

1.7.5 This paragraph does not restrict any right of Beneficiaries to occupy land under the Trusts of Land and Appointment of Trustees Act 1996.

1.8 *Trade*

The Trustees may carry on a trade, in any part of the world, alone or in partnership.

1.9 *Borrowing*

The Trustees may borrow money for investment or any other purpose. Money borrowed shall be treated as Trust Property.

1.10 *Delegation*

A Trustee or the Trustees jointly (or other Person in a fiduciary position) may authorise any Person to exercise all or any functions on such terms as to remuneration and other matters as they think fit. A Trustee (or other Person in a fiduciary capacity) shall not be responsible for the default of that Person (even if the delegation was not strictly necessary or convenient) provided he took reasonable care in his selection and supervision. None of the restrictions on delegation in sections 12 to 15 Trustee Act 2000 shall apply.

1.11 *Nominees and custodians*

1.11.1 The Trustees may appoint a Person to act as their nominee in relation to such of the assets of the trust as they may determine. They may take such steps as are necessary to secure that those assets are vested in the nominee.

1.11.2 The Trustees may appoint a Person to act as custodian in relation to such of the assets of the trust as they may determine. The Trustees may give the custodian custody of the assets and any documents or records concerning the assets. The Trustees are not obliged to appoint a custodian of securities payable to bearer.

1.11.3 The Trustees may appoint a Person to act as nominee or custodian on such terms as to remuneration and other matters as they may think fit.

1.12 *Place of administration*

The Trustees may carry on the administration of this Trust anywhere they think fit.

1.13 *Indemnities*

The Trustees may indemnify any Person for any liability relating to the Trust.

1.14 *Security*

The Trustees may mortgage or charge Trust Property as security for any liability incurred by them as Trustees (and may grant a floating charge so far as the law allows).

1.15 *Supervision of company*

The Trustees are under no duty to enquire into the conduct of a company in which they are interested, unless they have knowledge of circumstances which call for inquiry.

1.16 *Appropriation*

The Trustees may appropriate Trust Property to any Person or class of Persons in or towards the satisfaction of their interest in the Trust Fund.

1.17 *Receipt by charities*

Where Trust Property is to be paid or transferred to a charity or non-charitable association or company, the receipt of the treasurer or appropriate officer of the organisation shall be a complete discharge to the Trustees.

1.18 *Release of powers*

The Trustees (or other Person in a fiduciary position) may by deed release wholly or in part any of their rights or functions and (if applicable) so as to bind their successors.

1.19 *Ancillary powers*

The Trustees may do anything which is incidental or conducive to the exercise of their functions.

1.20 *Power to pay insurance premiums out of income*

The Trustees may pay premiums of any insurance policy out of income.

1.21 *Waiver of income*

The Trustees may waive the payment of income before it becomes due.

MINORS

1.22 Where the Trustees may apply income for the benefit of a minor, they may do so by paying the income to the minor's parent or guardian on behalf of the minor, or to the minor if the minor has attained the age of 16. The Trustees are under no duty to inquire into the use of the income unless they have knowledge of circumstances which call for inquiry. **1–111**

1.23 Where the Trustees may apply income for the benefit of a minor, they may do so by resolving that they hold that income on trust for the minor absolutely and:

1.23.1 The Trustees may apply that income for the benefit of the minor during his minority.
1.23.2 The Trustees shall transfer the residue of that income to the minor on attaining the age of 18.
1.23.3 For investment and other administrative purposes that income shall be treated as Trust Property.

MENTALLY HANDICAPPED BENEFICIARY

Where income or capital is payable to a Beneficiary who does not have the mental capacity to appoint an attorney under a lasting power of attorney which related to the property and affairs of the Beneficiary, the Trustees may (subject to the directions of the Court or a deputy appointed under the Mental Capacity Act whose powers include receiving such income or capital) apply that income or capital for the benefit of the Beneficiary. **1–112**

DISCLAIMER

A Person may disclaim his interest in this Trust wholly or in part. **1–113**

CONFLICTS OF INTEREST

1.24 In this paragraph: **1–114**

1.24.1 "**Fiduciary**" means a Person subject to fiduciary duties under the Trust.
1.24.2 "An Independent Trustee", in relation to a Person, means a Trustee who is not:

1.24.2.1 a brother, sister, ancestor, descendant or dependent of the Person;
1.24.2.2 a spouse or Civil Partner of paragraph .1.2.1 above, or a spouse or Civil Partner of the Person;
1.24.2.3 a company controlled by one or more of any of the above.

1.25 Subject to subparagraph 3 below a Fiduciary may:

1.25.1 enter into a transaction with the Trustees, or
1.25.2 be interested in an arrangement in which the Trustees are or might have been interested, or
1.25.3 act (or not act) in any other circumstances;

even though his fiduciary duty under the Trust conflicts with other duties or with his personal interest.

1.26 Subparagraph .2 above only has effect if:

1.26.1 the Fiduciary first discloses to the Trustees the nature and extent of any material interest conflicting with his fiduciary duties, and
1.26.2 there is in relation to the Fiduciary an Independent Trustee in respect of whom there is no conflict of interest, and he considers that the transaction arrangement or action is not contrary to the general interest of the Trust.

1.27 The powers of the Trustees may be used to benefit a Trustee (to the same extent as if he were not a Trustee) provided that there is in relation to that Trustee an Independent Trustee in respect of whom there is no conflict of interest.

ABSOLUTE DISCRETION CLAUSE

1–115 1.28 The powers of the Trustees may be exercised:

1.28.1 at their absolute discretion; and
1.28.2 from time to time as occasion requires.

1.29 The Trustees are not under any duty to consult with any Beneficiaries or to give effect to the wishes of any Beneficiaries.

TRUSTEE REMUNERATION

1–116 1.30 A Trustee acting in a professional capacity is entitled to receive reasonable remuneration out of the Trust Fund for any services that the Trustee provides to or on behalf of this Trust.

1.31 For this purpose, a Trustee acts in a professional capacity if the Trustee acts in the course of a profession or business which consists of or includes the provision of services in connection with:

1.31.1 the management or administration of trusts generally or a particular kind of trust, or
1.31.2 any particular aspect of the management or administration of trusts generally or a particular kind of trust.

1.32 The Trustees may make arrangements to remunerate themselves for work done for a company connected with the Trust Fund.

COMMISSIONS AND BANK CHARGES

1–117 1.33 A Person may retain any reasonable commission or profit in respect of any transaction relating to this Trust even though that commission or profit was procured by an exercise of fiduciary powers (by that Person or some other Person) provided that:

1.33.1 The Person would in the normal course of business receive and retain the commission or profit on such transaction.
1.33.2 The receipt of the commission or profit shall be disclosed to the Trustees.

1.34 A bank may make loans to the Trustees and generally provide banking services upon its usual terms and shall not be liable to account for any profit so made even though the receipt of such profit was procured by an exercise of fiduciary powers (by the bank or some other Person).

LIABILITY OF TRUSTEES

1–118 1.35 The duty of reasonable care (set out in s.1, Trustee Act 2000) applies to all the functions of the Trustees.

1.36 A Trustee shall not be liable for a loss to the Trust Fund unless that loss was caused by his own fraud or negligence.

1.37 A Trustee shall not be liable for acting in accordance with the advice of Counsel, of at least ten years' standing, with respect to the Trust. The Trustees may in particular conduct legal proceedings in accordance with such advice without obtaining a Court Order. A Trustee may recover from the Trust Fund any expenses where he has acted in accordance with such advice.

1.38 The above sub-paragraph does not apply:

1.38.1 if the Trustee knows or has reasonable cause to suspect that the advice was given in ignorance of material facts;
1.38.2 if proceedings are pending to obtain the decision of the court on the matter;
1.38.3 in relation to a Trustee who has a personal interest in the subject matter of the advice; or
1.38.4 in relation to a Trustee who has committed a breach of trust relating to the subject matter of the advice.

1.39 The Trustees may distribute Trust Property or income in accordance with this Trust but without having ascertained that there is no Person who is or may be entitled to any interest therein by virtue of a relationship unknown to the Trustees. The Trustees shall not be liable to such a Person unless they have notice of his claim at the time of the distribution.

1.40 This paragraph does not prejudice any right of any Person to follow property or income into the hands of any Person, other than a purchaser, who may have received it.

APPOINTMENT AND RETIREMENT OF TRUSTEES

1.41 A Person may be appointed Trustee of the Trust even though he has no connection with the United Kingdom. **1–119**

1.42 A Trustee may be discharged even though there is neither a trust corporation nor two Persons to act as trustees provided that there remains at least one trustee.

CHANGE OF GOVERNING LAW

The Trustees may during the Trust Period by deed with the consent of the Settlor during his life or of two Beneficiaries after his death declare that from the date of such declaration: **1–120**

1.43 The law of any Qualifying Jurisdiction governs the validity of this Trust, and its construction, effects and administration, or any severable aspect of this Trust; and

1.44 The courts of any Qualifying Jurisdiction have exclusive jurisdiction in any proceedings involving rights or obligations under this Trust.
In this paragraph a "Qualifying Jurisdiction" is one which recognises trusts (as defined in the Hague Convention on the Law Applicable to Trusts and on their Recognition).

**Questions**

1. Which party has most influence in the operation of a trust: the settlor, the trustee, or the beneficiary?
2. Does the nature of equity as a supplementary body of rules help us to understand the nature of the trust?
3. "Any attempt to provide a general definition of the trust is doomed to failure." Do you agree?
4. "Significantly, a trust, unlike a corporation, has no legal personality." **Discuss**.

# PART II

# CREATION OF EXPRESS TRUSTS

# 2
# CONSTITUTION OF TRUSTS

## 1. Introduction

In this chapter and the four that follow, we consider various rules governing the creation of express trusts. In this chapter, our focus is on the situation where a settlor wishes to create an express trust by transferring property to a trustee to hold on trust for a beneficiary. This is not the only means, however, by which a party may acquire a beneficial interest under a trust. Such a right will also arise if a settlor retains property, but declares that she holds that property on trust for the beneficiary. In addition, a party may instead acquire a beneficial interest not under an express trust, but under a trust imposed by law. It is important to keep those two possibilities in mind when considering cases where a settlor wishes to create an express trust by transferring property to a trustee to hold on trust for a beneficiary. If it turns out that the settlor has not successfully constituted the trust as intended, the planned beneficiary will still acquire a beneficial interest if she can show instead: (i) that the settlor in fact retained the property and declared a trust of it; or (ii) that a resulting or constructive trust of the property has arisen in her favour. **2–001**

In Chapter 3, we will examine the formality requirements that govern the means by which a party can acquire a beneficial interest under a trust. In Chapter 4, we will look at the rules which hold that three things must be certain before it can be said that a valid trust has been created: the settlor's intention to create the trust; the subject-matter of the trust; and the objects of the trust. In Chapter 5, we consider the principle that a valid trust must have a beneficiary. Consistently with this principle, trusts for private purposes are not generally valid under English law; exceptionally, however, trusts for charitable purposes are valid, and these are discussed in Chapter 6. **2–002**

## 2. Completely Constituted Trusts

### *A. Transferring Property to Trustees*

In this chapter, our focus is on the situation where a settlor wishes to create an express trust by transferring property to a trustee to hold on trust for a beneficiary. This means of creating a trust can can take effect (i.e. the trust can be "completely constituted") only if the property is indeed transferred to the trustee. So, if formality rules govern the transfer of such property, those formality rules must be satsfied. For example, if the subject matter of the trust is legal title to registered land, the conveyance to the trustees must take the form of a deed,[1] and the transfer must be entered onto the Land Register.[2] **2–003**

[1] Law of Property Act 1925 s.52.
[2] Land Registration Act 2002 ss.29 and 30.

Legal title to chattels must be transferred by delivery or by deed of gift. A bill of exchange must be transferred by endorsement[3] and a copyright by writing.[4] If the intended trust property is itself an equitable interest under another trust, then again the transfer must be in writing.[5]

**2-004** In the case of testamentary trusts, the deceased's property is transferred to the settlor's executors, or the administrators of her estate, by virtue of her death.[6] Once those personal representatives have paid all the debts owed by the deceased, as well as relevant taxes and expenses of administering the estate, they are placed under equitable obligations[7] to transfer the relevant property according to the terms of the deceased's will, or, in the event of intestacy, according to the statutory rules as to distribution.[8] So, if the deceased made a valid will instructing that property should go to trustees to hold for a beneficiary, that trust will be constituted by means of a transfer to the trustees, as long as debts, taxes and expenses do not exhaust the relevant property. This testamentary trust will be completely constituted even if the named trustee disclaims (i.e. refuses to accept the property) or is unable to take the property because of incapacity or death.[9] In such a case, whoever succeeds to the legal title to the property will take it subject to the trust: once a trust is constituted, equity will not allow it to fail for want of a trustee.[10]

## B. Self-Declaration of Trust

**2-005** If a settlor wishes to create an express inter vivos trust,[11] it is also possible to do so by retaining property and declaring that she will hold that property as trustee upon certain trusts. In such a case, of course, no transfer of the trust property is required. The three certainties must be present[12]: in particular, it must be clear that the settlor intended to hold the property subject to a duty to use it for the benefit of others, or for a charitable purpose. There is no need for a particular formula or phrase to be used and the settlor may indeed be unaware of the concept of a trust: the requirement, as we will see in Chapter 4,[13] is for some form of expression which in the circumstances shows that the settlor intended to hold the property subject to a binding duty.[14]

## C. The Basic Rule: An Unsuccessful Transfer to Trustees Is Not a Self-Declaration of Trust

**2-006** We have seen so far that there are two different ways in which a settlor may create an express trust: (i) by transfer to trustees; (ii) by self-declaration. Each method results in the acquisition of a beneficial interest by the beneficiary; but there is a fundamental difference between them. In the former case, the settlor no longer holds the property, and the beneficiary's rights are against the transferees of the property; in the latter case, the settlor retains the property, and the beneficiaries' rights are against

---

3 Bills of Exchange Act 1882 s.31; Cheques Act 1957 ss.1, 2.
4 Copyright Designs and Patents Act 1988 s.90(3).
5 Law of Property Act 1925 s.53(1)(c): see paras 3-050ff.
6 Administration of Estates Act 1925 ss.1, 9, 25, and 32.
7 *Commissioner of Stamp Duties v Livingston* [1965] A.C. 694; *Marshall v Kerr* [1995] 1 A.C. 148.
8 See Administration of Estates Act 1925 s.46.
9 *Sonley v Clock Makers' Co* (1780) 1 Bro. C.C. 81; *Re Smirthwaite's Trusts* (1871) L.R. 11 Eq. 251.
10 *Re Armitage* [1972] Ch. 438 at 445 (where it is pointed out that very exceptionally the trust can fail if the personality of the named trustee is vital to the carrying out of the trust).
11 An inter vivos trust takes effect during the settlor's life and so is different from a testamentary trust.
12 See Ch.4.
13 See para.4-014.
14 See, e.g. *Paul v Constance* [1977] 1 W.L.R. 527 (extracted at paras 4-017–4-029).

her. That crucial difference means that, if the settlor intends to create a trust by means of a transfer to trustees, but fails to make that transfer, those facts alone do *not* permit the intended beneficiary to claim that an express trust has arisen by means of a self-declaration of trust by the settlor. It is clear, after all, that the settlor had no such intention to hold property on trust for the beneficiary, as she rather intended to transfer the property to trustees to hold on trust. This very important principle is often known as the rule in *Milroy v Lord*.

*Milroy v Lord*

Court of Appeal in Chancery (1862) 4 De G. F. & J. 264

Thomas Medley executed what was treated as a voluntary deed,[15] which purported to assign 50 shares in the Louisiana Bank to Samuel Lord upon trust for the benefit of the plaintiffs. The shares were transferable only by entry in the books of the bank; but no such transfer was ever made. At the relevant time Samuel Lord held a general power of attorney authorising him to transfer Thomas Medley's shares, and Thomas Medley, after the execution of the settlement, gave him a further power of attorney authorising him to receive the dividends on the bank shares. Thomas Medley lived for three years after the execution of the deed, during which period the dividends were received by Samuel Lord and remitted by him to the plaintiffs, sometimes directly and sometimes through Thomas Medley. There was thus a perfect gift of the dividends. Shortly after the execution of the deed, the settlor had delivered to Samuel Lord the certificates for the shares; and on the death of the settlor, Samuel Lord gave up the certificates to the settlor's executor. The shares stood in the settlor's name before and at the time of his death. At first instance Stuart V.C. held that a trust had been created for the plaintiffs but this decision was reversed on an appeal by the executor. 2–007

TURNER L.J. (with whom KNIGHT-BRUCE L.J. agreed): Under the circumstances of this case, it would be difficult not to feel a strong disposition to give effect to this settlement to the fullest extent, and certainly I have spared no pains to find the means of doing so, consistently with what I apprehend to be the law of the court; but, after full and anxious consideration, I find myself unable to do so. I take the law of this court to be well settled, that, in order to render a voluntary settlement valid and effectual, the settlor must have done everything which, according to the nature of the property comprised in the settlement, was necessary to be done in order to transfer the property and render the settlement binding upon him. He may, of course, do this by actually transferring the property to the persons for whom he intends to provide, and the provision will then be effectual, and it will be equally effectual if he transfers the property to a trustee for the purposes of the settlement, or declares that he himself holds it in trust for those purposes; and if the property be personal, the trust may, as I apprehend, be declared either in writing or by parol; but, in order to render the settlement binding, one or other of these modes must, as I understand the law of this court, be resorted to, for there is no equity in this court to perfect an imperfect gift. The cases, I think, go further to this extent: that if the settlement is intended to be effectuated by one of the modes to which I have referred, the court will not give effect to it by applying another of those modes. If it is intended to take effect by transfer, the court will not hold the intended transfer to operate as a declaration of trust, for then every imperfect instrument would be made effectual by being converted into a perfect trust. These are the principles by which, as I conceive, this case must be tried. 2–008

Applying, then, these principles to the case, there is not here any transfer either of the one class of shares or of the other to the objects of the settlement, and the question therefore must be whether a valid and effectual trust in favour of those objects was created in the defendant Samuel Lord or in the settlor himself as to all or any of these shares. Now it is plain that it was not the purpose of this settlement, or the intention of the settlor, to constitute himself a trustee of the bank shares. The intention was that the trust should be vested in the defendant Samuel Lord, and I think therefore that we should not be justified in holding that by the settlement, or by any parol declaration made by the settlor, he himself became a trustee of these shares for the purposes of the settlement. By doing so we should be converting the settlement or the parol 2–009

15 The deed (apparently executed in Louisiana) was expressed to be made in consideration of one dollar. In *Prest v Petrodel Resources Ltd* [2013] 2 A.C. 415 at [49], a transfer for a nominal consideration of £1 was also treated as gratuitous for the purpose of applying presumptions as to resulting trusts: see para.4–025.

declaration to a purpose wholly different from that which was intended to be effected by it and, as I have said, creating a perfect trust out of an imperfect transaction. . .

2-010 The more difficult question is whether the defendant Samuel Lord did not become a trustee of these shares. Upon this question I have felt considerable doubt; but in the result, I have come to the conclusion that no perfect trust was ever created in him. The shares, it is clear, were never legally vested in him; and the only ground on which he can be held to have become a trustee of them is that he held a power of attorney under which he might have transferred them into his own name; but he held that power of attorney as the agent of the settlor; and if he had been sued by the plaintiffs as trustee of the settlement for an account under the trust, and to compel him to transfer the shares into his own name as trustee, I think he might well have said: "These shares are not vested in me; I have no power over them except as the agent of the settlor, and without his express directions I cannot be justified in making the proposed transfer, in converting an intended into an actual settlement." A court of equity could not, I think, decree the agent of the settlor to make the transfer, unless it could decree the settlor himself to do so, and it is plain that no such decree could have been made against the settlor. In my opinion, therefore, this decree cannot be maintained as to the fifty Louisiana Bank shares. . .

2-011 In a case such as *Milroy v Lord*, it is only natural for a judge to feel "a strong disposition to give effect to this settlement to the fullest extent"[16]; after all, the settlor did intend that the claimant would acquire a beneficial interest. The rule applied in that case must, however, be correct. Given that the settlor clearly intended to set up the trust by means of a transfer to a trustee, it would be inconsistent with that specific intention to find a self-declaration of trust by the settlor.

## *D. The Scope of the Basic Rule*

### i. Finding a Genuine Self-Declaration

2-012 The rule in *Milroy v Lord*, however, applies only if it is the case that the settlor intended to set up the trust by means of a transfer to trustees, and failed to make that transfer. The rule does not prevent a court from finding that, on the facts, the settlor instead intended to, and indeed did, make a self-declaration of trust. Of course, when interpreting the facts of a particular case, a court may be influenced by the "strong disposition" to give effect to the planned trust, and therefore find that the settlor intended a self-declaration rather than a transfer. That seems to have been the case, for example, in *T. Choithram International SA v Pagarani*.[17]

*T. Choithram International SA v Pagarani*

Privy Council [2001] 1 W.L.R. 1

2-013 Pagarani (referred to in the Privy Councils' advice as TCP) was a wealthy businessman who was dying of cancer. A month before he died, he organised an elaborate ceremony at his London bedside to establish a philanthropic foundation in the form of a Jersey trust of which he was settlor and one of the trustees. He executed the trust deed in the presence of three (of the other six) trustees and of his accountant and the First Secretary of the Indian High Commission. They recollected him as orally making an immediate absolute gift of all his wealth in his shareholdings and credit balances with four British Virgin Island companies by stating that: "I give to the Foundation". However, English law does not recognise foundations as legal persons like companies, and legal title to the property was not vested in the other trustees before Pagarani died. On his death some of his children therefore sought to establish that the attempted gift was ineffective.

2-014 LORD BROWNE-WILKINSON: . . . Their Lordships then turn to the central and most important question: on the basis that TCP intended to make an immediate absolute gift "to the foundation" but had not vested

[16] (1862) 4 De G.F. & J. 264 at 274 (extracted at para.2-008).

[17] See too *Paul v Constance* [1977] 1 W.L.R. 527, reproduced at paras 4-014ff.

the gifted property in all the trustees of the foundation, are the trusts of the foundation trust deed enforceable against the deposits and the shares or is this (as the judge and the Court of Appeal held) a case where there has been an imperfect gift which cannot be enforced against TCP's estate whatever TCP's intentions.

The judge and the Court of Appeal understandably took the view that a perfect gift could only be made in one of two ways, viz (a) by a transfer of the gifted asset to the donee, accompanied by an intention in the donor to make a gift; or (b) by the donor declaring himself to be a trustee of the gifted property for the donee. In case (a), the donor has to have done everything necessary to be done which is within his own power to do in order to transfer the gifted asset to the donee. If the donor has not done so, the gift is incomplete since the donee has no equity to perfect an imperfect gift:[18] Moreover, the court will not give a benevolent construction so as to treat ineffective words of outright gift as taking effect as if the donor had declared himself a trustee for the done.[19] So, it is said, in this case TCP used words of gift to the foundation (not words declaring himself a trustee): unless he transferred the shares and deposits so as to vest title in all the trustees, he had not done all that he could in order to effect the gift. It therefore fails. Further it is said that it is not possible to treat TCP's words of gift as a declaration of trust because they make no reference to trusts. Therefore the case does not fall within either of the possible methods by which a complete gift can be made and the gift fails. **2–015**

Though it is understandable that the courts below should have reached this conclusion since the case does not fall squarely within either of the methods normally stated as being the only possible ways of making a gift, their Lordships do not agree with that conclusion. The facts of this case are novel and raise a new point. It is necessary to make an analysis of the rules of equity as to complete gifts. Although equity will not aid a volunteer, it will not strive officiously to defeat a gift. This case falls between the two common form situations mentioned above. Although the words used by TCP are those normally appropriate to an outright gift—"I give to X"—in the present context there is no breach of the principle in *Milroy v Lord* if the words of TCP's gift (ie to the foundation) are given their only possible meaning in this context. The foundation has no legal existence apart from the trust declared by the foundation trust deed. Therefore the words "I give to the foundation" can only mean "I give to the trustees of the foundation trust deed to be held by them on the trusts of foundation trust deed". Although the words are apparently words of outright gift they are essentially words of gift on trust. **2–016**

But, it is said, TCP vested the properties not in *all* the trustees of the foundation but only in one, i.e. TCP. Since equity will not aid a volunteer, how can a court order be obtained vesting the gifted property in the whole body of trustees on the trusts of the foundation? Again, this represents an over-simplified view of the rules of equity. Until comparatively recently the great majority of trusts were voluntary settlements under which beneficiaries were volunteers having given no value. Yet beneficiaries under a trust, although volunteers, can enforce the trust against the trustees. Once a trust relationship is established between trustee and beneficiary, the fact that a beneficiary has given no value is irrelevant. It is for this reason that the type of perfected gift referred to in class (b) above is effective since the donor has constituted himself a trustee for the donee who can as a matter of trust law enforce that trust. **2–017**

What then is the position here where the trust property is vested in one of the body of trustees, viz. TCP? In their Lordship's view there should be no question. TCP has, in the most solemn circumstances, declared that he is giving (and later that he has given) property to a trust which he himself has established and of which he has appointed himself to be a trustee. All this occurs at one composite transaction taking place on 17 February. There can in principle be no distinction between the case where the donor declares himself to be sole trustee for a donee or a purpose and the case where he declares himself to be one of the trustees for that donee or purpose. In both cases his conscience is affected and it would be unconscionable and contrary to the principles of equity to allow such a donor to resile from his gift. Say, in the present case, that TCP had survived and tried to change his mind by denying the gift. In their Lordship's view it is impossible to believe that he could validly deny that he was a trustee for the purposes of the foundation in the light of all the steps that he had taken to assert that position and to assert his trusteeship. In their Lordship's judgment in the absence of special factors where one out of a larger body of trustees has the trust property vested in him he is bound by the trust and must give effect to it by transferring the trust property into the name of all the trustees.[20] **2–018**

18 *Milroy v Lord* (1862) 4 De G.F. & J. 264; *Richards v Delbridge* (1874) L.R. 18 Eq. 11; *Re Rose, Midland Bank Executor and Trustee Co Ltd v Rose* [1949] Ch. 78; *Rose v IRC* [1952] Ch. 499.

19 *Milroy v Lord* (1862) 4 De G.F. & J. 264.

20 As it happened, the relevant companies had altered their share registers after Pagarani's death so that legal title to the

2-019 As noted by Lord Browne-Wilkinson, the facts of the *Pagarani* case were somewhat unusual. It seems that Pagarani was regarded as having said, in effect: "As sole owner of the assets and as legal trustee of the Foundation I now hold my property on trust for the charitable purposes of the Foundation." The court was able to interpret his intention in this way because the case differed from *Milroy v Lord* in two important respects. First, it was not clear that the settlor intended to establish the trust by way of transfer as, although he had an intention to make a gift to the "Foundation", the Foundation had no legal personality in English law and so no transfer could be made to it.[21] Secondly, as the settlor was one of the trustees of the Foundation, it was possible to say that the settlor did in fact intend a self-declaration of trust, and the language of a gift to the "Foundation" in fact meant that the settlor intended to hold the property on the terms of the trust set out in the Foundation's trust deed. It was therefore possible to find, consistently with the rule in *Milroy v Lord*, that the settlor had intended, and succeeded, in constituting an express trust by means of a self-declaration.[22]

2-020 It is important to note that an intention to set up a trust by way of transfer does not preclude the possibility of the settlor *also* making a self-declaration of trust, to take effect immediately and to operate in the period pending the transfer. For example, as in *Re Ralli's Will Trusts*,[23] a settlor may both promise to transfer existing and future property to trustees to hold on trust *and* also declare that particular existing property held by the settlor is, pending transfer to the trustees, to be *immediately* subject to the planned trusts. In such a case, that declaration cannot create a trust over future property not currently in the hands of the settlor, but it will operate to bind the identified, existing property of the settlor, even if the promise to transfer the property to trustees is not honoured.[24]

2-021 It is also crucial to note that, in a case where a donor simply wants to make an absolute gift to a donee (so that no trust is intended), but fails to satisfy the requirements of a valid transfer, the intention to make an absolute gift does *not* suffice for the court to find a declaration of trust by the donor.[25] In a passage which has received judicial approval,[26] Maitland analysed this important principle by considering a case in which an intending donor attempts, but fails, to make a gift by transferring property to another[27]:

> It would be an imperfect gift, and being an imperfect gift the court will not regard it as a declaration of trust. I have made quite clear that I do not intend to make myself a trustee. I mean to give. The two intentions are very different—the giver means to get rid of his rights, the man who is intending to make himself a trustee intends to retain his rights but to come under an onerous obligation. The latter intention is far rarer than the former. Men often mean to give things to their kinsfolk, they do not often mean to constitute themselves trustees. An imperfect gift is no declaration of trust.

---

shares was actually vested in the remaining six trustees. Hence the Privy Council concluded that the administrators of Pagarani's intestate estate could not claim the shares or the deposit balances with the companies.

21 Compare the discussion at paras 5–079ff of gifts to unincorporated associations.

22 See, e.g. *Curtis v Pulbrook* [2011] 1 B.C.L.C. 638 at [43], where Briggs J regarded *Pagarani* as a case in which "by a benevolent construction and effective gift or implied declaration of trust may be teased out the words used". The suggestion in *Pennington v Waine* [2002] 1 W.L.R. 2075 at [59] that the trust in *Pagarani* was a constructive one therefore seems unnecessary: see further paras 2–097ff.

23 [1964] Ch. 288 (extracted at paras 2–048—2–056).

24 See *Re Ralli's W.T.* [1964] Ch. 288 (extracted at paras 2–048—2–056). Buckley J held that Helen's existing reversionary interest under the will of her deceased father was bound by the declaration of trust, so that when it passed into possession, the rights thus acquired were held subject to the terms of the trust benefitting the children of Helen's sister.

25 See, e.g. *Richards v Delbridge* (1874) L.R. 18 Eq. 11.

26 See, e.g. *Pennington v Waine* [2002] 1 W.L.R. 2075 at [53].

27 F.W. Maitland, *Equity – A Course of Lectures*, 2nd edn (Cambridge University Press, 1936), p.73.

### ii. Where the Settlor Has Done Everything in Her Power to Effect the Planned Transfer to Trustees

#### (1) The Rule in *Re Rose*

In *Milroy v Lord*, Turner LJ stated that: 2–022

> I take the law of this court to be well settled, that, in order to render a voluntary settlement valid and effectual, the settlor must have done everything which, according to the nature of the property comprised in the settlement, was necessary to be done in order to transfer the property and render the settlement binding upon him.

In a case where a transfer to trustees is planned, that statement can be interpreted in one of two ways: either: (i) the planned transfer must occur; or (ii) the settlor must have done everything in her power to effect the transfer.

The difference between those two interpretations was crucial in the following case, where the second interpretation of Turner LJ's statement was adopted. 2–023

*Re Rose, Midland Bank Executor & Trustee Co Ltd v Rose*

Chancery Division [1949] Ch. 78

The testator, Rose, had given a number of shares in his will to Hook, but the gift was subject to a qualification: "if such shares have not been transferred to him previously to my death". The question for the court was whether particular shares had already been transferred to Hook. Rose had intended to make an *inter vivos* transfer of certain shares to Hook and had executed a transfer document in the required form and handed it, with the share certificate, to Hook. By the time of Rose's death, however, Hook had not been registered as the new holder of the shares. As a result, it was clear that legal title to the shares remained in Rose at the time of his death. The residuary legatee under the will claimed the shares on the basis that: (i) Hook had no right in the shares at the time of Rose's death; but (ii) the testamentary gift to Hook was also ineffective, as the qualification applied, as the term "transfer", in that qualification, included Rose's execution of a transfer document. Jenkins J., however, accepted an argument made on Hook's behalf that, at his death, Rose held his legal title to the shares on trust for Hook. 2–024

JENKINS J.: It is argued on behalf of the residuary legatee that the testator's transfer of the 5,000 preference shares to Mr Hook, owing to the fact that the transfer was not registered in his lifetime, was at the time of the testator's death in the state of being an incomplete or inchoate gift. I was referred to the well known case of *Milroy v Lord*, and also to the recent case of *Re Fry*.[28] Those cases, as I understand them, turn on the fact that the deceased donor had not done all in his power, according to the nature of the property given, to vest the legal interest in the property in the donee. In such circumstances it is, of course, well settled that there is no equity to complete the imperfect gift. If any act remained to be done by the donor to complete the gift at the date of the donor's death the court will not compel his personal representatives to do that act and the gift remains incomplete and fails. 2–025

In *Milroy v Lord*, the imperfection was due to the fact that the wrong form of transfer was used for the purpose of transferring certain bank shares. The document was not the appropriate document to pass any interest in the property at all. . .In this case, as I understand it, the testator had done everything in his power to divest himself of the shares in question to Mr Hook. He had executed a transfer. It is not suggested that the transfer is not in accordance with the company's regulations. He had handed that transfer together with the cerificates to Mr Hook. There was nothing else the testator could do. It is true that Mr Hook's legal title would not be perfected until the directors passed the transfer for registration, but that was not an act which the testator had to do, it was an act which depended on the discretion of the directors. Therefore it seems to me that the present case is not *in pari materia* with the two cases to which I have been referred. . . 2–026

---

28 [1946] Ch. 312.

2-027 What actually happened was that the transfer having been executed and the certificates hadned over by the testator in his lifetime, Mr Hook's title under the transfer was in fact completed by registration after the testator's death. In my judgment, therefore, the position is that the shares had been transferred to Mr Hook previously to the testator's death within the meaning of clause 3(g) of the will, and his title under the transfer to him was perfected after the death by registration, and he takes the shares comprised in the transfer by the virtue of the transfer and not under the will.

2-028 The reasoning of Jenkins J was approved by the Court of Appeal in a different case, which also happened to involve a donor called Rose. In *Re Rose, Rose v IRC*,[29] it was again necessary to determine when a transfer had occurred. The question arose this time in relation to tax. Rose had transferred shares absolutely to his wife, and also to trustees on trust. The Crown claimed estate duty on the basis that the gifts had been completed only when the shares were registered in the names of the transferees. If, however, it could be shown that the gifts had been completed at an earlier point, that estate duty would not be payable. It was therefore argued that the gifts were, in the eyes of equity at least, complete when Rose completed the required transfer forms and handed them to the donees.

2-029 The Court of Appeal (the panel included Jenkins LJ) accepted that argument, adopting the "view of the limitations of *Milroy v Lord*" espoused by Jenkins J (as he then was) in the first *Re Rose* case.[30] Lord Evershed MR stated that[31]:

> If a man executes a document tranferring all his equitable interest, say, in shares, that document, operating, and intended to operate, as a transfer, will give rise to and take effect as a trust; for the assignor will then be a trustee of the legal estate in the shares for the person in whose favour he had made an assignment of his beneficial interest. And I do not think that the case of *Milroy v Lord* is an authority which compels the court to hold that in this case—where, in the terms of Turner L.J.'s judgment, the settlor did everything which, according to the nature of the property comprised in the settlement, was necessary to be done by him in order to transfer the property—the result necessarily negatives the conclusion that, pending registration, the settlor was a trustee of the legal interest for the transferee.

2-030 Jenkins LJ added his agreement[32]:

> I agree with [Lord Evershed M.R.] that the case of *Milroy v Lord* by no means covers the question with which we have to deal in the present case. If the deceased had in truth transferred the whole of his interest in these shares so far as he could transfer the same, including such right as he could pass to his transferee to be placed on the register in respect of the shares, the question arises, what beneficial interest had he then left? The answer can only be, in my view, that he had no beneficial interest left whatever: his only remaining interest consisted in the fact that his name still stood on the register as holder of the shares; but having parted in fact with the whole of his beneficial interest, he could not, in my view, assert any beneficial title by virtue of his postion of registered holder. In other words, in my view the effect of these transactions, having regard to the form and the operation of the transfers, the nature of the property transferred, and the necessity for registration I order to perfect the legal title, coupled with the discretionary power on the part of the directors to withhold registration, must be that, pending registration, the deceased was in the position of a trustee of the legal title in the shares for the transferees.

2-031 The analysis of Jenkins J and of the Court of Appeal in the two (otherwise unconnected) *Re Rose* cases thus makes it clear that the rule in *Milroy v Lord* is limited in this way: if a donor intends to make a transfer, and has done everything in her power to effect it, equity can regard the transfer as

---

29 [1952] Ch. 499.
30 ibid., at 511 per Lord Evershed MR.
31 ibid., at 510–511.
32 ibid., at 517–518. Morris LJ agreed with both Jenkins LJ and Lord Evershed MR.

complete, with the consequence that the donee has an immediate beneficial interest and the donor holds on trust for the transferee. This analysis can apply not only where the donor plans to make an absolute gift, but also where a settlor intends to transfer property to trustees to hold on trust for B: in the latter case, it seems that the settlor then holds the property for B, on the terms of the intended trust.[33]

In *Mascall v Mascall*,[34] for example, the Court of Appeal applied the principle where a father had attempted to transfer legal title to registered land to his son. The father had executed the relevant transfer form and handed over the land certificate: "all that remained was for the son, in the ordinary way of conveyancing, to submit the transfer for stamping and then to ask the Land Registry to register his title".[35] At that stage, the transfer was regarded in equity as complete and so, although the father and son later fell out and the transfer form was returned by the Inland Revenue (to whom it had been sent for stamp duty purposes) to the father, it was no longer possible for the father to revoke the gift. Browne-Wilkinson LJ stated that[36]: **2–032**

> The basic principle underlying all the cases is that equity will not come to the aid of a volunteer. Therefore, if a donee needs to get an order from a court of equity to complete his title, he will not get it. If, on the other hand, the donee has under his control everything necessary to constitute his title completely without any further assistance from the donor, the donee needs no assistance from equity and the gift is complete. It is on that principle, which is laid down in *Re Rose*, that in equity it is held that a gift is complete as soon as the settlor or donor has done everything that the donor has to do, that is to say, as soon as the donee has within his control all those things necessary to enable him, the donee, to complete his title.

As this statement shows, care must be taken when invoking the maxim that "equity will not assist a volunteer". There are many situations in which a claimant who has given no value can acquire rights in equity. The most obvious is where a settlor successfully exercises her power to set up a trust for the claimant, either by a transfer to trustees or by a self-declaration. Once a trust has been completely constituted, the courts will give effect to it and will enforce the rights of a beneficiary, regardless of whether the beneficiary has given any value in exchange for these rights.[37] As Lord Browne-Wilkinson subsequently noted in the *Choithram* case[38]: "Once a trust relationship is established between trustee and beneficiary, the fact that a beneficiary has given no value is irrelevant". The rule in *Re Rose* similarly depends on the idea that, as the donor has done what is necessary, in the eyes of equity at least, to complete the gift, the donee acquires an equitable interest, regardless of whether she has provided any value in exchange for it. **2–033**

### (2) Justifying the Rule in *Re Rose*

As noted above,[39] the approach taken in *Re Rose* depends on adopting the second of the two possible interpretations of a statement of Turner LJ in *Milroy v Lord*.[40] The first of those interpretations is equally consistent with the result in that case and might be thought to provide a clearer fit with the **2–034**

[33] In *Re Rose, Rose v IRC* [1952] Ch. 499, for example, Rose intended two distinct transfers of shares: one to his wife absolutely, another to trustees to hold on trust, and the Court of Appeal regarded its analysis as applying in the same way to each of those intended transfers.
[34] (1985) 50 P. & C.R. 119.
[35] ibid., at 125 per Lawton LJ.
[36] ibid., at 126.
[37] *Paul v Paul* (1882) 20 Ch.D. 742.
[38] *T. Choithram International SA v Pagarani* [2001] 1 W.L.R. 1 at 12.
[39] See para.2–023.
[40] (1862) 4 De G.F. & J. 264.

logic of the reasoning in the case: if a settlor intends to set up a trust by means of a transfer of property to a trustee, that express trust can take effect only if the property is in fact transferred. The complication introduced by *Re Rose* is that a transfer can be said to be effective *in equity*, even if the conditions for the transfer of the property at common law have not been met.

**2-035** There are, however, two obvious objections to the analysis adopted in *Re Rose*. First, property is either transferred or it is not; if there are rules as to what is necessary for such a transfer (such as the need for registration in relation to shares or land), then why should equity bypass those rules and directly contradict the common law by finding that a transfer has occurred? Moreover, if the common law rules are to be ignored, how can we then tell what is necessary in equity for a transfer to occur? In *Pennington v Waine*,[41] for example, a case that also concerned a planned gift of shares, Clarke LJ held that a transfer occurred in equity as soon as the donor executed the share transfer form, even if that form was not then given to the donee;[42] in contrast, Arden LJ (with whom Schiemann LJ agreed) stated that[43]: "the ratio of *Re Rose (Rose v IRC)* was as I read it that the gifts of shares in that case were completely constituted when the donor executed share transfers and delivered them to the transferees even though they were not registered in the register of members of the company until a later date."

**2-036** The second objection to the analysis adopted in *Re Rose* is that it seems to depend on a particular transaction being effective to transfer the donor's equitable interest in property, but not her legal interest. It is clear, however, that if the donor simply owns property absolutely, it is misleading to think of her as having both a distinct legal interest and a distinct equitable interest. Equity has no reason to intervene where A simply holds a legal right to property, and, in the absence of grounds for equitable intervention, there can be no distinct equitable interest. In Lord Browne-Wilkinson's words in *Westdeutsche Landesbank Girozentrale v Islington LBC*[44]:

> A person solely entitled to the full beneficial ownership of money or property, both at law and in equity, does not enjoy an equitable interest in that property. The legal title carries with it all rights. Unless and until there is a separation of legal and equitable estates, there is no separate equitable title.

**2-037** Can a different justification be found for the approach in *Re Rose*? There are two prominent possibilities. In *Mascall v Mascall*,[45] Browne-Wilkinson LJ focussed on the point that if "the donee has under his control everything necessary to constitute his title completely without any further assistance from the donor, the donee needs no assistance from equity and the gift is complete". The idea here may be that, if, as a result of the donor's actions, the donee obtains a power, through her own actions, to acquire the relevant property, then a trust arises. This view has some academic support, but it is far from being fully worked out in the case-law, and gives rise to some difficult questions. For example, once the donee factually has the power to complete the transfer (e.g. by registration) does that mean that the trust continues even if the donee then loses that factual power (as occurred in *Mascall*, when the transferee lost possession of the transfer form)? If so, why does the fact that the donee at one point had the power to complete the transfer subject the donor to an ongoing duty?

**2-038** It could alternatively be said that where the donor has done everything necessary to complete the transaction, it would then be unconscionable for her to attempt to rescind the gift and a constructive

---

41 [2002] 1 W.L.R. 2075; extracted at paras 2-098—2-113.

42 ibid., at [106] and [110].

43 ibid., at [65].

44 [1996] A.C. 669 at 706. The case is an important authority on resulting trusts, and so is examined in detail in Ch.4: as to this specific point, see paras 4-165—4-167.

45 (1985) 50 P. & C.R. 119 at 126.

trust of the property therefore arises to give effect to his duty to make the transfer. The reasoning of Arden LJ (with whom Schiemann LJ agreed) in *Pennington v Waine*[46] seems to be consistent with that analysis. The difficulty, however, is in explaining precisely why the mere fact that the donor *tried* to make a gift then makes it unconscionable for the donor to change her mind and decide not to proceed.[47] After all, if the maxim that "equity will not assist a volunteer" means anything,[48] it means that no duty is imposed on a donor simply because she intended, and tried, to make a gift.

### iii. Where the Planned Transfer Does not Occur, but the Property Ends Up in the Hands of the Intended Trustee by Other Means.

#### (1) The Basic Rule: Only the Settlor (or Her Authorised Agent) Can Constitute a Trust

Consider a case in which the settlor, S, plans to set up a trust by transferring property to a trustee, T, to hold on trust for a beneficiary, B. It may even be that S has made a gratuitous promise to T that she will transfer a specific painting to T to hold on trust for B. S dies, however, without having made that planned transfer of the painting. Clearly the rule in *Milroy v Lord* means that B cannot claim that S held the painting on trust for B. If, however, S's title to the painting came into T's hands by some other means, should the courts then regard that trust as completely, even if coincidentally, constituted, so that B acquires the planned beneficial interest? **2–039**

The basic answer is no: like the donor of a gift, the settlor (or her duly authorised agent) must be responsible for the trust property becoming duly vested in the trustees.[49] That answer obtains even if, as in our example, S made a gratuitous promise to T to make the transfer: the point is that the gratuitous promise does not create a duty owed by S and that, in the absence of a transfer authorised by S, the planned trust has not been completely constituted. This is the result of the approach taken in the following extract. **2–040**

*Re Brooks' Settlement Trusts*

Chancery Division [1939] Ch. 993

By the terms of a marriage settlement the income of the settled fund was directed to be paid to the wife during her life and the fund was to be held in trust for such of her issue as she might by deed or will appoint; in default of any appointment the fund was to be held in trust in equal shares for all her children who being sons should attain the age of twenty-one years or being daughters should attain that age or marry. In 1929 one of her children (AT) executed a voluntary settlement whereby he assigned to Lloyds Bank as trustees, "all the part or share, parts or shares and other interest whether vested or contingent to which the settlor is now or may hereafter become entitled whether in default of appointment, or under any appointment hereafter to be made or on failure of any such appointment of and in the trust property [under the marriage settlement]". By an appointment in pursuance of her power under the marriage settlement, AT's mother in 1939 appointed him a sum of £3,517 and released her life interest. Thereupon Lloyds Bank Ltd, who had by then become trustees of the marriage settlement as well as of AT's voluntary settlement, took out a summons asking whether they should pay AT the £3,517. Farwell J. held that AT was entitled to require payment of the sum appointed, and could not be compelled to permit the bank to retain the £3,517. **2–041**

FARWELL J.: When one looks at the voluntary settlement, at first sight the answer would seem to be quite clearly that the trustees' duty was to retain the sum of £3,517 as part of the funds which the son had voluntarily settled, and the language of the voluntary settlement would seem to leave no doubt on that **2–042**

[46] [2002] 1 W.L.R. 2075 at [64]–[65].
[47] See paras 2–097ff.
[48] See para.2–033.
[49] *Re Brooks's ST* [1939] 1 Ch. 993; *Re Adlard* [1954] Ch. 29.

score, because the settlor assigned to the bank "all the part or share parts or shares and other interest whether vested or contingent to which the settlor is now or may hereafter become entitled whether in default of appointment or under any appointment hereafter to be made or on failure of any such appointment of and in the trust property which is now or may at any time hereafter become subject to the trusts of the wife's settlement." One would say, looking at the language of the settlement, that it would be difficult to find words more apt to embrace in the voluntary settlement all the interests which the son had then or might thereafter have under the marriage settlement and that accordingly the answer should be that it is the duty of the trustees to retain this as part of the voluntary settlement fund. But, when one considers the legal position in this matter, a different aspect seems to appear. If the matter could be tested simply as one of construction, the answer would appear to be in favour of the trustees of the voluntary settlement; but the question is not one of construction only, and I have to consider whether the attempt to assign that which the son has now become entitled to by virtue of the exercise of the power is enforceable against him.

**2-043** The legal position in the case of a special power of appointment is not in any doubt at all. Referring to *Farwell on Powers*,[50] I find this statement of principle, which will be found in exactly the same language in earlier editions of the book, and therefore is not in any way the creation of the editor:

> "The exercise of a power of appointment divests (either wholly or partially according to the terms of the appointment) the estates limited in default of appointment and creates a new estate, and that, too, whether the property be real or personal."

The effect of this is that in the case of a special power the property is vested in the persons who take in default of appointment, subject, of course, to any prior life interest, but liable to be divested at any time by a valid exercise of the power, and the effect of such an exercise of the power is to defeat wholly or pro tanto the interests which up to then were vested in the persons entitled in default of appointment and to create new estates in those persons in whose favour the appointment had been made. That being so, it is, in my judgment, impossible to say that until an appointment has been made in favour of this son the son had any interest under his mother's settlement other than an interest as one of the people entitled in default of appointment; he had an interest in that; but that interest was liable to be divested, and, if an appointment was made in favour of the son, then to that extent the persons entitled in default were defeated and he was given an interest in the funds which he had never had before and which came into being for the first time when the power was exercised. No doubt it is quite true to say that the appointment has to be read in to the marriage settlement, but, in my judgment, that is not sufficient ground for saying that at the time when this voluntary settlement was made the son had any interest at all in the fund other than his vested interest in default of appointment; for the rest, he had nothing more than a mere expectancy, the hope that at some date his mother might think fit to exercise the power of appointment in his favour, but, until she did so choose, he had nothing other than his interest in default of appointment to which he could point and say: "That is a fund to which I shall become entitled in future or to which I am contingently entitled." Apart from this he was not contingently entitled at all; he had no interest whatever in the fund until the appointment had been executed.

**2-044** If that be the true view, as I believe it to be, the result must be that, whatever the language of the settlement may be, the settlor under the voluntary settlement was purporting to assign to the trustees something to which he might in certain circumstances become entitled in the future, but to which he was not then entitled in any sense at all, and if that be so, then it is plain on the authorities that the son cannot be compelled to hand over or to permit the trustees to retain this sum and that he is himself entitled to call upon them to pay it over to him. . .

**2-045** Notwithstanding the fact that the language of this voluntary settlement as a matter of construction is wide enough to comprise this interest, the principle of law which I have stated makes it impossible to enforce the settlement to that extent and prevents the settlor from being compelled by this Court to transfer or permit the trustees to retain this money as part of the funds subject thereto.

**2-046** In *Re Brooks' Settlement Trusts*, then, AT had made a gratuitous promise to make a transfer, of property he might receive under an existing marriage settlement, to Lloyds Bank to hold on trust. Lloyds Bank then became trustees of the marriage settlement, and, under its terms, were under a

[50] 3rd edn (1916), p.310 [edited by Farwell J himself].

duty to pay a sum of money to AT. Lloyds Bank could not instead immediately hold that money on the terms of AT's promised voluntary settlement: that trust would only be completely constituted if AT, or his agent, authorised Lloyds Bank to hold on the terms of the voluntary settlement[51]; AT was under no duty to do so as his promise was gratuitous. The case thus makes very clear that a trust will not be completely constituted if, in the absence of the planned transfer by the settlor, the planned trust property happens to end up in the hands of the planned trustee. The law is not, however, as clear as it might be, owing to some further decisions that we will now consider.

### (2) A Challenge to the Basic Rule: *Re Ralli's Will Trusts*

The first case to discuss is *Re Ralli's Will Trusts*,[52] where the approach taken by Buckley J in obiter dicta does not attempt to set up an exception to the basic rule, but seems rather to challenge its existence. **2–047**

*Re Ralli's Will Trusts*

Chancery Division [1964] Ch. 288

In 1899, Helen Ralli became entitled, under a trust set up in her father's will, to one-half of her father's residuary estate subject to her mother's life interest. The mother died in 1961 so Helen's reversionary interest then fell into possession. In 1924, Helen in her marriage settlement had covenanted to assign to the trustees thereof as soon as circumstances would admit all her existing and after-acquired property upon certain trusts for her children which failed (Helen dying a childless widow) and ultimately upon trusts for the benefit of the children of Helen's sister, Irene, who were volunteers. A subsequent clause in the marriage settlement was held on its proper construction to declare that all property currently held by Helen and comprised within the terms of the covenant should be subject immediately to the trusts of the marriage settlement, pending assignment to the trustees. Helen died in 1956 without having assigned her reversionary interest acquired in 1899 under her father's will. The plaintiff (who was married to Helen's sister) was the sole surviving trustee of the 1924 marriage settlement. It so happened that in 1946 he had also become a trustee of the Helen's father's will trust and was now also the sole surviving trustee of that trust. He therefore claimed that Helen's reversionary interest under the father's will trusts was now held by him on the trusts of the marriage settlement (which benefitted his daughters). The defendants, Helen's personal representatives, disputed this, claimed that her estate was entitled to the reversionary interest, as Helen had made no transfer of it to the trustees of the marriage settlement. **2–048**

BUCKLEY J. held that the vested reversionary interest, being existing property of Helen at the time she made what he construed as an independent declaration of trust pending assignment to the trustees of her marriage settlement, was held on the trusts of the marriage settlement.[53] He then continued: **2–049**

If this view is right, this disposes of the case, but I think I should go on to state what would be my view, if I were mistaken in the view I have expressed. The investments representing the share of residue in question stand in the name of the plaintiff. This is because he is now the sole surviving trustee of the [father's] will. Therefore, say the defendants, he holds these investments primarily on the trusts of the will, that is to say, in trust for them as part of Helen's estate. The plaintiff is, however, also the sole surviving covenantee under clause 7 of the [marriage] settlement, as well as the sole surviving trustee of that settlement. This, however, affords him no answer, say the defendants, to their claim under the will unless the plaintiff, having transferred the property to them in pursuance of the trusts of the will, could compel them to return it in pursuance of their obligation under the covenant, and this, they say, he could not do. . . . **2–050**

The plaintiff, on the other hand, contends that, as he already holds the investments, no question of his having to enforce the covenant arises. The fund having come without impropriety into his hands is now, **2–051**

[51] *Re Adlard* [1954] Ch. 29. Note that s.53(1)(c) of the Law of Property Act 1925 would apply in such a case to require AT's authority to be in signed: see *Grey v IRC* [1960] A.C. 1, discussed at paras 3–052ff. Any authority given to Lloyds Bank before its receipt of the property, if given gratuitously, and not otherwise irrevocable, could be revoked before receipt: *Re Bowden* [1936] Ch. 71, although cf. *Re Burton's Settlements* [1955] Ch. 82 at 104 per Upjohn J.

[52] [1964] Ch. 288.

[53] [See para.2–020.]

he says, impressed in his hands with the trusts on which he ought to hold it under the settlement; and because of the covenant it does not lie in the mouth of the defendants to say that he should hold it in trust for Helen's estate. He relies on *Re Bowden*[54] in which case a lady by a voluntary settlement purported to assign to trustees inter alia such property as she should become entitled to under the will of her father, who was still alive, and authorised the trustees to receive the property and give receipts for it. In due course her father died and the property to which the lady became entitled under his will was transferred to the trustees of the settlement. Many years later the lady claimed that the property belonged to her absolutely. Bennett, J. [held] that she was not entitled to the property. . .

**2-052** Counsel for the defendants says that *Re Bowden* and *Re Adlard's Settlement Trust*[55] are distinguishable from the present case because in each of those cases the fund had reached the hands of the trustees of the relevant settlement and was held by them in that capacity, whereas in the present case the fund is, as he maintains, in the hands of the plaintiff in the capacity of trustee of the will and not in the capacity of trustee of the settlement. He says that *Re Burton's Settlements*,[56] the complicated facts of which I forbear to set out here, should be distinguished on the ground that, when the settlement there in question was made, the trustee of that settlement and the trustee of the settlement under which the settlor had expectations was the same, so that the settlor by her settlement gave directions to the trustee of the settlement under which she had expectations, who then already held the relevant fund.

**2-053** Counsel for the plaintiff says that the capacity in which the trustee has become possessed of the fund is irrelevant. Thus in *Strong v Bird*,[57] an imperfect gift was held to be completed by the donee obtaining probate of the donor's will of which he was executor, notwithstanding that the donor died intestate as to her residue and that the donee was not a person entitled as on her intestacy. Similarly in *Re James*,[58] a grant of administration to two administrators was held to perfect an imperfect gift by the intestate to one of them, who had no beneficial interest in the intestate's estate.

**2-054** In my judgment the circumstance that the plaintiff holds the fund because he was appointed a trustee of the will is irrelevant. He is at law the owner of the fund and the means by which he became so have no effect on the quality of his legal ownership. The question is: for whom, if any one, does he hold the fund in equity? In other words, who can successfully assert an equity against him disentitling him to stand on his legal right? It seems to me to be indisputable that Helen, if she were alive, could not do so, for she has solemnly covenanted under seal to assign the fund to the plaintiff and the defendants can stand in no better position. It is, of course, true that the object of the covenant was not that the plaintiff should retain the property for his own benefit, but that he should hold it on the trusts of the settlement. It is also true that, if it were necessary to enforce performance of the covenant, equity would not assist the beneficiaries under the settlement, because they are mere volunteers; and that for the same reason the plaintiff, as trustee of the settlement, would not be bound to enforce the covenant and would not be constrained by the court to do so, and indeed, it seems, might be constrained by the court not to do so. As matters stand, however, there is no occasion to invoke the assistance of equity to enforce the performance of the covenant. It is for the defendants to invoke the assistance of equity to make good their claim to the fund. To do so successfully they must show that the plaintiff cannot conscientiously withhold it from them. When they seek to do this, he can point to the covenant which, in my judgment, relieves him from any fiduciary obligation that he would otherwise owe to the defendants as Helen's representatives. In so doing the plaintiff is not seeking to enforce an equitable remedy against the defendants on behalf of persons who could not enforce such a remedy themselves: he is relying on the combined effect of his legal ownership of the fund and his legal right to enforce the covenant. That an action on the covenant might be statute-barred is irrelevant, for there is no occasion for such an action.

**2-055** Had someone other than the plaintiff been the trustee of the will and held the fund, the result of this part of the case would, in my judgment, have been different; and it may seem strange that the rights of the parties should depend on the appointment of the plaintiff as a trustee of the will in 1946, which for present purposes may have been a quite fortuitous event. The result, however, in my judgment, flows—and flows, I think, quite rationally—from the consideration that the rules of equity derive from

54 [1936] Ch. 71.
55 [1954] Ch. 29.
56 [1955] Ch. 82.
57 (1874) L.R. 18 Eq. 315.
58 [1935] Ch. 449.

> the tenderness of a court of equity for the consciences of the parties. There would have been nothing unconscientious in Helen or her personal representatives asserting her equitable interests under trusts of the will against a trustee who was not a covenantee under clause 7 of the [marriage] settlement, and it would have been unconscientious for such a trustee to disregard those interests. Having obtained a transfer of the fund, it would not have been unconscientious in Helen to refuse to honour her covenant, because the beneficiaries under her settlement were mere volunteers: nor seemingly would the court have regarded it as unconscientious in the plaintiff to have abstained from enforcing the covenant either specifically or in damages, for the reason, apparently, that he would have been under no obligation to obtain for the volunteers indirectly what they could not obtain directly. In such circumstances Helen or her personal representatives could have got and retained the fund. In the circumstances of the present case, on the other hand, it is not unconscientious in the plaintiff to withhold from Helen's estate the fund which Helen covenanted that he should receive: on the contrary, it would have been unconscientious in Helen to seek to deprive the plaintiff of that fund, and her personal representatives can be in no better position. The inadequacy of the volunteers' equity against Helen and her estate consequently is irrelevant, for that equity does not come into play; but they have a good equity as against the plaintiff, because it would be unconscientious in him to retain as against them any property which he holds in consequence of the provisions of the settlement.
>
> For these reasons I am of opinion that in the events which have happened the plaintiff now holds the fund in question on the trusts of the marriage settlement, and I will so declare. **2–056**

The first important point to note about the foregoing analysis in *Re Ralli's Will Trusts* is that it is expressly stated to be obiter: the result in the case was determined by the fact that Helen had made an inter vivos self-declaration of trust that she would hold her current property (including her beneficial interest under the trusts of her father's will) on the trusts of the marriage settlement.[59] **2–057**

The second point to note is that, on the obiter analysis, everything turned on the coincidence that the plaintiff, Helen's brother-in-law, was both the trustee of Helen's father's will, under which Helen had a beneficial interest *and* the trustee of Helen's marriage settlement, and thus the party to whom Helen, if she had kept her promise to do so, would have transferred property (including her interest under her father's will) on trust to be held for the benefit of the plaintiff's daughters. Buckley J took the view that, whilst no-one could have sued Helen to force her to abide by her gratuitous promise to transfer property into the trusts marriage settlement, as property subject to that promise was now coincidentally in the hands of the trustee of that marriage settlement, Helen (and thus her personal representatives) could not now prevent the trustee from applying that property according to the terms of the marriage settlement trusts. **2–058**

On the facts of *Re Ralli* itself, this no doubt suited the trustee, as the beneficiaries of the marriage settlement trusts were his daughters; but the general approach of Buckley J could, in practice, cause grave difficulties for professional trustees who act as such in relation to a very large number of different trusts. It seems that, even if they received property to hold on the basis of one such trust, they may in fact hold it on the terms of another one of those trusts, if the beneficiary of the former trust made a promise (even a gratuitous one) to effect a transfer of it to the latter trust. **2–059**

Whatever its practical consequences might be, the obiter reasoning of Buckley J in *Re Ralli* appears to be a direct challenge to the reasoning in *Re Brook's Settlement Trusts*; but unfortunately it seems that the earlier decision was not cited to the court. Buckley J did however rely on *Strong v Bird*, and we will now consider that decision, though it seems at most to be an exception to the basic rule established in *Re Brook's*, rather than a rejection of that rule. **2–060**

59 See para.2–020.

### (3) An Exception to the Basic Rule? *Strong v Bird*

2-061 In itself, the decision in *Strong v Bird*[60] is of quite limited effect, but later cases have used it as the basis for an exception to the general rule that, where a settlor plans to set up a trust by means of a transfer to trustees, the trust will be completely constituted only if the planned transfer is made by the settlor or her authorised agent.

2-062 Consider a case in which a debtor (D) owes a creditor (C) £100. C dies and appoints D as her executor. What effect does this have on the debt? Generally, of course, it is the job of an executor to enforce outstanding debts owed to the deceased, but can we really say that C expected D, after C's death, to collect the debt that D himself owes to C? The common law certainly treated D's appointment[61] as executor as extinguishing or releasing his debt to C,[62] on the basis that C must have intended such a result.[63] As an administrator (who carries out the same essential role as an executor where the deceased dies intestate) is not specifically chosen by the deceased, the common law did not treat the appointment of the administrator as the release of any debt due to the deceased from the administrator.[64] In equity, however, the position was different: even if the debt had been formally extinguished D (whether C's executor or administrator) had to account for the debt to the estate, so that the £100 was available to pay off creditors of the estate or to be distributed among the beneficiaries.[65]

2-063 In *Strong v Bird*, the Court of Chancery resolved this difference by ruling that the logic of the common law's approach should prevail, so that D did not have to account to the estate for the debt, as long as C had indeed manifested an intent to forgive the debt in her lifetime and this intent had continued until C's death. So, C's merely saying to D, "I forgive this debt" would not by itself release the debt, either at law or in equity[66]; but as Sir George Jessel MR ruled in *Strong v Bird*, things are different if:

> [D] proves to the satisfaction of the court a continuing intention [of C] to give; and it appears to me that there being the continuing intention to give, and there being a legal act which transferred ownership or released the obligation—for it is the same thing—the transaction is perfected, and [D] does not want the aid of a court of Equity to carry it out, or make it complete, because it is complete already, and there is no equity against him to take the property away from him.

2-064 How then does *Strong v Bird* bear on the general rule that a trust by way of transfer to trustees is completely constituted only if the transfer is made by the settlor or her agent? First, it might be thought that the language of gifts and ownership seems strange when considering the release of a debt, but there is an obvious analogy between making a gift of £100 and releasing a debt of £100. The "gift" in *Strong v Bird* was considered complete as a result of C's having appointed D as executor with the intention of forgiving the debt. Secondly, however, it is important to note the limits of *Strong v Bird*: essentially, equity left the common law position undisturbed in a case where C appointed D as an executor and had an ongoing intention to release a debt. It certainly was not a case in which a donee invoked the assistance of equity in order to complete an imperfect gift, nor was it one in which an

---

60 (1874) L.R. 18 Eq. 315.

61 The appointment itself discharges the debt even if the executor dies before taking out probate: see, e.g. *Wankford v Wankford* (1704) 1 Salk. 299; *Re Applebee* [1891] 3 Ch. 422; *Jenkins v Jenkins* [1928] 2 K.B. 501.

62 See. e.g. *Re Bourne* [1906] 1 Ch. 697; *Bone v Stamp Duties Commissioner* (1974) 132 C.L.R. 38.

63 See, e.g. *Bone v Stamp Duties Commissioner* (1974) 132 C.L.R. 38 at 53 per Mason J.

64 *Wankford v Wankford* (1704) 1 Salk. 299; *Seagram v Knight* (1867) 2 Ch. App. 628; *Re Gonin* [1977] 2 All E.R. 720 at 734. Now see Administration of Estates Act 1925 s.21A added by Limitation Amendment Act 1980 s.10.

65 *Berry v Usher* (1805) 11 Ves. 87; *Jenkins v Jenkins* [1928] 2 K.B. 501.

66 *Strong v Bird* (1874) L.R. 18 Eq. 315 at 317–318 per Sir George Jessel MR: "It is what the law calls nudum pactum, a promise made without an actual consideration passing, and which consequently cannot be supported as a contract. It is not a release, because it is not under seal. Therefore the mere circumstance of saying 'I forgive you' will not do."

exception was recognised to the general rule that a trust by way of transfer to trustees is completely constituted only if the transfer is made by the settlor or her agent.

Later decisions, however, extended the impact of *Strong v Bird*. For example, in *Re Stewart*, Neville J said[67]: **2–065**

> Where a testator has expressed the intention of making a gift of personal estate to one who upon his death becomes his executor, the intention continuing unchanged, the executor is entitled to hold the property for his own benefit. The reasoning is first that the vesting of the property in the executor at the testator's death completes the imperfect gift made in the lifetime and secondly that the intention of the testator to give the beneficial interest to the executor is sufficient to countervail the equity of beneficiaries under the will, the testator having vested the legal estate in the executor.

*Re Stewart* has been followed many times at first instance[68] and treated as good law by the Court of Appeal.[69] In *Re James*,[70] Farwell J extended *Re Stewart* to perfect an imperfect gift of real property made by a donor to his housekeeper who, on the donor's intestacy, had herself appointed by the court one of two administratrices of the deceased donor's estate, thereby obtaining legal title to the house. This extension has been doubted by Walton J in *Re Gonin*[71] and rejected by the British Virgin Islands' Court of Appeal in *Re Pagarani*[72]: after all, it is the *choice* of the testator in appointing her debtor as her executor that extinguishes the debt at law, so that the fortuitous appointment by the court of an administrator who was a debtor of the intestate did not extinguish the debt. *Strong v Bird*, therefore, would have been differently decided if the defendant had been an administrator and not an executor. **2–066**

It thus seems that "the rule in *Strong v Bird*" has now developed far beyond the principle In the case itself, and may now allow an imperfect immediate[73] gift of specific[74] existing[75] real or personal property[76] to be perfected if the intended donee is appointed the testator's executor or administrator, alone or with others, so long as the intention to make the gift continues unchanged till the testator's death.[77] Whilst the perfection of the gift thus prevents any claim to the property by those beneficially entitled to the deceased's estate, it probably does not, however, bar a claim to that property by creditors of the deceased, since the common law rule as to the release of a debt by appointment of the debtor as executor did not avail against creditors.[78] **2–067**

It therefore seems that a limited exception, of doubtful pedigree, has been recognised to the general rule that a trust by way of transfer to trustees is completely constituted only if the transfer is made by the settlor or her agent. The exception applies where: (i) the settlor did not complete the **2–068**

---

67 [1908] 2 Ch. 251 at 254.

68 *Re Comberback* (1929) 73 Sol. Jo. 403; *Re James* [1935] Ch. 449; *Re Nelson* (1967) 91 Sol. Jo. 533: see also *Re Ralli's WT* [1964] Ch. 288; *Re Gonin* [1979] Ch. 16.

69 *Re Freeland* [1952] Ch. 110, counsel unreservedly accepting *Re Stewart*.

70 [1935] Ch. 449.

71 [1979] Ch. 16.

72 (1999) 2 O.F.L.R. 1. The issue was not considered by the Privy Council on the appeal from that decision: *T. Choithram International SA v Pagarani* [2001] 1 W.L.R. 1 (which is excerpted at paras 2–013—2–018).

73 *Re Innes* [1910] 1 Ch. 188; *Re Freeland* [1952] Ch. 110; *Re Gonin* [1979] Ch. 16; *Re Pink* [1912] 2 Ch. 528 at 536–539; *Simpson v Simpson* [1992] 1 F.L.R. 601. *Re Goff* (1914) 111 L.T. 34 is out of line since the donor only intended to forgive the debt if the donor predeceased the donee.

74 *Re Innes* [1910] 1 Ch. 188 at 193.

75 *Morton v Brighouse* [1927] 1 D.L.R. 1009.

76 *Re James* [1935] Ch. 449.

77 It seems that contrary expressions before death may be ignored if the intent to make the imperfect gift is confirmed in the will: *Re Stoneham* [1919] 1 Ch. 149 at 158. For cases on contrary intention see *Re Freeland* [1952] Ch. 110; *Re Eiser's WT* [1937] 1 All E.R. 244; *Re Wale* [1956] 1 W.L.R. 1346; *Morton v Brighouse* [1927] 1 D.L.R. 1009 (property imperfectly given to X subsequently specifically bequeathed to Y).

78 *Bone v Stamp Duties Commissioner* (1974) 132 C.L.R. 38.

planned transfer during her life; but (ii) the settlor appointed the planned trustee as an executor of her estate, or the planned trustee was appointed as an administrator of that estate[79]; and (iii) the settlor's intention to make the transfer on trust continued until her death, so that she had at that time "a present intention of giving".[80]

### E. Summary

**2-069** We have now considered the basic rule in *Milroy v Lord*, the scope of that rule, and its application in practice. It is perhaps helpful to summarise the results. First, the basic rule states that, if a settlor intends to set up a trust by making a transfer to trustees to hold on trust for B, but fails to make the planned transfer, the settlor's intention to benefit B does not suffice to allow B to claim that the settlor instead declared a trust and so held the property on trust for B. This is because there is a clear distinction between: (i) intending to benefit B by transferring to trustees to hold on trust for B; and (ii) intending to benefit B by retaining property and declaring a trust of that property in favour of B.[81] Secondly, however, if it can be found that the settlor did in fact declare that she held the property on trust for B, that declaration will be given effect to and, it seems, in a case where it was clear that the settlor wished to benefit B, a court may adopt a "benevolent" interpretation of the facts in order to find such a declaration.[82] Thirdly, if, although the requirements for a valid transfer of legal title to the property were not met, the settlor nonetheless did everything in her power to make that transfer, the transfer will be considered complete in equity, and the settlor will hold her legal title to the property subject to the planned trusts.[83] Fourthly, whilst the basic rule is that the planned transfer to trustees must be completed by the settlor or her agent,[84] an exception is permitted where the planned trustee receives the planned trust property as an executor or administrator on the death of the settlor, provided that the settlor had a continuing intention to set up the trust at the time of her death.[85]

## 3. Incompletely Constituted Trusts and Constructive Trusts

**2-070** Consider a case in which the settlor plans to set up a trust in B's favour by making a transfer to trustees to hold on trust for B. If such a transfer is not made,[86] B cannot claim to have acquired a beneficial interest under such a trust. If, equally, the settlor made no self-declaration of a trust in favour of B, then it will be impossible for B to show that the settlor created an express trust in her favour: there is no completely constituted express trust. As previously noted,[87] however, it may still be possible for B

---

79 Note that in *Carter v Hungerford* [1917] 1 Ch. 260 at 273, Astbury J suggested that the rule would also apply to protect an executor from the claims of those entitled under the settlor's will if the executor, mistakenly believing herself to be bound to do so, transferred property to the settlor's intended donees. This seems, however, to be an extension too far, as an executor, unlike a settlor, is subject to fiduciary duties and should not be able thus to defeat those entitled under the settlor's will purely in order to complete a transfer that the settlor died without completing.

80 *Re Innes* [1910] 1 Ch. 188 at 193, applied in, e.g. *Re Freeland* [1952] Ch. 110 at 116.

81 See *Milroy v Lord* (1862) 4 De G.F. & J. 264: see paras 2-006–2-011.

82 See, e.g. *T Choithram International SA v Pagarani* [2001] 1 W.L.R. 1: see paras 2-012–2-021.

83 *Re Rose, Rose v IRC* [1952] Ch. 499, approving *Re Rose, Midland Bank Executor & Trustee Co Ltd v Rose* [1949] Ch. 78.

84 *Re Brook's Settlement Trusts* [1939] Ch. 993: see paras 2-039–2-046; although note that the basic rule is challenged by *obiter* observations of Buckley J in *Re Ralli's Will Trusts* [1964] Ch. 288.

85 See *Re Stewart* [1908] 2 Ch. 251, giving a very expansive interpretation to the principle in *Strong v Bird* (1874) L.R. 18 Eq. 315: see paras 2-061–2-068.

86 Either under the general rule regulating the transfer of such property, or under the apparently different equitable rules applied in, e.g. *Re Rose, Rose v IRC* [1952] Ch. 499: see paras 2-034–2-035.

87 See para.2-001.

to claim a beneficial interest if she can show that a non-express trust has arisen, i.e. a trust that was not created by the settlor's successful exercise of a power to create a trust, but was rather imposed by law. There are many different bases on which such a constructive trust might arise,[88] and we will examine such trusts in more detail in Chapter 5. We will consider here only the types of constructive trust that are most likely to be relevant in cases of an incompletely constituted express trust.[89]

### A. The General Position: "Equity Will Not Assist a Volunteer"

The general position as to the possibility of B's claiming a right under a constructive trusts is very clear: the mere fact that the settlor intended, and perhaps even attempted, to set up a trust for B does not, in itself, suffice to give rise to a constructive trust. It is often said that such a trust can be imposed on a party holding property only in response to the prospect of unconscionable conduct by that party, and there is nothing unconscionable in the settlor's conduct if she either repents of the intention to set up a trust for B, or dies having failed to constitute the planned trust. This general position can be explained by invoking the maxim that "equity will not assist a volunteer".[90] It is far from clear, however, that the maxim is helpful. As noted above,[91] caution must be exercised as, *if* an express trust has been completely constituted, B will acquire a beneficial interest under that trust even if she provided nothing in exchange for the settlor's exercise of the power to set up a trust. The maxim does however reflect the basic point that equity has no reason to intervene and impose a constructive trust where B has simply failed to receive a gift. **2–071**

### B. Special Circumstances: When a Constructive Trust May Arise

#### i. Promise by the Settlor for which B Provides Consideration

The general position considered in the preceding paragraph applies where the settlor simply intended, and failed, to make a transfer to trustees to hold on trust for B. Things may be different, however, if the settlor also made a *promise* to make such a transfer and thus to set up a trust for B. If B is regarded as having provided consideration for that promise, and the settlor's promise relates to specific property which the settlor holds at the time of the promise, or later acquires, then a constructive trust may be imposed on that property in favour of B. This means, of course, that the property is then held by the settlor directly on trust for B, rather than (as planned) by trustees who received the property from the settlor. The rule in *Milroy v Lord* is not, however, departed from as that rule simply means that an unsuccessful attempt to set up a trust by means of a transfer to trustees cannot be recharacterised as a successful self-declaration of trust. The rule does not, therefore, prevent a constructive trust arising in favour of B and binding property held by the settlor. The operation of such a constructive trust can be seen in the following extract. **2–072**

---

88 For a general consideration of such circumstances, and their possible justifications, see Ch.15.

89 We will not consider resulting trusts here, as the circumstances in which a resulting trust may arise (considered in Ch.4) are very unlikely to assist B in our case where the settlor planned to set up an express trust.

90 See, e.g. *Re Plumptre's Marriage Settlement* [1910] 1 Ch. 609; *Re D'Angibau* (1880) 15 Ch.D. 228.

91 See para.2–033.

*Pullan v Koe*

Chancery Division [1913] 1 Ch. 9

2-073 A marriage settlement of 1859 contained a covenant by the husband and wife to transfer the wife's after-acquired property of the value of £100 or upwards to the trustees of the marriage settlement. In 1879 the wife received £285 and paid it into her husband's banking account, on which she had power to draw. Shortly afterwards part of the money was invested in two bearer bonds which remained at the bank until the husband's death in 1909. The bonds then passed into the hands of his executors. The plaintiffs, trustees of the marriage settlement, claimed against the defendants, the husband's executors that, as soon as the wife received the £285, it was held by her on a trust enforceable in favour of all persons within the marriage consideration, as such persons were to be considered as having provided consideration for the promise, contained in the covenant, to transfer such property to the trustees of the settlement. As a result, it was claimed, the bearer bonds were also then held subject to such a trust, even though, because of the expiry of the statutory limitation period, it was no longer possible for the trustees to enforce the wife's covenant at common law.

2-074 SWINFEN EADY J.: [The defendants] insisted that, although they still retained the bonds, they were under no liability to the plaintiffs. They put their case in this way—that the plaintiff trustees could not follow the bonds into their hands, that the only liability of the husband was upon his covenant, and the claim of the trustees was for damages only, and that as this claim accrued in 1879 it was long since barred by the Statutes of Limitation. . . .

2-075 [The husband] received the bonds, purchased with his wife's money, with full notice of the trusts of the settlement, and knowing that the £285 and the bonds purchased with part of it were bound by the covenant. The trustees having traced the property into his hands are entitled to claim it from his executors.

2-076 It was contended that the bonds never in fact became trust property, as both the wife and husband were only liable in damages for breach of covenant, and that the case was different from cases where property which has once admittedly become subject to the trusts of an instrument has been improperly dealt with, and is sought to be recovered. In my opinion as soon as the £285 was paid to the wife it became in equity bound by and subject to the trusts of the settlement. The trustees could have claimed that particular sum, could have obtained at once the appointment of a receiver of it, if they could have shown a case of jeopardy, and, if it had been invested and the investment could be traced, could have followed the money and claimed the investment.

2-077 This point was dealt with by Jessel M.R. in *Smith v Lucas*,[92] where he said:

> "What is the effect of such a covenant in equity? It has been said that the effect in equity of the covenant of the wife, as far as she is concerned, is that it does not affect her personally, but that it binds the property: that is to say, it binds the property under the doctrine of equity that that is to be considered as done which ought to be done. That is in the nature of specific performance of the contract no doubt. If therefore, this is a covenant to settle the future-acquired property of the wife, and nothing more is done by her, the covenant will bind the property."

Again in *Collyer v Isaacs*[93] Jessel M.R. said:

> "A man can contract to assign property which is to come into existence in the future, and when it has come into existence, equity, treating as done that which ought to be done, fastens upon that property, and the contract to assign thus becomes a complete assignment. If a person contract for value, e.g. in this marriage settlement, to settle all such real estate as his father shall leave him by will, or purports actually to convey by the deed all such real estate, the effect is the same. It is a contract for value which will bind the property if the father leaves any property to his son."

2-078 Again the trustees are entitled to come into a Court of Equity to enforce a contract to create a trust, contained in a marriage settlement, for the benefit of the wife and the issue of the marriage, all of whom are within the marriage consideration. The husband covenanted that he and his heirs, executors, and administrators should, as soon as circumstances would admit, convey, assign, and surrender to the

92 (1881) 18 Ch.D. 531 at 543.
93 (1882) 19 Ch.D. 342 at 351.

> trustees the real or personal property to which his wife should become beneficially entitled. The trustees are entitled to have that covenant specifically enforced by a Court of Equity. In *Re D'Angibau*[94] and in *Re Plumptre's Marriage Settlement*[95] it was held that the Court would not interfere in favour of volunteers, not within the marriage consideration, but here the plaintiffs are the contracting parties and the object of the proceeding is to benefit the wife and issue of the marriage.

The specific decision in *Pullan v Koe* thus depends in part on the special rules relating to marriage settlements: even though the promise made in the covenant of the husband and wife appears to be gratuitous, as it was made before and in consideration of marriage, it is regarded as having been made for value,[96] and that value is deemed to have been provided by the spouses, their children and remoter issue.[97] As a result, if the promise of the husband or wife relates to property later acquired by one of them, he or she is subject to an immediate duty to abide by the promise, and that duty can be enforced by the trustees of the marriage settlement, or by anyone who is deemed to have provided consideration for it. **2-079**

The general principle underlying *Pullan v Koe* is, however, much broader: we will consider it in more detail in Chapter 5.[98] As can be seen from the statement of Jessel MR in *Collyer v Isaacs*,[99] for example, it can apply to *any* promise, made for value, to transfer property to trustees to hold on trust. Indeed, the underlying principle of equity is broader still, as it applies to a simple promise for value to transfer property absolutely (such as a contract to transfer land) and also to a promise for value to hold rights as security,[100] or to, for example, grant a lease[101] or easement[102] over the promisor's land. That principle is often said to depend on the maxim that "equity looks on as done that which ought to be done"[103]: e.g. as the promisor in *Pullan v Koe* had promised to transfer the property on trusts, that transfer could be considered as completed, so that the planned beneficiaries under those trusts are regarded as having acquired an immediate beneficial interest. **2-080**

The maxim that "equity looks on as done that which ought to be done", like most equitable maxims, is, however, somewhat unhelpful.[104] The point in *Pullan v Koe*, for example, was not that the wife was under a moral obligation to honour the promise in the covenant; it was rather that the wife could be said to owe a duty to a party who could be regarded as the promisee, and as having provided consideration for the promise. As that duty related to specific property, and was a duty to use that property not for the wife's own benefit, but on the terms of the marriage settlement, the wife thus held the property on trust. The trust was a constructive one[105] as it did not depend on the wife's actually exercising her power to set up the promised trust; it rather arose immediately, as soon as she acquired the relevant property. **2-081**

---

94 (1880) 15 Ch.D. 228 at 242.

95 [1910] 1 Ch. 609 at 616.

96 If, for example, a trust is created after marriage and contains a true recital that it was made in pursuance of an ante-nuptial promise to create the trust it will be treated as having been made for value: *Re Holland* [1902] 2 Ch. 360.

97 Such parties are "within the marriage consideration". Old cases allowing children of a former marriage or a possible later remarriage or illegitimate children to be within the scope of marriage consideration can now only be supported on the basis that such children's interests were so closely interwoven with the interests of the children of the marriage that the latter could only benefit on terms allowing the former to benefit: *Rennell v IRC* [1962] Ch. 329 at 341; *Re Cook's S.T.* [1965] Ch. 902 at 914.

98 See paras 5-025—5-029.

99 (1882) 19 Ch.D. 342 at 351 (extracted at para.2-077).

100 The principle is therefore the basis of the modern law of secured lending: see, e.g. *Holroyd v Marshall* (1862) 10 H.L.C. 191 and *Tailby v Official Receiver* (1888) 13 App. Cas. 523.

101 See, e.g. *Walsh v Lonsdale* (1882) 21 Ch.D. 9.

102 See, e.g. *McManus v Cooke* (1887) 35 Ch.D. 681.

103 See, e.g. *Smith v Lucas* (1881) 18 Ch.D. 531 at 543 per Jessel MR (extracted at para.2-077).

104 See paras 5-022—5-024.

105 As acknowledged in, e.g. *Lysaght v Edwards* (1876) 2 Ch.D. 499 at 509–510 per Jessel MR.

### (1) The Principle and Future Property

2-082 *Pullan v Koe* demonstrates that, if a settlor makes a promise to set up a trust of property that she does not yet have ("after-acquired" or "future" property), a constructive trust of such property may arise at that point in the future when the settlor does acquire that property if, at that point, the settlor is under a duty, enforceable in equity, to honour the promise. The principle is therefore important when considering a settlor's attempts to deal with future property. It is of course impossible for a settlor, whatever her intentions may be, to set up an immediate trust of future property[106]: if the settlor does not have the property, then she cannot hold it on trust for B; nor can it can be transferred to trustees to hold on trust for B.

2-083 Some care is needed, however, as future property must be distinguished from an existing right held by a settlor to obtain property in the future.[107] For example, we noted above[108] that in *Re Ralli's Will Trusts*, Helen Ralli was able to declare an immediate trust of her right, acquired under her father's will, to have the benefit of property on the death of her mother. Under such a remainder interest, a party has direct access to the benefit of the property only on the occurrence of a particular event; but the interest is itself an existing right with which the party can deal, for example by declaring a trust. In contrast, no such existing right exists if a party simply has the hope of inheriting property upon the death of a relative, or of receiving property under the exercise of a power of appointment, or of acquiring royalties arising on sales of a book.

2-084 What happens then if the donor attempts to make an immediate gift of such future property? At law, an assignment of future property has no effect, as the donor has no right to transfer.[109] In equity, however, the principle underlying *Pullan v Koe* can apply *if* the donee gave valuable consideration: the failed attempt at an immediate assignment is then treated by equity as a *promise* to make such an assignment, with the effect that, if and when the donor acquires the property, she will hold it on constructive trust for the donee.[110] In a case where the settlor instead attempts to transfer future property to trustees to hold on trust for B, and B provides consideration, it therefore seems that, if and when the settlor acquires that property, she will hold it on trust for B. There is no contradiction of the rule in *Milroy v Lord*, as B's beneficial interest arises under a constructive trust, and does not depend on recharacterising the failed attempt to set up a trust by transfer as a self-declaration of trust. Similarly, if the settlor attempts to make an immediate self-declaration of trust in favour of B in relation to future property, then, if B provided consideration, a constructive trust can again arise if and when the settlor acquires that property.

### (2) Limits to the Principle: Covenants to Settle

2-085 The type of constructive trust recognised in *Pullan v Koe* depends on the settlor, S, being under a duty, enforceable in equity, to honour her promise to set up the trust in favour of the planned beneficiary, B. It does not arise, therefore, if the settlor's promise is gratuitous because a promise for which no consideration is provided is not regarded, in equity, as giving rise to an enforceable duty. This is the case even if the gratuitous promise was made in a deed[111] executed by the settlor and the planned trustee.

---

106 See, e.g. *Re Ellenborough* [1903] 1 Ch. 697; *Williams v C.I.R.* [1965] N.Z.L.R. 395.

107 See *Re Earl of Midleton's WT* [1969] 1 Ch. 600 at 607.

108 See para.2-020.

109 *Holroyd v Marshall* (1862) 10 H.L.Cas. 191 at 220; *Re Tilt* (1896) 74 L.T. 163.

110 See, e.g. *Re Lind* [1915] 2 Ch. 354 at 360. This principle is discussed further at paras 5-025–5-029.

111 Such a promise is often referred to as a covenant.

The use of a deed means that the planned trustee has a right at common law to sue the settlor for failing to honour the promise,[112] but it does not lead to a constructive trust in favour of the planned beneficiaries, as the promise is still gratuitous and so does not give rise to a duty enforceable in equity: this is, therefore, a further context in which the maxim that "equity will not assist a volunteer" has some weight.

For example, consider a case in which S covenants (i.e. promises in a deed) to pay £10,000 and to transfer her unique fifth dynasty Ming vase to B, a volunteer. The use of a deed means that B has a valid claim at law against S if S does not honour the promise. B cannot obtain specific performance of the promise to transfer the unique vase, as S's promise is gratuitous and so is not enforceable in equity. There is no reason, however, for equity to prevent B from enforcing his common law claim against S and recovering damages reflecting the value of the right that S promised to transfer.[113] **2-086**

What if S's promise, again gratuitous and again made in a deed, was instead made to T and was a promise to pay £10,000 to T and to transfer her unique fifth dynasty Ming vase to T, so that T would hold the cash and the vase on trust for B, a volunteer? Such a promise is often referred to as a "covenant to settle". In such a case, if S made the promise with the express or implied intent that T shall hold the benefit of the covenant on trust for B, then a completely constituted trust has been created in B's favour.[114] It is not a trust of the cash or the vase, but is rather a trust of T's right, at common law, to sue S. As we have seen,[115] once a trust has been completely constituted in B's favour, it is irrelevant that B is a volunteer who has given nothing in exchange: B can enforce the trust. It is worth noting that such a "trust of the benefit of a covenant" can arise even if the covenant relates solely to "after-acquired" or "future" property: i.e. property that S does not hold at the time of the covenant. The point is that whilst S cannot, of course, hold property that she does not yet have on trust for B or anyone else,[116] T has a right against S as soon as the covenant is made, and that existing chose in action may then be held by T on trust.[117] If such a trust is found, this means that, even if T does not wish to sue S, B can force T to do so,[118] and any damages acquired by T by means of that common law claim against S will then be held by T on trust for B. In such a case, of course, B's claim does not depend on a constructive trust; it is rather based on the existence of an express trust of T's cause of action against S. **2-087**

B can take advantage of this possibility, therefore, only if it can be shown that S intended to set up such a trust of T's right to sue S. The courts were, at one point, quite willing to infer such an intention, if only to give some means of redress to B in a case where S failed to honour the promise to transfer the property to T to hold on trust for B.[119] Since the middle of the twentieth century, however, it has instead **2-088**

---

112 See, e.g. *Cannon v Hartley* [1949] Ch. 213. For the requirements of a deed, see Law of Property (Miscellaneous Provisions) Act 1989 s.1. Note too s.56 of the Law of Property Act 1925, which allows B to acquire a right under a deed made between S and another even if B is not a party to it, if certain conditions are met: see *Beswick v Beswick* [1968] A.C. 58 and *Amsprop Trading Ltd v Harris Distribution Ltd* [1997] 1 W.L.R. 1025.

113 See *Cannon v Hartley* [1949] Ch. 213 (assuming of course that the promise made in the deed was not vitiated by, e.g. fraud, undue influence or unconscionable conduct).

114 See *Fletcher v Fletcher* (1844) 4 Hare 67. See too *Cox v Barnard* (1850) 8 Hare 310 at [312] and [313]; *Milroy v Lord* (1862) 4 De G.F. & J. 264 at 278.

115 See paras 2-033—2-071.

116 See paras 2-082.

117 See, e.g. *Kwok Chi Leung Karl v Commissioner of Estate Duty* [1988] 1 W.L.R. 1035 at 1040 per Lord Oliver: "A chose in action is no less a chose in action because it is not immediately recoverable by action", applied in *Re Landau* [1997] 3 All E.R. 322 at 328.

118 Procedurally, B's claim to force T to sue S, and T's claim against S, can be combined in one action by means of what is known as a *Vandepitte* procedure (named for *Vandepitte v Preferred Accident Insurance Corp of New York* [1933] A.C. 70).

119 See, e.g. *Fletcher v Fletcher* (1844) 4 Hare 67: the intention was not express but was inferred in rather special circumstances. Further examples of such inferences can be found: e.g. *Cox v Barnard* (1850) 8 Hare 310; *Watson v Parker* (1843) 6 Beav. 283; *Dowling v Dowling* [1917] V.L.R. 208.

been emphasised, quite justifiably, that such a trust of the benefit of a covenant can be found only if there was a genuine intention on the part of S and T to set up such a trust.[120] After all, S has made no promise directly to B, and the most likely interpretation of the parties' transaction is that S intended B to acquire a beneficial interest, but only in relation to the property referred to in the covenant, and only after a transfer of that property to T.[121]

**2–089** What is B's position then, if S has made a gratuitous promise in a deed to transfer property to T to hold on trust for B, and it cannot be shown that S intended T to hold the benefit of the right to enforce the covenant on trust for B? First, there is now the possibility that the Contract (Rights of Third Parties) Act 1999 may apply to give B a direct claim against S, even in the absence of a trust of the benefit of the covenant. The position is not, however, entirely clear[122]; and, in any case, such a claim does not involve any trust. If S does not perform the promise in the covenant, T does then have a right at common law to sue S and B might then claim that T holds such damages on trust for B, as the covenant was not intended to benefit T. The difficulty for B, however, is that S may well argue that substantial damages should not be paid: after all, the right to enforce the promise belongs to T, and T is unlikely to have suffered any loss as a result of S's failure to perform. In practice, it may be that S's promise was to transfer property into an existing settlement whereby T already holds some assets on trust for B. In such a case, T will have to consider whether her existing duties as trustee mean that she should sue S in an attempt to recover damages that can then be held on trust for B. T will of course wish to have access to the trust funds to meet any costs incurred in suing S, but, where T has asked for directions from the court in such a case, the courts have held that T cannot use the trust funds to claim common law damages from S.[123] In fact, this response is so well-established that there is now no need for a trustee in T's position to bother the court: T has a complete defence if B claims that T was in breach of trust by not suing S for damages.[124] It therefore seems that the courts have accepted that B would derive no benefit from T's suing S.[125] This reflects the fact that, although made in a deed, S's promise to set up a trust is simply a promise to make a gift.

### ii. Proprietary Estoppel

**2–090** The doctrine of proprietary estoppel provides another means by which a settlor's promise to make a gift to B, whether directly or by means of a trust in B's favour, may give rise to a constructive trust for B.

---

120 See, e.g. *Re Kay's Settlement* [1939] Ch. 329; *Re Schebsman* [1944] Ch 83; *Re Cook's ST* [1965] Ch. 902.

121 See, e.g. *Re Plumptre's MS* [1910] 1 Ch. 609; *Re Pryce* [1917] 1 Ch. 234. That interpretation is perhaps further supported if the covenant relates only to "after-acquired" property of S: i.e. property which S does not hold at the time of the covenant. It may be going too far, however, to suggest (as W.A. Lee (1969) 85 L.Q.R. 313 does) that there can never be the trust of the benefit of such a covenant: for example, in *Davenport v Bishop* (1843) 2 Y. & C.C.C. 451, Knight Bruce VC indicated at 460 that such a trust can arise. See too *Lloyd's v Harper* (1880) 16 Ch.D. 290 and *Royal Exchange Assurance v Hope* [1928] Ch. 179.

122 For discussion of this point, which turns ultimately on whether a promise, enforceable because made in a deed, counts as a contract, see, e.g. R. Stevens, "The Contracts (Rights of Third Parties) Act 1999" (2004) 120 L.Q.R. 292 at 313–314.

123 See, e.g. *Re Pryce* [1917] 1 Ch. 234; *Re Kay's Settlement* [1939] Ch. 329; *Re Cook's Settlement Trusts* [1965] Ch. 902.

124 *Re Ralli's WT* [1964] Ch. 288 at 301–302.

125 T might of course argue that T should receive substantial damages on his own behalf as T has a right to the value of the promised performance by S, and that value is substantial even if B would be the principal beneficiary of S's performance. The success of such a claim would depend on the application of rules as to damages (compare, e.g. the case, postulated by Lord Goff in *Alfred McAlpine Construction Ltd v Panatown* [2001] 1 A.C. 518 at 547, where "a wealthy man who lives in a village decides to carry out at his own expense major repairs to, or renovation, or even construction of the village hall, and himself enters a contract with a builder to carry out the work to the existing building which belongs to another"). As T's claim is then for damages for himself, and not for B, then of course it is right that T should not have access to the trust funds to bring such a claim, and so, even were substantial damages available on this basis, this prospect does not undermine the reasoning in the cases cited at fn.123.

The doctrine does not require B to have provided anything of value in exchange for S's promise. When applied to promises,[126] it has three principal requirements[127]: (i) the defendant (in our case, S) made a promise that B will acquire a right in relation to identified property and the promise is such as could be reasonably understood by the claimant (in our case, B) as seriously intended to be capable of being relied upon[128]; (ii) B reasonably relied on that promise by acting, or not acting, in a particular way[129]; and (iii) as a result of that reliance, B would now suffer a detriment if S were wholly free to renege on the promise.[130] Those three requirements are inter-related, and they are underpinned by the notion of unconscionability,[131] so that, if they appear to have been satisfied, but it would not "shock the conscience of the court" to refuse B's claim, then B's proprietary estoppel claim may still fail.[132] As stated by Robert Walker LJ in *Gillett v Holt*,[133]

> the doctrine of proprietary estoppel cannot be treated as subdivided into three or four watertight compartments . . . Moreover the fundamental principle that equity is concerned to prevent unconscionable conduct permeates all the elements of the doctrine. In the end the court must look at the matter in the round.

In contrast to promissory estoppel, proprietary estoppel may operate as a cause of action, and thus give B an independent means of making a claim against S. In *Thorner v Major*, Lord Walker stated that[134]: **2-091**

> In my opinion it is a necessary element of proprietary estoppel that the assurances given to the claimant (expressly or impliedly, or, in standing-by cases, tacitly) should relate to identified property owned (or, perhaps, about to be owned) by the defendant. That is one of the main distinguishing features between the two varieties of equitable estoppel, that is promissory estoppel and proprietary estoppel. The former must be based on an existing legal *relationship* (usually a contract, but not necessarily a contract relating to land). The latter need not be based on an existing legal relationship, but it must relate to *identified property* (usually land) owned (or, perhaps, about to be owned) by the defendant. It is the relation to identified land of the defendant that has enabled proprietary estoppel to develop as a sword, and not merely a shield.[135]

---

[126] The promise-based strand of proprietary estoppel is most relevant in the current context. It is also possible to identify an acquiescence-based strand and a representation-based strand of proprietary estoppel. The former can apply where the defendant has failed to take reasonable steps to correct the claimant's mistaken belief as to the claimant's current rights, even though the defendant knew of the claimant's belief and of the true position: see, e.g. *Willmott v Barber* (1880) 15 Ch. D. 96 at 105–106; *Fisher v Brooker* [2009] 1 W.L.R. 1764 at [62]. The latter can apply where one party has made a representation as to a matter of existing fact, or mixed fact and law, intending that the other party should rely on it, and the other party does so rely: see, e.g. *Hopgood v Brown* [1955] 1 W.L.R. 213.

[127] *Thorner v Major* [2009] 1 W.L.R. 776 at [29] per Lord Walker.

[128] See, e.g. *Thorner v Major* [2009] 1 W.L.R. 776 at [5] per Lord Hoffmann.

[129] It is often said, following the analysis of Lord Denning MR in *Greasley v Cooke* [1980] 1 W.L.R. 1306, that there is a "presumption of reliance", but it is very difficult to see why the burden of proving an element of the claim should not, as usual, be on the claimant, and the validity of such a presumption has been doubted, both in relation to estoppel generally (see, e.g. *Steria Ltd v Hutchison* [2007] I.C.R. 445 at [129] per Neuberger LJ) and in relation specifically to proprietary estoppel (see *Sidhu v van Dyke* (2014) 251 C.L.R. 505).

[130] See, e.g. *Gillett v Holt* [2001] Ch. 210 at 232.

[131] See *Gillett v Holt* [2001] Ch. 210 at 225 per Robert Walker LJ: the elements of proprietary estoppel "cannot be treated as subdivided into three or four watertight compartments".

[132] See *Cobbe v Yeoman's Row Management Ltd* [2008] 1 W.L.R. 1752 at [92] per Lord Walker. For example, a significant change of circumstances occurring since the time of S's promise may mean that it is no longer unconscionable for S to leave B to suffer a detriment as a result of B's reliance on S's promise: see, e.g. *Germanotta v Germanotta* [2012] Q.S.C. 116. For further discussion of the role of unconscionability in this context, see B. McFarlane, *The Law of Proprietary Estoppel* (Oxford University Press, 2014), paras 5–54 to 5–112.

[133] [2001] Ch. 210 at 225.

[134] [2009] 1 W.L.R. 776 at [61].

[135] See Lord Denning MR in *Crabb v Arun DC* [1976] 1 Ch. 179 at 187.

**2-092** If the doctrine of proprietary estoppel applies it may result in the enforcment of S's promise.[136] If it is thus found that S is under a duty to perfect the promised gift to B, S will hold the relevant property subject to that duty, and a constructive trust thus arises in B's favour. The doctrine does not, however, necessarily lead to the enforcement of S's promise. Certainly, it will not be enforced if the value of S's promise is "out of all proportion" to the extent of the potential detriment B will suffer as a result of her reliance if S reneges on the promise.[137] In such a case S will be under a lesser duty, such as a duty to pay a sum of money to B[138]: in that case, no constructive trust arises, as S holds no property on trust for B.

**2-093** In a case where S has made a promise to transfer specific, identifiable property to T to hold on trust for B, it therefore seems that, if B has reasonably relied on that promise and would as a result suffer a detriment were S to renege on the promise, the doctrine of proprietary estoppel may apply[139] and, depending on the extent of B's potential detriment, may lead to S's being under a duty to perform her promise, and thus to a constructive trust in B's favour.[140] In a case where S's promise was to transfer property into an existing settlement where T already holds on trust for B, and T has relied on the promise by, for example, incurring expenses on B's behalf in relation to the improvement or management of the property that T has promised to convey, it may be possible to regard such reliance as having been incurred on B's behalf and so as capable of supporting a proprietary estoppel claim by B.

### iii. Donatio Mortis Causa

**2-094** The doctrine of *donatio mortis causa* may apply where S attempts to make a deathbed gift, but fails to transfer property as planned to the donee.[141] Where it appli-es, its effect is that S, at her death, is regarded in equity as having made a valid transfer, and thus holds the subject matter of the planned gift subject to a constructive trust for the donee.[142] There is no reason in principle why the doctrine

---

[136] See, e.g. *Pascoe v Turner* [1979] 1 W.L.R. 431; *Thorner v Major* [2009] 1 W.L.R. 776. The decision in *Dillwyn v Llewellyn* (1862) 4 De G.F. & J. 517 appears to have been based on an analogy with part performance of a contract, but may perhaps today be seen as a proprietary estoppel case.

[137] See, e.g. *Jennings v Rice* [2003] 1 P. & C.R. 8; *Ottey v Grundy* [2003] W.T.L.R. 1253; *Henry v Henry* [2010] 1 All E.R. 988.

[138] See, e.g. *Jennings v Rice* [2003] 1 P. & C.R. 8; *Powell v Benney* [2007] EWCA Civ 1283. In *Campbell v Griffin* [2001] W.T.L.R. 981 and *McGuane v Welch* [2008] 2 P. & C.R. 24, the duty to pay a sum of money was secured by a charge on the land that had been promised to B.

[139] It seems to be the case, in general, that a proprietary estoppel claim, like a contractual claim, depends on S having made a promise to B rather than to a third party (see McFarlane, *The Law of Proprietary Estoppel* (2014), paras 8–34 to 8–36); however, on the facts of our hypothetical, where the promise is made to T in relation to a planned trust for B's benefit, then it may well still be possible for B to show that it was reasonable in the circumstances for B to have regarded S's promise as one that was seriously intended as capable of being relied on *by B*.

[140] Similarly, the doctrine may apply to assist B in a case where an attempted self-declaration of trust by S has failed or cannot be proved. In *McGuane v Welch* [2008] 2 P. & C.R. 24, for example, it was held that a document containing a self-declaration of trust in B's favour of a lease held by S could not be given in evidence, as the stamp duty on the declaration had not been paid, nor had any undertaking to pay that duty been given to the court by a solicitor (see per Mummery LJ at 27). It was held however that B could still rely on the doctrine of proprietary estoppel. Given the circumstances in which the B procured S's agreement to the parties' arrangement, and the limited detriment to B, it was held that S was not under a duty to give effect to that arrangement by holding the lease on trust for B, and instead was merely under a duty to compensate B for his expenditure incurred in reliance on the arrangement, such duty secured by a charge over S's lease: see, e.g. per Mummery LJ at 46.

[141] The origins, as well as the name, of the doctrine, can be traced to Roman law, but the English doctrine differs in its requirements from that recognised in Roman law: *Sen v Headley* [1991] Ch. 425 at 432.

[142] See, e.g. *Duffield v Elwes* (1827) 1 Bli. N.S. 497 at 543 per Lord Eldon: "this is a good *donatio mortis causa*, raising by operation of law a trust; a trust which being raised by operation of law is not within the Statute of Frauds". See too *Sen v Headley* [1991] Ch. 425 at 439 per Nourse LJ.

could not apply in a case where the planned deathbed gift was intended to have effect by means of a transfer to T to hold on trust for B: S would then hold that property on constructive trust for B.

The doctrine will apply if three requirements are met: (i) the donor (S) must have made the gift in contemplation, though not necessarily in expectation, of S's impending death; (ii) S must have delivered to the donee (B)[143] the subject-matter of the gift, or the means or part of the means of getting at that subject-matter (e.g. by delivering car keys[144] or a key to a box containing essential indicia of title,[145] intending to part with dominion over the property to which the key relates); (iii) the circumstances must have been such as to establish that the gift was to be absolute and complete only on S's death so as to be revocable before then. A condition to this effect need not be expressed and will normally be implied from the fact that the gift was made when the S was ill.[146] **2–095**

Where the planned gift relates, for example, to a chose in action, the doctrine may apply where S has delivered a document which is necessary to prove title to the chose in action.[147] It is not necessary that the document should contain all the terms on which the subject-matter of the chose in action is held.[148] The doctrine can also apply where there has been delivery of title deeds to land,[149] or of a share certificate,[150] or of a cheque payable to S.[151] The mere delivery by S to B of a cheque drawn by S on S's own account does not allow the doctine to apply, however, as the cheque is not a document giving B the right to any *specific* property held by S.[152] **2–096**

### iv.Other Cases of Unconscionable Conduct?

We have considered a number of means by which a constructive trust may arise and give B a beneficial interest in relation to property where S planned, but failed, to make a gift of that property to B (either directly or by means of a trust where T was to hold the property on trust for B). At an abstract level, it might be said that the need to prevent unconscionable conduct by S underlies the recognition of such constructive trusts and, indeed, of any trust imposed by law. However, a broad and unparticularised notion of unconscionability, if not given effect to through specific principles, is a very uncertain guide when attempting to establish rights in relation to property. This does not mean that the law cannot develop: new, specific principles can emerge, identifying and responding to particular forms of unconscionable conduct. Such principles need to be invoked, however, only if none of the existing rules give rise to a constructive trust. It is useful to bear these points in mind when considerig the following extract. **2–097**

*Pennington v Waine*

[2002] 1 W.L.R. 2075 (CA)

Ada owned 1,500 out of 2,000 shares in C Ltd. She told her nephew, Harold, who was company secretary, that she was going to give him 400 of those shares and wanted him to become a director. She then instructed Pennington, a partner in the firm of accountants which acted as the company auditors, **2–098**

---

143 Where S's plan was to transfer T to hold on trust for B, delivery to T would presumably suffice.
144 *Woodard v Woodard* (1991) 21 Fam. Law 470 (not necessary to hand over the car's log book).
145 *Re Lillingston* [1952] 2 All E.R. 184; *Sen v Headley* [1991] Ch. 425.
146 See *Re Mustapha* (1891) 8 T.L.R. 160; *Re Lillingston* [1952] 2 All E.R. 184.
147 *Moore v Darton* (1851) 4 De G. & Sm. 517; *Re Dillon* (1890) 44 Ch.D. 76; *Birch v Treasury Solicitor* [1951] Ch. 298.
148 *Birch v Treasury Solicitor* [1951] Ch. 298; disapproving dicta in *Re Weston* [1902] 1 Ch. 680 and *Delgoffe v Fader* [1939] Ch. 922.
149 *Sen v Headley* [1991] Ch. 425.
150 *Dufficy v Mollica* [1968] 3 N.S.W.L.R. 751 at 759.
151 *Re Mead* (1880) 15 Ch.D. 651.
152 *Re Beaumont* [1902] 1 Ch. 889; *Re Leaper* [1916] 1 Ch. 579.

to prepare a share transfer form. She executed the form and returned it to Pennington. He then put the form in the file relating to the company which he kept in his office. He subsequently told Harold of Ada's gift, saying that Harold need take no further action, and he asked Harold to sign the necessary form of consent to act as director now that he had qualifying shares. Harold signed the form and Ada as director countersigned it. Ada then made a will bequeathing 620 shares to Harold, assuming that after her death he would then have 1,020 of the 2,000 shares. A month later she died. The question was whether the 400 shares formed part of her estate or had instead been effectively given to Harold.

**2-099** ARDEN L.J. (with whom SCHIEMANN L.J. agreed): . . . The legal title to a share may today be conveyed by the execution and registration of an instrument of transfer (section 182(1) of the Companies Act 1985). However, the equitable interest in a share may pass under a contract of sale even if the contract is not completed by registration.[153] In addition, a share may also be the subject of a valid equitable assignment: see for example *Re Rose, Rose v IRC*.

**2-100** This appeal raises the question of what is necessary for the purposes of a valid equitable assignment of shares by way of gift. If the transaction had been for value, a contract to assign the share would have been sufficient: neither the execution nor the delivery of an instrument of transfer would have been required. However, where the transaction was purely voluntary, the principle that equity will not assist a volunteer must be applied and respected. This principle is to be found in *Milroy v Lord* and other cases. . . . Accordingly the gift must be perfected, or "completely constituted".

**2-101** . . .the principle that equity will not assist a volunteer at first sight looks like a hard-edged rule of law not permitting much argument or exception. Historically the emergence of the principle may have been due to the need for equity to follow the law rather than an intuitive development of equity. The principle against imperfectly constituted gifts led to harsh and seemingly paradoxical results. Before long, equity had tempered the wind to the shorn lamb (i.e. the donee). It did so on more than one occasion and in more than one way.

**2-102** First it was held that an incompletely constituted gift could be upheld if the gift had been completed to such an extent that the donee could enforce his right to the shares as against third parties without forcing the donor to take any further step. Accordingly, if a share transfer has been executed by the donor and duly presented to the company for registration, the donee would be entitled, if necessary, to apply to the court for an order for rectification of the share register under section 359 of the Companies Act 1985. Such an order would not, of course, be granted if for example the directors had a discretion to refuse to register the transfer and had timeously passed a valid resolution to decline to register the transfer.[154]

**2-103** That exception was extended in *Re Rose, Rose v IRC* and other cases by holding that for this exception to apply it was not necessary that the donor should have done all that it was necessary to be done to complete the gift, short of registration of the transfer. On the contrary it was sufficient if the donor had done all that it was necessary for him or her to do. . . .

**2-104** Secondly equity has tempered the wind (of the principle that equity will not assist a volunteer) to the shorn lamb (the donee) by utilising the constructive trust. This does not constitute a declaration of trust thus does not fall foul of the principle[155] that an imperfectly constituted gift is not saved by being treated as a declaration of trust. Thus, for example, in *T. Choithram International SA v Pagarani*,[156] the Privy Council held that the assets which the donor gave to the foundation of which he was one of the trustees were held upon trust to vest the same in all the trustees of the foundation on the terms of the trusts of the foundation. This particular trust obligation was not a term of the express trust constituting the foundation but a constructive trust adjunct to it.[157]. . .

**2-105** Thirdly, equity has tempered the wind to the shorn lamb by applying a benevolent construction to words of gift . . . In [*T. Choithram International SA v Pagarani*][158] [t]he Privy Council held that the gift to the

---

153 *Hawks v McArthur* [1951] 1 All E.R. 22.

154 See *Buckley on the Companies Acts*, 15th edn (2000) para.[359.277].

155 See *Milroy v Lord* (1862) 4 De G F & J 264 and *Jones v Lock* (1865) 1 Ch App 25.

156 [2001] 1 W.L.R. 1. See paras 2-012—2-021.

157 [Note that this analysis of the specific duty to vest the property in all the trustees does not mean that the core trust in *Pagarani* must be regarded as constructive: as made clear by Arden LJ in her judgment (see, e.g. at [60], extracted at para.2-105), and in her later judgment in *Shah v Shah* [2011] W.T.L.R. 519 at [14]-[20], that core trust in *Pagarani* depended on the finding that a valid self-declaration of trust had been made, and so the trust was thus express and not constructive.

158 [2001] 1 W.L.R. 1. See paras 2-012—2-021.

"Foundation" could only properly be construed as a gift to the purposes declared by the trust deed and administered by the trustees. [Arden L.J. then cited the paragraphs of Lord Browne-Wilkinson's advice extracted above[159]]. . .

Accordingly the principle that, where a gift is imperfectly constituted, the court will not hold it to operate as a declaration of trust, does not prevent the court from construing it to be a trust if that interpretation is permissible as a matter of construction, which may be a benevolent construction. The same must apply to words of gift. An equity to perfect a gift would not be invoked by giving a benevolent construction to words of gift or, it follows, words which the donor used to communicate or give effect to his gift. **2–106**

The cases to which counsel have referred us do not reveal any, or any consistent single policy consideration behind the rule that the court will not perfect an imperfect gift. The objectives of the rule obviously include ensuring that donors do not by acting voluntarily act unwisely in a way that they may subsequently regret. This objective is furthered by permitting donors to change their minds at any time before it becomes completely constituted. This is a paternalistic objective, which can outweigh the respect to be given to the donor's original intention as gifts are often held by the courts to be incompletely constituted despite the clearest intention of the donor to make the gift. Another valid objective would be to safeguard the position of the donor: suppose, for instance, that (contrary to the fact) it had been discovered after Ada's death that her estate was insolvent, the court would be concerned to ensure that the gift did not defeat the rights of creditors. But, while this may well be a relevant consideration, for my own part I do not consider that this need concern the court to the exclusion of other considerations as in the event of insolvency there are other potent remedies available to creditors where insolvents have made gifts to defeat their claims.[160] There must also be, in the interests of legal certainty, a clearly ascertainable point in time at which it can be said that the gift was completed, and this point in time must be arrived at on a principled basis. **2–107**

There are countervailing policy considerations which would militate in favour of holding a gift to be completely constituted. These would include effectuating, rather than frustrating, the clear and continuing intention of the donor, and preventing the donor from acting in a manner which is unconscionable. . . . **2–108**

If one proceeds on the basis that a principle which animates the answer to the question whether an apparently incomplete gift is to be treated as completely constituted is that a donor will not be permitted to change his or her mind if it would be unconscionable, in the eyes of equity, vis à vis the donee to do so, what is the position here? There can be no comprehensive list of factors which makes it unconscionable for the donor to change his or her mind: it must depend on the court's evaluation of all the relevant considerations. What then are the relevant facts here? Ada made the gift of her own free will: there is no finding that she was not competent to do this. She not only told Harold about the gift and signed a form of transfer which she delivered to Mr Pennington for him to secure registration: her agent also told Harold that he need take no action. In addition Harold agreed to become a director of the company without limit of time, which he could not do without shares being transferred to him. If Ada had changed her mind on (say) 10 November 1998, in my judgment the court could properly have concluded that it was too late for her to do this as by that date Harold signed the form 288A, the last of the events identified above, to occur. **2–109**

There is next the pure question of law: was it necessary for Ada deliver the form of transfer to Harold?. . . the ratio of *Re Rose, Rose v IRC* was as I read it that the gifts of shares in that case were completely constituted when the donor executed share transfers and delivered them to the transferees even though they were not registered in the register of members of the company until a later date. **2–110**

However, that conclusion as to the ratio in *Re Rose, Rose v IRC* does not mean that this appeal must be decided in the appellants' favour. Even if I am correct in my view that the Court of Appeal took the view in *Re Rose, Rose v IRC* that delivery of the share transfers was there required, it does not follow that delivery cannot in some circumstances be dispensed with. Here, there was a clear finding that Ada intended to make an immediate gift. Harold was informed of it. Moreover, I have already expressed the view that a stage was reached when it would have been unconscionable for Ada to recall the gift. It follows that it would also have been unconscionable for her personal representatives to refuse to hand over the share transfer to Harold after her death. In those circumstances, in my judgment, delivery of the share transfer before her death was unnecessary so far as perfection of the gift was concerned. **2–111**

It is not necessary to decide the case simply on that basis. After the share transfers were executed **2–112**

159 See paras 2–016—2–017.

160 See, e.g. ss.339 and 423 of the Insolvency Act 1986.

> Mr Pennington wrote to Harold on Ada's instructions informing him of the gift and stating that there was no action that he needed to take. I would also decide this appeal in favour of the respondent on this further basis. If I am wrong in the view that delivery of the share transfers to the company or the donee is required and is not dispensed with by reason of the fact that it would be unconscionable for Ada's personal representatives to refuse to hand the transfers over to Harold, the words used by Mr Pennington should be construed as meaning that Ada and, through her, Mr Pennington became agents for Harold for the purpose of submitting the share transfer to the Company. This is an application of the principle of benevolent construction to give effect to Ada's clear wishes. Only in that way could the result "This requires no action on your part" and an effective gift be achieved. Harold did not question this assurance and must be taken to have proceeded to act on the basis that it would be honoured.
>
> **2–113** [CLARKE L.J. gave a separate judgment holding that mere execution of the signed share transfer form on its own amounted to a valid equitable assignment,[161] but, if he were wrong on that, then he agreed with ARDEN L.J.'s reasons.]

**2–114** On one reading, *Pennington v Waine* thus opens the door to a beneficial interest arising in favour of B (presumably under a constructive trust) whenever "it would be unconscionable, in the eyes of equity, vis-à-vis [B]"[162] for S to change her mind and not proceed with a planned gift to B. There would then be no specific principle as to when B can thus claim a beneficial interest, as "[t]here can be no comprehensive list of factors which makes it unconscionable for the donor to change her mind. It must depend on the court's evaluation of all the relevant considerations."[163] As previously noted,[164] however, such an approach would leave the law in a very uncertain state, causing problems, for example, to third parties dealing with property which apparently belongs absolutely to S, but which might later turn out to have been impressed with a constructive trust arising because of S's earlier plan to make a gift of the property to B.

**2–115** Fortunately, such a broad interpretation has not been given to *Pennington v Waine* by subsequent courts (at least not yet). In *Curtis v Pulbrook*, for example, Briggs J gave the following analysis of the decision[165]:

> In *Pennington v Waine*, Arden L.J. (with whom Schiemann L.J. agreed) identified three routes by which, in the context of a defective voluntary transfer of shares, the court might avoid the rigorous application of the principle that equity will not compel the completion of an imperfect gift, in the absence of a valid declaration of trust. She described all three as methods whereby a court of equity might temper the wind to the shorn lamb. The first is where the donor has done everything necessary to enable the donee to enforce a beneficial claim without further assistance from the donor.[166] The second is where some detrimental reliance by the donee upon an apparent although ineffective gift may so bind the conscience of the donor to justify the imposition of a constructive trust.[167] The third is where by a benevolent construction an effective gift or implied declaration of trust may be teased out of the words used.[168] On its facts, *Pennington v Waine* appears to have been an example of sufficient detrimental reliance by the donee, who had agreed to become a director of the subject company upon an assumption that he had received an effective gift of qualifying shares in it.[169]

---

161 For a criticism of this analysis, see 2–035.
162 [2002] 1 W.L.R. 2075 at [64] (extracted at para.2–109).
163 ibid., at [64] (extracted at para.2–109).
164 See para.2–097.
165 [2011] EWHC 167 (Ch) at [43].
166 See [2002] 1 W.L.R. 2075 at [55]–[56] and *Rose v IRC* [1952] Ch. 499.
167 See [2002] 1 W.L.R. 2075 at [59] (extracted at para.2–104).
168 See [2002] 1 W.L.R. 2075 at [60]–[61] (extracted at paras 2–105—2–106), apparently based on *T. Choithram International SA v Pagarani* [2001] 1 W.L.R. 1.
169 See [2002] 1 W.L.R. 2075 at [64]–[66] (extracted at paras 2–109—2–111).

The analysis of Briggs J provides a useful limit to the impact of the decision in *Pennington v Waine*, in effect regarding it as an application of the doctrine of proprietary estoppel.[170] The difficulty with that reading on the facts may be that the extent of Harold's detriment, arising as a result of his act of becoming director, is likely to have been limited and so, if the doctrine of proprietary estoppel were applied, there would at least be a question of whether enforcing Ada's promise would be a disproportionate response. It should also be noted that the promise-based strand of proprietary estoppel is usually applied only where the promise relates, at least in part, to some land of the promisor.[171] **2–116**

It is of course easy to understand why, in a case such as *Pennington v Waine*, a court may wish to reach a result which upholds the clear intentions of S: in that case, Ada had clearly wished to ensure that, on her death, Harold would have a majority shareholding in the company, and that outcome depending on Harold having acquired, during Ada's life, a beneficial interest in the 400 shares that she intended to transfer to him. As Turner LJ noted in *Milroy v Lord*, it is only natural for a judge to feel "a strong disposition to give effect to [the donor's intentions] to the fullest extent".[172] As we will see in the next chapter, that same sentiment is often apparent in cases where a failure to comply with a formality rule threatens to frustrate S's clear intentions. However, the rules as to constitution of trusts, like formality rules, are there for a reason,[173] and, if they have not been satisfied, and neither a transfer to trustees nor a self-declaration of trust by S can be found on the facts, a constructive trust should be imposed only if there is a specific reason why S should hold property subject to a duty to B. Certainly, the frustration of S's intentions caused by a failure successfully to exercise a power to give B a beneficial interest should not, in itself, provide sufficent grounds for the imposition of a constructive trust. **2–117**

**Questions**

1 In *T. Choithram International SA v Pagarani*, Lord Browne-Wilkinson said that: "Although equity will not assist a volunteer, it will not strive officiously to defeat a gift." Is it possible to reconcile those two aspects of equity's approach to the constitution of trusts?

2. Sam is registered freehold owner of land in Wales, the registered shareholder of 10,000 OK Ltd shares, a depositor of £12,000 with Bigg Bank, and is entitled to XYZ Ltd shares held for him by Eric, executor of his father's will.

   Sam executes a transfer form in Dawn's favour in relation to the registered land, and gives it to his solicitor, who then posts it to Dawn's solicitor. It arrives at Dawn's solicitor's office, but the office is in the process of moving to new premises, and the form is lost. Sam orally tells Frances he is holding his OK Ltd shares on trust for her, tells George he is holding his Bigg account on trust for him, and tells Eric to transfer the XYZ shares absolutely to Jennifer. Eric signs a duly completed share transfer form and encloses it with the relevant share certificate in an envelope which he gives to Jennifer, who accidentally throws it out with some old newspapers and empty envelopes.

---

170 In *Shah v Shah* [2011] W.T.L.R. 519, the third of the three *Pennington v Waine* methods of "tempering the wind" was adopted: the donor of shares had sent a signed transfer form, but not the share certificate, to the donee, but had also stated that he held the shares on trust for the donee. The donee thus acquired a beneficial interest under a self-declaration of trust, which was sufficiently clear that no "benevolent construction" was needed: see per Arden LJ at [20].

171 See, e.g. *Thorner v Major* [2009] 1 W.L.R. 776 at [61]. Note that where, as in *Thorner* itself, the promise also relates to other property of S (such as livestock), a constructive trust arising through proprietary estoppel may also encompass such property.

172 (1862) 4 De G.F. & J. 264 at 274 (extracted at para.2–008).

173 As noted, e.g. by Arden LJ in *Pennington v Waine* [2002] 1 W.L.R. 2075 at [62] (extracted at para.2–107).

**One month later a financial disaster strikes Sam, who now wishes to sell all the above property and use the proceeds of sale to meet his debts. Advise him. Would your answer be different in respect of the OK Ltd shares if he had made a further declaration of trust of 3,000 OK shares in favour of Keith?**

3. Under Andy's father's will property is settled on trust for Wendy for life, remainder to his sons Andy and Ben equally, but Wendy has an express power to appoint the capital between Andy and Ben as she sees fit. Andy, in a signed document, assigns "All my interest under my father's will trusts to Bigg Bank on trust for Steve for life, remainder to Theresa".

   **Advise the bank if Wendy dies either: (i) without having made an appointment so that Andy receives £450,000 under his father's will trusts; or (ii) having appointed £500,000 to Andy a month before her death, so that Andy then also receives assets worth a further £200,000 under his father's will trusts.**

   **Would your advice differ if, instead, Andy had assigned to the Bank, inter alia "all such assets whatsoever as shall come into my possession on my mother's death under the terms of my father's will trusts"? Would any of your advice to the bank differ if unknown to Andy the bank happened to be trustee of his father's will trusts?**

4. "When it comes to Chancery judges directing trustees not to sue on covenants that are not themselves the subject-matter of a trust, the judges cannot justify their directions simply on the negative basis that 'Equity will not assist a volunteer' because Equity is positively intervening to prevent trustees exercising their common law rights." **Discuss.**

5. Is the following approach to questions arising in connection with completely and incompletely constituted trusts a sound one?

   (a) Ask if a trust has been completely constituted by property having been transferred by S to trustees on trust for B. In considering whether such a trust has been established by transfer, note that the rule in *Re Rose* may apply to allow a court to find that a transfer has occurred "in equity". Note too the general rule that the transfer has to be effected by S or S's agent, and the exception to that rule resulting from the extension of the *Strong v Bird* decision.

   (b) If a completely constituted trust by transfer cannot be found, ask if a trust has been completely constituted by a declaration of trust by S, of property currently held by S, in favour of B. Note that, in a case where it is clear that S intended a trust for B, a court may adopt a "benevolent construction" of the facts in order to find such a self-declaration. The mere fact, however, that S intended to set up a trust for B by means of a transfer to trustees cannot, in itself, justify a court in finding that S declared a trust.

   (c) If no completely constituted trust has arisen, either by tranfer to trustees or by self-declaration, then consider if a constructive trust has arisen in B's favour. The mere fact that S intended to make a gift to B cannot suffice for such a trust to arise, but, in suitable circumstances, B may be able to invoke the doctrine of proprietary estoppel or of donatio mortis causa. If B has provided consideration for S's promise to make a gift, B may be able to rely on the principle applied in *Pullan v Koe*.

   (d) If no express trust or constructive trust has arisen in relation to the property initially held by S, but S made a promise in a deed (a covenant) to T to make a transfer to T to hold on trust for B, then ask if S intended that T should hold the benefit of T's common law right to sue on that covenant on trust for B. If so, B can then compel T to sue S and claim substantial damages which will be held by T on trust for B.

# 3

# FORMAL REQUIREMENTS

## 1. Introduction

### A. Formality Rules

The law provides that certain transactions, such as the creation or transfer of property rights, must take a particular form, e.g. they must be carried out in writing. The underlying purposes of such rules are, first, to ensure that an owner of property seriously considers what she is doing before transferring beneficial ownership of the property to another person, and, secondly, to ensure that documentary evidence exists that will make fraud more difficult and forestall problems that might otherwise arise in determining who is entitled to what, especially after many years have elapsed, when memories have faded and the main actors may even have died.[1] This chapter will consider the content and scope of the formality rules governing the creation and transfer of equitable property interests under a trust, and the consequences of non-compliance with these rules. 3–001

We will focus on four formality rules. In relation to lifetime, or inter vivos, dealings with property, we will consider: (i) the Law of Property (Miscellaneous Provisions) Act 1989 s.2; (II) the Law of Property Act 1925 s.53(1)(b); and (iii) the Law of Property Act 1925 s.53(1)(c). The first of those is a general formality rule, not specific to trusts, that regulates contracts for the sale or other disposition of an interest in land. The second is specific to trusts, although it applies only in relation to land, as it regulates the means by which a party can prove a declaration of a trust of land. The third applies to the disposition of existing equitable interests, whether or not relating to land, and so is relevant, for example, when a beneficiary of trust seeks to assign her beneficial interest to another party. Additionally, in relation to testamentary dispositions, we will consider: (iv) the Wills Act 1837 s.9. This is a general formality rule, not specific to trusts, that regulates testamentary dispositions. 3–002

It may first be useful to make four points. First, there is a distinction between formal requirements that apply specifically to the creation of a trust and those that apply generally to the transfer of, or other dealings with, a particular type of property. For example, as we saw in Chapter 2, if a settlor wishes to transfer property to trustees to hold on trust, the general rule is that the intended trust will be constituted only if the transfer is made successfully. This may require compliance with formality rules, if such rules regulate the transfer of the type of property in question.[2] Such formality rules, however, apply whether or not a trust is intended. 3–003

---

1 See L. Fuller, "Consideration and Form" (1941) 41 Columbia L.R. 799, which makes similar points in connection with the formality rules governing the creation of contracts. See too P. Critchley, "Taking Formalities Seriously" in S. Bright and J. Dewar (eds), *Land Law: Themes and Perspectives* (Oxford University Press, 1998).

2 For example, if the settlor intends to transfer company shares to trustees to hold on trust, that trust will be constituted only when the trustees are registered as the holders of the shares.

3-004 Secondly, there are no formality rules that specifically govern the creation of a trust. If a settlor holds property other than land, and wishes to give another party a beneficial interest in that property, the settlor can do so simply by means of an *oral* declaration of trust. This is the case even if the beneficiary is a volunteer: a party who has provided no consideration and who simply benefits from the settlor's generosity. As Jeffrey Hackney has noted[3]:

> I can informally transfer to you my economic advantages in chattels of huge value by a few significantly chosen words, and once simply done that act cannot be revoked. No other device in the legal system approaches the massive power of these spoken words in Equity: 'I declare myself trustee of this for you.'[4]

Indeed, whilst the Law of Property Act s.53(1)(b) imposes a formality rule for the declaration of trusts in relation to land, that rule, as we will see,[5] regulates the means by which such trusts can be *proved*, not the means by which they can be created.

3-005 Thirdly, it is generally true that formality rules, where they apply, regulate attempts by a party to exercise a legal power, such as the power to make a transfer of particular property, or the power to dispose of property on her death. As a result, such rules may be relevant when considering, for example, a party's attempt to make a particular type of contract,[6] or a beneficiary's attempt to exercise the power to assign her beneficial interest to another.[7] In contrast, as noted in Chapter 1,[8] if a party claims that a trust has arisen by operation of law, and thus by means of a constructive or resulting trust, it is unlikely that a formality rule will be relevant, as such trusts do not depend on any party having exercised a power to set up a trust. It is therefore important to note that, even if a particular formality rule prevents the claimant from showing that a party successfully exercised a power to give her a beneficial interest in property, this does not necessarily prevent the claimant from showing that she acquired such an interest by means of a resulting or constructive trust.[9]

3-006 Fourthly, in understanding the operation of formality rules, it is important to distinguish between lifetime and testamentary dispositions, as the Wills Act 1837 regulates the latter but not the former. We will now examine how that distinction is made.

### *B. Lifetime and Testamentary Dispositions Distinguished*

3-007 A lifetime disposition is a disposition of property that takes effect during the lifetime of the person disposing of the property. A testamentary disposition is a disposition that takes effect after death, and will be effective only if made in the form of a valid will. A will is "an instrument by which a person makes a disposition of his property to take effect after his decease and which is in its own nature ambulatory and revocable during his life".[10] The party making the will is the testator or testatrix.

---

3 J. Hackney, *Understanding Equity and Trusts* (Fontana Press, 1987), p.109.

4 Note too that the settlor does not have to use any specific words or formula to set up the trust. The question is rather whether an objective intention to declare a trust has been sufficiently manifested: see, e.g. *Paul v Constance* [1977] 1 WLR 527.

5 At paras 3-026ff.

6 See the Law of Property (Miscellaneous Provisions) Act 1989 s.2.

7 See the Law of Property Act 1925 s.53(1)(c).

8 See paras 1-046—1-052.

9 See, e.g. Law of Property (Miscellaneous) Provisions Act 1989 s.2(5), providing that "nothing in [s.2] affects the creation or operation of resulting, implied or constructive trusts"; and Law of Property Act 1925 s.53(2), providing that "[t]his section does not affect the creation or operation of resulting, implied or constructive trusts", thereby putting such trusts outside the reach of the s.53(1)(b) and s.53(1)(c) formality rules.

10 *Baird v Baird* [1990] 2 A.C. 548 at 556, adopting T. Jarman, R. Jennings and J. Harper, *Jarman on Wills*, 8th edn (Sweet & Maxwell, 1951), p.26.

There are various reasons why it might matter whether a disposition is testamentary in character. One is that a testamentary disposition can always be revoked during the lifetime of the testator,[11] but a disposition which is not testamentary may or may not be revocable, depending on its terms. Another reason is that a disposition will be void if it is testamentary and the disponor fails to comply with the formality rules contained in the Wills Act 1837. If the disposition is void, the benefit of the property will go not to the intended recipient, but rather to the estate of the testator, and this provides a reason for a party taking a share of that estate to try to persuade a court to characterise a particular disposition as testamentary. **3–008**

In *Chopra v Bindra*,[12] for example, the deceased had owned a house with his sister, and they had executed a deed stating that, whilst they each held a distinct beneficial interest in the house as tenants in common, on either of their deaths, the survivor would be entitled to the whole proceeds of sale of the house. The wife of the deceased, who was the sole beneficiary under his will, claimed, inter alia, that this provision in the deed was invalid, as it was a testamentary disposition that did not comply with the formality requirements imposed by the Wills Act 1837. The Court of Appeal rejected that argument, as the deed "disposed of the proceeds of the unsold house with immediate effect and was irrevocable" whereas "[i]t is the essence of a testamentary disposition that it is only intended to take effect after the testator's death and is revocable during the testator's lifetime".[13] **3–009**

This does not mean, however, that every document intended to operate on death and containing a power of revocation is necessarily testamentary in character. In *Baird v Baird*,[14] for example, the deceased was employed by a company that provided its employees with a pension scheme, the rules of which stated that a member could (revocably) nominate a beneficiary to receive a "death benefit" if the member died while he was in employment; if no valid nomination was made then the death benefit would go to his spouse. The deceased nominated his brother, married, and then died without altering his nomination. His brother claimed the death benefit, but his widow argued that the nomination constituted a testamentary disposition, and was void for non-compliance with statutory formality rules applying to wills. The Privy Council held that the nomination was not a testamentary disposition. Such a disposition can occur only in relation to property that belongs to a testator in her lifetime, and the deceased had not owned any of the death benefit, having merely had the contractual right to require the trustees to pay it to his nominee after his death.[15] **3–010**

## 2. Lifetime Dispositions

### A. Law of Property (Miscellaneous Provisions) Act 1989 s.2

As noted above,[16] this is a formality rule, not specific to trusts, that regulates contracts for the sale or other disposition of an interest in land. **3–011**

---

11 See, e.g. *Baird v Baird* [1990] 2 A.C. 548 at 557 per Lord Oliver: "an essential characteristic of a will is that, during the lifetime of the testator, it is a mere declaration of his present intention and may be freely revoked or altered."

12 [2009] 2 F.L.R. 786.

13 ibid., at [15] per Rimer LJ.

14 [1990] 2 A.C. 548.

15 ibid., at 557, applying *Re Danish Bacon Co Ltd Staff Pension Fund Trusts* [1971] 1 W.L.R. 248.

16 See para.3–002.

**Law of Property (Miscellaneous Provisions) Act 1989 s.2**

3–012 (1) A contract for the sale or other disposition of an interest in land can only be made in writing and only by incorporating all the terms which the parties have expressly agreed in one document or, where contracts are exchanged, in each.

(2) The terms may be incorporated in a document either by being set out in it or by reference to some other document.

(3) The document incorporating the terms or, where contracts are exchanged, one of the documents incorporating them (but not necessarily the same one) must be signed by or on behalf of each party to the contract.

(4) Where a contract for the sale or other disposition of an interest in land satisfies the conditions of this section by reason only of the rectification of one or more documents in pursuance of an order of a court, the contract shall come into being, or be deemed to have come into being, at such time as may be specified in the order.

(5) This section does not apply in relation to—

(a) a contract to grant such a lease as is mentioned in section 54(2) of the Law of Property Act 1925 (short leases);
(b) a contract made in the course of a public auction; or
(c) a contract regulated under the Financial Services Act 1986;

and nothing in this section affects the creation or operation of resulting, implied or constructive trusts.

(6) In this section—

"disposition" has the same meaning as in the Law of Property Act 1925; "interest in land" means any estate, interest or charge in or over land or in or over the proceeds of sale of land.

(7) Nothing in this section shall apply in relation to contracts made before this section comes into force.

(8) Section 40 of the Law of Property Act 1925 (which is superseded by this section) shall cease to have effect.

## i. The Scope of s.2

3–013 A contract to create a trust of any interest in land,[17] and a contract to dispose of an equitable interest in land, e.g. a life interest or a co-owner's equitable interest under a trust of land, is governed by the Law of Property (Miscellaneous Provisions) Act 1989 s.2.[18] The section provides that the contract is void unless all the terms are in one document signed by both parties or in exchanged documents signed by each exchanger (or by a person acting on her behalf),[19] though it is possible to incorporate

[17] No formality rule applies to a contract to create a trust in relation to property other than land: see, e.g. *Chinn v Collins* [1981] A.C. 533 at 548; nor to a contract to transfer an existing beneficial interest in property other than land: see, e.g. *Neville v Wilson* [1997] Ch. 144, extracted at paras 3–106—3–117.

[18] The 1989 Act does not apply to the exercise of an option to purchase an interest in land (*Spiro v Glencrown Properties Ltd* [1991] Ch. 537) nor to a lock-out agreement not to consider any further offers if the purchaser exchanges contracts within two weeks (*Pitt v PHH Asset Management Ltd* [1994] 1 W.L.R. 327) nor to a collateral contract (*Record v Bell* [1991] 1 W.L.R. 853) nor to an agreement supplemental to a completed contract (*Tootal Clothing Ltd v Guinea Properties Management Ltd* (1992) 64 P. & C.R. 452). However it does apply to variations: *McCausland v Duncan Lawrie Ltd* [1997] 1 W.L.R. 38. If the parties omit an agreed term (of the sale contract, rather than of some collateral agreement: *North Eastern Properties Ltd v Coleman* [2010] 1 W.L.R. 2715) then rectification can sometimes (but not always) be obtained so that the rectified document complies with the 1989 Act: *Wright v Robert Leonard (Developments) Ltd* [1994] E.G.C.S. 69; cf. *Oun v Ahmad* [2008] EWHC 545 (Ch). For discussion of rectification, see paras 18–286ff.

[19] Old, liberal authorities on what constituted a sufficient signature for the Statute of Frauds 1677 and the Law of Property Act 1925 are no longer relevant: the 1989 Act has a different philosophy, and a signature for the purposes of the 1989 Act must be a personal signature: *Firstpost Homes Ltd v Johnson* [1995] 1 W.L.R. 1567.

terms set out in another document by referring to that document. The s.2 formality rule is also important to the law of trusts because, as we will see in Chapter 5,[20] a trust may arise as a result of a contract for the sale of an interest in land, even before that contract has been performed by the conveyance of the interest itself. Such a trust, however, depends on there being a valid contract, and so cannot arise if the formality rule has not been satisfied.

### ii. The Consequences of Non-Compliance

It is important to note that if s.2 is not complied with, there is no contract between the parties. Formerly, under both the Statute of Frauds 1677 s.4 and the Law of Property Act 1925 s.40, it was instead the case that an oral contract for the sale of an interest in land was valid, but unenforceable. The basic validity of the contract gave the courts the space to develop the equitable doctrine of part performance, under which specific performance of the contract could be ordered if some part of the contract had been performed and the claimant would therefore suffer some detriment if the contract were not enforced.[21] However, the nature and operation of the doctrine of part performance were unclear,[22] and one of the aims of the 1989 Act[23] was to avoid the complications of the doctrine by making clear that if the formality rule is not complied with, there is simply no contract between the parties. **3–014**

In the report which led to the enactment of the 1989 Act, the Law Commission, whilst emphasising the benefits of removing the doctrine of part performance from contracts, noted that there still might be situations where injustice could be caused if, in the absence of a contractual claim, a party were to have no recourse. It therefore noted that various non-contractual claims might be available to such a party: for example, a proprietary estoppel claim might be available if, as a result of reasonable reliance on the defendant's non-contractual promise, the claimant would now suffer a detriment if the defendant were wholly free to revoke that promise; and an unjust enrichment claim might arise if the claimant had transferred benefits to the defendant on the shared understanding that there was indeed a contract between the parties. **3–015**

It is indeed the case that, since the 1989 Act came into force, the courts have recognised that such non-contractual claims may arise in a case where s.2 has not been complied with.[24] The difficulty for the claimant, of course, lies in showing that she has established all the requirements of a non-contractual claim. **3–016**

In *Cobbe v Yeoman's Row Management Ltd*,[25] for example, the parties had made an oral agreement in principle that land would be sold to the claimant if planning permission were obtained and, in reliance on that agreement, and with the encouragement of the defendant vendor, the claimant had prepared the successful planning application. The judgment at first instance,[26] affirmed by the Court **3–017**

---

20 At paras 5–011—5–024.

21 *Steadman v Steadman* [1976] A.C. 536 as narrowly interpreted in *Re Gonin* [1979] Ch. 16.

22 For discussion of the doctrine see *Yaxley v Gotts* [2000] Ch. 162 at 171–172 per Robert Walker LJ, and for a helpful survey of the history and nature of the doctrine, see P. Matthews, "The Words Which Are Not There: A Partial History of the Constructive Trust" in C. Mitchell (ed.), *Constructive and Resulting Trusts* (Hart Publishing, 2010), pp.25–44.

23 See Law Commission, *The Transfer of Land: Formalities for Contracts of Sale etc. of Land* (HMSO, 1987), Law. Com. No.164, HC Paper No.2 (Session 1987–88) para.5.4 and *Yaxley v Gotts* [2000] Ch. 162 at 188 per Beldam LJ: "Section 2 of the 1989 Act was primarily intended to overcome the complexities which had arisen from the doctrine of part-performance and from problems caused by the interpretation of section 40 of the Law of Property Act 1925." Beldam LJ had been Chair of the Law Commission at the time of its work on the issue.

24 For a proprietary estoppel claim, see, e.g. *Yaxley v Gotts* [2000] Ch. 162; *Kinane v Mackie-Conteh* [2005] W.T.L.R. 345; *Herbert v Doyle* [2011] 1 E.G.L.R. 119; *Whittaker v Kinnear* [2011] EWHC 1479 (QB). For an unjust enrichment claim, see *Cobbe v Yeoman's Row Management Ltd* [2008] 1 W.L.R. 1752.

25 [2008] 1 W.L.R. 1752.

26 [2005] W.T.L.R. 625.

of Appeal,[27] was that the doctrine of proprietary estoppel applied and the defendant, who had refused to sell the land to the claimant, was ordered to pay the claimant a sum of around £2 million, equal to half of the increase in the value of the defendant's land resulting from the award of planning permission. The House of Lords, however, found that the ingredients of proprietary estoppel were absent: as Lord Neuberger later noted,[28] the parties' agreement in principle had left some important points outstanding, and it was therefore not possible for the claimant to show that he had reasonably relied on a promise which could be seen as one seriously intended by the defendant as capable of being relied upon. Nonetheless, the House of Lords held that a claim in unjust enrichment was made out,[29] as the claimant had performed valuable work for the defendant on the shared understanding that, if planning permission were obtained, that work would be rewarded. It was also held, however, that the extent of the claimant's award was not related to the increase in value of the defendant's land resulting from the claimant's work, but was limited instead to the usual market value of the services rendered by the claimant, plus other costs incurred: a sum estimated at around £150,000.[30]

**3-018** The decision of the House of Lords in the *Cobbe* case thus demonstrates that a failure to comply with s.2 does not rule out all claims. In that case, however, Lord Scott made the following statement[31]:

> There is one further point regarding proprietary estoppel to which I should refer. Section 2 of the 1989 Act declares to be void any agreement for the acquisition of an interest in land that does not comply with the requisite formalities prescribed by the section. Subsection (5) expressly makes an exception for resulting, implied or constructive trusts. These may validly come into existence without compliance with the prescribed formalities. Proprietary estoppel does not have the benefit of this exception. The question arises, therefore, whether a complete agreement for the acquisition of an interest in land that does not comply with the s. 2 prescribed formalities, but would be specifically enforceable if it did, can become enforceable via the route of proprietary estoppel. It is not necessary in the present case to answer this question, for the second agreement was not a complete agreement and, for that reason, would not have been specifically enforceable so long as it remained incomplete. My present view, however, is that proprietary estoppel cannot be prayed in aid in order to render enforceable an agreement that statute has declared to be void. The proposition that an owner of land can be estopped from asserting that an agreement is void for want of compliance with the requirements of s. 2 is, in my opinion, unacceptable. The assertion is no more than the statute provides. Equity can surely not contradict the statute.

**3-019** On the view adopted by Lord Scott, then, in a case where s.2 prevents a contractual claim, the claimant cannot turn to proprietary estoppel—although, owing to the express provision in s.2(5), the claimant may be able to rely on principles very similar to those of proprietary estoppel in order to show that a constructive trust has arisen.[32] Lord Scott's obiter suggestion[33] has not been received with universal enthusiasm[34] and, it is submitted, five key objections can be made.

**3-020** First, Lord Scott's view that s.2 renders an *agreement* void is incorrect: the section expressly regulates

---

27 [2006] 1 W.L.R. 2964.

28 *Thorner v Major* [2009] 1 W.L.R. 776 at [93]: "there was total uncertainty as to the nature or terms of any benefit (property interest, contractual right, or money) and, if a property interest, as to the nature of that interest (freehold, leasehold or charge), to be accorded to Mr Cobbe." That is perhaps putting matters at their highest, but it was certainly true that the parties had not decided whether the land was to be conveyed to Mr Cobbe, or to a company to be set up by him, nor how security was to be provided for a planned overage provision in the vendor's favour.

29 [2008] 1 W.L.R. 1752 at [40]–[44].

30 ibid., at [44], although note the reluctance of Lord Mance at [96] to support any such estimate.

31 ibid., at [29].

32 The links, for example, between proprietary estoppel and the "common intention" constructive trust will be considered at paras 5-140–5-144.

33 It was not necessary for the decision in the case, as the proprietary estoppel claim failed in any case: see para.3-017.

34 See *Whittaker v Kinnear* [2011] EWHC 1479 (QB) where Bean J stated at [30] that "notwithstanding Lord Scott's dicta in *Cobbe*, proprietary estoppel in a case involving the sale of land has survived the enactment of s.2 of the 1989 Act".

*contracts* and so it does not therefore rule out a non-contractual claim, even if that claim depends in part on the defendant's having made an oral promise to the claimant.

Secondly, and contrary to Lord Scott's view of the doctrine, proprietary estoppel does not operate to prevent the defendant from denying the existence of a contract, or the grant of a right; it rather provides a means by which an independent claim may be made.[35] Unlike a contractual claim, such a claim does not, for example, require the provision of consideration, or that the parties intended to make an immediately binding agreement;[36] and unlike a contractual claim, it does not necessarily lead to the promisor's being under a duty to put the claimant in the position that the claimant would have been in had the promise been performed.[37] It is therefore difficult to see how proprietary estoppel, if its requirements are properly applied, is inconsistent with either the express wording or underlying policy of the s.2 formality requirement. **3–021**

Thirdly,[38] Lord Scott's view leads to the strange position that, in a case where the parties have reached an agreement that would be contractually binding but for s.2, no proprietary estoppel claim can be made; whereas, in cases where it is clear that, even without s.2, there would be no contract between the parties, the courts have allowed proprietary estoppel claims without any consideration of the s.2 point.[39] Indeed, in *Yaxley v Gotts*,[40] the Court of Appeal was confronted with the unusual situation in which the *defendant* wished to show that he was party to an agreement to give the claimant a lease of particular flats, in order then to rely on s.2 to deny liability, whereas the claimant instead preferred to argue that a proprietary estoppel claim arose not because of any promise of the defendant, but rather as a result of the defendant standing by and acquiescing in the mistaken belief of the claimant that he had a contract with a third party.[41] **3–022**

Fourthly, as there is no reported case in which a proprietary estoppel claim has failed simply on the basis of a failure to comply with formality rules, the effect of Lord Scott's view would be to force courts to rely on s.2(5) by finding that a constructive trust has arisen even if, on the facts of the case, it is clear that the defendant does not in fact hold any property on trust for the claimant.[42] **3–023**

Finally, it was suggested above[43] that formality rules regulate situations where a party attempts to exercise a power, and it seems reasonably clear that the doctrine of proprietary estoppel operates to impose a liability on the defendant where necessary to prevent a particular form of unconscionable **3–024**

---

35 See, e.g. B. McFarlane and A. Robertson, "The Death of Proprietary Estoppel" [2008] L.M.C.L.Q. 449; T. Etherton, "Constructive Trusts and Proprietary Estoppel: The Search for Clarity and Principle" [2009] Conv. 104. Note that in the later case of *Thorner v Major* [2009] 1 W.L.R. 776 only one member of the panel of the House of Lords adopted Lord Scott's analysis of proprietary estoppel in *Cobbe*: Lord Scott.

36 See, e.g. *Walton v Walton* unreported, 14 April 1994; *Sutcliffe v Lloyd* [2007] 2 E.G.L.R. 13 at 38 per Wilson LJ.

37 See, e.g. *Jennings v Rice* [2003] 1 P. & C.R. 8; *Henry v Henry* [2010] 1 All E.R. 988.

38 This point is noted by, e.g. B. McFarlane, "Proprietary Estoppel and Failed Contractual Negotiations" [2005] Conv. 501 and Lord Neuberger, "The Stuffing of Minerva's Owl? Taxonomy and Taxidermy in Equity" [2009] C.L.J. 537, 546.

39 See, e.g. *Crabb v Arun DC* [1976] Ch. 179.

40 [2000] Ch. 162.

41 Note that Clarke LJ ([2000] Ch. 162 at 181) agreed with Beldam LJ's conclusion that there had, on the facts, been no agreement between the claimant and the defendant. As the presence of such an agreement (then, it was argued, rendered void by s.2) formed the basis of the defendant's appeal, the appeal failed. Given the differences in the analysis of Beldam LJ and Robert Walker LJ, it is significant that Clarke LJ took this view, as the appeal was thus dismissed on the basis that the first instance judge was correct to have found that a proprietary estoppel claim arose as a result of the defendant's acquiescence in the claimant's mistaken belief, not as a result of any agreement between the parties. See further B. McFarlane, *The Law of Proprietary Estoppel* (Oxford University Press, 2014), paras 6.54–6.63.

42 Note that there is already evidence of this problem in the case-law: e.g. in *Yaxley v Gotts* [2000] Ch. 162, there was said to be a constructive trust, yet it does not appear that the defendant held any property on trust, as the court's order was that the defendant should grant the claimant the promised lease, or pay him its value.

43 See para.3–005.

behaviour: as this form of liability is thus imposed by law it would be strange if it were regulated by a formality rule.

**3-025** It is therefore submitted that s.2 has no impact on a proprietary estoppel claim: if the requirements of such a claim are established, it should be permitted, whether or not a constructive trust can be found.[44] There is no need to resort to s.2(5), as the basic s.2 rule, which is limited to *contracts*, simply does not apply. As Lord Neuberger, writing extra-judicially, has put it[45]:

> [Where proprietary estoppel is concerned] I suggest that s. 2 has nothing to do with the matter. . . the estoppel rests on the finding that it would be inequitable for the defendant to insist on his strict legal rights. So the fact that, if there was a contract, it would be void is irrelevant: indeed the very reason for mounting the proprietary estoppel claim is that there is no enforceable contract.

## *B. Law of Property Act 1925 s.53(1)(b)*

**Law of Property Act 1925 s.53**

**3-026** (1) Subject to the provisions hereinafter contained with respect to the creation of interests in land by parol:

(a) No interest in land can be created or disposed of except by writing signed by the person creating or conveying the same, or by his agent thereunto lawfully authorised in writing, or by will, or by operation of law;

(b) A declaration of trust respecting any land or any interest therein must be manifested and proved by some writing signed by some person who is able to declare such trust or by his will;

(c) A disposition of an equitable interest or trust subsisting at the time of the disposition, must be in writing signed by the person disposing of the same, or by his agent thereunto lawfully authorised in writing or by will.

(2) This section does not affect the creation or operation of resulting, implied or constructive trusts.

### i. The Scope of s.53(1)(b)

**3-027** The formality rule imposed by s.53(1)(b) applies only to a declaration of trust "respecting any land or any interest therein". It varies from the rules imposed by s.53(1)(a) and s.53(1)(c) as it does not regulate the creation of rights, but only the means by which such creation can be proved.[46] So, for example, if an oral trust of land is declared, but later written evidence of the trust, signed by a party who is able to declare such a trust, comes into being, the beneficiary can prove that the trust existed *from the moment of its oral declaration*.[47]

**3-028** As the effect of a failure to comply with s.53(1)(b) thus differs from that in relation to s.53(1)(a), a

---

44 Note that in *McGuane v Welch* [2008] 2 P. & C.R. 24 at [35], it was held that the particular nature of the parties' agreement "left no space for the insertion of a constructive trust", yet a proprietary estoppel claim, based on that oral agreement, was nonetheless allowed to arise.

45 Lord Neuberger, "The Stuffing of Minerva's Owl? Taxonomy and Taxidermy in Equity" [2009] C.L.J. 537, 546.

46 As noted by W. Swadling, "The Nature of the Trust in *Rochefoucauld v Boustead*" in C. Mitchell (ed.), *Constructive and Resulting Trusts* (2010), p.108, s.53(1)(b) does not mean that the trust is unenforceable: rather, it simply regulates the means by which the trust can be proved.

47 See, e.g. *Gardner v Rowe* (1825) 2 S. & S. 346, affirmed (1828) 5 Russ. 258: the deed confirming the earlier oral declaration was executed only after the settlor went into insolvency, but it enabled proof of the declaration which was made before the insolvency, and the beneficial interest under the trust therefore bound the assignees in bankruptcy.

dividing line needs to be drawn between the two formality rules. It would seem that s.53(1)(a) must be interpreted as covering the creation of equitable interests in land other than equitable interests arising under a declaration of trust (e.g. restrictive covenants).[48] The fact that a slightly more lenient rule applies under s.53(1)(b) may perhaps be justified by the fact that, owing to the possibility of overreaching,[49] the existence of a beneficial interest under a trust of land causes fewer problems for third parties dealing with the land than the presence of a different type of equitable interest.

A settlor may create a trust of land either by declaring that she herself will henceforth hold the land on specified trusts, or by conveying the land to trustees and declaring specified trusts on which the trustees are to hold the land. In both cases, proof of the declaration of the trusts must be in writing specifying the beneficiaries, the trust property, and the nature of the trusts,[50] and the writing may be comprised in linked documents.[51] **3–029**

The signed writing must be "by some person who is able to declare such trust". So, for example, the sub-section would be satisfied if A conveyed Blackacre to B and at the same time declared signed written trusts for C. Again, if T1 and T2 held property on trust for A for life, remainder to B, but with power for the trustees to declare new trusts in favour of C or her issue, then the sub-section would be satisfied if T1 and T2 exercised this power in signed writing. In contrast to s.53(1)(a) or (c), there is no express reference in s.53(1)(b) to the possibility of an agent's signature, but this may simply be because a duly authorised agent, acting on behalf of a settlor, can be seen as "some person who is able to declare such trust". **3–030**

The signatory (or principal if signature by an agent is permitted) should be the person who, at the time of the signature, would be entitled to the enjoyment of the land if no declaration of trust had been made.[52] So, if A declares herself trustee of land for B, the relevant person would be A; and if, subsequently, B declares that she holds her equitable interest on trust for C, the relevant person would be B.[53] However, if A conveys land to B and orally declares a trust for C, then subsequent written evidence of the trust signed by B satisfies s.53(1)(b).[54] If A instead conveys land or transfers other property to B to hold to A's order and on some later date A then tells B to hold on trust for C, this amounts to A's disposing of her subsisting equitable interest to C, a disposition that, as we will see below,[55] will be void under s.53(1)(c) unless in writing signed by A or her agent.[56] **3–031**

### ii. The Consequences of Non-Compliance

If A either transfers land to B, or buys land in B's name, on an oral understanding with B that B will hold the land on trust for A, then case law assumes that, to satisfy s.53(1)(b), it is necessary for some **3–032**

---

48 In view of L.P.A. 1925 s.52(1), s.53(1)(a) cannot be restricted to legal interests and in order to prevent s.53(1)(a) from making s.53(1)(b) otiose, para.(b) should be construed in line with the maxim *generalia specialibus non derogant* (i.e. general clauses cannot derogate from special clauses), so that declarations of trust of land fall outside the scope of s.53(1)(a): *Hagan v Waterhouse* (1991) 34 N.S.W.L.R. 308 at 385–386.

49 See Trusts of Land and Appointment of Trustees Act s.6 and Law of Property Act 1925 ss.2 and 27. For an example of overreaching operating to protect such a third party, see *City of London Building Society v Flegg* [1998] A.C. 54.

50 *Smith v Matthews* (1861) 3 De G. F. & J. 139; *Morton v Tewart* (1842) 2 Y. & C. Ch. Cas. 67.

51 *Forster v Hale* (1798) 3 Ves. Jun. 696.

52 T. G. Youdan, "Formalities for Trusts of Land and the Doctrine in *Rochefoucauld v Boustead*" [1984] C.L.J. 306, 316–320.

53 *Tierney v Wood* (1854) 19 Beav. 330; *Kronheim v Johnson* (1877) 7 Ch.D. 60.

54 *Gardner v Rowe* (1828) 5 Russ. 258; *Smith v Matthews* (1861) 3 De G. F. & J. 139; *Mountain v Styak* [1922] N.Z.L.R. 131. If the oral trusts had been for A herself then she would have an equitable interest under a constructive trust which she could then sub-settle: *Tierney v Wood* (1854) 19 Beav. 330.

55 At paras 3–050ff.

56 *Grey v IRC* [1960] A.C. 1.

writing proving the trust to be signed by B.[57] What if B refuses to provide such writing, and instead attempts to keep the land for her own benefit? It would clearly be unconscionable for B, in such a case, to decide to keep the land for herself and to rely on the statute to prevent A proving any trust of the property: after all, the s.53(1)(b) formality rule derives from the Statute of Frauds,[58] which was enacted with the express purpose of *preventing* fraud. It is, fortunately, clear that, in such a case, A will be able to assert a beneficial interest against B. There is, however, a debate as to the best explanation for this undoubted position, and as to the nature of the trust that A can assert against B. There are two principal views.

**3-033** On the first view, the trust asserted by A is an express one, arising as a result of the oral declaration of trust. A is allowed to prove that declaration by means other than signed writing, as it would be fraudulent in the circumstances for B to rely on s.53(1)(b), and a "statute cannot be used as an instrument of fraud".[59] On this view, of course, the crucial issue is to define what conduct counts as fraud sufficient to prevent a party relying on the formality rule.[60] On the second view, the trust asserted by A is a constructive one, which does not arise as a result of the oral declaration of trust, but is rather imposed on the facts[61] to prevent the particular form of unconscionable conduct that would consist of B receiving property on the basis of a promise to hold it on trust, and then holding that property free from the promised trust. On this view, of course, the crucial issue is to define the precise form of unconscionable conduct involved.[62] Before considering those views in more detail, it is useful to examine a key authority.

*Rochefoucauld v Boustead*

Court of Appeal [1897] 1 Ch. 196

**3-034** In 1868, the plaintiff, the Comtesse de la Rochefoucauld, held an equity of redemption in coffee plantations in Ceylon (the Delmar Estates).[63] Legal title to the properties was held by the mortgagee, a Dutch company. The defendant, Mr Boustead, managed the plantations on behalf of the plaintiff. The Comtesse was unable to repay the mortgage debts and was concerend that the Dutch company would enforce its security by exercising its power to sell the land to a stranger. She therefore agreed with the defendant that, when the Dutch company auctioned off the estates, he would buy the titles to those estates at a price sufficient to cover the mortgage debt and expenses, and that he would hold those titles on trust for her, subject to a lien for his expenditure.[64] In 1873, the defendant bought the titles from the mortgagee,

---

[57] See, e.g. *Re Duke of Marlborough* [1894] 2 Ch. 133; *Smith v Matthews* (1861) 3 De G.F. & J. 139; *Gardner v Rowe* (1828) 5 Russ. 258; *Mountain v Styak* [1922] N.Z.L.R. 131.

[58] See Statute of Frauds 1677 s.7.

[59] For academic support for that view, see, e.g. W Swadling, "The Nature of the Trust in *Rochefoucauld v Boustead*" in C. Mitchell (ed.), *Constructive and Resulting Trusts* (2010). For discussion of the principle that "equity will not allow a statute to be used as an instrument of fraud" see G. Allan, "Once a Fraud, Forever a Fraud: The Time Honoured Doctrine of Parol Agreement Trusts" (2014) 34 L.S. 419.

[60] See further paras 5-030—5-045.

[61] For academic support for that view, see, e.g. B. McFarlane, "Constructive Trusts Arising on Receipt of Property *Sub Conditione*" (2004) 120 L.Q.R. 667; N. Hopkins, "Conscience, Discretion and the Creation of Property Rights" (2006) 26 L.S. 475; S. Gardner, "Reliance-Based Constructive Trusts" in C. Mitchell (ed.), *Constructive and Resulting Trusts* (2010); Y.K. Liew "*Rochefoucauld v Boustead* (1897)" in C. Mitchell and P. Mitchell (eds), *Landmark Cases in Equity* (Hart Publishing, 2012).

[62] Note that, whilst they agree that the trust is constructive and not express, there is no unanimity on this point between the commentators cited at fn.61. See further para.5-044.

[63] Note that *Rochefoucauld* itself involved land outside the English jurisdiction. The formality rule imposed by the Statute of Frauds 1677, s. 7 was still considered relevant as it was said to affect the means of proof, in an English court, of the trust: see [1897] 1 Ch 196, 207, relying on *Leroux v Brown* (1852) 12 CB 80, which dealt with Statute of Frauds 1677, s. 4. It is not clear that a modern court would adopt the same view of s. 53(1)(b): see L Collins et al (eds) *Dicey, Morris and Collins: The Conflict of Laws* (15th edn, 2013) at 7-031.

[64] Y K Liew, '*Rochefoucauld v Boustead* (1897)' in C Mitchell & P Mitchell (eds) *Landmark Cases in Equity* (2012) suggests, drawing on the Law Times report of the case, (1897) 75 LT 502, 504–505, that this route was adopted as the Comtessse

with the conveyance saying nothing of the planned trust for the plaintiff. Without her knowledge, he then mortgaged the titles to the estates to secure his own borrowings. In 1894, the plaintiff sought a declaration that he had bought the titles as trustee for her, for an account of his dealings as trustee with the estates, and for payment of the amount found to be due. By then, the titles had already been sold, but the plaintiff alleged that the proceeds of sale were sufficient to repay the defendant all she owed him, and that a surplus remained, which he should pay her.

The defendant denied that he had bought the titles as trustee for the plaintiff, and said that in any case the alleged trusts could not be proved by any writing signed by him, and that the Statute of Frauds 1677 s.7 (the predecessor of s. 53(1)(b) of the Law of Property Act 1925) precluded the admission of oral evidence to make good the plaintiff's allegation. Kekewich J. heard the plaintiff's oral testimony but did not admit it into evidence, on the ground that he was precluded from doing so by section 7. Hence he found that the plaintiff had not proved that the defendant had agreed to hold the titles on trust for her, and dismissed the claim. The Court of Appeal held that Kekewich J. had been wrong to use section 7 to keep out the claimant's evidence. Admitting that evidence, the court held that it proved the plaintiff's case. The defendant also sought to rely on the six-year limitation period in the Trustee Act 1888 s.8(1)(b), which governed claims for breach of trust against constructive trustees, but the court held that the trust was express, so that no limitation period applied. Hence the court granted the relief sought. **3–035**

LINDLEY L.J. delivered the judgment of the court (which consisted of LORD HALSBURY L.C., LINDLEY and A.L. SMITH L.JJ.): The question raised by this appeal is whether the plaintiff is entitled to an account from the defendant of the proceeds of sale of certain coffee estates in Ceylon. The estates in question are known as the Delmar estates. They formerly belonged to the plaintiff; they were mortgaged first to Barings and then to a Dutch company, and on May 27, 1873, they were sold and conveyed to the defendant. In form the conveyance was to him absolutely, but the plaintiff insists that the estates were conveyed to the defendant as a trustee for the plaintiff, subject, however, to the repayment to the defendant of the amount which he paid for them and of the expenses which he has incurred in managing the estates. The estates were sold by the defendant or his mortgagees many years ago without the knowledge of the plaintiff, and she says that the proceeds of sale were more than sufficient to repay to the defendant all his advances, and that a considerable surplus remained which the defendant ought to have paid over to her. The defendant, in answer to this claim, says (1.) the estates were conveyed to him, not as a trustee for the plaintiff, but as beneficial owner; (2.) the trusts alleged by the plaintiff cannot be proved by any writing signed by the defendant, and the Statute of Frauds affords a defence to the action; (3.) the plaintiff's claim, even if proved, is barred (a) by the defendant's bankruptcy, (b) by the Statute of Limitations, (c) by the plaintiff's laches, an the equitable doctrines applicable to delay independently of the statute. **3–036**

Kekewich J. decided against the plaintiff on the first ground—namely, that there was no trust in favour of the plaintiff. This view of the case rendered it unnecessary for him to consider the other defences. The plaintiff has appealed from this decision; and, as we have been unable to take the same view as the learned judge of the effect of the evidence, it will be necessary for us to deal with all the other defences relied upon by the defendant. **3–037**

The circumstances under which the Delmar estates were conveyed to the defendant are to be gathered from the verbal testimony of the plaintiff, the defendant, and Mr Duff, and a mass of correspondence both before and after the conveyance. The correspondence after the conveyance is relied upon by the plaintiff as being inconsistent with the defendant's contention that he acquired the estates for himself beneficially, free from any trust in favour of the plaintiff. **3–038**

[The Court then stated the leading facts in the history of the case, and examined the parties' correspondence, and summed up as follows:] We come, therefore, to the conclusion that the plaintiff has proved that the estates in question were conveyed to the defendant on May 27, 1873, upon trust for her, but subject to a charge in his favour in respect of all sums advanced by him in order to obtain the estates from the Dutch company in the first instance, and of all sums advanced by him in order to work them as coffee plantations after he had acquired them. **3–039**

This conclusion renders it necessary to consider whether the Statute of Frauds affords a defence to the plaintiff's claim. The section relied upon is s.7, which has been judicially interpreted in *Forster v Hale*[65] and **3–040**

was concerned about possible claims to her interest in the plantations by her recently-divorced husband, and she wanted her husband to believe that she no longer had any rights in the plantations.

65 (1798) 3 Ves. Jun. 696.

*Smith v Matthews*.[66] According to these authorities, it is necessary to prove by some writing or writings signed by the defendant, not only that the conveyance to him was subject to some trust, but also what that trust was. But it is not necessary that the trust should have been declared by such a writing in the first instance; it is sufficient if the trust can be proved by some writing signed by the defendant, and the date of the writing is immaterial. It is further established by a series of cases, the propriety of which cannot now be questioned, that the Statute of Frauds does not prevent the proof of a fraud; and that it is a fraud on the part of a person to whom land is conveyed as a trustee, and who knows it was so conveyed, to deny the trust and claim the land himself. Consequently, notwithstanding the statute, it is competent for a person claiming land conveyed to another to prove by parol evidence that it was so conveyed upon trust for the claimant, and that the grantee, knowing the facts, is denying the trust and relying upon the form of conveyance and the statute, in order to keep the land himself. . .

**3–041** The defence, based on the Statute of Frauds, is met by the plaintiff in two ways. First, she says that the documents signed by the defendant prove the existence of the trust alleged; secondly, she says that if those documents do not prove what the trust is with sufficient fulness and precision, the case is one of fraud which lets in other evidence, and that with the aid of other evidence the plaintiff's case is established. In our opinion the plaintiff is correct in this contention. We are by no means satisfied that the letters signed by the defendant do not contain enough to satisfy the Statute of Frauds. Whether this is so or not, the other evidence is admissible in order to prevent the statute from being used in order to commit a fraud; and such other evidence proves the plaintiff's case completely. . .

**3–042** Having come to the conclusion that the plaintiff has proved her case by evidence admissible by our law, it is necessary to consider the other defences raised. . .

**3–043** The next defence is the Statute of Limitations. The trust which the plaintiff has established is clearly an express trust within the meaning of that expression as explained in *Soar v Ashwell*.[67] The trust is one which both plaintiff and defendant intended to create. This case is not one in which an equitable obligation arises although there may have been no intention to create a trust. The intention to create a trust existed from the first. The defendant is not able in this case to claim the benefit of s.8 of the Trustee Act, 1888, and the statute which is applicable is the Judicature Act 1873 s.25, subs. 2, which enacts as follows: "No claim of a cestui que trust against his trustee for any property held on an express trust, or in respect of any breach of such trust, shall be held to be barred by any Statute of Limitations." The Statutes of Limitations, therefore, afford no defence if the plaintiff's action is to be regarded as one brought by a cestui que trust against his trustee seeking for an account of trust property.

**3–044** [The court also rejected the defence of laches, and concluded:] The appeal must be allowed and the judgment be reversed. It must be declared that the defendant purchased the Delmar estates as a trustee for the plaintiff, but subject to a charge for the amount paid to the Dutch company. An account must then be directed of the defendant's dealings and transactions with the Delmar estates. The account will be an account as between a trustee and his cestui que trust, not an account as between mortgagor and mortgagee, and there must be no account on the footing of wilful default. The defendant must be allowed all his advances and outlays, with colonial interest; but he ought only to be charged simple interest at 4 per cent on balances in his hands, unless it appears that he has made more. Minutes had better be prepared and signed, and, if necessary, they can be mentioned to the Court. The defendant must pay the costs of the action up to the hearing and the costs of the appeal.

**3–045** It might therefore seem clear that the Court of Appeal adopted the first view: the Comtesse was permitted to prove the expressly declared trust without producing any signed writing, as it was necessary to stop Boustead using the formality rule as an instrument of fraud.[68] There are, however, some difficulties with applying that view on the specific facts of *Rochefoucauld*.[69] Moreover, there are certainly later decisions in which the trust recognised in *Rochefoucauld* has been described as a

---

[66] (1861) 3 D. F. & J. 139.

[67] [1893] 2 Q. B. 390.

[68] That is certainly the argument made by W. Swadling, "The Nature of the Trust in *Rochefoucauld v Boustead*" in C. Mitchell (ed.), *Constructive and Resulting Trusts* (2010).

[69] See Y.K. Liew, "*Rochefoucauld v Boustead* (1897)" in C. Mitchell and P. Mitchell (eds), *Landmark Cases in Equity* (2012), preferring the second, constructive trust view of the case.

constructive trust.[70] We need to know more about constructive trusts in order to understand the debate, and so we will examine these and other points for and against each of the two views in more detail in Chapter 15.[71] At this point, however, it is useful to ask why it might matter which of the two views is to be preferred.

There is no difference between the views when it comes to considering the possible application of a limitation period to A's claim against B. On the express trust view, as made clear in *Rochefoucauld*, no statutory limitation period applies; but even on the constructive trust view, as the case is one in which B agreed to hold on trust, it is again accepted that no statutory limitation period applies.[72] There are, however, two broader reasons for asking which of the two views is to be preferred. **3–046**

First, consider a case in which A transfers land to B subject to an oral agreement that B is to hold the land on trust for C. Such a "three-party" case can be contrasted with the "two-party" case in which A transfers land to B subject to an oral agreement that B is to hold on trust for A. In the three-party case, it seems clear, on either of the two views, that B should not be free to use the land for her own benefit. On the first view, however, it may be that B's potential fraud can be adequately addressed by finding that B holds the land on a trust for *A*[73]; or, to the same effect, that no risk of fraud arises, because if the oral trust for C cannot be proved, and, to that extent, fails, then a resulting trust arises for A.[74] On the second view, in contrast, it may be that the form of unconscionable conduct to which equity responds consists of B's reneging on the promise subject to which the property was acquired: in that case, B's promise must be enforced, and so a constructive trust is imposed in favour of *C*.[75] On the first view, of course, if a resulting trust arises for A, A will then have another chance to give C the beneficial interest in the land; but A may die before then, or may change her mind, and in such a case, the difference between the two views may be of critical importance to C.[76] **3–047**

Secondly, consider a case in which A transfers land to B subject to an oral agreement that B will allow A (or C) to make some limited use of the land, as a licensee. On the first view, there is of course no express trust, as no party has attempted to set up a trust, and so the principle applying in *Rochefoucauld* provides no assistance for A or C. On the second view, however, if a constructive trust can arise where it would be unconscionable for B to renege on a promise subject to which she acquired property, then there is a strong argument that B's promise should be enforced whether or not it is a **3–048**

---

[70] See, e.g. *Paragon Finance v Thakerar* [1999] 1 All E.R. 400 at 409 per Millett LJ; *Gissing v Gissing* [1971] A.C. 886 at 905 per Lord Diplock; *Bannister v Bannister* [1948] 2 All E.R. 133.

[71] At paras 15–030—15–045.

[72] See, e.g. *Paragon Finance Plc v DB Thakerar & Co* [1999] 1 All E.R. 400 at 408–409. where Millett LJ distinguishes between different types of constructive trust when considering the relevant limitation rules. It is conceivable that a similar approach could be adopted when considering, for example, the application of conflicts of laws rules, so that a constructive trust arising in a case where the defendant had agreed to hold on trust would be treated in the same way as an express trust.

[73] As argued by, e.g. J.D. Feltham, "Informal Trusts and Third Parties" [1987] Conv. 246. N. Hopkins, *The Informal Acquisition of Rights in Land* (Sweet & Maxwell, 2000), pp.37–38 argues that the prevailing position should be a trust for A, and that a trust for C should arise only in "exceptional circumstances where intervention in C's favour is the only means of preventing fraud".

[74] See paras 4–102ff. and compare, e.g. *Hodgson v Marks* [1971] Ch. 892.

[75] As argued by, e.g. T. Youdan, "Formalities for Trusts of Land and the Doctrine in *Rochefoucauld v Boustead*" (1984) 43 C.L.J. 306 and "Informal Trusts and Third Parties: A Response" [1988] Conv. 267, as well as by, e.g. B. McFarlane, "Constructive Trusts Arising on Receipt of Property *Sub Conditione*" (2004) 120 L.Q.R. 667 and S. Gardner, "Reliance-Based Constructive Trusts" in C. Mitchell (ed.), *Constructive and Resulting Trusts* (2010). This view is supported by the analysis of Patten LJ in *de Bruyne v de Bruyne* [2010] EWCA Civ 519 at [51] referring to a principle giving rise to a constructive trust where the defendant's unconscionable conduct is "in the form of a denial or refusal to carry out the agreement to hold the property for the benefit of the third party which was the only basis upon which the property was transferred".

[76] Taxation rules may also apply differently if C's right is acquired not as a result of the initial transaction, but as a result of a later gift by A. As noted at para.1–062, the timing of a gift may be crucial, for example, in determining its consequences for inheritance tax.

promise to hold on trust.[77] Of course, in a case where B's promise is simply to allow A or C a licence, or other forms of personal right, no trust should arise[78]; but the principle may still be important in allowing a court to enforce B's promise even if it is not otherwise binding.[79]

**3-049** It is, therefore, of some importance to know not only that A can assert a beneficial interest in a case such as *Rochefoucauld*, but also *why* A is permitted to do so. The debate between the express and constructive views of the case will be examined further in Chapter 5.[80]

## *C. Law of Property Act 1925 s.53(1)(c)*

### Law of Property Act 1925 s.53

**3-050** (1) Subject to the provisions hereinafter contained with respect to the creation of interests in land by parol. . .

(c) A disposition of an equitable interest or trust subsisting at the time of the disposition, must be in writing signed by the person disposing of the same, or by his agent thereunto lawfully authorised in writing or by will.

(2) This section does not affect the creation or operation of resulting, implied or constructive trusts.

### i. The Scope of s.53(1)(c)

**3-051** For the purposes of s.53(1)(c), an "equitable interest" comprises an interest in land or in other property.[81] The formality rule, therefore, may potentially be relevant whenever a beneficiary of a trust intends to deal with her beneficial interest. It provides that any transaction which amounts to a disposition must be in signed writing or it is void. In contrast to declarations of trusts of land under s.53(1)(b), then, written evidence of oral dealings with equitable interests, created after the event, will not rescue a disposition from the effects of non-compliance with s.53(1)(c). Equally, if an initial oral attempt at a disposition is followed by a later signed document that is itself capable of making a disposition, the document will itself take effect and the date of its execution will determine the date of the disposition.[82] The signed writing may comprise linked documents.[83] If the assignee of an equitable interest is herself to hold the assigned equitable interest as a trustee, the writing need not contain the particulars of the trust: those details may be communicated orally,[84]

---

77 This argument can be used, for example, to explain the result in *Binions v Evans* [1972] Ch. 359 and the analysis of the relevant law adopted by the Court of Appeal in *Ashburn Anstalt v Arnold* [1989] Ch. 1, *Lloyd v Dugdale* [2002] 2 P. & C.R. 13 and *Chaudhary v Yavuz* [2013] Ch. 249. See further B. McFarlane, "Constructive Trusts Arising on Receipt of Property *Sub Conditione*" (2004) 120 L.Q.R. 667, 691–693.

78 Although note that in the cases cited at fn.77, the courts did continue to use the language of constructive trust. When applied to cases where B did not promise to hold on trust, however, this language is inappropriate, as noted by, e.g. W. Swadling, "Property" in A. Burrows (ed.), *English Private Law*, 3rd edn (Oxford University Press, 2013), para.4.126; S. Bright, "The Third Party's Conscience and Land Law" [2000] Conv. 398, 402.

79 If B's promise to A is contractually binding, then, even if it is made for C's benefit, C may acquire a right to enforce it under the Contract (Rights of Third Parties) Act 1999. But note that if B's oral promise is made as part of the contract of sale between A and B, then s.2 of the Law of Property (Miscellaneous Provisions) Act 1989 operates to ensure that it is not contractually binding, and so the 1999 Act cannot then assist C.

80 At paras 5-030—5-045.

81 Assumed in *Grey v IRC* [1960] A.C. 1; *Oughtred v IRC* [1960] A.C. 206; *Vandervell v IRC* [1967] 2 A.C. 291; and treated as well established in *Re Tyler's Fund Trusts* [1967] 1 W.L.R. 1269 at 1274. The context must oust L.P.A. 1925 s.205(1)(ii), (x).

82 This may of course have consequences for taxation purposes, as in *Grey v IRC* [1960] A.C. 1. See B. Green, "*Grey, Oughtred* and *Vandervell*—A Contextual Reappraisal" (1984) 47 M.L.R. 385, 391–392.

83 *Re Danish Bacon Co Ltd Staff Pension Fund* [1971] 1 W.L.R. 248.

84 *Re Tyler's Fund Trusts* [1967] 1 W.L.R. 1269.

although if the interest is in land then some subsequent written evidence will be necessary to satisfy s.53(1)(b).

The key question in establishing the scope of the s.53(1)(c) formality rule is as to the meaning of a "disposition". Its predecessor, the Statute of Frauds 1677 s.9, referred instead to "grants and assignments" of an equitable interest. Whilst a "disposition" undoubtedly includes "grants and assignments",[85] its meaning has been taken to be wider than this, and it includes other types of transaction, as can be seen from the decision of the House of Lords in *Grey v IRC*. 3-052

*Grey v Inland Revenue Commissioners*

House of Lords [1960] A.C. 1

On February 1, 1955, Hunter, as settlor, transferred 18,000 shares of £1 each to trustees (the appellants) as nominees for himself. The appellants were also the trustees of six other settlements, in favour of Hunter's children, which Hunter had previously created. On February 18, 1955, Hunter orally directed the trustees to divide the 18,000 shares into six parcels of 3,000 shares each and to appropriate the parcels to the trusts of the six settlements, one parcel to each settlement. On March 25, 1955, the trustees executed six deeds of declaration of trust (which Hunter also executed in order to testify to the oral direction previously given by him) declaring that since February 18, 1955, they had held each of the parcels of 3,000 shares on the trusts of the relevant settlement. The Commissioners of Inland Revenue assessed the deeds of declaration of trust to ad valorem stamp duty on the basis it was those deeds which had created the trusts of the shares, and they were therefore taxable as instruments transferring an interest in property. The appellants argued instead that the deeds had merely recorded and confirmed the earlier transfer, which had taken place as a result of Hunter's oral instructions, and so were not taxable. 3-053

The starting point and end point of the transaction can be explained by way of a diagram, with the arrow linking the trustees to the parties for whom they hold on trust: 3-054

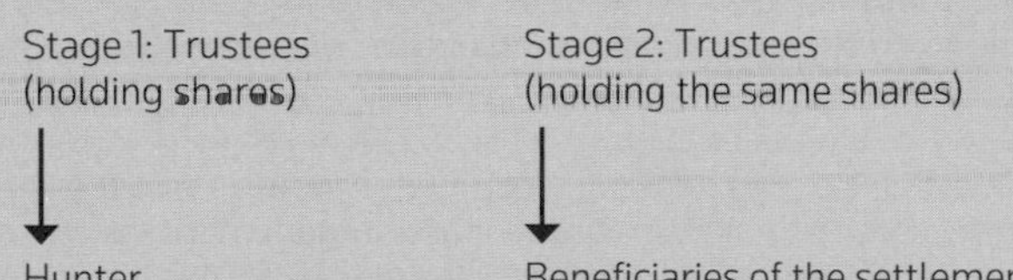


The question was whether, in order to get from Stage 1 to Stage 2, signed writing in compliance with s. 53(1)(c) was required. If so, the stamp duty was payable, as the written instrument made the transfer, it did not merely record it. A unanimous House of Lords, agreeing with a majority of the Court of Appeal, held that compliance with s. 53(1)(c) was indeed required to get from Stage 1 to Stage 2, and thus agreed with the IRC that stamp duty was payable.

VISCOUNT SIMONDS (with whom LORD REID agreed, stated the facts, continued): These facts give rise to the plain question whether the oral directions given by Mr Hunter, which are recited in each of the instruments, were effective or were, having regard to section 53(1)(c) of the Law of Property Act, 1925, wholly ineffective. In the former event the instruments would not, and in the latter would, be chargeable with ad valorem duty. . . 3-055

Briefly, then, were the several oral directions given by Mr Hunter dispositions by him of the equitable interest in the shares held by the appellants as nominees for him? 3-056

If the word "disposition" is given its natural meaning, it cannot, I think, be denied that a direction given by Mr Hunter, whereby the beneficial interest in the shares theretofore vested in him became vested in another or others, is a disposition. But it is contended by the appellants that the word "disposition" is to be given a narrower meaning and (so far as relates to inter vivos transactions) be read as if it were synonymous with "grants and assignments" and that, given this meaning, it does not cover such a direction as was given in this case. As I am clearly of the opinion, which I understand to be shared by your Lordships, that there is no justification for giving the word "disposition" a narrower meaning than it ordinarily bears, 3-057

85 *Halley v Law Society* [2003] W.T.L.R. 845 at [69]ff.

it will be unnecessary to discuss the interesting problem that would otherwise arise. It was for this reason that your Lordships did not think it necessary to hear learned counsel for the appellants in reply on this part of the case.

3-058 My Lords, the argument for narrowing the meaning of "disposition" was that the Law of Property Act 1925, was a consolidating Act, that among the Acts which it consolidated was the Statute of Frauds 1677 s.9, that that section enacted that "all grants and assignments of any trust or confidence shall likewise be in writing, signed by the party granting or assigning the same, or by such last will or devise, or else shall likewise be utterly void and of none effect," and that therefore the word "disposition" in section 53(1)(c) of the Act of 1925 is to be given the same meaning as would be given to "grants and assignments" in section 9 of the Statute of Frauds.

3-059 My Lords, the principles applicable to the construction of a consolidating Act are not in doubt. The presumption is that such an Act is not intended to alter the law, but this prima facie view must yield to plain words to the contrary.[86] If the Law of Property Act 1925 was a typical consolidating Act, the question would be whether the alteration from "grants and assignments" to "disposition" changed the law by enlarging the area of void transactions—a question that might not be easy to answer. But the Act of 1925 cannot be thus regarded. . .

3-060 LORD RADCLIFFE (with whom LORD COHEN and LORD KEITH agreed): My Lords, if there is nothing more in this appeal than the short question whether the oral direction that Mr Hunter gave to his trustees on February 18, 1955, amounted in any ordinary sense of the words to a "disposition of an equitable interest or trust subsisting at the time of the disposition", I do not feel any doubt as to my answer. I think that it did. Whether we describe what happened in technical or in more general terms, the full equitable interest in the eighteen thousand shares concerned, which at that time was his, was (subject to any statutory invalidity) diverted by his direction from his ownership into the beneficial ownership of the various equitable owners, present and future, entitled under his six existing settlements. . .

3-061 In my opinion, it is a very nice question whether a parol declaration of trust of this kind was or was not within the mischief of section 9 of the Statute of Frauds. The point has never, I believe, been decided and perhaps it never will be. Certainly it was long established as law that while a declaration of trust respecting land or any interest therein required writing to be effective a declaration of trust respecting personalty did not. Moreover, there is warrant for saying that a direction to his trustee by the equitable owner of trust property prescribing new trusts of that property was a declaration of trust. But it does not necessarily follow from that that such a direction, if the effect of it was to determine completely or pro tanto the subsisting equitable interest of the maker of the direction, was not also a grant or assignment for the purposes of section 9 and therefore required writing for its validity. Something had to happen to that equitable interest in order to displace it in favour of the new interests created by the direction: and it would be at any rate logical to treat the direction as being an assignment of the subsisting interest to the new beneficiary or beneficiaries or, in other cases, a release or surrender of it to the trustee.

3-062 I do not think, however, that that question has to be answered for the purposes of this appeal. It can only be relevant if section 53(1) of the Law of Property Act 1925 is treated as a true consolidation of the three sections of the Statute of Frauds concerned and as governed, therefore, by the general principle, with which I am entirely in agreement, that a consolidating Act is not to be read as effecting changes in the existing law unless the words it employs are too clear in their effect to admit of any other construction. But, in my opinion, it is impossible to regard section 53 of the Law of Property Act 1925 as a consolidating enactment in this sense.

3-063 The approach of the House of Lords in *Grey v IRC* can be summarised simply: the term "disposition" in s.53(1)(c) is apt to cover a case where a party ensures that his trustees now hold on trust for others, rather than for himself, and there is no need to consider whether such an arrangement would have fallen within the scope of the Statute of Frauds 1677 s.9, as Parliament in 1925 did not intend simply to replicate the effect of that earlier provision. In *Grey*, there was a disposition of an equitable interest as, at Stage 1, Hunter had the beneficial interest in the shares, whereas, at Stage 2, the beneficial interest in the same shares was shared by the beneficiaries of the six settlements.

---

86 See *Gilbert v Gilbert* [1928] P. 1 at 8, per Scrutton LJ.

In *Vandervell v IRC*, the House of Lords had to consider a slightly different situation, which it distinguished from that in *Grey v IRC*. 3–064

*Vandervell v Inland Revenue Commissioners*

House of Lords [1967] 2 A.C. 291

In 1958 Vandervell decided to make a gift to the Royal College of Surgeons to found a chair of pharmacology, using 100,000 shares in a private company held by a bank on trust for him. The shares would be transferred to the RCS. The RCS would then be entitled to the dividends declared on the shares, which would suffice to set up the chair. Vandervell could of course have received the dividends himself, and then paid them over to the RCS, but he would then have been assessed to surtax on the dividends. The RCS, as a charity, would not have to pay such tax on the dividends. Once the dividends had been declared, however, Vandervell wanted the RCS to release the shares to a trustee company which acted as trustee of a settlement he had made in favour of his children. Hence it was arranged that the shares would be transferred to RCS subject to an option, vested in the trustee company, to purchase the shares for £5,000. 3–065

Vandervell orally directed the bank to transfer full ownership of the shares to RCS, and during the tax years 1958–59 and 1959–60 dividends on the shares, amounting to £162,500 and £87,500, respectively, were paid. In October, 1961, the trustee company then exercised its option and paid RCS £5,000 for the shares. Vandervell was then assessed to surtax on the dividends on the basis that the transaction amounted to a settlement of property of which he had not absolutely divested himself, so that the dividends fell to be treated for surtax purposes as his income and not that of any other person. 3–066

It is important to note that the IRC made two main arguments. First, it was said that Vandervell's oral direction to the bank to transfer full ownership of the shares to the RCS was an attempted disposition of his beneficial interest in the shares, and was void as it did not comply with s. 53(1)(c). If that argument were accepted, Vandervell would retain the beneficial interest in the shares and be liable for the surtax. Second, even if the oral direction did not fall within s. 53(1)(c) and so was valid, Vandervell nonetheless had a sufficient interest in the shares to be liable for the surtax because the option to purchase the shares, vested in the trustee company, was in fact held on a resulting trust for Vandervell. 3–067

In the House of Lords, the IRC succeeded on the *second* argument: we will consider this aspect of the law of resulting trusts in Chapter 4.[87] Here, we will consider only the first argument, and so the following extracts concern the s.53(1)(c) point only. 3–068

The relevant stages of the transaction can again be explained by way of a diagram, with the arrow linking the trustees to the parties for whom they hold on trust: 3–069

Stage 1: Trustees (holding shares) Stage 2: RCS

↓

Vandervell

There is no arrow at Stage 2 as the RCS did not hold the shares on trust, although the trustee company did of course have an option to buy the shares from the RCS. The question was whether, in order to get from Stage 1 to Stage 2, signed writing in compliance with s. 53(1)(c) was required. A unanimous House of Lords held that compliance with s. 53(1)(c) was *not* required to get from Stage 1 to Stage 2.

LORD UPJOHN:. . . the object of [s. 53(1)(c)], as was the object of the old Statute of Frauds, is to prevent hidden oral transactions in equitable interests in fraud of those truly entitled, and making it difficult, if not impossible, for the trustees to ascertain who are in truth the beneficiaries. When the beneficial owner, however, owns the whole beneficial estate and is in a position to give directions to his bare trustee with regard to the legal as well as the equitable estate there can be no possible ground for invoking the section where the beneficial owner wants to deal with the legal estate as well as the equitable estate. 3–070

I cannot agree with Diplock L.J. [in the Court of Appeal decision in the case] that prima facie a transfer of the legal estate carries with it the absolute beneficial interest in the property transferred; this plainly is 3–071

87 See para.4–104.

not so, e.g. the transfer may be on a change of trustee; it is a matter of intention in each case. If, however, the intention of the beneficial owner in directing the trustee to transfer the legal estate to X is that X should be the beneficial owner, I can see no reason for any further document or further words in the document assigning the legal estate also expressly transferring the beneficial interest; the greater includes the less. X may be wise to secure some evidence that the beneficial owner intended him to take the beneficial interest in case his beneficial title is challenged at a later date but it certainly cannot, in my opinion, be a statutory requirement that to effect its passing there must be some writing under section 53(1)(c).

**3-072** Counsel for the Crown admitted that where the legal and beneficial estate was vested in the legal owner and he desired to transfer the whole legal and beneficial estate to another he did not have to do more than transfer the legal estate and he did not have to comply with section 53(1)(c); and I can see no difference between that case and this.

**3-073** As I have said, that section is, in my opinion, directed to cases where dealings with the equitable estate are divorced from the legal estate and I do not think any of their Lordships in *Grey v IRC*[88] and *Oughtred v IRC*[89] had in mind the case before your Lordships. To hold the contrary would make assignments unnecessarily complicated; if there had to be assignments in express terms of both legal and equitable interests that would make the section more productive of injustice than the supposed evils it was intended to prevent. . .

**3-074** LORD WILBERFORCE: On November 14, 1958, [Vandervell's] solicitor received from the bank a blank transfer of the shares, executed by the bank, and the share certificate. So at this stage [Vandervell] was the absolute master of the shares and only needed to insert his name as transferee in the transfer and to register it to become the full legal owner. He was also the owner in equity. On November 19, 1958, the solicitor. . . on behalf of [Vandervell], who intended to make a gift, handed the transfer to the College, which in due course, sealed it and obtained registration of the shares in the College's name. The case should then be regarded as one in which [Vandervell] himself has, with the intention to make a gift, put the College in a position to become the legal owner of the shares, which the College in fact became. If [Vandervell] had died before the College had obtained registration, it is clear on the principle of *Re Rose*[90] that the gift would have been complete, on the basis that he had done everything in his power to transfer the legal interest, with an intention to give, to the College. No separate transfer, therefore, of the equitable interest ever came to or needed to be made and there is no room for the operation of the subsection. What the position would have been had there simply been an oral direction to the legal owner (viz. the bank) to transfer the shares to the College, followed by such a transfer, but without any document in writing signed by [Vandervell] as equitable owner, is not a matter which calls for consideration here. . .

**3-075** It has been suggested that it is difficult to reconcile the decision in *Vandervell v IRC* with that in *Grey v IRC*.[91] Certainly, the argument rejected by the House of Lords in *Vandervell v IRC* was a fairly simple one: (i) *Grey v IRC* establishes that "disposition" is to be given its natural interpretation, and is not limited to "grants and assignments"; (ii) Vandervell initially had a beneficial interest in the shares (Stage 1 in the diagram above) and he wished to move to a situation where he no longer had that beneficial interest (Stage 2): as this involves his getting rid of (i.e. disposing) his beneficial interest, it must be a "disposition" of that interest.

**3-076** As seen in the extract above, the House of Lords gave two reasons for rejecting that argument. First, there is Lord Wilberforce's use of *Re Rose, Midland Bank Executor & Trustee Co Ltd v Rose*. That analysis, however, is far from convincing: in *Re Rose*, the taxpayer started with full ownership of the shares, whereas Vandervell had only a beneficial interest. In *Re Rose*, the taxpayer did all he could to transfer them by executing a share transfer and delivering the transfer and the share certificate to the transferee. To say that Vandervell had done all he could to vest the shares in the RCS was to beg the s.53(1)(c) question of what is required of an owner of a subsisting equitable interest to achieve a disposition of that interest.

---

88 [1960] A.C. 1.
89 [1960] A.C. 206.
90 *Re Rose, Midland Bank Executor & Trustee Co Ltd v Rose* [1949] Ch. 78: see paras 2-022ff.
91 See, e.g. B. Green, "*Grey, Oughtred* and *Vandervell*—A Contextual Appraisal" (1984) 47 M.L.R. 385.

Secondly, there is Lord Upjohn's analysis. Importantly, it looks to the *purposes* of the s.53(1)(c) formality rule, stating that the object of the rule is "to prevent hidden oral transactions in equitable interests in fraud of those truly entitled, and making it difficult, if not impossible, for the trustees to ascertain who are in truth the beneficiaries".[92] It could be argued that a special formality rule for the disposition of equitable interests is required to give a beneficiary, for example, protection against risks that are specific to her position as a beneficiary, such as the risk of the trustee performing the trust in favour of the wrong person. Equally, a trustee should be concerned about that risk, as performing the trust in favour of the wrong person may of course lead to the trustee's being under a liability to the true beneficiary. **3–077**

The formality rule contained in s.53(1)(c) can, on Lord Upjohn's analysis, be seen as protecting both the beneficiary and the trustee against this risk. Consider a case in which a fraudster, X, goes to the trustee, T, falsely claims that B transferred her beneficial interest to X, and demands that T perform the trust in favour of X. The advantage of s.53(1)(c) is that T can insist on X's producing some writing signed by B before acceding to that demand. **3–078**

On this view, then, Lord Upjohn's analysis can be seen as stating that the purpose of s.53(1)(c) is to protect both B and T from a risk that is peculiar to their position as beneficiary and trustee: the risk that the trustee will perform the trusts in favour of the wrong person. On that analysis, there is no need for writing to get from Stage 1 to Stage 2 in *Vandervell*, as the relevant transaction *necessarily involves the trustee*. The transaction required legal title to the shares to vest in the RCS, and that was only possible with the co-operation of the trustee who, of course, held such title to the shares. The case can therefore be distinguished from *Grey* as the transaction in that earlier case was not of a type that necessarily involves the trustee.[93] **3–079**

Lord Upjohn's analysis is also helpful when considering the somewhat controversial question of whether s.53(1)(c) applies where B, the beneficiary of an existing trust, declares that she holds that beneficial interest on trust for another, thus creating a sub-trust. If the aim of the formality rule were simply to protect B from the risk of fraud, there is an argument that such a declaration should be regarded as a "disposition": that would certainly make life harder for X, a fraudster seeking to get the economic value of B's beneficial interest by falsely claiming that B declared a sub-trust in X's favour.[94] But why should B receive special protection against the risk of such fraud? After all, *anyone* holding full ownership of property other than land is subject to the risk that X might falsely claim that an oral declaration of trust had been made in X's favour. Since there is no general formality rule regulating how such declarations of trust are to be made or proved, why should B, the holder of a purely equitable interest, receive special protection? **3–080**

There is, therefore, a strong argument that s.53(1)(c) does not apply to a declaration of a sub-trust by a party, B, with an existing beneficial interest.[95] Certainly, Lord Upjohn's analysis of the purpose of the formality rule supports that view. No writing is required in such a case, as none is needed to protect either B, or the existing trustee T, from the risk that T might perform the trust in favour of the **3–081**

---

[92] [1967] 2 A.C. 291 at 311 (extracted at para.3–070).

[93] See too R. Nolan, "*Vandervell v IRC*: A Case of Overreaching" [2002] C.L.J. 169, 188: Nolan's analysis is different from any considered by the House of Lords, but is based on the idea that, as the trustees transferred legal title to the shares with the consent of Vandervell, "[t]he gift of the shares also overreached Vandervell's equitable interest in them. Consequently, the Royal College acquired the shares free of that interest". There is a link with Lord Upjohn's analysis, as overreaching requires a transfer by the trustees (which they have power to make) and so the trustees are necessarily involved in the transaction.

[94] B. Green, "*Grey, Oughtred* and *Vandervell*—A Contextual Appraisal" (1984) 47 M.L.R. 385, 396–399 therefore argues that a declaration of a sub-trust should fall within the scope of s.53(1)(c). For a contrary view, see P. Matthews, "All About Bare Trusts—Part 2" [2005] P.C.B. 336, 336–340.

[95] See, e.g. *Sheffield v Sheffield* [2014] W.T.L.R. 1039 at [78]–[86].

wrong person. Consider a case in which X, a fraudster, falsely claims that B declared a sub-trust in X's favour. Crucially, even if B had made such a declaration, it would not give X a direct claim against T and so would not mean that T had to perform the trusts in favour of X. The point is that, as such a declaration would merely create a sub-trust (so that T holds on trust for B who then holds on trust for X), it would not change the fact that T's duty is owed to B, and so T cannot be forced to perform the trusts in favour of X,[96] unless B asks T to do so.

**3-082** It has instead been suggested that, at least in cases where the sub-trust declared by B in favour of X is purely "passive",[97] and so does not require the exercise of any powers by B, B should be treated as "dropping out of the picture", so that X would then have a direct claim against T.[98] If that were the case, then, applying Lord Upjohn's analysis, writing would be required for the declaration of such a passive sub-trust. The conclusion that B might thus drop out of the picture position is not, however, dictated by authority,[99] and it seems hard to defend in principle: the effect of declaring a trust, whether a sub-trust or not, is that the party declaring it continues to hold the trust property, but subject to duties to the beneficiary. As noted by Lawrence Collins LJ in *Nelson v Greening & Sykes (Builders) Ltd*,[100] even if the *practical* effect of the sub-trust is that B becomes merely a conduit to pass on the economic benefits of the trust property to X, that does not mean that its *legal* effect is to dispose of B's beneficial interest. On the contrary, B's beneficial interest must continue to exist, as otherwise there would be no subject-matter to the sub-trust for X.[101]

**3-083** As demonstrated by the decision of the Court of Appeal in the next instalment of the Vandervell saga, *Re Vandervell (No.2)*, there are further situations in which a dealing with a beneficial interest does not amount to a disposition, and so can be carried out orally.

---

96 In *Nelson v Greening & Sykes (Builders) Ltd* [2008] 1 E.G.L.R. 59 at [57], Lawrence Collins LJ noted that, in such a case, T may choose to deal directly with X, "as a matter of practicality", but also noted there that this does not mean that T holds directly for X.

97 It is certainly the case that s.53(1)(c) does not apply where B has powers to exercise under the sub-trust: see, e.g. *Onslow v Wallis* (1849) 1 Mac. & G. 506.

98 See, e.g. *Grey v IRC* [1958] Ch. 690 at 715 per Lord Evershed MR.

99 The conclusion is said to derive support from *Grainge v Wilberforce* (1889) 5 T.L.R. 436 and *Re Lashmar* [1891] 1 Ch. 258. The former case, however, simply decided that, in a claim for specific performance of a contract to convey land, an intermediate trustee under a settlement of that land did not need to be a party to the conveyance: that result can be explained on the basis that the planned conveyance would in any case overreach the interests of any intermediate beneficiaries. The latter case simply decided that a party with no beneficial interest in property, and with no duties to perform as trustee of that property, could not claim that property from the party holding legal title to it. So, as noted by Lawrence Collins LJ in *Nelson v Greening & Sykes (Builders) Ltd* [2008] 1 E.G.L.R. 59 at [57], the relevant cases "do not bind this court to hold that as a matter of law an intermediate trustee ceases to be a trustee". See too *Sheffield v Sheffield* [2014] W.T.L.R. 1039 at [82] where HHJ Pelling QC, analysing *Grainge v Wilberforce* and *Re Lashmar*, stated that "there is nothing in these authorities that is necessarily inconsistent with the conclusion of the Court of Appeal in *Nelson*".

100 [2008] 1 E.G.L.R. 59 at [57]: "saying (as Lord Evershed MR said) [in *Grey v IRC* [1958] Ch. 690 at 715] that the practical effect [of the sub-trust] would seem to amount to or be capable of amounting to the 'getting rid' of the trust of the equitable interest then subsisting, is not the same as saying that as a matter of law it does get rid of the intermediate trust. What he was saying was that in the case of a trust and sub-trust of personal property the trustees may decide that as a matter of practicality it is more convenient to deal directly with the beneficiary of the sub-trust."

101 In *Re Lehman Brothers International (Europe) Ltd* [2010] EWHC 2914 (Ch) at [397] (affirmed [2012] 2 B.C.L.C. 151) Briggs J referred to the "structure of trusts and sub-trusts between the legal owner and ultimate beneficial owner in relation to intermediated securities" (see para.1-071) and noted that under such a structure, the depositary holding legal rights to the shares recognises one party (B) as its beneficiary and that party in turn recognises another (B2) as its beneficiary: the implication is that, even though holding on a sub-trust for B2, B does not simply drop out of the picture. See further B. McFarlane and R. Stevens, "Interests in Securities: Practical Problems and Conceptual Solutions" in L. Gullifer and J. Payne (eds), *Intermediated Securities* (2010), pp.46-48.

*Re Vandervell (No.2)*

Court of Appeal [1974] Ch. 269

Recall that, on receiving full title to the shares, the RCS granted the Vandervell trustee company (VT) an option to buy those shares for £5,000. Remember too that, as we noted at para.3–068, the House of Lords in *Vandervell v IRC* decided that VT held that option on resulting trust for Vandervell. When, in October 1961, the possibility of such a trust became apparent to Vandervell, he orally instructed VT to exercise the option, using money held by VT on a trust benefitting Vandervell's children. VT did so. The intention of V and VT was that the shares would then be held on the same trust for Vandervell's children, and the dividends later declared on the shares were added to the fund held on the children's trusts. The revenue then suggested that, as s.53(1)(c) had not been complied with, Vandervell was still liable for surtax on the dividends declared after October 1961. In January 1965, to resolve any doubts as to the position from that point onwards, V executed a deed transferring any rights he had in the option, shares, or dividends to VT to hold on the trusts of the children's settlement. V died in 1967. Owing to their concern as to the possible surtax liabilty of Vandervell's estate for dividends declared between October 1961 and January 1965, his executors sought a declaration that Vandervell (and hence now his estate) had been entitled to all dividends on the shares during that period. The executors' argument was based on the contention that the attempted oral dealings with the shares in October 1961 did not dispose of Vandervell's beneficial interest. The argument was that, as he had the beneficial interest in the option, and the shares were acquired by the exercise of that option, any transfer of the beneficial interest in the shares to the children was a disposition of Vandervell's initial beneficial interest, and so s. 53(1)(c) applied, with the effect that the disposition occurred only in January 1965, when signed writing was used. 3–084

The relevant stages of the transaction can again be explained by way of a diagram, with the arrow linking the trustees to the parties for whom they hold on trust: 3–085

| Stage 1: VT (holding option) | Stage 2: VT (holding shares) |
|---|---|
| ↓ | ↓ |
| Vandervell | Vandervell's children |

The trust at Stage 1 is the resulting trust found to exist in relation to the option in *Vandervell v IRC*.

At first instance, Megarry J. accepted the argument of the executors and held that, until January 1965, VT held the shares on trust for Vandervell, although, in its capacity as trustees for the children's settlement, VT had a lien for £5,000 in order to recover the money, taken from the children's settlement in order to exercise the option. The Court of Appeal, however, held that compliance with s. 53(1)(c) was *not* required to get from Stage 1 to Stage 2. The judges were unanimous in their decision, but not as to their reasons. 3–086

LORD DENNING M.R.: . . .There is a complete fallacy in [the executors'] argument. A resulting trust for the settlor [such as the resulting trust of the option in favour of Vandervell] is born and dies without any writing at all. It comes into existence whenever there is a gap in the beneficial ownership. It ceases to exist whenever that gap is filled by someone becoming beneficially entitled. As soon as the gap is filled by the creation or declaration of a valid trust, the resulting trust comes to an end. In this case, before the option was exercised, there was a gap in the beneficial ownership. So there was a resulting trust for Mr. Vandervell. But, as soon as the option was exercised and the shares registered in the trustees' name, there was created a valid trust of the shares in favour of the children's settlement. Not being a trust of land, it could be created without any writing. . . 3–087

**Estoppel**

Even if [counsel for the executors] were right in saying that Mr Vandervell retained an equitable interest in the shares, after the exercise of the option, the question arises whether Mr Vandervell can in the circumstance be heard to assert that claim against his children. Just see what happened. He himself arranged for the option to be exercised. He himself agreed to the shares being transferred to the trustee company. He himself procured his products company to declare dividends on the shares and to pay them to the trustee company for the benefit of the children. Thenceforward the trustee company invested the money and treated it as part of the children's settlement. If he himself had lived, and not died, he could not have claimed it back. He could not be heard to say that he did not intend the children's trust to have it. Even a 3–088 court of equity would not allow him to do anything so inequitable and unjust. Now that he has died, his executors are in no better position.

**Conclusion**

3–089 [Counsel for the executors] realized that the claim of the executors here had no merit whatsoever. He started off by reminding us that 'hard cases make bad law'. He repeated it time after time. He treated it as if it was an ultimate truth. But it is a maxim which is quite misleading. It should be deleted from our vocabulary. It comes to this: 'Unjust decisions make good law': whereas they do nothing of the kind. Every unjust decision is a reproach to the law or to the judge who administers it. If the law should be in danger of doing injustice, then equity should be called into remedy it. Equity was introduced to mitigate the rigour of the law. But in the present case it has been prayed in aid to do injustice on a large scale—to defeat the intentions of a dead man—to deprive his children of the benefits he provided for them – and to expose his estate to the payment of tax of over £600,000. I am glad to find that we can overcome this most unjust result.

3–090 LAWTON L.J.: . . .On or about October 10, 1961, the trustee company acquired the shares with money taken by them from the children's settlement. In my judgment the inference from this course of conduct is that Mr. Vandervell intended that to happen which did happen and that when the directors of the trustee company used money from the children's settlement to pay for the shares he intended that company to hold the shares not for himself but for the trusts of the children's settlement. If the trustee company had used this money otherwise than for the benefit of the children they would have been in breach of trust, and as Mr. Vandervell knew what was happening and intended it to happen, he would have been guilty of aiding and abetting them.

3–091 The result in law is that after the transfer the trustee company held the shares for the benefit of the children's settlement as Mr. Vandervell had intended it should. This followed from the operation of the rule that if A uses B's money to buy property, in the absence of any evidence to show otherwise, A holds that property for the benefit of B. It follows that once the transfer of the shares had been registered the beneficial interest in them was held by the trustee company on the trusts of the children's settlement so that no declaration of trust was necessary.

3–092 STEPHENSON L.J.: I have had more doubt than Lord Denning M.R. and Lawton L.J. whether we can overturn the judgment of Megarry J. in what I have not found an easy case. . . Lord Denning M.R. and Lawton L.J. are able to hold that no such disposition [i.e. no written disposition complying with s. 53(1)(c)] is needed because (1) the option was held on such trusts as might thereafter be declared by the trustee company or Mr. Vandervell himself, and (2) the trustee company has declared that it holds the shares in the children's settlement. . . I should be more confident of the second if it had been pleaded or argued either here or below and we had had the benefit of Megarry J.'s views upon it. . . I see, as perhaps did counsel, difficulties in the way of a limited company declaring a trust by parole or conduct and without a resolution of the board of directors, and difficulties also in the way of finding any declaration of trust by Mr. Vandervell himself in October or November 1961, or any conduct then or later which would in law or equity estop him from denying that he made one.

3–093 However, Lord Denning M.R. and Lawton L.J. are of opinion that these difficulties, if not imaginary, are not insuperable and that these shares went into the children's settlement in 1961 in accordance with the intention of Mr. Vandervell and the trustee company—a result with which I am happy to agree as it seems to me to be in accordance with the justice and the reality of the case.

3–094 The decision of the Court of Appeal in *Re Vandervell (No.2)* is generally regarded as a difficult one to explain satisfactorily. Lord Denning MR's concern to do justice is of course understandable, but an inevitable consequence of formality rules is that they may seem to lead to unwelcome outcomes in specific cases and their justification lies instead in the benefits they provide in the vast majority of cases where the rule is complied with. There are certainly some problems with Lord Denning's reasoning as to resulting trusts: whilst it is true that such a trust can arise, and even be proved in relation to land, without any writing, it does not necessarily follow that no writing is required to dispose of an interest under such a trust. It is not obvious, for example, that the result in *Grey v IRC* would have been different if the initial trust of the shares for Hunter had arisen under a resulting trust.

As to estoppel, we noted above[102] that proprietary estoppel may assist a claimant in a case where a formality rule prevents an agreement from having contractual effect, and may, in a suitable case, lead to the imposition of a trust. It may therefore be relevant where there has been a failure to comply with s.53(1)(c), but only if the requirements of the doctrine have been made out on the facts. The principal difficulty with using proprietary estoppel reasoning, or any other form of estoppel reasoning, to explain *Re Vandervell (No.2)*, is that there was no evidence of any action in reliance by the beneficiaries of the children's settlement, nor of any detriment they would suffer (other than the absence of a gift). **3–095**

Lawton LJ's reasoning is perhaps more convincing, as it focusses on the potentially important fact that the option held by the trustee company was exercised by using part of the funds held by those trustees for the children's settlement. As Lawton LJ noted, where A uses B's money to buy property, a trust may arise and, as it is imposed by law, such a trust can arise without any formality. Such a constructive or resulting trust,[103] like proprietary estoppel, may therefore be relevant where there has been a failure to comply with s.53(1)(c), but, again, only if the requirements of the doctrine have been made out on the facts. The difficulty in *Re Vandervell (No.2)* is that, whilst money held on trust for the children was used to acquire the shares, the sum paid was far lower than the market value of the shares, thanks to the terms of the option. The existence of the option, held on trust for Vandervell, was therefore just as crucial to the acquisition of the shares as the payment of the £5,000, held on trust for the children. However, it may still be possible to support Lawton LJ's analysis, if it is combined with Stephenson LJ's point that Vandervell intended the children to have the beneficial interest in the shares: it could perhaps be said that Vandervell had abandoned any intention to acquire an interest in the shares, leaving the trust for the children to take effect; or, similarly, that Vandervell's oral attempt to dispose of the beneficial interest in the shares, whilst incapable of effecting such a disposition in itself, can still be used to rebut any presumption of resulting trust that might otherwise have arisen when the shares were acquired through the exercise of the option. **3–096**

In considering *Re Vandervell (No.2)*, it is also useful to return to Lord Upjohn's analysis of the purposes of the s.53(1)(c) formality rule.[104] If we view the relevant transaction in the case as consisting of just two stages,[105] it can be said that, as was also the case in *Vandervell v IRC*, but not in *Grey v IRC*, the transaction was of such a type that the trustee was *necessarily involved* in it. After all, the option could not be exercised without action by the trustee company (VT). However a difficulty arises if we take a different view of the transaction and break it down into a further stage. If the transaction is thus broken down then there are two possibilities. Case (i) is that the option must first have been exercised, so that VT then held the shares on trust for Vandervell, and that beneficial interest in the shares was then transferred from Vandervell to the children. In that case, *Grey v IRC* must apply at the second stage, to the transfer of the beneficial interest in the shares from Vandervell to the children. Case (ii) is that the beneficial interest in the option was first transferred from Vandervell to the children, so that VT held the option on trust for the children, and only then was the option exercised for their benefit. In that case, *Grey v IRC* must apply at the first stage, to the transfer of the beneficial interest in the option from Vandervell to the children. **3–097**

Nonetheless, even if it is accepted that the transaction has thus to be broken down into a further stage, it may just still be possible to explain the result in *Re Vandervell (No.2)*. One suggestion is that Vandervell did not simply transfer a beneficial interest to the children; rather, he surrendered or **3–098**

[102] At paras 3–017—3–025.

[103] There is some debate as to the classification of the trust arising in a case where B's money is used by A, without B's consent, to acquire property for A: see paras 5–196ff.

[104] Discussed at para.3–077.

[105] As in the diagram at para.3–085.

waived his beneficial interest (either in the option or in the shares), thereby creating a moment when the trustee company (VT) held the option or shares outright. At that point, VT could then orally declare a trust in favour of the children, as such a declaration certainly does not require writing. This suggestion depends on the view that a surrender of a beneficial interest to a trustee is outside the scope of s.53(1)(c): after all, as such a transaction, like the transfer of the shares in *Vandervell v IRC*, terminates a trust, it does not create any risk that the trustee will be confused as to the identity of the beneficiary.

**3–099** After this consideration of the three key decisions—*Grey v IRC*; *Vandervell v IRC*; and *Re Vandervell (No.2)*—it may be useful to summarise the scope of s.53(1)(c). First, it clearly applies to a simple transfer of a beneficial interest: such a transfer creates a risk that the trustees may be unaware of the identity of the new beneficiary and so falls within the mischief identified by Lord Upjohn in *Vandervell v IRC*. As a result, it also applies, as in *Grey v IRC*, to an instruction by the beneficiary to the trustees that they should now hold the trust property for a new beneficiary. It could be argued that, on the facts of *Grey*, there was no risk of the trustees' being confused, given that they received their instructions from Hunter. The problem, however, is that a transfer of a beneficial interest does not *necessarily* involve the trustees, and the usefulness of the s.53(1)(c) formality rule in limiting disputes would be undermined if an exception were permitted where it could be shown that the initial beneficiary had made an oral communication to the trustees.

**3–100** Secondly, as shown by *Vandervell v IRC*, s.53(1)(c) does not apply where the trustees, at the request of those beneficially entitled, transfer the trust property outright to a third party. Such a transaction terminates the trust and necessarily involves the trustees, and so it falls outside the mischief identified by Lord Upjohn. Green has argued that this gives rise to the unwelcome possibility, in a case such as *Grey v IRC*, that the initial beneficiary can direct the trustee to transfer the trust property to another trustee to hold on trust for new beneficiaries, and such a transaction, if carried through by the trustees, can occur without the need for compliance with s.53(1)(c).[106] That does indeed seem to be the effect of *Vandervell v IRC*,[107] but it is far from clear that the possibility is unwelcome: given that the trustees are necessarily involved in the transaction, the need for signed writing does not arise.

**3–101** Thirdly, it seems that a declaration of a sub-trust by a beneficiary does not fall within the scope of s.53(1)(c), as the beneficiary of the sub-trust has no direct claim against the head trustee so that, again, the need for signed writing does not arise, as the transaction does not change the identity of the party to whom the head trustees owe their duties under the trust.

**3–102** Fourthly, it has also been held that s.53(1)(c) does not apply in a case where B disclaims an existing beneficial interest, thereby putting an end to that interest: "a disclaimer operates by way of avoidance and not by way of disposition."[108] Since a disclaimer ends the trust, we can certainly say that it causes no risk that the trustee might perform the trust in favour of the wrong person, and so it seems to lie outside the mischief identified by Lord Upjohn in *Vandervell v IRC*.

**3–103** As for the scope of s.53(1)(c), it is also worth noting that the formality rule applies only where B's interest is "subsisting at the time of the disposition". So, if an employee exercises her contractual right to nominate a person to receive moneys payable under a pension trust fund in the event of the employee's death in service, s.53(1)(c) does not apply, as the employee has simply exercised a power to direct what will occur in the future, and has not dealt with an existing beneficial interest.[109]

---

106 B. Green, "*Grey, Oughtred* and *Vandervell*—A Contextual Appraisal" (1984) 47 M.L.R. 385, 411.

107 On the overreaching analysis of the case adopted by Nolan, the effect of *Vandervell v IRC* in such a case would depend on whether the transaction was seen as having two stages (an overreaching transfer to the new trustees, followed by a declaration of trust, neither of which require writing) or just one (in which case *Grey v IRC* might apply): R. Nolan, "*Vandervell v IRC*: A Case of Overreaching" [2002] C.L.J. 169, 186–187.

108 *Re Paradise Motor Co Ltd* [1968] 1 W.L.R. 1125 at 1143 per Danckwerts LJ.

109 *Re Danish Bacon Co Ltd Staff Pension Fund* [1971] 1 W.L.R. 248; *Baird v Baird* [1990] 2 A.C. 548. Similarly, if B takes out

Finally, s.53(1)(c) has been expressly disapplied in certain contexts where equitable interests are the subject of frequent financial trading, and the markets dependent on such trading would grind to a halt if signed writing were required for every disposition of such equitable interests. For example, a party with a stock portfolio including shares in a public company very rarely holds legal title to such shares: the shares are "dematerialised"[110] and the party instead holds a derivative equitable interest in the shares. Trading in such shares would be very inconvenient if every sale of such shares required signed writing.[111] So the Uncertificated Securities Regulations 2001[112] disapply s.53(1)(c). The sub-section has also been disapplied, for similar reasons, in relation to financial collateral arrangements,[113] and the scope of the exemption has been given a broad interpretation, so as to ensure the underlying aim of simplifying activities carried out under a financial collateral arrangement.[114] 3–104

### ii. The Effect of Non-Compliance

We have seen in this chapter that a failure to comply with a particular formality rule, whilst it may prevent the claimant from showing that a party successfully exercised a power to give the claimant a right, does not necessarily prevent the claimant from showing that she acquired a very similar right by some other means. This is also true of s.53(1)(c). In particular, it is important to note that, whilst the section requires signed writing for a disposition of a beneficial interest, no such writing is required for a *contract* for the disposition of such an interest, at least if the interest itself is not an interest in land. As we will consider in more detail in Chapter 5,[115] a contract for the transfer of property may, in certain circumstances, give rise to a constructive trust of that property in favour of the planned transferee. A combination of those two points means that, even in the absence of a written transfer of B's beneficial interest, a claimant may acquire valuable equitable proprietary rights by showing that, as a result of B's oral contractual promise to make such a transfer, B now holds that beneficial interest on constructive trust for the claimant. Some doubt was cast on this analysis by some of the members of the House of Lords in *Oughtred v IRC*,[116] but it was confirmed by the Court of Appeal in *Neville v Wilson*. 3–105

*Neville v Wilson*

Court of Appeal [1997] Ch. 144

Shareholders of a company (JEN) agreed to liquidate it informally and they also orally agreed to divide up between themselves that company's equitable interest in shares in a private company. 3–106

NOURSE L.J. (giving the judgment of the court to which ROSE and ALDOUS L.JJ also contributed):. . . The effect of the agreement, more closely analysed, was that each shareholder agreed to assign his interest in the other shares of JEN's equitable interest in exchange for the assignment by the other shareholders of their interests in his own aliquot share. Each individual agreement having been a disposition of a subsisting equitable interest not made in writing, there then arises the question whether it was rendered ineffectual by s.53 of the Law of Property Act 1925. . . 3–107

The simple view of the present case is that the effect of each individual agreement was to constitute 3–108

a policy on her life where rights to a money payment crystallise only on her death, B's nomination that on her death T is to receive the payment and hold it on trust for B2 does not require signed writing as it is not a disposition of a *subsisting* equitable interest.

110 See para.1–071.

111 See, e.g. Financial Markets Law Committee, "Property Interests in Investment Securities: Analysis of the Need for and Nature of Legislation relating to Property Interests in Indirectly Held Investment Securities" (July 2004) (Issue 3), para.6.9.

112 (SI 2001/3755). See reg.38(5).

113 Financial Collateral Arrangements (No.2) Regulations 2009 (SI 2009/2462), reg. 4(2).

114 See *Mills v Sportsdirect.com Retail Ltd* [2010] 2 B.C.L.C. 143 at [70].

115 See paras 5–011—5–024.

116 [1960] A.C. 206.

the shareholder an implied or constructive trustee for the other shareholders, so that the requirement for writing contained in sub-s.(1)(c) of s.53 was dispensed with by sub-s.(2). That was the view taken by Upjohn J. at first instance and by Lord Radcliffe in the House of Lords in *Oughtred v IRC*. In order to see whether it is open to us to adopt it in this court, we must give careful consideration to those views and to the other speeches in the House of Lords.

**3–109** In *Oughtred v IRC*[117] a mother and son were the tenant for life and absolute reversioner respectively under a settlement of shares in a private company. By an oral agreement made on 18 June 1956 they agreed that on 26 June the son would exchange his reversionary interest under the settlement for shares in the same company owned by the mother absolutely, to the intent that her life interest in the settled shares should be enlarged into an absolute interest. On 26 June the mother and the son released the trustees by a deed which recited, amongst other things, that the settled shares were "accordingly now held in trust for [the mother] absolutely", and that it was intended to transfer them to her. On the same day the trustees transferred the settled shares to the mother by deed, the consideration being expressed to be ten shillings. It was held by Lord Keith of Avonholm, Lord Denning and Lord Jenkins, (Lord Radcliffe and Lord Cohen dissenting), that the transfer was assessable to ad valorem stamp duty. The basis of decision adopted by the majority was that, even if the oral agreement was effective to pass the equitable interest in the settled shares to the mother, the transfer, as the instrument by which the transaction was completed, was none the less a conveyance on sale within s.54 of the Stamp Act 1891.

**3–110** Upjohn J., having said that s.53(2) of the 1925 Act was a complete answer to the argument that s.53(1)(c) applied, continued:[118]

> "This was an oral agreement for value, and, accordingly, on the making thereof Peter the vendor became a constructive trustee of his equitable reversionary interest in the trust funds for the appellant. No writing to achieve that result was necessary, for an agreement of sale and purchase of an equitable interest in personalty (other than chattels real) may be made orally, and s.53 has no application to a trust arising by construction of law."

**3–111** Lord Radcliffe, having expressed the view that the judgment of Upjohn J. was correct and agreeing with his reasons, said:[119]

> "The reasoning of the whole matter, as I see it, is as follows: On June 18, 1956, the son owned an equitable reversionary interest in the settled shares; by his oral agreement of that date he created in his mother an equitable interest in his reversion, since the subject-matter of the agreement was property of which specific performance would normally be decreed by the court. He thus became a trustee for her of that interest *sub modo*; having regard to sub-s.(2) of s.53 of the Law of Property Act, 1925, sub-s.(1) of that section did not operate to prevent that trusteeship arising by operation of law."

**3–112** Lord Cohen, the other member of the minority, said:[120]

> "Before your Lordships, counsel for the Crown was prepared to agree that, on the making of the oral agreement, Peter became a constructive trustee of his equitable reversionary interest in the settled funds for the appellant, but he submitted that, none the less, s. 53(1)(c) applied and, accordingly, Peter could not assign that equitable interest to the appellant except by a disposition in writing. My Lords, with that I agree, but it does not follow that the transfer was a conveyance of that equitable interest on which ad valorem stamp duty was payable under the Stamp Act, 1891."

Having held that the transfer was not such a conveyance, he dissented on that ground.

**3–113** Lord Denning said:[121]

> "I do not think it necessary to embark on a disquisition on constructive trusts; because I take the view that, even if the oral agreement of June 18, 1956, was effective to transfer Peter's reversionary interest to his mother, nevertheless, when that oral agreement was subsequently implemented by the transfer, then the transfer became liable to stamp duty. But I may say that I do not think the oral

---

117 [1960] A.C. 206.
118 [1958] Ch. 383 at 390.
119 [1960] A.C. 206 at 227.
120 Ibid. at 230.
121 Ibid. at 233.

> agreement was effective to transfer Peter's reversionary interest to his mother. I should have thought that the wording of s.53(1)(c) of the Law of Property Act 1925 clearly made a writing necessary to effect a transfer, and s.53(2) does not do away with that necessity."

The views of their Lordships as to the effect of s.53 can be summarised as follows. Lord Radcliffe, agreeing with Upjohn J., thought that sub-s.(2) applied. He gave reasons for that view. Lord Cohen and Lord Denning thought that it did not. Although neither of them gave reasons, they may be taken to have accepted the submissions of Mr. Wilberforce Q.C.[122] Lord Keith and Lord Jenkins expressed no view either way. We should add that when the case was in this court, Lord Evershed M.R., in delivering the judgment of himself, Morris and Ormerod L.JJ., said:[123] 3–114

> "In this court the case for the Crown has, we think, been somewhat differently presented, and in the end of all, the question under s.53 of the Law of Property Act [1925] does not, in our judgment, strictly call for a decision. We are not, however, with all respect to the learned judge, prepared to accept, as we understand it, his conclusion on the effect of s.53 of the Law of Property Act."

The basis of this court's decision was the same as that adopted by the majority of the House of Lords.

We do not think that there is anything in the speeches in the House of Lords which prevents us from holding that the effect of each individual agreement was to constitute the shareholder an implied or constructive trustee for the other shareholders. In this respect we are of the opinion that the analysis of Lord Radcliffe, based on the proposition that a specifically enforceable agreement to assign an interest in property creates an equitable interest in the assignee, was unquestionably correct.[124] A greater difficulty is caused by Lord Denning's outright rejection of the application of s.53(2), with which Lord Cohen appears to have agreed. 3–115

So far as it is material to the present case, what sub-s.(2) says is that sub-s.(1)(c) does not affect the creation or operation of implied or constructive trusts. Just as in *Oughtred v IRC* the son's oral agreement created a constructive trust in favour of the mother, so here each shareholder's oral or implied agreement created an implied or constructive trust in favour of the other shareholders. Why then should sub-s.(2) not apply? No convincing reason was suggested in argument and none has occurred to us since. Moreover, to deny its application in this case would be to restrict the effect of general words when no restriction is called for, and to lay the ground for fine distinctions in the future. With all the respect which is due to those who have thought to the contrary, we hold that sub-s.(2) applies to an agreement such as we have in this case. 3–116

For these reasons, we have come to the conclusion that the agreement entered into by the shareholders of JEN in about April 1969 was not rendered ineffectual by s.53 of the 1925 Act. 3–117

The reasoning in *Neville v Wilson* has been criticised.[125] For example, Chadwick LJ later stated, in an obiter observation, that: "I am far from persuaded that s.53(2) of the Law of Property Act 1925 can have any application in a case where it is sought to avoid the effect of s.53(1)(c) by relying on an oral contract to make the disposition which s.53(1)(c) requires to be in writing."[126] Nonetheless, there is further judicial support for the reasoning,[127] and there is nothing illogical in having a formality requirement that applies to a disposition of an equitable interest, but not to a contract to make such a disposition. For example, if a party has full legal title to shares, the transfer of that title may require registration, but no formality rule applies to a contract to make such a transfer. 3–118

---

122 See [1960] A.C. 206 at 220–222.

123 [1958] Ch. 678 at 687.

124 Cf. *London and South Western Rly Co v Gomm* (1882) 20 Ch.D. 562 at 581, per Jessel MR.

125 See, e.g. R. Nolan, "The Triumph of Technicality" [1996] C.L.J. 436; S. Worthington, *Equity*, 2nd edn (Oxford University Press, 2006), pp.233–234.

126 *United Bank of Kuwait Plc v Sahib* [1997] Ch. 107 at 129.

127 See, e.g. Upjohn J in *Oughtred v IRC* [1958] Ch. 383; Lord Radcliffe in *Oughtred v IRC* [1960] A.C. 206 at 227–228; Megarry J in *Re Holt's Settlement* [1969] 1 Ch. 100; and Goff and Shaw LJJ in *DHN Food Distributors Ltd v Tower Hamlets LBC* [1976] 1 W.L.R. 852 at 865, 867. See too Lord Cohen in *Oughtred v IRC* [1960] A.C. 206 at 230, stating that, at least when the purchase price has been paid, B can no longer claim, as against the purchaser, to be entitled to the benefit of the property.

3-119 There is an important practical question as to whether the principle in *Neville v Wilson* is limited, as was assumed by the Court of Appeal in that case,[128] to *specifically enforceable* contracts for the disposition of an equitable interest.[129] This was not in issue in the case itself: the shares were in a private company, and so the contract was specifically enforceable, as damages are an inadequate remedy where the claimant cannot acquire equivalent property on the open market.[130] The conventional view is that a contract for the transfer of property must indeed be specifically enforceable if it is to give rise to a constructive trust, but we will examine challenges to that view in Chapter 5,[131] when considering that particular type of constructive trust.[132]

## 3. Testamentary Dispositions: The Wills Act 1837

### A. Introduction

3-120 As noted above,[133] the Wills Act 1837, which is not specific to trusts, prescribes special formalities for the validity of testamentary dispositions.

#### Wills Act 1837 ss.9 and 15[134]

3-121 9. No will shall be valid unless—

(a) it is in writing, and signed by the testator, or by some other person in his presence and by his direction; and
(b) it appears that the testator intended by his signature to give effect to the will; and
(c) the signature is made or acknowledged by the testator in the presence of two or more witnesses present at the same time; and
(d) each witness either—
    (i) attests and signs the will; or
    (ii) acknowledges his signature, in the presence of the testator (but not necessarily in the presence of any other witness), but no form of attestation shall be necessary.

3-122 15. If any person shall attest the execution of any will to whom or to whose wife or husband any beneficial devise, legacy, estate, interest, gift, or appointment, of or affecting any real or personal estate (other than and except charges and directions for the payment of any debt or debts), shall be thereby given or made, such devise, legacy, estate, interest, gift, or appointment shall, so far only as concerns such person attesting the execution of such will, or the wife or husband of such person, or any person claiming under such person or wife or husband, be utterly null and void, and such person so attesting shall be admitted as a witness to prove the execution of such will, or to prove the validity or invalidity

---

128 [1997] Ch. 144 at 157 [extracted at para.3–115].

129 In *Chinn v Collins* [1981] A.C. 533, when considering non-specifically enforceable contractual dealings with an equitable interest in shares, Lord Wilberforce stated at 548 that: "Dealings related to the equitable interest in these [shares] required no formality. As soon as there was an agreement for their sale accompanied or followed by payment of the price, the equitable title passed at once to the purchaser and all that was needed to perfect his title was notice to the trustee or the nominee."

130 See para.18–118.

131 At paras See para.5–021.

132 Note that in *Chinn v Collins* [1981] A.C. 533 at 548, Lord Wilberforce assumed at 548 that, even in the absence of specific enforceability, dealings in an equitable interest in shares required no formality: "As soon as there was an agreement for their sale accompanied or followed by payment of the price, the equitable title passed at once to the purchaser and all that was needed to perfect his title was notice to the trustee or nominee."

133 See para.3–002.

134 Section 9 supersedes the Statute of Frauds 1677 s.5, and was itself substituted by the Administration of Justice Act 1982 s.17.

thereof, notwithstanding such devise, legacy, estate, interest, gift, or appointment mentioned in such will.[135]

## *B. The Scope of the Formality Requirements*

Under s.1 of the Wills Act 1837, the term "will" extends to any "testamentary disposition". It is important to note that the relevant formality requirements apply not just to a document identified as a will, but to any testamentary disposition. The meaning of that term is therefore crucial to the scope of the Wills Act, as we have already discussed.[136] It follows that if a party intends to set up a trust that will take effect on her death, but not before then, the starting point[137] is that the power to set up such a trust must be exercised in writing, signed by that party, and attested by two witnesses, with s.15 providing that certain persons cannot act as valid witnesses. **3–123**

The probate doctrine of incorporation by reference may assist in satisfying these formal requirements. For example, if the will states that: "I devise Blackacre to X upon trusts which I have communicated to her by letter dated November 11, 2008", then, as the will refers to a written instrument, already existing at the date of the will, and in such terms that the written instrument can be ascertained, the doctrine of incorporation applies.[138] Consequently the incorporated letter will be admitted to public probate as part of the testator's will, and the trust as set out in the letter can take effect as a simple express trust, arising as a result of the testator's successful exercise of her power to set up such a trust. **3–124**

## *C. The Effect of Non-Compliance: Secret Trusts and Mutual Wills*

We have seen throughout this chapter that a failure to comply with a particular formality rule, whilst it may prevent the claimant from showing that a party successfully exercised a power to give the claimant a right to property, does not necessarily prevent the claimant from showing that she acquired a very similar right by some other means. We will be concerned here with two particular doctrines that may assist a claimant when the deceased has not complied with the Wills Act. **3–125**

We will first consider the doctrine of secret trusts. The doctrine of fully secret trusts may assist the claimant where, for example, a will states that "I leave Blackacre to X absolutely", but X had in fact agreed with the testator to hold Blackacre on trust for the claimant. The doctrine of half secret trusts, which has slightly different requirements, may assist the claimant where, for example, a will states that "I leave Blackacre to X on trust" and, before the will was made, X had agreed with the testator to hold Blackacre on trust for the claimant. The point is that where a person has died, having been induced to leave property by will to X[139] on the oral understanding[140] that X will hold the property on trust for B, it would be unconscionable for X to decide to keep the property for her own benefit. As a **3–126**

---

135 Note that the Wills Act 1968 s.1 stipulates that: "For the purposes of section 15 of the Wills Act 1837 the attestation of a will by a person to whom to whose spouse there is given or made any such disposition as described in that section shall be disregarded if the will is duly executed without his attestation and without that of any other such person."

136 See paras 3–007—3–010.

137 Some express exceptions are made, e.g. under s.11 of the Wills Act 1837 for "any soldier being in actual military service, or any mariner or seaman at sea". See P. Critchley, "Privileged Wills and Testamentary Formalities: A Time to Die?" [1999] C.L.J. 49.

138 *In the Goods of Smart* [1902] P. 238; *Re Jones* [1942] Ch. 328, restricted by *Re Edwards WT* [1948] Ch. 440.

139 Or, indeed, to fail to make a will on the basis that X, the intestate successor, has agreed to hold the property thus received on trust for B.

140 A good practical precaution, if the deceased is concerned about the question of proof, is to have a document signed by X and put into the possession of B.

result, equity recognises that, despite the absence of the requisite formalities, X holds the property thus received on trust for B.

**3–127** There is, therefore, a clear link with the court's response to a case where land is transferred subject to an oral understanding that is to be held on trust[141] for the transferor, and thus with the doctrine applied in *Rochefoucald v Boustead*,[142] for example. Indeed, the courts have often justified the doctrine of secret trusts on the basis of the principle, also relied on in *Rochefoucald* in relation to what is now s.53(1)(b) of the Law of Property Act 1925, that a statute cannot be used as an instrument of fraud.[143] The important question is as to what counts, in this context, as fraud?[144] Different answers are given to that question in cases of fully and of half secret trusts, and so we will consider the two separately before comparing them.

**3–128** In considering secret trusts, it is important to realise that a will, when admitted to probate, is a public document. If a testator wishes to set up a particular trust on her death, but does not want others to know of that trust or its terms she may try to take advantage of the doctrine of secret trusts. It is tempting to think that such trusts were necessary only in a bygone age when, for example, a husband did not want his wife to know that he had made provision in his will for his mistress or her children. Today, however, both men and women who remarry may not want their new families to know that they have made testamentary provision for their children from previous marriages.

**3–129** The results of an empirical survey of private client practitioners carried out in 2001 suggest that secret trusts are still used, or at least considered, by modern day testators.[145] An unusual example is provided by *Re Freud, Deceased*,[146] where the court had to consider the interpretation of a clause in the will of Lucien Freud, the painter, which, on its face, gave his residuary estate (estimated to be worth, after tax, around £42 million) absolutely to two parties, his solicitor and one of his children, also acting as executrices of the will. A previous will had made the same bequest, but referred on its face to a trust, the terms of which were not set out in the will. The court accepted that "when considering the significance of this change of wording it is unrealistic to suggest that Lucien Freud did not have an appreciation of secret trusts."[147] The evidence of his solicitor was that the bequest was made subject to a secret trust and the court noted that "the law recognises secret trusts, it is common place for solicitors to be appointed as trustees, and one reasonable explanation for a clause which confers a beneficial gift on a solicitor is that the testator intended to impose a fully secret trust." In concluding that the terms of the will did not themselves impose any trust, the court effectively proceeded on the assumption that the solicitor's evidence was correct and that a secret trust was in place.

**3–130** We will also consider the doctrine of mutual wills. Consider a case in which two parties (H and W)[148] agree to make identical wills, so that, on the death of either party, their property will pass either to the

---

141 Note that the undertaking can take a variety of forms: the obligation of X may be, for example, to transfer the property to B, to hold on trust for B, to pass the property by will to B on X's death, or even to pass by will to B whatever property remains after X has had recourse to it in X's lifetime (as in *Ottaway v Norman* [1972] Ch. 698).

142 [1897] 1 Ch. 196. See paras 3–032—3–049. The link between that doctrine and secret trusts is drawn, for example, by Patten LJ in *de Bruyne v de Bruyne* [2010] EWCA Civ 519 at [51].

143 *Jones v Badley* (1868) 3 Ch. App. 362 at 364; *McCormick v Grogan* (1869) L.R. 4 H.L. 82 at 88–89; *Blackwell v Blackwell* [1929] A.C. 318 at 336–367.

144 Note too that, despite the references to fraud, it is not the case that the claimant, B, must necessarily meet the higher standard of proof applicable to allegations of deceit: the requirements of a secret trust need be proved only to the usual civil standard of the balance of probabilities: see *Re Snowden, deceased* [1979] Ch. 528 at 537 (disagreeing with *Ottaway v Norman* [1972] Ch. 698 at 712).

145 R. Meager, "Secret Trusts: Do They Have a Future?" [2003] Conv. 203.

146 [2014] W.T.L.R. 1453.

147 ibid., at [61]. Freud certainly did not lack access to legal advice: it is noted at [2] that he spoke to his solicitor, a partner in a reputable firm, "almost daily for about 20 years before he died".

148 The cases often involve a husband and a wife, but this is not, of course, a requirement of the doctrine.

survivor of the two, if there is one, or to B. The first party to die, H, abides by the agreement, and so his property passes under his will to the survivor, W. W then revokes her earlier will, and instead makes a new will, complying with all relevant formality requirements, leaving her property to Z. In such a case, B may have a claim to W's estate, even though W revoked the earlier will, and instead left her estate to Z. W's later will is admitted to probate, and the property vests in her personal representatives, but on trust to give effect to the terms of the agreement upon which the mutual wills were made, i.e. upon trust for B. There is a question as to whether or not the doctrine of mutual wills rests on the same underlying principle as the doctrine of secret trusts, and we will consider that question below.[149]

## D. Fully Secret Trusts

A fully secret trust is one where neither the existence of the trust nor its terms are disclosed by the will.[150] As noted by Brightman J in the following extract, there are three key requirements for such a trust to arise where the will, on its face, makes an absolute bequest to X: (i) the intention of the testator that X will hold property subject to a duty; (ii) communication of that intention to X; and (iii) acceptance of that duty by X, either expressly or by acquiescence. **3–131**

### *Ottaway v Norman*

### Chancery Division [1972] Ch. 698

A testator, Harry Ottaway, by will devised his bungalow (with fixtures, fittings and furniture) to his housekeeper Miss Hodges in fee simple, and gave her a legacy of £1,500 and half the residue of his estate. It was alleged that Miss Hodges had orally agreed with the testator to leave the bungalow, etc., by her will to the claimants, who were the testator's son and daughter-in-law, Mr and Mrs William Ottaway. Further, it was alleged that she had orally agreed to leave them whatever money was left at her death. By her will Miss Hodges left all her property away from the claimants, who therefore brought an action against Miss Hodges' executor, Mr Norman, for a declaration that he held the appropriate parts of Miss Hodges' estate on trust for them. Brightman J. upheld the claim except in respect of the money. **3–132**

BRIGHTMAN J.:. . . It will be convenient to call the person on whom such a trust is imposed the "primary donee" and the beneficiary under that trust the "secondary donee". The essential elements which must be proved are: (i) the intention of the testator to subject the primary donee to an obligation in favour of the secondary donee; (ii) communication of that intention to the primary donee; and (iii) the acceptance of that obligation by the primary donee either expressly or by acquiescence. It is immaterial whether these elements precede or succeed the will of the donor. I am informed that there is no recent reported case where the obligation imposed on the primary donee is an obligation to make a will in favour of the secondary donee as distinct from some form of inter vivos transfer. But it does not seem to me that that can really be a distinction which can validly be drawn on behalf of the defendant in the present case. The basis of the doctrine of a secret trust is the obligation imposed on the conscience of the primary donee and it does not seem to me that there is any materiality in the machinery by which the donor intends that that obligation shall be carried out. . . **3–133**

I find as a fact that Harry Ottaway intended that Miss Hodges should be obliged to dispose of the bungalow in favour of the plaintiffs at her death, that he communicated that intention to Miss Hodges and that Miss Hodges accepted the obligation. I find the same facts in relation to the furniture, fixtures and fittings which passed to Miss Hodges under clause 4 of Harry Ottaway's will. I am not satisfied that any similar obligation was imposed and accepted as regards any contents of the bungalow which had not devolved on Miss Hodges under clause 4 of Harry Ottaway's will. **3–134**

I turn to the question of money. In cross-examination William Ottaway said the trust extended to the house, furniture and money: **3–135**

[149] At paras 3-201–3-205.

[150] It can also arise in cases of intestacy: *Sellack v Harris* (1708) 2 Eq. Ca. Abr. 46.

"Everything my father left to Miss Hodges was to be in the trust. The trust comprised the lot. She could use the money as she liked. She had to leave my wife and me whatever money was left."

3–136 In cross-examination Mrs Ottaway said that her understanding was that Miss Hodges was bound to make a will giving her and her husband the bungalow, contents and any money she had left. "She could please herself about the money. She did not have to save it for us. She was free to spend it." It seems to me that two questions arise. First as a matter of fact what did the parties intend should be comprised in Miss Hodges's obligation? All money which Miss Hodges had at her death, including money which she had acquired before Harry's death and money she acquired after his death from all sources? Or, only money acquired under Harry's will? Secondly, if such an obligation existed would it as a matter of law create a valid trust? On the second question I am content to assume for present purposes but without so deciding that if property is given to the primary donee on the understanding that the primary donee will dispose by his will of such assets, if any, as he may have at his command at his death in favour of the secondary donee, a valid trust is created in favour of the secondary donee which is in suspense during the lifetime of the primary donee, but attaches to the estate of the primary donee at the moment of the latter's death. There would seem to be at least some support for this proposition in an Australian case to which I was referred: *Birmingham v Renfrew*.[151] I do not, however, find sufficient evidence that it was Harry Ottaway's intention that Miss Hodges should be compelled to leave all her money, from whatever source derived, to the plaintiffs. This would seem to preclude her giving even a small pecuniary legacy to any friend or relative. I do no think it is clear that Harry Ottaway intended to extract any such far-reaching undertaking from Miss Hodges or that she intended to accept such a wide obligation herself. Therefore the obligation, if any, is in my view to be confined to money derived under Harry Ottaway's will. If the obligation is confined to money derived under Harry Ottaway's will, the obligation is meaningless and unworkable unless it includes the requirement that she shall keep such money separate and distinct from her own money. I am certain that no such requirement was ever discussed or intended. If she had the right to mingle her own money with that derived from Harry, there would be no ascertainable property on which the trust could bite at her death.[152]

3–137 There is another difficulty. Does money in this context include only cash or cash and investments, or all moveable property of any description? The evidence is quite inconclusive. In my judgment the plaintiff's claim succeeds in relation to the bungalow and in relation to the furniture, fixtures and fittings which devolved under clause 4 of Harry Ottaway's will subject, of course, to normal wastage and fair wear and tear, but not to any other assets.

3–138 It is clear that nothing short of an express or implied acceptance by X will raise a trust.[153] Communication and acceptance must be of a definite legally binding obligation of X, not of a mere hope or confidence expressed by the testator.[154] In the case of a fully secret trust,[155] communication and acceptance[156] may be effected at any time during the life of the testator, whether before or after the execution of the will and communication may be made through an agent.[157] If X is told in the testator's lifetime that she is to hold the property on trust, but is not informed of the terms of the trust, she holds the property on a resulting trust for the testator's residuary legatee or devisee, or if there is

---

151 (1937) 57 C.L.R. 666.

152 On this principle see *Henry v Hammond* [1913] 2 K.B. 515 at 521; endorsed in *Re Chelsea Cloisters Ltd* (1980) 41 P. & C.R. 98 at 101, and followed in *Azam v Iqbal* [2008] Bus. L.R. 168.

153 *Wallgrave v Tebbs* (1855) 2 K. & J. 313.

154 See *Att.-Gen. v Chamberlain* (1904) 90 L.T. 581; *Re Snowden (Deceased)* [1979] Ch. 528 at 534; *Kasperbauer v Griffith* [2000] W.T.L.R. 333 at 343.

155 Compare the different position for a half-secret trust: see para.3–140.

156 The full extent of the property to be covered by the obligation must be communicated and accepted so that where a secret trust for a £5,000 legacy has been communicated to and accepted by the trustee, and the legacy is increased by £5,000 in a further codicil but nothing is said to the trustee, the further £5,000 is not caught by the secret trust: *Re Colin Cooper, (Deceased)* [1939] Ch. 580 at 586. The further £5,000 is taken beneficially by the fully secret "trustee".

157 *Moss v Cooper* (1861) 1 J. & H. 352. If the agent were unauthorised but the legatee did not approach the testator to clarify the matter would this amount to acquiescence?

no such person, or the property is residuary property, then for the testator's intestate successors.[158] Of course, if X is not told of the testator's intention to impose a trust at all, then no trust arises, as X does not act unconscionably by using the property for her own benefit.

## E. Half-Secret Trusts

A half-secret trust is one where the existence of the trust is disclosed by the will but the terms are not. It can be argued that such a case differs fundamentally from one in which a fully secret trust might arise. Where the existence of the trust is disclosed by the will, it is clear from the face of the will that X, the recipient of the bequest, is not free to use that property for her own benefit, and can only do so to the extent that she is permitted by the terms of the trust. So, if no half-secret trust can be established, X will hold the bequest on resulting trust for the testator's estate. It could then be argued that it should not be possible for B, the intended beneficiary, to avoid the formality requirements In the WIlls Act 1837 and to establish a beneficial interest, as such a result is not necessary to prevent unconscionable conduct by X. As X will in any case hold the property on resulting trust, where is the risk of fraud? **3–139**

In *Blackwell v Blackwell*,[159] however, the House of Lords considered and rejected that argument, concluding instead that there is a doctrine of half-secret trusts, which provides that they are governed by the same basic requirements as fully secret trusts (intention of the testator; communication to X; and acceptance by X). There is, however, at least one important difference between the two forms of secret trust[160]: in a fully secret trust, the communication and acceptance can occur at any point before the death of the testator; in relation to a half secret trust, it must occur before the will is made.[161] We will ask whether this difference is justified after considering the following extract from *Blackwell v Blackwell*. **3–140**

*Blackwell v Blackwell*

House of Lords [1929] A.C. 318

A testator by a codicil bequeathed £12,000 to five persons upon trust to invest according to their discretion and "to apply the income. . . for the purposes indicated by me to them." Before the execution of the codicil the objects of the trust were communicated in outline to four of the legatees and in detail to the fifth, and the trust was accepted by all of them. The fifth legatee also made a memorandum of the testator's instructions, on the same day as (though a few hours after) the execution of the codicil. The plaintiffs (the residuary legatees) now claimed a declaration that no valid trust in favour of the objects so communicated had been created, on the ground principally that parol evidence was inadmissible to establish the purposes indicated by the testator. Eve J. and the Court of Appeal held that the evidence was admissible, and here proved a valid secret trust for the persons named by the testator in his instructions to the legatees. The plaintiffs' appeal to the House of Lords was unsuccessful. **3–141**

---

[158] *Re Boyes* (1884) 26 Ch. D. 531. In *Re Keen* [1937] Ch. 236, which concerned a half-secret trust, X had agreed to be bound by the terms unknown to X and contained in a letter handed to him by the testator in an envelope to be kept sealed until after the testator's death: the half-secret trust failed on other grounds: see para.3–148.

[159] [1929] A.C. 318.

[160] It may be that, in *Re Freud, deceased* [2014] W.T.L.R. 1453 (for which see para.3–129) the testator changed his will so as to establish a fully secret trust, rather than a half-secret trust, precisely in order to avoid any disputes about the timing of the communication and acceptance.

[161] See, e.g. *Re Keen* [1937] Ch. 236; *Re Bateman's WT* [1970] 1 W.L.R. 1463. If a testator, having created a valid half-secret trust, subsequently tells the trustee not to hold for the old beneficiaries but to hold for new beneficiaries, then the trust for the new beneficiaries will fail (see, e.g. *Re Keen* [1937] Ch. 236). It is also possible that the revocation of the old trusts will fall on the basis that it was conditional on the creation of valid new trusts, although it should succeed if construed as unconditional (by analogy with, e.g. *Re Finnemore* [1992] 1 W.L.R. 793 on conditional revocation of wills), with the effect that the property will pass to the residuary legatee (or the statutory next-of-kin).

3–142 VISCOUNT SUMNER (with whom LORD HAILSHAM L.C., LORD BUCKMASTER, LORD CARSON, and LORD WARRINGTON agreed):. . . In itself the doctrine of equity, by which parol evidence is admissible to prove what is called "fraud" in connection with secret trusts, and effect is given to such trusts when established, would not seem to conflict with any of the Acts under which from time to time the legislature has regulated the right of testamentary disposition. A court of conscience finds a man in the position of an absolute legal owner of a sum of money, which has been bequeathed to him under a valid will, and it declares that, on proof of certain facts relating to the motives and actions of the testator, it will not allow the legal owner to exercise his legal right to do what he will with his own. This seems to be a perfectly normal exercise of general equitable jurisdiction. The facts commonly, but not necessarily, involve some immoral and selfish conduct on the part of the legal owner. The necessary elements, on which the question turns, are intention, communication and acquiescence. The testator intends his absolute gift to be employed as he and not as the donee desires; he tells the proposed donee of this intention and, either by express promise or by the tacit promise, which is satisfied by acquiescence, the proposed donee encourages him to bequeath the money in the faith that his intentions will be carried out. For the prevention of fraud equity fastens on the conscience of the legatee a trust, a trust, that is, which otherwise would be inoperative; in other words it makes him do what the will in itself has nothing to do with; it lets him take what the will gives him and then makes him apply it as the court of conscience directs, and it does so in order to give effect to wishes of the testator which would not otherwise be effectual.

3–143 To this, two circumstances must be added to bring the present case to the test of the general doctrine, first, that the will states on its face that the legacy is given on trust but does not state what the trusts are, and further contains a residuary bequest, and, second, that the legatees are acting with perfect honesty, seek no advantage to themselves, and only desire, if the court will permit them, to do what in other circumstances the court would have fastened it on their conscience to perform.

3–144 Since the current of decisions down to *Re Fleetwood*[162] and *Re Huxtable*[163] has established that the principles of equity apply equally when these circumstances are present as in cases where they are not, the material question is whether and how the Wills Act affects this case. It seems to me that, apart from legislation, the application of the principle of equity which was made in *Fleetwood's case* and *Huxtable's case* was logical, and was justified by the same considerations as in the cases of fraud and absolute gifts. Why should equity forbid an honest trustee to give effect to his promise, made to a deceased testator, and compel him to pay another legatee, about whom it is quite certain that the testator did not mean to make him the object of his bounty? In both cases the testator's wishes are incompletely expressed in his will. Why should equity, over a mere matter of words, give effect to them in one case and frustrate them in the other? No doubt the words "in trust" prevent the legatee from taking beneficially, whether they have simply been declared in conversation or written in the will, but the fraud, when the trustee, so called in the will, is also the residuary legatee, is the same as when he is only declared a trustee by word of mouth accepted by him. I recoil from interfering with decisions of long standing, which reject this anomaly, unless constrained by statute. . .

3–145 The limits, beyond which the rules as to unspecified trusts must not be carried, have often been discussed. A testator cannot reserve to himself a power of making future unwitnessed dispositions by merely naming a trustee and leaving the purposes of the trust to be supplied afterwards, nor can a legatee give testamentary validity to an unexecuted codicil by accepting an indefinite trust, never communicated to him in the testator's lifetime: *Johnson v Ball*,[164] *Re Boyes*,[165] *Riordan v Banon*,[166] *Re Hetley*.[167] To hold otherwise would indeed be to enable the testator to "give the go-by" to the requirements of the Wills Act, because he did not choose to comply with them. It is communication of the purpose to the legatee, coupled with acquiescence or promise on his part, that removes the matter from the provision of the Wills Act and brings it within the law of trusts, as applied in this instance to trustees, who happen also to be legatees. . .

---

162 (1880) 15 Ch.D. 594, where a testatrix by a codicil bequeathed to X all her personalty "to be applied as I have requested him to do." Before the execution of the codicil she had stated to X the trusts on which she intended the property to be held, and X made a memorandum of the details in her presence. Hall VC held that external evidence was admissible to prove the terms of the understanding between X and the testatrix.

163 [1902] 2 Ch. 793.

164 (1851) 5 De G. & Sm. 85.

165 (1884) 26 Ch.D. 531.

166 (1876) 10 I.R.Eq. 469.

167 [1902] 2 Ch. 866.

Viscount Sumner's reasoning thus purports to justify treating fully secret and half-secret trusts differently when it comes to the timing of the required communication and acceptance. The argument goes that a testator cannot be permitted, through the medium of a valid will which imposes a trust but does not set out the beneficial interests of that trust, to reserve to herself a power to create the beneficial interests in an informal non-testamentary manner, so giving the go-by to the requirements of the Wills Act 1837.[168] It seems odd, however, that this scruple as to undermining the formality rules should appear at this point, as it is clear from fully secret trust cases[169] that the need to enforce the understanding subject to which X has acquired property can, in general, be given effect to without jeopardising the Wills Act.[170] Indeed, there are a number of other jurisdictions that have not accepted the special rule as to the timing of communication and acceptance of half-secret trusts.[171] **3–146**

It has been suggested that there is another means of defending the rule that the communication and acceptance of a half-secret trust must occur before the will is made. It depends on seeing half-secret trusts as depending on the probate doctrine of incorporation by reference. It is certainly true that, as noted above,[172] that doctrine can apply only where the incorporated document exists at the time of the will referring to it. It is, however, hard to see why this should have any bearing on the operation of half-secret trusts. The essential point is that, whilst the doctrine of incorporation by reference operates within the scope of the formality requirements for testamentary dispositions, secret trusts are imposed precisely where those requirements have not been met: they operate independently of the Wills Act.[173] There are, further, some important differences between the doctrine of half-secret trusts and the probate doctrine of incorporation by reference[174]: in the former, for example, the terms of the trust, set out in the communication and acceptance, need not be in writing; and in the latter, for example, X does not need to be aware of the document incorporated. **3–147**

The distinction between half-secret trusts and incorporation by reference also casts doubt on another supposed special requirement for half-secret trusts: that the communication of the trusts and the terms of the trust must not conflict with the wording of the will, for to allow otherwise would be to allow oral evidence to contradict the express words of the will.[175] Thus, leaving property to four persons "to be dealt with in accordance with my wishes which I have made known to them" is ineffective to create a half-secret trust unless the wishes were communicated to all four.[176] Furthermore, if property is left by will to X as trustee, evidence is not admissible to show that X was meant to have some part of that property beneficially.[177] In contrast, if the wording of the will gives property "to **3–148**

---

168 See too *Re Keen* [1937] Ch. 236 at 246, 248.

169 See, e.g. *McCormick v Grogan* (1869) L.R. 4 H.L. 82; *Ottaway v Norman* [1972] Ch. 698.

170 Note too that the case from which the special rule as to half-secret trusts is often said to derive, *Johnson v Ball* (1851) 5 De G. & Sm. 85, has been persuasively criticised: see W. Holdsworth, "Secret Trusts" (1937) 53 L.Q.R. 501.

171 e.g. Ireland: *Re Browne* [1944] Ir. R. 90; *Re Prendiville* (unreported, but noted [1992] Conv. 202 by J. Mee); New South Wales: *Ledgerwood v Perpetual Trustee Co Ltd* (1997) 41 N.S.W.L.R. 532; U.S.A.: American Law Institute, *Restatement (3rd) of Trusts* (American Law Institute, 2003), §18, comment (b).

172 At para.3–124.

173 See, e.g. *Blackwell v Blackwell* [1929] A.C. 318 at 335 (extracted at para.3–145); *Re Snowden, deceased* [1979] Ch. 528 at 535. However, as P. Critchley in (1999) 115 L.Q.R. 631 at 641 correctly states, "the mistake is to confuse 'outside the will' with 'outside the Wills Act'": a disposition by way of secret trust is a testamentary disposition, being revocable and ambulatory, as made clear so as to fall within the Wills Act. It is the harmful effect of the secret trustee's wrongful conduct that justifies equity's intervention.

174 In addition, if the doctrine of incorporation by reference is to apply, the will itself must refer to the document to be incorporated with sufficient precision to enable it to be identified: *Re Edwards' WT* [1948] Ch. 440; and a beneficiary of a half-secret trust who witnesses the will, unlike a beneficiary-witness named in an incorporated document, does not forfeit his or her beneficial interest: *Re Young* [1951] Ch. 344.

175 *Re Keen* [1937] Ch. 236.

176 *Re Spence* [1949] W.N. 237, following *Re Keen* [1937] Ch. 236.

177 See, e.g. *Re Rees* [1950] Ch. 204; *Re Tyler* [1967] 1 W.L.R. 1269.

X absolutely" or "to X relying on her, but not by way of trust, to carry out my wishes . . ." then oral evidence is admissible to prove a fully-secret trust, contradicting the express words of the will, for to allow otherwise would be to allow the possibility of fraud.[178]

**3–149** It is, again, difficult to see why the rules should differ as between fully secret and half secret trusts. There is, doubtless, an argument that there should be no doctrine of half-secret trusts, as the prospect of unconscionability or fraud is adequately dealt with by the resulting trust that would arise if there were no such doctrine.[179] Given, however, that the House of Lords rejected that argument in *Blackwell v Blackwell*,[180] holding that the principle behind fully secret trusts is applicable, there is no obvious reason why that principle should be applied differently.

## *F. Fully and Half Secret Trusts: Applying the Concepts*

**3–150** Before looking at the basis and possible justification of secret trusts, it is useful to consider some specific points that have arisen in applying the relevant principles.

### i. Attestation of Will by Secret Beneficiary

**3–151** Section 15 of the Wills Act 1837 sets out the general position that a party cannot take an interest under a will if her attestation of the will as a witness is vital to its validity.[181] In *Re Young*[182] there was a bequest by a testator to his wife with a direction that on her own death she should leave the property for the purposes which had been communicated to her (i.e. on a half-secret trust). Before execution of his will, a direction was given by him, and accepted by his wife, that she would leave a legacy of £2,000 to the testator's chauffeur. The chauffeur then witnessed the testator's will. Danckwerts J held that the chauffeur had not forfeited his legacy under the Wills Act 1837 s.15:

> the whole theory of the formulation of a secret trust is that the Wills Act has nothing to do with the matter because the forms required by the Wills Act are entirely disregarded, since the persons do not take by virtue of the gift in the will, but by virtue of the secret trusts imposed upon the beneficiary who does in fact take under the will.

**3–152** Even if this view of secret trusts is accepted, however, there is still a strong policy argument in favour of applying s.15, as its function is presumably to ensure attestation by an impartial witness with nothing to gain or lose by her testimony. Danckwerts J, however, took a narrow view of the rule, no doubt because of its potential to frustrate the intentions of the testator.

### ii. Beneficiary Predeceasing the Testator

**3–153** If a testator leaves leaves property to X on trust for B, and B predeceases the testator, the gift to B will lapse, just as an inter vivos trust for B fails if B is not alive when the trust is created.[183] As a result, no beneficial interest passes to B's estate. The same result should apply whether the trust in B's favour is

---

178 *Re Spencer's Will* (1887) 57 L.T. 519; *Re Williams* [1933] 1 Ch. 244.

179 The argument is well made by, e.g. J. Hackney, *Understanding Equity & Trusts* (1987), p.103.

180 [1929] A.C. 318.

181 See para.3–122.

182 [1951] Ch. 344.

183 *Re Corbishley's Trusts* (1880) 14 Ch.D. 846; *Re Tilt* (1896) 74 L.T. 163; both concerned with personalty where a gift to B gave B an absolute interest: for realty a gift by will after 1837 to B gave an absolute interest whilst till 1925 a gift by deed to B gave B only a life interest in the absence of proper words of limitation.

set out expressly in the will, or is a secret trust. The point in each case is that B acquires no right until the death of the testator and so, if B dies before then, B has no right to pass on to her estate.

In *Re Gardner (No.2)*,[184] however, Romer J held that in a secret trust case B's interest did *not* lapse when B died before the testator, as B obtained an interest as soon as the terms of the secret trust were communicated to and accepted by X.[185] This reasoning was based on the idea that the source of B's right was not the will itself, but rather the obligation accepted by X. Even if this is accepted, however, the problem is that B's right under the trust can arise only when the trust is constituted by X's receipt of the trust property.[186] After all, until that point, a testator could simply change her mind and make a different testamentary disposition, or, indeed, die insolvent and with no unencumbered property to pass to X. The authority of *Re Gardner (No.2)* is thus very weak indeed. **3–154**

### iii. Bequest to Two on a Promise by One

The orthodox position was laid down in *Re Stead* by Farwell J[187]: **3–155**

> If A induced B either to make, or to leave unrevoked, a will leaving property to A and C as tenants in common, by expressly promising or tacitly consenting, that he and C will carry out the testator's wishes and C knows nothing of the matter until after the testator's death, A is bound, but C is not bound: *Tee v Ferris*;[188] the reason stated being, that to hold otherwise would be to enable one beneficiary to deprive the rest of their benefits by setting up a secret trust. If, however, the gift were to A and C as joint tenants, the authorities have established a distinction between those cases in which the will is made on the faith of an antecedent promise by A and those in which the will is left unrevoked on the faith of a subsequent promise. In the former case the trust binds both A and C: *Russell v Jackson*;[189] *Jones v Bradley*,[190] the reason stated being that no person can claim an interest under a fraud committed by another; in the latter case A and not C is bound: *Burney v Macdonald*[191] and *Moss v Cooper*,[192] the reason stated being that the gift is not tainted with any fraud in procuring the execution of the will. Personally, I am unable to see any difference between a gift made on the faith of an antecedent promise and a gift left unrevoked on the faith of a subsequent promise to carry out the testator's wishes; but apparently a distinction has been made by the various judges who have had to consider the question. I am bound, therefore, to decide in accordance with these authorities. . . .

The position in a case where A but not C accepted the secret trust is, therefore, that A's share is bound by the secret trusts, but C's share is not[193] *unless* it is the case that *both* (i) A and C take as joint tenants; and (ii) A's acceptance occurred before the will was made. In such a case, both A and C are bound, as the testator made the will on the basis of A's aceptance and if C were to take free from any trust, C would be profiting from A's fraud. As Perrins has suggested,[194] however, the timing of A's acceptance is not necessarily a reliable test as to whether the gift to C was induced by A's acceptance: it may be, for example, that the testator was induced not to amend an existing will by A's acceptance. **3–156**

---

184 [1923] 2 Ch. 230.
185 ibid., at 233.
186 See paras 2–082—2–084.
187 [1900] 1 Ch. 231 at 247. The principles here discussed apply only to fully secret trusts. In the case of half-secret trusts, if the will permits communication to be made to one only of several trustees, a communication made before or at the time of the execution of the will to one only of the trustees binds all of them, the trust being a joint office: *Blackwell v Blackwell* [1929] A.C. 318; *Re Spence* [1949] W.N. 237; *Ward v Duncombe* [1893] A.C. 369; *Re Gardom* [1914] 1 Ch. 662 at 673.
188 (1856) 2 K. & J. 357.
189 (1852) 10 Hare 204.
190 (1868) L.R. 3 Ch. 362.
191 (1845) 15 Sim. 6.
192 (1861) 1 J. & H. 352.
193 Where A and C take under the will as joint tenants, but A is bound and C is not, a severance of the joint tenancy is imposed.
194 B. Perrins, "Can You Keep Half a Secret?" (1972) 88 L.Q.R. 225, 228.

It is interesting to note, however, that the current law distinguishes between the fraud or unconscionable conduct necessary in general for a secret trust to arise, and the heightened form of fraud that consists in accepting the secret trust *before* the will is made, finding that the latter can have an impact not only on the accepting party but also on an innocent party receving property under the will jointly with that accepting party.

### iv. Trustee Disclaiming after Testator's Death, or Predeceasing the Testator

**3–157** Generally, a gift by will to X is said to lapse if X predeceases the testator.[195] However, if the gift is to X on trust for B and B survives the testator, X's predecease will not cause the gift to lapse, as equity will not allow a trust to fail for want of a trustee.[196] In *Re Maddock*, a case concerning a fully secret trust, Cozens-Hardy LJ suggested that "if the legatee renounces and disclaims, or dies in the lifetime of the testator, the persons claiming under the memorandum [i.e. the secret beneficiaries] can take nothing".[197]

**3–158** As to disclaimer after the testator's death,[198] if a person named as a half-secret trustee disclaimed the office then it would seem clear that the testator's personal representative would hold on the trusts for the secret beneficiaries. Notwithstanding the suggestion of Cozens-Hardy LJ, it is difficult, again, to argue for applying a different rule to a fully secret trust and, in *Blackwell v Blackwell*, Lord Buckmaster suggested that if a fully secret trustee disclaimed then "the court having once admitted the evidence of the trust, would interfere to prevent its defeat".[199]

**3–159** As to the predecease of X, however, it seems that Cozens-Hardy LJ's suggestion should apply, and to both fully and half-secret trusts. The point, again, is that the secret trust is constituted only when the trust property is acquired by a party who, as a result of the communication and acceptance of the testator's intention, is under a duty to the beneficiary. If X's pre-decease prevents X receiving the trust property, no such trust can arise.

### v. Secret Trusts of Interests in Land

**3–160** As discussed above,[200] the Law of Property Act 1925 s.53(1)(b) requires a declaration of trust respecting any land or any interest therein to be proved in signed writing. Does this formality rule apply to secret trusts, so that the acceptance of the trust by X must be proved by writing signed by either the testator or X? It is of course prudent for a testator, even if no land is involved, to ensure that some such signed document exists, in order to make it easier for the beneficiaries to prove the terms and existence of a secret trust. The impact of the absence of such writing, where land is involved, depends on the broader question as to the basis of secret trusts, which we will now examine. It will be suggested as a result of that analysis that no signed writing is required for proof of a secret trust of land: this is either because the fraud that prevents X from relying on the Wills Act 1837 to deny the trust also prevents X

---

195 Exceptionally, if issue predecease a testator leaving issue of their own surviving the testator, the gift takes effect in favour of the surviving issue: Wills Act 1837 s.33. The persons benefiting from this exception will not be able to disregard the deceased legatee-trustee's undertaking: cf. *Huguenin v Baseley* (1807) 14 Ves. Jun. 273.

196 The testator's personal representative will step in as trustee. See, e.g. *Mallott v Wilson* [1903] 2 Ch. 494; *Re Armitage, (Deceased)* [1972] Ch. 438.

197 [1902] 2 Ch. 220 at 231.

198 If X instead attempts to revoke his or her acceptance of the secret trust *before* the testator dies, the effect of the testator going ahead with the bequest to X may depend on whether or not X's revocation gave the testator sufficient time to consider whether to make, and then to make, any consequent change to the will.

199 [1929] A.C. 318 at 328.

200 At paras 3–027—3–033.

from relying on s.53(1)(b), or because the secret trust is a constructive one, arising to prevent a particular form of uncosncionable conduct by X, and so falls within s.53(2) of the Law of Property Act 1925.

## G. Justifying Secret Trusts

In the foregoing discussion, we noted[201] that judges have drawn a distinction between the transfer of property to X, which occurs as a result of the will, and the imposition of the secret trust on that property, which occurs outside the will, in response to X's conduct in agreeing to hold the property for the benefit of B.[202] In *Re Snowden*, for example, Megarry J stated that[203] **3–161**

> the whole basis of secret trusts . . . is that they operate outside the will, changing nothing that is written in it, and allowing it to operate according to its tenor, but then fastening a trust on the property in the hands of the recipient.

That analysis, whilst accurate, does not mean that secret trusts can be justified simply as express trusts,[204] arising outside the will[205] as a result of the testator's successful exercise of a power to set up a trust. As Patricia Critchley has persuasively argued, the important question is not whether a secret trust arises outside the will, but whether it arises outside the Wills Act.[206] The latter applies formality requirements to "testamentary dispositions" and the creation of an express trust arising only on the testator's death, whether or not contained in a will, is undoubtedly such a disposition. The fact that a secret trust arises outside the will is the phenomenon that we need to explain, not the explanation for the trust.

An alternative view, consistent with the analyses of the House of Lords in *McCormick v Grogan*[207] **3–162**
(as applied in *Ottaway v Norman*[208]) and in *Blackwell v Blackwell*,[209] is that secret trusts depend on the principle that equity will not allow a statute to be used as an instrument of fraud: X is not permitted to rely on the formality rules in the Wills Act 1837 if the result would be that X would be free to use property entirely for her own benefit, having agreed instead to hold that property on trust for B (or to hold it subject to some other condition). As noted above,[210] a similar analysis was applied by the Court of Appeal in *Rochefoucald v Boustead*,[211] when permitting a trust of land to be proved orally. On this view, secret trusts are essentially express trusts, arising as a result of the testator's successful exercise of her power to set up a trust.[212]

There is another view that can be taken, both of the type of trust recognised in *Rochefoucauld* and of **3–163**

[201] See, e.g. para.3–147.

[202] See, e.g. *Re Young* [1951] Ch. 344; *Re Gardner (No.2)* [1923] 2 Ch. 230; *Blackwell v Blackwell* [1929] 2 A.C. 318 at 340, 342.

[203] [1979] Ch. 528 at 535.

[204] If secret trusts are express trusts arising outside the will, then s.53(1)(b) would apply to require signed writing for the proof of an express trust of land, as suggested by, e.g. A.J. Oakley, *Constructive Trusts*, 3rd edn (Sweet & Maxwell, 1992), pp.262ff.

[205] This theory of secret trusts has sometimes been called the "dehors" theory, using the French word for "outside"; but as acerbically noted by J. Hackney, *Understanding Equity & Trusts* (1987), p.106: "Sloganising in French or Latin is plainly no substitute for analysis, and the notion lacks convincing explanation."

[206] P. Critchley, "Instruments of Fraud, Testamentary Dispositions, and the Doctrine of Secret Trusts" (1999) 115 L.Q.R. 631, 633–641.

[207] (1868) L.R. 4 H.L. 82 at 88–89.

[208] [1972] Ch. 698; extracted at paras 3–132—3–137.

[209] [1929] A.C. 318; extracted at paras 3–141—3–145.

[210] See para.3–045.

[211] [1897] 1 Ch. 196.

[212] This does not mean, however that, on this view, a secret trust of land must be proved in writing: the same fraud that prevents reliance on the Wills Act 1837 also prevents reliance on s.53(1)(b) of the Law of Property Act 1925.

secret trusts. On this view, the trusts are constructive trusts,[213] imposed to prevent the particular form of unconscionable conduct of X that consists of acquiring property as a result of a promise made in relation to that property, and then keeping the property whilst breaking the promise.[214] Constructive trusts are not expressly exempted from the Wills Act 1837 (which contains no equivalent to s.2(5) of the Law of Property (Miscellaneous Provisions) Act 1989 or s.53(2) of the Law of Property Act 1925),[215] but such trusts are imposed by law as a result of X's conduct and not as a result of the testator's successful exercise of a power to create a trust. As a result, the recognition of a constructive trust does not involve a "testamentary disposition".[216]

**3–164** The differences between these two views will be discussed further in Chapter 5,[217] as part of our general examination of constructive trusts. Three points are worth making here. First, on either view, the key question concerns the sufficiency of X's conduct—either to raise the prospect of using a statute as an instrument of fraud,[218] or to raise the prospect of a particular form of unconscionable conduct. As to the fraud analysis, it should be noted that fraud in this context cannot be coterminous with the tort of deceit, as a secret trust can arise even if X, when agreeing to the trust, fully intends to give effect to it.[219] As to the unconscionability analysis, it should be noted that different views can be taken of the particular mischief targeted by the doctrine: is it, for example, the prospect of the testator suffering the detriment of having her intentions frustrated as a result of relying on X's promise[220]; or is it the prospect of X enjoying the benefit of property contrary to the terms of the promise subject to which X acquired that property?[221]

**3–165** Secondly, on the fraud analysis, there is a question as to the constitutional validity of the maxim that a statute cannot be used as an instrument of fraud[222]: it could be argued, for example, that it is for Parliament expressly to determine the scope of a formality rule, and that the courts should not read in exceptions. On the unconscionability analysis, the constructive trust arising lies outside the

---

213 See, e.g. *Re Cleaver* [1981] 1 W.L.R. 939 at 947; *Re Basham* [1986] 1 W.L.R. 1498 at 1504; *Kasperbauer v Griffith* [2000] W.T.L.R. 333 at 342 per Peter Gibson LJ.

214 See, e.g. *Gillett v Holt* [2001] Ch. 210 at 228 per Robert Walker LJ, referring in obiter dicta to secret trusts: "There must be an agreement between A [the testator] and B [the secret trustee] as to conferring a benefit on C [the secret beneficiary] because it is the agreement (and not C's moral claims) which would make it unconscionable for B to resile from his agreement." See too *de Bruyne v de Bruyne* [2010] EWCA Civ 519 at [51] per Patten LJ, referring to a principle giving rise to a constructive trust where the defendant's unconscionable conduct is "in the form of a denial or refusal to carry out the agreement to hold the property for the benefit of the third party which was the only basis upon which the property was transferred".

215 On this view of secret trusts, of course, there is no requirement for a secret trust of land to be proved in writing, as it is a constructive trust and so excepted from s.53(1)(b) of the Law of Property Act 1925 by s.53(2).

216 In the same way, see para.3–005, where it is noted that formality rules are generally limited to cases where it is claimed that a party has successfully exercised a power to give the claimant a right.

217 At paras 5–030—5–045.

218 For an analysis of the possible requirements of "fraud" in the context of secret trusts, see, e.g. P. Critchley, "Instruments of Fraud, Testamentary Dispositions, and the Doctrine of Secret Trusts" (1999) 115 L.Q.R. 631, 646–653. For the general question of what it might mean to say that a statute cannot be used as an instrument of fraud, see further paras 5–036—5–045.

219 Indeed, even if X maintains that intention throughout, a secret trust still arises, and is necessary in a half-secret trust case to rebut the claims of the testator's estate, who might otherwise argue that the property is held on resulting trust, and in a fully secret trust case to show that X, when later, e.g. giving the benefits of the property to B, is not making a gift (with, e.g. consequences under the Inheritance Tax Act 1984) but is instead performing the terms of the trust established on the testator's death.

220 As suggested by, e.g. S. Gardner, "Reliance-Based Constructive Trusts" in C. Mitchell (ed.), *Constructive and Resulting Trusts* (2010).

221 As suggested by, e.g. B. McFarlane, "Constructive Trusts Arising on Receipt of Property *Sub Conditione*" (2004) 120 L.Q.R. 667.

222 As noted by, e.g. P. Critchley, "Instruments of Fraud, Testamentary Dispositions, and the Doctrine of Secret Trusts" (1999) 115 L.Q.R. 631, 653–654.

scope of the Wills Act 1837: it is imposed by law as a result of X's conduct, and therefore, as it does not arise as a result of the testator's power to deal with her property on death, it is not a "testamentary disposition".[223]

Thirdly, doubts as to the validity of the doctrine of secret trusts may stem from the fact that it seems to give testators a simple means to avoid the general rule that there must be a public record of what happens to their property on death. Whether the fraud or the constructive trusts argument is adopted, the facts triggering the secret trust—X's acceptance of the duty to hold property subject to conditions—are undoubtedly close to the facts involved in any express trust created by a transfer to a trustee.[224] However, this may contribute to a justification of secret trusts: if the power to create an express trust by transfer initially developed because equity considered that trustees should be bound by the conditions subject to which they received property, it is no surprise that equity should continue to intervene in such cases, even if a formality rule means that it cannot simply be said that the testator exercised a power to create a trust.[225] **3–166**

## *H. Mutual Wills*

### i. Introduction

As we have said,[226] the doctrine of mutual wills can operate to impose a trust that gives effect to a testator's earlier promise to dispose of her property on death in a certain way, even if she attempted to renege on that promise, and left a valid will disposing of the property differently. As Mummery LJ said in *Fry v Densham-Smith*[227]: **3–167**

> This illustrates the anomalous character of the doctrine of mutual wills: if and when it applies, absolute beneficial testamentary dispositions . . . do not take effect in accordance with their terms. The surviving party of a claimed mutual wills agreement is able to make further wills, but cannot, after the death of the first to die, effectively revoke dispositions already made in the mutual will. This irrevocable result can only be produced by an agreement made and acted on with that intention.

The key point therefore is that the survivor's promise was part of an agreement as to mutual testamentary dispositions made with a party who died earlier and who honoured that agreement. The doctrine of mutual wills thus shows "equity intervening to prevent unconscionable conduct",[228] and the precise form of unconscionable conduct targeted consists in breaching the terms of a binding agreement as to mutual testamentary dispositions, where the other party has acted on the basis of that agreement by disposing of her property in a particular way on death. **3–168**

Before looking in more detail at the requirements, effect, and possible justifications of the doctrine, it is useful to consider the analysis of the Court of Appeal in the following extract. **3–169**

---

223 See para.3–005, where it is noted that formality rules are generally limited to cases where it is claimed that a party has successfully exercised a power to give the claimant a right.

224 See W. Swadling, "The Nature of the Trust in *Rochefoucauld v Boustead*" in C. Mitchell (ed.), *Constructive and Resulting Trusts* (2010), p.107.

225 See B. McFarlane, "The Centrality of Constructive and Resulting Trusts" in C. Mitchell (ed.), *Constructive and Resulting Trusts* (2010), pp.199–201.

226 See para.3–130.

227 [2011] W.T.L.R. 387 at [30].

228 *Gillett v Holt* [2001] Ch. 210 at 228 per Robert Walker LJ.

*Re Walters*

Court of Appeal [2009] Ch. 212

3–170 MUMMERY L.J. (with whom DYSON and MAURICE KAY L.JJ. agreed): Norris J. held that in 1998 Mr Harold Walters and his late wife, Freda ("the deceased") made a mutual wills contract pursuant to which they executed similar codicils amending their wills. The deceased died in 2006 leaving her will and codicil unrevoked. Mr Walters inherited her estate, but disputed the application of the mutual wills doctrine to him or to the deceased's estate in his hands.

3–171 The judge applied the principles summarised by Dixon J. in *Birmingham v Renfrew*:[229]

> "It has long been established that a contract between persons to make corresponding wills gives rise to equitable obligations when one acts on the faith of such an agreement and dies leaving his will unrevoked so that the other takes property under its dispositions. It operates to impose upon the survivor an obligation regarded as specifically enforceable. It is true that he cannot be compelled to make and leave unrevoked a testamentary document and if he dies leaving a last will containing provisions inconsistent with his agreement it is nevertheless valid as a testamentary act. But the doctrines of equity attach the obligation to the property. The effect is, I think, that the survivor becomes a constructive trustee and the terms of the trust are those of the will he undertook would be his last will."

3–172 This appeal is about (1) the sufficiency of the evidence for the finding of a mutual wills contract between Mr Walters and the deceased, and (2) the sufficiency in law of its terms. The litigation is regrettable. A family apparently united around the grandparents is now divided on the question whether they made a mutual wills contract. The decision on this appeal may not bring the dispute to an end. If the appeal fails, further issues may arise about the effect of the mutual wills on the ability of Mr Walters to deal with the assets derived from the deceased's estate. As recent cases have shown this equitable doctrine dating from the 18th century[230] continues to be a source of contention for the families of those who have invoked it. The likelihood is that in future even fewer people will opt for such an arrangement and even more will be warned against the risks involved.

3–173 In its *22nd Report on the Making and Revocation of Wills* the Law Reform Committee noted particular problems with the mutual wills doctrine. It recommended that the difficulties would "be better clarified by judicial development than by legislation".[231] The novel aspect of this case is that the survivor of the alleged contract is alive and gave evidence denying the alleged contract and disputing the application of the doctrine and its consequences. This feature was absent from all the authorities cited to the court. . .[232]

**The Proceedings and the Judgment**

3–174 On 16 March 2007 Andrew [a grandson of Mr and Mrs Walters who was also a solicitor and who drafted their wills] began these proceedings to have the deceased's 1988 will and the 1998 codicil proved in solemn form and for a declaration that the deceased's codicil takes effect as a valid and effective mutual will. . .

3–175 The judge considered the effect of the agreement made between Mr Walters and the deceased. He held that a valid mutual will was made. He rejected submissions on behalf of Mr Walters that the agreement was not intended to be a binding agreement and that it did not satisfy the requirements for mutual wills, because it did not record any express agreement not to revoke the wills so made . . . [The judge] did not regard the absence of any explicit mention of revocation as rendering "the mutual testamentary dispositions" incapable of enforcement as mutual wills, a reading which was reinforced by a consideration of the surrounding circumstances, in particular the covering letter of explanation.

3–176 As for the form of the relief to be granted on the mutual wills aspect of the case, the judge held that the declaration should be that the codicils executed by the deceased and Mr Walters on 18 May 1998 "take effect as valid and effective mutual wills *so as to bind the deceased's estate*."[233] He explained the

---

229 (1937) 57 C.L.R. 666 at 683.

230 Lord Camden L.C.'s judgment in *Dufour v Pereira* (1769) 1 Dick. 419.

231 (Cmnd 7902, 1980) p.26, para.3.52.

232 *Re Oldham* [1925] Ch. 75; *Birmingham v Renfrew* (1937) 57 C.L.R. 666; *Re Cleaver, deceased* [1981] 1 W.L.R. 939; *Re Dale, deceased* [1994] Ch. 31; *Re Goodchild, deceased* [1996] 1 W.L.R. 694, affirmed [1997] 1 W.L.R. 1216; and *Birch v Curtis* [2002] 2 F.L.R. 847.

233 [2007] EWHC 3060 (Ch) at [41].

italicised words by the fact that he had made no findings or holdings as to the scope of the agreement relating to mutual wills, which he regarded as a question of construction of the agreement embodied in clause 2 of the codicil. He confirmed that, as reflected in the form of declaration, the deceased's estate was bound by the agreement "when in due course it passes to Mr Walters or his executors". He added that he regarded the issue of Mr Walters's own estate as simply not before him. The declaration was made as to the deceased's estate, but nothing else.

**Defendant's Submissions**

On the first ground of appeal—the insufficiency of the terms of the contract—Mr Steinfeld submitted that it was vital to know all the terms of the contract for mutual wills. How else could the subject matter and terms of the constructive trust arising from it be determined? The judge had erred in failing to decide with sufficient particularity the scope and terms of the contract. The survivor was entitled to know exactly what he could or could not do with the assets that he acquired on the death of the deceased, or, indeed, with his own assets. **3–177**

On the judge's findings it was unclear what property was affected by the supposed constructive trust and what Mr Walters was entitled to do with the deceased's property, which had been left to him absolutely under the 1988 will, and even what he was entitled to do with his own property during the rest of his life. There was a range of possibilities as to the scope of the contract which the judge had failed to determine. Was Mr Walters prevented from dealing with the deceased's estate at all in his lifetime? Or did the constructive trust only extend to the part of the deceased's estate left when he died? Did it extend to his estate at the date of the deceased's death? Or as at the date of his death? What was the position in relation to the Mill Hill house? What, if anything, could be done in relation to it? **3–178**

The problem arising from lack of contractual certainty was, Mr Steinfeld submitted, well illustrated in two ways: first, by the form of the *quia timet* injunction originally sought in the claim form, but later abandoned because of the difficulty of formulating it; and secondly, and more immediately, by a very recent exchange between the parties about whether, if Mr Walters lost his appeal and was ordered to pay the costs, he would be entitled to use property coming to him absolutely from the deceased's estate to pay those costs. It was said on behalf of Andrew that Mr Walters would not be entitled to make that use of the deceased's property or make any other disposition of it inter vivos that would subvert the purpose for which the constructive trust was imposed to give effect to the contract. **3–179**

It was also submitted by Mr Steinfeld that the terms of the declaration made by the judge were incorrect. The constructive trust did not affect the deceased's property in the hands of Mr Walters at all. The estate was expressly left to him absolutely. The trust would only bind his personal representatives as regards any property left by him on his death. The words "of the defendant" should be omitted from the declaration to make it clear that the constructive trust did not affect the assets of the deceased's estate in his hands. . . **3–180**

**Discussion and Conclusions**

I turn to the legal submission that the contract found by the judge is not in law a valid and binding contract for mutual wills and that the judge was accordingly wrong in law to make the declaration in the form that he did, or at all. **3–181**

In my judgment, Mr Steinfeld's submissions on insufficiency of the terms of the contract between Mr Walters and the deceased do not accurately reflect the fundamental principles of mutual wills. **3–182**

It is a legally necessary condition of mutual wills that there is clear and satisfactory evidence of a contract between two testators. However, the argument resting on the alleged insufficiency or uncertainty of the terms of this contract is misconceived. The case for the existence of mutual wills does not involve making a contractual claim for specific performance or other relief. The claimant in a mutual wills case is not even a party to the contract and does not have to establish that he was. **3–183**

The obligation on the surviving testator is equitable. It is in the nature of a trust of the property affected, so the constructive trust label is attached to it. The equitable obligation is imposed for the benefit of third parties, who were intended by the parties to benefit from it. It arises by operation of law on the death of the first testator to die so as to bind the conscience of the surviving testator in relation to the property affected. **3–184**

It is a legally sufficient condition to establish what the judge described as "its irreducible core", which he analysed as a contract between two testators, T1 and T2:[234] **3–185**

[234] [2007] EWHC 3060 (Ch) at [9].

> "that in return for T1 agreeing to make a will in form X and not to revoke it without notice to T2, then T2 will make a will in form Y and agree not to revoke it without notice to T1. If such facts are established then upon the death of T1 equity will impose upon T2 a form of constructive trust (shaped by the exact terms of the contract that T1 and T2 have made). The constructive trust is imposed because T1 has made a disposition of property on the faith of T2's promise to make a will in form Y, and with the object of preventing T1 from being defrauded."

**3–186** In my judgment, that is an accurate and clear statement of the equitable principles. Mr Steinfeld accepted that. He agreed that Mr Walters would be bound by a constructive trust, but only if sufficient terms of the contract were established to raise one.

**3–187** The answer to the sufficiency point is, I think, summed up in a single sentence in *Snell's Equity*:[235]

> "Mutual wills provide an instance of a trust arising by operation of law to give effect to an express intention of the two testators."

**3–188** The intentions of Mr Walters and the deceased were sufficiently expressed in the contract to lay the foundations for the equitable obligations that bind the conscience of Mr Walters, as the survivor, in relation to the deceased's estate. The judge found all that he needed to find in order to hold that, contrary to the contentions of Mr Walters, mutual wills existed. Possible, and as yet unexplored, legal consequences of the application of the equitable principles do not negative the existence of the foundation contract or prevent a constructive trust from arising by operation of law on the death of the deceased.

**3–189** It had been accepted on behalf of Mr Walters in submissions to Norris J. that, if there was a valid contract for mutual wills, the doctrine operated by imposing a constructive trust on him as the survivor, because the deceased had performed her promise to leave her estate to him. In my judgment, the trust is immediately binding on him in relation to the deceased's property left to him on the basis of the contract. It is not postponed to take effect only after the death of Mr Walters when the property, or what may be left of it, comes into the hands of his personal representatives.

**3–190** Disputes about the actual operation of the trust in practice usually turn on construction of the contract in all the relevant circumstances. Of course, the disagreements can be resolved without litigation, if all the beneficiaries are agreed and have legal capacity to do so. If not, the disputes can be determined on an application to the court by Mr Walters in proceedings to which those interested are made parties.

**3–191** In this case the issues before the judge were the validity of the codicil and the existence of the mutual wills contract, both of which were unsuccessfully contested by Mr Walters. The judge determined those issues against him for sound reasons in an excellent judgment. He was not asked to rule on the possible legal consequences of the declaration for Mr Walters or for the beneficiaries arising on the death of the deceased. The judge prudently declined to be drawn into determining matters, such as the scope or extent of the constructive trust, which were neither raised in the pleadings nor in the submissions of the parties. As Bowen L.J. said in *Cooke v New River Co*,[236] the teaching of experience is that judgments should be given on points that the judge is bound to decide. Deciding more than is necessary could, "like the proverbial chickens of destiny", come home to roost sooner or later. Unnecessary opinions can be a source of future embarrassment, or even worse when, as here, no other points have been pleaded, investigated or argued.

### ii. The Requirements of the Doctrine

**3–192** The doctrine does not apply simply because two parties make wills in almost identical terms. As Leggatt LJ stated in *Re Goodchild*[237]:

> Two wills may be in the same form as each other. Each testator may leave his or her estate to the other with a view to the survivor leaving both estates to their heir. But there is no presumption that a present plan will be immutable in the future. A key feature of the concept of mutual wills is the irrevocability of the mutual intentions. Not only must they be binding when made, but the testators must have undertaken, and so

---

[235] 31st edn (2005), para.22–31.

[236] (1888) 38 Ch. D. 56 at 71.

[237] [1997] 1 W.L.R. 1216 at 1225. See too *Birch v Curtis* [2002] 2 F.L.R. 847 at [64]ff.

> must be bound, not to change their intentions after the death of the first testator. The test must always be, suppose that during the lifetime of the surviving testator, the intended beneficiary did something which the survivor regarded as unpardonable, would he or she be free not to leave their combined estate to him? The answer must be that the survivor is so entitled unless the testators agreed otherwise when they executed their wills. Hence the need for a clear agreement.

The approach adopted in *Re Goodchild* is given effect to by Mummery LJ's statement in *Re Walters* that: "It is a legally necessary condition of mutual wills that there is clear and satisfactory evidence of a contract between two testators."[238] The need for such a contract may be explained by the fact that the mutual wills doctrine extends beyond that of secret trusts, as it can apply not only to property received by the survivor under the will of the first testator, but to *any* property which the survivor promised to dispose of in a particular way in her will.[239] Secret trusts, in contrast, do not require a contractual agreement as such, as the principle applied there relates to *receipt* of property subject to a promise to hold that property subject to particular conditions. As the doctrine of mutual wills can have a wider effect, and relate to property acquired by the survivor independently of any promise made to the deceased (the first testator), a binding contract is required. As a result, it must be shown that the parties' agreement to make specific dispositions of their property on death[240] was intended to be legally binding[241] and is sufficiently certain to be enforced.[242] **3–193**

It should therefore be noted that the doctrine of mutual wills can apply even if the agreement does not involve the survivor receiving any property under the will of the deceased[243] and even if the wills of the two parties do not mirror one another.[244] The parties are also free to set the terms of the agreement: it may be that the survivor is to receive a life interest in all or a specific part of property received from the first testator; it may be that the survivor is instead to have a life interest in all or a specific part of her own property as held at the date of death of the deceased.[245] Sometimes, it may appear that the survivor is to be absolute owner of all her property, subject only to a duty to bequeath to the agreed beneficiaries whatever she has left at the time of death.[246] If the parties fail to make it clear which property is subject to the trust then this uncertainty may make it impossible for the survivor to know what dispositions she is entitled to make during her life, in which case an application to the court for directions may be required.[247] **3–194**

Given that the doctrine of mutual wills requires a contractual agreement between the first and second testator, the question arises, whether s.2 of the Law of Property (Miscellaneous Provisions) Act 1989 has to be satisfied if the doctrine is to apply to any interest in land held by the survivor. In *Healey v Brown*,[248] the section was said to apply, with the effect that, whilst an interest in land acquired by the **3–195**

---

238 [2009] Ch. 212 at [36] (extracted at para.3–183). See too *Re Dale* [1994] Ch. 31 at 38 per Morritt J: there must be a "contract at law".

239 See, e.g. *Re Dale* [1994] Ch. 31.

240 It is sometimes said that the agreement must be "not to revoke" the wills, but revocation may well be permissible, so long as a substitute will is made giving effect to the agreed dispositions.

241 Hence it does not suffice if the parties make a non-contractual agreement trusting and confidently assuming that each will do as the other has asked: see, e.g. *Gray v Perpetual Trustee Ltd* [1928] A.C. 391; *Re Oldham* [1925] Ch. 75; *Re Goodchild* [1997] 1 W.L.R. 1216.

242 *Re Walters* [2009] Ch. 212 at [36].

243 *Re Dale* [1994] Ch. 31.

244 See, e.g. *Re Newey* [1994] 2 N.Z.L.R. 590.

245 *Re Hagger* [1930] 2 Ch. 190.

246 Such beneficiaries may well not have vested interests liable to be divested: the parties probably intend them to benefit only if alive on the survivor's death so that if they all predecease the second testator, his or her duty will cease.

247 As in *Edell v Sitzer* (2001) 4 I.T.E.L.R. 149, where the court declined to make an order as the parties had not made mutual wills. For further discussion, see P. Luxton, "*Walters v Olin*: Uncertainty of Subject Matter – An Insoluble Problem in Mutual Wills?" [2009] Conv. 498.

248 [2002] W.T.L.R. 849.

survivor under the will of the deceased was held on trust on the terms of the parties' oral agreement, an interest in land held independently by the survivor was not subject to any such trust, even though it was also covered by the oral agreement. This distinction reflects the different bases of the doctrines of secret trusts and of mutual wills. The preliminary question, however, is whether s.2 applies at all, and there are prior dicta inconsistent with the view taken on that point in *Healey*.[249] It can also be argued that, as Mummery LJ pointed out in *Re Walters*,[250] the doctrine of mutual wills is not concerned with enforcing a contract as such (after all, the beneficiary of the trust is not a party to the contract between the testators), but rather responds to the prospect of a specific form of unconscionable conduct. That unconscionable conduct consists of the survivor reneging on an agreement that is intended to be binding and on which the deceased is assumed to have relied when making her own testamentary dispositions. As the law stands, however, if a mutual will deals with land, the parties' agreement should be put in signed writing, signed by both parties, and containing all the terms of the parties' contract.

**3–196** It seems that the principles underlying mutual wills extend to an agreement not to revoke existing wills, made prior to the agreement,[251] and also to an agreement made between two joint tenants, who agree not to sever their joint tenancy (thus ensuring that the survivor takes the whole interest by survivorship) and also that the survivor will then dispose of that interest in an agreed manner on her death.[252]

### iii. Effects of the Doctrine

**3–197** Before the death of either party, the agreement is a purely contractual one made in consideration of the mutual promises of the two parties for the benefit of a third party.[253] If one of the parties attempts to revoke the agreement before either has died, that revocation, depending on the terms of the parties' agreement, may be a breach of contract and so actionable by the other party.[254] If, however, the revoking party gives notice in sufficient time before the death of the other party, it would seem that the doctrine should not apply, even if the non-revoking party rejects the revocation and attempts to affirm the contract.[255] Whilst it is true as a matter of general contract law that an unaccepted repudiation is of no effect, this may simply reflect the suggestion made above,[256] that the doctrine of mutual wills is not concerned with enforcing a contract as such,[257] but rather with responding to a particular form of unconscionable conduct, and it is difficult to regard the conduct of the survivor as unconscionable if sufficient notice was given to the deceased and she then failed to alter her will.

**3–198** If there is no revocation of the agreement then, as confirmed in *Re Walters*,[258] on the death of the first party, an immediate trust arises in favour of B (the party to whom the second testator has promised to leave the property on her death).[259] As Lewison J stated in *Thomas and Agnes Carvel Foundation v Carvel*[260]

---

249 See, e.g. *Birmingham v Renfrew* (1957) 57 C.L.R. 666 at 690 per Dixon J; *Lewis v Cotton* [2001] W.T.L.R. 1117 at 1131.
250 [2009] Ch. 212 at [36] (extracted at para.3–183).
251 *Dufour v Pereira* (1769) 1 Dick. 419; *Re Fox* [1951] Ontario R. 378; *Edell v Sitzer* (2001) 4 I.T.E.L.R. 149 at [68].
252 *Re Newey* [1994] 2 N.Z.L.R. 590; *Manitoba University v Sandeman* (1998) 155 D.L.R. (4th) 40.
253 *Dufour v Pereira* (1769) 1 Dick. 419 at 421; *Birmingham v Renfrew* (1937) 57 C.L.R. 666; *Re Walters* [2009] Ch. 212.
254 The breach is unlikely to give rise to substantial damages: *Lewis v Cotton* (2000) 3 I.T.E.L.R. 447 at [44]. B, the intended ultimate beneficiary, may have a claim under the Contract (Rights of Third Parties) Act 1989 if its requirements are met.
255 As stated in *Lewis v Cotton* (2000) 3 I.T.E.L.R. 447 at [44].
256 See para.3–195.
257 See, e.g. *Re Walters* [2009] Ch. 212 at [36] per Mummery LJ (see para.3–183).
258 [2009] Ch. 212 at [42] (see para.3–189).
259 See too, e.g. *Birmingham v Renfrew* (1937) 57 C.L.R. 666; *Re Dale* [1994] Ch. 31.
260 [2008] Ch. 395 at [27].

> the trust does not arise under the will of the surviving testator. Nor does it arise under any previous will of the surviving testator. It arises out of the agreement between the two testators not to revoke their wills, and the trust arises when the first of the two dies without having revoked his will.

As was also confirmed in *Re Walters*,[261] the trust is a constructive one, imposed by law to prevent unconscionable conduct by the second testator.[262]

If, therefore, B dies after the first testator, but before the surviving testator, B has an existing interest at the time of her death, which does not lapse and instead forms part of her estate.[263] B's interest is also unaffected if the surviving testator disclaims any benefits acquired under the will of the first testator.[264] It is the death of the first testator, who of course no longer has the opportunity to revoke her own will, which means that the agreement will necessarily be enforced in favour of B, even if the surviving testator revokes her will. **3–199**

Whilst B has an existing interest from the time of the death of the first testator, the terms of the parties' agreement may be such that there is a form of "floating trust" which crystallises (i.e. takes final form) only on the death of the survivor.[265] The question can therefore arise as to what use of any relevant property the survivor may make during her life. If, for example, the parties' agreement was that all of the survivor's estate should be left to B, is it permissible for the survivor to make a large lifetime gift to charity, thereby reducing the size of her estate? As observed by Mummery LJ in *Re Walters*,[266] such questions "usually turn on the construction of the contract in all the relevant circumstances", and are far from intractable, with an application to court always available in the event of disagreement. **3–200**

## *I. Justifying the Doctrine of Mutual Wills*

In *Re Cleaver*, Nourse J said that cases on mutual wills are: **3–201**

> only one example of a wider category of cases, for example secret trusts, in which a court of equity will intervene to impose a constructive trust. . . The principle of all these cases is that a court of equity will not permit a person to whom property is transferred by way of gift, but on the faith of a clear understanding that it is to be dealt with in a partiuclar way for the benefit of a third person, to deal with that property inconsistently with that agreement or understanding. If he attempts to do so after having received the benefit of the gift equity will intervene by imposing a constructive trust on the property which is the subject matter of the agreement or understanding.

That analysis has been echoed in a number of other decisions.[267] It is certainly important to note, when attempting to justify a trust arising under the doctrine of mutual wills, that the trust is constructive[268]: it does not arise in response to the deceased's successful exercise of a power to set up a trust, but is imposed by law to prevent a particular form of unconscionable conduct by the survivor. **3–202**

---

[261] [2009] Ch. 212 at [42] (see para.3–189).

[262] See, e.g. *Re Cleaver* [1981] 1 W.L.R. 939 at 947; *Re Basham* [1986] 1 W.L.R. 1498 at 1504; *Gillett v Holt* [2001] Ch. 210 at 228; *Birmingham v Renfrew* (1937) 57 C.L.R. 666 at 680.

[263] *Re Hagger* [1930] 2 Ch. 190.

[264] *Dufour v Pereira* (1769) 1 Dick. 419 at 421; *Stone v Hoskins* [1905] P. 194 at 197; *Re Hagger* [1930] 2 Ch. 190.

[265] See, e.g. *Re Goodchild* [1996] 1 W.L.R. 694 at 702 (affirmed [1997] 1 W.L.R. 1216), drawing on *Birmingham v Renfrew* (1937) 57 C.L.R. 666 at 689.

[266] [2009] Ch. 212 at [43]–[44] (see paras 3–190—3–191).

[267] See, e.g. *Re Basham* [1986] 1 W.L.R. 1498 at 1504; *Gillett v Holt* [2001] Ch. 210 at 228; *de Bruyne v de Bruyne* [2010] EWCA Civ 519 at [51].

[268] In addition to the cases cited at n.267, the characterisation of the trust as constructive has also been accepted in, e.g. *Charles v Fraser* [2010] W.T.L.R. 1489 at [59] and *Shovelar v Lane* [2012] 1 W.L.R. 637 at [37].

This is clear, for example, from the fact that, whilst the parties' agreement may simply be that B should acquire absolute title to property on the death of the survivor, the doctrine instead recognises that a trust arises in B's favour on the death of the first testator.

**3–203** Besides Nourse J's analysis, there is also some academic support for the idea that the doctrine of mutual wills has the same basis as that of secret trusts.[269] Care is needed, however. The doctrines seem to have different requirements, as well as a different scope. As noted above,[270] the requirement of a binding contract may explain why mutual wills, unlike secret trusts, can affect not only property acquired by the survivor under the will of the first testator, but also any other property that the survivor promised to bequeath in a particular way. Whereas the analysis of Nourse J assumes that mutual wills, like secret trusts, affect only property *transferred* to the defendant subject to an agreement, the mutual wills doctrine is in fact broader, and can affect property independently held by the defendant.[271]

**3–204** The more limited scope of secret trusts means that, in considering that doctrine, it is possible to suggest a justification which looks to the need to prevent the defendant from taking the benefit of property where that property was acquired subject to a promise to use it for the benefit of another person: it would be unconscionable for the defendant to keep the property and break the promise subject to which it was acquired. The mutual wills doctrine, however, can apply in the absence of any such receipt by the survivor, and so it seems that we cannot base a justification on the prospect of an unjust benefit to the survivor. Further, although a contract is required, basic contract law[272] cannot provide the justification for mutual wills because, of course, the beneficiary of the trust is not the other contracting party (the first testator), but a third party to whom the survivor promised to leave the property.

**3–205** It may therefore be necessary to look not only to the parties' agreement, but also to the reliance on it by the deceased, who honoured that agreement by making the agreed bequest. That reliance is certainly required for the doctrine to operate. The question then is why equity responds to the prospect of the deceased suffering a detriment through such reliance by enforcing the survivor's promise in favour of the beneficiary, rather than, for example, by giving a remedy to the estate of the deceased. Certainly, as we saw in Chapters 2 and 3,[273] the doctrine of proprietary estoppel may be seen as concerned with avoiding the prospect of detriment arising through reliance, and it gives a claim to the party who has relied, and often limits the right arising by considering the extent of such detriment: there is no guarantee that the defendant's promise will be enforced. In the context of mutual wills, however, the definitive nature of the deceased's reliance means that she has irrevocably lost the opportunity to make a different testamentary disposition of her own estate and so the general principle suggested by Simon Gardner seems apposite[274]: the deceased has suffered a "loss of opportunity" and "if the law is to correct this loss, it must in fact require [the survivor] to hold the

[269] See, e.g. S. Gardner, "Reliance-Based Constructive Trusts" in C. Mitchell (ed.), *Constructive and Resulting Trusts* (2010), p.75.

[270] See para.3–193.

[271] As apparent from *Re Dale* [1994] Ch. 31.

[272] Those basic rules have now been supplemented by the Contract (Rights of Third Parties) Act 1999, but of course the doctrine long predated the Act and, in any case, there are differences between the operation of a contractual claim (or a claim under the 1999 Act) and the doctrine of mutual wills: see paras 3–195 and 3–197.

[273] See paras 2–090—2–093 and 3–017—3–025.

[274] S. Gardner, "Reliance-Based Constructive Trusts" in C. Mitchell (ed.), *Constructive and Resulting Trusts* (2010), p.79. Gardner argues there that one general principle, concerned with enforcing detrimentally-relied on agreements, underpins a broad range of constructive trusts. It is however possible to accept the principle in the particular context of mutual wills, but not in relation to all the forms of constructive trust where Gardner suggests it applies. For the difficulties of applying this principle to certain cases of such trusts, see para.5–168.

property in question on a constructive trust along the lines of his undertaking". The enforcement of the parties' agreement is also justified by the fact that, in contrast to proprietary estoppel, the doctrine of mutual wills requires a contract between the deceased and the survivor.[275] Once the contract and the deceased's reliance on it provides a justification for the survivor's being under a duty to honour the agreement, a trust necessarily arises, as the duty of the survivor relates to specific property held by the survivor, and involves a basic duty not to use that property for her own benefit.[276]

**Questions**

1. T1 and T2 hold shares on trust for X. What formalities are required in the following situations?
   (a) X assigns her equitable interest to Y;
   (b) X directs T1 and T2 to hold the property on trust for Y;
   (c) X directs T1 and T2 to transfer the property to T3 and T4 to hold on trust for Y;
   (d) X contracts with Y to transfer her equitable interest to him;
   (e) X declares herself a trustee of her interest for Y; and
   (f) X directs T1 and T2 that they henceforth have power to appoint the property to such of Y, his spouse and issue as they may see fit. A month later T1 and T2 declare that they therefore hold the property on trust for Y for life, remainder to his children equally.

2. Two years ago Brian transferred his cottage to Tom, orally telling Tom to hold it for Brian for life and then for Clarissa absolutely. He also transferred 10,000 ICI Plc shares, 8,000 Hanson Plc shares and 6,000 British Gas shares to his sister, Susan, orally telling her to hold them for himself or for such of their relatives as she might select. He soon told her to hold the ICI shares for Clarissa absolutely. Susan complied but said that she was now going to hold the Hanson shares for her cousin, Joy. Brian then told her to transfer the British Gas shares to Tom, who had already orally agreed to hold them on the same trusts as he held the cottage. Susan did so transfer the shares. A year ago Brian had a row with Clarissa and so told Tom: "Hold the cottage and the shares for me absolutely until I decide what to do about them." Last month he wrote a letter to Tom: "When I die I want you to transfer the cottage and the shares to Joy." A fortnight ago Brian died, having, by will, left everything to Eric.

   **Advise Eric.**

3. Is this a sound approach to gifts by will where secret trusts or mutual wills may be involved?
   (a) Consider if there appears to be: (i) incorporation by reference; (ii) a half-secret trust; (iii) a fully secret trust; or (iv) mutual wills.
   (b) If (i) ask whether the will refers to an ascertainable already existing document or attempts to incorporate a future document or an assortment of present and future documents.
   (c) If (ii) ask whether the terms of the obligation were communicated before or after the will and, if before, ask if they were communicated in accordance with the will, to a person who accepted them.
   (d) If (iii) ask whether there was an intention outside of the will to create a binding obligation,

---

[275] This suggests that, as noted by Robert Walker LJ in *Gillett v Holt* [2001] Ch. 210 at 228, it would be a mistake to go "too far in seeking a parallel between those principles [of mutual wills] and those of proprietary estoppel".

[276] See further para.15–219 and B. McFarlane, "The Centrality of Constructive and Resulting Trusts" in C. Mitchell (ed.), *Constructive and Resulting Trusts* (2010).

and whether the terms of the obligation were communicated in the testator's lifetime to a person who accepted the obligation.

(e) If (iv) ask whether the parties accepted that the survivor would be legally obliged to carry out the arrangements.

4. In 2006 Alan made his will as follows: "Whatever I die possessed of I give to my wife Brenda." The will was witnessed by two of Alan's daughters, Diana and Edwina. Shortly afterwards, Alan asked Brenda if she would hold half the property she received under his will for their three daughters, Diana, Edwina and Freda equally. Brenda assented to this. In 2010 Freda ran away with a merchant seaman, Wayne. As a result Alan told Brenda to keep Freda's share for herself. A year ago Diana died, childless, and a week later Alan died after a long illness.

   **How should his £150,000 estate be distributed? Would it make any difference if Brenda disclaimed all benefits due to pass to her under the will and relied, instead, upon her rights under the intestacy rules?**

# 4

# THE THREE CERTAINTIES

## 1. Introduction

4-001 An express trust can exist only if the trust property is held by the trustee (i.e. the trust must be completely constituted),[1] any requisite formalities have been complied with,[2] and the "three certainties" are present: certainty of intention to create a trust; certainty of subject matter of the trust; and certainty of objects. The three certainties are required to ensure that trustees hold specific property in respect of which they owe duties to beneficiaries which are capable of being enforced in practice by the courts. The existence of such duties is crucial to the existence of trusts. As Millett LJ stated in *Armitage v Nurse*[3]:

> there is an irreducible core of obligations owed by the trustees to the beneficiaries and enforceable by them which is fundamental to the concept of a trust. If the beneficiaries have no rights enforceable against the trustees there are no trusts.

4-002 Certainty of subject matter and of objects are requirements of *all* trusts. If, for example, B claims that she has a beneficial interest under a constructive or resulting trust, then she needs to show that the defendant holds specific property subject to a duty to B. Certainty of intention, however, is a requirement only where a settlor exercises her power to set up a trust. Hence it does not apply to trusts imposed by law. In cases of the latter sort, the defendant still holds specific property subject to a duty to B, but that duty arises for some other reason, not because of the settlor's successful creation of an express trust.

4-003 There is a further difference between certainty of intention on the one hand and certainty of subject matter and of objects on the other. In the former case, we are concerned with the simple question of whether or not the settlor intended to create a trust. In relation to certainty of subject matter and of objects, however, we are not simply seeking a "Yes" or "No" answer when considering the acts of the settlor: we must ask, rather, what property was meant to be subject to the trust, and which people were meant to benefit (or not meant to benefit) from its performance? Whilst certainty of intention can be seen as relating to the preliminary question of whether the supposed trustee is under a duty *at all*, certainty of subject matter requires us to find specific property to which that duty relates, and certainty of objects requires us to be able to identify the content of that duty.

---

1 See Ch.2.
2 See Ch.3.
3 [1998] Ch. 241 at 253.

## 2. Certainty of Intention

4-004 An express trust can arise only if it can be shown that the settlor (S) intended to create a trust, either by transferring property to trustees to hold on trust,[4] or by declaring herself to be the trustee of property that she owns.[5] Certainty of intention is required because the key event that gives rise to the trust is the settlor's exercise of a power to set up the trust. The beneficiary has no necessary role to play in the creation of an express trust: S can successfully set up a trust for B without B having any knowledge that S has exercised her power to do so.[6]

4-005 Where a trust has been constituted by S having transferred property to T to hold on trust for B, the trust will take effect even if T, having received the property, refuses to act as trustee. The same is true where S sets up a testamentary trust whereby T is to hold on trust for B, and T refuses to accept the property from S's personal representatives. In each case, if necessary,[7] a new trustee will be found,[8] and the property will be vested in that new trustee: "equity never allows a trust to fail for want of a trustee."[9] The express trust can thus be complete, and B's beneficial interest under it can come into existence, without T necessarily having consented to act as trustee.[10] In the vast majority of cases, however, the trustees receive the property having previously agreed with the settlor that they will be trustees, and the beneficiaries know that they will be beneficiaries.

### *A. The Test*

4-006 S's intention to create a trust cannot, by itself, have that effect. Rather, an express trust arises where S has exercised her power to create a trust, and that requires not only intention, but also some external communication of that intention. It is important to note that, as in other parts of the law where rights can arise as a result on one party's exercise of a power to create such rights, S's intention must be judged objectively, as emphasised by the judgment set out in the following extract.

*Byrnes v Kendle*

High Court of Australia (2011) 243 C.L.R. 253

4-007 Kendle held legal title to a property but had signed an acknowledgment of trust in 1997 declaring that he held a half share of the interest in the property on trust for Byrnes, his estranged wife. It was now claimed that Kendle had committed breaches of his duties as trustee, by letting the house out to his son for five years for only a nominal rent. That claim was allowed by the High Court of Australia. One of the arguments made by Kendle in attempting to resist the claim was that he was not in fact a trustee as, although he had signed the acknowledgement of trust, he did not in fact have the required intention to create a trust

---

4 See paras 2-003–2-005.

5 See para.2-005.

6 See, e.g. *Fletcher v Fletcher* (1844) 4 Hare 67; *Re Lewis* [1904] 2 Ch. 656; *Rose v Rose* (1986) 7 N.S.W.L.R. 679 at 686; *Re Kayford* [1975] 1 W.L.R. 279. Indeed, there may be no beneficiaries for a period while income is being accumulated and the ultimate contingent beneficiary may not be born or otherwise ascertained for some time, especially for jurisdictions other than England where the accumulation period can be as long as the perpetuity period.

7 Where B is the sole beneficiary and absolutely entitled under the trust, and is also adult and of sound mind, she will be able to exercise the *Saunders v Vautier* (1841) 4 Beav. 115 power to terminate the trust: see paras 7-04ff) and so an order for the transfer of the property itself to B may well be appropriate.

8 Note that under Trustee Act 1925 s.36, S's personal representative will hold the property on trust for B, but with a power to appoint new trustees.

9 *Bisrat v Kebede* [2015] EWHC 840 (Ch) at [30]. See too, e.g. *Re Robinson* [1892] 1 Ch. 95 at 100: "If the gift is good in other respects the Court will take care that it shall not fail for want of a trustee." See too, e.g. *Mallott v Wilson* [1903] 2 Ch. 494; *Harris v Sharp* [2003] W.T.L.R. 1541; *Kynnersley v Wolverhampton CC* [2008] W.T.L.R. 65.

10 *Fletcher v Fletcher* (1844) 4 Hare 67; *Childers v Childers* (1857) 1 De G. & J. 482.

of the property. That argument was rejected by all of the judges in the High Court decision. This extract reproduces the reasons for doing so given by Heydon and Crennan JJ., in a joint judgment.

HEYDON AND CRENNAN JJ.: In this court [Kendle] submitted that it was necesssary for [Byrnes] to establish a subjective intention by [Kendle] to create a trust. . . This submission is incorrect. The trial judge's estimate of [Kendle's] evidence about subjective intention, and the evidence itself, was irrelevant. The submission rests on a fundamental but very common misconception. . . **4–008**

The authorities establish that in relation to trusts, as in relation to contracts, the search for "intention" is only a search for the intention as revealed in the words the parties, used, amplified by facts known to both parties. Thus in 1881 Sir George Jessel M.R. said:[11] **4–009**

> "The settlement is one which I cannot help thinking was never intended by the framer of it to have the effect I am going to attribute to it; but, of course, as I very often say, one must consider the meaning of the words used, not what one may guess was the intention of the parties."

In 1934 Lord Wright said, speaking of a failed attempt to settle property on trust:[12] **4–010**

> "the court, while it seeks to give effect to the intention of the parties, must give effect to that intention as expressed, that is, it must ascertain the meaning of the words actually used. There is often an ambiguity in the use of the word 'intention' in cases of this character. The word is constantly used as meaning motive, purpose, desire, as a state of mind, and not as meaning intention as expressed. The words actually used must no doubt be construed with reference to the facts known to the parties and in contemplation of which the parties must be deemed to have used them . . . But allowing for these and other rules of the same kind, the principle of the common law has been to adopt an objective standard of construction and to exclude general evidence of actual intention of the parties; the reason for this has been that otherwise all certainty would be taken from the words in which the parties have recorded their agreement or their dispositions of property."

Neither in England nor in Australia has the application of the principles for establishing and defining a trust been analysed with the sophistication devoted in England to their application in contract. However, in both English and Australia law the surrounding circumstances are material to the questions whether the words used created a trust and what its terms are. Accordingly, Conaglen was correct to say: **4–011**

> "The court's focus when construing the terms of [a] bilateral arrangement [creating a trust] is on the objective meaning that those terms would convey to a reasonable person, just as it is when construing contractual arrangements."

The question is what the settlor or settlors did, not what they intended to do.

That truth tends to be obscured by constant repetititon of the need to search for an "intention to create a trust". That search can be seen as concerning the first of the three "certainties" . . . But the "intention" referred to is an intention to be extracted from the words used, not a subjective intention which may have existed but which cannot be extracted from those words. This is as true of unilateral declarations of alleged trust as it is of bilateral covenants to create an alleged trust. It is as true of alleged trusts which are not wholly in writing as it is of alleged trusts which are wholly in writing. In relation to alleged trusts which are not wholly in writing, the need to draw inferences from circumstances in construing the terms of convresations may in practice widen the extent of the inquiry, but it does not alter its nature. **4–012**

As with contracts, subjective intention is only relevant in relation to trusts when the transaction is open to some challenge or some application for modification[13] . . . But subjective intention is irrelevant both to the question of whether a trust exists and to the question of what its terms are. **4–013**

---

11 *Smith v Lucas* (1881) 18 Ch. D. 531 at 542.

12 *IRC v Raphael* [1935] A.C. 96 at 142–143.

13 [Three of the examples given of such a challenge or application were "an equitable challenge for mistake" (see para.4-068); an "allegation of 'sham'" (see paras 4–057ff); and a "claim for rectification" (see paras 18–286ff).]

## B. Applying the Test in Practice

### i. A General Donative Intention is Insufficient

**4-014** No technical expressions of particular formulae are needed to create a trust: the circumstances must show however that the person holding the relevant property is intended to be subject to a legally binding *duty* to hold that property for others (or for herself and others). As Jessel MR said in *Richards v Delbridge*, when considering the rules applying to a self-declaration of trust[14]:

> It is true that [the settlor] need not use the words 'I declare myself trustee', but he must do something which is equivalent to it, and use expressions which have that meaning; for, however anxious the Court may be to carry out a man's intention, it is not at liberty to construe words otherwise than according to their proper meaning . . . The cases in which the question has arisen are nearly all cases in which a man, by documents insufficient to pass a legal interest, has said 'I give or grant certain property to B.' . . . The true distinction appears to me to be plain, and beyond dispute: for a man to make himself a trustee there must be an expression of intention to become a trustee, whereas words of present gift show an intention to give property over to another, and not retain it in the donor's own hands for any purpose, fiduciary or otherwise.

**4-015** As Jessel MR went on to note,[15] this approach accords with the principle in *Milroy v Lord*,[16] which was discussed in Chapter 2[17]: if S attempts to set up a trust for B by means of a transfer to trustees to hold for B, but that attempt fails, as the property remains with S, a court cannot then use S's undoubted general intention to benefit B as the basis on which to find a declaration of trust by S, as clearly S did *not* intend to hold the property herself on trust for B. If a declaration is to be found in such a case, there must be some additional evidence, such as some statement by S that justifies a court in finding that S exercised the power to bind the property in her own hands[18]; although where S clearly intended some form of gift to B, it has been suggested that it may be possible for a court, in some cases at least, to look at the words used by S and, "by a benevolent construction . . . tease out" an implied declaration of trust.[19]

**4-016** Besides the cases referred to by Jessel MR, where S has said "I give or grant certain property to B", there may also be cases, particularly in a domestic context, where legal title to property is vested in one party only (S), but there is some evidence that the property was treated, in practice, as held for the benefit of that party and another (B). Where the property involved is land, s.53(1)(b) of the Law of Property Act 1925 means that B can prove such a declaration only by means of signed writing,[20] and in the absence of such writing, B may then have to resort to a constructive or resulting trust in order to claim a beneficial interest.[21] In relation to property other than land, no such formality requirement applies. The question in such cases is simply whether any statement of S can be found which, when

---

14 (1874) L.R. 18 Eq. 11 at 14, reaffirmed in *Clarence House Ltd v National Westminster Bank Plc* [2010] 1 W.L.R. 1216 at [43] per Ward LJ.

15 (1874) L.R. 18 Eq. 11 at 15.

16 (1862) 4 De G.F. & J. 264.

17 See paras 2-006—2-011.

18 As was found to be the case in, e.g. *Re Ralli's W.T.* [1964] Ch. 288 and *T Choithram International SA v Pagarani* [2001] 1 W.L.R. 1: see paras 2-012—2-021.

19 *Curtis v Pulbrook* [2011] 1 B.C.L.C. 638 at [43] per Briggs J, applying *Pennington v Waine* [2002] 1 W.L.R. 2075. It is worth noting, however, that in *T Choithram International SA v Pagarani* [2001] 1 W.L.R. 1 at 11 per Lord Browne-Wilkinson, citing *Milroy v Lord* (1862) 4 De G.F. & J. 264, specifically said that "the court will not give a benevolent construction so as to treat ineffective words of outright gift as taking effect as if the donor had declared himself a trustee for the donee". Further discussion at paras 2-019—2-021.

20 See paras 3-026ff.

21 See paras 15-030—15-045.

interpreted against the relevant facts (which include the nature of the parties' relationship), shows an objective intention that S should hold the property subject to a legal duty not to use it wholly for S's own benefit, but to use it for B's benefit too. The next extract provides an example of how that question may be resolved in practice.

*Paul v Constance*

Court of Appeal [1977] 1 W.L.R. 527

SCARMAN L.J. (with whom BRIDGE and CAIRNS L.J. agreed): Mr Dennis Albert Constance was a wage earner living in Cheltenham until he died on March 9, 1974. He was married to Bridget Frances Constance, the defendant in this action. But they parted in June 1965. In 1967 Mr Constance met Mrs Doreen Grace Paul, who is the plaintiff in this action. The two of them set up house together in December of that year, and they lived to all appearances as man and wife up to the date of Mr Constance's death. The house in which they lived was the property of the plaintiff. **4–017**

In August 1969 Mr Constance was injured at his work. He claimed damages against his employers . . . his claim was disposed of by the payment to him of a sum of £950. This money he received by cheque early in 1973. He discussed with the plaintiff what to do with the money, and the evidence is clear that they decided it was to go into a bank account. The two of them went to see the manager of the St George's Square branch of Lloyds Bank in Cheltenham, and there they had a discussion about opening a bank account. According to the notes of evidence which the trial judge made, the two of them had a discussion with the bank manager. He explained to them the different sorts of accounts which they could open, and the decision was taken to open a deposit account. At that stage Mr Constance revealed that they were not married. It is perhaps of some significance in understanding this interview if one recalls the evidence that was given by a Mr Thomas, a fellow employee of Mr Constance's, who said that he knew that they were not married but most people did not. After Mr Constance had told the manager that they were not married the manager said: "Well, it will be in your name only then?" Mr Constance said: "Yes." Then Mr Constance asked the manager what was to happen if the plaintiff wanted to draw on the account, or if he wanted the plaintiff to draw on it, and the manager said that that could be done if she used a note with Mr Constance's signature on it authorising her to draw on the account. **4–018**

The account that was opened on that day in February 1973 is at the very heart of this case. The account was maintained in Mr Constance's name from that date until the date of his death. Over the period between 1973 and his death, some 13 months later in 1974, further sums were paid into the account including, in particular, some sums which represented "bingo" winnings. It is clear from the evidence that Mr Constance and the plaintiff did play "bingo", and they played it really as a joint venture. They did have winnings from time to time, and at any rate three of such winnings—none of them very great—were paid into the account. It is clear from the plaintiff's evidence that they thought of those winnings as "their winnings": neither hers nor his alone, but theirs. Nevertheless, when the account was closed on the death of Mr Constance the ultimate balance, after the addition of interest, consisted largely of the initial sum of £950 representing Mr Constance's damages as a result of his injury at work. There was one withdrawal during this period, a sum of £150, and the evidence was that that money was divided between the two of them after part of it had been used for buying Christmas presents and some food. **4–019**

The plaintiff began her action after the death of Mr Constance against his lawful wife, the defendant, who took out letters of administration for his estate since he died intestate. The plaintiff claims that the bank account in his name, to which I have referred, was held by him on trust for the benefit of himself and the plaintiff jointly. She claims that it was an express trust declared orally by him on numerous occasions. The defendant maintains that the whole fund contained in the account was the beneficial property of the deceased at the time of his death, and, as such, became part of his estate after death. **4–020**

The matter came on for trial and on August 12 the Judge found in favour of the plaintiff. He found the existence of an express trust, a trust for the benefit of the plaintiff and the deceased jointly, and he ordered that the sum of £499.21 be paid to the plaintiff as representing one half share of the fund to which she was beneficially entitled. **4–021**

The only point taken by the defendant on her appeal to this court goes to the question whether or not there was, in the circumstances of this case, an express declaration of trust. **4–022**

Counsel for the defendant drew the attention of the court to the so-called three certainties that have **4–023** to be established before the court can infer the creation of a trust. We are concerned only with one of the three certainties, and it is this:[22]

> "The words [that is the words of the declaration relied on] must be so used that on the whole they ought to be construed as imperative. [A little later on the learned author says:] No particular form of expression is necessary for the creation of a trust, if on the whole it can be gathered that a trust was intended. A trust may well be created, although there may be an absence of any expression in terms imposing confidence. A trust may thus be created without using the word 'trust' for what the court regards is the substance and effect of the words used."

**4–024** Counsel for the defendant has taken the court through the detailed evidence and submits that one cannot find anywhere in the history of events a declaration of trust in the sense of finding the deceased man, Mr Constance, saying: "I am now disposing of my interest in this fund so that you, Mrs Paul, now have a beneficial interest in it." Of course, the words which I have just used are stilted lawyers' language, and counsel for the plaintiff was right to remind the court that we are dealing with simple people, unaware of the subtleties of equity, but understanding very well indeed their own domestic situation. It is right that one should consider the various things that were said and done by the plaintiff and Mr Constance during their time together against their own background and in their own circumstances.

**4–025** Counsel for the defendant drew our attention to two cases [*Jones v Lock*[23] and *Richards v Delbridge*[24]], and he relies on them as showing that, though a man may say in clear and unmistakable terms that he intends to make a gift to some other person, for instance his child or some other member of his family, yet that does not necessarily disclose a declaration of trust; and, indeed, in the two cases to which we have been referred the court held that, though there was a plain intention to make a gift, it was not right to infer any intention to create a trust. . .

**4–026** There is no suggestion of a gift by transfer in this case. The facts of those cases do not, therefore, very much help the submission of counsel for the defendant, but he was able to extract from them this principle: that there must be a clear declaration of trust, and that means there must be clear evidence from what is said or done of an intention to create a trust, or as counsel for the defendant put it, "an intention to dispose of a property or a fund so that somebody else to the exclusion of the disponent acquires the beneficial interest in it." He submitted that there was no such evidence.

**4–027** When one looks to the detailed evidence to see whether it goes as far as that—and I think that the evidence does have to go as far as that—one finds that from the time that Mr Constance received his damages right up to his death he was saying, on occasions, that the money was as much the plaintiff's as his. When they discussed the damages, how to invest them or what to do with them, when they discussed the bank account, he would say to her: "The money is as much yours as mine." The judge, rightly treating the basic problem in the case as a question of fact, reached this conclusion. He said:

> "I have read through my notes, and I am quite satisfied that it was the intention of [the plaintiff] and Mr Constance to create a trust in which both of them were interested."

**4–028** In this court the issue becomes: was there sufficient evidence to justify the judge reaching that conclusion of fact? In submitting that there was, counsel for the plaintiff draws attention first and foremost to the words used. When one bears in mind the unsophisticated character of Mr Constance and his relationship with the plaintiff during the last few years of his life, counsel for the plaintiff submits that the words that he did use on more than one occasion namely: "This money is as much yours as mine", convey clearly a present declaration that the existing fund was as much the plaintiff's as his own. The judge accepted that conclusion. I think he was well justified in doing so and, indeed, I think he was right to do so. There are, as counsel for the plaintiff reminded us, other features in the history of the relationship between the plaintiff and Mr Constance which support the interpretation of those words as an express declaration of trust. I have already described the interview with the bank manager when the account was opened. I have mentioned also the putting of the "bingo" winnings into the account, and the one withdrawal for the benefit of both of them.

**4–029** The question, therefore, is whether in all the circumstances the use of those words on numerous

22 *Snell's Equity* 27th edn, p.111.
23 (1865) 1 Ch.App. 25.
24 (1874) L.R. 18 Eq. 11.

> occasions as between Mr. Constance and the plaintiff constituted an express declaration of trust. The judge found that they did. For myself, I think he was right so to find. I therefore would dismiss the appeal.

A question that went unaddressed by the court in *Paul v Constance* was as to the precise terms of the trust declared by Constance (S).[25] If the initial trust was such that S was holding on trust for himself and Paul (B) as joint tenants, and this beneficial joint tenancy was not severed before S's death then, on S's death, B would become solely entitled to the beneficial interest, and so could have claimed the full sum credited to the bank account. It seems to have instead been assumed that the initial trust involved S holding on trust for himself and B as beneficial tenants in common, each with an individual (but undivided) half share of the beneficial interest, so that on S's death, and in the absence of a will by S, his 50 per cent share passed under the intestacy rules. The answer to this question as to the terms of the initial trust must also depend on S's objective intention, but of course, particularly where the parties are not alive to the technicalities, there is unlikely to be any clear intention on this point. **4–030**

As we will see in Chapter 15,[26] when considering the common intention constructive trust of the family home, the courts are now willing to accept that, if an intention that the parties' beneficial entitlements should vary from their legal interests has been established either through express statements or by a process of inference, then the extent of the parties' beneficial entitlements can depend on the parties' *imputed* (i.e. fictional) intention. Even then, however, in a case such as *Paul v Constance* where the relevant intention is that the property is "as much mine as yours", it is probably necessary to have a default answer to the question of whether such an intention gives rise to a joint tenancy or a tenancy in common. It is probably right to say that, consistently with the result in *Paul v Constance*, a tenancy in common should be preferred as it ensures that each party has an individual interest that can be passed on her death,[27] and so avoids the "gamble of the tontine".[28] **4–031**

### ii. An Intention to Impose a Legally Binding Duty is Necessary

A trust arises only when the trustee holds property subject to a legally binding duty and so an express trust can arise only where S's objective, expressed intention was that such a duty should arise. This point is important if S transfers property to T expressing confidence, a wish, or a hope that T will use the property for the benefit of B. Such transfers are most likely to occur in a testamentary context. Originally, the courts were only too ready to treat such words as creating a trust,[29] but the following extract is from a case which signalled a change in approach. **4–032**

*Lambe v Eames*

Court of Appeal in Chancery (1870–71) L.R. 6 Ch. App. 597

John Lambe left his entire estate, including a freehold, to his widow "to be at her disposal in any way she may think best for the benefit of herself and family." When the widow died, she left the freehold on trust for one of her daughters, Elizabeth Eames, but subject to an annual payment for Henry Lambe, an illegitimate **4–033**

---

25 Note that this question has also been overlooked, even by the House of Lords and Supreme Court, in relation to the common intention constructive trust of land: see, e.g. A. Briggs (2012) 128 L.Q.R. 183, commenting on *Jones v Kernott* [2012] 1 A.C. 776 and *Stack v Dowden* [2007] 2 A.C. 432.

26 At paras 15–051ff.

27 A joint tenancy carries with it the doctrine of survivorship which has been described as "odious in equity" (*R. v Williams* (1735) Bunb. 342 at 343) owing to its effect that the surviving joint tenant is wholly entitled.

28 That is, the point that a joint tenancy, if not severed, means that the survivor takes all, whereas those who die earlier take nothing.

29 *Eade v Eade* (1820) 5 Madd. 118 at 121; *Palmer v Simmonds* (1854) 2 Drew. 221; *Gutty v Cregoe* (1857) 24 Beav. 185.

son of one of Lambe's sons. Elizabeth refused to make the annual payment to Henry, arguing that, by the terms of John's will, the widow had received the freehold subject to a trust for the benefit of herself and family, and that Henry, as an illegitimate child, did not qualify as "family". Henry argued instead that John's will had made an absolute gift of the freehold to his widow.

**4-034** JAMES L.J.: If this will had to be construed irrespective of any authority, the construction would, in my opinion, not be open to any reasonable doubt . . . [The] question is whether [the words "to be at her disposal in any way she may think best for the benefit of herself and family"] create any trust affecting the property; and in hearing case after case cited, I could not help feeling that the officious kindness of the Court of Chancery in interposing trusts where in many cases the father of the family never meant to create trusts, must have been a very cruel kindness indeed. I am satsifed that the testator in this case would have been shocked to think that any person caling himself a next friend could file a bill in this Court, and, under pretence of benefitting the children, have taken the administration of the estate from his wife. I am satisfied that no such trust was intended, and that it would be a violation of the clearest and plainest wishes of the testator if we decided otherwise. . .

**4-035** It is possible that in this case there may be some obligation on the widow to do something for the benefit of the children; but assuming that there is such an obligation, it cannot be extended to mean a trust for the widow for her life, and after her death for the children, in such shares as she may think fit to direct . . . [And] if there be any such obligation, I think it has been fairly discharged by the way in which she has made her will—giving part for the benefit of one member of the family, and part to a natural son, whom she might reasonably think it her duty to benefit.

**4-036** The "very cruel kindness" consisted of the courts' former willingness, in interpreting a provision such as that in John Lambe's will, to find that the widow held the property subject to a trust for the benefit of herself and her children: this would secure a benefit to the children, but would equally hamper the widow's ability to deal with the property. The point made by James LJ is that a testator, particularly one such as John Lambe who made his will "in the prime of life, with a wife and young children", might well prefer his widow to have complete freedom to deal with the property, and so to be able to react to unforeseen events, trusting that she would discharge any moral duties to provide for other family members but not imposing any legal limits on her dealings.

**4-037** Since the 1870s, the courts have therefore drawn an important distinction between words which express a hope or desire that T *will* act in a certain way[30] and words which impose a duty that T *must* act in a certain way. The former, by themselves, do not give rise to a trust[31]; although of course the question is always whether, viewed in context, the true expressed, objective intention of S was to impose a duty on T.[32] For example, in *Re Adams and Kensington Vestry*,[33] a testamentary transfer from a husband to his widow "in full confidence that she will do what is right as to the disposal thereof between [S's] children" did not manifest an intention to impose a legally binding duty on T and so did not give rise to not trust.[34]

---

30 Such words are sometimes referred to as "precatory", with "precatory words" then being words that do not, by themselves, create a trust: see, e.g. *Re Brace* [1954] 1 W.L.R. 955 at 958; *Re Freud (Deceased)* [2014] W.T.L.R. 1453 at [43], [46]. However, the term "precatory" is not very helpful, as some cases also refer to "precatory trusts": e.g. *Re Steele's WT* [1948] Ch. 603 at 607–608.

31 See, e.g. *Re Adams and Kensington Vestry* (1884) 27 Ch.D. 394: a testamentary transfer to T "in full confidence that [T] will do what is right as to the disposal of the money between [S's] children" did not manifest an intention to impose a legally binding duty on T and so gave rise to not trust.

32 By the Administration of Justice Act 1982 s.21, extrinsic evidence, including evidence of the testator's intention, may be admitted to assist in its interpretation: (a) in so far as any part of the will is meaningless; (b) in so far as the language used in any part of it is ambiguous on the face of it; and (c) in so far as evidence, other than evidence of the testator's intention, shows that the language used in any part of it is ambiguous in the light of the surrounding circumstances.

33 (1884) 27 Ch.D. 394.

34 See too, e.g. *Mussoorie Bank Ltd v Raynor* (1882) 7 App. Cas. 321 (no trust where the will gives property to T "feeling confident that she will act justly to our children in dividing the same when no longer required by her"); *Re Diggles* (1888) 39 Ch.D. 253 (no trust where the will states: "it is my desire that she allows A.G. an annuity of £25 during her life) "; *Re Johnson*

In the specific context of a testamentary transfer to a spouse, the Administration of Justice Act 1982 s.22, states that: **4–038**

> Except where a contrary intent is shown, it shall be presumed that if a testator devises or bequeaths property to his spouse in terms which in themselves would give an absolute interest to the spouse but by the same instrument purports to give his issue an interest in the same property, the gift to the spouse is absolute notwithstanding the purported gift to the issue.

So, for example, if a testator leaves "all my property to my wife and after her death to our children", the wife will take the property absolutely and is under no obligation to hold it on trust for the children.[35]

It is important to bear in mind that if S, by a will or an inter vivos transfer, transfers property to B, but some mention is also made of that property benefitting C, then (at least) five constructions are possible. Taken in ascending order as to the strength of C's right to the property (if any), the words indicating that a benefit should go to C may be treated as: **4–039**

(i) merely indicating S's motive, so that B takes an absolute beneficial interest, and C has no legal right[36];

(ii) creating a condition subsequent that affects the property in B's hands making B liable to forfeit the property if the condition is broken[37];

(iii) creating a personal obligation binding B to C so that if B accepts the property she must then perform the obligation in C's favour[38] (even if it costs her more than the value of the property[39]);

(iv) creating a charge in C's favour on the property given to B, so that B takes the property beneficially subject to the charge for securing payment of money to C[40]; or

(v) creating a trust either in favour of C absolutely or in favour of B and C.[41]

Options (iii) and (iv) demonstrate that S's intention to impose *some* duty on B does not necessarily give rise to a trust; for a trust to arise, B's duty must relate specifically to the trust property, and must be such that B has a duty not to use the property for her own benefit, unless and to the extent that B too is a beneficiary of the trust. In option (iii), there is no trust as B's duty to C does not need to be satisfied **4–040**

---

[1939] 2 All E.R. 458 (no trust where the will states that "I request that C on her death leave her property to my four sisters").

35 The statutory presumption contained in s.22 can be displaced. See, e.g. *Re Harrison* [2006] 1 W.L.R. 1212: the testator had expressed a sufficiently clear intention that his widow had a life interest in the relevant property which was held on trust for the children in equal shares.

36 e.g. *Re Brace* [1954] 1 W.L.R. 955 (bequest of particular land to daughter "on condition that she will always provide a home for [another daughter] at the above address").

37 e.g. *Ellis v Chief Adjudication Officer* [1998] 1 F.L.R. 184 (inter vivos transfer of flat to daughter subject to condition that she repays the mortgage and allows the donor to remain in the property: when the daughter later evicted the mother, thus breaching the condition, the gift failed and the property reverted to the donor).

38 e.g. *Re Lester* [1942] Ch. 324 (bequest of shares "subject to the payment" of certain annuities).

39 e.g. *Re Hodge* [1940] Ch. 260.

40 See, e.g. *Re Oliver* (1890) 62 L.T. 533. This would be the effect, for example, of a bequest of land "to B, subject to paying from the rents thereof £10,000 each year to C". In such a case, B is under no personal obligation to make up any deficiency caused by insufficiency of the property charged.

41 See, e.g. *Re Harrison* [2006] 1 W.L.R. 1212 (bequest in a homemade will leaving a bungalow "in trust" to B (S's wife) with the provision that on her death the proceeds of sale are to be divided equally between S's four children, and an additional clause stating: "No doubt if mum runs into money problems you can sort something out. Like selling the bungalow." The bequest was interpreted as imposing a trust for the children in equal shares under which B had a life interest.)

by using the specific property received by B. In option (iv), there is no trust because, provided that the specific duty to pay C is satisfied, B is otherwise free to use the property as she wishes.

### iii. The Relevance of Segregation of the Alleged Trust Property

**4-041** In ascertaining whether S's expressed objective intention was to set up a trust of particular property, one relevant factor may be as to how that property was to be treated by the supposed trustee, T. If there is nothing to indicate that T (or, in the event of a claimed self-declaration, S) was to treat the property as separate from her own, that will be, at least, a strong indication that no trust was intended. After all, a key feature of a trust is that the trustee is not free to use the property entirely for her own benefit. As Channell J put it in *Henry v Hammond*[42]:

> It is clear that if the terms upon which the person receives the money are that he is bound to keep it separate, either in a bank or elsewhere, and to hand that money so kept as a separate fund to the person entitled to it, then he is a trustee of that money and must hand it over to the person who is his [beneficiary]. If on the other hand he is not bound to keep the money separate, but is entitled to mix it with his own money and deal with it as he pleases, and when called upon to hand over an equivalent sum of money, then, in my opinion, he is not a trustee of the money, but merely a debtor.

**4-042** This point may be important in determining the nature of an agency relationship. For example, consider a case where an agent (A) collects money from customers on behalf of her principal (P). If the arrangement between A and P is that A is free to pay that money into her own bank account, but must settle up with P on a monthly basis by paying an equivalent sum over to P, then A simply owes a debt to P (i.e. A must pay P a particular sum of money) and does not hold the money received from customers on trust for P. In contrast, if the arrangement between A and P is, for example, that A must pay the money into a separate bank account, then it may be possible to find an intention that A was to hold that money on trust for P. In that case, A's duty is not simply a personal obligation to pay a sum of money to P; rather A holds *specific* rights (the chose in action constituted by the bank account) on trust for P. The difference between those two cases will of course be crucial if, for example, A goes into insolvency[43]: if P can identify money held by A on trust for P, P can simply claim that money; whereas if A is a collecting agent, P is simply an unsecured creditor who will have to settle for receiving a proportion of the total sum due from A.

**4-043** The distinction between an agent who owes a debt to P and an agent who instead holds funds received on trust is also crucial when considering if a statutory limitation period applies to an action by P to recover sums due from A. P's claim against a collecting agent is purely contractual, and so is barred six years from the date of A's breach of contract.[44] In contrast, if a trust exists, P's claim is "to recover from the trustee trust property" and no statutory limitation period applies.[45] That difference

---

[42] *Henry v Hammond* [1913] 2 K.B. 515 at 521 per Channell J. See too, e.g. *R. v Clowes (No.2)* [1994] 2 All E.R. 316 at 325; *Commissioners of Customs & Excise v Richmond Theatre Management Ltd* [1995] S.T.C. 257.

[43] See, e.g. *Azam v Iqbal* [2008] Bus. L.R. 168: the claimant paid money to the defendant on the basis that the defendant would then credit the claimant's relatives in Pakistan with rupees at an agreed exchange rate. A receiver was appointed over the defendant's assets before the defendant had made the payment to the relatives. It was held that there had been no trust of the claimant's payment, as the defendant's duty had simply been to make the agreed payment to the claimant's relatives and the defendant was free to use the money paid by the claimant as it wished (just as a bank receiving money paid into an account does not hold that money on trust for the account holder).

[44] Limitation Act 1980 s.5. The contractual limitation applies even if the claim is an action for an account, as s.23 stipulates that: "An action for an account shall not be brought after the expiration of any time limit under this Act which is applicable to the claim which is the basis of the duty to account."

[45] Limitation Act 1980 s.21(1)(b).

was in issue in *Nelson v Rye*,[46] a decision discussed by Millett LJ in the following extract from *Paragon Finance plc v DB Thakerar & Co*[47]:

> In *Nelson v Rye* the plaintiff was a solo musician who appointed the defendant his manager on terms that he would collect the fees and royalties which were due to him and pay his expenses and account to him annually for his net income after deducting his own commission. When the relationship came to an end the plaintiff claimed an account, and the question was whether the account should be limited to the six years before the issue of the writ or wheher it should extend over the whole period of the relationship. . . **4–044**
>
> . . . [The] defendant's liability to account for more than six years before the issue of the writ in *Nelson v Rye* depended on whether he was, not merely a fiduciary (for every agent owes fiduciary duties to his principal), but a trustee, that is to say, on whether he owed fiduciary duties in relation to the money. **4–045**
>
> Whether he was in fact a trustee of the money may be open to doubt. Unless I have misunderstood the facts or they were very unusual it would appear that the defendant was entitled to pay receipts into his own account, mix them with his own money, use them for his own cash flow, deduct his own commission, and account for the balance to the plaintiff only at the end of the year. It is fundamental to the existence of a trust that the trustee is bound to keep the trust property separate from his own and apply it exclusively for the benefit of the beneficiary. Any right on the part of the defendant to mix the money which he received with his own and use it for his own cash flow would be inconsistent with the existence of a trust. So would a liaibility to account annually, for a trustee is obliged to account to his beneficiary and pay over the trust property on demand. . . **4–046**
>
> Unless the defendant was a trustee of the money which he received, however, the claim for an account was barred after six years. . .Accordingly, in so far as it decided that the defendant was liable to account without limit of time even if the money was not trust money, *Nelson v Rye* was wrongly decided. **4–047**

The basic point is that a trust requires T to be under a duty in relation to specific property: a duty just to pay B a sum of money, where that money can come from any source, does not count as a trust. There is, therefore, an overlap with the requirement of certainty of subject matter, and we wlll see below that the courts, particularly in modern commerical contexts, have been willing to find a trust even where T has a broad power to use and mix the trust funds.[48] It should therefore be emphasised that the overarching question is one as to the settlor S's expressed and objectively understood intention. The mere fact that T is permitted to mix funds does not, by itself, prevent the finding of a trust. **4–048**

For example, the mingling of funds received from S1 and S2 will not be fatal to the finding of a trust where T receives such funds to make investments for the parties which are to be held separately from T's own assets: an investment, such as a block of securities, can be held by T on trust for S1 and S2 in their proportionate shares.[49] Similarly, where T adds funds of S1 and S2 to funds of T's own, and then makes investments to be held separately from T's own assets, those investments can be held on trust for S1, S2 and T in proportionate shares.[50] If T were then to sell such investments and, without authority from S1 and S2, to pay the proceeds into T's own bank account, S1 and S2 would each then have a right to trace into T's right to the bank account and claim a proportionate share of that right[51]: once a trust has been established, unauthorised mingling by T does not, by itself, terminate the trust.[52] **4–049**

---

46 [1996] 1 W.L.R. 1378.
47 [1999] 1 All E.R. 400 at 415–416.
48 See para.4–082.
49 *R. v Clowes (No.2)* [1994] 2 All E.R. 316; *Re Goldcorp Exchange* Ltd [1995] 1 A.C. 74.
50 *Re Lewis's of Leicester Ltd* [1995] 1 B.C.L.C. 428.
51 See, e.g. *Foskett v McKeown* [2001] 1 A.C. 102.
52 For discussion of the rules of tracing, and of the limits of the ability of a beneficiary to assert a claim in relation to assets acquired through an unauthorised use of trust assets, see paras 12–016ff.

### iv. The Distinction between a Trust and a Power

**4–050** In answering the key question of whether S had an expressed, objective intention to impose on T the required duty in relation to the trust property, it is useful to bear in mind the distinction between a trust and a power.[53] The distinction can be somewhat tricky to apply in practice. There may be cases in which T clearly is a trustee, and B is clearly a beneficiary of that trust, but T also has authority to use the trust property so as to benefit C. The question then is whether T has merely been given a *power* to act so as to benefit C, or whether instead the terms of the settlement impose a *duty* on T to act in that way: only in the latter case does C acquire a beneficial interest under the trust; only in the latter case will the court be required to execute the trust if T fails to act for C's benefit. As we will see below,[54] the distinction between a power and a trust is also crucial in determining which particular test is to be applied in determining if the parties benefitting from the exercise of the power or trust have been defined with sufficient certainty.

**4–051** The conceptual distinction between a power and a trust is clear, although it is complicated slightly by the fact that S may have intended T to hold a power in a fiduciary capacity, so that T has particular duties in relation to the exercise of the power, such as a duty to consider seriously and fairly whether to exercise it. The existence of such duties distinguish a fiduciary power from a bare power: a bare power exists where T has no duty to consider seriously and fairly whether to exercise the power.

**4–052** In practice, however, in the context of a specific settlement, there may be only a very fine line between seeing a term that potentially benefits C as giving T a fiduciary power or as instead imposing a trust under which C, as well as B, has a beneficial interest. For example, consider the following two cases: (i) T holds funds on trust for B, but with a power to make distributions of interest to C, X, Y or Z; and (ii) T holds funds on a discretionary trust for B and C, but with a power to distribute a certain proportion of those funds to X, Y or Z. It may not always be simple in practice to determine which of those two interpretations best accords with S's expressed, objective intentions: as Lord Wilberforce put it in *Re Baden's Deed Trusts (No.1)*: "A layman and, I suspect, also a logician, would find it hard to understand what difference there is."[55]

**4–053** There are of course further possibilities. For example, if S makes a testamentary disposition to trustees on trust to B for life, S may combine that with a bare power for B to appoint the capital among such of S and B's children as B may see fit. If, then, that power is not exercised, the capital will be held on a resulting trust for S's estate, as S has not directed any other parties for whose benefit the trustees should hold the property if the power is not exercised.[56] A different result obtains, of course, if S instead intended that, in default of B exercising the power to appoint among the children, the property should then be held for the children in equal shares: in that case there is a fixed trust for all of the children, but the beneficial interest of each child is subject to B's exercising the power to appoint the property wholly to the other children.[57]

---

53 Discussed at paras 1–042—1–043.

54 See paras 4–117ff.

55 [1971] A.C. 424 at 448 (also known as *McPhail v Doulton*; extracted at paras 4–119—4–136).

56 See, e.g. *Re Weekes's Settlement* [1897] 1 Ch. 289: a bequest to B, S's husband, was made with a "power to dispose of all such property by will amongst our children in accordance with the power granted to him as regards the other property which I have under my marriage settlements" with no express gift over in default of B's exercise of that power. Romer J refused to infer that S intended that, should B fail to exercise the power, the property should be divided equally between the children, stating at 292: "The authorities do not show, in my opinion, that there is a hard and fast rule that a gift to A for life with a power to A to appoint among a class and nothing more must, if there is no gift over in the will, be held a gift by implication to the class in default of the power being exercised." See too *Re Combe* [1925] 1 Ch. 210; *Re Poulton's WT* [1987] 1 All E.R. 1068.

57 See, e.g. *Wilson v Duguid* (1883) 24 Ch.D. 244, where, in contrast to *Re Weekes's Settlement* [1897] 1 Ch. 289, it was found

There may be a very fine line between cases in which the court is, and is not, willing to infer that S intended such a fixed trust in the event of B's not fully exercising the power to appoint.[58] One relevant factor will be the width of the class: whilst a trust for equal division between the objects of an unexercised power of appointment may be a practical solution if the objects are all members of a narrow class (e.g. S's children), such a trust would be very unlikely to reflect S's intention if the class were very broad (e.g. all S's employees, ex-employees and their relatives and dependants). As Lord Wilberforce noted in *Re Baden (No.1)* in considering that very class[59]: **4–054**

> Equal division is surely the last thing the settlor ever intended: equal division among all may, probably would, produce a result beneficial to none. Why suppose that the court would lend itself to a whimsical execution?. . .Equal division may be sensible and has been decreed, in cases of family trusts, for a limited class, here there is life in the maxim 'equality is equity', but the cases provide numerous examples where this has not been so. . .

In relation to a broad class of objects, it is of course possible for S to set up a discretionary trust, so that T does have to distribute the trust property, but there is no duty to divide it equally amongst members of the class. The difference between a discretionary trust and a power of appointment is that, in the former, T has a *duty* to distribute. There is therefore an extremely fine line between the cases where: (i) T holds on a discretionary trust for X, Y and Z, but subject to the possible exercise of a power of appointment by T in favour of C; and (ii) T has a power to appoint to X, Y and Z, and T is to hold on trust for C if the power of appointment is not exercised. **4–055**

Further, in our example where S makes a testamentary disposition to trustees on trust to B for life, with a bare power for B to appoint the capital among such of S and B's children as B may see fit, it would also be possible for S to provide expressly that, if B does not exercise that power of appointment, the trustees will then hold on discretionary trust for S and B's children. It is however very difficult for a court to *infer* such an intention to create a discretionary trust in default. Consequently the basic choice, if no express provision is made for the case where B does not exercise the power of appointment, is between a resulting trust for S's estate[60] and a trust for equal division amongst S and B's children.[61] The court will have to decide which of those possiblities best reflects S's expressed, objective intention. **4–056**

---

on the facts that an inference could be made that S had intended a gift to the children equally if B did not exercise the power of appointment. Similarly, each child has an immediate beneficial interest, but one which is liable to be divested by B's exercise of the power, if there is a bequest "to W for life, remainder to our children equally, but so that W may instead appoint the capital between our children in such shares as she may see fit": see, e.g. *Re Llewellyn's Settlement* [1921] 2 Ch. 281; *Re Arnold* [1947] Ch. 131.

58 It is of course also possible for S, for example, to stipulate that, in default of the exercise of the power of appointment, the trustees will hold on a discretionary trust, with the children as objects of that trust; but it would be very difficult for a court to *infer* such an intention if it is not clearly expressed in the settlement. For the consequences where trustees holding on discretionary trust do not perform their duty to allocate the trust property amongst the objects of the trust, see paras 4–138—4–139.

59 [1971] A.C. 424 at 451 (also known as *McPhail v Doulton*). See further paras 4–138—4–139. Lord Wilberforce's comments were made when considering how a court would execute a discretionary trust for such a class, but his point is clearly relevant to the question of establishing the likely intentions of S in relation to such a class.

60 As was found in, e.g. *Re Weekes's Settlement* [1897] 1 Ch. 289.

61 As was found in, e.g. *Wilson v Duguid* (1883) 24 Ch.D. 244.

## C. Shams

### i. The Doctrine

4-057 As emphasised by Heydon and Crennan JJ in the passage from *Byrnes v Kendle* set out above,[62] the court's focus when determining if S has exercised her power to set up a trust is on S's expressed, objective intention. In that judgment, however, an "allegation of sham" was recognised as one of the situations in which subjective intention may be relevant, as "the tranasation is open to some challenge".[63]

4-058 In *Midland Bank Plc v Wyatt*,[64] for example, Mr and Mrs Wyatt, beneficial owners of their family home, signed a trust deed which stated that Mr Wyatt now held his beneficial share on trust for Mrs Wyatt and his two daughters. Mr Wyatt relied on this deed when the bank attempted to enforce a charging order against his interest in the home: he argued that his debts could not be enforced against that property, as he held it on trust for his wife and daughter. In the usual case, the signed deed would of course be conclusive evidence that S had indeed exercised his power to set up a trust.[65] It was held by the judge, however, that "the trust deed was executed by [Mr Wyatt], not to be acted upon but to be put in the safe for a rainy day" and the judge stated that: "I do not believe Mr Wyatt had any intention when he executed the trust deed of endowing his children with the interest, which at that time was his only real asset."[66] The finding then was that Mr Wyatt had intended only to rely on the trust deed if it was necessary to protect his interest in the home from execution by a creditor; despite signing the deed, he had had no subjective intention to set up a trust and so he had not in fact exercised his power to do so. As a result, his interest in the home was subject to no trust, and so the bank could proceed to enforce their charging order over that interest.

4-059 The sham doctrine may also apply to a document signed by S apparently setting up a trust by way of a transfer to T. In *Rahman v Chase Bank (CI) Trust Co Ltd*,[67] for example, Rahman purported to set up a trust, governed by Jersey law, where any capital remaining in the trust fund on an appointed day was to be divided between certain of his relatives. Until that point, both the trustees and Rahman had various powers in relation to the trust property, including a power to make appointments to Rahman. The court, looking at what had happened in practice after the date of the document, found that, to the extent that it suggested that Rahman had set up a trust for the benefit of others, the document was a sham: in fact, the trustees held the property as nominees for Rahman, who therefore had the beneficial interest in the trust property. The judge held that "the trustee was never made the master of the assets. [Rahman] intended to and in fact retained control of the capital and income of the trust fund throughout this lifetime".[68] The terms of the document could therefore be disregarded:[69] the trustee in fact held the property on a bare trust for Rahman.

---

62 (2011) 243 C.L.R. 253 at [42], [50]–[62] (extracted at paras 4-007—4-013).

63 ibid., at [63]. Note that s.423 of the Insolvency Act 1986 (which deals with transactions defrauding creditors, whether those transactions take the form of a trust or not) can apply where S acts with a substantial purpose of putting assets beyond the reach of actual or future creditors, allowing a court to make an order restoring the property to S for the benefit of S's creditors. That provision may of course apply even if there was no sham, and a trust was set up by S. Similarly, s.37 of the Matrimonial Causes Act 1973 gives the court a jurisdiction to set aside dispositions made with the intention of defeating a spouse's claim to ancillary relief.

64 [1995] 1 F.L.R. 697.

65 See, e.g. *National Westminster Bank Plc v Jones* [2001] 1 B.C.L.C. 98 at [59] per Neuberger J: "there is a very strong presumption that parties intend to be bound by the provisions of agreements into which they enter, and, even more, intend the agreements they enter into to take effect."

66 [1995] 1 F.L.R. 696 at 707.

67 [1991] J.L.R. 103.

68 ibid., at 112.

69 Note that there are cases, and *Rahman* may well have been one, where, even if the document is treated at face value,

The onus of proving that a document which appears to create a proper trust is actually a sham is on the person making the allegation.[70] It is important to note that, even if S has retained some signficant practical control over the exercise of powers by T, this may be perfectly consistent with the finding that S intended to create a trust for the benefit of others, rather than a trust solely for S's own benefit[71]: after all, one of the main attractions of a trust (as opposed to an outright gift) is that it may be used by settlors as a means of benefitting other people whilst also keeping some control over the use of the trust property. 4–060

The finding of a sham can have very significant consequences for S, the apparent settlor. As can be seen from *Midland Bank v Wyatt*, it means that property which, according to the terms of the document, is held by S for others is in fact at S's free disposition and so is available to meet the claims of S's creditors. Similarly, in a case such as *Rahman*, the finding of a sham means that T holds the property on a bare trust for S: such an interest is again available to S's creditors and must be taken into account when assessing S's tax liability. As well as insulating assets from general creditors or trying to limit a tax bill, S may have wished to put assets beyond the reach of any claims by a spouse, or by a relative who would be entitled on S's death under a particular jurisdiction's "forced heirship" rules. 4–061

Whilst it is rarely invoked, the sham doctrine is therefore generally relied upon *against* S, by a party such as one of S's creditors.[72] Certainly, it is not open to a purported settlor to deny the objective effect of her own acts by relying on her secret dishonest intention to produce a different outcome.[73] In *Official Assignee v Wilson*[74] the New Zealand Court of Appeal concluded from this that S's trustee in bankruptcy was also precluded from alleging the existence of a sham, as he could be in no better position than the "settlor" herself. However, it seems strongly arguable that, as the trustee in bankruptcy acts on behalf of S's creditors, her ability to have a transaction declared a sham should not be compromised by any deception practised by S; although, of course, the interests of any innocent third parties who have relied on the apparent trust must be taken into account.[75] 4–062

## ii. Defining a Sham

The notion of a sham is not, of course, specific to the law of trusts. In *Snook v London and West Riding Investments Ltd*, Diplock LJ, albeit reluctantly,[76] suggested the following definition of the concept[77]: 4–063

---

and the sham doctrine is not applied, it can still be said that the rights and powers given to S by the document are so extensive that S in fact has a beneficial interest in the trust property. Certain offshore jurisdictions, however, not wanting to deter potential settlors, have legislated to ensure that the reservation of certain types of rights and powers will not lead to a finding that S has a beneficial interest in the property, e.g. the Bermuda Trusts (Special Provisions) Act 1989 s.2 (as amended by the Trusts (Special Provisions) Amendment Act 2014).

70 *A v A* [2007] 2 F.L.R. 467 at [69]; *National Westminster Bank Plc v Jones* [2001] 1 B.C.L.C. 98 at [68]. It is a serious allegation involving dishonesty, and "the more serious the allegation the less likely it is that the event occurred and, hence, the stronger should be the evidence before the court concludes that the allegation is established on the balance of probability": *Re H (Minors)* [1996] A.C. 563 at 586.

71 Similarly, the mere fact that T in practice acquiesced in S's wishes without considering the terms of the trust does not render the document setting up the trust a sham, as it may be that T is simply acting in breach of the trust genuinely set up in that document: see *A v A* [2007] 2 F.L.R. 467 at [42].

72 See too, e.g. *Hitch v Stone* [2001] S.T.C. 214. Note too that, even if there is no sham and S did set up such a trust, such creditors may then attempt to rely on the "claw-back" provisions of the Insolvency Act 1986, as discussed at para.1–064.

73 See, e.g. *Shalson v Russo* [2005] Ch. 281 at [190]. In *Commissioner of Stamp Duties v Jolliffe* (1920) 28 C.L.R. 178, the High Court of Australia allowed S to rely on his own sham as against a taxing authority, but the dissent of Isaacs J has since been preferred: see, e.g. *Byrnes v Kendle* (2011) 243 C.L.R. 253.

74 [2008] 3 N.Z.L.R. 45.

75 See, e.g. *Carman v Yates* [2005] B.P.I.R. 476 at [219]–[220]; *National Westminster Bank Plc v Jones* [2001] 1 B.C.L.C. 98 at [60].

76 The statement set out here was prefaced by Diplock LJ's comment that: "it is, I think, necessary to consider what, if any, legal concept is involved in the use of this popular and pejorative word": [1967] 2 Q.B. 786 at 802.

77 [1967] 2 Q.B. 786 at 802. The reference to documents cannot mean that either all of a document is sham, or none of

> it means acts done or documents executed by the parties to the 'sham' which are intended by them to give to third parties or to the court the appearance of creating between the parties legal rights and obligations different from the actual legal rights and obligations (if any) which the parties intended to create. . .for acts or documents to be a 'sham', with whatever legal consequences follow from this, all the parties thereto must have a common intention that the acts or documents are not to create the legal rights and obligations which they give the appearance of creating. No unexpressed intentions of a 'shammer' affect the rights of a party whom he deceived.

**4–064** It is therefore clear that a degree of dishonesty is involved in a sham.[78] Whose intention is relevant when considering if a document apparently setting up a trust is a sham? In *Re Esteem Settlement*, the Royal Court of Jersey held that, where the apparent trust was set up by S's transfer of property to T to hold on trust,[79]

> in order to find a sham, the court must find that both the settlor and the trustee had the intention that the true position should be otherwise than as set out in the trust deed which they both executed.

**4–065** That reasoning was also adopted by Rimer J in *Shalson v Russo*[80]:

> When a settlor creates a settlement he purports to divest himself of assets in favour of the trustee, and the trustee accepts them on the basis of the trusts of the settlement. The settlor may have an unspoken intention that the assets are in fact to be treated as his own and that the trustee will accede to his every request on demand. But unless that intention is from the outset shared by the trustee (or later becomes so shared), I fail to see how the settlement can be regarded as a sham. Once the assets are vested in the trustee, they will be held on the declared trusts, and he is entitled to regard them as so held and to ignore any demands from the settlor as to how to deal with them. I cannot understand on what basis a third patry could claim, merely by reference to the unilateral intentions of the settlor, that the settlement was a sham and that the assets in fact remained the settlor's property. One might as well say that an apparently outright gift made by a donor can subsequently be held to be a sham on the basis of some unspoken intention of the donor not to part with the property in it. But if the donee accepted the gift on the footing that it was a genuine gift, the donor's undeclared intentions cannot turn an ostensibly valid disposition of his property into no disposition at all. To set that sort of case up the donee must also be shown to be a party to the alleged sham. In my judgment, in the case of a settlement executed by a settlor and a trustee, it is insufficient in considering whether or not it is a sham to look merely at the intentions of the settlor. It is essential also to look at those of the trustee.

**4–066** In *A v A*, Munby J similarly stated that[81]:

> [there should be no finding of sham where] the trust property has been vested in someone who accepts that he holds the property as trustee on the trusts of a document which he believes to be a genuine instrument. He has no intention that the arrangement should be a sham . . . What is required is a common *intention* [of S and T], but reckless indifference will be taken to constitute the necessary intention. [82]

---

it: see *Hitch v Stone* [2001] S.T.C. 214. Rather, each apparent creation of rights within a document must be seen as a relevant "act", and will only be valid if accompanied by the necessary intention that those rights should genuinely be created.

78 See, e.g. *National Westminster Bank Plc v Jones* [2001] 1 B.C.L.C. 98 at [46], [59], endorsed in *A v A* [2007] 2 F.L.R. 467 at [53].

79 [2003] J.L.R. 188 at [54].

80 [2005] Ch. 281 at [190].

81 [2007] 2 F.L.R. 467 at [46], [52].

82 Munby J. considered *Midland Bank v Wyatt* to be a case in which that test was satisfied, as Mrs Wyatt could be seen as having gone along with the sham "neither knowing or caring what [she was] signing": [2007] 2 F.L.R. 467 at [52], approving the analysis in *Re Esteem Settlement* [2003] J.L.R. 188 at [58].

There may seem to be a discrepancy between this requirement of common intention and the point made above,[83] that a settlor setting up an express trust is exercising her own power to do so, and can therefore act unilaterally.[84] However this tension can be resolved by seeing the sham doctrine as essentially evidential[85]: the court is asking when, in considering the intention of the settlor, it is possible to look beyond a signed document seemingly setting out that intention and instead to take account of factors such as the subsequent conduct of the relevant parties. Where that document has been executed by two parties, it seems that it can be disregarded only when both of those parties are, to some degree at least, involved in the deception. However, if a case were to involve a deed executed unilaterally and purporting to declare a trust of S's property, it is difficult to see how the intention of anyone other than S could be relevant.[86] Once the document is disregarded, the court can establish S's true intention. At that point, having made a decision as to the relevant evidence, and having undertaken an assessment of that evidence, the court can apply the standard test for the existence of an express trust.[87] **4–067**

### D. Mistakes

We have seen that S's intention to set up a trust has to be judged objectively, but that S's subjective intention to deceive will be relevant when considering if a document apparently setting up a trust can be disregarded as a sham. S's inward thought processes may also be relevant where S did express a genuine intention to set up a trust, but her decision to exercise her power to set up a trust was vitiated by a mistake. In these circumstances the court may allow her to rescind the settlement, provided that her decision to create the trust was caused by her mistake, and she made a mistake sufficiently serious to render the trust voidable.[88] When deciding whether to allow rescission, the court will also take into account matters such as the interests of third parties. This is all examined in more detail in Chapter 18.[89] **4–068**

## 3. Certainty of Subject-Matter

### A. The Nature of the Test

A trust can exist only if a trustee (T) is under a duty in relation to specific property held by T. To establish a valid express trust the settlor (S) must therefore make it certain what property is to be held on trust.[90] For example, in *Boyce v Boyce*,[91] S bequeathed two houses to T on trust to convey whichever **4–069**

83 See para.4–004.

84 This point is explored by J. Palmer [2008] N.Z.L.J. 319, although note the reply to Palmer's analysis by M. Conaglen, "Trusts and Intention" in E. Simpson and M. Stewart (eds), *Sham Transactions* (2013), paras 7.36–7.66.

85 This seems to be the effect of the analysis in M. Conaglen, "Sham Trusts" [2008] CL.J. 176 and M. Conaglen, "Trusts and Intention", ibid.

86 See, e.g. *Painter v Hutchison* [2008] B.P.I.R. 170 at [111]–[112]. At [115], Lewison J offered one way of explaining this point: "where there is a simple unilateral declaration of trust, the settlor and the trustee are one and the same person. So even if it is necessary to consider the intention of both the settlor and the trustee, in practice that amounts to the same thing as considering the intention of the settlor alone."

87 This the argument of B. McFarlane and E. Simpson, "Tackling Avoidance" in J. Getzler (ed.), *Rationalizing Property, Equity and Trusts: Essays in Honour of Edward Burn* (Oxford University Press, 2003).

88 *Pitt v Holt* [2013] 2 A.C. 108.

89 See paras 18–253ff.

90 *Palmer v Simmonds* (1854) 2 Drew. 221 at 227 ("the bulk of my residuary estate" cannot satisfy the certainty requirement though "my residuary estate" can); *Re London Wine Co (Shippers) Ltd* [1986] P.C.C. 121 (settlor cannot declare itself trustee of unascertained 20 out of 80 bottles of Château Lafite 1970 in its cellar though it could declare it held its holding of 80 bottles on trust as for three-quarters for itself and one-quarter for X).

91 (1849) 16 Sim. 476.

house Maria should choose to Maria and to convey the other to Charlotte. Maria died before S and so could not make a selection. It was held that the trust in favour of Charlotte was void for uncertainty of subject matter.

**4–070** The need to identify the specific property to which B's right relates is certainly not unique to trusts: it is present in any case where B claims a legal or equitable property right. For example, no matter what the intention of the parties may have been, no property can pass in a sale of goods unless the specific goods have been identified, either by the terms of the parties' contract or by later ascertainment and appropriation.[92] As noted by Lord Mustill in *Re Goldcorp Exchange Ltd*,[93] this need for identification (as well as intention) is not some "arid legal technicality" but rather depends on "the very nature of things".[94] In that case, for example, the vendor had promised to sell a particular quantity of gold bullion to each customer, but the promise did not relate to any *specific* bullion, and so, even if a customer paid in advance, she could acquire no legal title. Seeking protection from the consequences of the vendor's insolvency, such customers instead claimed that a trust had arisen. This claim, as far as it related to any particular bullion,[95] failed for exactly the same reason: the subject-matter of the supposed equitable property right could not be identified.

## B. Applying the Test

**4–071** The test does not require the subject matter of a gift or trust to be identified before the time when the gift or trust takes effect. In a will, therefore, S can validly make a disposition of "the residue of my estate" as the property comprised in that residue will be clear by the time when the gift or trust takes effect, as the executors will have met any debts and taxes due from the estate and have distributed any specific legacies. Similarly, of course, a gift or trust in relation to "half of the residue of my estate" would be valid; a disposition of "the bulk of my residuary estate" would however be too uncertain,[96] unless clear guidance could be found as to a particular meaning of the term "bulk" intended by S.

**4–072** Where S makes a lifetime transfer of property to T to hold on trust for B, the identity of the trust property will necessarily be certain by virtue of the transfer. However, identifiability problems can arise in cases where S purports to declare herself trustee of some of her property without clearly identifying that property. For example, if S purports to declare herself trustee for B of 20 of her 80 gold bars, then (just as would be the case if a contract for sale was made on those terms) B acquires no interest until 20 bars have been ascertained and appropriated to the transaction with B.[97]

**4–073** The position is different, however, if S declares a trust under which B has a 25 per cent share of S's interest in the 80 gold bars. In such a case, the subject-matter of B's equitable property right *is* identified: it is the all of the 80 gold bars. B's interest allows her a share in the benefit of S's single right to the identified 80 bars. For the same reason, property can pass immediately in a contract for the sale of a 25 per cent share in S's right to the 80 bars.

---

92 Sale of Goods Act 1979 s.16.

93 [1995] 1 A.C. 74 at 90.

94 This is in turn a reference to C. Blackburn, *The Effect of the Contract of Sale* (William Benning and Co, 1845), p.123.

95 The customers also attempted to claim that the pre-payment of the price was held on a trust imposed by law. No such trust could arise, however, as the contract had not imposed any limit on the use the vendors could make of the money: the claimed trust of the money therefore failed for the same reason as the trust claimed in *Westdeutsche Landesbank Girozentrale v Islington LBC* [1996] A.C. 669: see paras para.14–028.

96 *Palmer v Simmonds* (1854) 2 Drew 221.

97 *Re London Wine Co Shippers Ltd* [1986] P.C.C. 121; *Re Stapylton Fletcher Ltd* [1995] 1 All E.R. 192; *Re Goldcorp Exchange* [1995] 1 A.C. 74. Some of the practical problems in the sale of goods context have now been remedied by Sale of Goods (Amendment) Act 1995.

In *Hunter v Moss*,[98] the question was whether a trust could arise as a result of a declaration that S held 50 of his 950 shares in a particular private company on trust for B. The Court of Appeal affirmed the view of the first instance judge that there was sufficient certainty of subject-matter and so a trust arose. Dillon LJ stated that [99]: **4–074**

> Just as a person can give, by will, a specified number of his shares of a certain class in a certain company, so equally, in my judgment, he can declare himself a trustee of 50 of his ordinary shares in [a company] and that is effective to give a beneficial proprietary interest to the beneficiary under the trust.

This particular reasoning can be criticised. If S has made a will, then on her death, S's rights in all her assets are transferred to her executor, who is then obliged to implement S's wishes subject to payment of debts, expenses and taxes. At no point does the executor have the free enjoyment of the property for herself. In contrast, where S purports to declare an inter vivos trust of property of which she is currently the full beneficial owner, it could be said that her attempt to constitute a trust of some of this property should be complete only when she has taken the further step of identifying the specific property to be held on trust. It could be argued that, until then, S has simply made an imperfect gift. **4–075**

It may nonetheless be possible to support the approach in *Hunter v Moss* on different grounds. The principle in the case was usefully summarised by Briggs J in *Re Lehman Brothers International (Europe)*,[100] who then went on to discuss the nature of the trust recognised in that case: **4–076**

> A trust of part of a fungible mass without the appropriation of any specific part of it for the beneficiary does not fail for uncertainty of subject matter, provided that the mass itself is sufficiently indentified and provided also that the beneficiary's proportionate share of it is not itself uncertain . . . *Hunter v Moss* has not been without its academic and judicial critics, but its conclusion that there is no objection on the grounds of uncertainty to a trust of part of a shareholding of a trustee has been generally followed, in this country,[101] in Hong Kong,[102] and in Australia.[103] . . . The difficulty with applying the Court of Appeal's judgment in *Hunter v Moss* to any case not on almost identical facts lies in the absence of any clearly expressed rationale as to how such a trust works in practice. There has not been unanimity among those courts which have followed *Hunter v Moss*, nor among the many academics who have commented on it, as to the correct approach. The analysis which I have found the most persuasive is that such a trust works by creating a beneficial co-ownership share in the identifed fund, rather than in the conceptually much more difficult notion of seeking to identify a particular part of that fund which the beneficiary owns outright.[104]

On this view, the key point in *Hunter v Moss* is that S was dealing with shares and not, for example, with gold. A share, by definition, is simply a proportionate part of a total set of entitlements, held by the complete body of shareholders, in relation to a company.[105] So, if dealing with a shareholding of shares of the same type, S is already dealing in proportions. A declaration of trust of 50 of S's 950 shares can therefore be interpreted as a declaration of trust under which B becomes beneficially **4–077**

---

98 [1994] 1 W.L.R. 452; criticised by D.J. Hayton (1994) 110 L.Q.R. 335; followed in an undefended case as applicable to intangibles but not tangibles: *Re Harvard Securities Ltd* [1997] 2 B.C.L.C. 369.

99 [1994] 1 W.L.R. 452 at 459.

100 [2010] EWHC 2914 (Ch) at [225]. The decision of Briggs J. was affirmed by the Court of Appeal: [2012] 2 B.C.L.C. 151.

101 *Re Harvard Securities Ltd (in liq.)* [1997] 2 B.C.L.C. 369.

102 *Re CA Pacific Finance Ltd* [2000] 1 B.C.L.C. 494.

103 [2006] NSWSC 1379 [after a very thorough analysis of the authorities and of academic views].

104 [Reference was made here to R. Goode, "Are Intangible Assets Fungibles?" [2003] L.M.C.L.Q. 309 and the judgment of Campbell J in *White v Shortall* [2006] NSWSC 1379 at [212].]

105 See R. Goode "Are Intangible Assets Fungibles?" [2003] L.M.C.L.Q. 309, although note the contrary argument (in relation to private companies such as that in *Hunter v Moss*) made by G. Morton in *Commercial Law and Commercial Practice*, edited by S. Worthington (Hart Publishing, 2003), pp.296–302.

entitled to a 1/19th share of S's chose in action against the company constituted by all of the 950 shares: it is thus the same as a declaration of trust of a 25 per cent share of 80 gold bars.[106] In contrast, if S instead declares a trust of 20 of her 80 gold bars, that *cannot*, by itself, be interpreted as a declaration of trust of a 25 per cent share of S's right to the whole 80 bars, as each gold bar is a specific thing, and has a specific existence independent of any broader right.

**4–078** There is certainly some evidence that, following *Hunter v Moss*, the courts have been readier to find that the requirement for certainty of subject-matter has been met. In *Re Lehman Brothers International (Europe),*[107] for example, it was reasonably clear that the parties had intended to create a system where T, acting as a hub for buying and selling shares and other securities for all Lehman affiliate companies in Europe, would acquire rights from third parties on behalf of the affiliates, and would then hold those rights on trust for the affiliates. On the collapse of Lehman Brothers, different companies within the group had different creditors, and some of those creditors disputed whether the parties' arrangements had indeed created a trust, instead arguing that T in fact held full title to the securities.

**4–079** This argument was based on the fact that the parties had agreed that, although T held the securities for and on account of the affiliates, T was also free to deal with those securities for its own benefit (for example by lending them, or by transferring them to third parties in order to satisfy its own contracts with such third parties) provided that, when the affiliate accounts were settled at the end of each day, T was able to provide the correct number and type of securities to each affiliate. It was therefore argued that the apparent trust lacked certainty of subject-matter, as T's ultimate duty related purely to the number and type of securities and so did not relate to any specific property held by T, as that duty could be satisfied by using securities acquired from elsewhere, not the securities initially acquired on behalf of a particular affiliate.

**4–080** Briggs J, whilst noting that the facts of the case were much more complicated than those in *Hunter v Moss*,[108] held that the certainty of subject matter requirement had nonetheless been satisfied. The point was that if, for example, T at one point acquired 100 ordinary ICI shares on behalf of an individual affiliate company (B), the subject matter of the trust would then be T's total holding of such shares, as well as any rights of T arising as a result out of its future dealings with such shares (such as rights against third parties to whom T might lend the shares or sell the shares). It was argued that problems could arise if there was, at any point, a shortfall, so that the current rights held by T did not suffice to meet its duties to the affiliates; but Briggs J found that, as all the parties had consented to the arrangement, and thus to the possibility of a shortfall, it could be implied that they had consented to "bear the consequences of the shortfall equally".[109]

**4–081** Moreover, whilst there might be points in time when T had disposed of shares without gaining any rights against third parties as a result, and so (consistently with the terms of the agreement) would have to reconstitute the fund by acquiring such shares, "a trust does not fail for want of certainty merely because its subject matter is to consist of after-acquired property"[110] as even though at a particular point its subject matter might be uncertain, the trust can be valid if "the terms of the trust are sufficient to identify its subject matter in the future."[111] On this point, it is worth noting that the

---

106 Note that where S is dealing with shares in a public company, it is almost certain (see paras 1–071 and 3–104) that S has only an equitable interest, as the shares are held through intermediaries, and S's equitable interest is very likely to be a proportionate one in a bigger pool of such shares held by an intermediary higher up the chain: in such a case, any declaration of trust of S's shares is necessarily a dealing in relation to co-ownership of a bigger pool of such shares.
107 [2010] EWHC 2914 (Ch) at [225]. The decision of Briggs J was affirmed by the Court of Appeal: [2012] 2 B.C.L.C. 151.
108 ibid., at [239]
109 ibid., at [244].
110 ibid., at [235].
111 ibid., at [225].

arrangement between the parties was not gratuitous: T had a binding contractual duty to reconstitute the fund by acquiring the necessary shares. It may therefore be possible to draw on the principle applied in cases such as *Pullan v Koe*,[112] and to find that a trust therefore arose immediately on T's acquisition of such shares.[113]

The broader issue in *Lehman Brothers*, which has arisen in a number of contexts, is the extent to which commercial parties can secure the advantages that come from establishing a trust, whilst at the same time giving the supposed trustee a wide power to deal with the trust property, or giving parties other than the supposed beneficiaries significant powers in relation to the decisions made by the trustees.[114] Briggs J's approach to this broader question is evident from his statement that[115]: **4–082**

> The law does not lightly allow contracting parties' purposes and intentions to be defeated by supposed uncertainty, and there is in my judgment no reason why the law should do so any more readily than normal merely because the issue is as to the validity of an intended trust. On the contrary, the law commonly recognises the creation of a trust as a necessary consequence of an intention that parties should share property beneficially, in circumstances where the parties themselves have given no thought at all to the terms of the consequential trust, if indeed they even recognised its existence. In all such cases the law fills the consequential gaps by impliaction, and by importation of generally applicable principles.

Indeed, as shown by Briggs J's drawing of an analogy with common intention constructive trusts of the family home,[116] this judicial desire to give effect, where possible, to an intention to establish a trust can be seen beyond the commercial sphere. *Hunter v Moss* itself provides an example of the court's willingness to take a practical, rather than an overly-technical, approach when applying the test for certainty of subject-matter. Rimer QC, deciding the case at first instance, stated that[117] **4–083**

> the question of whether in any particular case there is such certainty depends, or ought to depend, not on the application of any Immutable principle based on the requirements of a need for segregation or appropriation, but rather on whether immediately after the purported declaration of trust, the court could, if asked, make an order for the execution of the purported trust. In any particular case it could and will only do so if, inter alia, the subject matter of the trust is identified with sufficient certainty.

In *Re Golay's Will Trusts*,[118] for example, a gift in a will directing that B should receive "a reasonable income" was upheld as valid, as the testator was regarded as having "given a sufficient indication of his intention to provide an effective determinant of what he intends so that the court in applying that determinant can give effect to the testator's intention". This was because the term was interpreted as requiring an objective assessment of reasonableness, such as courts are accustomed to making, which did not depend on the testator's subjective or personal view. As we will now see, this emphasis on whether the terms of the supposed gift or trust are clear enough to enable the court to ensure that those terms have been complied with is also evident when considering the third of the three certainties. **4–084**

---

112 [1913] 1 Ch. 9. See paras 2–072ff.

113 But note, strictly speaking, this trust is a constructive one.

114 See too *Citibank NA v MBIA Assurance SA* [2007] 1 All E.R. (Comm) 475.

115 [2010] EWHC 2914 (Ch) at [245].

116 Briggs J went on to note ([2010] EWHC 2914 (Ch) at [245]) that, in the "protracted and difficult debate" as to the common intention constructive trust of the family home (as to which, see paras 16–046ff), it has never been suggested that the parties' failure to specify the extent of B's beneficial interest causes the trust to fail for uncertainty.

117 *Hunter v Moss* [1993] 1 W.L.R. 934 at 945 (affirmed on appeal: [1994] 1 W.L.R. 452).

118 [1965] 1 W.L.R. 969 at 971.

## 4. Certainty of Objects

### A. The Nature of the Tests

4-085 The third of the three certainities, which can also be referred to as requiring "certainty of objects", is, again, based on an underlying principle that is not unique to the law of trusts. A trust necessarily involves T holding property subject to a duty; a contract, for example, also involves a contracting party (call her D) being under a duty to another. Such a duty can exist only where it is possible for a court to enforce it. This means two things. First, a court must be able to *police* the duty: it must be able to tell if particular action by T (or D) is or is not a breach of the duty. Secondly, a court must be able to *enforce* the duty: in the event of T (or D)'s failure to perform the duty, the court must be able to make an order that gives effect to the content of the duty. A valid trust, like a valid contract, must therefore provide a court with sufficient information to police and enforce the supposed duty imposed on T or on D. This form of certainty is therefore a requirement of a valid contract as well as of a valid trust.

4-086 There may also be relationships which a court must police, but need not enforce. This is the case where T has a *power* to act in a certain way, but no duty to act. For example, S may transfer property to T to hold on trust for B, but with a power for T to appoint up to one half of the property to "any of [S's] old friends". T has no duty to make any such appointment, and so a court will never be called upon to enforce the power. The court does need to ensure, however, that any purported exercise of the power by T is valid. This means that if T chooses, for example, to exercise the power in favour of X, and B challenges the exercise of that power, the court needs to be able to tell if X is, or is not, an "old friend" of S. If the term "old friend" is so uncertain that a court will simply be unable to make such an assessment, then the power cannot be policed, and so it will be invalid.

4-087 It is therefore clear that when a court deals with questions of certainty of objects, we first need to ask what limits S intended to impose on T, in order to see what information is required for a court to police and (if necessary) enforce such limits. We must first, therefore, consider the different possibilities. We will start with arrangements with the least demanding certainty of objects requirements, and move up to those with the most demanding.

### B. Identifying the Test to be Applied

#### i. Gifts Subject to a Condition Precedent

4-088 In *Re Barlow's Will Trusts*,[119] a testatrix (S) instructed her executor "to allow any member of my family and any friends of mine who may wish to do so to purchase" particular paintings in her estate at a low valuation. The term "friend" seems like a clear example of an uncertain term: how could a court tell in practice if X is or is not within that class? However, Browne-Wilkinson J held the disposition to be valid. His reasoning turned on the fact that the testatrix had effectively made a series of individual gifts to persons answering the description of her blood relations or friends, since the effect of the disposition was to confer on such persons a series of options to purchase at a low price. This was important as, if the disposition was invalidated, this would result in the loss of property to any person who clearly

119 [1979] 1 W.L.R. 278. This was the test suggested by Lord Denning in *Re Gulbenkian's ST* [1968] Ch. 126 at 134 for judging certainty of powers and rejected by the House of Lords on appeal. "Jewish faith and parentage" was held void for uncertainty in *Clayton v Ramsden* [1943] A.C. 320 but in *Re Tepper's WT* [1987] Ch. 358 Scott J was reluctant to find "Jewish faith" uncertain and so adjourned the case to see if evidence of the Jewish faith as practised by the testator would clarify the matter. Both cases involved conditions subsequent.

was, on any view, a member of S's family or friend of S. This suggested that as long as S had just one friend (on anyone's definition of that word), invaliding the instruction to S's executor as regards friends would, in effect, deprive that person of a clear property right.

Certainly, there was no need to have a complete list of all family members and friends, as all that was required was for the executors to be able to say of any individual coming forward whether or not she had proved that she was a relation or friend. The risk of the executors allowing someone not truly entitled to buy a painting (e.g. X, who was not in fact a friend of S) could therefore be dealt with by other means, e.g. by presuming that, if X cannot show that she is clearly within the class of "member of my family" or "friends", then X is not within that class and no gift need be made to her.[120] Such an approach may create some practical difficulties for the executors, who may have awkward decisions to make, but that disadvantage, it seems, is the price of ensuring that the vested property rights of any clear friends are upheld. **4–089**

In *Re Barlow's Will Trusts*, Browne-Wilkinson J relied on *Re Allen*,[121] where the Court of Appeal had upheld a bequest "to the eldest of the sons of [S] who shall be a member of the Church of England and an adherent to the doctrine of that Church". By upholding this gift, the court gave the eldest son the chance to establish that he met the condition imposed on the gift. It was not necessary for the executors to be able to tell of a hypothetical X whether or not X met the condition: they simply had to consider, in turn according to age, each of the sons of S. As Lord Evershed MR observed in *Re Allen*,[122] a gift to "B if he is a tall man" should not be invalidated, as B, if he is 6ft 6ins, should not be deprived of the gift. **4–090**

Certainly, if there are a small number of ascertainable possible recipients of the gift, it seems reasonable that each should be given the chance to show that she comes within the "core" meaning of the qualifying condition, even if that term is conceptually uncertain, in the sense that a clear meaning, enabling marginal cases to be decided, cannot be found.[123] **4–091**

### ii. Non-Fiduciary Powers

It is possible for a settlor S to give a party who is not a trustee a power in relation to trust property. For example, S could give property to trustees to hold on trust for B, whilst also giving P, S's sister, a power to order the trustees to advance up to half of the trust fund to any of S's friends. In such a case, there is a question as to whether S intended P to be under any duties in relation to the exercise of that power—such as, for example, a duty to consider periodically whether or not to exercise that power. Such duties are generally assumed to arise where S gives a power to a trustee, T, because T, as a trustee, is a fiduciary. If, instead, S gives a power to someone such as P who is not expected to have similar responsibilties, then there is no such presumption.[124] **4–092**

Where P has no such duties, P may be called a holder of a "non-fiduciary power" or "bare power". In such a case, the court's only concern in policing the exercise of the power is to ensure that P does not exercise the power in favour of someone who is outside the class specified by S. This means that the court needs to be able to tell of any given person whether or not that person is inside the class: should **4–093**

---

120 That was the approach taken to relatives by Megaw and Sachs LJJ in *Re Baden's Deed Trusts (No.2)* [1973] Ch. 9: see paras 4–167—4–170.

121 [1953] Ch. 810.

122 [1953] Ch. 810 at 817.

123 See, e.g. L. McKay [1980] Conv. 263 at 277; C.T. Emery (1982) 98 L.Q.R. 551 at 564.

124 Indeed, if the power given to P is one which P can also exercise for her own benefit, then it will be difficult to see it as a fiduciary power, as the ability to act in one's own self-interest is inconsistent with the basic nature of fiduciary duties: see paras 9–018—9–019.

P exercise the power in favour of X, and B then challenges that disposition, the court will then be able to tell if the exercise of the power was valid. This test is often called the "given postulant" test or the "is or is not" test. It is of great importance in practice, as it also applies in the much more common case where a power is given to a trustee.

**4–094** It seems that a power to make dispositions in favour of any "friend" of S will not pass this "is or is not" test, as the term is not sufficiently certain to enable a court to decide, in a marginal case, if X is nor is not in the class. This may be unfortunate for C, a party who was, on any view of the concept of friendship, a friend of S. It is important to note, however, that the invalidity of the power does not deprive C of any vested property right, but only of the possibility that P would have exercised the power in C's favour. This explains why the more relaxed test applied to conditional gifts[125] does not apply to powers. In *Re Gulbenkian's Settlement Trusts*,[126] the House of Lords therefore rejected the view of Lord Denning MR in the Court of Appeal that, in the case of a power,[127] it was only necessary to show that any one person is clearly within the class. Lord Upjohn stated that[128]

> with respect to mere powers, while the court cannot compel the trustees to execise their powers, yet those entitled to the fund in default must clearly be entitled to restrain the trustees from exercising it save among those within the power. So the trustees, or the court, must be able to say with certainty who is within and who is without the power.

### iii. Fiduciary Powers

**4–095** Consider a case in which a settlor S gives property to a trustee T to hold on trust for a beneficiary B, whilst also giving T a power to advance up to half of the trust fund to any of S's friends. As in the case of a non-fiduciary power, the court will have to police the power by ensuring that it is not exercised in favour of anyone outside that class, and so the "is or is not" test will be applied. In this case, however, T's power is a fiduciary one because she holds it in her capacity as trustee. This means that T will be under further duties: the question is whether the existence of such duties means that a higher standard of certainty is required than in the case of a non-fiduciary power. Those questions were considered by Megarry VC in the following extract, which draws an explicit link between the nature of the duties that S seeks to impose and the certainty required of S's settlement.

**4–096** At various points in the extract Megarry VC refers to a "mere power" vested in trustees, by which he means a fiduciary power that the trustees need not exercise. Megarry VC uses this term to differentiate the power from a power that the trustees owe a duty to exercise in some way. Confusingly, the latter type of power is sometimes called a "trust power",[129] but, as it gives rise to a discretionary trust, we will examine it further below.[130]

> *Re Hay's Settlement Trusts*
>
> Chancery Division [1982] 1 W.L.R. 202
>
> **4–097** By clause 4 of Lady Hay's settlement made in 1958, trustees held the trust fund
>
> > "on trust for such persons or purposes for such interests and with such gifts over and (if for persons) with such provisions for their respective maintenance or advancement at the discretion of the Trustees

---

[125] See paras 4–088—4–091.
[126] [1970] A.C. 508.
[127] The case itself concerned fiduciary powers, but the reasoning also applies to non-fiduciary powers.
[128] [1970] A.C. 508 at 525.
[129] As in, e.g. *Re Baden (No.1)* [1971] A.C. 424 (extracted below at paras 4–119—4–136).
[130] See paras 4–117ff.

> or of any other persons as the Trustees shall by any deed or deeds revocable or irrevocable (but if revocable not after the expiration of 21 years from the date hereof) executed within 21 years from the date hereof appoint . . . and in default of such appointment in trust for the nieces and nephews of the Settlor now living in equal shares."

A proviso precluded any appointment being made to the settlor, any husband of her, and any trustee or past trustee. For the first five years income was to be accumulated and then the income was to be held on discretionary trusts for the nieces and nephews or charities until the clause 4 power of appointment was exercised or ceased to be exercisable (by expiry of the 21 years). In 1969 a deed of appointment was executed, clause 1 conferring a power of appointment on the trustees (exercisable till expiry of the 21-year period in the 1958 settlement) to hold "the trust fund and the income thereof on trust for such persons and such persons as shall be appointed." Clause 2 directed that the undisposed-of income (until full exercise of the clause 1 power) be held on discretionary trusts for the benefit of any persons whatsoever (the settlor, any husband of her, any existing or former trustee excepted) or for any charity. The questions arose: (i) whether or not the very wide power of appointment in the 1958 settlement was valid; and (ii) if it was valid then whether its purported exercise by the trustees in 1969 was void in creating a very wide discretionary trust that was either an impermissible delegation by the trustees of their power under the 1958 settlement, or was in itself void as th planned discretionary trust was administratively unworkable? The first question is our focus here, and it was decided in favour of validity; on the second question, however, it was decided that the very wide discretionary trust involved an impermissible delegation by the trustees of their powers under the 1958 settlement.

MEGARRY V.-C.: . . . The starting point must be to consider whether the power created by the first limb of clause 4 of the settlement is valid. . . . The essential point is whether a power for trustees to appoint to anyone in the world except a handful of specified persons is valid. Such a power will be perfectly valid if given to a person who is not in a fiduciary position: the difficulty arises when it is given to trustees, for they are under certain fiduciary duties in relation to the power, and to a limited degree they are subject to the control of the courts. . . **4–098**

In *Re Manisty's Settlement*[131] a settlement gave trustees a discretionary power to apply the trust fund for the benefit of a small class of the settlor's near relations, save that any member of a smaller "excepted class" was to be excluded from the class of beneficiaries. The trustees were also given power at their absolute discretion to declare that any person, corporation or charity (except a member of the excepted class or a trustee) should be included in the class of beneficiaries. Templeman J. held that this power to extend the class of beneficiaries was valid. . . **4–099**

I propose to approach the matter by stages. First, it is plain that if a power of appointment is given to a person who is not in a fiduciary position, there is nothing in the width of the power which invalidates it per se. The power may be a special power with a large class of persons as objects; the power may be what is called a "hybrid" power, or an "intermediate" power, authorising appointment to anyone save a specified number or class of persons; or the power may be a general power. Whichever it is, there is nothing in the number of persons to whom an appointment may be made which will invalidate it. The difficulty comes when the power is given to trustees as such, in that the number of objects may interact with the fiduciary duties of the trustees and their control by the court. The argument of counsel for the defendants carried him to the extent of asserting that no valid intermediate or general power could be vested in trustees. **4–100**

That brings me to the second point, namely, the extent of the fiduciary obligations of trustees who have a mere power vested in them, and how far the court exercises control over them in relation to that power. In the case of a trust, of course, the trustee is bound to execute it, and if he does not, the court will see to its execution. A mere power is very different. Normally the trustee is not bound to exercise it, and the court will not compel him to do so. That, however, does not mean that he can simply fold his hands and ignore it, for normally he must from time to time consider whether or not to exercise the power, and the court may direct him to do this. **4–101**

When he does exercise the power, he must, of course (as in the case of all trusts and powers) confine himself to what is authorised, and not go beyond it. But that is not the only restriction. Whereas a person who is not in a fiduciary position is free to exercise the power in any way that he wishes, unhampered by any fiduciary duties, a trustee to whom, as such, a power is given is bound by the duties of his office **4–102**

---

131 [1974] Ch. 17.

in exercising that power to do so in a responsible manner according to its purpose. It is not enough for him to refrain from acting capriciously; he must do more. He must "make such a survey of the range of objects or possible beneficiaries" as will enable him to carry out his fiduciary duty. He must find out "the permissible area of selection and then consider responsibly, in individual cases, whether a contemplated beneficiary was within the power and whether, in relation to the possible claimants, a particular grant was appropriate"[132] . . .

4-103 That brings me to the third point. How is the duty of making a responsible survey and selection to be carried out in the absence of any complete list of objects? This question was considered by the Court of Appeal in *Re Baden (No.2)*. That case was concerned with what, after some divergences of judicial opinion, was held to be a discretionary trust and not a mere power; but plainly the requirements for a mere power cannot be more stringent than those for a discretionary trust. The duty, I think, may be expressed along the following lines. The trustee must not simply proceed to exercise the power in favour of such of the objects as happen to be at hand or claim his attention. He must first consider what persons or classes of persons are objects of the power within the definition in the settlement or will. In doing this, there is no need to compile a complete list of the objects, or even to make an accurate assessment of the number of them: what is needed is an appreciation of the width of the field, and thus whether a selection is to be made merely from a dozen or, instead, from thousands or millions. . . . Only when the trustee has applied his mind to "the size of the problem" should he then consider in individual cases whether, in relation to other possible claimants, a particular grant is appropriate. In doing this, no doubt he should not prefer the undeserving to the deserving; but he is not required to make an exact calculation whether, as between deserving claimants, A is more deserving than B.[133]

4-104 If I am right in these views, the duties of a trustee which are specific to a mere power seem to be threefold. Apart from the obvious duty of obeying the trust instrument, and in particular of making no appointment that is not authorised by it, the trustee must, first, consider periodically whether or not he should exercise the power; second, consider the range of objects of the power; and third, consider the appropriateness of individual appointments. I do not assert that this list is exhaustive; but as the authorities stand it seems to me to include the essentials, so far as relevant to the case before me.

4-105 On this footing, the question is thus whether there is something in the nature of an intermediate power which conflicts with these duties in such a way as to invalidate the power if it is vested in a trustee. . .I do not see how mere numbers can inhibit the trustees from considering whether or not to exercise the power, as distinct from deciding in whose favour to exercise it.

4-106 The second ground of [claimed invalidity] seems to be that the power is so wide that it would be impossible for the trustees to consider in any sensible manner how to exercise it, and also impossible for the court to say whether or not they were properly exercising it. With respect, I do not see how that follows. If I have correctly stated the extent of the duties of trustees in whom a mere power is vested, I do not see what there is to prevent the trustees from performing these duties. [In *Re Baden (No.2)*,[134] the Court of Appeal explained] how the trustees should make a survey and consider individual appointments in cases where no complete list of objects could be compiled. I also have in mind that the settlor in the present case is still alive, though I do not rest my decision on that.

4-107 From what I have said it will be seen that I cannot see any ground on which the power in question can be said to be void. Certainly it is not void for linguistic or semantic uncertainty; there is no room for doubt in the definition of those who are or are not objects of the power. Nor can I see that the power is administratively unworkable. The words of Lord Wilberforce in *Re Baden (No.1)*[135] are directed to discretionary trusts, not powers. Nor do I think that the power is void as being capricious. In *Re Manisty's Settlement*[136] Templeman J. appears to be suggesting that a power to benefit "residents in Greater London" is void as being capricious "because the terms of the power negative any sensible intention on the part of the settlor". In saying that, I do not think that the judge had in mind a case in which the settlor was, for instance, a former chairman of the Greater London Council, as subsequent words of his on that page indicate. In any case, as he pointed out earlier, this consideration does not apply to intermediate powers, where no class which could

---

132 *Re Baden (No.1)* [1971] A.C. 424 at 449 and 457, per Lord Wilberforce.
133 See *Re Gestetner, deceased* [1953] Ch. 672 at 688, approved in *Re Baden (No.1)* [1971] A.C. 424 at 453.
134 [1973] Ch. 9.
135 [1971] A.C. 424 at 457.
136 [1974] Ch. 17 at 27.

be regarded as capricious has been laid down. Nor do I see how the power in the present case could be invalidated as being too vague, a possible ground of invalidity considered in *Re Manisty's Settlement*.[137] Of course, if there is some real vice in a power, and there are real problems of administration or execution, the court may have to hold the power invalid: but I think that the court should be slow to do this. Dispositions ought if possible to be upheld, and the court ought not to be astute to find grounds on which a power can be invalidated. Naturally, if it is shown that a power offends against some rule of law or equity, then it will be held to be void: but a power should not be held void on a peradventure. In my judgment, the power conferred by clause 4 of the settlement is valid.

[Megarry VC then accepted the argument that "clause 2 of the deed of appointment is void as being an excessive execution of the power" as it involved an impermissible delegation of that power by the trustees of the 1958 settlement to the trustees of the 1969 discretionary trust]. . . **4–108**

That, I think, suffices to dispose of the case. I have not dealt with the submission which counsel for the defendants put in the forefront of his argument. This was that even if the power had been wide enough to authorise the creation of the discretionary trust, that trust was nevertheless as bad as being a trust in favour of "so hopelessly wide" a definition of beneficiaries "as not to form anything like a class so that the trust is administratively unworkable".[138] I do not propose to go into the authorities on this point. I consider that the duties of trustees under a discretionary trust are more stringent than those of trustees under a power of appointment,[139] and as at present advised I think that I would, if necessary, hold that an intermediate trust such as that in the present case is void as being administratively unworkable. In my view there is a difference between a power and a trust in this respect. The essence of that difference, I think, is that beneficiaries under a trust have rights of enforcement which mere objects of a power lack. **4–109**

[He then held that the nieces and nephews living at the date of the settlement had become entitled to the trust fund on the expiration of 21 years from the date of the settlement by virtue of the gift over in default of any valid appointment within the 21 years.] **4–110**

The analysis of Megarry VC is very helpful as it makes clear the link between the certainty of objects test and the nature of the duties owed by the holder of a power. Like the holder of a non-fiduciary power, the holder of a fiduciary power is unable to exercise the power in favour of someone outside the permitted class, and so the "is or is not" certainty test must be met.[140] In addition, however, the holder of a fiduciary power also has, at least,[141] the three duties identified by Megarry VC[142]: (i) to consider periodically whether or not he should exercise the power; (ii) to consider the range of objects of the power; and (iii) to consider the appropriateness of individual appointments. **4–111**

As held by Megarry VC,[143] the width of the class does not in itself prevent T from fulfilling those duties. It is important that T can carry them out without having a complete list of all potential objects. In *Re Baden (No.2)*,[144] for example, Megaw LJ stated that (even in relation to a discretionary trust), there is no need for T to ascertain all of the possible objects: as long as a substantial number of objects can clearly be identified, T can proceed to consider how to exercise the power to select particular objects as recipients of part of the fund. **4–112**

It could instead be argued, in the words of Lord Upjohn in *Re Gulbenkian's Settlement Trusts*,[145] that: **4–113**

---

137 [1974] Ch. 17 at 24.
138 *Re Baden (No.1)* [1971] A.C. 424 at 457 per Lord Wilberforce.
139 See *Re Baden (No.1)* [1971] A.C. 424 at 457.
140 This may be the point that Templeman J had in mind in *Re Manisty's Settlement Trusts* [1974] Ch. 17 at 24 when stating that a power may be invalid if "too vague".
141 Note Megarry VC's statement that "I do not assert that this list is exhaustive": [1982] 1 W.L.R. 202 at 210 (extracted at para.4–104).
142 [1982] 1 W.L.R. 202 at 210 (extracted at para.4–104).
143 Preferring the analysis of Templeman J in *Re Manisty's Settlement Trusts* [1974] Ch. 17 to the obiter views of Buckley LJ in *Blausten v IRC* [1972] Ch. 256.
144 [1973] Ch. 9 at 24.
145 [1970] A.C. 508 at 524.

> The trustees have a duty to select the donees of the donor's bounty from among the class designated by the donor; he has not entrusted them with any power to select the donees merely from known claimants who are within the class, for that is constituting a narower class and the donor has given them no power to do this.

The practical difficulty, however, is that if a complete list of all potential objects were required, the flexibility available to S by conferring a power on trustees would be severely reduced. The most significant way of departing from S's intentions, of course, is to find that a power is invalid with the effect that those entitled in default of the exercise of the power take absolutely, without any chance for the power to be exercised. It is therefore reasonable for a court to presume that, in order for the power to be valid, S would be content with T, when considering the exercise of the power, to have an "appreciation of the width of the field",[146] rather than a duty to survey the whole field. This coincides with the point that we noted above in relation to certainty of subject matter[147]: the courts are prepared to take a practical view of certainty requirements in order to uphold, if possible, the intended arrangement. As Megarry VC phrased it[148]:

> Dispositions ought if possible to be upheld, and the court ought not to be astute to find grounds on which a power can be invalidated.

**4–114** Megarry VC did however consider whether the terms of the power were such as to make it "void as being capricous". In *Re Manisty's Settlement Trusts*,[149] Templeman J's view was that this ground of invalidity would arise if "the terms of the power negative any sensible intention on the part of the settlor." The point seems to be that, in discharging the three duties identified by Megarry VC, T needs to bear in mind the (expressed, objective) intention of the settlor: it will clearly be a key factor, for example, in considering the appropriateness of a particular possible distribution. If, however, the terms of the trust provide T with no evidence as to that intention, and there is no other evidence that T could draw on in considering what might be a sensible approach to the exercise of the power, then the power will be invalid. It would seem that this need for a "sensible intention on the part of the settlor" is not a requirement for a non-fiduciary power, as the holder of such a power is free in any case simply to refuse to consider whether to exercise it.

**4–115** It therefore seems that the need for the power to be non-capricious (i.e. for there to be evidence of a sensible intention on the part of the settler, either from the terms of the power or from other circumstances) is a further requirement for the validity of a fiduciary power which does not apply to a non-fiduciary power. It should be emphasised, however, that this additional hurdle is extremely unlikely to cause any practical problems for S. After all, in practice, people do not tend to use settlements (especially ones drawn up with professional advice) as a means to act irrationally or mysteriously. Indeed, it is worth noting that the power in question in *Re Manisty's Settlement* was itself upheld, and the example given by Templeman J of a capricious power (a power to benefit "residents in Greater London") was queried by Megarry VC in *Re Hay's Settlement Trusts*,[150] on the basis that a sensible intention of the settlor might be evident if "the settlor was, for instance, a former chairman of the Greater London Council". Megarry VC also limited the potential reach of the non-capricious requirement by stating that it cannot apply where the power is an intermediate one (i.e. exercisable in

---

[146] *Re Hay's Settlement Trusts* [1982] 1 W.L.R. 202 at 210 (extracted at para.4–103).
[147] See para.4–084.
[148] *Re Hay's Settlement Trusts* [1982] 1 W.L.R. 202 at 212 (extracted at para.4–107).
[149] [1974] Ch. 17 at 27.
[150] [1982] 1 W.L.R. 202 at 212 (extracted at para.4–107).

favour of anyone in the world, bar those specifically excepted) as in such a case, "no class which could be regarded as capricious has been laid down".

Megarry VC also considered, and rejected, the argument that a fiduciary power will be invalid if it is "administratively unworkable", stating that this requirement applied only to discretionary trusts.[151] We will now consider the rules applying in the latter type of case. **4–116**

## iv. Discretionary Trusts

The distinction between a fiduciary power and a discretionary trust consists in the fact that the latter involves a duty on a trustee (T) to exercise the power in some way, and hence make some distribution of the trust property.[152] When holding property on a discretionary trust, T can be prevented from exercising her power in favour of a party outside the permitted class of objects and, as a fiduciary, she also has the duties outlined above.[153] The "is or is not" test and the non-capricious requlrement must therefore apply to discretionary trusts as they do to a fiduciary power. The question is whether the addition of the duty to make some distribution should lead to further certainty requirements that apply to a discretionary trust but not to a fiduciary power. **4–117**

This critical question was considered by the House of Lords in *Re Baden's Deed Trusts (No.1)*, which is also known as *McPhail v Doulton*.[154] It had been previously held by the Court of Appeal that a discretionary trust can be valid only if a complete list can be drawn up of all the objects of the trust, i.e. of all possible recipients of the trust property.[155] The majority of the House of Lords rejected that view and instead found that discretionary trusts should, with some small differences,[156] be subject to the same certainty test as applied by the House of Lords to fiduciary powers in *Re Gulbenkian's Settlement Trusts*:[157] the "is or is not" test. It should be noted that Lord Wilberforce in the following extract refers to a discretionary trust as a "trust power"[158] to distinguish it from what in *Re Hay's Settlement Trusts* Megarry VC called a "mere power" held in a fiduciary capacity.[159] **4–118**

*Re Baden's Deed Trusts (No.1), McPhail v Doulton*

House of Lords [1971] A.C. 424

The facts and the issues appear clearly in the following speech of LORD WILBERFORCE with which LORD REID and VISCOUNT DILHORNE concurred, although dissenting speeches were delivered by LORD HODSON and LORD GUEST. **4–119**

LORD WILBERFORCE: My Lords, this appeal is concerned with the validity of a trust deed dated July 17, 1941, by which Mr. Bertram Baden established a fund for the benefit, broadly, of the staff of the respondent company Matthew Hall & Co Ltd. **4–120**

The critical clauses are as follows: **4–121**

"9. (a) The Trustees shall apply the net income of the Fund in making at their absolute discretion grants to or for benefit of any of the officers and employees or ex-officers or ex-employees of the Company or any relatives or dependants of any such persons in such amounts at such times and on such

---

[151] [1982] 1 W.L.R. 202 at 213 (extracted at para.4–109).

[152] A discretionary trust need not be exhaustive however: the duty need not be to distribute all of the trust fund. For discussion see, e.g. Y. Grbich, "*Baden*: Awakening the Conceptually Moribund Trust" (1974) 37 M.L.R. 643, 643.

[153] See para.4–111.

[154] [1971] A.C. 424.

[155] *IRC v Broadway Cottage Trusts* [1955] Ch. 20.

[156] See further paras 4–140—4–143.

[157] [1970] A.C. 508.

[158] See too, e.g. *Re Baden (No.1)* [1971] A.C. 424 (extracted below at paras 4–119—4–136).

[159] See paras 4–101 and 4–103.

conditions (if any) as they think fit and any such grant may at their discretion be made by payment to the beneficiary or to any institution or person to be applied for his or her benefit and in the latter case the Trustees shall be under no obligation to see to the application of the money.

"(b) The Trustees shall not be bound to exhaust the income of any year or other period in making such grants as aforesaid and any income not so applied shall be dealt with as provided by clause 6(a) hereof enabling moneys to be placed with any Bank or to be invested.

"(c) The Trustees may realise any investments representing accumulations of income and apply the proceeds as though the same were income of the Fund and may also (but only with the consent of all the Trustees) at any time prior to the liquidation of the Fund realise any other part of the capital of the Fund which in the opinion of the Trustees it is desirable to realise in order to provide benefits for which the current income of the Fund is insufficient.

"10. All benefits being at the absolute discretion of the Trustees, no person shall have any right title or interest in the Fund otherwise than pursuant to the exercise of such discretion, and nothing herein contained shall prejudice the right of the Company to determine the employment of any officer or employee."

**4–122** Clause 11 defines a perpetuity period within which the trusts are, in any event, to come to an end and clause 12 provides for the termination of the fund. On this event the trustees are directed to apply the fund in their discretion in one or more of certain specified ways of which one is in making grants as if they were grants under clause 9(a) . . .

**4–123** In this House, the appellants contended that the provisions of clause 9(a) constitute a trust and not a power. If that is held to be the correct result both sides agree that the case must return to the Chancery Division for consideration, on this footing, whether this trust is valid. But here comes a complication. In the present state of authority, the decision as to validity would turn on the question whether a complete list (or on another view a list complete for practical purposes) can be drawn up of all possible beneficiaries. This follows from the Court of Appeal's decision in *Inland Revenue Comrs v Broadway Cottages Trust*[160] as applied in later cases by which, unless this House decides otherwise, the Court of Chancery would be bound. The respondents invite your Lordships to review this decision and challenge its correctness. So the second issue which arises, if clause 9(a) amounts to a trust, is whether the existing test for its validity is right in law and if not, what the test ought to be.

**4–124** Before dealing with these two questions some general observations, or reflections, may be permissible. It is striking how narrow and in a sense artificial is the distinction, in cases such as the present, between trusts or as the particular type of trust is called, trust powers, and powers. It is only necessary to read the learned judgments in the Court of Appeal[161] to see that what to one mind may appear as a power of distribution coupled with a trust to dispose of the undistributed surplus, by accumulation or otherwise, may to another appear as a trust for distribution coupled with a power to withhold a portion and accumulate or otherwise dispose of it. A layman and, I suspect, also a logician, would find it hard to understand what difference there is.

**4–125** It does not seem satisfactory that the entire validity of a disposition should depend on such delicate shading. And if one considers how in practice reasonable and competent trustees would act, and ought to act, in the two cases, surely a matter very relevant to the question of validity, the distinction appears even less significant. To say that there is no obligation to exercise a mere power and that no court will intervene to compel it, whereas a trust is mandatory and its execution must be compelled, may be legally correct enough, but the proposition does not contain an exhaustive comparison of the duties of persons who are trustees in the two cases. A trustee of an employees' benefit fund, whether given a power or a trust power, is still a trustee and he would surely consider in either case that he has a fiduciary duty; he is most likely to have been selected as a suitable person to administer it from his knowledge and experience, and would consider he has a responsibility to do so according to its purpose. It would be a complete misdescription of his position to say that, if what he has is a power unaccompanied by an imperative trust to distribute, he cannot be controlled by the court if he exercised it capriciously, or outside the field permitted by the trust.[162] Any trustee would surely make it his duty to know what is the permissible area of selection and

160 [1955] Ch. 20.

161 [1969] 2 Ch. 388.

162 cf. G. Farwell, *Farwell on Powers*, 3rd edn (Stevens & Son, 1916), p.524.

then consider responsibly, in individual cases, whether a contemplated beneficiary was within the power and whether, in relation to other possible claimants, a particular grant was appropriate.

Correspondingly a trustee with a duty to distribute, particularly among a potentially very large class, would surely never require the preparation of a complete list of names, which anyhow would tell him little that he needs to know. He would examine the field, by class and category; might indeed make diligent and careful enquiries, depending on how much money he had to give away and the means at his disposal, as to the composition and needs of particular categories and of individuals within them; decide on certain priorities or proportions, and then select individuals according to their needs or qualifications. If he acts in this manner, can it really be said that he is not carrying out the trust? **4–126**

Differences there certainly are between trusts (trust powers) and powers, but as regards validity should they be so great as that in one case complete, or practically complete ascertainment is needed, but not in the other? Such distinction as there is would seem to lie in the extent of the survey which the trustee is required to carry out; if he has to distribute the whole of a fund's income, he must necessarily make a wider and more systematic survey than if his duty is expressed in terms of a power to make grants. But just as, in the case of a power, it is possible to underestimate the fiduciary obligation of the trustee to whom it is given, so, in the case of a trust (trust power), the danger lies in overstating what the trustee requires to know or to enquire into before he can properly execute his trust. The difference may be one of degree rather than of principle; in the well-known words of Sir George Farwell[163] trusts and powers are often blended, and the mixture may vary in its ingredients. **4–127**

I now consider whether the provisions of clause 9(a) constitute a trust or a power. Naturally read, the intention of the deed seems to me clear: clause 9(a), whose language is mandatory ("shall"), creates, together with a power of selection, a trust for distribution of the income, the strictness of which is qualified by clause 9(b) which allows the income of any one year to be held up and (under clause 6(a)) either placed, for the time, with a bank, or, if thought fit, invested. Whether there is, in any technical sense, an accumulation seems to me in the present context a jejune enquiry; what is relevant is that clause 9(c) marks the difference between "accumulations" of income and the capital of the fund: the former can be distributed by a majority of the trustees, the latter cannot. As to clause 10, I do not find in it any decisive indication. If anything it seems to point in favour of a trust, but both this and other points of detail are insignificant in the face of the clearly expressed scheme of clause 9. I therefore declare that the provisions of clause 9(a) constitute a trust and remit the case to the Chancery Division for determination whether on this basis clause 9 is (subject to the effects of section 164 of the Law of Property Act 1925) valid or void for uncertainty. **4–128**

This makes it necessary to consider whether, in so doing, the court should proceed on the basis that the relevant test is that laid down in the *Broadway Cottages* case[164] or some other test. That decision gave the authority of the Court of Appeal to the distinction between cases where trustees are given a power of selection and those where they are bound by a trust for selection. In the former case the position, as decided by this House, is that the power is valid if it can be said with certainty whether any given individual is or is not a member of the class and does not fail simply because it is impossible to ascertain every member of the class. (The *Gulbenkian* case.[165]) But in the latter case it is said to be necessary, for the trust to be valid, that the whole range of objects (I use the language of the Court of Appeal) should be ascertained or capable of ascertainment. **4–129**

The respondents invited your Lordships to assimilate the validity test for trusts to that which applies to powers. Alternatively, they contended that in any event the test laid down in the *Broadway Cottages* case was too rigid, and that a trust should be upheld if there is sufficient practical certainty in its definition for it to be carried out, if necessary with the administrative assistance of the court, according to the expressed intention of the settlor. I would agree with this, but this does not dispense from examination of the wider argument. The basis for the *Broadway Cottages* case principle is stated to be that a trust cannot be valid unless, if need be, it can be executed by the court, and that the court can only execute it by ordering an equal distribution in which every beneficiary shares. So it is necessary to examine the authority and reason for this supposed rule as to the execution of trusts by the court. **4–130**

Assuming, as I am prepared to do for present purposes, that the test of validity is whether the trust can be executed by the court, it does not follow that execution is impossible unless there can be equal division. **4–131**

---

163 G. Farwell, *Farwell on Powers*, 3rd edn (1916), p.10.

164 [1955] Ch. 20.

165 [1970] A.C. 508.

As a matter of reason, to hold that a principle of equal division applies to trusts such as the present is certainly paradoxical. Equal division is surely the last thing the settlor ever intended; equal division among all may, probably would, produce a result beneficial to none. Why suppose that the court would lend itself to a whimsical execution? And as regards authority, I do not find that the nature of the trust, and of the court's powers over trusts, calls for any such rigid rule. Equal division may be sensible and has been decreed, in cases of family trusts for a limited class, here there is life in the maxim "equality is equity," but the cases provide numerous examples where this has not been so, and a different type of execution has been ordered, appropriate to the circumstances. . . .

**4–132** So I come to *Inland Revenue Comrs v Broadway Cottage Trusts*.[166] This was certainly a case of trust, and it proceeded on the basis of an admission, in the words of the judgment, "that the class of 'beneficiaries' is incapable of ascertainment." In addition to the discretionary trust of income, there was a trust of capital for all the beneficiaries living or existing at the terminal date. This necessarily involved equal division and it seems to have been accepted that it was void for uncertainty since there cannot be equal division among a class unless all the members of the class are known. . .

**4–133** . . . I think we are free to review the *Broadway Cottages* case. The conclusion which I would reach, implicit in the previous discussion, is that the wide distinction between the validity test for powers and that for trust powers, is unfortunate and wrong, that the rule recently fastened on the courts by the *Broadway Cottages* case ought to be discarded, and that the test for the validity of trust powers ought to be similar to that accepted by this House in *Re Gulbenkian's Settlement Trusts* for powers, namely that the trust is valid if it can be said with certainty that any given individual is or is not a member of the class.

**4–134** Assimilation of the validity test does not involve the complete assimilation of trust powers with powers. As to powers, I agree with my noble and learned friend Lord Upjohn in *Re Gulbenkian's Settlement* that although the trustees may, and normally will, be under a fiduciary duty to consider whether or in what way they should exercise their power, the court will not normally compel its exercise. It will intervene if the trustees exceed their powers, and possibly if they are proved to have exercised it capriciously. But in the case of a trust power, if the trustees do not exercise it, the court will; I respectfully adopt as to this the statement in Lord Upjohn's opinion.[167] I would venture to amplify this by saying that the court, if called on to execute the trust power, will do so in the manner best calculated to give effect to the settlor's or testator's intentions. It may do so by appointing new trustees, or authorising or directing representative persons of the classes of beneficiaries to prepare a scheme of distribution, or even, should the proper basis for distribution appear, by itself directing the trustees so to distribute. The books give many instances where this has been done and I see no reason in principle why they should not do so in the modern field of discretionary trusts.[168] Then, as to the trustees' duty of enquiry or ascertainment, in each case the trustees ought to make such a survey of the range of objects or possible beneficiaries as will enable them to carry out their fiduciary duty.[169] A wider and more comprehensive range of enquiry is called for in the case of trust powers than in the case of powers.

**4–135** Two final points: first, as to the question of certainty, I desire to emphasise the distinction clearly made and explained by Lord Upjohn,[170] between linguistic or semantic uncertainty which, if unresolved by the court, renders the gift void, and the difficulty of ascertaining the existence or whereabouts of members of the class, a matter with which the court can appropriately deal on an application for directions. There may be a third case where the meaning of the words used is clear but the definition of beneficiaries is so hopelessly wide as not to form "anything like a class" so that the trust is administratively unworkable or in Lord Eldon L.C.'s words one that cannot be executed.[171] I hesitate to give examples for they may prejudice future cases, but perhaps "all the residents of Greater London" will serve. I do not think that a discretionary trust for "relatives" even of a living person falls within this category . . .

**4–136** [The appeal was therefore allowed. It was declared that the provisions of clause 9(a) constituted a trust. The case was remitted for determination whether, on the basis of the test set out by the majority of the

---

166 [1955] Ch. 20.
167 [1970] A.C. 508 at 525.
168 See *Brunsden v Woolredge* (1765) Amb. 507; *Supple v Lowson* (1773) Amb. 729; *Liley v Hey* (1842) 1 Hare 580; and *Lewin on Trusts* (16th edn, 1964), p.630.
169 cf. *Liley v Hey* (1842) 1 Hare 580.
170 [1970] A.C. 508 at 524.
171 *Morice v Bishop of Durham* (1805) 10 Ves 521 at 527 (see paras 5–001—5–006).

> House of Lords, clause 9 was valid or void for uncertainty. On this remittal, Brightman J. held that the trust was valid, and this was confirmed by the Court of Appeal in *Re Baden's Deed Trusts (No.2)*.[172]]

We noted above that the certainty of objects test is based on the need for the court to police limits and enforce duties. The important point about a discretionary trust, as opposed to a fiduciary power, is that the trustee has a duty to make at least some distribution, and the court may need to enforce that duty. It is therefore vital to know what form such enforcment might take. If the only option for the court is to order the trustee to divide the relevant property equally between all those within the class then, as Lord Wilberforce noted, it is necessary to have a complete list of all such objects.[173] That seems to have been the assumption behind the Court of Appeal's view, in *IRC v Broadway Cottage Trusts*,[174] that a discretionary trust is valid only if a complete list of objects can be drawn up. **4–137**

Lord Wilberforce's rejection of that view depends on the (surely correct) point that a court is not so limited when it comes to enforcing a discretionary trust. Indeed, in a case such as *Re Baden (No.1)*, where the settlor has nominated a very wide class of objects, such equal division, which would perhaps see each party acquiring only a very small sum of money, is "surely the last thing the settlor ever intended; equal division among all may, probably would, produce a result beneficial to none".[175] As other means of enforcement are available,[176] the potential need to enforce the trustee's duty to make some distribution does not require a complete list of objects to be drawn up. **4–138**

As Lord Wilberforce also noted, given the difficulties in some cases of distinguishing between a fiduciary power and a discretionary trust, it is also sensible to align the certainty tests applying in each case.[177] Indeed, it has since been held, by the Privy Council in *Schmidt v Rosewood Trust Ltd*,[178] that even if a party is only an object of a fiduciary power, rather than of a discretionary trust, that party "may also be entitled to protection from a court of equity, although the circumstances in which he may seek protection, and the nature of the protection he may expect to obtain, will depend on the court's discretion".[179] It therefore seems that, in exceptional cases at least, it may be possible for a court to step in and execute a fiduciary power.[180] **4–139**

This does not mean, however, that the certainty tests to be applied to a fiduciary power and to a discretionary trust are necessarily identical. First, as to policing T's duties, Lord Wilberforce suggested, in relation to T's duty to survey the range of objects of the power, that: "A wider and more comprehensive range of enquiry is called for in the case of trust powers [ie a discretionary trust] than in the case of powers."[181] Secondly, as to enforcing T's duties, Lord Wilberforce suggested that there may be cases in which **4–140**

> the meaning of the words used is clear but the definition of beneficiaries is so hopelessly wide as not to form 'anything like a class' so that the trust is administratively unworkable or in Lord Eldon L.C.'s words one that cannot be executed.[182]

---

172 [1973] Ch. 9 (extracted at paras 4–149—4–165).
173 [1971] A.C. 424 at 450 (extracted at paras 4–130—4–131).
174 [1955] Ch. 20.
175 [1971] A.C. 424 at 451 (extracted at para.4–131).
176 [1971] A.C. 424 at 451 (extracted at para.4–131).
177 [1971] A.C. 424 at 448–449 (extracted at paras 4–127—4–131).
178 [2003] 2 A.C. 709.
179 [2003] 2 A.C. 709 at [51] per Lord Walker.
180 See *Mettoy Pension Trustees Ltd v Evans* [1991] 2 All E.R. 513 at 549, approved in *Schmidt v Rosewood Trust Ltd* [2003] 2 A.C. 709 at [42], [51].
181 [1971] A.C. 424 at 457 (extracted at para.4–134).
182 [1971] A.C. 424 at 457 (extracted at para.4–135).

**4–141** The first of Lord Wilberforce's points is hard to understand and seems to have had no practical effect: in later cases, such as *Re Hay's*, no distinction has been made between fiduciary powers and discretionary trusts in considering the nature of a fiduciary's duty to survey the range of objects. Even if the need for the discretionary trustee to make some exercise of the power justifies a somewhat higher duty in this respect, it is very difficult to translate it into a tangibly different certainty test.

**4–142** The second of Lord Wilberforce's points, in contrast, has had an impact, and there are cases in which discretionary trusts have failed on the grounds of administrative unworkability. The example hesitantly given by Lord Wilberforce was of a class of "all the residents of Greater London".[183] In *R v District Auditor, Ex p. West Yorkshire MCC*,[184] an attempt to set up a discretionary trust "for the benefit of any or all or some of the inhabitants of the County of West Yorkshire" failed on the basis of administrative unworkability.[185] It has been assumed that the requirement of administative workability applies only to discretionary trusts, and not to powers, even if fiduciary.[186]

**4–143** The requirement of administratively workability does therefore seem to be a distinction between discretionary trusts and fiduciary powers. It is not of great practical importance, even in the rare case where a trust or power in relation to such a class is set up. This is because fiduciary powers are subject to the non-capricious requirement,[187] and this may well also apply where the apparent arrangement would be administratively unworkable. The distinction does appear to be defensible as a matter of principle, if it is related to the fact that the discretionary trustee, unlike a fiduciary power-holder, has a duty to make some distribution, and the court may need to enforce that duty. It may then be possible to say that there are some decisions as to distribution that a fiduciary power-holder may validly make but which a court would not wish to undertake, as the role of the courts as even-handed purveyors of justice means that they should not also be involved in broad polycentric disputes as to, for example, how a large sum of money should be spent amongst the 2.5 million inhabitants of West Yorkshire.[188]

## v. Fixed Trusts

**4–144** If a settlor (S), for example, transfers property to a trustee (T) to hold on trust for various beneficiaries, each of whom is to receive a fixed share of the benefit of the property, then of course the identity of each beneficiary must be certain. This requirement causes no practical problems as S will naturally have identified the beneficiaries: if one or more of the beneficiaries cannot be found, this will not invalidate the trust and jeopardise the rights of the ascertainable beneficiaries, as the trustees can simply pay the shares of the missing beneficiaries into court, or otherwise ask the court for directions.[189]

---

183 [1971] A.C. 424 at 457 (extracted at para.4–135).

184 (1986) R.V.R. 24.

185 See too *Re Harding (Deceased)* [2008] Ch. 235 at [15]: it is "common ground that a private trust for such a large class as the black community in four London Boroughs would be so large as to make a private trust unworkable, and hence void".

186 See, e.g. *Re Hay's Settlement Trusts* [1982] 1 W.L.R. 202 at 212 (extracted at para.4–109).

187 See para.4–114.

188 For example, whilst it might be permissible for T, as a private individual, to choose to spend the money on sports facilities for local residents, a court might not want to have to take a view as to whether the money should be spent on that purpose or instead on schools, or hospitals, or transport, etc.

189 See too Trustee Act 1925 s.27, which gives trustees and personal representatives who have advertised properly and waited for beneficiaries to come forward immunity from liability if funds are then distributed only amongst ascertainable beneficiaries. Note too that, by means of a *Benjamin* order (named for *Re Benjamin* [1902] 1 Ch. 723), a court may allow a trustee or executor to distribute even if not all of the beneficiaries have been ascertained. See, e.g. *Re Green's W.T.* [1985] 3 All E.R. 455. The purpose in each case is to protect the trustees or executor from liability for the distribution; the beneficial interests of any unascertained beneficiaries do continue unless and until, for example, the relevant property is acquired by a bona fide purchaser for value without notice.

A difficulty may arise, however, if the trust calls for equal division amongst members of a certain class, and the number within that class cannot be established, as that uncertainty means that the extent of any individual's beneficial interest cannot be established. In such a case, then, the "complete list" test, which no longer applies to discretionary trusts, must apply. 4–145

### vi. Gifts Subject to a Condition Subsequent

We started this discussion by considering gifts subject to a condition precedent, such as where S transfers property to T to hold on trust for B *if* B meets a certain condition. A condition subsequent is imposed where, instead, B acquires her right but that right is forfeited if the condition occurs. We saw that the certainty test applied in the case of a condition precedent is very easy to satisfy, as, if there is a situation in which one person might clearly qualify for the gift, then that person should not lose her property right by means of the gift's being seen as invalid. The same concern, of protecting B's entitlement, leads to a very strict certainty test's being applied in the case of a gift subject to a condition subsequent. The condition must be described in such a way that the court can see from the outset precisely and distinctly upon the happening of what event the interest is to be forfeited.[190] The circumstances involving forfeiture must be clearly known in advance so that B knows precisely where she stands. The condition will also be invalid if it is repugnant to the essential alienability of the interest given[191] or if it is void on the grounds of public policy.[192] 4–146

## *C. Applying the Relevant Test*

### i. Applying the "Is or Is Not" Test

We have seen that the "is or is not" test, which states that a power or discretionary trust will not be valid if it is not possible to tell of any given person whether that person is or is not in the permitted class, is crucial in determining the validity of powers (both non-fiduciary and fiduciary) and discretionary trusts. Having determined by a majority that the test should apply to the discretionary trust that S attempted to set up in *Re Baden's Deed Trusts (No.1)*, the House of Lords remitted the case to the High Court so the test could be applied. 4–147

The critical clause in the trust deed (cl.9(a)) provided for grants "to or for the benefit of any of the officers and employees or ex-officers or ex-employees of [the defined company] or to any relatives or dependants of any such persons".[193] Brightman J decided at first instance that this class did pass the "is or is not" test, although in reaching that conclusion he held that the trustees and a court could assume that anyone who could not show that she was in the class was in fact outside the class. The Court of Appeal confirmed that result but each of the three judges provided different reasons for his decision. 4–148

---

190 *Clavering v Ellison* (1859) 7 H.L.Cas. 707; *Blathwayt v Lord Cawley* [1976] A.C. 397 at 429.

191 *Re Scientific Investment Pension Plan Trusts* [1999] Ch. 53 at 59.

192 See, e.g. *Church Property Trustees of Newcastle Diocese v Ebbeck* (1960) 104 C.L.R. 394: a condition that B must "profess Protestant faith" was void for public policy as it was designed by the testator to encourage his three sons to divorce their Catholic wives. A condition designed to restrain marriage altogether will also be void as contrary to public policy: see, e.g. *Lloyd v Lloyd* (1852) 2 Sim. N.S. 255.

193 See [1973] Ch 9 at 12.

*Re Baden's Deed Trusts (No.2)*

Court of Appeal [1973] Ch. 9

4–149 SACHS L.J.: It is first to be noted that the deed must be looked at through the eyes of a businessman seeking to advance the welfare of the employees of his firm and those so connected with the employees that a benevolent employer would wish to help them. He would not necessarily be looking at the words he uses with the same eyes as those of a man making a will. Accordingly, whether a court is considering the concept implicit in relevant words, or whether it is exercising the function of a court of construction, it should adopt that same practical and common-sense approach which was enjoined by Upjohn J. in *Re Sayer*[194] and by Lord Wilberforce in *Re Baden (No.1)*,[195] and which would be used by an employer setting up such a fund.

4–150 The next point as regards approach that requires consideration is the contention, strongly pressed by Mr Vinelott [counsel for S's executors, arguing that the trust was invalid], that the court must always be able to say whether any given postulant is not within the relevant class as well as being able to say whether he is within it. In construing the words already cited from the speech of Lord Wilberforce in *Re Baden (No.1)*,[196] (as well as those of Lord Reid and Lord Upjohn in *Re Gulbenkian's Settlement Trusts*)[197], it is essential to bear in mind the difference between conceptual uncertainty and evidential difficulties. That distinction is explicitly referred to by Lord Wilberforce in *Re Baden (No.1)*,[198] when he said:

> ". . . as to the question of certainty. I desire to emphasise the distinction clearly made and explained by Lord Upjohn[199] between linguistic or semantic uncertainty which, if unresolved by the court, renders the gift void, and the difficulty of ascertaining the existence or whereabouts of members of the class, a matter with which the court can appropriately deal on an application for directions."

4–151 As Mr. Vinelott himself rightly observed, "the court is never defeated by evidential uncertainty," and it is in my judgment clear that it is conceptual certainty to which reference was made when the "is or is not a member of the class" test was enunciated. (Conceptual uncertainty was in the course of argument conveniently exemplified, rightly or wrongly matters not, by the phrase "someone under a moral obligation" and contrasted with the certainty of the words "first cousins.") Once the class of persons to be benefited is conceptually certain it then becomes a question of fact to be determined on evidence whether any postulant has on inquiry been proved to be within it: if he is not so proved, then he is not in it. That position remains the same whether the class to be benefited happens to be small (such as "first cousins") or large (such as "members of the X Trade Union" or "those who have served in the Royal Navy"). The suggestion that such trusts could be invalid because it might be impossible to prove of a given individual that he was *not* in the relevant class is wholly fallacious—and only Mr. Vinelott's persuasiveness has prevented me from saying that the contention is almost unarguable.

4–152 It was suggested that some difficulty arises from the passage in the speech of Lord Wilberforce in *Re Baden (No. 1)*,[200] where he referred to the need of trustees "to make such a survey of the range of objects or possible beneficiaries as will enable them to carry out their fiduciary duty." The word "range," however, in that context has an inbuilt and obvious element of considerable elasticity, and thus provides for an almost infinitely variable range of vision suitable to the particular trust to be considered. In modern trusts of the category now under consideration it may be sufficient to know whether the range of potential postulants runs into respectively dozens, hundreds, thousands, tens of thousands or even hundreds of thousands. I cannot imagine that the above-quoted passage was intended to cast doubt, for instance, on the validity of wide-ranging discretionary trusts such as those of the Army Benevolent Fund. When looked at in the context of the rest of the speech this particular passage does not seem to me to cause any difficulty. In my judgment it refers to something quite different, to a need to provide a list of individuals or to provide a closely accurate enumeration of the numbers in the class: it relates to that width of the field from which

---

194 [1957] Ch. 423 at 436.
195 [1971] A.C. 424 at 452.
196 [1971] A.C. 424 at 450: "can it be said with certainty that any given individual is or is not a member of the class?".
197 [1970] A.C. 508, at 518, 521 and 525.
198 [1971] A.C. 424 at 457.
199 *Re Gulbenkian's Settlement Trusts* [1970] A.C. 508 at 524.
200 [1971] A.C. 424 at 457.

beneficiaries may be drawn and which the trustees should have in mind so that they can adapt to it their methods of discretionary selection. Assessing in a businesslike way "the size of the problem" is what the trustees are called on to do. . .

In agreement with the practical approach of Brightman J.,[201] I consider that the trustees, or if necessary the court, are quite capable of coming to a conclusion in any given case as to whether or not a particular candidate could properly be described as a dependant—a word that, as the judge said, "conjures up a sufficiently distinct picture." I agree, too, that any one wholly or partly dependent on the means of another is a "dependant." There is thus no conceptual uncertainty inherent in that word and the executors' contentions as to the effect of its use fail. **4–153**

As regards "relatives" Brightman J., after stating, "It is not in dispute that a person is a relative of an . . . employee . . ., if both trace legal descent from a common ancestor:" a little later said: "In practice, the use of the expression 'relatives' cannot cause the slightest difficulty."[202] With that view I agree for the reasons he gave when he correctly set out the evidential position. **4–154**

MEGAW L.J.: If this trust were to be held void for uncertainty because of the inclusion of the "dependants" in clause 9 (a), I think that few trusts would stand. I do not find any greater uncertainty in it than is inherent in, or can by ingenuity be conjured up in relation to, any ordinary, well understood word. . . **4–155**

Then it is said that the deed is invalid because of the inclusion of the word "relatives." Brightman J.,[203] approached that question on the basis that: "It is not in dispute that a person is a relative of an officer or employee or ex-officer or ex-employee, if both trace legal descent from a common ancestor." He held that the executors' argument on this issue also failed. I agree, for the reasons given by the judge. **4–156**

[The test set out by Lord Wilberforce in *Re Baden (No.1)*[204]] is this: **4–157**

> ". . . the power is valid if it can be said with certainty whether any given individual is or is not a member of the class and does not fail simply because it is impossible to ascertain every member of the class."

The executors' argument concentrates on the words "or is not" in the first of the two limbs of the sentence quoted above: "if it can be said with certainty whether any given individual is *or is not* a member of the class." It is said that those words have been used deliberately, and have only one possible meaning; and that, however startling or drastic or unsatisfactory the result may be—and Mr. Vinelott does not shrink from saying that the consequence is drastic—this court is bound to give effect to the words used in the House of Lords' definition of the test. It would be quite impracticable for the trustees to ascertain in many cases whether a particular person was *not* a relative of an employee. The most that could be said is: "There is no proof that he is a relative." But there would still be no "certainty" that such a person was not a relative. Hence, so it is said, the test laid down by the House of Lords is not satisfied, and the trust is void. For it cannot be said with certainty, in relation to any individual, that he is not a relative. **4–158**

I do not think it was contemplated that the words "or is not" would produce that result. It would, as I see it, involve an inconsistency with the latter part of the same sentence: "does not fail simply because it is impossible to ascertain every member of the class." The executors' contention, in substance and reality, is that it does fail "simply because it is impossible to ascertain every member of the class.". . . **4–159**

In my judgment, much too great emphasis is placed in the executors' argument on the words "or is not." To my mind, the test is satisfied if, as regards at least a substantial number of objects, it can be said with certainty that they fall within the trust; even though, as regards a substantial number of other persons, if they ever for some fanciful reason fell to be considered, the answer would have to be, not "they are outside the trust," but "it is not proven whether they are in or out." What is a "substantial number" may well be a question of common sense and of degree in relation to the particular trust: particularly where, as here, it would be fantasy, to use a mild word, to suggest that any practical difficulty would arise in the fair, proper and sensible administration of this trust in respect of relatives and dependants. **4–160**

STAMP L.J.: There are, however, in my judgment serious difficulties in the way of a rejection of Mr. Vinelott's submission. . . **4–161**

The first difficulty, as I see it, is that the rejection of Mr. Vinelott's submission involves holding that the trust is good if there are individuals—or even one—of whom you can say with certainty that he is a member **4–162**

---

201 [1972] Ch. 607 at 625.
202 [1972] Ch. 607 at 625.
203 [1972] Ch. 607 at 625.
204 [1971] A.C. 424 at 450 and 454.

of the class. That was the test adopted by and the decision of the Court of Appeal in *Re Gulbenkian's Settlement Trusts*[205] where what was under consideration was a power of distribution among a class conferred upon trustees as distinct from a trust for distribution: but when the case came before the House of Lords that test was decisively rejected and the more stringent test upon which Mr. Vinelott insists was adopted. Clearly Lord Wilberforce in expressing the view that the test of validity of a discretionary trust ought to be similar to that accepted by the House of Lords in the *re Gulbenkian's Settlement Trusts*[206] did not take the view that it was sufficient that you could find individuals who were clearly members of the class; for he himself remarked, towards the end of his speech as to the trustees' duty of inquiring or ascertaining, that in each case the trustees ought to make such a survey of the range of objects or possible beneficiaries as will enable them to carry out their fiduciary duty. It is not enough that trustees should do nothing but distribute the fund among those objects of the trust who happen to be at hand or present themselves. . .

**4–163** If the matter rested there, it would in my judgment follow that, treating the word "relatives" as meaning descendants from a common ancestor, a trust for distribution such as is here in question would not be valid. Any "survey of the range of the objects or possible beneficiaries" would certainly be incomplete, and I am able to discern no principle upon which such a survey could be conducted or where it should start or finish. The most you could do, so far as regards relatives, would be to find individuals who are clearly members of the class—the test which was accepted in the Court of Appeal, but rejected in the House of Lords, in *Re Gulbenkian's Settlement Trusts*.[207]

**4–164** The matter does not, however, rest there. . .[Stamp L.J. then referred to *Harding v Glyn*,[208] in which a court executed a discretionary trust for relations by distributing to the testator's next of kin in equal shares]. . . Does it then make any difference that here the discretionary trust for relations was a reference not to the relations of a deceased person but of one who was living? I think not. The next of kin of a living person are as readily ascertainable at any given time as the next of kin of one who is dead. A trust for the next of kin of a person, without more, was not a trust for the next of kin according to the statutes which would regulate the distribution of the personal property of a deceased person had he died intestate, but a trust for his nearest blood relations.[209] To execute a discretionary trust for the relations or relatives of a living person by distribution among his nearest blood relations appears to me a satisfactory method of so doing; and, if it were necessary to give a construction to the word "relatives" in relating to a living person in an inter vivos settlement, to construe it as a reference to his nearest blood relations would be far more likely to give effect to the intention than a construction which embraced all who were descended from one of his ancestors. . .nothing could be more improbable than that [S] should have intended the trustees to be at liberty to make grants to a relative of an employee of whose very existence that employee might be ignorant. "Nearest blood relations or dependants" makes more sense. . .

**4–165** The only other challenge to the validity of the trust is directed against the use of the word "dependants" which it is said introduces a linguistic or semantic uncertainty. That in the context the word connotes financial dependence I do not doubt, and although in a given case there may be a doubt whether there be a sufficient degree of dependence to satisfy the qualification of being a "dependant," that is a question which can be determined by the court and does not introduce linguistic uncertainty.

**4–166** Stamp LJ's approach can be seen as more faithful to the specific language used by Lord Wilberforce in *Re Baden (No.1)*: it must be possible to tell of any given person whether she is *or is not* in the class. In other words, in considering if a given postulant, X, in a relative or dependant, it must be possible to put X in either in the "Yes" box or the "No" box. A discretionary trust would therefore be void if X had to go into a "Don't know" box. On that approach, the trust was valid (in a world before DNA testing) only because Stamp LJ was prepared to treat relatives as meaning "next-of-kin" or "nearest blood relations" in which case any postulant would fall within the "Yes" box or the "No" box.

205 [1968] Ch. 126.
206 [1970] A.C. 508.
207 [1970] A.C. 508.
208 (1739) 1 Atk. 469.
209 *Re Gray's Settlement* [1896] 2 Ch. 802.

The approach of Sachs and Megaw LJJ (as well as that of Brightman J at first instance)[210] could be seen as more faithful to the underlying policy of Lord Wilberforce's speech in *Re Baden (No.1)*, which was to develop the law so as to give S the flexibility to set up a discretionary trust with a potentially very wide class of objects. It is also consistent with the pragmatic, rather than overly-technical, approach to certainty tests that we have seen at a number of points in this chapter.[211] A key part of their approach is the assumption that if it cannot be shown that X is in the class, X must be treated as being out of the class. This may introduce an element of artificiality, but it enables a court to police the trustees, who know that they are at risk if exercising a power in favour of a party who has not demonstrated that she is within the permitted class. **4–167**

Once such an assumption is adopted, however, the question arises of whether anything in fact remains of the certainty test: might any class, even "friends" be valid on the basis that anyone not clearly in the class must be treated as outside it? The practical problem in such a case might be that so few people would clearly qualify that T would not be able to exercise a genuine choice when deciding how to exercise the power. Megaw LJ sought to deal with this by imposing a requirement that there must be a "substantial" core of objects who are clearly within the class. This raises again the point raised by Lord Upjohn in *Re Gulbenkian' Settlement Trusts*:[212] the consequence is that the class is narrowed from that which the S stated; but at least the trust is validated. **4–168**

Sachs LJ, in contrast, sought to give some content to the certainty test by adopting the distinction between conceptual and evidential uncertainty.[213] This provides another means of invalidating a discretionary trust for "friends": the term in itself is inherently uncertain, as no stable definition can be provided. In practical terms, though, it is difficult to see why thls matters: if it could be shown that sufficient people were clearly within the class (as the uncertain term nonetheless has a core meaning) then, given the assumption that anyone who cannot show she is in the class is outside it, the duties of the trustees could, it seems, be discharged in practice. **4–169**

It might be thought that, given the differing approaches adopted in *Re Baden (No.2)*, the law is in an unsatisfactory state. It is certainly not the case, however, that the courts have subsequently had to deal with problems arising from the application of the "is or is not" test to powers and discretionary trusts, nor that the use of such wide powers and trusts has diminished. It seems rather that, with the confirmation in *Re Baden (No.2)* that key terms such as "relative" and "dependant" are sufficiently certain, well-advised settlors have felt no need to investigate the boundaries of the certainty test through the sort of idiosyncratic terms that are beloved of examiners but extremely rare in practice. **4–170**

## ii. Resolving Apparent Uncertainty

It is possible for a settlor S to attempt to avoid certainty problems by identifying a party who can resolve a dispute as to whether X is or is not in the permitted class, or has or has not met a particular condition. It is clear that such a party's decisions may assist in relation to evidential uncertainty although, following *Re Baden (No.2)*,[214] such uncertainty is in any case unlikely to invalidate the planned arrangement. The more important question is as to the impact of such a party's decision on potential conceptual uncertainty caused by the inherent vagueness of the terms used to define a class. **4–171**

---

210 [1972] Ch. 607 at 626.

211 See paras 4–049—4–084.

212 [1970] A.C. 508 at 524 (extracted at para.4–094).

213 For further discussion of this distinction, see C. Emery, "The Most Hallowed Principle—Certainty of Beneficiaries of Trusts and of Powers of Appointment" (1982) 98 L.Q.R. 551.

214 [1973] Ch. 9: see paras 4–149—4–170.

4–172 In *Re Tuck's Settlement Trusts*, for example, S's settlement provided for payment of an income to B "if and when and so long as he shall be of the Jewish faith and be married to an approved wife". An approved wife was defined as "a wife of Jewish blood by one or both of her parents and who has been brought up in and has never departed from and at the date of the marriage continues to worship according to the Jewish faith". It was also provided that as to such facts, in the case of dispute or doubt, the decision of the Chief Rabbi in London of either the Sephardim or Ashkenazim communities "shall be conclusive". It was held by the Court of Appeal that these terms were conditions precedent and, given the lenient test applied in such cases,[215] they were certain enough even without the reference to the Chief Rabbi.

4–173 In an obiter discussion, Lord Denning MR rejected the argument of counsel that the appointment of a party to resolve doubt could not save a settlement from conceptual (as opposed to evidential) uncertainty, stating instead that[216]:

> I see no reason why a testator or settlor should not provide that any dispute or doubt should be resolved by his executors or trustees, or even by a third person . . . [If] the appointed person is ready and willing to resolve the doubt or difficulty, I see no reason why he should not do so. So long as he does not misconduct himself or come to a decision which is wholly unreasonable, I think his decision should stand. After all, that was plainly the intention of the testator or settlor.

4–174 Lord Denning's analysis can be contrasted with that of Jenkins J in *Re Coxen*[217]:

> If the testator had insufficiently defined the state of affairs on which the trustees were to form their opinion he would not have saved the condition from invalidity on the ground of uncertainty merely by making their opinion the criterion, although the declaration by the trustees of this or that opinion would be an event about which in itself there could be no uncertainty.

4–175 This view was followed in *Re Jones*[218] and then in *Re Wright's Will Trusts*[219] where a gift of property to trustees "to use the same at their absolute discretion for such people and institutions as they think have helped me or my late husband" failed for uncertainty. The point is that S had not intended the trustees to be able to appoint to anyone at all: a condition is attached and the trustees need some means of making sense of that condition.

4–176 It may be that Lord Denning's approach can be reconciled to this by finding that, if a party is appointed by S to resolve doubts, this does not mean that the arrangement will necessarily be certain. After all, the court[220] must have some means of reviewing any decision by the appointed party: in *Dundee General Hospital Board v Walker*,[221] a case heavily relied on by Lord Denning in *Re Tuck*,[222] Lord Reid pointed out (in a case where such a power had been given to trustees), that their decision could be challenged

> if it can be shown that the trustees considered the wrong question, or that, although they purported to consider the right question, they did not really apply their minds to it or perversely shut their eyes to the facts, or that they did not act honestly or in good faith.

---

215 See paras 4–088—4–091.
216 [1978] Ch. 49 at 61–62.
217 [1948] Ch. 747 at 761–762.
218 [1953] Ch. 125: "if at any time B shall in the uncontrolled opinion of the trustee have social or other relationship with C."
219 [1981] L.S. Gaz. 841. Also see *Tatham v Huxtable* (1950) 81 C.L.R. 639 at 653.
220 The jurisdiction of the court cannot be ousted: *Re Raven* [1915] 1 Ch. 673: *Re Wynn's WT* [1952] Ch. 271.
221 [1952] 1 All E.R. 896.
222 [1978] Ch. 49 at 61.

It must similarly be the case that the decision can be challenged if it was so unreasonable that no reasonable person could have made it. In order to consider such challenges, it seems, the court will need *some* information as to the criteria to be used by the appointed party when making the decision, and so, whilst a decision by the third party may assist in resolving some doubts, it would be a mistake to think that the underlying definition of the class can be wholly uncertain.

**Questions**

1. A testator who died a month ago by his will made the following bequests:
   (a) £10,000 to Alan and at his death the remaining part of what is left that he does not want for his own use to be divided equally between Xerxes and Yorick;
   (b) £50,000 to my trustees Tom and Tim to distribute among such of the inhabitants of Cambridge as they shall in their unfettered discretion think fit;
   (c) £100,000 to my said trustees to distribute among Brian, Charles, David, Ellen, Oswald, Peter, Quentin and Roger and such of my other business associates and old friends as they shall see fit;
   (d) £100,000 to my said trustees to use the income for 80 years from my death as the applicable perpetuity period or such other period as the law allows if less for providing holidays for employees and ex-employees their spouses and relatives of ICI Plc and of companies on whose boards of directors, directors of ICI Plc sit, and thereafter to use the income for the education of my relatives; and
   (e) residue to my son Simon trusting that he will see to it that my old friends shall have the contents of my wine cellar; and in case of any doubts he shall have power to designate who are my business associates and old friends.

   **Consider the validity of these bequests, the testator having lived in Cambridge all his life.**

2. Are the certainty tests applicable to fiduciary powers identical to those applying to discretionary trusts? Should they be?

3. Simon Settlor, who was 4ft 11ins tall, has just died. In his home-made will, he directed his executors:
   (a) to pay £2,000 to each of my small relatives;
   (b) to distribute £8,000 as they see fit among such persons as they consider to be friends of mine; and
   (c) to hold my residuary estate on trust to pay the income therefrom to my four daughters equally in their respective lifetimes but if a daughter marries a supporter of Watford Football Club the share of such daughter shall accrue to the other daughters, as shall also be the case on the death of a daughter, but on the death of my last surviving daughter they shall distribute the capital within one year among such persons connected with me who have been benefited by me in my lifetime as they shall see fit.

   **Advise on the validity of the above bequests.**

# 5

# THE BENEFICIARY PRINCIPLE

## 1. The Basic Principle

A trust can exist only where the trustee holds certain property subject to a duty, and that duty must be capable of enforcement. As a result, a court will not uphold any alleged trust that cannot be effectively supervised and sanctioned by the court at the behest of someone in whose favour performance can be decreed. As the Master of the Rolls stated in *Morice v Bishop of Durham*[1]: 5–001

> There can be no trust, over the exercise of which this Court will not assume a control; for an uncontrollable power of disposition would be ownership, and not a trust.

Or, as the Lord Chancellor put it in later proceedings between the same parties[2]:

> As it is a maxim that the execution of a trust shall be under the control of the Court, it must be of such a nature, that it can be under that control, so that the administration of it can be reviewed by the Court; or, if the trustee dies, the Court itself can execute the trust.

The decision in *Morice v Bishop of Durham* is often associated with the beneficiary principle: a trust "to be effective must have ascertained or ascertainable beneficiaries".[3] Note, however, that an exception is made for charitable trusts, as explained by Viscount Simonds in *Leahy v Attorney General for New South Wales*[4]: 5–002

> A gift can be made to persons (including a corporation) but it cannot be made to a purpose or to an object: so, also, a trust may be created for the benefit of persons as cestuis que trust but not for a purpose or object unless the purpose or object be charitable. For a purpose or object cannot sue, but, if it be charitable, the Attorney-General can sue to enforce it.

The beneficiary principle is thus synonymous with the rule of English law that there can be no private (i.e. non-charitable) purpose trusts. A simple example of the rule's operation is provided by *Re Shaw*.[5] George Bernard Shaw, in his will, directed that funds should be held on trust for the purpose of undertaking research into the possibility of a 40-letter alphabet. As this purpose was found not to 5–003

1 (1804) 9 Ves. Jun. 399 at 405 per Sir William Grant MR. For a discussion of the case in its historical context, see J. Getzler, "*Morice v Bishop of Durham* (1805)" in C. Mitchell and P. Mitchell (eds), *Landmark Cases in Equity* (Hart Publishing, 2012).

2 (1805) 10 Ves. Jun. 521 at 539 per Lord Eldon LC. See too *Re Astor's S.T.* [1952] Ch. 534 at 549 per Roxburgh J: "A court of equity does not recognise as valid a trust which it cannot both enforce and control."

3 *Re Endacott* [1960] Ch. 232 at 246 per Lord Evershed MR.

4 [1959] A.C. 457 at 479.

5 [1957] 1 W.L.R. 729.

be charitable, this attempt to set up a purpose trust failed and it was held that the recipients held the funds on resulting trust for Shaw's estate.[6]

**5–004** It is, therefore, relatively simple to state the basic principle. It contains, however, an important ambiguity. The foregoing statements from *Morice v Bishop of Durham* are focussed on the need for there to be a party who can call on the court to enforce the trust, but do not explain why that party should be a beneficiary. Might it be possible instead to set up a trust where the duty of the trustee is owed to a party who does not personally benefit from performance of that duty? There would be no beneficiary, but that party would have standing to enforce the terms of the trust. If that proposition were accepted in English law, we would no longer have a beneficiary principle, and instead we would have an "enforcer principle". The crucial distinction between a beneficiary and an enforcer is that the latter need not benefit from the performance of the duties of the trustees.

**5–005** We examine the arguments for and against an enforcer principle below,[7] after we have considered the current law. Two points are nonetheless worth making at this stage. First, charitable trusts conform with the enforcer principle, since they are enforceable in the public interest by the Attorney General or by the Charity Commission, but they do not conform to the beneficiary principle, as they are always trusts for an abstract purpose (even if the accomplishment of that purpose benefits particular individuals). However, this does not conclusively prove that English law has accepted the enforcer principle, since it is clear, as we will see in Chapter 6, that charitable trusts differ in significant ways from other trusts. Secondly, it is important to remember that English law is not the only law of trusts and, in other jurisdictions, non-charitable purpose trusts are permitted.[8] Indeed, under the terms of the Recognition of Trusts Act 1987,[9] the basic position is that an English court, if dealing with a dispute where the settlor of a trust has stipulated that the trust is to be governed by the law of such a jurisdiction, would have to apply that foreign law and recognise a private purpose trust as valid.[10]

**5–006** It is reasonably clear that the current English law of non-charitable trusts, unless and until this is re-interpreted by a bold Supreme Court, adopts the beneficiary principle rather than the enforcer principle.[11] In *Armitage v Nurse*, Millett LJ stated that[12]:

---

6 An appeal in the case was however settled on the basis that permission was given by those entitled under the resulting trust for use of the money as intended by the testator for 21 years: see *Re Shaw* [1958] 1 All ER 245n. For a more recent example of the failure of a non-charitable purpose trust leading to a resulting trust for a donor of property, see *Re St Andrew's (Cheam) Lawn Tennis Club Trust* [2012] 1 W.L.R. 3487. Resulting trusts are considered in Ch.14.

7 At paras 5–101—5–109.

8 Foreign laws permitting non-charitable purpose trusts include, for example, the laws of Jersey, the Isle of Man, the British Virgin Islands and the Cayman Islands. The Scottish Law Commission says that such trusts are valid under current Scottish law (a proposition for which there is little evidence) and should be permitted by any reformed trusts law of Scotland: Scottish Law Commission, *Report on Trust Law* (TSO, 2014), Scots Law Com. No.239, 2014, paras 14.2–14.10. For a helpful overview of developments outside England, see D. Hayton, "'Trusts' in Private International Law" (2014) 366 Recueil des Cours 17, 29–39.

9 Giving effect in English law to the Hague Convention on the Law Applicable to Trusts and their Recognition. The terms of art.2 of the Hague Convention are broad enough to include a non-charitable purpose trust: these are extracted at para.1–039.

10 Although note that under arts 15, 16 and 18 of the Hague Convention, there are circumstances in which a court can refuse to give effect to a trust even if it is valid under the governing law and even if it falls within the definition of a trust in art.2. This point is discussed at paras 16–045—16–049.

11 See, e.g. *Re Wood* [1949] Ch. 498 at 501; *Re Endacott* [1960] Ch. 232 at 250; *Re Denley's Trust Deed* [1969] 1 Ch. 373 at 382–383 (extracted at para.5–016); *Re Horley Town Football Club* [2006] W.T.L.R. 1817 at [89]; *Re St Andrew's (Cheam) Lawn Tennis Club Trust* [2012] 1 W.L.R. 3487 at [45]: "It is trite law that a valid trust must either vest the trust property absolutely in ascertainable persons within the perpetuity period or be for exclusively charitable purposes."

12 [1998] Ch. 241 at 253.

> there is an irreducible core of obligations owed by the trustees to the beneficiaries and enforceable by them which is fundamental to the concept of a trust. If the beneficiaries have no rights enforceable against the trustees there are no trusts.

The current assumption is that this requirement applies to all non-charitable trusts, and not merely the sub-set of such trusts which happen to have beneficiaries. There are some situations, however, which may seem to constitute exceptions to the beneficiary principle. We will examine these now, and we will see that there is a strong argument that, properly understood, they are not true exceptions to the rule.

## 2. Exceptions to the Beneficiary Principle?

### A. "Anomalous" Testamentary Purpose Trusts

The Court of Appeal[13] has held that there are some anomalous cases, not to be extended, where testamentary trusts infringing the beneficiary principle have been held valid as concessions to human sentiment.[14] The rule against inalienability remains applicable and so the trust must be restricted directly or indirectly[15] to the common law perpetuity period. The anomalous cases are: **5-007**

- trusts for the maintenance of particular animals[16];
- trusts for the erection or maintenance of graves and sepulchral monuments[17];
- trusts for the saying of masses in private[18]; and
- trusts for the promotion and furtherance of fox-hunting.[19]

These trusts are sometimes referred to as trusts of imperfect obligation: there is no-one who can apply to the court to enforce the trust and so the trustees are not in fact under a duty to carry out the specified purpose. The concession made by the courts is that the testamentary disposition is not regarded as invalid, and so the property is not held on an immediate resulting trust for the deceased's estate. The recipients of the property instead have a *power* to carry out the specified purpose. If they do not exercise that power, the property can be claimed by the party otherwise entitled (i.e. who would have had the benefit of the resulting trust had the disposition failed immediately).[20] As a result, the **5-008**

---

13 *Re Endacott* [1960] Ch. 232 (residuary gift to a parish council "for the purpose of providing some useful memorial to" the testator held void for uncertainty and for infringing the beneficiary principle).

14 Note that such trusts would also infringe an enforcer principle, in the absence of provisions appointing any party as an enforcer.

15 *Pedulla v Nasti* (1990) 20 N.S.W.L.R. 720. If a will restricts a bequest expressly "so far as the law allows" this is construed as restricting the period to 21 years so satisfying the rule against inalienability: *Re Hooper* [1932] 1 Ch. 38. The court will not imply such a term: *Re Compton* [1946] 1 All E.R. 117. If the legacy does not have to be kept intact as endowment capital but can be spent as soon as practicable on the purpose then the rule against inalienability has no application: *Trimmer v Danby* (1856) 25 L.J. Ch. 424; *Mussett v Bingle* [1876] W.N. 170.

16 *Pettingall v Pettingall* (1842) 11 L.J. Ch. 176; *Re Dean* (1889) 41 Ch.D. 552. Such trusts are not charitable as they are confined to specific animals; many trusts for animals generally are charitable: *Re Wedgwood* [1915] 1 Ch. 113; and see para.6–293.

17 *Re Hooper* [1932] Ch. 38; *Mussett v Bingle* [1876] W.N. 170; *Pirbright v Salwey* [1896] W.N. 86; *Trimmer v Danby* (1856) 25 L.J. Ch. 424.

18 *Bourne v Keane* [1919] A.C. 815 at 874–875. The saying of public masses would be a charitable purpose.

19 *Re Thompson* [1934] Ch. 342, but the default beneficiary, a charity, only objected pro forma.

20 See, e.g. *Re Thompson* [1934] Ch. 342 at 344, where Clauson J ordered that the fund should be paid to the recipient on his

purported testamentary purpose trust is not given effect to; it is rather recharacterised as a trust for the benefit of the party otherwise entitled, where the trustees have a power to spend the fund on the specified purpose.

**5–009** It may be questioned whether these cases do in fact constitute exceptions to the beneficiary principle. The point is that the trustees are not under a duty to apply the property to the specified purpose; they merely have a power to do so. The true concession consists in the courts having created limited exceptions to the principle that they will not treat words purporting to create a trust as in fact creating a power.[21]

**5–010** It is also possible to query how anomalous these trusts really are.[22] As for the maintenance of specific animals, such animals belong to specific individuals and, as will be seen below,[23] there are further cases in which an apparent purpose trust has been characterised as a trust for those parties who benefit from the performance of the purpose. The maintenance of private graves may be possible in any case under the Parish Councils and Burial Authorities (Miscellaneous Provisions) Act 1970 s.1, and if the construction is part of the fabric of a church then the trust will be charitable and valid on that ground.[24] Gifts for the saying of masses in private are very close to gifts for the saying of masses in public, which are charitable, and it is only the dubious rule in *Re Hetherington*[25] that divides the two, by holding that the saying of prayers can only be for the public benefit (and thus legally charitable) if persons other than the priest can hear them being said and are thereby benefited by this edifying example.[26] Trusts for the promotion of fox-hunting may be truly anomalous, but the form of fox-hunting involved in the relevant case has now been made illegal by the Hunting Act 2004.

## *B. Apparent Purpose Trusts Benefitting Particular People*

### i. Absolute Gift with a Motive

**5–011** It may be possible to characterise an apparent purpose trust as, in fact, an absolute gift to a specific person or persons, with the supposed purpose in fact constituting the donor's motive for the gift. In such a case, the gift will be valid, and cannot be challenged by, for example, a residuary legatee, but the recipient will take absolutely and will be under no duty to apply the money only for the specified purpose. In *Re Andrew's Trust*,[27] for example, a fund was subscribed solely for the education of the seven children of a deceased clergyman and not for the exclusive use of one child or for equal division among them but as necessary. After the formal education of the children had been completed, Kekewich J held that the children were entitled to the balance equally. He construed "education" in the broadest sense as an ongoing process that did not come to an end with the conclusion of formal education, and he treated the reference to education as expressing merely the motive of the gift, holding that[28]:

---

undertaking to apply the money for the specific purpose, with the residuary legatee to have a power to apply for the funds if not spent on that purpose.

21 See, e.g. *IRC v Broadway Cottage Trust* [1955] Ch. 20 at 36; *Re Shaw* [1957] 1 W.L.R. 729 at 746.

22 As argued in P. Matthews, "The New Trust: Obligations Without Rights?" in A.J. Oakley (ed.), *Trends in Contemporary Trust Law* (Oxford University Press, 1997).

23 At paras 5–011—5–014.

24 *Hoare v Osborne* (1866) L.R. 1 Eq. 585.

25 [1990] Ch. 1.

26 See paras 6–233—6–242 for discussion.

27 [1905] 2 Ch. 48.

28 ibid., at 52–53, citing Page-Wood V.C. in *Re Sanderson's Trust* (1857) 3 K. & J. 497 at 503.

If a gross sum be given, or if the whole income of property be given, and a special purpose be assigned for the gift this court [rebuttably] regards the gift as absolute and the purpose merely as the motive of the gift, and therefore holds that the gift takes effect as to the whole sum or the whole income as the case may be.

This approach was applied by the Court of Appeal in *Re Osoba*,[29] in holding that a bequest to the testator's widow upon trust "for her maintenance and for the training of my daughter Abiola up to university grade and for the maintenance of my aged mother" was a trust for the three women absolutely as joint tenants, with the reference to maintenance and training bearing solely on the testator's motive for the gift. As the widow and the mother had died by that point, the daughter was absolutely entitled as the sole surviving joint tenant. Similarly in *Re Bowes*[30] a trust to spend £5,000 on planting trees for shelter on the Wemmergill Estate was held to be a trust for the estate owners absolutely with the motive of having trees planted. The trust was therefore valid, but as the owners were absolutely entitled they could choose to spend the money as they wished. **5–012**

It is clear that these cases, again, do not constitute an exception to the beneficiary principle. In each, there was a clear beneficiary or beneficiaries and there was no duty on the trustees to spend the fund solely for the specified purpose.[31] The difficulty in the cases is a factual rather than a legal one: is it right to say that, on the facts of the case, the donor intended the recipient to be free to spend the money as she wished, with the apparent purpose being only a motive for such a gift? It may be that the court has strained to apply that interpretation, as the alternative is that the donor's intended purpose trust will fail, and the recipient will receive nothing (unless she happens also to be the person entitled should a resulting trust arise). **5–013**

A more likely candidate as an exception to the beneficiary rule is *Re Abbott*.[32] A fund had been subscribed for the maintenance and support of two deaf and mute women. Stirling J held, not solely as a matter of construction of the documents by which the subscriptions had been sought, but as an inference from all the facts, that the surplus left after both women had died was held on resulting trust for the subscribers. His view, therefore, was that the subscribers had not intended the funds to be held on trust absolutely for the benefit of the women, with the reference to maintenance and support providing only a motive, but had rather intended the funds to be used for their benefit only whilst at least one survived. It may then be argued that, before the death of the survivor, the funds were held subject to a purpose trust, before resulting back to the donors on that death. The result is, however, also consistent with the analysis suggested above for the anomalous testamentary purpose trusts:[33] the attempted purpose trust failed immediately, and so the funds were held on resulting trust for the donors from that point, but the trustees had a power to spend the money on the specified purpose, such power ending only when the purpose could no longer be achieved. **5–014**

### ii. *Re Denley's Trust Deed*

*Re Denley's Trust Deed*

Chancery Division [1969] 1 Ch. 373

In 1936 land was conveyed by a company to trustees so that, until the expiration of 21 years from the death of the last survivor of certain specified persons, the land should under clause 2(c) of a trust deed "be **5–015**

---

29 [1979] 2 All E.R. 393.

30 [1896] 1 Ch. 507.

31 Note too that it is possible to make an absolute gift to a recipient, with the value of the gift to be set by the money spent by that person on a specific purpose: *Re Sanderson's Trust* (1857) 3 K. & J. 497.

32 [1900] 2 Ch. 326.

33 See para.5–009.

maintained and used as and for the purpose of a recreation or sports ground primarily for the benefit of the employees of the company and secondarily for the benefit of such other person or persons (if any) as the trustees may allow to use the same." The main question was dealt with as follows:

5-016 GOFF J: It was decided in *Re Astor's Settlement Trusts*,[34] that a trust for a number of non-charitable purposes was not merely unenforceable but void on two grounds; first that they were not trusts for the benefit of individuals, which I refer to as "the beneficiary principle", and, secondly, for uncertainty.

5-017 Counsel for the first defendant has argued that the trust in clause 2(c) in the present case is either a trust for the benefit of individuals, in which case he argues that they are an unascertainable class and therefore the trust is void for uncertainty; or it is a purpose trust, that is a trust for providing recreation, which he submits is void on the beneficiary principle; or alternatively it is something of a hybrid having the vices of both kinds.

5-018 I think that there may be a purpose or object trust, the carrying out of which would benefit an individual or individuals, where that benefit is so indirect or intangible or which is otherwise so framed as not to give those persons any locus standi to apply to the court to enforce the trust, in which case the beneficiary principle would, as it seems to me, apply to invalidate the trust, quite apart from any question of uncertainty or perpetuity. Such cases can be considered if and when they arise. The present is not, in my judgment, of that character, and it will be seen that clause 2(d) of the trust deed expressly states that, subject to any rules and regulations made by the trustees, the employees of the company shall be entitled to the use and enjoyment of the land.

5-019 Apart from this possible exception, in my judgment the beneficiary principle of *Re Astor*,[35] which was approved in *Re Endacott (decd.)*,[36] see particularly by Harman L.J.,[37] is confined to purpose or object trusts which are abstract or impersonal. The objection is not that the trust is for a purpose or object per se, but that there is no beneficiary or cestui que trust. The rule is so expressed in *Lewin on Trusts*,[38] and, in my judgment, with the possible exception which I have mentioned, rightly so. In *Re Wood*[39] Harman J. said:

> "There has been an interesting argument on the question of perpetuity, but it seems to me, with all respect to that argument, that there is an earlier obstacle which is fatal to the validity of this bequest, namely, that a gift on trust must have a cestui que trust, and there being here no cestui que trust the gift must fail."

5-020 Again, in *Leahy v Att.-Gen. of New South Wales*[40] Viscount Simonds, delivering the judgment of the Privy Council, said:

> "A gift can be made to persons (including a corporation) but it cannot be made to a purpose or to an object: so, also [and these are the important words] a trust may be created for the benefit of persons as cestuis que trust but not for a purpose or object unless the purpose or object be charitable. For a purpose or object cannot sue, but, if it be charitable, the Attorney-General can sue to enforce it."

5-021 Where, then, the trust, though expressed as a purpose, is directly or indirectly for the benefit of an individual or individuals, it seems to me that it is in general outside the mischief of the beneficiary principle.

5-022 I am fortified in this conclusion by the dicta of Lord Evershed M.R. and Harman L.J. in *Re Harpur's Will Trusts, Haller v Att.-Gen*.[41]

5-023 Some further support for my conclusion is, I think, to be found in *Re Aberconway's Settlement Trusts*[42] where it was assumed that a trust for the upkeep and development of certain gardens which were part of a settled estate was valid.

5-024 I also derive assistance from what was said by North J. in *Re Bowes*.[43] That was a bequest of a sum of money on trust to expend the same in planting trees for shelter on certain settled estates. It happened

---

34 [1952] Ch. 534.
35 [1952] Ch. 534.
36 [1960] Ch. 232.
37 [1960] Ch. 232 at 250.
38 16th edn, p.17.
39 [1949] Ch. 498 at 501.
40 [1959] A.C. 457 at 478.
41 [1962] Ch. 78 at 91, 96.
42 [1953] Ch. 647.
43 [1896] 1 Ch. 507.

that there was a father and a son of full age, tenant for life in possession and tenant in tail in remainder respectively; so that, subject to the son disentailing, they were together absolutely entitled, and the actual decision was that they could claim the money, but North J. said[44]:

> "If it were necessary to uphold it, the trees can be planted upon the whole of it until the fund is exhausted. Therefore, there is nothing illegal in the gift itself . . .";

and:[45]

> "I think there clearly is a valid trust to lay out money for the benefit of the persons entitled to the estate."

The trust in the present case is limited in point of time so as to avoid any infringement of the rule against perpetuities and, for the reasons which I have given, it does not offend against the beneficiary principle; and unless, therefore, it be void for uncertainty, it is a valid trust. **5–025**

There is, however, one other aspect of uncertainty which has caused me some concern; that is, whether this is in its nature a trust which the court can control, for, as Lord Eldon L.C. said in *Morice v Bishop of Durham*:[46] **5–026**

> "As it is a maxim that the execution of a trust shall be under the control of the court, it must be of such a nature that it can be under that control; so that the administration of it can be reviewed by the court; or, if the trustee dies, the court itself can execute the trust: a trust, therefore, which, in case of maladministration could be reformed; and a due administration directed; and then, unless the subject and the objects can be ascertained upon principles familiar in other cases, it must be decided that the court can neither reform maladministration nor direct a due administration."

In my judgment, however, it would not be right to hold the trust void on this ground. The court can, as it seems to me, execute the trust both negatively by restraining any improper disposition or use of the land, and positively by ordering the trustees to allow the employees and such other persons (if any) as they may admit to use the land for the purpose of a recreation or sports ground. Any difficulty there might be in practice in the beneficial enjoyment of the land by those entitled to use it is, I think, really beside the point. The same kind of problem is equally capable of arising in the case of a trust to permit a number of persons—for example, all the unmarried children of a testator or settlor—to use or occupy a house or to have the use of certain chattels; yet no one would suggest, I fancy, that such a trust would be void. **5–027**

In my judgment, therefore, the provisions of clause 2(c) are valid. **5–028**

Goff J thus considered that the attainment of the trust purposes was sufficiently for the benefit of certain individuals that the settlor should be taken to have intended that those individuals should have locus standi to enforce the trust positively in their favour.[47] In effect, the trust was primarily for the benefit of particular people (the employees), with the specified way in which they were to be benefited being a secondary consideration.[48] **5–029**

A *Re Denley*-type trust typically involves a relatively large, fluctuating class of beneficiaries and so varies, in its factual context, from the trusts which have previously been discussed. If, however, the class of parties benefitting from performance of the purpose is too widely drawn, the *Re Denley* analysis cannot apply, as it is then difficult to argue that the trust has any ascertainable beneficiaries.[49] It is, **5–030**

---

44 [1896] 1 Ch. 507 at 510.

45 [1896] 1 Ch. 507 at 511.

46 (1805) 10 Ves. 522 at 539.

47 See too *Re Saxone Shoe Co's Trust Deed* [1962] 1 W.L.R. 934 (which would now be valid under the *McPhail v Doulton* [1971] A.C. 424 test for discretionary trusts); *Wicks v Firth* [1983] A.C. 214; *Grender v Dresden* [2009] W.T.L.R. 379 at [18]. Persons named in a trust deed and benefiting directly or indirectly (e.g. as employees) but not intended to have a right to enforce the trust have no locus standi to apply to the court: *Shaw v Lawless* (1838) 5 Cl. & Fin. 129 at 153; *Gandy v Gandy* (1885) 30 Ch.D. 57 at 69–70.

48 Note that as the trust in *Re Denley* was expressly limited to a life in being plus 21 years, and a gift over was provided, it satisfied the rule against perpetuities: see paras 7–085—7–089.

49 See *Re Lipinski's Will Trusts* [1976] Ch. 235 at 248, discussed at paras 5–094—5–097.

therefore, far from clear whether the *Re Denley*-type trust constitutes an exception to the beneficiary principle which was, after all, expressly invoked in Goff J's judgment.[50] Certainly, it is clear that the duties of the trustees can be enforced by parties who benefit from the perfomance of those duties, and who can thus be seen as beneficiaries rather than as enforcers.

**5-031** Differing views have been expressed as to whether it is possible, in theory, for the beneficiaries of a *Re Denley*-type trust, acting together, to combine to terminate the trust and call for a transfer to them of the trust property, thus exercising the *Saunders v Vautier* power.[51] The answer depends on which of two competing views of the *Re Denley*-type trust is taken.[52] On the first, the beneficiaries do have the power, if acting together, to terminate the trust. The existence of the power may be merely theoretical, given the practical difficulties in gaining unanimity amongst the large, fluctuating class of beneficiaries, but the same can be said of a discretionary trust with a large class of actual or potential objects. On this view, the *Re Denley*-type trust is a standard trust for persons.[53] On the second view, the beneficiaries only have the power to ensure that the terms of the trust are complied with, and have no power to terminate the trust.[54]

**5-032** If this second view were accepted, the *Re Denley*-type trust, whilst not technically constituting an exception to the beneficiary principle, might be seen nonetheless as an exception to another general rule of English[55] trusts law, which may even underpin the beneficiary principle. That rule, given effect to in *Saunders v Vautier*,[56] is that the beneficiaries, acting together, have ultimate control of the trust property.[57] It may be that the beneficiary rule reflects a commitment in English law to the view that it is the proprietary entitlement of a beneficiary that generates a right to enforce the terms of the trust, and that therefore a settlor who appoints an enforcer who lacks any such proprietary entitlement has not succeeded in setting up a trust. As we will note below,[58] this debate as to the basis of the beneficiary principle is thus tied to the broader debate about the nature of a beneficiary's rights under a trust, which we will examine in Chapter 17.

## C. Quistclose Trusts

**5-033** In *Barclays Bank Ltd v Quistclose Investments Ltd*,[59] Quistclose lent money to Rolls Razor, another company in the same corporate group, so that Rolls Razor could pay a dividend to its shareholders. Rolls Razor became insolvent before the dividend was paid.[60] The House of Lords held that the money

---

50 [1969] 1 Ch. 373 at 382–383 (extracted at para.5-016). In *Grender v Dresden* [2009] W.T.L.R. 379 at [18], Norris J described the trust arising there as "a trust for a definable class of persons of the type recognized in *Re Denley*".

51 (1841) 4 Beav. 115: see paras 1-037 and 7-004ff.

52 The method of applying the rule against perpetuities to a *Re Denley*-type trust may also turn on which of these two views is adopted: see paras 7-085—7-089.

53 This view was taken of a *Re Denley*-type trust in *Re Grant's WT* [1980] 1 W.L.R. 360.

54 The treatment of *Re Denley* in *Re Lipinski's Will Trusts* [1976] Ch. 235 at 247–249 is consistent with this second view.

55 The rule does not form part of, for example, the trusts law of jurisdictions in the United States: see, e.g. *Claflin v Claflin* 149 Mass. 19 (1889); *Shelton v King* 229 U.S. 90 (1913).

56 (1841) 4 Beav. 115. For discussion of that rule and its importance to English trusts law, see P. Matthews, "The Comparative Importance of the Rule in *Saunders v Vautier*" (2006) 122 L.Q.R. 266 and para.7-004ff.

57 This is why Lawrence Collins J stated obiter in *Re Horley Town Football Club* [2006] W.T.L.R. 1817 at [131] that "there are difficulties with regard to termination of [a *Re Denley*-type trust] which make it an unsafe basis for decision". In contrast to *Re Denley* itself, no gift over was provided in the *Re Horley Town Football Club* case. It might nonetheless be argued that, as long as the purpose is limited to a suitable perpetuity period, the resulting trust taking effect at the end of such a period, in the absence of a gift over, ensures that the rule against inalienability (see paras 7-088—7-091) is not infringed: see, e.g. L. Tucker, N. Le Poidevin and J. Brightwell, *Lewin on Trusts*, 19th edn (Sweet & Maxwell, 2015), para.8-070.

58 At paras 5-101—5-109.

59 [1970] A.C. 567. See too *Re ETVR* [1987] B.C.L.C. 646.

60 For an entertaining account of the factual background, see R. Stevens, "Rolls Razor Ltd" in W. Swadling (ed.), *The Quistclose Trust* (Hart Publishing, 2004).

was held by Rolls Razor on trust for Quistclose, so that it was not available to Rolls Razor's other creditors. Lord Wilberforce, with whom the rest of the panel agreed, reached that result by finding that the money had been initially held by Rolls Razor on a trust to pay the dividends and that, when it went into insolvency, that purpose failed and a second trust arose in favour of Quistclose.[61]

Lord Wilberforce's analysis thus depended on a primary trust having arisen which, on one view, was a non-charitable purpose trust.[62] There are, however, some difficulties with that explanation. First, of course, it would constitute a departure from the beneficiary principle, which would be surprising given the lack of discussion of that principle in Lord Wilberforce's speech. Secondly, the trust in favour of the lender would then arise only on the insolvency of the borrower, and a key principle of insolvency law is that proprietary interests should not arise for the first time on insolvency, given their effect on other creditors.[63] Thirdly, why should the secondary trust arise at all, given that the insolvency does not by itself prevent payment of the money to the shareholders?[64] **5–034**

In *Twinsectra Ltd v Yardley*, Lord Millett, building on his own extra-judicial analysis of the so-called *Quistclose* trust,[65] as well as other academic criticisms of Lord Wilberforce's reasoning,[66] put forward a different interpretation of the case, which was generally[67] accepted by the other members of the House of Lords' panel, and has been applied in subsequent cases.[68] **5–035**

*Twinsectra Ltd v Yardley*

House of Lords [2002] 2 A.C. 164

Yardley needed a loan to complete a purchase of land. Twinsectra, the claimant, offered to lend him £1 million, but only if the loan was secured by a solicitor's personal undertaking (a very unusual requirement). Yardley's solicitor, Leach, refused to give the undertaking. Sims, another solicitor known to Yardley, but who was not acting for him in the purchase of the land, did agree to give the undertaking. By this point, Yardley had found another source of finance for the purchase of the land. He and Sims nonetheless decided to take up the offer of the £1 million loan from Twinsectra. As between them, the plan was that Sims would give the money to Yardley, to discharge a debt owed to Yardley, and Sims would then be primarily liable for repaying Twinsectra. Twinsectra was not told of this plan, nor was it told that the money was no longer to be used for buying the land. It paid the money to Sims on the basis that it would be used for acquiring property, and Sims promised (1) to keep the money until it was applied in buying land on behalf of Yardley, and (2) that the money would be used *solely* for that purpose. In breach of those conditions, Sims, on receiving the money from Twinsectra, released it to Leach, who received it on behalf of Yardley, and credited it to a client account. The money was then paid out in accordance with the instructions of Yardley or one of his co-directors. Some of the money was spent on the acquisition of property, but other **5–036**

---

61 [1970] A.C. 567 at 582: "the intention to create a secondary trust for the benefit of the lender, to arise if the primary trust, to pay the dividend could not be carried out, is clear and I can find no reason why the law should not give effect to it."

62 On the facts of *Quistclose* itself, it could be argued that the trust was for the benefit of the parties who would receive dividends (although for the problems of such an analysis, see Lord Millett in *Twinsectra v Yardley* [2002] 2 A.C. 164 at [82]–[89], extracted at paras 5–053—5–057). A *Quistclose* trust was, however, also found to arise in cases where the money was to be used solely for an abstract purpose: see, e.g. *Re EVTR* [1987] B.C.L.C. 646 and Lord Millett in *Twinsectra* at [89], extracted at para.5–057.

63 See R. Stevens, "Insolvency" in *The Quistclose Trust* (2004).

64 A point made by Lord Millett in *Twinsectra v Yardley* [2002] 2 A.C. 164 at [98], extracted at para.5–066. Of course, an insolvent company cannot choose to pay debts that are due to some of its creditors and refuse to pay debts due to others, but, as Lord Millett notes, ibid, on the hypothesis that a primary trust exists, the money was not in any case beneficially owned by the company.

65 P. J. Millett QC, "The *Quistclose* Trust: Who Can Enforce It?" (1985) 101 L.Q.R. 269.

66 See, e.g. R. Chambers, *Resulting Trusts* (Oxford University Press, 1997), pp.68–89.

67 Although note that on Lord Hoffmann's analysis at [11], the trust is express rather than resulting: see further para.5–072.

68 See, e.g. *Templeton Insurance Ltd v Penningtons Solicitors* [2007] W.T.L.R. 1103. In *Cooper v PRG Powerhouse Ltd* [2008] 2 All E.R. (Comm) 964, Evans-Lombe J also purported to follow *Twinsectra*, notwithstanding references throughout his judgment to "the purpose trust".

sums (totalling £357,720.11) were not. Neither Yardley nor Sims repaid Twinsectra. Twinsectra therefore wished to sue Leach. It claimed that the money it advanced to Sims had been impressed with a *Quistclose* trust, that Sims had breached this trust, and that Leach had dishonestly assisted in the breach by advancing sums to Yardley that were not used in the acqusition of property. The House of Lords held unanimously that the loan money had indeed been impressed with a *Quistclose* trust, and the parts of Lord Millett's speech dealing with this issue are reproduced here. Their Lordships also held by a majority (Lord Millett dissenting) that Leach was not liable in dishonest assistance, as he had not acted with the requisite degree of dishonesty. This was a controversial finding, and the definition of dishonesty in this context was later revisited by the Privy Council in *Barlow Clowes International Ltd v Eurotrust International Ltd*.[69]

LORD MILLETT:

**Was there a *Quistclose* trust?**

5-037 Money advanced by way of loan normally becomes the property of the borrower. He is free to apply the money as he chooses, and save to the extent to which he may have taken security for repayment the lender takes the risk of the borrower's insolvency. But it is well established that a loan to a borrower for a specific purpose where the borrower is not free to apply the money for any other purpose gives rise to fiduciary obligations on the part of the borrower which a court of equity will enforce. In the earlier cases the purpose was to enable the borrower to pay his creditors or some of them, but the principle is not limited to such cases.

5-038 Such arrangements are commonly described as creating "a *Quistclose* trust", after the well known decision of the House in *Barclays Bank Ltd v Quistclose Investments Ltd*[70] in which Lord Wilberforce confirmed the validity of such arrangements and explained their legal consequences. When the money is advanced, the lender acquires a right, enforceable in equity, to see that it is applied for the stated purpose, or more accurately to prevent its application for any other purpose. This prevents the borrower from obtaining any beneficial interest in the money, at least while the designated purpose is still capable of being carried out. Once the purpose has been carried out, the lender has his normal remedy in debt. If for any reason the purpose cannot be carried out, the question arises whether the money falls within the general fund of the borrower's assets, in which case it passes to his trustee in bankruptcy in the event of his insolvency and the lender is merely a loan creditor; or whether it is held on a resulting trust for the lender. This depends on the intention of the parties collected from the terms of the arrangement and the circumstances of the case.

5-039 In the present case Twinsectra contends that paragraphs 1 and 2 of the undertaking which Mr Sims signed on 24 December created a *Quistclose* trust. Mr Leach denies this and advances a number of objections to the existence of a trust. He says that Twinsectra lacked the necessary intention to create a trust, and relies on evidence that Twinsectra looked exclusively to Mr Sims' personal undertaking to repay the loan as its security for repayment. He says that commercial life would be impossible if trusts were lightly inferred from slight material, and that it is not enough to agree that a loan is to be made for a particular purpose. There must be something more, for example, a requirement that the money be paid into a segregated account, before it is appropriate to infer that a trust has been created. In the present case the money was paid into Mr Sims' client account, but that is sufficiently explained by the fact that it was not Mr Sims' money but his client's; it provides no basis for an inference that the money was held in trust for anyone other than Mr Yardley. Then it is said that a trust requires certainty of objects and this was lacking, for the stated purpose "to be applied in the purchase of property" is too uncertain to be enforced. Finally it is said that no trust in favour of Twinsectra could arise prior to the failure of the stated purpose, and this did not occur until the money was misapplied by Mr Yardley's companies.

**Intention**

5-040 The first two objections are soon disposed of. A settlor must, of course, possess the necessary intention to create a trust, but his subjective intentions are irrelevant. If he enters into arrangements which have the effect of creating a trust, it is not necessary that he should appreciate that they do so; it is sufficient that he intends to enter into them. Whether paragraphs 1 and 2 of the undertaking created a *Quistclose* trust turns on the true construction of those paragraphs.

5-041 The fact that Twinsectra relied for its security exclusively on Mr Sims's personal liability to repay goes to Twinsectra's subjective intention and is not relevant to the construction of the undertaking, but it is in any

69 [2006] 1 W.L.R. 1476; discussed at paras 11–134—11–136.
70 [1970] A.C. 567.

case not inconsistent with the trust alleged. Arrangements of this kind are not intended to provide security for repayment of the loan, but to prevent the money from being applied otherwise than in accordance with the lender's wishes. If the money is properly applied the loan is unsecured. This was true of all the decided cases, including the *Quistclose* case itself.

**The Effect of the Undertaking**

A *Quistclose* trust does not necessarily arise merely because money is paid for a particular purpose. A lender will often inquire into the purpose for which a loan is sought in order to decide whether he would be justified in making it. He may be said to lend the money for the purpose in question, but this is not enough to create a trust; once lent the money is at the free disposal of the borrower. Similarly payments in advance for goods or services are paid for a particular purpose, but such payments do not ordinarily create a trust. The money is intended to be at the free disposal of the supplier and may be used as part of his cashflow. Commercial life would be impossible if this were not the case. **5–042**

The question in every case is whether the parties intended the money to be at the free disposal of the recipient.[71] His freedom to dispose of the money is necessarily excluded by an arrangement that the money shall be used exclusively for the stated purpose, for as Lord Wilberforce observed in the *Quistclose* case:[72] **5–043**

> "A necessary consequence from this, by a process simply of interpretation, must be that if, for any reason, [the purpose could not be carried out,] the money was to be returned to [the lender]: the word 'only' or 'exclusively' can have no other meaning or effect."

In the *Quistclose* case a public quoted company in financial difficulties had declared a final dividend. Failure to pay the dividend, which had been approved by the shareholders, would cause a loss of confidence and almost certainly drive the company into liquidation. Accordingly the company arranged to borrow a sum of money "on condition that it is used to pay the forthcoming dividend". The money was paid into a special account at the company's bank, with which the company had an overdraft. The bank confirmed that the money "will only be used for the purpose of paying the dividend due on 24 July 1964". The House held that the circumstances were sufficient to create a trust of which the bank had notice, and that when the company went into liquidation without having paid the dividend the money was repayable to the lender.

In the present case paragraphs 1 and 2 of the undertaking are crystal clear. Mr Sims undertook that the money would be used solely for the acquisition of property and for no other purpose; and was to be retained by his firm until so applied. It would not be held by Mr Sims simply to Mr Yardley's order; and it would not be at Mr Yardley's free disposition. Any payment by Mr Sims of the money, whether to Mr Yardley or anyone else, otherwise than for the acquisition of property would constitute a breach of trust. **5–044**

Mr Leach insisted that such a payment would, no doubt, constitute a breach of contract, but there was no reason to invoke equitable principles merely because Mr Sims was a solicitor. But Mr Sims's status as a solicitor has nothing to do with it. Equity's intervention is more principled than this. It is unconscionable for a man to obtain money on terms as to its application and then disregard the terms on which he received it. Such conduct goes beyond a mere breach of contract. As North J. explained in *Gibert v Gonard*:[73] **5–045**

> "It is very well known law that if one person makes a payment to another for a certain purpose, and that person takes the money knowing that it is for that purpose, he must apply it to the purpose for which it was given. He may decline to take it if he likes; but if he chooses to accept the money tendered for a particular purpose, it is his duty, and there is a legal obligation on him, to apply it for that purpose."

The duty is not contractual but fiduciary. It may exist despite the absence of any contract at all between the parties, as in *Rose v Rose*;[74] and it binds third parties as in the *Quistclose* case itself. The duty is fiduciary in character because a person who makes money available on terms that it is to be used for a particular purpose only and not for any other purpose thereby places his trust and confidence in the recipient to ensure that it is properly applied. This is a classic situation in which a fiduciary relationship arises, and since it arises in respect of a specific fund it gives rise to a trust.

---

71 *Re Goldcorp Exchange Ltd* [1995] 1 A.C. 74 at 100 per Lord Mustill.
72 [1970] A.C. 567 at 580.
73 (1884) 54 L.J. Ch. 439 at 440.
74 (1986) 7 N.S.W.L.R. 679.

### The Nature of the Trust

5-046 The latter two objections cannot be so easily disposed of. They call for an exploration of the true nature of the *Quistclose* trust, and in particular the location of the beneficial interest while the purpose is still capable of being carried out.

5-047 This has been the subject of much academic debate. The starting point is provided by two passages in Lord Wilberforce's speech in the *Quistclose* case. He said:[75]

> "That arrangements of this character for the payment of a person's creditors by a third person, give rise to a relationship of a fiduciary character or trust, in favour, as a primary trust, of the creditors, and secondarily, if the primary trust fails, of the third person, has been recognised in a series of cases over some 150 years."

Later, he said:[76]

> "when the money is advanced, the lender acquires an equitable right to see that it is applied for the primary designated purpose (see *In re Rogers*[77] where both Lindley L.J. and Kay L.J. recognised this) . . .".

5-048 These passages suggest that there are two successive trusts, a primary trust for payment to identifiable beneficiaries, such as creditors or shareholders, and a secondary trust in favour of the lender arising on the failure of the primary trust. But there are formidable difficulties in this analysis, which has little academic support. What if the primary trust is not for identifiable persons, but as in the present case to carry out an abstract purpose? Where in such a case is the beneficial interest pending the application of the money for the stated purpose or the failure of the purpose? There are four possibilities: (i) in the lender; (ii) in the borrower; (iii) in the contemplated beneficiary; or (iv) in suspense.

5-049 *(i) The lender.*

In "The *Quistclose* Trust: Who Can Enforce It?",[78] I argued that the beneficial interest remained throughout in the lender. This analysis has received considerable though not universal academic support.[79] It was adopted by the New Zealand Court of Appeal in *General Communications Ltd v Development Finance Corp of New Zealand Ltd*[80] and referred to with apparent approval by Gummow J. in *In re Australian Elizabethan Theatre Trust*.[81] Gummow J. saw nothing special in the *Quistclose* trust, regarding it as essentially a security device to protect the lender against other creditors of the borrower pending the application of the money for the stated purpose.

5-050 On this analysis, the *Quistclose* trust is a simple commercial arrangement akin (as Professor Bridge observes) to a retention of title clause (though with a different object) which enables the borrower to have recourse to the lender's money for a particular purpose without entrenching on the lender's property rights more than necessary to enable the purpose to be achieved. The money remains the property of the lender unless and until it is applied in accordance with his directions, and insofar as it is not so applied it must be returned to him. I am disposed, perhaps pre-disposed, to think that this is the only analysis which is consistent both with orthodox trust law and with commercial reality. Before reaching a concluded view that it should be adopted, however, I must consider the alternatives.

5-051 *(ii) The borrower.*

It is plain that the beneficial interest is not vested unconditionally in the borrower so as to leave the money at his free disposal. That would defeat the whole purpose of the arrangements, which is to prevent the money from passing to the borrower's trustee in bankruptcy in the event of his insolvency. It would also

---

75 [1970] A.C. 567 at 580.
76 At 581.
77 (1891) 8 Morr. 243.
78 (1985) 101 L.Q.R. 269.
79 See for example Priestley L.J. "The *Romalpa* Clause and the *Quistclose* Trust" in *Equity and Commercial Relationships*, edited by P. D. Finn (1987), pp. 217, 237; and M. Bridge "The *Quistclose* Trust in a World of Secured Transactions" (1992) 12 O.J.L.S. 333, 352; and others.
80 [1990] 3 N.Z.L.R. 406.
81 (1991) 102 A.L.R. 681.

be inconsistent with all the decided cases where the contest was between the lender and the borrower's trustee in bankruptcy, as well as with the *Quistclose* case itself.[82]

The borrower's interest pending the application of the money for the stated purpose or its return to the lender is minimal. He must keep the money separate; he cannot apply it except for the stated purpose; unless the terms of the loan otherwise provide he must return it to the lender if demanded; he cannot refuse to return it if the stated purpose cannot be achieved; and if he becomes bankrupt it does not vest in his trustee in bankruptcy. If there is any content to beneficial ownership at all, the lender is the beneficial owner and the borrower is not. 5-052

In the present case the Court of Appeal adopted a variant, locating the beneficial interest in the borrower but subject to restrictions. I shall have to return to this analysis later.

*(iii) In the contemplated beneficiary.* 5-053

In the *Quistclose* case itself, as in all the reported cases which preceded it, either the primary purpose had been carried out and the contest was between the borrower's trustee in bankruptcy or liquidator and the person or persons to whom the borrower had paid the money; or it was treated as having failed, and the contest was between the borrower's trustee-in-bankruptcy and the lender. It was not necessary to explore the position while the primary purpose was still capable of being carried out and Lord Wilberforce's observations must be read in that light.

The question whether the primary trust is accurately described as a trust for the creditors first arose in *Re Northern Developments (Holdings) Ltd*,[83] where the contest was between the lender and the creditors. The borrower, which was not in liquidation and made no claim to the money, was the parent company of a group one of whose subsidiaries was in financial difficulty. There was a danger that if it were wound up or ceased trading it would bring down the whole group. A consortium of the group's banks agreed to put up a fund of more than £500,000 in an attempt to rescue the subsidiary. They paid the money into a special account in the name of the parent company for the express purpose of "providing money for the subsidiary's unsecured creditors over the ensuing weeks" and for no other purpose. The banks' object was to enable the subsidiary to continue trading, though on a reduced scale; it failed when the subsidiary was put into receivership at a time when some £350,000 remained unexpended. Relying on Lord Wilberforce's observations in the passages cited above, Sir Robert Megarry V.C. held that the primary trust was a purpose trust enforceable (inter alios) by the subsidiaries' creditors as the persons for whose benefit the trust was created. 5-054

There are several difficulties with this analysis. In the first place, Lord Wilberforce's reference to *Re Rogers* makes it plain that the equitable right he had in mind was not a mandatory order to compel performance, but a negative injunction to restrain improper application of the money; for neither Lindley L.J. nor Kay L.J. recognised more than this. In the second place, the object of the arrangements was to enable the subsidiary to continue trading, and this would necessarily involve it in incurring further liabilities to trade creditors. Accordingly the application of the fund was not confined to existing creditors at the date when the fund was established. The company secretary was given to understand that the purpose of the arrangements was to keep the subsidiary trading, and that the fund was "as good as share capital". Thus the purpose of the arrangements was not, as in other cases, to enable the debtor to avoid bankruptcy by paying off existing creditors, but to enable the debtor to continue trading by providing it with working capital with which to incur fresh liabilities. There is a powerful argument for saying that the result of the arrangements was to vest a beneficial interest in the subsidiary from the start. If so, then this was not a *Quistclose* trust at all. 5-055

In the third place, it seems unlikely that the banks' object was to benefit the creditors (who included the Inland Revenue) except indirectly. The banks had their own commercial interests to protect by enabling the subsidiary to trade out of its difficulties. If so, then the primary trust cannot be supported as a valid non-charitable purpose trust.[84] 5-056

The most serious objection to this approach is exemplified by the facts of the present case. In several of the cases the primary trust was for an abstract purpose with no one but the lender to enforce performance or restrain misapplication of the money. In *Edwards v Glyn*[85] the money was advanced to a bank to enable 5-057

---

[82] See in particular *Toovey v Milne* (1819) 2 B. & Ald. 683; *In re Rogers, Ex p. Holland & Hannen* (1891) 8 Morr. 243.

[83] Unreported, October 6, 1978.

[84] See *Re Grant's Will Trusts* [1980] 1 W.L.R. 360 and cf. *Re Denley's Trust Deed* [1969] 1 Ch. 373.

[85] (1859) 2 E. & E. 29.

the bank to meet a run. In *Re EVTR*,[86] it was advanced "for the sole purpose of buying new equipment". In *General Communications Ltd v Development Finance Corp of New Zealand Ltd*[87] the money was paid to the borrower's solicitors for the express purpose of purchasing new equipment. The present case is another example. It is simply not possible to hold money on trust to acquire unspecified property from an unspecified vendor at an unspecified time. There is no reason to make an arbitrary distinction between money paid for an abstract purpose and money paid for a purpose which can be said to benefit an ascertained class of beneficiaries, and the cases rightly draw no such distinction. Any analysis of the *Quistclose* trust must be able to accommodate gifts and loans for an abstract purpose.

5-058 *(iv) In suspense.*

As Peter Gibson J. pointed out in *Carreras Rothmans Ltd v Freeman Matthews Treasure Ltd*[88] the effect of adopting Sir Robert Megarry V.C.'s analysis is to leave the beneficial interest in suspense until the stated purpose is carried out or fails. The difficulty with this (apart from its unorthodoxy) is that it fails to have regard to the role which the resulting trust plays in equity's scheme of things, or to explain why the money is not simply held on a resulting trust for the lender.

5-059 Lord Browne-Wilkinson gave an authoritative explanation of the resulting trust in *Westdeutsche Landesbank Girpcentrale v Islington Borough Council*[89] and its basis has been further illuminated by Dr Robert Chambers in his book *Resulting Trusts* published in 1997. Lord Browne-Wilkinson explained that a resulting trust arises in two sets of circumstances. He described the second as follows: "Where A transfers property to B on express trusts, but the trusts declared do not exhaust the whole beneficial interest." The *Quistclose* case was among the cases he cited as examples. He rejected the argument that there was a resulting trust in the case before him because, unlike the situation in the present case, there was no transfer of money on express trusts. But he also rejected the argument on a wider and, in my respectful opinion, surer ground that the money was paid and received with the intention that it should become the absolute property of the recipient.

5-060 The central thesis of Dr Chambers's book is that a resulting trust arises whenever there is a transfer of property in circumstances in which the transferor (or more accurately the person at whose expense the property was provided) did not intend to benefit the recipient. It responds to the absence of an intention on the part of the transferor to pass the entire beneficial interest, not to a positive intention to retain it. Insofar as the transfer does not exhaust the entire beneficial interest, the resulting trust is a default trust which fills the gap and leaves no room for any part to be in suspense. An analysis of the *Quistclose* trust as a resulting trust for the transferor with a mandate to the transferee to apply the money for the stated purpose sits comfortably with Dr Chambers' thesis, and it might be thought surprising that he does not adopt it.

5-061 *(v) The Court of Appeal's analysis.*

The Court of Appeal were content to treat the beneficial interest as in suspense, or (following Dr Chambers's analysis) to hold that it was in the borrower, the lender having merely a contractual right enforceable by injunction to prevent misapplication. Potter L.J. put it in these terms:[90]

> "The purpose imposed at the time of the advance creates an enforceable restriction on the borrower's use of the money. Although the lender's right to enforce the restriction is treated as arising on the basis of a 'trust', the use of that word does not enlarge the lender's interest in the fund. The borrower is entitled to the beneficial use of the money, subject to the lender's right to prevent its misuse; the lender's limited interest in the fund is sufficient to prevent its use for other than the special purpose for which it was advanced."

This analysis, with respect, is difficult to reconcile with the court's actual decision in so far as it granted Twinsectra a proprietary remedy against Mr Yardley's companies as recipients of the misapplied funds. Unless the money belonged to Twinsectra immediately before its misapplication, there is no basis on which a proprietary remedy against third party recipients can be justified.

---

86 [1987] B.C.L.C. 646.
87 [1990] 3 N.Z.L.R. 406.
88 [1985] Ch. 207 at 223.
89 [1996] A.C. 669 at 708.
90 [1999] Lloyd's Rep. Bank. 438 at 456.

Dr Chambers's "novel view" (as it has been described) is that the arrangements do not create a trust at all; the borrower receives the entire beneficial ownership in the money subject only to a contractual right in the lender to prevent the money being used otherwise than for the stated purpose. If the purpose fails, a resulting trust in the lender springs into being. In fact, he argues for a kind of restrictive covenant enforceable by negative injunction yet creating property rights in the money. But restrictive covenants, which began life as negative easements, are part of our land law. Contractual obligations do not run with money or a chose in action like money in a bank account. 5–062

Dr Chambers's analysis has attracted academic comment, both favourable and unfavourable. For my own part, I do not think that it can survive the criticism levelled against it by Lusina Ho and P. St. J. Smart [in their article] "Reinterpreting the *Quistclose* Trust: A Critique of Chambers' Analysis".[91] It provides no solution to cases of non-contractual payment; is inconsistent with Lord Wilberforce's description of the borrower's obligation as fiduciary and not merely contractual; fails to explain the evidential significance of a requirement that the money should be kept in a separate account; cannot easily be reconciled with the availability of proprietary remedies against third parties; and while the existence of a mere equity to prevent misapplication would be sufficient to prevent the money from being available for distribution to the creditors on the borrower's Insolvency (because the trustee in bankruptcy has no greater rights than his bankrupt) it would not prevail over secured creditors. If the bank in the *Quistclose* case had held a floating charge (as it probably did) and had appointed a receiver, the adoption of Dr. Chambers's analysis should have led to a different outcome. 5–063

Thus all the alternative solutions have their difficulties. But there are two problems which they fail to solve, but which are easily solved if the beneficial interest remains throughout in the lender. One arises from the fact, well established by the authorities, that the primary trust is enforceable by the lender. But on what basis can he enforce it? He cannot do so as the beneficiary under the secondary trust, for if the primary purpose is fulfilled there is no secondary trust: the precondition of his claim is destructive of his standing to make it. He cannot do so as settlor, for a settlor who retains no beneficial interest cannot enforce the trust which he has created. 5–064

Dr Chambers insists that the lender has merely a right to prevent the misapplication of the money, and attributes this to his contractual right to specific performance of a condition of the contract of loan. As I have already pointed out, this provides no solution where the arrangement is non-contractual. But Lord Wilberforce clearly based the borrower's obligation on an equitable or fiduciary basis and not a contractual one. He was concerned to justify the co-existence of equity's exclusive jurisdiction with the common law action for debt. Basing equity's intervention on its auxiliary jurisdiction to restrain a breach of contract would not have enabled the lender to succeed against the bank, which was a third party to the contract. There is only one explanation of the lender's fiduciary right to enforce the primary trust which can be reconciled with basic principle: he can do so because he is the beneficiary. 5–065

The other problem is concerned with the basis on which the primary trust is said to have failed in several of the cases, particularly *Toovey v Milne* and the *Quistclose* case itself. Given that the money did not belong to the borrower in either case, the borrower's insolvency should not have prevented the money from being paid in the manner contemplated. A man cannot pay some only of his creditors once he has been adjudicated bankrupt, but a third party can. A company cannot pay a dividend once it has gone into liquidation, but there is nothing to stop a third party from paying the disappointed shareholders. The reason why the purpose failed in each case must be because the lender's object in making the money available was to save the borrower from bankruptcy in the one case and collapse in the other. But this in itself is not enough. A trust does not fail merely because the settlor's purpose in creating it has been frustrated: the trust must become illegal or impossible to perform. The settlor's motives must not be confused with the purpose of the trust; the frustration of the former does not by itself cause the failure of the latter. But if the borrower is treated as holding the money on a resulting trust for the lender but with power (or in some cases a duty) to carry out the lender's revocable mandate, and the lender's object in giving the mandate is frustrated, he is entitled to revoke the mandate and demand the return of money which never ceased to be his beneficially. . . . 5–066

As Sherlock Holmes reminded Dr Watson, when you have eliminated the impossible, whatever remains, however improbable, must be the truth. I would reject all the alternative analyses, which I find unconvincing for the reasons I have endeavoured to explain, and hold the *Quistclose* trust to be an entirely orthodox 5–067

[91] (2001) 21 O.J.L.S. 267.

> example of the kind of default trust known as a resulting trust. The lender pays the money to the borrower by way of loan, but he does not part with the entire beneficial interest in the money, and in so far as he does not it is held on a resulting trust for the lender from the outset. Contrary to the opinion of the Court of Appeal, it is the borrower who has a very limited use of the money, being obliged to apply it for the stated purpose or return it. He has no beneficial interest in the money, which remains throughout in the lender subject only to the borrower's power or duty to apply the money in accordance with the lender's instructions. When the purpose fails, the money is returnable to the lender, not under some new trust in his favour which only comes into being on the failure of the purpose, but because the resulting trust in his favour is no longer subject to any power on the part of the borrower to make use of the money. Whether the borrower is obliged to apply the money for the stated purpose or merely at liberty to do so, and whether the lender can countermand the borrower's mandate while it is still capable of being carried out, must depend on the circumstances of the particular case.
>
> **Certainty**
>
> **5–068** After this over-long exposition, it is possible to dispose of the remaining objections to the creation of a *Quistclose* trust very shortly. A trust must have certainty of objects. But the only trust is the resulting trust for the lender. The borrower is authorised (or directed) to apply the money for a stated purpose, but this is a mere power and does not constitute a purpose trust. Provided the power is stated with sufficient clarity for the court to be able to determine whether it is still capable of being carried out or whether the money has been misapplied, it is sufficiently certain to be enforced. If it is uncertain, however, then the borrower has no authority to make any use of the money at all and must return it to the lender under the resulting trust. Uncertainty works in favour of the lender, not the borrower; it cannot help a person in the position of Mr Leach.
>
> **When the Trust in Favour of the Lender Arises**
>
> **5–069** Like all resulting trusts, the trust in favour of the lender arises when the lender parts with the money on terms which do not exhaust the beneficial interest. It is not a contingent reversionary or future interest. It does not suddenly come into being like an 18th century use only when the stated purpose fails. It is a default trust which fills the gap when some part of the beneficial interest is undisposed of and prevents it from being "in suspense".
>
> **Conclusion**
>
> **5–070** In my opinion the Court of Appeal were correct to find that the terms of paragraphs 1 and 2 of the undertaking created a *Quistclose* trust. The money was never at Mr Yardley's free disposal. It was never held to his order by Mr Sims. The money belonged throughout to Twinsectra, subject only to Mr Yardley's right to apply it for the acquisition of property. Twinsectra parted with the money to Mr Sims, relying on him to ensure that the money was properly applied or returned to it. Mr Sims act in paying the money over to Mr Leach was a breach of trust, but it did not in itself render the money incapable of being applied for the stated purpose. In so far as Mr Leach applied the money in the acquisition of property, the purpose was achieved.

**5–071** In essence, Lord Millett held that where A lends money to B on the condition that B applies the money only for a specific purpose, a trust of the money immediately arises in A's favour, but this trust is defeasible by the exercise of a power vested in B to apply the money to the specified purpose.[92] If and when the money is so applied, the trust ends and B simply owes A a personal duty to repay the loan on the terms agreed between the parties. It is important to note that this analysis, whereby the holder of property has a power to spend it on a particular purpose, but no purpose trust arises, is consistent with the analysis suggested above for the anomalous testamentary purpose trust cases and for *Re Abbott*.[93]

**5–072** It seems from his extra-judicial writings that Lord Millett formerly thought that the initial trust

---

[92] The nature of this power is discussed in L. Smith, "Understanding the Power" in *The Quistclose Trust* (2004).

[93] [1900] 2 Ch. 326. See paras 5–009 and 5–014 respectively.

for B would always be an express trust, arising as a result of A's exercise of a power to set up a trust. His speech in *Twinsectra*, however, suggests that he was persuaded by Professor Chambers' general work on resulting trusts to modify this opinion,[94] so that in cases where the transferor does not declare an express trust for herself, a resulting trust can arise in her favour.[95] This is consistent with the general rule that, if A gives money to B intending B to hold it on a non-charitable purpose trust, such a trust immediately fails and B holds that money on resulting trust for A. However, it would be easy to exaggerate the signficance of Lord Millett's shift from an express trust to a resulting trust analysis. As we discuss in Chapter 4, A's intention to create a trust has an important role to play in each type of trust.[96] Each of the express and resulting trust analyses is consistent with Lord Millett's point that the "question in every case is whether the parties intended the money to be at the free disposal of the recipient"[97] and so the governing factor in finding a trust is "the intention of the parties collected from the terms of the arrangement and the circumstances of the case".[98]

## *D. Gifts for the Purposes of Unincorporated Bodies*

### i. Unincorporated Bodies

An unincorporated body, whether called an association, club, society, or anything else, lacks legal personality as a body: it cannot hold legal rights nor be subject to legal duties, and so it cannot own property or enter into contracts.[99] Legally, such a body consists simply of its individual members at any given time. **5–073**

### ii. Holding of Property by Unincorporated Bodies

Whilst an unincorporated body cannot itself hold property, trustees or others nominated under the body's constitution may hold property on a bare trust for the members of the body. The existence of such a trust ensures that the property is insulated from the general creditors of those holding it. Such a trust does not, of course, constitute an exception to the beneficiary principle, as the beneficiaries are the members of the body. The particular rights of the beneficiaries will depend on the body's constitution and the express or implied contractual arrangements between the members.[100] As trustees, **5–074**

94 Although not his analysis of the *Quistclose* case, which his Lordship thought vulnerable to the criticisms made in L. Ho and P. St.J. Smart "Reinterpreting the *Quistclose* Trust: A Critique of Chambers' Analysis" (2001) 21 O.J.L.S. 267. Chambers answers these criticisms, and restates his position on *Quistclose*, in "Restrictions on the Use of Money" in Swadling, ibid., See too J. Glister, "The Nature of *Quistclose* Trusts: Classification and Reconciliation" [2004] C.L.J. 632.

95 As noted in J. Penner, "Lord Millett's Analysis" in Swadling, ibid., pp.50–56. See also Lord Millett's own comments in the foreword at p.ix. Whether the recipient is an express trustee or a resulting trustee with knowledge of X's equitable interest, Y must account to X for the money from the moment of receipt, and must pay X any profit she obtains by misapplication of the money: *Abraaj Investment Management Ltd v Bregawn Jersey Ltd* [2010] EWHC 630 (Comm) at [28]–[32].

96 As we will see at paras 14–161ff, Lord Millett's analysis of the resulting trust, which depends not on a positive intention, but rather on "the absence of an intention on the part of the transferor to pass the entire beneficial interest", is something of a minority position within the current law, and is inconsistent with the House of Lords' approach in the leading case of *Westdeutsche Landesbank Girozentrale v Islington LBC* [1996] A.C. 669.

97 [2002] 2 A.C. 164 at [74] (extracted at para.5–043).

98 ibid., at [69] (extracted at para.5–038).

99 Trade unions are unincorporated associations (if not incorporated as a special register body) but by the Trade Union and Labour Relations Consolidation Act 1992 s.10 they can make contracts in their own names, may sue or be sued in their own names, judgments can be enforced against them as if they were bodies corporate, and property may be vested in trustees on trust "for the union".

100 *Re Bucks Constabulary Fund Friendly Society (No.2)* [1979] 1 W.L.R. 936.

those holding the property may enter into contracts, thereby putting the property at risk vis-à-vis the claims of creditors, and may even be authorised to declare trusts binding the body's property.[101]

### iii. Acquisition of Property by Unincorporated Bodies

**5-075** Consider a simple case where A wishes to make a gift of £500 to her local tennis club, which is an unincorporated body and is not devoted to exclusively charitable purposes. It may be that her intention is for the money, like a subscription paid by a member, simply to become part of the general funds of the club, held by the trustees on trust for the current members, and to be spent as soon as convenient on general expenses. However, she may intend that the fund be held as a separate endowment, so that income but not capital is spent, managed separately from the body's general assets. The difficulty then is in giving effect to this fairly simple intention. The beneficiary principle means that the money cannot be held on a non-charitable purpose trust. If it is found that the only possible interpretation of the facts is that A intended to set up such a trust, the gift will fail and there will be a resulting trust to A or A's estate.[102]

#### (1) Lifetime Gifts: The Mandate Analysis

**5-076** In *Conservative Central Office v Burrell*,[103] Brightman LJ suggested that where A contributes funds to a body, for example by advancing them to its treasurer, she may choose to keep ownership of that property but give the treasurer a mandate to add the money to the general funds of the association and spend it accordingly. Once that has been done the mandate becomes irrevocable, but until then she has the right to restrain or have made good a misapplication of the fund. This construction is consistent with the beneficiary principle, as ownership of the property remains with the donor, and it also gives the donor some degree of control over the use of the property. It should also be noted that it is consistent with the power analysis that we have already seen applied to other situations,[104] as the basic model is that the recipient has a power but not a duty to apply funds to a particular purpose.

#### (2) Testamentary Gifts

**5-077** The mandate analysis works well where A makes a lifetime transfer, but it cannot apply to a testamentary transfer as "no agency could be set up at the moment of death between a testator and his chosen agent".[105] Hence the analysis does not assist in the fairly common case where A wishes to leave funds in her will to a local club. As has been judicially noted, however, "It would astonish a layman to be told there was a difficulty in his giving a legacy to an unincorporated non-charitable society which he had, or could have, supported without trouble during his lifetime".[106] In *Neville Estates Ltd v Madden*,[107] Cross J set out three possible interpretations of a testamentary gift to an unincorporated association: the first is an

---

[101] Anything they do may be ratified by the members since unincorporated bodies have no legal capacity to be limited and so unlike companies they cannot act in an ultra vires way (although the ultra vires doctrine for companies has been abolished where outsiders dealing with the company are concerned: Companies Act 2006 s.39).

[102] As occurred in, e.g. *Re St Andrew's (Cheam) Lawn Tennis Club Trust* [2012] 1 W.L.R. 3487, in relation to land given to the club.

[103] [1982] 1 W.L.R. 522 at 529–530.

[104] See paras 5-009, 5-014 and 5-071.

[105] As accepted by Brightman LJ in *Conservative Central Office v Burrell* [1982] 1 W.L.R. 522 at 530. See too *Re Wilson* [1908] 1 Ch. 839.

[106] *Re Recher's Will Trusts* [1972] Ch. 526 at 536.

[107] [1962] Ch. 526 at 540.

absolute gift to the current members as joint tenants[108]; the second is an absolute gift to the members where those members will hold the property subject to the terms of the contract between them in their capacity as members;[109] the third is a gift in trust to be applied for the purposes of the body.[110]

(a) *Absolute gift to current members*

It is of course possible that A might wish to make an absolute gift solely to the current members of the club.[111] In such a case, each member can claim her proportionate share and, as a simple gift to individuals has been made, there is again no question of any breach of the beneficiary principle. The interpretation used in a case such as *Re Andrew's Trust*[112] can thus be applied, with any reference to the purposes of the club merely providing the motive for A's decision to make an absolute gift, rather than a binding restraint on the members' rights to the funds. An interesting question arises if there is a contract between the donees as members of the body (e.g. the consitution of the club by which they all agree with one another to be bound) which requires gifts to members as members to be treated as an accretion to the body's fund to be dealt with according to the body's rules.[113] In such a case, it seems that the donor's property will have to be so treated[114]: presumably, proportionate shares of the property are initially acquired but are then held by the members subject to a constructive trust, arising as a result of the members' contractual duties to each other.[115] **5–078**

If A's gift can thus be interpreted as an absolute gift to existing members of the club, it will be valid, and there is no question of a resulting trust arising. There is also, of course, no perpetuities problem, as the property vests immediately and absolutely in the existing members of the club. Indeed, in *Leahy v Attorney General of New South Wales*,[116] Viscount Simonds stated that, if nothing else is known about A's intentions, a simple gift to an unincorportated body without more is a gift to the members of the club at the date of the gift. As in the *Leahy* case itself, however, this presumption is easily displaced. In the usual case, it is clear that the gift is intended not as an absolute one to the individuals who happen to make up the club's membership at the time the gift takes effect, under which any of those individuals would immediately be free to take a proportionate part of the property. The gift is rather to the members *as members*. However there is also a difficulty in saying that the money is to be held for the benefit of current *and future* members. A's intent to benefit future members requires the capital to be kept intact and held on trust for only the income to be used, so that the capital would remain available for the benefit of future members.[117] If the gift were construed as a gift to the body on trust for carrying out purposes, with the gift being an endowment fund to be used for those purposes only, it would, again, be an invalid attempt to set up a non-charitable purpose trust, and the funds would be held on resulting trust for A or A's estate.[118] **5–079**

---

108 Considered at paras 5–078—5–080.
109 Considered at paras 5–081—5–092.
110 Considered at paras 5–093—5–098.
111 In *Neville Estates Ltd v Madden* [1962] Ch. 832, Cross J noted that a gift to existing members as joint tenants is one possible interpretation of a gift to an unincorporated body, but that interpretation can be applied only if consistent with A's actual intention.
112 [1905] 2 Ch. 48: see para.5–011.
113 Like property caught by a donee's covenant to settle after-acquired property: *Pullan v Koe* [1913] 1 Ch. 9.
114 *Leahy v Attorney General for New South Wales* [1959] A.C. 457 at 478 per Viscount Simonds: "If it is a gift to individuals, each of them is entitled to his distributive share (unless he has previously bound himself by the rules of the society that it should be devoted to some other purpose)."
115 Compare, e.g. *Pullan v Koe* [1913] 1 Ch. 9, for which see paras 2–074ff. See too paras 16–025—16–029.
116 [1959] A.C. 457 at 477.
117 *Leahy v Attorney General for New South Wales* [1959] A.C. 457.
118 There is equally a potential perpetuity problem with a gift for future members: unless a suitable time limit is imposed, and a gift over is provided, the gift infringes the rule against remoteness of vesting: see paras 7–080—7–087.

5-080 It would be very unfortunate if the law could not accommodate such a simple desire as the wish to give money to a local club. Means have therefore been found to analyse the effect of a donation to an unincorporated association. It is important to bear in mind that these means are *not* exceptions to the beneficiary principle: they are rather ways of escaping the effect of that principle. We will now examine the principal interpretations that the courts have used in order to uphold a transfer of property to the trustees or other officers of an unincorporated body, and to avoid the conclusion that an invalid purpose trust was intended.

(b) *The "contract-holding"*[119] *analysis: an absolute gift of legal title to the current members, taking effect as an accretion to the body's funds which is to be dealt with (under a bare trust) according to the rules of the body by which the members are all contractually bound*

5-081 In *Conservative Central Office v Burrell*,[120] the Court of Appeal considered the correct analysis of donations made to the Conservative Party. Brightman LJ noted that, if the Conservative Party had been "an unincorporated association with an identifiable membership bound together by identifiable rules" with the Central Office holding the party funds, then any contribution to the Party would:

> take effect in favour of the members of the unincorporated association known as the Conservative Party as an accretion to the funds which are the subject matter of the contract which such members have made inter se: see, for example, *Re Recher's Will Trusts*.[121]

5-082 This analysis, described by Brighman LJ as the "easy answer"[122] to the problem of validating a gift to an unincorporated body, thus depends on finding a contractual link between all the members, so that they are subject to mutual rights and duties, whether set out in a constitution or found by implication. There is, of course, no perpetuities problem, as the property vests immediately in the existing members of the club, and they have the power to alienate the property by, if necesssary, altering the terms of their contract. The acquisition of property by such a club can then be explained as in the following extract.

*Re Recher's Will Trusts*

Chancery Division [1972] Ch. 526

5-083 By will dated May 23, 1957, a testator gave a share of her residue to what the judge interpreted as "the London and Provincial Anti-Vivisection Society" which had ceased to exist on January 1, 1957. The testator died in 1962. Consideration was first given to the question whether the gift would have been valid if the unincorporated society had existed at the time of her death.

5-084 BRIGHTMAN J.: Having reached the conclusion that the gift in question is not a gift to the members of the London and Provincial Society at the date of death, as joint tenants or tenants in common so as to entitle a member as of right to a distributive share, nor an attempted gift to present and future members beneficially, and is not a gift in trust for the purpose of the society, I must now consider how otherwise, if at all, it is capable of taking effect.

5-085 As I have already mentioned, the rules of the London and Provincial Society do not purport to create any trusts except insofar as the honorary trustees are not beneficial owners of the assets of the society, but are trustees on trust to deal with such assets according to the directions of the committee.

5-086 A trust for non-charitable purposes, as distinct from a trust for individuals, is clearly void because there

---

119 The term "contract-holding" is used as a shorthand for this analysis by e.g. Lawrence Collins J in *Re Horley Town Football Club* [2006] W.T.L.R. 1817 at [43]–[46], [114].

120 [1982] 1 W.L.R. 522 at 529–530.

121 [1972] Ch. 526.

122 [1982] 1 W.L.R. 522 at 529.

is no beneficiary. It does not, however, follow that persons cannot band themselves together as an association or society, pay subscriptions and validly devote their funds in pursuit of some lawful non-charitable purpose. An obvious example is a members' social club. But it is not essential that the members should only intend to secure direct personal advantages to themselves. The association may be one in which personal advantages to the members are combined with the pursuit of some outside purpose. Or the association may be one which offers no personal benefit at all to the members, the funds of the association being applied exclusively to the pursuit of some outside purpose. Such an association of persons is bound, I would think, to have some sort of constitution; i.e. the rights and liabilities of the members of the association will inevitably depend on some form of contract inter se, usually evidenced by a set of rules. In the present case it appears to me clear that the life members, the ordinary members and the associate members of the London Provincial Society were bound together by a contract inter se. Any such member was entitled to the rights and subject to the liabilities defined by the rules. If the committee acted contrary to the rules, an individual member would be entitled to take proceedings in the courts to compel observance of the rules or to recover damages for any loss he had suffered as a result of the breach of contract. As and when a member paid his subscription to the association, he would be subjecting his money to the disposition and expenditure thereof laid down by the rules. That is to say, the member would be bound to permit, and entitled to require, the honorary trustees and other members of the society to deal with that subscription in accordance with the lawful directions of the committee. Those directions would include the expenditure of that subscription, as part of the general funds of the association, in furthering the objects of the association. The resultant situation, on analysis, is that the London and Provincial Society represented an organisation of individuals bound together by a contract under which their subscriptions became, as it were, mandated towards a certain type of expenditure as adumbrated in rule 1. Just as the two parties to a bipartite bargain can vary or terminate their contract by mutual assent, so it must follow that the life members, ordinary members and associate members of the London and Provincial Society could, at any moment of time, by unanimous agreement (or by majority vote if the rules so prescribe), vary or terminate their multipartite contract. There would be no limit to the type of variation or termination to which all might agree. There is no private trust or trust for charitable purposes or other trust to hinder the process. It follows that if all members agreed, they could decide to wind up the London and Provincial Society and divide the net assets among themselves beneficially. No one would have any locus standi to stop them so doing. The contract is the same as any other contract and concerns only those who are parties to it, that is to say, the members of the society.

The funds of such an association may, of course, be derived not only from the subscriptions of the contracting parties but also from donations from non-contracting parties and legacies from persons who have died. In the case of a donation which is not accompanied by any words which purport to impose a trust, it seems to me that the gift takes effect in favour of the existing members of the association as an accretion to the funds which are the subject-matter of the contract which such members have made inter se, and falls to be dealt with in precisely the same way as the funds which the members themselves have subscribed. So, in the case of a legacy. In the absence of words which purport to impose a trust, the legacy is a gift to the members beneficially, not as joint tenants or as tenants in common so as to entitle each member to an immediate distributive share, but as an accretion to the funds which are the subject-matter of the contract which the members have made inter se. **5–087**

In my judgment the legacy in the present case to the London and Provincial Society ought to be construed as a legacy of that type, that is to say, a legacy to the members beneficially as an accretion to the funds subject to the contract which they had made inter se. Of course, the testatrix did not intend the members of the society to divide their bounty between themselves, and doubtless she was ignorant of that remote but theoretical possibility. Her knowledge or absence of knowledge of the true legal analysis of the gift is irrelevant. The legacy is accordingly in my view valid, subject only to the effect of the events of January 1, 1957. **5–088**

The analysis in *Re Recher's Will Trusts*, sometimes referred to as the "second of Cross J's categories",[123] is very important as it provides the standard way of understanding the effect of a gift to an unincorporated **5–089**

---

[123] See, e.g. *Hanchett-Stamford v Attorney General* [2009] Ch. 173 at [29], referring to Cross J's analysis in *Neville Estates Ltd v Madden* [1962] Ch. 526 at 540, set out at para.5–077.

body in the usual case where it is possible to find an express or implied contract between the members.[124] It is important to note that the analysis can apply even where the purposes of the body are "outward-looking" and so the donor's expectation is that the members will not in fact use the funds for their own benefit.[125] The point is that even if the donor's aim is to achieve that purpose, the legal means of fulfilling the aim is to "make a gift to an association formed for the pursuit of that purpose in the expectation that the subject matter of the gift will be so used, without imposing or attempting to impose any trust or obligation on the members, or the trustees, or the committee of the association".[126]

**5-090** It is also worth emphasising that the analysis does not constitute an exception to the beneficiary principle: Brightman J makes clear in *Re Recher's Will Trusts* that in the standard case, where the gift does not include "any words which purport to impose a trust" the gift is made "to the members beneficially, not as joint tenants or tenants in common so as to entitle each member to an immediate distributive share, but as an accretion to the funds which are the subject matter of the contract which the members have made inter se". As Brightman J acknowledges, this does mean that the members at any point may decide to vary their contract and so "could decide to wind up the [club] and divide the net assets among themselves beneficially". The point here is the same as that examined above,[127] in relation to gifts subject to a motive: whilst it may be the case that the members thus choosing to wind up the club and take the money would be contrary to the donor's likely intention, this solution does at least permit the gift to be valid, and so avoids the resulting trust for the donor (or, in the case of a testamentary gift, to the donor's estate) that would arise if the gift were interpreted instead as an attempt to set up a non-charitable purpose trust.

**5-091** It is clear that the analysis in *Re Recher's Will Trusts* is the courts' preferred means of validating a gift to an unincorporated body, and that they will use it even if this requires a somewhat flexible interpretation of the facts of the case.[128] There are, nonetheless, some situations in which the contract-holding analysis cannot be applied. First, it cannot apply if, on the facts, it is impossible to find any express or implied contract that binds all the members of the body.[129] Secondly, it cannot apply if, on the facts, it is not within the power of the members of the body, acting together, to agree to end any restrictions on the use of the body's property and to divide that property amongst themselves.[130] This is because, in the absence of such a power, it is impossible to find that a gift to the members, albeit subject to the members' contract, has been made.[131]

**5-092** Each of those two restrictions has caused difficulties for a political party. In *Conservative Central Office v Burrell*,[132] the first problem arose: the standard contract-holding analysis could not be applied

---

124 As noted by Lewison J in *Hanchett-Stamford v Attorney General* [2009] Ch. 173 at [29].

125 See *Re Recher's WT* [1972] Ch. 526 at 542, doubting the approach adopted by the High Court of Australia in *Bacon v Pianta* (1966) 114 C.L.R. 634, where a gift to the Communist Party of Australia for "its sole use and benefit" was interpreted as an invalid attempt to set up a purpose trust.

126 As noted by Vinelott J in *Re Grant's WT* [1980] 1 W.L.R. 360 at 367.

127 At para.5-013.

128 In *Re Horley Town Football Club* [2006] W.T.L.R. 1817, for example, land was conveyed by a deed (referred to in the judgment as "the Deed") on trust "for the primary purpose of securing a permanent ground for The Horley Town Football Club", for a defined period consistent with the perpetuities rules, but Lawrence Collins J (at [114]) was nonetheless "satisfied that the Deed should be construed as a gift to the Club, as a 'contract-holding' gift to the Club and its members for the time being within category (2) in *Neville Estates v Madden*".

129 See, e.g. *Conservative Central Office v Burrell* [1982] 1 W.L.R. 522.

130 See, e.g. *Re Grant's WT* [1980] 1 W.L.R. 360; *Re St Andrew's (Cheam) Lawn Tennis Club Trust* [2012] 1 W.L.R. 3487.

131 See *Re Grant's WT* [1980] 1 W.L.R. 360 at 368 per Vinelott J: "It must, as I see it, be a necessary characteristic of any gift within the second category that the members of the association can by an appropriate majority, if the rules so provide, or acting unanimously if they do not, alter the rules so as to provide that the funds, or part of them, should be applied for some new purpose, or even distributed amongst the members for their own benefit."

132 [1982] 1 W.L.R. 522 at 529–530.

to gifts made to the Central Office for the Conservative Party, as the Party included both members of local constituency associations and members of Parliament and there was no contractual link between those members. In *Re Grant's Will Trusts*,[133] the second problem arose: a gift was made for the benefit of a local constituency party of the Labour Club, but its members did not have full potential control of the property, as the constituency party's rules were:

> capable of being altered by an outside body [the Annual Party Conference or the National Executive Committee] which could direct an alteration under which the general committee of the [local party] would be bound to transfer any property for the time being held for the benefit of the [local party] to the National Labour Party for national purposes.[134]

(c) *Trust for the purposes of the association*

Even if the members of the unincorporated body are bound by a contract, and have full potential control of the property, it may be that the terms of A's bequest make it clear that she intended the property to be held on trust for a particular purpose. In *Re Recher's Will Trusts*, for example, in applying the contract-holding analysis, Brightman J emphasised that it applied "[i]n the case of a donation which is not accompanied by any words which purport to impose a trust".[135] **5–093**

Care must be taken, however. The fact that A's gift is expressed as a gift for a purpose does not necessarily mean that A will be viewed as having intended to set up a trust, and so it does not preclude the application of the contract-holding analysis.[136] Just as in the cases such as *Re Bowes*,[137] that were discussed earlier,[138] the reference to the purpose can be seen as a motive for the gift to the members subject to their contract, not as evidence of an intention to impose an absolute restriction of the use of the property. Further, just as in cases such as *Re Thompson*,[139] a court may well be keen to find that no trust was intended, in order to ensure that the gift can be validated under the contract-holding approach.[140] For example, in *Re Lipinski's Will Trusts*,[141] the testator's gift was made "for the Hull Judeans (Maccabi) Association in memory of my late wife, to be used solely in the work of constructing the new buildings for the association and/or improvements to the said buildings". Oliver J stated that[142]: **5–094**

> Where the donee association is itself the beneficiary of the prescribed purpose, there seems to me to be the strongest argument in common sense for saying that the gift should be construed as an absolute one within the second category[143]—the more so where, if the purpose is carried out, the members can by appropriate action vest the resulting property in themselves, for here the trustees and the beneficiaries are the same persons.

---

133 [1980] 1 W.L.R. 360.
134 ibid., at 374.
135 [1972] Ch. 526 at 539, extracted at para.5–087.
136 See *Re Grant's WT* [1980] 1 W.L.R. 360 at 367 where Vinelott J refers to *Re Turkington* [1937] 4 All E.R. 501 and *Re Lipinski's W.T.* [1976] Ch. 235.
137 [1896] 1 Ch. 507.
138 See paras 5–011—5–014.
139 [1934] Ch. 342. See paras 5–007—5–010.
140 See, e.g. *Re Horley Town Football Club* [2006] W.T.L.R. 1817.
141 [1976] Ch. 235.
142 ibid., at 246.
143 i.e. the contract-holding analysis set out at paras 5–081—5–092, which is the second of the three categories identified by Cross J in *Neville Estates Ltd v Madden* [1962] Ch. 832 at 849: see para.5–077.

Oliver J also relied on cases where a purpose stated by the donor was seen as a motive for a gift, not as a binding restriction on the recipient's use of the property.[144]

**5–095** If, nonetheless, the gift is interpreted as a trust for a specific purpose then, if that purpose is charitable, there is no difficulty, since the beneficiary principle and the rule against inalienability will not apply. However, the funds will need to be kept separate from any non-charitable funds of the body and will remain subject to the charitable purpose, even after dissolution of the body.[145]

**5–096** However, if the gift is interpreted as a trust for a *non-charitable* purpose, the beneficiary principle will apply and the attempted gift will fail, unless, following the approach in *Re Denley's Trust Deed*,[146] the gift can be seen as in fact for specific individuals who benefit from the fulfillment of the purpose, and as conforming to the applicable perpetuities rules.[147] For example, in *Re Grant's Will Trusts*,[148] where the contract-holding analysis could not apply, Vinelott J held that the property was meant to be kept intact as endowment capital on trust for Labour Party purposes and so was void for infringing the beneficiary principle and the rule against inalienability.[149]

**5–097** To escape this outcome it would have to be argued that the fulfilment of the association's non-charitable purpose enures to the benefit of a sufficiently certain class of individuals for the trust to be regarded as a *Re Denley*-type trust.[150] In *Re Lipinski's Will Trusts*, for example, Oliver J was prepared to apply *Re Denley*[151] as the beneficiaries of the purpose were the members of the association and therefore "ascertainable at any one time",[152] whereas he would not have applied *Re Denley* if the purpose had instead been for the benefit of "the whole Jewish community in Hull" as it would then have been "difficult to argue that there was any ascertainable beneficiary".[153]

**5–098** Alternatively, and subject to the discussion of the enforcer principle below,[154] it might be argued that a trust for the association's non-charitable purposes could be rescued by the appointment of an

---

144 [1976] Ch. 235 at 249, relying on *Re Bowes* [1896] 1 Ch. 507.

145 *Brooks v Richardson* [1986] 1 All E.R. 952; *Re Finger's WT* [1972] Ch. 300 revealing the predisposition of the court to treat a gift to an unincorporated charitable body as a trust for charitable purposes, so as to prevent the gift lapsing if the body had been earlier dissolved and the second construction had been applied.

146 [1969] 1 Ch. 373: see paras 5–015–5–032.

147 As to the question of the application of the perpetuity rules to a *Re Denley*-type trust, see paras 7–084—7–087. Note that the trust in *Re Denley* itself was confined to a suitable period, with a gift over provided. In *Radmanovich v Nedeljkovic* [2001] N.S.W.S.C. 492, the *Re Denley* analysis was not applied where property was given to an unincorporated body with a provision that, on dissolution, it was to pass to the Serbian Orthodox Church. As noted in Tucker, Le Poidevin and Brightwell, *Lewin on Trusts* (2015), para.4–045, the real difficulty in that case was as to remoteness of vesting, as the property might have vested in the Church outside the permitted perpetuity period.

148 [1980] 1 W.L.R. 360. See para.5–092.

149 See too *Re St Andrew's (Cheam) Lawn Tennis Club Trust* [2012] 1 W.L.R. 3487: the rules of the tennis club, set up for members of a local church, prevented the members from dividing the property amongst themselves and could not be amended without the consent of the church. As no argument was made that a *Re Denley*-type trust had been set up, Arnold J stated at [62] that the gifts failed because they were for the purposes of the club, and those purposes were not charitable.

150 In *Re Horley Town Football Club* [2006] W.T.L.R. 1817 at [131], Lawrence Collins J stated obiter that "there are difficulties with regard to termination of [a *Re Denley*-type trust] which make it an unsafe basis for decision". This reflects the doubt raised at para.5–031 as to whether or not the parties who benefit from the performance of such a trust can combine to exercise a *Saunders v Vautier* power to terminate the trust.

151 Apparently as an alternative basis for his decision to uphold the testator's bequest, which he also held was valid on the contract-holding analysis.

152 There was moreover no problem of inalienability such as to infringe the rule against perpetuities, as the association was free to spend the capital: [1976] Ch. 235 at 245.

153 [1976] Ch. 235 at 248. In *Re Horley Town Football Club* [2006] W.T.L.R. 1817 at [131], Lawrence Collins J, having found that the relevant gift was valid on the contract-holding analysis, stated that it was not necessary to consider the possible application of *Re Denley*. He noted though that the existence of associate and temporary members of the club would not prevent the application of *Re Denley*: "the existence of those members could properly be overlooked on the basis that they are not within the class of persons for whose benefit the property is held on trust."

154 At paras 5–101—5–109.

enforcer, e.g. the chairman from time to time of the club. If this argument were to be accepted, then the trust would need to be restricted from the outset to a common law perpetuity period so as not to infringe the rule against inalienability, and the purposes would need to be sufficiently certain to enable the restrictions on the use of the income to be identified and enforced.[155]

## E. Conclusion: Are There Any Exceptions to the Beneficiary Principle?

In *Re Horley Town Football Club*, Lawrence Collins J stated the principle that: "In general, in order to be valid, a non-charitable trust must have an ascertainable beneficiary in whose favour performance of the trust may be decreed."[156] We have considered four possible types of exception to this general principle, and have found that, in terms of the legal concepts involved, none constitutes a true exception. The point is not that the courts have recognised the existence of a non-charitable purpose trust; it is rather that they have adopted a different legal characterisation of a transfer made by A, in order to ensure that the transfer does not fail and lead to a resulting trust for A or A's estate. In the "anomalous" testamentary cases,[157] it seems that the property is held by the recipients on trust for the specific beneficiaries who would have acquired the property if the gift had failed, but with a power for the recipients to spend the funds on the purpose specified by A. In the case of an absolute gift with a motive, the property is held on trust for the specific beneficiaries, who are then free to terminate the trust and use that property as they wish. In a *Re Denley*-type trust,[158] the specific beneficiaries consist of the defined individuals who benefit from the performance of the stipulated purpose. In the case of a *Quistclose* trust, the property is held on trust for the lender, with the recipient having the power to spend the property on the stipulated purpose. This mandate analysis may also be applied to an inter vivos gift to an unincorporated body, although the standard analysis in such a case, which may also apply to a testamentary bequest to an unincorporated body, is that the property is held by the members outright, subject to their mutual contract to comply with the terms of the body's constitution and apply the property in accordance with that contract. **5–099**

The fact that English law can currently be seen to conform closely to the beneficiary principle is not, however, a conclusive argument in favour of the principle. First, the analyses outlined in the preceding paragraph, whilst enabling the courts to avoid invalidating a transfer which might appear to involve a non-charitable purpose trust, may not always represent the true intention of A, the party making the transfer. Certainly, in some cases, A might be surprised to learn, for example, that the apparent purpose is regarded merely as a motive for an absolute gift, or that the current or future members of a club are free to decide to dissolve the club and divide A's gift amongst themselves, rather than spending it on the purposes of the club. Secondly, of course, the ingenuity needed to devise such analyses would not be required were at least some private purpose trusts to be permitted, assuming that the purpose trust in each case conformed to the relevant perpetuity rules. Thirdly, as we will now consider, many other jurisdictions have departed decisively from the beneficiary principle, and can be seen to have replaced it with an enforcer principle. **5–100**

---

155 cf. *Twinsectra Ltd v Yardley* [2000] W.T.L.R. 527 at 560 (reversed on other grounds [2002] 2 A.C. 164) on the certainty of analogous *Quistclose*-type trust restrictions: where the purposes are spelled out in certain workable fashion one could have all the club members as enforcers.

156 [2006] W.T.L.R. 1817 at [89], citing *Leahy v Attorney General for New South Wales* [1959] A.C. 457 at 478 and *Re Denley's Trust Deed* [1969] 1 Ch. 373.

157 See para.5–009.

158 See *Re Denley's Trust Deed* [1969] 1 Ch. 373.

## 3. An Enforcer Principle?

5–101 It seems difficult to argue against the proposition that there must be *someone* at whose behest a court can enforce a trust; if not, the apparent duty of the trustee to conform to the terms of the trust is a mere illusion. The question, however, is whether that person must be a beneficiary with an equitable proprietary interest in the trust assets. On one view, noted above,[159] the decision in *Re Denley's Trust Deed* has already relaxed that requirement, by allowing the party enforcing the trust to be one of a defined group of individuals who directly benefits from the performance of a defined non-charitable purpose.[160] A more radical departure would entail the English courts permitting the "enforcer",[161] the party with a right to hold the trustees to account, to be someone who has no beneficial interest in the trust assets, and who does not benefit directly from the performance of the trust.

5–102 A large number of offshore jurisdictions have embraced this enforcer model. They can be seen as having responded to a gap in the trusts "market" by enacting legislation validating non-charitable purpose trusts so long as the trust instrument appoints an enforcer (who could be the settlor or an independent or related third party) with provision for further enforcers after the enforcer's death or retirement. An example is provided by the following provisions of Bermuda law.[162]

### Bermuda Trusts (Special Provisions) Act 1989 ss.12A and 12B[163]

5–103 **12A. Purpose Trusts**

(1) A trust may be created for a non-charitable purpose or purposes provided that the conditions set out in subsection (2) are satisfied; and in this Part such a trust is referred to as a "purpose trust".
(2) The conditions are that the purpose or purposes are—

(a) sufficiently certain to allow the trust to be carried out,
(b) lawful, and
(c) not contrary to public policy.

(3) A purpose trust may only be created in writing.
(4) The rule of law (known as the rule against excessive duration or the rule against perpetual trusts) which limits the time during which the capital of a trust may remain unexpendable to the perpetuity period under the rule against perpetuities shall not apply to a purpose trust.
(5) The rule against perpetuities (also known as the rule against remoteness of vesting) as modified by the Perpetuties and Accumulations Act 1989 shall apply to a purpose trust.

5–104 **12B. Enforcement and Variation of Purpose Trust by the Court**

(1) The Supreme Court may make such order as it considers expedient for the enforcement of a purpose trust on the application of any of the following persons—

(a) any person appointed by or under the trust for the purposes of this subsection;

---

159 At para.5–032.
160 As noted at para.5–031, however, that is not the only possible interpretation of the decision in *Re Denley's Trust Deed*.
161 Scottish Law Commission, *Report on Trust Law*, para.14.28 prefers to use the word "supervisor" to refer to such a party.
162 The Bermudan legislation is chosen as it was the first jurisdiction to permit non-charitable purpose trusts, but many other offshore jurisdictions have followed suit, some would say in a "race to the bottom". Note that the original Bermudan legislation, unlike the current version set out above, required an enforcer to be expressly appointed. Much of the current legislation on purpose trusts, e.g. that of Guernsey and the Bahamas, has been influenced by the Special Trusts (Alternative Regime) Law 1997 (Cayman Islands), (STAR), now contained in that jurisdiction's Trusts Law (2011 Revision), Part VIII. For discussion of the STAR trust regime, see, e.g. A. Duckworth, "STAR Trusts" (2013) 19 T. & T. 215.
163 Inserted by the Bermuda Trusts (Special Provisions) Amendment Act 1998.

(b) the settlor, unless the trust instrument provides otherwise;
(c) a trustee of the trust;
(d) any other person whom the court considers has sufficient interest in the enforcement of the trust;

and where the Attorney-General satisfies the court that there is no such person who is able and willing to make an application under this subsection, the Attorney-General may make an application for enforcement of the trust.

(2) On an application in relation to a purpose trust by any of the following persons—

(a) any person appointed by or under the trust for the purposes of this subsection;
(b) the settlor, unless the trust instrument provides otherwise;
(c) a trustee of the trust,

the court may if it thinks fit approve a scheme to vary any of the purposes of the trust, or to enlarge or otherwise vary any of the powers of the trustees of the trust.

(3) Where any costs are incurred in connection with any application under this section, the Supreme Court may make such order as it considers just as to payment of those costs (including payment out of the property of the trust).

A clear aim of such legislation is to make the particular jurisdiction appealing to settlors. This is achieved not only by permitting non-charitable purpose trusts but also, for example, by altering the effect of the rule against perpetuities[164] (as in s.12A(4) of the Bermuda Trusts (Special Provisions) Act 1989, set out above), and by permitting settlors to reserve wide rights and powers without imperilling the validity of the trust, or leading the trust to be regarded as a sham.[165] Of course, settlors are not attracted to such jurisdictions because the purpose trust regime allows them to make donations to their local tennis club. The key attraction of such a trust is, rather, that it allows property to be insulated both from the creditors of the trustees and of the settlor (as it is of course trust property) but also, more importantly,[166] from the creditors of any other party (as no party has a beneficial entitlement to the property). This means, first, that such a trust may appeal to a wealthy individual who wishes to place wealth offshore, where it will receive a more favourable tax treatment, and who can benefit from dispositions made by the trustees in exercise of the wide powers conferred on them, or on a party such as an enforcer, under the trust. It also means, secondly, that a private purpose trust can be employed to good effect in various financing arrangements, such as securitisations, or to facilitate commercial transactions.[167] A non-charitable purpose trust may be used, for example, to allow shares to be vested in an entity that holds those shares for a limited purpose,[168] or simply in allowing property to be held by trustees (and potentially distributed following the exercise of a power) without any beneficial interests arising. Offshore jurisdictions are keen to cater for such needs as they derive benefits not only **5–105**

---

164 Still more radical departures from the rule have been permitted in jurisdictions in the United States: see, e.g. the survey by M. Schanzenbach and R. Sitkoff, "Perpetuities or Taxes? Explaining the Rise of the Perpetual Trust" (2006) 27 Cardozo Law Review 2465.

165 See, e.g. Bermuda Trusts (Special Provisions) Amendment Act 2014, building on s.2(3) of the 1989 Act.

166 There may of course be cases where a court has a statutory power to make orders against a creditor (e.g. a divorcing spouse in ancillary relief proceedings) that relate not only to the property of that spouse, but also to property he or she is likely to receive in the future through the exercise of a power: see, e.g. *Whaley v Whaley* [2012] 1 F.L.R. 735. Note too *Tasarruf Mevduati Sigorta Fonu v Merrill Lynch Bank and Trust Co (Cayman) Ltd* [2012] 1 W.L.R. 1721.

167 See, e.g. Scottish Law Commission, *Report on Trust Law*, para.14.7, giving the example of a purpose trust established to allow assets to be held for the purpose of providing security for as yet unidentified parties who may otherwise suffer loss in relation to a commercial project.

168 It may, for example, hold those shares simply for the purpose of holding a controlling interest in a private company: see, e.g. Virgin Islands Special Trusts Act 2003.

from the establishment of such trusts, for example by requiring that only licensed companies can act as trustees, but also from related financial services.[169]

**5–106** Two questions arise from the permissibility of non-charitable purpose trusts in offshore jurisdictions. First, what would happen if an English court were faced with a non-charitable purpose trust governed by a foreign law that treats such a trust as valid where the terms of the trust appoint an enforcer? The answer of course depends on the English conflict of laws rules, and so will be discussed in more detail in Chapter 16.[170] The basic conclusion there is that, as such a trust is consistent with the definition of a trust under the Recognition of Trusts Act 1987, an English court would have to enforce it unless its operation could be regarded as inconsistent with fundamental policies of English law. It may perhaps be possible to mount such an argument if the trust is a pure purpose trust and relates to English land (it is worth noting, for example, that some offshore jurisdictions specifically prevent their private purpose regimes from applying to land in that jurisdiction)[171]; but there is otherwise a strong case for saying that, as English law is not so insular as to refuse to recognise any aspect of foreign law that is different from English law,[172] the English court should recognise the validity of trusts whenever they clearly supply a mechanism for the positive enforcement of the trust so that the trustees are under an obligation to account to someone in whose favour the court can positively decree performance, whether this person is a beneficiary with a proprietary interest in the trust assets or an enforcer with no such proprietary interest.[173]

**5–107** The second question relates purely to English domestic law: should it too move to replace the beneficiary principle with an enforcer principle? Two, linked sets of issues must be considered: policy matters and the conceptual nature of the trust in English law. As for policy, there may be a desire to "compete" with other trusts jurisdictions by catering for settlors who wish to set up non-charitable purpose trusts.[174] On the other hand, there may be a concern that such trusts can be used as a means to shield assets, by ensuring that the assets (for the maximum period permitted by any perpetuity rule adopted) remain free from the claims of *any* creditors. After all, the beneficiary principle, when coupled with the rule against perpetuities, does ensure that trust assets, whilst protected from creditors of the trustees, will be available at some point to the creditors of those who eventually receive the trust assets.

**5–108** As for the conceptual nature of the trust, two basic views can be contrasted. The question is as to which of those views is regarded as best reflecting the *English* law of trusts.[175] We will examine these views in more detail in Chapter 17. On the first view, the essence of the trust lies in the holding of property

---

169 As noted by e.g. D. Waters, "The Trust: Continual Evolution of a Centuries-Old Idea" [2007] JTCP 207, there is thus keen competition between such jurisdictions to appeal to potential settlors.

170 See para.16–049.

171 See, e.g. the position in the Cayman Islands: Trusts Law (2011 Revision) s.109.

172 The inalienability of an alimentary life interest under Scots law was accepted by the Court of Appeal in *Re Fitzgerald* [1904] 1 Ch. 573 though English life interests cannot be inalienable.

173 D.J. Hayton, "Developing the Obligation Characteristic of the Trust" (2001) 117 L.Q.R. 96. cf. P. Matthews "From Obligation to Property, and Back Again" in D.J. Hayton (ed.), *Extending the Boundaries of Trusts and Similar Ring-Fenced Funds* (Kluwer Law International, 2002), who argues that arrangements of the latter sort may be valid under English law on contract law principles, but cannot be trusts because trusts necessarily entail equitable property ownership by a beneficiary.

174 For example, the Scottish Law Commission, *Report on Trust Law*, paras 14.2–14.10 argues for legislation affirming the non-charitable purpose trust in Scottish law, and at para.1.3 the report says that it is "essential that Scottish trust law should be, and should be perceived as being, suitable for use in contemporary financial and economic conditions".

175 It is undoubtedly true of some other trusts jurisdictions that a proprietary view of the trust (see para.5–109) is *not* adopted: this can be seen, for example, in offshore legislation permitting non-charitable purpose trusts. For a general consideration of different views of the basis of the trust adopted in different jurisdictions, see, e.g. D. Clarry, "Fiduciary Ownership and Trusts in a Comparative Perspective" (2014) 63 I.C.L.Q. 901.

subject to an equitable duty relating to the use of that property.[176] The question then is as to the nature of that duty: is there any reason why it must be owed to a party who benefits directly from its performance? There may be practical reasons for arguing that the answer is yes, and for doubting whether an enforcer will have sufficient incentive properly to supervise the trustees of a non-charitable purpose trust.[177] There may also be the conceptual concern that, in private law generally, duties tend to be owed to those who benefit from their performance, and an enforcer principle instead applies a more "public law" approach, under which the trustees' duties are seen not as correlative to a right of another, but rather as a burden of their office, or as a limit on their powers.[178] Nonetheless, if one views the trust in English law as consisting of the holding of property subject to a duty, the replacement of the beneficiary principle with an enforcer principle would not require a rethinking of the fundamental basis of the trust.[179]

On the second view, the essence of the trust instead lies in the equitable proprietary rights of the beneficiaries, such rights being proprietary in the sense of giving the beneficiaries the ultimate right to control the use of the trust property, even if that right is residual and may, for its realisation, require the termination of the trust through the exercise of a *Saunders v Vautier* power.[180] On this view, replacing the beneficiary principle with an enforcer principle would indeed involve a fundamental shift in the conceptual nature of the English law of trusts.[181] **5–109**

**Questions**

1. By his will Tony left:
   (a) "£1,000,000 to my executor and trustee Eric to use the income to further the purposes of the UK Socialist Party so far as the law allows, such trust to be enforceable by the Leader from time to time of such Party";
   (b) "£50,000 to the Treasurer of the Salford University Law Society to deal with it as the Society wishes";
   (c) "£50,000 to the Treasurer of the Manchester Literary and Philosophical Society on trust to apply the income for the benefit of its members";
   (d) "the proceeds of sale of my residuary estate to the Treasurer of the Manchester Mavericks

---

176 See, e.g. D.J. Hayton, "Developing the Obligation Characteristic of the Trust" (2001) 117 L.Q.R. 96.

177 The question arises whether the enforcer owes a duty to enforce the trust, and if so, to whom that duty is owed. It is interesting to note that under s.106(2) of the Cayman Islands Trust Law (2011 Revision), in relation to a pure purpose trust, the trust assets are to be regarded, as against the trustee and the enforcer as property "belonging to others" and if a trustee or enforcer has an intention "to defeat the trust" this shall be "regarded accordingly as an intention to deprive others of property" thereby potentially exposing the enforcer (or trustee) to criminal charges for theft.

178 For an illuminating discussion of the different possible conceptions of "duty" in relation to the law of trusts, see J. Harris, "Trust, Power and Duty" (1971) 87 L.Q.R. 31.

179 On this view, even though there is no party with a beneficial interest in the property under the trust, it could be said that there is no resulting trust for the settlor, as, in general, if the settlor has "expressly, or by necessary implication, abandoned any beneficial interest in the trust property, there is in my view no resulting trust" (*Westdeutsche Landesbank v Islington LBC* [1966] A.C. 669 at 708, per Lord Browne-Wilkinson) and that is true in a case where the settlor sets up a non-charitable purpose trust with an enforcer. That is certainly the case under, for example, a Cayman Islands STAR trust set up for a purpose: A. Duckworth, "STAR Trusts" (2013) 19 T. & T. 215, 218.

180 This view seems to underpin the analysis of Vinelott J in *Re Grant's WT* [1980] 1 W.L.R. 360. For academic support for this view, see P. Matthews, "The Comparative Importance of the Rule in *Saunders v Vautier*" (2006) 122 L.Q.R. 266, 273–74, extracted at paras 7-015—7-029. See too Matthews "From Obligation to Property, and Back Again", *Extending the Boundaries of Trusts and Similar Ring-Fenced Funds* (2002).

181 e.g. A. Duckworth, "STAR Trusts" (2013) 19 T. & T. 215, 215 describes that regime as one in which "the trust is freed at last from the idea that the trust is a matter of equitable ownership, a relationship between title-holder (trustee) and equitable owners (beneficiaries)". It is therefore inconsistent with the view that "if there are no equitable owners, there can be no trust—other than a resulting trust for the settlor".

> Darts Club to apply half the income for the purposes of the Club and half the income for providing educational assistance to the children of Club members."

Statute prevents the members of the Literary and Philosophical Society from winding up the Society and dividing its assets between themselves, while this is possible in the case of the Darts Club only if membership falls below five, although the rules can be changed by a 90 per cent majority vote.

**Advise on the validity of the above bequests.**

2. Does Lord Millett's analysis in *Twinsectra* end the debate as to the nature of the *Quistclose* trust?
3. To what extent, if at all, does a *Re Denley*-type trust depart from traditional rules of trusts law?
4. Do you have any anxieties over a legal structure where a £20 million portfolio of shares, land and paintings is owned by a company, all of whose shares are held by a private trust company holding the shares on trust for the purpose of developing the value of the shares, and where the shares in the trust company are held by individuals on trust for the purpose of running the business of the trust company as trustee of only one trust?

# 6

# CHARITABLE TRUSTS

## 1. Legal Forms Used by Charities

The Charities Act 2011 s.1(1) defines a charity as "an institution which (a) is established for charitable purposes only, and (b) falls to be subject to the control of the High Court in the exercise of its jurisdiction with respect to charities". Charities often take the legal form of a charitable trust,[1] i.e. a trust with legally charitable purposes. The law which determines whether particular purposes are legally charitable forms the main subject matter of this chapter. **6–001**

Charities can take other legal forms besides the trust. They can take the form of an unincorporated association,[2] a chartered corporation,[3] a friendly society,[4] an industrial and provident society,[5] a company limited by guarantee (which differs from a company limited by shares, the form used by businesses which distribute profits as dividends to their shareholders),[6] or a Charitable Incorporated Organisation (CIO).[7] **6–002**

All of these bodies typically have written provisions detailing their purposes and the rules governing their administration. Confusingly, these provisions count as "trusts" for the purposes of the charities **6–003**

1 The Charity Commission has published a model trust deed for a charitable trust: Charity Commission, "Charitable Trusts: Model Trust Deed (GD2)" (November 2013), *https://www.gov.uk/government/uploads/system/uploads/attachment_data/file/269509/gd2text.pdf* [Accessed 1 June 2015].

2 The Charity Commission has published a model constitution for a charitable unincorporated association: Charity Commission, "Charitable Associations: Model Constitution" (November 2013), *https://www.gov.uk/government/uploads/system/uploads/attachment_data/file/278200/gd3text.pdf* [Accessed 1 June 2015].

3 There are only a few of these, and they are all very well-established charities with large funds, e.g. the older universities, the Church Commissioners, and the British Museum.

4 Friendly societies are incorporated mutual assurance associations which provide social or financial benefits, e.g. life assurance, funeral benefits. They are charitable only if their purpose is the relief of poverty.

5 A form generally used by housing associations. An industrial and provident society is a corporate body with members whose purpose is to carry on industry or conduct business, either as a co-operative (in which case it will not be charitable) or for the benefit of the community (in which case it will be charitable).

6 J. Gray, "Guarantee Companies in the Voluntary Sector" in A. Dunn (ed.), *The Voluntary Sector, the State and the Law* (Hart Publishing, 2000). The Charity Commission has published model articles of association of a charitable company limited by guarantee at *https://www.gov.uk/government/uploads/system/uploads/attachment_data/file/269508/gd1textc.pdf* [Accessed 1 June 2015].

7 A legal form introduced in 2010 which enables charities to acquire the benefits of incorporation without attracting the disadvantage of dual regulation by Companies House and the Charity Commission. There are two types: "foundation CIOs" whose only voting members are the charity trustees and which resemble an incorporated charitable trust, run by a small group of people (the charity trustees) who make all the key decisions; and "association" CIOs with a wider membership, including voting members other than the charity trustees. Model constitutions have been published by the Charity Commission, "Constitution of a Charitable Incorporated Organisation whose only voting members are its charity trustees" (August 2014), *https://www.gov.uk/government/uploads/system/uploads/attachment_data/file/390171/FoundationModelConstitution.pdf* [Accessed 1 June 2015]; "Constitution of a Charitable Incorporated Organisation with voting members other than its charity trustees" (August 2014), *https://www.gov.uk/government/uploads/system/uploads/attachment_data/file/390170/AssociationModelConstitution.pdf* [Accessed 1 June 2015].

legislation whether or not they take effect by way of trust.[8] Similarly, their officers are referred to as "trustees" in the legislation and in the Charity Commission literature, whether or not they are the trustees of a charitable trust.[9]

## 2. The Advantages of Charitable Status

**6-004** Whatever legal form they take, charities enjoy various fiscal and legal advantages over institutions formed for private or commercial reasons, reflecting the fact that charitable purposes enure to the public good.

### *A. Tax Advantages*

**6-005** United Kingdom[10] charities do not pay income or corporation tax on their property income and investment income which is applicable to charitable purposes only and is in fact applied solely for those purposes.[11] Nor do they pay capital gains tax in respect of gains made upon disposals by them, again provided that the gain is applied solely to charitable purposes.[12] Charities can obtain 80 per cent relief as of right in respect of non-domestic rates for premises wholly or mainly used for charitable purposes and some discretionary relief in respect of the rest.[13] Charities are also exempt from stamp duty.[14] However they only have a few reliefs from value added tax in prescribed circumstances, e.g. relating to medical supplies, fuel for lifeboats, etc.[15]

**6-006** Charities are exempt from tax on their trading income if the profits are used solely for charitable purposes, and either the trade is exercised in the course of the carrying out of a primary purpose of the charity, or the work in connection with the trade is mainly carried out by beneficiaries of the charity, or the charity can bring itself within a small scale trading exemption because its annual turnover falls below £5,000.[16] Charities can also avoid paying tax on trading that is not within these exemptions, by incorporating subsidiary trading companies and causing them to donate all their profits to the charities, with the result that their taxable profits are effectively kept at zero.[17]

**6-007** No inheritance tax is payable on gifts to charities,[18] nor does a charge to capital gains tax arise on disposals of property to charities.[19] Individuals who make gifts of shares, securities and real property

---

8 Charities Act 2011 s.353.

9 Charities Act 2011 s.177.

10 *Camille and Henry Dreyfus Foundation Inc v IRC* [1956] A.C. 39; *Routier v HMRC* [2015] S.T.C. 451. Under EC law, charities established in one Member State may be entitled to the benefit of tax advantages in another, as in, e.g. *Commission v Spain* (Case C-153/08) [2010] 1 C.M.L.R. 30.

11 Income Tax Act 2007 ss.531, 532; Corporation Tax Act 2010 Pt 11. See *IRC v Educational Grants Association Ltd* [1967] Ch. 123.

12 Taxation of Chargeable Gains Act 1992 s.256.

13 Local Government Finance Act 1988 ss.43(5) and (6), 47 and 64(10).

14 Finance Act 1982 s.129.

15 Value Added Tax Act 1994 Sch.8, Groups 4, 5, 6, 8, 12 and 15 and Sch.9, Groups 6, 7, 10, 12 and 13. See HMRC, *"VAT for Charities"*, *https://www.gov.uk/vat-charities/overview* [Accessed 1 June 2015].

16 Income Tax Act 2007 ss.524–526; Corporation Tax Act 2010 ss.478, 479.

17 A company donating its taxable profits to charity can get a tax deduction equal to the amount of the profits, so that no corporation tax is payable. In the hands of the charity the donation is taxable as income but is exempt from tax if it is applied for charitable purposes: Income Tax Act 2007 s.522; Corporation Tax Act 2010 s.473(1). Discussion in Charity Commission, "CC 35: Trustees, Trading and Tax" (2007), *https://www.gov.uk/government/uploads/system/uploads/attachment_data/file/366991/cc35text.pdf* [Accessed 1 June 2015]; HMRC, *"Charities—Trading and Business Activities"*, *https://www.gov.uk/government/publications/charities-detailed-guidance-notes/annex-iv-trading-and-business-activities-basic-principles* [Accessed 1 June 2015].

18 Inheritance Tax Act 1984 s.23.

19 Taxation of Chargeable Gains Act 1992 s.257.

to charities are given relief from income tax by deducting a corresponding amount when calculating their net income for the tax year in which the gift is made.[20] Charities can also recover basic rate tax in respect of any gifts made to them under the gift aid scheme.[21]

In the tax year 2013/14, there were about 164,000 registered charities in England and Wales, with a total annual income of about £64 billion.[22] The cost of tax reliefs to charities during this period in terms of tax payments lost to the Treasury was about £3 billion, and the cost of tax reliefs to individual donors was about £1.1 billion.[23] **6–008**

## *B. Trust Law Advantages*

Charitable trusts are not subject to the rule against inalienability[24] that applies exclusively to pure purpose trusts and, where a charity is constituted as a company, it enjoys a limited exemption from the rule against remoteness of vesting.[25] At common law a gift over from one person to another that might possibly take effect outside the perpetuity period was void.[26] But a gift over from one charity to another charity was valid, the property being treated as belonging to charity throughout so as not to be caught by the rule against remoteness.[27] If the gift were a gift over from a charity to a non-charity[28] or from a non-charity to a charity[29] then the rule against remoteness of vesting applied. Since 1964, however, it has been possible in the two latter instances to wait and see when the gift over takes effect[30]: if it takes effect within the perpetuity period then it is good; if not then it is bad and the first gift becomes absolute, no longer subject to defeasance or determination. **6–009**

The Perpetuities and Accumulations Act 2009 s.13 abolished the statutory restrictions which previously affected the accumulation of income within private trusts.[31] Under s.14, however, where the trustees of a charitable trust have a duty or power to accumulate income for a period of more than 21 years, this duty or power ceases to have effect. This section was introduced on the recommendation of the Law Commission, which feared that otherwise charity trustees might accumulate income indefinitely.[32] The result of the 2009 legislation is that the privilege of indefinite duration accorded to charitable trusts continues to apply only to their endowment capital. **6–010**

A charitable trust is valid although it is a purpose trust because the Attorney General can enforce it, taking action against defaulting trustees where necessary. It is also the Attorney General's responsibility to represent charities in disputes over the construction or validity of wills and of trust **6–011**

---

20 Income Tax Act 2007 ss.431ff.

21 Income Tax Act 2007 ss.413ff.

22 Charity Commission, "Recent Charity Register Statistics" (September 2014), *https://www.gov.uk/government/publications/charity-register-statistics/recent-charity-register-statistics-charity-commission* [Accessed 1 June 2015].

23 HMRC Statistics 2014, Table 10.2, "Costs of Tax Relief" (April 2015), *https://www.gov.uk/government/uploads/system/uploads/attachment_data/file/388557/Table_10_2.pdf* [Accessed 1 June 2015].

24 e.g. *Re Banfield* [1968] 1 W.L.R. 846 compared with *Re Warre's WT* [1953] 1 W.L.R. 725 or *Re Gwyon* [1930] 1 Ch. 255.

25 For the perpetuity rules affecting private trusts, see paras 7–079—7–101.

26 *Re Frost* (1889) 43 Ch. D. 246.

27 *Christ's Hospital v Grainger* (1849) 1 Mac. & G. 460; *Re Tyler* [1891] 3 Ch. 252.

28 *Re Bowen* [1893] 2 Ch. 491.

29 *Re Peel's Release* [1921] 2 Ch. 218; *Re Dalziel* [1943] Ch. 277.

30 Perpetuities and Accumulations Act 1964 s.3. See now Perpetuities and Accumulations Act 2009 s.7.

31 See para.7–092.

32 Law Commission, *The Rules against Perpetuities and Excessive Accumulations* (TSO, 1998) Law Com. No.251, HC Paper No.579, para.10.19. Trustees often wish to build up their charity's reserves against future contingencies: C. Mitchell, "Saving for a Rainy Day: Charity Reserves" (2002) 8 C.L.P.R. 35. The Panacea Society provides an unusual example: they were a religious community (which came to an end in 2012) who believed that they should accumulate assets in preparation for the Second Coming of Christ. In 2001, the Charity Commission controversially imposed a scheme amending the charity's objects to include the relief of poverty and sickness in Bedford.

deeds where there is a charitable interest at stake, to intervene where necessary in disputes over the use or sale of charitable property, to direct schemes for the administration of charities where necessary, and to direct charitable bequests in cases where a charity has not been identified or no longer exists.[33]

**6-012** In the case of a charitable trust, the requirement of certainty of objects is satisfied so long as the settlor has manifested a sufficiently clear general charitable intention to enable a *cy-près* scheme to be formulated for giving effect to her intention as nearly as possible.[34] Thus a charitable trust "for world-wide charitable purposes" or "for the poor" is valid, although a private discretionary trust for everyone in the UK would be void for uncertainty of objects. The *cy-près* doctrine is peculiar to charitable trusts and will be dealt with at the end of this chapter.[35]

**6-013** Two further differences between charitable purpose trusts and private trusts for persons can be mentioned. Charity trustees can act by a majority instead of unanimously, which is required of private trustees unless they are the trustees of a pensions trust,[36] or the trust deed authorises majority decisions;[37] and the six-year limitation period in the Limitation Act 1980 s.21(3) applies to an action against the trustees by a beneficiary under a private trust for persons,[38] but not to an action by the Attorney General to enforce a charitable trust for the benefit of the public.[39]

## *C. Policing and Advice*

**6-014** Concerns over the negligent and corrupt mismanagement of charitable funds led to the appointment of the Charity Commissioners in the 1850s,[40] public officials who were charged with the investigation and regulation of charities. Legislation over the past 50 years has expanded their duties and strengthened their powers,[41] and has given the Charity Commission legal status as a corporate body.[42]

**6-015** In theory, the Charity Commission is an independent regulator, a non-ministerial government department which is accountable to the Home Secretary for its efficiency, but not for the manner in which it pursues its objectives.[43] In practice, the Commission has come under pressure to pursue a politicised agenda from time to time, for example, from those who believe that the voluntary sector should be more heavily regulated,[44] from those who consider that the Commission should not strictly enforce the legal rules against political campaigning by charities,[45] and from those who wish the

---

33 Attorney General's Office, *Annual Review 2008–9* at 14. In practice responsibility for the Attorney General's charity business is delegated to the Solicitor General.

34 *Morice v Bishop of Durham* (1804) 9 Ves. Jun. 399 at 405; *Re Harding, deceased* [2008] Ch. 235 at [21]–[22].

35 See paras 6-298—6-320.

36 Pensions Act 1995 s.32.

37 *Re Whiteley* [1910] 1 Ch. 600 at 608.

38 See paras 10-247—10-251.

39 *Attorney General v Cocke* [1988] Ch. 414; though the six-year limitation period may apply to an action to enforce a charitable trust for the benefit of a defined class, even if the Attorney General is the claimant: *President and Scholars of the College of St Mary Magdalen, Oxford v Attorney General* (1857) 6 H.L. Cas. 189.

40 Charitable Trusts Acts 1853, 1855 and 1860. See R. Tompson, *The Charity Commission and the Age of Reform* (Routledge, 1979).

41 Charities Acts 1960, 1992, 1993, 2006 and 2011.

42 See now Charities Act 2011 s.13.

43 Charities Act 2011 s.13(4). For the Commission's objectives, functions, duties and incidental powers, see Charities Act 2011 ss. 14–17 and 20.

44 See, e.g. Select Committee on Public Accounts, *28th Report: Charity Commission—Regulation and Support of Charities* (TSO, 1998), HC Paper No.408 (Session 1997–98), discussed in C. Mitchell, "Reviewing the Register" in C. Mitchell and S. Moody (eds), *Foundations of Charity* (Hart Publishing, 2000), pp.188–190.

45 e.g. Cabinet Office Strategy Unit, *Private Action, Public Benefit* (Cabinet Office, September 2002), pp.45–46, critiqued in S. Brodie, "The Charity Commission—Politicised and Politicising" (2010) 30 Economic Affairs 9; and see paras 6-118—6-142.

Commission to force charities to broaden access to their facilities and services on pain of losing their charitable status.[46]

Most, though not all, charities are required by statute to register with the Charity Commission,[47] and those registered charities with a gross annual income exceeding £250,000 must submit annual accounts and returns to the Commission,[48] which must ensure that these have been prepared accurately and honestly. All charities are also selectively targeted by HM Revenue and Customs to ensure that their accounts are in proper order, and that they are eligible for the tax exemptions which they claim. **6–016**

The Charity Commission has wide powers to institute inquiries into the administration of charities, to require that people furnish them with information relevant to these inquiries, and to obtain information relating to charities from the police and other public bodies.[49] Where misconduct or mismanagement in a charity's administration is discovered, the Commission can suspend or remove any of the charity's officers and appoint new ones as it thinks necessary.[50] It also has powers, corresponding to and concurrent with those possessed by the Attorney General, to go to the courts for the enforcement of obligations owed by charity trustees and others.[51] **6–017**

Appeals can be made from decisions, directions, and orders made by the Commission to the First-tier Tribunal (Charity), an independent judicial body first established in 2008.[52] The Tribunal was introduced to provide charities and their officers with a cheaper and swifter mechanism for reviewing the Commission's decisions than is offered by the High Court. Since its creation, however, it has had much less business than other tribunals, possibly because the Commission often settles complaints, possibly also because charities believe the Tribunal's services to be expensive,[53] although (since there is no costs-shifting within the Tribunal and each party must bear its own costs) this is true only if charities are legally represented and is not true if they appear as litigants in person (as frequently occurs in other tribunals).[54] Appeals lie from the First-tier Tribunal (Charity) to the Upper Tribunal (Tax and Chancery Chamber) and from there to the High Court. **6–018**

As well as investigating possible misconduct and abuse of charitable funds with a view to taking remedial action, the Commission also provides charities with guidance and information in publications that can be accessed on its website. It is empowered to give advice to charity trustees to **6–019**

---

46 e.g. House of Lords and House of Commons Joint Committee on the Draft Charities Bill, *The Draft Charities Bill* (TSO, 2004), HL 167 and HC 660, pp.19–33; and see paras 6–063—6–100. below.

47 Charities Act 2011 Pt 4.

48 Charities Act 2011 Pt 8.

49 Charities Act 2011 Pt 5.

50 Charities Act 2011 ss.76–83. During the 2014/15 Parliamentary session the Government brought forward a draft Protection of Charities Bill designed to give the Commission further powers against guilty trustees; a Joint Select Committee issued a broadly favourable report on the draft bill in February 2015: Joint Committee on the Draft Protection of Charities Bill, *Draft Protection of Charities Bill* (TSO 2015), HL Paper 108, HC 813, 2015.

51 Charities Act 2011 s.114.

52 Charities Act 2011 Pt 17 and Sch.6.

53 For this reason the Commission unusually agreed to revisit its decision of 7 June 2012 not to register Preston Down Trust as a charity rather than letting the matter go to the First-tier Tribunal, "Decision on Preston Down Trust's Application for Registration" (Charity Commission, 3 January 2014), *https://www.gov.uk/government/uploads/system/uploads/attachment_data/file/336112/preston_down_trust_full_decision.pdf* [Accessed 1 June 2015].

54 A. McKenna, "Appealing the Regulator: Experience from the Charity Tribunal for England and Wales" in M. Harding, A. O'Connell and M. Stewart (eds), *Not-for-Profit Law: Theoretical and Comparative Perspectives*, (Cambridge University Press, 2014), p.350. See too D. Morris, "The First-tier Tribunal (Charity): Enhanced Access to Justice for Charities or a Case of David versus Goliath?" (2010) 29 C.J.Q. 491, 502–504 and 505–506. And cf. Law Commission, *Technical Issues in Charity Law: A Consultation Paper* (Law Commission, 2015), L.C.C.P. No.220, ch.16, recommending that trustees should not have to obtain permission from the Commission before they can bring proceedings and that they should in some cases be entitled to a *Beddoe* order entitling them to be indemnified out of charity funds against personal liability for litigation costs.

make the administration of their charity more effective,[55] and a trustee acting on such advice is deemed to have acted in accordance with the terms of the trust, provided that no court decision has been obtained on the matter and the trustee has not withheld material facts when seeking the Commission's directions.[56] The Commission can also make schemes and orders to modernise the purposes and administration of charities, and give the trustees additional powers.[57]

**6–020** Between 2007/08 and 2015/16 the Commission's operating budget was reduced from £32.6 million to £20.2 million. This led to staff cuts and a narrowing of the Commission's focus to concentrate on policing the sector. Previously the Commission often gave one-to-one advice to charity trustees on such matters as how to simplify their administration, alter their trusts, amend their governing documents, transfer property, and appoint new trustees.[58] Now it provides generic guidance through its website but gives one-to-one advice only in a very limited range of circumstances.[59] The Commission argues that this is consistent with a new policy of promoting self-reliance by trustees and supporting the pro bono provision of advice by volunteers,[60] but there is a danger that the retrenchment "will result in under-confident trustees . . . and that an unregulated market of advice providers will be created to the detriment of public trust and confidence".[61]

## 3. Determining Charitable Status

### A. Decision-Making Bodies

**6–021** It will be seen from the foregoing discussion that institutions with charitable status enjoy advantages which cost the state money, in the form of foregone tax revenues and the costs of charity regulation. This suggests that decisions on legal entitlement to charitable status should be taken by a body with a democratic mandate, charged with undertaking a cost–benefit analysis of purposes to determine whether they merit the advantages flowing from charitable status.[62] However while Parliament has occasionally legislated to provide that a purpose is legally charitable,[63] decisions on charitable status are not generally taken by Parliament or indeed any other democratically accountable body, and are instead taken by various unelected bodies, whose basic approach is to decide the question as though it were a "pure" question of law divorced from fiscal considerations.

**6–022** The courts are asked from time to time to decide whether testamentary purpose trusts are charitable; HM Revenue and Customs must frequently decide whether an institution is a "charity" for the purposes of determining its entitlement to tax reliefs; local government rating departments must decide whether institutions are entitled to rates relief; and most significantly, the Charity Commission must decide applications by bodies to be included on the Register of Charities which it owes a statutory duty to maintain. The effect of registration by the Commission is that for all purposes other than rectification of the Register, a body is conclusively presumed to be or to have been a charity at any time

---

55 Charities Act 2011 s.110.
56 Charities Act 2011 s.110(2).
57 Charities Act 2011 s.69.
58 Charity Commission, *Report for 1996*, paras 123–125.
59 Charity Commission, *Risk Framework: Application of the Charity Commission's Risk Framework* (January 2012), p.17.
60 S. Younger, "The Charity Commission's Strategy" [2013] P.C.B. 84.
61 A. Dunn, "Regulatory Shifts: Developing Sector Participation in Regulation for Charities in England and Wales" (2014) 34 L.S. 660, 665.
62 C. Mitchell, "Redefining Charity in English Law" (1999) 13 Tru L.I. 21, 39–41.
63 e.g. Recreational Charities Act 1958 (reenacted as Charities Act 2011 s.5); Charities Act 2006 s.2 (reenacted as the Charities Act 2011 s.3), which was meant to codify the pre-existing law on charitable status, but which was amended to deem certain purposes to be charitable which had not previously been charitable. See para.6–056.

when it is or was registered.[64] In the event that it refuses to register a body as a charity, an appeal can be made from its decision to the First-tier Tribunal (Charity).[65]

## B. Methodology

### i. Analogising with Existing Charitable Purposes

When deciding the question whether the purposes of a trust or organisation are charitable, the courts and Charity Commission first consider whether such purposes have previously been held to be legally charitable. If not, then they ask whether an analogy can be drawn between the purposes under review and purposes which have previously been held to be legally charitable. For example, in *Scottish Burial Reform & Cremation Society Ltd v Glasgow Corporation*,[66] the House of Lords held that the operation of crematoria was charitable by analogy with the provision of burial grounds, which itself had been held charitable by analogy with the upkeep of churchyards, which itself had been held charitable by analogy with the repair of churches. By these steps successive courts began with an essentially religious charitable purpose and ended up by recognising as charitable an essentially secular purpose focused on public health provision. **6–023**

The same process of analogising from one purpose to another is employed by the Charity Commission when deciding whether to register as charities institutions whose purposes have not previously been recognised as charitable.[67] It is also recognised by the Charities Act 2011 s.3(1)(m)(ii) which provides that purposes are charitable if they "may reasonably be regarded as analogous to, or within the spirit of" the purposes identified in s.3(1) as being charitable; s.3(1)(m)(iii) further states that purposes are charitable if they "may reasonably be regarded as analogous to, or within the spirit of" purposes held by a decision-maker to be charitable under s.3(1)(m)(ii). **6–024**

This approach to determining charitable status has been criticised as a formalistic charade that disguises the value judgments made by decision-makers as to the desirability of using public money to underwrite the pursuit of particular purposes. A vivid example of this artificiality is the Canadian Federal Court of Appeal's decision in *Vancouver Regional FreeNet Association v MNR*,[68] that the provision of free public access to the "information super-highway", including the internet, is a charitable purpose by way of analogy to the charitable purpose of repairing bridges, ports, causeways and highways. Reasoning of this kind brings the legal process into disrepute. **6–025**

A further peculiarity of the law is that to a large extent the precedental value of decisions on charitable status is not altered by the fact that the consequences of charitable status have changed over time.[69] Several well-known cases extending charitable status to particular purposes were decided **6–026**

---

64 Charities Act 2011 s.37. The courts are bound by this provision when considering the validity of a gift to a body which has attained or subsequently attains registration: *Re Murawski's WT* [1971] 1 W.L.R. 707. It also binds rating authorities: *Wynn v Skegness UDC* [1967] 1 W.L.R. 52. But tax relief may be refused to registered charities which spend their money on non-charitable purposes: *IRC v Educational Grants Assoc Ltd* [1967] Ch. 123.

65 As in, e.g. *Full Fact v Charity Commission* CA/2011/0001, 26 July 2011, published online at: *http://www.charity.tribunals.gov.uk/Documents/FullFactdecision_26Jul11.pdf* [Accessed 1 June 2015]; *Uturn UK CIC v Charity Commission* CA/2011/0006, 27 February 2012, published online at: *http://www.charity.tribunals.gov.uk/documents/decisions/Uturn_UK_Decision.pdf* [Accessed 1 June 2015]; *Human Dignity Trust v Charity Commission* CA/2013/0013, 9 July 2014, published online at: *http://www.charity.tribunals.gov.uk/documents/decisions/human-dignity-trust-v-charity-commission-judgment.pdf* [Accessed 1 June 2015].

66 [1968] A.C. 138.

67 As discussed in Charity Commission, "RR1a: Recognising New Charitable Purposes" (October 2001), *https://www.gov.uk/government/uploads/system/uploads/attachment_data/file/358849/rr1atext.pdf* [Accessed 1 June 2015].

68 [1996] 3 F.C.R. 880.

69 Although to some extent changing social and economic circumstances are now taken into account when assessing the import of previous case law: see paras 6–027—6–029.

during the currency of the Mortmain and Charitable Uses Act 1736, which invalidated gifts of land to charitable purposes (unless the recipient was an exempted university or school). Examples are *Trustees of the British Museum v White*[70] and *Thornton v Howe*.[71] At the time when they were decided, the expansive view taken in these cases of (respectively) education and religion worked to the disadvantage of bodies with such purposes to whom gifts of land were made, as it meant that the gifts were rendered void.[72] However it now works to the advantage of voluntary bodies with such purposes when they seek charitable status.

### ii. Changing Social and Economic Circumstances

**6-027** When deciding whether purposes are legally charitable neither the courts nor the Charity Commission purport to consider whether one purpose is a better use of public money than another, nor do they attempt to align their findings on charitable status with current government policy, and they have declined to hold that a purpose is necessarily charitable merely by reason of the fact that Parliament has provided for it to be undertaken.[73] Since the 1990s, however, the Commission has laid more stress on the question whether changes in social and economic circumstances have made it more (or less) desirable for particular purposes to be pursued,[74] and it has departed from previous court decisions on this ground, a practice which it considers to be justified by the fact that the courts have done the same thing.[75] Examples are its 1993 finding that rifle clubs were no longer charitable[76] and its 2001 finding that the General Medical Council was a charity.[77]

**6-028** To the extent that such decisions reveal something of the decision-makers' policy calculations about public resource allocation, they do at least bring some transparency to the decision-making process. But the question remains whether it is desirable for the Commission and the courts to formulate policy in this area at all? In *Dingle v Turner*, Lord Cross held that "in answering the question whether any given trust is a charitable trust the courts . . . cannot avoid having regard to the fiscal

---

70 (1826) 2 Sim. & St. 594.

71 (1862) 31 Beav. 14.

72 G. Jones, *History of the Law of Charity 1532–1827* (Cambridge University Press, 1969) Ch.7; P. Ridge, "Legal Neutrality, Public Benefit and Religious Charitable Purposes: Making Sense of *Thornton v Howe*" (2010) 31 J.L.H. 177, esp. at 191–195.

73 *General Nursing Council for England and Wales v St Marylebone Corp* [1959] A.C. 540 (nurses' self-regulatory body was authorised by Parliament but was not a charity because the nurses took a private benefit from its activities); followed in *Helena Partnerships Ltd v HMRC* [2012] 4 All E.R. 111 at [67]–[71] (provision of social housing by housing association was not charitable because the members took a private benefit). Cf. *Latimer v IRC* [2004] 1 W.L.R. 1466 at [37]: the Government's "money is applicable and is applied for numerous non-charitable purposes. It is true that these are public purposes rather than private purposes; . . . but not all public purposes are charitable purposes."

74 But cf. the Commission's refusal to register Good News for Israel: Charity Commission, "Application for Registration of Good News for Israel" (5 February 2004), *https://www.gov.uk/government/uploads/system/uploads/attachment_data/file/324278/gnfidecision.pdf* [Accessed 1 June 2015] (establishment of the state of Israel did not justify departing from *Keren Kayemeth Le Jisroel Ltd v IRC* [1931] 2 K.B. 465 to hold that the settlement of Jewish people in the Holy Land could be accepted as furthering a religious purpose when previously it could not).

75 e.g. *National Anti-Vivisection Soc v IRC* [1948] A.C. 31, departing from *Re Foveaux* [1895] 2 Ch. 501 to hold that anti-vivisection was not a charitable purpose. See too *IRC v McMullen* [1981] A.C. 1 at 15, per Lord Hailsham LC: "both the legal conception of charity, and within it the educated man's ideas about education, are not static, but moving and changing . . . with changes in ideas about social values." These dicta mark a departure from the Victorian judges' view that once a purpose had been held legally charitable, it would always be legally charitable, whatever contemporary social opinion might be about the usefulness of the purpose: *Philpott v St George's Hospital* (1859) 27 Beav. 107 at 111–112. *Re Foveaux* [1895] 2 Ch. 501 at 505.

76 (1993) 1 Ch. Com. Dec. 4, departing from *Re Stephens* (1892) 8 T.L.R. 792.

77 Departing from *GMC v IRC* [1928] All E.R. 252; published online at: Charity Commission, "Decision Of The Charity Commissioners For England And Wales Made On 2nd April 2001 Application For Registration As A Charity By The General Medical Council" (2 April 2001), *https://www.gov.uk/government/uploads/system/uploads/attachment_data/file/324270/GMC.pdf* [Accessed 1 June 2015].

privileges accorded to charities",[78] but three other law lords in the case disassociated themselves from these remarks, considering that questions of public resource allocation are unsuited for judicial determination.[79] However, ignoring the issue does not make it go away: like it or not, the courts and the Charity Commission have effectively been left to decide such questions because successive governments have not wished to take responsibility for doing so.

In *Amateur Youth Soccer Association v Canada Revenue Agency*,[80] the Supreme Court of Canada acknowledged the fiscal implications of decisions on charitable status, but treated these as a reason for denying charitable status on the basis that such decisions are "best left to Parliament".[81] As Adam Parachin has written[82]: **6–029**

> for better or for worse, Parliament delegated the task of defining charity to courts knowing full well that charity decisions would carry with them revenue implications. Deferring the tough decisions back to Parliament on the basis of resource considerations arguably calls into question the legislative decision to deliver a state subsIdy on the basis of a judicially administered common law test for charitable status.

Parachin argues that the courts would do better to hold that fiscal considerations are not a determining factor when deciding questions of charitable status, and to direct their minds instead towards the question whether particular purposes live up to a conceptual or philosophical "ideal" of charity.[83] However it is very doubtful that the courts, rather than Parliament, are the appropriate body to decide what that ideal might be.

### iii. Purposes and Activities

Where the purposes of an institution are clearly described in an establishing document (e.g. a declaration of trust or a company's objects clause), legal orthodoxy states that the question whether the purposes are charitable must be decided solely by reference to the document, and that information regarding the institution's present or future activities should be disregarded, even where this information is available.[84] However, as Jonathan Garton writes in the following extract, this orthodoxy rests on the fallacious premise that a bright line divides charitable purposes and charitable activities. Moreover, it is clear that in various situations the courts and the Charity Commission do take account of a body's activities when determining whether its purposes are charitable, and there are good reasons for believing this to be appropriate and justifiable. **6–030**

## J. Garton, "Charitable Purposes and Activities"

(2014) 67 C.L.P. 373, 387–399

[The orthodoxy that purposes, and not activities, are relevant to charitable status] presupposes a bright line dividing purposes from activities, which is . . . fallacious. Where a constitution describes a purpose in **6–031**

---

78 [1972] A.C. 601 at 624.
79 ibid. at 614.
80 [2007] 3 S.C.R. 217.
81 ibid. at [44].
82 A. Parachin, "The Role of Fiscal Considerations in the Judicial Interpretation of Charity" in *Not-for-Profit Law: Theoretical and Comparative Perspectives* (2014), p.128.
83 ibid., p.116.
84 *Tennants Plays Ltd v IRC* [1948] 1 All E.R. 506 at 509; *Incorporated Council of Law Reporting for England and Wales v Attorney General* [1972] Ch. 73 at 99; *Attorney General v Ross* [1986] 1 W.L.R. 252 at 263; *R (on the application of Independent Schools Council) v Charity Commission* [2012] Ch. 214 at [188].

terms of the specific activity that is to be carried on, the question whether the purpose is charitable effectively becomes the question whether the activity is charitable, or at least whether the activity is one which can be seen as furthering a purpose that falls within the categories of charity: compare, for example, an institution whose stated purpose is simply 'the advancement of education' with one whose stated purpose is specific about how this is to be achieved, e.g. 'the schooling of children' or, to borrow an example from the Attorney-General's reference in the *Independent Schools Council* case, the schooling of children 'whose families can afford to pay fees representing the cost of the provision of their education'.[85] The more precise the wording of an organization's purpose, the more it becomes necessary for the court to engage with the nature of the activities that will be carried on thereunder. Sometimes, the distinction between a purpose and an activity is merely a question of degree: where a body is established to carry on a range of endeavours in pursuit of a particular purpose, then each individual endeavour is likely to be treated as an activity tending to the purpose, but where a body focusses on one endeavour this may be treated as a purpose in its own right, as in *National Anti-Vivisection Society v IRC*,[86] where the argument that the Society's quest for the repeal of the Cruelty to Animals Act 1876 was 'merely ancillary' to its purpose of prohibiting vivisection was rejected:[87] the evidence was that campaigning for the repeal was effectively all that the Society did, and so this was treated as its main purpose.[88] In certain other cases, the distinction between purpose and activity appears to be nothing more than a question of construction, as in the gift in *Re Hood*,[89] where the second of two ostensibly discrete purposes—the promotion of Christian principles and the promotion of temperance—was interpreted by the court as merely one possible means of achieving the former . . .

**6–032** . . . In fact, despite the orthodoxy, it is clear that there are certain circumstances when it is appropriate to look to a would-be charity's activities in order to shed light on the nature of its purposes. The reality, though, is that the case law is confused and, while some authorities suggest that consideration of on organization's activities is never appropriate, others suggest otherwise, and in doing so attach varying degrees of significance to those activities. Some semblance of order can be imposed if we consider that there are six different ways in which activities could potentially play a role in determining charitable status. Activities could be used to:

- determine the purpose of an organization in the absence of complete written information;
- determine the true purpose of an organization where the written information is inaccurate;
- determine whether that purpose falls within the categories of charity, in the case of a novel purpose;
- determine whether that purpose is a charitable purpose even though it is otherwise clear, e.g. from precedent, that it falls within the categories of charity;
- distinguish between the dominant and subsidiary purposes of an organization with more than one stated purpose (there being no need for the subsidiary purpose to be charitable); or
- determine whether an organization with an exclusively charitable purpose meets any further requirements of charitable status.

### Determining the Purpose of an Organization

**6–033** The orthodox position presupposes that every potential charity has some form of written constitution that can be consulted for definitive information about the purpose for which the organization is established. However, this is not necessarily the case, particularly in the case of inter vivos charitable trusts, the creation of which requires no particular formalities.[90] This was acknowledged in the *Independent Schools Council* case,[91] where the Upper Tribunal observed that in the absence of a written constitution, or where the written constitution is incomplete, 'all the circumstances' may be taken into account in order to determine

---

85 [2012] Ch. 214 at [114].

86 [1948] A.C. 31.

87 As per Lord Greene M.R.'s dissent in the Court of Appeal: [1946] K.B. 185 at 207.

88 [1948] A.C. 31 at 61, per Lord Simonds, and at 77, per Lord Normand. See also *McGovern v Att.-Gen.* [1982] Ch. 321 at 341, per Slade J.

89 [1931] 1 Ch. 240 at 252, per Lawrence L.J.

90 *Lyell v Kennedy* (1889) 14 App. Cas. 437. Though where the trust property is land, it will be unenforceable—though still valid—unless evidenced in signed writing: Law of Property Act 1925, s.53(1)(b).

91 [2012] Ch. 214.

the organization's purposes.[92] So, in *Re Resch's W.T.*,[93] where a fee-charging hospital had no written constitution or document identifying its general purposes, the Privy Council examined how the hospital operated in practice in order to determine that its purpose was the provision of healthcare to those in need,[94] while in *Re Banfield*,[95] a gift of residue for the purposes of the Pilsdon Community House, which had no founding instrument or other governing documents, was upheld as charitable on the basis that its various activities bore out the assertion of its representative that the House advanced religion.[96] . . .

**Correcting Inaccurate Information**

Even where an organization has an apparently complete written constitution, the courts have on occasion taken activities into account as evidence that the constitution does not accurately state the organization's true purposes. Despite Lord Halsbury L.C.'s caution against reading into a document words that were in the creator's mind but did not make it onto the page,[97] the court may exceptionally do so where there has been a mistake or where there is an intention to create a sham. Regarding the former, the court has an equitable discretion in the case of a trust instrument or contract, although not a company's articles or memorandum of association,[98] to rectify or set aside the document where it is not an accurate reflection of what was intended by the parties to it.[99] Where donations or voluntary subscriptions are held on a valid but vague charitable trust and the trustees exercise their implied right to 'prescribe accurately' its terms in a new trust instrument,[100] this instrument may also be rectified or set aside for inaccuracy if it goes beyond the purposes contemplated by the donors.[101] . . . 6–034

Activities may also be taken into consideration where there is a deliberate sham, i.e. 'the appearance of creating . . . legal rights and obligations different from the actual legal rights and obligations (if any) which the parties intend to create'.[102] Where there is suspicion of a sham,[103] the court is entitled to look beyond the governing documents—now 'no more than a piece of paper'[104]—and consider, inter alia, both the subjective intentions of the founders and the trustees and their 'subsequent conduct'.[105] Unlike rectification of a trust instrument, a sham requires dishonesty on the part of the founders and trustees.[106] This will clearly be satisfied in the case of a would-be charity where there is an attempt to procure donations under false pretences, such as an organization ostensibly established for the relief of poverty overseas but which in reality is set up to finance acts of terrorism,[107] or where there is an intention to defraud the tax authorities.[108] 6–035

**Determining a Novel Charitable Purpose**

In the *Independent Schools Council* case, the Upper Tribunal reasserts the orthodoxy that, at least where there is a complete written constitution, it is inappropriate to consider the activities subsequently carried 6–036

---

92 Ibid. at [193].
93 [1969] 1 A.C. 514.
94 Ibid. at 540.
95 [1968] 1 W.L.R. 846.
96 Ibid. at 850, per Goff J.
97 *Hunter v Att.-Gen.* [1899] A.C. 309 at 317–18.
98 *Scott v Frank F Scott (London) Ltd* [1940] Ch. 794.
99 *Re Butlin's S.T.* [1976] Ch. 251.
100 *Att.-Gen. v Mathieson* [1907] 2 Ch. 383 at 394, per Cozens-Hardy M.R.
101 Ibid.; *Shergill v Khaira* [2014] UKSC 33 at [26], per Lords Neuberger, Sumption and Hodge, with whom Lords Mance and Clarke agreed.
102 *Snook v London and West Riding Investment Ltd* [1967] 2 Q.B. 786 at 802, per Diplock L.J.; *Hitch v Stone (Inspector of Taxes)* [2001] S.T.C. 214 at [1], per Arden L.J.; approved in the trust law context in *Midland Bank plc v Wyatt* [1995] 1 B.C.L.C. 242 at 245, per David Young Q.C.; *Re Abacus (CI) Ltd* [2004] W.T.L.R. 1 at [42]–[45], per Birt D.B.
103 The burden of proof lies with the person who alleges the sham: *National Westminster Bank plc v Jones* [2001] 1 B.C.L.C. 98 at [68], per Neuberger J.; *A v A* [2007] 2 F.L.R. 467 at [69], per Munby J.
104 *National Westminster Bank plc v Jones* [2001] 1 B.C.L.C. 98 at [68], per Neuberger J.
105 *Hitch v Stone (Inspector of Taxes)* [2001] S.T.C. 214 at [65], per Arden L.J.; *Re Abacus (CI) Ltd* [2004] W.T.L.R. 1 at [44], per Birt D.B.
106 *National Westminster Bank plc v Jones* [2001] 1 B.C.L.C. 98 at [46] and [59], per Neuberger J.; *A v A* [2007] 2 F.L.R. 467 at [53], per Munby J.; *MacKinnon v Regent Trust Co Ltd* [2005] W.T.L.R. 1369 at [19]–[20], per Richard Southwell Q.C.
107 On which see Charity Commission, *Counter-Terrorism Strategy* (April 2012).
108 See, outside the charity context, *Hitch v Stone (Inspector of Taxes)* [2001] STC 214.

on by an organization when determining whether it was established for exclusively charitable purposes, both at common law and under the Charities Act 2011.[109] However, this overlooks the fact that there is a clear distinction to be made between the task of identifying what the specific purposes of an organization are, on the one hand, and whether those purposes fall within the categories of charity, on the other. Both of these questions must be answered in order to find that an organization is established for charitable purposes. The distinction is made clear by the *Incorporated Council of Law Reporting* case: although the Court of Appeal . . . stressed that it could look only to the written constitution—which was neither incomplete nor inaccurate—to determine the purposes for which the council was established, its activities were nevertheless relevant when considering the nature of those purposes.

6-037 . . . Accordingly, whilst the court did not look to the council's activities to determine that it was established for the purpose of preparing and publishing law reports, it did consider them in order to conclude that this was a charitable purpose falling under the second or fourth heads of *Pemsel*.[110] The same approach was applied in *IRC v Oldham Training and Enterprise Council*,[111] where Lightman J. considered the proposed or actual activities of Oldham TEC—which promoted trade, commerce, and enterprise—to be 'irrelevant' in determining its purposes and yet 'graphic evidence' of the charitableness of those purposes.[112]

**Determining a Purpose with Precedent**

6-038 It is one thing to take account of activities, proposed or actual, in order to determine whether a clearly stated purpose falls within the categories of charity in the case of a novel purpose, quite another to do this where there is precedent that the purpose is charitable. In the latter case, there can be no question, at least in the absence of significant social change, of proposed or actual activities displacing the fact that, as a matter of law, the organization in question is established for a charitable purpose; to suggest otherwise is to misunderstand the nature of the legal definition of charity. . .

**Distinguishing Dominant and Subsidiary Purposes**

6-039 Activities may be taken into account in order to determine which purposes, in the case of an organization with more than one, constitute its main objects and which, if any, are subsidiary to these. This is particularly significant given that a charity may legitimately have non-charitable objects where these are subsidiary to a dominant charitable purpose. So, in *Chartered Insurance Institute v London Corporation*,[113] Devlin J. considered it necessary to look beyond the objects clause of an organization, which listed 13 discrete purposes, some educational and some not, in order to determine whether its main purpose was the advancement of education; rather than balance the educational objects against the others in the abstract, he focussed on 'the way in which those objects have actually been achieved or attempted'.[114] Consideration of activities as a matter of course when determining dominant purposes was advocated by Lord Denning in *National Deposit Friendly Society v Skegness UDC*,[115] who suggested that 'in order to ascertain the "main objects" of an organization, you are entitled, I think, to look not only at its rules but also to consider the way in which it has conducted its affairs',[116] although other authorities have taken a more circumspect approach such that activities are relevant only when the distinction between the dominant and the subsidiary is unclear from the governing documents.[117]

**Further Requirements of Charity**

6-040 Even if a body's activities were not relevant to the question of whether it has a charitable purpose . . . it would not follow that they are not relevant to charitable status at all. It is easy to forget, particularly given the emphasis that the Charities Act 2011 places both on the nature of a charitable purpose and on the

109 [2012] Ch. 214 at [187]–[188].
110 The court was unanimous that this purpose fell under the fourth head; however, Russell L.J. did not share the majority view that this was also an educational purpose: ibid. at 89.
111 [1996] S.T.C. 1218.
112 Ibid. at 1234–35.
113 [1957] 1 W.L.R. 867.
114 Ibid. at 875.
115 [1959] A.C. 293.
116 Ibid. at 320.
117 See *Berry v St Marylebone BC* [1958] Ch. 406 at 417, per Romer L.J.; *Victory (Ex-Services) Association Ltd v Paddington BC* [1960] 1 All E.R. 498 at 500, per Lord Parker C.J.

> public benefit in a charitable purpose, that although an exclusively charitable purpose is a requirement of charitable status, it is not the only requirement. It is clear that a body with an exclusively charitable purpose will only have charitable status if that purpose is such that its benefits are open to enjoyment by a sufficient section of the community[118] and it does not create more than incidental benefits for private individuals.[119] The distinction between charitable purpose and charitable status was made explicit in *Oppenheim v Tobacco Securities Trust*,[120] where the House of Lords recognized that the purpose of the trust in question, being for the advancement of education, was charitable, although its restricted class of beneficiaries meant that the trust was denied charitable status.[121] . . .
>
> When determining whether a sufficient section of the public is able to enjoy the carrying out of a particular charitable purpose, or whether it will generate more than incidental benefit for a private class, which the public benefit requirement also prohibits, consideration of an organization's activities, where relevant information is available, is certainly relevant insofar as this sheds light on these questions. . . **6–041**

## 4. Legally Charitable Purposes

The Charities Act 2011 s.2 provides that a purpose is legally charitable if it is one of the purposes listed in s.3 and it satisfies the public benefit requirement in s.4. The legislation therefore follows the case law in distinguishing between the question of whether a purpose is inherently beneficial and the question of whether it will enure to the benefit of the whole public, or a substantial part of it, rather than to the private advantage of a group of individuals.[122] The latter question emerged as a distinct issue in the Victorian period when the courts first developed a "public benefit" rule as a means of denying charitable status to trusts for purposes which had previously been held legally charitable.[123] However, it was not until the twentieth century that the courts systematically distinguished inherently beneficial purposes and legally charitable purposes, "the former being merely one (albeit necessary) element of the latter together with the requirement that the purpose be carried on for the benefit of a sufficient section of the community".[124] **6–042**

Jonathan Garton has suggested that each question can itself be sub-divided. The first question encompasses these questions: (a) whether broadly described set of purposes are inherently beneficial in the abstract; and (b) whether a particular purpose identified in a trust deed or body's governing documents falls within a set of purposes that have been identified as inherently beneficial. Hence, for example, if a trust deed provided that the trust funds should be applied to the provision of advice on debt management, one would need to ask: (a) whether the relief and prevention of poverty are inherently beneficial purposes; and (b) whether the provision of debt management advice can be characterised as falling within the scope of relieving and preventing poverty. The second question divides into: (c) what constitutes a sufficient section of the public to justify treating a purpose as legally **6–043**

---

118 *Goodman v Saltash Corporation* (1882) 7 App. Cas. 633; *Oppenheim v Tobacco Securities Trust Co Ltd* [1951] A.C. 297.

119 *IRC v Oldham Training and Enterprise Council* [1996] S.T.C. 1218.

120 [1951] A.C. 297.

121 Ibid. at 309, per Lord Normand, and at 313, per Lord Macdermott. cf. *Gilmour v Coats* [1949] A.C. 426 at 449, per Lord Simonds, and at 462, per Lord Reid, where cloistered nuns were held not to have a charitable purpose, despite clearly advancing religion.

122 Respectively described as a "qualitative" and a "quantitative" question (while noting that the latter "is not simply . . . a matter of numbers") in J. Jaconelli, "Adjudicating on Charitable Status—A Reconsideration of the Elements" [2013] Conv. 96, 96–07.

123 *Cocks v Manners* (1871) L.R. 12 Eq. 574 at 585; *Yeap Cheah Neo v Ong Cheng Neo* (1875) L.R. 6 P.C. 381 at 396; *Re White* [1893] 2 Ch. 41 at 53. Discussion in P. Ridge, "Legal Neutrality, Public Benefit and Religious Charitable Purposes: Making Sense of *Thornton v Howe*" (2010) 31 J.L.H. 177, 199–202.

124 J. Garton, *Public Benefit in Charity Law: Principles and Practice* (Oxford University Press, 2013), para.1–22, identifying *Oppenheim v Tobacco Securities Trust Co Ltd* [1951] A.C. 297 as the case in which this step was decisively taken. The distinction was not clearly drawn in *Verge v Somerville* [1924] A.C. 496, although the case turned on the question whether a trust was legally charitable if it benefited those who were not poor.

charitable; and (d) when does the pursuit of a purpose lead to more than an incidental benefit to a private class so that charitable status should be denied?[125]

**6–044** Unfortunately, the courts have not distinguished these connected but conceptually different issues as clearly as they might have done. Confusingly, they have used the same terminology of "public benefit" when discussing all of them, a practice which has caused significant confusion and misunderstandings. Some steps towards clarification were taken in the *Independent Schools Council* case, however, where the difference between the two main questions was explained in the following passage.

*R (on the application of the Independent Schools Council) v Charity Commission*

Upper Tribunal (Tax and Chancery) [2012] Ch. 214 at [44]

**6–045** WARREN J. (CHAMBER PRESIDENT), UPPER TRIBUNAL JUDGES McKENNA AND OVEY: It is possible . . . to discern from the cases two related aspects of public benefit. The first aspect is that the nature of the purpose itself must be such as to be a benefit to the community: this is public benefit in the first sense. In that sense, the advancement of education, referred to in the Preamble under the guise of "schools of learning, free schools and scholars in universities", has the necessary element of benefit to the community . . . The second aspect is that those who may benefit from the carrying out of the purpose must be sufficiently numerous, and identified in such manner as, to constitute what is described in the authorities as "a section of the public": this is public benefit in the second sense. The decision in *Oppenheim's case*[126] illustrates these two aspects, which we will refer to as public benefit in "the first sense" and "the second sense". The advancement of education, as such, was of a nature which was beneficial to the community (and so of public benefit in the first sense); but the practical restriction of the benefits to children of employees of certain employers was in effect to render the trust a private trust, because it was not for the benefit of a sufficient section of the public. It was therefore not charitable.

**6–046** Conversely, as the Upper Tribunal also noted, "a trust to train pickpockets would not be charitable" even if the training were offered to everyone in the country, as in this case the anti-social nature of the trust's educational purpose would mean that it was not for the public benefit in the first sense, and so could never be legally charitable.[127]

**6–047** In the following overview of the law governing legally charitable purposes we shall first consider the purposes identified by the Charities Act 2011 s.3 as being inherently beneficial ("for the public benefit" in the first sense identified in the *Independent Schools Council* case) and then discuss the requirement in the Charities Act 2011 s.4 that legally charitable purposes must additionally be for the benefit of a significant section of the community ("for the public benefit" in the second sense identified in the case).

## *A. Inherently Beneficial Purposes*

**6–048** The modern law of charity can be traced back to the Statute of Charitable Uses 1601. This statute appointed poor law commissioners to investigate misappropriations of charity property. The preamble to the statute contained a list of objects which were understood to be legally charitable at that time, and which the courts later came to use as a reference point for the determination of cases, with the result that, in addition to the objects listed in the preamble, other objects analogous to them or within the spirit and intendment of the preamble also came to be regarded as legally charitable.

---

[125] ibid., at para.2–15.

[126] *Oppenheim v Tobacco Securities Trust Co Ltd* [1951] A.C. 297.

[127] *R (Independent Schools Council) v Charity Commission* [2012] Ch. 214 at [48]. See too *Re Pinion* [1965] Ch. 85 at 105.

## Preamble to the Statute of Charitable Uses 1601

Whereas lands, chattels, money have been given by sundry well disposed persons: some for the relief of aged, impotent and poor people; the maintenance of sick and maimed soldiers and mariners, schools of learning, free schools, and scholars in universities; the repair of bridges, ports, havens, causeways, churches, sea banks and highways; the education and preferment of orphans; the relief, stock, or maintenance for houses of correction; the marriage of poor maids; the supportation aid and help of young tradesmen, handicraftsmen and persons decayed; the relief or redemption of prisoners or captives; the aid or ease of any poor inhabitants concerning payment of fifteens, setting out of soldiers and other taxes; which lands, chattels and money have not been employed according to the charitable intent of the givers by reason of frauds, breaches of trust and negligence. . . **6-049**

In *Morice v Bishop of Durham*, the Preamble was identified by Sir William Grant MR and by Lord Eldon LC as the starting point for any judicial examination of the question whether the purposes of a trust were legally charitable.[128] They also stressed that popular notions of charity were beside the point when answering this question. According to Grant MR, the word charity[129]: **6-050**

> in its widest sense denotes all the good affections, men ought to bear towards each other; in its most restricted and common sense, relief of the poor. In neither of these senses is it employed in this Court. Here its signification is derived chiefly from the Statute of Elizabeth. Those purposes are considered charitable, which that Statute enumerates, or which by analogies are deemed within its spirit and intendment; and to some such purpose every bequest to charity generally shall be applied.

Lord Eldon agreed, and approved a classification of legally charitable objects proposed by counsel[130] that was founded on the Preamble. In Lord Eldon's words[131]: **6-051**

> There are four objects, within one of which all charity, to be administered in this Court, must fall: 1st, relief of the indigent; in various ways: money: provisions: education: medical assistance: &c.; 2dly, the advancement of learning: 3dly, the advancement of religion; and, 4thly, which is the most difficult, the advancement of objects of general public utility.

This four-part classification of legally charitable objects was to prove hugely influential. It was taken up at the end of the nineteenth century by Lord Macnaghten in *Special Commissioners for the Purposes of Income Tax v Pemsel*, where he said that[132]: **6-052**

> 'Charity' in its legal sense comprises four principal divisions: trusts for the relief of poverty; trusts for the advancement of education; trusts for the advancement of religion; and trusts for other purposes beneficial to the community, not falling under any of the preceding heads.

The four "*Pemsel* heads of charity", as they were known thereafter, subsequently formed the starting-point for the courts and the Charity Commission throughout the twentieth century, up until the enactment of the Charities Act 2006 s.2. Intended as a codifying measure, this section set out a list of 13 charitable purposes, retaining the first three *Pemsel* heads, and sub-dividing the fourth into ten new heads, including a residual category of purposes which swept in all the existing charitable purposes

---

128 The facts and arguments in the case, and the judges' decisions, are all well explained in J. Getzler, "*Morice v Bishop of Durham* (1805)" in C. Mitchell and P. Mitchell (eds), *Landmark Cases in Equity* (Hart Publishing, 2010).

129 (1804) 9 Ves. Jun. 399 at 405.

130 Samuel Romilly, who later became Solicitor-General and earned fame for his reforms of the criminal law.

131 (1805) 10 Ves. Jun. 522 at 532.

132 [1891] A.C. 531 at 583.

which did not fall under any of the other 12 heads, and which also allowed for the recognition of new charitable purposes by a version of the analogising process familiar from the case law.

**6–053** The Charities Act 2006 s.2 was later reenacted as the Charities Act 2011 s.3, which is reproduced here along with s.5, which has replaced the Recreational Charities Act 1958, legislation which deemed the provision of recreational facilities to be a charitable purpose and thereby reversed the effect of *IRC v Baddeley*,[133] in which the House of Lords had held that the promotion of social well-being was not a charitable purpose falling within the fourth *Pemsel* head, and had thereby threatened the status of village halls which had generally been assumed to been charitable prior to the court's decision.[134]

## Charities Act 2011 ss. 3 and 5

### 3 Descriptions of purposes

**6–054** (1) A purpose falls within this subsection if it falls within any of the following descriptions of purposes –

(a) the prevention or relief of poverty;
(b) the advancement of education;
(c) the advancement of religion;
(d) the advancement of health or the saving of lives;
(e) the advancement of citizenship or community development;
(f) the advancement of the arts, culture, heritage or science;
(g) the advancement of amateur sport;
(h) the advancement of human rights, conflict resolution or reconciliation or the promotion of religious or racial harmony or equality and diversity;
(i) the advancement of environmental protection or improvement;
(j) the relief of those in need because of youth, age, ill-health, disability, financial hardship or other disadvantage;
(k) the advancement of animal welfare;
(l) the promotion of the efficiency of the armed forces of the Crown or of the efficiency of the police, fire and rescue services or ambulance services;
(m) any other purposes—

(i) that are not within paragraphs (a) to (l) but are recognised as charitable purposes by virtue of section 5 (recreational and similar trusts, etc.) or under the old law,

(ii) that may reasonably be regarded as analogous to, or within the spirit of, any purposes falling within any of paragraphs (a) to (l) or sub-paragraph (i), or
(iii) that may reasonably be regarded as analogous to, or within the spirit of, any purposes which have been recognised, under the law relating to charities in England and Wales, as falling within sub-paragraph (ii) or this sub-paragraph.

(2) In subsection (1)—

(a) in paragraph (c), "religion" includes—

(i) a religion which involves belief in more than one god, and
(ii) a religion which does not involve belief in a god,

(b) in paragraph (d), "the advancement of health" includes the prevention or relief of sickness, disease or human suffering,
(c) paragraph (e) includes—

(i) rural or urban regeneration, and

---

133 [1955] A.C. 572.
134 Discussion at paras 6–026—6–027.

(ii) the promotion of civic responsibility, volunteering, the voluntary sector or the effectiveness or efficiency of charities,

(d) in paragraph (g), "sport" means sports or games which promote health by involving physical or mental skill or exertion,
(e) paragraph (j) includes relief given by the provision of accommodation or care to the persons mentioned in that paragraph, and
(f) in paragraph (l), "fire and rescue services" means services provided by fire and rescue authorities under Part 2 of the Fire and Rescue Services Act 2004.

(3) Where any of the terms used in any of paragraphs (a) to (l) of subsection (1), or in subsection (2), has a particular meaning under the law relating to charities in England and Wales, the term is to be taken as having the same meaning where it appears in that provision.
(4) In subsection (1)(m)(i), "the old law" means the law relating to charities in England and Wales as in force immediately before 1 April 2008.

**5 Recreational and similar trusts, etc.**

(1) It is charitable (and is to be treated as always having been charitable) to provide, or assist in the provision of, facilities for— **6–055**

(a) recreation, or
(b) other leisure-time occupation,

if the facilities are provided in the interests of social welfare.
(2) The requirement that the facilities are provided in the interests of social welfare cannot be satisfied if the basic conditions are not met.
(3) The basic conditions are –

(a) that the facilities are provided with the object of improving the conditions of life for the persons for whom the facilities are primarily intended, and
(b) that –

(i) those persons have need of the facilities because of their youth, age, infirmity or disability, poverty, or social and economic circumstances, or
(ii) the facilities are to be available to members of the public at large or to male, or to female, members of the public at large.

(4) Subsection (1) applies in particular to—

(a) the provision of facilities at village halls, community centres and women's institutes, and
(b) the provision and maintenance of grounds and buildings to be used for purposes of recreation or leisure-time occupation,

and extends to the provision of facilities for those purposes by the organising of any activity. But this is subject to the requirement that the facilities are provided in the interests of social welfare.
(5) Nothing in this section is to be treated as derogating from the public benefit requirement.

The terms in which the statutory heads of charity are expressed in s.3, such as "the advancement of religion", must be read in line with their meanings at common law under s.3(3). This is consistent with the Government's stated intention when putting the Charities Bill 2005 before Parliament, which was to codify the existing common law rules. In some respects, however, the statute went further than that, and changed the law, partly as a result of changes to the wording of the bill as it went through Parliament. Section 3(1)(a) recognises the prevention of poverty as a stand-alone charitable purpose, the first *Pemsel* head having previously been confined to the relief of poverty; s.3(2)(a)(ii) defines "religion" to include "a religion which does not involve belief in a god", a departure from cases which defined religion to mean belief in a god; and s.3(2)(d) defines "sport" to include "sports or games **6–056** which promote health by involving . . . mental skill or exertion", the law previously having held that sporting purposes were charitable only to the extent that they involved physical effort and skill.

**6-057** Some of the categories in s.3(1) overlap, so that some purposes might fit within two or more of the descriptions of purposes listed there. Examples are trusts for the relief of those suffering from financial hardship, which could fall within s.3(1)(a) and (j); trusts for the promotion of the arts, which could fall within s.3(1)(b) and (f); and trusts for the advancement of health and care of the sick, which could fall within s.3(1)(d), (g), (j) and (l). Since the Government's purpose in enacting the section was to make the law simpler and more accessible, this is unfortunate.

## *B. Benefit to a Significant Section of the Community*

### i. Common Law Development

**6-058** As noted above,[135] the rule first emerged in the nineteenth century that a valid charitable trust must provide an identifiable and demonstrable benefit for the community at large, or at least a significant section of it, as opposed to a private class of individuals. It is clear that a trust need not benefit every person in the country to be charitable, but the courts have struggled to articulate a test to distinguish between charitable trusts which benefit a group of people qua members of the public and private trusts which benefit a group of people qua private individuals.

**6-059** The House of Lords in *Oppenheim v Tobacco Securities Trust Co Ltd*[136] used the personal nexus test put forward in *Re Compton*[137]: they held that except in "poverty" cases no class of beneficiaries can constitute a section of the public if the distinguishing quality which links them together is a relationship to a particular person, e.g. through a common ancestor or a common employer. Thus a trust for the education of the children of employees of British American Tobacco Co Ltd or any of its subsidiary or allied companies was not a valid charitable trust. This was despite the fact that there were over 110,000 current employees. If the trust in *Oppenheim* had been for the education of those employed or formerly employed in the tobacco industry, it would have been valid, as it would if the provision of education had been confined to children of those engaged in the tobacco industry in a particular place.

**6-060** The weaknesses of the personal nexus test are revealed in the dissenting speech of Lord MacDermott in *Oppenheim*, with whose approach the House of Lords were in obiter agreement in *Dingle v Turner*.[138] In the latter case, Lord Cross said that whether or not the potential beneficiaries of a trust can fairly be said to constitute a section of the public is a question of degree in all the circumstances of the case, and that much must depend on the purposes of the trusts. If that is correct, it means that whether a purpose is inherently socially beneficial and whether the pursuit of the purpose enures to a significant section of society are interconnected issues, and that it is possible for the court to hold, e.g. that a trust for the relief of poverty is charitable although it enures to the benefit of many fewer people than would be required for a trust for the advancement of education to be charitable.[139]

**6-061** Owing to the conflicting views expressed in the Lords in *Oppenheim* and *Dingle*, the lower courts and the Charity Commission have faced a dilemma in cases that compel a choice between the two views. The narrow personal nexus approach, although conducive to certainty, also leads to artificial manipulation of the legal forms so as to obtain fiscal advantages, e.g. in the case of a trust for the

---

135 See para.6-042.
136 [1951] A.C. 297.
137 [1945] Ch. 123.
138 [1972] A.C. 601.
139 See also *Attorney General v Charity Commission* [2012] W.T.L.R. 977 at [64], where the Upper Tribunal (Tax and Chancery Chamber) came to exactly this conclusion.

education of children of inhabitants of Bourneville, which might be invalidated under the broad approach as being in substance a trust benefiting employees of Cadbury Schweppes Plc. The broad approach, though less predictable in outcome, at least concerns itself with the substance of the matter and is not unduly preoccupied with form.

Note also that an institution's purposes cannot be for the public benefit if they do more harm than good, i.e. if the detriment resulting from their pursuit is greater than the benefit which they bring. This was established in *National Anti-Vivisection Society v IRC*,[140] where the House of Lords held that the appellant society's purpose of campaigning for the abolition of vivisection was not charitable because the harm that would result if the society's goals were achieved would outweigh the good. **6–062**

## ii. Statutory Developments and Their Aftermath

In 2006 the Labour Government sought to alter the law in this area by enacting ss.3 and 4 of the Charities Act 2006. The Government believed there to be a common law presumption that the purposes of relieving poverty, advancing education, and advancing religion were "for the public benefit" in the second sense described in the *ISC* case.[141] Section 3(2) of the 2006 Act was enacted with the intention of abrogating this supposed rule. At the same time s.4 placed the Charity Commission under a new duty to issue guidance "to promote awareness and understanding" of the public benefit requirement, to which charity trustees would henceforth be required to "have regard" when exercising relevant powers and duties. **6–063**

The Government stated that these measures were intended to simplify the law and to strengthen the Commission's ability as sector regulator to clarify and publicise the legal rules governing charitable status. The Government also had a political objective: it wished to empower the Commission to revisit the charitable status of fee-charging charities, and particularly fee-charging schools and hospitals, whose purposes, in the Government's view, enured to the benefit of an insufficiently broad section of society to justify their having such status. **6–064**

Sections 3 and 4 were later reenacted without any substantive change to their wording as ss.4 and 17 of the Charities Act 2011 (a consolidating statute). These are reproduced below, along with the Charities Act 2011 s.14, which lists the Commission's (rather nebulous) institutional objectives, and which was also copied across from the 2006 Act. **6–065**

### Charities Act 2011 ss. 4, 14 and 17

**4 The public benefit requirement**

(1) In this Act "the public benefit requirement" means the requirement in section 2(1)(b) that a purpose falling within section 3(1) must be for the public benefit if it is to be a charitable purpose. **6–066**
(2) In determining whether the public benefit requirement is satisfied in relation to any purpose falling within section 3(1), it is not to be presumed that a purpose of a particular description is for the public benefit.
(3) In this Chapter any reference to the public benefit is a reference to the public benefit as that term is understood for the purposes of the law relating to charities in England and Wales.
(4) Subsection (3) is subject to subsection (2).

[140] [1948] A.C. 31. See too *R (Independent Schools Council) v Charity Commission* [2012] Ch. 214 at [106].
[141] See para.6–045. For the Government's understanding of the law, see, e.g. Hansard, HC Vol.448, cols 50–51 (26 June 2006), A. Milburn MP.

**14 The Commission's objectives**

6–067 The Commission has the following objectives—

*1 The public confidence objective*
The public confidence objective is to increase public trust and confidence in charities.

*2 The public benefit objective*
The public benefit objective is to promote awareness and understanding of the operation of the public benefit requirement.

*3 The compliance objective*
The compliance objective is to promote compliance by charity trustees with their legal obligations in exercising control and management of the administration of their charities.

*4 The charitable resources objective*
The charitable resources objective is to promote the effective use of charitable resources.

*5 The accountability objective*
The accountability objective is to enhance the accountability of charities to donors, beneficiaries and the general public.

**17 Guidance as to operation of public benefit requirement**

6–068 (1) The Commission must issue guidance in pursuance of its public benefit objective (see paragraph 2 of section 14).
(2) The Commission may from time to time revise any guidance issued under this section.
(3) The Commission must carry out such public and other consultation as it considers appropriate –
  (a) before issuing any guidance under this section, or
  (b) (unless it considers that it is unnecessary to do so) before revising any guidance under this section.
(4) The Commission must publish any guidance issued or revised under this section in such manner as it considers appropriate.
(5) The charity trustees of a charity must have regard to any such guidance when exercising any powers or duties to which the guidance is relevant.

6–069 The Government's objectives in enacting these sections were not achieved. There are several reasons for this. One is that the Charities Act 2006 s.3(2) was premised on a mistaken view of the common law. There was no common law rule that the first three *Pemsel* purposes should be presumed to be "for the public benefit" in the second sense. The view that such a rule existed depended on a misreading of Lord Wright's dictum in *National Anti-Vivisection Society v IRC* that[142]:

> The test of benefit to the community goes through the whole of Lord Macnaghten's classification [in the *Pemsel* case], though, as regards the first three heads, it may be prima facie assumed unless the contrary appears.

However, as the Upper Tribunal later noted in the *Independent Schools Council* case,[143] Lord Wright was speaking in this passage of "public benefit" in the first rather than the second sense.

6–070 Lord Wright's point was that purposes falling within the first three *Pemsel* heads can be assumed to be inherently beneficial, but that the contrary may appear if they are framed in an anti-social way (e.g.

---

142 [1948] A.C. 31 at 42.

143 *R (Independent Schools Council) v Charity Commission* [2012] Ch. 214 at [63]. See too P. Luxton, "A Three-Part Invention: Public Benefit Under the Charity Commission" (2009) 11 C.L. & P.R. 19, 23.

running a school for pickpockets, relieving poverty by killing the homeless). And as the Upper Tribunal also noted, even this was not to say that there is a "presumption" that the first three *Pemsel* heads are "for the public benefit" in the first sense, for in each case the court[144]:

> will form its own view on the evidence before it whether the trust is for the public benefit and will do so, not by way of assumption, but by way of decision. It will no doubt take account of other decided cases; and it will take judicial notice of facts where appropriate. This is far from a 'presumption' in the usual sense.

Since Lord Wright did not say that purposes falling within the first three *Pemsel* heads are presumed to deliver benefits to a wide section of society, s.3(2) cannot have abolished a presumption that such purposes are "for the public benefit" in the second sense: no such presumption has ever existed. And if instead the sub-section abolished a presumption that such purposes are "for the public benefit" in the first sense, then this can have made "little, if any, difference" to the law,[145] because this was a "presumption" only in a very attenuated sense of the word.

Problems were also caused by the measures taken by the Charity Commission in pursuit of its duty under the Charities Act 2006 s.4 to promote awareness and understanding of the public benefit requirement.[146] These can be partly attributed to the Commission's ambiguous status as a regulator with de facto law-making powers. Critics have contended that as an independent regulator the Commission is empowered only to apply the law defining public benefit as it is laid down by the courts and legislature, and that it has no authority to make or develop the law.[147] However, that is to ignore the reality that when deciding applications by voluntary bodies for registration the Commission has frequently made new law by analogising between old and new charitable purposes and by departing from previous court decisions in light of changing social and economic circumstances.[148] Asking whether the Charities Act 2006 s.4 gave the Commission a new law-making power in relation to public benefit therefore misses the point that it already had such a power, although it is unfortunate that the government did not clarify this issue in the 2006 legislation, given the politically contentious nature of the policy towards fee-charging charities that it expected the Commission to apply. **6–071**

Following enactment of the 2006 Act, the Commission undertook a consultation process, and then published a generic guidance document[149] and supplementary documents on issues specific to various charitable purposes[150] and on fee charging.[151] These documents set out certain principles for which there was little clear authority in the pre-existing case law. Most notably, the Commission asserted that "where benefit is to a section of the public, the opportunity to benefit must not be unreasonably restricted . . . by ability to pay any fees charged" (principle 2b) and also that "people in poverty must not be excluded from the opportunity to benefit" (principle 2c). Part of the Commission's fee-charging document is reproduced below, to illustrate its approach. **6–072**

---

144 [2012] Ch. 214, at [68]. See too *Attorney General v Charity Commission* [2012] W.T.L.R. 977 at [39].

145 [2012] Ch. 214, at [88].

146 A. Dunn, "Using the Wrong Policy Tools: Education, Charity, and Public Benefit" (2012) 39 J.L.S. 491.

147 P. Luxton, *Making Law: Parliament v The Charity Commission* (2009); C. Decker and M. Harding, "Three Challenges in Charity Regulation: The Case of England and Wales" in *Not-for-Profit Law: Theoretical and Comparative Perspectives* (2014).

148 See paras 6–023—6–029.

149 Charity Commission, *Charities and Public Benefit* (January 2008).

150 Charity Commission, *The Prevention or Relief of Poverty for the Public Benefit* (December 2008); *The Advancement of Religion for the Public Benefit* (December 2008); *The Advancement of Education for the Public Benefit* (December 2008 version).

151 *Public Benefit and Fee-Charging* (December 2008).

## Charity Commission, *Public Benefit and Fee-Charging* (December 2008)

### C. Fee-charging as a public benefit issue

6–073 . . . Fee-charging is likely to be a public benefit issue where:

> the service or facility that is charged for forms a significant part of the charity's aims, or the way it carries out those aims; and/or
> the fees that are charged for that service or facility are high.

6–074 *A significant part of the charity's aims:* where a charity's sole or main aim, or way it carries out its aims, is to provide a service or facility for which it charges, the level of fees it charges is significant when assessing whether the organisation is carrying out those aims for the public benefit. This is because it has a bearing on who has the opportunity to benefit from that service or facility and, in particular, the extent to which the charity can show that its aims meet public benefit principles 2b and 2c.

6–075 Where the service or facility that is charged for is an insignificant aspect of what the charity does, or is just one of many ways in which the charity carries out its aims, many of which are not charged for, then fee-charging is generally less of a public benefit issue. . . .

6–076 *Charities charging low fees:* where a charity charges low fees that most people can afford, then the fee-charging is unlikely to give rise to public benefit difficulties. In most cases it will not be necessary for those charities to demonstrate any further opportunities to benefit since the low fees do not prevent people from having the opportunity to benefit from the charity's services or facilities. . . .

6–077 *Charities charging high fees:* where a charity charges high fees that many people could not afford, the trustees must ensure that:

> the benefits are not unreasonably restricted by a person's ability to pay; and that
> people in poverty are not excluded from the opportunity to benefit.

The charity trustees must therefore demonstrate that there is sufficient opportunity for people who cannot afford those fees to benefit in a material way that is related to the charity's aims. . . .

6–078 *Opportunities to benefit*: there must be sufficient *opportunity* to benefit for people who cannot afford to pay the fees charged for the services or facilities provided by the charity. It does not mean that people who cannot afford the fees must actually benefit. What is important is that they must not be excluded from the opportunity to benefit, whether or not they actually choose to do so. However, the opportunity to benefit should be genuine and meaningful. If the opportunity to benefit that is provided is not genuine, or is meaningless or trivial, then it would count for very little in a public benefit assessment.

6–079 . . . Some fee-charging charity trustees might wish to argue that there are wider or remote benefits to the public at large that arise from carrying out their charity's aims and that these benefits should be regarded as opportunities to benefit for people who cannot afford the fees.

6–080 For example, this might include wider or remote benefits such as:

> the general relief of public expenditure from a charity doing something that the state would otherwise have to provide, such as relieving the exchequer of the cost of educating children at state schools or treating patients at NHS hospitals; or
> benefits to the nation from educating students who go on to become, for example, successful entrepreneurs or scientists; or
> other sorts of wider or remote benefits to the public that might be claimed by any charity carrying out a charitable aim, such as encouraging charitable giving or volunteering.

6–081 In cases where such public benefits are clear and related to the charity's aims, they might be relevant when considering the public benefit of a fee-charging charity in relation to public benefit principle 1a. . . . However, we do not consider that they are opportunities to benefit in a "material way" for people who cannot afford the fees. For that reason we do not consider they are relevant when considering the extent to which a charity meets public benefit principles 2b and 2c. . . .

6–082 Fee-charging charities must ensure that there are sufficient opportunities to benefit for people who cannot afford the fees. There are many different ways of doing this.

6–083 This might be by:

*offering free or subsidised access*: enabling people who cannot afford the fees to access the service or facility by offering it at a reduced rate or for no fee, or via schemes or arrangements which offer financial assistance to help meet the cost of the fees;
*providing other significant opportunities to benefit*: providing other significant opportunities to benefit that do not involve free or subsidised access to the service or facility that is charged for.

*Trustees' discretion*: it is for the charity's trustees to decide what sorts of opportunities to benefit they wish, and are able, to provide for people who cannot afford the fees, taking into consideration what is appropriate in their charity's circumstances. However, what is provided must be sufficient to satisfy principles 2b and 2c. 6–084

**Satisfying Principles 2b and 2c:** 6–085

where a charity provides a sufficient amount of free or subsidised access (in the context of the charity's circumstances) to people who cannot afford the fees, this will satisfy principles 2b and 2c;
where a charity provides a combination of free or subsidised access and other significant opportunities to benefit, we can take into account the totality of the opportunities to benefit it provides;
where a charity provides other significant opportunities to benefit, but offers no free or subsidised access, the trustees must be able to demonstrate in what other ways the opportunities to benefit that the charity provides clearly satisfy principles 2b and 2c.

We will look at each case on its own merits and in the context of the individual charity's circumstances.

*Totality of benefits*: in assessing whether a charity provides sufficient opportunity to benefit for people who cannot afford the fees, we will consider the totality of the opportunities to benefit that the charity provides. . . . 6–086

*Percentage of free or subsidised access*: there is no "one-size-fits-all" amount, or percentage, of free or subsidised access that fee-charging charities must offer. 6–087

We cannot specify how many concessionary tickets a theatre should offer, or suggest a percentage of bursaries that all independent schools should offer, or say how many free beds should be available at a hospital. 6–088

It is primarily for the trustees of the charity to decide for themselves the extent to which they offer free or subsidised access, and how much to offer to how many people, provided they can show that people who cannot afford the fees have sufficient opportunity to benefit in a material way that is related to the charity's aims. 6–089

We have to consider what is reasonable and appropriate in each particular charity's circumstances. Offering free or subsidised access costs money and so can clearly impact on the financial situation of a charity. What is appropriate and sufficient will vary from charity to charity, depending upon, amongst other things: its charitable aims; the level of the fees charged; any relevant local needs or factors; and the resources available to the charity. 6–090

It is unusual for a charity that charges high fees to offer no free or subsidised access. Typically, most such charities offer concessions on fees, or assistance with fees, and might also provide other significant opportunities to benefit alongside offering some free or subsidised access. . . . 6–091

*Measures aimed at people who cannot afford the fees*: measures that are designed specifically, and exclusively, to assist people who cannot afford the fees are likely to provide greater opportunity to benefit than other measures. 6–092

For example, in the context of charitable independent schools, it means that bursaries (which are usually specifically aimed at assisting children from poorer families) are likely to provide a greater opportunity to benefit to people who cannot afford the fees than would be the case with scholarships (which are usually open to anyone to apply for and which are awarded solely on academic merit). 6–093

Bursaries usually still require the applicant to show academic merit (e.g. to meet entrance requirements) but should guarantee that children, whose parents or guardians are unable to pay the fees, are given sufficient opportunity to benefit. . . . 6–094

*Providing other significant opportunities to benefit that meet local needs:* it is possible that, in looking to ensure that the public benefit requirement is met, trustees will seek opportunities to work with other service and facility providers. We do not want charities, as a result of the public benefit requirement, to provide opportunities to benefit that are not desired or valued. Charity trustees should have regard to whether the way in which they propose providing other significant opportunities to benefit are relevant and desired. 6–095

6–096 If trustees decide to explore providing other significant opportunities to benefit to meet local needs, we recommend that they engage with their partners and local communities. This is so that they can properly and sufficiently discuss and evaluate local needs when deciding what sort of services, facilities or collaboration to provide. Trustees might want to use peer review or other forms of quality assessment to assist them.

6–097 Examples of other significant opportunities to benefit that are not wanted or required, because they do not meet the needs of the intended beneficiaries, might include:

> a charitable hospital that argues that it offered the local NHS hospital the use of a consultant specialising in children's illnesses but the NHS hospital refused the offer. Where the local NHS hospital caters only for elderly patients, or if it already has sufficient medical staff, the opportunity offered by the charity would have no effect in showing that it provides other significant opportunities to benefit. In this case, the charitable hospital might provide more significant opportunities to benefit if it consults the local NHS hospital about what it could offer that would be of more assistance to the NHS hospital and to benefit people locally;
> a charitable independent school that offers to provide teaching staff to the local state school for certain subjects but the subject areas offered are not required by the local state school. In this case, it would be more beneficial for the trustees of the independent school to consult other education providers locally about how to achieve the maximum impact from sharing resources. It could then target the charity's assistance to state schools and other educational establishments most in need of help in ways that are likely to make most difference to their students.

6–098 Following the publication of its public benefit guidance, the Commission undertook "public benefit assessments" of certain fee-paying schools and invoked principles 2b and 2c to justify their stance that such bodies could be assured of charitable status only if they created means-tested bursaries and made access to their facilities available to the public at large.[152] This policy was said to apply not only to new schools seeking to be registered as charities for the first time but also to existing schools which could lose their charitable status if they failed to comply with the public benefit requirement.

6–099 In 2012, proceedings for judicial review were brought against the Commission by a body representing around 1,000 charitable fee-paying schools. In *R (Independent Schools Council) v Charity Commission*,[153] the applicant sought an order to quash principles 2b and 2c as founded on errors of law. The Upper Tribunal held among other things that an organisation is not charitable if it excludes the poor and that fee-charging charities owe a duty to provide benefits to members of the public who cannot afford their fees.[154] But it also held that it is for the trustees to decide, and not for the Charity Commission to proscribe, the nature and extent of such benefits provided that these exceed a de minimis level.[155] Moreover, if the trustees of an existing charity do not ensure that it delivers benefits to a sufficiently broad section of the public then it follows not that the charity should lose its charitable status, but that the trustees are in breach of their duty to apply the body's resources to its charitable purposes.[156] Consequently the statement relating to fees in principle 2b was incorrect and although principle 2c was correctly stated, its significance was incorrectly explained in the guidance. Hence the Upper Tribunal ordered that these parts of the guidance should be quashed unless they were withdrawn by the Commission. In the event this was done and the guidance was rewritten.

6–100 Both sides claimed a victory. The applicant pointed to the Upper Tribunal's repudiation of the

---

152 Charity Commission, "Highfield Priory School Ltd: Public Benefit Assessment Report" (July 2009), *http://forms.charity-commission.gov.uk/media/93747/assesshigh.pdf* [Accessed 1 June 2015].

153 [2012] Ch. 214.

154 ibid., at [178]

155 ibid., at [215]–[220].

156 ibid., at [191]–[195]. But note the possibility discussed at [194] that an institution might cease "to be able ever to carry out its objects in a manner which would be for the public benefit" so that its original character is "blotted out": in this case, "there may arise an obligation for its trustees to apply for a cy-près scheme".

Commission's over-proscriptive approach, its affirmation of trustee autonomy and its findings with respect to the consequences of non-compliance with the public benefit requirement. The Commission claimed to have been vindicated by the Upper Tribunal's finding that a trust is not charitable if it excludes the poor. However, it is very doubtful that this proposition is correct in law. The Upper Tribunal itself conceded that although they believed it to be "right as a matter of principle", "there is no case which decides [the] point",[157] and as Mary Synge demonstrates in the following extract, there are in fact many cases which hold, on the contrary, that some purposes can be for the public benefit in the second sense although they do not benefit the poor.

## M. Synge, "Poverty: An Essential Element in Charity after All?"

[2011] C.L.J. 649 at 651–656

Whether or not poverty, and the needs of the poor, must be addressed in all cases of charity has proved to be a contentious aspect of charity law. On the one hand, there have been clear authoritative statements to the effect that poverty does not always need to be considered. Most notably, perhaps, in a Privy Council decision in 1924,[158] Lord Wrenbury made it clear that poverty is not "a necessary element" in charities under the fourth head[159] and, similarly, that education and religion "do not require any qualification of poverty to be introduced to give them validity."[160] On the other hand, the relevance of poverty has been argued on occasion, principally in relation to charities dealing with the aged or infirm and where fees are charged for the charity's services. **6–101**

To say that poverty is not an essential element of charity is to say, first, that the relief of poverty does not need to be one of the purposes of the organisation and, secondly, that there is no requirement in charity law for the poor to be given the opportunity to benefit from an organisation's charitable purposes. It may well not accord with popular notions of charity, but that is because "charity" has a distinct legal meaning that is "clear and distinct, peculiar to the law" and "not depending upon or coterminous with the popular or vulgar use of the word".[161] The technical nature of the legal definition of charity was not changed by the Act. **6–102**

The beneficiaries of a charity's purposes might comprise all poor, all rich, or a combination of poor and rich. For our purposes, "rich" means "not poor" and "poor" means "not rich". The two terms are thus mutually exclusive and require no further definition.[162] Whilst accepting the principle that a class need not be confined to the poor and that the rich may also benefit, the Commission maintains that, where all the beneficiaries may be rich, the poor must also be given material opportunities to benefit. **6–103**

A class comprising only the rich might arise in the following ways: **6–104**

- By an indifference to whether those who actually benefit are rich or poor
- By declaring that purposes are aimed at the rich or with a proviso or qualification that the poor shall not benefit (an "express exclusion on the terms")
- By describing a class of beneficiaries in such a way that only the rich could possibly fall within it (an "implied exclusion on the terms")
- By declaring purposes which can only benefit the rich because high fees are charged (an "implied exclusion in practice")

Except where purposes are clearly aimed at relieving poverty, very often there is no intention that a potential beneficiary's wealth should be taken into account in considering his eligibility to receive the benefits **6–105**

---

157 ibid., at [178].

158 *Verge v Somerville* [1924] A.C. 496.

159 At 499–500, referring to the four heads of charity (relief of poverty, education, religion and other purposes beneficial to the community) outlined in *Commissioners for Special Purposes of the Income Tax v Pemsel* [1891] A.C. 531 at 583.

160 Ibid. at 503. See too *Re Compton* [1945] Ch. 123 at 139.

161 *Pemsel's case* [1891] A.C. 531 at 581, per Lord Macnaghten.

162 Thus avoiding the inevitably tortuous problems of scope and definition which the Commission fails to resolve: since the law does not rule out rich beneficiaries, there is no need to address any other class on the sliding scale between the wealthy and the impoverished.

of the charitable purposes[163] and this lack of concern on the part of the donor is reflected in the courts' attitudes. It seems unlikely that an express exclusion on the terms would arise in practice and even less likely, if it did, that charitable status would be advocated or defended with any vigour.[164] An implied exclusion on the terms is more likely to arise and, indeed, has arisen in some cases[165] and, of course, an implied exclusion in practice is commonplace where fees are charged.

**1. The relief of poverty**

6–106 Clearly poverty is an essential element under the first head of charity. In the case of membership organisations, which are potentially non-charitable because of their non-public character, charitable status will only exist if the purpose, or one of the dominant purposes, is to relieve poverty.[166] Thus in *Re Hobourn Aero Components Limited's Air Raid Distress Fund*,[167] the Court of Appeal held that a fund which was primarily for contributing employees who had suffered from air raids did not constitute a charitable trust, principally on the ground that it was of a private and not public nature.[168] Had there been a requirement of poverty in those eligible for assistance, the trust would have been charitable, whereas the relief of distress from air raids (which would be capable of being charitable in a public context) would not render a private arrangement charitable.[169]

**2. Advancement of education**

6–107 In *Attorney-General v The Earl of Lonsdale*,[170] the Vice-Chancellor, Sir John Leach, dismissed outright an argument by counsel that a free school for the education of gentlemen's sons could not be charitable. He conceded that such an object would not be charitable "in popular language" but then stated that "in the view of the statute of Elizabeth, all schools for learning are so to be considered".[171] Nearly a century later, Lord Cozens Hardy M.R. refused to accept that a trust for the advancement of education could not be charitable unless there was an element of poverty: "There is no foundation for it in authority nor is there any foundation for it in reason."[172]

6–108 Many fee-paying schools were founded for the education of the poor.[173] Fee-paying boarders were initially few in number, or introduced at a later date, but, typically, became the sole or main category of pupils. This evolution in educational provision led to many repeated calls for independent schools to be closed, or for fiscal privileges and/or charitable status to be removed,[174] but it did not hinder the unswerving attitude of the judiciary in attributing charitable status to them in the nineteenth and twentieth centuries.[175]

6–109 Provided purposes are actually seen as tending to advance education,[176] they have been held to be charitable without any consideration of the presence or absence of poverty.[177] A failure to attract charitable status, on the other hand, has not been due to the absence of poverty but other reasons, most notably lack of public character where education has been intended for relatives or employees.[178]

---

163 For example, the services offered by a charitable lifeboat organisation are available to all distressed seamen, without regard to their means.

164 Some judicial dicta (below) which suggest that charitable status would be denied if the poor were excluded appear to be limited to such an express exclusion (it is submitted that this covers any exclusion of persons less rich than those included [so that, again, there is no need to consider various degrees of wealth]).

165 e.g. a school for the sons of gentlemen: *Attorney General v Earl of Lonsdale* (1827) 1 Simons 105.

166 *Splller v Maude* 1864. S. 22n.; *Re Lacy* [1899] 2 Ch. 149.

167 [1946] Ch. 194.

168 Ibid. at p.203.

169 Ibid. at p.210; nor will restricting a non-charitable purpose to a particular locality: *Williams' Trustees v. IRC* [1947] A.C. 447 at 456.

170 57 E.R. 518 (in 1827).

171 Ibid. at p.520 (referring to the Charitable Uses Act 1601).

172 *R v Special Commissioners of Income Tax, ex parte University College of North Wales* (1909) 78 L.J.K.B. 576, 578.

173 Including Eton and Winchester.

174 See, for example, I. Williams, *The Alms Trade* (London 1989).

175 *Brighton College v Marriott* [1926] A.C. 192; *Abbey Malvern* [1951] Ch. 728.

176 The courts have interpreted "education" widely but not without limitation: *Re Pinion* [1965] Ch. 85; *Re Shaw* [1957] 1 W.L.R. 729.

177 e.g. *Re Gott* [1944] Ch. 193; *Re Koeppler Will Trusts* [1986] Ch. 423; *Smith v Kerr* [1902] 1 Ch. 774; *IRC v McMullen* [1981] A.C. 1.

178 *Re Compton* [1945] Ch. 123; *Oppenheim v. Tobacco Securities Trust Co. Ltd*. [1951] A.C. 297 at 306; *IRC v Educational Grants Association* [1967] Ch. 993.

### 3. Advancement of religion

The relevance of poverty was central to *Pemsel's* case,[179] where the House of Lords held that the purposes of "advancing the missionary establishments among heathen nations of the Protestant Episcopal Church"[180] were charitable and entitled to income tax allowances. Three of their Lordships dismissed the "restricted"[181] view that charity implies the relief of poverty and that the testator must be found to have had an intention to provide such relief. They found the purposes to be charitable, notwithstanding that there was no intention to discriminate between rich and poor heathens. **6–110**

As with education, the presence or absence of poverty has not been a determining factor in purposes for the advancement of religion.[182] **6–111**

### 4. Cases falling under the fourth head

After identifying the fourth head of charity in *Pemsel's* case, Lord Macnaghten added that trusts within that category "are not the less charitable in the eye of the law, because incidentally they benefit the rich as well as the poor, as indeed, every charity that deserves the name must do either directly or indirectly".[183] Of course, in itself, this tells us only that the beneficiaries of a charitable trust are not required to be exclusively poor and not that poverty is an irrelevant consideration. Whilst it is authority for the proposition that the rich may benefit incidentally, it is not authority for saying that the rich cannot benefit in ways that are not merely incidental.[184] To suggest that it requires at least some poor to benefit, regardless of purpose and charges, would be to ignore the historical and factual context of the case. **6–112**

Later dicta address more explicitly the relevance of poverty in charities under the fourth head. In *IRC v Baddeley*,[185] trusts were declared to be non-charitable because the purposes were not recognised by law as exclusively charitable. Lord Reid was clearly of the opinion that, had the purposes been exclusively within the fourth head, "the element of poverty is not necessary to make them valid charitable purposes".[186] In *Re Resch*,[187] Lord Wilberforce referred to Lord Wrenbury having "held generally that poverty is not a necessary qualification in trusts beneficial to the community". **6–113**

Again, numerous purposes have been found to be charitable under this head without any consideration of poverty[188] and charitable status has been denied on a number of grounds but not the absence of poverty.[189] **6–114**

### 5. Relief of the aged or infirm

The significance of poverty has been especially prominent where the purposes are concerned with the aged or infirm.[190] In these cases are to be found some of the most notable suggestions of a judicial reluctance[191] to accord charitable status to purposes that do not include an element of poverty. In the mid-twentieth century, academics debated whether a trust for the relief of "aged peers" or "impotent millionaires" would be charitable. Megarry noted the evolving cases of the time and identified the nub of the problem as it seeming "to accord ill with the spirit of the Statute to open the doors of charity to those who are **6–115**

---

179 [1891] A.C. 531.
180 Ibid. at p.532.
181 Ibid. at p.571, per Lord Herschell.
182 e.g. *Re Manser* [1905] 1 Ch. 68; *Re Hood* [1931] 1 Ch. 240; *Farley v Westminster Bank* [1939] A.C. 430; *Cocks v. Manners* (1871) L.R. 12 Eq. 574.
183 [1891] A.C. 531 at 583.
184 Recognised by Lord Wrenbury in *Verge v Somerville* [1924] A.C. 496 at 503.
185 [1955] A.C. 572.
186 Ibid. at 604.
187 [1969] 1 A.C. 514 at 542.
188 e.g. *Re Good* [1905] 2 Ch. 60; *Scottish Burial and Cremation Society Ltd v Glasgow Corporation* [1968] A.C. 138.
189 e.g. *National Anti-Vivisection Society v IRC* [1948] A.C. 31; *IRC v City of Glasgow Police Athletic Association* [1953] A.C. 380 (likewise the "animal cases" contain no consideration of poverty: *Re Wedgwood* [1915] 1 Ch. 113; *Re Grove-Grady* [1929] 1 Ch. 557).
190 Perhaps because the preamble to the 1601 Act includes the relief of the "aged, impotent and poor people", without indicating whether a conjunctive or disjunctive interpretation was intended.
191 Or "great disinclination": *Re Lewis (Deceased)* [1955] Ch. 104 at 107.

wealthy and well able to provide for themselves, merely because they are aged".[192] Brunyate,[193] however, considered the example of a rich blind man and distinguished between gifts of money on the one hand and curing blindness or providing braille services on the other.[194] Taking a bolder approach than some, he noted: "to regard a rich man who is blind or maimed as in no sense a proper object of charity would surely be taking a very worldly view of human suffering".[195] The cases which addressed this issue over the following two decades[196] reflected this view and to relieve the needs of aged or impotent persons came to be regarded as charitable without any need for poverty, just as other prima facie charitable purposes had not been disqualified through an absence of poverty.

**6–116** After a period of reticence, where judges appeared to be reassured to find evidence which suggested that the testator had intended to benefit aged people who were also poor[197] or indigent,[198] a new confidence emerged in *Re Robinson*,[199] where Vaisey J. held, without hesitation, that a gift to people aged over 65 was charitable without any need for poverty. The requirement for some relief of a need attributable to age, however, was favoured as an approach and emphasised in *Joseph Rowntree Memorial Trust v Attorney General*.[200] Peter Gibson J. in that case considered a number of schemes for the provision of special housing for the elderly and found that the relief of that need was prima facie charitable without any qualification of poverty. Basing his decision on logic as well as judicial authority, he expressed his conclusion with utmost clarity: "It would be as absurd to require that the aged must be impotent or poor as it would be to require the impotent to be aged or poor, or the poor to be aged or impotent."[201]

**6–117** The question of whether poverty is essential in gifts for the relief of the infirm was to the fore in *Re Lewis*.[202] Roxburgh J., in construing gifts of £100 to blind boys and girls, boldly decided to "grasp the nettle" and decide whether or not the absence of "any element of poverty whatsoever" was fatal to finding that the gifts were charitable.[203] He was also happy to endorse the disjunctive interpretation (and its necessary consequences) adopted by Danckwerts J. and Vaisey J.[204] Like Peter Gibson J,[205] Roxburgh J. pointed to the illogical nature of the counter-argument that would mean that a trust for poor people would not be charitable unless they were also aged or infirm. . .

## *C. Political Purposes*

**6–118** In the context of charity law, "political purposes" have been defined by the courts to include attempts to change the law by legislation or oppose proposed changes to the law and attempts to influence local or national government home or foreign policy.[206] In *National Anti-Vivisection Society v IRC*, excerpted below, the House of Lords held that trusts for political purposes cannot be charitable because the courts have no means of judging whether a proposed change in the law would or would not be for the public benefit,[207] and because the law cannot stultify itself by holding that it is for the

192 (1951) 67 L.Q.R. 164.
193 (1945) 61 L.Q.R. 268; see too *Attorney General v Duke of Northumberland* (1877–78) L.R. 7 Ch. D. 745, 749.
194 Echoed by Peter Gibson J. in *Joseph Rowntree Memorial Trust Housing Association Ltd v Attorney-General* [1983] Ch. 159, 171.
195 61 L.Q.R. at p. 272. See too P.S. Atlyah, "Public Benefit in Charities" (1958) 21 M.L.R. 138, at p.140.
196 Briefly, but helpfully, reviewed in the *Joseph Rowntree* case, at pp. 172–173.
197 *Re Lucas* [1922] 2 Ch. 52.
198 *Re Glyn's Will Trusts* [1950] 2 All E.R. 1150n.
199 [1951] Ch. 198. See too *Re Neal* (1966) 110 S.J. 549; *Re Bradbury* [1950] W.N. 558.
200 [1983] Ch. 159. This emphasis on need is also discernible in *Re Resch*.
201 [1983] Ch. 159 at 171. See too *McGovern v Attorney General* [1982] Ch. 321 at 333 where the principle was reiterated without question.
202 [1955] Ch. 104.
203 Ibid. at p. 107.
204 In *Re Glyn's Will Trust* and *Re Robinson*.
205 In the *Joseph Rowntree* case.
206 See *Baldry v Feintuck* [1972] 1 W.L.R. 552; *Webb v O'Doherty* (1991) 3 Admin. L.R. 731; *Re Koeppler's WT* [1984] Ch. 243. In *Southwood v Attorney General* [2000] W.T.L.R. 1199 the Court of Appeal held that a trust to educate the public to accept that peace is best secured by demilitarisation and disarmament was political and non-charitable.
207 See also *Bowman v Secular Society* [1917] A.C. 406 at 442, per Lord Parker.

public benefit that the law itself should be changed.[208] These reasons are found to be inadequate by Jonathan Garton in a critique of the decision that is also excerpted below.

*National Anti-Vivisection Society v IRC*

House of Lords [1948] A.C. 31

The question was whether the appellant society was a body established for charitable purposes only, within the meaning of the Income Tax Act 1918, s.37, and accordingly entitled to exemption from income tax on the income it derived from its investments. The Special Commissioners for the Purposes of Income Tax held that the society was so entitled, but this decision was reversed by McNaghten J.,[209] whose judgment was upheld by the Court of Appeal.[210] The society appealed unsuccessfully. **6–119**

LORD WRIGHT: . . . The claim of the appellant society . . . must fail . . . because its object is to secure legislation to give legal effect to it. It is, in my opinion, a political purpose within the meaning of Lord Parker's pronouncement in *Bowman v. Secular Society Ltd.*[211] Lord Parker was discussing in a different connexion the same question of the true criterion for deciding if charitable gifts are for the benefit of the public in the legal sense; he was there referring to the objects enumerated in the memorandum of association of the Secular Society Ltd. He said: **6–120**

> "Now, if your Lordships will refer for a moment to the society's memorandum of association you will find that none of its objects, except, possibly, the first, are charitable. The abolition of religious tests, the disestablishment of the church, the secularization of education the alteration of the law touching religion or marriage, or the observation of the Sabbath, are purely political objects. Equity has always refused to recognize such objects as charitable. It is true that a gift to an association formed for their attainment may, if the association be unincorporated, be upheld as an absolute gift to its members, or, if the association be incorporated, as an absolute gift to the corporate body; but a trust for the attainment of political objects has always been held invalid, not because it is illegal, for everyone is at liberty to advocate or promote by any lawful means a change in the law, but because the court has no means of judging whether a proposed change in the law will or will not be for the public benefit, and therefore cannot say that a gift to secure the change is a charitable gift."

While I was preparing this part of my opinion my noble and learned friend Lord Simonds was kind enough to draw to my attention the passage which, in due course, your Lordships will hear quoted by him from a work of authority, *Tyssen on Charitable Bequests* . . . It is, I think, a very important contribution to this question. It appears to me to go to explain and justify Lord Parker's opinion. I refer especially to Tyssen's words: "the law could not stultify itself by holding that it was for the public benefit that the law itself should be changed" and again: "each court . . . must decide on the principle that the law is right as it stands." I am reminded of the words of a great common law judge who warned the courts against usurping the functions of the legislature. I do not regard the statements of Lord Parker and Tyssen as inconsistent but as complementary. In my opinion, the respondents' objection under this head is well founded. . . **6–121**

LORD SIMONDS: . . . The first and shorter point is whether a main purpose of the society is of such a political character that the court cannot regard it as charitable. To this point little attention was directed in the courts below . . . As will appear in the course of this opinion, it is worthy of more serious debate. **6–122**

My Lords, on the first point the learned Master of the Rolls cites in his judgment[212] a passage from the speech of Lord Parker in *Bowman v Secular Society Ltd*:[213] **6–123**

> "A trust for the attainment of political objects has always been held invalid, not because it is illegal . . . but because the court has no means of judging whether a proposed change in the law will or will not be for the public benefit."

---

[208] See also *Bonar Law Memorial Trust v IRC* (1933) 49 T.L.R. 220 (Conservative); *Re Ogden* [1933] Ch. 678 (Liberal); *Re Hopkinson* [1949] W.N. 29 (Socialist); *Re Strakosch* [1949] Ch. 529 (appeasing racial feeling); *Re Bushnell* [1975] 1 W.L.R. 1596 (furthering socialised medicine in a socialist state).

[209] [1945] 2 All E.R. 529.

[210] [1946] K.B. 185.

[211] [1917] A. C. 406 at 442.

[212] [1946] K. B. 185 at 207.

[213] [1917] A. C. 406 at 442.

Lord Parker is here considering the possibility of a valid charitable trust and nothing else and when he says "has always been held invalid" he means "has always been held not to be a valid charitable trust." The learned Master of the Rolls found this authoritative statement upon a branch of the law, with which no one was more familiar than Lord Parker, to be inapplicable to the present case for two reasons, first, because he felt difficulty in apvplying the words to "a change in the law which is in common parlance a 'non-political' question", and secondly, because he thought they could not in any case apply, when the desired legislation is "merely ancillary to the attainment of what is *ex hypothesi* a good charitable object."

**6–124** My Lords, if I may deal with this second reason first, I cannot agree that in this case an alteration in the law is merely ancillary to the attainment of a good charitable object. In a sense no doubt, since legislation is not an end in itself, every law may be regarded as ancillary to the object which its provisions are intended to achieve. But that is not the sense in which it is said that a society has a political object. Here the finding of the commissioners is itself conclusive. "We are satisfied," they say, "that the main object of the society is the total abolition of vivisection . . . and (for that purpose) the repeal of the Cruelty to Animals Act, 1876, and the substitution of a new enactment prohibiting vivisection altogether." This is a finding that the main purpose of the society is the compulsory abolition of vivisection by Act of Parliament. What else can it mean? and how else can it be supposed that vivisection is to be abolished? Abolition and suppression are words that connote some form of compulsion. It can only be by Act of Parliament that that element can be supplied . . . Coming to the conclusion that it is a main object, if not the main object, of the society, to obtain an alteration of the law, I ask whether that can be a charitable object, even if its purposes might otherwise be regarded as charitable.

**6–125** My Lords, I see no reason for supposing that Lord Parker in the cited passage used the expression "political objects" in any narrow sense or was confining it to objects of acute political controversy. On the contrary he was, I think, propounding familiar doctrine, nowhere better stated than in a text-book, which has long been regarded as of high authority but appears not to have been cited for this purpose to the courts below (as it certainly was not to your Lordships), *Tyssen on Charitable Bequests*. The passage is worth repeating at length:[214]

> "It is a common practice for a number of individuals amongst us to form an association for the purpose of promoting some change in the law, and it is worth our while to consider the effect of a gift to such an association. It is clear that such an association is not of a charitable nature. However desirable the change may really be, the law could not stultify itself by holding that it was for the public benefit that the law itself should be changed. Each court in deciding on the validity of a gift must decide on the principle that the law is right as it stands. On the other hand, such a gift could not be held void for illegality."

**6–126** Lord Parker uses slightly different language but means the same thing, when he says that the court has no means of judging whether a proposed change in the law will or will not be for the public benefit. It is not for the court to judge and the court has no means of judging. The same question may be looked at from a slightly different angle. One of the tests, and a crucial test, whether a trust is charitable, lies in the competence of the court to control and reform it. I would remind your Lordships that it is the King as *parens patriæ* who is the guardian of charity and that it is the right and duty of his Attorney-General to intervene and inform the court, if the trustees of a charitable trust fall short of their duty. So too it is his duty to assist the court, if need be, in the formulation of a scheme for the execution of a charitable trust. But, my Lords, is it for a moment to be supposed that it is the function of the Attorney-General on behalf of the Crown to intervene and demand that a trust shall be established and administered by the court, the object of which is to alter the law in a manner highly prejudicial, as he and His Majesty's Government may think, to the welfare of the state? This very case would serve as an example, if upon the footing that it was a charitable trust it became the duty of the Attorney-General on account of its maladministration to intervene. There is undoubtedly a paucity of judicial authority on this point . . . But in truth the reason of the thing appears to me so clear that I neither expect nor require much authority. I conclude upon this part of the case that a main object of the society is political and for that reason the society is not established for charitable purposes only.

---

[214] (1st edn, 1898) at p.176.

## J. Garton, "National Anti-Vivisection Society v Inland Revenue Commissioners (1948)"

in C. Mitchell and P. Mitchell (eds), Landmark Cases in Equity (Hart Publishing, 2012), pp.542–550

. . . Given that the House was not bound by precedent to recognise any rule to the effect that an otherwise valid charitable trust – i.e. one that had an exclusively charitable purpose and demonstrable public benefit – would fail if it had a political purpose, we might expect that their Lordships would have offered convincing justifications for the rule. The majority gave three reasons for their decision: 6–127

a) the court's inability to judge the public benefit of a change in law;
b) the inappropriateness of the court's usurping the legislature; and
c) the problem of requiring the Attorney-General to enforce a political trust.

Each is fallacious.

Our main concern must lie with the dictum of Lord Parker in *Bowman*, which was cited with approval by each of the majority judges in the *National Anti-Vivisection Society* case[215] and was clearly instrumental in their Lordships' reaching the conclusion that they did:[216] 6–128

> "[A] trust for the attainment of political objects has always been held invalid, not because it is illegal, for everyone is at liberty to advocate or promote by any lawful means a change in the law, but because the court has no means of judging whether a proposed change in the law will or will not be for the public benefit, and therefore cannot say that a gift to secure the change is a charitable gift."

Public benefit in this context refers to the common law requirement that for a purpose to be charitable, It must not only fall within the spirit and intendment of the list of charitable purposes contained in the Preamble to the Statute of Charitable Uses 1601 but must, conceptually,[217] be one which benefits the public. To the extent that an inability to determine public benefit is the stumbling block preventing a charitable purpose that is also political from being valid, we may say a number of things.

The traditional criticism levelled is that the court ought to be perfectly able to judge whether a change in the law would be for the public benefit, for this is what it is to be a judge in the common law tradition. The position was summed up neatly by Leslie Sheridan 40 years ago:[218] 6–129

> "Granted that a judge must decide cases on the basis of the law as it stands, he does not have to approve the eternal correctness of all our law . . . Nothing could be more stultifying of the legal system than the judges always sticking to precedent, never breaking new ground, taking no notice of changing social conditions, applying a rule in 1972 solely because there is a precedent of 1372."

The reality is that of course the court has on more than one occasion shown that it is capable of judging whether a change in the law would be for the public benefit, and two examples from both ends of the spectrum should suffice by way of illustration:[219] in the *National Anti-Vivisection Society* case itself . . . the change in the law sought out by the Society was found on the evidence to be "greatly to the public disadvantage";[220] whilst Slade J. in *McGovern v Attorney-General* would later describe Amnesty International's three main objects—securing the release of prisoners of conscience, opposing the detention 6–130

---

[215] At 61 (Lord Simonds, with whom Viscount Simon concurred), 50 (Lord Wright) and 77 (Lord Normand).

[216] *Bowman v Secular Society* [1917] A.C. 406 at 442.

[217] It is another matter whether in practice a charity pursues its conceptually beneficial purpose in such a way as to meet the further requirement, confusingly also referred to as public benefit, that if access to its benefits is in any way restricted then an "appreciably important" section of the public must still be able to enjoy them: *Verge v Somerville* [1924] A.C. 496 at 499 (Lord Wrenbury).

[218] L.A. Sheridan, "Charity versus Politics" (1973) 2 Anglo-American Law Review 4757. See too L.A. Sheridan, "The Political Muddle – A Charitable View" (1977) 19 Malaya Law Review 42, 65; C.E.F. Rickett, 'Charity and Politics' (1982) 10 New Zealand University Law Review 169, 172.

[219] See also F. Gladstone, *Charity, Law and Social Justice* (1982) 100–01, who wonders, in the context of a community association's campaign to procure the construction of a pedestrian crossing, "how many old-age pensioners would need to be knocked down before a court could judge that [the] crossing would be for the public benefit".

[220] At 65 (Lord Simonds).

without trial of prisoners of conscience and political prisoners, and opposing the death penalty, torture and inhumane treatment of all prisoners—as "philanthropic purposes of an excellent character",[221] despite the fact that they necessitated changes to the laws or the government policies in jurisdictions where relevant abuses occurred.

6–131 However, an important aspect of Lord Parker's dictum has hitherto been overlooked. When read in the light of the House's comments in the *National Anti-Vivisection Society* case, that the court must weigh the benefits and detriments of a purpose in the balance when considering whether it is for the public benefit, the only logical conclusion is that the court is capable of judging on the evidence whether a purpose is charitable if pursued outside the political arena, but incapable of judging whether the same purpose is charitable if pursued through political action. This means we may conceive of a situation where the court can say that a society established for a particular purpose tends towards the public benefit (and is therefore charitable) because it seeks to effect that purpose through non-political means, but it is unable to say one way or the other whether another society established for the same purpose tends towards the public benefit (and is therefore not charitable) because it seeks to effect that purpose politically. If the purpose is the same in both cases, and if the end result is the same if either society is successful, then why does the public benefit, or rather the court's ability to judge the public benefit, disappear?

6–132 If we assume no other variables then the only logical conclusion is that there must be something about the political process itself that has the potential to introduce a detriment capable of outweighing the public benefit otherwise inherent in a given purpose—*potential* here being key, as we know that there is nothing in the political process that *necessarily* outweighs the public benefit of an otherwise charitable purpose, for this would mean that a political purpose is not, on balance, for the public benefit, and Lord Parker's dictum is clear: the court cannot say either way whether a political purpose is for the public benefit.

6–133 This is difficult, not least because Lord Simonds[222] and Lord Wright[223] both make it clear in their speeches that it is not the process but the end result—the change in the law—that is the problem. . .

6–134 Lord Wright suggests that a second justification for the prohibition is that if the court were to recognise political purposes as charitable then this would usurp the functions of the legislature.[224] The idea is not pursued in any detail, and it is clear that approving as charitable an organisation with political objects would not in reality involve the court stepping on the shoes of Parliament. There are several reasons for this.

6–135 First, the decision whether to grant an organisation with political objects charitable status is, in itself, unlikely to be determinative of whether the organisation in fact goes on to pursue those objects. Unless structured around a testamentary purpose trust, which would fail if denied charitable status,[225] its trustees would still be free to carry on its political objects, though there may be resource implications in failing to obtain charitable status.

6–136 Secondly, even if a charity were to campaign for a change in the law as a result of a decision of the court, it would not follow that Parliament must respond by effecting that change, as Francis Gladstone observes:[226]

> "Apart from anything else, granting charitable status to such trusts is not at all the same thing as actually granting the reforms they seek. There is no guarantee that they will be successful; and if they are, it will be because they have convinced public opinion and Parliament of the need for reform, not because the judiciary has usurped the prerogative of Parliament."

6–137 Thirdly, it is fallacious to suggest that by granting charitable status to an institution campaigning for a change in the law, the court itself is advocating that change: in the spirit of Voltaire, the court could permit a charity to pursue a purpose in a manner of which it does not necessarily approve, so long as the purpose is otherwise charitable and there is public benefit. Furthermore, just as we have argued why two charities with the same broad purpose might seek to achieve it through different means and with different effects in the interests of the diversity of organised civil society, so too might two charities legitimately take different

---

221 *McGovern v Attorney-General* [1982] Ch. 321 at 329.
222 At 62.
223 At 50.
224 At 50.
225 Although an *inter vivos* purpose trust would also fail, the settlor would of course be in a position to select an alternative vehicle, such as a company or a society, to carry out the desired objects.
226 Gladstone at p.102.

> positions on the desirability or otherwise of a proposed change in the law; allowing one to pursue its object by campaigning for the change would not prevent the court from allowing the other to pursue the same object by campaigning against it.[227] Neither charity would be able to claim the "approval" of the court.
>
> Additional support is lent to this argument if we contrast the court's attitude towards political trusts 6–138
> following the *National Anti-Vivisection Society* case with its long-standing attitude towards religious trusts, where it has no problem recognising the validity of trusts without approving or disapproving of any particular set of religious beliefs[228]. . .
>
> The final argument against political purposes in the *National Anti-Vivisection Society* case, hitherto 6–139
> largely overlooked, is that if a political trust were to be upheld as charitable and its trustees defaulted or acted in breach of trust, this might place the Attorney-General, who has jurisdiction at common law to enforce charitable trusts, in a difficult position . . . Such a situation, the argument goes, would clearly give rise to a conflict of interest, and there would be strong incentive for the Attorney-General either to refuse to exercise his discretion to intervene[229] or to mount an ineffectual action for the sake of form. In other cases, where the object of the charitable trust was to advocate maintaining the status quo, the Attorney-General would presumably happily pull out all the stops to hold the trustees to account. The same line of reasoning could be applied today with regard to enforcement by the Charity Commission . . . This argument has been largely ignored by critics of the prohibition, but it can be easily dismissed: it overlooks the simple fact that charities are already free to pursue their purposes in ways that might conceivably bring them into conflict with the views of the government of the day—the activities that a charity carries out do not require State approval and, save where they reveal something about the true nature of the institution's purposes, . . . do not come under meaningful scrutiny. So whilst it is true that the Attorney-General and the Charity Commission might have an incentive to enforce certain political purposes over others, so too do they have a similar incentive with other charitable purposes under the current law.

The rule that political purposes are not charitable has been followed by the English courts and the 6–140
Charity Commission[230] and by the courts of other Commonwealth jurisdictions. It remains the law in Canada.[231] However, it was repudiated by the High Court of Australia in *Aid/Watch Incorporated v Federal Commissioner of Taxation*,[232] where the court held that "the encouragement of public debate" on matters falling within an existing charitable head is a charitable purpose in its own right because it contributes to the culture of free political expression on which a representative system of government depends.[233] This decision was affirmed by federal legislation.[234] The rule denying chartable status to political purposes was also rejected by the New Zealand Supreme Court in *Re Greenpeace of New Zealand Inc*,[235] although the court did not whole-heartedly accept the *Aid/Watch* finding that the promotion of political debate is a charitable purpose in itself,[236] and instead they held that courts must assess whether the achievement of a political purpose will enure to the public good.[237]

---

227 See Rickett at p.171.

228 *O'Hanlon v Logue* [1906] 1 I.R. 247 at 259 (Lord Walker L.C.). See also *Gilmour v Coats* [1949] A.C. 426 at 457 (Lord Reid): '[S]ince diversity of religious beliefs arose and became lawful the law has shown no preference in this matter to any church and other religious body. Where a belief is accepted by some and rejected by others the law can neither accept nor reject, it must remain neutral'.

229 Note *Central Bayside General Practice Association Ltd v Commissioner of State Revenue* (2006) 228 C.L.R. 168 at [179], where by implication Callinan J. contemplates a similar situation, given that he argues that there would be no such conflict where a charity's objects are in line with those of the State.

230 e.g. *McGovern v Attorney General* [1982] Ch. 321; *The Margaret Thatcher Foundation* [1991] Ch. Comm. Rep. 39; *Southwood v Attorney General* [2000] W.T.L.R. 1199; *Hanchett-Stamford v Attorney General* [2009] Ch. 173.

231 *Vancouver Society of Immigrant and Visible Minority Women v M.N.R.* [1999] 1 S.C.R. 10.

232 (2010) 241 C.L.R. 539.

233 ibid., at [44]–[47].

234 Charities Act 2013 (Cth) s.12(1)(l); but note s.11(b): the purpose of promoting or opposing a political party or a candidate for political office is not charitable in itself.

235 (2014) 17 I.T.E.L.R. 296.

236 Their comments about this at [62] and [103] are ambiguous.

237 At [72]–[76].

**6–141** Of the two approaches, *Aid/Watch* is preferable to *Greenpeace*, since it rightly recognises the promotion of public debate as a social good in itself and obviates the need for courts to become embroiled in contentious arguments about the merits or demerits of particular changes to the legal status quo.[238] We must therefore hope that the English courts and Charity Commission will move English law in the same direction, something which would be consistent with the emphasis that the Commission now places in its guidance document on the benefits flowing from the advocacy and campaigning work done by charities.[239] This is currently permissible to the extent that it is not done as an end in itself but as an ancillary means towards the achivement of a purpose that is itself charitable.[240] So, for example, Shelter, a charity which aims to relieve the homeless, can legitimately press for changes in the Government's housing policy.

**6–142** The recognition of political campaigning as a charitable purpose in itself has also been brought closer by the Charities Act 2011 s.3(1)(h), which states the advancement of human rights to be a charitable purpose.[241] The import of this sub-section was considered by the First-tier Tribunal (Charity) in 2013, in the course of deciding that the purposes of the Human Dignity Trust were not political, although these entailed campaigning for foreign states to amend their domestic laws to align them with international human rights norms, and bringing litigation against foreign states with this goal in mind.[242] The First-tier Tribunal reasoned that these norms were embodied in treaties to which the relevant states were signatories and were guaranteed by the states' constitutions. Hence litigation aimed at upholding the constitutional rights of the citizens of these states did not seek to change the states' laws but to enforce and uphold rights guaranteed by their constitutions. Technically this must have been correct, but the finding that bodies such as the Human Dignity Trust are legally charitable makes it harder to deny the same status to bodies who use the same means to accomplish similar ends, particularly if the *Aid/Watch* argument is accepted, that campaigning is a social good regardless of the outcomes which it produces.

### *D. Discriminatory Purposes*

**6–143** The Equality Act 2010 prohibits direct or indirect discrimination in relation to the "protected characteristics" of age, disability, gender reassignment, marriage and civil partnership, pregnancy and maternity, race, religion or belief, sex, and sexual orientation. However, the Equality Act 2010 s.193(2), reproduced below, permits charities to restrict benefits to a class of people defined by reference to a "protected characteristic" if this is either a "proportionate means of achieving a legitimate aim" or is "for the purpose of preventing or compensating for a disadvantage" connected to that characteristic.

---

238 M. Harding, "An Antipodean View of Political Purposes and Charity Law" (2015) 131 L.Q.R. 181 at 183.

239 Charity Commission, "CC 9: Speaking Out—Guidance on Campaigning and Political Activities by Charities" (March 2008), *https://www.gov.uk/government/uploads/system/uploads/attachment_data/file/300222/cc9text.pdf* [Accessed 1 June 2015]. The Commission has not always taken such a positive view of political activities by charities and in the past has sharply criticised bodies such as Oxfam and War on Want for overstepping the line.

240 *McGovern v Attorney General* [1982] Ch. 321 at 351; Charity Commission, *Decision to Register English PEN as a Charity*, 21 July 2008, reported at [2008] W.T.L.R. 1799. But note that the ability of charities to campaign for political changes during the run-up to an election or referendum has been circumscribed by the Transparency of Lobbying, Non Party Campaigning and Trade Union Administration Act 2014: Charity Commission, "Guidance: Charities, Elections and Referendums" (July 2014), *https://www.gov.uk/government/uploads/system/uploads/attachment_data/file/346058/elect.pdf* [Accessed 1 June 2015].

241 For an interesting case study of the decision taken by War on Want to rewrite its objectives so as to bring itself within s.3(1)(h), see H. Miller, "A Change in Charity Law for England and Wales: Examining War on Want's Foremost Adoption of the New Human Rights Charitable Purpose" (2012) 16 I.J.H.R. 1003.

242 *Human Dignity Trust v Charity Commission*, First-tier Tribunal (Charity), 9 July 2014, *http://www.charity.tribunals.gov.uk/documents/decisions/human-dignity-trust-v-charity-commission-judgment.pdf* [Accessed 1 June 2015].

6–144 This was considered in *Catholic Care (Diocese of Leeds) v Charity Commission*,[243] which concerned a charitable Catholic adoption agency that wished to amend its objects so as to limit its provision of adoption services to prospective foster parents who were heterosexuals. The agency argued that its proposed discrimination was proportionate to the achievement of a legitimate aim, namely "the prospect of increasing the number of children (particularly 'hard to place' children) placed with adoptive families". It argued that if it did not discriminate against same sex couples, it would lose funding from its Catholic supporters and be forced to close. This would mean that fewer children would be adopted, and the harm to them would exceed the harm suffered by same sex couples who could not adopt through the agency. Sitting in the Upper Tribunal (Tax and Chancery Chamber), Sales J accepted that the agency's aim was a legitimate aim for the purposes of the Act. However he did not accept that the evidence bore out the agency's case that the number of children placed in adoptive care would be increased by its continued work, since there was a surplus of potential adopters available through other adoption agencies. Hence the it could not prove the "weighty and convincing reasons" required to justify its proposed discrimination against homosexuals.[244]

6–145 The Equality Act 2010 s.193(3) permits charities to treat people with disabilities more favourably than others when providing them with employment, so that, e.g. the Royal National Institute for the Blind can prefer employing visually impaired persons. Section 193(4) forbids charities to restrict the provision of benefits to a class defined by colour, and any trust that purports to do so will be read as though the reference to colour was absent. Thus a trust for "the black community of Hackney, Haringey, Islington and Tower Hamlets" was upheld as a valid charitable trust, but only on the basis that the word "black" was deleted.[245] Section 193(5) permits charities to discriminate in favour of, although not against, people defined by reference to their religious beliefs. Section 193(7) permits charities to benefit persons of one sex only, e.g. Boy Scouts or Girl Guides.

**Equality Act 2010 s.193**

6–146

(1) A person does not contravene this Act only by restricting the provision of benefits to persons who share a protected characteristic if—

(a) the person acts in pursuance of a charitable instrument, and
(b) the provision of the benefits is within subsection (2).

(2) The provision of benefits is within this subsection if it is—

(a) a proportionate means of achieving a legitimate aim, or
(b) for the purpose of preventing or compensating for a disadvantage linked to the protected characteristic.

(3) It is not a contravention of this Act for—

(a) a person who provides supported employment to treat persons who have the same disability or a disability of a prescribed description more favourably than those who do not have that disability or a disability of such a description in providing such employment;
(b) a Minister of the Crown to agree to arrangements for the provision of supported employment which will, or may, have that effect.

(4) If a charitable instrument enables the provision of benefits to persons of a class defined by reference to colour, it has effect for all purposes as if it enabled the provision of such benefits—

243 [2013] 1 W.L.R. 2105, discussed in D. Morris, "Charities and the Modern Equality Framework—Heading for a Collision?" (2012) 65 C.L.P. 295.
244 ibid., at [55] per Sales J.
245 *Re Harding (Deceased)* [2008] Ch. 235, applying the statutory precursor to s.193(4), the Race Relations Act 1976 s.34(1).

(a) to persons of the class which results if the reference to colour is ignored, or
(b) if the original class is defined by reference only to colour, to persons generally.

(5) It is not a contravention of this Act for a charity to require members, or persons wishing to become members, to make a statement which asserts or implies membership or acceptance of a religion or belief; and for this purpose restricting the access by members to a benefit, facility or service to those who make such a statement is to be treated as imposing such a requirement.

(6) Subsection (5) applies only if—

(a) the charity, or an organisation of which it is part, first imposed such a requirement before 18 May 2005, and
(b) the charity or organisation has not ceased since that date to impose such a requirement.

(7) It is not a contravention of section 29 for a person, in relation to an activity which is carried on for the purpose of promoting or supporting a charity, to restrict participation in the activity to persons of one sex. . .

## *E. Purposes Must Be Exclusively Charitable*

### i. The Basic Rule

**6–147** If, consistently with a trust's terms, the property may be applied for purposes which are not charitable, it is a non-charitable trust even though, consistently with the trust's terms, the property may be applied exclusively for purposes which are charitable. Hence these trusts are not exclusively charitable and so are void: "for worthy causes", for "charitable or benevolent purposes",[246] for purposes "connected with the education and welfare of children"[247] or "for the public good".[248] The same principle was applied in *Uturn UK CIC v Charity Commission*,[249] where the First-tier Tribunal affirmed the Commission's decision that it was not a charitable purpose to promote "street associations" where there was no guarantee that the associations themselves would undertake exclusively charitable activities and would not deliver private benefits to individuals.

### ii. Exceptions

**6–148** Notwithstanding the basic rule, a benignant construction can sometimes save a charitable trust as in *Guild v IRC*[250] where the trust deed required funds to be used for a sports centre in North Berwick qualifying as a valid recreational charity under the Recreational Charities Act 1958 "or some similar purpose in connection with sport", and where the House of Lords held such "similar purpose" must likewise be a charitable purpose. Again, in *Armenian Patriarch of Jerusalem v Sorsino*,[251] a trust for the "education and advancement in life of Armenian children" was construed conjunctively and so for the charitable purpose of education.

**6–149** If the purpose of a trust is charitable but it undertakes non-charitable activities which are incidental to the effective promotion of its purpose, then it is established for charitable purposes only.[252]

---

246 *Chichester Diocesan Fund v Simpson* [1944] A.C. 341; *Latimer v CIR* [2004] 1 W.L.R. 1466 at [32].

247 *Attorney General of the Bahamas v Royal Trust Co* [1986] 1 W.L.R. 1001 (welfare purposes not restricted to educational welfare purposes so as to qualify as charitable).

248 *Attorney General of Cayman Islands v Wahr-Hansen* [2001] 1 A.C. 75.

249 27 February 2012, *http://www.charity.tribunals.gov.uk/documents/decisions/Uturn_UK_Decision.pdf* [Accessed 1 June 2015].

250 [1992] 2 A.C. 310.

251 (2002) 5 I.T.E.L.R. 125.

252 *Royal College of Surgeons of England v National Provincial Bank Ltd* [1952] A.C. 631; *Re Coxen* [1948] Ch. 747; *London Hospital Medical College v IRC* [1976] 1 W.L.R. 613.

However, if a trust has a non-charitable object as one of its purposes then it is not established for exclusively charitable purposes. In Slade J's words[253]:

> The distinction is between (a) those non-charitable activities authorised by the trust instrument which are merely incidental or subsidiary to a charitable purpose and (b) those non-charitable activities so authorised which themselves form part of the trust purpose. In the latter but not the former case the reference to non-charitable activities will deprive the trust of its charitable status.

Where a trustee is directed to apportion between charitable and non-charitable objects the trust is always good as to the charitable objects. The trust will be valid *in toto* if the non-charitable objects are certain and valid,[254] and, in the absence of apportionment by the trustee, the court will divide the fund equally between both classes of objects in accordance with the maxim that "equality is equity".[255] If the non-charitable objects are uncertain, then the trust will be good as to the charitable objects only, provided they are sufficiently well defined to reveal a general charitable intention.[256] **6–150**

## 5. The Thirteen Heads of Charity

The following discussion proceeds in accordance with the classificatory scheme of the Charities Act 2011 s.3(1), which has been reproduced above.[257] For expository purposes, the discussion of the first three heads is divided so as to deal in turn with the question whether particular purposes fall within each head, and the question whether carrying out such purposes enures to a sufficiently broad section of the community. **6–151**

### *A. Section 3(1)(a): "The Prevention or Relief of Poverty"*

#### i. Inherently Beneficial Purposes

Section 3(1)(a) has its origins in that part of the preamble to the Statute of Charitable Uses 1601 which speaks of "the relief of aged, impotent and poor people". At common law, these words had to be read disjunctively so that a trust was charitable if the beneficiaries were either elderly, or ill, or poor.[258] Under the Charities Act 2011, the relief of those in need by reason of age and ill-health has been separated from relief of the poor and appears in s.3(1)(j). **6–152**

The "relief" of poverty and the "prevention" of poverty exist along a continuum of measures that can be taken for the benefit of the needy, and many charities aim to do both. But there is a difference between the two, in that prevention entails addressing the causes, while relief entails addressing the consequences of poverty, and this is recognised by the wording of s.3(1)(a) which treats each as a stand-alone purpose. The prevention of poverty might be undertaken, for example, by charities that provide money management and debt counselling advice. **6–153**

"Poverty" is a relative term and the expression "poor people" is not necessarily confined to the destitute poor: it includes persons who have to "go short" in the ordinary acceptation of that term, due **6–154**

---

253 *McGovern v Attorney General* [1982] Ch. 321 at 341.

254 *Re Douglas* (1887) 35 Ch. D. 472.

255 *Salusbury v Denton* (1857) 3 K. & J. 529.

256 *Re Clarke* [1923] 2 Ch. 407. The *cy-près* doctrine is available if required; as to this see paras 6–028ff.

257 See para.6–054.

258 Age: *Re Robinson* [1951] Ch. 198; *Re Glyn's WT* [1950] 2 All E.R. 1150n.; *Re Bradbury* [1950] 2 All E.R. 1150n.; *Rowntree Memorial Trust Housing Association v Attorney General* [1983] Ch. 159; impotence: *Re Elliott* (1910) 102 L.T. 528; *Re Hillier* [1944] 1 All E.R. 480; *Re Lewis* [1955] Ch. 104.

regard being had to their station in life and so forth.[259] Thus, a trust fund for "poor and needy" relatives could be used to assist those who may need a helping hand from time to time in order to overcome an unforeseen crisis: the failure of a business venture, urgent repairs to a dwelling house or expenses brought on by reason of failing health. The "working classes" do not ipso facto constitute a section of the poor,[260] but in *Re Niyazi's WT*[261] a gift of residue worth about £15,000 for "the construction of or as a contribution towards the construction of a working men's hostel" in Famagusta was held charitable. The size of the gift, the grave housing shortage in Famagusta, and the term "working men's hostel" provided a sufficient connotation of poverty to make the gift charitable. The Charity Commission now advises that[262]:

> For a charity carrying out its aims in England and Wales, 'people in poverty' might typically mean households living on less than 60% of median income who go short in some unacceptable way. This includes those people who, despite working, might still fall into this category and people may qualify for assistance from a poverty charity whether or not they are eligible for state benefits.

## ii. Provision of Benefit to the Community

**6–155** Trusts for the relief of poverty (but not for the relief of elderly[263] or ill persons[264]) form an exception to the principle that the people benefiting from a charitable trust must not be a private class of individuals defined by reference to a personal nexus with a particular person. The exception covers both the poor relations of a named individual[265] and the poor employees of a particular employer and their families.[266] However, there must be a primary intent to relieve poverty, albeit among a particular class of person. If the primary intent is to benefit particular persons (e.g. A, B, C and their children for their relief in needy circumstances) the trust is a private one and not charitable.[267]

**6–156** These principles are derived from *Dingle v Turner*,[268] parts of which are reproduced below. Following the enactment of the Charities Act 2006 s.3, which has been discussed above,[269] doubts were raised as to the continued validity of these principles. In particular, the Charity Commission doubted whether it remained a charitable purpose to provide financial assistance to a settlor's poor relations. The Attorney General therefore made a non-adversarial reference to determine whether the 2006 Act had altered the common law rules on this point, and in *Attorney General v Charity Commission*,[270] which is also excerpted below, the Upper Tribunal (Tax and Chancery Chamber) held that it had not.

---

[259] *Re Segelman* [1996] Ch. 171; *Re Coulthurst* [1951] Ch. 661 at 666; *Re Young* [1953] 3 All E.R. 689: Charity Commission, *Decision to Register the AITC Foundation* (19 February 2004).

[260] *Re Sanders' WT* [1954] Ch. 265, ("dwellings for the working classes and their families resident in the area of Pembroke Dock or within a radius of 5 miles therefrom" held not charitable).

[261] [1978] 3 All E.R. 785.

[262] Charity Commission, *The Prevention or Relief of Poverty for the Public Benefit* (December 2008 version), Pt C1.

[263] *Re Dunlop* [1984] N.I. 408 (trust to found a home for old Presbyterian persons held to be for sufficient section of public to be charitable under fourth head of charity).

[264] *Re Resch's WT* [1969] 1 A.C. 514.

[265] *Re Scarisbrick* [1951] Ch. 622.

[266] *Dingle v Turner* [1972] A.C. 601. See, too, *Cawdron v Merchant Taylors' School* [2010] P.T.S.R. 507 at [29]–[34] (trust to benefit sons of the school's old boys killed or disabled in the First World War).

[267] *Re Scarisbrick* [1951] Ch. 662; *Re Cohen* [1973] 1 W.L.R. 415; *Re Segelman* [1995] 3 All E.R. 676 at 686–692 (26 persons in the class which would increase with the birth of further members).

[268] [1972] A.C. 601.

[269] See paras 6–063ff.

[270] [2012] W.T.L.R. 977.

*Dingle v Turner*

House of Lords [1972] A.C. 601

VISCOUNT DILHORNE: My Lords, I agree with Lord Cross that this appeal should be dismissed and with the reasons he gives for the conclusion. 6–157

With Lord MacDermott, I too do not wish to extend my concurrence to what my noble and learned friend Lord Cross has said with regard to the fiscal privileges of a legal charity. Those privileges may be altered from time to time by Parliament and I doubt whether their existence should be a determining factor in deciding whether a gift or trust is charitable. 6–158

LORD MACDERMOTT: My Lords, the conclusion I have reached on the facts of this case is that the gift in question constitutes a public trust for the relief of poverty which is charitable in law. I would therefore dismiss the appeal. 6–159

I do not find it necessary to state my reasons for this conclusion in detail. In the first place, the views which I have expressed at some length in relation to an educational trust in *Oppenheim v Tobacco Securities Trust Co Ltd*[271] seem to me to apply to this appeal and to mean that it fails. And, secondly, I have had the advantage of reading the opinion prepared by my noble and learned friend, Lord Cross of Chelsea, and find myself in agreement with his conclusion for the reasons he has given. But I would prefer not to extend my concurrence to what my noble and learned friend goes on to say respecting the fiscal privileges of a legal charity. This subject may be material on the question whether what is alleged to be a charity is sufficiently altruistic in nature to qualify as such, but beyond that, and without wishing to express any final view on the matter, I doubt if these consequential privileges have much relevance to the primary question whether a given trust or purpose should be held charitable in law. 6–160

LORD HODSON: My Lords, I agree with my noble and learned friend, Lord Cross of Chelsea, that this appeal should be dismissed and with his reasons for that conclusion. With this reservation: that I share the doubts expressed by my noble and learned friends, Lord MacDermott and Viscount Dilhorne, as to the relevance of fiscal considerations in deciding whether a gift or trust is charitable. 6–161

LORD SIMON OF GLAISDALE: My Lords, I have had the advantage of reading the opinion of my noble and learned friend, Lord Cross of Chelsea, with which I agree. 6–162

LORD CROSS OF CHELSEA: My Lords, . . . Clause 8(e) was in the following terms: 6–163

> "(e) To invest the sum of ten thousand pounds in any of the investments for the time being authorised by law for the investment of trust funds in the names of three persons (hereinafter referred to as 'the Pension Fund Trustees') to be nominated for the purpose by the persons who at the time at which my Executors assent to this bequest are directors of E. Dingle & Company Limited and the Pension Fund Trustees shall hold the said sum and the investments for the time being representing the same (hereinafter referred to as 'the Pensions Fund') upon trust to apply the income thereof in paying pensions to poor employees of E. Dingle & Company Limited or of any other company to which upon any reconstruction or amalgamation the goodwill and the assets of E. Dingle & Company Limited may be transferred who are of the age of Sixty years at least or who being of the age of Forty five years at least are incapacitated from earning their living by reason of some physical or mental infirmity provided always that if at any time the Pension Fund Trustees shall for any reason be unable to apply the income of the Pension Fund in paying such pensions to such employees as aforesaid the Pension Fund Trustees shall hold the Pensions Fund and the income thereof upon trust for the aged poor in the Parish of St. Andrew, Plymouth."

Finally by clause 8(g) the testator directed his trustees to hold the ultimate residue of his estate on the trusts set out in clause 8(e).

The testator died on January 10, 1950. His widow died on October 8, 1966, having previously released her testamentary power of appointment over her husband's shares in E. Dingle & Co Ltd, which accordingly fell into the residuary estate. When these proceedings started in July 1970, the value of the fund held on the trusts declared by clause 8(e) was about £320,000 producing a gross income of about £17,800 per annum. 6–164

E. Dingle and Co Ltd was incorporated as a private company on January 20, 1935. Its capital was owned by the testator and one John Russell Baker and it carried on the business of a departmental store. At the 6–165

[271] [1951] A.C. 297.

time of the testator's death the company employed over 600 persons and there was a substantial number of ex-employees. On October 23, 1950, the company became a public company. Since the testator's death its business has expanded and when these proceedings started it had 705 full-time and 189 part-time employees and was paying pensions to 89 ex-employees.

6–166 The trustees took out an originating summons asking the court to determine whether the trust declared by clause 8(e) were valid and if so to determine various subsidiary questions of construction—as, for example, whether part-time employees or employees of subsidiary companies were eligible to receive benefits under the trust. To this summons they made defendants (1) representatives of the various classes of employees or ex-employees, (2) those who would be interested on an intestacy if the trusts failed, and (3) Her Majesty's Attorney-General. It has been common ground throughout that the trust at the end of clause 8(e) for the aged poor in the Parish of St Andrew Plymouth is dependent on the preceding trust for poor employees of the company so that although it will catch any surplus income which the trustees do not apply for the benefit of poor employees it can have no application if the preceding trust is itself void.

6–167 The contentions of the appellant and the respondents may be stated broadly as follows. The appellant says that in the *Oppenheim* case this House decided that in principle a trust ought not to be regarded as charitable if the benefits under it are confined either to the descendants of a named individual or individuals or the employees of a given individual or company and that although the "poor relations" cases may have to be left standing as an anomalous exception to the general rule because their validity has been recognised for so long, the exception ought not to be extended to "poor employees" trusts which had not been recognised for long before their status as charitable trusts began to be called in question. The respondents, on the other hand, say, first, that the rule laid down in the *Oppenheim* case with regard to educational trusts ought not to be regarded as a rule applicable in principle to all kinds of charitable trust and, secondly, that in any case it is impossible to draw any logical distinction between "poor relations" trusts and "poor employees" trusts, and, that as the former cannot be held invalid today after having been recognised as valid for so long, the latter must be regarded as valid also.

6–168 By a curious coincidence within a few months of the decision of this House in the *Oppenheim* case the cases on gifts to "poor relations" had to be considered by the Court of Appeal in *Re Scarisbrick*.[272] Most of the cases on this subject were decided in the eighteenth or early nineteenth centuries and are very inadequately reported but two things at least were clear. First, that it never occurred to the judges who decided them that in the field of "poverty" a trust could not be a charitable trust if the class of beneficiaries was defined by reference to descent from a common ancestor. Secondly, that the courts did not treat a gift or trust as necessarily charitable because the objects of it had to be poor in order to qualify, for in some of the cases the trust was treated as a private trust and not a charity. The problem in *Re Scarisbrick* was to determine on what basis the distinction was drawn. The Court of Appeal held that in this field the distinction between a public or charitable trust and a private trust depended on whether as a matter of construction the gift was for the relief of poverty amongst a particular description of poor people or was merely a gift to particular poor persons. The fact that the gift took the form of a perpetual trust would no doubt indicate that the intention of the donor could not have been to confer private benefits on particular people whose possible necessities he had in mind; but the fact that the capital of the gift was to be distributed at once did not necessarily show that the gift was a private trust. . .

6–169 [His Lordship then reviewed the earlier cases leading up to *Gibson v South American Stores* and continued:] The facts in *Gibson v South American Stores (Gath & Chaves) Ltd*[273]—the case followed by Megarry J. in this case—were that a company had vested in trustees a fund derived solely from its profits to be applied at the discretion of the directors in granting gratuities, pensions or allowances to persons—

> "who . . . are or shall be necessitous and deserving and who for the time being are or have been in the company's employ . . . and the wives widows husbands widowers children parents and other dependants of any person who for the time being is or would if living have been himself or herself a member of the class of beneficiaries."

6–170 The Court of Appeal held that this trust was a valid charitable trust but it did so without expressing a view of its own on the question of principle involved, because the case of *Re Laidlaw*[274] which was unearthed

[272] [1951] Ch. 622.
[273] [1950] Ch. 177.
[274] (January 11, 1935) unreported, the decision (and not the reasoning) only being available.

in the course of the hearing showed that the Court of Appeal had already accepted the decision in *Re Gosling*[275] as correct.

In *Oppenheim v Tobacco Securities Trust Co Ltd*[276] this House had to consider the principle laid down by the Court of Appeal in *Re Compton*.[277] There the trustees of a fund worth over £125,000 were directed to apply its income and also if they thought fit all or any part of the capital— **6–171**

> "in providing for or assisting in providing for the education of children of employees or former employees of British-American Tobacco Co, Ltd . . . or any of its subsidiary or allied companies . . .".

There were over 110,000 such employees. The majority of your Lordships—namely Lord Simonds (in whose judgment Lord Oaksey concurred), Lord Normand and Lord Morton of Henryton—in holding that the trust was not a valid charitable trust gave unqualified approval to the Compton principle. They held, that is to say, that although the "poverty" cases might afford an anomalous exception to the rule, it was otherwise a general rule applicable to all charitable trusts that no class of beneficiaries can constitute a "section of the public" for the purpose of the law of charity if the distinguishing quality which links them together is relationship to a particular individual either through common descent or common employment. My noble and learned friend, Lord MacDermott, on the other hand, in his dissenting speech, while not challenging the correctness of the decisions in *Re Compton* or in the *Hobourn Aero* case[278] said that he could not regard the principle stated by Lord Greene M.R. as a criterion of general applicability and conclusiveness. He said[279]: **6–172**

> ". . . I see much difficulty in dividing the qualities or attributes which may serve to bind human beings into classes into two mutually exclusive groups, the one involving individual status and purely personal, the other disregarding such status and quite impersonal. As a task this seems to me no less baffling and elusive than the problem to which it is directed, namely, the determination of what is and what is not a section of the public for the purposes of this branch of the law."

He thought that the question whether any given trust was a public or a private trust was a question of degree to be decided in the light of the facts of the particular case and that viewed in that light the trust in the *Oppenheim* case was a valid charitable trust . . .

The *Oppenheim* case was a case of an educational trust and although the majority evidently agreed with the view expressed by the Court of Appeal in the *Hobourn Aero* case,[280] that the *Compton* rule was of universal application outside the field of poverty, it would no doubt be open to this House without overruling *Oppenheim* to hold that the scope of the rule was more limited. If ever I should be called on to pronounce on this question—which does not arise in this appeal—I would as at present advised be inclined to draw a distinction between the practical merits of the *Compton* rule and the reasoning by which Lord Greene M.R. sought to justify it. That reasoning—based on the distinction between personal and impersonal relationships—has never seemed to me very satisfactory and I have always—if I may say so—felt the force of the criticism to which my noble and learned friend Lord MacDermott subjected it in his dissenting speech in the *Oppenheim* case.[281] For my part I would prefer to approach the problem on far broader lines. The phrase "a section of the public" is in truth a phrase which may mean different things to different people. In the law of charity judges have sought to elucidate its meaning by contrasting it with another phrase "a fluctuating body of private individuals". But I get little help from the supposed contrast for as I see it one and the same aggregate of persons may well be describable both as a section of the public and as a fluctuating body of private individuals. The ratepayers in the Royal Borough of Kensington and Chelsea, for example, certainly constitute a section of the public; but would it be a misuse of language to describe them as a "fluctuating body of private individuals"? After all, every part of the public is composed of individuals and being susceptible of increase or decrease is fluctuating. So at the end of the day one is left where one started with the bare contrast between "public" and "private". No doubt some classes are more naturally describable as sections of the public than as private classes while other classes are more **6–173**

---

275 (1900) 48 W.R. 300.
276 [1951] A.C. 297.
277 [1945] Ch. 123.
278 [1946] Ch. 194.
279 [1951] A.C. 297 at 317.
280 [1946] Ch. 194.
281 [1951] A.C. 297. See also G. Cross, as Lord Cross then was, (1956) 72 L.Q.R. 187.

naturally describable as private classes than as sections of the public. The blind, for example, can naturally be described as a section of the public; but what they have in common—their blindness—does not join them together in such a way that they could be called a private class. On the other hand, the descendants of Mr Gladstone might more reasonably be described as a "private class" than as a section of the public, and in the field of common employment the same might well be said of the employees in some fairly small firm. But if one turns to large companies employing many thousands of men and women most of whom are quite unknown to one another and to the directors the answer is by no means so clear. One might say that in such a case the distinction between a section of the public and a private class is not applicable at all or even that the employees in such concerns as ICI or GEC are just as much "sections of the public" as the residents in some geographical area. In truth the question whether or not the potential beneficiaries of a trust can fairly be said to constitute a section of the public is a question of degree and cannot be by itself decisive of the question whether the trust is a charity. Much must depend on the purpose of the trust. It may well be that, on the one hand, a trust to promote some purpose, prima facie charitable, will constitute a charity even though the class of potential beneficiaries might fairly be called a private class and that, on the other hand, a trust to promote another purpose, also prima facie charitable, will not constitute a charity even though the class of potential beneficiaries might seem to some people fairly describable as a section of the public.

**6–174** In answering the question whether any given trust is a charitable trust the courts—as I see it—cannot avoid having regard to the fiscal privileges accorded to charities. As counsel for the Attorney-General remarked in the course of the argument the law of charity is bedevilled by the fact that charitable trusts enjoy two quite different sorts of privilege. On the one hand, they enjoy immunity from the rules against perpetuity and uncertainty and although individual potential beneficiaries cannot sue to enforce them the public interest arising under them is protected by the Attorney-General. If this was all there would be no reason for the courts not to look favourably on the claim of any "purpose" trust to be considered as a charity if it seemed calculated to confer some real benefit on those intended to benefit by it whoever they might be and if it would fail if not held to be a charity. But that is not all. Charities automatically enjoy fiscal privileges which with the increased burden of taxation have become more and more important and in deciding that such and such a trust is a charitable trust the court is endowing it with a substantial annual subsidy at the expense of the taxpayer. Indeed, claims of trusts to rank as charities are just as often challenged by the Revenue as by those who would take the fund if the trust was invalid. It is, of course, unfortunate that the recognition of any trust as a valid charitable trust should automatically attract fiscal privileges, for the question whether a trust to further some purpose is so little likely to benefit the public that it ought to be declared invalid and the question whether it is likely to confer such great benefits on the public that it should enjoy fiscal immunity are really two quite different questions. The logical solution would be to separate them and to say—as the Radcliffe Commission proposed—that only some charities should enjoy fiscal privileges. But as things, are, validity and fiscal immunity march hand in hand and the decisions in the *Compton*[282] and *Oppenheim*[283] cases were pretty obviously influenced by the consideration that if such trusts as were there in question were held valid they would enjoy an undeserved fiscal immunity. To establish a trust for the education of the children of employees in a company in which you are interested is no doubt a meritorious act; but however numerous the employees may be the purpose which you are seeking to achieve is not a public purpose.[284] It is a company purpose and there is no reason why your fellow taxpayers should contribute to a scheme which by providing "fringe benefits" for your employees will benefit the company by making their conditions of employment more attractive. The temptation to enlist the assistance of the law of charity in private endeavours of this sort is considerable—witness the recent case of the Metal Box scholarships—*Inland Revenue Comrs v Educational Grants Association Ltd*[285]—and the courts must do what they can to discourage such attempts. In the field of poverty the danger is not so great as in the field of education—for while people are keenly alive to the need to give their children a good education and to the expense of doing so, they are generally optimistic enough not to entertain serious fears of falling on evil days much before they fall on them. Consequently the existence of company "benevolent funds", the income of which is free of tax does not constitute a very attractive "fringe benefit".

---

282 [1945] Ch. 123.
283 [1951] A.C. 297.
284 For a critical view of this approach see T.G. Watkin [1978] Conv. 277.
285 [1967] Ch. 993.

This is a practical justification—although not, of course, the historical explanation—for the special treatment accorded to poverty trusts in charity law. For the same sort of reason a trust to promote some religion among the employees of a company might perhaps safely be held to be charitable provided that it was clear that the benefits were to be purely spiritual. On the other hand, many "purpose" trusts falling under Lord Macnaghten's fourth head if confined to a class of employees would clearly be open to the same sort of objection as educational trusts. As I see it, it is on these broad lines rather than for the reasons actually given by Lord Greene M.R. that the *Compton* rule can best be justified.

My Lords, I would dismiss this appeal. 6–175

*Appeal dismissed.* 6–176

*Attorney General v Charity Commission*

Upper Tribunal (Tax and Chancery Chamber) [2012] W.T.L.R. 977

WARREN J. (CHAMBER PRESIDENT) AND UPPER TRIBUNAL JUDGE MCKENNA: These proceedings concern a Notice of Reference . . . made by Her Majesty's Attorney General on 27 January 2011, by which he sought the Tribunal's determination of a number of issues relating to charities for the relief of poverty, in which the potential beneficiaries are connected by a family relationship to the founder, common employment or former employment, or their membership of an unincorporated organisation. . . 6–177

**The Pre 2006 Act Position**

The concept of public benefit prior to the 2006 Act was considered at [42]ff of the decision in *I.S.C.* [i.e. *R (Independent Schools Council) v Charity Commission*[286]] . . . which explains . . . how it is possible to discern from the cases two related aspects of public benefit. The first aspect is that the nature of the purpose itself must be such as to be a benefit to the community: this was referred to as public benefit in the first sense . . . The second aspect is that those who may benefit from the carrying out of the purpose must be sufficiently numerous, and identified in such manner, as to constitute what is described in the authorities as "a section of the public": this is public benefit in the second sense. 6–178

. . . In our view, the purposes of the institutions with which we are concerned insofar as they relate to the relief of poverty . . . which were all charitable institutions prior to the 2006 Act, are all purposes which are for the public benefit in the first sense. The relief of poverty is, we consider, ordinarily to be seen a purpose of a nature which is for the public benefit just as ordinary education is of a nature which is for the public benefit. It is a purpose which is expressly mentioned in the Preamble and thus of a nature which is charitable. But just as there may be educational purposes which are not charitable because they are not for the public benefit in the first sense—the school for pickpockets again: see [48b] of the decision in *ISC* – it is possible that there could be a trust for the relief of poverty which is not for the public benefit in the first sense either. Indeed, in his speech in *National Anti- Vivisection Society v IRC*,[287] Lord Simonds gave practical examples of such a possibility and observed:[288] 6–179

> "If today a testator made a bequest for the relief of the poor and required that it should be carried out in one way only and the court was satisfied by evidence that that way was injurious to the community, I should say that it was not a charitable gift, though three hundred years ago the court might upon different evidence or in the absence of any evidence have come to a different conclusion."

. . . In the light of the discussion at [45] to [71] of *ISC* we do not think that the abolition of the presumption of public benefit in section 3(2) of the 2006 Act has had any impact on whether a trust for the relief of poverty is charitable or not. There is no presumption that a trust for the relief of poverty is for the public benefit, any more than there is a presumption that education is for the public benefit. In either case, the Court or Tribunal will form its own view on the evidence before it whether the trust is for the public benefit and it will do so, not by way of assumption, but by way of decision. It will no doubt take account of other decided cases; and it will take judicial notice of facts where appropriate. But as the Tribunal said at [68] of the decision in *ISC*, this is far from a "presumption" in the usual sense. 6–180

286 [2012] Ch. 214; see para.6–045.
287 [1948] A.C. 31 at 60.
288 Ibid. at 69–70.

6–181 [The judges reviewed *Gibson v South American Stores (Gath & Chaves) Ltd*,[289] *Oppenheim v Tobacco Securities Trust Co Ltd*,[290] *Re Scarisbrick*,[291] and *Dingle v Turner*,[292] and drew these conclusions]: (a) First, to state the obvious, there is nothing in the [foregoing cases] which raises the slightest doubt that what we have referred to as public benefit in the first sense is a necessary requirement for a purpose to qualify as a charitable purpose. (b) Secondly, there is nothing in [the foregoing cases] which leads to the conclusion that what we have referred to as public benefit in the first sense has nothing to do with the public benefit requirement, but is (only) a separate and distinct requirement which has to be satisfied if a purpose is to be charitable.

6–182 Accordingly, it is an element of the "public benefit" as that term is understood for the purposes of charity law that the nature of the purpose has to be one which is capable of being of benefit to the community. Before the 2006 Act, the purposes of a trust, in order to be charitable, had to fall within, or within the spirit of, the Preamble. After the 2006 Act, the purposes of the trust must fall within section 2(2). But in each case, there is (or was) a requirement that the purpose is (or was) also one which is of its nature capable of being for the benefit of the community. Thus, a school for pickpockets fails the test even though it is educational; and there may be a trust for the relief of poverty which is to be carried out in such a way that it fails the test too.

**The Post-2006 Act Position**

6–183 We now turn back to . . . [the position following the 2006 Act]. For an institution to be a charity, its purposes have to be "for the public benefit" and reference to the "public benefit" is a reference to the public benefit as that term is understood for the purposes of the law relating to charities in England and Wales. Mr Dibble submits that each limb of the public benefit test must be satisfied in relation to an institution if it is to be charitable. Accordingly, even if the purpose of a trust for the relief of poverty is for the public benefit in the first sense, it is not, if restricted to a narrow class, for the public benefit in the second sense and is therefore not charitable.

6–184 We reject that submission. It is clear, we consider, that whether or not an institution satisfies the public benefit requirement must be assessed by reference to the criteria which are relevant to its purposes. For instance, as is clear from the cases, what is or is not a sufficient section of the public to satisfy the second aspect of public benefit varies depending on the nature of the charity: a sufficient section of the public in relation to an educational institution may not be sufficient in relation to a religious institution and vice versa. Accordingly, it does not make sense to address in abstract the public benefit requirement under the 2006 Act. Rather, it has to be asked what that requirement is in relation to the particular institution under consideration. In the case of a trust for the relief of poverty which had a narrow class of direct beneficiary, the trust was nonetheless charitable under the law prior to the 2006 Act even though the class was not wide enough to establish public benefit in the second sense as applied to poverty trusts. In order that a trust for the relief of poverty with a narrow class of beneficiary should be charitable, the public benefit requirement as applied to such a trust required only that public benefit in the first sense be established. The 2006 Act has not, in our judgment, changed that. The "public benefit" as that term was understood for the purposes of the law of charity required, in the context of a trust for the relief of poverty, only that public benefit in the first sense should be shown. Of course, a trust for the relief of poverty might be one which is also for the public benefit in the second sense because the class of potential beneficiary is, on any view, a sufficient section of the community. But it does not follow from that consideration that every trust for the relief of poverty must be for the public benefit in the second sense. . .

## B. Section 3(1)(b): "The Advancement of Education"

### i. Inherently Beneficial Purposes

6–185 This group of charitable trusts has its origins in those parts of the preamble to the Statute of Charitable Uses 1601 which speak of "the maintenance of schools of learning, free schools and scholars in

[289] [1949] Ch. 572; [1950] Ch. 177.
[290] [1951] A.C. 297.
[291] [1951] Ch. 622.
[292] [1972] A.C. 601.

universities" and "the education and preferment of orphans". Providing students with a school or university education remains the purpose that most obviously falls within s.3(1)(b), but the advancement of education takes in a wider range of purposes than this. In *IRC v McMullen*,[293] the House of Lords held that it is charitable to provide sports facilities for children and young people at school and university because physical education and development are an integral part of the education of the young. This decision is reproduced below for the court's discussion of education as a legally charitable purpose.[294] At the time when the case was decided, the promotion of sport was not in itself a charitable object, but the law in this area has moved on, and s.3(1)(g) now recognises the advancement of amateur sport as a beneficial purpose.[295]

Various cases show that education also includes the encouragement of the arts and graces of life, including *Re Shaw's Will Trusts*[296] ("the teaching, promotion and encouragement in Ireland of self-control, elocution, oratory, deportment, the arts of personal contact, of social intercourse, and the other arts of public, private, professional and business life"); *Royal Choral Society v IRC*[297] (choral singing in London); *Re Levien*[298] (organ music); *Re Delius*[299] (the music of the composer Delius); *Re Dupree's Deed Trusts*[300] (encouragement of chess-playing among young people in Portsmouth); and *Re South Place Ethical Society*[301] (the study and dissemination of ethical principles and the cultivation of a rational religious sentiment). Some of these purposes would now appear to fall within other sub-sections, most notably s.3(1)(f), which recognises as a charitable purpose "the advancement of the arts, culture, heritage or science". **6–186**

The Charity Commission has upheld as charitable Public Concern at Work (concerned with promoting business ethics and advising and protecting employees faced with ethical dilemmas at work)[302] and Full Fact (concerned with ensuring that factual inaccuracies in public statements are corrected by making correction requests and promoting general improvements to information made available to the public).[303] In the latter decision, the Commission accepted that[304]: **6–187**

> the structured provision of information which is factually accurate may be capable of being educational, where is it provided in furtherance of a genuinely educational purpose, to advance the knowledge or abilities of the recipients in a meaningful way and . . . is not promoting particular opinions or propaganda.

Note, however, that the Commission will pay particular attention to the quality of instruction offered by organisations which claim to be training their users outside formal educational establishments, and

---

293 [1981] A.C. 1.

294 See paras 6–194ff.

295 For discussion see paras 6–285—6–286.

296 [1952] Ch. 163.

297 [1943] 2 All E.R. 101; contrast *Associated Artists Ltd v IRC* [1956] 1 W.L.R. 752 (production of artistic dramatic works).

298 [1955] 1 W.L.R. 964.

299 [1957] Ch. 299; contrast *Re Pinion* [1965] Ch. 85 (bequest of worthless works of art to found a museum); *Sutherland's Trustees v Verschoyle* 1968 S.L.T. 43.

300 [1945] Ch. 16.

301 [1980] 1 W.L.R. 1565.

302 [1994] 2 Ch. Comm Decisions 5.

303 Charity Commission, "Decision to Register Full Fact" (17 September 2014), *https://www.gov.uk/government/uploads/system/uploads/attachment_data/file/372962/Full_Fact_Decision.pdf* [Accessed 1 June 2015]. The Commission had previously rejected Full Fact's application to register in 2009 under the head of "advancement of citizenship and civic responsibility" (see now s.3(1)(e) and (2)(c)(ii)), but accepted that its purposes were educational following a statement to that effect by the First-tier Tribunal, *"Full Fact v Charity Commission"* (26 July 2011), *http://www.charity.tribunals.gov.uk/Documents/FullFactdecision_26Jul11.pdf* [Accessed 1 June 2015].

304 ibid., at [23].

will decline to register them if it considers their activities to amount to nothing more the unstructured imparting of information.[305]

6–188 The decision of Harman J in *Re Shaw*[306] (denying charitable status where George Bernard Shaw had bequeathed funds for pursuing inquiries into a new 40-letter alphabet) appeared to render doubtful the validity of trusts for the advancement of research, at any rate where no element of teaching was involved; but *Re Hopkins' Will Trusts* removes most of the doubts. There Wilberforce J held that[307]:

> the word 'education', as used by Harman J., must be used in a wide sense, certainly extending beyond teaching, and that the requirement is that, in order to be charitable, research must either be of educational value to the researcher or must be so directed as to lead to something which will pass into the store of educational material or so as to improve the sum of communicable knowledge in an area which education may cover . . . research of a private character, for the benefit only of the members of a society, would not normally be educational or otherwise charitable but I do not think that the research in the present case [into the works of Francis Bacon and whether he might have been the author of plays ascribed to Shakespeare] can be said to be of private character, for it is inherently inevitable and manifestly intended that the result of any discovery should be published to the world.

6–189 In *McGovern v Attorney General*, Slade J summarised the governing principles as follows[308]:

> (1) A trust for research will ordinarily qualify as a charitable trust if, but only if (a) the subject matter of the proposed research is a useful subject of study; and (b) it is contemplated that knowledge acquired as a result of the research will be disseminated to others; and (c) the trust is for the benefit of the public, or a sufficiently important section of the public. (2) In the absence of a contrary context, however, the court will be readily inclined to construe a trust for research as importing subsequent dissemination of the results thereof. (3) Furthermore, if a trust for research is to constitute a valid trust for the advancement of education, it is not necessary either (a) that a teacher/pupil relationship should be in contemplation, or (b) that the persons to benefit from the knowledge to be acquired should be persons who are already in the course of receiving 'education' in the conventional sense.

6–190 The rule that trusts for research purposes are charitable only if it is contemplated that the research will be published was revisited by the Charity Commission in its guidance document on *Public Benefit and the Advancement of Education*, where it stated that[309]:

> This does not mean that research has to be presented in a way that is understandable by everyone. It might only be capable of being understood by people who are experts in the field. What is important is that it is published and made publicly available so that everyone who is capable of understanding it has access to it, and its benefits or usefulness are widely available to everyone.

6–191 Trusts to disseminate particular political opinions are not charitable where this amounts to propaganda rather than education.[310] The rule that political purposes are not charitable has been discussed above.[311]

---

305 Charity Commission, *Decision on the Millennium College UK Ltd's Application for Registration as a Charity* (27 April 2004); *Decision on Living in Radiance's Application for Registration as a Charity* (24 August 2005).

306 [1965] Ch. 699; [1957] 1 W.L.R. 729.

307 [1965] Ch. 669 at 680–681.

308 [1982] Ch. 321 at 352.

309 (December 2008 version) para.E2.

310 *Bonar Law Memorial Trust v IRC* (1933) 49 T.L.R. 220; *Re Hopkinson* [1949] 1 All E.R. 346; *Southwood v Attorney General* [2000] W.T.L.R. 1199; cf. *Re McDougall* [1957] 1 W.L.R. 81 (study of methods of government is a charitable object). For the same reason, a trust to persuade people to accept particular religious beliefs is not a charitable trust for an education purpose: Charity Commission, *Decision on the Gnostic Centre's Application for Registration as a Charity* (16 December 2009), paras 12–18.

311 See paras 6–118—6–142.

## ii. Provision of Benefit to the Community

Trusts supporting the educational activities of schools are charitable, even if the schools are fee-charging institutions, provided that they do not make profits, or if they do, that these are used solely for the charitable purposes of the institution.[312] In *R (Independent Schools Council) v Charity Commission*,[313] the Upper Tribunal held that the trustees of fee-charging schools must make provision for the community as a whole that goes beyong a "de minimis or token level", but that it is for the trustees to decide what that should be "in all the circumstance of the particular school under consideration".[314] This case has already been discussed.[315] **6–192**

In *Oppenheim v Tobacco Securities Trust Co Ltd*,[316] reproduced below, the House of Lords held that a trust for the education of beneficiaries who are ascertained by reference to some personal tie (e.g. of blood or contract), such as the relations of a particular individual, the members of a particular family, the employees of a particular firm or the members of a particular trade union, lacks the necessary element of public benefit and is not charitable. In contrast, a trust to educate the residents of a town[317] or the children of members of a particular profession[318] will be valid. **6–193**

*IRC v McMullen*

House of Lords [1981] A.C. 1

LORD HAILSHAM: Four questions arose for decision below. In the first place neither the parties nor the judgments below were in agreement as to the proper construction of the trust deed itself. Clearly this is a preliminary debate which must be settled before the remaining questions are even capable of decision. In the second place the trustees contend and the Crown disputes that, on the correct construction of the deed, the trust is charitable as being for the advancement of education. Thirdly, the trustees contend and the Crown disputes that if they are wrong on the second question the trust is charitable at least because it falls within the fourth class of Lord Macnaghten's categories as enumerated In *Income Tax Special Purposes Comrs v Pemsel*[319] as a trust beneficial to the community within the spirit and intendment of the preamble to the statute 43 Eliz. I, c.4.[320] Fourthly, the trustees contend and the Crown disputes that, even if not otherwise charitable, the trust is a valid charitable trust as falling within section 1 of the Recreational Charities Act 1958, that is as a trust to provide or to assist in the provision of facilities for recreation or other leisure time occupation provided in the interests of social welfare. **6–194**

Since we have reached the view that the trust is a valid educational charity their Lordships have not sought to hear argument nor, therefore, to reach a conclusion on any but the first two disputed questions in the dispute. Speaking for myself, however, I do not wish my absence of decision on the third or fourth points to be interpreted as an indorsement of the majority judgments in the Court of Appeal nor as necessarily dissenting from the contrary views contained in the minority judgment of Bridge L.J. For me at least the answers to the third and fourth questions are still left entirely undecided. **6–195**

I now turn to the question of construction, for which it is necessary that I reproduce the material portions of the deed . . . The objects of the Trusts are:— **6–196**

"(a) to organise or provide or assist in the organisation and provision of facilities which will enable and encourage pupils of Schools and Universities in any part of the United Kingdom to play Association

---

[312] *Abbey Malvern Wells Ltd v Ministry of Local Government* [1951] Ch. 728; *Oppenheim v Tobacco Securities Trust Co Ltd* [1951] A.C. 297 at 306; *Customs & Excise Commissioners v Bell Concord Education Trust* [1990] 1 Q.B. 1040.

[313] [2012] Ch. 214 at [69].

[314] ibid., at [215].

[315] See paras 6–071—6–100.

[316] [1951] A.C. 297.

[317] *Re Tree* [1945] Ch. 325: a restriction to Methodists or members of the Church of England would seem valid.

[318] *Hall v Derby Sanitary Authority* (1885) 16 Q.B.D. 163 approved in *Oppenheim v Tobacco Securities Trust Co* [1951] A.C. 297.

[319] [1891] A.C. 531 at 583.

[320] Charitable Uses Act 1601.

Football or other games or sports and thereby to assist in ensuring that due attention is given to the physical education and development of such pupils as well as to the development and occupation of their minds and with a view to furthering this object (i) to provide or assist in the provision of Association Football or games or sports equipment of every kind for the use of such pupils as aforesaid (ii) to provide or assist in the provision of courses lectures demonstrations and coaching for pupils of Schools and Universities in any part of the United Kingdom and for teachers who organise or supervise playing and coaching of Association Football or other games or sports at such Schools and Universities as aforesaid (iii) to promote provide or assist in the promotion and provision of training colleges for the purpose of training teachers in the coaching of Association Football or other games or sports at such Schools and Universities as aforesaid (iv) to lay out manage equip and maintain or assist in the laying out management equipment and maintenance of playing fields or appropriate indoor facilities or accommodation (whether vested in the Trustees or not) to be used for the teaching and playing of Association Football or other sports or games by such pupils as aforesaid.

"(b) to organise or provide or assist in the organisation or provision of facilities for physical recreation in the interests of social welfare in any part of the United Kingdom (with the object of improving the conditions of life for the boys and girls for whom the same are provided) for boys and girls who are under the age of twenty-one years and who by reason of their youth or social and economic circumstances have need of such facilities."

**6–197** I pause here only to say that no question arises as to clause 3(b) above which clearly corresponds to the language of the Recreational Charities Act 1958. Controversy therefore revolves solely around clause 3(a), since it is obvious that, if this cannot be shown to be solely for charitable purposes, the whole trust ceases to be a charitable trust. . .

**6–198** I agree with [the judgment of Bridge LJ] . . . that what the deed means is that the purpose of the settlor is to promote the physical education and development of pupils at schools and universities as an addition to such part of their education as relates to their mental education by providing the facilities and assistance to games and sports in the manner set out at greater length and in greater detail in the enumerated sub-clauses of clause 3(a) of the deed . . .

**6–199** On a proper analysis, therefore, I do not find clause 3(a) ambiguous. But, before I part with the question of construction, I would wish to express agreement with a contention made on behalf of the trustees and of the Attorney-General, but not agreed to on behalf of the Crown, that in construing trust deeds the intention of which is to set up a charitable trust, and in others too, where it can be claimed that there is an ambiguity, a benignant construction should be given if possible. This was the maxim of the civil law: *semper in dubiis benigniora praeferenda sunt*. There is a similar maxim in English law: *ut res magis valeat quam pereat*. It certainly applies to charities when the question is one of uncertainty (*Weir v Crum-Brown*[321]) and, I think, also where a gift is capable of two constructions one of which would make it void and the other effectual (cf. *Bruce v Deer Presbytery*,[322] *Houston v Burns*[323] and *Bain, Public Trustee v Ross*[324]). In the present case I do not find it necessary to resort to benignancy in order to construe the clause, but, had I been in doubt, I would certainly have been prepared to do so. . . .

**6–200** I must now turn to the deed, construed in the manner in which I have found it necessary to construe it, to consider whether it sets up a valid charitable trust for the advancement of education.

**6–201** It is admitted, of course, that the words "charity" and "charitable" bear, for the purposes of English law and equity, meanings totally different from the senses in which they are used in ordinary educated speech, or for instance, in the Authorised Version of the Bible. But I do not share the view, implied by Stamp and Orr L.JJ. in the instant case,[325] that the words "education" and "educational" bear, or can bear, for the purposes of the law of charity, meanings different from those current in present day educated English speech. I do not believe that there is such a difference. What has to be remembered, however, is that, as Lord Wilberforce pointed out in *Re Hopkins' Will Trusts*[326] and in *Scottish Burial Reform and Cremation Society*

[321] [1908] A.C. 162 at 167.
[322] (1867) L.R. 1 Sc. & Div. 96 at 97.
[323] [1918] A.C. 337 at 341–342.
[324] [1930] 1 Ch. 224 at 230.
[325] [1979] 1 W.L.R. 130 at 135, 139.
[326] [1965] Ch. 669 at 678.

*Ltd v Glasgow City Corpn*,[327] both the legal conception of charity, and within it the educated man's ideas about education are not static, but moving and changing. Both change with changes in ideas about social values. Both have evolved with the years. In particular in applying the law to contemporary circumstances it is extremely dangerous to forget that thoughts concerning the scope and width of education differed in the past greatly from those which are now generally accepted.

In saying this I do not in the least wish to cast doubt on *Re Nottage*,[328] which was referred to in both courts below and largely relied on by the Crown here. Strictly speaking *Re Nottage* was not a case about education at all. The issue there was whether the bequest came into the fourth class of charity categorised in Lord Macnaghten's classification of 1891.[329] The mere playing of games or enjoyment of amusement or competition is not per se charitable, nor necessarily educational, though they may (or may not) have an educational or beneficial effect if diligently practised. Neither am I deciding in the present case even that a gift for physical education per se and not associated with persons of school age or just above would necessarily be a good charitable gift. That is a question which the courts may have to face at some time in the future. But in deciding what is or is not an educational purpose for the young in 1980 it is not irrelevant to point out what Parliament considered to be educational for the young in 1944 when, by the Education Act of that year in sections 7 and 53 (which are still on the statute book), Parliament attempted to lay down what was then intended to be the statutory system of education organised by the state, and the duties of the local education authorities and the Minister in establishing and maintaining the system. Those sections are so germane to the present issue that I cannot forbear to quote them both. Section 7 provides (in each of the sections the emphasis being mine): **6–202**

> "The statutory system of public education shall be organised in three progressive stages to be known as primary education, secondary education, and further education; and it shall be the duty of the local education authority for every area, so far as their powers extend, to contribute towards the spiritual, moral, mental, and physical development of the community by securing that efficient education throughout those stages shall be available to meet the needs of the population of their area"

and in section 53 of the same Act it is said:

> "(1) It shall be the duty of every local education authority to secure that the facilities for primary, secondary and further education provided for their area include adequate facilities for recreation and social and physical training, and for that purpose a local education authority, with the approval of the Secretary of State, may establish maintain and manage, or assist the establishment, maintenance, and management of camps, holiday classes, playing fields, play centres and other places (including playgrounds, gymnasiums, and swimming baths not appropriated to any school or college), at which facilities for recreation and for such training as aforesaid are available for persons receiving primary, secondary or further education, and may organise games, expeditions and other activities for such persons, and may defray or contribute towards the expenses thereof."

. . . I find the first instance case of *Mariette*,[330] a decision of Eve J., both stimulating and instructive. Counsel for the Crown properly reminded us that this concerned a bequest effectively tied to a particular institution. Nevertheless, I cannot forbear to quote a phrase from the judgment, always bearing in mind the danger of quoting out of context. Eve J. said:[331] **6–203**

> "No one of sense could be found to suggest that between those ages [10 to 19] any boy can be properly educated unless at least as much attention is given to the development of his body as is given to the development of his mind."

Apart from the limitation to the particular institution I would think that these words apply as well to the settlor's intention in the instant appeal as to the testator's in *Re Mariette*, and I regard the limitation to the pupils of schools and universities in the instant case as a sufficient association with the provision of formal education to prevent any danger of vagueness in the object of the trust or irresponsibility or capriciousness **6–204**

327 [1968] A.C. 138 at 154.
328 [1895] 2 Ch. 649.
329 See *Income Tax Special Purposes Comrs v Pemsel* [1891] A.C. 531 at 583.
330 [1915] 2 Ch. 284.
331 [1915] 2 Ch. 284 at 288.

in application by the trustees. I am far from suggesting either that the concept of education or of physical education even for the young is capable of indefinite extension. On the contrary, I do not think that the courts have as yet explored the extent to which elements of organisation, instruction or the disciplined inculcation of information, instruction or skill may limit the whole concept of education. I believe that in some ways it will prove more extensive, in others more restrictive than has been thought hitherto. But it is clear at least to me that the decision in *Re Mariette*[332] is not to be read in a sense which confines its application for ever to gifts to a particular institution. It has been extended already in *Re Mellody*[333] to gifts for annual treats for schoolchildren in a particular locality (another decision of Eve J.), to playgrounds for children (*Re Chester*,[334] possibly not educational, but referred to in *Inland Revenue Comrs v Baddeley*[335]); to a children's outing (*Re Ward's Estate*[336]), to a prize for chess to boys and young men resident in the City of Portsmouth (*Re Dupree's Deed Trusts*,[337] a decision of Vaisey J.) and for the furthering of the Boy Scouts' movement by helping to purchase sites for camping, outfits, etc. (*Re Webber*,[338] another decision of Vaisey J.).

**6–205** It is important to remember that in the instant appeal we are dealing with the concept of physical education and development of the young deliberately associated by the settlor with the status of pupillage in schools or universities (of which, according to the evidence, about 95 per cent are within the age-group 17 to 22). We are not dealing with adult education, physical or otherwise, as to which some considerations may be different.

**6–206** I am at pains to disclaim the view that the conception of this evolving, and therefore not static, view of education is capable of infinite abuse or, even worse, proving void for uncertainty. Quite apart from the doctrine of the benignant approach to which I have already referred, and which undoubtedly comes to the assistance of settlors in danger of attack for uncertainty, I am content to adopt the approach of my predecessor Lord Loreburn L.C. in *Weir v Crum-Brown*,[339] to which attention was drawn by counsel for the Attorney-General, that if the bequest to a class of persons, is as here capable of application by the trustees, or, failing them, the court, the gift is not void for uncertainty. Lord Macnaghten also said:[340]

> "The testator has taken pains to provide competent judges. It is for the trustees to consider and determine the value of the service on which a candidate may rest his claim to participate in the testator's bounty."

**6–207** Mutatis mutandis, I think this kind of reasoning should apply here. Granted that the question of application may present difficulties for the trustees, or, failing them, for the court, nevertheless it is capable of being applied, for the concept in the mind of the settlor is an object sufficiently clear, is exclusively for the advancement of education, and, in the hands of competent judges, is capable of application.

**6–208** My Lords, for these reasons I reach the conclusion that the trust is a valid charitable gift for the advancement of education, which, after all, is what it claims to be. The conclusion follows that the appeal should be allowed.

**6–209** LORD DIPLOCK and LORD SALMON merely concurred while LORD RUSSELL and LORD KEITH concurred and gave brief speeches.

### *Oppenheim v Tobacco Securities Trust Co Ltd*

### House of Lords [1951] A.C. 297

**6–210** Investments were held by the respondents, Tobacco Securities Trust Co Ltd, on trust to apply the income in providing for "the education of children of employees or former employees of British-American Tobacco Co Ltd . . . or any of its subsidiary or allied companies without any limit of time being specified". The High

---

332 [1915] 2 Ch. 284.
333 [1918] 1 Ch. 228.
334 (July 25, 1934) unreported.
335 [1955] A.C. 572 at 596.
336 [1937] 81 Sol. Jo. 397.
337 [1945] Ch. 16.
338 [1954] 1 W.L.R. 1500.
339 [1908] A.C. 162 at 167.
340 [1908] A.C. 162 at 169.

Court and Court of Appeal held the trust void for perpetuity because it was not charitable on the ground that it lacked public benefit.

LORD SIMONDS (with whom LORD NORMAND, LORD OAKSEY and LORD MORTON agreed): In the case of trusts for educational purposes the condition of the public benefit must be satisfied. The difficulty lies in determining what is sufficient to satisfy the test, and there is little to help your Lordships to solve it. **6–211**

If I may begin at the bottom of the scale, a trust established by a father for the education of his son is not a charity. The public element, as I will call it, is not supplied by the fact that from that son's education all may benefit. At the other end of the scale the establishment of a college or university is beyond doubt a charity. "Schools of learning and free schools, and scholars of universities" are the very words of the preamble to the [Charitable Uses Act 1601 (43 Eliz. I, c.4)]. So also the endowment of a college, university or school by the creation of scholarships or bursaries is a charity, and nonetheless because competition may be limited to a particular class of persons. It is on this ground, as Lord Greene M.R. pointed out in *Re Compton*,[341] that the so-called "founder's kin" cases can be rested. The difficulty arises where the trust is not for the benefit of any institution either then existing or by the terms of the trust to be brought into existence, but for the benefit of a class of persons at large. Then the question is whether that class of persons can be regarded as such a "section of the community" as to satisfy the test of public benefit. These words "section of the community" have no special sanctity, but they conveniently indicate (1) that the possible (I emphasise the word "possible") beneficiaries must not be numerically negligible, and (2) that the quality which distinguishes them from other members of the community, so that they form by themselves a section of it, must be a quality which does not depend on their relationship to a particular individual. It is for this reason that a trust for the education of members of a family or, as in *Re Compton*, of a number of families cannot be regarded as charitable. A group of persons may be numerous, but, if the nexus between them is their personal relationship to a single *propositus* or to several *propositi*, they are neither the community nor a section of the community for charitable purposes. **6–212**

I come, then, to the present case where the class of beneficiaries is numerous, but the difficulty arises in regard to their common and distinguishing quality. That quality is being children of employees of one or other of a group of companies. I can make no distinction between children of employees and the employees themselves. In both cases the common quality is found in employment by particular employers. The latter of the two cases, by which the Court of Appeal held itself to be bound, the *Hobourn* case, is a direct authority for saying that such a common quality does not constitute its possessors a section of the public for charitable purposes. In the former case, *Re Compton*, Lord Greene M.R. had by way of illustration placed members of a family and employees of a particular employer on the same footing, finding neither in common kinship nor in common employment the sort of nexus which is sufficient. My Lords, I am so fully in agreement with what was said by Lord Greene in both cases, and by my noble and learned friend, then Morton L.J., in the *Hobourn* case, that I am in danger of repeating without improving upon their words. It appears to me that it would be an extension [of the legal definition of charity], for which there is no justification in principle or authority, to regard common employment as a quality which constitutes those employed a section of the community. It must not, I think, be forgotten that charitable institutions enjoy rare and increasing privileges, and that the claim to come within that privileged class should be clearly established. With the single exception of *Re Rayner*,[342] which I must regard as of doubtful authority, no case has been brought to the notice of the House in which such a claim as this has been made, where there is no element of poverty in the beneficiaries, but just this and no more, that they are the children of those in a common employment. **6–213**

Learned counsel for the appellant sought to fortify his case by pointing to the anomalies that would ensue from the rejection of his argument. For, he said, admittedly those who follow a profession or calling—clergymen, lawyers, colliers, tobacco-workers and so on—are a section of the public; how strange then it would be if, as in the case of railwaymen, those who follow a particular calling are all employed by one employer. Would a trust for the education of railwaymen be charitable,[343] but a trust for the education of men employed on the railways by the Transport Board not be charitable? And what of service of the Crown, whether in the civil service or the armed forces? Is there a difference between soldiers and soldiers of the King? My Lords, I am not impressed by this sort of argument and will consider on its merits if the **6–214**

[341] [1945] Ch. 123.
[342] (1920) 89 L.J. Ch. 369.
[343] As to this see *Hall v Derby Sanitary Authority* (1885) 16 Q.B.D. 163.

occasion should arise, the case where the description of the occupation and the employment is in effect the same, where in a word, if you know what a man does, you know who employs him to do it. It is to me a far more cogent argument, as it was to my noble and learned friend in the *Hobourn* case, that, if a section of the public is constituted by the personal relation of employment, it is impossible to say that it is not constituted by a thousand as by 100,000 employees, and if by a thousand, then by a hundred, and, if by a hundred, then by ten. I do not mean merely that there is a difficulty in drawing the line, though that, too, is significant. I have it also in mind that, though the actual number of employees at any one moment might be small, it might increase to any extent, just as, being large, it might decrease to any extent. If the number of employees is the test of validity, must the court take into account potential increase or decrease, and, if so, as at what date? . . .

**6–215** LORD MACDERMOTT (dissenting): The question is whether it is of a public nature, whether, in the words of Lord Wrenbury in *Verge v Somerville*,[344] "it is for the benefit of the community or of an appreciably important class of the community." The relevant class here is that from which those to be educated are to be selected. The appellant contends that this class is public in character; the respondent bank (as personal representative of the last surviving settlor) denies this and says that the class is no more than a group of private individuals.

**6–216** Until comparatively recently the usual way of approaching an issue of this sort, at any rate where educational trusts were concerned, was, I believe, to regard the facts of each case and to treat the matter very much as one of degree. No definition of what constituted a sufficient section of the public for the purpose was applied, for none existed; and the process seems to have been one of reaching a conclusion on a general survey of the circumstances and considerations regarded as relevant rather than of making a single, conclusive test. The investigation left the course of the dividing line between what was and what was not a section of the community unexplored, and was concluded when it had gone far enough to establish to the satisfaction of the court whether or not the trust was public; and the decision as to that was, I think, very often reached by determining whether or not the trust was private.

**6–217** If it is still permissible to conduct the present inquiry on these broad if imprecise lines, I would hold with the appellant. The numerical strength of the class is considerable on any showing. The employees concerned number over 110,000, and it may reasonably be assumed that the children, who constitute the class in question, are no fewer. The large size of the class is not, of course, decisive but in my view it cannot be left out of account when the problem is approached in this way. Then it must be observed that the propositi are not limited to those presently employed. They include former employees (not reckoned in the figure I have given) and are, therefore, a more stable category than would otherwise be the case. And, further, the employees concerned are not limited to those in the service of the "British American Tobacco Co Ltd or any of its subsidiary or allied companies"—itself a description of great width—but include the employees, in the event of the British American Tobacco Co Ltd being reconstructed or merged on amalgamation, of the reconstructed or amalgamated company or any of its subsidiary companies. No doubt the settlors here had a special interest in the welfare of the class they described, but, apart from the fact that this may serve to explain the particular form of their bounty, I do not think it material to the question in hand. What is material, as I regard the matter, is that they have chosen to benefit a class which is, in fact, substantial in point of size and importance and have done so in a manner which, to my mind, manifests an intention to advance the interests of the class described as a class rather than as a collection or succession of particular individuals . . .

**6–218** The respondent bank, however, contends that the inquiry should be of quite a different character to that which I have been discussing. It advances as the sole criterion a narrower test derived from the decisions of the Court of Appeal in *Compton*,[345] and in *Hobourn*.[346] The basis and nature of this test appear from the passage in the judgment of the court in *Compton*,[347] where Lord Greene M.R., says:

> "In the case of many charitable gifts it is possible to identify the individuals who are to benefit, or who at any given moment constitute the class from which the beneficiaries are to be selected. This circumstance does not, however, deprive the gift of its public character. Thus, if there is a gift to relieve the poor inhabitants of a parish the class to benefit is readily ascertainable. But they do not enjoy the

---

[344] [1924] A.C. 496 at 499.

[345] [1945] Ch. 123.

[346] [1946] Ch. 194.

[347] [1945] Ch. 123 at 129–130.

> benefit, when they receive it, by virtue of their character as individuals but by virtue of their membership of the specified class. In such a case the common quality which unites the potential beneficiaries into a class is essentially an impersonal one. It is definable by reference to what each has in common with the others, and that is something into which their status as individuals does not enter. Persons claiming to belong to the class do so not because they are A.B., C.D. and E.F., but because they are poor inhabitants of the parish. If, in asserting their claim, it were necessary for them to establish the fact that they were the individuals A.B., C.D. and E.F., I cannot help thinking that on principle the gift ought not to be held to be a charitable gift, since the introduction into their qualification of a purely personal element would deprive the gift of its necessary public character. It seems to me that the same principle ought to apply when the claimants, in order to establish their status, have to assert and prove, not that they themselves are A.B., C.D., and E.F., but that they stand in some specified relationship to the individuals A.B., C.D., and E.F., such as that of children or employees. In that case, too, a purely personal element enters into and is an essential part of the qualification, which is defined by reference to something, i.e., personal relationship to individuals or an individual which is in its essence non-public."

The test thus propounded focuses upon the common quality which unites those within the class concerned and asks whether that quality is essentially impersonal or essentially personal. If the former, the class will rank as a section of the public and the trust will have the element common to and necessary for all legal charities; but, if the latter, the trust will be private and not charitable. It is suggested in the passage just quoted, and made clear beyond doubt in *Hobourn*,[348] that in the opinion of the Court of Appeal employment by a designated employer must be regarded for this purpose as a personal and not as an impersonal bond of union. In this connection and as illustrating the discriminating character of what I may call "the *Compton*[349] test" reference should be made to that part of the judgment of the learned Master of the Rolls in *Hobourn*,[350] in which he speaks of the decision in *Hall v Derby Borough Urban Sanitary Authority*.[351] The passage runs thus: **6–219**

> "That related to a trust for railway servants. It is said that if a trust for railway servants can be a good charity, so too a trust for railway servants in the employment of a particular railway company is a good charity. That is not so. The reason, I think, is that in the one case the trust is for railway servants in general and in the other case it is for employees of a particular company, a fact which limits the potential beneficiaries to a class ascertained on a purely personal basis."

My Lords, I do not quarrel with the result arrived at in the *Compton* and *Hobourn* cases, and I do not doubt that the *Compton* test may often prove of value and lead to a correct determination. But, with the great respect due to those who have formulated this test, I find myself unable to regard it as a criterion of general applicability and conclusiveness. In the first place I see much difficulty in dividing the qualities or attributes, which may serve to bind human beings into classes, into two mutually exclusive groups, the one involving individual status and purely personal, the other disregarding such status and quite impersonal. As a task this seems to me no less baffling and elusive than the problem to which it is directed, namely, the determination of what is and what is not a section of the public for the purposes of this branch of the law. After all, what is more personal than poverty or blindness or ignorance? Yet none would deny that a gift for the education of the children of the poor or blind was charitable; and I doubt if there is any less certainty about the charitable nature of a gift for, say, the education of children who satisfy a specified examining body that they need and would benefit by a course of special instruction designed to remedy their educational defects. **6–220**

But can any really fundamental distinction, as respects the personal or impersonal nature of the common link, be drawn between those employed, for example, by a particular university and those whom the same university has put in a certain category as the result of individual examination and assessment? Again, if the bond between these employed by a particular railway is purely personal, why should the bond between those who are employed as railway men be so essentially different? Is a distinction to be drawn in this respect between those who are employed in a particular industry before it is nationalised and those **6–221**

348 [1946] Ch. 194.
349 [1945] Ch. 123.
350 [1946] Ch. 194 at 206.
351 (1885) 16 Q.B.D. 163.

who are employed therein after that process has been completed and one employer has taken the place of many? Are miners in the service of the National Coal Board now in one category and miners at a particular pit or of a particular district in another? Is the relationship between those in the service of the Crown to be distinguished from that obtaining between those in the service of some other employer? Or, if not, are the children of, say, soldiers or civil servants to be regarded as not constituting a sufficient section of the public to make a trust for their education charitable?

6–222 It was conceded in the course of the argument that, had the present trust been framed so as to provide for the education of the children of those engaged in the tobacco industry in a named county or town, it would have been a good charitable disposition, and that even though the class to be benefited would have been appreciably smaller and no more important than is the class here. That concession follows from what the Court of Appeal has said. But if it is sound and a personal or impersonal relationship remains the universal criterion I think it shows, no less than the queries I have just raised in indicating some of the difficulties of the problem, that the *Compton* test is a very arbitrary and artificial rule. This leads me to the second difficulty that I have regarding it. If I understand it aright it necessarily makes the quantum of public benefit a consideration of little moment; the size of the class becomes immaterial and the need of its members and the public advantage of having that need met appear alike to be irrelevant. To my mind these are considerations of some account in the sphere of educational trusts for, as already indicated, I think the educational value and scope of the work actually to be done must have a bearing on the question of public benefit.

6–223 Finally, it seems to me that, far from settling the state of the law on this particular subject, the *Compton* test is more likely to create confusion and doubt in the case of many trusts and institutions of a character whose legal standing as charities has never been in question. Take, for instance, a trust for the provision of university education for boys coming from a particular school. The common quality binding the members of that class seems to reside in the fact that their parents or guardians all contracted for their schooling with the same establishment or body. That the school in such a case may itself be a charitable foundation seems altogether beside the point and quite insufficient to hold the *Compton* test at bay if it is well founded in law.

6–224 I therefore return to what I think was the process followed before the decision in *Compton's case*, and, for the reasons already given, I would hold the present trust charitable and allow the appeal. I have only to add that I recognise the imperfections and uncertainties of that process. They are as evident as the difficulties of finding something better. But I venture to doubt if it is in the power of the courts to resolve those difficulties satisfactorily as matters stand. It is a long cry to the age of Elizabeth and I think what is needed is a fresh start from a new statute.

6–225 *Appeal dismissed.*

## C. Section 3(1)(c): "The Advancement of Religion"

### i. Inherently Beneficial Purposes

6–226 This category has its origin in the preamble to the 1601 Statute which spoke of "the repair of churches". The courts soon held that the equity of the Statute extended to trusts advancing the religious purposes of the Church of England, and for a time these were the only religious purposes that were legally charitable. Trusts for the advancement of other religions were illegal and void,[352] and in cases where the settlor's words were held to manifest a general charitable intention, the property was liable to be redirected into Anglican purposes by application of the *cy-près* doctrine.[353] These rules came to be moderated with the advent of greater religious toleration. Trusts for Protestant Nonconformist

[352] e.g. *Mitford v Reynolds* (1842) 1 Phillips 185 at 193, where Lord Lyndhurst LC held that a trust to build a Hindu temple in Dakka would not be charitable because "an application of the fund for the purpose of encouraging idolatry could [not] be for the benefit of the native inhabitants".

[353] As in *Da Costa v Da Pas* (1754) Amb. 228, where the prerogative *cy-près* power was exercised to apply a void legacy to

purposes were made legally charitable by the Toleration Act 1688, subject to the proviso that nothing in them should assist persons denying the Trinity; this proviso was removed by the Unitarian Relief Act 1813. Trusts to advance Judaism were made legally charitable by the Jewish Relief Act 1846. The Catholic Relief Act 1791 abolished penalties for public adherence to Catholicism, but trusts for the furtherance of Catholicism remained void because they were illegal per se.[354] The Roman Catholic Charities Act 1832 then retrospectively validated gifts for many Catholic purposes, including schools and churches, but gifts for the saying of requiem masses remained invalid as they were still deemed to be for a "superstitious use".[355] The hardship of this was abated by the Roman Catholic Charities Act 1860 s.1, by which the courts were empowered to apply funds settled for a "superstitious" use to other Catholic purposes at their discretion.

During the twentieth century the purposes of an increasingly wide range of theistic religions were recognised as legally charitable, including the Plymouth Brethren,[356] Sikh,[357] Islamic,[358] Hindu[359] and Spiritualist[360] religions. The Unification Church (the "Moonies") has been accorded charitable status,[361] and so has the Druid Network, a group with animistic beliefs in Nature.[362] **6–227**

In rejecting the claim of an ethical society to be a charity for the advancement of religion Dillon J said[363]: **6–228**

> Religion is concerned with man's relations with God, and ethics are concerned with man's relations with man. The two are not the same, all are not made the same by sincere inquiry into the question: what is God? If reason leads people not to accept Christianity or any known religion, but they do believe in the excellence of qualities, such as truth, beauty and love, or believe in the platonic concept of the ideal, their beliefs may seem to them to be the equivalent of a religion, but viewed objectively they are not religion. . . . It seems to me that two of the essential attributes of religion are faith and worship: faith in a god and worship of that god. The Oxford English Dictionary gives as one of the definitions of religion: 'A particular system of faith and worship.' Then: 'Recognition on the part of man of some higher unseen power as having control of his destiny, and as being entitled to obedience, reverence and worship.'

On this definition, however, Buddhism is not a religion since it is a "realised" rather than a "revealed" religion, and its adherents do not revere the Buddha as a "god", but instead believe that they should follow a spiritual path that he laid out which can ultimately lead to spiritual awakening. Dillon J failed to resolve this in his judgment, and although the Charity Commissioners subsequently registered various Buddhist trusts as charitable, they were criticised for acting inconsistently with Dillon J's approach. The issue is now settled by the Charities Act 2011 s.3(2)(a)(ii), which provides that for the purposes of s.3(1) religion includes "a religion which does not involve belief in a god". **6–229**

---

found a Jewish yeshiva (religious school) to pay for a Christian preacher at the Foundling Hospital. The *cy-près* doctrine is discussed below at paras 6–298ff.

354 *Cary v Abbot* (1802) 7 Ves. Jun. 490.

355 *West v Shuttleworth* (1835) 2 My. & K. 684; *Heath v Chapman* (1854) 2 Drew. 423; but cf. *Re Michel's Trust* (1860) 28 Beav. 39 at 42–43.

356 *Holmes v Attorney General The Times*, 12 February 1981; Charity Commission, "Decision on Preston Down Trust's Application for Registration" (3 January 2014), *https://www.gov.uk/government/uploads/system/uploads/attachment_data/file/336112/preston_down_trust_full_decision.pdf* [Accessed 1 June 2015].

357 cf. *Khaira v Shergill* [2014] 3 W.L.R. 1.

358 cf. *Liverpool Muslim Society v HMRC* [2015] S.T.I. 142.

359 cf. *Varsani v Jesani* [1999] Ch. 219.

360 Charity Commission, *Decision on the Application for Registration of the Sacred Hands Spiritual Centre* (5 September 2003).

361 [1982] Charity Commissioners *Annual Report*, paras 36–38. The Attorney General dropped his action to deprive them of charitable status: *Hansard*, HC Vol.126, col.977 (3 February 1988).

362 Charity Commission, "Decision to Register the Druid Network as a Charity" (21 September 2010), *https://www.gov.uk/government/uploads/system/uploads/attachment_data/file/324236/druiddec.pdf* [Accessed 1 June 2015].

363 *Re South Place Ethical Society* [1980] 1 W.L.R. 1565 at 1571. The society was charitable under the second and fourth heads of charity. Lord Denning defined religion in a similar way in *R v Registrar General, Ex p. Segerdal* [1970] 2 Q.B. 697 at 707.

6–230 These sub-sections were first enacted in the Charities Act 2006, and while that legislation was at bill stage, efforts were unsuccessfully made by the Humanist peer Lord Wedderburn and others to have the advancement of moral but non-religious belief systems included alongside the advancement of religious belief systems in the sub-section. This was resisted by the Government on the basis that this purpose could be charitable by another route, e.g. the promotion of moral and spiritual welfare, which was recognised as a charitable purpose at common law and which is now covered by s.3(1)(m).[364]

6–231 The Charity Commission has refused to register the Church of Scientology, in a decision that is reproduced below.[365] The Commission considered that although Scientologists believe in a supreme being, this belief does not find expression in conduct indicative of reverence or veneration for the supreme being: study and therapy or counselling did not amount to such worship. This decision is criticised by Peter Edge and Joan Loughrey in an article that is also excerpted below, and it may have to be revisited following the Supreme Court's decision in *R (Hodkin) v Registrar General of Births, Deaths and Marriages*.[366] The court held there that a chapel of the Church of Scientology was a "place of meeting for religious worship" for the purposes of the the Places of Worship Registration Act 1855 s.2. Lord Toulson drew support for this conclusion from the wording of the Charities Act 2011 s.3(2)(a), which was not in point, but which he thought was an "indication that the understanding of religion in today's society is broad".

6–232 Trusts for adding to or repairing the fabric of a church[367] or for the upkeep of a churchyard[368] are charitable but not for the erection or upkeep of a particular tomb in a churchyard.[369] If a gift is made to an ecclesiastic in her official name and by virtue of her office then if no purposes are expressed in the gift the gift is for charitable religious purposes inherent in the office.[370] However, if the purposes are expressed in terms not confining them to exclusively charitable purposes then the charitable character of the trustee will not make the gift charitable.[371]

### ii. Provision of Benefit to the Community

6–233 In *Gilmour v Coats*,[372] which is reproduced below, the House of Lords held that a trust for a contemplative order of nuns who did not leave their cloisters nor allow the public into them was not charitable. The court does not have to accept as proved whatever a particular religion believes, and the benefits of the nuns' edifying example and their intercessory prayers were too vague and incapable of being proved to be of tangible benefit for the public. Similarly, in *Re Hetherington*[373] it was held that a trust for Masses for the repose of particular souls was charitable only by implicitly restricting it to Masses that had to be held in public.

---

364 *Hansard*, HL Vol.673, cols 136–152 (28 June 2005) and Vol.674, cols 292–298 (12 October 2005).

365 Decision of 17 November 1999, reproduced below at para.6–243.

366 [2014] A.C. 610. Note also that the Church of Scientology has achieved recognition as a religious charity in other jurisdictions, e.g. Australia: *Church of the New Faith v Commissioner of Pay-roll Tax* (1983) 154 C.L.R. 120.

367 *Hoare v Osborne* (1866) L.R. 1 Eq. 585; *Re Raine* [1956] Ch. 417.

368 *Re Vaughan* (1866) 33 Ch. D. 187 at 192; *Re Douglas* [1905] 1 Ch. 279.

369 *Lloyd v Lloyd* (1852) 2 Sim. (N.S.) 225; *Re Hooper* [1932] 1 Ch. 38; see Parish Councils and Burial Authorities (Miscellaneous Provisions) Act 1970 s.1 (a burial or local authority may contract to maintain a grave or memorial for not exceeding 99 years).

370 *Re Rumball* [1956] Ch. 105.

371 *Re Simson* [1946] Ch. 299 (gift to vicar "for his work in the parish" charitable); *Farley v Westminster Bank* [1939] A.C. 430 (gift to vicar "for parish work" not charitable) applying *Dunn v Byrne* [1912] A.C. 407.

372 [1949] A.C. 426.

373 [1990] Ch. 1 criticised by C. Rickett [1990] Conv. 34; further see *Nolan v Downes* (1917) 23 C.L.R. 546 and *Carrigan v Redwood* (1910) 30 N.Z.L.R. 244.

It cannot be said, however, that the courts and the Charity Commission have taken a very consistent line towards religious bodies which conduct their religious services in private. The foregoing cases can be contrated with *Neville Estates Ltd v Madden* where Cross J upheld as charitable a trust for the members from time to time of the Catford Jewish Synagogue although access to its services was restricted, because he felt "entitled to assume that some benefit accrues to the public from the attendance at places of worship of persons who live in this world and mix with their fellow citizens".[374] The Charity Commission has also registered as charitable both the Society of the Precious Blood[375] and the Preston Down Trust.[376] The first of these was an enclosed contemplative society of Anglican nuns, whose activities within their walls included holding services open to the public, providing religious and secular education of the public and relieving suffering, sickness, poverty and distress through their counselling service. The second is a trust for the advancement of the purposes of the Plymouth Brethren Christian Church, a body whose beliefs centre on the doctrine of separation from evil and whose practices include not only holding services for members only but also imposing physical separation between members and non-members in their daily lives. **6–234**

*Gilmour v Coats*

House of Lords [1949] A.C. 426

The income of a trust fund was to be applied to the purposes of a Carmelite convent, if those purposes were charitable. The convent was comprised of an association of strictly cloistered and purely contemplative nuns who were concerned with prayers and meditation, and who did not engage in any activities for the benefit of people outside the convent. In the view of the Roman Catholic Church, however, their prayers and meditation caused the intervention of God for the benefit of members of the public, and their life inside the convent provided an example of self-denial and concentration on religious matters which was beneficial to the public. At first instance and in the Court of Appeal it was held that the trust was not a charitable one, and the House of Lords dismissed an appeal from this conclusion. **6–235**

LORD SIMONDS (with whom LORD DU PARCQ, LORD NORMAND, LORD MORTON, and LORD REID agreed): I need not go back beyond the case of *Cocks v Manners*,[377] which was decided nearly eighty years ago by Wickens V.C. In that case the testatrix left her residuary estate between a number of religious institutions, one of them being the Dominican convent at Carisbrooke, a community not differing in any material respect from the community of nuns now under consideration. The learned judge used these words,[378] which I venture to repeat, though they have already been cited in the courts below: **6–236**

> "On the Act [the statute of Elizabeth] unaffected by authority I should certainly hold that the gift to the Dominican convent is neither within the letter nor the spirit of it; and no decision has been referred to which compels me to adopt a different conclusion. A voluntary association of women for the purpose of working out their own salvation by religious exercises and self-denial seems to me to have none of the requisites of a charitable institution, whether the word 'charitable' is used in its popular sense or in its legal sense. It is said, in some of the cases, that religious purposes are charitable, but that can only be true as to religious services tending directly or indirectly towards the instruction or the edification of the public; an annuity to an individual, so long as he spent his time in retirement and constant

---

374 [1962] Ch. 832 at 853. Clearly, the benefited class was small, and in *Dingle v Turner* [1972] A.C. 601 at 625 Lord Cross said, "A trust to promote some religion among the employees of a company might perhaps be held to be charitable, provided it was clear that the benefits were to be purely spiritual." *Re Warre's WT* [1953] 1 W.L.R. 725 (retreat house not charitable) is of dubious authority.

375 Charity Commission, *Annual Report* (1989), paras 56–62; Decisions, Vol.3, p.11.

376 Charity Commission, "Decision on Preston Down Trust's Application for Registration" (3 January 2014), *https://www.gov.uk/government/uploads/system/uploads/attachment_data/file/336112/preston_down_trust_full_decision.pdf* [Accessed 1 June 2015]. This was a controversial decision, not least because the Commission had reached the opposite conclusion only two years' previously.

377 (1871) L.R. 12 Eq. 574.

378 ibid. at 585.

devotion, would not be charitable, nor would a gift to ten persons, so long as they lived together in retirement and performed acts of devotion, be charitable. Therefore the gift to the Dominican convent is not, in my opinion, a gift on a charitable trust."

**6–237** Apart from what I have called the final argument, which I will deal with later, the contention of the appellant rests, not on any change in the lives of the members of such a community as this, nor, from a wider aspect, on the emergence of any new conception of the public good, but solely on the fact that for the first time certain evidence of the value of such lives to a wider public together with new arguments based on that evidence has been presented to the court. Never before, it was urged, has the benefit to be derived from intercessory prayer and from edification been brought to the attention of the court; if it had been, the decision in *Cocks v Manners* would, at least should, have been otherwise.

**6–238** My Lords, I would speak with all respect and reverence of those who spend their lives in cloistered piety, and in this House of Lords spiritual and temporal, which daily commences its proceedings with intercessory prayers, how can I deny that the Divine Being may in His Wisdom think fit to answer them? But, my Lords, whether I affirm or deny, whether I believe or disbelieve, what has that to do with the proof which the court demands that a particular purpose satisfies the test of benefit to the community? Here is something which is manifestly not susceptible of proof. But, then it is said, this is a matter not of proof but of belief, for the value of intercessory prayer is a tenet of the Catholic faith, therefore, and in such a prayer there is benefit to the community. But it is just at this "therefore" that I must pause. It is, no doubt, true that the advancement of religion is, generally speaking, one of the heads of charity, but it does not follow from this that the court must accept as proved whatever a particular church believes. The faithful must embrace their faith believing where they cannot prove: the court can act only on proof. A gift to two or ten or a hundred cloistered nuns in the belief that their prayers will benefit the world at large does not from that belief alone derive validity any more than does the belief of any other donor for any other purpose. The importance of this case leads me to state my opinion in my own words but, having read again the judgment of the learned Master of the Rolls, I will add that I am in full agreement with what he says on this part of the case.

**6–239** I turn to the second of the alleged elements of public benefit, edification by example, and I think that this argument can be dealt with very shortly. It is, in my opinion, sufficient to say that this is something too vague and intangible to satisfy the prescribed test. The test of public benefit has, I think, been developed in the last two centuries. Today it is beyond doubt that that element must be present. No court would be rash enough to attempt to define precisely or exhaustively what its content must be. But it would assume a burden which it could not discharge if now for the first time it admitted into the category of public benefit something so indirect, remote, imponderable and, I would add, controversial as the benefit which may be derived by others from the example of pious lives.

**6–240** I must now refer to certain cases on which the appellant relied. They consist of a number of cases in the Irish courts and *Re Caus*,[379] a decision of Luxmoore J. A consideration of the Irish cases shows that it has there been decided that a bequest for the saying of masses, whether in public or in private, is a good charitable bequest: see, e.g., *Att.-Gen. v Hall*[380] and *O'Hanlon v Logue*.[381] And in *Re Caus* Luxmoore J. came to the same conclusion. I would expressly reserve my opinion on the question whether these decisions should be sustained in this House. So important a matter should not be decided except on a direct consideration of it. It is possible that, particularly in regard to the celebration of masses in public, good reason may be found for supporting a gift for such an object as both a legal and a charitable purpose. But it follows from what I have said in the earlier part of this opinion that I am unable to accept the view, which at least in the Irish cases is clearly expressed, that in intercessory prayer and edification that public benefit which is the condition of legal charity is to be found. Of the decision of Luxmoore J. in *Re Caus*, I would only say that his ratio decidendi is expressly stated to be,[382] "first, that it (i.e., a gift for the saying of masses) enables a ritual act to be performed which is recognised by a large proportion of Christian people to be the central act of their religion, and, secondly, that it assists in the endowment of priests whose duty it is to perform the ritual act." The decision, therefore, does not assist the appellant's argument in the present case and I make no further comments on it.[383]

[379] [1934] Ch. 162.
[380] [1897] 2 I.R. 426.
[381] [1906] 1 I.R. 247.
[382] [1934] Ch. 162 at 170.
[383] See *Re Hetherington* [1990] Ch. 1 on *Re Caus*.

It remains, finally, to deal with the argument that the element of public benefit is supplied by the fact that qualification for admission to membership of the community is not limited to any group of persons but is open to any woman in the wide world who has the necessary vocation. Thus, it is said, just as the endowment of a scholarship open to public competition is a charity, so also a gift to enable any woman (or, presumably, any man) to enter a fuller religious life is a charity. To this argument, which, it must be admitted, has a speciously logical appearance, the first answer is that which I have indicated earlier in this opinion. There is no novelty in the idea that a community of nuns must, if it is to continue, from time to time obtain fresh recruits from the outside world. That is why a perpetuity is involved in a gift for the benefit of such a community, and it is not to be supposed that, to mention only three masters of this branch of the law, Wickens V.C., Lord Lindley or Lord Macnaghten failed to appreciate the point. Yet, by direct decision or by way of emphatic example, a community such as this is by them regarded as the very type of religious institution which is not charitable. I know of no consideration applicable to this case which would justify this House in unsettling a rule of law which has been established so long and by such high authority. But that is not the only, nor, indeed, the most cogent reason why I cannot accede to the appellant's argument. It is a trite saying that the law is life, not logic. But it is, I think, conspicuously true of the law of charity that it has been built up, not logically, but empirically. It would not, therefore, be surprising to find that, while in every category of legal charity some element of public benefit must be present, the court had not adopted the same measure in regard to different categories, but had accepted one standard in regard to those gifts which are alleged to be for the advancement of religion, and it may be yet another in regard to the relief of poverty. To argue by a method of syllogism or analogy from the category of education to that of religion ignores the historical process of the law. Nor would there be lack of justification for the divergence of treatment which is here assumed. For there is a legislative and political background peculiar to so-called religious trusts, which has, I think, influenced the development of the law in this matter.[384] **6–241**

*Appeal dismissed.* **6–242**

## Charity Commission, *Decision on Application for Registration of the Church of Scientology*, 17 December 1999

### The Legal Test of Public Benefit under the Third Head of Charity

The Commissioners noted that it is clear (from the dicta of Lord Greene M.R. in *Coats v Gilmour*) that the burden is upon the religious organisation in question to demonstrate both its impact upon the community and that the impact is beneficial, if public benefit is to be demonstrated. **6–243**

Some clear principles emerge from the decided cases: **6–244**

> A gift for the advancement of religion must be beneficial to the public (or a sufficient section of the public)[385] and not simply for the benefit of the adherents of the particular religion themselves.[386]
>
> It is settled law that the question whether a particular gift satisfies the requirement of public benefit must be determined by the court and the opinion of the donor or testator is irrelevant.[387]
>
> The court must decide whether or not there is a benefit to the community in the light of evidence of a kind cognisable by the court.[388]

The presence or absence of the necessary element of public benefit has also been considered in a number of cases. The essential distinguishing feature seems to be whether or not the practice of the religion is essentially public. The case *Re Hetherington decd.*[389] focused on the question of public benefit in relation to **6–245**

---

384 The Nathan Committee on Charitable Trusts rejected the suggestion of the representatives of the Roman Catholic Church that trusts for the advancement of religion should be defined to include "the advancement of religion by those means which that religion believes and teaches are means by which it does advance it": (1952) Cmnd. 8710, paras 129–130.

385 *National Anti-Vivisection Society v IRC* [1948] A.C. 31.

386 *Holmes v AG*, *The Times*, February 12, 1981.

387 *Re Hummeltenberg* [1923] 1 Ch. 237 and *National Anti-Vivisection Society v IRC* (above).

388 *Gilmour v Coats* [1949] A.C. 426.

389 [1990] Ch. 1.

religion. In that case the Judge summarised the principles established by the legal authorities. In concluding that a gift for the celebration of masses (assumed to be in public) was charitable he drew upon cases concerning a variety of religious practices and concluded as follows:

1. a trust for the advancement of education, the relief of poverty or the advancement of religion is charitable and assumed to be for the public benefit. The assumption can be rebutted by showing that in fact the particular trust in question cannot operate so as to confer a legally recognised benefit on the public—as in *Gilmour v Coats;*
2. the celebration of a religious rite in public does confer sufficient public benefit because of the edifying and improving effect of such celebration on the members of the public who attend; and
3. the celebration of a religious rite in private does not contain the necessary element of public benefit since any benefit of prayer or example is incapable of proof in the legal sense and any element of edification is limited to a private not public class of those present at the celebration. Following *Gilmour v Coats,*[390] *Yeap Cheah Neo v Ong Cheng Neo*[391] and *Hoare v Hoare*[392]; and
4. where there is a gift for a religious purpose which could be carried out in a way which is beneficial to the public, (i.e. by public masses) but could also be carried out in a way which would not have a sufficient element of public element (i.e. by private masses) the gift is to be construed as a gift to be carried out by methods that are charitable, all non charitable methods being excluded.

It is clear from *In re Hetherington decd*[393] and the cases cited there that it is the public nature of the religious practice which is essential to the gift being charitable.

6–246 The Commissioners concluded that the decided cases indicated that where the practice of the religion is essentially private or is limited to a private class of individuals not extending to the public generally, the element of public benefit will not be established.[394]

**The Legal Test of Public Benefit under the Fourth Head**

6–247 The Commissioners turned next to the legal test of public benefit under the fourth head of charity and considered the test to be that set out by Lord Wright in *National Anti-Vivisection Society v IRC.*[395] Lord Wright said that:

> "I think the whole tendency of the concept of charity in a legal sense under the fourth head is towards tangible and objective benefits, and at least, that approval by the common understanding of enlightened opinion for the time being, is necessary before an intangible benefit can be taken to constitute a sufficient benefit to the community to justify admission of the object into the fourth class."

6–248 It seemed to the Commissioners that the benefit that arises from the moral or spiritual welfare or improvement of the community is likely to be an intangible rather than a tangible one. The Commissioners considered the test in respect of an intangible benefit to mean a common consensus of opinion among people who were fair minded and free from prejudice or bias.

6–249 The Commissioners considered in particular whether the representations which it had received about Scientology generally and CoS [Church of Scientology] in particular, both favourable and unfavourable amounted to such "common understanding" and concluded that they did not. The representations were not easily substantiated and in effect represented opposing ends of the spectrum of opinion about CoS or Scientology generally.

6–250 The Commissioners further indicated that a key factor in assessing whether the test in that case was met (i.e. whether there was a common understanding of enlightened opinion that public benefit flowed from the advancement of Scientology by CoS), was the extent to which the core practices of Scientology were readily accessible by the public generally.

6–251 Accordingly, the Commissioners would need to consider whether there was approval by the common

---

390 [1949] A.C. 426.
391 (1875) L.R. 6 P.C. 381.
392 (1886) 56 L.T. 147.
393 [1990] Ch. 1.
394 *In re Hetherington decd* (above); *Coats v Gilmour* [1948] Ch. 340 at 347, per Lord Evershed.
395 [1948] A.C. 31 at 49.

understanding of enlightened opinion that pursuit of Scientology doctrines and practices is beneficial to the community such that CoS may be regarded as charitable under the fourth head.

**Consideration of CoS's Arguments as to Public Benefit under the Fourth Head of Charity**

The Commissioners noted CoS's arguments in this respect. One interpretation of CoS's legal arguments was to the effect that public benefit under the fourth head of charity does not have to be proved, but that it is only necessary to show that the organisation's activities may have that result. **6–252**

The Commissioners considered CoS's argument apparently based upon *Berry v St Marylebone Corporation*[396] concerning the Theosophical Society in England seeking relief from paying rates under section 8 of the Ratings and Valuation (Miscellaneous Provisions) Act 1955. The Commissioners noted that CoS appeared to rely on dicta of Romer L.J. in that case as support for the proposition that public benefit under the fourth head of charity need not be proven but should only be shown. **6–253**

The Commissioners did not accept this argument, as it was not clear to them that the case cited—*Berry v St Marylebone Corporation*—was authority for this proposition, rather it seemed to the Commissioners that it was authority for the proposition that it was necessary to show that the purpose (in that case the advancement of religion) may be likely to be advanced. This they had considered above. In any event the case related specifically to the requirements of section 8 of the Ratings and Valuation (Miscellaneous Provisions) Act 1955 and was not a discussion about charitable status such that the judge's comments were not directly applicable to charity law. **6–254**

In relation to the question of public benefit it seemed clear to the Commissioners from the dicta of Lord Wright in *National Anti-Vivisection Society v IRC* that public benefit must positively be shown under the fourth head of charity. Lord Wright's comments in that case that the whole tendency of the concept of charity under the fourth head is towards tangible and objective benefits, seemed to the Commissioners to indicate quite clearly that the benefits must be identifiable and demonstrable, and that a common consensus of approval is necessary before an intangible benefit can be regarded as sufficient to satisfy the requirement of public benefit. **6–255**

**Whether CoS is Established for the Public Benefit, whether under the Third or Fourth Heads of Charity**

The Commissioners next sought to address the question of whether CoS had shown itself to be established for the public benefit. The Commissioners considered the considerable volume of evidence supplied by CoS in support of its arguments that CoS was established for the public benefit whether under the third or fourth heads of charity because **6–256**

> "Individual churches of Scientology conduct numerous religious services freely accessible by members of the public.
>
> CoS sufficiently benefits the public through extensive charitable and public benefit programmes including anti drug campaigns, eradicating illiteracy, disaster relief and raising public morality.
>
> The Company (CoS) is limited by guarantee and its members make no profit.
>
> It is of the essence of Scientology "like most other religions" to seek to make itself available to all.
>
> Many of Mr Hubbard's teachings are already recognised as charitable and applied by existing registered charities.
>
> The Scientology movement engages in other activities which could potentially give rise to public benefit e.g. volunteer and relief programmes; rituals and practices such as "assists" (described as a form of healing); work in the field of criminal rehabilitation; observance of a moral code by individual Scientologists and promulgation of that moral code through the "Way to Happiness Foundation"."

The Commissioners considered that the evidence and arguments supplied by CoS may indicate ways in which Scientology organisations, and individual Scientologists, seek to benefit the wider community. They noted that in terms of English charity law some of that work may potentially be charitable in its own right, albeit not as promoting the moral or spiritual welfare or improvement of the community nor as advancing religion.[397] However, the Commissioners noted that the evidence and argument put to them by CoS **6–257**

---

[396] [1959] Ch. 406.

[397] Much Scientology activity appeared to the Commissioners to be in the fields of education and what might broadly be termed "relief in need".

did not address the central question of whether the advancement of Scientology (whether as a religion or as a non-religious belief system) confers recognisable benefit upon the public in English charity law. CoS states that its principal activities are auditing and training and that it is through these core activities that Scientology is advanced. In the Commissioners view it therefore had to be demonstrated that the advancement of Scientology through auditing and training is beneficial to the public. The Commissioners considered that it is to the central activities of auditing and training that the question of public benefit should be addressed.

6–258 The Commissioners went on to consider whether it was demonstrated that public benefit flowed from the core practices of Scientology. The Commissioners again noted that the test of public benefit was slightly different in relation to the third and fourth heads of charity. In relation to the third head the decided cases indicated that the public or private nature of the "religious practice" of the organisation in question was central to determining the presence or absence of public benefit. In relation to the purpose of promoting the moral or spiritual welfare or improvement of the community under the fourth head of charity the legal test was that set out by Lord Wright in the *National Vivisection Society v IRC* case.

6–259 *In relation to the test of public benefit for the advancement of religion the Commissioners concluded that:*

**(1) The Central "Religious" Practices of Scientology are Conducted in Private and not in Public**

6–260 The "religious practices" of Scientology are auditing and training. Scientologists regard these as worship. Auditing is conducted in private on a one to one basis. It appears akin to a form of counselling and is described by Scientologists as such.[398] Training is essentially a private activity requiring the study of specialist material and access to specialist trainers. Whilst members of the public may sign up for a course of auditing and training, generally upon payment of the appropriate requested donation, these activities are not carried out "in public". Further, progression beyond introductory or initial levels of auditing and training necessitated membership of the Church.

6–261 Attendance at a session of auditing or training by members of the public generally does not appear to be a possibility. The Commissioners found it difficult therefore to see how any edifying and improving effects upon the public generally might flow from the "religious" practices of Scientology.

6–262 In relation to the fourth proposition in *Re Hetherington decd*, there was no suggestion that auditing and training could be carried out in a way that was public rather than private. It did not seem possible to construe auditing and training as religious rites which could be conducted in public rather than in private such as to render them charitable.

**(2) Auditing and Training are in their Nature Private rather than Public Activities**

6–263 The Commissioners considered that even if a member of the public could attend an auditing and/or training session other than as a participant but rather as an observer, these Scientology services are by their very nature directed to the particular individual receiving them. Auditing appears akin to a form of counselling and is described by Scientologists who receive it as "counselling". It is directed to the private needs of the individual receiving it. The Commissioners found it difficult to see how the public could be edified or otherwise benefited by attending and observing at such a session.

6–264 Both the above factors—that Scientology services are conducted in private, and are in their nature private being directed to the needs of the private individual in receipt of them seemed to the Commissioners to indicate that these actual activities are of a private rather than a public kind. In any event it seemed to the Commissioners that any benefit to the public that may flow from auditing and training is incapable of proof, any edification or improving effect being limited to the private individual engaging in the auditing or training. Accordingly, the Commissioners concluded that these activities conferred no legally recognised benefit on the public.

6–265 In addition the Commissioners noted that the apparent dependence of participation in those activities upon payment of the requested donation referred to by CoS strengthened their perception that these activities were of a private rather than a public kind. Whilst CoS states that there are ways in which adherents can and do participate in auditing and training without making any form of monetary contribution, so that a lack of financial means is no bar to a member's progress in Scientology, access to auditing and

[398] Video presentation "The Church of Scientology at Saint Hill—A Special presentation to the Charity Commission of England and Wales".

training through requested donations is the norm. The Commissioners noted that the fact that a practice existed of requesting and making these payments strengthened the Commissioners in their perception that the activities were of a private rather than a public kind.

The Commissioners further noted that in its published and promotional literature, including the book "What is Scientology?", Scientology on balance presented its benefits in private rather than public terms. **6–266**

In addition the Commissioners noted that a not insignificant number of individual Scientologists described the benefits of Scientology in private and personal terms this being borne out both by a number of the statements printed in Scientology's published literature and by a significant proportion of the letters of support for CoS received from individual Scientologists. **6–267**

The fact that Scientology describes its benefits in private rather than public terms in its published and promotional literature, and that individual Scientologists described the benefits of Scientology to them in private and personal terms confirmed the Commissioners conclusion that CoS is not established for the public benefit. **6–268**

*In relation to the test of public benefit under the fourth head of charity law for the moral or spiritual welfare or improvement of the community the Commissioners concluded that:* **6–269**

The question of accessibility by the public was key to the existence of public benefit.

As indicated above, the Commissioners had already concluded that the central practices of Scientology (auditing and training) were conducted in private rather than in public, and were in their nature private rather than public activities. In addition there was the practice of requesting donations in advance of receipt of those services. This led the Commissioners to conclude that the restricted access to those practices meant that any benefit flowing from Scientology as advanced by CoS is of a private rather than a public kind. In addition the description of the benefits of Scientology, both in Scientology published and promotional literature and by individual Scientologists, as already acknowledged by the Commissioners, confirmed them in this conclusion.

The Commissioners concluded that it could not be said that CoS had demonstrated that it was established for the public benefit so as to satisfy the legal test of public benefit of a charitable purpose for the advancement of religion or for the moral or spiritual welfare or improvement of the community. **6–270**

## P.W. Edge and J.M. Loughey, "Religious Charities and the Juridification of the Charity Commission"

(2001) 21 L.S. 36, 47–51.

. . . [In *Gilmour v Coates*, the House of Lords] appear to have taken it as read that the courts have no jurisdiction to accept some spiritual benefits which are not proven by conventional means, and reject others, on the basis that some religious systems are true, and others are not.[399] Rather, they sought to deal with the different issue of whether the courts should treat all religions the same by accepting all spiritual benefits, or by rejecting all spiritual benefits. The House opted very firmly for rejecting all spiritual benefits.[400] This element of the decision seems inevitable in a legal system which no longer wishes to exercise a jurisdiction in spiritual truth, but which seeks only to support as charitable activities which benefit the public as a whole. It does, however, shift attention from first order benefits from religious practices (i.e. spiritual) to second order benefits from religious practices (i.e. civic, or leading to greater opportunities to gain first order benefits), even to the point where the courts will avoid debate about the efficacious or otherwise effects of particular spiritual purposes claimed to have an immediate, secular, effect.[401] This shift poses serious problems for the courts in deciding what evidence it should have regard to in determining whether these benefits exist.[402] . . . **6–271**

In the Scientology decision, the Commissioners stated that religious systems were both theistical,[403] **6–272**

399 A point made most clearly by Lord Reid [1949] A.C. 426 at 457.

400 See also *Re Joy* (1889) 60 L.T. 175; *Att.-Gen. v Delaney* (1876) Ir.R. 10 C.L. 104.

401 See *Re Le Cren Clarke (decd)* [1996] 1 All E.R. 715 at 723.

402 See J.C. Brady, "Public Benefit and Religious Trusts: Fact or Fiction" (1974) 25 N.I.L.Q. 174 at p.177.

403 *Decision on Application for Registration of the Church of Scientology*, 17 December 1999 (hereafter "*CoS*") at 21.

and involved an element of worship—drawing on *South Place Ethical Society*, it was not possible to worship an ethical or philosophical ideal with reverence.[404] These criteria do not, however, adequately justify all decisions taken by the Commissioners. For example, some branches of Buddhism are non-theistical, yet Buddhist trusts are registered as trusts for the advancement of religion. It is unclear what rationale underlies those decisions which appear to fall outside the criteria in the Scientology decision. It is probable that the Commissioners have taken a number of their decisions on the basis of extra-doctrinal factors.[405] Society is generally assumed to recognise Buddhism, and at least some polytheistic belief systems, as religions and the Commissioners have indicated that they will take account of public opinion and 'a common understanding of enlightened opinion' in determining what is charitable.[406] In ascertaining public opinion they refer to dictionaries, the decisions of other public bodies, and academic commentary.[407] Relying upon popular consensus as a factor in decision making, however, can result in the Commissioners having no coherent structures to draw upon in those hard cases where public opinion is divided. Additionally, the methods by which the Commissioners gauge public opinion, in particular how they separate enlightened and unenlightened opinion without prejudging the case, are subject to criticism. Anticipating these objections, the Commissioners have stated that they will not allow public opinion to be used as an obstacle to registration.[408] This only partly answers the criticisms, however, as an unpopular group may fail to be registered because of a strict application of the legal requirements, while a more popular group with identical deficiencies may be registered. For instance, the Commissioners have accepted Buddhist trusts despite the requirement of theism and worship in the definition of religion. Reliance upon unreasoned obiter dicta,[409] or perceived public opinion, does not indicate whether there should be other exceptions to these requirements.

**6–273** . . . The Scientology decision turned upon the concept of worship, which the Commissioners stated was an essential element of religion, and defined as conduct which indicated reverence or veneration for the supreme being and submission to the object worshipped.[410] They rejected defining worship as 'formal observation of the tenets of the belief system or canons of conduct giving effect to the belief in question'.[411] The central practices of auditing and training by the Church of Scientology did not include reverence or veneration of a supreme being and were not akin to acts of worship recognised by English case law. Consequently, despite a belief in a supreme being, Scientology was not a religion in English law.[412] There are a number of problems with this approach. First, as already indicated, the Commissioners are inconsistent in the application of these principles: it is unclear that worship in such a sense is always a feature of Buddhism. Secondly, as argued before the Commissioners, the requirement of and definition of worship is heavily reliant on Judaeo-Christian concepts.[413] Although the Commissioners indicated that this requirement was a clear and objective criterion,[414] they can be criticised for an inarticulate drawing upon the traditions of a subset of religious systems in order to formulate a requirement applicable to all. Thirdly, by shifting one way in which religion can be advanced to the definition of religion the Commissioners emphasised one type of religious practice over others without clearly indicating why worship is so paramount. . .

**6–274** The benefit derived from the advancement of religion has often been left unspecified, but has been described as edification and improving effects,[415] instruction of the public,[416] or moral uplift and spiritual

---

404 *CoS* at 24.

405 By which we mean factors beyond the application of the doctrinal legal rules of charity law; rather than factors beyond the content of the beliefs or fundamental values and rules of the belief systems.

406 Charity Commission, *Framework for the Review of the Register of Charities* (1998) (hereafter "Framework") Annex E 33, paras 3 and 4.

407 For an example of this approach, see *CoS* at 19.

408 Framework, Annex E, p 33, para 4.

409 *Re South Place Ethical Society* [1980] 3 All E.R. 918; *R v Registrar General, ex parte Segerdal* [1970] 2 Q.B. 697.

410 *CoS* at 15.

411 *CoS* at 24 citing from and rejecting *Fellowship of Humanity v County of Alameda* 153 Cal. App. 2d 673, 315 P. 2d 394 (1957) and *Church of the New Faith v Commissioner for Payroll Tax (Vic)* (1983) 49 A.L.R. 65 respectively.

412 *CoS* at 25.

413 See discussion at *CoS* at 22–23.

414 *CoS* at 24.

415 *Re Hetherington* [1990] 1 Ch. 1 at 12.

416 *Cocks v Manners* [1871] L.R. 12 Eq. 574 at 585.

comfort.[417] Charities have not been called upon to prove these benefits. Consequently, where the practices of a religion appear to have a detrimental effect, the Commissioners have no means of weighing a demonstrable public detriment against an unproven presumption of public benefit. This was demonstrated on the sole occasion upon which they attempted to address the issue. In 1974 the Commissioners established an enquiry into the practices of the Exclusive Brethren, and in particular the practice of the separation of evil.[418] The inquiry found this practice was inimical to the public interest and as such, a religion based on that doctrine could not be charitable. The Commissioners could, however

> "derive no help from any decided court cases to enable them to determine whether the consequences which have in some cases arisen from the practice of this doctrine are sufficient in themselves to negative the presumption of public benefit arising from the establishment of a trust for the advancement of religion."[419]

They therefore withheld registration of the trust pending a court's determination. When the matter came before the High Court, Walton J. found that a public benefit element was present because the Exclusive Brethren proselytised and allowed the public to attend their meetings, although he went on to state that, following *Thornton v Howe*, he was not concerned 'in any way to evaluate the precise amount of benefit'.[420] The Commissioners have shown a similar reluctance to make judgments as to the balance between beneficial and detrimental impact of religions whose charities are already registered,[421] although it seems likely that the Commissioners would take account of criminal activities on the basis that registration would sanction breaches of the law, rather than by balancing the disbenefit of the criminal activity against the presumed benefits. **6–275**

Although the Commissioners have proven unwilling to apply their law-making powers to the bare question of public benefit, they have substituted for most practical purposes a test of public interaction, avoiding the difficulties inherent in assessing public benefit. The issue of whether a group interacts with the public is susceptible of proof whether the public benefit from such interaction is less so. Applying this test, the Cornmissioners have recognised St Cuthbert's Retreat House for members of the clergy[422] and the Caldey Abbey community as benefiting the community and therefore charitable. In relation to the latter, a sufficient level of public benefit existed because the central act of worship of the community was held in public and had its effect on the public, the abbey church was open to the public at all times and, in addition, priests were sent out to serve in parishes on the mainland.[423] In relation to the former, the benefit lay in enabling ministers to better carry out their public ministry. Subsequently, the Commissioners determined that a trust in favour of the Church of Scientology was not for the advancement of religion because of the lack of public interaction. The Commissioners stated that the question which had to be answered was whether the advancement of Scientology benefited the public and consequently only those public practices of a religion which could be said to advance Scientology would be relevant to the question of public benefit. Relying on an apparent concession by the Church of Scientology that Scientology was advanced by the core practices of auditing and training they concluded that therefore it had to be shown that these activities were public and it was irrelevant that other practices were.[424] The Commissioners concluded, on the basis that these activities were by their nature private and charges were levied, that they did not.[425] It was insufficient that the practice of a religion took place in public unless the practice was one **6–276**

---

417 M. Chesterman, *Charities, Trusts and Social Welfare* (London: Weidenfield & Nicholson, 1979) p. 160.

418 [1974] Ch. Comm Rep., para. 81.

419 [1976] Ch. Comm. Rep, p. 36, para. 8 of Press Release.

420 *The Kingston Meeting Rooms Trust (Feltham); Holmes v Attorney General (The Exclusive Brethren)* (1981) Times, 12 February; [1981] Ch. Comm. Rep., paras 26–30.

421 [1981] Ch. Comm. Rep., paras 72–73: see *Orme v Associated Newspapers Group Ltd* (1982) Times, 20 December, C.A.; [1982] Ch. Comm. Rep., Appendix C; [1976] Ch. Comm. Rep., para. 108.

422 [1965] Ch. Comm. Rep. Appendix C, Part A, para. 16.

423 [1969] Ch. Comm. Rep., para. 19; although not referred to, this decision follows *Re Caus* [1934] Ch. 162.

424 *CoS* at 47; given that the Church of Scientology gave evidence that, inter alia, numerous religious services were carried out in public (*CoS* at 46) it seems highly unlikely that the Church intended to concede that only training and auditing advanced the practice of Scientology: nevertheless the Commissioners' finding can only be justified on this ground or alternatively upon the ground that the other public practices did not advance the religion, possibly upon the basis that they were not core practices of the religion. Such a distinction was not, however, expressed and would, it is submitted, be unprincipled.

425 *CoS* at 48 and 49.

> by which the religion advanced itself and it followed by implication that not all practices of a religion which took place in public could be said to advance that religion.[426]
>
> 6–277 This was an important innovation, which fits poorly with the decided cases. As well as discounting the beneficial effects of public religious ceremonies such as naming ceremonies and Sunday services which were carried out in public,[427] the Commissioners do not appear to have taken into account the case of *Neville v Madden*,[428] where the court assumed that public benefit arose where members of a religious order lived in the world and mixed with their fellow citizens.[429] Similarly, in relation to the Exclusive Brethren, outsiders were not permitted to attend the celebration of the Eucharist, presumably a core religious act of worship. They could however attend meetings and the Exclusive Brethren also occasionally proselytised. Taking these two factors together, Walton J. concluded that 'it was quite impossible' to conclude a lack of public benefit.[430]
>
> 6–278 This emphasis on the need for public interaction has the effect of shifting attention from the central activities of the religion, which may still confer a public benefit, to those activities which take place in public. . .

### *D. Section 3(1)(d): "The Advancement of Health or the Saving of Lives"*

**6–279** The Charities Act 2011 s.3(2)(b) states that for the purposes of s.3(1)(d) "the advancement of health" includes "the prevention or relief of sickness, disease or human suffering". This encompasses measures to ease the suffering, or to assist the recovery, of people who are sick, convalescent, disabled or infirm;[431] and a person may relevantly be "sick" if she suffers from a mental disorder or an addiction.[432] The advancement of health:

> includes conventional methods as well as complementary, alternative or holistic methods which are concerned with healing mind, body and spirit in the alleviation of symptoms and the cure of illness.[433]

However the Charity Commission also says that[434]:

> to be charitable there needs to be sufficient evidence of the efficacy of the method to be used. Assessing the efficacy of different therapies will depend upon what benefits are claimed for it (i.e. whether it is diagnostic, curative, therapeutic and/or palliative) and whether it is offered as a complement to conventional medicine or as an alternative. Each case is considered on its merits but the House of Lords Report on complementary and alternative medicine provides a useful guide.[435]

**6–280** Section 3(1)(d) takes in the provision of medical and nursing services, whether in the community,[436] or in hospitals, hospices, care homes, rest homes, etc.[437] It also includes the promotion of health by the

---

426 This follows from the discussion at *CoS* at 46 and 47.

427 *CoS* at 6.

428 [1962] 1 Ch. 832.

429 See also *Re Le Cren Clarke (decd)* [1996] 1 All E.R. 715.

430 [1981] Ch. Comm Rep., para. 27.

431 *Re Lewis* [1955] Ch. 104 (blind); *Motability* [1977] Ch. Com. Rep. paras [51]–[56] (physically disabled); *Sarah Mary Collard Fund for the Provision of Guide Dogs* [1983] Ch. Com. Rep. paras [57]–[58].

432 *Needham v Bowers* (1888) 21 Q.B.D. 436 ("institution for the reception of insane persons"); *Cawse v Committee of the Nottingham Lunatic Hospital* [1891] 1 Q.B. 585 ("lunatic hospital").

433 Charity Commission, *Commentary on the Descriptions of Charitable Purposes in the Charities Act 2006* (August 2009) para. [25]. See too *Re Le Cren Clarke* [1996] 1 All E.R. 715 (faith healing); Charity Commission, *Decision on the Application for Registration of NSFH Charitable Trust Ltd* (15 August 2002) (spiritual healing).

434 Charity Commission, *Commentary on the Descriptions of Charitable Purposes in the Charities Act 2006* (August 2009), para.[25].

435 *6th Report of the House of Lords Select Committee on Science and Technology, Session 1999–2000*.

436 *IRC v Peebleshire Nursing Assoc* 1927 S.C. 215; *Re Webster* [1912] 1 Ch. 106 (midwives).

437 *Biscoe v Jackson* (1887) 35 Ch. D. 460; *Re Weir Hospital* [1910] 2 Ch. 124; *Re Welsh Hospital (Netley) Fund* [1921] 1 Ch. 655;

provision of other services, items and facilities for patients,[438] the welfare of health professionals,[439] the education and training of health professionals,[440] and the organisation and regulation of their activities.[441] The pursuit of medical research also falls within the scope of s.3(1)(d),[442] as does the education of the public with regard to health and safety matters.[443] However these last few purposes also fall within s.3(1)(b), and the saving of lives by rescue services, which falls under this head,[444] also falls under s.3(1)(l).

In *Re Resch's WT*, Lord Wilberforce stated that a hospital may not be a charitable body if "the benefits it provides are not for the public, or a sufficiently large class of the public to satisfy the necessary tests of public character". However, he also considered that a private hospital which "provides only for persons of means who are capable of paying the substantial fees required as a condition of admission" does not necessarily fall foul of this rule, because "to provide, in response to public need, medical treatment otherwise inaccessible but in its nature expensive, without any profit motive, might well be charitable" albeit that "to limit admission to a nursing home to the rich would not be so".[445] **6–281**

This case was distinguished by the Charity Commission in its decision to refuse registration as a charity to Odstock Private Care Ltd.[446] The applicant company was formed, by means of a loan from an NHS foundation trust, to promote the undertaking of private patient work at the trust's district hospital. It did this by entering agreements with patients and insurance companies for the provision of private care, and then contracting with the trust to provide staffed facilities to enable this work to be carried out by clinicians. The company argued that its overall aim was to provide low-cost treatment to patients, using facilities which were available to the public at large and ploughing any surpluses back into additional NHS facilities at the hospital. However, the Commission took the view that the scheme was not available to the public at large, but only to those who could pay the fees, and so people living in poverty would not have access to its services. As the company did not provide financial assistance to patients on low incomes, they would need to fall back on insurance, but the cost of such insurance had not been shown to be affordable to all members of the community.[447] **6–282**

---

*Kytherian Association of Queensland v Sklavos* (1958) 101 C.L.R. 56; *Re Smith, (Deceased)* [1962] 1 W.L.R. 763; *Re Resch's WT* [1969] 1 A.C. 514.

438 *Attorney General v Belgrave Hospital* [1910] 1 Ch. 73; *Re Adams* [1968] Ch. 80; Charity Commission, *Annual Report for 1966*, p.32. By extension a gift to provide accommodation for relations coming to visit patients is also charitable: *Re Dean's WT* [1950] 1 All E.R. 882.

439 *Armagh County Infirmary Committee v Commissioner for Valuation for NI* [1940] N.I. 1 (house for visiting surgeon); *Re White's WT* [1951] 1 All E.R. 528 (rest home for nurses). See too *Re Pettit* [1988] 2 N.Z.L.R. 513 (relief of doctors' widows).

440 *Re Lysaght* [1966] 1 Ch. 191 (medical studentships); *London Hospital Medical College v IRC* [1976] 1 W.L.R. 613 (student union at medical school).

441 Including the promulgation and enforcement of professional standards: Charity Commission, *Decision on the Application for Registration as a Charity by the General Medical Council* (2 April 2001).

442 *Taylor v Taylor* (1910) 10 C.L.R. 218; *Re Osmund* [1944] Ch. 206; *National Trust Co v Canadian Diabetes Assoc* (1993) 109 D.L.R. (4th) 232.

443 *Re Hood* [1931] 1 Ch. 240 (temperance); *McGregor v Commissioner of Stamp Duties* [1942] N.Z.L.R. 164 (obstetrics and maternal welfare); *The League of Highway Safety and Safe Drivers Ltd* [1965] Ch. Com. Rep. 27 (road safety); *The Royal Association for Disability and Rehabilitation* [1977] Ch. Com. Rep. [57] (causes of disablement and the ways in which these may be reduced or eliminated); *Auckland Medical Aid Trust v CIR* [1979] 1 N.Z.L.R. 382 (human reproduction).

444 *Thomas v Howell* (1874) L.R. 18 Eq. 198 (lifeboat); *Re Wokingham Fire Brigade Trusts* [1951] Ch. 373 (fire brigade).

445 [1969] 1 A.C. 514 at 540–541.

446 25 September 2007.

447 For further discussion of private hospitals, see D. Morris, "Fee-Paying Hospitals and Charitable Status: A New Dawn or Lost Opportunities?" (2007) 18 K.L.J. 455.

### E. Section 3(1)(e): "The Advancement of Citizenship or Community Development"

**6–283** This head takes in a broad group of charitable purposes which are directed towards support for community and social infrastructure and whose focus is on the community rather than the individual. These include the promotion of urban and rural regeneration,[448] the promotion of community capacity building,[449] and the promotion of the voluntary sector.[450]

### F. Section 3(1)(f): "The Advancement of the Arts, Culture, Heritage, or Science"

**6–284** Charities concerned with the advancement of art and culture, such as museums[451] and art galleries,[452] must satisfy a criterion of educational or artistic merit.[453] The advancement of "heritage" takes in the preservation and conservation of historic land and buildings,[454] as well as the preservation of historical traditions by folk clubs, country dancing societies, eisteddfods, etc. The advancement of science includes scientific research projects and charities connected with learned societies and institutions, e.g. the Royal College of Surgeons[455] and the Royal Geographical Society.[456]

### G. Section 3(1)(g): "The Advancement of Amateur Sport"

**6–285** For many years, the promotion of sport was upheld as charitable only where it was ancillary to the pursuit of a charitable purpose.[457] Until 2003, however, the promotion of sport as such was not a charitable object.[458] The law was then changed by the Charity Commission's decision to recognise as charitable "the promotion of community participation in healthy recreation by providing facilities for playing particular sports".[459] In this context, "facilities" meant not just lands, building, and equipment, but also the organising of sporting activity such as that undertaken by community amateur sports clubs (CASCs). A CASC could therefore be a charity provided that: (1) the sport in question was capable of improving physical health and fitness; and (2) the club had an open membership, i.e. access to the club's facilities was genuinely available to anyone who wished to take advantage

---

448 Charity Commission, *RR 2: Promotion of Rural and Urban Regeneration* (March 1999 version). cf. *Re Tenant* [1996] 2 N.Z.L.R. 633 (provision of creamery).

449 Charity Commission, *RR 5: The Promotion of Community Capacity Building* (November 2000 version).

450 Charity Commission, *RR 13: Promotion of the Voluntary Sector for the Benefit of the Public* (September 2004 version). See too Charity Commission, *Decision on the Application for Registration of the Charity Bank Ltd* (17 April 2002); Charity Commission, *Decision on the Application for Registration of Guidestar UK* (7 March 2003); Charity Commission, *RR 14: Promoting the Efficiency and Effectiveness of Charities and the Effective Use of Charitable Resources for the Benefit of the Public* (September 2004 version).

451 *Trustees of the British Museum v White* (1826) 2 Sim. & St. 594; *Re Holburne* (1885) 53 L.T. 212.

452 *Abbott v Fraser* (1874) L.R. 6 P.C. 96.

453 Charity Commission, *RR 10: Museums and Art Galleries* (August 2002 version), paras 6–12 and Annex A. See too *Re Pinion* [1965] Ch. 85.

454 *Re Verrall* [1916] 1 Ch. 100 (National Trust); *Re Cranstoun* [1932] 1 Ch. 537 (Elizabethan cottages); *Settle & Carlisle Railway Trust* [1990] Ch. Com. Rep. 23–26 (railway line). See too Charity Commission, *RR 9: Preservation and Conservation* (February 2001 version).

455 *Royal College of Surgeons of England v National Provincial Bank Ltd* [1952] A.C. 631.

456 *Beaumont v Oliviera* (1869) L.R. 4 Ch. 309.

457 School sports: *Re Mariette* [1915] 2 Ch. 284; *IRC v McMullen* [1981] A.C. 1, reproduced at paras 6–194—6–209. University and medical school sports: *London Hospital Medical College v IRC* [1976] 2 All E.R. 113. See too *Attorney General v Ross* [1985] 3 All E.R. 334. Army sports: *Re Gray* [1925] Ch. 362 (but doubted in *IRC v City of Glasgow Police Athletic Assoc* [1953] A.C. 380 at 391 and 401).

458 *Re Nottage* [1885] 2 Ch. 649 (yacht racing); *Re Clifford* (1911) 106 L.T. 14 (angling); *Re Patten* [1929] 2 Ch. 276 (cricket); *Re Birchfield Harriers* [1989] Ch. Com. Rep. paras 48–52 (athletics).

459 Charity Commission, *RR 11: Charitable Status and Sport* (April 2003 version).

of them.[460] Some restrictions on club membership were tolerated, e.g. limited facilities and health of applicants,[461] but others were not, e.g. tests of skill for admission and membership subscriptions which are unaffordable for most of the community served by the club.[462]

In 2006 the law was changed again by the Charities Act 2006. The Government's intention was simply to codify the pre-existing law, but an amendment was agreed to the legislation during its passage through Parliament, with the result that s.3(2)(d) now provides that for the purposes of s.3(1)(g) "'sport' means sports or games which promote health by involving physical or mental skill or exertion". Hence it can now be a charitable purpose to undertake sport and games involving mental as well as physical skill or exertion—assuming that these activities "promote health". In a guidance document published in 2003, the Charity Commission stated that the following sports did not appear to meet its criteria for "healthy recreation": angling; ballooning; billiards, pool and snooker; crossbow shooting; rifle and pistol shooting; flying; gliding; motor sports; and parachuting.[463] It seems likely that the Commission will take a similar line when construing the Charities Act 2011 s.3(2)(d). This is borne out by its 2015 decision not to register the Cambridgeshire Target Shooting Association as a charity, because although the evidence supported the contention that target shooting involves "physical and mental skill or exertion" it did not support the contention that target shooting "promotes health".[464] This may be contrasted with its 2011 decision to register the Hitchin Bridge Club after accepting evidence that "playing bridge among seniors . . . lower[s] the risk of developing Alzheimer's disease and other dementia by as much as 75%".[465] **6–286**

## *H. Section 3(1)(h): "The Advancement of Human Rights, Conflict Resolution or Reconciliation or the Promotion of Religious or Racial Harmony or Equality and Diversity"*

The promotion of human rights can be accomplished in various ways including monitoring human rights abuses, obtaining redress for the victims of such abuses, and campaigning in favour of the recognition of human rights, to the extent that political activity of this kind is ancillary to the charity's main purposes.[466] The advancement of conflict resolution or reconciliation includes the resolution of international conflicts, the promotion of international co-operation,[467] and relieving the suffering and distress arising through conflict on a national and international scale. It also includes mediation and conciliation services,[468] and the promotion of restorative justice, where all the parties affected by a particular criminal offence come together to resolve collectively how to deal with its aftermath.[469] **6–287**

The appeasement of racial feelings between Dutch- and English-speaking South Africans was held **6–288**

---

460 *RR11* at para.7.
461 *RR11* at paras 16–17.
462 *RR11* at paras 18–19.
463 Charity Commission, *RR11: Charitable Status and Sport* (April 2003 version), para.11.
464 Charity Commission, *Decision on Application for Registration by Cambridgeshire Target Shooting Association*, 2 February 2015, paras 21–31.
465 Charity Commission, *Decision on Application for Registration by Hitchin Bridge Club*, 1 March 2011, para.19.
466 See further Charity Commission, *RR 12: The Promotion of Human Rights* (January 2005 version). For discussion of political activities, see para.6–118. And for a survey of charities working in this field, see Charity Commission, *RS 16: Charities Working in the Field of Human Rights* (December 2007 version).
467 cf. *Re Koeppler's WT* [1986] Ch. 423 (trust to fund conferences to promote co-operation in Europe charitable as for the advancement of education).
468 *Mediation in Divorce (Richmond-upon-Thames); The National Family Conciliation Council* [1983] Ch. Com. Rep. paras 28–34.
469 Charity Commission, *Decision on Application for Registration by Restorative Justice Consortium Ltd* (15 January 2003).

not to be a charitable purpose in *Re Strakosch*,[470] essentially because the court considered it to be a political purpose. Social attitudes subsequently underwent a considerable shift, however, and the enactment of the Race Relations Act 1968 indicated that Parliament considered the promotion of harmonious race relations to be for the public benefit. For this reason, the Charity Commissioners departed from *Re Strakosch* in 1983, when they stated that "promoting race relations, endeavouring to eliminate discrimination on grounds of race, and encouraging equality of opportunity" are charitable purposes.[471]

**6–289** The purposes of human rights organisations frequently have a strong political slant, and so the the question often arises whether they fall foul of the rule that political purposes cannot be charitable? This has been discussed above.[472]

### *I. Section 3(1)(i): "The Advancement of Environmental Protection or Improvement"*

**6–290** This head includes[473] the conservation of particular species of flora and fauna, of particular geographical areas,[474] and of the environment more generally,[475] along with the promotion of sustainable development and bio-diversity and the promotion of recycling and renewable energy resources.[476] Charities for the conservation of species or of particular land must produce independent expert evidence that the species or land in question are worthy of conservation.[477]

**6–291** In *Re Grove-Grady*,[478] the Court of Appeal struck down a trust to establish a sanctuary for wild birds and animals from which the public would be excluded, because the court could perceive no benefit to mankind in leaving the animals to their own devices in this way. However, ideas about environmental protection and the survival of endangered species have moved on. The Charity Commission's current approach to wildlife sanctuaries is to presume that they are not for the public benefit unless the public is given physical access to the site, but to take a flexible approach to the level of access needed, acknowledging that access "needs to be consistent with the aims of the charity so that visitors should not be allowed access at the expense of deterioration of a fragile . . . environment".[479] If an organisation can make out a case for limiting or excluding public access, it may still be able to satisfy the public benefit requirement, e.g. by allowing access to parts of the site, publishing books and videos about its activities, etc.[480]

---

470 [1949] Ch. 529.

471 [1983] Ch. Com. Rep. paras 15–20. See too *Community Security Trust* (1995) 4 Decisions of the Charity Commissioners 8. The promotion of gender equality is also a charitable purpose: *Halpin v Seear* Ch. D. 27 February 1976; *Women's Service Trust* [1977] Ch. Com. Rep. paras 34–36.

472 See paras 6–118ff.

473 For a survey of charities working in this field, see Charity Commission, *Going Green: Charities and Environmental Responsibility* (December 2008 version), Pt 5.

474 *The Upper Teesdale Defence Fund* [1969] Ch. Comm. Rep. paras 23–24 (fund for preservation of flora and fauna of Upper Teesdale).

475 Charity Commission, *Decision on the Application for Registration of Environment Foundation* (24 January 2003).

476 Charity Commission, *Decision on the Application for Registration of Recycling in Ottery* (April 2002).

477 Charity Commission, *RR 9: Preservation and Conservation* (February 2001 version), paras A10–A15.

478 [1929] 1 Ch. 557.

479 Charity Commission, *RR 9: Preservation and Conservation* (February 2001 version) para.A19.

480 *RR9* para.A20. cf. *Attorney General. for New South Wales v Sawtell* [1978] 2 N.S.W.L.R. 200.

## J. Section 3(1)(j): "The Relief of Those in Need by Reason of Youth, Age, Ill-health, Disability, Financial Hardship or other Disadvantage"

As previously noted,[481] "the relief of aged, impotent and poor people" was specified as charitable in the Preamble to the Statute of Charitable Uses 1601, but because these words are to be construed disjunctively,[482] the relief of those in need by reason of age,[483] and the relief of those in need by reason of ill-health or disability, are stand-alone charitable purposes—though they belong more obviously under s.3(1)(d). The Preamble also mentions "the education and preferment of orphans", and by analogy with this purpose, the promotion of the welfare of children generally is also a charitable purpose.[484] **6–292**

## K. Section 3(1)(k): "The Advancement of Animal Welfare"

Trusts for the protection or welfare of animals have been upheld as charitable provided that they benefit, or promote the moral improvement of, the community.[485] Note, however, that in *National Anti-Vivisection Society v IRC*,[486] the House of Lords held among other things that anti-vivisection is not a charitable purpose because the practical benefits to mankind of retaining vivisection outweighed the moral benefits of abolishing it. **6–293**

## L. Section 3(1)(l): "The Promotion of the Efficiency of the Armed Forces of the Crown, or of the Efficiency of the Police, Fire and Rescue Services or Ambulance Services"

This sub-section was introduced by amendment as the Charities Bill 2005 went through Parliament primarily in order to safeguard the charitable status of the 15,000-odd service funds whose purposes are (broadly speaking) to further *esprit de corps* in the armed services.[487] Typically these include funds for increasing the physical fitness of members of the services through the provision of sporting facilities, equipment, and sporting competitions; funds to support messes (NCOs and Officers) and institutes (other ranks), including the provision of plate, etc.; benevolent funds for serving members, ex-serving members, widows/widowers of serving or ex-serving members, and the dependents of serving or ex-serving members who are in need; and so on. **6–294**

## M. Section 3(1)(m): Other Purposes

Section 3(1)(m)(i) deems other purposes to be charitable which do not fall under any other head, but which either fall within s.5 or were recognised as charitable in the case law predating the **6–295**

---

[481] See para.6–152.

[482] *Re Robinson* [1951] Ch. 198; *Joseph Rowntree Memorial Trust Housing Assoc Ltd v Attorney General* [1983] Ch. 159.

[483] *Re Dunlop* [1984] N.I. 408 (home for elderly Presbyterians); *Joseph Rowntree Memorial Trust Housing Assoc Ltd v Attorney General* [1983] Ch. 159 (sheltered accommodation for the elderly). The Charities Act 2006 s.2(3)(e) specifies that "relief" of those in need under this head includes the provision of accommodation or care.

[484] *D v NSPCC* [1978] A.C. 171 at 228. See too *Re Sahal's WT* [1958] 1 W.L.R. 1243 (gift of house as children's home); Charity Commission, *Decision on the Application for Registration of the Internet Content Rating Association* (12 September 2002) (protection of children and young people from harm arising from contact with unsuitable material on the internet).

[485] *Re Wedgwood* [1915] 1 Ch. 113 (promotion of humane methods of slaughtering livestock); *Re Moss* [1949] 1 All E.R. 495 (welfare of cats and kittens); *Re Green's WT* [1985] 3 All E.R. 455 (rescue, maintenance, and benefit of cruelly treated animals).

[486] [1948] A.C. 31.

[487] *Hansard*, HL Vol.673, cols 131ff (28 June 2005).

coming into force of the Charities Act 2006. Purposes falling into the latter category include: the payment of rates and taxes[488]; the provision of public works and public amenities[489]; the promotion of agriculture,[490] and of industry and commerce,[491] provided that the public benefit outweighs any private benefits derived by those involved[492]; the relief of unemployment[493]; the promotion of moral or spiritual welfare[494]; the relief of refugees[495]; and the relief of victims of accidents and disasters.[496]

**6–296** Section 5 concerns the provision of facilities for recreation or other leisure-time occupation. At common law, trusts of land for public use as a recreation ground had long been charitable,[497] but doubts about the provision of recreational facilities were created by the House of Lords' decision in *IRC v Baddeley*.[498] This concerned a trust to promote the moral, social and physical well-being of Methodists resident in West Ham and Leyton by the provision of facilities for moral, social and physical training and recreation. The court held that this was not a charitable trust, first, because the intended beneficiaries did not comprise a sufficient section of the community for the trust to merit charitable status, and, secondly, because the promotion of social well-being was not a charitable purpose. This decision prompted fears that village halls and similar institutions which had previously been considered legally charitable might not be charitable after all, and so the Recreational Charities Act 1958 was enacted to remove any doubt on this point. The 1958 Act has now been replaced by the Charities Act 2011 s.5.

**6–297** The section provides that it is a charitable purpose to provide facilities in the interests of social welfare, and that two criteria must both be satisfied before this can be said. The first is constant: the object of providing the facilities must be to improve the intended beneficiaries' conditions of life; but the second may be satisfied in alternative ways—by showing either that the beneficiaries have need of the facilities by reason of the factors enumerated in s.5(3)(b)(i), or that the facilities are available to members of the public at large, or to either male or to female members of the public at large

---

488 Dating back to the Preamble which refers to the "aid or ease of any poor inhabitants concerning payment of fifteens, setting out of soldiers and other taxes." See, e.g. *Nightingale v Goulburn* (1848) 2 Ph. 594.

489 *Attorney General v Heelis* (1824) 2 Sim. & St. 67 (town lighting, paving, drains and sewers); *Attorney General v Shrewsbury Corp* (1843) 6 Beav. 220 (repair and improvement of town's bridges, towers and walls); *Scottish Burial Reform and Cremation Soc v Glasgow Corp* [1968] A.C. 138 (crematorium); *Oxford Ice-Skating Assoc Ltd* [1984] Ch. Com. Rep. paras 19–25 (ice-rink). Because the provision of amenities and services of this kind is nowadays frequently undertaken by public authorities, many trusts for their provision have been made the subject of schemes under the Charities Act 1993 s.13. See further *Charities for the Maintenance of Highways, Bridges, and Similar Works* [1968] Ch. Com. Rep. paras 66–72.

490 *IRC v Yorkshire Agricultural Soc* [1928] 1 K.B. 611.

491 *IRC v White* (1980) 55 T.C. 61 (improvement of standards of craftsmanship); *Business in the Community* [1987] Ch. Com. Rep. paras 16–19. Note that the regulation of a trade is not a charitable purpose: *Wine Standards Board of the Vintners' Company* [1978] Ch. Com. Rep. paras 95–98.

492 *IRC v Oldham Training and Enterprise Council* [1996] S.T.C. 1218.

493 *Oldham TEC* at 1234; Charity Commission, *RR 3: Charities for the Relief of Unemployment* (March 1999 version).

494 *Re South Place Ethical Society* [1980] 1 W.L.R. 1565; *Public Concern at Work* (1994) 2 Decisions of the Charity Commissioners 5 (assistance to employees faced with moral and ethical issues of whistle-blowing). But cf. Charity Commission, *Decision on the Gnostic Centre's Application for Registration as a Charity* (16 December 2009), paras 50–57: furtherance of the applicant body's non-religious philosophical beliefs was not charitable because it had no demonstrable impact on the community.

495 *Re Morison* (1967) 117 N.L.J. 757.

496 *Re Hartley Colliery Accident Relief Fund* (1908) 102 L.T. 165n.; *Re North Devon and Somerset Relief Fund Trusts* [1953] 1 W.L.R. 1260. Disaster funds are entitled to charitable status only if the help is given to those in need: Charity Commission, *CC 40: Disaster Appeals* (January 2002 version).

497 *Re Hadden* [1932] 1 Ch. 133 (park); *Re Morgan* [1955] 1 W.L.R. 738 (recreation ground); *Brisbane CC v Attorney General for Queensland* [1979] A.C. 411 (park); *Bath and North Eastern Somerset Council v Attorney General* (2002) 5 I.T.E.L.R. 274 (recreation ground).

498 [1955] A.C. 572. See too *Londonderry Presbyterian Church House Trustees v IRC* [1946] N.I. 178; *Williams Trustees v IRC* [1947] A.C. 447.

(see s.5(3)(b)(ii)). Organisations which might typically be expected to fall within the scope of these provisions include village halls, community centres and women's institutes.

## 6. The *Cy-près* Doctrine

Where a private trust is initially ineffective or subsequently fails there arises a resulting trust for the settlor (or her estate if she is dead).[499] Similarly, where a charitable trust is impossible or impracticable from the outset there is a resulting trust in favour of the settlor (or her estate if she is dead), unless she had a general charitable intention.[500] However, if she had a general charitable intention, the property will be applied *cy-près* under a scheme by the court or the Charity Commission.[501] This means that it will be applied to another charitable purpose which resembles the intended purpose as nearly as possible (the term "*cy-près*" derives from the French "*aussi près que possible*"). Likewise, where a settlor creates an initially effective charitable trust that later becomes impossible or impracticable the property will be applied *cy-près*—and in this case it does not matter whether the settlor had a general charitable intention, because the law holds that once property has been effectively dedicated to charity it must be applied to charitable purposes in perpetuity,[502] unless the settlor stated at the outset that in the event of subsequent failure the property should result to her estate.[503] **6–298**

There are two key questions in every case where a *cy-près* application of charitable funds is proposed. First, is it impossible to apply the funds to the purpose for which they were originally intended? Secondly, is the new purpose to which it is now proposed to apply the funds as close as possible to the original purpose? Over the past 150 years,[504] the courts and the Charity Commissioners have approached these two questions with varying degrees of strictness, according to the weight which they have accorded, on the one hand, to the consideration that the original intentions of donors should be respected, and, on the other hand, to their desire to apply charitable funds in accordance with current ideas about the desirability and effectiveness of different methods of welfare provision. **6–299**

Inevitably, their ideas about this have not been particularly consistent. For example, with regard to the first question, the courts and the Charity Commissioners have given different answers at different times to the question whether a scheme can legitimately be made to apply increased charity income to new purposes although increased expenditure on the trust's original purposes remains practicable.[505] And with regard to the second question, they have varied widely in their views on the "nearness" to the settlor's original purpose that a new purpose must achieve. For example, a strict approach to this question was taken in cases such as *Attorney General v Whiteley*,[506] where Lord Eldon held that a gift for "grammar school education" could not be used to fund tuition in languages other **6–300**

---

499 See paras 14–102ff.

500 An elaborate set of rules of construction are now used to determine whether a testatrix had a general charitable intention in cases where she has left money to an institution that has never existed or has ceased to exist between the writing of the will and the testatrix's death.

501 *Mayor of Lyons v Advocate-General of Bengal* (1876) 1 App. Cas. 91 at 112–114; *Biscoe v Jackson* (1887) 35 Ch. D. 460; *Re Rymer* [1895] 1 Ch. 19; *Re Stemson* [1970] Ch. 16.

502 *Attorney General v Mayor of Bristol* (1820) 2 J. & W. 295; *Attorney General v Earl of Craven* (1856) 21 Beav. 292; *Re Slevin* [1891] 2 Ch. 236.

503 *Re Randell* (1888) 38 Ch. D. 213, following *Walsh v Secretary of State for India* (1863) 10 H.L.C. 367.

504 The Charity Commissioners first acquired a concurrent jurisdiction with the court to make schemes under the Charitable Trusts Act 1860.

505 *Attorney General v Boultbee* (1794) 2 Ves. Jun. 380 at 387–388; *Attorney General v Rochester Corp.* (1854) 5 De G. M. & G. 797 at 813; *Re Campden Charities*. (1881) 18 Ch. D. 310; *Twenty-eighth Report of the Charity Commissioners for England and Wales*, PP 1881 (HC No 2862), pp.9–10; *Re Weir Hospital* [1910] 2 Ch. 124 at 131.

506 (1805) 11 Ves. Jun. 241.

than Latin and Greek; *Attorney General v Wansay*,[507] where a fund to buy apprenticeships for poor Presbyterian boys could not be used to benefit poor boys of other religions; *Re Prison Charities*,[508] where a gift for poor prisoners could not be applied to found a school for prisoners' children; and *Re Bridewell Hospital*,[509] where income from a trust for the reformation of vagrants by compulsory labour could not be used to relieve the destitute unless they were required to work. Yet in *Attorney General v Ironmongers' Co*,[510] a gift for the redemption of English captives in Barbary was applied to educational purposes in England, despite Lord Campbell's pithy observation that "if education in England be next to redemption of slaves in Barbary, it is next at a great interval"[511]; in *Re Ashton's Charity*[512] a gift for almswomen was used to found a school; and in *Re Campden Charities*,[513] a dole fund was used for a variety of educational purposes.

6–301 The Charities Act 2011 ss.62 and 67 now give the courts and the Charity Commission a broad discretion when approaching each question, authorising them to take into account both the "spirit of the gift" concerned and the "the social and economic circumstances prevailing at the time of the proposed alteration of the original purposes". These sections are excerpted below, along with a Charity Commission Operational Guidance document in which the meaning of the two sections is expounded. In practice, most schemes are now made by the Charity Commission, and even in cases where the court directs a scheme to be made it will often ask the Commission to draft the scheme, under the Charities Act 2011 s.69(3).

## Charities Act 2011 ss. 62 and 67

### 62 Occasions for applying property cy-près

6–302 (1) Subject to subsection (3), the circumstances in which the original purposes of a charitable gift can be altered to allow the property given or part of it to be applied cy-près are—

(a) where the original purposes, in whole or in part—

(i) have been as far as may be fulfilled, or
(ii) cannot be carried out, or not according to the directions given and to the spirit of the gift,

(b) where the original purposes provide a use for part only of the property available by virtue of the gift,
(c) where—
(i) the property available by virtue of the gift, and
(ii) other property applicable for similar purposes,can be more effectively used in conjunction, and to that end can suitably, regard being had to the appropriate considerations, be made applicable to common purposes,

(d) where the original purposes were laid down by reference to—

(i) an area which then was but has since ceased to be a unit for some other purpose, or
(ii) a class of persons or an area which has for any reason since ceased to be suitable,

---

507 (1808) 15 Ves. Jun. 231.
508 (1873) L.R. 16 Eq. 129.
509 (1860) 8 W.R. 718; also reported at (1860) 30 L.J. (N.S.) Ch. 99.
510 (1844) 10 Cl. & F. 908. Money from this large trust was applied to educational purposes in 700 parishes around the country: *Report from the Select Committee on Charitable Trusts Acts*, PP 1884 (HC No 306) 23 (Q 311, Henry Longley).
511 ibid., at 925.
512 (1859) 27 Beav. 115.
513 (1881) 18 Ch. D. 310.

regard being had to the appropriate considerations, or to be practical in administering the gift, or

(e) where the original purposes, in whole or in part, have, since they were laid down—

(i) been adequately provided for by other means,
(ii) ceased, as being useless or harmful to the community or for other reasons, to be in law charitable, or
(iii) ceased in any other way to provide a suitable and effective method of using the property available by virtue of the gift, regard being had to the appropriate considerations.

(2 In subsection (1) "the appropriate considerations" means—

(a) (on the one hand) the spirit of the gift concerned, and
(b) (on the other) the social and economic circumstances prevailing at the time of the proposed alteration of the original purposes.

**67 Cy-près schemes**

(1) The power of the court or the Commission to make schemes for the application of property cy-près must be exercised in accordance with this section. **6–303**

(2) Where any property given for charitable purposes is applicable cy-près, the court or the Commission may make a scheme providing for the property to be applied—

(a) for such charitable purposes, and
(b) (if the scheme provides for the property to be transferred to another charity) by or on trust for such other charity, as it considers appropriate, having regard to the matters set out in subsection (3).

(3) The matters are—

(a) the spirit of the original gift,
(b) the desirability of securing that the property is applied for charitable purposes which are close to the original purposes, and
(c) the need for the relevant charity to have purposes which are suitable and effective in the light of current social and economic circumstances. The "relevant charity" means the charity by or on behalf of which the property is to be applied under the scheme.

(4) If a scheme provides for the property to be transferred to another charity, the scheme may impose on the charity trustees of that charity a duty to secure that the property is applied for purposes which are, so far as is reasonably practicable, similar in character to the original purposes. . .

## Charity Commission, *Operational Guidance OG2: Application of Property Cy-près* (14 March 2012)

**1. Circumstances for cy-près**

*1.1 The legal framework*

Section 62(1) of the 2011 Act sets out the circumstances in which the purposes of a charitable gift can be altered so that it may be applied cy-près. . . **6–304**

. . . The "spirit of the gift" in the context of s.62 means the basic intention underlying the original gift as a whole: *Re Lepton's Charity* [1972] Ch 276. The intention may be clear from the terms of the governing document of the charity: if not, records available at the time the charity was established, or even the way in which the charity has been administered and managed over the years, may be relevant. **6–305**

The meaning of "social and economic circumstances prevailing at the time of the proposed alteration" is not defined, but is about evaluating the ongoing usefulness of the charity's trusts. This provision enables the Commission to consider other relevant factors alongside the spirit of the original gift in deciding whether a cy-près occasion has arisen, placing equal emphasis on the wording of the original purposes and the needs and circumstances of current beneficiaries. It is clear from the Parliamentary debates on the **6–306**

Charities Bill that the phrase "social and economic circumstances" is intended to be interpreted broadly, and to encompass all relevant circumstances that the trustees or the Commission might need to take into account when deciding how or whether the purposes of the charity should be altered. Other authorities have suggested that this could therefore include environmental, legal, scientific or technological considerations.

6–307 We might take into account, for example, the following:

- In some cases the provision of specific articles such as food or fuel may no longer be the most practical means of relieving financial hardship or other forms of disadvantage.
- Provision of care for people with disabilities is now generally based around enabling them to live in their own homes rather than housing them in institutions.
- In some cases the social or economic circumstances that led to the setting up of a charity (e.g. to provide education or housing) for members of one sex only may have changed over time.
- The objects of some charities may imply outdated social or moral judgements about potential beneficiaries, such as 'deserving poor' (historically, poor people who could work but didn't were officially classed as 'idle' and therefore undeserving). These may unnecessarily restrict the beneficiary class. Some objects contain language that could now be offensive or off-putting to potential beneficiaries or donors, such as 'crippled', 'handicapped', 'invalid' or 'insane'. . .

*1.2 Failure of objects not always required*

6–308 As explained above, a cy-près occasion would arise under section 62(1)(a) if the charity's purposes failed. The term 'failure' has often been used as convenient shorthand to refer to any of the circumstances set out in section 62(1). However, it is important to note that the circumstances which permit a cy-près application of a charity's property are not restricted to 'failure' and therefore the trustees do not necessarily have to demonstrate that the charity's purposes are incapable of being carried out or wholly impracticable, particularly when current social and economic circumstances are also taken into account.

6–309 In some cases a cy-près application may be justified under the other provisions of section 62(1), even though the purposes of the charity can still be carried out. For example, we can make cy-pres Schemes without the current objects 'failing' under:

- s.62(1)(b), where a charity's objects may be completely workable but do not provide a use for all of the available income or property;
- s.62(1)(c), where a charity is proposing to amalgamate with another charity with similar objects; the question of 'failure' is irrelevant; or
- s.62(1)(e), which may allow a charity to make a case that the purposes have ceased in any way to be a suitable and effective method of using the charity's property (bearing in mind the spirit of the gift and current social and economic circumstances).

6–310 For example, an almshouse charity for 'poor persons with a preference for a poor gentlefolk couple' could merge with another almshouse charity in the same geographical area whose beneficiaries are 'poor persons who (except in special cases to be approved by the Commission) have been resident in the area of benefit for not less than five years'. In this example, the trustees of both charities were the same, and in practice, administered together. The aim of the merger was to provide greater efficiency and effectiveness in the administration of the charities. Although the first charity does not specify an area of benefit, the objects are sufficiently similar for a merger under s.62(1)(c). In practice the area of benefit for the first charity would be similar to the second charity. In this example, the merged charity's beneficiaries were amended to 'poor persons in particular, but not limited to, those resident in the area of benefit'. . .

**3. Application of cy-près doctrine**

*3.1 The legal framework*

6–311 Section 67 of the 2011 Act sets out how the Commission's and the court's power to make schemes to apply charity property cy-près is to be exercised. . .

*3.2 Our policy*

6–312 We should be flexible and imaginative in applying the cy-près doctrine, balancing usefulness and practicality with respect for the existing purposes and beneficiaries. The purpose of making a cy-près Scheme is to enable a charity to continue being effective, useful and relevant to its beneficiaries' needs in modern society, where without our intervention it would not be. We should, however, exercise caution where a proposed change might be a significant departure from the founder's intentions or might exclude existing beneficiaries (unless, for example, the problem is that the existing beneficial class has ceased to exist). We should always take account of the trustees' views when deciding how to amend a charity's objects.

Section 67(3) directs us to take account of three factors. Generally we should give equal weight to these factors, but there may be circumstances where it is reasonable to emphasise one factor over the other two. For example, if a charity for the relief of poverty operates in an area where poverty is no longer an issue, it would be reasonable to focus almost entirely on finding purposes that are relevant to the current issues in the area of benefit. If on the other hand there is evidence that the values of the founder and of all those associated with the charity mean that the spirit of the gift is important to the future existence of the charity, we should consider how we can ensure that the new objects continue to reflect those factors. **6–313**

Careful thought should be given to identifying the spirit of the original gift. Understanding the real purpose of the charity should give us greater flexibility. It would be reasonable to assume that the founder(s) of the charity would be more concerned about who they wanted to benefit, and the kind of charitable benefit provided (e.g. relief of poverty, education generally or in a particular subject, religious belief, recreational or community facilities) than any specific method of delivering that benefit. **6–314**

We have applied the following principles in making cy-près Schemes since at least 1989 when they were published in the Commission's annual report, and they are still relevant. The changes introduced by the Charities Act 2006 and carried forward into the 2011 Act, give us even greater flexibility: **6–315**

Descriptions or classifications of charitable purposes should not be treated as rigid or mutually exclusive. This was particularly important before the 2006 Act, when charities were classified within four 'heads' (the Macnaghten classification), but the principle should still be upheld. There is considerable scope for overlap between many of the 13 descriptions of charitable purposes in the Charities Act 2011 and it is acceptable to include new objects which bring in additional purposes as defined within the Act. For example, we could agree new objects for a charity for the relief of poverty that deal with related issues, for example, prevention of poverty, advancement of education, advancement of health or community development (including regeneration). Alternatively, if the charity's income is more than sufficient to relieve poverty in the area we could provide an additional object for surplus income to be applicable for any charitable purpose. The key consideration is to find new objects that serve existing beneficiaries in an up-to-date and appropriate way and which enable the charity to use any surplus funds effectively having regard to the spirit of the gift and current social and economic circumstances. **6–316**

Legal points should be balanced by practical considerations. For example, in the case of a proposed merger, the purposes of the merging charities are required to be similar, not identical. Or taking too narrow a view of what is similar to existing purposes may limit a charity's future usefulness. This principle is all the more important when considering the social utility of new purposes; we should consider carefully the views of the trustees as to what will be useful to beneficiaries and allow the charity to be effective in view of current social and economic circumstances. **6–317**

Care should be taken not to place undue emphasis on one part of a charity's trusts over another. Where the beneficiaries of a charity are defined by reference to a number of elements (for example poor women resident in a particular locality) care should be taken not to give greater emphasis to one element than another without good reason for doing so. (For example, the charity's foundation or governing document might indicate whether any element is particularly important.) **6–318**

In some circumstances it may be acceptable to exclude part of a charity's existing purposes. For example, a merger of charities should not be discounted because part of the area of benefit or beneficiary group of one charity would be lost as a result. **6–319**

No part of a charity's trusts is unalterable. There is no point in trying to preserve a particular aspect of a charity's trusts if the new purposes would not, as a result, be suitable and effective in the light of current social and economic circumstances. **6–320**

**Questions**

1. "Because of the tax exemptions enjoyed by registered charities, decisions on charitable status entail decisions on resource allocation by the State. So they should be taken by a democratically elected body, with reference to Government policy on public resource allocation." **Discuss.**

2. "The courts and the Charity Commission have yet to produce a compelling reason why trusts of a political nature must fail. So long as it is otherwise exclusively charitable, and the appropriate public benefit test is satisfied, a trust for a political purpose should be upheld." **Discuss.**

3. "The Charity Commission cannot make new law, and can only state and apply existing law, when deciding whether to register voluntary bodies as charities, when issuing guidance to charities on the public benefit requirement, and when assessing registered charities to determine whether their activities are for the public benefit." **Discuss.**

4. Sam Smith is a rich industrialist who owns a majority shareholding in a large private company, Taurus Ltd. The company employs approximately one thousand people manufacturing widgets at an industrial plant in Manchester. Sam dies, leaving a valid will under which his residuary estate goes to his son Ben, and in which he also makes gifts, each of £500,000, to trustees to invest and apply the income therefrom to each of the following purposes:

   (a) to relieve poverty in Manchester, provided that past and present employees of Taurus Ltd and their relatives and dependents shall have priority over others when the money is applied;
   (b) to bring the residents of Manchester to a better understanding of the desirability of unilateral nuclear disarmament in the UK;
   (c) to arrange the legal adoption of children in Manchester by heterosexual couples who will bring them up in the Roman Catholic faith; and
   (d) to venerate the memory of Elvis Presley, who is not a deity, but a better appreciation of whose music will help us all to find our 'inner centres' and live in better harmony with one another.

   **Advise Ben as to the validity of these bequests.**

# PART III

# VARIATION AND TERMINATION OF EXPRESS TRUSTS

# 7

# VARIATION AND TERMINATION OF EXPRESS TRUSTS

## 1. Introduction

Obviously trusts come to an end when the trustees distribute all of the trust property to the beneficiaries. Settlors can also reserve powers of revocation, appointment and amendment of the trust to themselves, or confer such powers on others, and the effect of exercising such powers can be to vary or terminate the trust. Various legal rules can also affect the variation and termination of trusts: the rule in *Saunders v Vautier*[1] provides that in some circumstances the absolutely entitled sui juris beneficiaries of a trust can demand a transfer of legal title to the trust property; the courts have a limited equitable jurisdiction to vary trusts, and statutory powers of variation under the Variation of Trusts Act 1958; and the perpetuities legislation can bring some trusts to an end once a fixed period of time has elapsed. **7–001**

## 2. Powers of Revocation, Appointment and Amendment

The settlor of a trust has no power to revoke the trust after it has been completely constituted unless she expressly reserves such a power to herself.[2] In the UK a settlor would be very unlikely to do this as she would then be treated for tax purposes as having retained an interest in the property so that she would be liable for tax on capital gains and income generated within the settlement.[3] Moreover, if the effect of the trust were to give her control of the property during her lifetime but to cause beneficial enjoyment of the property to pass to others on her death, it is likely that the court would find it to be a testamentary disposition with the result that it would be void if it failed to comply with the attestation rules.[4] **7–002**

A settlor may also confer a power of revocation on the trustees (or others), and it is common practice **7–003**

---

1 (1841) 4 Beav. 115.

2 For general discussion of the reservation of powers by settlors, see W.D. Goodman QC, "Retention of Powers by Settlor" in J. Glasson (ed.), *The International Trust* (Jordan Publishing Ltd, 2002); G. Thomas, "Shams, Revocable Trusts and Retention of Control" in J. Glasson and G. Thomas (eds), *The International Trust*, 2nd edn (Jordan Publishing Ltd, 2006), pp.606–614.

3 The position is different in many offshore jurisdictions and in the US: C. McKenzie, "Having and Eating the Cake: A Global Survey of Settlor Reserved Power Trusts" [2007] P.C.B. 336, 428.

4 Following Sir John Wilde's statement in *Cocke v Cooke* (1866) L.R. 1 P.D. 241 at 243 that "whatever may be the form of a duly executed instrument, if the person executing it intends that it shall not take effect until after his death, and it is dependent on his death for its full vigour and effect, it is testamentary". But note that in the US courts have accepted that such devices are not testamentary and they are widely used to avoid cumbersome and expensive probate processes: J. Langbein, "The Nonprobate Revolution and the Future of the Law of Succession" (1984) 97 Harvard L.R. 1108; A. Newman, "Revocable Trusts and the Law of Wills: An Imperfect Fit" (2008) 43 Real Property, Trust and Estate Law Journal 523.

to give them such a power along with an overriding power of appointment,[5] since the latter power cannot effectively be exercised without first exercising of a power of revocation.[6] Trustees may also be given an overriding power of advancement,[7] the exercise of which may also be to vary, or even terminate, the interests under the settlement, and the same result may also follow if the trustees (e.g. of a pension trust or an insurance premiums trust deed) exercise an overriding power of amendment of the trust. However powers of the latter sort are confined to such amendments as can reasonably be considered to have been within the contemplation of the parties,[8] and where such powers are given to trustees they must avoid exercising them in a way that would prioritise the trustees' interests over the beneficiaries' interests.[9]

## 3. The Rule in *Saunders v Vautier*

**7-004** *Saunders v Vautier*,[10] reproduced below, holds that if a beneficiary of full capacity has a vested, and not a contingent, interest in the trust property,[11] then she can call for a transfer of legal title from the trustees, irrespective of any material purpose that the settlor might have had in mind. As a matter of property law an absolutely entitled beneficiary can do whatever she wants with the property, and any restriction on her enjoyment is inconsistent with the absolute nature of her interest.[12] The settlor cannot oust this principle, even by express declaration.[13] Hence beneficiaries who are entitled in succession (e.g. a life tenant and remainderman) may combine to call for a transfer, provided that they are of full capacity and are collectively entitled absolutely.[14] "This is a matter of present entitlement, and does not depend on any exercise of any dispositive power of appointment or advancement by the trustees."[15] Likewise, if all the beneficiaries of a discretionary trust are of full capacity and are entitled absolutely to the property between them, then they too may call for a transfer, provided that they act together.[16] Indeed, the rule in *Saunders v Vautier* applies even where there are nothing more than powers of appointment with a gift over in default of appointment.[17]

---

5 As in, e.g. *Abacus Trust Co (Isle of Man) Ltd v Barr* [2003] Ch. 409; *Stow v Stow* [2008] Ch. 461; *Howell v Lees-Millais* [2009] W.T.L.R. 1163. See too *Barclays Bank Ltd v Quistclose Investments Ltd* [1970] A.C. 567, as interpreted in *Twinsectra Ltd v Yardley* [2002] A.C. 164: where money is lent for a specific purpose, it may be held on trust for the lender, subject to a power vested in the borrower to apply the money to the agreed purpose, full or partial exercise of which will defeat the lender's beneficial interest under the trust. This is discussed at paras 5-033ff.

6 *Re Thursby's Settlement* (1855) 6 De G.M. & G. 654 at 671; *Saunders v Evans* (1861) 8 H.L.C. 721 at 739.

7 As in, e.g. *Re Hancock* [1896] 2 Ch. 173; *Pilkington v IRC* [1966] A.C. 612.

8 *Hole v Garnsey* [1930] A.C. 472 at 500; *Lord Napier and Ettrick v R.F. Kershaw Ltd (No.2)* [1999] 1 W.L.R. 756 at 767–778.

9 *Hillsdown Holdings Plc v Pensions Ombudsman* [1997] 1 All E.R. 862; *Urenco UK Ltd v Urenco UK Pension Trustee Co Ltd* [2012] Pens. L.R. 307 at [45].

10 (1841) 4 Beav. 115, affirmed (1841) 1 Cr. & Ph. 240. The principle articulated in the case was not new; previous decisions to the same effect included: *Lord Pawlet's case* (1685) 2 Vent. 366; *Love v L'Estrange* (1727) 5 Bro. P.C. 59; *Barnes v Rowley* (1797) 3 Ves. Jun. 305; *Barton v Briscoe* (1822) Jac. 603; *Dawson v Hearn* (1831) 1 Russ. & My. 606.

11 For the principles of construction which determine whether a beneficiary has a vested or contingent interest, see *Harrison v Tucker* [2003] W.T.L.R. 883.

12 *Weatherall v Thornburgh* (1878) 5 Ch.D. 261 at 270 per Cotton LJ.

13 *Stokes v Cheek* (1860) 28 Beav. 620.

14 *Barton v Briscoe* (1822) Jac. 603; *Haynes v Haynes* (1866) 35 L.J. Ch. 303; *Re Millner* (1872) L.R. 14 Eq. 245; *Anson v Potter* (1879) 13 Ch.D. 141; *Re Bowes* [1896] 1 Ch. 507; *Re White* [1901] 1 Ch. 570.

15 *Hughes v Bourne* [2012] W.T.L.R. 1333 at [34] per Henderson J.

16 *Re Nelson* [1928] Ch. 920n.; *Re Smith* [1928] Ch. 915; *Sir Moses Montefiore Jewish Home v Howell & Co (No.7) Pty Ltd* [1984] 2 N.S.W.L.R. 406 at 410.

17 *Schmidt v Rosewood Trust* [2003] 2 A.C. 709 at [41].

*Saunders v Vautier*

Master of the Rolls (1841) 4 Beav. 115

A testator bequeathed his stock on trust to accumulate the dividends until V should attain the age of twenty-five, and then to transfer the principal, together with the accumulated dividends, to V. V, having attained twenty-one, claimed to have the fund transferred to him. It was contended for him that he had "a vested interest, and that as the accumulation and postponement of payment was for his benefit alone, he might waive it and call for an immediate transfer of the fund." **7–005**

LORD LANGDALE M.R.: I think that principle has been repeatedly acted upon; and where a legacy is directed to accumulate for a certain period, or where the payment is postponed the legatee, if he has an absolute indefeasible interest in the legacy, is not bound to wait until the expiration of that period, but may require payment the moment he is competent to give a valid discharge. **7–006**

On a question raised, with reference to a previous order for maintenance, as to whether there was a vested interest in V before he attained twenty-five, the petition stood over, with liberty to apply to the Lord Chancellor. Held, by the Lord Chancellor, the fund was intended wholly for the benefit of V, although the enjoyment of it was postponed: it vested Immediately, and he could now claim the transfer. **7–007**

*Stephenson v Barclays Bank Ltd,*[18] reproduced below, further establishes that if several beneficiaries are together absolutely entitled as co-owners of the trust property, the rule in *Saunders v Vautier* applies to each beneficiary separately, provided that his share can be severed from the trust fund without harm to the remainder.[19] The rule also applies to severable parts of, or interests in, the trust fund. So, for example, if income is payable during a certain period to such of A, B and C as the trustees shall select, with separate trusts affecting the capital, then A, B and C can jointly demand that the income be paid as they direct.[20] **7–008**

*Stephenson v Barclays Bank Ltd*

Chancery Division [1975] 1 W.L.R. 882

WALTON J.: I think it may be desirable to state what I conceive to be certain elementary principles. (1) In a case where the persons who between them hold the entirety of the beneficial interests in any particular trust fund are all sui juris and acting together ("the beneficial interest holders"), they are entitled to direct the trustees how the trust fund may be dealt with. (2) This does not mean, however, that they can at one and the same time override the pre-existing trusts and keep them in existence. Thus, in *Re Brockbank*[21] itself the beneficial interest holders were entitled to override the pre-existing trusts by, for example, directing the trustees to transfer the trust fund to X and Y, whether X and Y were the trustees of some other trust or not, but they were not entitled to direct the existing trustees to appoint their own nominee as a new trustee of the existing trust. By so doing they would be pursuing inconsistent rights. (3) Nor, I think, are the beneficial interest holders entitled to direct the trustees as to the particular investment they should make of the trust fund. I think this follows for the same reasons as the above. Moreover, it appears to me that once the beneficial interest holders have determined to end the trust they are not entitled, unless by agreement, to the further services of the trustees. Those trustees can of course be compelled to hand over the entire trust assets to any person or persons selected by the beneficiaries against a proper discharge, but they cannot be compelled, unless they are in fact willing to comply with the directions, to do anything else with the trust fund which they are not in fact willing to do. (4) Of course, the rights of the beneficial interest holders are always subject to the right of the trustees to be fully protected against such matters as **7–009**

18 [1975] 1 W.L.R. 882. See too *Pearson v Lane* (1809) 17 Ves. 101; *Re Marshall* [1914] 1 Ch. 192; *Re Sandeman's WT* [1937] 1 All E.R. 368; *Crowe v Appleby* [1975] 1 W.L.R. 1539 at 1543.

19 For cases concerning shareholdings in a private company where this was an issue, see e.g. *Re Weiner's WT* [1956] 1 W.L.R. 579; *Lloyds Bank Plc v Duker* [1987] 1 W.L.R. 1324.

20 *Re Smith* [1928] Ch. 915; *Re AEG Unit Trust* [1957] Ch. 415 at 422.

21 [1948] Ch. 206.

duty, taxes, costs or other outgoings; for example, the rent under a lease which the trustees have properly accepted as part of the trust property.

7-010 So much for the rights of the beneficial interest holders collectively. When the situation is that a single person who is sui juris has an absolutely vested beneficial interest in a share of the trust fund, his rights are not, I think, quite as extensive as those of the beneficial interest holders as a body. In general, he is entitled to have transferred to him (subject, of course, always to the same rights of the trustees as I have already mentioned above) an aliquot share of each and every asset of the trust fund which presents no difficulty so far as division is concerned. This will apply to such items as cash, money at the bank or an unsecured loan, stock exchange securities and the like. However, as regards land, certainly, in all cases, as regards shares in a private company in very special circumstances (see *Re Weiner's Will Trusts*[22]) and possibly (although the logic of the addition in facts escapes me[23]) mortgage debts (see *Re Marshall*[24] per Cozens-Hardy M.R.) the situation is not so simple, and even a person with a vested interest in possession in an aliquot share of the trust fund may have to wait until the land is sold, and so forth, before being able to call on the trustees as of right to account to him for his share of the assets.

7-011 The rule in *Saunders v Vautier* does not apply where a beneficiary has only a contingent interest: i.e. where his entitlement under the trust does not arise until the happening of a specified event, such as the beneficiary attaining 25 years of age.[25] Nor does it apply where there is a fluctuating body of beneficiaries from time to time within a class,[26] even where the likelihood of another beneficiary being born before the fund is exhausted is remote.[27] Nor does it apply where other persons have an interest in the accumulations of income which the beneficiaries would like to stop.[28]

7-012 Where trusts arise out of contractual relationships it is possible for the parties who are beneficiaries to contract out of their *Saunders v Vautier* rights. So, for example, unit-holders in a unit trust cannot terminate the trust and claim the trust property while the trust is operating as a going concern and before it is wound up as agreed pursuant to the trust deed. Also the rule does not apply if the trust property consists of a non-assignable contract under which there are outstanding obligations to be performed by the trustee.[29]

7-013 The rule in *Saunders v Vautier* does not give beneficiaries the right to control the trustee in the exercise of any discretion conferred upon him by statute or the trust instrument.[30] However, if property is held on trust for beneficiaries all of whom are ascertained and of full capacity then the beneficiaries, acting collectively, may force the trustees to retire in favour of new trustees whom they have nominated.[31]

7-014 In a 2006 article, part of which is reproduced below, Paul Matthews explained that the rule in

---

22 [1956] 1 W.L.R. 579.

23 In *Crowe v Appleby* [1975] 1 W.L.R. 1539 at 1543, Goff J. endorsed Walton J.'s views and pointed out that "the logic of the addition of mortgages is that they include not only the debt but the estate and powers of the mortgagee."

24 [1914] 1 Ch. 192 at 199.

25 *Re Couturier* [1907] 1 Ch. 470 at 473, where Joyce J points out the distinction between giving a person an interest *contingent* on her reaching a specified age, and giving her a *vested* interest and postponing the enjoyment of it to a specified age. See too *Gosling v Gosling* (1859) John 265; *Re Lord Nunburnholme* [1912] 1 Ch. 489; *Thorpe v HMRC* [2010] S.T.C. 964. If a contingent interest is given, but the specified event does not occur, then either the trust deed will specify that someone else then becomes entitled to the trust property, as in, e.g. *Re Bellville's ST* [1964] Ch. 163, or it will go to the settlor or her estate on a resulting trust.

26 *Re Levy* [1960] Ch. 346 at 363; *Re Westphal* [1972] N.Z.L.R. 792 at 794–795.

27 *Thorpe v HMRC* [2009] S.T.C. 2107 at [14]–[15].

28 *Berry v Geen* [1938] A.C. 575.

29 *Don King Productions Inc v Warren* [2000] Ch. 291 at 321, citing *Re Brockbank* [1948] Ch. 206.

30 *Re Brockbank* [1948] Ch. 206; *Re George Whichelow Ltd* [1954] 1 W.L.R. 5; *Holding and Management Ltd v Property Holdings Plc* [1990] 1 All E.R. 938 at 948.

31 Trusts of Land and Appointment of Trustees Act 1996 ss.19 and 20 (assuming that no-one else has the power to nominate new trustees). See further paras 8-010ff.

*Saunders v Vautier* is linked with the further rule of English law that prohibits restraints on the inalienability of trust interests.[32] Yet neither rule forms part of the law of many American states, which have tended instead to follow the Massachusetts case of *Claflin v Claflin*,[33] to hold either that the rule in *Saunders v Vautier* does not apply at all, or else that it cannot be applied to bring a trust to an end if some material purpose of the settlor remains to be carried out.[34] The fact that so many states manage satisfactorily without the rule in *Saunders v Vautier* suggests that it is not a necessary part of the trust concept, however integral a part of this concept English lawyers may believe it to be, and lends support to critics who say that the rationale offered by the English courts for the rule is syllogistic: it is premised on an understanding of equitable property rights that is asserted but not justified.[35]

## P. Matthews, "The Comparative Importance of the Rule in *Saunders v Vautier*"

(2006) 122 L.Q.R. 266, 273–281

. . . Why does this rule matter? First, it illustrates and exemplifies the idea of beneficial (or "equitable") ownership or property. But we must be careful what we mean by this. It is true that the rights of trust beneficiaries are good against many—if not in practice most—third parties. They fail only when the asset concerned[36] reaches the hands of a bona fide purchaser for value without notice. And a property right need not be absolute. Indeed, in most civil law systems, good faith purchase by a third party defeats the original owner's proprietary claim to a stolen asset,[37] although in some cases it may give rise to an option for the original owner to repurchase it from the third party.[38] At all events, persistence of rights in a thing against third parties is the hallmark of the property idea,[39] and equity lawyers have therefore found it convenient to borrow from the common law the language and vocabulary of ownership.[40] 7–015

However, it is not this aspect of "property" that the rule in *Saunders v Vautier* illustrates.[41] Instead, it is the idea of exclusive decision-making. If I give something to you, then the "property" idea should mean that it is yours to deal with as you please. "Property" means—indeed, etymologically, has to mean—that you decide. I should not be able, consistently with the idea of property, to make something your "property", and then tell you how to deal with it.[42] So equity used the same idea, and for example, generally forbade 7–016

---

32 For which see *Brandon v Robinson* (1811) 18 Ves. 429; *Green v Spicer* (1830) Russ. & My. 395; *Re Dugdale* (1888) 38 Ch.D. 176 at 182.

33 20 N.E. 454 (1889).

34 The wider socio-economic implications of this are examined in J. Getzler, "Transplantation and Mutation in Anglo-American Trust Law" (2009) 10 Theoretical Inquiries in Law 355.

35 As contended in J.H. Langbein, "Why the Rule in *Saunders v Vautier* is Wrong" in P.G. Turner (ed.), *Equity and Administration* (Cambridge University Press, 2015).

36 We are not here concerned with the debate over how the position changes when the asset is itself a personal right, e.g. an institutional or governmental bond.

37 *Code Civil*, art.2279; *Codice Civile*, art.1153.

38 *Code Civil*, art.2280; *Código Civil*, art.464.

39 See, e.g. Birks, in Bright and Dewar (eds), *Land Law: Themes and Perspectives* (1998), p.473; Smith in Birks and Pretto (eds), *Breach of Trust* (2002), pp.112–114.

40 See generally Matthews, "From Obligation to Property and Back Again? The Future of Non Charitable Purpose Trusts" in Hayton (ed.), *Extending the Boundaries of Trusts and Other Ring-Fenced Funds* (2002). Whether there is a numerus clausus principle at work here is another matter, and beyond the scope of this paper. But see, e.g. Merrill and Smith (2000) 110 Yale L.J. 1; Hansmann and Kraakman (2002) 31 J. Leg. Stud. 383.

41 Cf. Underhill and Hayton, *Trusts and Trustees*, 16th edn (2003), p.52. The rights of trust beneficiaries only became exigible against third parties later on in the development of the trust idea, but there is no a priori reason why imposing obligations on third parties should have altered the nature of the beneficiaries' relationship with the trustee. More likely, the right of the beneficiaries to collapse the trust was developed independently of the third- party idea, and may even have been present from the beginning.

42 See, e.g. *Ware v Cann* (1830) 10 B. & C. 433; *Hood v Oglander* (1865) 34 Beav. 513; *Re Rosher* (1884) 26 Ch.D. 801; *Corbett v Corbett* (1889) 14 P.D. 7; *Harbin v Masterman* [1894] 2 Ch. 184, affd [1895] A.C. 186; *Re Nelson* [1928] Ch. 920n; *Re Brown* [1954] Ch. 39. Cf. the similar idea in civil law systems: e.g. the French *Code Civil*, art.544.

the attempt to impose a restraint on the alienation of an equitable interest.[43] *Saunders v Vautier* is in one sense merely an application of the same principle: if there is only one beneficiary of a particular trust, that beneficiary must be entitled to take the property subject to the trust and decide what he wishes to do with it.[44] The same is true if two or more persons are interested, and they are agreed on what should happen.[45] In English law the settlor cannot oust this principle even by express declaration.[46] Related to this is the principle that a settlor or testator cannot create a trust to destroy property, or to waste it, as by blocking up a house for 20 years,[47] or by throwing money into the sea.[48] Whatever the subject-matter of the trust, it no longer belongs to the settlor or (obviously) the testator, and the decision whether to enjoy it or destroy it is no longer one for him. Instead it is ultimately a decision for those who benefit from the trust.[49]

**7-017** A second point is that the rule reflects a fundamental rule of English private trust law. This is that the trust must be for the benefit of persons rather than for purposes.[50] These persons will at some time be able to operate the rule in *Saunders v Vautier*.[51] They are the owners in equity of the trust assets.[52] On the other hand, a trust which is for pure purposes is normally void.[53] The *Saunders v Vautier* power cannot be exercised, and will never be capable of exercise. The assets have no owner in equity.[54] The only genuine exception[55] in English law to this rule is the charitable trust. But the charitable trust is unusual, being for the benefit of society as a whole, rather than for that of private individuals. It is an instrument of public law rather than of private law.

**7-018** A third point relates to the rule requiring certainty of objects in a trust, and through that the rules about disclosure of information to them. We have seen that beneficiaries under fixed trusts, discretionary trusts or powers are all needed to join together in order to exercise the "equitable ownership" right under *Saunders v Vautier*. This means that they are all equitable owners of some kind, albeit that in some cases it is impossible to say just how much of the equitable interest they each own individually. In such circumstances it is desirable, and perhaps indeed necessary, that the rules on certainty of objects should be the same for all three categories.

**7-019** Accordingly, in one decision in 1955 the Court of Appeal held that the same test of certainty should apply for beneficiaries under fixed trusts and discretionary trusts.[56] The court did not have to deal with mere powers in that case. In a later decision, the House of Lords held that the tests for the beneficiaries of discretionary trusts and for the objects of powers should be the same, but that it should be a different test from that put forward by the Court of Appeal in its earlier decision.[57] So the Court of Appeal's decision was overruled to that extent. The House of Lords, however, was not concerned in that case with the test for fixed trusts. Most trust commentators consider that the Court of Appeal's decision accordingly still applies to such trusts.[58] I do not. In my view the Court of Appeal was right to apply the same test to fixed trusts and discretionary trusts, but wrong in the test it applied. And the House of Lords was equally right to apply the same test to discretionary trusts as to powers, but, unlike the Court of Appeal, quite right in the test it applied.[59] In my view there is no sensible basis for applying a different test of certainty for different kinds

---

43 *Brandon v Robinson* (1811) 18 Ves. 429; *Re Dugdale* (1888) 38 Ch.D 176 at p.182.

44 See, e.g. *Younghusband v Gisborne* (1844) 1 Coll. 400; *Stokes v Cheek* (1860) 28 Beav. 620; *Weatherall v Thornburgh* (1878) 8 Ch.D 261 at 270; *Re Johnston* [1894] 3 Ch. 204; *Re Robbins* [1907] 2 Ch. 8, CA; *Re Brunning* [1909] 1 Ch. 276; *Re Lipinski's WT* [1976] Ch. 235.

45 *Barton v Briscoe* (1822) Jac. 603; *Re Bowes* [1896] 1 Ch. 507.

46 *Stokes v Cheek* (1860) 28 Beav. 620.

47 *Brown v Burdett* (1882) 21 Ch.D. 667.

48 *McCaig v University of Glasgow* 1907 S.C. 231.

49 The civilian idea of property includes the power to destroy it (abuses): see, e.g. Mazeaud and Mazeaud, *Leçons de Droit Civil, Biens* (5th edn, 1994), Vol.II, paras 1332–1333; cf. Mattei, *La Proprietà* (2001), pp.259–262.

50 See generally, Matthews, "The New Trust: Obligations without Rights?" in Oakley (ed.), *Trends in Contemporary Trust Law* (1996), Ch.1.

51 *Schmidt v Rosewood Trust Ltd* [2003] UKPC 26; [2003] 2 A.C. 709 (at [41]).

52 *Gosling v Gosling* (1859) Johns. 265; *Re Nelson* [1928] Ch. 920.

53 *Bowman v Secular Society* [1917] A.C. 406 at 441; *Re Wood* [1949] Ch. 498 at 501.

54 See *Schmidt v Air Products Canada Ltd* [1992] 2 S.C.R. 611 at 640.

55 See *Re Endacott* [1960] Ch. 232 for certain quasi-exceptions.

56 *IRC v Broadway Cottages Trust* [1955] Ch. 20.

57 *McPhail v Doulton* [1971] A.C. 424.

58 e.g. Hayton and Martin [1984] Conv. 304; *Lewin on Trusts* (17th edn, 2000), para.4–30.

59 See Matthews [1984] Conv. 22.

of equitable owners. The size or stability of the equitable interest concerned is not a sufficient reason. All interests having a *Saunders v Vautier* value (however big or small) should be judged by the same criteria of certainty.

So, too, and as a fourth point, the courts have now reached a similar position in relation to the disclosure of trust information to beneficiaries of trusts and objects of powers. No beneficiary or object has an absolute right to such information, and the trustee's obligation to disclose is simply an aspect of the court's supervisory role in relation to trusts.[60] The court will judicially exercise its discretion to order disclosure where this is appropriate in the context of holding the trustee to account. Beneficiaries under fixed and discretionary trusts, and objects of powers, are all on the same footing. The court may order disclosure to them all. Once more the rule in *Saunders v Vautier* brings together those with similar rights. **7–020**

. . . However, there is much more to it than this. There is the whole law of perpetuities. When ownership is split up between different persons, it becomes in practice inalienable, or at any rate harder to deal with. Market liquidity suffers, as do the land itself and the creditors of its owner. These are all matters of public interest. In (for example) French, Italian, Spanish and Swiss law, as in Roman law before them,[61] the basic rule of property law is that there should be one owner of all the rights in one thing at the same time.[62] That is the idea of dominium. Of course there are exceptions: co-ownership, for instance. But the French law of coownership has a simple rule that "*nul ne peut être contraint de demeurer dans l'indivision*"—no one is bound to remain a co-owner.[63] Or, in other words, if the co-owners cannot agree, then the property must be sold and the proceeds divided. Similarly in Italian, Spanish and Swiss law.[64] In that way the tying up and stultifying of property is avoided, or at least minimised. English law has rules with the same idea. One is the rule in the 1925 property legislation that there can no longer be a tenancy in common of land at law, only in equity behind a trust.[65] Another is the rule—from the same source—that life estates and future interests can no longer be created at law, but (again) only in equity behind a trust.[66] **7–021**

More important are the complications presented by the English system of estates and interests, allowing the fragmentation of property rights amongst a number of people, completely contrary to the civilian rule which I have just mentioned. In particular interests, especially future interests, belonging to unborn or unascertained persons are less marketable, even unmarketable, under ordinary circumstances. **7–022**

The wishes of rich men, especially landowners, throughout the centuries have been to control the destiny of their property after death, for as long as possible into the future.[67] This is often called the "dead hand" principle. So long as one person remains absolute owner of the asset, there is no problem. The land is readily marketable, the proceeds of its sale are fungible, and creditors may seize it or them in satisfaction of their debts. Even if the current owner refuses to sell, he is mortal, and one day will die.[68] His heir or heirs may take a different view. But if, on or before his death, the ownership is fragmented between many persons, including future persons, it takes the asset out of the market for as long as the fragmentation continues, because the future persons are not in a position to agree to sell. **7–023**

This is objected to as potentially damaging to society, on at least three grounds. First, the asset itself may be incapable of being sold or otherwise dealt with (e.g. used as security—which was one of the problems which led in 19th-century England and Ireland to the Settled Land Acts).[69] Secondly, even if the trustees have power to vary the actual investments for the time being, it may be argued that the economic value is nonetheless sterilised, and in particular the historically conservative rules on trustee investments[70] **7–024**

---

60 *Schmidt v Rosewood Trust Ltd* (above).

61 Watkin, *Historical Introduction to the Civil Law* (1999), p.25; Buckland, *Textbook of Roman Law* (3rd edn, 1963), p.187; Thomas, *Textbook of Roman Law* (1976), pp.134–5.

62 *Code Civil*, art.544; *Codice Civile*, art.832; *Código Civil*, art.348; *Swiss Civil Code*, art.641; Watkin, above, pp.227–228.

63 *Code Civil*, art.815.

64 *Codice Civile*, art.1111; *Código Civil*, art.400; Swiss Civil Code, art.650.

65 Law of Property Act 1925; ss.1(6), 34; Settled Land Act 1925, s.36(4).

66 Law of Property Act 1925, s.1(1)-(3).

67 See, e.g. Basnage, *Oeuvres* (4th edn) Vol.1, p.337.

68 Hence the old prohibitions on the holding of land by corporations (which of course could not die): see, e.g. Raban, *Mortmain Legislation and the English Church 1279–1500* (1982); Oesterhoff (1972) 27 U.T.L.J. 257.

69 See, e.g. Megarry and Wade, *Law of Real Property* (5th edn,1984), pp.312–313 (more detailed on this point than 6th edn).

70 See *Lewin on Trusts* (17th edn, 2000), Ch.35, in the context of the more liberal investment rules after the Trustee Act 2000, though the trustees' duty is still to invest prudently.

mean that that value is withdrawn both from the risk capital available to a capitalist society,[71] and from the free capital available for consumer spending.[72] In a country where a significant amount of the available wealth was contained in settlements (as was certainly the case in England in the late 17th century),[73] the first of these would be a serious matter. In a modern consumer society, where consumer spending not only can be a useful contributor to a country's economic well-being but can also assist in creating a climate of confidence in which economic progress can be made (which is certainly the case for England in the 21st century), the second of these would also be a serious matter. Thirdly, the interests of creditors may be damaged by being unable easily to access assets to pay debts. This seems to have been a particularly potent point in civil law countries,[74] and is now dawning on lawyers in common law ones.[75] Hence, for example, the enormous interest of U.S. lawyers (and, to some extent, common lawyers elsewhere) in so-called "asset protection trusts" designed to shield assets from otherwise legitimate creditors' claims.[76]

7-025 To combat these apparently disadvantageous consequences,[77] rules relating to tying up assets for the future would be needed. In England and other common law jurisdictions these rules are the rules on perpetuities and accumulations.[78] They compromise between allowing land to be tied up forever, and not allowing it to be tied up at all. The rules could have been based on arrangements not exceeding a certain number of years, or not exceeding a certain number of generations (as they were in Roman law[79] and the pre-Revolutionary French law[80]). As it happens, the English rules as finally settled[81] are based on a different and indeed relatively simple idea. This is that, within a certain period (known as the "perpetuity period")[82] from this state of unmarketability coming into being there must be a restoration of marketability. But the simple idea was implemented in a rather complex way, using the notion of "vesting in interest". This technical term—to be distinguished from "vesting in possession"—refers to the resolution of the uncertainty of certain contingencies inherent in the original gift. However, it is important to notice that the notion of a thing being or not being marketable was based, at common law,[83] not on there being a sole owner with all the property rights, but instead on (the idea behind) the rule in *Saunders v Vautier*. Subject to one important qualification . . . if at a given moment the rule in *Saunders v Vautier* was capable of being operated (even if it was not in fact so operated), the land or other asset was (at least in theory) marketable, and so ceased to be subject to the rules against perpetuities.[84]

7-026 Take a simple example. Suppose assets are settled on trust for A for life with remainder to B for life with remainder to B's eldest son on attaining 21 absolutely, with a gift over to C absolutely if B has no son. Suppose also that A, B and C are lives in being, but B has no son yet. The common law[85] considered that there was no doubt in such a case that either B must have a son who attains 21, or it must otherwise become clear that B will never do so (if at all), within the perpetuity period (i.e. lives in being plus 21 years),

---

71 Simes, "The Policy Against Perpetuities" (1955) 103 U. Penn. L.R. 707; Morris and Leach, Rule Against Perpetuities (2nd edn, 1962), pp.13–18; Haskell (1988) 66 North Carolina L.Rev. 545 at 558–559.

72 Simes, above.

73 At the time of the leading case on the subject, *The Duke of Norfolk's case* (1683) 3 Ch. Ca. 1.

74 De Wulf, *The Trust and Corresponding Institutions in Civil Law* (1965), pp.70–71.

75 See Moritz, "Dynasty Trusts and the Rule against Perpetuities" (2003) 116 Harv. L.R. 2588 at 2607–2608.

76 See, e.g. Matthews [1995] K.C.L.J. 62, reprinted (1996) 5 O.T.P.R. 57.

77 It is not necessary here to assess the economic validity of any of these claims. Indeed, there are good reasons for supposing that the second of them at least is mistaken, as based on an insufficient understanding of markets for funds. Our purpose is simply to point out the kinds of arguments which led to the invention of the so-called perpetuity rules. Whether we would today invent such rules from scratch (for these or other reasons) is an entirely different matter.

78 See generally, e.g. Morris and Leach, *Rule Against Perpetuities* (2nd edn, 1962); Maudsley, *Modern Law of Perpetuities* (1979); Megarry and Wade, *Law of Real Property* (6th edn, 2000), Ch.7.

79 See Buckland, *Equity in Roman Law* (1911), pp.84–85; Buckland, *Textbook of Roman Law* (3rd edn, 1963), p.364; Thomas, *Textbook of Roman Law* (1976), pp.513–514.

80 *Ordonnance d'Orléans*, 1560; *Ordonnance des Moulins*, 1566; *Ordonnance des Substitutions*, 1747; *Code Civil*, 1804, art.896.

81 On this (lengthy) process see Holdsworth, *History of English Law*, Vol.vii, pp.193–238, and Simpson, *Introduction to the History of Land Law* (1961), Ch.9.

82 See *The Duke of Norfolk's case* (1683) 3 Ch. Ca. 1 at 20, 28, 48.

83 Statute has since intervened; in particular the Variation of Trusts Act 1958.

84 *MacVean v MacVean* (1899) 24 Vict. L.R. 835 at 839.

85 We need say nothing here of the modern technological advances, such as artificial insemination donation, that may enable a man to have a child many years after his own death; as Leach put it in (1962) 48 A.B.A.J. 942 at 943 fn.3, "*en ventre son frigidaire*". See generally on this subject Atherton (1999) 19 Legal Studies 140.

and the gift is therefore valid. But the property is in effect inalienable at common law until B has a son who attains 21, or it is otherwise clear that that will never happen. At that time, even if A and B are still alive, and the trust continues, the rule in *Saunders v Vautier* can be operated.[86] Indeed, that is essentially what happened in the old strict settlement days. In every generation there would be a termination and resettlement using (what came to be known as) the rule in *Saunders v Vautier*.[87]

I said "at common law" because the courts in England—and in other common law jurisdictions which have followed its example[88]—now have power by statute to give consent to an arrangement to vary the trusts on behalf of unborn and minor beneficiaries. Essentially this modern technique relies on the rule in *Saunders v Vautier*, in that all the adult beneficiaries agree that the trusts should be varied in a particular way, and the judge supplies the consent for those who cannot do so for themselves.[89] But the court cannot supply consent for adults who refuse to give it.[90] . . . **7–027**

In recent years many common law jurisdictions have revisited their perpetuity rules, and have made liberalising reforms. These include England, which in 1964 introduced the so-called "wait and see" rule (i.e. to treat an interest as valid until it became clear it was void), and the possibility of specifying a fixed period of up to 80 years as the applicable perpetuity period.[91] The English model has been followed elsewhere in the Commonwealth.[92] Since then, some jurisdictions have extended the "fixed period" of 80 years to a perpetuity period of 120 or 150 years.[93] Some have abolished the rule altogether.[94] At least 22 U.S. states (and the District of Columbia) have radically reformed their perpetuity rules, though in a number of different ways (some in more than one). These include: complete abolition without replacement,[95] limiting the time during which the power to alienate can be suspended,[96] extending the perpetuity period,[97] enabling settlors to "opt out" of the rule,[98] and restricting the rule in future so that it only applies to non-trust property,[99] or only to real property.[100] Other states have made lesser reforms, mitigating the severity of the common law rule.[101] Some, however, have tried to reform and so far failed.[102] Even the English Law Commission, no revolutionaries they, have recommended a liberalising reform of the English perpetuity rules, including the adoption of a fixed perpetuity period of 125 years.[103] . . . **7–028**

. . . [So] we see that the wider aspect of the rule in *Saunders v Vautier* was not a 19th-century innovation. Instead it represents a logical—albeit not the only possible—consequence of the early development of **7–029**

86 *MacVean v MacVean*, above; cf. *Curtis v Lukin* (1842) 5 Beav. 147 (trust for accumulation would have been valid, as rule in *Saunders v Vautier* could have been operated, but trust property inherently uncertain).

87 Williams, *Settlement of Real Estates* (1865), Lect.XV; Megarry and Wade, *Law of Real Property* (6th edn, 2000), para.8-003; Baker, *Introduction to English Legal History* (4th edn, 2002), pp.293–295.

88 In particular Australia (except New South Wales and Tasmania), Canada (except Quebec and Newfoundland), New Zealand, Hong Kong, Jersey, Guernsey, Isle of Man, the Bahamas, Belize, Bermuda, BVI, Cayman Islands, Cook Islands, Cyprus (international trusts only), Gibraltar, Turks and Caicos Islands, Mauritius and Barbados.

89 Variation of Trusts Act 1958; *Re Holt's Settlement* [1969] 1 Ch. 100; *Goulding v James* [1997] 2 All E.R. 239, CA.

90 See *Lewin on Trusts* (17th edn, 2000), para.45–44; *Buschau v Rogers Communications Inc* (2004) 236 D.L.R. (4th) 18; 6 I.T.E.L.R. 919.

91 Perpetuities and Accumulations Act 1964.

92 See Perpetuities Act 1964 (New Zealand); Perpetuities and Accumulations Act 1968 (Victoria); Perpetuities and Accumulations Act 1968 (Isle of Man); Property Law Act 1969 (Western Australia); Perpetuities and Accumulations Ordinance 1970 (Hong Kong); Property Law Act 1974 (Queensland); Revised Statutes of British Columbia 1979 (c.321); Perpetuities Act 1984 (New South Wales); in Canada, Ontario, Yukon & North West Territories and Alberta adopted "wait and see", but not the 80-year alternative.

93 e.g. Belize (Trusts Act 1992, s.6: 120 years); St Vincent (International Trusts Act 1996, s.8: 120 years); Cayman Islands (Perpetuities Law 1995, ss.4, 11A: 150 years).

94 e.g. Anguilla (Trusts Ordinance 1994, s.6); Cook Islands (International Trusts Act 1984, s.6); Nauru (Foreign Trusts Estates and Wills Act 1972, s.3); Turks and Caicos Islands (Trusts Ordinance 1990, s.14); Manitoba (Perpetuities and Accumulations Act, C.C.S.M. c.P. 33).

95 Rhode Island.

96 Alaska, Delaware, Idaho, Illinois, Maine, Maryland, Missouri, Ohio, New Jersey, South Dakota and Wisconsin.

97 Florida (360 years), Washington (150 years), Utah, Wyoming (1,000 years).

98 Illinois, Indiana, Maine, Maryland, Ohio and Virginia.

99 Delaware, Arizona, District of Columbia, Colorado, Nebraska.

100 Delaware, Idaho and Virginia.

101 California, Colorado, Montana, Nevada.

102 Nevada, New York, Texas.

103 Law Com. No.251 (1998), 97–108.

English trust law.[104] To stigmatise it as novel,[105] or as a wrong turn, deserves the same riposte as Gray gave to the American criticism[106] of the parallel rule against restraints on alienability of trust interests:

"The decisions of the English Chancery which have been cited[107] do not set forth . . . any novel doctrines. They are simply applications of a principle older than *Taltaram's case*.[108] They are a part of the struggle of the law against feudalism, and against the attempt to give the enjoyment of wealth without its responsibilities. They are modern only because the special form of dishonesty, family pride, and sentimentalism at which they are aimed is modern."[109]

## 4. Judicial Variation of Trusts

### A. Equitable Jurisdiction

7-030 The rule in *Saunders v Vautier* applies only where all the trust beneficiaries are of full capacity so that they can use their rights under the rule to demand a transfer of legal title. Where they are not of full capacity, the decision of the House of Lords in *Chapman v Chapman*[110] in 1954 made it clear that the court did not possess plenary powers to alter a trust on the ground that alteration would be advantageous to infant or unborn beneficiaries. However, there were some limited exceptions to this principle. Some of these related to acts done by the trustees in regard to the trust property in the administration of the trust, while others went beyond this and conferred a limited power to remould the beneficial interests when this was to the advantage of the beneficiaries.

#### i. Trustees' Administrative Acts

**(1) Salvage**

7-031 This group of cases involved the alienation of infants' property and established the proposition that the court could sanction a mortgage or sale of part of an infant's beneficial interest for the benefit of the part retained in cases of absolute necessity.[111]

**(2) Emergency**

7-032 This exception can be regarded as an extension of the salvage cases. The salvage cases required proof of absolute necessity. The principle of the emergency cases was somewhat wider and enabled the court to sanction departure from the terms of a trust where an emergency had arisen which the settlor had not foreseen and which required to be dealt with by the conferment of extraordinary powers on the trustees.[112]

---

104 See, e.g. Waters, *Law of Trusts in Canada* (2nd edn, 1984), p.962.

105 See Chesterman in Rubin and Sugarman (eds), *Law Economy and Society: Essays in the History of English Law 1750–1914* (1984), p.154; Moffat, *Trusts Law, Text and Materials* (3rd edn, 1999), p.250.

106 See, e.g. *Nichols v Eaton*, 91 U.S. 716, 725 (1875), per Miller J.

107 i.e. *Brandon v Robinson* (1811) 18 Ves. 429; *Graves v Dolphin* (1826) 1 Sim. 66; *Rochford v Hackman* (1852) 9 Hare 474.

108 i.e. *Hunt v Smyth* (1472), Kiralfy, *Sourcebook of English Law* (1957), pp.86–99 (judicial recognition of the common recovery as an effective procedure to bar a fee tail).

109 Gray, *Restraints on the Alienation of Property* (2nd edn, 1895), pp.161–162.

110 [1954] A.C. 429. Legislation was later enacted to undo the bad effects of this decision, in the shape of the Variation of Trusts Act 1958, and the variation of trust sought by the applicants in *Chapman* was subsequently granted under the statute: *Re Chapman's ST (No.2)* [1959] 1 W.L.R. 372.

111 *Re Jackson* (1882) 21 Ch.D. 786; *Conway v Fenton* (1888) 40 Ch.D. 512; cf. *Re De Teissier* [1893] 1 Ch. 153; *Re Montagu* [1897] 2 Ch. 8.

112 *Re New* [1901] 2 Ch. 534; *Re Tollemache* [1903] 1 Ch. 457; *Saipem SpA v Rafidain Bank* [1994] C.L.C. 253.

### (3) Trustee Act 1925 s.57

Section 57 rested the court's jurisdiction on expediency—a basis which, it is conceived, is wider than that of salvage or emergency. 7–033

## Trustee Act 1925 s.57

**Power of court to authorise dealings with trust property**

(1) Where in the management or administration of any property vested in trustees, any sale, lease, mortgage, surrender, release or other disposition or any purchase, investment, acquisition, expenditure, or other transaction is in the opinion of the court expedient, but the same cannot be effected by reason of the absence of any power for that purpose vested in the trustees by the trust instrument, if any, or by law, the court may by order confer upon the trustees, either generally or in any particular instance, the necessary power for the purpose, in such terms, and subject to such provisions and conditions, if any, as the court may think fit and may direct in what manner any money authorised to be expended, and the costs of any transaction, are to be paid or borne as between capital and income. . . 7–034

Section 57 is an overriding section, the provisions of which are read into every settlement.[113] The powers of the court are limited only by expediency, though the proposed transaction must be for the benefit not of one beneficiary but of the whole trust.[114] The power has been used to authorise the sale of chattels settled on trusts which prevent sale,[115] the sale of land on trusts which prevent sale,[116] the sale of land where a consent requisite to sale has been refused,[117] the development of land where the trustees lacked a power to trade,[118] the partitioning of land where there was no power to partition,[119] the blending of two charitable funds into one,[120] the investment of funds in assets of any kind as if the trustees were beneficial owners subject to obtaining professional investment advice,[121] and the making of distributions out of an "exempt approved" pension fund in the form of taxable payments.[122] 7–035

The question whether s.57 empowers the courts to reallocate the beneficial interests under a trust is considered by Mummery LJ in the following passage of his judgment in *Sutton v England*. 7–036

*Sutton v England*

Court of Appeal [2012] 1 W.L.R. 326 at [6]–[8]

MUMMERY L.J.: There is no jurisdiction under section 57(1) to confer a power to depart from the beneficial interests under the trusts by rewriting, remoulding or rearranging them. Variations of the beneficial interests under the trusts are not, as such, matters of "the management or administration" of the trust property and "trust property" cannot be equated with beneficial interests in the trust property. Rulings to that effect in *Re Downshire Settled Estates*[123] and *Chapman v Chapman*[124] led to the passing of the Variation of Trusts Act 1958. . . 7–037

---

113 *Re Mair* [1935] Ch. 218.
114 *Re Craven's Estate (No.2)* [1937] Ch. 431.
115 *Re Hope's WT* [1929] 2 Ch. 136.
116 *Alexander v Alexander* [2012] W.T.L.R. 187.
117 *Re Beale's ST* [1932] 2 Ch. 15.
118 *Re Portman Estate* [2015] W.T.L.R. 871.
119 *Re Thomas* [1930] 1 Ch. 194. A power to partition is now given by the Trusts of Land and Appointment of Trustees Act 1996 s.13, on which see *Rodway v Landy* [2001] Ch. 703.
120 *Re Harvey* [1941] 3 All E.R. 284.
121 *Anker-Petersen v Anker-Petersen* [2000] W.T.L.R. 581.
122 *NBPF Pension Trustees Ltd v Warnock-Smith* [2008] 2 All E.R. (Comm) 740.
123 [1953] Ch. 218 at 248.
124 [1954] A.C. 429.

7-038 It has been held, on the other hand, that an application under section 57(1) to confer powers for the purpose of a proposed transaction is within the jurisdiction of the court, if the exercise of the powers conferred by the court under section 57(1) might only incidentally affect the beneficial interests in the trust property.[125]

7-039 The court must decide, on the particular facts of each case, on which side of the line the application falls. That may be difficult, especially when, as is the case here, the application is not opposed. The court is nervous about the fundamental matter of jurisdiction if it is asked to act without the benefit of adversarial argument that normally disciplines its decision-making processes.

7-040 The *Sutton* case concerned a family trust under which the beneficiaries were entitled to the benefit of the income and capital of the whole of the trust property. Some beneficiaries were resident in the UK and some in the US. To avoid the US resident beneficiaries incurring a double tax burden the trustees proposed partitioning the trust property to create a sub-trust of separated funds for the benefit of the US resident beneficiaries, to be administered by US trustees. Since they had no power to partition the trust funds they applied for an order under s.57, which Mann J refused to give them, reasoning that it would amount to a variation of the beneficial interests under the trust since the US beneficiaries would become entitled to a share of the income of part of the fund instead of the whole fund.[126] This was reversed on appeal, on the basis that the partitioning would have only an incidental impact on the beneficiaries' interests.

## ii. Remoulding of the Beneficial Interests

7-041 Under the courts' equitable jurisdiction they also have some limited scope for remoulding the beneficial interests under a settlement.

### (1) Maintenance[127]

7-042 Where a settlor made a provision for a family but postponed the enjoyment, either for a particular purpose or generally for the increase of the estate, it was assumed that she did not intend that the children should be left unprovided for, or in a state of such moderate means that they could not be educated properly for the position which she intended them to have, and the court accordingly broke in upon the accumulation and provided maintenance for the children. The exercise of this jurisdiction resulted in an alteration of beneficial interests since income was applied in maintaining beneficiaries notwithstanding the fact that the settlor had directed that it should be accumulated or applied in reduction of incumbrances. The jurisdiction was not confined to cases of emergency or necessity.[128]

### (2) Compromise

7-043 It has long been clear that where the rights of the beneficiaries under a trust are the subject of doubt or dispute, the court has jurisdiction on behalf of all interested parties, whether adult, infant or unborn, to sanction a compromise by substituting certainty for doubt.[129] The issue in *Re Downshire,*

---

[125] See the *Downshire* case, at 248, per Lord Evershed M.R.

[126] [2010] W.T.L.R. 335.

[127] *Erratt v Barlow* (1807) 14 Ves. Jun. 202; *Greenwell v Greenwell* (1800) 5 Ves. Jun. 194; *Havelock v Havelock* (1880) 17 Ch.D. 807; *Re Collins* (1886) 32 Ch.D. 229; *Re Walker* [1901] 1 Ch. 879.

[128] *Haley v Bannister* (1820) 4 Madd. 275.

[129] *Brooke v Mostyn* (1864) 2 De G. J. & S. 415; *Re Barbour's Settlement* [1974] 1 All E.R. 1188.

*Re Blackwell* and *Re Chapman* before the Court of Appeal,[130] and in the last-named case[131] before the House of Lords, was whether the court had jurisdiction to do the same with regard to rights which were admittedly not in dispute. Their Lordships emphatically rejected the view that the courts had so ample a jurisdiction.

### (3) The Settled Land Act 1925 s.64

Section 64(1) provides that any transaction affecting or concerning the settled land, or any part thereof, or any other land (not being a transaction otherwise authorised by the Act, or by the settlement) which in the opinion of the court would be for the benefit of the settled land, or any part thereof, or the persons interested under the settlement, may, under an order of the court, be effected by a tenant for life, if it is one which could have been validly effected by an absolute owner. "Transaction" is defined by subs.(2) to include "any sale, extinguishment of manorial incidents, exchange, assurance, grant, lease, surrender, reconveyance, release, reservation or other disposition, any purchase or other acquisition, any covenant, contract, or option, and any application of capital money . . . and any compromise or other dealing or arrangement". 7–044

"Transaction" is a word of very wide import, and enables beneficial interests to be altered even without the consent of beneficiaries of full age and capacity. Section 64 has been held wide enough to enable trustees to transfer part of their trust property to another settlement of which they were trustees even though benefiting some other persons,[132] and to enable the 11th Duke of Marlborough to convey the Blenheim estate to trustees of a new settlement giving his troublesome son a protected life interest instead of a fee tail, such interest being under a trust for sale and not under an Settled Land Act trust so that the son had no power as tenant for life.[133] 7–045

### (4) Trustee Act 1925 s.53

Section 53 provides that where an infant is beneficially entitled to any property the court may with a view to the application of the capital or income thereof for the maintenance, education or benefit of the infant make an order appointing a person to convey such property upon such terms as the court may think fit. The effect of this section may be summarised as follows. Where: (a) an infant is beneficially entitled to any interest in property, whether real or personal; (b) the interest itself is not under the settlement applicable for his maintenance, education or benefit, nor is it producing any income which is so applicable; and (c) a proposal is made that the court should authorise a "conveyance"[134] of the infant's interest with a view to the application of the capital or income, arising out of such conveyance, for the maintenance, education or benefit of the infant; then the court has jurisdiction to sanction the proposal upon such terms as it thinks fit. Thus the sale of an infant's contingent reversionary interest to the life-tenant in order to minimise liability to estate duty was made with a view to, and was, an application of the proceeds of sale for the infant's benefit, where they amounted to more than he would have been likely to receive if no sale had taken place, and they were to be settled upon[135] and not paid outright to him.[136] 7–046

---

130 [1953] Ch. 218.
131 [1954] A.C. 429.
132 *Raikes v Lygon* [1988] 1 W.L.R. 28.
133 *Hambro v Duke of Marlborough* [1994] Ch. 158.
134 Including a mortgage: *Re Gower's Settlement* [1934] Ch. 365; *Re Bristol's Settled Estates* [1965] 1 W.L.R. 469.
135 *Re Meux* [1958] Ch. 154.
136 *Re Heyworth's Contingent Reversionary Interest* [1956] Ch. 364.

## B. The Variation of Trusts Act 1958

### i. Introduction

7-047 The Variation of Trusts Act 1958 was enacted on the recommendation of the Law Reform Committee,[137] which considered that the decision in *Chapman v Chapman*[138] had left the law in an unsatisfactory state. In essence, the 1958 Act empowers the court on behalf of persons who cannot themselves give their approval (e.g. because unborn, unascertainable or minors) to approve arrangements varying or revoking beneficial and administrative provisions under trusts so long as these are for the benefit of the persons in question. Exceptionally, in the case of persons with contingent discretionary interests under protective trusts, where the interest of the protected beneficiary has not failed or determined, the court can give an approval on behalf of (and against the will of) ascertained adults and no benefit to them is required.[139]

#### Variation of Trusts Act 1958 s.1

7-048 (1) Where property, whether real or personal, is held on trusts arising, whether before or after the passing of this Act, under any will, settlement or other disposition, the court may if it thinks fit by order approve on behalf of—

(a) any person having, directly or indirectly, an interest, whether vested or contingent, under the trusts who by reason of infancy or other incapacity is incapable of assenting,[140] or
(b) any person (whether ascertained or not) who may become entitled, directly or indirectly, to an interest under the trusts as being at a future date or on the happening of a future event a person of any specified description[141] or a member of any specified class of persons, so however that this paragraph shall not include any person who would be of that description, or a member of that class, as the case may be, if the said date had fallen or the said event had happened at the date of the application to the court,[142] or
(c) any person unborn, or
(d) any person[143] in respect of any discretionary interest of his under protective trusts where the interest of the principal beneficiary has not failed or determined,

any arrangement (by whomsoever proposed,[144] and whether or not there is any other person beneficially interested who is capable of assenting thereto) varying or revoking all or any of the trusts, or enlarging[145] the powers of the trustees of managing or administering any of the property subject to the trusts:

---

137 Law Reform Committee, *Sixth Report, "Court's Power to Sanction Variation of Trusts"* (HMSO, 1957), Cmnd.310.
138 [1954] A.C. 429. See para.7–030.
139 Variation of Trusts Act 1958 s.1(1)(d) and proviso. Here the settlor's intentions have much significance: *Re Steed's WT* [1960] Ch. 407; *Goulding v James* [1997] 2 All E.R. 239 at 250.
140 Objects of a discretionary trust are included: *Re Clitheroe's ST* [1959] 3 All E.R. 784; but not objects of a power of appointment: *Knocker v Youle* [1986] 1 W.L.R. 934.
141 Unascertained future spouses are included: *Re Steed's WT* [1960] Ch. 407.
142 This refers inter alia to the potential next-of-kin of a living person, who must make up their own minds whether to give their consent: *Re Suffert's Settlement* [1961] Ch. 1.
143 Including an unascertained or unborn person: *Re Turner's WT* [1960] Ch. 122. This approval may be given without the need to show "benefit".
144 The arrangement need not be in the nature of a contract between the parties: *Re Steed's WT* [1959] Ch. 354; but must not amount to a completely new settlement: *Re T's ST* [1964] Ch. 158; *Re Ball's ST* [1968] 1 W.L.R. 899; and it must be practical and business-like: *Re Van Jenisen's WT* [1964] 1 W.L.R. 449.
145 e.g. conferring wider investment powers: *Re Coates's Trusts* [1959] 1 W.L.R. 375; *Re Byng's WT* [1959] 1 W.L.R. 375; *Re Allen's ST* [1960] 1 W.L.R. 6; *Re Royal Naval and Royal Marine Children's Homes, Portsmouth* [1959] 1 W.L.R. 755.

Providing that except[146] by virtue of paragraph (d) of this subsection the court shall not approve an arrangement on behalf of any person unless the carrying out thereof would be for the benefit[147] of that person.

(2) In the foregoing subsection "protective trusts" means the trusts specified in paragraphs (i) and (ii) of subsection (1) of section thirty-three of the Trustee Act 1925 or any like trusts, "the principal beneficiary" has the same meaning as in the said subsection (1) and "discretionary interest" means an interest arising under the trust specified in paragraph (ii) of the said subsection (1) or any like trust.[148]

(3) The jurisdiction conferred by subsection (1) of this section shall be exercisable by the High Court, except that the question whether the carrying out of any arrangement would be for the benefit of a person falling within paragraph (a) of the said subsection (1) who lacks capacity (within the meaning of the Mental Capacity Act 2005) to give his assent is to be determined by the Court of Protection. . . .

(5) Nothing in the foregoing provisions of this section shall apply to trusts affecting property settled by Act of Parliament.

(6) Nothing in this section shall be taken to limit the powers conferred by section sixty-four of the Settled Land Act 1925, section fifty-seven of the Trustee Act 1925, or the powers of the Court of Protection.

The Act has been useful for saving tax by exporting trusts and by partitioning the trust fund between the life tenant (who might have a protected interest) and the remaindermen (who might be minors, unborn or unascertained). However, where no alteration of beneficial interests is sought, and it is only sought to expand the trustees' administrative powers, it is simpler and cheaper to invoke the Trustee Act 1925 s.57, which also obviates the need to obtain the consent of every adult beneficiary.[149] **7–049**

### ii. An Example

To illustrate the courts' general approach when deciding applications under the 1958 Act, we reproduce *Wright v Gater* here. The facts appear from Norris J's judgment. **7–050**

*Wright v Gater*

Chancery Division [2012] 1 W.L.R. 802

NORRIS J.: Edward Greenstreet died intestate on 28 October 2009. His entire estate, which had a net value of some £514,600, passed to his son Kieran. No inheritance tax was payable because the deceased was entitled to a doubled-up nil rate band. Edward Greenstreet's estate remains unadministered. **7–051**

Unfortunately, Kieran himself died intestate on 17 May 2010. His entire estate (which includes his inheritance from Edward Greenstreet) passes to his son Rory by his partner Ellen. Rory was born on 27 May 2008 and so is now three years old. Kieran's own net estate amounts to some £6,000. The inheritance tax payable on the combined estates on Kieran's death is about £89,000. Nobly, Ellen does not intend to make any claim against Kieran's estate (being content with the joint property that passed to her by survivorship and with the death benefit which she received). The position therefore is that the aggregated estates of Edward Greenstreet and Kieran are held upon the statutory trusts contained in **7–052**

146 Even in the excepted case the court must exercise its discretion judicially: *Re Burney's Settlement* [1961] 1 W.L.R. 545; *Re Baker's ST* [1964] 1 W.L.R. 336.

147 The court will not approve an arrangement which is a fraud on a power (*Re Robertson's WT* [1960] 1 W.L.R. 1050) or is contrary to public policy (*Re Michelham's WT* [1964] Ch. 550). Nor will the court use the Act as a justification for rectifying a settlement on the basis of mistake (*Re Tinker's Settlement* [1960] 1 W.L.R. 1011) or for making an order which can be made without the aid of the Act (*Re Pettifor's WT* [1966] Ch. 257 where the female beneficiary was 70 years old and so well past child-bearing age).

148 For "like" trusts, see *Re Wallace's Settlement* [1968] 1 W.L.R. 711 at 716.

149 *Anker-Petersen v Anker-Petersen* [2000] W.T.L.R. 581.

section 47 of the Administration of Estates Act 1925. This means that they are held on trust for Rory contingently on his attaining 18 (or marrying or forming a civil partnership under that age), and in the meantime the statutory power of maintenance under section 31 of the Trustee Act 1925 and of advancement under section 32 of that Act will be available. If Rory does not attain a vested interest then the aggregated estates would be held upon the statutory trusts for the persons identified in section 46(1)(v) of the Administration of Estates Act 1925. At the hearing it was established that this meant that the aggregated estates would be held upon statutory trusts for Kieran's uncles and aunts (the brothers or sisters of the whole blood of a parent of Kieran living at Kieran's death). I will call this group "the ultimate beneficiaries".

**7-053** If Rory were to take Edward Greenstreet's estate directly (instead of via Kieran's estate) all inheritance tax would be avoided. An arrangement varying the dispositions taking effect on Edward Greenstreet's death to substitute Rory for Kieran is entirely straightforward (it now being established by *Re Bernstein*[150] that there is jurisdiction under the Variation of Trusts Act 1958 to vary the trusts of an unadministered estate).

**7-054** But a complication has been introduced. By para 11 of her witness statement Ellen says:

> "I have been advised of the consequences of the 'relevant property' regime under the Inheritance Tax Act 1984 as amended, and also of the income [tax] treatment of accumulated income. Nevertheless I am strongly of the view that it is extremely undesirable that Rory should be entitled to income, let alone capital, as soon as he is 18. I do not think it is to the benefit of any child to be in absolute control of that kind of income or capital in their early twenties. I consider that the consequences of the fund being deemed 'relevant property' are far outweighed by the risk of his being entitled to such significant funds before he is 30, or at the very earliest 25."

**7-055** Ellen and Kieran's uncle Michael Greenstreet (who are together the administrators, for the use and benefit of Rory, of Kieran's estate) have therefore commenced proceedings under the Variation of Trusts Act 1958 for the approval of an arrangement under which they will hold Edward Greenstreet's estate as trustees: (a) upon trust for Rory contingently upon his attaining the age of 30 years; (b) subject to an unrestricted power to accumulate the whole of the income until Rory attains 30; (c) subject to a power to apply income to or for the benefit of Rory until he reaches the age of 30; (d) with the benefit of an enlarged power of advancement under section 32; (e) subject to those trusts and powers upon trust as to both capital and income for any widow or civil partner of Rory at Rory's death and any children of Rory in such shares as the trustees should appoint within six months after Rory's death; and (f) with an ultimate trust in favour of the ultimate beneficiaries along with Ellen and the issue of Lesley (an aunt who predeceased Kieran). (There is a power to appoint within this class, and in default of complete exercise of that power there is a trust for equal division.) I do not know the ages of the members of this class, so that it is not possible to form a view as to its likely composition 27 years hence.

**7-056** . . . [The] proposed arrangement is promoted by Ellen (as one of Kieran's personal representatives); but she is also Rory's litigation friend. Nobody can doubt the sincerity of the views she has expressed, and it is absolutely plain that she seeks no personal advantage for herself in any of the proposals (notwithstanding she features in the ultimate trust). But I consider it improper to have placed her in this position. She cannot possibly both advocate the arrangement and subject it to independent scrutiny in the sole interest of Rory. The difficulties in her position were mirrored by those of counsel, who found himself both drafting the arrangement and writing an independent opinion in support of it on behalf of Rory, without the advantage of any of the proposals being tested in negotiation or subjected to contrary argument. This is a small (and united) family so that the representation of Rory's individual interest is not easy. But I would have been assisted if Rory's litigation friend had been a family friend or a professional (such as a solicitor) who had instructed separate counsel to undertake entirely independent scrutiny. The instruction of separate counsel is in my view a fundamental requirement.

**7-057** . . . Section 1(1) of the 1958 Act empowers the court "if it thinks fit by order [to] approve on behalf of—(a) any person having . . . an interest, whether vested or contingent, under [a trust] who by reason of infancy . . . is incapable of assenting" an arrangement which varies or revokes the trusts in whole or in part. But the proviso of subsection (1) declares that "the court *shall not* approve an arrangement on behalf of any person unless the carrying out thereof would be for the benefit of that person" (emphasis supplied) . . . [So]

---

[150] [2010] W.T.L.R. 559.

I must be satisfied that the arrangement . . . is for Rory's benefit, otherwise I have no power or discretion to approve the arrangement.

In undertaking that task I have applied the following principles. 7–058

(a) I approach the task with what Megarry J. in *Re Wallace's Settlements* described as "a fair, cautious and inquiring mind".[151]
(b) What I am doing is not redistributing property according to some wise scheme of which I approve. The Court of Chancery never claimed a power to direct a settlement of the property of a minor, and the 1958 Act did not alter this.[152] Rather, I am supplying consent on behalf of Rory.[153] The question to be asked is therefore: "Should Rory consent to this arrangement?" That question is answered in the sense "Only if the judge is satisfied that it is for his benefit". So it is never enough that the proposal does Rory no real harm: to elicit his consent it must always confer on him a real benefit.
(c) "Benefit" is generally financial in nature: and when it is the court will be concerned in "a practical and business-like consideration of the arrangement, including the total amounts of the advantages which the various parties obtain, and their bargaining strength". The court will ask whether, if the persons on whose behalf consent is to be given were themselves competent and reasonable, the bargain is one that they would enter.[154] If the outcome of the arrangement cannot be predicted with certainty then the court is prepared to take on behalf of a minor a risk that an adult would be prepared to take.[155]
(d) But "benefit" need not be financial: and when it is not (or where non-financial benefit falls to be weighed against financial disadvantage) business-like considerations do not provide a sure guide, though the recognition of risk will still have some part to play. In such cases the assessment of benefit and advantage must be approached with caution (as Wilberforce J. recognised in *Re T's Settlement Trusts*[156]) lest the process simply becomes a reflection of the perceptions and preferences of the individual judge. The difficulties inherent in the task are perhaps illustrated by *Re Weston's Settlements*.[157]
(e) One step towards objectifying the assessment of non-financial benefit would be to pose the question based on that posed under different legislation in *Re Irving*[158]: would a prudent adult, motivated by intelligent self-interest, and after sustained consideration of the proposed trusts and powers and the circumstances in which they may fall to be implemented, be likely to accept the proposal?

In the instant case the financial benefit is the achievement of an immediate saving of inheritance tax of £89,000. That falls to be weighed against the significant financial disadvantage which Rory will suffer over time through being deprived of his right to income for 12 years, through the alteration in the contingency upon which he becomes absolutely entitled and through the disadvantageous tax regime which will apply once such trusts are brought into existence. It is said that that financial disadvantage is cancelled out by the moral benefit conferred on Rory by preventing him being in absolute control of income or capital until he is 30. Is such deferment beneficial? 7–059

The cases show that a deferment of vesting is capable of constituting "benefit" for the purposes of the 1958 Act. In *Re T's Settlement Trusts*[159] a strong case was made out on the facts that a beneficiary (who in 18 days was to become absolutely entitled to substantial funds) was "alarmingly immature and irresponsible as regards money" and that the possession of a large sum of free capital would expose her and her fortune to considerable hazards. Wilberforce J. deferred vesting and imposed protective trusts in the meanwhile. Such specifically fact-based cases can be put on one side, for in the instant case the proffered evidential basis for the proposed deferment is simply Ellen's view that it would not be good for her three-year-old son to have access to substantial sums of money before attaining 30. 7–060

---

151 [1968] 1 W.L.R. 711 at 718.
152 See *Re T's Settlement Trusts* [1964] Ch. 158 at 161.
153 *S v T* [2006] W.T.L.R. 1461 at para.16.
154 *Re Van Gruisen's Will Trusts* [1964] 1 W.L.R. 449 at 450, per Ungoed-Thomas J.
155 *Re Cohen's Will Trusts* [1959] 1 W.L.R. 865.
156 [1964] Ch. 158 at 161.
157 [1969] 1 Ch. 223.
158 (1975) 66 D.L.R. (3d) 387.
159 [1964] Ch 158 at 160.

7-061 [The judge considered *Re Holt's Settlement*,[160] *Re CL*,[161] *Re Remnant's Settlement Trusts*,[162] *Re RGST Settlement Trust*,[163] and *Re Bernstein*,[164] and continued:] . . . I do not consider that these cases warrant the conclusion that the court should regard postponement of vesting beyond the age of majority as "beneficial" in principle. I think in each case the court will have to be persuaded that a variation incorporating such a feature is justified on the facts of a particular case; perhaps because of the proven personal characteristics of the beneficiary; or perhaps because the size of the fund, the circumstance in life of the beneficiary, the family context in which the existing trusts will be implemented or some similar feature (the list is not exhaustive) gives rise to risks which any reasonable person would regard as real, and to which the proposed variation provides a sufficient and proportionate response. I accept that it is of benefit to a beneficiary to make provision for eliminating, or moderating or compensating for realistically assessed risks to which he or she is exposed, at least to a degree that is no more than necessary.

7-062 Adopting the approach indicated, I considered that I could not provide consent on Rory's behalf to the originally proposed arrangement. First, it seemed to me to come dangerously close to (if not to cross) the line between "variation" and "resettlement". Nothing remained of the original statutory trust. Second, there was nothing in the character or setting in the life of this three-year-old toddler to suggest that that was a real risk that he would be incapable of dealing with any income or capital inherited from his grandfather without supervision before he attained 30. I pictured myself trying to explain to a 28-year-old Rory who was married and with children and who wanted to embark on a particular career why he could only do so with the approval of his mother and uncle (or the persons they had appointed to succeed them), and why I had taken away his access to his inherited funds. Third, it seemed to me wrong to approve the establishment of a long-term trust where close family members controlled the purse strings. Whilst accepting without hesitation that Ellen and Michael Greenstreet were genuinely seeking to do what they perceived to be the best for Rory (and would no doubt continue to do so), I consider that Rory has the right to have his independence and autonomy as a young adult respected (an independence and autonomy which may cause tension between himself and his family and which suggests that in these financial matters there should be a distinction between his close family and his trustees).

7-063 I consider that I can approve the revised arrangement. Under this arrangement: (a) the trustees of the fund are to be Ellen, Michael Greenstreet and Mr Gater (a solicitor); (b) Rory will become entitled to the income of the fund contingently on his attaining the age of 18 (albeit not on the contingency of earlier marriage); (c) Rory will become entitled to 10% of the fund as it then stands (including accumulations but without bringing any previous advances into hotchpot) contingently on attaining the age of 21; (d) Rory will become entitled to the balance of the fund contingently on his attaining the age of 25; (e) if Rory fails to obtain 18 then the fund will be held for the ultimate beneficiaries; (f) if Rory attains 18 but dies before reaching 25 the fund is held for any widow or civil partner of Rory's and any issue of his in such shares as he may by deed or will have appointed, and in default of such appointment then in such shares as the trustees may within a limited period appoint; (g) there is a default trust in favour of the ultimate beneficiaries, Ellen and the issue of Lesley (with Rory again having a power to appoint within the class, the trustees then having a time-limited power, and an ultimate trust for stirpital division); (h) there are the usual (enlarged) powers to apply income and advance capital.

7-064 I approved an arrangement in this form for these reasons. First, I consider it constitutes a variation and not a resettlement.

7-065 Second, Ellen has strong views about postponing any entitlement for Rory for the longest period possible: and if the existing trusts remain unaltered then she and Michael Greenstreet could implement those views to the extent permitted by the statutory power of advancement by effecting a resettlement. By approving an arrangement which specifically addresses what is for Rory's benefit I think that (on the footing that no fundamental character flaws emerge as Rory grows up) sensible trustees will regard the proper degree of postponement of his entitlement as settled, and will not seek to exercise the power of advancement to achieve further postponement.

160 [1969] 1 Ch. 100.
161 [1969] 1 Ch. 587.
162 [1970] Ch. 560.
163 [2008] S.T.C. 1883.
164 [2010] W.T.L.R. 559.

> Third, assuming an accumulation rate of 2.5%, if the statutory trusts remain unaltered Rory will have unrestricted access to about £750,000 at his eighteenth birthday. In my judgment any reasonable person would regard that as posing risks for Rory, being brought up in a family not accustomed to significant wealth, and without his father; a context which makes Ellen's ability to discipline and guide him more difficult and which exposes Rory to significant temptation and the realistic possibility of exploitation. I take judicial notice of the frequency with which testators and donors acting on competent advice employed "accumulation and maintenance trusts" to moderate these risks (at least before the Finance Act 2006) so that it became "established sensible estate planning practice".[165] 7–066
>
> Fourth, I am satisfied that the sort of person contemplated by the "*Irving* test" would consider that the revised arrangement provides proportionate measures to address those risks and goes no further than is necessary to do so. A degree of mental contortion is required, but going through the process enabled me to conclude that the revised arrangement is beneficial (even if I might have had a personal preference for straightforward protective trusts). Certainly Parliament has looked favourably upon trusts of the type contained in the arrangement: see, most recently, section 71D of the Inheritance Tax Act 1984 (inserted by section 156 of and paragraph 1(1) of Schedule 20 to the Finance Act 2006). The practical effect of the arrangement will be to introduce Rory gradually to control of his wealth, and afford those who care deeply for him the opportunity to bring the matter before the court again if he shows signs of going off the rails (subject to the input of a professional lawyer)... 7–067

## iii. The Courts' Jurisdiction under the Act

### (1) Variation Cannot Be Resettlement

It is often said that the Act does not extend beyond a variation to a completely new resettlement.[166] However, in *Re Ball's Settlement* Megarry J stated[167]: 7–068

> If an arrangement changes the whole substratum of the trust, then it may well be that it cannot be regarded merely as varying that trust. But if, an arrangement, whilst leaving the substratum, effectuates the purpose of the trust by other means, it may still be possible to regard that arrangement as merely varying the original trusts, even though the means employed are wholly different and even though the form is completely changed... in essence the court is merely contributing on behalf of infants and unborn and unascertained persons the binding assets which they, unlike an adult beneficiary, cannot give. So far as is proper, the power of the court to give that consent should be assimilated to the wide powers which the ascertained adults have.

In the case a settlement conferred a life interest on the settlor (subject to a power of appointment in favour of his sons and grandchildren) and the capital was in default of appointment to be divided between the two sons of the settlor or their issue *per stirpes* if either son predeceased the settlor. The approved arrangement revoked the beneficial and administrative provisions of the settlement and replaced them with new provisions whereby each half of the trust fund was held on trust for one of the sons for life and, subject thereto, for such of that son's children equally as were born before a certain date. This jurisdictional limit is thus unlikely in practice to cause much difficulty. 7–069

---

165 Tiley, *Revenue Law*, 6th ed (2008), p.1384.

166 *Re T's Settlement Trusts* [1964] Ch. 158 at 162; *Re Holt's Settlement* [1969] 1 Ch. 100 at 117; *Wyndham v Egremont* [2009] W.T.L.R. 1473 at [21].

167 [1968] 1 W.L.R. 899 at 905.

### (2) Benefit

7–070 "Benefit" may be financial, moral or social[168] or the facilitation of the administration of the settlement.[169] Unfortunately, the reported cases all too often show, as one commentator has put it,[170] "that benefit and the measure of it is simply what the court says it is". For example, in *Re Remnant's WT*[171] Pennycuik J deleted a forfeiture clause in a testamentary trust which would have deprived the settlor's Catholic grandchildren of an interest in the trust property and passed this to the Protestant grandchildren. The judge acceded to the application in the interests of family harmony and freedom of marital choice, notwithstanding that this was contrary to the settlor's clear intentions and worked to the disadvantage of the Protestant grandchildren.

7–071 So long as the arrangement is for the benefit of the incapable or unborn beneficiaries it does not matter that it is contrary to the settlor's wishes,[172] the operation of the rule in *Saunders v Vautier* entitling the beneficiaries collectively to deal with their property as they want and the court's approval operating as the collective consent of the unborn or incapable beneficiaries. Exceptionally, in the case of protective trust cases under s.1(1)(d) of the 1958 Act, where it is immaterial that there is no benefit for the class of contingent beneficiaries, the settlor's purpose to protect the protected life tenant from improvident dealings is a significant consideration.[173]

7–072 The court may sanction a proposed arrangement which involves an element of risk to infant or unborn beneficiaries if the risk is one which an adult might well be prepared to take.[174] It will not sanction an arrangement involving an appointment made under a special power considered to be a fraud on the power. Thus, if a life tenant exercises a power to appoint capital to his two minor children to the exclusion of any of his future children, with the ulterior intent of receiving a larger share of the capital than otherwise would be possible this can be invalidated.[175]

7–073 The court may be willing to approve an arrangement varying the trusts of a settlement with a view to mitigating potential tax burdens,[176] but it is likely to be unwilling to approve an arrangement which has adverse tax consequences for those on whose behalf it is concerned to give its approval, unless those consequences are more than outweighed by other benefits.[177]

7–074 In *Re Cohen's WT*,[178] Danckwerts J said that the court could take a risk on behalf of an infant if it was a risk an adult would be prepared to take. In a later case of the same name, however,[179] Stamp J stressed that: (i) the court had to be satisfied that there was a benefit in the case of each individual infant and not merely of the whole class to which the infant belonged; and (ii) while the court need not be satisfied that each individual infant is bound to be better off than she would otherwise have been, it must be sure that she is making a bargain which is a reasonable one which an adult would be prepared to make. It seems, further, that the court may take a broad reasonable view but not a galloping gambling view.[180]

---

168 *Re Towler's ST* [1964] Ch. 158; *Re Holt's Settlement* [1969] 1 Ch. 100; *Re Weston's Settlement* [1969] 1 Ch. 224; *Re Remnant's ST* [1970] 1 Ch. 560; but cf. *Re Tinker's Settlement* [1960] 1 W.L.R. 1011.

169 *Re University of London Charitable Trusts* [1964] Ch. 282; *Re Seale's Marriage Settlement* [1961] Ch. 574.

170 R.B.M. Cotterell (1971) 34 M.L.R. 96, 98.

171 [1970] 1 Ch. 560.

172 *Goulding v James* [1997] 2 All E.R. 239.

173 *Goulding* at 249–251, based on *Re Steed's WT* [1960] Ch. 407.

174 *Re Cohen's WT* [1959] 1 W.L.R. 865; *Re Holt's Settlement* [1969] 1 Ch. 100; *Re Robinson's ST* [1976] 1 W.L.R. 806.

175 *Re Brook's Settlement* [1968] 1 W.L.R. 1661; and cf. *Re Wallace's Settlements* [1963] 1 W.L.R. 711.

176 *Ridgewell v Ridgewell* [2008] S.T.C. 1883; *Wright v Gater* [2012] 1 W.L.R. 802; *Allfrey v Allfrey* [2015] EWHC 1717 (Ch).

177 *Wyndham v Egremont* [2009] W.T.L.R. 1473 at [25].

178 [1959] 1 W.L.R. 865 at 868; criticised at (1960) 76 L.Q.R. 22 (R. E. M.).

179 *Re Cohen's WT* [1965] 1 W.L.R. 1229.

180 *Re Robinson's ST* [1976] 1 W.L.R. 806.

### (3) Parties to the Application

Application is by claim form (under Pt 8 of the Civil Procedure Rules) supported by affidavits to which a draft scheme of arrangement will be exhibited. The proper claimants are the adult beneficiaries and not the trustees.[181] The trustees are supposed to be "watch-dogs" concerned with the interests of those who may possibly be adversely affected by the arrangement proposed. The defendant should be the trustees, the settlor, any beneficiary not a claimant, and any person who may become entitled to an interest under the trusts as being at a future date or on the happening of a future event a person of any specified description or a member of any specified class (e.g. next-of-kin of S, still alive) who would be of that description or of that class if the said date had fallen or the said event had happened (e.g. S's death) at the date of the application to the court, being the date of issue of the claim form.[182] No other persons who might eventually fulfil that description or be members of that class (e.g. distant relatives who might be next-of-kin if the nearer relatives conveniently died) need be made parties, nor need possible objects of a power of appointment which has not actually been exercised in their favour, or persons whose only interest is under discretionary trusts in a protective trust where the interest of the protected beneficiary has not failed or determined. However, a person who has an actual interest conferred directly on him by a settlement, however remote or contingent, has been held not to be a person who may become entitled to an interest so the court cannot approve on his behalf.[183] **7–075**

### (4) Effect of the Court's Approval

The variation takes effect as soon as the order of the court is made without any further instrument,[184] and the order may be liable to stamp duty.[185] A fundamental question is whether it is the order of the court or the arrangement which that order approves which has the effect of varying the trusts. The former view was taken in *Re Hambleden's WT*.[186] The latter view is supported by dicta of Lords Reid and Wilberforce in *Re Holmden's Settlement*.[187] **7–076**

In *Re Holt's Settlement*,[188] decided before *Re Holmden's Settlement* was reported, Megarry J rejected the view taken in *Re Hambleden's WT*, canvassed the difficulties arising from such rejection and accepted counsel's submission that,[189] "when the adults by their counsel assented to the arrangement and the court on behalf of the infants by order approved the arrangement then there was an arrangement which varied the trusts". The variation is thus effected by the consent of all parties on *Saunders v Vautier*[190] principles, the court supplying the consents of the unborn, the unascertained and infants. This was endorsed in *Goulding v James* by Mummery LJ, who said that[191]: **7–077**

---

181 *Re Druce's ST* [1962] 1 W.L.R. 363. Trustees should only act as claimants where they are satisfied that the proposed arrangement is beneficial and that no beneficiary is willing to make the application.
182 *Knocker v Youle* [1986] 1 W.L.R. 934 at 938.
183 *Knocker v Youle* [1986] 1 W.L.R. 934.
184 *Re Holmden's Settlement* [1968] A.C. 685; *Re Holt's Settlement* [1969] 1 Ch. 100.
185 Practice Note [1966] 1 W.L.R. 345; *Re Holt's*, above; *Thorn v IRC* [1976] 1 W.L.R. 915, although, note that ad valorem duty on gifts was abolished by the Finance Act 1985 s.82.
186 [1960] 1 W.L.R. 82.
187 [1968] A.C. 685 at 701, 702, 710 and 713.
188 [1969] 1 Ch. 100.
189 [1969] 1 Ch. 100 at 115.
190 See paras 7–004ff.
191 [1997] 2 All E.R. 239 at 247.

> The court is merely contributing on behalf of infants and unborn and unascertained persons the binding assents to the arrangements which they, unlike an adult beneficiary, cannot give. The 1958 Act has thus been viewed by the courts as a statutory extension of the consent principle embodied in the rule in *Saunders v Vautier*. The principle recognises the rights of beneficiaries who are sui juris and together absolutely entitled to the trust property, to exercise their proprietary rights to overbear and defeat the intention of a testator or settlor.

### *C. The Matrimonial Causes Act 1973*

**7-078** Under the Matrimonial Causes Act 1973 ss.21(2)(c) and 24(1)(c), the court has very extensive powers to make an order varying any "ante-nuptial or post-nuptial"[192] settlement made on the parties to the marriage for the benefit of the parties and/or the children of the marriage, so long as it is for the benefit of some of them. An order extinguishing or reducing the interest of either of the spouses may even be made under s.24(1)(d). The trustees should be made parties and may be replaced, while the terms of the settlement may be completely rewritten.[193]

## 5. The Rules against Perpetuities

**7-079** The law holds that private (i.e. non-charitable) trusts may not continue indefinitely.[194] Reference is often made to a trust offending the rule against perpetuities without it being made clear whether the trust infringes the rule against remoteness of vesting, directed at persons' interests vesting at too remote a time, or infringes the rule against inalienability, directed at immediately effective interests which can go on for too long, so tying up the use of the income of trust property for too long. The two rules are mutually exclusive, the former applying to "people" trusts and the latter to "purpose" trusts. The Perpetuities and Accumulations Act 2009, which has now superseded the 1964 legislation in this area, helps to validate people trusts, but does not affect the rule against inalienability that can invalidate private purpose trusts.

### *A. The Rule against Remoteness of Vesting*

#### i. The Common Law Rule

**7-080** Where capital is set on one side to be kept intact ("endowment" capital) with only the income thereof being used, this cannot last indefinitely. A settlor cannot be allowed to rule the living from her grave for thousands of years nor to compel capital to be used for ever as "safe" trust capital instead of absolutely owned capital available for risky entrepreneurial ventures. Thus, where a settlor created successive interests a future interest (contingent on birth or whatever) was, under the common law rule, void unless at the creation of the trust it was absolutely certain that the contingency would be satisfied—and so the interest would become "vested in interest"—within the perpetuity period.

---

[192] *Brooks v Brooks* [1996] A.C. 375; but pension schemes that amount to nuptial settlements are now outside the MCA 1973 because pension-splitting is now possible under the Welfare Reform and Pensions Act 1999.

[193] *E v E (Financial Provision)* [1990] 2 F.L.R. 233; *T v Y (Joinder of Third Parties)* [1996] 2 F.L.R. 357.

[194] For discussion of the reasons for this and an overview of the legal position prior to the enactment of the Perpetuities and Accumulations Act 2009, see Law Commission, *The Rules Against Perpetuities and Excessive Accumulations*, reviewed in Gallanis (2000) 59 C.L.J. 284. See also the passage from Paul Matthews' article that has been reproduced above at paras 7-021–7-028.

The perpetuity period cannot exceed 21 years from the death of some expressly or impliedly relevant life in being at the creation of the trust. A settlor can expressly stipulate that his beneficiaries are only those described by him who take a vested interest before the expiry of 21 years from the death of the last survivor of all the descendants of King George VI living at the date of the settlement (a "royal lives" clause). If T died, leaving his estate on trust for his widow, W, for life, remainder to S, his only child, for life, remainder to such of his grandchildren who attained 21 years of age, all the trusts are valid. W has a life interest "vested in possession" (a present right of present enjoyment), S has a life interest "vested in interest" (a present right to future enjoyment), while grandchildren under 21 have contingent interests (a contingent right to future enjoyment), which must become vested in interest within 21 years of the deaths of S and his spouse, even though in the case of class gifts a member's interest does not vest in interest (for perpetuity purposes) until the size of the share is fixed when the last class member is ascertained. The grandchildren's parents' lives are impliedly causally relevant in restricting the period within which the contingent interests inevitably must, if at all, become vested interests. **7–081**

### ii. The Statutory "Wait and See" Rule

If, by any stretch of the imagination, a contingent interest might possibly not become vested in interest within the perpetuity period, it was void. To mitigate this harshness the Perpetuities and Accumulations Act 1964 radically reformed the rule against remoteness. Where a contingent future interest would have been void at common law, the statute provided that one should instead "wait and see" what actually happened in a statutory perpetuity period.[195] The interest was valid until it became clear that it must vest in interest (if at all) outside the period prescribed by statute, which replaced causally relevant common law lives by a list of statutory lives in being[196] and, as an alternative, expressly allowed a specified period of years not exceeding 80 to be chosen as the perpetuity period.[197] Common practice was to use the 80-year period because one then knew in advance exactly when the trust would terminate. **7–082**

In 1998 the Law Commission published a report recommending reform of the rules against perpetuities and accumulations.[198] Among other things, it recommended that the range of permitted perpetuity periods should be replaced by a single period of 125 years. Legislation to this effect was enacted in the form of the Perpetuities and Accumulations Act 2009 s.5. The "wait and see" rule is preserved by s.7, and applies in all cases where, at the outset, it is possible that an interest will not vest within the perpetuity period. Hence the relevant provision will be treated as entirely valid unless and until it becomes clear that the interest cannot vest, or the relevant power will not be exercised, or fully exercised, within the perpetuity period. **7–083**

Section 8 further provides that, where it is or becomes clear that the inclusion of future or potential members of a class of beneficiaries would cause the interest to be void for remoteness, those members are automatically excluded from the class unless the effect of so doing would be to exhaust the class. Sections 9 and 10 remove some inconvenient consequences that would otherwise flow from the "wait and see" rule. Section 9 validates any interest, that would otherwise be valid, that follows or is dependent on a disposition which is void for remoteness, and enables such an interest to be accelerated. Section 10 substantially re-enacts ss.3 and 12 of the 1964 Act, and provides that, where the gift **7–084**

195 Perpetuities and Accumulations Act 1964 s.3(1), (2), (3).
196 s.3(5).
197 s.1.
198 Law Commission, *The Rules Against Perpetuities and Excessive Accumulations* (1998) Law Com. No.251.

over expectant on a determinable interest is void for remoteness, the determinable interest becomes absolute. Section 11 defines differing kinds of special powers of appointment, which are among the dispositions to which the "wait and see" rule applies.

### iii. *Re Denley*-Type Locus Standi Purpose Trusts

**7–085** As discussed in Chapter 5,[199] *Re Denley*[200] upheld a trust of land to be maintained and used as a recreation or sports ground for the benefit of employees from time to time of a particular company, while in *Wicks v Firth*[201] the House of Lords assumed that there can be a valid trust to award scholarships to assist in the education of children of employees of a company from time to time. Both trusts were limited expressly to a valid perpetuity period, but what would have happened if such trusts were left open-ended to last indefinitely?

**7–086** It seems likely that for perpetuity purposes such a trust would have been regarded as analogous to a discretionary trust before the 1964 Act.[202] Thus, because the powers of the trustees to benefit the beneficiaries were not bound to have been exhaustively exercised within the common law perpetuity period the trusts would have been void. Under the statutory "wait and see" rule, however, the trusts are valid to the extent that the trustees exercise their powers of appointment within the statutory perpetuity period. At the end of the period the property will then be held on resulting trust for the settlor.

**7–087** An alternative approach would be to say that *Re Denley*-type purpose trusts should be treated like other permitted non-charitable purpose trusts[203] and so be subject not to the rule against remoteness but to the rule against inalienability.[204] This would make them void unless at the outset it is certain that by the end of the perpetuity period the trust fund will be wholly alienable by some absolute owners.[205] However, in light of the modern judicial tendency to facilitate, rather than frustrate, the intentions of settlors and testators, it seems likely that the courts will not invoke the harsh rule against inalienability that applies to purpose trusts but will regard *Re Denley*-type purpose trusts as trusts for those persons with locus standi to sue.[206]

## *B. The Rule against Inalienability (or Perpetual Purpose Trusts)*

**7–088** The common law rule against remoteness ensured that endowment trusts for persons were void unless one could be absolutely sure from the outset that by the end of the perpetuity period the beneficiaries would have obtained vested interests enabling them to deal with the trust fund as they wished. Under the rule in *Saunders v Vautier*[207] if trustees hold property on trust for A absolutely or for B for life, remainder to C absolutely, then (assuming that each is sui juris) A or B and C, as the case may be, can direct the trustees how to deal with the property, e.g. vest it in A absolutely or divide it absolutely between B and C in the shares agreed by B and C. Persons like B must obtain vested

---

199 See para.5–015.
200 [1969] 1 Ch. 373.
201 [1983] A.C. 214.
202 See *Re Grant's WT* [1979] 3 All E.R. 359 at 368.
203 See paras 5–007ff.
204 *Re Northern Developments (Holdings) Ltd* unreported 6 October 1978: see (1991) 107 L.Q.R. 608 at 611.
205 See next sub-heading.
206 See Vinelott J in *Re Grant's WT* [1979] 3 All E.R. 359 at 368; P.J. Millett QC (now Lord Millett) (1985) 101 L.Q.R. 268 at 281–282.
207 (1841) 4 Beav. 115.

interests before the end of the perpetuity period but there is no requirement that their interests must terminate within the perpetuity period so that someone must become absolutely entitled to the relevant property in such period.[208] Thus, if at the end of the period B has a life interest the trust continues untill C acquires the property on B's death.

The rule against inalienability makes the few permitted[209] non-charitable endowment purpose trusts void unless from the outset it is certain that persons will become absolutely entitled beneficiaries by the end of the perpetuity period,[210] i.e. 21 years from the death of the last survivor of any causally relevant lives in being.[211] Such a rule was necessary because purposes unlike individuals can last forever and because a rule against remoteness of vesting is inappropriate when interests cannot vest in purposes as opposed to persons. Thus, testamentary trusts to erect and then maintain a sepulchral monument, or to say private masses for the testator, are void unless restricted to a specified perpetuity period, which will be 21 years unless, say, a royal lives clause is used. **7–089**

Whatever happen from time to time to be the particular trust assets comprised in the trust fund will be alienable under the Settled Land Act 1925, or the Law of Property Act 1925, or the Trustee Act 2000. However, if trust income has to be used for a particular purpose then the trust fund producing that income must be kept intact for as long as the income is required for that purpose. The inalienability of the trust income inevitably leads to the inalienability of the trust fund. The rule against inalienability is concerned to ensure that the length of time for which trustees must retain the trust fund (in whatever assets it is from time to time invested) does not exceed the perpetuity period. **7–090**

If the trustees do not have to keep the capital intact and use only the income thereof but can spend trust money on the trust purposes without the need to consider whether or not the money represents capital or income and whether the purpose is a "capital" or "income" type of purpose, then the rule against inalienability has no application.[212] Usually, the settlor will make it clear if the trustees are to hold her property on trust only to use the income within a specified perpetuity period for particular purposes and at the end of the period to distribute the capital to beneficiaries. Exceptionally, she may make it clear that her property is to be used without distinction between capital and income until fully consumed. **7–091**

## *C. The Rule against Excessive Accumulations*

Fearful of the implications for the English economy if very wealthy men like Peter Thellusson could by will[213] have the income of their estate accumulated for the full perpetuity period of royal lives plus 21 years—and more fearful for the finances of themselves and their children—English **7–092**

---

208 *Re Chardon* [1928] Ch. 464; *Re Gage* [1898] 1 Ch. 498; *Wainwright v Miller* [1897] 2 Ch. 255.

209 See para.5–007.

210 *Leahy v Attorney General for New South Wales* [1959] A.C. 457; *Cocks v Manners* (1871) L.R. 12 Eq. 574.

211 *Re Astor's ST* [1952] Ch. 534; *Re Khoo Cheng Teow* [1932] Straits Settlement Reports 226. The statutory period of 125 years introduced by the 2009 Act applies only to the rule against remoteness: see s.18 which provides that "This Act does not affect the rule of law which limits the duration of noncharitable purpose trusts".

212 *Re Lipinski's WT* [1976] Ch. 235 at 245; *Re Drummond* [1914] 2 Ch. 90 at 98; *Re Prevost* [1930] 2 Ch. 383 at 388; *Re Price* [1943] Ch. 422 at 428, 430; *Re Macaulay's Estate* [1943] Ch. 435 at 436. In *Leahy v Attorney General for New South Wales* [1959] A.C. 457 at 483. Viscount Simonds doubted whether a society's liberty to spend the capital and income of a gift as it saw fit saved a gift on trust to the society unless its members are treated as the immediate beneficiaries capable of disposing of the gifted property. This is too restrictive a view of the beneficiary principle: there can be *Re Denley*-type purpose trusts benefiting individuals within a fluctuating class who have no right to make the trust property their own but do have a right to ensure that the property is used for their benefit.

213 *Thellusson v Woodford* (1799) 4 Ves. 227, for a full account of which, see P. Polden, *Peter Thellusson's Will of 1797 and Its Consequences on Chancery Law* (Edwin Mellen Press, 2002).

MPs passed the Accumulations Act 1800 (the "Thellusson Act") to restrict the period for which income could be accumulated. Subsequent legislation in the area meant that until 2009, where it was sought to give trustees a power to accumulate, it was crucial to restrict the accumulation to one of the six periods allowed by ss.164–166 of the Law of Property Act 1925 and s.13 of the 1964 Act.[214] However, the rule against excessive accumulation was abolished for most purposes by the Perpetuities and Accumulations Act 2009 s.13, which repeals the relevant sections of the 1925 and 1964 statutes. The effect of this should be to provide settlors and testators with considerable freedom to accumulate income within settlements, although the rule against perpetuities effectively limits the life of a trust and so provides an upper limit on any accumulation.

## Perpetuities and Accumulations Act 2009

### 1. Application of the Rule

7-093 (1) The rule against perpetuities applies (and applies only) as provided by this section.
(2) If an instrument limits property in trust so as to create successive estates or interests the rule applies to each of the estates or interests.
(3) If an instrument limits property in trust so as to create an estate or interest which is subject to a condition precedent and which is not one of successive estates or interests, the rule applies to the estate or interest.
(4) If an instrument limits property in trust so as to create an estate or interest subject to a condition subsequent the rule applies to –

(a) any right of re-entry exercisable if the condition is broken, or
(b) any equivalent right exercisable in the case of property other than land if the condition is broken.

(5) If an instrument which is a will limits personal property so as to create successive interests under the doctrine of executory bequests, the rule applies to each of the interests.
(6) If an instrument creates a power of appointment the rule applies to the power. . .
(8) This section has effect subject to the exceptions made by section 2 and to any exceptions made under section 3.

### 2. Exceptions to Rule's Application

7-094 (1) This section contains exceptions to the application of the rule against perpetuities.
(2) The rule does not apply to an estate or interest created so as to vest in a charity on the occurrence of an event if immediately before the occurrence an estate or interest in the property concerned is vested in another charity.
(3) The rule does not apply to a right exercisable by a charity on the occurrence of an event if immediately before the occurrence an estate or interest in the property concerned is vested in another charity.
(4) The rule does not apply to an interest or right arising under a relevant pension scheme.
(5) The exception in subsection (4) does not apply if the interest or right arises under—

(a) an instrument nominating benefits under the scheme, or
(b) an instrument made in the exercise of a power of advancement arising under the scheme. . . .

### 5. Perpetuity Period

7-095 (1) The perpetuity period is 125 years (and no other period).
(2) Subsection (1) applies whether or not the instrument referred to in section 1(2) to (6)

[214] Unless s.31 of the Trustee Act 1925 allowed accumulations during a beneficiary's minority.

specifies a perpetuity period; and a specification of a perpetuity period in that instrument is ineffective.

**6. Start of perpetuity period**

(1) The perpetuity period starts when the instrument referred to in section 1(2) to (6) takes effect; but this is subject to subsections (2) and (3). 7–096

(2) If section 1(2), (3) or (4) applies and the instrument is made in the exercise of a special power of appointment the perpetuity period starts when the instrument creating the power takes effect; but this is subject to subsection (3).

(3) If section 1(2), (3) or (4) applies and—

(a) the instrument nominates benefits under a relevant pension scheme, or

(b) the instrument is made in the exercise of a power of advancement arising under a relevant pension scheme,

the perpetuity period starts when the member concerned became a member of the scheme.

(4) The member concerned is the member in respect of whose interest in the scheme the instrument is made.

**7. Wait and See Rule**

(1) Subsection (2) applies if (apart from this section and section 8) an estate or interest would be void on the ground that it might not become vested until too remote a time. 7–097

(2) In such a case—

(a) until such time (if any) as it becomes established that the vesting must occur (if at all) after the end of the perpetuity period the estate or interest must be treated as if it were not subject to the rule against perpetuities, and

(b) if it becomes so established, that does not affect the validity of anything previously done (whether by way of advancement, application of intermediate income or otherwise) in relation to the estate or interest.

(3) Subsection (4) applies if (apart from this section) any of the following would be void on the ground that it might be exercised at too remote a time—

(a) a right of re-entry exercisable if a condition subsequent is broken;

(b) an equivalent right exercisable in the case of property other than land if a condition subsequent is broken;

(c) a special power of appointment.

(4) In such a case—

(a) the right or power must be treated as regards any exercise of it within the perpetuity period as if it were not subject to the rule against perpetuities, and

(b) the right or power must be treated as void for remoteness only if and so far as it is not fully exercised within the perpetuity period.

(5) Subsection (6) applies if (apart from this section) a general power of appointment would be void on the ground that it might not become exercisable until too remote a time.

(6) Until such time (if any) as it becomes established that the power will not be exercisable within the perpetuity period, it must be treated as if it were not subject to the rule against perpetuities.

**8. Exclusion of Class Members to Avoid Remoteness**

(1) This section applies if— 7–098

(a) it is apparent at the time an instrument takes effect or becomes apparent at a later time that (apart from this section) the inclusion of certain persons as members of a class would cause an estate or interest to be treated as void for remoteness, and

(b) those persons are potential members of the class or unborn persons who at birth would become members or potential members of the class.

(2) From the time it is or becomes so apparent those persons must be treated for all the purposes of the instrument as excluded from the class unless their exclusion would exhaust the class.
(3) If this section applies in relation to an estate or interest to which section 7 applies, this section does not affect the validity of anything previously done (whether by way of advancement, application of intermediate income or otherwise) in relation to the estate or interest.
(4) For the purposes of this section—

(a) a person is a member of a class if in that person's case all the conditions identifying a member of the class are satisfied, and
(b) a person is a potential member of a class if in that person's case some only of those conditions are satisfied but there is a possibility that the remainder will in time be satisfied. . . .

**9. Saving and Acceleration of Expectant Interests**

7-099 (1) An estate or interest is not void for remoteness by reason only that it is ulterior to and dependent on an estate or interest which is so void.
(2) The vesting of an estate or interest is not prevented from being accelerated on the failure of a prior estate or interest by reason only that the failure arises because of remoteness.

**10. Determinable Interests Becoming Absolute**

7-100 (1) If an estate arising under a right of reverter on the determination of a determinable fee simple is void for remoteness the determinable fee simple becomes absolute.
(2) If an interest arising under a resulting trust on the determination of a determinable interest is void for remoteness the determinable interest becomes absolute.

**11. Powers of Appointment**

7-101 (1) Subsection (2) applies to a power of appointment exercisable otherwise than by will (whether or not it is also exercisable by will).
(2) For the purposes of the rule against perpetuities the power is a special power unless –

(a) the instrument creating it expresses it to be exercisable by one person only, and
(b) at all times during its currency when that person is of full age and capacity it could be exercised by that person so as immediately to transfer to that person the whole of the interest governed by the power without the consent of any other person or compliance with any other condition (ignoring a formal condition relating only to the mode of exercise of the power).

(3) Subsection (4) applies to a power of appointment exercisable by will (whether or not it is also exercisable otherwise than by will).
(4) For the purposes of the rule against perpetuities the power is a special power unless –

(a) the instrument creating it expresses it to be exercisable by one person only, and
(b) that person could exercise it so as to transfer to that person's personal representatives the whole of the estate or interest to which it relates.

(5) Subsection (6) applies to a power of appointment exercisable by will or otherwise.
(6) If for the purposes of the rule against perpetuities the power would be a special power under one but not both of subsections (2) and (4), for the purposes of the rule it is a special power.

**Questions**

1. "Where there is a trust for A, B and C absolutely, A, B and C are in a strong position." **Discuss**.
2. "It has been said that the courts have no jurisdiction under the Variation of Trusts Act 1958 to approve a resettlement, but in reality they have approved arrangements which amount to resettlements in all but name." **Discuss**.

3. Brian leaves his cricket field and pavilion to trustees to hold on trust solely for the present and future members of Slogworthy Cricket Club. Consider in the light of the Perpetuities and Accumulations Act 2009. Would the position be different if such property had been left on trust to further the playing of cricket by persons resident in Slogworthy?
4. What would happen if the facts in *Re Denley* resulted from a 2015 conveyance which omitted to restrict the trusts to any specified perpetuity period?

# PART IV

# RIGHTS AND DUTIES OF EXPRESS TRUSTEES

# 8

# APPOINTMENT, RETIREMENT, REMOVAL AND PAYMENT OF TRUSTEES

## 1. Introduction

It is vital to ensure that the appointment, retirement and removal of trustees are correctly carried out. If they are not, various problems may ensue: the old trustees will remain liable to account to the beneficiaries as trustees, while the new "trustees" will become liable to account as trustees *de son tort*[1]; also the new "trustees" may not be the legal owners of the trust property, with potentially significant consequences for the validity of their purported dispositions of trust property, and for the tax treatment of the settlement.[2] **8–001**

Consistently with the rule that trustees should avoid conflicts between their personal interests and the beneficiaries' interests,[3] they are not generally entitled to be paid for their services. But there are some exceptions to this rule, and trustees are also entitled to be indemnified for costs which they incur in the course of carrying out the trust affairs. **8–002**

## 2. Appointment of Trustees

### A. Express Powers of Appointment

When a settlor creates a trust in her lifetime, she will usually appoint the first trustees of the trust, e.g. by declaring herself trustee, or by including a clause in the trust instrument appointing herself and/or others as the trustees. Once the trust has come into existence, however, the settlor has no right to appoint new trustees unless she reserves a power of appointment to herself in the trust instrument. Alternatively she may give such a power to another person.[4] In the case of a testamentary trust, the settlor obviously can do no more than appoint the first trustees, but again she may give a power to appoint new trustees to another person. **8–003**

It is often said that a power to appoint new trustees and a power to remove existing trustees are both fiduciary powers, with the result that they cannot be exercised by the donee of the power in a **8–004**

1 See paras 11–014—11–016.
2 e.g. *Jasmine Trustees Ltd v Wells & Hind (a firm)* [2008] Ch. 194.
3 See paras 9–018ff.
4 e.g. *Re Walker and Hughes* (1883) 24 Ch.D. 698; *Re Sheppard's ST* [1888] W.N. 234.

way that creates an actual or potential conflict between her personal interest and the interests of the beneficiaries. Authority for this rule is commonly said to be *Re Skeats Settlement*,[5] a case concerning a marriage settlement under which the husband and wife were empowered to appoint the trustees; they appointed the husband and Kay J set this appointment aside. However, David Pollard and Dawn Heath have persuasively argued that this decision was context-specific and should not necessarily be followed in every case.[6] The question of whether a power is fiduciary must turn on the circumstances of the case, and in the context of pension scheme trusts there are good reasons for thinking that a power of appointment vested in an employer will often not be fiduciary, including: the ongoing interests of the employer in the scheme; the fact that employer powers under pension schemes are generally not fiduciary; and the existence of other limits on employer's powers, and especially its implied duty of good faith.[7]

**8-005** If no power to appoint new trustees is conferred by the trust instrument, either generally or in some specific situation, then they may be appointed either under the statutory powers contained in the Trustee Act 1925 s.36 or the Trusts of Land and Appointment of Trustees Act 1996 s.19, or by the court.

**8-006** Note that a person appointed trustee may disclaim the office, for "a man cannot have an estate put into him in spite of his teeth". The disclaimer of a trust by a person appointed trustee must be a disclaimer of the whole trust; it cannot be partial.[8] Ideally it should be in writing (or by deed), but it may also be oral,[9] by conduct,[10] by mere inactivity (it seems),[11] or signified on behalf of the person appointed trustee by counsel at the Bar.[12] If a person is appointed both executrix and trustee and she proves the will, she thereby accepts the trust. But if she renounces probate, she does not thereby necessarily disclaim the trust.[13]

**8-007** Note, too, that trusts do not fail for want of trustees. If a testator creates a trust in her will, but fails to appoint trustees or appoints trustees who refuse or are unable to act or have ceased to exist, then the trust does not fail[14] (unless its operation was conditional upon a specific trustee undertaking the trust[15]). Nor does it fail if the intended trustees disclaim ownership of shares or land secretly transferred into their names by a settlor. The property or the beneficial interest therein remains in the settlor or the personal representatives of the testator to be held upon the trusts of the settlement or the will as the case may be.[16]

**8-008** On the death of a sole or sole surviving trustee, the trust property vests in her personal representatives subject to the trusts and by the Trustee Act 1925 s.18(2), they are capable of exercising or performing any power or trust which the deceased trustee could have exercised or performed. They are not bound to accept the position and duties of trustees and may exercise their power of appointing

---

5 (1889) L.R. 42 Ch.D. 522.

6 D. Pollard and D. Heath, "The Power of Employers to Appoint or Remove Trustees of Occupational Pension Schemes: Is It Fiduciary?" (2011) 25 Tru. L.I. 184.

7 Arising under *Imperial Group Pension Trust Ltd v Imperial Tobacco Ltd* [1991] 2 All E.R. 597.

8 *Re Lord and Fullerton* [1896] 1 Ch. 228.

9 *Bingham v Clanmorris* (1828) 2 Moll. 253; doubted by Wood VC in *Re Ellison* (1856) 2 Jur. 62.

10 *Stacey v Elph* (1883) 1 My. & K. 195; *Re Birchall* (1889) 40 Ch.D. 436.

11 *Re Clout and Frewer* [1924] 2 Ch. 230.

12 *Landbroke v Bleaden* (1852) 16 Jur. (O.S.) 630; *Foster v Dawber* (1860) 8 W.R. 646.

13 *Mucklow v Fuller* (1821) Jac. 198; *Ward v Butler* (1824) 2 Moll. 533; *Dix v Burford* (1854) 19 Beav. 409 at 412, per Romilly MR.

14 *Re Willis* [1921] 1 Ch. 44; *Re Armitage* [1972] Ch. 438; *Re Morrison* (1967) 111 S.J. 758.

15 *Re Lysaght* [1966] 1 Ch. 191.

16 *Mallot v Wilson* [1903] 2 Ch. 494, accepted as good law by the Court of Appeal in *Harris v Sharp* [2003] W.T.L.R. 1541. P. Matthews [1981] Conv. 141 contends that disclaimer of an inter vivos transfer to a trustee should make the transfer void and the trust fail; but one may treat the transferor as constructive trustee by *Re Rose* [1952] Ch. 499 principles, for which see paras 2-022ff. See also *Standing v Bowring* (1885) 31 Ch.D. 282 at 288; *Tett v Phoenix* [1984] B.C.L.C. 599; and on the unilateral and bilateral nature of gifts see J. Hill (2001) 117 L.Q.R. 127.

new trustees under s.36 with a right to payment of the costs thereof from the trust moneys.[17] If need be the court may appoint new trustees under s.41[18] or itself execute the trust.[19]

What happens if a deceased trustee's powers devolve upon her personal representative who then dies herself, without having appointed new trustees? If she accepted the trustee role under s.18(2) then she should herself be treated as a trustee for her powers to devolve under s.18(2) to her own personal representative.[20] If she was an executor of the deceased trustee and she appointed an executor under her own will, then this executor would be executor by representation of the trustee[21] and so have the s.18(2) powers in any event. **8–009**

## *B. Statutory Powers of Appointment*

The Trustee Act 1925 s.36 gives a power to appoint new trustees to the following persons in the following order: (i) the person(s) nominated in the trust instrument (s.36(1)(a)); (ii) if there is no such person, or no such person able or willing to act, the surviving and continuing trustees (s.36(1)(b)); or (iii) if there is no surviving or continuing trustee, the personal representatives of the last or only surviving trustee (s.36(1)(b)). **8–010**

Where the power to appoint new trustees vests in the current trustees, it is a fiduciary power[22] and when exercising it they must pay due regard to the interests of the trust and of the conflicting interests of the beneficiaries. Their function is a paternalistic one requiring them to protect the beneficiaries from themselves.[23] Thus, before 1996 even if the beneficiaries were all of full capacity and between them absolutely entitled, they still could not compel the trustees under s.36 to appoint their nominee: the trustees were entitled to exercise their independent judgment.[24] All that the beneficiaries could do was put an end to the existing settlement under the rule in *Saunders v Vautier*[25] and then create a new settlement of which, as settlors, they could appoint new trustees—but this had fiscal disadvantages. **8–011**

However, the position was changed by the enactment of the Trusts of Land and Appointment of Trustees Act 1996 s.19, which provides that if all the beneficiaries are ascertained and of full age and capacity then they have a right to require the trustees to retire and to direct the trustees to appoint specified persons to be new trustees, such right not existing where a person nominated in the trust instrument (not the current trustees) has the power to appoint new trustees.[26] **8–012**

The provision in the Trustee Act 1925 s.36(1) which enables a trustee who remains out of the UK for more than 12 months to be replaced does not make persons resident abroad ineligible to be appointed as trustees, as held by Pennycuick VC in *Re Whitehead's WT*.[27] However, while accepting that the appointment of non-resident trustees had been a proper valid one in the case before him, **8–013**

---

17 *Re Benett* [1906] 1 Ch. 216.
18 *Jones v Jones* (1874) 31 L.T. 538.
19 *McPhail v Doulton* [1971] A.C. 424 at 457.
20 P.W. Smith, "The Chains of Trusteeship" (1977) 41 Conv. 423.
21 Administration of Estates Act 1925 s.7.
22 Indeed, even if the power of appointing new trustees is reserved to the settlor while alive it will be presumed to be a fiduciary power: *IRC v Schroder* [1983] S.T.C. 480; *Re Osiris Trustees Ltd* [2000] W.T.L.R. 933. The settlor needs to act in altruistic good faith.
23 *Head v Gould* [1898] 2 Ch. 250.
24 *Re Brockbank* [1948] Ch. 206.
25 (1841) 4 Beav. 115. See paras 7–004ff.
26 s.19(1)(a). s.19 is inapplicable to a pre-Act trust if the settlor subsequently executes a deed stating it is to be inapplicable: s.21(6).
27 [1971] 1 W.L.R. 833.

he went on to say that in the absence of special circumstances (e.g. the beneficiaries having taken up permanent residence in a foreign country where the newly-appointed trustees reside) the appointment of non-residents was improper (though neither void nor illegal) so that the court would be likely to interfere at the instance of the beneficiaries.[28]

**8-014** This approach is now out of date where the trustees are exercising their discretion to appoint foreign trustees and are merely seeking the declaratory authorisation of the court for their own protection. In *Richard v Mackay*,[29] Millett J stated:

> The appropriateness is for the trustees to decide, and different minds may have different views on what is appropriate in particular circumstances. Certainly, in the conditions of today when one can have an international family with international interests and where they are as likely to make their home in one country as in another and as likely to choose one jurisdiction as another for the investment of their capital, I doubt that the language of Sir John Pennycuick is really in tune with the times. In my judgment, where the trustees retain their discretion, as they do in the present case, the court should need to be satisfied only that the proposed transaction is not so inappropriate that no reasonable trustee could entertain it.

**8-015** Thus, the trustees (in case UK exchange control was reintroduced) could properly transfer part of the trust fund to the trustees of a trust to be established in Bermuda with Bermudan resident trustees, Bermuda having a stable English system of law and very experienced corporate trustees, even though the beneficiaries had no connection with Bermuda. Although the proposal was not to appoint new trustees of an existing trust nothing turns on the distinction, as recognised in *Re Whitehead's WT*.[30]

**8-016** However, Millett J contrasted cases where the court is asked to exercise a discretion of its own (e.g. under the Variation of Trusts Act 1958[31] or the Trustee Act 1925 s.41[32]) with cases where the trustees are exercising their own discretion. In the former situation the applicants have to make out a positive case for the court's exercise of its discretion "and the court is unlikely to assist them where the scheme is nothing more than a device to avoid tax and has no other advantages of any kind".

**8-017** Tax-saving is, of course, a proper consideration for trustees[33] and where it is clear that the proposed transaction is not so inappropriate that no reasonable trustee could entertain it the appointment of foreign trustees can now proceed without seeking any confirmation from the court.

**8-018** Under the Trustee Act 1925 s.37(1)(c) "a trustee shall not be discharged from his trust unless there will be either a trust corporation or at least two persons to act as trustees to perform the trust." This sub-section was amended (with prospective effect only) in 1996, having previously specified that at least two "individuals" must have been appointed if resigning trustees were to be discharged, the word "individuals" meaning natural persons only, so that resigning trustees were not discharged following the appointment as the new trustees, e.g. of a human being and a company that was not a trust corporation.[34] This trap was eliminated in 1996 by the replacement of the word "individuals" with the word "persons". Note, however, that "trust corporation" still cannot cover a company that is not incorporated in a Member State of the EU,[35] and that if a sole corporate trustee is appointed then

---

[28] It thus seems that the appointment is voidable by the beneficiaries, and that: the Revenue will have no locus standi to object unless the appointment was void as part of a criminal conspiracy to defraud the Revenue.

[29] (1997) 11 Tru. L. I. 22, noted by R. Bramwell QC in (1990) 1 O.T.P.R. 1, and followed in *Re Beatty's WT (No.2)* (1997) 11 Tru. L.I. 77.

[30] [1971] 1 W.L.R. 833 at 838.

[31] See paras 7-047ff.

[32] See para.8-026.

[33] [1971] 1 W.L.R. 833 at 839.

[34] *Jasmine Trustees Ltd v Wells & Hind (a firm)* [2008] Ch. 194 at [22]-[32]. For trust corporations, see para.8-037.

[35] See Trustee Act 1925 s.68(18).

the purportedly replaced trustees remain as trustees if the new corporate trustee does not rank as a "trust corporation".[36]

However, it seems that s.37(1)(c) is subject to express contrary intention so that the trust instrument can expressly authorise the discharge of trustees from the trusts by replacing them with the appointment as sole trustee of a corporation ranking as a trust corporation by the law of the state of its incorporation, except for trust property consisting of land in England and Wales.[37] After all, a valid receipt for the proceeds of sale of such land can only be given by a trust corporation or two persons acting as trustees.[38] **8–019**

## Trustee Act 1925 ss.36 and 37

### 36. Power of appointing new or additional trustees

(1) Where a trustee,[39] either original or substituted, and whether appointed by a court or otherwise, is dead, or remains out of the United Kingdom for more than twelve months, or desires to be discharged from all or any of the trusts or powers reposed in or conferred on him, or refuses or is unfit to act therein, or is incapable of acting therein, or is an infant, then, subject to the restrictions imposed by this Act on the number of trustees[40]— **8–020**

(a) the person or persons nominated for the purpose of appointing new trustees by the instrument, if any, creating the trust; or

(b) if there is no such person, or no such person able and willing to act, then the surviving or continuing[41] trustees or trustee for the time being, or the personal representatives of the last surviving or continuing trustee[42]:

may, by writing, appoint one or more other persons (whether or not being the persons exercising the power) to be a trustee or trustees in the place of the trustee so deceased, remaining out of the United Kingdom, desiring to be discharged, refusing, or being unfit or being incapable, or being an infant, as aforesaid.

(2) Where a trustee has been removed under a power contained in the instrument creating the trust, a new trustee or new trustees may be appointed in the place of the trustee who is removed, as if he were dead, or, in the case of a corporation, as if the corporation desired to be discharged from the trust, and the provisions of this section shall apply accordingly, but subject to the restrictions imposed by this Act on the number of trustees.

(3) Where a corporation being a trustee is or has been dissolved, either before or after the commencement of this Act, then, for the purposes of this section and of any enactment replaced thereby, the corporation shall be deemed to be and to have been from the date of the dissolution incapable of acting in the trusts or powers reposed in or conferred on the corporation.

---

36 e.g. *Adam & Co International Trustees Ltd v Theodore Goddard* (2000) 2 I.T.E.L.R. 634, [2000] W.T.L.R. 349.

37 Trustee Act 1925 ss.69(2), 71(3); *London Regional Transport Pension Fund Trust Co v Hatt* [1993] P. L.R. 227 at 260, accepted in *Adam & Co*, above.

38 Trustee Act 1925 s.14(2), (3); Law of Property Act 1925 s.27(2).

39 "Trustee" is used as to exclude personal representatives. Accordingly, no power is conferred to appoint executors. By the Administration of Estates Act 1925 s.7, an executor of a sole or last surviving executor of a testator is the executor by representation of that testator.

40 Maximum of four trustees except for charities: Trustee Act 1925 s.34 and see s.36(5).

41 A continuing trustee is one who is to continue to act after completion of the intended appointment: *Re Coates to Parsons* (1886) 34 Ch.D. 370.

42 Persons appointed executors and trustees of wills of land must formally assent in favour of themselves qua trustees so as to take advantage of s.40: *Re King's WT* [1964] Ch. 542. An executor who has not proved his testator's will can exercise the power but the trustee appointed in such circumstances can only prove her title by reference to a proper grant of representation so that such a grant is, in practice, vital: *Re Crowhurst Park* [1974] 1 W.L.R. 583. If a will creates trusts but the trustees predecease the testator then s.36 is inapplicable: *Nicholson v Field* [1893] 2 Ch. 511.

(4) The power of appointment given by subsection (1) of this section or any similar previous enactment to the personal representatives of a last surviving or continuing trustee shall be and shall be deemed always to have been exercisable by the executors for the time being (whether original or by representation) of such surviving or continuing trustee who have proved the will of their testator or by the administrators for the time being of such trustee without the concurrence of any executor who has renounced or has not proved.

(5) But a sole or last surviving executor intending to renounce, or all the executors where they all intend to renounce, shall have and shall be deemed always to have had power, at any time before renouncing probate, to exercise the power of appointment given by this section, or by any similar previous enactment, if willing to act for the purpose and without thereby accepting the office of executor.

(6) Where, in the case of any trust, there are not more than three trustees

(a) the person or persons nominated for the purpose of appointing new trustees by the instrument, if any creating the trust; or

(b) if there is no such person, or no such person able and willing to act, then the trustee or trustees for the time being;

may, by writing, appoint another person or other persons to be an additional trustee or additional trustees, but it shall not be obligatory to appoint any additional trustee, unless the instrument, if any, creating the trust, or any statutory enactment provides to the contrary, nor shall the number of trustees be increased beyond four by virtue of any such appointment.

[Sub-sections (6A) to (6D) deal with the position of an attorney for a trustee making an appointment on behalf of the trustee].

(7) Every new trustee appointed under this section as well before as after all the trust property becomes by law, or by assurance, or otherwise, vested in him, shall have the same powers, authorities, and discretions, and may in all respects act as if he had been originally appointed a trustee by the instrument, if any, creating the trust.

(8) The provisions of this section relating to a trustee who is dead include the case of a person nominated trustee in a will but dying before the testator, and those relative to a continuing trustee include a refusing or retiring trustee, if willing to act in the execution of the provisions of this section.

(9) Where a trustee lacks capacity to exercise his functions as trustee and is also entitled in possession to some beneficial interest in the trust property, no appointment of a new trustee in his place shall be made by virtue of paragraph (b) of subsection (1) of this section unless leave to make the appointment has been given by the Court of Protection.

**37. Supplemental provisions as to appointment of trustees.**

8–021 (1) On the appointment of a trustee for the whole or any part of trust property—

(a) the number of trustees may, subject to the restrictions imposed by this Act on the number of trustees, be increased; and

(b) a separate set of trustees, not exceeding four, may be appointed for any part of the trust property held on trusts distinct from those relating to any other part or parts of the trust property, notwithstanding that no new trustees or trustee are or is to be appointed for other parts of the trust property, and any existing trustee may be appointed or remain one of such separate set of trustees, or, if only one trustee was originally appointed, then, save as hereinafter provided, one separate trustee may be so appointed; and

(c) it shall not be obligatory, save as hereinafter provided, to appoint more than one new trustee where only one trustee was originally appointed, or to fill up the original number of trustees where more than two trustees were originally appointed, but, except where only one trustee was originally appointed, and a sole trustee when appointed will be able to give valid receipts for all capital money, a trustee shall not be discharged from his trust unless there will be either a trust corporation or at least two persons to act as trustees to perform the trust; and

(d) any assurance or thing requisite for vesting the trust property, or any part thereof, in a sole trustee, or jointly in the persons who are the trustees, shall be executed or done.

(2) Nothing in this Act shall authorise the appointment of a sole trustee, not being a trust corporation where the trustee, when appointed, would not be able to give valid receipts for all capital money arising under the trust.

## Trusts of Land and Appointment of Trustees Act 1996 ss.19–21

**19. Appointment and retirement of trustee at instance of beneficiaries**

(1) This section applies in the case of a trust where— 8–022

(a) there is no person nominated for the purpose of appointing new trustees by the instrument, if any, creating the trust, and
(b) the beneficiaries under the trust are of full age and capacity and (taken together) are absolutely entitled to the property subject to the trust.

(2) The beneficiaries may give a direction or directions of either or both of the following descriptions—

(a) a written direction to a trustee or trustees to retire from the trust, and
(b) a written direction to the trustees or trustee for the time being (or, if there are none, to the personal representative of the last person who was a trustee) to appoint by writing to be a trustee or trustees the person or persons specified in the direction.

(3) Where—

(a) a trustee has been given a direction under subsection (2)(a),
(b) reasonable arrangements have been made for the protection of any rights of his in connection with the trust,
(c) after he has retired there will be either a trust corporation or at least two persons to act as trustees to perform the trust, and
(d) either another person is to be appointed to be a new trustee on his retirement (whether in compliance with a direction under subsection (2)(b) or otherwise) or the continuing trustees by deed consent to his retirement,

he shall make a deed declaring his retirement and shall be deemed to have retired and be discharged from the trust.

(4) Where a trustee retires under subsection (3) he and the continuing trustees (together with any new trustee) shall (subject to any arrangements for the protection of his rights) do anything necessary to vest the trust property in the continuing trustees (or the continuing and new trustees).
(5) This section has effect subject to the restrictions imposed by the Trustee Act 1925 on the number of trustees.

**20. Appointment of substitute for incapable trustee**

(1) This section applies where— 8–023

(a) a trustee lacks capacity (within the meaning of the Mental Capacity Act 2005) to exercise his functions as trustee,
(b) there is no person who is both entitled and willing and able to appoint a trustee in place of him under section 36(1) of the Trustee Act 1925, and
(c) the beneficiaries under the trust are of full age and capacity and (taken together) are absolutely entitled to the property subject to the trust.

(2) The beneficiaries may give to—

(a) a deputy appointed for the trustee by the Court of Protection,
(b) an attorney acting for him under the authority of an enduring power of attorney or lasting power of attorney registered under the Mental Capacity Act 2005, or
(c) a person authorised for the purpose by the Court of Protection under Part VII of the Mental Health Act 1983

a written direction to appoint by writing the person or persons specified in the direction to be a trustee or trustees in place of the incapable trustee.

**21. Supplementary**

8–024 (1) For the purposes of s.19 or 20 a direction is given by beneficiaries if—

(a) a single direction is jointly given by all of them, or
(b) (subject to subsection (2)) a direction is given by each of them (whether solely or jointly with one or more, but not all, of the others),

and none of them by writing withdraws the direction given by him before it has been complied with.

(2) Where more than one direction is given each must specify for appointment or retirement the same person or persons.
(3) Subsection (7) of section 36 of the Trustee Act 1925 (powers of trustees appointed under that section) applies to a trustee appointed under section 19 or 20 as if he were appointed under that section.
(4) A direction under section 19 or 20 must not specify a person or persons for appointment if the appointment of that person or those persons would be in contravention of section 35(1) of the Trustee Act 1925 or section 24(1) of the Law of Property Act 1925 (requirements as to identity of trustees).
(5) Sections 19 or 20 do not apply in relation to a trust created by a disposition in so far as provision that they do not apply is made by the disposition.
(6) Sections 19 and 20 do not apply in relation to a trust created before the commencement of this Act by a disposition in so far as provision to the effect that they do not apply is made by a deed executed—

(a) in a case in which the trust was created by one person and he is of full capacity, by that person, or
(b) in a case in which the trust was created by more than one person, by such of the persons who created the trust as are alive and of full capacity.

(7) A deed executed for the purpose of subsection (6) is irrevocable.
(8) Where a deed is executed for the purposes of subsection (6)—

(a) it does not affect anything done before its execution to comply with a direction under section 19 or 20, but
(b) a direction under section 19 or 20 which has been given but not complied with before its execution shall cease to have effect.

## *C. Appointment of Trustees by the Court*

8–025 The court has power to appoint new trustees under the Trustee Act 1925 s.41,[43] but an application should not be made to the court if the power of appointing new trustees contained in s.36(1) of the Act can be exercised.[44] The principles which guide the court in making an appointment are set out in *Re Tempest*,[45] which is reproduced below. If non-resident trustees are to be appointed the beneficiaries must usually[46] have a real and substantial connection with the country where the proposed trustees are resident.

---

43 Under the section a trustee may be displaced against her will: *Re Henderson* [1940] Ch. 764. The section authorises removal of trustees by replacement but not otherwise: *Re Harrison's ST* [1965] 3 All E.R. 795 at 799.

44 *Re Gibbon's Trusts* (1882) 30 W.R. 287; 45 L.T. 756. Otherwise, if it is uncertain whether the power under s.36(1) of the Act is exercisable: *Re May's Will Trusts* [1941] Ch. 109.

45 (1866) L.R. 1 Ch. 485.

46 But cf. *Re Chamberlain* (1976) 126 N.L.J. 1034 (reported in article by J. B. Morcom) the court approved Guernsey trustees where the beneficiaries were domiciled and resident some in France some in Indonesia.

## Trustee Act 1925 s.41

**41. Power of court to appoint new trustees.**

(1) The court, may, whenever it is expedient to appoint a new trustee or new trustees, and it is found inexpedient, difficult or impracticable so to do without the assistance of the court, make an order appointing a new trustee or trustees either in substitution for or in addition to any existing trustee or trustees, or although there is no existing trustee. 8–026

In particular and without prejudice to the generality of the foregoing provision, the court may make an order appointing a new trustee in substitution for a trustee who is lacks capacity to exercise his functions as trustee, or is a bankrupt, or is a corporation which is in liquidation or has been dissolved.

*Re Tempest*

Court of Appeal in Chancery (1865–66) L.R. 1 Ch. 485

TURNER L.J. (with whom KNIGHT-BRUCE L.J. agreed): In making such appointments the court acts upon and exercises its discretion; and this, no doubt, is generally true; but the discretion which the court has and exercises in making such appointments is not, as I conceive, a mere arbitrary discretion, but a discretion in the exercise of which the court is, and ought to be, guided by some general rules and principles, and, in my opinion, the difficulty which the court has to encounter in these cases lies not so much in ascertaining the rules and principles by which it ought to be guided, as in applying those rules and principles to the varying circumstances of each particular case. The following rules and principles may, I think, safely be laid down as applying to all cases of appointments by the court of new trustees. 8–027

First, the court will have regard to the wishes of the persons by whom the trust has been created, if expressed in the instrument creating the trust, or clearly to be collected from it. I think this rule may be safely laid down, because if the author of the trust has in terms declared that a particular person, or a person filling a particular character, should not be a trustee of the instrument, there cannot, as I apprehend, be the least doubt that the court would not appoint to the office a person whose appointment was so prohibited, and I do not think that upon a question of this description any distribution can be drawn between express declarations and demonstrated intention. The analogy of the course which the court pursued in the appointment of guardians affords, I think, some support to this rule. The court in those cases attends to the wishes of the parents, however informally they may be expressed. 8–028

Another rule which may, I think, safely be laid down is this—that the court will not appoint a person to be trustee with a view to the interest of some of the persons interested under the trust, in opposition either to the wishes of the testator or to the interests of others of the cestuis que trust. I think so for this reason, that it is of the essence of the duty of every trustee to hold an even hand between the parties interested under the trust. Every trustee is in duty bound to look to the interests of all, and not of any particular member or class of members of his cestuis que trust. 8–029

A third rule which, I think, may safely be laid down is that the court in appointing a trustee will have regard to the question whether his appointment will promote or impede the execution of the trust, for the very purpose of the appointment is that the trust may be better carried into execution. . . . 8–030

There cannot, I think, be any doubt that the court ought not to appoint a trustee whose appointment will impede the due execution of the trust; but, on the other hand, if the continuing or surviving trustee refuses to act with a trustee who may be proposed to be appointed . . . I think it would be going too far to say that the court ought, on that ground alone, to refuse to appoint the proposed trustee; for this would, as suggested in the argument, be to give the continuing or surviving trustee a veto upon the appointment of the new trustee. In such a case, I think it must be the duty of the court to inquire and ascertain whether the objection of the surviving or continuing trustee is well founded or not, and to act or refuse to act upon it accordingly. . . . 8–031

## *D. Protection of a Purchaser of Land of which New Trustees Have Been Appointed*

### Trustee Act 1925 s.38

**Evidence as to a vacancy in a trust**

8-032 (1) A statement, contained in any instrument coming into operation after the commencement of this Act by which a new trustee is appointed for any purpose connected with land, to the effect that a trustee has remained out of the United Kingdom for more than twelve months or refuses or is unfit to act, or is incapable of acting, or that he is not entitled to a beneficial interest in the trust property in possession, shall, in favour of a purchaser of a legal estate, be conclusive evidence of the matter stated.

(2) In favour of such purchaser any appointment of a new trustee depending on that statement, and any vesting declaration, express or implied, consequent on the appointment, shall be valid.

Where an appointment is invalid the general rule is that the old trustee remains trustee with the powers and liabilities of a trustee[47] though the invalidly appointed new trustee will become liable as trustee *de son tort* if he intermeddles with the property.[48]

## *E. Vesting of Trust Property in New or Continuing Trustees*

**8-033** The Trustee Act 1925 s.40 automatically vests trust property in new and/or continuing trustees as joint tenants without the need for any formal conveyance or assignment. The section is widely drafted to cover choses in action as well interests in land or chattels.[49]

### Trustee Act 1925 s.40

**Vesting of trust property in new or continuing trustees**

8-034 (1) Where by a deed a new trustee is appointed to perform any trust, then—

(a) if the deed contains a declaration by the appointor to the effect that any estate or interest in any land subject to the trust, or in any chattel so subject, or the right to recover or receive any debt or other thing in action so subject, shall vest in the persons who by virtue of the deed become or are the trustees for performing the trust, the deed shall operate, without any conveyance or assignment, to vest in those persons as joint tenants and for the purposes of the trust the estate interest or right to which the declaration relates; and

(b) if the deed is made after the commencement of this Act and does not contain such a declaration, the deed shall, subject to any express provision to the contrary therein contained, operate as if it had contained such a declaration by the appointor extending to all the estates interests and rights with respect to which a declaration could have been made.

(2) Where by a deed a retiring trustee is discharged under the statutory power without a new trustee being appointed, then—

(a) if the deed contains such a declaration as aforesaid by the retiring and continuing trustees, and by the other person, if any, empowered to appoint trustees, the deed shall, without any conveyance or assignment, operate to vest in the continuing trustees alone, as joint

---

47 *Adam & Co International Trustees Ltd v Theodore Goddard* (2000) 2 I.T.E.L.R. 634, [2000] W.T.L.R. 389.

48 *Pearce v Pearce* (1856) 22 Beav. 248.

49 As noted in *Gregson v HAE Trustees Ltd* [2009] 1 All E.R. (Comm) 457 at [48].

tenants, and for the purposes of the trust, the estate, interest, or right to which the declaration relates; and

(b) if the deed is made after the commencement of this Act and does not contain such a declaration, the deed shall, subject to any express provision to the contrary therein contained, operate as if it had contained such a declaration by such persons as aforesaid extending to all the estates, interests and rights with respect to which a declaration could have been made.

(3) An express vesting declaration, whether made before or after the commencement of this Act, shall, notwithstanding that the estate, interest or right to be vested is not expressly referred to, and provided that the other statutory requirements were or are complied with, operate and be deemed always to have operated (but without prejudice to any express provision to the contrary contained in the deed of appointment on discharge) to vest in the persons respectively referred to in subsections (1) and (2) of this section, as the case may require, such estates, interests and rights as are capable of being and ought to be vested in those persons.

(4) This section does not extend—

(a) to land conveyed by way of mortgage for securing money subject to the trust, except land conveyed on trust for securing debentures or debenture stock;

(b) to land held under a lease which contains any covenant, condition or agreement against assignment or disposing of the land without licence or consent, unless, prior to the execution of the deed containing expressly or impliedly the vesting declaration, the requisite licence or consent has been obtained, or unless, by virtue of any statute or rule of law, the vesting declaration, express or implied, would not operate as a breach of covenant or give rise to a forfeiture;

(c) to any share, stock, annuity or property which is only transferable in books kept by a company or other body, or in manner directed by or under an Act of Parliament.

In this subsection "lease" includes an underlease and an agreement for a lease or underlease.

(5) For purposes of registration of the deed in any registry, the person or persons making the declaration expressly or impliedly, shall be deemed the conveying party or parties, and the conveyance shall be deemed to be made by him or them under a power conferred by this Act. . . .

## *F. Special Types of Trustee*

Although most trustees are appointed by the settlors of express trusts, and are charged with active duties to hold and manage the trust property for the benefit of the beneficiaries, some special types of trustee are appointed in different circumstances and/or owe a different range of duties. **8–035**

### i. Custodian Trustees[50]

Custodian trustees are distinct from the usual managing trustees. They hold the trust property and the trust documents of title (e.g. title deeds, share certificates) and all sums payable to or out of the income or capital of the trust property are paid to or by them except that dividends and other income derived from the trust property may be paid to such other persons as they direct, e.g. the managing trustees or a beneficiary.[51] The day-to-day running of the trust is left to the managing trustees whose instructions must be obeyed by the custodian trustee unless aware that they involve a breach of trust.[52] The following may be appointed custodian trustees: the Public Trustee, the Official Custodian **8–036**

---

[50] Generally see S.G. Maurice (1960) 24 Conv. (N.S.) 196; P. Pearce (1972) 36 Conv. (N.S.) 260–261; G. Keeton's *Modern Developments in the Law of Trusts* (Northern Ireland Legal Quarterly, 1971), Ch.3; P. Matthews, "All About Bare Trusts: Part 1" [2005] P.C.B. 266, 266–269.

[51] Public Trustee Act 1906 s.4(2).

[52] Public Trustee Act 1906 s.4(2). Exceptionally, in the case of an authorised unit trust, the trustee, which must be a corporate EU trustee independent of the manager of the unit trust, has to take reasonable care to ensure that the manager acts

for Charities and trust corporations.[53] A trustee cannot be custodian trustee and managing trustee of the same trust.[54]

### ii. Trust Corporations

**8–037** A trust corporation can act alone where otherwise two trustees would be required, e.g. receipt of capital moneys on a sale of land. The following are trust corporations[55]: the Public Trustee, the Treasury Solicitor, the Official Solicitor, certain charitable corporations and corporations either appointed by the court in any particular case or entitled to act as custodian trustees under the Public Trustee Act 1906. Corporations so entitled include those constituted under UK law or the law of an EU state and having a place of business in the UK and empowered to undertake trust business, which are either incorporated by special Act or Royal Charter or else registered UK or other EU state companies with an issued capital of at least £250,000 (or its foreign equivalent) of which at least £100,000 (or its equivalent) has been paid up in cash.

### iii. The Public Trustee in the Official Solicitor's Office

**8–038** The Public Trustee was established in 1906 as a corporation sole available to deal with the difficulty persons might have in finding someone willing to act as trustee especially of low value trusts. However, it cannot accept charitable trusts, insolvent estates or, normally, trusts involving the carrying on of a business. It can act as personal representative, ordinary managing trustee, custodian trustee or judicial trustee. Since 1 April 2001, the Official Solicitor is also the Public Trustee.

### iv. Judicial Trustees

**8–039** The Judicial Trustees Act 1896 established judicial trustees in order "to provide a middle course in cases where the administration of the estate by the ordinary trustees had broken down and it was not desired to put the estate to the expense of a full administration" by the court.[56] Judicial trustees can only be appointed by the court upon a claim in existing proceedings or an original Pt 8 claim. Trouble-shooting accountants are often appointed to sort out the muddled situation. The judicial trustee is an officer of the court so that she can at any time obtain the court's directions as to the way in which she should act without the necessity of a formal application by summons though she has as much authority as ordinary trustees to act on her own initiative, and, for example, compromise claims.[57]

### v. Can There Be a "Controlling Trustee"?

**8–040** The basic position is that all trustees are equal and must act unanimously, trusteeship being a joint office par excellence, so that one trustee cannot be "controlling trustee" whom the other trustees can safely leave on her own to deal with all trust matters.[58] However, as where two trustees are needed to

---

within its powers, keeps adequate records and manages the scheme in accordance with the Financial Service Authority's Regulations for Collective Investment Schemes.

53 Public Trustee Rules 1912 r.30.

54 *Forster v Williams Deacon's Bank Ltd* [1935] Ch. 359; *Arning v James* [1936] Ch. 58.

55 Law of Property Act 1925 s.205(1)(xxviii); Trustee Act 1925 s.68(18); Law of Property (Amendment) Act 1925 s.3 (including trustees in bankruptcy).

56 *Re Ridsdel* [1947] Ch. 597 at 605, per Jenkins J. See *Judicial Trustee Rules 1983 and Practice Note* [2003] 3 All E.R. 974.

57 *Re Ridsdel* [1947] Ch. 597.

58 It is a breach of trust to leave matters to a co-trustee: all co-trustees must positively involve themselves with all trust matters; see paras 9–002, 10–258.

give a good receipt for capital moneys derived from land, the trust instrument can effectively provide for T2 always to do whatever T1 decides without being liable in any way for any breach of trust unless T2 was aware that she was assisting T1 to commit a breach of trust.[59] Similarly, there is no reason why a trust instrument might not effectively provide for T1 to have a casting vote if T1 and T2 cannot agree on a trust matter.[60]

## 3. Retirement of Trustees

Where a trustee retires and a new trustee is appointed to fill the vacancy,[61] the retirement and new appointment are effected under s.36(1) of the Trustee Act 1925. Where all the beneficiaries require retirement under s.19 of the 1996 Act, the retiring trustee must execute a deed discharging herself under s.19(3). Where a new trustee is not appointed to fill the vacancy, the retirement is effected under s.39. **8–041**

Independently of statute, a trustee may also retire under a power of retirement contained in the trust instrument,[62] or by the consent of all the beneficiaries, the latter being of full capacity,[63] or by authority of the court, to which the trustee has a right to apply to be discharged from the trust (although costs will depend on whether she has reasonable grounds for desiring to be discharged).[64] **8–042**

Normally, retirement will be effected by the one deed executed by the retiring trustee and the remaining trustees—*and* any person (an "appointor") empowered to appoint new trustees. If, by mistake, with the oral consent of her co-trustees, a trustee simply retires by executing a deed retiring from the trust, then it seems that matters can be regularised by a subsequent deed executed by the remaining trustees and the appointor, if any.[65] **8–043**

### Trustee Act 1925 s.39

**Retirement of trustee without a new appointment**

(1) Where a trustee is desirous of being discharged from the trust, and after his discharge there will be either a trust corporation or at least two individuals to act as trustees to perform the trust, then, if such trustee as aforesaid by deed declares that he is desirous of being discharged from the trust, and if his co-trustees and such other person, if any, as is empowered to appoint trustees, by deed consent to the discharge of the trustee, and to the vesting in the co-trustees alone of the trust property, the trustee desirous of being discharged shall be deemed to have retired from the trust, and shall, by the deed, be discharged therefrom under this Act, without any new trustee being appointed in his place. **8–044**

(2) Any assurance or thing requisite for vesting the trust property in the continuing trustees alone shall be executed or done.

## 4. Removal of Trustees

If the conditions in s.36(1) for replacing a trustee with another person cannot be satisfied for the removal of such trustee, then removal will require an express power in the trust instrument or an **8–045**

---

59 *Re Arnott* [1899] I.R. 201.

60 After all, the settlor can provide for trustees to act by majority decisions, but if only an even number of trustees subsists then the chairman of the trustees is to have a casting vote where the trustees are equally divided.

61 If no one else can be found the Public Trustee will usually be willing to act.

62 *Camoys v Best* (1854) 19 Beav. 414.

63 *Wilkinson v Parry* (1828) 4 Russ. 472 at 476.

64 *Gardiner v Dounes* (1856) 22 Beav. 395; *Barker v Peile* (1865) 2 Dr. & Sm. 340; *Re Chetwynd* [1902] 1 Ch. 692.

65 *Re Epona Trustees Ltd and Pentera Trustees Ltd* [2009] W.T.L.R. 87 (Jersey Royal Ct).

application to the court. The trust instrument may confer a power of removal,[66] though if it is conferred on a majority of the trustees and they are not unanimous then a meeting will need to be held.[67] It should be borne in mind that the benefit of property passing from the old trustees to the new trustees under s.40 only applies if a new trustee is appointed in place of the old trustee and not if the old trustee is simply removed.

**8–046** The court has a jurisdiction, independent of statute, to remove trustees, as illustrated by *Letterstedt v Broers*,[68] which appears below. This case makes it clear that while dishonest misconduct will certainly lead the court to remove a trustee, want of proper capacity to execute the duties of trustee will also suffice.[69] However a breakdown of personal relations between trustee and beneficiary is not enough in itself to justify the removal of a trustee, for the reason stated by Sales J in *National Westminster Bank Plc v Lucas*[70]:

> There are many contexts in which trustees or those in equivalent positions, such as personal representatives of a deceased person, have to make judgments which involve striking a balance between different competing interests and which may thus adversely affect some persons claiming under the trust or in respect of the estate of the deceased. It is to be expected that in such cases there will often be an element of friction between the trustee or personal representative and those disappointed by their decisions. This is not in itself a good ground to remove the trustee or personal representative from their office.

Nevertheless, in cases where personal hostility between trustee and beneficiary have made the proper administration of the trust impossible, this is a factor that the court can take into account when deciding whether the trustee should be removed.[71]

**8–047** Under s.41, the court may also remove a trustee on appointing a new trustee. On appointment of a new trustee under s.36 the appointors may remove a trustee. If hostility between trustees prevents them from acting unanimously (as they must do unless the trust instrument authorises otherwise) then one or all should be removed and replaced.[72]

**8–048** In an emergency, trustees may be removed on an ex parte interim application and a receiver appointed of the trust assets until appointment of new trustees at an inter partes hearing.[73]

**8–049** The Occupational Pensions Regulatory Authority has power under the Pensions Act 1995 ss.4 to 9 to suspend or remove trustees and appoint new trustees in the case of pension trust schemes, while the Charity Commission has similar powers under the Charities Act 2011 ss.76 to 81.[74]

### *Letterstedt v Broers*

### Privy Council (1884) 9 App. Cas. 371

**8–050** The Board of Executors of Cape Town were the sole surviving executors and trustees of a will under which the appellant was a beneficiary. The appellant alleged misconduct in the administration of the trust, and

---

66 A power of removal, e.g. vested in a protector, will be presumed a fiduciary power not to be exercised for the personal benefit of the power-holder but for the beneficiaries as a whole or perhaps even for the benefit of the settlor (although the trust instrument should spell this out): *Von Knierem v Bermuda Trust Co* (1994) Butts, O.C.M. Vol.1 at 116; *Re Osiris* [2000] W.T.L.R. 933.

67 *Att.-Gen. v Scott* (1750) 1 Ves. Sen. 413.

68 (1884) 9 App. Cas. 371.

69 See too *Thomas and Agnes Carvel Foundation v Carvel* [2008] Ch. 395 at [51]; *Jones v Firkin-Flood* [2008] EWHC 2417 (Ch) at [283]ff.

70 [2014] W.T.L.R. 637 at [83], affirmed [2015] W.T.L.R. 635.

71 *Scott v Scott* [2012] W.T.L.R. 1439; *Brudenell-Bruce v Moore* [2015] W.T.L.R. 373.

72 *Re Consiglis' Trusts (No.1)* (1973) 36 D.L.R. (3d) 658. On the exercise of the court's jurisdiction see *Titterton v Oates* [2001] W.T.L.R. 319.

73 *Clarke v Heathfield* (1985) 82 Law Soc. Gaz. 599; [1985] I.C.R. 203.

74 Considered in *Weth v Att.-Gen. (No.2)* [1999] 1 W.L.R. 686; *Seray-Wurie v Charity Commission* [2008] EWHC 1091 (Ch).

claimed that the Board were unfit to be entrusted with the management of the estate and should be removed in favour of a new appointment. The Supreme Court of the Cape of Good Hope had refused the application to remove the Board. The beneficiary appealed successfully.

LORD BLACKBURN: . . . the whole case has been argued here, and, as far as their Lordships can perceive, in the court below, as depending on the principles which should guide an English court of equity when called upon to remove old trustees and substitute new ones. It is not disputed that there is a jurisdiction "in cases requiring such a remedy", as is said in Story's *Equity Jurisprudence*, s.1287, but there is very little to be found to guide us in saying what are the cases requiring such a remedy; so little that their Lordships are compelled to have recourse to general principles **8–051**

Story says, section 1289: "But in cases of positive misconduct, courts of equity have no difficulty in interposing to remove trustees who have abused their trust; it is not indeed every mistake or neglect of duty, or inaccuracy of conduct of trustees, which will induce courts of equity to adopt such a course. But the acts or omissions must be such as to endanger the trust property or to show a want of honesty, or a want of proper capacity to execute the duties, or a want of reasonable fidelity." **8–052**

It seems to their Lordships that the jurisdiction which a court of equity has no difficulty in exercising under the circumstances indicated by Story is merely ancillary to its principal duty, to see that the trusts are properly executed. This duty is constantly being performed by the substitution of new trustees in the place of original trustees for a variety of reasons in non-contentious cases. And therefore, though it should appear that the charges of misconduct were either not made out, or were greatly exaggerated, so that the trustee was justified in resisting them, and the court might consider that in awarding costs, yet if satisfied that the continuance of the trustee would prevent the trusts being properly executed, the trustee might be removed. It must always be borne in mind that trustees exist for the benefit of those to whom the creator of the trust has given the trust estate. **8–053**

The reason why there is so little to be found in the books on this subject is probably that suggested by Mr Davey in his argument. As soon as all questions of character are as far settled as the nature of the case admits, if it appears clear that the continuance of the trustee would be detrimental to the execution of the trusts, even if for no other reason than that human infirmity would prevent those beneficially interested, or those who act for them, from working in harmony with the trustee, and if there is no reason to the contrary from the intentions of the framer of the trust to give this trustee a benefit or otherwise, the trustee is always advised by his own counsel to resign, and does so. If, without any reasonable ground, he refused to do so, it seems to their Lordships that the court might think it proper to remove him; but cases involving the necessity of deciding this, if they ever arise, do so without getting reported. It is to be lamented that the case was not considered in this light by the parties in the court below, for, as far as their Lordships can see, the Board would have little or no profit from continuing to be trustees, and as such coming into continual conflict with the appellant and her legal advisers, and would probably have been glad to resign, and get out of an onerous and disagreeable position. But the case was not so treated. **8–054**

In exercising so delicate a jurisdiction as that of removing trustees, their Lords do not venture to lay down any general rule beyond the very broad principle above enunciated, that their main guide must be the welfare of the beneficiaries. Probably it is not possible to lay down any more definite rule in a matter so essentially dependent on details often of great nicety. . . . **8–055**

It is quite true that friction or hostility between trustees and the immediate possessor of the trust estate is not of itself a reason for the removal of the trustees. But where the hostility is grounded on the mode in which the trust has been administered, where it has been caused wholly or partially by substantial overcharges against the trust estate, it is certainly not to be disregarded. **8–056**

Looking, therefore, at the whole circumstances of this very peculiar case, the complete change of position, the unfortunate hostility that has arisen, and the difficult and delicate duties that may yet have to be performed, their Lordships can come to no other conclusion than that it is necessary, for the welfare of the beneficiaries, that the Board should no longer be trustees. **8–057**

Probably if it had been put in this way below they would have consented. But for the benefit of the trust they should cease to be trustees, whether they consent or not . . . **8–058**

## 5. Remuneration of Trustees

8-059 The basic rule is that trustees must administer the trust gratuitously for otherwise "the trust estate might be loaded and made of little value".[75] There is an obvious conflict between their self-interest and their duty, but the position has been much liberalised and modernised by the Trustee Act 2000. The cases in which the trustee is entitled to payment for her services are as follows.

8-060 First, in a suitable case the court has an inherent jurisdiction to authorise a trustee to receive remuneration prospectively or retrospectively and it may also increase the remuneration authorised by the trust deed. To do so the court must be satisfied that the trustee's services have been or will be of exceptional benefit to the estate.[76] On occasion the power to award remuneration has been exercised even in favour of a trustee who has been ordered to disgorge unauthorised profits,[77] but it is difficult to predict when such awards will be made, following Lord Goff's statement in *Guinness Plc v Saunders*, that the exercise of the courts' jurisdiction should be restricted to cases where an award would not have the effect of encouraging fiduciaries to put themselves in a position of conflict.[78] The court, when appointing a corporation (other than the Public Trustee) to act, also has a statutory jurisdiction[79] under s.42 of the Trustee Act 1925 to authorise it to charge for its services.

8-061 Secondly, if the settlement authorises the trustee to charge for her services then she is entitled to be paid, but charging clauses used to be construed strictly with the onus on the trustee to show that the charge which she proposes to make is covered by the terms of the settlement. Thus, where a solicitor-trustee was authorised to make "professional charges", and even where the words "for his time and trouble" were added, he was not allowed to charge for time and trouble expended other than in his position as solicitor.[80] But where a will authorised the solicitor-trustee to make "the usual professional or other proper and reasonable charges for all business done and time expended in relation to the trusts of the will, whether such business is usually within the business of a solicitor or not", the solicitor was permitted to charge for business not strictly of a professional nature transacted by him in relation to the trust,[81] though, apparently, not for work altogether outside his professional vocation that a layman could do.[82]

8-062 However, the Trustee Act 2000 s.28(2) now treats a trustee entitled under the trust instrument to charge for services provided by her as entitled to receive payment "in respect of services even if they are services which are capable of being provided by a lay trustee", so long as the trustee is "a trust corporation or is acting in a professional capacity".[83] A trustee acts in a professional capacity[84] "if he

---

75 *Robinson v Pett* (1734) 3 P. Wms. 249 at 251.

76 *Marshall v Holloway* (1820) 2 Swans. 432; *Docker v Somes* (1834) 2 My. & K. 655; *Re Freeman* (1887) 37 Ch.D. 148; *Re Macadam* [1946] Ch. 73; *Re Masters* [1953] 1 W.L.R. 51; *Re Worthington (Deceased)* [1954] 1 W.L.R. 526; *Re Duke of Norfolk's ST* [1982] Ch. 61; *Foster v Spencer* [1996] 2 All E.R. 672; *Brudenell-Bruce v Moore* [2015] W.T.L.R. 373; *Re Portman's Estate* [2015] W.T.L.R. 871.

77 *Boardman v Phipps* [1967] 2 A.C. 46 at 104, 112; *O'Sullivan v Management Agency and Music Ltd* [1985] Q.B. 42; *Badfinger Music Ltd v Evans* [2001] W.T.L.R. 1. See also paras 13-101—13-102.

78 *Guinness Plc v Saunders* [1990] 2 A.C. 663 at 701, followed in, e.g. *Quarter Master UK Ltd (in liq) v Pyke* [2005] 1 B.C.L.C. 245 at [76]–[77], though cf. *Nottingham University v Fishel* [2000] I.C.R. 1462 at 1499–1500. See too *Imageview Management Ltd v Jack* [2009] Bus. L.R. 1034 at [54]–[60].

79 The Public Trustee has a statutory right to charge under the Public Trustee Act 1906 s.9, as have custodian trustees acting as custodian trustees *only* under the Public Trustee Act 1906 s.4: *Forster v Williams Deacon's Bank* [1935] Ch. 359. Judicial trustees may charge under the Judicial Trustees Act 1896 s.1.

80 *Re Chapple* (1884) 27 Ch.D. 584; *Re Orwell's WT* [1982] 1 W.L.R. 1337.

81 *Re Ames* (1883) 25 Ch.D. 72.

82 *Clarkson v Robinson* [1900] 2 Ch. 722.

83 Trustee Act 2000 s.31(1).

84 Trustee Act 2000 s.28(5).

acts in the course of a profession or business which consists of or includes the provision of services in connection with: (a) the management or administration of trusts generally or a particular kind of trust; or (b) any particular aspect of the management or administration of trusts generally or a particular kind of trust." A person acts as a "lay trustee" if she does not act in a professional capacity and is not a trust corporation.[85]

Thirdly, by s.29 of the Trustee Act 2000 (unless provision as to entitlement to remuneration has been made by the trust instrument or by primary or subordinate legislation[86]—and unless the trust is a charitable trust[87]) a trustee which is a trust corporation is entitled to "reasonable remuneration",[88] while a trustee who acts in a "professional capacity" (as defined in the last paragraph) and is not a sole trustee, is also entitled to reasonable remuneration if each other trustee has agreed in writing that she may be remunerated for the services she provides to the trust,[89] including services capable of being provided by a lay trustee.[90] The power for a trustee to agree that another trustee be remunerated for her services is a power to be exercised in the interests of the beneficiaries as a whole and not for the personal benefit of the trustee to be remunerated or of the person exercising the power,[91] hoping perhaps for a reciprocal agreement for her to be remunerated. **8–063**

Since it is the legislation that has placed a trustee in an invidious position where there is a sensible possibility of a conflict between her personal interest and the beneficiaries' interest, the exercise of the power to agree remuneration of a trustee is not impeachable by reason only that a conflict situation has arisen.[92] However, where T1 and T2 are to be trustees they would be well advised not to rely on s.29 and to rely instead on an express remuneration clause: in the absence of the latter, T1 and T2 agreeing to each other being remunerated would be vulnerable to attack by disaffected beneficiaries so that to protect themselves T1 and T2 would want to obtain the prior consent of adult beneficiaries or the authorisation of the court. **8–064**

Fourthly, although charity trustees cannot generally be paid for their services as trustees, the Charity Commission occasionally allows this to be done on a case-by-case basis.[93] Furthermore, the Charities Act 2011 ss.185–188 allow for charity trustees to be paid for other services in the absence of an express power to pay them, provided that certain conditions are met. These are: (a) the number of trustees receiving payment must be in a minority; (b) the amount paid must be reasonable and set out in a written agreement between the trustee and the charity; and (c) the governing document must not contain any specific provision forbidding this type of payment. **8–065**

The payment of charity trustees is a contentious issue because many people working in the charity sector believe that voluntarism is a fundamental feature of their activities, but at the same time large charities often wish to employ skilled professionals who cannot afford to take on a role as charity trustee unless they are paid for their work as trustees. The Hodgson Report on the Charities Act 2006 **8–066**

---

85 Trustee Act 2000 s.28(6).

86 Trustee Act 2000 s.29(5).

87 Trustee Act 2000 s.29(1)(b) and (2)(b).

88 As defined in s.29(3).

89 Trustee Act 2000 s.29(2).

90 Trustee Act 2000 s.29(4).

91 Law Commission, *Report on Trustees' Powers and Duties* (HMSO, 1999), Law Com. No.260, HC Paper No.538 (Session 1998–99), para.7.10 and Explanatory Note to Trustees Act 2000, para.103.

92 *Edge v Pensions Ombudsman* [1998] Ch. 512.

93 The Charity Commission will normally approve such payments only where "a charity's complexity of operation has led to an unusually high burden of trusteeship", something that will "usually involve a trustee exercising a higher degree of responsibility and supervision in a complex field of activity, perhaps because of the breadth and range of activities undertaken by the charity": *CC11 Trustee Expenses and Payments* (1 March 2012) para.6.3., *https://www.gov.uk/government/publications/trustee-expenses-and-payments-cc11/trustee-expenses-and-payments#paying-trustees-for-services* [Accessed 1 June 2015].

recommended that large charities should be empowered to pay their trustees, subject to disclosure requirements on the quantum and terms of any remuneration in the individual charity's annual report and accounts.[94] However the Government rejected this recommendation, stating that[95]:

> Feedback received from the majority of charities and their representatives has not been in favour of de-regulation in this case. Many have argued that permitting remuneration of charity trustees would undermine the voluntary nature of charity trusteeship, which is a defining feature of the charity sector. Some have also argued that there is currently insufficient evidence that paying trustees would result in more effective governance. Charities that wish to pay their trustees for acting as such can already make a case to do so and seek approval from the Charity Commission. The Charity Commission has said that applications of this sort are infrequent. We therefore consider that, for the time-being at least, and until there is stronger evidence that would support an easing of the general presumption against trustee remuneration, we should retain the status quo, but monitor the number of applications the Charity Commission receives and the number it grants or refuses.

**8-067** Fifthly, if the beneficiaries are all of full capacity and between them absolutely entitled to the trust estate, they may authorise the trustee to be paid. If the beneficiaries then sue the trustee for breach of trust in paying trust moneys to herself the trustee has their authorisation as a defence unless undue influence was exercised by her.

**8-068** Sixthly, the general rule of gratuitous service was particularly severe in the case of solicitor-trustees. Thus in *Christophers v White*,[96] it was held that a solicitor-trustee's firm was not entitled to charge for professional services rendered to the trust by a partner in the firm even though the partner was not one of the trustees.[97] But where a solicitor-trustee employed his partner, as distinct from his firm, under an express agreement that the partner should be individually entitled to charges, these were allowed on the ground that where such an agreement is carried out there is no infringement of the rule that a trustee may not make his office a source of remuneration.[98] Moreover, the severity of the rule was relaxed by the case of *Cradock v Piper*,[99] in which a solicitor-trustee acted as solicitor for himself and his co-trustees in legal proceedings relating to the trust, and was held to be entitled to his usual charges. The rule is that unlike a sole trustee acting as solicitor to the trust, a solicitor-trustee acting in legal proceedings[100] for a body of trustees, of whom she herself is one, is entitled to her usual charges if the fact of her appearing for herself and her co-trustees jointly has not increased the costs which would have been incurred if she had appeared for those co-trustees only.

**8-069** Seventhly, where the trust property is situated abroad and the law of the foreign country permits payment, the trustee is entitled to keep any remuneration which she has received. Thus in *Re Northcote*,[101] a testator who left assets both in this country and in the USA died domiciled in England, and the principal forum of administration was therefore English. The executors took out an English grant, and on doing so they were put on terms by the Revenue, the English effects being insufficient

---

94 *Trusted and Independent: Giving charity back to charities—Review of the Charities Act 2006* (TSO, 2012), Ch.4, recommendation 10.

95 *Government Responses to: 1) The Public Administration Select Committee's Third Report of 2013–14: The role of the Charity Commission and "public benefit": Post-legislative scrutiny of the Charities Act 2006; 2) Lord Hodgson's statutory review of the Charities Act 2006: Trusted and Independent, Giving charity back to charities* (TSO, 2013), Cmnd.8700, p.13.

96 (1847) 10 Beav. 523.

97 See also *Re Gates* [1933] Ch. 913 and *Re Hill* [1934] Ch. 623.

98 *Cluck v Carlon* (1861) 30 L.J. Ch. 639.

99 (1850) 1 Mac. & G. 664; discussed in C. Stebbings, "The Rule in *Cradock v Piper*: Exception or Principle?" (1998) 19 J.L.H. 189.

100 Legal proceedings need not necessarily be hostile litigation but may be friendly proceedings in chambers: *Re Corsellis* (1887) 34 Ch.D. 675. It must be work in connection with a writ or an originating summons rather than general advisory work relating to legal proceedings.

101 [1949] 1 All E.R. 442; see also *Chambers v Goldwin* (1802) 9 Ves. 271.

to pay the English duty, to undertake themselves personally to obtain a grant in New York in respect of the American assets. In due course they obtained such a grant, and got in the assets. Under the law of New York they were entitled to commission for so doing, and Harman J held that they were under no duty to account for it to the beneficiaries.

## Trustee Act 2000 ss.28 and 29

**28. Trustee's entitlement to payment under trust instrument**

(1) Except to the extent (if any) to which the trust instrument makes inconsistent provision, subsections (2) to (4) apply to a trustee if— 8–070

(a) there is a provision in the trust instrument entitling him to receive payment out of trust funds in respect of services provided by him to or on behalf of the trust, and
(b) the trustee is a trust corporation or is acting in a professional capacity.

(2) The trustee is to be treated as entitled under the trust instrument to receive payment in respect of services even if they are services which are capable of being provided by a lay trustee.

(3) Subsection (2) applies to a trustee of a charitable trust who is not a trust corporation only—

(a) if he is not a sole trustee, and
(b) to the extent that a majority of the other trustees have agreed that it should apply to him.

(4) Any payments to which the trustee is entitled in respect of services are to be treated as remuneration for services (and not as a gift) for the purposes of—

(a) section 15 of the Wills Act 1837 (gifts to an attesting witness to be void), and
(b) section 34(3) of the Administration of Estates Act 1925 (order in which estate to be paid out).

(5) For the purposes of this Part, a trustee acts in a professional capacity if he acts in the course of a profession or business which consists of or includes the provision of services in connection with—

(a) the management or administration of trusts generally or a particular kind of trust, or
(b) any particular aspect of the management or administration of trusts generally or a particular kind of trust,

and the services he provides to or on behalf of the trust fall within that description.

(6) For the purposes of this Part, a person acts as a lay trustee if he—

(a) is not a trust corporation, and
(b) does not act in a professional capacity.

**29. Remuneration of certain trustees**

(1) Subject to subsection (5), a trustee who— 8–071

(a) is a trust corporation, but
(b) is not a trustee of a charitable trust,

is entitled to receive reasonable remuneration out of the trust funds for any services that the trust corporation provides to or on behalf of the trust.

(2) Subject to subsection (5), a trustee who—

(a) acts in a professional capacity, but
(b) is not a trust corporation, a trustee of a charitable trust or a sole trustee,

is entitled to receive reasonable remuneration out of the trust funds for any services that he provides to or on behalf of the trust if each other trustee has agreed in writing that he may be remunerated for the services.

(3) "Reasonable remuneration" means, in relation to the provision of services by a trustee, such remuneration as is reasonable in the circumstances for the provision of those services to or on behalf of that trust by that trustee and for the purposes of subsection (1) includes, in relation to the provision of services by a trustee who is an authorised institution under the Banking Act 1987 and provides the services in that capacity, the institution's reasonable charges for the provision of such services.

(4) A trustee is entitled to remuneration under this section even if the services in question are capable of being provided by a lay trustee.

(5) A trustee is not entitled to remuneration under this section if any provision about his entitlement to remuneration has been made—

(a) by the trust instrument, or
(b) by any enactment or any provision of subordinate legislation.

(6) This section applies to a trustee who has been authorised under a power conferred by Part IV or the trust instrument—

(a) to exercise functions as an agent of the trustees, or
(b) to act as a nominee or custodian,

as it applies to any other trustee.

## 6. Indemnity of Trustees

### *A. Indemnity out of, and Lien over, the Trust Estate*

**8–072** Few individuals would become trustees unless they could recoup themselves out of the trust funds for the liabilities they incur while managing the trust affairs, and this is provided for by the Trustee Act 2000 s.31. Trustees can also reimburse their agents for expenses out of the trust funds under the Trustee Act 2000 s.32.

### Trustee Act 2000 ss.31 and 32

**31. Trustees' expenses.**

**8–073** (1) A trustee—

(a) is entitled to be reimbursed from the trust funds, or
(b) may pay out of the trust funds,

expenses properly incurred by him when acting on behalf of the trust.

(2) This section applies to a trustee who has been authorised under a power conferred by Part IV or any other enactment or any provision of subordinate legislation, or by the trust instrument—

(a) to exercise functions as an agent of the trustees, or
(b) to act as a nominee or custodian,

as it applies to any other trustee.

**32. Remuneration and expenses of agents, nominees and custodians**

**8–074** (1) This section applies if, under a power conferred by Part IV or any other enactment or any provision of subordinate legislation, or by the trust instrument, a person other than a trustee has been—

(a) authorised to exercise functions as an agent of the trustees, or
(b) appointed to act as a nominee or custodian.

(2) The trustees may remunerate the agent, nominee or custodian out of the trust funds for services if—

> (a) he is engaged on terms entitling him to be remunerated for those services, and
> (b) the amount does not exceed such remuneration as is reasonable in the circumstances for the provision of those services by him to or on behalf of that trust.
>
> (3) The trustees may reimburse the agent, nominee or custodian out of the trust funds for any expenses properly incurred by him in exercising functions as an agent, nominee or custodian.

These provisions reflect the established position that trustees only have power to pay "proper costs incident to the execution of the trust".[102] As Lord Selborne LC stated in *Stott v Milne*[103]: **8–075**

> The right of trustees to indemnity against all costs and expenses properly incurred by them in the execution of the trust is a first charge on all the trust properly, both income and corpus. The trustees, therefore, had a right to retain the costs out of the income until provision could be made for raising them out of the corpus.

However, no indemnity can be claimed by a trustee in respect of a liability improperly incurred,[104] e.g. because of lack of power under the trust instrument; or because of lack of due authorisation under internal requirements[105]; or because the transaction entails a breach of duty by the trustee, e.g. to diversify investments, to supervise agents, or to invest with the statutory duty of care.[106] Moreover, a trustee cannot reimburse herself out of the trust fund if she is indebted to the trust by reason of some unconnected breach of trust, since her right to reimbursement depends ultimately on the state of accounts between her and the beneficiaries and it is limited to the balance, if any, in her favour.[107] Finally, no right of indemnity exists to the extent that this has been excluded in the trust instrument, as may happen where the trustee has a liberal right to remuneration under a charging clause intended to cover expenses.[108] **8–076**

The trustee can protect herself against the problems created by her lack of power or authority by taking the advice of lawyers or even the guidance of the court but this takes time and money. She can also protect herself against allegations that, in breach of her equitable duties, she involved herself as claimant or defendant in an action involving the trust and a third party, so that she should personally pay her own costs and the costs of the other (winning) side in the action. To do this, she seeks in private a *Beddoe's* order[109] from the court which will entitle her to be reimbursed costs out of the trust fund no matter the result of the litigation, so long as full and frank disclosure is made to the court. However, where the claim seeks to undermine the trust wholly or partly (e.g. claims by the settlor's creditors or **8–077**

---

102 *Holding and Management Ltd v Property Holding and Investment Trust Plc* [1989] 1 W.L.R. 1313 at 1324 per Nicholls LJ See too *Re Grimthorpe* [1958] Ch. 615 at 623.

103 (1884) 25 Ch.D. 710 at 715. See too S. Donald, "The 'Proper' Approach to a Trustee's Right to Indemnity out of Trust Assets" (2014) 8 J.Eq. 283.

104 Exceptionally, if the trustee acted in good faith and the transaction benefited the trust fund he should have a right of indemnity to the extent of the benefit to prevent unjust enrichment of the beneficiaries: *Vyse v Foster* (1872) 8 Ch. App. 309 at 336–337; *Conway v Fenton* (1888) 11 Ch.D. 512 at 518—or the trust deed might expressly permit indemnity even beyond the extent of the benefit to the whole expense.

105 e.g. for trustee unanimity, or for the beneficiaries' consent, or for a meeting to be duly held before any decision is taken.

106 *Spencer v Fielder* [2014] EWHC 2768 (Ch) at [26].

107 *Ex p. Edmonds* (1862) 4 De G.F. & J. 488 at 498; *Re Johnson* (1880) 15 Ch.D. 548; *Re British Power Traction & Lighting Co Ltd* [1910] 2 Ch. 470.

108 *Ex p. Chippendale, Re German Mining Co* (1854) 4 De G.M. & G. 19 at 52; *McLean v Burns Philip Trustee Co Pty. Ltd* [1985] 2 N.S.W.L.R. 623 (the right to indemnity excluded in unit trusts so as not to affect the marketability of units).

109 Named after *Re Beddoe* [1893] 1 Ch. 547: this is in a separate action and the judge who hears it will not hear the main action. For details see L. Tucker, N. Le Poidevin and J. Brightwell, *Lewin on Trusts*, 19th edn (Sweet & Maxwell, 2015), paras 27–236—27–262.

trustee in bankruptcy[110]) the trustee may be required to be neutral and only have a right of indemnity for the costs of acting neutrally,[111] unless no other person is appropriate to represent the interests of beneficiaries who are unborn or otherwise unascertained.[112]

**8–078** The right of indemnity of a trustee is bolstered by an equitable proprietary right in the nature of a non-possessory lien,[113] which enables the trustee to retain assets against actual, contingent or possible liabilities[114] or to seek a sale of the assets[115] if in the ownership of a successor trustee. The equitable lien will continue to bind successor trustees,[116] but it will not bind beneficiaries to whom the assets are distributed unless expressly preserved by the distributing trustee(s), the recipient beneficiary normally receiving the assets (whether expressly or by necessary implication) discharged from the interests of other beneficiaries and from the prior equitable interests of trustees.[117]

**8–079** Trustees should reimburse themselves as soon as possible because they are not entitled to interest on the money they have paid out to meet expenses.[118] This rule probably derives from the practical consideration that it would be inconvenient if interest were to accrue on each item of a trustee's expenditure on a piecemeal basis, but it can cause hardship and injustice to trustees where costs have mounted up over an extended period.[119] It seems, though, that the courts have a discretion to award interest in hard cases.[120]

### *B. Indemnity by the Beneficiary Personally*

**8–080** A trustee's right of indemnity in respect of expenses properly incurred—e.g. in respect of costs, a call on shares, solicitor's, stockbroker's or auctioneer's charges—is a right of indemnity against the trust estate, not against the beneficiary. Hence, the trustees of an ordinary club are entitled to be indemnified out of the club property, not by the club members,[121] unless, as is often the case, the club rules allow this. But a trustee's indemnity extends beyond the trust estate to the beneficiary personally where the trustee accepted the trust at the request of the settlor who is also a beneficiary so as to raise an implied contract of indemnity[122] and also where the beneficiary is a sole beneficiary sui juris

---

110 Insolvency Act 1986 ss.339–342, 423–425.

111 *Alsop Wilkinson v Neary* [1996] 1 W.L.R. 1220.

112 *Re Hall* [1994–95] Cayman I.L.R. 456, *Lloyds Bank v Bylevan Corp SA* [1994–95] C.I.L.R. 519.

113 *Jennings v Mather* [1902] 1 K.B. 1 at 6, 9; *Stott v Milne* (1884) L.R. 25 Ch.D. 710 at 715; *Commissioner of Stamp Duties v ISPT* (1999) 2 I.T.E.L.R. 1 at 18; *Octavo Investments Pty Ltd v Knight* (1979) 114 C.L.R. 360; *Dimos v Dikeatos Nominees Ltd* (1997) 149 A.L.R. 113.

114 *X v A* [2000] 1 All E.R. 490.

115 *Re Pumfrey* (1882) 22 Ch.D. 255 at 262.

116 *Dimos v Dikeatos Nominees Ltd* (1997) 149 A.L.R. 113.

117 Australian cases (like *Dimos* and *Chief Commissioner of Stamp Duties v Buckle* (1998) 72 A.L.J.R. 242) treat the trustee's right not as an "encumbrance" but as a proprietary right equivalent to (but ranking ahead of) the equitable interests of beneficiaries.

118 *Gordon v Trail* (1820) 8 Price 416; *Foster v Spencer* [1996] 2 All E.R. 672 at 678.

119 *Foster v Spencer* [1996] 2 All E.R. 672 at 678.

120 *Re German Mining Co* (1853) 4 De G.M. & G. 19 at 36 and 43; *Murray's Executors' Case* (1854) 5 De G.M. & G. 746 at 753.

121 *Wise v Perpetual Trustee Co* [1903] A.C. 139, establishing a presumption that the members of an unincorporated association do not intend to pledge their personal credit for any larger sum than the amount of their membership dues. For critical comment, see T.C. Williams (1903) 19 L.Q.R. 386; R.W. Rideout, "Limited Liability of Unincorporated Associations" (1996) 49 C.L.P. 187, 198–204; R. Flannigan, "Contractual Responsibility in Non-Profit Associations" (1998) 18 O.J.L.S. 631, 641–644.

122 *Ex parte Chippendale* (1854) 4 De G.M. & G. 19 at 54; *Jervis v Wolferstan* (1874) L.R. 18 Eq. 18, as explained by Lord Blackburn in *Fraser v Murdoch* (1881) 6 App. Cas. 855 at 872; *Matthews v Ruggles-Brise* [1911] 1 Ch. 194. In that case it was also held that where a beneficiary is personally liable to indemnify her trustee, an assignment by her of her beneficial interest does not affect that liability as it stood at the date of the assignment.

and entitled absolutely,[123] or where there are several beneficiaries who are sui juris and between them collectively entitled absolutely.[124]

This can prove very useful where a trustee for such beneficiaries properly borrows money to carry out authorised trading or investing and the borrowings exceed the assets when things go dreadfully wrong as occurred in *JW Broomhead (Vic) Pty Ltd (in liq.) v JW Broomhead Pty Ltd*[125] where McGarvie J held that "where there are several beneficiaries entitled to separate benefits, a beneficiary who gets a proportion of the benefit should bear that proportion of its burdens unless he can show why the trustee should bear the proportion of them himself". He further held that where a beneficiary is insolvent the loss in respect of his proportion falls on the trustee and not the other beneficiaries. He also accepted that "a request from a beneficiary to the trustee to assume the office of trustee or to incur liabilities obviously justifies the imposition of a personal liability to indemnify on the beneficiary and this should be so even if the beneficiary has only a limited interest". **8–081**

The beneficiary's obligation to indemnify the trustee does not depend on the beneficiary having requested the trustee to incur the liability, but arises out of the principle that "the cestui que trust who gets all the benefit of the property should bear its burden"[126]—although consistently with this the beneficiary can escape her liability by disclaiming her interest in the trust property.[127] It also follows that a beneficiary who takes an interest by assignment from the original beneficiary is bound to indemnify the trustee,[128] although in this case the original beneficiary also remains liable to indemnify.[129] Note that the trustee's right to be indemnified by the beneficiaries is separate from her right to be indemnified out of the trust assets, and it is no answer to a trustee's claim to be indemnified by the beneficiaries personally that she should have recouped herself out of the trust property when she had a chance to do so.[130] **8–082**

## *C. Subrogation of Third Parties and the Trustees' Indemnity Rights*[131]

In carrying out the trusts or powers, a trustee is personally liable to the extent of her whole fortune or patrimony for debts, contracts, torts or taxes arising in respect of her acts or omissions as trustee. After all, the trust property is not an entity that can be regarded as a person to be made liable. Having transferred her property, usually by way of gift, to the trustees the settlor has disappeared from the picture. The trustees are not agents for the beneficiaries nor are they in a partnership with them so there is no legal connection between the beneficiaries and any creditors. Thus, the trustees are personally liable and remain so even after retiring as trustees: hence the need for an indemnity from the new trustees or reliance upon their equitable lien. **8–083**

As a matter of contract law, a trustee and a third party may agree that the trustee may limit or **8–084**

---

123 *Hardoon v Belilios* [1901] A.C. 118.

124 *Buchan v Ayre* [1915] 2 Ch. 474 at 477; *Re Reid* (1971) 17 D.L.R. (3d) 199; *Balkin v Peck* (1997) 43 N.S.W.L.R. 766 (English executor recovered from Australian beneficiaries when he overlooked the tax payable on proceeds remitted to Australia).

125 [1985] V.R. 891 at 936–939.

126 *Hardoon v Belilos* [1901] A.C. 118 at 125 per Lord Lindley. See too *Balkin v Peck* (1997) 43 N.S.W.L.R. 706 at 711–712, per Mason P.

127 *Hardoon* at 125.

128 *Hardoon* at 125.

129 *Matthews v Ruggles-Brise* [1911] 1 Ch. 194 at 203.

130 *Balkin v Peck* (1997) 43 N.S.W.L.R. 706 at 714 per Mason P.

131 In 1999, the Trust Law Committee, an English law reform body based at King's College London, published a report recommending various statutory reforms of the law in this area: Trust Law Committee, *Rights of Creditors against Trustees and Trust Funds* (June 1999), *http://www.kcl.ac.uk/law/research/centres/trustlawcommittee/otherpapersandreports/TLCCredRightsReport1404991.pdf* [Accessed 1 June 2015]. For general discussion, see too C. Mitchell and S. Watterson, *Subrogation: Law and Practice* (2007), Ch. 12.

exclude her personal liability and that the trustee shall pay the debt out of the trust property under her statutory right of indemnity.[132] The onus lies on the trustee to displace the strong presumption of personal liability so that contracting descriptively "as trustee" is not sufficient,[133] but contracting "as trustee and not otherwise" will suffice since the phrase would be meaningless if not excluding personal liability.[134]

**8-085** Where a trustee does not pay a creditor out of her own moneys or out of trust moneys available under her statutory right of indemnity the creditor may have a claim by way of subrogation to the trustee's right of indemnity.[135] The problem is that the creditor's right is derivative: she stands in the shoes of the trustee and has no better right than the trustee.[136] Thus, for the creditor to be paid out of the trust assets she will need to show that the right of indemnity was not excluded by the trust instrument,[137] that the debt was properly incurred in the authorised carrying on of the trust, and that the state of accounts between the trustee and the beneficiaries (taking into account any losses caused by any breach of trust on the trustee's part) is such that there is some balance in the trustee's favour to which the right of indemnity may attach. However, where there are two or more trustees and one of them does not have a clear account (e.g. because of an outstanding claim against her for a breach of trust) the creditor can rely on the right to indemnity enjoyed by the other trustee.[138]

**8-086** In addition to her proprietary right of indemnity, a trustee in some limited circumstances (already discussed above) may have a personal right of indemnity against a beneficiary personally. The right of subrogation in respect of the proprietary right of a trustee to an indemnity from the trust property arose out of the Court of Chancery's practice in administration of trust estates in an administration action. There was no similar practice for allowing a right of subrogation in respect of a trustee's right of indemnity against a beneficiary personally but, in principle, there should be such a right of subrogation.

**8-087** A person contracting with a trustee is in a particularly invidious position due to her derivative right being worthless if the trustee happens to be or become indebted to the trust fund for some unconnected breach of trust or if the trustee happens to be in breach of some equitable duty of care in negotiating the contract. In the absence of a power to create a fixed charge over specific assets or to create an equitable interest in the fluctuating trust fund in the nature of a floating charge, what can be done to protect the creditor's interests?

**8-088** To deal with the unconnected indebtedness problem it seems possible to negotiate as part of the price of the contract a necessarily incidental, but express, term that the trustee is in no way personally liable upon the contract, but the creditor shall have a personal non-proprietary direct independent

---

[132] *Muir v City of Glasgow Bank* (1879) 4 App. Cas. 337 at 355. It is possible for the trustee, if authorised, to go further and charge the trust property with payment of the debt: such an intention to create a charge is not likely to be inferred merely from an agreement that the creditor is to look to the trust property and not to the trustee for payment: cf. *Swiss Bank Corp v Lloyds Bank* [1980] 2 All E.R. 419 at 426; affirmed [1981] 2 All E.R. 449.

[133] *Watling v Lewis* [1911] 1 Ch. 414 at 424; *Marston Thompson & Evershed Plc v Benn* [2007] W.T.L.R. 315.

[134] *Re Robinson's Settlement* [1912] 1 Ch. 717 at 729; *Muir v City of Glasgow Bank* (1879) 4 App. Cas. 337 at 362.

[135] *Re Johnson* (1880) 15 Ch.D. 548 at 552; *Re Blundell* (1889) 44 Ch.D. 1 at 11; *Re Raybould* [1900] 1 Ch. 199; *Vacuum Oil Pty Ltd v Wiltshire* (1945) 72 C.L.R. 319 at 325, 336; *Franknelly Nominees Pty Ltd v Abrugiato* [2013] WASCA 285.

[136] *Ex p. Edmonds* (1862) 4 De G.F. & J. 488 at 498; *Re Johnson* (1880) 15 Ch.D. 548; *Re British Power Traction & Lighting Co Ltd* [1910] 2 Ch. 470.

[137] Unlike the Trustee Act 1925 s.69(2) which expressly allowed s.30(2) to be subject to contrary intent, no provision in Trustee Act 2000 allows this in respect of s.31 (the successor to s.30(2) of the 1925 Act), but it is considered that no court would permit a trustee to exploit s.31 if its generous remuneration was premised upon no recovery of expenses. A court could hold s.31 inapplicable on the basis the trustee was acting not "on behalf of the trust" but on behalf of itself in order to earn its generous remuneration or could hold the benefit of the remuneration was only available as burdened by the obligation not to claim expenses.

[138] *Re Frith* [1902] 1 Ch. 342 at 346.

right of recourse to the trust fund, so that it is immaterial whether or not the trustee's right of indemnity has been extinguished by indebtedness to the trust fund. It would be better, however, if statute were to provide that the indebtedness of a trustee to the trust at the time a contractual creditor (or a victim of a tort) seeks an indemnity out of the trust fund should not be a reason for refusing such an indemnity to such creditor (or victim).

Dealing with a trustee who may be in breach of her equitable duty of care is fraught with danger. If the creditor believes she is getting too good a bargain perhaps she should disclose this to help ensure that the trustee satisfies the equitable duty—but this would seem to place intending contractors with trustees under a fiduciary obligation which seems inappropriate and impractical in the commercial context. Perhaps, the House of Lords or even the Court of Appeal might restrict "properly incurred" to mean incurred by virtue of authority in the trust instrument and complying with any internal procedures so that it would be immaterial[139] that there had been a breach of equitable duties of care in investing or in supervising agents. It would be better if statute were to provide that a trustee's breach of equitable duties should not prevent a creditor having a right of indemnity out of the trust fund unless dishonestly implicated in such breach. Furthermore, where a trustee's conduct made her a tortfeasor and such conduct amounted to a breach of her equitable duties (e.g. of care) this should not prevent the victim from having a right of indemnity out of the trust fund. In *Re Raybould*,[140] reproduced below, it was fortunate for the claimant that the subsidence damage was caused by the proper management of the colliery by the trustee. In *Re Christian Brothers of Ireland in Canada*[141] the Brothers operated schools where some of the teachers unlawfully sexually abused pupils, and it was held that all the property of the charity was available to satisfy pupils' claims. 8–089

### *Re Raybould*

Chancery Division [1900] 1 Ch. 199

The surviving trustee and executor of a deceased's estate properly worked one of the testator's collieries. Earthworks caused a subsidence damaging the buildings and machinery of the adjoining owners, Roberts & Cooper. They obtained a judgment against the trustee for damage and costs. In the present proceedings they sought an order that this amount and cost be paid out of the testator's estate. 8–090

BYRNE J.: The first question I have to consider is whether the same principle ought to be applied to the case of a trustee claiming a right to indemnity for liability for damages for a tort, as is applied to the simpler case of claims made against a trustee by ordinary business creditors, where they have been allowed the benefit of his right to indemnity, by proving directly against the assets: the kind of case of which *Dowse v Gorton*[142] is a recent illustration. It has been argued that there is no authority to justify me in holding that, where damages have been recovered against a trustee in respect of a tort, the person so recovering can avail himself of the trustee's right to indemnity, and so go direct against the trust estate; but the authority of *Bennett v Wyndham*[143] goes to show that if a trustee in the course of the ordinary management of his testator's estate, either by himself or his agent, does some act whereby some third person is injured, and that third person recovers damages against the trustee in an action for tort, the trustee, if he has acted with due diligence and reasonably, is entitled to be indemnified out of his testator's estate. When once a trustee is entitled to be this indemnified out of his trust estate, I cannot myself see why the person who has recovered judgment against the trustee should not have the benefit of this right to indemnify and go direct against the trust estate or the assets, as the case may be, just as an ordinary creditor of a business carried on by a trustee or executor has been allowed to do, instead of having to go through the double process 8–091

---

139 Assuming the problem of indebtedness to the trust fund for such breach of trust was overcome.

140 [1900] 1 Ch. 199.

141 (2000) 184 D.L.R. (4th) 445, noted D.R. Wingfield (2003) 119 L.Q.R. 44, and discussed in M.H. Ogilvie, "Vicarious Liability and Charitable Immunity in Canadian Sexual Torts Law" (2004) 4 O.U.C.L.J. 167.

142 [1891] A.C. 190.

143 (1862) 4 De G.F. & J. 259.

of suing the trustee, recovering the damages from him and leaving the trustee to recoup himself out of the trust estate. I have the parties interested in defending the trust estate before me, and I have also the trustee, and he claims indemnity, and, assuming that a proper case for indemnifying him is made out by the evidence, I think his claim should be allowed.

8-092 The next question I have to decide is whether this trustee has worked the colliery in such a way as to be entitled to be indemnified. Having considered all the evidence, I am not prepared to say that the injury done to the applicants' land was occasioned by reckless or improper working, or otherwise than by the ordinary and reasonable management of the colliery; and I therefore come to the conclusion that the trustee is entitled to be indemnified out of the assets against the damages and costs which he has been ordered to pay to Messrs Roberts & Cooper. It follows, therefore, for the reasons already given, that Messrs Roberts & Cooper are entitled to stand in the trustee's place for the purpose of obtaining this indemnity direct from this testator's estate. The result, therefore, is that this summons succeeds. . . .

**Questions**

1. Given that the absolutely entitled beneficiaries of a trust can use their *Saunders v Vautier* rights to wind up the trust if they are unhappy with their trustees, what is the practical significance of their rights to force the trustees to retire and appoint new ones under the Trusts of Land and Appointment of Trustees Act 1996?
2. If a trustee wants to retire how can this be achieved, and what are the risks for her and the remaining trustees?
3. What happens when: (a) one of two trustees dies; and then (b) the survivor dies?
4. How does trust property become vested in new trustees?
5. Can the courts ever award an equitable allowance for services to a defaulting fiduciary, given Lord Goff's statement in *Guinness Plc v Saunders* that such awards should not be made if they will encourage fiduciaries to put themselves in a position of conflict?
6. Michael and Naomi are the trustees of a large family trust, who run the trust affairs out of an office which they rent from Larry. Michael and Naomi commit various negligent and fraudulent breaches of trust and then become bankrupt.

   **Advise Larry whether he can recover rent arrears out of the trust fund or from the beneficiaries.**

# 9

# DUTIES OF TRUSTEES

## 1. Introduction

### A. Distributive and Administrative Roles of Trustees

Trustees have two roles to perform: a distributive role, concerned with distributing income and capital to authorised beneficiaries (or applying them to authorised purposes), and an administrative role, concerned with safeguarding and developing the value of the trust fund. When performing her distributive role a trustee must ensure that trust property is distributed only to those entitled to benefit under the trust (or applied only to those purposes authorised by the trust).[1] She must act in the beneficiaries' exclusive interest and must not favour her own, or anyone else's, interests over theirs when taking decisions about the trust affairs.[2] She must exercise her discretionary powers impartially, taking account of all and only relevant factors,[3] and must not exercise such powers capriciously or in a way that is contrary to the sensible expectations of the settlor.[4] When performing her administrative role, the trustee must comply with the limits of her authority, act in the exclusive interest of the beneficiaries and act with reasonable care.[5] 9–001

### B. Co-Trustees

Where there is more than one trustee, as is usually the case, each trustee is personally responsible for acts performed in the administration of the trust and so should personally consider each act that needs to be done: if things turn out badly, it is no defence for a trustee to say that she was a "sleeping trustee" blindly relying on her co-trustees.[6] Nor can trustees collectively delegate their duties to another person, except where this is authorised by the trust instrument or by the Trustee Act 2000, which gives them broad powers to delegate their managerial, but not their distributive, functions.[7] The trustees must act unanimously except where the settlement or the court directs 9–002

1 *AIB Group (UK) Plc v Mark Redler & Co* [2014] 3 W.L.R. 1367 at [51].

2 *Keech v Sandford* (1726) Sel. Cas. temp. King 61; *Boardman v Phipps* [1967] 2 A.C. 46 at 123.

3 *Pitt v Holt* [2013] 2 A.C. 108.

4 *Re Hay's ST* [1982] 1 W.L.R. 202 at 209; *Re Beatty's WT* [1990] 3 All E.R. 844 at 846; *McPhail v Doulton* [1971] A.C. 424 at 449, *Re Manisty's Settlement* [1994] Ch. 17 at 26.

5 *Re Whiteley* (1886) 33 Ch.D. 347 at 355; Trustee Act 2000 s.1.

6 *Munch v Cockerell* (1840) 5 Myl. & Cr. 178; *Bahin v Hughes* (1886) 31 Ch.D. 390; *Re Turner* [1897] 1 Ch. 536; *Head v Gould* [1898] 2 Ch. 250. There is no automatic vicarious liability for a co-trustee's breaches of trust, but a trustee will be liable for her own breach of trust if she fails to act jointly with the others and take reasonable steps to monitor their conduct: see, e.g. *Re Lucking's WT* [1968] 1 W.L.R. 866.

7 Trustee Act 2000 Pt IV. An individual trustee may delegate her own functions, including distributive functions, under the Trustee Delegation Act 1999. For further discussion see paras 9–277.

otherwise,[8] although the trustees of charitable trusts and pension trusts may act by a majority.[9] For example, if there is a trust to sell land with a power to postpone sale, the postponement power is only effective if all the trustees wish to exercise it: if one wishes the trust to sell then the sale must be carried out, all the trustees being under a duty to sell unless the power to postpone sale is exercised unanimously.[10] Conversely, if there is a trust to hold land with a power to sell,[11] exercise of the sale power must be exercised unanimously, and if that is not possible an application to the court will be required.[12]

## C. New Trustees

**9–003** When accepting office as a trustee a person should ascertain the terms of the trust and check that she has been properly appointed.[13] She should inspect all the trust documents and ensure that all the trust property is properly invested and is in the joint names of herself and her co-trustees,[14] or in the name of a duly authorised nominee or custodian.[15] It is often best to have title deeds or share certificates deposited at a bank in the joint names of the trustees, but in the absence of special circumstances the court will not order one trustee who has possession of the documents to do this.[16] A person who is appointed as a new trustee of an existing trust must investigate any suspicious circumstances which suggest that a breach of trust may have occurred prior to her appointment, so that action can be taken to recoup the trust fund if necessary.[17]

## D. Overview of the Chapter

**9–004** We begin in section 2, below, with a discussion of the three main duties owed by trustees: the duty to comply with the terms of the trust instrument and the general law, the fiduciary duty to act exclusively in the beneficiaries' interest, and the duty to take reasonable care. We then consider a series of practical actions which trustees must typically take in order to make the trust work, and the rules which affect their performance of these actions. Section 3 concerns the notification of beneficiaries and the provision of trust information; section 4 concerns the reduction of the trust property into possession; section 5 concerns the investment of trust property; section 6 concerns the balance that must be struck between capital and income beneficiaries; section 7 concerns the distribution of trust property; section 8 concerns the exercise of discretionary powers by trustees; and section 9 concerns the delegation of trustee duties and powers.

---

8 *Luke v South Kensington Hotel Ltd* (1879) 11 Ch.D. 121; *Re Butlin's ST* [1976] Ch. 251 (rectification to allow majority decisions).

9 *Re Whiteley* [1910] 1 Ch. 600 at 608 (charitable trusts); Pensions Act 1995 s.32 (pension trusts).

10 *Re Mayo* [1943] Ch. 302. However, the letter of the trust will not be enforced if so to do would defeat the spirit of the trust: *Jones v Challenger* [1961] 1 Q.B. 176.

11 This is normal for co-ownership under Trusts of Land and Appointment of Trustees Act 1996.

12 Trusts of Land and Appointment of Trustees Act 1996 ss.14, 15.

13 *Harvey v Oliver* (1887) 57 L.T. 239 at 241; *Jones v Firkin-Flood* [2008] EWHC 2417 (Ch) at [240].

14 *Hallows v Lloyd* (1888) 39 Ch.D. 686 at 691; *Harvey v Olliver* (1887) 57 L.T. 239; *Tiger v Barclays Bank* [1952] W.N. 38; *Lewis v Nobbs* (1878) 8 Ch.D. 591. For those classes of property not vesting in the new trustee under Trustee Act 1925 s.40, the ordinary modes of transferring the property will have to be used.

15 Trustee Act 2000 ss.16–23.

16 *Re Sisson's Settlements* [1903] 1 Ch. 262. Bearer securities have to be deposited with a custodian unless otherwise authorised by the trust instrument: Trustee Act 2000 s.18.

17 *Re Strahan* (1856) 8 De G.M. & G. 291; *Re Forest of Dean Coal Co* (1878) 10 Ch.D. 250.

## 2. Main Duties Owed by Trustees

### A. Duty to Comply with the Terms of the Trust and the General Law

A trustee owes a duty to hold the trust property in an authorised form for the beneficiaries (or for the charitable purposes) identified by the settlor, and to account to them for her dealings with the property (or in the case of charitable trusts, to the Charity Commission and Attorney General). To enable the trustee to carry out her managerial and distributive roles, she is typically given powers—to buy and sell trust property, to accumulate income, to distribute income and capital, and so on—but she must not exercise these powers in a manner that would be inconsistent with the terms of the trust, for example by distributing property to anyone who is not a beneficiary (or by applying charitable funds to some unauthorised purpose[18]). Additional limits may also be placed on the trustee's powers by the settlor or by the general law: for example, she may be forbidden to sell particular trust assets, or to buy particular types of property for investment purposes. **9–005**

When describing such limits on the trustee's powers it can be said that she owes a duty to comply with the terms of the trust and the general law. So, in *Youyang Pty Ltd v Minter Ellison Morris Fletcher* the High Court of Australia said that "perhaps the most important duty of a trustee is to obey the terms of the trust",[19] and in *AIB Group (UK) Plc v Mark Redler & Co*, Lord Toulson spoke of a trustee owing "a duty to preserve the assets of the trust except in so far as the terms of the trust permit [her] to do otherwise".[20] However, this is not a duty breach of which generally leads to an award of compensation in the same way that breach of a primary obligation to perform a contract triggers a secondary obligation to pay compensatory damages.[21] Hence it may be more illuminating to say that the rules constraining the exercise of trustees' powers disable them from carrying out unauthorised transactions. **9–006**

This is not merely a semantic point. The reason why it matters becomes clear when one considers the claims which beneficiaries can bring, and the remedies to which they are entitled, in cases where the trustee purports to dispose of trust property in an unauthorised transaction. In such cases, the courts do not generally say that the trustee has committed a breach of duty, and then fix the trustee with a personal compensatory liability that is quantified by asking what loss has been caused by this breach. Instead they generally treat the unauthorised disposal of trust property as ineffective to discharge the trustee from her continuing duty to keep the trust property in an authorised form, with the result that she must either return the misapplied assets *in specie*, or obtain and deliver replacement property, or pay in the current monetary value of the missing property. The mechanics of this, and the ways in which the beneficiaries' remedy differs from an award of damages, are discussed in Chapter 10. **9–007**

The duty owed by trustees and other stewards of property[22] to obey instructions and comply with the terms of their authority when dealing with the property is quite often described as a "fiduciary **9–008**

---

18 cf. Charity Commission, *CC 12: Managing Financial Difficulties and Insolvency in Charities* (Charity Commission, September 2004), para.34: "It is a breach of trust to use restricted funds for purposes other than those for which they were given"; Charity Commission, *The Prevention or Relief of Poverty for the Public Benefit* (Charity Commission, December 2008), para G1: "a breach of trust can arise where trustees act outside their duties or powers, including using their charity's property and other resources for something that falls outside the charity's aims."

19 (2003) 212 C.L.R. 484 at [32].

20 [2014] 3 W.L.R. 1367 at [51].

21 See Lord Diplock's exposition in *Moschi v Lep Air Services Ltd* [1973] A.C. 331 at 350, and *Photo Production Ltd v Securicor Transport Ltd* [1980] A.C. 827 at 848–849.

22 "Stewardship" is not a legal term of art and is used here in a loose sense to describe the control and management of property for another person's benefit. For judicial usage of the word in this sense, see, e.g. *Bairstow v Queens Moat*

duty", to express the idea that it is a duty exemplified by the duty which a trustee owes to the beneficiaries to act in this way. Company directors, for example, are often said to owe "fiduciary duties" to the company in this sense. However, as Charles Mitchell explains in the following passage, it would be best if the courts were to avoid this usage, as it creates a serious risk of confusion with a different duty that is even more commonly termed a "fiduciary duty", namely the duty owed by a person in whom trust and confidence are reposed to act exclusively in the interests of her principal. This second duty is discussed in the next section.

### C. Mitchell, "Stewardship of Property and Liability to Account"

[2014] Conv. 215 at pp.216–218

9–009 Lawyers often use the term "fiduciary duty" to describe a duty of undivided loyalty owed by a person who has assumed a position of trust and responsibility towards a principal: he must subordinate his personal interests to the interests of his principal and must not serve several principals with conflicting interests. Lawyers also use the term in a different sense, to describe any duty owed by a trustee or a person resembling a trustee. These meanings of the term "fiduciary duty" can overlap, as trustees and other stewards often owe a duty of undivided loyalty to their beneficiaries and principals. But the meanings are not identical, since trustees and other stewards also owe other duties.[23]

9–010 For example, they owe a duty of care. This differs from their duty of undivided loyalty, which is why Millett L.J. said in *Bristol & West Building Society v Mothew* that it would be "inappropriate to apply the expression ["fiduciary"] to the obligation of a trustee . . . to use proper skill and care in the discharge of his duties."[24] There would be no objection to describing a trustee's duty of care as a "fiduciary duty", if it were clear that this meant no more than "duty of care owed by a trustee". But in many cases, this is not clear, because the term might also mean "duty of undivided loyalty". So this usage is best avoided.

9–011 The same point can be made about the rule that a steward of property must comply with the terms of his authority. Express trustees are required to do this. Indeed, the High Court of Australia has said that "perhaps the most important duty of a trustee is to obey the terms of the trust".[25] Hence one could describe this limit on their powers as a "fiduciary duty of compliance with instructions", meaning no more than "a duty of compliance owed by a trustee". But, again, this language may create the false impression that the rules which prevent stewards from exceeding their authority coincide with the rules which require them to be loyal. So, again, this usage should be avoided.

9–012 Consider these dicta. In *HMRC v Holland* Lord Walker referred to "the fiduciary duty that a company director owes to his company not to make an unauthorised distribution of capital";[26] in *Pitt v Holt* Mummery L.J. said that if a "disposition [by a power-holder] is a misapplication of property outside the scope of the power . . . that will be a breach of fiduciary duty";[27] in *Sinclair Investments (UK) Ltd v Versailles Trade Finance Ltd* Lord Neuberger M.R. said that "a person entrusted with another person's money for a specific purpose has fiduciary duties to the other person in respect of the use to which those moneys are put";[28] and in *Ross River Ltd v Waveley Commercial Ltd* Lloyd L.J. said that "the essence of the fiduciary duty" owed by a director was that the company's "assets should have been kept intact, without being depleted by unauthorised payments".[29]

9–013 In all of these passages, their Lordships describe unauthorised disposals of property as breaches of "fiduciary duty". What they mean is that a person charged with administering and applying property for another person's benefit may not exceed the terms of his authority when dealing with the property, and

*Houses Plc* [2001] 2 B.C.L.C. 531 at [53]; *Ultraframe (UK) Ltd v Fielding* [2005] EWHC 1638 (Ch) at [513]; *AIB Group (UK) Plc v Mark Redler & Co* [2014] 3 W.L.R. 1367 at [39].

23 M. Conaglen, *Fiduciary Loyalty: Protecting the Due Performance of Non-Fiduciary Duties* (2010), Ch.3.

24 [1998] Ch. 1 at 16.

25 *Youyang Pty Ltd v Minter Ellison Morris Fletcher* (2003) 212 C.L.R. 484 at [32].

26 [2011] Bus. L.R. 111 at [121].

27 [2012] Ch. 132 at [237].

28 [2012] Ch. 453 at [34].

29 [2013] EWCA Civ 910 at [118].

that if he does this he will be required to restore the missing property in the same way that a trustee is required to reconstitute a trust fund depleted by unauthorised disposals. What their Lordships do not mean is that acting beyond one's powers is in itself necessarily a disloyal thing to do.

Of course, one can imagine cases where a steward of property might exceed his powers with a disloyal intention. If a trustee or director misappropriates the trust funds or the company's property for himself then he may simultaneously exceed his authority and improperly prioritise his personal interests over the interests of the beneficiaries or the company. But in this situation there are two problems with the transaction and not one. **9–014**

One way to see this is to notice that some unauthorised transactions are not entered for a disloyal purpose. Consider the case where a trustee uses trust money to buy an unauthorised investment because he believes this to be in the beneficiaries' best interests. Even if the investment turns out well, a "carping beneficiary could insist that the unauthorised investment be sold and the proceeds invested in authorised investments".[30] The reason is that the trustee has exceeded his powers, and it does not matter that there was no conflict between the trustee's interests and the beneficiaries' interests. **9–015**

In *Bairstow v Queens Moat Houses plc* Robert Walker L.J. emphasised the difference between **9–016**

> "a breach of fiduciary duty in the wrongful disbursement of funds of which the fiduciary has [a] sort of trustee-like stewardship and a breach of fiduciary duty of a different character (for instance a solicitor's failure to disclose a conflict of interest . . .)."[31]

His Lordship was right to notice the difference between these two types of case, but it might have been still more desirable to have used the term "fiduciary duty" to describe the duty of loyalty alone, or to have dropped it altogether.[32]

In this connection, there is a lesson to be learnt from the Companies Act 2006. Section 171 places directors under a duty to act within their powers. Section 175 places them under a duty to avoid conflicts of interest. These are clearly stated in the legislation to be different duties, and neither is described as a "fiduciary" duty. **9–017**

## *B. Fiduciary Duty to Act Exclusively in the Beneficiaries' Interests*

### i. The Duty Stated

A trustee must not allow her personal interest to come into conflict with the beneficiaries' interests, for example by contracting to buy trust property,[33] or by taking some other profit-making opportunity for herself that was offered to her in her capacity as trustee.[34] This is why trustees may not generally take payment for their services, although as we have seen in Chapter 8, charging clauses are frequently inserted into trust deeds, to enable the employment of professional trustees and trustee companies.[35] **9–018**

The remedies available to beneficiaries when trustees act in breach of the "no conflicts" rule are discussed in Chapter 13, where we also make the point that other people besides trustees can also owe a duty to act exclusively in a principal's interest.[36] This duty is what people most commonly mean when they refer to a "fiduciary duty", and this is the sense in which the term is used in this book. Those who owe such a duty (including trustees) are commonly referred to as "fiduciaries". **9–019**

---

30 *Target Holdings Ltd v Redferns (a firm)* [1996] A.C. 421 at 433 per Lord Browne-Wilkinson.

31 [2001] 2 B.C.L.C. 531 at [53].

32 Cf. R. Grantham, "Company Directors and Compliance with the Company's Constitution" (2003) 20 New Zealand Universities Law Review 450, esp. at p.461.

33 *Fox v Mackreth* (1791) 2 Cox Eq. Cas. 320; *Re Thompson's Settlement* [1986] Ch. 99 at 115; *Tito v Waddell (No 2)* [1977] Ch. 106 at 246–250; *Barnsley v Noble* [2014] EWHC 2657 (Ch) at [261]ff.

34 *Keech v Sandford* (1726) Sel. Cas. temp. King 61; *Aberdeen Town Council v Aberdeen University* (1877) 2 App. Cas. 544; *Re Knowles's W.T.* [1948] 1 All E.R. 866. The same rules apply to charity trustees: *Mountstar (PTC) Ltd v Charity Commission* First-tier Tribunal (General Regulatory Chamber), 17 October 2013 at [17]–[20].

35 See paras 8–061ff for discussion.

36 See paras 13–007—13–054.

### ii. The Duty Distinguished from Other Duties

9-020 In the following passage of Millett LJ's judgment in *Bristol and West Building Society v Mothew*,[37] he stresses the importance of distinguishing clearly between fiduciary duties and the other duties which trustees and other fiduciaries can owe. The defendant solicitor acted for the purchasers of a house and also for the claimant building society which made the purchasers a loan towards the purchase on condition that the balance of the purchase price would be paid by the purchasers without further borrowing. The loan was to be secured by a mortgage over the house. The claimant instructed the defendant to report any proposal by the purchasers to create a second mortgage or otherwise borrow money to finance part of the purchase price. The solicitor knew they were arranging to create a second charge on the property to secure an existing debt, but failed to report this, due to an oversight. The claimant lent the money, the purchase was completed, the borrowers defaulted on their mortgage repayments, the claimant foreclosed and the house was sold at a loss. The claimant sought to recover its loss on the transaction from the defendant. The Court of Appeal held that the claimant could recover damages for negligence, but that the defendant had committed no breach of fiduciary duty since his reporting failure was unconnected to the fact that he was also acting for the purchasers.

*Bristol and West Building Society v Mothew*

Court of Appeal [1998] Ch. 1 at 16 and 18

9-021 MILLETT L.J.: Despite the warning given by Fletcher Moulton L.J. in *Re Coomber*,[38] this branch of the law has been bedevilled by unthinking resort to verbal formulae. It is therefore necessary to begin by defining one's terms. The expression "fiduciary duty" is properly confined to those duties which are peculiar to fiduciaries and the breach of which attracts legal consequences differing from those consequent upon the breach of other duties. Unless the expression is so limited it is lacking in practical utility. In this sense it is obvious that not every breach of duty by a fiduciary is a breach of fiduciary duty. I would endorse the observations of Southin J. in *Girardet v Crease & Co*.[39]:

> "The word 'fiduciary' is flung around now as if it applied to all breaches of duty by solicitors, directors of companies and so forth. . . . That a lawyer can commit a breach of the special duty [of a fiduciary] . . . by entering into a contract with the client without full disclosure . . . and so forth is clear. But to say that simple carelessness in giving advice is such a breach is a perversion of words."

These remarks were approved by La Forest J. in *LAC Minerals Ltd v International Corona Resources Ltd* where he said: "not every legal claim arising out of a relationship with fiduciary incidents will give rise to a claim for breach of fiduciary duty."[40]

9-022 It is similarly inappropriate to apply the expression to the obligation of a trustee or other fiduciary to use proper skill and care in the discharge of his duties. If it is confined to cases where the fiduciary nature of the duty has special legal consequences, then the fact that the source of the duty is to be found in equity rather than the common law does not make it a fiduciary duty. The common law and equity each developed the duty of care, but they did so independently of each other and the standard of care required is not always the same. But they influenced each other, and today the substance of the resulting obligations is more significant than their particular historic origin. . .

9-023 This leaves those duties which are special to fiduciaries and which attract those remedies which are peculiar to the equitable jurisdiction and are primarily restitutionary or restorative rather than compensatory. A fiduciary is someone who has undertaken to act for or on behalf of another in a particular matter in circumstances which give rise to a relationship of trust and confidence. The distinguishing obligation of a

37 [1998] Ch. 1 at 16.
38 [1911] 1 Ch. 723 at 728.
39 (1987) 11 B.C.L.R. (2d) 361 at 362.
40 (1989) 61 D.L.R. (4th) 14 at 28.

> fiduciary is the obligation of loyalty. The principal is entitled to the single-minded loyalty of his fiduciary. This core liability has several facets. A fiduciary must act in good faith; he must not make a profit out of his trust; he must not place himself in a position where his duty and his interest may conflict; he may not act for his own benefit or the benefit of a third person without the informed consent of his principal. This is not intended to be an exhaustive list, but it is sufficient to indicate the nature of fiduciary obligations. They are the defining characteristics of the fiduciary. As Dr. Finn pointed out in his classic work *Fiduciary Obligations*,[41] he is not subject to fiduciary obligations because he is a fiduciary; it is because he is subject to them that he is a fiduciary.

### iii. Content of the Duty

It is uncontroversial that a fiduciary cannot validly act where there is a conflict between her personal interests and her principal's interests,[42] and that she cannot validly act where there is a conflict between the interests of two different principals whom she serves.[43] Whether fiduciary duties have a larger content than this is debated, but Matthew Conaglen has argued that they do not, because the other duties owed by fiduciaries are also owed by people who are not fiduciaries, and so they cannot be fiduciary duties on the principle stated in *Mothew*, that fiduciary duties are "those duties which are peculiar to fiduciaries".[44] **9–024**

So, for example, Conaglen argues that the duty to act for a proper purpose cannot be a fiduciary duty because it is a duty owed by all power-holders, whether or not they hold their powers in a fiduciary capacity—a conclusion with which we agree as we believe that that this duty is best understood not as an aspect of the rules forbidding conflicts of interest, but as an aspect of the rules affecting the "excessive execution" of powers. In other words, the purported exercise of a power for an improper purpose[45] is void for the same reason that the purported exercise of a power is void if it is undertaken by a person who does not actually possess the power in question.[46] **9–025**

Conaglen also contends, rightly in our view, that the rule which forbids fiduciaries from making an unauthorised profit from their position is an extension of the "no conflicts" rule, and should not be understood as a separate rule underpinned by another principle.[47] Others think differently,[48] however, and this matters because it affects our understanding of the reasons why constructive trusts are imposed on the proceeds of a breach of fiduciary duty. This is a difficult issue and, as we discuss further below,[49] it is complicated by the further question of whether the rule requiring fiduciaries to disgorge profits is a "duty-based" rule or a "disability-based" rule. **9–026**

---

41 (1977), p. 2.

42 *Bray v Ford* [1896] A.C. 44 at 51; *Boardman v Phipps* [1967] 2 A.C. 46 at 123; *Swain v Law Society* [1982] 1 W.L.R. 17 at 30–31; *FHR European Ventures LLP v Cedar Capital Partners LLC* [2015] A.C. 250 at [5].

43 *Bristol & West Building Society v Mothew* [1998] Ch. 1 at 19; *FHR European Ventures LLP v Cedar Capital Partners LLC* [2015] A.C. 250 at [5].

44 Conaglen, *Fiduciary Loyalty: Protecting the Due Performance of Non-Fiduciary Duties* (2010), Ch.3.

45 As in, e.g. *Re Pauling's S.T.* [1964] Ch. 303. The origin of the duty to exercise powers for a proper purpose lies in the equitable doctrine of fraud on a power, which is discussed below at paras 9–205—9–235.

46 As in, e.g. *Re Keele Estates (No.2) Ltd* [1952] Ch. 603 at 622–626. Note, however, that although Farwell LJ held in *Cloutte v Storey* [1911] 1 Ch. 18 that the exercise of a power for an improper purpose is "void", his definition of "voidness" looked very like "voidability", prompting Lord Walker to suggest in *Pitt v Holt* [2013] 2 A.C. 108 at [62] that "a fraudulent appointment (that is, one shown to have been made for a positively improper purpose) may need a separate pigeon-hole somewhere between the categories of excessive execution and inadequate deliberation." See further para.9–235.

47 See Conaglen, *Fiduciary Loyalty: Protecting the Due Performance of Non-Fiduciary Duties* (2010), pp.39–40, 113–125. For judicial statements of the same view, see *Boardman v Phipps* [1967] 2 A.C. 46 at 123; *FHR European Ventures LLP v Cedar Capital Partners LLC* [2015] A.C. 250 at [5].

48 e.g. L. Smith, "Fiduciary Relationships: Ensuring the Loyal Exercise of Judgement on Behalf of Another" (2014) 130 L.Q.R. 608, 625ff.

49 See paras 9–073ff, 13–185ff.

### iv. "No Conflicts" Rule Strictly Applied in Practice

**9–027** At this stage it is desirable to give two examples of cases in which the courts have found trustees and other fiduciaries to have breached the "no conflicts" rule. *Keech v Sandford*[50] and *Boardman v Phipps*,[51] reproduced below, both illustrate the firm line that has traditionally been taken by the courts against fiduciaries (including trustees): they have held that a fiduciary can be liable for breaching the "no conflicts" rule although she has acted in good faith, although her actions have left her principal better off than he would have been if the fiduciary had done nothing, and although there was only a potential (rather than an actual) conflict between the fiduciary's interest and the interests of her principal.[52]

*Keech v Sandford*

Lord Chancellor (1726) Sel. Cas. T. King 61

**9–028** A person being possessed of a lease of the profits of a market devised his estate to a trustee in trust for his infant. Before the expiration of the term the trustee applied to the lessor for a renewal, for the benefit of the infant, which he refused, since the lease being only of the profits of a market, there could be no distress, and its enforcement must rest in covenant, by which the infant could not be bound. The infant sought to have the lease assigned to him, and for an account of the profits, on the principle that wherever a lease is renewed by a trustee or executor it shall be for the benefit of the cestui que use, which principle was agreed on the other side, though endeavoured to be differenced on account of the express proof of refusal to renew to the infant.

**9–029** LORD KING L.C.: I must consider this as a trust for the infant, for I very well see, if a trustee, on the refusal to renew, might have a lease to himself, few trust estates would be renewed to cestui que use. Though I do not say there is fraud in this case, yet he should rather have let it run out than to have had the lease to himself. This may seem hard, that the trustee is the only person of all mankind who might not have the lease; but it is very proper that the rule should be strictly pursued, and not in the least relaxed; for it is very obvious what would be the consequences of letting trustees have the lease on refusal to renew to cestui que use.

**9–030** So decreed, that the lease should be assigned to the infant, and that the trustee should be indemnified from any covenants comprised in the lease, and an account of the profits made since the renewal.

*Boardman v Phipps*

House of Lords [1967] 2 A.C. 46

**9–031** The respondent, John Phipps, was one of the residuary legatees under the will of his father, who died in 1944. The residuary estate included 8,000 out of 30,000 issued shares in a private company, Lester & Harris Ltd. By his will the testator left an annuity to his widow and, subject to her interest, 5/18ths of his residuary estate to each of his three sons and 3/18ths to his only daughter. At the end of 1955 the trustees of the will were the testator's widow (who was senile and took no part in the affairs of the trust), his only daughter, Mrs Noble, and an accountant, Fox. The first appellant, Boardman, was at all material times solicitor to the trustees and also to the children of the testator (other than the respondent). The second appellant, Tom Phipps, was the younger brother of John and in the transactions which gave rise to the case he was associated with and represented by the first appellant, Boardman.

**9–032** In 1956 Boardman and Fox decided that the recent accounts of Lester & Harris Ltd were unsatisfactory and with a view to improving the position the appellants attended the annual general meeting of the company in December 1956 with proxies obtained from two of the trustees, Mrs Noble and Fox. They were

[50] (1726) Sel. Cas. T. King 61.

[51] [1967] 2 A.C. 46.

[52] See also *Parker v McKenna* (1874) L.R. 10 Ch. App. 96; *Regal (Hastings) Ltd v Gulliver* [1942] 1 All E.R. 378, [1967] 2 A.C. 134n., for discussion of which see R. Nolan, "*Regal (Hastings) Ltd v Gulliver* (1942)" in C. Mitchell and P. Mitchell (eds), *Landmark Cases in Equity* (Hart Publishing, 2012).

not satisfied with the answers given at the meeting regarding the state of the company's affairs. Shortly after this meeting the appellants decided with the knowledge of Mrs Noble and Fox to try to obtain control of Lester & Harris Ltd by themselves making an offer for all the outstanding shares in that company other than the 8,000 held by the trustees. The trustees had no power to invest in the shares of the company without the sanction of the court and Fox said in evidence that he would not have considered seeking such sanction. The appellants originally offered £2 5s per share, which they later increased to £3, but by April 1957 they had received acceptances only in respect of 2,925 shares and it was clear that as things then stood they would not go through with their offer. This ended the first phase in the negotiations which ultimately led to the acquisition by the appellants of virtually all the outstanding shares in Lester & Harris Ltd. During this phase the appellants attended the annual general meeting as proxies of the two trustees and obtained information from the company as to the prices at which shares had recently changed hands; but they made the offer to purchase on their own behalf.

The second phase lasted from April 1957 to August 1958. Throughout this period Boardman carried on negotiations with the chairman of Lester & Harris Ltd with a view to reaching agreement on the division of the assets of that company between the Harris family and the directors on the one hand and the Phipps family on the other. During this phase Boardman obtained valuable information as to the value of the company's assets and throughout he purported to act on behalf of the trustees. These negotiations proved abortive. **9–033**

The third phase began in August 1958 with the suggestion by Boardman that he and Tom Phipps should acquire for themselves the outstanding shares in the company. The widow died in November 1958 and a conditional agreement for the sale of the shares was made on March 10, 1959. On May 26, 1959, the appellants gave notices making the agreements unconditional to buy 14,567 shares held by the chairman of the company and his associates at £4 10s per share. This, in addition to the earlier agreements to purchase 2,925 shares at £3 each and the purchase of a further 4,494 shares at £4 10s each, made the appellants holders of 21,986 shares. **9–034**

Thereafter the business of the company was reorganised, part of its assets was sold off at considerable profit, and substantial sums of capital, amounting in the aggregate to £5 17s 6d per share, were returned to the shareholders, whose shares were still worth at least £2 each after the return of capital. The appellants acted honestly throughout. **9–035**

The respondent, like the other members of the Phipps family, was asked by Boardman whether he objected to the acquisition of control of the company by the appellants for themselves; but Boardman did not give sufficient information as to the material facts to succeed in the defence of consent on the part of the respondent. At first the respondent expressed his satisfaction but later he became antagonistic and issued a writ claiming (i) that the appellants held 5/18ths of the above-mentioned 21,986 shares as constructive trustees for him (subject to a lien for their outlay on the purchase of the shares) and (ii) an account of the profits made by the appellants out of the said shares. **9–036**

Wilberforce J. granted this relief,[53] his decision was affirmed by the Court of Appeal,[54] and their decision was affirmed in turn by a majority of the House of Lords (Lords Cohen, Hodson and Guest; Viscount Dilhorne and Lord Upjohn dissenting). **9–037**

LORD COHEN: . . . As Wilberforce J. said,[55] the mere use of any knowledge or opportunity which comes to the trustee or agent in the course of his trusteeship or agency does not necessarily make him liable to account. In the present case had the company been a public company and had the appellants bought the shares on the market, they would not, I think have been accountable. The company, however, is a private company and not only the information but also the opportunity to purchase these shares came to them through the introduction which Mr Fox gave them to the board of the company and, in the second phase, when the discussions related to the proposed split up of the company's undertaking, it was solely on behalf of the trustees that Mr Boardman was purporting to negotiate with the board of the company. The question is this: when in the third phase the negotiations turned to the purchase of the shares at £4 10s a share, were the appellant debarred by their fiduciary position from purchasing on their own behalf the 21,986 shares in the company without the informed consent of the trustees and the beneficiaries? **9–038**

53 [1964] 1 W.L.R. 993.
54 [1965] Ch. 992 (Lord Denning M.R., Pearson and Russell L.JJ.).
55 [1964] 1 W.L.R. 993 at 1011.

9–039 Wilberforce J.[56] and, in the Court of Appeal,[57] both Lord Denning M.R. and Pearson L.J. based their decision in favour of the respondent on the decision of your Lordships' House in *Regal (Hastings) Ltd v Gulliver*.[58] I turn, therefore, to consider that case. Counsel for the respondent relied on a number of passages in the judgments of the learned Lords who heard the appeal, in particular on (i) a passage in the speech of Lord Russell of Killowen where he said[59]:

> "The rule of equity which insists on those, who by use of a fiduciary position make a profit, being liable to account for that profit, in no way depends on fraud, or absence of bona fides; or upon such questions or considerations as whether the profit would or should otherwise have gone to the plaintiff, or whether the profiteer was under a duty to obtain the source of the profit for the plaintiff, or whether he took a risk or acted as he did for the benefit of the plaintiff, or whether the plaintiff has in fact been damaged or benefited by his action. The liability arises from the mere fact of a profit having, in the stated circumstances, been made"

(ii) a passage in the speech of Lord Wright where he says[60]:

> "That question can be briefly stated to be whether an agent, a director, a trustee or other person in an analogous fiduciary position, when a demand is made upon him by the person to whom he stands in the fiduciary relationship to account for profits acquired by him by reason of his fiduciary position, and by reason of the opportunity and the knowledge, or either, resulting from it, is entitled to defeat the claim upon any ground save that he made profits with the knowledge and assent of the other person. The most usual and typical case of this nature is that of principal and agent. The rule in such cases is compendiously expressed to be that an agent must account for net profits secretly (that is, without the knowledge of his principal) acquired by him in the course of his agency. The authorities show how manifold and various are the applications of the rule. It does not depend on fraud or corruption."

These paragraphs undoubtedly help the respondent but they must be considered in relation to the facts of that case. In that case the profit arose through the application by four of the directors of Regal for shares in a subsidiary company which it had been the original intention of the board should be subscribed for by Regal. Regal had not the requisite money available but there was no question of it being ultra vires Regal to subscribe for the shares. In the circumstances Lord Russell of Killowen said[61]: "I have no hesitation in coming to the conclusion, upon the facts of this case, that these shares, when acquired by the directors, were acquired by reason, and only by reason, of the fact that they were directors of Regal, and in the course of their execution of that office." He went on to consider whether the four directors were in a fiduciary relationship to Regal and concluded that they were. Accordingly, they were held accountable. Counsel for the appellants argued that the present case is distinguishable. He puts his argument thus. The question one asks is whether the information could have been used by the principal for the purpose for which it was used by his agents. If the answer to that question is no, the information was not used in the course of their duty as agents. In the present case the information could never have been used by the trustees for the purpose of purchasing shares in the company; therefore purchase of shares was outside the scope of the appellants' agency and they are not accountable.

9–040 This is an attractive argument, but it does not seem to me to give due weight to the fact that the appellants obtained both the information which satisfied them that the purchase of the shares would be a good investment and the opportunity of acquiring them as a result of acting for certain purposes on behalf of the trustees. Information is, of course, not property in the strict sense of that word and, as I have already stated, it does not necessarily follow that, because an agent acquired information and opportunity while acting in a fiduciary capacity, he is accountable to his principals for any profit that comes his way as the result of the use he makes of that information and opportunity. His liability to account must depend on the facts of the case. In the present case much of the information came the appellants' way when Mr Boardman was acting on behalf of the trustees on the instructions of Mr Fox, and the opportunity of bidding for the shares

56 ibid.
57 [1965] Ch. 992.
58 [1942] 1 All E.R. 378.
59 ibid. at 386.
60 ibid. at 392.
61 ibid. at 387.

came because he purported for all purposes except for making the bid to be acting on behalf of the owners of the 8,000 shares in the company. In these circumstances it seems to me that the principle of the Regal case applies and that the courts below came to the right conclusion.

That is enough to dispose of the case but I would add that an agent is, in my opinion, liable to account for profits which he makes out of the trust property if there is a possibility of conflict between his interest and his duty to his principal. Mr Boardman and Mr Tom Phipps were not general agents of the trustees, but they were their agents for certain limited purposes. The information which they had obtained and the opportunity to purchase the 21,986 shares afforded them by their relations with the directors of the company—an opportunity they got as the result of their introduction to the directors by Mr Fox—were not property in the strict sense but that information and that opportunity they owed to their representing themselves as agents for the holders of the 8,000 shares held by the trustees. In these circumstances they could not, I think, use that information and that opportunity to purchase the shares for themselves if there was any possibility that the trustees might wish to acquire them for the trust. Mr Boardman was the solicitor whom the trustees were in the habit of consulting if they wanted legal advice. Granted that he would not be bound to advise on any point unless he were consulted, he would still be the person they would consult if they wanted advice. He would clearly have advised them that they had no power to invest in shares of the company without the sanction of the court. In the first phase he would also have had to advise on the evidence then available that the court would be unlikely to give such sanction: but the appellants learnt much more during the second phase. It may well be that even in third phase the answer of the court would have been the same but, in my opinion, Mr Boardman would not have been able to give unprejudiced advice if he had been consulted by the trustees and was at the same time negotiating for the purchase of the shares on behalf of himself and Mr Tom Phipps. In other words, there was, in my opinion, at the crucial date (March 1959) a possibility of a conflict between his interest and his duty. **9–041**

In making these observations I have referred to the fact that Mr Boardman was the solicitor to the trust. Mr Tom Phipps was only a beneficiary and was not as such debarred from bidding for the shares, but no attempt was made in the courts below to differentiate between them. Had such an attempt been made it would very likely have failed, as Mr Tom Phipps left the negotiations largely to Mr Boardman, and it might well be held that, if Mr Boardman was disqualified from bidding, Mr Tom Phipps could not be in a better position. Be that as it may, counsel for the appellants rightly did not seek at this stage to distinguish between the two. He did, it is true, say that Mr Tom Phipps as a beneficiary would be entitled to any information that the trustees obtained. This may be so, but nonetheless I find myself unable to distinguish between the two appellants. They were, I think, in March 1959, in a fiduciary position vis-à-vis the trust. That fiduciary position was of such a nature that (as the trust fund was distributable) the appellants could not purchase the shares on their own behalf without the informed consent of the beneficiaries: it is now admitted that they did not obtain that consent. They are therefore, in my opinion, accountable to the respondent for his share of the net profits which they derived from the transaction. **9–042**

I desire to repeat that the integrity of the appellants is not in doubt. They acted with complete honesty throughout, and the respondent is a fortunate man in that the rigour of equity enables him to participate in the profits which have accrued as the result of the action taken by the appellants in March 1959 in purchasing the shares at their own risk. As the last paragraph of his judgment clearly shows, the trial judge evidently shared this view. He directed an inquiry as to what sum was proper to be allowed to the appellants or either of them in respect of their or his work and skill in obtaining the said shares and the profits in respect thereof. The trial judge concluded by expressing the opinion that payment should be on a liberal scale. With that observation I respectfully agree. . . . **9–043**

LORD HODSON: . . . The proposition of law involved in this case is that no person standing in a fiduciary position, when a demand is made on him by the person to whom he stands in the fiduciary relationship to account for profits acquired by him by reason of his fiduciary position and by reason of the opportunity and the knowledge, or either, resulting from it, is entitled to defeat the claim on any ground save that he made profits with the knowledge and assent of the other person . . . **9–044**

. . . it is said on behalf of the appellants that information as such is not necessarily property and it is only trust property which is relevant. I agree, but it is nothing to the point to say that in these times corporate trustees, e.g. the Public Trustee and others, necessarily acquire a mass of information in their capacity of trustees for a particular trust and cannot be held liable to account if knowledge so acquired enables them to operate to their own advantage, or to that of other trusts. Each case must depend on its own facts, and I dissent from the view that information is of its nature something which is not properly to be described as property. We are aware that what is called "know-how" in the commercial sense is property which may **9–045** be very valuable as an asset. I agree with the learned judge[62] and with the Court of Appeal[63] that the confidential information acquired in this case, which was capable of being and was turned to account, can be properly regarded as the property of the trust. It was obtained by Mr Boardman by reason of the opportunity which he was given as solicitor acting for the trustees in the negotiations with the chairman of the company, as the correspondence demonstrates. The end result was that, out of the special position in which they were standing in the course of the negotiations, the appellants got the opportunity to make a profit and the knowledge that it was there to be made. . . .

**9–046** *Regal (Hastings) Ltd v Gulliver* differs from this case mainly in that the directors took up shares and made a profit thereby, it having been originally intended that the company should buy these shares. Here there was no such intention on the part of the trustees. There is no indication that they either had the money or would have been ready to apply to the court for sanction enabling them to do so. On the contrary, Mr Fox, the active trustee and an accountant who concerned himself with the details of the trust property, was not prepared to agree to the trustees buying the shares and encouraged the appellants to make the purchase. This does not affect the position. As *Keech v Sandford* shows, the inability of the trust to purchase makes no difference to the liability of the appellants, if liability otherwise exists. The distinction on the facts as to intention to purchase shares between this case and *Regal (Hastings) Ltd v Gulliver* is not relevant. The company (Regal) had not the money to apply for the shares on which the profit was made. The directors took the opportunity which they had presented to them to buy the shares with their own money and were held accountable. Mr Fox's refusal as one of the trustees to take any part in the matter on behalf of the trust, so far as he was concerned, can make no difference. Nothing short of fully informed consent, which the learned judge found not to have been obtained, could enable the appellants in the position which they occupied, having taken the opportunity provided by that position, to make a profit for themselves. . .

**9–047** The confidential information which the appellants obtained at a time when Mr Boardman was admittedly holding himself out as solicitor for the trustees was obtained by him as representing the trustees, the holders of 8,000 shares of Lester & Harris Ltd. As Russell L.J. put it[64]: "The substantial trust shareholding was an asset of which one aspect was its potential use as a means of acquiring knowledge of the company's affairs, or of negotiating allocations of the company's assets, or of inducing other shareholders to part with their shares." That aspect was part of the trust assets. Whether this aspect is properly to be regarded as part of the trust assets is, in my judgment, immaterial. The appellants obtained knowledge by reason of their fiduciary position, and they cannot escape liability by saying that they were acting for themselves and not as agents of the trustees. Whether or not the trust, or the beneficiaries in their stead, could have taken advantage of the information is immaterial, as the authorities clearly show. No doubt it was but a remote possibility that Mr Boardman would ever be asked by the trustees to advise on the desirability of an application to the court in order that the trustees might avail themselves of the information obtained. Nevertheless, whenever the possibility of conflict is present between personal interest and the fiduciary position the rule of equity must be applied. . . .

**9–048** LORD GUEST: . . . I take the view that from first to last Mr Boardman was acting in a fiduciary capacity to the trustees. This fiduciary capacity arose in phase 1 and continued into phase 2, which glided into phase 3. In saying this I do not for one moment suggest that there was anything dishonest or underhand in what Mr Boardman did. He has obtained a clean certificate below and I do not wish to sully it; but the law has a strict regard for principle in ensuring that a person in a fiduciary capacity is not allowed to benefit from any transactions into which he has entered with trust property. If Mr Boardman was acting on behalf of the trust, then all the information that he obtained in phase 2 became trust property. The weapon which he used to obtain this information was the trust holding; and I see no reason why information and knowledge cannot be trust property. . . .

**9–049** LORD UPJOHN (dissenting): On the evidence there was never any suggestion at any subsequent stage [after 1956] that Mr Fox or any other trustee would ever have contemplated any purchase of further shares. . . . In *Aberdeen Railway Co v Blaikie Bros*[65] Lord Cranworth L.C. said, "and it is a rule of universal application that no-one having such duties to discharge shall be allowed to enter into engagements in which he has or can have a personal interest conflicting or which possibly may conflict with the interests of

62 [1964] 1 W.L.R. 993 at 1008–1011.
63 [1965] Ch. 992.
64 [1965] Ch. 992 at 1031.
65 [1843–1860] All E.R. Rep. 249 at 252.

those whom he is bound to protect." The phrase "possibly may conflict" requires consideration. In my view it means that the reasonable man would think that there was a real sensible possibility of conflict; not that you could imagine some situation arising which might, in some conceivable possibility in events not contemplated as real sensible possibilities by any reasonable person, result in a conflict . . . [*Regal (Hastings) Ltd v Gulliver* and *Keech v Sandford* bear no relation to this case].

This case, if I may emphasise it again, is one concerned not with trust property or with property of which the persons to whom the fiduciary duty was owed were contemplating a purchase but, in contrast to the facts in *Regal*, with property which was not trust property or property which was ever contemplated as the subject-matter of a possible purchase by the trust. . . . **9–050**

This question whether the appellants were accountable requires a closer analysis than it has received in the lower courts. This analysis requires detailed consideration: **9–051**

(1) The facts and circumstances must be carefully examined to see whether in fact a purported agent and even a confidential agent is in a fiduciary relationship to his principal. It does not necessarily follow that he is in such a position.
(2) Once it is established that there is such a relationship, that relationship must be examined to see what duties are thereby imposed on the agent, to see what is the scope and ambit of the duties charged on him.
(3) Having defined the scope of those duties one must see whether he has committed some breach thereof by placing himself within the scope and ambit of those duties in a position where his duty and interest may possibly conflict. It is only at this stage that any question of accountability arises.
(4) Finally, having established accountability it only goes so far as to render the agent accountable for profits made within the scope and ambit of his duty.

Before applying these principles to the facts, however, I shall refer to the judgment of Russell L.J. which proceeded on a rather different basis. He said: **9–052**

> "The substantial trust shareholding was an asset of which one aspect was its potential use as a means of acquiring knowledge of the company's affairs, or of negotiating allocations of the company's assets, or of inducing other shareholders to part with their shares. That aspect was part of the trust assets."

My Lords, I regard that proposition as untenable.

In general, information is not property at all. It is normally open to all who have eyes to read and ears to hear. The true test is to determine in what circumstances the information has been acquired. If it has been acquired in such circumstances that it would be a breach of confidence to disclose it to another, then courts of equity will restrain the recipient from communicating it to another. In such cases such confidential information is often and for many years has been described as the property of the donor, the books of authority are full of such references; knowledge of secret processes, "know-how", confidential information as to the prospects of a company or of someone's intention or the expected results of some horse race based on stable or other confidential information. But in the end the real truth is that it is not property in any normal sense, but equity will restrain its transmission to another if in breach of some confidential relationship. **9–053**

With all respect to the views of Russell L.J., I protest at the idea that information acquired by trustees in the course of their duties as such is necessarily part of the assets of trust property which cannot be used by the trustees except for the benefit of the trust. Russell L.J. referred to the fact that two out of three of the trustees could have no authority to turn over this aspect of trust property to the appellants except for the benefit of the trust; this I do not understand, for if such information is trust property not all the trustees acting together could do it for they cannot give away trust property. **9–054**

We heard much argument on the impact of the fact that the testator's widow was at all material times incapable of acting in the trust owing to disability. Of course trustees must act all of them and unanimously in matters affecting trust affairs, but they never performed any relevant act on behalf of the trust at all; I quoted Mr Fox's answer earlier for this reason. At no time after going to the meeting in December 1956, did Mr Boardman or Tom rely on any express or implied authority or consent of the trustees in relation to trust property. They understood rightly that there was no question of the trustees acquiring any further trust property by purchasing further shares in the company, and it was only in the purchase of other shares that they were interested. **9–055**

9-056 There is, in my view, and I know of no authority to the contrary, no general rule that information learnt by a trustee during the course of his duties is property of the trust and cannot be used by him. If that were to be the rule it would put the Public Trustee and other corporate trustees out of business and make it difficult for private trustees to be trustees of more than one trust. This would be the greatest possible pity for corporate trustees and others may have much information which they may initially acquire in connection with some particular trust but without prejudice to that trust can make it readily available to other trusts to the great advantage of those other trusts.

9-057 The real rule is, in my view, that knowledge learnt by a trustee in the course of his duties as such is not in the least property of the trust and in general may be used by him for his own benefit or for the benefit of other trusts unless it is confidential information which is given to him (i) in circumstances which, regardless of his position as a trustee, would make it a breach of confidence for him to communicate to anyone, for it has been given to him expressly or impliedly as confidential; or (ii) in a fiduciary capacity, and its use would place him in a position where his duty and his interest might possibly conflict. Let me give one or two simple examples. A, as trustee of two settlements X and Y holding shares in the same small company, learns facts as trustee of X about the company which are encouraging. In the absence of special circumstances (such, for example, that X wants to buy more shares) I can see nothing whatever which would make it improper for him to tell his co-trustees of Y who feel inclined to sell that he has information that this would be a bad thing to do. Another example: A as trustee of X learns facts that make him and his co-trustees want to sell. Clearly he could not communicate this knowledge to his co-trustees of Y until at all events the holdings of X have been sold for there would be a plain conflict, reflected in the prices that might or might possibly be obtained.

9-058 My Lords, I do not think for one moment that Lord Brougham in *Hamilton v Wright*,[66] quoted in the speech of my noble and learned friend, Lord Guest, was saying anything to the contrary; one has to look and see whether the knowledge acquired was capable of being used for his own benefit to injure the trust (my italics). That test can have no application to the present. There was no possibility of the information being used to injure the trust. The knowledge obtained was used not in connection with trust property but to enhance the value of the trust property by the purchase of other property in which the trustees were not interested. . . .

9-059 As a result of the information the appellants acquired, admittedly by reason of the trust holding, they found it worthwhile to offer a good deal more for the shares than in phase 1 of chapter 2. I cannot see that in offering to purchase non-trust shares at a higher price they were in breach of any fiduciary relationship in using the information which they had acquired for this purpose. I cannot see that they have, from start to finish, in the circumstances of this case, placed themselves in a position where there was any possibility of a conflict between their duty and interest.

9-060 I have dealt with the problems that arise in this case at considerable length but it could, in my opinion, be dealt with quite shortly. In *Barnes v Addy*,[67] Lord Selborne L.C., said:

> "It is equally important to maintain the doctrine of trusts which is established in this court, and not to strain it by unreasonable construction beyond its due and proper limits. There would be no better mode of undermining the sound doctrines of equity than to make unreasonable and inequitable applications of them."

That, in my judgment, is applicable to this case.

9-061 The trustees were not willing to buy more shares in the company. The active trustees were very willing that the appellants should do so themselves for the benefit of their large minority holding. The trustees, so to speak, lent their name to the appellants in the course of prolonged and difficult negotiations and, of course, the appellants thereby learnt much which would have otherwise been denied to them. The negotiations were in the end brilliantly successful. How successful Tom was in his reorganisation of the company is apparent to all. They ought to be very grateful.

9-062 In the long run the appellants have bought for themselves with their own money shares which the trustees never contemplated buying and they did so in circumstances fully known and approved of by the trustees. To extend the doctrines of equity to make the appellants accountable in such circumstances is, in my judgment, to make unreasonable and inequitable applications of such doctrines.

---

66 (1842) 9 Cl. & Fin. 111.

67 (1874) 9 Ch. App. 244 at 251.

*Boardman* possesses some difficult features that have been well explained by Michael Bryan in his study of the case.[68] One is that none of the courts which heard the case gave a convincing explanation of the reason why Boardman and Tom Phipps were fiduciaries for John Phipps. Boardman gave advice on various matters as a solicitor to the trustees and beneficiaries but he was not on a permanent retainer; nor were he or Tom ever appointed as an agent either for the trustees or the beneficiaries with instructions to deal with the company management. Bryan concludes that the only basis on which they can have been fiduciaries is that they were "self-appointed agents", in Wilberforce J's term,[69] i.e. intermeddlers in the trust affairs who took it on themselves to act as though they were agents for the beneficiaries and who were accordingly treated as though they had been regularly appointed. **9–063**

Another difficult point is that John Phipps's statement of claim did not expressly allege a conflict of interest and the idea that Boardman had placed himself in a position where his personal interest prevented him from giving disinterested advice to the trustees appeared for the first time in Lord Denning MR's judgment in the Court of Appeal.[70] He reasoned that the articles of the company gave existing shareholders a right of pre-emption when another shareholder wished to sell his shares; hence when the directors were negotiating the sale of the company shares with Boardman and Tom Phipps, the trustees might have asked Boardman for advice as to whether they should exercise their pre-emption rights and if they had done so, there would then have been a conflict between his personal interests and his principal's interests. In the House of Lords the majority spoke in vague terms of a conflict of interests without identifying even this precisely what the conflict was. In this respect, *Boardman* can only be seen as a harsh decision, which most probably turned on a potential rather than an actual conflict of interest; furthermore this was a conflict that did not directly affect the claimant, who was not a trustee with pre-emption rights as a shareholder and was merely a beneficiary of the trust. **9–064**

### v. Loyalty and Exclusivity

It is often said that the essence of fiduciary duties is the notion of undivided loyalty.[71] However, for the reasons given by James Penner in the following excerpt, the rules requiring fiduciaries to act exclusively in the interests of their principals are not really concerned with loyalty, as that idea is commonly understood. Hence it may be more apt to speak of fiduciaries owing a duty of "deliberative exclusivity", meaning that when exercising their judgment on behalf of their principals they are not required to identify subjectively with their principal's interests, but they are required to exclude their own, and any third party's, interests from consideration. **9–065**

#### J. E. Penner, "Distinguishing Fiduciary, Trust, and Accounting Relationships"

(2014) 8 J.Eq. 201, 206–208

... I do not agree that the concept of loyalty, or at least not any concept of loyalty which relates to the commonsense concept of loyalty, has anything really to do with understanding the fiduciary relationship.[72] **9–066**
In my view, the application of the rules governing fiduciaries, in particular the no-conflict rule (including

68 M. Bryan, "*Boardman v Phipps* (1967)" in C. Mitchell and P. Mitchell (eds), *Landmark Cases in Equity* (2012).

69 [1964] 1 W.L.R. 993 at 1007.

70 [1965] Ch. 992 at 1020.

71 e.g. *Boardman v Phipps* [1967] 2 A.C. 46 at 123; *Grimaldi v Chameleon Mining NL (No.2)* (2012) 200 F.C.R. 296 at [174]; *FHR European Ventures LLP v Cedar Capital Partners LLC* [2015] A.C. 250 at [5]; *AIB Group (UK) Plc v Mark Redler & Co* [2014] 3 W.L.R. 1367 at [51].

72 J.E. Penner, "Is Loyalty a Virtue, and Even If It Is, Does It Really Help Explain Fiduciary Liability?" in A. Gold and P. Miller (eds), *Philosophical Foundations of Fiduciary Law* (2014).

> the special applications of that rule, the self-dealing and fair-dealing rules, and the 'no-profit' rule), is not about ensuring loyalty. The rule addresses the fact that where an exercise of a power is taken in cases where the trustee's judgment is impaired, that exercise can be set aside. This idea of impairment follows from the recognition that, even with the best intentions in the world, where one is interested in a transaction one cannot even oneself be sure that one has made an unbiased decision; judgment in these circumstances is moreover compromised by the human propensity to rationalise a decision favouring oneself. That is it, and one needn't invoke any notion of loyalty to explain the law. There are also positive reasons to reject loyalty as an underlying organising value or virtue for the fiduciary relationship. To summarise them:
>
> 9-067 (1) The notion of loyalty is both over- and under-inclusive. Many wrongs that are properly characterised as disloyal have nothing to do with fiduciary relationships.[73] A low-level employee who steals from his employer can certainly be characterized as disloyal, but there is no breach of any fiduciary relationship here for there is none.[74] Conversely, fiduciaries who have been found liable under the rules do not necessarily act disloyally. In no way could the actions of Boardman in the leading U.K. case of *Boardman v Phipps* be said to have been 'disloyal'.[75]
>
> 9-068 (2) To act disloyally, which would be required for fiduciary liability on this view, is to reveal a state of mind, an animus against the principal; disloyalty is an offence requiring mens rea. As *Boardman* also tells us,[76] this is not required for fiduciary liability.
>
> 9-069 (3) To be loyal to someone is to give them "deliberative priority" in relation to others to whom one is not expected to be loyal. To be loyal to my friends requires me to take their interests more seriously than those of people who are not my friends. But to act loyally does not require one not to take one's own interests into account. To act loyally is not to act selflessly. A principal, by contrast, is entitled to the "deliberative exclusivity" of his fiduciary. The powers the fiduciary exercises are exercised in the interests of their principal, and no one else. This is most obviously the case with a trustee-fiduciary. They must exercise the trust discretions with only the trust beneficiaries in mind because it is beneficially their property, not his.
>
> 9-070 (4) Lastly, loyalty concerns a relationship in which the loyal person must emotionally identify with the object of her loyalty, such that she understands her life to go better when the life of the object of her loyalty goes better. Moreover, relations of loyalty give rise to the possibility of "epistemic bias"; the identification involved lends itself to forming favourable but false or at least dubious beliefs about the object of loyalty . . . While there is a weak sense in which fiduciaries should identify with their principals, generally thinking that their role in serving their principals is worthwhile, discharging the role of fiduciary does not require any sympathy or identification of this kind, in the sense that how the life of the fiduciary will go tracks in any really important way whether her principal flourishes. Being a fiduciary is just a job, after all. Once again, the case of the trustee-fiduciary makes this point particularly clearly. One of the main tasks of the family trustee-fiduciary is to stand back and take a clear-eyed view of the beneficiaries, untainted by personal "identification", drawing upon personal knowledge of the beneficiaries of course, but not being swayed by likes or dislikes . . . Indeed, in the case of family trusts, one of the whole purposes of placing powers in the hands of impartial trustees is to provide an antidote to the false beliefs which persons close to the beneficiaries might form based on their identification with them. . .

### vi. Why Are Fiduciary Duties Imposed?

9-071 Penner's comments lead into the larger question of why fiduciary duties are imposed.[77] On one view of this question, the point of fiduciary duties is to force fiduciaries to act altruistically, which

---

73 At least on the discretionary model which both Smith and I endorse.

74 Or at least none in respect of a duty not to steal. In Australia, the employer-employee relationship has been described as a fiduciary one. . . . most recently in *Commonwealth Bank v Barker* (2014) 312 A.L.R. 356 at [16], [30]. With respect, it would seem correct to treat only those employees as fiduciaries who undertake an advisory or agent-like role vis-à-vis their employers.

75 [1967] 2 A.C. 46.

76 See also *Regal (Hastings) Ltd v Gulliver* [1967] 2 A.C. 134.

77 For an overview of the literature, see P.B. Miller, "Justifying Fiduciary Duties" (2013) 58 McGill L.J. 969.

is desirable because the inter-personal trust engendered by altruistic behaviour is a social good with an inherent moral value, because trust is critical to the individual flourishing of socially interdependent human beings, and because trust enables people to co-operate effectively towards the achievement of larger, socially desirable goals.[78] However, there are problems with this understanding of fiduciary duties. The idea of "trust" is only vaguely explained by those who place it at the centre of their analysis. Moreover it is a purposive concept: we trust people to do things for us, and this creates the difficulty that if the things we trust them to do are bad rather than good, then trusting people to do them may itself be a bad rather than a good thing. Also, imposing fiduciary duties by law does not seem a good way to reinforce trust between the members of society: if people avoid conflicts of interest only because the law requires them to, how far can they be trusted?

On another view, the point of fiduciary duties is to enable fiduciaries to make better decisions for their principals by requiring them to exercise disinterested judgment[79]; another, more elaborate, version of this argument holds that the point of fiduciary duties is to support the proper performance of other duties owed by fiduciaries by insulating them from temptation[80]: the idea here is that a fiduciary charged with taking decisions in her principal's interest will find it easier to do this carefully if she is not distracted by the prospect of personal advancement. Instrumental arguments of this sort do not treat conflicts of interest as morally problematic in themselves. Yet the terms in which the courts speak of fiduciary breaches, and the stringency with which breaching fiduciaries are treated, suggest that they are perceived—by the courts at least—as morally wrongful. Furthermore, if the point of fiduciary duties is to reduce the risk of fiduciaries breaching their non-fiduciary duties, then why do their breaches of fiduciary duty attract more stringent treatment than their breaches of the non-fiduciary duties which it is supposedly the job of their fiduciary duties to support?[81] **9–072**

### vii. From "Disability" to "Duty"

We have spoken of the "duty" owed by fiduciaries to act in their principals' interests. However, just like a trustee's "duty" to comply with the terms of the trust deed, this "duty" was not originally conceived of as a primary duty, breach of which could trigger a secondary duty to pay compensation or disgorge gains. The origins of fiduciary duties lie in equitable rules that were understood to operate differently, to disable fiduciaries from entering certain types of transaction. In recent years, however, fiduciary duties have been partially reconceptualised by all of the Commonwealth courts, with the result that the law is now in an uneasy state of transition. This development is described by Charles Mitchell in the following passage. **9–073**

---

[78] See, e.g. T. Frankel, "Fiduciary Law" (1983) 71 California L.R. 795; R. Flannigan, "The Fiduciary Obligation" (1989) 9 O.J.L.S. 285; M. Harding, "Trust and Fiduciary Law" (2013) 33 O.J.L.S. 81.

[79] See, e.g. I. Samet, "Guarding the Fiduciary's Conscience—A Justification of a Stringent Profit-Stripping Rule" (2008) 28 O.J.L.S. 763; L. Smith, "Deterrence, Prophylaxis and Punishment in Fiduciary Obligations" (2013) 7 J.Eq. 87; L. Smith, "Fiduciary Relationships: Ensuring the Loyal Exercise of Judgment on Behalf of Another" (2014) 130 L.Q.R. 608; J.E. Penner, "Distinguishing Fiduciary, Trust, and Accounting Relationships" (2014) 8 J.Eq. 201; Miller, "The Fiduciary Relationship" in *Philosophical Foundations of Fiduciary Law* (2015).

[80] The leading proponent of this argument is Matthew Conaglen, in his article "The Nature and Function of Fiduciary Loyalty" (2005) 121 L.Q.R. 121 and his book, *Fiduciary Loyalty: Protecting the Due Performance of Non-Fiduciary Duties* (2010). See also P. Birks, "The Content of Fiduciary Obligation" (2000) 34 Israel L.R. 3.

[81] R. Lee, "In Search of the Nature and Function of Fiduciary Loyalty: Some Observations on Conaglen's Analysis" (2007) 27 O.J.L.S. 327.

## C. Mitchell, "Equitable Compensation for Breach of Fiduciary Duty"

(2013) 66 C.L.P. 307 at pp.313–316

9–074 In his famous judgment in *Earl of Chesterfield v Janssen*, delivered in 1751, Lord Hardwicke L.C. said that the Chancery court would "relieve against every species of fraud", including fraud

> "which may be presumed from the circumstances and condition of [two] parties contracting: and this goes farther than the rule of law; which is, that it must be proved, not presumed; but it is wisely established in this court to prevent taking surreptitious advantage of the weakness or necessity of another . . . ."[82]

Here is another source of modern fiduciary doctrine, and also of the modern doctrine of undue influence. These are now understood to be separate, though overlapping, doctrines,[83] but a century after Lord Hardwicke's judgment they were still hardly distinguishable in Joseph Story's great treatise on *Equity Jurisprudence*, where he wrote of "constructive frauds . . . which arise from some peculiar confidential, or fiduciary relation between the parties".[84] Story included relations between parents and children, attorneys and solicitors and clients, principals and agents, guardians and wards—and trustees and beneficiaries. Contracts of sale between such parties were prohibited, and in cases where "confidence [was] reposed, and one party [had] it in his power, in a secret manner, for his own advantage, to sacrifice those interests, which he [was] bound to protect', that party was not 'permitted to hold any such advantage".[85]

9–075 Story did not think that this rule placed fiduciaries under a duty to refrain from disloyal behaviour, and his discussion of "trustee duties" makes no mention of the rule.[86] In this he was followed by other treatise writers of the nineteenth century, such as James Hill and Thomas Lewin. They saw things differently, writing that trustees and other fiduciaries were "incapable" of entering legally binding contracts with their principals, or that they could not do so because they were subject to an "equitable disability".[87] The same language appears in cases throughout the nineteenth and twentieth centuries.[88] It embodies a particular idea of the rules affecting fiduciaries' disloyal behaviour.[89] This is that fiduciary relationships are governed by a set of proscriptive rules that disable fiduciaries from acting in certain ways, rather than a set of prescriptive rules requiring them to perform certain duties, breaches of which trigger secondary obligations to disgorge profits or pay compensation. In modern times this idea of fiduciary disability has been championed by Lord Millett, who has emphasised in extra-judicial writings that an order directing a fiduciary to account for unauthorised profits 'is not a monetary award for wrongdoing',[90] but an order that gives effect to a rule that the fiduciary is legally incapable of keeping such gains for himself.

---

82 (1751) 2 Ves. Sen. 125 at 155–56.

83 R.P. Meagher, J.D. Heydon and M.J. Leeming, *Meagher, Gummow and Lehane's Equity: Doctrines and Remedies* (2002) para 15–100; D. O'Sullivan, S. Elliott, and R. Zakrzewski, *The Law of Rescission* (2008) paras 8.07–8.08; M. Conaglen 'Fiduciaries' in J. McGhee (gen. ed.), *Snell's Equity* (32nd edn, 2010), 239–41. But note R. Bigwood, *Exploitative Contracts* (2003) ch. 8, esp 406–23, cautioning against the potentially misleading nature of such statements.

84 J. Story, *Commentaries on Equity Jurisprudence as Administered in England and America* (1836) vol I 304.

85 Ibid. vol. I 320.

86 Ibid. vol. II 509 ff.

87 Ibid. vol. II 506; J. Hill, *A Practical Treatise on the Law Relating to Trustees* (1845) 554–57; T. Lewin, *A Practical Treatise on the Law of Trusts* 3rd edn (1857) 460–73. Cf. A. Underhill, *A Practical and Concise Manual of the Law Relating to Private Trusts and Trustees* 5th edn (1901) 243 and 250; E. Vinter, *A Treatise on the History and Law of Fiduciary Relationship* (1932) ch. 1; L.A. Sheridan, *Fraud in Equity: A Study in English and Irish Law* (1957) 185; O'Sullivan et al, paras 8.09–8.10.

88 *Ex parte Bennett* (1805) 10 Ves. Jun. 381 at 385; *Downes v Grazebrook* (1817) 3 Mer. 200 at 200; *Carter v Palmer* (1842) 7 Cl. & F. 657 at 707; *Re Bloye's W.T.* (1849) 1 Mac. & G. 488 at 495; *Grand Junction Canal Co v Dimes* (1850) 2 H & T 92, 100; *Franks v Bollans* (1868) L.R. 3 Ch. App 717 at 718; *McPherson v Watt* (1877) 3 App. Cas. 254 at 266; *Re Canadian Oil Works Corp* (1875) L.R. 10 Ch. App. 593 at 601; *Clare v Joseph* [1907] 2 K.B. 369 at 378–9; *Bath v Standard Land Co Ltd* [1911] 1 Ch. 618 at 634; *Transvaal Lands Co v New Belgium (Transvaal) Land and Development Co* [1914] 2 Ch. 488 at 502; *Taylor v Davies* [1920] A.C. 636 at 647; *Furs Ltd v Tomkies* (1936) 54 C.L.R. 583 at 592; *Re Bulmer* [1937] Ch. 499 at 503; *Scott v Scott* (1963) 109 C.L.R. 649; *Regal (Hastings) Ltd v Gulliver* [1967] 2 A.C. 134 at159; *Tito v Waddell (No. 2)* [1977] Ch. 106 at 248; *Guinness plc v Saunders* (1987) 3 B.C.C. 271 at 287; and [1990] 2 A.C. 663 at 669 (arguendo); *HR v JAPT* [1997] O.P.L.R. 123 at [29].

89 And also of the doctrine of undue influence: *Henchman v East India Co* (1797) 8 Bro. P.C. 85; *Agnew v Länsförsäkringsbolagens AB* [2001] 1 A.C. 223 at 264.

90 Lord Millett, "Book Review" (2002) 2 *Oxford University Commonwealth Law Journal* 291, 295. See too Sir P Millett, "Bribes

> A different way of thinking about fiduciary duty emerged in the case law of the late twentieth century. . . . This envisages that a fiduciary owes a positive duty "not to promote his personal interest . . . in circumstances in which there is a conflict or a real or substantial possibility of a conflict between his personal interests and those of the persons whom he is bound to protect".[91] Breach of this duty is conceptualised as a civil wrong that triggers a secondary duty to account for unauthorised gains,[92] or to pay compensation for loss.[93] 9–076
>
> This new idea sits very uneasily alongside the old thinking. The courts have held that it does not matter which version of fiduciary obligation is correct for the purposes of the causation rules[94] and limitation rules[95] governing claims for unauthorised profits. Nor does this clearly affect the question whether the principal's claim to such profits is proprietary or merely personal . . . But it goes to the heart of the question whether a principal can have compensation for loss, and now that the courts have moved to the position that he can, the disability model has come under great pressure. As Conaglen has written, the authorities currently require us to think that the 'remedies of rescission, accounts of profits and proprietary constructive trusts operate on the basis that the fiduciary was under a disability', but that 'where a compensatory remedy is sought the claim . . . takes on the characteristics of a duty-based claim'.[96] It is doubtful that this can be sustained. There is a strong likelihood that the number of compensatory claims will increase over the next few years, and that one effect of this will be that the disability model yields to the breach of duty model in the context of claims for unauthorised gains.[97] This in turn may have knock-on consequences for issues such as the proper classification of such claims for the purposes of the limitation rules, a topic that is anyway in need of a serious rethink. . . 9–077

## C. Duty of Care

When performing her managerial role, a trustee is generally required to display no higher degree of diligence than a person of ordinary prudence would exercise in the management of her own private affairs.[98] In the investment sphere, however, the trustee's duty is 9–078

> not to take such care only as a prudent man would take if he had only himself to consider; the duty rather is to take such care as an ordinary prudent man would take if he were minded to make an investment for the benefit of other people for whom he felt morally bound to provide.[99]

Moreover, with the advent of professional paid trustees and trust companies it has become established that a higher degree of care is expected of them, so that they are judged according to the

and Secret Commissions" [1993] *Restitution Law Review* 7, 20, endorsed in *A-G for Hong Kong v Reid* [1994] 1 A.C. 324 at 337; Lord Millett, "Proprietary Restitution" in S. Degeling and J. Edelman (eds) *Equity in Commercial Law* (2005) 324; Lord Millett, "Bribes and Secret Commissions Again" (2012) 71 *Cambridge Law Journal* 583, 585 and 591–92.

91 *Hospital Products Ltd v United States Surgical Corp* (1984) 156 C.L.R. 41 at 103.

92 *New Zealand Netherlands Society 'Oranje' Inc v Kuys* [1973] 1 W.L.R. 1126 at 1129; *Chan v Zacharia* (1984) 154 C.L.R. 178 at 189; *Maguire v Makaronis* (1997) 188 C.L.R. 449 at 468; *United Pan-Europe Communications NV v Deutsche Bank AG* [2000] 2 B.C.L.C. 461 at [44]; *Walsh v Deloitte & Touche Inc* [2002] 4 L.R.C. 454 at [13]; *Lindsley v Woodfull* [2004] 2 B.C.L.C. 131 at [28]–[30].

93 [Many Commonwealth cases have been decided in the past 20 years in which equitable compensation for breach of fiduciary duty has been awarded or its availability has been recognized in principle. English cases include *Swindle v Harrison* [1997] 4 All E.R. 705; *Nationwide Building Society v Balmer Radmore (a firm)* [1999] P.N.L.R. 606; *Longstaff v Birtles* [2002] 1 W.L.R. 470 at [35]–[37]; *DEG-Deutsche Investitions und Entwicklungsgesellschaft mbH v Koshy* [2004] 1 B.C.L.C. 131 at [142]–[147]; *Také Ltd v BSM Marketing Ltd* [2009] EWCA Civ 45; *Bank of Ireland v Jaffery* [2012] EWHC 1377 (Ch).]

94 *Murad v Al-Saraj* [2005] W.T.L.R. 1573 at [49].

95 *Koshy* at [104]–[109].

96 Conaglen at pp. 221–22.

97 Another likely effect will be the increasing use of the term 'damages' to describe compensatory awards for breach of fiduciary duty. This usage is already widespread and there is no sign of the courts 'stamp[ing it] out', as advocated in P Millett, 'Equity's Place in the Law of Commerce' (1998) 114 *Law Quarterly Review* 214, at p.225.

98 *Learoyd v Whiteley* (1887) 12 A.C. 727 at 733 per Lord Watson.

99 *Re Whiteley* (1886) 33 Ch.D. 347 at 355 per Lindley LJ, endorsed in *Cowan v Scargill* [1985] Ch. 270 at 289; *Nestlé v National Westminster Bank Plc* [1994] 1 All E.R. 118 at 126, 140.

standards of care which they profess,[100] although they should presumably be afforded the margin available to those called on to exercise their professional judgment in like circumstances.[101]

**9-079** In 2000, the equitable duty of care was replaced by a statutory duty of care which now applies to all trustee activities relating to investments, using agents, nominees and custodians, compounding liabilities, insuring, valuing, and auditing. The content of the statutory duty does not appear to differ from the content of the equitable duty, but s.1 of the Trustee Act 2000 states very clearly what approach should be taken by the courts when assessing whether a trustee has acted to a reasonably careful standard.

## Trustee Act 2000 s.1

**The duty of care**

**9-080** (1) Whenever the duty under this subsection applies to a trustee, he must exercise such care and skill as is reasonable in the circumstances, having regard in particular—

(a) to any special knowledge or experience that he has or holds himself out as having, and
(b) if he acts as trustee in the course of a business or profession, to any special knowledge or experience that it is reasonable to expect of a person acting in the course of that kind of business or profession.

**9-081** Note that s.1(1)(a) involves a subjective element relating to any extra knowledge or experience of the trustee personally, while s.1(1)(b) objectively relates to persons engaged in the trustee's business or profession generally. In (b) there is a distinction between a trustee who carries on trust business in the course of practising generally as a solicitor or accountant, and a trustee who specialises in trust work in the course of the specific business of being a trustee: the latter will normally be governed by a higher standard. Note, too, that the statutory duty of care laid down in section 1 may be excluded by an express term of the trust instrument.[102]

**9-082** If a trustee performs her managerial and administrative functions with an appropriate degree of skill and care then she will not be liable for loss which occurs as a result of her actions (also assuming that these are authorised). So, for example, she will not be liable for resulting losses if she takes a reasonable decision to buy investments which then depreciate in value following a drop in the securities market. Nor will she be liable for profits that she would have made if she had been more dynamic and skilful, e.g. in more actively selling and buying shares. When determining whether trustees have breached their duties of skill and care in making decisions (e.g. on selling or buying particular investments) the court will treat them in the same way as other professionals, who would only be:

> liable for damage caused by their advice, acts or omissions in the course of their professional work which no member of the profession who was reasonably well-informed and competent would have given or done or omitted to do.[103]

---

[100] *Bartlett v Barclays Bank Trust Co* [1980] 1 All E.R. 139 at 152. See too Lord Nicholls, "Trustees and Their Broader Community: Where Duty, Morality and Ethics Converge" (1995) 9 Tru. L.I. 71, 73.

[101] Cf. *Rubinstein v HSBC Bank Plc* [2013] P.N.L.R. 9 at [89], accepting the principle that professionals are entitled to such a margin, although the defendant could not take advantage of this on the facts.

[102] Trustee Act 2000 Sch.1 para.7. For general discussion of exemption clauses, see paras 10-201—10-211.

[103] *Saif Ali v Sydney Mitchell & Co* [1980] A.C. 198 at 218, per Lord Diplock, applied in *Wight v Olswang (No.2)* [2000] W.T.L.R. 783, and on appeal [2001] W.L.T.R. 291. See too *Bristol & West BS v Mothew* [1998] Ch. 1 at 17–18.

## 3. Notification of Beneficiaries and Provision of Trust Information

### A. Notification of Beneficiaries

In *Armitage v Nurse*, Millett LJ stated that[104]: 9–083

> there is an irreducible core of obligations owed by the trustees to the beneficiaries and enforceable by them which is fundamental to the concept of a trust. If the beneficiaries have no rights enforceable against the trustees there are no trusts.

If a trust is purportedly created for a beneficiary who can never exercise her rights against the trustee because she does not know that she is a beneficiary, then it cannot meaningfully be said that she has any enforceable rights, and so it cannot be said that there is a trust at all. Hence, to give substance to the beneficiary's core right to performance of the trust, a sui juris beneficiary has the right to be told that she is a beneficiary, and the trustee owes a concomitant duty to notify her of this fact.[105] In the case of charitable purpose trusts, one might also think of the registration requirements under the Charities Act 2011 Pt 4 as a duty placed on the trustees to inform the Attorney General and Charity Commission in their capacity as enforcers of the trustees' duties about the existence of the trust.

Note that a trustee's duty of notification is only a duty to take reasonable steps in all the circumstances, and in a case where the objects of a power of appointment vested in trustees consist of more than one category of person, the court may consider that by necessary implication the settlor only intended that the trustee should inform the primary objects of her bounty.[106] Suppose, for example, that a settlor declares a discretionary trust for her descendants, her other relatives known to her trustees, and employees and ex-employees of X Co Ltd (which she founded). In this case, the latter two classes are likely to be treated as peripheral with the result that they do not have as extensive rights as the former two classes. Similarly, if there was also a power of appointment vested in the trustees in favour of English charities benefiting children, such charities' interests should also be considered peripheral. Conversely, however, suppose that there is a discretionary trust to accumulate income for the trust period and then distribute the capital between such English charities as the trustees then see fit in their discretion, but with a power, instead, to appoint income or capital from time to time to the descendants of the settlor and their spouses or cohabitants. In this case, the descendant-objects are likely to be the primary focus of the settlor's bounty with the charities only having a peripheral interest in the capital, if any, left at the end of the period. Much must depend on the circumstances of a settlement, however, and in the words of David Fox[107]: 9–084

> Where the interests of different beneficiaries were opposed to each other (as where they were the respective objects of a special power and a gift over), then the due accountability of the donee of the power might require some of each group to be notified of their status. To leave all the powers of enforcement in, say, the beneficiary of a gift over might not be sufficient to ensure the donee was effectively accountable in respect of his distinctive duties to the objects of the power.

---

104 [1998] Ch. 241 at 253. See too D.J. Hayton, "The Irreducible Core Content of Trusteeship" in A.J. Oakley (ed.), *Trends in Contemporary Trust Law* (Clarendon Press, 1996).

105 *Brittlebank v Goodwin* (1868) L.R.5 Eq. 541 at 550; *Hawkesley v May* [1956] 1 Q.B. 304; *Foreman v Kingston* [2005] W.T.L.R. 823 at [85]. The beneficiary also has the right to be told the name and address of the trustee to whom a request can be made for a discretionary distribution: *Re Murphy's ST* [1999] 1 W.L.R. 282, where the judge treated the claimant as a primary object of a power of appointment in a discretionary trust.

106 *Re Manisty's Settlements* [1974] Ch. 17 at 25.

107 D. Fox, "Non-Excludable Trustee Duties" (2011) 17 T.&T. 17, 21.

## B. Provision of Trust Accounts

**9–085** A beneficiary has the right, exercisable at reasonable intervals, to inspect accounts prepared by the trustees explaining the current whereabouts of the trust property and the history of their dealings with it.[108] The trustees owe a correlative duty to keep proper accounts and to produce these on demand, along with supporting oral or documentary information.[109] Trustees "who indefensibly fail to produce accounts may be ordered to pay not only the costs of proceedings to obtain the accounts but also the costs of taking the account which is ordered".[110] Note that "every beneficiary is entitled to see the trust accounts, whether his interest is in possession or not".[111] Thus, any beneficiary with a future interest,[112] including (so far as practicable) a person who is merely the likely object of a discretionary trust or power which may never actually be exercised in her favour,[113] has the means to discover a breach of trust which she may then take action to redress.[114] Again, in the context of charitable trusts, we can understand the provisions of the Charities Act 2011 Pt 8 as serving a similar function: these sections provide that charity trustees must file accounts with the Charity Commission, the level of required detail varying with the size of the charity's annual income.

## C. Other Trust Documents

**9–086** In *Re Londonderry's Settlement*,[115] the Court of Appeal drew a distinction between trust accounts and other "trust documents" which could be inspected by a beneficiary, and material which did not count as "trust documents", and which was therefore not available for inspection, for example correspondence between the trustees themselves, or between the trustees and beneficiaries, and the agenda for trustees' meetings. Moreover, while "trust documents" included minutes of trustees' meetings and other documents of the trustees disclosing their deliberations on the exercise of their discretions or their reasons for any particular exercise of their discretions or "the material upon which such reasons were or might have been based", these were exempt from the beneficiaries' right to inspect trust documents. Otherwise, the right of trustees not to be obliged to give reasons for the exercise of their discretionary distributive functions would be undermined.[116] This still enabled beneficiaries to see a factual aide-memoire on the state of the fund, past distributions and future possibilities, and legal advice as to the law relating to the manner in which trustees were entitled to exercise their discretions;

---

[108] She can take copies of these accounts at her own expense or pay the trustee for copies provided by the trustee for an agreed sum representing the cost to the trustee: *Kemp v Burn* (1863) 4 Giff. 348; *Re Watson* (1904) 49 Sol. Jo. 54.

[109] *White v Lady Lincoln* (1803) 8 Ves. Jun. 363; *Pearse v Green* (1819) 1 Jac. & W. 135 at 140; *Eglin v Sanderson* (1862) 3 Giff. 434 at 440; *Re Cowin* (1886) 33 Ch.D. 179; *Re Rabaiotti's 1989 Settlement* [2000] W.T.L.R. 953; *Schmidt v Rosewood Trust Ltd* [2003] 2 A.C. 709; *Re EA Scott 1991 Children's Settlement No.1* [2012] W.T.L.R. 1439.

[110] *Mason v Coleman* [2007] EWHC 3149 (Ch) at [93]. See too *Kemp v Burn* (1863) 4 Giff 348; *Jefferys v Marshall* (1870) 23 L.T. 548; *Re Skinner* [1904] 1 Ch. 289; *Re Den Haag Trust* (1997/98) 1 O.F.L.R. 495.

[111] *Armitage v Nurse* [1998] Ch. 241 at 261 per Millett LJ. Unless there is a possibility of income being accumulated and added to capital it seems that a capital beneficiary is, however, not entitled to see the income accounts disposing of income to income beneficiaries: *Nestlé v National Westminster Bank* [2000] W.T.L.R. 795 at 822; but she must be entitled to check that the investment policy keeps an equitable balance between income and capital beneficiaries: see paras 9–159ff.

[112] Including contingent interests: *Re Tillott* [1892] 1 Ch. 86; *Attorney General of Ontario v Stavro* (1995) 119 D.L.R. (4th) 750.

[113] *Chaine-Nickson v Bank of Ireland* [1976] I.R. 393; *Spellson v George* (1987) 11 N.S.W.L.R. 300 at 315–316; *Hartigan Nominees Pty Ltd v Rydge* (1992) 29 N.S.W.L.R. 405; *Re Rabbaiotti's 1989 Settlement* [2000] W.T.L.R. 953; *Schmidt v Rosewood Trust Ltd* [2003] 2 A.C. 709.

[114] Although time does not begin to run against her until she obtains a present interest in the trust property because she "should not be compelled to litigate (at considerable personal expense) in respect of an injury to an interest which [she] may never live to enjoy": *Armitage* [1998] Ch. 241 at 261.

[115] [1965] Ch. 818.

[116] *Re Beloved Wilkes' Charity* (1851) 3 Mac. & G. 440; *Wilson v Law Debenture Trust Corp* [1995] 2 All E.R. 337.

but there was no right to see legal advice obtained by a trustee obtained at her own expense for her own protection when aware of likely proceedings against her,[117] or to any evidence on a *Beddoe's* application by trustees for directions whether to take proceedings against a beneficiary.[118]

In *Re Londonderry's Settlement*, the court was attracted by the argument that beneficiaries are the equitable owners of trust documents which have been created by the expenditure of trust money, suggesting that they should be entitled to see them.[119] As the court recognised, however, this analysis made it hard to explain why any trust documents should be kept confidential, although the court thought that in some situations there are good reasons why they should be. A further problem with the court's "proprietary" analysis is that it suggests that a person who is not a beneficiary, but who is an object of a power of appointment vested in the trustees, should not be entitled to disclosure of trust documents, although she was the primary object of the settlor's bounty. **9–087**

This problem was addressed in *Schmidt v Rosewood*, where the Privy Council put the petitioner's right to disclosure on a different basis, characterising it an incident of the court's inherent jurisdiction to supervise the administration of trusts. It seems likely that in future all claims for disclosure of trust information will be argued on this basis, although it remains the case that the courts may refuse to order the disclosure of confidential information, and may decline to override an express clause in the trust deed preventing the trustees from disclosing information except in certain circumstances.[120] The court's recognition in *Schmidt* that the objects of a power of appointment can have a real and direct interest in the trust fund may also strengthen their claims to have locus standi to challenge trustee actions.[121] **9–088**

*Schmidt v Rosewood Trust Ltd*

Privy Council [2003] 2 A.C. 709

The petitioner sought disclosure of documents relating to two settlements of which his late father was a settlor. He was himself a possible object of a power of appointment vested in the trustees, and the administrator of his father's estate, his father also having been a possible object of a power of appointment vested in the trustees. The trustees resisted disclosure, arguing that trust documents only need to be disclosed to trust beneficiaries by virtue of the beneficiaries' proprietary interests in the documents, with the result that they need not be disclosed to the objects of powers of appointment. This proprietary analysis of disclosure rights was rejected by the Privy Council. **9–089**

LORD WALKER (giving the judgment of the court): . . .

**Disclosure to Discretionary Beneficiaries: A Proprietary Basis?**

Much of the debate before the Board addressed the question whether a beneficiary's right or claim to disclosure of trust documents should be regarded as a proprietary right. Mr Brownbill argued that it should be classified in that way, and from that starting point he argued that no object of a mere power could have any right or claim to disclosure, because he had no proprietary interest in the trust property. . . . **9–090**

Their Lordships are therefore in general agreement with the approach adopted in the judgments of Kirby P. and Sheller J.A. in the Court of Appeal of New South Wales in *Hartigan Nominees Pty Ltd v Rydge*.[122] . . . It will be observed that Kirby P. said that for an applicant to have a proprietary right might be sufficient, but was not necessary. In the Board's view it is neither sufficient nor necessary. Since *Re Cowin*[123] well over **9–091**

---

117 *Talbot v Marshfield* (1865) 2 Dr. & Sm. 549; *Bacon v Bacon* (1876) 3 4 L.T. 349.

118 *Re Eaton* [1964] 1 W.L.R. 1269; *Midland Bank Trust Co Ltd v Green* [1980] Ch. 590 at 604–609.

119 See too *O'Rourke v Derbishire* [1920] A.C. 581 at 626, per Lord Wrenbury: "The beneficiary is entitled to see all trust documents because they are trust documents and because he is a beneficiary. They are in a sense his own."

120 cf. *Re Application for Information about a Trust* (2014) 16 I.T.E.L.R. 955 (Bermuda C.A.).

121 As in, e.g. *Re Hall (Deceased)* [2014] NICh 23 (object of power of appointment has standing to challenge excessive trustee remuneration). See also para.9–204.

122 (1992) 29 N.S.W.L.R. 405.

123 (1886) 33 Ch.D. 179.

a century ago the court has made clear that there may be circumstances (especially of confidentiality) in which even a vested and transmissible beneficial interest is not a sufficient basis for requiring disclosure of trust documents; and *Re Londonderry's Settlement*[124] and more recent cases have begun to work out in some detail the way in which the court should exercise its discretion in such cases. There are three such areas in which the court may have to form a discretionary judgment: whether a discretionary object (or some other beneficiary with only a remote or wholly defeasible interest) should be granted relief at all; what classes of documents should be disclosed, either completely or in a redacted form; and what safeguards should be imposed (whether by undertakings to the court, arrangements for professional inspection, or otherwise) to limit the use which may be made of documents or information disclosed under the order of the court. . .

**Conclusion**

**9–092** Their Lordships have already indicated their view that a beneficiary's right to seek disclosure of trust documents, although sometimes not inappropriately described as a proprietary right, is best approached as one aspect of the court's inherent jurisdiction to supervise (and where appropriate intervene in) the administration of trusts. There is therefore in their Lordships' view no reason to draw any bright dividing-line either between transmissible and non-transmissible (that is, discretionary) interests, or between the rights of an object of a discretionary trust and those of the object of a mere power (of a fiduciary character). The differences in this context between trusts and powers are (as Lord Wilberforce demonstrated in *McPhail v Doulton*[125]) a good deal less significant than the similarities. The tide of Commonwealth authority, although not entirely uniform, appears to be flowing in that direction.

**9–093** However the recent cases also confirm (as had been stated as long ago as *Re Cowin* in 1886) that no beneficiary (and least of all a discretionary object) has any entitlement as of right to disclosure of anything which can plausibly be described as a trust document. Especially when there are issues as to personal or commercial confidentiality, the court may have to balance the competing interests of different beneficiaries, the trustees themselves, and third parties. Disclosure may have to be limited and safeguards may have to be put in place. Evaluation of the claims of a beneficiary (and especially of a discretionary object) may be an important part of the balancing exercise which the court has to perform on the materials placed before it. In many cases the court may have no difficulty in concluding that an applicant with no more than a theoretical possibility of benefit ought not to be granted any relief.

## *D. Letters of Wishes*

**9–094** Difficult issues arise where a settlor provides the trustees with a letter of wishes that she intends to guide them when they exercise their discretionary powers (e.g. to appoint property to the beneficiaries of a discretionary trust). Such letters have special significance after the settlor's death, because while alive the settlor should in any event be consulted by the trustees before a significant exercise of their discretionary distributive functions.[126] Such letters are brought into existence for the purposes of the operation of the trust, and they must be handed on from a retiring trustee to the new trustee, some regard needing to be had to them before a discretionary decision is taken on any matter to which they refer, even if the trustees exercising their independent discretion then decide to ignore a particular wish.[127] Thus, a letter of wishes is a trust document that is legally significant, although not so significant as the trust deed itself unless, exceptionally, the settlor intends the letter to be legally binding so as to override the trust deed to the extent necessary to give effect to what was laid down in the letter.[128]

---

[124] [1965] Ch. 918.

[125] [1971] A.C. 424.

[126] *Abacus Trust Co v Barr* [2003] Ch. 409 at [23]–[25].

[127] *Bank of Nova Scotia Trust Co (Bahamas) Ltd v Ricart de Barletta* 1 Butterworths Offshore Cases & Materials 5, discussed by H. Thompson in (1994) 3 Jo. Int. T. & Corp. p.35. Further see D.J. Hayton (1999) 32 Vanderbilt Jo. of Transnat. Law 555, 573–576.

[128] *Chase Manhattan Equities Ltd v Goodman* [1991] B.C.L.C. 897 at 923.

Nevertheless, in *Breakspear v Ackland*,[129] Briggs J held that letters of wishes are generally subject to the *Londonderry* principle that the exercise by trustees of their dispositive discretionary powers should be regarded, from start to finish, as an essentially confidential process. A document brought into existence for the sole or predominant purpose of being used in such a process is itself properly to be regarded as confidential, so that the trustees ordinarily need not disclose it to beneficiaries merely because they ask to see it, unless, in the trustees' view, disclosure is in the interests of the sound administration of the trust, and the exercise of their discretions. **9–095**

*Breakspear v Ackland*

Chancery Division [2009] Ch. 32

The settlor of a family discretionary trust gave a non-binding "wish letter" to the trustees in which he requested that they take stated matters into account when exercising their dispositive powers. Three of the beneficiaries (who were the settlor's children) asked the trustees to disclose the contents of the letter in order to evaluate their future expectations under the trust, but the trustees refused on the ground that the wish letter was confidential and its disclosure would cause family discord. The beneficiaries successfully brought an action for disclosure of the letter. The passages of Briggs J.'s judgment reproduced here concern the general principles governing disclosure of letters of wishes. **9–096**

BRIGGS J.: . . . Since few would argue that clearly and rationally expressed wishes and relevant information included by settlors in wish letters could be treated by trustees as wholly irrelevant to the exercise of their discretionary powers, it is inescapable that their content will potentially be relevant, both to beneficiaries in monitoring the performance by trustees of their fiduciary obligations, and to the court in enforcing that performance where necessary and appropriate. Furthermore, the contents of a relevant wish letter may make all the difference to a beneficiary in understanding, in the context of an otherwise broadly drafted discretionary trust, what are or may be his or her expectations of benefit from the assets of a family settlement. While such expectations may on occasion be damaging, in particular to young beneficiaries, a broad knowledge of their prospects may be of significant advantage to them in planning both their own lives, and the education and maintenance of their children and other dependants. It is incidentally for this latter purpose that the claimants say that they have made their claim to disclosure. **9–097**

There is therefore an inevitable tension between on the one hand the advantages of confidentiality, and on the other hand, the advantages of disclosure, in relation to wish letters. It is precisely this tension which has generated the controversy evident in the Australian, New Zealand and Channel Islands authorities. It is tempting to say that the infinitely variable weight to be given to those competing considerations in any particular case is best resolved by the exercise of discretion by the judge resorted to for the resolution of the impasse, rather than by the laying down of rules or even guidelines. But in my judgment this superficially attractive solution has real disadvantages. The first is that unless the principles are generally understood, settlors are likely to treat the uncertainty as to the general confidentiality of wish letters as a disincentive to their beneficial use. The second is that the uncertainty is likely to lead to more rather than less applications to court to resolve questions of disclosure, and will therefore be a recipe for litigation. In the context of the likely asset base of even wealthy families, the attendant cost should be avoided if at all possible. . . . **9–098**

[Briggs J reviewed a series of cases,[130] then drew the following conclusions]: The first question is whether it is either permissible or appropriate in the light of *O'Rourke v Darbishire* and the *Londonderry* case for me to decide at first instance that the basis upon which trustees and the court should approach a request for disclosure of a wish letter (or of any other document in the possession of trustees in their capacity as such) is one calling for the exercise of discretion rather than the adjudication upon a proprietary right. In my judgment it is both permissible and appropriate to answer that question in the affirmative. My review of **9–099**

---

129 [2009] Ch. 32. See too *Re Rabbaiotti's 1989 Settlement* [2000] W.T.L.R. 953; *Hartigan Nominees Pty Ltd v Rydge* (1992) 29 N.S.W.L.R 405.

130 *Re Beloved Wilkes's Charity* (1851) 3 Mac. & G. 440; *O'Rourke v Darbishire* [1920] A.C. 581; *Re Londonderry's Settlement* [1965] Ch. 918; *Hartigan Nominees Pty Ltd v Rydge* (1992) 29 N.S.W.L.R. 405; *Wilson v Law Debenture Trust Corp Plc* [1995] 2 All E.R. 337; *Re Rabaiotti's Settlements* [2000] W.T.L.R. 953; *Schmidt v Rosewood Trust Ltd* [2003] 2 A.C. 709; *Foreman v Kingstone* [2005] W.T.L.R. 823; *Countess Bathurst v Kleinwort Benson (Channel Islands) Trustees Ltd* [2007] W.T.L.R. 959.

the authorities demonstrates that there is now virtual unanimity in the relevant common law jurisdictions to that effect. Furthermore, as I have sought to demonstrate, even the Court of Appeal in the *Londonderry* case itself found the proprietary analysis to be both inconclusive and unsatisfactory, by comparison with the recognition of a clear, principled basis for refusing disclosure even in cases where there appeared to be a prima facie proprietary right to disclosure.

**9–100** On that basis, the second question is whether the *Londonderry* principle remains good law, at least in England. In my opinion, it is still good law and, in any event, law by which a first instance judge remains bound, unless and until released by some higher judicial or parliamentary authority.

**9–101** At the heart of the *Londonderry* principle is the unanimous conclusion (most clearly expressed by Danckwerts L.J.) that it is in the interests of beneficiaries of family discretionary trusts, and advantageous to the due administration of such trusts, that the exercise by trustees of their dispositive discretionary powers be regarded, from start to finish, as an essentially confidential process. It is in the interests of the beneficiaries because it enables the trustees to make discreet but thorough inquiries as to their competing claims for consideration for benefit without fear or risk that those inquiries will come to the beneficiaries' knowledge. They may include, for example, inquiries as to the existence of some life-threatening illness of which it is appropriate that the beneficiary in question be kept ignorant. Such confidentiality serves the due administration of family trusts both because it tends to reduce the scope for litigation about the rationality of the exercise by trustees of their discretions, and because it is likely to encourage suitable trustees to accept office, undeterred by a perception that their discretionary deliberations will be subjected to scrutiny by disappointed or hostile beneficiaries, and to potentially expensive litigation in the courts.

**9–102** I recognise the force of the contrary proposition, best enunciated by the editors of *Underhill & Hayton*,[131] that the conferral of a general confidentiality upon the exercise by trustees of their discretionary powers may in particular cases reduce the practical extent to which they can be held to account. Trustees undoubtedly are accountable for the exercise of those powers, but it seems to me quite wrong to suppose that the courts have been mindless of the existence of that core principle of accountability, during the period of more than 150 years when the law has been that it is better for confidentiality to be afforded. While Kirby P. and those who sympathise with his views may be right in recognising that, in society generally, the principle of fiduciary accountability has gained ground in recent years, it seems to me that this is better described as a process whereby the strict principles whereby a trustee has always been accountable have spread to other areas of society, where the concept of fiduciary obligations by those who hold property or exercise power or authority on behalf of others, or over their affairs, has come to be more generally recognised.

**9–103** Nor can I see any persuasive basis for thinking that the reasoning which led the English courts to think it appropriate in the interests of beneficiaries, and in the administration of trusts, to confer confidentiality on the exercise by family trustees of their discretionary dispositive powers has ceased to hold good. It is not obvious that the potentially disastrous consequences of a resort to civil litigation about the administration of family trust property, in terms of the expenditure of time and cost, are much less of a potential evil than they were in the 19th century. Nor is there any less need today than there always has been to avoid deterring suitable family trustees from accepting an arduous unpaid office. Of course there is a risk that the conferral of such confidentiality may enable unworthy trustees to use it as a shield for the concealment of their culpable inadequacies, but this risk cannot have been ignored in the 19th century, and now that it is recognised that the general principle of confidentiality is subject to being overridden as a matter of discretion by the court, it may fairly be supposed that the risk has if anything become more rather than less manageable.

**9–104** My reason for concluding that, regardless of my own opinion, I am bound to continue to treat the *Londonderry* principle as still being good law is simply because it formed part of the ratio of that decision, it has never been overruled, and because, if anything, it received a general endorsement rather than criticism in *Schmidt v Rosewood Trust Ltd*.[132]

**9–105** While in a sense a wish letter is the companion of the trust deed, it by no means follows that it therefore needs or ought to be afforded similar treatment in the hands of the trustees. The trust deed is a document which confers and identifies the trustees' powers. There is in principle nothing confidential about the existence and precise boundaries of those powers. By contrast, the wish letter, operating exclusively within

---

[131] *Underhill & Hayton's Law of Trusts and Trustees*, 17th edn (Butterworths, 2007), para.60.5.

[132] [2003] 2 A.C. 709.

> those boundaries and purely in furtherance of the trustees' confidential exercise of discretionary powers, may properly be afforded a status of confidentiality which the trust deed itself entirely lacks. . . .
>
> Where a beneficiary makes a request for disclosure, that in my judgment merely triggers an occasion upon which the trustees need to exercise (or reconsider the exercise of) that discretion, giving such weight to the making of and reasons for that request as they think fit. Having made their decision the trustees are not obliged to give reasons for it, any more than in relation to any other exercise of their discretionary powers. In a difficult case the trustees may, as always, seek the directions of the court on the question whether to disclose but, bearing in mind the inevitable cost associated with doing so, the trustees will need to think twice before concluding that the difficulty of the question justifies the expenditure. It is by no means a matter for criticism (of the type levelled against the trustees in this case) that trustees do not either give reasons or apply to the court for directions, if minded not to accede to a beneficiary's request for disclosure. **9–106**
>
> At the second stage (i.e. determination of the disclosure issue by the court in proceedings brought solely for that purpose), the matter may be presented, at least in theory, in four different ways. In its simplest form the trustees may seek to surrender their discretion to the court, in which case (if it permits the surrender, which it is not obliged to do) the court is exercising its own discretion afresh, rather than reviewing any negative exercise of discretion by the trustees. Alternatively, the trustees may, without surrendering their discretion, invite the court in effect to bless their refusal. Thirdly the case may be brought by the disappointed beneficiary by way of a challenge to the trustees' negative exercise of their discretion to disclose. Finally, the beneficiary may seek simply to invoke an original discretion in the court, as part of its jurisdiction in the administration of trusts. **9–107**
>
> The second and third of those types of application involve a review of the trustees' negative exercise of their discretion to disclose. If the trustees themselves apply, then it is in practice inevitable that they will have to disclose their reasons. If the disappointed beneficiary applies, then it seems to me that the *Londonderry* principle will entitle the trustees, if they choose to do so, to decline to give reasons, and to defend the challenge upon the basis that, if it be the case, the disappointed beneficiary has disclosed no grounds for impugning either the fairness or the honesty of their decision, their reasoning being off-limits for that purpose. **9–108**
>
> Finally, if the disappointed beneficiary seeks to invoke the court's administrative jurisdiction, then it will be incumbent upon him to demonstrate, by reference to whatever facts may be available to him, that an occasion has arisen which calls for the interference of the court. A mere refusal to disclose a wish letter, unaccompanied by reasons or evidence of *mala fides* or unfairness, would not ordinarily justify such intervention. Of course, if the trustees volunteer reasons for their refusal, the court may investigate those reasons, and call for such factual material or further explanation from the trustees as may be thought fit. **9–109**
>
> The third stage (where disclosure is sought from the court to facilitate the determination of an issue to which the wish letter is alleged to be relevant) gives rise to different considerations, governed by the law and practice as to disclosure in civil proceedings. For those purposes, the relevance of the foregoing detailed analysis of the status of a wish letter is that identified by Danckwerts L.J. in the *Londonderry* case,[133] namely that if the document in question does no more than illuminate the trustees' reasons for the making of a discretionary decision, it may be simply irrelevant, unless the trustees by a partial disclosure of their reasons have put into play the issue as to their rationality. . . . **9–110**

## *E. Beneficiaries' Rights to Disclosure in Course of Civil Litigation*

So far, we have been concerned with the rights of a beneficiary or object of a fiduciary power, to whom the trustee must account for the trusteeship to obtain disclosure of trust documents and supporting information under the law of trusts. Quite separately, under the Civil Procedure Rules governing civil litigation,[134] if a beneficiary can make out a properly particularised claim (so that it cannot be struck **9–111**

---

133 [1965] Ch. 918 at 936.

134 CPR Pt 31 and the related Practice Direction. It is also possible to obtain pre-action disclosure of specific documents discoverable under standard disclosure post-action: see CPR r.31.16 and *Black v Sumitomo Corp* [2002] 1 W.L.R. 156 (if desirable to save costs or dispose fairly of the proceedings or assist the dispute to be resolved without proceedings).

down as a mere "fishing expedition" to see if material can be found to support a claim) then this triggers standard disclosure of documents that can advance or hinder either party's case. Subsequent applications can also be made in relation to specific disclosure of documents not disclosed pursuant to standard disclosure. Previously, a similar procedure was known as "discovery", and the order in *Re Londonderry's Settlement* was expressly made "without prejudice to any right of the defendant to discovery in separate proceedings against the plaintiffs". As Robert Walker J pointed out in *Scott v National Trust*[135]:

> If a decision taken by trustees is directly attacked in legal proceedings, the trustees may be compelled either legally (through discovery or subpoena) or practically (in order to avoid adverse inferences being drawn) to disclose the substance of the reasons for their decision.

## 4. Reduction of the Trust Property into Possession

9–112 It has already been noted that upon accepting trusteeship a new trustee should ensure that all trust property is put into the joint names of herself and her co-trustees or into the name of a duly authorised nominee.[136] However she also needs to be aware of the following statutory powers.

### Trustee Act 1925 ss.15 and 22

**15. Power to Compound Liabilities**

9–113 A personal representative or two or more trustees acting together, subject to the restrictions[137] imposed in regard to receipts by a sole trustee not being a trust corporation, a sole acting trustee where by the instrument, if any, creating the trust, or by statute, a sole trustee is authorised to execute the trusts and powers reposed in him, may, if and as he or they think fit—

(a) accept any property, real or personal, before the time at which it is made transferable or payable; or
(b) sever and apportion any blended trust funds or property; or
(c) pay or allow any debt or claim on any evidence that he or they think sufficient; or
(d) accept any composition or any security, real or personal, for any debt or for any property, real or personal, claimed; or
(e) allow any time of payment of any debt; or
(f) compromise, compound, abandon, submit to arbitration, or otherwise settle any debt, account, claim or thing whatever relating to the testator's or intestate's estate or to the trust;

and for any of those purposes may enter into, give, execute, and do such agreements, instruments of composition or arrangement, releases, and other things as to him or them seem expedient, without being responsible for any loss occasioned by any act or thing so done by him or them if he has or they have discharged the duty of care set out in section 1(1) of the Trustee Act 2000.

**22. Reversionary Interests, Valuations and Audit**

9–114 (1) Where trust property includes any share or interest in property not vested in the trustees, or the proceeds of the sale of any such property, or any other thing in action, the trustees on the same falling into possession, or becoming payable or transferable may—

(a) agree or ascertain the amount or value thereof or any part thereof in such manner as they may think fit;

---

[135] [1998] 2 All E.R. 705 at 719, and to similar effect Buxton LJ in *Taylor v Midland Bank Trust Co* (2000) 2 I.T.E.L.R. 439 at 459–461.
[136] See para.9–10.
[137] See the Law of Property Act 1925 s.27; Trustee Act 1925 s.14.

> (b) accept in or towards satisfaction thereof, at the market or current value, or upon any valuation or estimate of value which they may think fit, any authorised investments;
> (c) allow any deductions for duties, costs, charges and expenses which they may think proper or reasonable; (d) execute any release in respect of the premises so as effectually to discharge all accountable parties from all liability in respect of any matter coming within the scope of such release;
>
> without being responsible in any such case for any loss occasioned by any act or thing so done by them if they have discharged the duty of care set out in section 1(1) of the Trustee Act 2000.
>
> (2) The trustees shall not be under any obligation and shall not be chargeable with any breach of trust by reason of any omission—
>
> (a) to place any distringas notice or apply for any stop or other like order upon any securities or other property out of or on which such share or interest or other thing in action as aforesaid is derived, payable or charged; or
> (b) to take any proceedings on account of any act, default, or neglect on the part of the persons in whom such securities or other property or any of them or any part thereof are for the time being, or had at any time been, vested;
>
> unless and until required in writing so to do by some person, or the guardian of some person, beneficially interested under the trust, and unless also due provision is made to their satisfaction for payment of the costs of any proceedings required to be taken.
> Provided that nothing in this subsection shall relieve the trustees of the obligation to get in and obtain payment or transfer of such share or interest or other thing in action on the same falling into possession.
>
> (3) Trustees may, for the purpose of giving effect to the trust, or any of the provisions of the instrument, if any, creating the trust or of any statute, from time to time (by duly qualified agents) ascertain and fix the value of any trust property in such manner as they think proper, and any valuation so made shall be binding upon all persons interested under the trust if the trustees have discharged the duty of care set out in section 1(1) of the Trustee Act 2000.
>
> (4) Trustees may, in their absolute discretion, from time to time, but not more than once in every three years unless the nature of the trust or any special dealings with the trust property make a more frequent exercise of the right reasonable, cause the accounts of the trust property to be examined or audited by an independent accountant, and shall, for that purpose, produce such vouchers and give such information to him as he may require; and the costs of such examination or audit, including the fee of the auditor, shall be paid out of the capital or income of the trust property, or partly in one way and partly in the other, as the trustees, in their absolute discretion, think fit, but, in default of any direction by the trustees to the contrary in any special case, costs attributable to capital shall be borne by capital and those attributable to income by income.

## 5. Investment of the Trust Property

The trustees must invest and manage the trust fund so that there is adequate income and capital available when they exercise their distributive function. They must familiarise themselves with their powers of investment so that they know which investments are within or outside their powers. When deciding whether to sell or purchase investments within the authorised range of investments, they must also comply with further duties: in this section we consider their duty of care and their duty to obtain the best financial return for all the beneficiaries, and in the next section we discuss their duty to act even-handedly between different classes of beneficiaries. **9–115**

## A. The Range of Authorised Investments

**9–116** Trustees are under a fundamental duty to invest the trust funds in investments authorised expressly or impliedly by the trust instrument, or by the court,[138] or in default by the Trustee Act 2000. A properly drafted trust instrument will contain very extensive powers of investment so that there is no need to apply to the court for wider powers, or otherwise to rely upon the Trustee Act 2000 which applies to pre-existing trusts (from 1 February 2001) as well as new trusts. If a testator by specific gift leaves certain investments (e.g. "my apartments in Tenerife") to trustees for A for life, then B absolutely, this impliedly authorises the trustees to retain such investments but not to purchase any more.[139] If personal representatives appropriate property to trustees under the Administration of Estates Act 1925 s.41, then the property is thereafter treated as an authorised investment for purposes of retention but not for purchasing more of the same.

## B. Duties when Investing

### i. To Act like a Prudent Person Conducting Another's Affairs

**9–117** Trustees must exhibit the statutory duty of care laid down by the Trustee Act 2000 s.1,[140] which is reproduced above.[141] When exercising her powers of investment, a trustee must act like a prudent person investing for other people, reviewing the portfolio of investments regularly,[142] and if lacking investment knowledge seeking professional advice and considering such advice before acting upon it.[143] A prudent person might reasonably select some speculative investments for herself that she should avoid if investing for the benefit of another person who depends on the trust fund as a safe basis for securing her future. Thus, the 2000 Act has not affected the following risk averse approach summarised by Lord Nicholls.

**Lord Nicholls, "Trustees and Their Broader Community: Where Duty, Morality and Ethics Converge"**

(1995) 9 Tru. L.I. 71 at 73–74.

**9–118** . . . It is not enough that a trustee should act honestly. Promotion of the trust purpose requires a trustee to be prudent and exercise the degree of care he would in conducting his own affairs but mindful, when making investment decisions, that he is dealing with another's property. The classic formulation of this standard of conduct was enunciated by Lindley L.J. in *Re Whiteley*.[144] The duty of a trustee is not to take such care only as a prudent man would take if he had only himself to consider; the duty is rather to take such care as an ordinary prudent man would take if he were minded to make an investment for the benefit of other people for whom he felt morally bound to provide. . . . This "ordinary prudent person conducting another's affairs" is the equitable counterpart of the reasonable man who is so ubiquitous in the common law. . . . A comment is needed here on the ordinary prudent person. His standards are the minimum

---

[138] The court's powers are in the Trustee Act 1925 s.57, and the Variation of Trusts Act 1958.

[139] *Re Pugh* [1887] W.N. 143; *Re Whitfield* (1920) 125 L.T. 61.

[140] The duty may be excluded or modified by the trust deed: Trustee Act 2000 Sch.1 para.7.

[141] At para.9–080.

[142] *Nestlé v National Westminster Bank Plc* [1994] 1 All E.R. 118.

[143] *Cowan v Scargill* [1985] Ch. 279; *Jones v AMP Perpetual Trustee Co NZ Ltd* [1994] 1 N.Z.L.R. 690. Pension trustees are required to seek advice by the Pensions Act 1995 s.36, for breach of which duty the defendant trustees were held liable in *Adams v Bridge* [2009] Pens. L.R. 153.

[144] (1886) 33 Ch.D. 347 at 355.

standards expected of trustees. If the trustee is a person professing particular expertise in the management of trusts, and he has been appointed for that reason, his conduct will be judged by the standards he professes. A professional person, a trust corporation, held out as an expert, will be expected to display the degree of skill and care and diligence such an expert would have.

Investment policy is aimed at producing a portfolio of investments which is balanced overall and suited to the needs of the particular trust. Different investments are accompanied by different degrees of risk, which are reflected in the expected rate of return. A large fund with a widely diversified portfolio of securities might justifiably include modest holdings of high risk securities which would be imprudent and out of place in a smaller fund. In such a case it would be inappropriate to isolate one particular investment out of a vast portfolio and enquire whether that can be justified as a trust investment. Such a 'line by line' approach is misplaced. The inquiry, rather, should be to look at a particular investment and enquire whether that is justified as a holding in the context of the overall portfolio. Traditional warnings against the need for trustees to avoid speculative or hazardous investments are not to be read as inhibiting trustees from maintaining portfolios of investments which contain a prudent and sensible mixture of low risk and higher risk securities. They are not to be so read, because they were not directed at a portfolio which is a balanced exercise in risk management. 9–119

Modern trustees acting within their investment powers are thus entitled to be judged by the standards of current portfolio theory, which emphasises the risk level of the entire portfolio rather than the risk attaching to each investment taken in isolation.[145] This requires portfolio securities having a low co-variance with each other, where a positive co-variance means that the values of two assets are likely to move in the same direction, and a low co-variance means that the values are likely to move in opposite directions. Having dissimilar investments is not sufficient: land and government bonds are different, but movements in interest rates affect both types of investment in the same way. The proportions of different types of asset within the portfolio are crucial for achieving the purposes of the fund, the most basic proportion being that between equity and debt, i.e. between shares and fixed interest securities, e.g. 60 per cent to 40 per cent or vice versa. 9–120

Sections 4 and 5 of the Trustee Act 2000 now expressly impose such duties upon trustees, although trustees might legitimately decide against diversification if instructed by the settlor to retain particular assets within the trust fund.[146] Where the trust assets include real estate, the trustees' s.4 duty requires them to consider from time-to-time whether the property should be sold.[147] 9–121

## Trustee Act 2000 ss.4 and 5

**4. Standard investment criteria**

(1) In exercising any power of investment, whether arising under this Part or otherwise, a trustee must have regard to the standard investment criteria. 9–122
(2) A trustee must from time to time review the investments of the trust and consider whether, having regard to the standard investment criteria, they should be varied.
(3) The standard investment criteria, in relation to a trust, are—
   (a) the suitability to the trust of investments of the same kind as any particular investment proposed to be made or retained and of that particular investment as an investment of that kind, and
   (b) the need for diversification of investments of the trust, in so far as is appropriate to the circumstances of the trust.

[145] On modern portfolio theory, see J. Langbein, "The Uniform Prudent Investor Act and the Future of Trust Investing" (1996) 81 Iowa L.R. 641; I.N. Legair, "Modern Portfolio Theory: A Primer" (2000) 14 Tru L.I. 75.
[146] *Gregson v HAE Trustees Ltd* [2009] 1 All E.R. (Comm.) 457 at [70]–[92].
[147] *Jeffrey v Gretton* [2011] W.T.L.R. 809.

**5. Advice**

9–123 (1) Before exercising any power of investment, whether arising under this Part or otherwise, a trustee must (unless the exception applies) obtain and consider proper advice about the way in which, having regard to the standard investment criteria, the power should be exercised.

(2) When reviewing the investments of the trust, a trustee must (unless the exception applies) obtain and consider proper advice about whether, having regard to the standard investment criteria, the investments should be varied.

(3) The exception is that a trustee need not obtain such advice if he reasonably concludes that in all the circumstances it is unnecessary or inappropriate to do so.

(4) Proper advice is the advice of a person who is reasonably believed by the trustee to be qualified to give it by his ability in and practical experience of financial and other matters relating to the proposed investment.

### ii. To Do the Best They Can Financially for the Beneficiaries as a Whole

9–124 It is often said that trustees owe a duty to act in the best interests of the beneficiaries. Writing extra-judicially, however, Lord Nicholls has made the point that this "is to do nothing more than formulate in different words a trustee's obligation to promote the purpose for which the trust was created".[148] Hence, it

> is necessary first to decide what is the purpose of the trust and what benefits were intended to be received by the beneficiaries before being in a position to decide whether a proposed course is for the benefit of the beneficiaries or in their best interests.[149]

In the context of a private trust this is generally interpreted by the courts to mean the beneficiaries' best financial interests, but in the context of a charitable trust it makes it possible to say that certain types of investment would be contrary to the trust's purposes.

9–125 Failure to render trust property financially productive is a breach of trust. So, as Heydon and Crennan JJ said in an Australian case, *Byrnes v Kendle*[150]:

> It is the duty of a trustee to obtain income from the trust property if it is capable of yielding an income. If the property is money, it should be invested at interest or used to purchase income-yielding assets like shares. If the property consists of business assets, it should be employed in a business. If the property is lettable land, it should be let for rent.[151]

When lending trust money the trustees must secure a commercial rate of interest for it is "a breach of trust to offer a loan on 'soft', uncommercial terms to a person who is not a beneficiary".[152] When selling trust property it is the overriding duty of a trustee to get the best possible price for the beneficiaries.[153] She must therefore secure by every means in her power a proper competition for the property in order to obtain the best price,[154] and she must not make a sale with a view to advancing the particular purposes of one beneficiary at the expense of another.[155]

---

148 Lord Nicholls, "Trustees and Their Broader Community: Where Duty, Morality and Ethics Converge" (1995) 9 Tru. L.I. 71.

149 *Re Merchant Navy Ratings Pension Fund* [2015] EWHC 448 (Ch) at [228]–[229].

150 (2011) 243 C.L.R. 253 at [119], followed in *Brudenell-Bruce v Moore* [2015] W.T.L.R. 373 at [88].

151 Citing *Earl of Egmont v Smith* (1877) 6 Ch. D. 469 at 476; *Re Byrne* (1902) 19 W.N. (N.S.W.) 141.

152 *Baxendale-Walker v Middleton* [2011] EWHC 998 (QB) at [60].

153 *Downes v Graysbrook* (1817) 3 Mer. 200; *Re Cooper and Allen's Contract* (1876) 4 Ch. D. 802; *Killearn v Killearn* [2011] EWHC 3775 (Ch) at [16].

154 *Harper v Hayes* (1862) Giff. 210.

155 *Ord v Noel* (1820) 5 Madd. 438.

If trustees have agreed to sell so as to be morally bound but not yet legally bound by a contract, they are under a duty to gazump (i.e. to negotiate with someone putting in a serious higher offer) so as to obtain a higher price for the beneficiaries, even if as honourable people they would prefer to implement the bargain to which they felt in honour bound. This is the ratio of *Buttle v Saunders*.[156] **9–126**

If trustees have strong opinions against alcohol or smoking or the arms trade, then if such investments would be likely to be more beneficial financially than other proposed investments they must purchase those investments even though they find them disagreeable. This is the ratio of *Cowan v Scargill*, which is reproduced below. However, if trustees obtain professional advice that particular investments other than in companies engaging in such activities are equally satisfactory from a financial point of view then they can buy those investments. Thus, Lord Nicholls has written extra-judicially that[157]: **9–127**

> In practice in these cases where trustees or [beneficiaries] have strong views about particular investments on non-financial grounds it should be possible for trustees to exercise their investment powers in a manner avoiding embarrassment to all concerned without upsetting the balance of the portfolio . . . The range of investment is so extensive that there is scope for trustees to give effect to moral considerations without thereby prejudicing beneficiaries' financial interests.

### *Cowan v Scargill*

### Chancery Division [1985] Ch. 270

Under a mineworkers' pension scheme set up by the National Coal Board, a committee of management was formed of ten trustees (five appointed by the Board and five by the National Union of Mineworkers) to control and administer funds provided by members' contributions to the scheme and by contributions by the Board of approximately the same amount. The funds totalled some £3,000 million, with some £200 million available for investment each year. The committee had wide powers of investment which they used with the assistance of an advisory panel of experts. An investment plan was submitted by a sub-committee for approval, but the five union trustees on the committee of management objected to investments in oil, investments overseas, and the acquisition of land overseas. The five Board trustees sought the court's directions as to whether the union trustees were in breach of duty in holding up the adoption of the investment plan. Megarry V.-C. held that they were, because their objections could not be justified on broad economic grounds, and were only remotely in the interests of the beneficiaries, for whom there would be no advantage in excluding investments overseas or investments in competition with the coal industry. **9–128**

MEGARRY V.-C.: . . . I turn to the law. The starting point is the duty of trustees to exercise their powers in the best interests of the present and future beneficiaries of the trust, holding the scales impartially between different classes of beneficiaries. This duty of the trustees towards their beneficiaries is paramount. They must, of course, obey the law; but subject to that, they must put the interests of their beneficiaries first. When the purpose of the trust is to provide financial benefits for the beneficiaries, as is usually the case, the best interests of the beneficiaries are normally their best financial interests. In the case of a power of investment, as in the present case, the power must be exercised so as to yield the best return for the beneficiaries, judged in relation to the risks of the investments in question; and the prospects of the yield of income and capital appreciation both have to be considered in judging the return from the investment. **9–129**

The legal memorandum that the union obtained from their solicitors is generally in accord with these views. In considering the possibility of investment for "socially beneficial reasons which may result in lower returns to the fund", the memorandum states that "the trustees' only concern is to ensure that the return is the maximum possible consistent with security"; and then it refers to the need for diversification. However, it continues by saying: **9–130**

---

[156] [1950] 2 All E.R. 193.

[157] Lord Nicholls, "Trustees and Their Broader Community: Where Duty, Morality and Ethics Converge" (1995) 9 Tru. L.I. 71, 75.

"Trustees cannot be criticised for failing to make a particular investment for social or political reasons, such as in South African stock for example, but may be held liable for investing in assets which yield a poor return or for disinvesting in stock at inappropriate times for non-financial criteria."

**9–131** This last sentence must be considered in the light of subsequent passages in the memorandum which indicate that the sale of South African securities by trustees might be justified on the ground of doubts about political stability in South Africa and the long-term financial soundness of its economy, whereas trustees could not properly support motions at a company meeting dealing with pay levels in South Africa, work accidents, pollution control, employment conditions for minorities, military contracting and consumer protection. The assertion that trustees could not be criticised for failing to make a particular investment for social or political reasons is one that I would not accept in its full width. If the investment in fact made is equally beneficial to the beneficiaries, then criticism would be difficult to sustain in practice, whatever the position in theory. But if the investment in fact made is less beneficial, then both in theory and in practice the trustees would normally be open to criticism.

**9–132** This leads me to the second point, which is a corollary of the first. In considering what investments to make trustees must put on one side their own personal interests and views. Trustees may have strongly held social or political views. They may be firmly opposed to any investment in South Africa or other countries, or they may object to any form of investment in companies concerned with alcohol, tobacco, armaments or many other things. In the conduct of their own affairs, of course, they are free to abstain from making any such investments. Yet under a trust, if investments of this type would be more beneficial to the beneficiaries than other investments, the trustees must not refrain from making the investments by reason of the views that they hold.

**9–133** Trustees may even have to act dishonourably (though not illegally) if the interests of their beneficiaries require it. Thus where trustees for sale had struck a bargain for the sale of trust property but had not bound themselves by a legally enforceable contract, they were held to be under a duty to consider and explore a better offer that they received, and not to carry through the bargain to which they felt in honour bound.[158] In other words, the duty of trustees to their beneficiaries may include a duty to "gazump", however honourable the trustees. As Wynn-Parry J. said trustees "have an overriding duty to obtain the best price which they can for their beneficiaries".[159] . . .

**9–134** Powers must be exercised fairly and honestly for the purposes for which they are given and not so as to accomplish any ulterior purpose, whether for the benefit of the trustees or otherwise.[160]

**9–135** Third, by way of a caveat I should say that I am not asserting that the benefit of the beneficiaries which a trustee must make his paramount concern inevitably and solely means their financial benefit, even if the only object of the trust is to provide financial benefits. Thus if the only actual or potential beneficiaries of a trust are all adults with very strict views on moral and social matters, condemning all forms of alcohol, tobacco and popular entertainment, as well as armaments, I can well understand that it might not be for the "benefit" of such beneficiaries to know that they are obtaining rather larger financial returns under the trust by reason of investments in those activities than they would have received if the trustees had invested the trust funds in other investments. The beneficiaries might well consider that it was far better to receive less than to receive more money from what they consider to be evil and tainted sources. "Benefit" is a word with a very wide meaning, and there are circumstances in which arrangements which work to the financial disadvantage of a beneficiary may yet be for his benefit.[161] But I would emphasise that such cases are likely to be very rare, and in any case I think that under a trust for the provision of financial benefits the burden would rest, and rest heavy, on him who asserts that it is for the benefit of the beneficiaries as a whole to receive less by reason of the exclusion of some of the possibly more profitable forms of investment. Plainly the present case is not one of this rare type of case. Subject to such matters, under a trust for the provision of financial benefits, the paramount duty of the trustees is to provide the greatest financial benefits for the present and future beneficiaries.

**9–136** Fourth, the standard required of a trustee in exercising his powers of investment is that he must

---

158 *Buttle v Saunders* [1950] 2 All E.R. 193.

159 *Buttle* at 195.

160 See *Duke of Portland v Topham* (1864) 11 H.L. Cas. 32, a case on a power of appointment that must apply a fortiori to a power given to trustees as such.

161 See, for example, *Re Towler's Settlement Trusts* [1964] Ch. 158; *Re CL* [1969] 1 Ch. 587.

"take such care as an ordinary prudent man would take if he were minded to make an investment for the benefit of other people for whom he felt morally bound to provide".[162]

That duty includes the duty to seek advice on matters which the trustee does not understand, such as the making of investments, and on receiving that advice to act with the same degree of prudence. This requirement is not discharged merely by showing that the trustee has acted in good faith and with sincerity. Honesty and sincerity are not the same as prudence and reasonableness. Some of the most sincere people are the most unreasonable; and Mr Scargill told me that he had met quite a few of them. Accordingly, although a trustee who takes advice on investments is not bound to accept and act on that advice, he is not entitled to reject it merely because he sincerely disagrees with it, unless in addition to being sincere he is acting as an ordinary prudent man would act.

Fifth, trustees have a duty to consider the need for diversification of investments . . . The degree of diversification that is practicable and desirable for a large fund may plainly be impracticable or undesirable (or both) in the case of a small fund. **9–137**

In the case before me, it is not in issue that there ought to be diversification of the investments held by the fund. The contention of the defendants, put very shortly, is that there can be a sufficient degree of diversification without any investment overseas or in oil, and that in any case there is no need to increase the level of overseas investments beyond the existing level. Other pension funds got on well enough without overseas investments, it was said, and in particular the N.U.M.'s own scheme had, in 1982, produced better results than the scheme here in question. . . **9–138**

I shall not pursue this matter. Even if other funds in one particular year, or in many years, had done better than the scheme which is before me, that does not begin to show that it is beneficial to this scheme to be shorn of the ability to invest overseas. . . **9–139**

Sixth, there is the question whether the principles that I have been stating apply, with or without modification, to trusts of pension funds. Mr. Stamler asserted that they applied without modification, and that it made no difference that some of the funds came from the members of the pension scheme, or that the funds were often of a very substantial size. Mr. Scargill did not in terms assert the contrary. He merely said that this was one of the questions to be decided, and that pension funds may be subject to different rules. I was somewhat unsuccessful in my attempts to find out from him why this was so, and what the differences were. What it came down to, I think, was that the rules for trusts had been laid down for private and family trusts and wills a long time ago; that pension funds were very large and affected large numbers of people; that in the present case the well-being of all within the coal industry was affected; . . . **9–140**

I can see no reason for holding that different principles apply to pension fund trusts from those which apply to other trusts. Of course, there are many provisions in pension schemes which are not to be found in private trusts, and to these the general law of trusts will be subordinated. But subject to that, I think that the trusts of pension funds are subject to the same rules as other trusts. The large size of pension funds emphasises the need for diversification, rather than lessening it, and the fact that much of the fund has been contributed by members of the scheme seems to me to make it even more important that the trustees should exercise their powers in the best interests of the beneficiaries. In a private trust, most, if not all, of the beneficiaries are the recipients of the bounty of the settlor, whereas under the trusts of a pension fund many (though not all) of the beneficiaries are those who, as members, contributed to the funds so that in due time they would receive pensions. It is thus all the more important that the interests of the beneficiaries should be paramount, so that they may receive the benefits which in part they have paid for. I can see no justification for holding that the benefits to them should run the risk of being lessened because the trustees were pursuing an investment policy intended to assist the industry that the pensioners have left, or their union. . . **9–141**

I reach the unhesitating conclusion that the trusts of pension funds are in general governed by the ordinary law of trusts, subject to any contrary provision in the rules or other provisions which govern the trust. In particular, the trustees of a pension fund are subject to the overriding duty to do the best that they can for the beneficiaries, the duty that in the United States is known as "the duty of undivided loyalty to the beneficiaries".[163] **9–142**

---

[162] See *Re Whiteley* (1886) 33 Ch.D. 347 at 355, per Lindley L.J. and see also at 350, 358; *Learoyd v Whiteley* (1887) 12 App. Cas. 727.

[163] *Blankenship v Boyle* 329 F. Supp. 1089 (1971) at 1095.

9–143 In considering that duty, it must be remembered that very many of the beneficiaries will not in any way be directly affected by the prosperity of the mining industry or the union. Miners who have retired, and the widows and children of deceased miners, will continue to receive their benefits from the fund even if the mining industry shrinks: for the scheme is fully funded, and the fund does not depend on further contributions to it being made . . . I cannot regard any policy designed to ensure the general prosperity of coal mining as being a policy which is directed to obtaining the best possible results for the beneficiaries, most of whom are no longer engaged in the industry, and some of whom never were. The connection is far too remote and insubstantial. Further, the assets of even so large a pension fund as this are nowhere near the size at which there could be expected to be any perceptible impact from the adoption of the policies for which Mr Scargill contends. . .

9–144 A settlor, of course, can always restrict the trustees' powers of investment by excluding certain types of investments and she can always reduce the duties owed by the trustees, e.g. by permitting or directing the trustees to invest only in companies whose products or policies are ecologically more beneficial than those of other competing companies in the opinion of the trustees and by exempting the trustees from any liability so long as they acted in good faith.[164]

9–145 The duties of charity trustees were considered by Nicholls VC in *Harries v Church Commissioners*.[165] He held that the basic rule for them is the same as for other trustees: they can pursue an ethical investment policy only if they can achieve this without jeopardising the financial return they get on the trust capital. But he also held that there are two situations in which charity trustees might be justified in departing from this rule. The first is where investment in a particular type of business would conflict with the aims of the charity. So, for example, the trustees of a charity with objects for the protection of the environment might legitimately decide not to invest in businesses which pollute the environment; and the trustees of a charity concerned with the rehabilitation of alcoholics and prevention of alcoholism could legitimately choose not to invest in companies manufacturing and distributing alcoholic drinks. There must, however, be a real practical conflict between the charity's aims and the activities of potential recipients of charity investment; moral disapproval of their activities is not enough in itself.

9–146 The second situation is where an investment might hamper a charity's work, by making potential beneficiaries unwilling to be helped because of the source of the charity's funding, or by alienating donors. For example, donors to a charity for cancer relief would not wish the trustees to invest in tobacco companies. However, the Charity Commission have said that this requires a balancing exercise. On one side are the difficulties which the charity would encounter, or the likely cost of lost support, if it were to hold the relevant investments. On the other side there may be a risk of financial underperformance if those investments are excluded from its portfolio. The greater the risk of underperformance, the more certain the trustees need to be of the countervailing disadvantages to the charity of such an exclusion before they incur that risk.

## Charity Commission, *CC14: Charities and Investment Matters: A Guide for Trustees* (October 2011)

### 3.3 Can a charity decide to make ethical investments?

*The short answer*

9–147 Yes. Trustees of any charity can decide to invest ethically, even if the investment might provide a lower rate of return than an alternative investment. Ethical investment means investing in a way that reflects a charity's values and ethos and does not run counter to its aims. However, a charity's trustees must be

[164] On exemption clauses see paras 10–201ff.

[165] [1992] 1 W.L.R. 1241.

able to justify why it is in the charity's best interests to invest in this way. The law permits the following reasons:

- particular investment conflicts with the aims of the charity; or
- the charity might lose supporters or beneficiaries if it does not invest ethically; or
- there is no significant financial detriment.

*In more detail*

Trustees must ensure that any decision that they take about adopting an ethical investment approach can be justified within the criteria above. They must be clear about the reasons why certain companies or sectors are excluded or included. Trustees should also evaluate the effect of any proposed policy on potential investment returns and balance any risk of lower returns against the risk of alienating support or damage to reputation. This cannot be an exact calculation but trustees will have to assess the risk to their charity. **9–148**

An ethical investment approach may involve one or a combination of the following approaches: **9–149**

Negative screening: this means avoiding investment in companies or sectors or companies undertaking a particular activity or operating in a way which may be harmful to the charity's interests

Positive screening: this means investing all or part of an investment portfolio in companies or sectors which reflect a charity's values in areas like environmental protection, health, employment or human rights, or in a wider range of companies that demonstrate good corporate social responsibility and governance. For example, positive screening might involve only investing in companies that have targets/proven records for reducing their carbon footprint

Stakeholder activism: this is where a charity, as a shareholder, exercises its voting rights in order to influence a company's policies in a way that reflects its values and ethos. This could mean that a charity might invest in companies whose environmental policies it does not approve of in order to encourage more responsible business practices within those companies. It is also possible to engage in stakeholder activism as a programme related or mixed motive investment. . .

*Examples of ethical investment strategies*

(1) An environmental charity with aims to protect wildlife and the environment decides to adopt an ethical investment policy. It decides to avoid investing in companies that have a poor environmental record (for example, recent cautions or convictions for pollution offences). (This approach would be referred to as negative screening.) **9–150**

(2) A charity established with the aim of educating the public in the causes and prevention of heart disease decides to adopt an ethical approach to the investment of its funds by choosing to invest in companies that promote healthy living through their products and services. This might include running gyms, production of sports equipment or the production of healthy food products. (This approach would be referred to as positive screening.) **9–151**

## *C. The Trustee Act 2000 Default Powers*

In the absence of wider express powers in the trust instrument, and subject to any restriction or exclusion in such instrument or in primary or subordinate legislation, the Trustee Act 2000 (after repealing most of the Trustee Investments Act 1961) confers on trustees of old or new trusts[166] first, a "general power of investment", extending to loans secured on land (whether by way of legal or equitable mortgage or charge) but not to acquiring land, and second, a power to acquire legal estates in freehold or leasehold land in the UK as an investment or for occupation by a beneficiary or for any other reason. **9–152**

By s.3(1) "a trustee may make any kind of investment that he could make if he were absolutely entitled to the assets of the trust", but by subs.(3) "the general power of investment does not permit a trustee to make investments in land other than in loans secured on land". Investments can thus **9–153**

[166] Trustee Act 2000 ss.7(1), 10(2).

properly be made in assets anywhere in the world, including loans secured on foreign land, so long, of course, as the various equitable and statutory duties of care are observed. An "investment" was originally considered to be an asset acquired for the sake of the income it was expected to yield[167] but, nowadays, with the emphasis on "total return",[168] taking account of income yield and capital appreciation in accordance with modern portfolio theory, an investment is considered to cover an asset acquired for the sake of either or both an income yield or a likely capital profit.[169] It follows, for example, that the purchase of depreciating chattels for a villa owned by the trustees or of a depreciating vehicle for use by a beneficiary or of a lottery ticket fall outside the general power of investment, so that the beneficiary will need to have trust income or capital properly distributed to her and then use it to purchase the chattels or vehicle or lottery ticket for herself.

**9–154** By s.8(1) "a trustee may acquire freehold or leasehold land in the United Kingdom (a) as an investment, (b) for occupation by a beneficiary, or (c) for any other reason". In England and Wales "freehold or leasehold land"[170] means a legal estate in land and, particularly in purchasing leases, the trustees will need to ensure that they observe their equitable and statutory duties of care. Then, by s.8(3), "for the purpose of exercising his functions as a trustee, a trustee who acquires land under this section has all the powers of an absolute owner in relation to the land". For trustees who have acquired land other than under s.8(3), e.g. because the settlor settled land[171] on the trustees, the Trusts of Land and Appointment of Trustees Act 1996 s.6(3) provides: "The trustees of land have power to acquire land under the power conferred by section 8 of the Trustee Act 2000." Under s.8(3) it seems that the use of the present tense enables trustees to acquire the land with the assistance of a mortgage thereon and, to that extent, "gear up" the value of the trust fund. Otherwise, gearing up by money borrowed on the security of existing assets to acquire new assets needs express authorisation.[172]

## *D. Express Investment Clauses*

**9–155** Express investment clauses are found in virtually all express trusts although clauses in trust instruments more than 50 years old are usually much more limited than clauses drafted in modern conditions where a wide variety of financial products are now on offer. In default of express powers of investment, the Trustee Act 1925 and the Trustee Investments Act 1961 gave trustees powers to acquire investments detailed on a safe list of authorised investments. However such powers became increasingly outdated and ineffective to safeguard and develop the value of the trust fund.

**9–156** Draftsmen have developed their own sophisticated investment clauses and continue to use these (rather than rely on the default powers conferred by the Trustee Act 2000) so as to confer the broadest possible powers on the trustees, whose opportunities, however broad their powers, are narrowed by the equitable and statutory duties of care imposed upon them (save to the extent that these are modified or excluded by the trust instrument). To confer the broadest possible investment powers, draftsmen will often employ clauses like:

---

167 *Re Wragg* [1919] 2 Ch. 58 at 64, 65; *Re Power's WT* [1947] Ch. 572; *Tootal Broadhurst Lee Co Ltd v IRC* [1949] 1 All E.R. 261 at 265.

168 *Cowan v Scargill* [1985] Ch. 270 at 287; *Harries v Church Commissioners* [1992] 1 W.L.R. 1241 at 1246; *JW v Morgan Trust Co of the Bahamas Ltd* (2000) 4 I.T.E.L.R. 541.

169 In *Cook v Medway Housing Soc* [1997] S.T.C. 90 at 98, "investment" was said to amount to the "laying out of moneys in anticipation of a profitable capital or income return". See too *Weston v IRC* [2001] W.T.L.R. 1217 at [18].

170 Trustee Act 2000 s.8(2). Interests in foreign land may be acquired by acquiring shares in a company that owns foreign land.

171 But land that is within the Settled Land Act 1925 is governed exclusively by such Act: Trustee Act 2000 s.10(1).

172 *Re Suenson-Taylor's Settlement Trusts* [1974] 1 W.L.R. 1280.

> to apply or invest in the purchase or acquisition of assets or investments of whatsoever nature and wherever situated, and whether or not yielding income or being appreciating or depreciating assets, and including the acquisition of derivatives but only for the purpose of limiting risks and not for the purpose of speculation.

However, if most exceptionally, speculation is desired, the draftsman can insert "or speculate" after "or invest" and omit the limitation on the acquisition of derivatives, while providing that in exercising such flexible powers the trustees "are under a duty to speculate with the trust fund as would an absolute beneficial owner who could afford to lose an amount equivalent to the value of the trust fund without it affecting his standard of living in any way whatever" and "are not to be liable for any conduct unless acting dishonestly".[173]

The draftsman can also confer an express power to "gear up" the trust fund by borrowing on the security of existing trust property to acquire further property for the trust[174] and an express power to lend merely on the security of a personal promise of the borrower to repay,[175] when a high interest rate will be payable because a personal promise to repay provides no security in the event of non-payment. Ethical investment clauses can also be inserted to give the trustees a wide discretion, e.g. "to select only those investments which the trustees in their absolute discretion consider to be ethically acceptable". **9–157**

At one stage the courts took a narrow restrictive approach to the interpretation of investment clauses as extending the default statutory investment powers as little as possible, but for the last 50 years the courts have been interpreting investment clauses according to the natural and proper meaning of the words used in their context so as to empower investment in a fairly construed wide range of investments. However, they have been strict in refusing to treat the conferment of a power for a trustee to invest in her absolute discretion in all respects as if she were the absolute beneficial owner of the trust fund as exempting the trustee from the need to act with an appropriate degree of care.[176] **9–158**

## 6. Capital and Income: The Trustee's Duty of Impartiality

### A. Introduction

There are several reasons why it is often essential for trustees to distinguish between capital and income when they manage the trust property. First, this distinction is crucial for taxation purposes. Secondly, where investments are held on trust for interests in succession (e.g. "A for life, remainder to B"), investment returns will be allocated to the life tenant or the remainderman according to whether they are classified as income or capital receipts. This consideration is likely to affect the investment strategy adopted by the trustees, given their duty to maintain a fair balance between the needs of differing classes of beneficiaries when investing the trust funds. Thirdly, where property forms part of the permanent endowment of a charitable trust, a receipt classified as capital will usually form part of that endowment and will not normally be available to be spent for charitable purposes. This consideration is also likely to affect the trustees' investment strategy. Fourthly, the distinction between capital and income can affect the allocation of trustee expenses to different parts of the trust fund. Fifthly, while trust law does not give trustees any general flexibility in classifying the **9–159**

---

173 Such exemption clauses are valid if known and approved by the settlor: *Armitage v Nurse* [1998] Ch. 241; *Bogg v Raper* (1998) 1 I.T.E.L.R. 267. See paras 10–201ff.

174 Otherwise not permitted: *Re Suenson-Taylor's Settlement Trusts* [1974] 1 W.L.R. 1280,

175 Otherwise not permitted: *Khoo Tek Keong v Ch'ng Joo Neoh* [1934] A.C. 529; *Dalraida Trustees Ltd v Faulds* [2012] Pens. L.R. 15 at [61]–[63].

176 *Re Maberly* (1886) 33 Ch. D. 455 at 458; *Bartlett v Barclays Bank Trust Co Ltd* [1980] Ch. 515 at 536.

returns from investments, it has developed certain equitable rules of apportionment which require the sharing of certain returns and outgoings between capital and income, and in some cases impose a duty to sell certain trust property. These matters will all be discussed in turn. It should be noted at the outset that they were all reviewed in a report published by the Law Commission in 2009 on *Capital and Income in Trusts: Classification and Entitlement*,[177] in response to which certain legislative changes were made to the law in this area by the Trusts (Capital and Income) Act 2013.

## *B. Classification of Receipts*

**9-160** Broadly speaking, property which can be categorised as the "tree" is capital, and the "fruit" it produces is categorised as income, e.g. rents, interest payments, dividends from shares. However, receipts by trustees from companies raise special problems.

**9-161** Except for the purposes of taxation, no distinction is made between a company's trading profits (being the excess of trading receipts over the costs of trading) and a company's capital profits (arising from selling an asset in excess of its balance sheet value). Both sorts are available for distribution to shareholders, but the company's capital itself can only be distributed to shareholders[178] on liquidation of the company or under an authorised reduction of share capital (or a payment out of a special share premium account[179]) or a bonus issue of stock or shares which capitalises company profits. What is paid out by the company as capital goes to benefit remaindermen: what is paid out as dividend goes to the life tenant.

**9-162** Distributions of capital profits can cause great unfairness. For example, in *Re Sechiari*,[180] a trust fund included shares in Thomas Tilling & Co Ltd. The company was nationalised, and was obliged to sell its road transport interests to the British Transport Commission (BTC) in return for BTC stock. It decided to distribute £5 of BTC stock for each £1 of stock held by its shareholders. This led to a 75 per cent drop in the value of its shares. The life tenant was held to be entitled to the distribution as income, thus receiving much more than was fair in view of the drastic diminution in value of the capital for the remaindermen.

**9-163** In the consultation paper which prefigured its report,[181] the Law Commission proposed the introduction of powers that would enable trustees to engage in "total return investment", i.e. to pursue an investment strategy that viewed income yield and capital growth as the combined investment objective for the fund without attempting to balance the different interests of income and capital beneficiaries. Trustees would instead have been empowered to strike that balance by the exercise of a new power to allocate all receipts between capital and income as a matter of their discretion. This would have made the current rules for classifying trust receipts default rules only. However, the proposal was dropped for all trusts except charitable trusts with a permanent endowment. These are now covered by the Charities Act 2011 ss.104A and 104B, which enable the trustees to make a resolution opting for new Charity Commission regulations to apply in place of the investment restrictions that currently prevent total return investment.

---

[177] Law Commission, *Capital and Income in Trusts: Classification and Entitlement* (TSO, 2009), Law Com. No.315, HC Paper No.426, (Session 2009–10).

[178] *Hill v Permanent Trustee Company of New South Wales Ltd* [1930] A.C. 720.

[179] Tantamount to an authorised reduction of capital: *Re Duff's Settlements* [1951] Ch. 923.

[180] [1950] 1 All E.R. 417 based on the rule in *Bouch v Sproule* (1885) 12 App. Cas. 385.

[181] Law Commission, *Capital and Income in Trusts: Classification and Apportionment* (TSO 2004), Law Com. Consultation Paper. No.175.

## C. Investment Policy

As Hoffmann J stated in *Nestlé v National Westminster Bank Plc*,[182] a "trustee must act fairly in making investment decisions which may have different consequences for differing classes of beneficiaries." Where there is a life tenant the distinction between capital and income is crucial, since the trustees have a discretion to choose whether to buy income-producing investments or capital-growth investments, and opting for an investment policy which lays too much stress on one objective or the other would unfairly favour the life tenant over the remainderman or vice versa.[183] The point can be illustrated by reference to a New Zealand case, *Re Mulligan*.[184] The settlor's widow was both a trustee and a life tenant, and she browbeat her co-trustees (a firm of solicitors who should have known better) into joining her in an investment strategy that was designed to maximise income, to the detriment of the remainderman. After her death the remainderman successfully sued her co-trustees, who were liable to compensate him for the decline in capital value suffered by the trust fund. **9–164**

Again, suppose that trustees use their power under the Trustee Act 2000 s.8, to purchase or retain a short lease of premises leased out so that the life-tenant can receive all rents during the last 10 or 12 years of the authorised lease, leaving nothing for the remainderman. In such a case, depending on what other assets form part of the trust fund, the trustees might be in breach of their overriding duty to keep an even hand between the beneficiaries, and they may also be in breach of their duty to invest prudently.[185] They would probably be in breach of this duty for purchasing such a lease in the first place,[186] and it would also be imprudent to retain it until it expires or for any longer period than reasonably necessary to sell the depreciating leases.[187] The owner of the remainder interest could also invoke ss.14 and 15 of the Trusts of Land and Appointment of Trustees Act 1996 for the court to compel the trustees to sell or she could take advantage of her inherent right to call for conversion if the land was held on trust for sale.[188] **9–165**

Where there is a power to appoint capital to the life tenant, the trustees will have the flexibility to invest a greater part than otherwise would be possible in assets yielding little or no income but where much capital growth is expected, so that they can then sell some of the assets and appoint the proceeds (capital) to the life tenant to make up for the income lost by investing in fewer assets yielding a good income. This would entail taking a "total return" approach to the trust investments. On this approach, if £1 million of trust assets appreciate to be worth £1,100,000 at the end of the year and yield income of £40,000, then the total return of £140,000, less an amount for inflation, could be spent without the trust fund being any worse off than it was at the outset. To make allowance for **9–166**

---

[182] [2000] W.T.L.R. 795 at 803. In an exceptional case it may even be necessary for the trustees to balance fairly the interests of beneficiaries belonging to the same class, e.g. several beneficiaries who are entitled to fixed shares of the capital. So where a trust fund included 999 shares in a private company, the trustees could reject the claim of a beneficiary entitled to 46/80 of a trust fund to have 574 of the shares, since such a majority shareholding is worth much more than 46/80 of the proceeds of sale of the 999 shares. In such a case the only fair course is to sell all the shares and divide the proceeds pro rata: *Lloyds Bank Plc v Duker* [1987] 1 W.L.R. 1324.

[183] In the case of charitable trusts which have a permanent endowment, which must be kept intact as capital, a balance also needs to be kept between capital and income.

[184] [1998] 1 N.Z.L.R. 481.

[185] For which see paras 9–117—9–123.

[186] e.g. *Re Maberly* (1886) 33 Ch.D. 455 (should not invest as directed in Irish land but in statutorily authorised investments).

[187] e.g. *Beauclerk v Ashburnham* (1845) 8 Beav. 322; 14 L.J.Ch. 241 where trustees were authorised and required by and with the consent and direction in writing of the life-tenant to invest in leaseholds. Obviously, the trustees could not object to investment in leaseholds as such, but they had a discretion whether or not to agree to a particular investment proposed "because it must be agreed at once that it would not be fit for them to lay out the trust moneys in a low, bad and deteriorating situation", per Lord Langdale MR at 8 Beav. 328.

[188] *Thornton v Ellis* (1852) 15 Beav. 193; *Wightwick v Lord* (1857) 6 H.L.C. 217; and cf. *Page v West* [2010] EWHC 504 (Ch).

annual ups and downs of the stock market it may be advisable to have a policy, if the terms of the trust allow it, to pay out the equivalent of five per cent of the value of the fund at the end of the year including the income produced that year. This can be done for well-drafted discretionary trusts or even well-drafted fixed interest trusts where the trustees have power to appoint capital to any beneficiary.

## D. Expenses

**9–167** In the absence of express provision in the trust deed, it is a matter for the general law to determine whether an expense incurred in the course of trust administration (e.g. accountancy fees or building repairs) should be charged against income or capital. The answer can have significant tax implications, because an expense that is properly chargeable to income reduces the income tax payable.

**9–168** The leading authority is *Carver v Duncan*,[189] which concerned the proper classification of various trust expenses including insurance premiums and investment advisers' fees, for the purposes of the statutory precursor to the Income Tax Act 2007 s.484.[190] The House of Lords held that these expenses had been incurred for the benefit of the whole estate and were therefore properly chargeable to capital. Lord Templeman stated that[191]:

> Trustees are entitled to be indemnified out of the capital and income of their trust fund against all obligations incurred by the trustees in the due performance of their duties and the due exercise of their powers. The trustees must then debit each item of expenditure either against income or against capital. The general rule is that income must bear all ordinary outgoings of a recurrent nature, such as rates and taxes, and interest on charges and encumbrances. Capital must bear all costs, charges and expenses incurred for the benefit of the whole estate.

**9–169** These principles were revisited by the Court of Appeal in *HMRC v Trustees of the Peter Clay Discretionary Trust*.[192] One issue was whether the executive trustees' fees should be treated as a trust expense for tax purposes—a question to which Lindsay J gave a positive answer at first instance, from which no appeal was made. The case also concerned the question whether a range of expenses incurred by the trustees should be debited against capital or income: investment management fees, bank charges, custodian charges, accountancy and administration fees, and trustees' remuneration. The Court of Appeal held that only those expenses which relate wholly and exclusively to income can be attributed to income: an expense which relates both to income and to capital must be charged wholly to capital. However, where trustees can show that part of a single fee relates to work done for income alone, then the trustees can apportion the expense, detaching the income element and charging it to income. That is the case whether or not the invoice is itemised; apportionment is possible provided an evidence-based estimate can be made.

## E. The Apportionment Rules

**9–170** Until recently, various rules of apportionment have required the sharing of certain returns and outgoings between capital and income. The point of these rules is to prevent any one beneficiary from benefiting to a disproportionate amount at the expense of another. However, they are technical and sometimes counter-intuitive (treating income as capital and vice versa), they have often caused

---

189 [1985] A.C. 1082.
190 Finance Act 1973 s.16, later the Income and Corporation Taxes Act 1988 s.686.
191 *Carver* [1985] A.C. 1082 at 1120.
192 [2009] Ch. 296.

administrative difficulties and they have required trustees to engage in complex calculations for small sums of money. They are generally excluded in trust documents and, if not, they are often ignored. For all these reasons they have been disapplied for trusts created or arising on or after October 2013, by the Trusts (Capital and Income) Act 2013 s.1. The section is reproduced below, followed by a brief explanation of each of the rules to which it refers, which still apply to older trusts.

### Trusts (Capital and Income) Act 2013 s.1

**Disapplication of apportionment etc. rules**

(1) Any entitlement to income under a new trust is to income as it arises (and accordingly section 2 of the Apportionment Act 1870, which provides for income to accrue from day to day, does not apply in relation to the trust). **9–171**

(2) The following do not apply in relation to a new trust—

(a) the first part of the rule known as the rule in *Howe v Earl of Dartmouth* (which requires certain residuary personal estate to be sold);
(b) the second part of that rule (which withholds from a life tenant income arising from certain investments and compensates the life tenant with payments of interest);
(c) the rule known as the rule in *Re Earl of Chesterfield's Trusts* (which requires the proceeds of the conversion of certain investments to be apportioned between capital and income);
(d) the rule known as the rule in *Allhusen v Whittell* (which requires a contribution to be made from income for the purpose of paying a deceased person's debts, legacies and annuities).

(3) Trustees have power to sell any property which (but for subsection (2)(a)) they would have been under a duty to sell.

(4) Subsections (1) to (3) have effect subject to any contrary intention that appears—

(a) in any trust instrument of the trust, and
(b) in any power under which the trust is created or arises.

(5) In this section "new trust" means a trust created or arising on or after the day on which this section comes into force (and includes a trust created or arising on or after that day under a power conferred before that day).

## i. The Apportionment Act 1870 s.2

Income beneficiaries are only entitled to the proportion of trust income which is deemed to have accrued during their period of entitlement. Section 2 of the 1870 Act provides that any payments received by the trustees in the nature of income (e.g. dividends) should be treated as accruing to the income beneficiaries at the date when they arise, removing the need for any apportionment. **9–172**

## ii. The Rule in *Allhusen v Whittell*[193]

Where a testator's residuary estate is left on trust for A for life, remainder to B absolutely, debts, expenses, and legacies have to be paid out of residue in the course of the year traditionally allowed to the executor to wind up distribution of the deceased's estate. These payments are treated under the rule in *Allhusen v Whittell* as coming partly from income and partly from capital. One must ascertain that sum which together with interest for the year would amount to the total expended on debts, expenses and legacies: such sum is borne by B as out of capital, while the excess of the total **9–173**

[193] (1867) 4 Eq. 295. See too *Re Wills* [1915] 1 Ch. 769.

expenditure over that sum is borne by A. The rate of interest is based on the ratio subsisting between the actual net income after tax for the year and the gross capital value of the estate.[194]

### iii. The Rule in *Howe v Earl of Dartmouth*[195]

**9–174** Once the net residue has been ascertained there are problems if A is receiving too high an income from unauthorised investments of a wasting or hazardous nature or if A is receiving too little income because some assets are non-income-producing (e.g. an equitable reversionary interest under another trust where the income is going to the prior life tenant). Under the first part of the rule in *Howe v Earl of Dartmouth* the unauthorised investments must be sold and the life tenant provided with a fair income calculated as a percentage of the value of the property, excess income having to be invested in authorised securities. Under the second part of the rule, the trustees must apportion property fairly between the income and capital beneficiaries until conversion. For new trusts, s.1(3) of the 2013 Act replaces the trustees' duty to sell with a power to sell.

### iv. The Rule in *Re Earl of Chesterfield's Trusts*[196]

**9–175** Once a capital value has materialised for the non-income-producing asset, whether by selling it or waiting until the death of the life tenant in the case of a reversionary interest, then the capital is apportioned between income and capital. One must ascertain that sum which, invested at four per cent from the date of the testator's death and accumulating at compound interest with yearly rests, would, with the accumulations, have produced the amount of capital to be apportioned: that ascertained sum is treated as capital and the excess as income.

## 7. Distribution of the Trust Property

### *A. Powers of Appointment*

**9–176** Trustees may not appoint trust property to anyone who is not a beneficiary. In *Eaves v Hickson*,[197] trustees were induced by a forgery to pay trust funds to persons not entitled, and Romilly MR held that, as between trustee and beneficiary, the loss falls on the former.[198] Note, however, that the Trustee Act 1925 s.61 is now available as a defence to a trustee who honestly and reasonably makes a wrongful payment through circumstances like those in *Eaves v Hickson*, or through a mistaken construction of the trust deed.[199]

**9–177** Before paying trust funds to an alleged assignee from a beneficiary a trustee must investigate the assignee's title. If she relies merely on the alleged assignee's statement, she is not acting reasonably. But although the trustee must investigate the assignee's title, she cannot require actual delivery up to her of the assignee's document of title.[200]

---

194 *Re Oldham* [1927] W.N. 113.
195 (1802) 7 Ves. Jun. 137.
196 (1883) 24 Ch.D. 643.
197 (1861) 30 Beav. 136. However, only if the forger or the wrong recipients could not compensate the beneficiary.
198 See also *Ashby v Blackwell* (1765) 2 Eden 299 at 302; *Sutton v Wilders* (1871) L.R. 12 Eq. 373; *Boulton v Beard* (1853) 3 De G.M. & G. 608; *Sporle v Barnaby* (1864) 10 Jur. 1142.
199 *Re Smith* (1902) 71 L.J. Ch. 411; *National Trustees Company of Australasia v General Finance Co of Australasia* [1905] A.C. 373, PC (Aus) *Re Allsop* [1914] 1 Ch. 1. For discussion of s.61, see paras 10–176—10–200.
200 *Re Palmer* [1907] 1 Ch. 486; see *Warter v Anderson* (1853) 11 Hare 301.

If a trustee-beneficiary underpays herself, then, according to *Re Horne*,[201] she suffers by her mistake, although it may be that, nowadays, she should be allowed to recoup herself out of trust property in her hands.[202] 9–178

## *B. Powers of Maintenance*

Under the Trustee Act 1925 s.31, trustees have a power to apply trust income to the maintenance of minor beneficiaries. This power is of fundamental importance in the administration of trusts for the assistance it may provide to minors, for the taxation repercussions flowing from the way in which it can convert what are vested interests under the terms of the trust into contingent interests and also flowing from a beneficiary's entitlement to income at 18 years of age. Section 31 was amended by the Inheritance and Trustees' Powers Act 2014 s.8, to clarify that the amount of the income used is a matter for the trustees' discretion, and is not limited by an objective standard of reasonableness, and to remove restrictions that were formerly imposed by s.31 on the amount of income which the trustees could pay out. 9–179

### Trustee Act 1925 s.31

**Power to apply income for maintenance and to accumulate surplus income during a minority**

(1) Where any property is held by trustees in trust for any person for any interest whatsoever, whether vested or contingent, then, subject to any prior interests or charges affecting that property— 9–180

(i) during the infancy of any such person, if his interest so long continues, the trustees may, at their sole discretion, pay to his parent or guardian, if any, or otherwise apply for or towards his maintenance, education, or benefit, the whole or such part, if any, of the income of that property as the trustees may think fit, whether or not there is—

(a) any other fund applicable to the same purpose; or
(b) any person bound by law to provide for his maintenance or education; and

(ii) if such person on attaining the age of eighteen years has not a vested interest in such income, the trustees shall thenceforth pay the income of that property and of any accretion thereto under subsection (2) of this section to him, until he either attains a vested interest therein or dies, or until failure of his interest.

(2) During the infancy of any such person, if his interest so long continues, the trustees shall accumulate all the residue of that income by investing it, and any profits from so investing it from time to time in authorised investments, and shall hold those accumulations as follows—

(i) If any such person—

(a) attains the age of eighteen years, or marries under that age or forms a civil partnership under that age, and his interest in such income during his infancy, or until his marriage or his formation of a civil partnership, is a vested interest or;
(b) on attaining the age of eighteen years or on marriage, or formation of a civil partnership, under that age becomes entitled to the property from which such income arose in fee simple, absolute or determinable, or absolutely, or for an entailed interest;

the trustees shall hold the accumulations in trust for such person absolutely, but without prejudice to any provision with respect thereto contained in any settlement by him made under any statutory

---

201 [1905] 1 Ch. 76.
202 See *Re Reading* [1916] W.N. 262.

> powers during his infancy, and so that the receipt of such person after marriage or formation of a civil partnership, and though still an infant shall be a good discharge, and
>
> (ii) In any other case the trustees shall, notwithstanding that such person had a vested interest in such income, hold the accumulations as an accretion to the capital of the property from which such accumulations arose, and as one fund with such capital for all purposes, and so that, if such property is settled land, such accumulations shall be held upon the same trusts as if the same were capital money arising therefrom;
>
> but the trustees may, at any time during the infancy of such person if his interest so long continues, apply those accumulations, or any part thereof, as if they were income arising in the then current year.
>
> (3) This section applies in the case of a contingent interest only if the limitation or trust carries the intermediate income of the property, but it applies to a future or contingent legacy by the parent of, or a person standing in loco parentis to, the legatee, if and for such period as, under the general law, the legacy carries interest for the maintenance of the legatee, and in any such case as last aforesaid the rate of interest shall (if the income available is sufficient, and subject to any rules of court to the contrary) be five pounds per centum per annum.
>
> (4) This section applies to a vested annuity in like manner as if the annuity were the income of property held by trustees in trust to pay the income thereof to the annuitant for the same period for which the annuity is payable, save that in any case accumulations made during the infancy of the annuitant shall be held in trust for the annuitant or his personal representatives absolutely.
>
> (5) This section does not apply where the instrument, if any, under which the interest arises came into operation before the commencement of this Act.

**9–181** The general law governing trustee decision-making applies to exercises of the s.31 power: trustees must consciously decide whether to exercise the power in good faith after due consideration of all and only relevant circumstances. In *Wilson v Turner*[203] trustees paid over trust income to a minor beneficiary's father without any request from him and without any attempt to ascertain whether any income was required for the minor's maintenance: the father was ordered to repay the income. Trustees should particularly review the situation a month or two before the minor attains 18 years since the statutory power to apply income and its accumulations over the years expires on her 18th birthday.

**9–182** Under the statutory power, so long as income is legally available,[204] there is a duty to accumulate the income for the period of the beneficiary's minority, so far as it is not used under a power to apply it for the maintenance, education or benefit of the beneficiary. During this period accumulations may be used as if they were current income despite having accrued to the capital.[205] Once the beneficiary attains 18, however, the trustees must pay the income from the capital (including the accumulations which become part of the capital) to the beneficiary even if the beneficiary's interest is still contingent under the trust terms, e.g. to B if she attains 25 years.

**9–183** Section 31(2) may convert what appear to be indefeasible vested interests into defeasible or contingent interests, since accumulations of income will not pass to a beneficiary with a vested interest in income under the terms of the trust unless she satisfies a contingency within s.31(2)(i), or unless she is entitled not just to income but also to capital to which the accumulations automatically accrue, as where personalty is settled on a minor not just for life but absolutely (s.31(2)(ii)).

**9–184** In the case of a minor with a vested interest s.31 requires income to be accumulated except insofar as it is applied for the maintenance of the minor unless the income is disposed of in favour of someone else

---

[203] (1883) 22 Ch. D. 521.

[204] A trust instrument may oust s.31 expressly or by necessary implication and s.31 only applies in the case of a contingent interest if the interest carries the intermediate income.

[205] Section 31(2).

or directed only to be accumulated.[206] But if the minor's interest is contingent, then by s.31(3) income is not required to be dealt with in this way, unless the limitation or trust carries the intermediate income.

## C. Powers of Advancement

Under the Trustee Act 1925 s.32, trustees have the power to advance trust capital for the benefit of beneficiaries who have a requisite type of entitlement to the capital of the trust fund. The section was amended by the Inheritance and Trustees' Powers Act 2014 s.9, to remove the limit that was previously placed on the statutory power of advancement, that trustees could only advance up to one-half of the capital to which the relevant beneficiary was entitled: they now have a discretion to advance up to (but not exceeding) the whole of the beneficiary's prospective share. The section has also been amended to make it clear that the trustees are able not only to pay out cash in the exercise of their statutory power of advancement but also to transfer or apply property. **9–185**

### Trustee Act 1925 s.32

**Power of advancement**

(1) Trustees may at any time or times pay or apply any capital money subject to a trust, or transfer or apply any other property forming part of the capital of the trust property, for the advancement or benefit, in such manner as they may, in their absolute discretion, think fit, of any person entitled to the capital of the trust property or of any share thereof, whether absolutely or contingently on his attaining any specified age or on the occurrence of any other event, or subject to a gift over on his death under any specified age or on the occurrence of any other event, and whether in possession or in remainder or reversion, and such payment, transfer or application may be made notwithstanding that the interest of such person is liable to be defeated by the exercise of a power of appointment or revocation, or to be diminished by the increase of the class to which he belongs: Provided that— **9–186**

(a) property (including any money) so paid, transferred or applied for the advancement or benefit of any person must not, altogether, represent more than the presumptive or vested share or interest of that person in the trust property; and

(b) if that person is or becomes absolutely and indefeasibly entitled to a share in the trust property the money or other property so paid, transferred or applied shall be brought into account as part of such share; and

(c) no such payment, transfer or application shall be made so as to prejudice any person entitled to any prior life or other interest, whether vested or contingent, in the money or other property paid, transferred or applied unless such person is in existence and of full age and consents in writing to such payment, transfer or application.

(1A) In exercise of the foregoing power trustees may pay, transfer or apply money or other property on the basis (express or implied) that it shall be treated as a proportionate part of the capital out of which it was paid, transferred or applied, for the purpose of bringing it into account in accordance with proviso (b) to subsection (1) of this section.

(2) This section does not apply to capital money arising under the Settled Land Act 1925.

(3) This section does not apply to trusts constituted or created before the commencement of this Act.

When exercising their s.32 power trustees must be careful, for a mistake will mean that both capital and income will disappear, probably for good. *Re Pauling's Settlement Trusts*[207] provides a salutary **9–187**

---

[206] *Re Turner's W.T.* [1937] Ch. 15; *Re Ransome* [1957] Ch. 348; *Re Reade-Revell* [1930] 1 Ch. 52; *Re Stapleton* [1946] 1 All E.R. 323.

[207] [1964] Ch. 303.

tale for compulsory reading by trustees before they exercise their power of advancement. The father of the beneficiaries was so charming and so forceful that the trustees were persuaded to fritter away much of the trust capital in ways that enabled the beneficiaries' mother's overdraft to be paid off, a house to be bought for the parents absolutely and an overly high standard of living to be maintained for the family. The lesson to be drawn is that requests for advancement of capital by young adults who are unemancipated from their parents' influence must be treated with caution and that when moneys are requested for particular purposes they should be applied to those purposes by the trustees themselves if experience suggests that they will otherwise be spent by the parents on something else. Further points are made about the exercise of powers of advancement in the following extract from Tipping J's judgment in *Kain v Hutton*.

*Kain v Hutton*

New Zealand Supreme Court [2008] 3 N.Z.L.R. 589 at [56]–[59]

**9–188** Importantly, a power of advancement may be exercised only if there is some "good reason" to exercise it at the time and in the manner proposed.[208] That good reason must of course be of benefit to the person the subject of the advancement. But in spite of the width of the concept of benefit, *Pauling's* case shows that it is insufficient simply to make an advancement on the basis that any receipt of money or other property ahead of the date of vesting in possession must be of benefit to the recipient. The concept of benefit is wide but not wholly unrestricted.

**9–189** For example, proposed advancements close to the date of vesting in possession should be viewed cautiously. Trustees must make sure that there really is a good reason to advance the date.[209] Similarly, advancements when the trustees are or should be aware that the beneficiary may be going to use the money or other property unwisely should also be viewed with caution, unless the advancement is by means of a protective trust.[210]

**9–190** Need, as such, is not the touchstone but if there is a total absence of material or moral need the interests of those who take in default should be preferred to those of the proposed advancee. The position, in short, is that trustees may exercise their discretionary power to make an advancement only if they have formed the considered view that there is good reason to do so and it truly will be of benefit to the advanced beneficiary to exercise the power in the manner contemplated.[211]

**9–191** In this respect powers of advancement are different from powers of appointment.[212] A person exercising a power of appointment is exercising a discretionary power to select who should take from a group of potential beneficiaries. That is a materially different task from that required of someone exercising a power of advancement. There, the essential question is whether a distribution should be made ahead of the time at which the beneficiary would otherwise receive possession of property in which they already have an interest.

**9–192** An advancement may be by way of settlement that benefits someone other than the beneficiary so long as the beneficiary receives significant benefit,[213] e.g. receiving a life interest in the advanced moneys, remainder to her widower for life, remainder to her children equally. To deal with a dictum of Upjohn J[214] and cases narrowly construing powers of appointment in outdated fashion, the power of advancement has often been expressly extended to permit delegation of duties and

---

208 See *Re Paulings Settlement Trusts* [1964] Ch. 303 at 333 per Willmer L.J.

209 See *Lewin on Trusts* (18th ed, 2008), para [32–18] and *Pilkington v IRC* [1964] A.C. 612 at 640–641.

210 See Thomas and Hudson, *The Law of Trusts* (2004), para [14-31].

211 See Thomas and Hudson, para [14–30] citing *Phillips v Phillips* (1853) Kay 40; *Re Kershaw's Trusts* (1840) L.R. 6 Eq. 322 and *Re Moxon's Will Trusts* [1958] 1 W.L.R. 165.

212 Unless of course the express terms of the power circumscribe its exercise by reference to benefit in which case that will be an additional criterion as well as the standard requirement that the appointee be an object of the power.

213 *Pilkington v IRC* [1964] A.C. 612; *Re Hampden* [2001] W.T.L.R. 195.

214 *Re Wills' Trusts* [1959] Ch. 1 at 13.

discretions to make clear that a re-settlement may be by way of discretionary trusts or by way of protective trusts which may end up after forfeiture as discretionary trusts. However, the modern consensus, supported by Viscount Radcliffe in *Pilkington v IRC*,[215] is that no question of delegation of the trustees' functions arises where they transfer property to be held on new trusts which may contain discretionary trusts and powers, because the new trustees are not exercising delegated functions but are exercising new original functions of their own as a result of the outright advancement.

It is necessary to ensure that the rule against remoteness is not infringed, for the perpetuity period relevant to the exercise of the power of advancement runs from the date of the settlement and not from the date of the exercise of the power.[216] If part of the exercise of the power of advancement is void for remoteness and the resultant effect of the intended advancement is such that it could not reasonably be regarded as being beneficial to the beneficiary intended to be advanced, then the advancement fails for it cannot be authorised as within the powers of the trustees under s.32; otherwise the part of the advancement not void for remoteness will stand as within the trustees' powers,[217] e.g. C's life interest stands where the advancement is to trustees for C for life with remainders to her issue where the remainders are void for remoteness. The fact that in such a case no effective beneficial trusts of capital are created does not mean that there has been no payment or application of capital as required by s.32: the transfer of capital to the trustees of the settlement for C for life is an application of capital within s.32.[218] **9–193**

## 8. Exercise of Discretionary Powers

### A. Overview

Trustees are frequently vested with discretionary powers, which may be distributive (e.g. powers of appointment) or managerial (e.g. powers of investment). Various legal rules affect the exercise of such powers.[219] First, there are mandatory rules of law governing the *creation* of powers in the first place, e.g. the rules against perpetuity which prevent certain powers being created at all,[220] and the rules on certainty of objects which invalidate powers of appointment if the class of objects is conceptually uncertain.[221] Secondly, there are rules determining the *extent* of powers, e.g. the rules of construction which enable the court to determine a power's scope, the rules which hold that a power of appointment must be exercised in favour of a person who is within the class of objects, and within the limits laid down by the power itself,[222] and the doctrine of fraud on a power, which holds that a purported exercise of a power is a nullity if the trustee acts for an improper purpose. Thirdly, there are rules which go to the trustee's *exercise* of a power, under which the court may review the trustee's decision-making and set a transaction to one side if they find that this is flawed, for example by invoking the rule in **9–194**

---

215 [1964] A.C. 612 at 639.

216 *Pilkington v IRC* [1964] A.C. 612. For the purposes of the Perpetuities and Accumulations Act 2009 the exercise of a power of advancement is treated as the exercise of a special power.

217 *Re Abraham's WT* [1969] 1 Ch. 463.

218 *Re Hastings-Bass* [1975] Ch. 25.

219 P. Matthews, "The Doctrine of Fraud on a Power, Part 1" [2007] P.C.B. 131; R.C. Nolan, "Controlling Fiduciary Power" (2009) 68 C.L.J. 293. *Pilkington, Abraham's* and *Hastings-Bass* must all now be read in the light of *Pitt v Holt* [2012] Ch. 132 at [33]–[67] and [2013] 2 A.C. 108 at [18]–[25].

220 *Re De Sommery* [1912] 2 Ch. 622 at 630.

221 *Re Gulbenkian's Settlement Trusts* [1970] A.C. 508; *Re Hay's Settlement Trusts* [1982] 1 W.L.R. 202. For discussion, see paras 4–092—4–116.

222 *Re Keele Estates (No.2) Ltd* [1952] Ch. 603; *Re Brinkley's Will Trusts* [1968] Ch. 407.

*Re Hastings-Bass*,[223] which holds that trustees must consider relevant matters and exclude irrelevant matters from consideration when exercising discretionary powers.

**9–195** Under a family discretionary trust the trustees have a duty to exercise their discretion by distributing income (or, ultimately, capital) in some sort of amounts to some of the beneficiaries (unless, under a power to accumulate, they have decided to accumulate income). If the trustees neglect or refuse or are unable to discharge their duty, the court will let them remedy this[224] or will positively have the settlor's intentions carried out, "by appointing new trustees or by authorising or directing representative persons of the classes of beneficiaries to prepare a scheme for distribution, or even, should the proper basis for distribution appear, by itself directing the trustees so to distribute".[225]

**9–196** In the case of distributive powers of appointment, advancement or maintenance, the trustees have a duty to consider from time to time whether or not to exercise the power but they need not exercise the power.[226] So if a power to distribute income to X instead of to trust beneficiaries is not exercised within a reasonable period (in default of a specified period), the power lapses in respect of that income so that the income devolves on the trust beneficiaries entitled in default of a valid exercise of the power.[227]

**9–197** If a trustee's attitude is that she will not bother using any powers to benefit a beneficiary for capricious reasons, the court will intervene to remove the trustee or direct a payment that no trustee could refuse to make unless being spiteful or malicious. This is the ratio of *Klug v Klug*,[228] where legacy duty had to be paid by a beneficiary whose income was insufficient to pay the instalments. One of the trustees (the beneficiary's mother) declined to exercise the power of appointment in her favour to enable her to pay the duty and so she applied to the court. Neville J said[229]:

> When the summons was previously before me, I decided that the trustees could in the exercise of their discretion under the powers of advancement, if they thought fit, advance out of capital a sum sufficient to pay this legacy duty. The public trustee thinks that their discretion should be so exercised, but his co-trustee, the mother, declines to join him in so doing, not because she has considered whether or not it would be for her daughter's welfare, that the advance should be made, but because her daughter has married without her consent, and her letters show, in my opinion, that she has not exercised her discretion at all. . . . In such circumstances, it is the duty of the court to interfere and to direct a sum to be raised out of capital sufficient to pay off . . . the legacy duty.

**9–198** The exercise by trustees of a discretionary power was also considered by Templeman J in his judgment in *Re Manisty's Settlement*.

*Re Manisty's Settlement*

Chancery Division [1974] Ch. 17 at [25]–[27]

**9–199** TEMPLEMAN J.: The court cannot insist on any particular consideration being given by the trustees to the exercise of the power. If a settlor creates a power exercisable in favour of his issue, his relations and the

---

223 [1975] Ch. 25.

224 *Re Locker's Settlement Trusts* [1978] 1 All E.R. 216.

225 *McPhail v Doulton* [1971] A.C. 424 at 451, per Lord Wilberforce.

226 *Re Hay's Settlement Trusts* [1981] 3 All E.R. 786 at 792–793.

227 *Re Allen-Meyrick's WT* [1966] 1 W.L.R. 499.

228 [1918] 2 Ch. 67. See too Re *Lofthouse* (1885) 29 Ch.D. 921 (where trustees had refused to pay maintenance to a beneficiary under a discretionary power and Bacon VC ordered £400 p.a. to be paid; on appeal his order was discharged without more ado since the trustees were agreeable to pay £250 p.a.). There was an interventionist attitude in some 19th century cases concerning powers to benefit a beneficiary, especially if the beneficiary was a ward of court: *Re Hodges* (1878) 7 Ch.D. 754; *Re Roper's Trusts* (1879) 11 Ch.D. 271.

229 *Klug* [1918] 2 Ch. 67 at 71.

employees of his company, the trustees may in practice for many years hold regular meetings, study the terms of the power and the other provisions of the settlement, examine the accounts and either decide not to exercise the power or to exercise it only in favour, for example, of the children of the settlor. During that period the existence of the power may not be disclosed to any relation or employee and the trustees may not seek or receive any information concerning the circumstances of any relation or employee. In my judgment it cannot be said that the trustees in those circumstances have committed a breach of trust and that they ought to have advertised the power or looked beyond the persons who are most likely to be the objects of the bounty of the settlor. The trustees are, of course, at liberty to make further inquiries, but cannot be compelled to do so at the behest of any beneficiary. The court cannot judge the adequacy of the consideration given by the trustees to the exercise of the power, and it cannot insist on the trustees applying a particular principle or any principle in reaching a decision.

If a person within the ambit of the power is aware of its existence he can require the trustees to consider exercising the power and in particular to consider a request on his part for the power to be exercised in his favour. The trustees must consider this request, and if they decline to do so or can be proved to have omitted to do so, then the aggrieved person may apply to the court which may remove the trustees and appoint others in their place. This . . . is the only right and only remedy of any object of the power. . . **9–200**

The court may also be persuaded to intervene if the trustees act "capriciously", that is to say, act for reasons which I apprehend could be said to be irrational, perverse or irrelevant to any sensible expectation of the settlor; for example, if they chose a beneficiary by height or complexion or by the irrelevant fact that he was a resident of Greater London . . . [Reasonable] trustees will endeavour, no doubt, to give effect to the intention of the settlor in making the settlement and will derive that intention not from the terms of the power necessarily or exclusively, but from all the terms of the settlement, the surrounding circumstances and their individual knowledge acquired or inherited . . . [They] have an absolute discretion and cannot be obliged to take any form of action, save to consider the exercise of the power and a request from a person who is within the ambit of the power. **9–201**

Exceptionally in the pensions fund context the courts have themselves been prepared positively to exercise fiduciary powers to augment pensions of beneficiaries where there is no one who can exercise the power, the employer-trustee being a company in liquidation and the liquidator being in the irreconcilable position of acting for the creditors interested in a non-exercise of the power to benefit the ordinary beneficiary-members of the pension scheme, while simultaneously acting as trustee required to look after such members' interests.[230] The court[231] acts in the manner in which a reasonable trustee could be expected to act in the light of all the material circumstances so as to do what is just and equitable. **9–202**

One accepts this in the pensions context where the member-beneficiaries have earned their entitlements as deferred pay and as settlors have some justified expectations that powers to augment their entitlement out of surpluses will be seriously considered for exercising in certain circumstances. In the private family trust context, however, where the trustees are in a position to exercise their powers in favour of persons who are not beneficiaries at all but only objects of a power of appointment, and the trustees choose not to exercise them, stating that they have fairly considered exercising their powers but have chosen not to, then one might expect that should be the end of the matter. **9–203**

However, in *Schmidt v Rosewood Trust Ltd*[232] Lord Walker asserted the court's inherent jurisdiction to supervise, and if necessary to intervene in, the administration of trusts, whether dealing with the rights of beneficiaries under discretionary trusts or the rights of objects of fiduciary powers of appointment. Thus, in an extreme case where, in the light of the settlor's letters of wishes, the trustees are **9–204**

230 *Mettoy Pension Trustees Ltd v Evans* [1990] 1 W.L.R. 1587; *Bridge Trustees Ltd v Noel Penny (Turbines) Ltd* [2008] Pens. L.R. 345; *Scully v Coley* [2009] UKPC 29 at [29].

231 *Thrells Ltd v Lomas* [1993] 1 W.L.R. 456. Now, under Pensions Act 1995 s.25(2) an independent person as trustee exists to exercise the power.

232 [2003] 2 A.C. 709 at [51].

not exercising their fiduciary powers of appointment in the manner intended by the settlor, the trustees can be replaced by more amenable trustees or even a particular exercise of the power could be directed by the court if it would be perverse to any sensible expectation of the settlor to exercise—or no rational trustee could possibly exercise—the power other than in the directed fashion.[233]

## *B. The Doctrine of Fraud on a Power*[234]

9–205 The doctrine of "fraud on a power" provides that the donee of a power may not exercise it in order to produce a result that is contrary to the purposes of the donor. The language of "fraud" is misleading in this context as it is possible for the donee to commit a fraud on the power although she acts in good faith. In *Vatcher v Paull* Lord Parker said that[235]:

> The term [fraud] in connection with frauds on a power does not necessarily denote any conduct on the part of the appointor amounting to fraud in the common law meaning of the term or any conduct which could properly be termed dishonest or immoral. It merely means that the power has been exercised for a purpose, or with an intention, beyond the scope of or not justified by the instrument creating the power.

9–206 A trustee would fall foul of the doctrine if she purported to exercise a power to achieve a purpose that was impermissible on the face of the power. For example, she might purport to appoint property to a person who was not a beneficiary.[236] A trustee might also commit a fraud on a power if she purported to exercise it in a way that produced a permissible outcome on its face, but with the bad faith intention of achieving a larger purpose that was impermissible. For example, it could constitute a fraud on a power for trustees to appoint property to a beneficiary who has previously agreed to apply the property for the benefit of a person who is not an object, as in *Wong v Burt*.[237] Or again, as Lord Parker noted in *Vatcher*,[238] it would constitute a fraud on a power for a father to exercise a power of appointment in favour of his child, although such an appointment is basically valid,[239] if he does so when the child is ill and with the intention of taking the child's estate for himself on the child's death—and in such a case, the appointment will constitute a fraud on the power even if the child subsequently recovers.[240]

### *Wong v Burt*

### New Zealand Court of Appeal [2005] 1 N.Z.L.R. 91

9–207 HAMMOND J.: The essential facts relating to this issue can be shortly stated.

9–208 Clause 5 of William Wong's will, in summary, provided as follows:

- The residuary estate was to be held in trust with the net annual income payable to Estelle Wong until her death.
- After the death of Estelle Wong, the net annual income was to be payable in equal shares to those of Phillipa and Wong Liu Sheung who were still alive. It is of singular importance to this case that

---

233 cf. *Klug v Klug* [1918] 2 Ch. 67.

234 See P. Matthews, "The Doctrine of Fraud on a Power, Parts 1 and 2" [2007] P.C.B. 131 and 191.

235 [1915] A.C. 372 at 378. See too *Duke of Portland v Topham* (1864) 11 H.L. Cas. 32 at 54.

236 *Kain v Hutton* [2008] 3 N.Z.L.R. 589 at [18].

237 [2005] 1 N.Z.L.R. 91. See too *Lane v Page* (1755) Amb. 233; *Re Turner's Settled Estates* (1884) 28 Ch.D. 205; *Re Greaves* [1954] Ch. 434. But cf. *Netherton v Netherton* [2000] W.T.L.R. 1171, followed in *Re X Trust* (2003) 5 I.T.E.L.R. 119; *Kain v Hutton* [2008] 3 N.Z.L.R. 589.

238 *Vatcher* [1915] A.C. 372 at 379–380.

239 See too *Henty v Wrey* (1882) 21 Ch.D. 232.

240 See too *Lord Hinchbrooke v Seymour* (1789) 1 Bro. C.C. 395.

there was no substitutionary provision in favour of grandchildren, if one of those daughters predeceased Estelle; in that event, all the income was to be paid to the other surviving daughter.

- After the death of the last surviving child, the estate is to be distributed among the children, or grandchildren, or great grandchildren of Phillipa. The exclusion of Wong Liu Sheung's children appears to have been quite deliberate, as a result of a family falling out.

Clause 6 of the will conferred upon the trustees a discretion to pay to Estelle, out of the capital of the estate: **9–209**

> ". . . such sum or sums as they in their absolute discretion may think fit if they shall consider it necessary, desirable or expedient so to do by reason of the state of my wife's health or her desire to travel or to acquire a home or by reason of a fall in the purchasing power of money or for any other reasons whatsoever whether similar or dissimilar to the foregoing."

When Phillipa Wong died in 1995 Mrs Estelle Wong became concerned as to the position of Mei-Ling and Matthew. She viewed the inability of these two children to take their mother's share of the estate income, in the event of their mother's death, as inappropriate, and unfair. **9–210**

To overcome this disability, in 1996 the trustees distributed $250,000 of the capital of the William Wong estate to Estelle. Estelle then lent this sum of $250,000 to the Phillipa Estelle Wong Trust (PEW Trust). The beneficiaries of PEW are Mei-Ling and Matthew. **9–211**

In effecting this payment of $250,000, the trustees relied on their powers under clause 6 of the will. The debt was then periodically forgiven over a period of years, and by this will. **9–212**

**The Claim in the High Court**

Wong Liu Sheung bought proceedings in the High Court claiming that, in so proceeding, the trustees: **9–213**

- had acted ultra vires the terms of the trust;
- breached their duty to exercise their discretion for a proper purpose; and
- breached their duty to act impartially and even handedly towards all classes of beneficiaries.

**The Judgment in the High Court**

Ronald Young J. dismissed this claim, in its entirety, in a judgment delivered on 6 May 2003. . . . **9–214**

**The Grounds of Appeal**

Ms Peters argued that the exercise of the discretion by the trustees in the impugned respect was for an improper purpose. This submission rested essentially on two propositions. First, that the sole purpose of the exercise of the discretion was to "remedy" a perceived inequality that had arisen under clause 5 of the will (the appellants really say as a device to circumvent the plain meaning of clause 5). Second, that the distribution made was to benefit a person who was not an object of the clause 6 discretion (i.e. not Estelle). **9–215**

As to remedies, Ms Peters submitted that the $250,000 can be traced to the PEW Trust, and as such, the trustees of that trust hold the funds as constructive trustees for the William Wong estate. **9–216**

Alternatively, the appellants submit that the trustees are personally liable. The essential issue both under clause 13 of the will (the exoneration provision) and s.73 is whether the trustees acted dishonestly. The appellants submit that the trustees' actions, particularly when they were specifically warned that the will prohibited the course of conduct proposed, amounted (at least) to "recklessness". . . . **9–217**

**The Law**

The notion of a fraud on a power itself rests on the fundamental juristic principle that any form of authority may only be exercised for the purposes conferred, and in accordance with its terms. This principle is one of general application. **9–218**

The particular expression, a "fraud on a power", applies to both a power and a discretion. The word "fraud" here denotes an improper motive, in the sense that a power given for one purpose is improperly used for another purpose. **9–219**

Over the years a number of attempts have been made to categorise the circumstances in which a fraud on a power will arise. For instance, Hanbury and Martin, *Modern Equity*[241] divides the cases into **9–220**

---

[241] 16th edn, 2001, p.188.

three categories. The first arises where the appointment is made as a result of a prior agreement or bargain with the appointee as to what he or she will do with the proceeds. Secondly, there are those cases where the power is exercised improperly so as to benefit the appointor. The third category are those cases in which an appointment is drafted so that the intent appears to benefit objects of the power, but the real intent is to benefit non-objects.

9–221 These distinctions are useful for analytic and descriptive purposes, but it is necessary to recall that the sine qua non which makes the exercise of a discretion or power "improper" is the improper intention of the person exercising it. The central principle is that if the power is exercised with the intention of benefiting some non-object of the discretionary power, whether that person is the person exercising it, or anybody else for that matter, the exercise is void. If, on the other hand, there is no such improper intention, even although the exercise does in fact benefit a non-object, it is valid.[242]

9–222 In the case of a discretionary power to be exercised in favour of one of its objects, but in the "hope" that the recipient will benefit a non-object, the validity of such an exercise will depend upon whether the recipient had legal and moral freedom of action.[243]

9–223 The case law in this area is difficult, not so much for the underlying principles, which seem plain enough, but in their application to often quite complex estates, or interrelated transactions. Assume, for instance, a case in which a discretionary power is exercisable in favour of an adult male (X) who states that, if it is in fact exercised in his favour, he will give part of the relevant fund to his parents, Y and Z, who are not objects of the discretionary power. If the true intention of the appointment is to benefit the parents, the exercise is invalid. If that is not the case, but X is under some distinct pressure to benefit Y and Z, the exercise would also be invalid.[244] On the other hand, if X has genuine freedom of action and wishes to give Y and Z a benefit, then it appears that the exercise of the power would be good.[245]

9–224 As to the effect of a finding of a fraud on a power, it has long been held that where a power is successfully impugned, its exercise is totally invalid,[246] unless the improper element in the appointment can be severed from the remainder of that appointment.[247]

**This Case**

9–225 It is necessary at this point to add some further facts. On the evidence, Mrs Estelle Wong was devastated by the death from cancer of her daughter Phillipa, in August of 1995. Phillipa was then only 43 years old, and Matthew and Mei-Ling were teenagers. Estelle was very close to Phillipa. Although Phillipa's family were in Australia, Estelle spoke regularly to Phillipa, and she would frequently go to Australia to visit her daughter.

9–226 On one occasion, after she had returned from Australia, Estelle expressed concern to Mr Burt (who is now a retired chartered accountant and had a long association with the Wong family) "about the effect of Bill Wong's will". Estelle suddenly came to appreciate that, under the will, Phillipa's share of the income would not pass to her children.

9–227 It was in those circumstances that advice was sought from Chapman Tripp on this issue. It seems that it was Mr Burt who calculated various figures, and "concluded that $250,000 would partly redress the situation and should be loaned to the PEW Trust, and successively forgiven". As Mr Burt put it, "the purpose of the loan and forgiveness programme was to restore the expected benefit that Mei-Ling and Matthew would have received on their mother's death had they been entitled under Bill's will to her life interest in the PW Estate Trust. . . .

9–228 In their opinion (which was disclosed to the Court) Chapman Tripp advised that clause 5 must be read in "its plain words". The solicitors said, "In other words there is no statutory remedy to allow Phillipa's two children to receive the income that she would have received". The solicitors then detailed three options which, as they saw it, were "available to remedy this matter". One was to resort to the discretionary power available to the trustees under clause 6 of the will, which "[Estelle] could then invest in [her] own name". Estelle could then amend her will to provide for that sum to be left equally to Mei-Ling and Matthew. Secondly, the capital sum received from the estate could be loaned to the PEW Trust and then, on Estelle's

242 See *Vatcher v Paull* [1915] A.C. 372 at 378, per Lord Parker.

243 *Birley v Birley* (1858) 25 Beav. 299.

244 *Re Dick* [1953] Ch. 343.

245 *Re Marsden's Trusts* (1859) 4 Drew. 594; and see Parker and Mellows, *The Modern Law of Trusts* (8th edn, Oakley), p.222.

246 *Re Cohen* [1911] 1 Ch. 37.

247 *Topham v Duke of Portland* (1858) 1 De G.J. & S. 517.

death, the assets of that trust automatically vest in Mei-Ling and Matthew. A third option was identified as being an interest-free loan from the husband's estate, but repayable on Janice's death.

Although some disadvantages in each of these alternatives were identified, it was at no point suggested by the solicitors that the potential difficulties relating to a fraud on a power might have to be addressed in relation to the first option. **9–229**

The evidence in the case in this respect is well documented and quite clear. In summary, on Phillipa's premature death, Mrs Estelle Wong became concerned that there was no gift-over provision as to income for Phillipa's children. A member of Chapman Tripp recorded in a file note: "this is of great concern to Mrs Wong and although she accepts that her late husband may never have anticipated their daughter predeceasing Mrs Wong she is adamant that it would have been his intention for Phillipa's share of the income to pass to her children". Thus it was that a scheme was settled by Mrs Wong, with the trustees, and after taking legal advice, which had the overt and pre-determined idea that the trustees would utilise clause 6 of the will to avoid the effect of clause 5 of the will, in the circumstances which had arisen. This exercise was not undertaken as a distinct, or separate advance to Mrs Wong or in the "hope" that Estelle Wong would benefit a non-object. The exercise was already constrained by a pre-considered course of action which also avoided Mrs Estelle Wong having to resort to any assets under her control or direction to assist her grandchildren. **9–230**

In our view, this deliberate, and pre-conceived, device amounted to a fraud on the power. If Mrs Estelle Wong had simply been advanced the money out of the estate and had then exercised genuine freedom of action to benefit the children (as for instance by setting up a trust for them), that would not have been unlawful. But what was knowingly erected was a deliberate scheme to subvert the terms of the will. What was overlooked was that the property was vested in those entitled in default of the exercise of the power, subject to its being divested by a proper exercise of the power in clause 6, and the steps in fact taken gave rise to a fraud on those entitled in default. **9–231**

*Held*: to the extent that the $250,000 could not be recovered by tracing into the PEW Trust, the trustees were personally accountable and were not protected by an exemption clause which provided that they should "not liable for any loss not attributable to dishonesty". **9–232**

To determine what the proper purpose of a power is, the courts will refer to the settlor's (objectively understood) expectations,[248] although trustees must beware of slavishly following a settlor's directions and exercising no independent judgment of their own as this could lead to a finding that the purported trust is a sham.[249] **9–233**

If a personal power is released so as to benefit the person entitled in default of the exercise of such power so that she can then benefit the person who has released the power, this is outside the fraud on a power doctrine, the person who released the power not being in a conflict of interest situation and the default beneficiary being the owner of the property (subject to divestment by exercise of the power) and capable of dealing with it as she likes.[250] However, if the donee of a personal power of appointment positively exercises it, then like the donee of a fiduciary power, she is subject to the fraud on a power doctrine, since it would constitute a wrong against those entitled in default of appointment for the donee to exercise the power for an improper purpose.[251] **9–234**

In *Pitt v Holt*,[252] Lloyd LJ aligned the doctrine of fraud on a power with the rule that power-holders cannot validly act outside the scope of their authority. This was consistent with *Cloutte v Storey*,[253] in **9–235**

---

[248] *Re Manisty's Settlement* [1974] Ch. 17 at 26; *Re Hay's Settlement Trusts* [1982] 1 W.L.R. 202 at 209; *Re Beatty's Will Trusts* [1990] 1 W.L.R. 1503 at 1506.

[249] See paras 4–057—4–067.

[250] *Re Somes* [1896] 1 Ch. 250. Similarly revocation of a revocable appointment made under a personal special power of appointment, even coupled with a release of the power, falls outside the fraud on a power doctrine unless the revocation is solely for the purpose of making a new appointment which is a fraud on the power: *Re Greaves* [1954] Ch. 434.

[251] *Mettoy Pension Trustees Ltd v Evans* [1990] 1 W.L.R. 1587 at 1613–1614, citing *Re Mills* [1930] 1 Ch. 654 and *Re Greaves* [1954] Ch. 434. See too *Hillsdown Holdings Plc v Pensions Ombudsman* [1997] 1 All E.R. 862.

[252] [2012] Ch. 132 at [96]–[98].

[253] [1911] 1 Ch. 18.

which Farwell LJ held that transactions entered in fraud on a power are void (like purported exercises of a power which the supposed power-holder does not possess). However, Lloyd LJ expressed some unhappiness with Farwell LJ's decision,[254] and this was echoed by Lord Walker when *Pitt* went to the Supreme Court.[255] The cause of their unhappiness was Farwell LJ's definition of "voidness" which appears rather to describe voidability. He said this[256]:

> If an appointment is void at law, no title at law can be founded on it; but this is not so in equity: the mere fact that the appointment is void does not prevent a Court of Equity from having regard to it: e.g., an appointment under a limited power to a stranger is void, but equity may cause effect to be given to it by means of the doctrine of election.

It appears that Lloyd LJ and Lord Walker would both have preferred to say that fraud on a power renders transactions voidable, i.e. that they validly transfer legal title to property unless they are retrospectively rescinded.[257] This would be consistent with cases such as *Hunter v Senate Support Services Ltd*[258] which hold that a company director's exercise of power for an improper purpose is "voidable", unlike her purported exercise of a power which she does not possess, which is "void".

## C. The Rule in *Hastings-Bass*[259]

**9–236** The case from which the rule in *Hastings-Bass* takes its name did not apply the rule in the form which it now takes, after a series of cases starting with *Mettoy Pension Trustees Ltd v Evans*[260] and culminating in *Pitt v Holt*.[261] For this reason, as Lord Walker said in *Pitt*, "the label 'the rule in *Hastings-Bass*' is a misnomer"[262]; however, he also said that it "is by now so familiar that it is best to continue to use it" and so we will follow that practice, while hoping that future courts will prefer to speak of "the 'rule in *Pitt v Holt*'".

**9–237** *Re Hastings-Bass (Deceased)*[263] concerned a tax avoidance scheme that went wrong. Hastings-Bass had a life interest under a settlement. Under applicable inheritance tax legislation, estate duty of 75 per cent was payable on any property in which he had a life interest at the time of his death. To avoid this, the trustees used their power under the Trustee Act 1925 s.32 to advance property out of the settlement into a second settlement created by Hastings-Bass's sister, on trust for Hastings-Bass's son for life, with remainder interests to the son's children. This would have worked but for the House of Lords' later decision in a case about perpetuities, *Pilkington v IRC*.[264] The effect of this decision was that all of the interests in the sub-settlement of the fund in *Hastings-Bass*, other than the son's life interest, were void for perpetuity. Following Hastings-Bass's death, the Revenue argued that there had been no valid exercise of the trustees' power of advancement, because their purported exercise of the power had produced a result different from the one they had intended. Hence the sub-settlement had been a nullity, Hastings-Bass's life interest in the fund had continued until his death, and estate duty was payable.

---

254 [2012] Ch. 132 at [98]: not "as cogent as that judge's decisions so often are".
255 [2013] 2 A.C. 108 at [62]: "may have to be revisited some day".
256 ibid., at [31].
257 The proprietary effects of rescission are discussed at paras 18–250—18–252.
258 [2005] 1 B.C.L.C. 175 at 173–179, cited with other authorities in P.L. Davies and S. Worthington, *Gower and Davies' Principles of Modern Company Law*, 9th edn (Sweet & Maxwell, 2012), p.533, n.114.
259 See M. Ashdown, *Trustee Decision Making: The Rule in Re Hastings-Bass* (Oxford University Press, 2015).
260 [1990] 1 W.L.R. 1587.
261 [2013] 2 A.C. 108.
262 ibid., at [1].
263 [1975] Ch. 25.
264 [1964] A.C. 612 at 639.

The Court of Appeal held as a matter of law that where a trustee acts in good faith the court should not hold his action to be ineffective[265]: 9–238

> notwithstanding that it does not have the full effect which he intended, unless (1) what he has achieved is unauthorised by the power conferred on him or (2) it is clear that he would not have acted as he did (a) had he not taken into account considerations which he should not have taken into account or (b) had he not failed to take into account considerations which he ought to have taken into account.

The Revenue argued that this test was satisfied, and that the court should therefore hold that the sub-settlement had been ineffective, because the trustees would not have appointed property into the sub-settlement if they had known that the remainder interests would be void for perpetuity. However the Court of Appeal held that even if the trustees had known this, they would still have advanced the capital in order to benefit Hastings-Bass's son for his life as this would itself have achieved the tax saving which the trustees had sought to achieve. Hence the appointment had been valid to the extent that it had benefited the son, Hastings-Bass had had no interest at the time of his death because he had disposed of it to his son, and the tax was not payable.

The Court of Appeal's statement of the circumstances in which the courts will treat the exercise of powers by trustees as ineffective was framed in a negative way—"the courts will not interfere unless"—but their formulation of principle was taken out of context and put into a positive form in *Mettoy Pension Trustees v Evans* where Warner J said that[266]: 9–239

> where a trustee acts under a discretion given to him by the terms of the trust, the court *will interfere* with his action if it is clear that he would not have acted as he did had he not failed to take into account considerations which he ought to have taken into account.

This positive formulation of the rule (or some variant of it) was then successfully invoked by trustees in a series of cases to escape the unforeseen tax consequences of transactions they had entered, in some cases on negligent advice received from their tax advisors.[267] By winning a declaration that such transactions should be set aside, the trustees were able to avoid paying the tax, obviating the need for them to sue their advisors for negligence, and for their advisors to claim on their insurance policies. For more than a decade HMRC made no attempt to intervene in these cases, but it came to be felt in many quarters that (in Lord Neuberger's memorable phrase) it was unfair for "Doctor Equity [to] administer a magical morning-after pill to trustees suffering from post-transaction remorse, but not to anyone else".[268] In two conjoined appeals, *Pitt v Holt* and *Futter v Futter*,[269] the Supreme Court then took corrective action to limit the scope of the *Hastings-Bass* rule. 9–240

*Pitt v Holt; Futter v Futter*

Supreme Court [2013] 2 A.C. 108

These were conjoined appeals from two cases where the rule in *Hastings-Bass* had been successfully invoked at first instance. In *Pitt v Holt*, Pitt was injured in a road accident and received compensation. His wife was appointed as a receiver on his behalf under the Mental Health Act 1983, and the decisions she 9–241

---

265 [1975] Ch. 25 at 41.

266 [1990] 1 W.L.R. 1587 at 1621 (emphasis added).

267 e.g. *Abacus Trust Co (Isle of Man) Ltd v NSPCC* [2001] S.T.C. 1344; *Green v Cobham* [2002] S.T.C. 820; *Burrell v Burrell* [2005] S.T.C. 569; *Sieff v Fox* [2005] 1 W.L.R. 3811; *Jiggens v Low* [2010] S.T.C. 1899.

268 Lord Neuberger, "Aspects of the Law of Mistake: *Re Hastings-Bass*" (2009) 15 T. & T. 189, 192. See also *Breadner v Granville- Grossman* [2001] Ch. 523 at [61]; *Futter v Futter* [2010] S.T.C. 982 at [1].

269 [2013] 2 A.C. 108.

took in this capacity were subject to the same rules as decisions taken by a trustee. She decided, on advice, to put the money into a settlement that was worded in such a way that a significant inheritance tax charge would be triggered on Pitt's death. This result could easily have been avoided if the trust instrument had been worded in a slightly different way.

9–242 *Futter* concerned an offshore trust which held stockpiled gains. On advice, losses were triggered within the settlement with a view to setting these off against the gains when they were distributed to the beneficiary onshore. However, the trustees' advisors who had recommended this course of action had overlooked the Taxation of Chargeable Gains Act 1994, s 2(4), which prevented offsetting in this way. Hence a significant tax charge was incurred when the distributions were made.

9–243 In both cases,[270] the judges at first instance held that the rule in *Hastings-Bass* applied and that the relevant transactions would be rescinded with the result that no tax was payable. HMRC appealed, and the Court of Appeal held in both cases that the claims for relief based on the rule in *Hastings-Bass* should fail.[271] Lloyd L.J. held that the *Hastings-Bass* rule applies only where the trustees have breached a duty to consider all and only relevant considerations when exercising their discretion, and that trustees do not breach this duty in cases where they act on advice given by professional advisers who have been selected with reasonable care.

9–244 The Court of Appeal's decision on this point was upheld by the Supreme Court, but in *Pitt* the court also held that Mrs Pitt could rescind the settlement on the ground of mistake; rescission for mistake was not pleaded in *Futter*. The following excerpt is concerned only with the application of the rule in *Hastings-Bass* to both cases. The portion of Lord Walker's judgment concerning rescission of the settlement in *Pitt* on the ground of mistake is reproduced at paras 18–254—18–281.

LORD WALKER (with whom LORD NEUBERGER, BARONESS HALE, LORD MANCE, LORD CLARKE, LORD SUMPTION and LORD CARNWATH agreed):

**Introduction**

9–245 These appeals raise important and difficult issues in the field of equity and trust law. Both appeals raise issues about the so-called rule in *Hastings-Bass*. One appeal (*Pitt v Holt*) also raises issues as to the court's jurisdiction to set aside a voluntary disposition on the ground of mistake. It is now generally recognised that the label "the rule in *Hastings-Bass*" is a misnomer. The decision of the Court of Appeal in *Re Hastings-Bass, decd*[272] can be seen, on analysis, to be concerned with a different category of the techniques by which trust law controls the exercise of fiduciary powers. That decision is concerned with the scope of the power itself, rather than with the nature of the decision-making process which led to its being exercised in a particular way.[273] The rule would be more aptly called "the rule in *Mettoy*", from the decision of Warner J. in *Mettoy Pension Trustees Ltd v Evans*.[274] But the misnomer is by now so familiar that it is best to continue to use it, inapposite though it is.

9–246 As *Mettoy's* case illustrates, the rule is concerned with trustees who make decisions without having given proper consideration to relevant matters which they ought to have taken into consideration. It has also been applied to other fiduciaries (in *Pitt v Holt* Mrs Pitt was acting as a receiver appointed by the Court of Protection). *Mettoy's* case was concerned with the rules of an occupational pension scheme, as are some other cases on the rule. But since the turn of the century there have been several cases concerned with family trusts, and in particular with tax-planning arrangements involving trusts, where the arrangements have for one reason or another proved unexpectedly disadvantageous, and the court has been asked to restore the status quo ante under the *Hastings-Bass* rule. . .

9–247 [Lord Walker reviewed the case-law, and explained the facts and first instance decisions in the cases at issue, before turning to the decision of the Court of Appeal:] I have already indicated my general agreement with Lloyd L.J.'s judgment on the *Hastings-Bass* issue [with which Longmore and Mummery LJJ agreed] . . . In the core of his judgment Lloyd L.J. correctly spelled out the very important distinction between an error by trustees in going beyond the scope of a power (for which I shall use the traditional term "excessive execution") and an error in failing to give proper consideration to relevant matters in making

---

270 *Pitt v Holt* [2010] 1 W.L.R. 1199; *Futter v Futter* [2010] S.T.C. 982.
271 [2012] Ch. 132.
272 [1975] Ch. 25.
273 See R.C. Nolan, "Controlling Fiduciary Power" [2009] C.L.J. 293, especially pp. 294–295, 306–309.
274 [1990] 1 W.L.R. 1587.

a decision which is within the scope of the relevant power (which I shall term "inadequate deliberation"). *Hastings- Bass* and *Mettoy* were, as he rightly observed, cases in quite different categories. The former was a case of excessive execution and the latter might have been, but in the end was not, a case of inadequate deliberation. . .

Lloyd L.J. then addressed the difficult question of how a fraudulent appointment (that is, an appointment ostensibly within the scope of a power, but made for an improper purpose) is to be fitted into the classification. The exercise of an equitable power may be fraudulent in this sense whether or not the person exercising it is a fiduciary. A well-known example of trustees exercising a power for an improper purpose is provided by *Re Pauling's S.T.*,[275] in which a power ostensibly exercisable for the benefit of young adult beneficiaries was used to distribute trust capital to be frittered away on their improvident parents' living expenses. **9–248**

There is Court of Appeal authority that a fraudulent appointment is void rather than voidable: *Cloutte v Storey*.[276] In that case the appointee under an improper appointment had charged his equitable interest as security for a loan (and in doing so made two false statutory declarations as to the genuineness of the appointment). It was held that the lender had no security, even though it had no notice of the equitable fraud. It is an authority which has bedevilled discussion of the true nature of the *Hastings-Bass* rule. Lightman J. in *Abacus Trust Co (Isle of Man) v Barr*[277] found the judgment of Farwell L.J. problematic and Lloyd L.J. shared his reservations.[278] So do I. It is hard to know what to make of Farwell L.J.'s observations:[279] **9–249**

> "If an appointment is void at law, no title at law can be founded on it; but this is not so in equity: the mere fact that the appointment is void does not prevent a Court of Equity from having regard to it: eg, an appointment under a limited power to a stranger is void, but equity may cause effect to be given to it by means of the doctrine of election."

The decision in *Cloutte v Storey* may have to be revisited one day. For present purposes it is sufficient to note that a fraudulent appointment (that is, one shown to have been made for a positively improper purpose) may need a separate pigeon-hole somewhere between the categories of excessive execution and inadequate deliberation.

Lloyd L.J. considered the duties of trustees in exercising their discretion, and in particular the relevance of tax considerations.[280] He referred to some well-known authorities including *Re Baden's Deed Trusts*.[281] That case was directly concerned with the correct test for certainty of objects of a discretionary trust (or trust power) but the speech of Lord Wilberforce contains[282] a general discussion of fiduciary discretions which has been very influential in the development of the law. This includes a passage[283] as to the court's intervention if trustees fail to exercise a trust power (that is, a discretion which it is their duty to exercise in some way). After referring to Lord Upjohn's opinion Lord Wilberforce said: **9–250**

> "I would venture to amplify this by saying that the court, if called upon to execute the trust power, will do so in the manner best calculated to give effect to the settlor's or testator's intentions. It may do so by appointing new trustees, or by authorising or directing representative persons of the classes of beneficiaries to prepare a scheme of distribution, or even, should the proper basis of distribution appear by itself directing the trustees so to distribute."

Lloyd L.J. did not refer to that particular passage, but Warner J. had done so in *Mettoy's* case,[284] since in that case a decision as to the exercise of the power to augment benefits would have to be taken by someone. The passage serves as a reminder that where trustees have been in breach of duty by exercising

---

275 [1964] Ch. 303.
276 [1911] 1 Ch. 18.
277 [2003] Ch. 409 at [31].
278 [2012] Ch. 132 at [98].
279 [1911] 1 Ch. 18 at 31.
280 At [102]–[118].
281 [1971] A.C. 424.
282 At 448–457.
283 At 456–457.
284 [1990] 1 W.L.R. 1587 at 1617–1618.

a discretion with inadequate deliberation, setting aside their decision may not be the only course open to the court.

9–251 . . . Lloyd L.J.[285] reaffirmed the view that he had expressed in *Sieff v Fox* that "fiscal consequences may be relevant considerations which the trustees ought to take into account".[286] I agree. In the private client world trusts are mostly established by and for wealthy families for whom taxes (whether on capital, capital gains or income) are a constant preoccupation. It might be said, especially by those who still regard family trusts as potentially beneficial to society as a whole, that the greater danger is not of trustees thinking too little about tax, but of tax and tax avoidance driving out consideration of other relevant matters.

9–252 That is particularly true of offshore trusts. They are usually run by corporate trustees whose officers and staff (especially if they change with any frequency) may know relatively little about the settlor, and even less about the settlor's family. The settlor's wishes are always a material consideration in the exercise of fiduciary discretions. But if they were to displace all independent judgment on the part of the trustees themselves (or in the case of a corporate trustee, by its responsible officers and staff) the decision-making process would be open to serious question. . .

9–253 It is a striking feature of the development of the *Hastings-Bass* rule that it has led to trustees asserting and relying on their own failings, or those of their advisers, in seeking the assistance of the court . . . There may be cases in which there is for practical purposes no other suitable person to bring the matter before the court, but I agree with Lloyd L.J.'s observation[287] that in general it would be inappropriate for trustees to take the initiative in commencing proceedings of this nature. They should not regard them as uncontroversial proceedings in which they can confidently expect to recover their costs out of the trust fund.

9–254 Lloyd L.J. stated the correct principle, as he saw it [as follows]:[288]

> "It seems to me that the principled and correct approach to these cases is, first, that the trustees' act is not void, but that it may be voidable. It will be voidable if, and only if, it can be shown to have been done in breach of fiduciary duty on the part of the trustees. If it is voidable, then it may be capable of being set aside at the suit of a beneficiary, but this would be subject to equitable defences and to the court's discretion. The trustees' duty to take relevant matters into account is a fiduciary duty, so an act done as a result of a breach of that duty is voidable. Fiscal considerations will often be among the relevant matters which ought to be taken into account. However, if the trustees seek advice (in general or in specific terms) from apparently competent advisers as to the implications of the course they are taking, and follow the advice so obtained, then, in the absence of any other basis for a challenge, I would hold that the trustees are not in breach of their fiduciary duty for failure to have regard to relevant matters if the failure occurs because it turns out that the advice given to them was materially wrong. Accordingly, in such a case I would not regard the trustees' act, done in reliance on that advice, as being vitiated by the error and therefore voidable."

*The requirement for breach of duty*

9–255 . . . [Mr Robert Ham QC's] submissions centred on whether the court's jurisdiction under the *Hastings-Bass* rule is exercisable only if there is a breach of fiduciary duty on the part of the trustees (or other relevant fiduciary). He argued that this is a novel requirement which leads to arbitrary and unfair distinctions, especially in cases where incorrect advice on tax has been given by professional advisers who may or may not themselves be trustees. Mr Ham also had subsidiary but important arguments about the attribution to trustees of fault on the part of their advisers, and about the identification of relevant considerations for the purposes of the rule.

9–256 Mr Ham contended that the supposed need for establishing a breach of fiduciary duty, before the *Hastings-Bass* rule can come into play, was a novel requirement introduced in 2003 by Lightman J. in his judgment in *Barr's* case.[289] . . . In my view Lightman J. was right to hold that for the rule to apply the inadequate deliberation on the part of the trustees must be sufficiently serious as to amount to a breach of fiduciary duty. Breach of duty is essential (in the full sense of that word) because it is only a breach of duty on the part of the trustees that entitles the court to intervene . . . It is not enough to show that the trustees'

285 [2012] Ch. 132 at [115].
286 [2005] 1 W.L.R. 3811 at [86].
287 At [130]
288 At [127].
289 [2003] Ch. 409 at [16]–[20].

deliberations have fallen short of the highest possible standards, or that the court would, on a surrender of discretion by the trustees, have acted in a different way. Apart from exceptional circumstances (such as an impasse reached by honest and reasonable trustees) only breach of fiduciary duty justifies judicial intervention.

. . . Mr Ham's fallback position was that if a breach of duty was an essential requirement, there could be a breach without fault on the part of any individual trustee being established . . . It is undoubtedly correct that trustees may be liable for breach of trust even though they have acted in accordance with skilled professional advice. Such advice cannot protect trustees from potential liability for a loss to the trust fund resulting from a decision that is, judged objectively, beyond the trustees' powers and detrimental to the trust (though professional advice may lead to their obtaining relief under section 61 of the Trustee Act 1925). An example mentioned in argument is *Dunn v Flood*,[290] in which trustees had sold by auction 73 plots of freehold land at Reading, subject to special conditions which the court held to be severely depreciatory (as Fry L.J. put it,[291] "eminently calculated to frighten away purchasers"). The Court of Appeal, upholding North J., refused to force a doubtful title on a reluctant purchaser. The fact that the trustees had consulted respectable solicitors was no excuse. It was not a reasonable exercise of discretion.[292] But the trustee's breach of duty was not in the manner of their decision-making (as to which we know nothing other than that they consulted respectable solicitors) but the loss to the trust property that their unreasonable decision appeared to have caused. **9–257**

Further examples are provided by the decision of the Court of Appeal in *Perrins v Bellamy*[293] and that of the Privy Council, on appeal from the Supreme Court of Victoria, in *National Trustees Co of Australasia Ltd v General Finance Co of Australasia Ltd*.[294] These cases, discussed by Lloyd L.J. [in] his judgment,[295] were both examples of action taken by trustees on professional advice which was unequivocally incorrect: one a sale of leaseholds when the trustees had no power of sale; the other a distribution (resulting from "some extraordinary slip" by solicitors of high standing) of a deceased beneficiary's vested share to persons who were not entitled to it under the intestacy law of Victoria in force at the beneficiary's death. As Lloyd L.J. observed, the issue in these cases: **9–258**

> "is altogether different, as it seems to me, from the question whether, if trustees take advice properly, and act on that advice in a matter which is within their powers, the fact that the advice has misled them as to the true position in a relevant respect means that they acted in breach of fiduciary duty."

I respectfully agree. Trustees may be liable, even if they have obtained apparently competent professional advice, if they act outside the scope of their powers (excessive execution), or contrary to the general law (for example, in the Australian case, the law regulating entitlement on intestacy). That can be seen as a form of strict liability in that it is imposed regardless of personal fault. Trustees may also be in breach of duty in failing to give proper consideration to the exercise of their discretionary powers, and a failure to take professional advice may amount to, or contribute to, a flawed decision-making process. But it would be contrary to principle and authority to impose a form of strict liability on trustees who conscientiously obtain and follow, in making a decision which is within the scope of their powers, apparently competent professional advice which turns out to be wrong. **9–259**

Such a result cannot be achieved by the route of attributing any fault on the part of professional advisers to the trustees as their supposed principals. Solicitors can and do act as agents in some clearly defined functions, usually of a ministerial nature, such as the receipt and transmission of clients' funds, and the giving and taking of undertakings on behalf of clients. But they do not and may not act as agents in the exercise of fiduciary discretions . . . **9–260**

. . . In *Futter v Futter* Mr Cutbill, a partner in a London firm of solicitors, was involved both as a trustee and as a solicitor advising the trustees. The facts as to his involvement were found at first instance by Norris J.[296] It so happened, as already mentioned, that the judgment of Mr Engelhart Q.C. in *Pitt v Holt* was **9–261**

---

[290] (1885) 28 Ch. D. 586.
[291] Ibid. at 594.
[292] Ibid. at 592 per Baggallay and Bowen L.JJ. and at 593-4 per Fry L.J.
[293] [1899] 1 Ch 797.
[294] [1905] AC 373.
[295] At [124].
[296] [2010] S.T.C. 982.

given on 18 January 2010, the first day of the hearing in *Futter v Futter*. In *Pitt v Holt* it had been common ground[297] that there was no need to identify a breach of duty by the trustees. It is not clear from Norris J.'s judgment whether the same incorrect concession was made and accepted before him. But Norris J. seems to have accepted *Sieff v Fox* as the leading authority from which to obtain guidance, and *Barr's* case received only a passing mention . . . in his judgment. Norris J. did not therefore make any clear finding about breach of fiduciary duty. He simply recorded and accepted Mr Cutbill's written evidence, which included the statement that "[Mr Futter] and I failed to pay any regard to the provisions of section 2(4) [TCGA] at the time, and therefore failed to consider the full tax implications".

**9–262** The Court of Appeal was therefore in as good a position as Norris J. to make a finding about breach of duty on the part of the trustees. This court has before it all the written evidence and exhibits that were before the judge, and in the absence of concurrent findings below it is also in a position to make findings, if necessary, on that issue. I will return to it below when dealing with the disposal of the *Futter* appeal.

**9–263** Finally, on this part of the case, there is the submission that the trustees' duty to take account of relevant considerations is to be interpreted as a duty to act on advice only if it is correct—in effect, a duty to come to the right conclusion in every case. I have left this submission until the end because it is to my mind truly a last-ditch argument. It involves taking the principle of strict liability for ultra vires acts . . . out of context and applying it in a different area, so as to require trustees to show infallibility of judgment. Such a requirement is quite unrealistic. It would tip the balance much too far in making beneficiaries a special favoured class, at the expense of both legal certainty and fairness. It is contrary to the well-known saying of Lord Truro L.C. in *Re Beloved Wilkes's Charity*[298]

> "that in such cases as I have mentioned it is to the discretion of the trustees that the execution of the trust is confided, that discretion being exercised with an entire absence of indirect motive, with honesty of intention, and with a fair consideration of the subject. The duty of supervision on the part of this court will thus be confined to the question of the honesty, integrity, and fairness with which the deliberation has been conducted, and will not be extended to the accuracy of the conclusion arrived at, except in particular cases."

The trustees' duty does not extend to being right ("the accuracy of the conclusion arrived at") on every occasion. . .

**9–264** As a first footnote on the topic of fault, I would mention that in his judgment,[299] Lloyd L.J. observed that a claim by beneficiaries against trustees may often be precluded by an exoneration clause in the trust instrument. Mr Philip Jones Q.C. (for the Revenue) disputed this, pointing out that even if a trustee is exonerated from liability to pay equitable compensation, he is still liable to injunctive relief to prevent a threatened breach of trust, and personal and proprietary remedies may be available against persons who receive assets distributed in breach of trust. Moreover an exoneration clause does not protect a trustee against removal from office by order of the court. The Futter No. 3 and No. 5 settlements contain exoneration clauses in conventional terms, stating that "in the professed execution of the trusts and powers hereof no trustee shall be liable for a breach of trust arising from a mistake or omission made by him in good faith". I would not treat that clause as ousting the application of the *Hastings-Bass* rule, if it were otherwise applicable.

**9–265** As a second footnote, there was some discussion in the course of argument as to the significance, in situations of this sort, of a possible claim for damages against professional advisers for financial loss caused by incorrect advice (or incorrect implementation of instructions). Mr Nugee referred to *Walker v Geo H Medlicott & Son*,[300] in which a strong Court of Appeal dismissed on two grounds a claim for damages for professional negligence in preparing a will. The second ground was that the aggrieved claimant's proper course was to mitigate his damage by seeking rectification of the will. That decision may reflect the court's view of the particular facts of the case, and the feeling that if the drafting of the will had gone wrong other beneficiaries under it should not obtain adventitious benefits. In principle the possibility that trustees may have a claim for damages should have no effect on the operation of the *Hastings-Bass* rule. In practice it will be rare for trustees to have so strong a claim that they can be confident of obtaining a full indemnity for their beneficiaries' loss and their own costs. In the *Pitt* case this court was told that

---

[297] [2010] 1 W.L.R. 1199 at [22].
[298] (1851) 3 Mac. & G. 440 at 448.
[299] At [128].
[300] [1999] 1 W.L.R. 727.

the claim against Frenkel Topping has been settled. Had it gone to trial the claim, even if successful in establishing duty and breach, might have faced difficulties over causation, since Mrs Pitt executed the SNT under the authority of an order of the Court of Protection, which had considered its terms. That court's apparent lack of awareness of the importance of section 89 of the Inheritance Tax Act 1984 is one of the most remarkable features of the whole sorry story. . .

*Void or voidable?*

Counsel on both sides readily admitted that they had hesitated over this point, but in the end they were all in agreement that Lloyd L.J. was right in holding that[301] 9–266

> "if an exercise by trustees of a discretionary power is within the terms of the power, but the trustees have in some way breached their duties in respect of that exercise, then (unless it is a case of a fraud on the power) the trustees' act is not void but it may be voidable at the instance of a beneficiary who is adversely affected."

In my judgment that is plainly right, and in the absence of further argument on the point it is unnecessary to add much to it. The issue has been clouded, in the past, by the difficult case *Cloutte v Storey*,[302] a case on appointments that are fraudulent in the equitable sense, that is made for a positively improper purpose. Here we are concerned not with equitable fraud, nor with dispositions which exceed the scope of the power, or infringe the general law (such as the rule against perpetuity). We are in an area in which the court has an equitable jurisdiction of a discretionary nature, although the discretion is not at large, but must be exercised in accordance with well-settled principles. . .

*Disposal of the Hastings-Bass issues*

In *Futter v Futter* the essential issue was whether the trustees of the No. 3 and No. 5 settlements, in deciding to take the steps which they took in March and April 2008, failed in their duty to take relevant considerations into account. Capital gains tax was a relevant consideration. Indeed, it is fairly plain that it was the paramount consideration, and the trustees thought about it a great deal. But the tax advice which they received and acted on was wrong, because an amendment to section 2(4) of TCGA had been overlooked. As Lloyd L.J. put it succinctly: "They did not overlook the need to think about CGT. They were given advice on the right point. The problem was that the advice was wrong."[303] 9–267

The only complication was that Mr Cutbill (the solicitor-trustee) was a member of both teams: the solicitors giving the erroneous advice, and the trustees receiving and acting on it. I agree with the Court of Appeal that it would be artificial to distinguish between the two trustees, who acted together in making and effectuating their decisions. I would if necessary go further and hold that the documentary evidence indicates that most if not all of the technical tax advice given by his firm came not from Mr Cutbill but from the assistant solicitor who was working with him, from January 2008, in a review of a number of different Futter family settlements. Until 27 March 2008 it was supposed, wrongly, that the No. 3 settlement's stockpiled gains were relatively small, and the fact that they amounted to about £188,000 led to a last-minute change of plan. On 28 March 2008 there was a telephone conversation between the assistant solicitor and Mr Bunce, Mr Futter's accountant, at which, without reference to Mr Cutbill, she definitely confirmed that Mr Futter's personal losses could be set off against the section 87 gains. Mr Cutbill seems to have been, very properly, reluctant to put the blame on a junior member of his firm, and of course his firm must take legal responsibility for any actionable mistake by any of its fee-earners. But the documents in exhibit "CDC 1" to Mr Cutbill's witness statement tend to confirm that he should not, as a trustee of the No. 3 and No. 5 settlements, be treated as having been personally in breach of fiduciary duty. 9–268

In *Pitt v Holt* the position was even clearer. As her husband's receiver under the Mental Health Act 1983 Mrs Pitt was in a fiduciary position but there is no suggestion that she had any professional qualifications. She devoted herself, alternating with a carer, to looking after her disabled husband. As anyone in that position would, she took professional advice from solicitors and specialist consultants. After hearing from her legal advisers and the Official Solicitor the Court of Protection made an order on 1 September 1994 authorising (not directing) her to execute the SNT and she acted on that authority on 1 November 1994 . . . She 9–269

---

301 At [99].

302 [1911] 1 Ch. 18.

303 At [138].

> had taken supposedly expert advice and followed it. There is no reason to hold that she personally failed in the exercise of her fiduciary duty. Unfortunately the advice was unsound.
>
> 9–270 I would therefore dismiss the appeal in *Futter v Futter*, and the appeal in *Pitt v Holt* so far as it turns on the *Hastings-Bass* rule.

**9–271** Some points should be made about this decision. First, Lord Walker followed Lloyd LJ in characterising *Re Hastings-Bass* itself as a case of "excessive execution" rather than as a case of "inadequate deliberation". Their reason was that the Court of Appeal had decided the case "on the ground that the advancement, so far as not struck down by the rule against perpetuities, must stand unless it could not, in that attenuated form, reasonably be regarded as beneficial to the advancee".[304] This meant that Buckley LJ had stated the ratio of *Hastings-Bass* too broadly in his judgment,[305] and so there had never been a real foundation for *Mettoy* and the cases which followed in its wake.

**9–272** Secondly, Lord Walker and Lloyd LJ both considered that the so-called "rule in *Hastings-Bass*", as it had evolved following *Mettoy*, was enabling trustees and their beneficiaries to escape the consequences of botched tax avoidance schemes too easily. The device they adopted to limit the scope of the rule, drawing on Lightman J's decision in *Abacus Trust Co (Isle of Man) Ltd v Barr*,[306] was to hold that it applies only when the trustees' failure to exercise their powers properly amounts to a breach of their duty to consider all and only relevant matters, and that trustees do not breach this duty where, in Lloyd LJ's words, they "seek advice (in general or in specific terms) from apparently competent advisers as to the implications of the course they are taking, and follow the advice so obtained".[307] The effect of this finding is that the rule in *Hastings-Bass* can no longer be invoked in many cases that would formerly have fallen within its scope, because the trustees have taken advice from apparently competent advisers. If the advice was negligent, the trustees can sue their advisers for tort or breach of contract.[308] Otherwise there is no remedy.

**9–273** In the Court of Appeal, Lloyd LJ said that "the trustees' duty to take relevant matters into account is a fiduciary duty",[309] meaning that it is a duty which they owe in their capacity as trustees. This explained why the court intervenes when they breach the duty, in the exercise of its supervisory jurisdiction over trust affairs. Given that he agreed with Lloyd LJ's reasoning, this must also have been what Lord Walker meant when he said that "the inadequate deliberation on the part of the trustees must be sufficiently serious as to amount to a breach of fiduciary duty."[310] We must therefore hope that in future cases his words are not taken out of context and misinterpreted to mean that the trustees must have breached some other duty, e.g. their duty to exercise their judgment in the exclusive interest of their principals[311] (suggesting incorrectly that the rule in *Hastings-Bass* applies only where there has been a conflict of interest),[312] or their duty of care (suggesting incorrectly that the exercise of discretionary dispositive powers can be impugned for having been made carelessly).[313]

---

304 [2013] 2 A.C. 108 at [24], affirming [2012] Ch. 132.

305 In the passage quoted above at para.9–238.

306 [2003] Ch. 409. In *Sieff v Fox* [2005] 1 W.L.R. 3811, Lloyd LJ had previously declined to follow Lightman J on this point, but in *Pitt v Holt* he changed his mind.

307 [2012] Ch. 132 at [127].

308 As to which, see T. Rosen Peacocke, "Liability of Professionals Retained by Settlors and Trustees following *Pitt v Holt/Futter v Futter*" (2011) 27 P.N. 200.

309 [2012] Ch. 132 at [127].

310 [2013] 2 A.C. 108 at [73].

311 For which, see paras 9–018ff.

312 Moreover, as Richard Nolan points out in (2013) 129 L.Q.R. 469, 470, "the conflicts rules already provide for a transaction that was made in conflict of duty and interest to be prima facie voidable, so the [rule in *Hastings-Bass*] would be redundant if limited to breaches of fiduciary duty in that narrow sense."

313 This is Richard Wilson's understanding of the duty in [2014] P.C.B. 20, 22. We agree with him that a trustee might owe a

Thirdly, Lloyd LJ envisaged that a broad spectrum of matters might be relevant to the exercise of a discretionary power, but understandably did not wish to be prescriptive as to what these might be as the circumstances of cases are various. He identified tax matters, the settlor's wishes and the beneficiaries' wishes, circumstances and needs.[314] Other cases have identified other matters material to the exercise of particular powers.[315] Further cases will no doubt provide further examples. **9–274**

Fourthly, in a passage of his judgment that was endorsed by Lord Walker, Lloyd LJ said that "one practical consequence" of his reconceptualisation of the rule in *Hastings-Bass* as turning on a breach of duty would be that[316]: **9–275**

> if in future it is desired to challenge an exercise by trustees of a discretionary power on this basis, it will be necessary for one or more beneficiaries to grasp the nettle of alleging and proving a breach of fiduciary duty on the part of the trustees. Only rarely would it be appropriate for the trustees to take the initiative in the proceedings. . .

It might be thought that trustees who have not acted fraudulently, and who are protected by an exemption clause from compensatory liability,[317] would have no financial reason to fear bringing proceedings with a view to establishing their own breach of duty (though reputational considerations might deter them from doing so). One might also have thought that if trustees were to bring such litigation this would be consistent with cases which hold that they not only have the power to sue one another for their breaches of duty but also have a positive duty to do so.[318] However, while the Trustee Act 2000 s.31 entitles trustees to recover expenses incurred in the course of trust business out of the trust fund, they are not usually entitled to be indemnified for their costs where they are successfully sued for breach of duty.[319] Could the trustees ask for a *Beddoe* order,[320] i.e. permission to bring proceedings on the basis of a pre-emptive indemnity out of the estate for their costs? Lord Walker seems to have ruled this out, stating that trustees "should not . . . confidently expect" to get one.[321]

Fifthly, if the absolutely entitled legal owner of property decides to do something with her property that triggers adverse tax consequences, she may well be unable to go back on this decision afterwards and say that it does not count. Why should trust beneficiaries be entitled to more favourable treatment when their trustees do the same thing? The answer given by trust lawyers is that the beneficiaries are vulnerable to flawed exercises of power by trustees, but arguably that is a problem for them that is internal to the trust relationship into which the settlor has put them, and it should be dealt with by giving them an action against the trustees. *Pitt* makes it harder for trustees and beneficiaries to use the rule in *Hastings-Bass*, but it remains controversial that they should be allowed to use it under any circumstances, given that other taxpayers are not so privileged.[322] **9–276**

---

duty to take care when gathering information prior to taking her decision – and indeed when communicating her decision to an agent after it has been made (cf. *Abacus Trust Co (Isle of Man) v Barr* (2003] Ch. 409)—but we do not agree that the exercise of a discretionary dispositive power is itself an action that can be tested against a standard of care. Further discussion in Ashdown, *Trustee Decision Making: The Rule in Re Hastings-Bass* (2015), paras 4.08ff.

314 [2012] Ch. 132 at [114]–[118].

315 e.g. *Edge v Pensions Ombudsman* [2000] Ch. 602 at 626–627, listing matters that could be relevant to pension trustees deciding whether to exercise a power to increase benefits.

316 [2012] Ch. 132 at [130].

317 As to which see paras 10–201ff.

318 *Walker v Symonds* (1818) 3 Swans. 1 at 71–72; *Butler v Butler* (1877) 7 Ch. D. 116; *Carson v Sloane* (1884) 13 L.R. Ir. 139 at 147; *Young v Murphy* [1996] 1 V.R. 279.

319 See para.8–076.

320 Named for *Re Beddoe* [1893] 1 Ch. 547.

321 [2013] 2 A.C. 108 at [69].

322 M. Bhandari, "Undoing Transactions for Tax Purposes: The *Hastings-Bass* Principle" in S. Elliott, B. Häcker and C. Mitchell (eds), *Restitution of Overpaid Tax* (Hart Publishing, 2013).

## 9. Delegation of Duties and Powers

### A. Introduction

9-277 The law's attitude towards the delegation of trustee duties has shifted over time. The classical rule of equity was *delegatus non potest delegare* ("a delegate is not able to delegate"), reflected in Langdale MR's comment in *Turner v Corney*[323] that:

> trustees who take on themselves the management of property for the benefit of others have no right to shift their duty on other persons; and if they employ an agent, they remain subject to the responsibility towards their cestuis que trust, for whom they have undertaken the duty.

In other words, trustees owed a continuing duty to account for the trust property to the beneficiaries that could not be discharged by transferring the property into the hands of an agent. If trustees did this, and the agent dealt with the property to good effect, then the beneficiaries could ratify the trustees' acts; but if the agent absconded with the property or negligently lost it, then the beneficiaries could hold the trustees liable to account for its value because the transfer to the agent was an unauthorised transaction that would be struck out on a taking of accounts—i.e. the accounts would be "falsified" to show that the transfer had never taken place, leaving the trustees with an ongoing duty to hold the property for the beneficiaries that they would have to perform substitutively by paying its market value into the trust fund.[324]

9-278 By the 1880s, however, the courts had become concerned that this rule operated too harshly against trustees who needed to be able to delegate their investment functions to professionals with expertise in investing in an increasingly sophisticated financial marketplace. Hence in *Speight v Gaunt*[325] the Court of Appeal, affirmed by the House of Lords, held that trustees had an implied authority to delegate their managerial responsibilities to an agent if, in the circumstances, delegation was either reasonably necessary or in the ordinary course of affairs. If these conditions were satisfied then the trustees would owe no continuing duty to account for property transferred to the agent. However, the trustees still had to be prudent in their selection and supervision, and could not employ an agent to do an act outside the scope of the agent's normal business.[326] It followed that the trustees could still be made liable for loss arising through an agent's default if they failed to exercise reasonable care in selecting and supervising the agent.[327] Moreover, they would not be relieved from such liability by an express or statutory provision[328] authorising a wide use of agents in ministerial matters and exempting them from liability for loss caused by the acts or defaults of an agent unless the loss occurred through the trustees' "wilful default".[329]

9-279 The Trustee Act 1925 radically enlarged trustees' collective powers to delegate implementation of their decisions to an agent because s.23(1) enabled them to delegate whether or not there was any reasonable need for this, and lazy trustees could therefore delegate matters they could have seen to personally. However, they could not delegate the exercise of their own discretion to decide what

---

323 (1841) 5 Beav. 515 at 517.

324 *Attorney General v Scott* (1749) 1 Ves. Sen. 413 at 417; *Clough v Bond* (1838) 3 My. & Cr. 440 at 496–497; *Rowland v Witherden* (1851) 3 Mac. & G. 568. Falsification of accounts and substitutive performance claims are discussed in Ch.10.

325 (1883) 22 Ch.D. 727, affirmed (1883) 9 App. Cas. 1; discussed in C. Stebbings, *The Private Trustee in Victorian England* (Cambridge University Press, 2001), Ch.5, esp. pp.151–155.

326 *Fry v Tapson* (1884) 28 Ch.D. 268.

327 *Matthews v Brise* (1845) 10 Jur. (O.S.) 105.

328 *Underwood v Stevens* (1816) 1 Mer. 712; Trustee Act 1925 s.30(1). The position is now governed by the Trustee Act 2000 s.23.

329 *Re Brier* (1884) 26 Ch.D. 238 at 243 per Lord Selborne LC Also see *Re Chapman* [1896] 2 Ch. 763 at 776 per Lindley LJ: "Wilful default which includes want of ordinary prudence on the part of the trustees must be proved." In *Speight v Gaunt* (1883) 9 App. Cas. 1 at 13–15, 22–23, the HL treated wilful default as including want of ordinary prudence.

should be done except, as before, in the case of managing overseas property (although under s.23(2) they could now do this whether or not there was any reasonable necessity for it).

Following the enactment of the 1925 legislation, it was uncertain whether trustees still owed a duty to select and supervise agents with the care of the prudent business person. Traditionalists considered that they did, and would be liable if they were personally guilty of wilful default in the traditional equitable sense which covered deliberate, reckless and negligent conduct.[330] Modernists believed in a literal, rather than a history-based, interpretation of s.23(1) so that in cases where use of agents was permissible trustees should not be personally "responsible for the default of any such agent if employed in good faith", although there could be personal liability for trustees guilty of wilful default in the common law sense of deliberate or reckless conduct.[331] In *Armitage v Nurse*,[332] the Court of Appeal, without full consideration of the arguments favouring the traditional approach, accepted the modernists' interpretation. **9–280**

## *B. Collective Delegation under the Trustee Act 2000*

The Trustee Act 2000 ss.11 to 27 confer the following powers on trustees collectively, subject to the following duties, and subject also to any restriction or exclusion imposed by the trust instrument or by any other legislation.[333] **9–281**

### i. Agents

#### Trustee Act 2000 s.11

**Power to employ agents**

(1) Subject to the provisions of this Part, the trustees of a trust may authorise any person to exercise any or all of their delegable functions as their agent. **9–282**

(2) In the case of a trust other than a charitable trust, the trustees' delegable functions consist of any function other than—

(a) any function relating to whether or in what way any assets of the trust should be distributed,

(b) any power to decide whether any fees or other payment due to be made out of the trust funds should be made out of income or capital,

(c) any power to appoint a person to be a trustee of the trust, or

(d) any power conferred by any other enactment or the trust instrument which permits the trustees to delegate any of their functions or to appoint a person to act as a nominee or custodian.

(3) In the case of a charitable trust, the trustees' delegable functions are—

(a) any function consisting of carrying out a decision that the trustees have taken;

(b) any function relating to the investment of assets subject to the trust (including, in the case of land held as an investment, managing the land and creating or disposing of an interest in the land);

(c) any function relating to the raising of funds for the trust otherwise than by means of profits of a trade which is an integral part of carrying out the trust's charitable purpose;

(d) any other function prescribed by an order made by the Secretary of State.

---

330 G.H. Jones, "Delegation by Trustees: A Reappraisal" (1959) 22 M.L.R. 381; J.H. Stannard, "Wilful Default" [1979] Conv. 345.

331 *Re Vickery* [1931] 1 Ch. 572.

332 [1998] Ch. 241.

333 Trustee Act 2000 s.26.

(4) For the purposes of subsection (3)(c) a trade is an integral part of carrying out a trust's charitable purpose if the profits are applied solely to the purposes of the trust and either—

(a) the trade is exercised in the course of the actual carrying out of a primary purpose of the trust, or
(b) the work in connection with the trade is mainly carried out by beneficiaries of the trust.

**9-283** It will be seen that s.11 is concerned with trustees' management or administrative functions, and not their discretionary distributive functions. It extends to a sole trustee,[334] but not to trustees of authorised unit trusts,[335] nor to enable pension trustees to delegate investment functions.[336]

## Trustee Act 2000 s.12

**Persons who may act as agents**

**9-284** (1) Subject to subsection (2), the persons whom the trustees may under section 11 authorise to exercise functions as their agent include one or more of their number.
(2) The trustees may not authorise two (or more) persons to exercise the same function unless they are to exercise the function jointly.
(3) The trustees may not under section 11 authorise a beneficiary to exercise any function as their agent (even if the beneficiary is also a trustee).
(4) The trustees may under section 11 authorise a person to exercise any function as their agent even though he is also appointed to act as their nominee or custodian (whether under section 16, 17 or 18 or any other power).

**9-285** It is important that the trustees can employ one of themselves for particular tasks so long as she is not a beneficiary, there then being conflict of interest possibilities with a beneficiary-agent being vulnerable to the charge of preferring her own interests to those of other beneficiaries. Exceptionally under s.9(1) of the Trusts of Land and Appointment of Trustees Act 1996:

> The trustees of land may, by power of attorney, delegate to any beneficiary or beneficiaries of full age and beneficially entitled to an interest in possession in land subject to the trust any of their functions as trustees which relate to the land.

This power of attorney may be for any period or indefinite,[337] must be given by all the trustees jointly, may be revoked by any one or more of them and will be revoked by the appointment of a new trustee.[338] Such power can be exercised to enable a life tenant to decide upon sale or lease of the land but cannot enable the life tenant to receive or give receipts for capital money,[339] two trustees being required for this purpose[340] (considering the practical danger of permitting an income beneficiary to receive capital moneys). Beneficiaries exercising delegated functions are in the same position as trustees (with the same duties and liabilities) but are not regarded "as trustees for any other purposes (including the purposes of any enactment permitting the delegation of functions by trustees or imposing requirements relating to the payment of capital money)".[341]

---

334 Trustee Act 2000 s.25.
335 Trustee Act 2000 s.37.
336 On which see the Pensions Act 1995 ss.34–36.
337 Trusts of Land and Appointment of Trustees Act 1996 (TOLATA) s.9(5).
338 TOLATA s.9(3).
339 TOLATA s.9(7).
340 Law of Property Act 1925 s.27; Trustee Act 1925 s.14.
341 TOLATA s.9(7).

As to be expected, an agent employed under s.11 to carry out a function (e.g. investment) is made subject to the same duties and restrictions attached to the function (e.g. having regard to the standard investment criteria) as if the trustees themselves were exercising the function.[342] **9–286**

## Trustee Act 2000 s.15

**Asset management: special restrictions**

(1) The trustees may not authorise a person to exercise any of their asset management functions as their agent except by an agreement which is in or evidenced in writing. **9–287**

(2) The trustees may not authorise a person to exercise any of their asset management functions as their agent unless—

  (a) they have prepared a statement that gives guidance as to how the functions should be exercised ("a policy statement"), and

  (b) the agreement under which the agent is to act includes a term to the effect that he will secure compliance with—

    (i) the policy statement, or

    (ii) if the policy statement is revised or replaced under section 22, the revised or replacement policy statement.

(3) The trustees must formulate any guidance given in the policy statement with a view to ensuring that the functions will be exercised in the best interests of the trust.

(4) The policy statement must be in or evidenced in writing.

(5) The asset management functions of trustees are their functions relating to—

  (a) the investment of assets subject to the trust,

  (b) the acquisition of property which is to be subject to the trust, and

  (c) managing property which is subject to the trust and disposing of, or creating or disposing of an interest in, such property.

Section 15 authorises the useful, if not essential, practice of employing a discretionary portfolio manager; it also extends to employing an estate agent to sell a trust property at the best price. Note that the section applies to all asset management delegation, whether under the Act or otherwise (e.g. under the terms of the trust instrument). **9–288**

## Trustee Act 2000 s.14

**Terms of agency**

(1) Subject to subsection (2) and sections 15(2) and 29 to 32, the trustees may authorise a person to exercise functions as their agent on such terms as to remuneration and other matters as they may determine. **9–289**

(2) The Trustees may not authorise a person to exercise functions as their agent on any of the terms mentioned in subsection (3) unless it is reasonably necessary for them to do so.

(3) The terms are—

  (a) a term permitting the agent to appoint a substitute;

  (b) a term restricting the liability of the agent or his substitute to the trustees or any beneficiary;

  (c) a term permitting the agent to act in circumstances capable of giving rise to a conflict of interest.

---

[342] Trustee Act 2000 s.13.

9–290 It will be seen that an objective test of what is "reasonably necessary" in all the circumstances applies to use of s.14 to authorise the potentially detrimental terms specified in s.4(3). An express power may liberally permit trustees to authorise any terms if the trustees subjectively bona fide believe such terms to be reasonably necessary in the best interests of the beneficiaries. It is doubtful whether a term ousting the liability of an agent (e.g. by excluding some otherwise applicable duty) is covered as "a term restricting the liability of" an agent[343] although, in any event, it may be difficult to justify any such ouster as "reasonably necessary".

9–291 In engaging a discretionary portfolio manager it may well be reasonably necessary to permit it to appoint a substitute for a foreign portfolio of shares, to permit it to exclude liability for negligence, to permit it as a market-maker in shares in a particular company to sell such shares to the trustees and to permit it to place business with a subsidiary or associated company entitled to charge for its services. At the time of the engagement it will be good practice for the trustees to record the factors making them consider that particular terms were reasonably necessary.

## Trustee Act 2000 s.32

**Remuneration and expenses of agents, nominees and custodians**

9–292 (1) This section applies if, under a power conferred by Part IV or any other enactment or any provision of subordinate legislation, or by the trust instrument, a person other than a trustee has been—

(a) authorised to exercise functions as an agent of the trustees, or
(b) appointed to act as a nominee or custodian.

(2) The trustees may remunerate the agent, nominee or custodian out of trust funds for services if—

(a) he is engaged on terms entitling him to be remunerated for those services, and
(b) the amount does not exceed such remuneration as is reasonable in the circumstances for the provision of those services by him to or on behalf of that trust.

(3) The trustees may reimburse the agent, nominee or custodian out of the trust funds for any expenses properly incurred by him in exercising functions as an agent, nominee or custodian.

9–293 If a trustee has been appointed agent, nominee or custodian, then she can claim properly incurred expenses out of the trust fund, but entitlement to remuneration for her services will be based on a clause in the trust instrument or, otherwise, the Trustee Act 2000 s.29.

9–294 Trustees are under the statutory duty of care[344] when selecting the person who is to act, when determining any terms on which that person is to act, and, if that person is to exercise asset management functions, when preparing a policy statement under s.15, such duty applying whether the appointment is made under the Trustee Act 2000 or otherwise[345] (e.g. under the terms of the trust instrument, except, of course, to the extent that the statutory duty is modified or excluded in the trust instrument[346]).

9–295 Under the Trustee Act 2000 s.22, while the agent continues to act for the trustees: (a) they must keep under review any arrangements under which the agent acts and how those arrangements are being put into effect; (b) if circumstances make it appropriate to do so, they must consider whether

[343] Ouster of one particular duty, however, may be said to reduce or restrict the overall possible liability of the agent.
[344] Trustee Act 2000 s.1; see para.9–080.
[345] Trustee Act 2000 Sch.1, para.3, and s.21(3).
[346] Trustee Act 2000 Sch.1, para.7.

there is a need to exercise any power of intervention that they have (e.g. a power to revoke the appointment or to give directions to the agent); and (c) if they consider there is a need to exercise such a power, they must do so. The position is the same where trustees of land delegate their functions under s.9 of the Trusts of Land and Appointment of Trustees Act 1996.[347]

In the case of an agent authorised to exercise asset management functions, the trustees' duties include a duty to consider whether there is any need to revise or replace the s.15 policy statement, a duty to revise or replace it if they consider there is such a need, and a duty to assess whether the current policy statement is being complied with.[348] The revision or replacement must be in, or evidenced in, writing and must be formulated with a view to ensuring that the delegated functions will be exercised in the best interests of the beneficiaries as a whole.[349] The statutory duty of care applies to the exercise of these supervisory duties. **9–296**

In deciding whether or not to exercise their powers of delegation under the Trustee Act 2000 the trustees can suit themselves and do not need to prove it was reasonably necessary to exercise the power or that exercise of the power was in the best interests of the beneficiaries. However the statutory duty of care applies to trustees of land when they decide whether or not to delegate any of their extensive functions under s.9 of the Trusts of Land and Appointment of Trustees Act 1996 to a beneficiary with an interest in possession[350]—because the extensive powers conferred upon such a beneficiary can be exercised with little restraint and much impact. **9–297**

### ii. Nominees and Custodians

The need for speedy settlement of share dealings within three days, the introduction of dematerialised holding and transfer of shares via the London Stock Exchange CREST system, and the use of computerised clearing systems in other financial markets make it vital that trustees are given broad powers to use nominees and custodians. These are contained in ss.16, 17 and 18 of the Trustee Act 2000. **9–298**

Trustees are under the statutory duty of care when selecting the nominee or custodian and determining its terms of engagement, whether under the Trustee Act 2000 or otherwise[351] (e.g. under the trust instrument, unless it provides otherwise). They also need to keep under review the arrangements under which the nominee or custodian acts and how those arrangements are being put into effect, considering whether any power of intervention needs to be exercised and then exercising it if called for.[352] The statutory duty of care applies to this reviewing duty[353] but not to deciding whether or not to exercise the powers to utilise the services of custodians or nominees. **9–299**

## *C. Delegation by Individual Trustees*

Section 25 of the Trustee Act 1925 for the first time allowed an individual trustee to delegate all or any of her discretionary functions, whether distributive functions or administrative functions, if she would be absent from the UK for more than a month. The Powers of Attorney Act 1971 then amended s.25 of the 1925 Act so that the facility was generally available to a trustee (whether or not absent abroad for a period) but the period for delegation was confined to 12 months, although another power of attorney **9–300**

---

347 TOLATA s.9A(2)–(5).
348 Trustee Act 2000 s.23(2).
349 Trustee Act 2000 s.15.
350 TOLATA s.9A(1).
351 Trustee Act 2000 s.21(3) and Sch.1 para.3.
352 Trustee Act 2000 s.22.
353 Trustee Act 2000 Sch.1 para.3.

could then forthwith be created for another 12 months and so on, if appropriate. The Trustee Delegation Act 1999 slightly further amended s.25 and repealed s.3(3) of the Enduring Powers of Attorney Act 1985. This subsection had been a last-minute amendment to the 1985 Act, to reverse a particular recent case involving co-owners of land[354] but it accidentally had the vastly greater effect of enabling a trustee by an enduring power of attorney to delegate all her trusteeships to another person for an unlimited period. The 1999 Act further made special provision[355] for co-owners of land so that a trustee who also has a beneficial interest in trust land (or the proceeds thereof) can simply grant an ordinary power of attorney under the Powers of Attorney Act 1971 to her co-owner, enabling such co-owner to make a valid overreaching sale of the land. The amended s.25 of the Trustee Act 1925 is reproduced below.

## Trustee Act 1925 s.25

**Delegation of trustee's functions by power of attorney.**

9-301 (1) Notwithstanding any rule of law or equity to the contrary, a trustee may, by power of attorney, delegate the execution or exercise of all or any of the trusts, powers and discretions vested in him as trustee either alone or jointly with any other person or persons.

(2) A delegation under this section—

(a) commences as provided by the instrument creating the power or, if the instrument makes no provision as to the commencement of the delegation, with the date of the execution of the instrument by the donor; and

(b) continues for a period of twelve months or any shorter period provided by the instrument creating the power.

(3) The persons who may be donees of a power of attorney under this section include a trust corporation.

(4) Before or within seven days after giving a power of attorney under this section the donor shall give written notice of it (specifying the date on which the power comes into operation and its duration, the donee of the power, the reason why the power is given and, where some only are delegated, the trusts, powers and discretions delegated) to—

(a) each person (other than himself), if any, who under any instrument creating the trust has power (whether alone or jointly) to appoint a new trustee; and

(b) each of the other trustees, if any; but failure to comply with this subsection shall not, in favour of a person dealing with the donee of the power, invalidate any act done or instrument executed by the donee.

(5) A power of attorney given under this section by a single donor—

(a) in the form set out in subsection (6) of this section; or

(b) in a form to the like effect but expressed to be made under this subsection, shall operate to delegate to the person identified in the form as the single donee of the power the execution and exercise of all the trusts, powers and discretions vested in the donor as trustee (either alone or jointly with any other person or persons) under the single trust so identified.

(6) The form referred to in subsection (5) of this section is as follows—"THIS GENERAL TRUSTEE POWER OF ATTORNEY is made on [date] by [name of one donor] of [address of donor] as trustee of [name or details of one trust]. I appoint [name of one donee] of [address of donee] to be my attorney [if desired, the date on which the delegation commences or the period for which it continues (or both)] in accordance with section 25 (5) of the Trustee Act 1925. [To be executed as a deed]".

---

354 *Walia v Michael Naughton Ltd* [1985] 1 W.L.R. 1115; *Hansard*, HL Vol.465, cols 548–549 (24 June 1985).

355 Trustee Delegation Act 1999 ss.1, 2, 3.

(7) The donor of a power of attorney given under this section shall be liable for the acts or defaults of the donee in the same manner as if they were the acts or defaults of the donor.
(8) For the purpose of executing or exercising the trusts or powers delegated to him, the donee may exercise any of the powers conferred on the donor as trustee by statute or by the instrument creating the trust, including power, for the purpose of the transfer of any inscribed stock, himself to delegate to an attorney power to transfer, but not including the power of delegation conferred by this section.

The amended s.25 applies to powers of attorney created from 1 March 2000 onwards. The duration of the delegation cannot exceed 12 months reckoned from the specified date or, in default, from the date of execution of the power. It is now possible to delegate to a single co-trustee but, unless this is a trust corporation, such sole attorney-co-trustee can give no valid overreaching receipt for capital moneys arising from a disposition of land.[356] Sub-delegation by the attorney is still prohibited. A statutory short form of attorney is available for use but, if used, a separate one must be used for each trust fund to which the delegation is to apply. However there is nothing to stop a partner in a firm of solicitors who is a trustee of ten trusts from executing one power of attorney delegating to a fellow partner the trusteeship powers of all ten trusts while she takes a period of leave. **9–302**

Delegation under s.25 is intended to be a temporary measure, the donor of the power being automatically liable for the acts and defaults of the donee as if they were the donor's, and also having to give written notification to the person, if any, having power to appoint new trustees and to the donor's co-trustees, who have the same power in default of any such person. They might then consider it more appropriate to replace the donor as trustee. If not, the delegation lasts till the expiry of the 12 months (or shorter specified period) unless the donor earlier dies or becomes mentally incompetent. **9–303**

### Questions

1. What are the connections between the rules on certainty of objects affecting the validity of discretionary trusts and powers of appointment and the rules governing the exercise of powers of appointment by trustees and donees of powers?

2. "There is no general requirement for trustees to give reasons for their actions, but the right to call trustees to account, at least, is an essential characteristic of the trust mechanism." **Discuss.**

3. "The law took a seriously wrong turn when the courts began to let trustees use the rule in *Re Hastings-Bass* to avoid dispositions of trust property with unforeseen tax consequences. In *Pitt v Holt*, the Supreme Court put the law back on the right course." **Discuss.**

4. Five years ago, Sam transferred assets worth £5 million to Vic and Waldo, to hold on trust for Sam himself for his life, and thereafter to hold on a discretionary trust for Sam's children, Rachel and Tom, and their issue. The trust instrument also gives the trustees a power to appoint property out of the trust fund to Eve, Sam's wife.

   At the time of settling the trust, Sam wrote a letter of wishes to the trustees in which he stated: (i) that he would make generous provision to Eve in his will and that after his death the trustees should only exercise their power of appointment in her favour if she found herself in serious financial need; (ii) that he did not want his children to become dependent on the trust and that

356 Trustee Delegation Act 1999 s.7.

he wanted them to make their own way in the world; and (iii) that particular care should be taken in relation to Tom as he was a feckless young man with no ambition beyond spending other people's money.

Three years ago, Sam died. Since then, Vic and Waldo have made regular distributions out of trust income to Rachel, but paid nothing to Tom. Tom has now complained about this, has demanded that they justify their "unfair" attitude towards distributing the trust property, and has said that unless they pay him a sizeable annual income henceforth he will have them replaced as trustees.

Last year Eve remarried. Her new husband, Jeremy, is a highly successful businessman. He has suggested to her, and she has now suggested to Vic and Waldo, that the trustees should appoint £2 million out of the trust fund to Eve which she could then give to Jeremy to invest in his business.

**Advise Vic and Waldo.**

# PART V

# REMEDIES FOR BREACH OF TRUST AND BREACH OF FIDUCIARY DUTY

# 10

# PERSONAL COMPENSATORY LIABILITY OF TRUSTEES FOR BREACH OF TRUST

## 1. Introduction

### A. What is a Breach of Trust?

A breach of trust is any act or omission by a trustee that is contrary to the duties which are imposed upon her by law and are not excluded by the trust instrument.[1] A trustee's breach of fiduciary duty is therefore a breach of trust just like a breach of any other duty owed by the trustee. However, for reasons of expository convenience, compensatory remedies for breach of fiduciary duty are not discussed in this chapter and are treated separately in Chapter 13. **10–001**

A breach of trust can occur in a wide variety of situations. In Millett LJ's words[2]: **10–002**

> A breach of trust may be deliberate or inadvertent; it may consist of an actual misappropriation or misapplication of the trust property or merely of an investment or other dealing which is outside the trustees' powers; it may consist of a failure to carry out a positive obligation of the trustees or merely of a want of skill and care on their part in the management of the trust property; it may be injurious to the interests of the beneficiaries or be actually to their benefit.

Trustees are liable only for their own breaches of duty and are not liable for the breaches of duty of their co-trustees. However, it is a breach of duty for a trustee to leave the trust affairs in the hands of a co-trustee to be dealt with as she sees fit,[3] or to leave trust property in her sole control,[4] or to stand by with knowledge that she is committing a breach of duty,[5] or to do nothing to obtain redress on becoming aware that she has committed a breach of trust,[6] or to retire from being a trustee with the object of facilitating a breach of trust which the remaining, or new, trustees then commit.[7] **10–003**

---

1 Exemption clauses are discussed at para.10–201.

2 *Armitage v Nurse* [1998] Ch. 241 at 250.

3 *Wynne v Tempest* (1897) 13 T.L.R. 360; *Re Lucking's Will Trusts* [1968] 1 W.L.R. 866. This assumes that there has been no proper delegation, e.g. under the Trustee Act 2000 ss.11, 12.

4 *Lewis v Nobbs* (1878) 8 Ch.D. 591. This assumes that the co-trustee is not an authorised nominee or custodian under the Trustee Act 2000 s.19.

5 *Booth v Booth* (1838) 1 Beav. 125; *Gough v Smith* [1872] W.N. 18.

6 *Wilkins v Hogg* (1861) 8 Jur. 25 at 26.

7 *Head v Gould* [1898] 2 Ch. 250; *Kingdom v Castleman* (1877) 36 L.T. 141.

10-004 Trustees who cause the same damage to their beneficiaries by their respective breaches of duty are jointly and severally liable, i.e. the beneficiaries can require two or more of the trustees jointly, or one of them individually, to discharge the whole of their common liability.[8] If a trustee is obliged to pay more than her fair share of a common liability for breach of trust, she can recover a contribution from the others, or require them to reimburse her in full.[9]

## *B. Who Can Sue for a Breach of Trust?*

10-005 Proceedings to have a breach of trust redressed "may be taken by a beneficiary against a trustee or a former trustee or the estate of a former trustee".[10] This includes the beneficiary of a discretionary trust, who can obtain an injunction to compel the proper administration of the trust although her interest is a mere expectancy.[11] Proceedings to redress a breach of trust can also be taken by a trustee against a co-trustee or former trustee,[12] without joining the beneficiaries,[13] and it is no answer to such a claim that the trustee herself participated in the breach.[14] Indeed, trustees are under a positive duty to take action to rectify breaches of duty by other trustees of which they are, or reasonably should be, aware, and failure to do so will itself constitute a breach of duty.[15] Where a beneficiary's equitable interest under a trust is settled on a sub-trust, the trustees of the sub-trust have standing to sue the trustees of the main trust for breach of duty.[16] A party who has no beneficial interest in the trust property has no standing to sue the trustees for breach of trust, even if she has an indirect interest in the trust affairs, e.g. as settlor of the trust or as a beneficiary's relation.

## *C. Remedies for Breach of Trust*

10-006 The focus of discussion in this chapter is on the personal compensatory remedies that can be awarded against a defaulting trustee, i.e. orders that the trustee should pay money to compensate the beneficiaries for loss. Note, however, that other remedies can also be awarded where a trustee has committed a breach of trust.

10-007 For example, where a trustee misapplies trust property, either by taking it for herself or by transferring it to a third party, the beneficiaries may be able to follow and/or trace the property and/or its proceeds into the hands of the trustee or the third party, and they may then be entitled to assert a

---

8 *Charitable Corp v Sutton* (1742) 2 Atk 400 at 406; *Walker v Symonds* (1818) 3 Swan 1 at 75; *Ashurst v Mason* (1875) L.R. 20 Eq. 225 at 233; *Re Duckwari Plc* [1999] Ch. 253 at 262.

9 See paras 10-256ff.

10 *Young v Murphy* [1996] 1 V.R. 279 at 281. See too *Re Cross* (1881) 20 Ch.D. 109; *Space Investments Ltd v Canadian Imperial Bank of Commerce Trust Co. (Bahamas) Ltd* [1986] 1 W.L.R. 1072 at 1074.

11 *Gartside v IRC* [1968] A.C. 553 at 617. See too *Spellson v George* (1987) 11 N.S.W.L.R. 300 at 316, considered in *Schmidt v Rosewood Trust Ltd* [2003] 2 A.C. 709 at [59]–[60]; *Armitage v Nurse* [1998] Ch. 241 at 261; *Johns v Johns* [2004] 3 N.Z.L.R. 202 at [34]; *Whalley v Whalley* [2012] 1 F.L.R. 735 at [112].

12 *Young v Murphy* [1996] 1 V.R. 279 at 281; *Dalriada Trustees Ltd v Woodward* [2012] W.T.L.R. 1489 at [37].

13 *Young* at 283. See too *Greenwood v Wakeford* (1839) 1 Beav 576; *Re Cross* (1881) 20 Ch.D. 109; *Williams v Barton* [1927] 2 Ch. 9; *Montrose Investment Ltd v Orion Nominees Ltd* [2004] W.T.L.R. 133 at [24]. If a trustee pursues proceedings against a co-trustee to judgment, the beneficiaries are generally bound by the outcome of the proceedings and forbidden to bring subsequent proceedings in their own right against the same defendant in respect of the same breach of trust: *Norton v Levy* (1883) 48 L.T. 703 at 704; *Re De Leeuw* [1922] 2 Ch. 540 at 550–551.

14 *Young* at 283. See too *Franco v Franco* (1796) 3 Ves. Jun. 76; *Price v Blakemore* (1843) 6 Beav. 507; *Baynard v Woolley* (1855) 20 Beav. 583 at 585; *Butler v Butler* (1877) 7 Ch.D. 116 at 120–121; *Carson v Sloane* (1884) 13 L.R. Ir. 139 at 147.

15 *Walker v Symonds* (1818) 3 Swans. 1 at 71–72; *Re Forest of Dean Coal Mining Co* (1878) 10 Ch. D. 450 at 451.

16 *Brown v InnovatorOne Plc* [2012] EWHC 1321 (Comm) at [974]–[975], approving the statement to this effect in J. Mowbray, *Lewin on Trusts*, 18th edn (Sweet & Maxwell, 2008), para.42–89.

proprietary claim to the property or its traceable proceeds.[17] In such a case the beneficiaries have a free choice whether to make a proprietary claim against the trustee or to sue her for compensation[18]; they also have a free choice whether to make a proprietary claim against the third party, and there is no rule requiring them to exhaust their remedies against the trustee before they do so.[19]

Trustees who have committed a breach of trust can be removed and new trustees appointed.[20] Judicial trustees and, exceptionally, receivers of trust property[21] can also be appointed, where this is needed to preserve the trust assets and no other remedy (such as appointing new trustees) is feasible. **10–008**

Remedies are also available where the beneficiaries have reasonable grounds for thinking that a trustee will commit a breach of trust in the future if she is not restrained. Prohibitory injunctions can be issued, restraining trustees from committing a breach.[22] Declarations binding on the trustee can be made, setting out the nature and extent of the beneficiaries' interests,[23] or the trustee's duties and powers.[24] A trustee who is uncertain whether a proposed course of action lies within her powers may herself seek prior authorisation from the court,[25] which should act cautiously in such a case, and be mindful that such an order will "deprive the beneficiaries of any opportunity of alleging that [the trustee's action] constitutes a breach of trust and seeking compensation for any loss which may flow from that wrong".[26] **10–009**

Can an award of exemplary damages be made in a case of outrageous misconduct by a trustee? In *Re Brogden*,[27] North J said that "the court will not punish a trustee pecuniarily for his breach of trust except so far as loss has resulted therefrom to the trust estate", and to date no English court has awarded exemplary damages against a defaulting trustee.[28] It was once thought that the English courts could not award exemplary damages in respect of equitable wrongdoing because there was no case pre-dating 1964 where this had been done, as required by the "cause of action" test for the award of exemplary damages laid down in *AB v South West Water Services Ltd*.[29] However, the discrediting **10–010**

---

17 See Ch.12.

18 *Re MF Global U.K. Ltd (No.5)* [2014] Bus. L.R. 1156 at [7]–[8].

19 Denning J, "The Recovery of Money" (1949) 65 L.Q.R. 37, 44; *Hagan v Waterhouse* (1994) 34 N.S.W.L.R. 308 at 369–370; *Foskett v McKeown* [2001] 1 A.C. 102 at 130; *Wong v Burt* (2004) 7 I.T.E.L.R. 263 at [59].

20 See paras 8–045—8–058 and 8–003—8–031 respectively.

21 *Att.-Gen. v Schonfield* [1980] 1 W.L.R. 1182; *Clarke v Heathfield* [1985] I.C.R. 203; *Derby & Co. Ltd v Weldon (Nos 3 and 4)* [1990] Ch. 65 (appointment in aid of a freezing injunction).

22 *Fox v Fox* (1870) L.R. 11 Eq. 142 (improper distribution of assets); *Dance v Goldingham* (1873) L.R. 8 Ch. App. 902; *Buttle v Saunders* [1950] 2 All E.R. 193 (sale of assets at an undervalue); *Walbrook Trustees (Jersey) Ltd v Fattal* [2010] 1 All E.R. (Comm.) 526 (interim injunction restraining disposal of property by trustees before trial).

23 The courts have an unfettered discretion to make binding declarations under CPR r.40.20, but will not normally entertain theoretical questions with no practical application: *Padden v Arbuthnot Pensions and Investments Ltd* [2004] EWCA Civ 582 at [24], [31]. The proper form of a declaration of equitable interest under r.40.20 is discussed in *Powell v Wilshire* [2005] 1 Q.B. 117 at [39]–[45]. The Trusts of Land and Appointment of Trustees Act 1996 s.14(2)(b) enables a person with an interest in property subject to a trust of land to a declaration of the nature or extent of her interest, as in, e.g. *Oxley v Hiscock* [2005] Fam. 211 and *Vinaver v Milton Ashbury Ltd* [2006] W.T.L.R. 1675.

24 *Cowan v Scargill* [1985] Ch. 270; *University of London v Prag* [2014] EWHC 3564 (Ch).

25 By proceedings pursuant to C.P.R. Pt 64.

26 *Richard v Mackay*, Ch.D. 4 March 1987, reported [2008] W.T.L.R. 1667 at 1671 per Millett J. See too *Public Trustee v Cooper* [2001] W.T.L.R. 901 at 922, per Hart J, quoting from an unreported judgment of Robert Walker J given in 1995; *X v A* [2006] 1 W.L.R. 741 at [30]; *Tamlin v Edgar* [2011] EWHC 3949 (Ch) at [25]; *Cotton v Earl of Cardigan* [2015] W.T.L.R. 39.

27 (1886) 38 Ch.D. 546 at 557. See too *Attorney General v Alford* (1855) 4 De G.M. & G. 843; *Vyse v Foster* (1872) L.R. 3 Ch. App. 309 at 333, affirmed (1874) L.R. 7 H.L. 318.

28 The Pensions Act 1995 s.10 permits penalty fines for maladministration of occupational pension schemes, but to date no such fine has been imposed in a reported case.

29 [1993] Q.B. 507. See too Law Commission, *Aggravated, Exemplary, and Restitutionary Damages* (1997), Law Com. No.247, HC Paper No.346 (Session 1997–98), paras [5.54]–[5.56], recommending legislation to give the courts a power to award exemplary damages in relation to breaches of equitable duty. This recommendation has not been acted upon by Parliament.

of this test in *Kuddus v Chief Constable of Leicestershire*[30] means that the English courts could now revisit their position if they wished to do so.

10–011 The Canadian and New Zealand courts have held that an award of exemplary damages can be made in response to a breach of fiduciary duty.[31] In Australia, the leading case on this topic is *Harris v Digital Pulse Pty Ltd*,[32] where Heydon JA opposed the award of exemplary damages for equitable wrongdoing, but Mason P favoured their award in suitable cases. Supporters of the latter view argue that similar cases should not be treated differently merely because they have historically fallen within the separate jurisdictions of the common law and Chancery courts, and that breaches of trust and fiduciary duty resemble torts for which exemplary damages can be awarded.[33]

10–012 It might be countered that to the extent that trustees and other fiduciaries voluntarily assume their duties, breaches of trust and breaches of fiduciary duty more closely resemble breaches of contract, for which exemplary damages are not available under English law.[34] More fundamentally, it can also been argued that exemplary damages should never be awarded and should be abolished in every case because they disrupt the internal rationality of private law by looking outside the relationship between the claimant and the defendant to policy goals of deterrence and punishment that are more appropriately dealt with in the public law sphere.[35]

## 2. Compensation Claims against Trustees

10–013 Equity recognises two different types of compensation claim against trustees, which will be termed substitutive performance claims and reparation claims, adopting terminology that was first proposed by Steven Elliott, some of whose work is excerpted below.[36] Substitutive performance claims are discussed below in part A.[37] They are claims for a money payment as a substitute for performance of the trustees' core obligation to hold and deliver trust assets on demand. Claims of this sort are apposite when trust property has been misapplied, and the amount claimed is the objective value of the property which the trustees should have been able to produce when asked to do so. Reparation claims are discussed below in part B.[38] They are claims for a money payment to make good the damage caused by a breach of trust, and the amount claimed is measured by reference to the loss sustained by the beneficiaries. Claims of this sort are often brought where trustees have carelessly mismanaged

---

30 [2002] 2 A.C. 122.

31 Canada: *Norberg v Wynrib* [1992] 2 S.C.R. 226; *KM v HM* [1992] 3 S.C.R. 6; *Whiten v Pilot Insurance Co* [2002] 1 S.C.R. 595; *Chudy v Merchant Law Group* (2008) 300 D.L.R. (4th) 56. New Zealand: *Aquaculture Corp v New Zealand Green Mussel Co. Ltd* [1990] 3 N.Z.L.R 299; *Cook v Evatt (No.2)* [1992] 1 N.Z.L.R. 676.

32 (2003) 56 N.S.W.L.R. 298.

33 e.g. A. Burrows, "Remedial Coherence and Punitive Damages in Equity" in S. Degeling and J. Edelman (eds), *Equity in Commercial Law* (Law Book Company, 2005).

34 *Johnson v Unisys Ltd* [2003] 1 A.C. 518 at [15]; *Devenish Nutrition Ltd v Sanofi-Aventis S.A.* [2009] Ch. 390 at [143].

35 A. Beever "The Structure of Aggravated and Exemplary Damages" (2003) 23 O.J.L.S. 87.

36 See paras 10–015—10–019. The fullest account of Elliott's work can be found in his Oxford DPhil thesis: S.B. Elliott, *Compensation Claims against Trustees* (University of Oxford, 2002). Parts of this are published as: S.B. Elliott, "Restitutionary Compensatory Damages for Breach of Fiduciary Duty?" [1998] R.L.R. 135; S.B. Elliott, "Fiduciary Liability for Client Mortgage Frauds" (1999) 13 Tru. L.I. 74; S.B. Elliott, "Remoteness Criteria in Equity" (2002) 65 M.L.R. 588; S.B. Elliott and C. Mitchell, "Remedies for Dishonest Assistance" (2004) 67 M.L.R. 16, esp. 23–34; S.B. Elliott and J. Edelman, "Money Remedies against Trustees" (2004) 18 Tru. L.I. 116. Various legal scholars have adopted Elliott's analysis in their own work, including C. Rickett, "Understanding Remedies for Breach of Trust" (2008) 11 Otago L.R. 603; L. Smith, "The Measurement of Compensation Claims against Trustees and Fiduciaries" in E. Bant and M. Harding (eds), *Exploring Private Law* (Cambridge University Press, 2010).

37 See paras 10–020—10–101.

38 See paras 10–102—10–121.

trust property, but they lie more generally wherever a trustee has caused loss to the beneficiaries by committing a breach of duty.

Both types of claim have traditionally been mediated through proceedings for an account, which are discussed below in part C.[39] However the claims are different in nature, essentially because the second type of claim depends on the assertion that the trustees have committed a breach of trust, while the first type of claim does not. Each type of claim is sometimes described as a "restitutionary" claim.[40] However this usage is best avoided, both to avoid confusing the two types of claim with one another, and to avoid confusing both of them with liability in unjust enrichment when it is clear that in this context the word "restitution" is used to mean "compensation".[41] **10–014**

## S. Elliott and C. Mitchell, "Remedies for Dishonest Assistance"

(2004) 67 M.L.R. 14, 23–25

### Money Claims against Trustees

. . . Equity allows two types of claim against errant trustees that may be described as compensatory. Both types of claim have traditionally been mediated through the trustee's account, but they are claims of fundamentally different types. One is a claim that the trustee perform his primary obligations to apply the trust property in accordance with the trust deed, by a payment of monetary compensation where he cannot perform *in specie*.[42] This is a type of performance claim. The other is a claim that the trustee make good loss suffered by the beneficial interests by reason of his breach of trust. This is a type of reparation claim, because the compensation he must pay is calculated to repair the loss. . . **10–015**

### Compensation and Loss

Claims for performance and claims for reparation may both yield compensatory relief, but the relief is compensatory in different senses of the word. Both concepts of compensation carry the idea of an equivalent,[43] but the object of the equivalence is different in each case. A failure to discriminate between these two senses has become a prime source of confusion in this branch of equity. **10–016**

In its dominant sense compensation consists in a money equivalent to the injury or loss that a person has suffered. This may be called reparative compensation because it is calculated to repair the loss. The measure of reparative compensation is the difference between the claimant's present position and the position he would have occupied if he had not sustained the wrong.[44] This hypothetical comparison is drawn pursuant to a causal inquiry linking the defendant's misconduct with deterioration in the claimant's position. Reparative compensation matches injury caused by the defendant's misconduct. In its second sense compensation consists in a money equivalent to property of which a person has been deprived or denied. This may be called substitutive compensation because it is calculated to provide a substitute for **10–017**

---

39 See paras 10–022—10–135.

40 In substitutive performance claims it is often said that the trustee must effect "restitution" or "restoration" of the trust assets for which she has failed to account, or their money equivalent: e.g. *Re Dawson* [1966] 2 N.S.W.R. 211 at 216; *Bartlett v Barclays Bank Trust Co. Ltd (No.2)* [1980] Ch. 515 at 543; *Target Holdings Ltd v Redferns* [1996] A.C. 421 at 433; *Hall v Libertarian Investments Ltd* (2013) 16 HKCFAR 681 at [168]. But in reparation claims, too, it is sometimes said that the trustee's liability is "restitutionary": e.g. *Hodgkinson v Simms* [1994] 3 S.C.R. 377 at 440; *Re Mulligan* [1998] 1 N.Z.L.R. 481 at 507; *Swindle v Harrison* [1997] 4 All E.R. 705 at 733.

41 *Bartlett v Barclays Bank Trust Co. Ltd (No.2)* [1980] Ch. 515 at 545, per Brightman LJ. See too S.B. Elliott, "Restitutionary Compensatory Damages for Breach of Fiduciary Duty?" [1998] R.L.R. 135.

42 Where the primary obligation is performed by payment of substitutive compensation, it is performed transformatively rather than in terms. We are grateful to Dr Rafal Zakrzewski for this insight.

43 J.A. Simpson and E.S.C. Weiner (gen eds), *Oxford English Dictionary* (Oxford: O.U.P., 2nd ed., 1989) s.v. 'Compensation', sense 2a; J. Burke (ed), *Jowitt's Dictionary of English Law* (London: Sweet & Maxwell, 2nd ed., 1977) s.v. 'Compensation'.

44 *Livingston v Rawlands Coal Co.* (1880) 5 App. Cas. 25 at 39. The measure is formulated differently in claims for breach of contract, where it is the difference between the claimant's present position and the position she would have occupied, had the agreement been performed.

> the property. Substitutive compensation is a familiar object of relief in expropriation cases: compensation is given in lieu of the property being taken.[45] Causal connection between the claimant's injury and the defendant's act is not to the point where compensation is used in the substitutive sense because the compensation is an equivalent to the property and not to whatever injury there may be.
>
> 10-018 These two concepts of compensation imply correspondingly different concepts of loss. Reparative compensation responds to loss in the figurative sense of injury or damage. Loss in this sense is subjective in that it is concerned with injury or damage to a particular claimant. It is harm to the claimant's interests such that his position is worse than it would have been if he had not suffered the wrong or if his contract had been performed. This idea includes foregone gains as well as consequential losses. Loss of this sort may be called reparable loss.
>
> 10-019 Substitutive compensation, by contrast, meets the loss of property to the claimant, whether by deprivation or denial. Substitutive compensation is measured by the property's objective value or by the objective value of some deterioration or diminution. How the property is to be valued is always a question for decision. Whether the claimant's overall financial position or personal well-being is diminished or improved by the deprivation of the property is not material to that valuation. Consequential loss is likewise conceptually inapposite to compensation of the substitutive variety.

## *A. Substitutive Performance Claims*

### i. Basic Principles

> 10-020 The duty of a trustee is properly to preserve the trust fund, to pay the income and the corpus to those who are entitled to them respectively, and to give all his cestuis que trust on demand information with respect to the mode in which the trust fund has been dealt with, and where it is.[46]

The beneficiaries have corresponding rights to obtain trust accounts and to insist that the trust assets are maintained or disbursed solely in accordance with the trust instrument.[47] The beneficiaries can obtain a court order commanding the trustees to perform their duties,[48] and to obtain such an order they need not assert that the trustees have done anything wrong. Their claim resembles a claim for specific performance of the primary obligations owed under a contract,[49] rather than a claim for damages for breach of contract or tort.[50]

10-021 If a trustee cannot perform her core obligation to account for and deliver a trust asset *in specie*, for example because she has misapplied it, then the court can order her instead to pay money as a

---

45 The distinction between these two types of compensation is drawn in the famous U.S. Supreme Court case *Monoghela Navigation Co. v United States*, 148 U.S. 312 (1893) 326.

46 *Low v Bouverie* [1891] 3 Ch. 82 at 99, per Lindley LJ.

47 *Target Holdings Ltd v Redferns* [1996] A.C. 421 at 434. These rights and duties arise immediately that the trustee receives trust assets in a fiduciary capacity: *Attorney General v Cocke* [1988] Ch. 414 at 420.

48 *Re Locker's Settlement Trusts* [1977] 1 W.L.R. 1323 (trustees ordered to exercise obligatory discretionary power of appointment). The courts can also make a vesting order directing trustees to transfer trust assets to an absolutely entitled beneficiary: Trustee Act 1925 ss.44(vi), 51(1)(d); *Re Knox's Trusts* [1895] 2 Ch. 483; cf. *Quinton v Proctor* [1998] 4 V.R. 469; *Davis v Williams* [2003] NSWCA 371 at [41]. Where one or more beneficiaries are absolutely beneficially entitled to land held on a trust of land, so that they have rights to replace the trustees under the Trusts of Land and Appointment of Trustees Act 1996 s.19, the English courts should also be willing to vest the land directly in the beneficiaries, preferring the approach in *Re Godfrey's Trusts* (1883) 23 Ch.D. 205 to that in *Re Holland* (1881) 16 Ch.D. 672 and *Re Carrie* (1878) 10 Ch.D. 93.

49 A claim for specific performance may succeed even though it is issued before the date when contractual performance is required, so that by definition no breach of contract can yet have occurred: *Hasham v Zenab* [1960] A.C. 316, noted R.E. Megarry (1960) 76 L.Q.R. 200.

50 Compare the statement in *Ex p. Adamson* (1878) 8 Ch. App. 807 at 819, that Chancery suits for breach of trust were always for "an equitable debt or liability in the nature of a debt", with the comment in *Jervis v Harris* [1996] Ch. 195 at 202–203, that: "The plaintiff who claims payment of a debt need not prove anything beyond the occurrence of the event or condition on the occurrence of which the debt becomes due. He need prove no loss; the rules as to remoteness of damage and mitigation of loss are irrelevant."

substitute for performance of her duty. In this situation, the trustee has committed a breach of trust, but there is no need for the beneficiaries to plead or prove this breach of trust in order to obtain their remedy.[51] The reason is that their claim is still a claim for performance of the trustee's primary obligation to deliver the asset, but with the difference that it is a claim for substitute performance of this obligation by the payment of a money sum. It is not a claim for money to compensate the beneficiaries for any harm which they may have suffered as a consequence of the trustee's failure to perform her obligation *in specie*.

The amount payable is accordingly measured by the objective value of the property which the trustee should have delivered: it "looks not so much to the loss suffered as to what is required to restore the trust fund".[52] The amount is calculated by requiring the trustee to produce accounts which omit no relevant incomings and record only authorised outgoings, by inspecting these to determine what property makes up the trust fund, and then, if the trustee cannot produce this property *in specie*, by ordering her to pay over a money substitute—either directly to the beneficiaries, or more usually, into the trust fund so that the trust can remain on foot. Thus, as Kekewich J held in *Head v Gould*[53]: **10-022**

> As against a trustee who, on the accounts being taken, is shewn to have improperly applied part of the trust estate, the right of a cestui que trust is to have those accounts set straight—that is, to compel the trustee to pay such a sum as will make them balance.

Because their claim is not founded on an assertion that the trustee has committed a breach of duty, the beneficiaries need not prove that the trustee's actions or omissions have caused them a loss,[54] nor do the concepts of remoteness[55] and contributory negligence[56] have any bearing on their claim. Moreover, no deduction will be made for tax which would have been payable by the trustees on the relevant property but for their default,[57] and the beneficiaries' tax liabilities do not enter the picture because they arise when capital or income is distributed out of the fund, and not when the trustee pays the value of the relevant asset back into the trust fund. **10-023**

The amount due from the trustee to make the accounts balance may be the value of misapplied (or wrongfully retained) trust income,[58] or of a misapplied capital sum plus interest.[59] Where some **10-024**

---

51 *Bacon v Clarke* (1837) 2 My. & Cr. 294; Re Stevens [1898] 1 Ch. 162; *Ahmed Angullia bin Hadjee Mohamed Salleh Angullia v Estate and Trust Agencies (1927) Ltd* [1938] A.C. 624 at 637.

52 *New Cap Reinsurance Corp Ltd v General Cologne Re Australia Ltd* (2004) 7 I.T.E.L.R. 295 at [55], per Young CJ in Eq. See too *Re Anglo-French Co-operative Soc* (1882) 21 Ch.D. 492 at [506]; *Re Windsor Steam Coal Co (1901) Ltd* [1929] 1 Ch. 151 at 166–167; *Knight v Haynes Duffell, Kentish & Co (a firm)* [2003] EWCA Civ 223 at [36]–[39]; *Re Lehman Brothers International (Europe) (in admin.) (No.2)* [2009] EWHC 2141 (Ch) at [53], per Blackburne J: a beneficiary's remedy for breach of trust is "principally directed to securing performance of the trust, rather than to the recovery of compensation or damages".

53 [1898] 2 Ch. 250 at 266. See too *Wiglesworth v Wiglesworth* (1852) 16 Beav. 269 at [272]; *Chaplin v Young* (1864) 33 Beav. 330 at 343.

54 *Cocker v Quayle* (1830) 1 Russ. & M. 353; *Salway v Salway* (1831) 2 Russ. & M. 215; *White v Baugh* (1835) 3 C. & F. 44 at [66]; *Youyang Pty Ltd v Minter Ellison Morris Fletcher* (2003) 212 C.L.R. 484 at [63], [69].

55 *Clough v Bond* (1838) 3 My. & Cr. 490; *Magnus v Queensland National Bank* (1888) 37 Ch.D. 466; *Re Dawson* [1966] 2 N.S.W.R. 211 at 214; *Re Duckwari Plc (No.2)* [1999] Ch. 268 at 272; *McCann v Switzerland Insurance Australia Ltd* (2000) 203 C.L.R. 579 at [621]–[622].

56 *Alexander v Perpetual Trustees (WA) Ltd* (2004) 216 C.L.R. 109 at [44] and esp. [104]: contributory negligence is inapt because "the basic principle that a fiduciary's liability to a beneficiary for breach of trust is one of restoration."

57 *Bartlett v Barclays Bank Trust Co Ltd (No.2)* [1980] Ch. 515 at 543; *Re Bell's Indenture* [1980] 1 W.L.R. 1217; *John v James* [1986] S.T.C. 352 at 361.

58 *Sharma v Farlam Ltd* [2009] EWHC 1622 (Ch) at [401]ff.

59 *Docker v Somes* (1834) 2 My. & K. 655; *Burdick v Garrick* (1870) 5 Ch. App. 233; *Re Davis* [1902] 2 Ch. 314; *Gordon v Gonda* [1955] 1 W.L.R. 885; *Kemp v Sims* [2009] Pens. L.R. 83.

other property than money has been misapplied, the trustee may be liable to pay the market value of the property at the date of misapplication plus interest,[60] or, if this is a higher sum, the market value of the property at the date of judgment,[61] along with the amount of any income that would otherwise have been generated by the property between the date of misapplication and the date of judgment.[62]

**10-025** When deciding whether a trustee's payments are justified and should therefore be allowed to stand on the taking of the account, the court will generally disallow unauthorised disbursements, with the result that unauthorised purchases are treated as having been made with the trustee's own money.[63] However, there are exceptional cases where unauthorised disbursements are allowed, and the trustee is exonerated from performance of her duty to hold the relevant property for the beneficiaries. One such case is where the beneficiaries elect to adopt the trustee's actions and ask the court to treat these as though they had been authorised all along. Beneficiaries would wish to do this where the trustee has bought an unauthorised investment which has increased in value,[64] or where the trustee has wrongfully sold trust property whose current market value is lower than the value of the sale proceeds plus interest.[65]

**10-026** Sometimes the courts also relieve a trustee from the performance of her duty where they consider that insisting on this would be inequitable. For example, in *Jones v Lewis*, Lord Hardwicke LC held that[66]:

> if a trustee is robbed, that robbery properly proved shall be a discharge, provided he keeps [the trust property] so as he would keep his own.

It is tempting, but wrong, to conclude from the fact that trustees need not account for stolen trust property which they kept with reasonable care that the courts will never require trustees to reach into their own pockets unless they have committed a breach of duty. Various cases have already been cited for the rule that substitutive performance claims do not depend on the assertion that the trustee has committed a breach of duty. Another is *Eaves v Hickson*,[67] where Romilly MR declined to relieve a trustee who made unauthorised distributions on presentation of a forged document. No finding was made that the trustee had failed to examine this document carefully, and although counsel cited *Jones* and other robbery cases,[68] his Lordship concluded that the trustee was still "bound to pay the trust fund to the right person".[69]

**10-027** In the following extract the foregoing principles are reviewed by an Australian judge, Street J, whose statement of the law has been endorsed by the English courts.[70]

---

60 *Shepherd v Mouls* (1845) 4 Hare 500 at 504.

61 *Re Massingberd's Settlement* (1890) 63 L.T. 296; *Re Bell's Indenture* [1980] 1 W.L.R. 1217.

62 *Kellaway v Johnson* (1842) 5 Beav. 319 at 324; *Hewett v Foster* (1843) 6 Beav. 259; *Dixon v Dixon* (1878) 9 Ch.D. 587.

63 *Jackson v Dickinson* [1903] 1 Ch. 947, esp. at 951–952 (where the consequences of this rule are fully explored).

64 *Re Patten* (1883) 52 L.J. Ch. 787; *Re Jenkins* [1903] 2 Ch. 362; *Wright v Morgan* [1926] A.C. 788 (PC) 799. If the beneficiaries choose to adopt the investment, they cannot *also* demand that the trustees pay in the difference between the current value of the investment and the (higher) current value of an authorised asset that was sold to make the purchase: *Thornton v Stokill* (1855) 1 Jur. 751, which should be preferred on this point to *Re Lake* [1903] 1 K.B. 439.

65 *Harrison v Harrison* (1740) 2 Atk. 121; *Bostock v Blakeney* (1794) 2 Bro. C.C. 653 at 656; *Pocock v Reddington* (1801) 5 Ves. Jun. 794 at 800.

66 (1750) 2 Ves. Sen. 240 at 241. See too *Morley v Morley* (1678) 2 Chan. Cas. 2; *Jobson v Palmer* [1893] 1 Ch. 71. And cf. *Ex p. Belchier* (1754) Amb. 218 at 219 (trustee not answerable for property lost on banker's bankruptcy); *Job v Job* (1875) 6 Ch.D. 562 at 563–564 (similar rule for executors).

67 (1861) 30 Beav 136. See also *Ashby v Blackwell* (1765) 2 Eden 299; *Bostock v Flyer* (1865) L.R. 1 Eq. 26; *Sutton v Wilders* (1871) L.R. 12 Eq. 373.

68 *Eaves* at 139.

69 *Eaves* at 141.

70 e.g. *Bartlett v Barclays Bank Trust Co. Ltd (No.2)* [1980] Ch. 515 at 543 per Brightman LJ.

*Re Dawson*

New South Wales Supreme Court [1966] 2 N.S.W.R. 211

STREET J.: The obligation of a defaulting trustee is essentially one of effecting a restitution to the estate. The obligation is of a personal character and its extent is not to be limited by common law principles governing remoteness of damage. In *Caffrey v Darby*,[71] trustees were charged with neglect in failing to recover possession of part of the trust assets. The assets were lost and it was argued by the trustees that the loss was not attributable to their neglect. The Master of the Rolls, in stating his reasons, asked "will they be relieved from that by the circumstance that the loss has ultimately happened by something that is not a direct and immediate consequence of their negligence?" His answer to this question was that, even supposing that "they could not look to the possibility" of the actual event which occasioned the loss, "yet, if they have already been guilty of negligence they must be responsible for any loss in any way to that property; for whatever may be the immediate cause the property would not have been in a situation to sustain that loss if it had not been for their negligence. If they had taken possession of the property it would not have been in his possession. If the loss had happened by fire, lightning, or any other accident, that would not be an excuse for them, if guilty of previous negligence. That was their fault." *Caffrey v Darby* is consistent with the proposition that if a breach has been committed then the trustee is liable to place the trust estate in the same position as it would have been in if no breach had been committed. Considerations of causation, foreseeability and remoteness do not readily enter into the matter. To the same effect is the case of *Clough v Bond*.[72] It was argued before Lord Cottenham L.C. that "the principle of the court is to charge persons in the situation of trustees as parties to the breach of trust, wherever they have acted irregularly, and the irregularity, however well intended, has in the result enabled their co-trustees to commit a breach of trust, or has been, however remotely, the origin of the loss." . . . The principles embodied in this approach do not appear to involve any inquiry as to whether the loss was caused by or flowed from the breach. Rather the inquiry in each instance would appear to be whether the loss would have happened if there had been no breach. **10–028**

. . . The cases to which I have referred demonstrate that the obligation to make restitution, which courts of equity have from very early times imposed on defaulting trustees and other fiduciaries, is of a more absolute nature than the common-law obligation to pay damages for tort or breach of contract. . . . Moreover the distinction between common law damages and relief against a defaulting trustee is strikingly demonstrated by reference to the actual form of relief granted in equity in respect of breaches of trust. The form of relief is couched in terms appropriate to require the defaulting trustee to restore to the estate the assets of which he deprived it. Increases in market values between the date of breach and the date of recoupment are for the trustee's account: the effect of such increases would, at common law, be excluded from the computation of damages but in equity a defaulting trustee must make good the loss by restoring to the estate the assets of which he deprived it notwithstanding that market values may have increased in the meantime. The obligation to restore to the estate the assets of which he deprived it necessarily connotes that, where a monetary compensation is to be paid in lieu of restoring assets, that compensation is to be assessed by reference to the value of the assets at the date of restoration and not at the date of deprivation. In this sense the obligation is a continuing one and ordinarily, if the assets are for some reason not restored in specie, it will fall for quantification at the date when recoupment is to be effected, and not before. **10–029**

### ii. Disapplication of the Basic Rules Where the Trust Has Been Exhausted and the Fund Has Become Absolutely Vested in Possession and/or Where Money Has Been Paid out of a Bare Trust Arising as an Incident of a Wider Commercial Transaction

In *Target Holdings Ltd v Redferns*,[73] which is excerpted below,[74] the claimant company agreed to lend money to a borrower to purchase property. Repayment of the loan was to be secured by a charge **10–030**

[71] (1801) 6 Ves. 488.
[72] (1838) 3 My. & Cr. 490.
[73] [1996] 1 A.C. 421.
[74] See paras 10–033ff.

on the property. The money was placed with the defendant solicitors on trust for payment to the borrower's order, once a duly executed charge over the property and supporting documents of title were delivered. The solicitors paid the money over to the borrower's order without first obtaining the charge or other documents, although these were later delivered. The borrower defaulted on the loan and it then transpired that the property had been fraudulently overvalued, so that the claimant was left substantially out of pocket after it had exercised its power of sale. The Court of Appeal held that the solicitors had committed a breach of trust by releasing the money before receiving the documents, and that at this moment there had been "an immediate loss placing the trustee under an immediate duty to restore the moneys to the trust fund".[75] The court concluded that the solicitors were liable for the full amount of the money, but to prevent double recovery they required the claimant to give credit for the amount realised by the sale of the property.

**10–031** The House of Lords agreed that there had been a breach of trust, but disagreed that the clock should be stopped at the date of breach for the purpose of quantifying the solicitors' liability. Their Lordships held that the relevant date was the date of judgment, i.e. after the transaction had been completed, and that the solicitors would therefore be liable only if the claimant could prove that its loss would not have occurred but for the early payment of the money without taking any security. Hence the case was sent back to the High Court for determination of this point.

**10–032** In his leading speech Lord Browne-Wilkinson recognised that the principles stated in the previous section comprise the basic rules governing liability to reconstitute the funds of a "traditional" trust depleted by an unauthorised disposal of the trust funds. However, the application of these rules would have led to a result that he wished to avoid, namely that the solicitors would then have had to pay for the claimant's entire loss, including loss caused by the fact that the property had been fraudulently overvalued. It appears that the solicitors may have known of the "flipping" transactions through which this had been achieved, suggesting a lack of good faith on their part. Nevertheless, Lord Browne-Wilkinson held that they would be liable for the difference between the amount of the purchase money which they had released in breach of trust and the amount which was realised by sale of the property only if it could be shown that the claimant would not have sustained this loss if the defendants had not made their unauthorised payment.

*Target Holdings Ltd v Redferns (a firm)*

House of Lords [1996] 1 A.C. 421

**10–033** The claimant mortgagee alleged that it had been the victim of a mortgage fraud as part of which the insolvent second defendant had overvalued the mortgaged property at £2 million. The first defendant, a firm of solicitors, had acted not just for the claimant but also for the mortgagor, Crowngate Ltd, and also for two other companies, Kohli Ltd and Panther Ltd. The owner of the property, Mirage Ltd, had agreed to sell to Crowngate for £775,000, but Crowngate had arranged matters so that Mirage would sell to Panther for £775,000, which would then sell the property on to Kohli for £1,250,000, which would then sell to Crowngate for £2 million. The claimant knew nothing of these arrangements, the point of which was to create a false impression of the property's value.

**10–034** The claimant paid £1,525,000 to the defendant solicitors to be held on a bare trust to pay the money to Crowngate's order only when the property was transferred to Crowngate and charges over it were executed in the claimant's favour. In breach of trust the money was paid over a month before the charges were executed. Crowngate became insolvent and the claimant sold the property for only £500,000. The claimant sued the defendant solicitors for breach of their duty of care as the claimant's solicitor in failing to alert the claimant to the suspicious circumstances, and also for breach of trust in paying the money

[75] [1994] 1 W.L.R. 1089 at 1103 per Peter Gibson LJ.

away without authority. The claimant sought summary judgment for breach of trust; Warner J. granted leave to defend, conditional upon payment into court of £1 million. The Court of Appeal granted summary judgment.

LORD BROWNE-WILKINSON (with whom LORD KEITH, LORD ACKNER, LORD JAUNCEY and LORD LLOYD agreed): Peter Gibson L.J., with whom Hirst L.J. agreed, held that the basic liability of a trustee in breach of trust is not to pay damages but to restore to the trust fund that which has been lost to it or to pay compensation to the beneficiary for what he has lost. He held that, in assessing the compensation payable to the beneficiary, causation is not irrelevant but common law rules of causation, as such, do not apply: the beneficiary is to be put back in the position he would have been in but for the breach of trust. He held that in cases where the breach of trust does not involve paying away trust money to a stranger (e.g. making an unauthorised investment), the answer to the question whether any loss has been thereby caused and the quantification of such loss will depend upon events subsequent to the commission of the breach of trust. But he held that in cases such as the present where the trustee has paid away trust moneys to a stranger, there is an immediate loss to the trust fund and the causal connection between the breach and the loss is obvious: the trustee comes under an immediate duty to restore the moneys to the trust fund. He held that the remedies of equity are sufficiently flexible to require Target (as it has always accepted) to give credit for the moneys received on the subsequent realisation of its security. But otherwise Redferns' liability was to pay to Target the whole of the moneys wrongly paid away. . . 10–035

Before considering the technical issues of law which arise, it is appropriate to look at the case more generally. Target alleges, and it is probably the case, that it was defrauded by third parties (Mr Kohli and Mr Musafir and possibly their associates) to advance money on the security of the property. If there had been no breach by Redferns of their instructions and the transaction had gone through, Target would have suffered a loss . . . [which] would have been wholly caused by the fraud of the third parties. The breach of trust committed by Redferns left Target in exactly the same position as it would have been if there had been no such breach: Target advanced the same amount of money, obtained the same security and received the same amount on the realisation of that security. In any ordinary use of words, the breach of trust by Redferns cannot be said to have caused the actual loss ultimately suffered by Target unless it can be shown that, but for the breach of trust, the transaction would not have gone through, e.g. if Panther could not have obtained a conveyance from Mirage otherwise than by paying the purchase money to Mirage out of the moneys paid out, in breach of trust, by Redferns to Panther on 29 June. If that fact can be demonstrated, it can be said that Redferns' breach of trust was a cause of Target's loss: if the transaction had not gone through, Target would not have advanced the money at all and therefore Target would not have suffered any loss. But the Court of Appeal decided,[76] and it is common ground before your Lordships, that there is a triable issue as to whether, had it not been for the breach of trust, the transaction would have gone through. Therefore the decision of the Court of Appeal in this case can only be maintained on the basis that, even if there is no causal link between the breach of trust and the actual loss eventually suffered by Target (i.e. the sum advanced less the sum recovered) the trustee in breach is liable to bear (at least in part) the loss suffered by Target. . . . 10–036

At common law there are two principles fundamental to the award of damages. First, that the defendant's wrongful act must cause the damage complained of. Second, that the plaintiff is to be put "in the same position as he would have been in if he had not sustained the wrong for which he is now getting his compensation or reparation".[77] Although, as will appear, in many ways equity approaches liability for making good a breach of trust from a different starting point, in my judgment those two principles are applicable as much in equity as at common law. Under both systems liability is fault based: the defendant is only liable for the consequences of the legal wrong he has done to the plaintiff and to make good the damage caused by such wrong. He is not responsible for damage not caused by his wrong or to pay by way of compensation more than the loss suffered from such wrong. The detailed rules of equity as to causation and the quantification of loss differ, at least ostensibly, from those applicable at common law. But the principles underlying both systems are the same. On the assumptions that had to be made in the present case until the factual issues are resolved (i.e. that the transaction would have gone through even if there had been no breach of trust), the result reached by the Court of Appeal does not accord with those principles. Redferns as trustees have been held liable to compensate Target for a loss caused otherwise than by 10–037

---

76 See [1994] 1 W.L.R. 1089 at 1100 and 1104, per Ralph Gibson and Peter Gibson L.JJ.

77 See *Livingstone v Rawyards Coal Co.* (1880) 5 App. Cas. 25 at 39, per Lord Blackburn.

the breach of trust. I approach the consideration of the relevant rules of equity with a strong predisposition against such a conclusion.

10-038 The considerations urged before your Lordships, although presented as a single argument leading to the conclusion that the views of the majority in the Court of Appeal are correct, on analysis comprise two separate lines of reasoning, viz.:

(A) an argument developed by Mr Patten Q.C. (but not reflected in the reasons of the Court of Appeal) that Target is now (i.e. at the date of judgment) entitled to have the "trust fund" restored by an order that Redferns reconstitute the trust fund by paying back into client account the moneys paid away in breach of trust. Once the trust fund is so reconstituted, Redferns as bare trustee for Target will have no answer to a claim by Target for the payment over of the moneys in the reconstituted "trust fund". Therefore, Mr Patten says, it is proper now to order payment direct to Target of the whole sum improperly paid away, less the sum which Target has received on the sale of property; and

(B) the argument accepted by the majority of the Court of Appeal that, because immediately after the moneys were paid away by Redferns in breach of trust there was an immediate right to have the "trust fund" reconstituted, there was then an immediate loss to the trust fund for which loss Redferns are now liable to compensate Target direct.

10-039 The critical distinction between the two arguments is that argument (A) depends upon Target being entitled now to an order for restitution to the trust fund whereas argument (B) quantifies the compensation payable to Target as beneficiary by reference to a right to restitution to the trust fund at an earlier date and is not dependent upon Target having any right to have the client account reconstituted now.

10-040 Before dealing with these two lines of argument, it is desirable to say something about the approach to the principles under discussion. The argument both before the Court of Appeal and your Lordships concentrated on the equitable rules establishing the extent and quantification of the compensation payable by a trustee who is in breach of trust. In my judgment this approach is liable to lead to the wrong conclusions in the present case because it ignores an earlier and crucial question, viz. is the trustee who has committed a breach under any liability at all to the beneficiary complaining of the breach? There can be cases where, although there is an undoubted breach of trust, the trustee is under no liability at all to a beneficiary. For example, if a trustee commits a breach of trust with the acquiescence of one beneficiary, that beneficiary has no right to complain and an action for breach of trust brought by him would fail completely. Again there may be cases where the breach gives rise to no right to compensation. Say, as often occurs, a trustee commits a judicious breach of trust by investing in an unauthorised investment which proves to be very profitable to the trust. A carping beneficiary could insist that the unauthorised investment be sold and the proceeds invested in authorised investments: but the trustee would be under no liability to pay compensation either to the trust fund or to the beneficiary because the breach has caused no loss to the trust fund. Therefore, in each case the first question is to ask what are the rights of the beneficiary: only if some relevant right has been infringed so as to give rise to a loss is it necessary to consider the extent of the trustee's liability to compensate for such loss.

10-041 The basic right of a beneficiary is to have the trust duly administered in accordance with the provisions of the trust instrument, if any, and the general law. Thus, in relation to a traditional trust where the fund is held in trust for a number of beneficiaries having different, usually successive, equitable interests (e.g. A for life with remainder to B), the right of each beneficiary is to have the whole fund vested in the trustees so as to be available to satisfy his equitable interest when, and if, it falls into possession. Accordingly, in the case of a breach of such a trust involving the wrongful paying away of trust assets, the liability of the trustee is to restore to the trust fund, often called "the trust estate", what ought to have been there.

10-042 The equitable rules of compensation for breach of trust have been largely developed in relation to such traditional trusts, where the only way in which all the beneficiaries' rights can be protected is to restore to the trust fund what ought to be there. In such a case the basic rule is that a trustee in breach of trust must restore or pay to the trust estate either the assets which have been lost to the estate by reason of the breach or compensation for such loss. Courts of Equity did not award damages but, acting in personam, ordered the defaulting trustee to restore the trust estate.[78] If specific restitution of the trust property is not possible, then the liability of the trustee is to pay sufficient compensation to the trust estate to put it back

78 See *Nocton v Lord Ashburton* [1914] A.C. 932 at 952, per Viscount Haldane L.C.

to what it would have been had the breach not been committed.[79] Even if the immediate cause of the loss is the dishonesty or failure of a third party, the trustee is liable to make good that loss to the trust estate if, but for the breach, such loss would not have occurred.[80] Thus the common law rules of remoteness of damage and causation do not apply. However, there does have to be some causal connection between the breach of trust and the loss to the trust estate for which compensation is recoverable, viz. the fact that the loss would not have occurred but for the breach.[81]

Hitherto I have been considering the rights of beneficiaries under traditional trusts where the trusts are still subsisting and therefore the right of each beneficiary, and his only right, is to have the trust fund reconstituted as it should be. But what if at the time of the action claiming compensation for breach of trust those trusts have come to an end? Take as an example again the trust for A for life with remainder to B. During A's lifetime B's only right is to have the trust duly administered and, in the event of a breach, to have the trust fund restored. After A's death, B becomes absolutely entitled. He of course has the right to have the trust assets retained by the trustees until they have fully accounted for them to him. But if the trustees commit a breach of trust, there is no reason for compensating the breach of trust by way of an order for restitution and compensation to the trust fund as opposed to the beneficiary himself. The beneficiary's right is no longer simply to have the trust duly administered: he is, in equity, the sole owner of the trust estate. Nor, for the same reason, is restitution to the trust fund necessary to protect other beneficiaries. Therefore, although I do not wholly rule out the possibility that even in those circumstances an order to reconstitute the fund may be appropriate, in the ordinary case where a beneficiary becomes absolutely entitled to the trust fund the court orders, not restitution to the trust estate, but the payment of compensation directly to the beneficiary. The measure of such compensation is the same, i.e. the difference between what the beneficiary has in fact received and the amount he would have received but for the breach of trust. . . . 10–043

**Argument (A)**

As I have said, the critical step in this argument is that Target is now entitled to an order for reconstitution of the trust fund by the repayment into client account of the moneys wrongly paid away, so that Target can now demand immediate repayment of the whole of such moneys without regard to the real loss it has suffered by reason of the breach. 10–044

Even if the equitable rules developed in relation to traditional trusts were directly applicable to such a case as this, as I have sought to show, a beneficiary becoming absolutely entitled to a trust fund has no automatic right to have the fund reconstituted in all circumstances. Thus, even applying the strict rules so developed in relation to traditional trusts, it seems to me very doubtful whether Target is now entitled to have the trust fund reconstituted. But in my judgment it is in any event wrong to lift wholesale the detailed rules developed in the context of traditional trusts and then seek to apply them to trusts of quite a different kind. In the modern world the trust has become a valuable device in commercial and financial dealings. The fundamental principles of equity apply as much to such trusts as they do to the traditional trusts in relation to which those principles were originally formulated. But in my judgment it is important, if the trust is not to be rendered commercially useless, to distinguish between the basic principles of trust law and those specialist rules developed in relation to traditional trusts which are applicable only to such trusts and the rationale of which has no application to trusts of quite a different kind. 10–045

This case is concerned with a trust which has at all times been a bare trust. Bare trusts arise in a number of different contexts: e.g. by the ultimate vesting of the property under a traditional trust, nominee shareholdings, and, as in the present case, as but one incident of a wider commercial transaction involving agency. In the case of moneys paid to a solicitor by a client as part of a conveyancing transaction, the purpose of that transaction is to achieve the commercial objective of the client, be it the acquisition of property or the lending of money on security. The depositing of money with the solicitor is but one aspect of the arrangements between the parties, such arrangements being for the most part contractual. Thus, the circumstances under which the solicitor can part with money from client account are regulated by the instructions given by the client: they are not part of the trusts on which the property is held. I do not intend to cast any doubt on the fact that moneys held by solicitors on client account are trust moneys or that the 10–046

---

79 See *Caffrey v Darby* (1801) 6 Ves. 488 and *Clough v Bond* (1838) 3 My. & Cr. 490.

80 See Underhill and Hayton, *Law of Trusts and Trustees* 14th edn (1987), pp. 734–736, *Re Dawson (decd)* [1966] 2 N.S.W.R. 211 and *Bartlett v Barclays Bank Trust Co. Ltd (No.2)* [1980] 2 Ch. 515.

81 See also *Re Miller's Deed Trusts* (1978) 75 L.S. Gaz. 454 and *Nestlé v National Westminster Bank Plc* [1993] 1 W.L.R. 1260.

basic equitable principles apply to any breach of such trust by solicitors. But the basic equitable principle applicable to breach of trust is that the beneficiary is entitled to be compensated for any loss he would not have suffered but for the breach. I have no doubt that, until the underlying commercial transaction has been completed, the solicitor can be required to restore to client account moneys wrongly paid away. But to import into such trust an obligation to restore the trust fund once the transaction has been completed would be entirely artificial. The obligation to reconstitute the trust fund applicable in the case of traditional trusts reflects the fact that no one beneficiary is entitled to the trust property and the need to compensate all beneficiaries for the breach. That rationale has no application to a case such as the present. To impose such an obligation in order to enable the beneficiary solely entitled (i.e. the client) to recover from the solicitor more than the client has in fact lost flies in the face of common sense and is in direct conflict with the basic principles of equitable compensation. In my judgment, once a conveyancing transaction has been completed the client has no right to have the solicitor's client account reconstituted as a "trust fund".

**Argument (B)**

10–047 . . . The key point in the reasoning of the Court of Appeal is that where moneys are paid away to a stranger in breach of trust, an immediate loss is suffered by the trust estate: as a result, subsequent events reducing that loss are irrelevant. They drew a distinction between the case in which the breach of trust consisted of some failure in the administration of the trust and the case where a trustee has actually paid away trust moneys to a stranger. There is no doubt that in the former case, one waits to see what loss is in fact suffered by reason of the breach, i.e. the restitution or compensation payable is assessed at the date of trial, not of breach. However, the Court of Appeal considered that where the breach consisted of paying away the trust moneys to a stranger it made no sense to wait: it seemed to Peter Gibson L.J. obvious that in such a case "there is an immediate loss, placing the trustee under an immediate duty to restore the moneys to the trust fund".[82] The majority of the Court of Appeal therefore considered that subsequent events which diminished the loss in fact suffered were irrelevant, save for imposing on the compensated beneficiary an obligation to give credit for any benefit he subsequently received. In effect, in the view of the Court of Appeal one "stops the clock" at the date the moneys are paid away: events which occur between the date of breach and the date of trial are irrelevant in assessing the loss suffered by reason of the breach.

10–048 A trustee who wrongly pays away trust money, like a trustee who makes an unauthorised investment, commits a breach of trust and comes under an immediate duty to remedy such breach. If immediate proceedings are brought, the court will make an immediate order requiring restoration to the trust fund of the assets wrongly distributed or, in the case of an unauthorised investment, will order the sale of the unauthorised investment and the payment of compensation for any loss suffered. But the fact that there is an accrued cause of action as soon as the breach is committed does not in my judgment mean that the quantum of the compensation payable is ultimately fixed as at the date when the breach occurred. The quantum is fixed at the date of judgment, at which date, according to the circumstances then pertaining, the compensation is assessed at the figure then necessary to put the trust estate or the beneficiary back into the position it would have been in had there been no breach. I can see no justification for "stopping the clock" immediately in some cases but not in others: to do so may, as in this case, lead to compensating the trust estate or the beneficiary for a loss which, on the facts known at trial, it has never suffered.

10–049 Moreover, in my judgment the distinction is not consistent with the decision in *Re Dawson (decd)*.[83] In that case a testator had established separate executors for his New Zealand and his Australian estates. In 1939 the New Zealand estate was under the administration of attorneys for, among others, PSD. PSD arranged that New Zealand £4,700 should be withdrawn from the New Zealand estate and paid away to a stranger, X, who in turn was supposed to lend the moneys to an Australian company in which PSD was interested. X absconded with the money. In that case, therefore, the trust money had been paid away to a stranger. Street J. had to decide whether the liability of PSD to compensate the estate was to be satisfied by paying sufficient Australian pounds to buy New Zealand £4,700 at the rate of exchange at the date of breach (when there was parity between the two currencies) or at the date of judgment (when the Australian pound had depreciated against the New Zealand pound). He held that the rate of exchange was to be taken as at the date of judgment. Although, contrary to the present case, this decision favoured the beneficiaries at the expense of the defaulting trustee, the principle is of general application whether

[82] [1994] 1 W.L.R. 1089 at 1103.
[83] [1966] 2 N.S.W.R. 211.

operating to the benefit or the detriment of the beneficiaries. The equitable compensation for breach of trust has to be assessed as at the date of judgment and not at an earlier date.

In *Canson Enterprises Ltd v Boughton & Co.*[84] the plaintiffs had bought some property in a transaction in which they were advised by the defendant, a solicitor. To the knowledge of the solicitor, but not of the plaintiffs, there was an improper profit being made by the vendors. If the plaintiffs had known that fact, they would not have completed the purchase. The defendant solicitor was in breach of his fiduciary duties to the plaintiffs. After completion the plaintiffs built a warehouse on the property, which due to the negligence of engineers and builders, was defective. The question was whether the defendant solicitor was liable to compensate the plaintiffs for the defective building, the plaintiffs contending that "but for" the defendant's breach of fiduciary duty they would not have bought the property and therefore would not have built the warehouse. Although the Supreme Court of Canada were unanimous in dismissing the claim, they reached their conclusions by two differing routes. The majority considered that damages for breach of fiduciary duty fell to be measured by analogy with common law rules of remoteness, whereas the minority considered that the equitable principles of compensation applied. Your Lordships are not required to choose between those two views. But the judgment of McLachlin J. (expressing the minority view) contains an illuminating exposition of the rules applicable to equitable compensation for breach of trust. Although the whole judgment deserves study, I extract the following statements: 10–050

> "While foreseeability of loss does not enter into the calculation of compensation for breach of fiduciary duty, liability is not unlimited. Just as restitution in specie is limited to the property under the trustee's control, so equitable compensation must be limited to loss flowing from the trustee's acts in relation to the interest he undertook to protect. Thus, Davidson states 'It is imperative to ascertain the loss *resulting from breach of the relevant equitable duty*'.[85] . . .
>
> "A related question which must be addressed is the time of assessment of the loss. In this area tort and contract law are of little help. . . . The basis of compensation at equity, by contrast, is the restoration of the actual value of the thing lost through the breach. The foreseeable value of the items is not in issue. As a result, the losses are to be assessed as at the time of trial, *using the full benefit of hindsight*[86] . . .
>
> "In summary, compensation is an equitable monetary remedy which is available when the equitable remedies of restitution and account are not appropriate. By analogy with restitution, it attempts to restore to the plaintiff what has been lost as a result of the breach, i.e. the plaintiff's lost opportunity. The plaintiff's actual loss as a consequence of the breach is to be assessed with the full benefit of hindsight. Foreseeability is not a concern in assessing compensation, but it is essential that the losses made good are only those which, *on a common sense view of causation*, were caused by the breach."[87]

In my view this is good law. Equitable compensation for breach of trust is designed to achieve exactly what the word compensation suggests: to make good a loss in fact suffered by the beneficiaries and which, using hindsight and common sense, can be seen to have been caused by the breach. . . . 10–051

Mr Patten for Target relied on *Nant-y-glo and Blaina Ironworks Co. v Grave*[88] as showing that a trustee can be held liable to recoup to the trust fund the value of shares at the highest value between the date of breach and the date of judgment. In my view that case has no relevance. The claim there was not for breach of trust but for account of profits made by a fiduciary (a company director) from shares which he had improperly received in breach of his duty. The amount recoverable in an action claiming an account of profits is dependent upon the profit made by the fiduciary, not the loss suffered by the beneficiary. 10–052

Mr Patten also relied on *Jaffray v Marshall*,[89] where the principles applicable in an action for an account of profits were, to my mind wrongly, applied to a claim for compensation for breach of trust. In my judgment that case was wrongly decided not only because the wrong principle was applied but also because the judge awarded compensation by assessing the quantum on an assumption (viz. that the house in 10–053

---

84 [1991] 3 S.C.R. 534.

85 I. Davidson, "The Equitable Remedy of Compensation" (1982) 3 Melb. U.L.R. 349, 354 (McLachlin J.'s emphasis).

86 McLachlin J.'s emphasis.

87 Lord Browne-Wilkinson's emphasis.

88 (1878) 12 Ch.D. 738.

89 [1993] 1 W.L.R. 1285.

question would have been sold at a particular date) when he found as a fact that such sale would not have taken place even if there had been no breach of trust.

10-054 For these reasons I reach the conclusion that, on the facts which must currently be assumed, Target has not demonstrated that it is entitled to any compensation for breach of trust. Assuming that moneys would have been forthcoming from some other source to complete the purchase from Mirage if the moneys had not been wrongly provided by Redferns in breach of trust, Target obtained exactly what it would have obtained had no breach occurred, i.e. a valid security for the sum advanced. Therefore, on the assumption made, Target has suffered no compensatable loss. Redferns are entitled to leave to defend the breach of trust claim.

10-055 However, I find it very difficult to make that assumption of fact. There must be a high probability that, at trial, it will emerge that the use of Target's money to pay for the purchase from Mirage and the other intermediate transactions was a vital feature of the transaction. The circumstances of the present case are clouded by suspicion, which suspicion is not dissipated by Mr Bundy's untruthful letter dated 30 June informing Target that the purchase of the property and the charges to Target had been completed. If the moneys made available by Redferns' breach of trust were essential to enable the transaction to go through, but for Redferns' breach of trust Target would not have advanced any money. In that case the loss suffered by Target by reason of the breach of trust will be the total sum advanced to Crowngate less the proceeds of the security. It is not surprising that Mr Sumption Q.C. was rather muted in his submission that Redferns should have had unconditional leave to defend and that the order for payment into court of £1m. should be set aside. In my judgment such an order was fully justified.

10-056 I would therefore allow the appeal, set aside the order of the Court of Appeal and restore the order of Warner J.

10-057 McLaughlin J's judgment in *Canson Enterprises Ltd v Boughton*[90] was a weak starting-point for Lord Browne-Wilkinson's analysis, since the case concerned a compensatory claim for breach of fiduciary duty rather than a compensatory claim following an unauthorised disposal of trust funds, and McLachlin J's own analysis suffers from a failure to distinguish between the different rules by which such claims are respectively governed.[91] In extra-judicial writing that is excerpted below, Lord Millett makes two further criticisms of Lord Browne-Wilkinson's judgment. First, he questions the relevance of the distinction drawn by Lord Browne-Wilkinson between ongoing "traditional" trusts, terminated "traditional" trusts with a single absolutely entitled beneficiary, and "bare" trusts in a commercial transaction.[92] Secondly, he argues that Lord Browne-Wilkinson's approach was unsatisfactory because claims for substitutive compensation are not claims for loss founded on the assertion that the trustee has committed a breach of duty, so that it is incoherent to introduce a requirement into such claims that there must be a causal link between a breach of duty by the trustee and a loss by the beneficiaries.

## P.J. Millett, "Equity's Place in the Law of Commerce"

(1998) 114 L.Q.R. 214, 224–227

10-058 Lord Browne-Wilkinson distinguished between traditional family trusts on the one hand and the bare trust which has become a valuable device in commercial and financial dealings. He accepted that the fundamental principles of equity apply as much to such trusts as they do to the traditional trust in relation to which those principles were originally formulated. But he suggested that it was important, if the trust concept was not to be rendered commercially useless, to distinguish between the basic principles of trust

90 [1991] 3 S.C.R. 534.

91 See paras 13–049—13–051.

92 See too J. Edelman, "Money Awards of the Cost of Performance" (2010) 4 J. Eq. 122: "[Lord Browne-Wilkinson's] assertion that the commercial trust would be rendered 'commercially useless' was unsupported by any reference to any empirical study."

law and those specialist rules developed in relation to traditional trusts which are applicable only to such trusts and the rationale of which has no application to trusts of a quite different kind.

It is difficult to know what to make of this. It is impossible to dissent from the proposition that equity is flexible and that circumstances alter cases. It is also true that, as Lord Browne-Wilkinson pointed out, the circumstances in which the solicitor [in *Target Holdings*] was entitled to part with his client's money were regulated by the client's instructions and were not part of the trusts on which the money was held. This is plainly correct. The only trust was a bare trust for the client; its instructions were superimposed on that trust. It was a form of *Quistclose* trust. But nothing turns on this, except that it made the instructions revocable. Application of trust money in such circumstances otherwise than in accordance with the unrevoked instructions of the beneficial owner is still a breach of trust. Likewise trustee investment powers are not part of the trusts on which trust money is held, but an unauthorised investment of trust money is still a breach of trust. . . **10–059**

Lord Browne-Wilkinson's speech is, with respect, disappointing in a second respect. He begins his analysis by referring to the basic right of a beneficiary to have the trust duly administered in accordance with the provisions of the trust instrument, if any, and the general law, and of the trustee's liability to pay compensation for any loss to the trust estate which may be occasioned by his breach of trust. From there he proceeds to speak exclusively in terms of causation, introducing the "but for" test while at the same time rejecting other tests of causation and remoteness of damage which have been adopted by the common law. This fails to explain why the trustee's liability is strict, or why equity should not adopt the common law rules of causation and remoteness in toto. **10–060**

It is misleading to speak of breach of trust as if it were the equitable counterpart of breach of contract at common law; or to speak of equitable compensation for breach of fiduciary duty as if it were common law damages masquerading under a fancy name. Forty years ago, the Chancery Judges bore down heavily on such solecisms. Woe betide a Chancery Junior who spoke of "damages for breach of trust" or "damages for breach of fiduciary duty". The judges knew that misuse of language often conceals a confusion of thought. Nowadays these misleading expressions are in common use. It is time that the usage was stamped out. **10–061**

Lord Diplock has said that a contracting party is under a primary obligation to perform his contract and a secondary obligation to pay damages if he does not.[93] It is tempting, but wrong, to assume that a trustee is likewise under a primary obligation to perform the trust and a secondary obligation to pay equitable compensation if he does not. The primary obligation of a trustee is to account for his stewardship. The primary remedy of the beneficiary—any beneficiary no matter how limited his interest—is to have the account taken, to surcharge and falsify the account, and to require the trustee to restore to the trust estate any deficiency which may appear when the account is taken. The liability is strict. The account must be taken down to the date on which it is rendered. That is why there is no question of "stopping the clock". **10–062**

If the beneficiary is dissatisfied with the way in which the trustee has carried out his trust—if, for example, he considers that the trustee has negligently failed to obtain all that he should have done for the benefit of the trust estate, then he may surcharge the account. He does this by requiring the account to be taken on the footing of wilful default. In this context "wilful default" bears a special and unusual meaning; it means merely lack of ordinary prudence or due diligence.[94] The trustee is made to account, not only for what he has in fact received, but also for what he might with due diligence have received. Since the trustee is, in effect, charged with negligence, and the amount by which the account is surcharged is measured by the loss occasioned by his want of skill and care, the analogy with common law damages for negligence is almost exact.[95] Although he is a fiduciary, his duty of care is not a fiduciary duty.[96] In this context it must be right to adopt the common law rules of causation and remoteness of damage to their fullest extent. The trustee's liability is enforced in the course of taking the trust account rather than by an action for damages, but the obligation of skill and care is identical to the common law duty of care. **10–063**

*Target Holdings Ltd v Redferns* was concerned with the other side of the account. Where the beneficiary complains that the trustee has misapplied trust money, he falsifies the account, that is to say, he asks for the disbursement to be disallowed. If, for example, the trustee lays out trust money in an unauthorised **10–064**

---

93 *Moschi v Lep Air Services Ltd* [1973] A.C. 331.

94 See e.g. *Re Chapman* [1896] 2 Ch. 763.

95 See *Henderson v Merrett Syndicates Ltd* [1995] 2 A.C. 145 at 205 per Lord Browne-Wilkinson.

96 See *Permanent Building Society v Wheeler* (1994) 14 A.C.S.R. 109 at 157–158 per Ipp J. approved in *Bristol & West B. S. v. Mothew* [1997] 2 WLR 436 at 448–449.

investment which falls in value, the beneficiary will falsify the account by asking the court to disallow both the disbursement and the corresponding asset on the other side of the account. The unauthorised investment will then be treated as having been bought with the trustee's own money and on his own behalf. He will be required to account to the trust estate for the full amount of the disbursement – not for the amount of the loss. That is what is meant by saying that the trustee is liable to restore the trust property; and why common law rules of causation and remoteness of damage are out of place.

**10–065** If the unauthorised investment has appreciated in value, then the beneficiary will be content with it. He is not obliged to falsify the account which the trustee renders; he can always accept it. (It goes without saying that the trustee cannot simply "borrow" the trust money to make a profitable investment for his own account and then rely on the fact that the investment was unauthorised to avoid bringing the transaction into the account. He must account for what he has done with the trust money, not merely for what he has properly done with it.) Where the beneficiary accepts the unauthorised investment, he is often said to affirm or adopt the transaction. That is not wholly accurate. The beneficiary has a right to elect, but it is merely a right to decide whether to complain or not.

**10–066** Where the beneficiary accepts the unauthorised investment, the account must be taken as if the investment were fully authorised in every respect. The investment is shown as a trust asset and the cost of acquisition as an authorised disbursement. But the converse is equally true. Where the beneficiary elects to falsify the account, the unauthorised investment is not shown as an asset, the disbursement is disallowed, and the trustee is accountable in every respect as if he had not disbursed the money. He is liable to restore the money to the trust estate; as notionally restored it remains subject to all the trusts powers and provisions of the trust as if it had never been disbursed; and the account is taken accordingly.

**10–067** All this is elementary, but it provides the solution to the problem in *Target Holdings Ltd v Redferns*. The solicitor held the plaintiff's money in trust for the plaintiff but with its authority to lay it out in exchange for an executed mortgage and the documents of title. He paid it away without obtaining these documents. This was an unauthorised application of trust money which entitled the plaintiff to falsify the account. The disbursement must be disallowed and the solicitor treated as accountable as if the money were still in his client account and available to be laid out in the manner directed. It was later so laid out. The plaintiff could not object to the acquisition of the mortgage or the disbursement by which it was obtained; it was an authorised application of what must be treated as trust money notionally restored to the trust estate on the taking of the account. To put the point another way; the trustee's obligation to restore the trust property is not an obligation to restore it in the very form in which he disbursed it, but an obligation to restore it in any form authorised by the trust.

**10–068** Lord Millett's analysis leaves intact Lord Browne-Wilkinson's finding that although a trustee who disposes of trust property in an unauthorised transaction comes under an immediate liability to restore the property, the quantum of the trustee's liability is not determined at the date of breach. However, this does not mean that the court can look at events occurring after the breach to see whether the beneficiaries would ultimately have suffered the same loss anyway.[97] Its significance lies rather in the fact that the court can look to see whether the trustee has rectified matters in an authorised fashion since the date of breach.[98] Also, if the trustee has not done this, the value of her obligation to hand over the property will vary according to its current market value, or, where the property is money, according to the amount of interest accrued on the money between the date of breach and the date of judgment.

**10–069** Lord Millett's analysis was considered by the High Court of Australia in *Youyang Pty Ltd v Minter Ellison Morris Fletcher*,[99] the facts of which were materially identical to those of *Target Holdings*, with the important difference that the defaulting trustee in *Youyang* never "cured" the breach of trust it had committed.

---

97 *Cocker v Quayle* (1830) 1 Russ. & M. 535.

98 M. Conaglen, "Explaining *Target Holdings v Redferns*" (2010) J.Eq. 288, noting that the question whether the trustee has cured her breach in an authorised way is a different question from whether the beneficiaries have adopted her unauthorised actions, a point misunderstood in J. Edelman, "Money Awards of the Cost of Performance" (2010) 4 J.Eq. 122, 128.

99 (2003) 212 C.L.R. 484, noted S. Elliott and J. Edelman "Target Holdings Considered in Australia" (2003) 119 L.Q.R. 545.

Citing Lord Millett's article, the court distinguished *Target Holdings* on this ground and ordered the trustee to pay the whole amount of its unauthorised disbursements as compensation,[100] although some of the trust money would have been lost even if the trustee had complied with its instructions.

The result and reasoning in *Youyang* encouraged the claimant lender in *A.I.B. Group (UK) Plc v Mark Redler & Co (a firm)*[101] to make the same argument. Again, the facts of *A.I.B.* were materially identical to those of *Target Holdings*, with the difference that the defendant solicitors had not put things right by the time that proceedings were issued. The claimant sought to distinguish *Target Holdings* on the ground that the breach of trust had not been "cured" by the defendants; it also argued that the cases were distinct because in *A.I.B.* the transaction in respect of which the lender had advanced its money had never relevantly been "completed". For the reasons set out in the following excerpt, however, the Supreme Court rejected both of these arguments. **10–070**

*A.I.B. Group (UK) Plc v Mark Redler & Co (a firm)*

Supreme Court [2014] 3 W.L.R. 1367

The defendant solicitors acted for the claimant bank in connection with a remortgage advance of £3.3 million on the security of the borrowers' home, which was then worth £4.25 million. The claimant instructed the solicitors that an existing mortgage over the property securing two loans totalling £1.5 million by Barclays Bank should be discharged and that a first charge over the property in the claimant bank's favour should be acquired before the funds were paid over. The solicitors negligently paid only one of the Barclays loans, worth £1.2 million, out of the advance, and paid the rest of the advance to the borrowers. Barclays' mortgage therefore remained as a first charge on the property to secure repayment of the £300,000 it was still owed, and the claimant's charge had to be registered as a second charge. The borrowers defaulted and became insolvent, the property was sold for £1.2 million after a collapse in the property market, and the claimant received only £900,000 after Barclays had been paid. **10–071**

The claimant sued the solicitors for £2.4 million, arguing that they had committed a breach of trust when they disbursed the £3.3 million without obtaining a first charge on the property in accordance with their instructions; that they were therefore liable to reconstitute the trust fund in full, subject to a credit for the £900,000 which had been recovered. The solicitors replied that if there had been a breach of trust (which they denied), their liability should be limited to the loss in value of the claimant's security caused by the solicitors' partial failure to pay off Barclays, quantified as the sum paid to Barclays from the sale proceeds (£300,000). **10–072**

The trial judge held that the solicitors had committed a breach of trust, but that they had partially satisfied the conditions on which the money could legitimately have been released, and payment to the borrowers had therefore been a breach of trust only to the extent that the solicitors had received a security that was worth £300,000 less than it should have been. The claimant's proper remedy was therefore restoration of that amount. The Court of Appeal upheld this result but on different reasoning. The court held that payment of the entire £3.3 million had been a breach of trust. Following *Target*, however, the measure of compensation payable by the solicitors should be calculated by asking what loss had been caused by the breach of trust. This should be done by asking the counterfactual question, what would have happened if there had been no breach of trust? The answer was that Barclays would have been paid off in full, the claimant would have acquired a first charge, and would have recovered the whole of the proceeds when the property was sold. Hence the only recoverable loss which the claimant had suffered was £300,000. This result and reasoning were upheld by the Supreme Court. **10–073**

LORD TOULSON (with whom LORD NEUBERGER, LADY HALE, LORD WILSON agreed; LORD REED gave a concurring judgment): . . . The determination of this appeal involves two essential questions. The more important question in the appeal is whether Lord Browne-Wilkinson's statement in *Target Holdings* of the fundamental principles which guided him in that case should be affirmed, qualified or (as the bank would put it) reinterpreted. Depending on the answer to that question, the second is whether the Court of Appeal properly applied the correct principles to the facts of the case. **10–074**

100 ibid., at [45]–[48].

101 [2014] UKSC 58, [2014] 3 W.L.R. 1367.

10-075 Two main criticisms have been made of Lord Browne-Wilkinson's approach. They have been made by a number of scholars, most recently by Professor Charles Mitchell in a lecture on "Stewardship of Property and Liability to Account" delivered to the Chancery Bar Association on 17 January 2014,[102] in which he described the Court of Appeal's reasoning in this case as incoherent. He expressed the hope that "if the case reaches the Supreme Court their Lordships will recognise that Lord Browne-Wilkinson took a false step in *Target* when he introduced an inapt causation requirement into the law governing . . . substitutive performance claims." He added that if it is thought too harsh to fix the solicitors in this case with liability to restore the full amount of the loan (subject only to a deduction for the amount received by the sale of the property), the best way to achieve this is "not to bend the rules governing substitutive performance claims out of shape", but to use the Trustee Act 1925, section 61, to relieve them from some or all of their liability.

10-076 The primary criticism is that Lord Browne-Wilkinson failed to recognise the proper distinctions between different obligations owed by a trustee and the remedies available in respect of them. The range of duties owed by a trustee include:

(1) a custodial stewardship duty, that is, a duty to preserve the assets of the trust except insofar as the terms of the trust permit the trustee to do otherwise;
(2) a management stewardship duty, that is, a duty to manage the trust property with proper care;
(3) a duty of undivided loyalty, which prohibits the trustee from taking any advantage from his position without the fully informed consent of the beneficiary or beneficiaries.

10-077 Historically the remedies took the form of orders made after a process of accounting. The basis of the accounting would reflect the nature of the obligation. The operation of the process involved the court having a power, where appropriate, to "falsify" and to "surcharge".

10-078 According to legal scholars whose scholarship I have no reason to doubt, in the case of a breach of the custodial stewardship duty, through the process of an account of administration in common form, the court would disallow (or falsify) the unauthorised disposal and either require the trust fund to be reconstituted in specie or order the trustee to make good the loss in monetary terms. The term "substitutive compensation" has come to be used by some to refer to a claim for the value of a trust asset dissipated without authority. (See the erudite judgment in *Agricultural Land Management Ltd v Jackson (No.2)*[103] of Edelman J., who attributes authorship of the term to Dr Steven Elliott.)

10-079 In a case of breach of a trustee's management stewardship duty, through the process of an action on the basis of wilful default, a court could similarly falsify or surcharge so as to require the trustee to make good the loss resulting from the breach. The phrase "wilful default" is misleading because, as Brightman L.J. explained in *Bartlett v Barclays Bank Trust Co. Ltd (Nos 1 and 2)*,[104] conscious wrongdoing is not required. In this type of case the order for payment by the trustee of the amount of loss is referred to by some as "reparative compensation", to differentiate it from "substitutive compensation", although in a practical sense both are reparative compensation.

10-080 In a case of breach of the duty of undivided loyalty, there are possible alternative remedies. If the trustee has benefited from it, the court will order him to account for it on the application of the beneficiary. In *Bristol and West Building Society v Mothew*[105] Millett L.J. described such relief as "primarily restitutionary or restorative rather than compensatory". Alternatively, the beneficiary may seek compensation in respect of his loss.

10-081 The history of the account of profits is more complex than this summary might suggest, and the whole concept of equitable compensation has developed and become far more prominent in the law since *Nocton v Lord Ashburton*. However, what I have said is sufficient to identify the main criticism advanced against Lord Browne-Wilkinson's approach in *Target Holdings*. It is said that he treated equitable compensation in too broad-brush a fashion, muddling claims for restitutive compensation with claims for reparative compensation.

10-082 The relevant principle, it is suggested, in a case of unauthorised dissipation of trust funds is that "the amount of the award is measured by the objective value of the property lost, determined at the date when

[102] Authors' note: this lecture has been published as C. Mitchell, "Stewardship of Property and Liability to Account" [2014] Conv. 215.
[103] [2014] WASC 102.
[104] [1980] Ch. 515 at 546.
[105] [1998] Ch. 1.

the account is taken and with the benefit of hindsight", per Millett N.P.J. in *Libertarian Investments Ltd v Hall*.[106] In determining the value of what has been lost, the court must take into account any offsetting benefits received, but it is not relevant to consider what the trustee ought to have done. The court is concerned only with the net value of the lost asset.

. . . According to the bank's argument, [the solicitors are] . . . responsible for loss which it would have suffered on the judge's findings if they had done what they were instructed to do. This involves effectively treating the unauthorised application of trust funds as creating an immediate debt between the trustee and the beneficiary, rather than conduct meriting equitable compensation for any loss thereby caused. I recognise that there are statements in the authorities which use that language to describe the trustee's liability. For example, in *Ex parte Adamson*,[107] James and Baggallay L.JJ. said that the Court of Chancery never entertained a suit for damages occasioned by fraudulent conduct or for breach of trust, and that the suit was always for "an equitable debt, or liability in the nature of a debt". This was long before the expression "equitable compensation" entered the vocabulary. Equitable monetary compensation for what in that case was straightforward fraud was clothed by the court in the literary costume of equitable debt, the debt being for the amount of the loss caused by the fraud. Whatever label is used, the question of substance is what gives rise to or is the measure of the "equitable debt or liability in the nature of a debt", or entitlement to monetary compensation, and what kind of "but for" test is involved. It is one thing to speak of an "equitable debt or liability in the nature of a debt" in a case where a breach of trust has caused a loss; it is another thing for equity to impose or recognise an equitable debt in circumstances where the financial position of the beneficiaries, actual or potential, would have been the same if the trustee had properly performed its duties. **10–083**

. . . There are arguments to be made both ways, as the continuing debate among scholars has shown, but absent fraud, which might give rise to other public policy considerations that are not present in this case, it would not in my opinion be right to impose or maintain a rule that gives redress to a beneficiary for loss which would have been suffered if the trustee had properly performed its duties. **10–084**

The same view was expressed by Professor Andrew Burrows in Burrows and Peel (eds.), *Commercial Remedies*, 2003, pp. 46–47, where he applauded *Target Holdings* for impliedly rejecting older cases that may have supported the view that the accounting remedy can operate differently from the remedy of equitable compensation. Despite the powerful arguments advanced by Lord Millett and others, I consider that it would be a backward step for this court to depart from Lord Browne-Wilkinson's fundamental analysis in *Target Holdings* or to "re-interpret" the decision in the manner for which the bank contends. **10–085**

All agree that the basic right of a beneficiary is to have the trust duly administered in accordance with the provisions of the trust instrument, if any, and the general law. Where there has been a breach of that duty, the basic purpose of any remedy will be either to put the beneficiary in the same position as if the breach had not occurred or to vest in the beneficiary any profit which the trustee may have made by reason of the breach (and which ought therefore properly to be held on behalf of the beneficiary). Placing the beneficiary in the same position as he would have been in but for the breach may involve restoring the value of something lost by the breach or making good financial damage caused by the breach. But a monetary award which reflected neither loss caused nor profit gained by the wrongdoer would be penal. **10–086**

The purpose of a restitutionary order is to replace a loss to the trust fund which the trustee has brought about. To say that there has been a loss to the trust fund in the present case of £2.5m by reason of the solicitors' conduct, when most of that sum would have been lost if the solicitors had applied the trust fund in the way that the bank had instructed them to do, is to adopt an artificial and unrealistic view of the facts. **10–087**

I would reiterate Lord Browne-Wilkinson's statement, echoing McLachlin J.'s judgment in *Canson*, about the object of an equitable monetary remedy for breach of trust, whether it be sub-classified as substitutive or reparative. As the beneficiary is entitled to have the trust properly administered, so he is entitled to have made good any loss suffered by reason of a breach of the duty. **10–088**

A traditional trust will typically govern the ownership-management of property for a group of potential beneficiaries over a lengthy number of years. If the trustee makes an unauthorised disposal of the trust property, the obvious remedy is to require him to restore the assets or their monetary value. It is likely to be the only way to put the beneficiaries in the same position as if the breach had not occurred. It is a real loss which is being made good. By contrast, in *Target Holdings* the finance company was seeking to be put in a **10–089**

---

106 [2014] 1 HKC 368 at [168].

107 (1878) 8 Ch.D. 807 at 807 and 819.

better position on the facts (as agreed or assumed for the purposes of the summary judgment claim) than if the solicitors had done as they ought to have done.

10-090 Other considerations reinforce my view that the House of Lords did not take a wrong step in *Target Holdings*.

10-091 Most critics accept that on the assumed facts of *Target Holdings* the solicitors should have escaped liability. But if causation of loss was not required for them to be liable, some other way had to be found for exonerating them from liability (unless the court was to use section 61 of the 1925 Act as a deus ex machina). The solution suggested by the bank is that the solicitors in *Target Holdings* should be treated as if the moneys which had been wrongly paid out had remained in or been restored to the solicitors' client account and had then been properly applied after the solicitors had obtained the necessary paperwork. There is something wrong with a state of the law which makes it necessary to create fairy tales.

10-092 As to the criticism of the passage in *Target Holdings* where Lord Browne-Wilkinson said that it would be "wrong to lift wholesale the detailed rules developed in the context of traditional trusts" and apply them to a bare trust which was "but one incident of a wider commercial transaction involving agency", it is a fact that a commercial trust differs from a typical traditional trust in that it arises out of a contract rather than the transfer of property by way of gift. The contract defines the parameters of the trust. Trusts are now commonly part of the machinery used in many commercial transactions, for example across the spectrum of wholesale financial markets, where they serve a useful bridging role between the parties involved. Commercial trusts may differ widely in their purpose and content, but they have in common that the trustee's duties are likely to be closely defined and may be of limited duration. Lord Browne-Wilkinson did not suggest that the principles of equity differ according to the nature of the trust, but rather that the scope and purpose of the trust may vary, and this may have a bearing on the appropriate relief in the event of a breach. Specifically, Lord Browne-Wilkinson stated that he did not cast doubt on the fact that monies held by solicitors on client account are trust monies, or that basic equitable principles apply to any breach of such trust by solicitors. What he did was to identify the basic equitable principles. In their application, the terms of the contract may be highly relevant to the question of fact whether there has been a loss applying a "but for" test, that is, by reference to what the solicitors were instructed to do. If the answer is negative, the solicitors should not be required to pay restitutive monetary compensation when there has in fact been no loss resulting from their breach. That is not because special rules apply to solicitors, but because proper performance of the trustee's obligations to the beneficiary would have produced the same end result.

10-093 I agree with the view of Professor David Hayton, in his chapter "Unique Rules for the Unique Institution, the Trust" in Degeling & Edelman (eds), *Equity in Commercial Law* (2005), pp. 279–308, that in circumstances such as those in *Target Holdings* the extent of equitable compensation should be the same as if damages for breach of contract were sought at common law. That is not because there should be a departure in such a case from the basic equitable principles applicable to a breach of trust, whether by a solicitor or anyone else. (If there were a conflict between the rules of equity and the rules of the common law, the rules of equity would prevail by reason of section 49(1) of the Senior Courts Act 1981, derived from the provisions of the Judicature Act 1875.) Rather, the fact that the trust was part of the machinery for the performance of a contract is relevant as a fact in looking at what loss the bank suffered by reason of the breach of trust, because it would be artificial and unreal to look at the trust in isolation from the obligations for which it was brought into being. I do not believe that this requires any departure from proper principles.

10-094 There remains the question whether the Court of Appeal properly applied the reasoning in *Target Holdings* to the facts of the present case. It was argued on behalf of the bank that this case falls within Lord Browne-Wilkinson's statement that "[u]ntil the underlying commercial transaction has been completed, the solicitor can be required to restore to the client account monies wrongly paid away."

10-095 This argument constricts too narrowly Lord Browne-Wilkinson's essential reasoning. Monetary compensation, whether classified as restitutive or reparative, is intended to make good a loss. The basic equitable principle applicable to breach of trust, as Lord Browne-Wilkinson stated, is that the beneficiary is entitled to be compensated for any loss he would not have suffered but for the breach. In this case, proper performance of the obligations of which the trust formed part would have resulted in the solicitors paying to Barclays the full amount required to redeem the Barclays mortgage, and, as Patten L.J. said, the bank would have had security for an extra £300,000 or thereabouts of its loan.

10-096 When Lord Browne-Wilkinson spoke of completion he was talking about a commercial transaction. The solicitors did not "complete" the transaction in compliance with the requirements of the CML Handbook. But as a commercial matter the transaction was executed or "completed" when the loan monies were released to the borrowers. At that moment the relationship between the borrowers and the bank became

> one of contractual borrower and lender, and that was a fait accompli. The Court of Appeal was right in the present case to understand and apply the reasoning in *Target Holdings* as it did.

Lord Toulson's reasoning in *A.I.B.*, like Lord Browne-Wilkinson's reasoning in *Target Holdings*, attaches special significance to the fact that the case concerned a trust of short duration created as an incident of a commercial arrangement between the parties. It is hard to make out the scope of this idea, to discern when the *Target Holdings/A.I.B.* rule will apply and when it will not. Nor can the answer to this question be inferred from the content of their Lordships' rule, since they did not clearly explain this either. Both problems with the *A.I.B.* judgment are noted by James Penner in the next passage. **10–097**

### J.E. Penner, "Distinguishing Fiduciary, Trust, and Accounting Relationships"

(2014) 8 J.Eq. 202, 225

The ratio decidendi [of *A.I.B.*] appears to be that in certain circumstances, very unclearly specified, a beneficiary of a trust will be disentitled from falsifying the account—the unauthorised expenditure will be regarded as an expenditure of the beneficiary's funds for the beneficiary's purposes. However, the trustee's breach in expending the funds on an unauthorised asset will be a wrong sufficient to support a claim to surcharge the account, so that if the expenditure as wrongly made causally gives rise to a lower asset value than would have been obtained had the intended, authorised, asset been acquired, the trustee will be liable for the difference. The court did not put their decision in these terms; indeed, it is not clear that the judges anywhere really discussed the logic of falsification, explaining why it should be rejected in this case; nevertheless, it is submitted that this is the clearest way of describing what the judgments decide. **10–098**

As in *Target Holdings*, the idea that this was a commercial trust of short duration, rather than a "traditional" trust expected to last a long time, somehow seemed to figure in the decision[108] not to allow the beneficiary to falsify the account, on the reasoning that where it would make no sense actually to reconstitute the trust, but instead, to pay "equitable compensation" directly to the beneficiary, the claim could only be one of compensation for loss, on a "but for" causal basis. But whether a trust is a traditional trust or a bare, commercial trust is a red herring. The right to falsify the account where the trustee makes an unauthorised expenditure has nothing to do with whether the trustee's subsequent liability is to "restore" the trust by ensuring he, or a successor trustee, is put in funds to hold on trust where the trust continues, or whether, given the circumstances, there would be no point in reconstituting a trust because the trust was part of a commercial transaction that has been completed or has failed. In both cases the falsification determines the basis of the defaulting trustee's personal liability.[109] **10–099**

The question arises, whether the result in *A.I.B.* could have been reached by the application of orthodox principle? Building on his earlier extra-judicial analysis of *Target Holdings*, Lord Millett has argued extra-judicially that it could.[110] His argument runs as follows. Although the solicitors were not authorised to pay the £3.3 million, and were therefore under a continuing duty to produce this cash *in specie*, they could have obtained a discharge from this duty if they had instead produced an authorised substitute for the money. The second charge which they obtained from the borrowers was an authorised substitute for the £3.3 million, save to the extent that it was subordinated to the Barclays' charge securing the borrowers' outstanding £300,000 liability. Hence, if the solicitors had paid A.I.B. £300,000 out of their own pocket at the time when the second charge was created, **10–100**

---

108 See *A.I.B.* [2014] UKSC 58 at [31], [33], [65], [67], [70], [71], and [74] per Lord Toulson, and [106], [107], [127], [130]–[132], and [137] per Lord Reed.

109 As the High Court of Australia correctly appreciated in *Youyang Pty Ltd v Minter Ellison Morris Fletcher* (2003) 212 C.L.R. 484. See also *Agricultural Land Management* (2014) 285 F.L.R. 121 at [333]–[385] per Edelman J.

110 Lord Millett, "Reflections on the Decision of the Supreme Court in *AIB v Redler*", lecture to the Professional Negligence Bar Association, 27 January 2015.

A.I.B. would then effectively have occupied the same position as the one they had instructed the solicitors to get them into. Hence a substitutive performance claim for £300,000 was the most to which A.I.B. should have been entitled.

**10–101** This analysis depends on a dubious characterisation of what should have counted as an "authorised substitute" for the misapplied trust money. This is a question of fact, to be determined by reference to the terms of the trust and any other instructions relevantly given to the trustee by the beneficiaries. As has been stated, the Court of Appeal in *A.I.B.* held as a fact, and the Supreme Court (rather reluctantly) decided the case on the agreed basis,[111] that payment of the whole £3.3 million constituted a breach of trust for the reason that the Barclays charge was never extinguished. The notion that the second charge obtained by the solicitors was an authorised substitute for the money save for the continued existence of the Barclays charge is inconsistent with this factual finding. It effectively entails dividing the solicitors' duties into parts and saying that most of them were carried out. That is what the trial judge said when he held that only the payment of £300,000 to the borrowers constituted a breach of trust, and the Court of Appeal held that to be factually incorrect. In their view, the solicitor's duties were entire, and that being so, their substitutive performance obligation should also have had to entail payment of the entire sum which they wrongly paid away.

## *B. Reparation Claims*

**10–102** Reparation claims are claims that trustees should make good the harm which the beneficiaries have suffered as a consequence of the trustees' breach of duty. They depend on the assertion that the trustees have committed a wrong,[112] and the award made is calculated by reference to the loss suffered by the beneficiaries,[113] including the loss of a chance to avoid a detriment or make a gain.[114] The beneficiaries must prove that their loss has been factually caused by the trustees' breach of duty, using a "but-for" causation test in all cases, regardless of whether the breach was innocent, negligent or fraudulent.[115] Canadian authorities also indicate that their claims are subject to the principle of novus actus interveniens,[116] and that where the beneficiaries have become aware that their trustees are not to be trusted, losses flowing from clearly unreasonable behaviour by the beneficiaries thereafter will be judged to have been caused by this behaviour and not by the breach.[117]

**10–103** A reparation claim might be brought, for example, where a trustee fails to exhibit an appropriate degree of care in negligently making an authorised investment which subsequently declines in value,[118] or again, where she has failed to do something, e.g. to collect the rents payable on the trust

---

[111] [2014] 3 W.L.R. 1367 at [16], [140].

[112] *Partington v Reynolds* (1858) 4 Drew 253 at 255–256; *Dowse v Gorton* [1891] A.C. 190 at 202; *Re Stevens* [1898] 1 Ch. 162 at 170.

[113] *Elder's Trustee and Executor Co. Ltd v Higgins* (1963) 113 C.L.R. 426 at 453; *Fales v Canada Permanent Trust Co.* [1977] 2 S.C.R. 302 at 320.

[114] *Sanders v Parry* [1967] 1 W.L.R. 753 at 767; *Nestlé v National Westminster Bank Plc* [1993] 1 W.L.R. 1260 at 1269; *Colour Control Centre Pty Ltd v Ty* N.S.W. Sup. Ct. (Eq. Div.) 24 July 1995; *Bank of New Zealand v New Zealand Guardian Trust Co Ltd* [1999] 1 N.Z.L.R. 664 at 685–686.

[115] *Target Holdings Ltd v Redferns* [1996] A.C. 421 at 436; *Collins v Brebner* [2000] Lloyds Rep. P.N. 587; *Hulbert v Avens* [2003] EWHC 76 (Ch) at [56]; *Gwembe Valley Development Co. Ltd v Koshy (No.3)* [2004] 1 B.C.L.C. 131 at [147]. But cf. *Bairstow v Queen's Moat Houses Plc* [2001] 2 B.C.L.C. 531 at [53]–[54]. On the question whether reparation claims are subject to a remoteness cap, see S.B. Elliott, "Remoteness Criteria in Equity" (2002) 65 M.L.R. 588; and also *Olszanecki v Hillocks* [2004] W.T.L.R. 975.

[116] *Hodgkinson v Simms* [1994] 3 S.C.R. 377 at 443; *Waxman v Waxman* (2004) 7 I.T.E.L.R. 162 at [663].

[117] *Canson Enterprises Ltd v Boughton & Co* [1991] 3 S.C.R. 534 at 554, endorsed in *Corporaçion del Cobre de Chile v Sogemin Metals Ltd* [1997] 1 W.L.R. 1396 at 1403–1404. See too *Lipkin Gorman v Karpnale Ltd* [1992] 4 All E.R. 331 at 361.

[118] In these circumstances no question can arise of the beneficiaries choosing whether to adopt or reject the transaction: the

property,[119] or to diversify investments,[120] or to sell particular assets,[121] or to monitor the activities of a 99 per cent owned company, as in *Bartlett v Barclays Bank Trust Co Ltd (No.2)*,[122] which is excerpted below.[123] In cases of this sort, it must be shown that the loss could not have occurred, but for the trustee's failure to do what no reasonable trustee (viz., a properly informed trustee exhibiting the due standard of care) could have failed to do. Proving this can be difficult,[124] but it seems that a claim would lie where trustees take a positive decision to take specific action, e.g. to sell particular shares as soon as practicable, and then fail to implement their decision without any conscious reason. Another way of analysing this situation, however, would be to draw an analogy with the case where a trust instrument requires a particular original investment to be sold as soon as practicable. If the trustees fail to perform this duty, then a substitutive performance claim will lie against them for the amount that would have been realised if they had sold investment within a reasonable time.[125]

In the *Bartlett* case, Brightman LJ thought that where trustees are ordered to pay money to make good the harm caused to the beneficiaries by the trustees' negligence, the award is "not readily distinguishable from damages except with the aid of a powerful legal microscope".[126] This comment was later echoed by Millett LJ in *Bristol & West BS v Mothew*, who held that[127]: **10–104**

> Equitable compensation for breach of the duty of skill and care [owed by a fiduciary] resembles common law damages in that it is awarded by way of compensation to the plaintiff for his loss. There is no reason in principle why the common law rules of causation, remoteness of damage and measure of damages should not be applied by analogy in such a case.

These dicta were followed by Newey J in *Brudenell-Bruce v Moore*,[128] where he held that a trustee who carelessly allows trust property to fall into disrepair is not liable for the costs of reinstatement where these would be much greater than the resulting enhancement of the property's value. In so holding, the judge drew an analogy with *Ruxley Electronics Ltd v Forsyth*,[129] a case concerning compensatory liability for breach of contract.

It is a controversial question whether trustees and other fiduciaries who harm their principals by their negligent acts or omissions should be treated in the same way as contract-breakers or tortfeasors at common law, or whether the fact that they are fiduciaries justifies treating them more stringently. When considering this question it is important to distinguish clearly between substitutive performance claims and reparation claims, and to bear in mind that either type of claim might lie on some sets of facts, e.g. where trustees make an unauthorised negligent investment. As Millett LJ stresses in the passage quoted above, analogies with tort claims are simply inapt if a substitutive performance claim is brought, but we may legitimately ask whether a reparation claim should be **10–105**

---

investment forms part of the trust estate, but the trustee may be personally liable to pay compensation for the loss caused by her negligence: *Re Salmon* (1888) 42 Ch.D. 351 at 369, 371.

119 *M'Donnel v White* (1865) 9 HLC 570 at 584.

120 *Nestlé v National Westminster Bank* [1993] 1 W.L.R. 1265 at 1281; *Re Mulligan* [1998] 1 N.Z.L.R. 181.

121 *Wight v Olswang (No.2)* [2000] W.T.L.R. 783, reversed [2001] W.T.L.R. 291; *Re Ambrazevicius Estate* (2002) 164 Man. R. (2d) 5.

122 [1980] Ch. 515.

123 At paras 10–108ff.

124 Consider *Nestlé v National Westminster Bank* [1993] 1 W.L.R. 1265, reproduced below at paras 10–151ff.

125 *Fry v Fry* (1859) 27 Beav. 144; *Fales v Canada Permanent Trust Co.* (1976) 70 D.L.R. (3d) 257 at 274.

126 [1980] Ch. 515 at 545.

127 [1998] Ch. 1 at 18, adopting *Permanent B.S. v Wheeler* (1994) 11 W.A.R. 187 at 237. See too *Bank of New Zealand v New Zealand Guardian Trust Co Ltd* [1999] 1 N.Z.L.R. 664 at 687; *Hilton v Barker Booth & Eastwood (a firm)* [2005] 1 W.L.R. 1597 at [29]; *Langlands v S.G. Hambros Trust Co (Jersey) Ltd* [2007] EWHC 627 (Ch) at [25].

128 [2014] EWHC 3679 (Ch) at [144]–[155].

129 [1996] A.C. 344.

governed by rules of causation, remoteness and contributory negligence which are identical with, or more claimant-friendly than, the rules which apply to tort claims for compensatory damages.

10–106 The authorities are divided on this point. Some stress that a fiduciary and her principal are not "independent and equal actors, concerned primarily with their own self-interest" but parties in a special relationship under which one "pledges itself to act in the best interest of the other", so that "when breach occurs, the balance favours the person wronged".[130] Others deny that there is a valid reason to treat a trustee or other fiduciary differently from anyone else who injures another person by her negligence, and that "regardless of the doctrinal underpinning, plaintiffs should not be able to recover higher damage awards merely because their claim is characterised as a breach of fiduciary duty, as opposed to breach of contract or tort".[131]

10–107 This debate is often conducted in all-or-nothing terms, but in our view the best way forward is for the courts to acknowledge that it can be appropriate to treat different kinds of trustee in different ways.[132] For example, there is an important difference between traditional family trusts and modern commercial trusts for absolutely entitled beneficiaries where the parties are on a more equal footing and the management role of the trustee is extensive and complex. In the latter case at least, the justification is much weaker for imposing a more stringent liability for negligent conduct than the trustee would incur at common law.

*Bartlett v Barclays Bank Trust Co Ltd*

Chancery Division [1980] Ch. 515

10–108 The claimant sued the trustees for failing to exercise proper supervision over the management of the family company, "BTL", which they controlled through possession of a 99.8 per cent shareholding. Subsequently BTL became a wholly-owned subsidiary of another company, "BTH", which the trustees also controlled through a 99.8 per cent shareholding. The trustees' failure to supervise BTL and then BTH led to the company losing over £1/2 million in a disastrous property speculation.

10–109 BRIGHTMAN J.: The situation may be summed up as follows. BTH made a large loss as a result of the involvement of itself and BTL in the Old Bailey project. This loss reduced the value of the BTH shares and thereby caused a loss to the trust fund of the 1920 settlement. The bank, had it acted in time, could be reason of its shareholding have stopped the board of BTL embarking on the Old Bailey project; and, had it acted in time, could have stopped the board of BTL and later the board of BTH (it is unnecessary to differentiate) from continuing with the project; and could, had it acted in time, have required BTH to sell its interest in Far to Stock Conversion on the no-loss or small-loss terms which (as I find) were available for the asking. This would not have necessitated the draconian course of threatening to remove, or actually removing, the board in favour of compliant directors. The members of the board were reasonable persons, and would (as I find) have followed any reasonable policy desired by the bank had the bank's wishes been

---

130 *Canson Enterprises Ltd v Boughton & Co.* [1991] 3 S.C.R. 534 at 543, per McLachlin J, quoted with approval in *Youyang Pty Ltd v Minter Ellison Morris Fletcher* (2003) 212 C.L.R. 484 at [40]. See too *Norberg v Wynrib* [1992] 2 S.C.R. 226 at [272], quoted with approval in *Pilmer v Duke Group Ltd (In Liquidation)* (2001) 207 C.L.R. 165 at [71]; *Maguire v Makaronis* (1997) 188 C.L.R. 449 at 473. The argument that equity should exert prophylactic pressure on fiduciaries by stringent treatment of their breaches of skill and care as well as their breaches of fiduciary duty has been made by Joshua Getzler in three articles: "Equitable Compensation and the Regulation of Fiduciary Relationships" in P. Birks and F.D. Rose (eds), *Restitution and Equity: Resulting Trusts and Equitable Compensation* (Mansfield Press, 2000); "Duty of Care" in P. Birks and A. Pretto (eds), *Breach of Trust* (Hart Publishing, 2002); "Am I My Beneficiary's Keeper? Fusion and Loss-Based Fiduciary Remedies" in *Equity in Commercial Law* (2005).

131 *Martin v Goldfarb* (1998) 41 O.R. (3d) 161 at 173, per Finlayson JA. See too *Day v Mead* [1987] 2 N.Z.L.R. 443 at 451; *Canson Enterprises Ltd v Boughton & Co.* [1991] 3 S.C.R. 534 at 585–589, per La Forest J; *Waxman v Waxman* (2004) 7 I.T.E.L.R. 162 at 660–662; J. Edelman and S. B. Elliott, "Money Remedies against Trustees" (2004) 18 Tru L.I. 116, 119–122; A.S. Burrows, *Remedies for Torts and Breach of Contract*, 3rd edn (Oxford University Press, 2004), pp.600–606.

132 See further C.E.F. Rickett, "Compensating for Loss in Equity: Choosing the Right Horse for Each Course" in P. Birks and F.D. Rose (eds), *Restitution and Equity* (Informa, 2000), Vol.1; D.J. Hayton "Unique Rules for the Unique Institution, the Trust" in *Equity in Commercial Law* (2005).

indicated to the board. The loss to the trust fund could have been avoided (as I find) without difficulty or disruption had the bank been prepared to lead, in a broad sense, rather than to follow.

What, then, was the duty of the bank and did the bank fail in its duty? It does not follow that because a trustee could have prevented a loss it is therefore liable for the loss. The questions which I must ask myself are: (i) what was the duty of the bank as the holder of 99.8 per cent of the shares in BTL and BTH? (2) Was the bank in breach of duty in any and if so what respect? (3) If so, did that breach of duty cause the loss which was suffered by the trust estate? (4) If so, to what extent is the bank liable to make good that loss? In approaching these questions, I bear in mind that the attack on the bank is based, not on wrongful acts, but on wrongful omissions, that is to say, non-feasance not misfeasance. **10–110**

The cases establish that it is the duty of a trustee to conduct the business of the trust with the same care as an ordinary prudent man of business would extend towards his own affairs.[133] In applying this principle, Lindley L.J. added in *Re Whiteley*:[134] **10–111**

> ". . . care must be taken not to lose sight of the fact that the business of the trustee, and the business which the ordinary prudent man is supposed to be conducting for himself, is the business of investing money for the benefit of persons who are to enjoy it at some future time, and not for the sole benefit of the person entitled to the present income. The duty of a trustee is not to take such care only as a prudent man would take if he had only himself to consider; the duty rather is to take such care as an ordinary prudent man would take if he were minded to make an investment for the benefit of other people for whom he felt morally bound to provide. The is the kind of business the ordinary prudent man is supposed to be engaged in; and unless this is borne in mind the standard of a trustee's duty will be fixed too low; lower than it has ever yet been fixed, and lower certainly than the House of Lords or this Court endeavoured to fix it in [*Re Speight*]."

. . . If the trust had existed without the incorporation of BTL, so that the bank held the freehold and leasehold properties and other assets of BTL directly on the trusts of the settlement, it would in my opinion have been a clear breach of trust for the bank to have hazarded trust money in the Old Bailey development project in partnership with Stock Conversion. The Old Bailey project was a gamble, because it involved buying into the site at prices in excess of the investment values of the properties, with no certainty or probability, with no more than a chance, that planning permission could be obtained for a financially viable redevelopment, that the numerous proprietors would agree to sell out or join in the scheme, that finance would be available on acceptable terms, and that the development would be completed, or at least become a marketable asset, before the time came to start winding up the trust. However one looks at it, the project was a hazardous speculation on which no trustee could properly have ventured without explicit authority in the trust instrument. I therefore hold that the entire expenditure in the Old Bailey project would have been incurred in breach of trust, had the money been spent by the bank itself. The fact that it was a risk acceptable to the board of a wealthy company like Stock Conversion has little relevance. **10–112**

I turn to the question, what was the duty of the bank as the holder of shares in BTL and BTH? I will first answer this question without regard to the position of the bank as a specialist trustee, to which I will advert later. The bank, as trustee, was bound to act in relation to the shares and to the controlling position which they conferred, in the same manner as a prudent man of business. The prudent man of business will act in such manner as is necessary to safeguard his investment. He will do this in two ways. If facts come to his knowledge which tell him that the company's affairs are not being conducted as they should be, or which put him on enquiry, he will take appropriate action. Appropriate action will no doubt consist in the first instance of enquiry of and consultation with the directors, and in the last but most unlikely resort, the convening of a general meeting to replace one or more directors. What the prudent man of business will not do is to content himself with the receipt of such information on the affairs of the company as a shareholder ordinarily receives at annual general meetings. Since he has the power to do so, he will go further and see that he has sufficient information to enable him to make a responsible decision from time to time either to let matters proceed as they are proceeding, or to intervene if he is dissatisfied. This topic was considered by Cross J. in *Re Lucking's Will Trusts*.[135] In that case nearly 70 per cent of the shares in **10–113**

---

133 See *Re Speight* (1883) 22 Ch.D. 727 at 739, per Jessel M.R., and 762, per Bowen L.J.; affirmed on appeal (1883) 9 App. Cas. 1., and see Lord Blackburn at 19.

134 (1886) 33 Ch.D. 347 at 355.

135 [1968] 1 W.L.R. 866.

the company were held by two trustees, L and B, as part of the estate of the deceased; about 29 per cent belonged to L in his own right, and 1 per cent belonged to L's wife. The directors in 1954 were Mr and Mrs L and D, who was the manager of the business. In 1956 B was appointed trustee to act jointly with L. The company was engaged in the manufacture and sale of shoe accessories. It had a small factory employing about 20 people, and one or two travellers. It also had an agency in France. D wrongfully drew some £15,000 from the company's bank account in excess of his remuneration, and later became bankrupt. The money was lost. Cross J. said this:[136]

> "The conduct of the defendant trustees is, I think, to be judged by the standard applied in *Re Speight*, namely, that a trustee is only bound to conduct the business of the trust in such a way as an ordinary prudent man would conduct a business of his own. Now, what steps, if any, does a reasonably prudent man who finds himself a majority shareholder in a private company take with regard to the management of the company's affairs? He does not, I think, content himself with such information as to the management of the company's affairs as he is entitled to as shareholder, but ensures that he is represented on the board. He may be prepared to run the business himself as managing director or, at least, to become a non-executive director while having the business managed by someone else. Alternatively, he may find someone who will act as his nominee on the board and report to him from time to time as to the company's affairs. In the same way, as it seems to me, trustees holding a controlling interest ought to ensure so far as they can that they have such information as to the progress of the company's affairs as directors would have. If they sit back and allow the company to be run by the minority shareholder and receive no more information than shareholders are entitled to, they do so at their risk if things go wrong."

**10–114** I do not understand Cross J. to have been saying that in every case where trustees have a controlling interest in a company it is their duty to ensure that one of their number is a director or that they have a nominee on the board who will report from time to time on the affairs of the company. He was merely outlining convenient methods by which a prudent man of business (as also a trustee) with a controlling interest in a private company, can place himself in a position to make an informed decision whether any action is appropriate to be taken for the protection of his asset. Other methods may be equally satisfactory and convenient, depending on the circumstances of the individual case. Alternatives which spring to mind are the receipt of the copies of the agenda and minutes of board meetings if regularly held, the receipt of monthly management accounts in the case of a trading concern, or quarterly reports. Every case will depend on its own facts. The possibilities are endless. It would be useless, indeed misleading, to seek to lay down a general rule. The purpose to be achieved is not that of monitoring every move of the directors, but of making it reasonably probable, so far as circumstances permit, that the trustee or (as in *Re Lucking's Will Trusts*) one of them will receive an adequate flow of information in time to enable the trustees to make use of their controlling interest should this be necessary for the protection of their trust asset, namely the shareholding. The obtaining of information is not an end in itself, but merely a means of enabling the trustees to safeguard the interest of their beneficiaries.

**10–115** . . . So far, I have applied the test of the ordinary prudent man of business. Although I am not aware that the point has previously been considered, except briefly in *Re Waterman's Will Trusts*,[137] I am of opinion that a higher duty of care is plainly due from someone like a trust corporation which carries on a specialised business of trust management. A trust corporation holds itself out in its advertising literature as being above ordinary mortals. With a specialist staff of trained trust officers and managers, with ready access to financial information and professional advice, dealing with and solving trust problems day after day, the trust corporation holds itself out, and rightly, as capable of providing an expertise which it would be unrealistic to expect and unjust to demand from the ordinary prudent man or woman who accepts, probably unpaid and sometimes reluctantly from a sense of family duty, the burdens of a trusteeship. Just as, under the law of contract, a professional person possessed of a particular skill is liable for breach of contract if he neglects to use the skill and experience which he professes, so I think that a professional corporate trustee is liable for breach of trust if loss is caused to the trust fund because it neglects to exercise the special care and skill which it professes to have. The advertising literature of the bank was not in evidence (other than the scale of fees) but counsel for the bank did not dispute that trust corporations, including the bank,

---

136 [1968] 1 W.L.R. 866 at 874–875.

137 [1968] 1 W.L.R. 866.

hold themselves out as possessing a superior ability for the conduct of trust business, and in any event I would take judicial notice of that fact. Having expressed my view of the higher duty required from a trust corporation, I should add that the bank's counsel did not dispute the proposition.

In my judgment the bank wrongfully and in breach of trust neglected to ensure that it received an adequate flow of information concerning the intentions and activities of the boards of BTL and BTH. It was not proper for the bank to confine itself to the receipt of the annual balance sheet and profit and loss account, detailed annual financial statements and the chairman's report and statement, and to attendance at the annual general meetings and the luncheons that followed, which were the limits of the bank's regular sources of information. Had the bank been in receipt of more frequent information it would have been able to step in and stop, and ought to have stopped, Mr Roberts and the board embarking on the Old Bailey project. That project was imprudent and hazardous and wholly unsuitable for a trust whether undertaken by the bank direct or through the medium of its wholly owned company. Even without the regular flow of information which the bank ought to have had, it knew enough to put it on enquiry. There were enough obvious points at which the bank should have intervened and asked questions. Assuming, as I do, that the questions would have been answered truthfully, the bank would have discovered the gamble on which Mr Roberts and his board were about to embark in relation to the Old Bailey site, and it could have, and should have, stopped the initial move towards disaster, and later on arrested further progress towards disaster. . . . 10–116

I hold that the bank failed in its duty whether it is judged by the standard of the prudent man of business or of the skilled trust corporation. The bank's breach of duty caused the loss which was suffered by the trust estate. If the bank had intervened as it could and should have, that loss would not have been incurred. By "loss", I mean the depreciation which took place in the market value of the BTL and BTH shares, by comparison with the value which the shares would have commanded if the loss on the Old Bailey project had not been incurred, and reduction of dividends through loss of income. The bank is liable for the loss so suffered by the trust estate, except to the extent that I shall heareafter indicate. . . . 10–117

The bank also relies on clause 18 of the settlement. Clause 18 entitled the bank to: 10–118

> "act in relation to [BTL] or any other company and the shares securities and properties thereof in such way as it shall think best calculated to benefit the trust premises and as if it was the absolute owner of such shares securities and property."

In my judgment this a clause which confers on the bank power to engage in a transaction which might otherwise be outside the scope of its authority; it is not an indemnity protecting the bank against liability for a transaction which is a breach of trust because it is one that a prudent man of business would have eschewed. . . .

Section 61 of the Trustee Act 1925 is pleaded. There is no doubt that the bank acted honestly. I do not think it acted reasonably. Nor do I think it would be fair to excuse the bank at the expense of the beneficiaries. 10–119

There remains this defence, which I take from paragraph 26 of the amended pleading: 10–120

> "In about 1963 the Old Company purchased a site at Woodbridge Road, Guildford, pursuant to the policy pleaded in paragraph 19 hereof, for the sum of £79,000, and re-sold the same for £350,000 to MEPC Ltd in 1973. The net profit resulting from such sale was £271,000. If, which is denied, the Defendant is liable for breach of trust, whether as alleged in the amended Statement of Claim or otherwise, the Defendant claims credit for such sum of £271,000 or other sum found to be gained in taking any accounts or inquiries."

The general rule as stated in all the textbooks, with some reservations, is that where a trustee is liable in respect of distinct breaches of trust, one of which has resulted in a loss and the other in a gain, he is not entitled to set off the gain against the loss, unless they arise in the same transaction. . . . The relevant cases are, however, not altogether easy to reconcile. All are centenarians and none is quite like the present. The Guildford development stemmed from exactly the same policy and (to a lesser degree because it proceeded less far) exemplified the same folly as the Old Bailey project. Part of the profit was in fact used to finance the Old Bailey disaster. By sheer luck the gamble paid off handsomely, on capital account. I think it would be unjust to deprive the bank of this element of salvage in the course of assessing the cost of the shipwreck. My order will therefore reflect the bank's right to an appropriate set-off. . . . 10–121

## C. Accountability

10–122 At the core of an express trust is the trustees' duty to account to the beneficiaries for what they have done with the trust property.[138] Beneficiaries are entitled to ask their trustees for such an account as a matter of right, but they can also obtain a court order directing the trustees to account for the trust property in the course of proceedings to enforce their rights to (specific or substitutive) performance of the trustees' primary duties or to recover reparative compensation for losses flowing from the trustees' breaches of duty.[139] In this context, the taking of the account is the first step in a two-step process that starts with the identification of deficits in the trust fund (usually undertaken by a Chancery Master or district judge) and is followed by the issuing of judgment for the balance found to be due. Sitting as a judge in the Hong Kong Final Court of Appeal, Lord Millett NPJ explained this process in *Libertarian Investments Ltd v Hall*.[140]

*Libertarian Investments Ltd v Hall*

Hong Kong Court of Final Appeal (2013) 16 H.K.C.F.A.R. 681 at [167]–[172]

10–123 LORD MILLETT N.P.J.: . . . It is often said that the primary remedy for breach of trust or fiduciary duty is an order for an account, but this is an abbreviated and potentially misleading statement of the true position. In the first place an account is not a remedy for wrong. Trustees and most fiduciaries are accounting parties, and their beneficiaries or principals do not have to prove that there has been a breach of trust or fiduciary duty in order to obtain an order for account. Once the trust or fiduciary relationship is established or conceded the beneficiary or principal is entitled to an account as of right. Although like all equitable remedies an order for an account is discretionary, in making the order the court is not granting a remedy for wrong but enforcing performance of an obligation.

10–124 In the second place an order for an account does not in itself provide the plaintiff with a remedy; it is merely the first step in a process which enables him to identify and quantify any deficit in the trust fund and seek the appropriate means by which it may be made good. Once the plaintiff has been provided with an account he can falsify and surcharge it. If the account discloses an unauthorised disbursement the plaintiff may falsify it, that is to say ask for the disbursement to be disallowed. This will produce a deficit which the defendant must make good, either in specie or in money. Where the defendant is ordered to make good the deficit by the payment of money, the award is sometimes described as the payment of equitable compensation; but it is not compensation for loss but restitutionary or restorative. The amount of the award is measured by the objective value of the property lost determined at the date when the account is taken and with the full benefit of hindsight.

10–125 But the plaintiff is not bound to ask for the disbursement to be disallowed. He is entitled to ask for an inquiry to discover what the defendant did with the trust money which he misappropriated and whether he dissipated it or invested it, and if he invested it whether he did so at a profit or a loss. If he dissipated

---

[138] Other parties besides trustees may also owe an obligation to account for what they have done with property belonging to another party, e.g. directors (*Re Lands Allotment Co* [1894] 1 Ch. 616 at 638; *H.M.R.C. v Holland* [2011] Bus. L.R. 111 at [56]); agents (*A.-G. v Cocke* [1988] Ch. 414 at 420); and receivers (*Mirror Group Newspapers Plc v Maxwell (No.1)* [1998] 1 B.C.L.C. 638 at 648–649). It does not necessarily follow from this that proceedings for an equitable account can be brought against them: *Barnett v Creggy* [2014] EWHC 3080 (Ch) at [74]. But that does not alter the substantive content of their liability for unauthorised action, which is the same as that owed by trustees: C. Mitchell, "Stewardship of Property and Liability to Account" [2014] Conv. 215; J.E. Penner, "Distinguishing Fiduciary, Trust, and Accounting Relationships" (2014) 8 J.Eq. 202.

[139] cf. *Doss v Doss* (1843) 3 Moo. Ind. App. 175 at 196–197: "a decree for an account is not a mere direction to inquire and report. It proceeds, and must always proceed, upon the assumption that the party calling for it is entitled to the sum found due. It is a decree affirming his rights, only leaving it to be inquired into, how much is due to him from the party accounting." Note that trustees "who indefensibly fail to produce accounts may be ordered to pay not only the costs of proceedings to obtain the accounts but also the costs of taking the account which is ordered": *Mason v Coleman* [2007] EWHC 3149 (Ch) at [93]. See too *Kemp v Burn* (1863) 4 Giff. 348; *Jefferys v Marshall* (1870) 23 L.T. 548.

[140] (2013) 16 H.K.C.F.A.R. 681; noted L. Ho and R. Lee (2014) 130 L.Q.R. 542. See too *Ultraframe (UK) Ltd v Fielding* [2007] W.T.L.R. 835 at [1513].

> it or invested it at a loss, the plaintiff will naturally have the disbursement disallowed and disclaim any interest in the property in which it was invested by treating it as bought with the defendant's own money. If, however, the defendant invested the money at a profit, the plaintiff is not bound to ask for the disbursement to be disallowed. He can treat it as an authorised disbursement, treat the property in which it has been invested as acquired with trust money, and follow or trace the property and demand that it or its traceable proceeds be restored to the trust in specie.
>
> If on the other hand the account is shown to be defective because it does not include property which the defendant in breach of his duty failed to obtain for the benefit of the trust, the plaintiff can surcharge the account by asking for it to be taken on the basis of "wilful default", that is to say on the basis that the property should be treated as if the defendant had performed his duty and obtained it for the benefit of the trust. Since ex hypothesi the property has not been acquired, the defendant will be ordered to make good the deficiency by the payment of money, and in this case the payment of "equitable compensation" is akin to the payment of damages as compensation for loss. **10–126**
>
> In an appropriate case the defendant will be charged, not merely with the value of the property at the date when it ought to have been acquired or at the date when the account is taken, but at its highest intermediate value. This is on the footing either that the defendant was a trustee with power to sell the property or that he was a fiduciary who ought to have kept his principal informed and sought his instructions. **10–127**
>
> At every stage the plaintiff can elect whether or not to seek a further account or inquiry. The amount of any unauthorised disbursement is often established by evidence at the trial, so that the plaintiff does not need an account but can ask for an award of the appropriate amount of compensation. Or he may be content with a monetary award rather than attempt to follow or trace the money, in which case he will not ask for an inquiry as to what has become of the trust property. In short, he may elect not to call for an account or further inquiry if it is unnecessary or unlikely to be fruitful, though the court will always have the last word. **10–128**

Before the Judicature Acts, beneficiaries could only make hostile claims against their trustees by bringing an administration suit. This was a suit for the judicial execution of the trust, asking the court to assume responsibility for the trust's performance. Beneficiaries can still bring full execution proceedings, but they can now also bring narrower proceedings for discrete relief by asking the court for an order that the trustees should present an account of their dealings for judicial scrutiny, adding the common form plea for administration of the trust estate "if and so far as necessary".[141] **10–129**

There are three types of accounting order which a court might make.[142] An order for an account in common form is the most common, as the name suggests. The trustees are directed to submit a set of accounts which identify the original trust property, what the trustees have received, what they have disbursed for costs and expenses,[143] what they have distributed to the beneficiaries, and what they have left in hand. These accounts can be challenged by the beneficiaries, but the fact that a court has ordered trustees to present accounts in this form need not imply that they have done anything wrong, as orders for common accounts can be made simply in order to clarify matters.[144] In contrast, an order for an account on the basis of wilful default is entirely grounded on the trustees' misconduct,[145] and requires them to account not only for what they have received but also for what they would have received if they had not committed a breach of duty.[146] The term "wilful default" is a misleading one in this context since **10–130**

---

141 *Iliffe v Trafford* [2002] W.T.L.R. 507 at [8].

142 As discussed by Austin J in *Glazier v Australian Men's Health (No.2)* [2001] NSWSC 6. See too S. Elliott, "Accounting in Equity" in *Snell's Equity*, J. McGhee (ed.), 32nd edn (Sweet & Maxwell, 2010), pp.592–599.

143 Note the Trustee Act 2000 s.31, discussed at paras 8–72ff., which empowers trustees to take properly incurred expenses out of the trust funds. For discussion of the question whether trustees can recover an indemnity for expenses incurred in the course of unauthorised conduct, see *Fitzwood Pty Ltd v Unique Goal Pty Ltd (In Liquidation)* (2001) 188 A.L.R. 566.

144 *Partington v Reynolds* (1858) 4 Drew 253 at 256.

145 *Partington* at 256.

146 *Re Tebbs* [1976] 1 W.L.R. 924; *Bartlett v Barclays Bank Co Ltd* [1980] Ch. 15; *Coulthard v Disco Mix Club Ltd* [1999] 2 All E.R. 457 at 481; *Armitage v Nurse* [1998] Ch. 241 at 252; *Iliffe v Trafford* [2002] W.T.L.R. 507 at [9].

it encompasses all breaches of duty, running from inadvertent non-compliance with the terms of the trust through to deliberate fraud.[147] Finally, an order for an account of profits requires the trustees to account for specific gains which they have made in the course of administering the trust affairs.

**10–131** An account of profits will be ordered in connection with a claim that the trustees should be required to hand over gains. An account on the basis of wilful default will be ordered in connection with a claim that the trustees should be required to pay reparative compensation for loss caused by the trustees' breach of duty. An account in common form can be ordered where the beneficiaries make a claim for specific or substitutive performance of the trustee's duty to produce the trust property when called upon to do so, but can also be used where the beneficiaries seek reparation.

**10–132** In all cases, where there is a dispute between trustees and beneficiaries as to whether the trustees have acted properly "the beneficiary carries the burden of proving surcharges and the [trustee] carries the burden of proving [her] discharge"; hence the trustee must be able to document each item, and presumptions may be made against her if she has not kept proper records or has destroyed them.[148] In the event that a court decides, following its scrutiny of the trustees' accounts, that they owe the beneficiaries a personal liability, different forms of order can be made against them, according to the nature of the trust. Where the trust is absolute and there is no need to reconstitute the fund, the court can simply order them to transfer trust assets or pay money directly to the beneficiaries.[149] Where the trust is still on foot, the trustees will be ordered to reconstitute the fund in a proper state, or where they have been replaced by new trustees, to transfer assets or pay money to the new trustees, to be held by them under the terms of the trust.[150]

**10–133** The various types of claim which can be brought against trustees are mediated through proceedings for an account in different ways. In the case of a substitutive performance claim where the trustees have made an unauthorised distribution, the court will not permit the trustees to enter the distribution into the accounts as an outgoing as it will not let them say they acted in breach of duty.[151] Instead, they will be treated as though they have spent their own money and kept the trust assets intact. The accounts will be "falsified" to delete the unauthorised outgoing, and the trustees will be ordered to produce the relevant trust property *in specie* or pay a money substitute out of their own pockets.[152] Reparation claims are brought into the conceptual scheme of the accounts in a rather different way. The loss claimed by the beneficiaries is translated into an accounting item by "surcharging" the trustees with the amount of the loss as if the trustees had already received this amount for the beneficiaries. They must then pay an equivalent amount into the trust funds out of their pockets in order to balance the accounts.[153] Essentially the same procedure is followed in the case of a claim for profits made in breach of fiduciary duty: the trustees are deemed to have received the relevant sum for the beneficiaries, and the accounts are surcharged with the amount of the trustees' gain.[154]

---

147 *Walker v Symonds* (1818) 3 Swans 1 at [69]; *Re Chapman* [1896] 2 Ch. 763 at 776, 779–780. See too J.H. Stannard "Wilful Default" [1979] Conv. 345, esp. 348.

148 *Snell's Equity* (2010), p.593, quoted with approval in *Exsus Travel Ltd v Turner* [2014] EWCA Civ 1331 at [22]. See too *Campbell v Gillespie* [1899] 1 Ch. 225 at 229; *Campbell v Hogg* [1930] 3 D.L.R. 673 (PC); *Maintemp Heating & Air Conditioning Inc v Monat Developments Inc* (2002) 59 O.R. (3d) 270 at [40]–[44]; *Sinclair v Sinclair* [2009] EWHC 926 (Ch) at [39]–[41].

149 *Target Holdings Ltd v Redferns* [1996] A.C. 421 at 435; *Roxborough v Rothmans of Pall Mall Australia Ltd* (2002) 185 A.L.R. 335 at 353.

150 *Partridge v Equity Trustees Executors and Agency Co. Ltd* (1947) 75 C.L.R. 149; *Hillsdown Plc v Pensions Ombudsman* [1997] 1 All E.R. 862 at 897; *Chellaram v Chellaram (No.2)* [2002] 3 All E.R. 17 at [159]; *Patel v London Borough of Brent* [2004] W.T.L.R. 577 esp. at [32].

151 *Re Smith* [1896] 1 Ch. 71 at 77; *Re Biss, (Deceased)* [1903] 2 Ch. 40.

152 *Knott v Cottee* (1852) 16 Beav. 77 at 79–80; *Re Bennion* (1889) 60 L.T. 859; *Re Salmon* (1889) 42 Ch. D. 351 at 357.

153 *Meehan v Glazier Holdings Pty. Ltd* (2002) 54 N.S.W.L.R. 146 at 149–150; *Re Ambrazevicius Estate* (2002) 164 Man. R. (2d) 5.

154 For discussion of the liability owed by trustees and other fiduciaries to account for gains made by breaching their fiduciary duties, see paras 13–066ff.

## D. Examples

### i. Making Unauthorised Investments

Where trustees make an unauthorised investment they are liable for the amount of the money improperly invested, but they are entitled to claim a credit for the sale proceeds of the property when it is sold, as held in *Knott v Cottee*.[155] **10–134**

*Knott v Cottee*

Master of the Rolls (1852) 16 Beav. 77

A testator who died in January 1844 directed his executor-trustees to invest in "the public or Government stocks or funds of Great Britain, or upon real security in England and Wales." In 1845 and 1846, the defendant executor-trustee invested part of the estate in Exchequer bills, which in 1846 were ordered into court, and in the same year sold at a loss. By a decree made in 1848, the court declared that the investment in Exchequer bills was improper. If, however, the investment had been retained, its realisation at the time of the decree of 1848 would have resulted in a profit. The judge held that "the executor ought to be charged with the amount improperly invested, and credited with the produce of the Exchequer bills in 1846." **10–135**

ROMILLY M.R.: Here is an executor who had a direct and positive trust to perform, which was, to invest the money upon government stocks or funds, or upon real securities, and accumulate at compound interest all the balances after maintaining the children. He has made certain investments, which the court has declared to be improper. The case must either be treated as if these investments had not been made, or had been made for his own benefit out of his own moneys, and that he had at the same time retained moneys of the testator in his hands. I think, therefore, that there must be a reference back, to ascertain what balances the executor retained from time to time, it being clear that he has retained some balances. . . . **10–136**

As to the mode of charging the executor in respect of the Exchequer bills, I treat the laying out in Exchequer bills in this way: The persons interested were entitled to earmark them, as being bought with the testator's assets, in the same manner as if the executor had bought a house with the trust funds; and though they do not recognise the investment, they had a right to make it available for what was due; and though part of the property of the executor, it was specifically applicable to the payment. When the Exchequer bills were sold and produced £3,955, the court must consider the produce as a sum of money refunded by the executor to the testator's estate on that day; and on taking the account, the master must give credit for this amount as on the day on which the Exchequer bills were sold. . . . **10–137**

### ii. Improper Retention of Unauthorised Investments

Where trustees retain an unauthorised investment which depreciates in value,[156] they are liable for the difference between the price obtainable on sale at the proper time and the proceeds of sale of the unauthorised investment when eventually sold. **10–138**

*Fry v Fry*

Master of the Rolls (1859) 27 Beav. 144

A testator who died in March 1834, after devising his residuary real estate to two trustees on trust to pay the rents (except those of the Langford Inn) to his wife during her widowhood, with remainder over, and bequeathing his residuary personal estate upon trust for conversion for his wife during her widowhood, with remainder over, directed the trustees: "And as for and concerning all that messuage or dwelling-house **10–139**

[155] (1852) 16 Beav. 77.

[156] Where the investment increases in value the beneficiaries can adopt its purchase and the gain will then belong to the trust: *Piety v Stace* (1799) 4 Ves. 620 at 622–623.

called Langford Inn . . . upon trust, as soon as convenient after my decease, to sell and dispose of the same, either by auction or private sale, and for the most money that could be reasonably obtained for the same." In April 1836 the trustees advertised the Langford Inn for sale for £1,000. They refused an offer of £900, made in 1837. One of the trustees died in 1842. A railway opened in 1843 caused the property to depreciate in value through the diversion of traffic. The property was again advertised for sale in 1845, but no offer was received. The other trustee died in 1856. Langford Inn was still unsold and could not be sold except at a low price.

**10–140** Held, by ROMILLY M.R., that the trustees had committed a breach of trust by reason of their negligence in not selling the property for so many years, that the property must be sold, and that the estates of the trustees were "liable to make good the deficiency between the amount which should be produced by the sale of the inn and the sum of £900, in case the purchase-money thereof should not amount to that sum."[157]

**10–141** It was held by the Court of Appeal in *Re Chapman*[158] and in *Rawsthorne v Rowley*,[159] that a trustee is not liable for a loss arising through the retention of an authorised investment unless she was guilty of wilful default,[160] which requires proof of want of ordinary prudence on the part of the trustee.[161] The position is now governed by the Trustee Act 2000 ss.1, 4, and 5. The trustees must from time to time obtain and consider proper advice on whether retention of the investment is satisfactory having regard to the need for diversification and the suitability of the investments. In deciding what to do the statutory duty of care needs to be observed (except to the extent excluded).

### iii. Improper Realisation of Proper Investments

**10–142** It is a breach of trust if trustees sell an authorised investment for the purpose of investing in an unauthorised investment or for the purpose of paying the proceeds to the life-tenant in breach of trust. In such cases the trustees are liable to replace the authorised investment or the proceeds of sale of the authorised investment, whichever is the greater burden.[162] Replacement of the authorised investment will be at its value at the date it is actually replaced or at the date of the court judgment if not earlier replaced or, exceptionally, at the date the authorised investment would, in any event, have been sold.[163]

*Phillipson v Gatty*

Vice-Chancellor (1848) 6 Hare 26, affirmed (1850) 7 Hare 516

**10–143** The trustees of a sum of consols, who had power to convert and reinvest in the public funds or upon real security, realised part of the stock and invested it in an unauthorised investment.

**10–144** WIGRAM V.C.: . . . Then comes another material question—are the trustees to replace the stock, or the money produced by the sale? Mr Wood argued that they were liable to make good the money only, distinguishing the sale, which he said was lawful, from the investment, which I have decided to have been

---

157 See also *Grayburn v Clarkson* (1868) 3 Ch. App. 605; *Dunning v Gainsborough* (1885) 54 L.J. Ch. 891. Where the proper time during which the unauthorised investments, e.g. shares, should have been sold is a period during which fluctuations occur in the value of the shares one may take half the sum of the lowest and highest prices at which the shares might have been sold in the period commencing when the shares could first have been sold to advantage and ending at the date by which they should reasonably have been sold: *Fales v Canada Permanent Trust Co.* (1976) 70 D.L.R. (3d) 257 at 274.

158 [1896] 2 Ch. 763.

159 [1909] 1 Ch. 409n.

160 See also *Baud v Fardell* (1855) 4 W.R. 40; *Henderson v Hunter* (1843) 1 L.T. (O.S.) 359 at 385; *Robinson v Murdoch* (1881) 45 L.T. 417; *Re Oddy* (1910) 104 L.T. 128 at 131; *Re Godwin* (1918) 87 L.J. Ch. 645.

161 *Re Chapman* [1896] 2 Ch. 763 at 776 per Lindley LJ.

162 Thus, if an authorised investment is sold for £10,000, then invested in an unauthorised investment sold for £8,000 and when matters are discovered the authorised investment can be repurchased for £7,000, the trustees must top up the £8,000 to £10,000, the true figure that should be in the accounts (after falsifying them) as retained for the beneficiaries: *Shepherd v Mouls* (1845) 4 Hare 500 at 504; *Watts v Girdlestone* (1843) 6 Beav. 188.

163 *Re Bell's Indenture* [1980] 3 All E.R. 425 at 437–439, pointing out that in *Re Massingberd* (1890) 63 L.T. 296 the reference to the date of the writ for ascertaining the value of the property sold in breach of trust was per incuriam and should be the date of the judgment.

> a breach of trust. My opinion is, that the trustees must replace the stock. There was no authority to sell, except with a view to the reinvestment; and here the sale was made with a view to the investment I have condemned. It was all one transaction, and the sale and investment must stand or fall together. . . .
>
> Held, therefore, that the trustees must replace the stock improperly realised. Affirmed on appeal.[164] **10–145**

### iv. Non-Investment of Trust Funds

A trustee ought not to leave trust moneys uninvested for an unreasonable length of time. If she unnecessarily retains trust moneys which she ought to have invested, she is chargeable with interest.[165] While an investment is being sought, however, a trustee has statutory powers to pay trust moneys into an interest-bearing account.[166] If a trustee, having been directed to invest in a specific investment, makes no investment at all, and the price of the specified investment rises, she may be required to purchase so much of that investment as would have been obtained by a purchase at the proper time.[167] This applies equally where she is directed to invest in a specific investment but makes some investment other than the one specified.[168] However, if she is directed to invest in a specified range of investments, and makes no investment at all, then she is chargeable only with the trust fund itself, and not with the amount of one or other of the investments which might have been purchased.[169] The reason was stated by Wigram VC in *Shepherd v Mouls* as follows[170]: **10–146**

> The discretion given to the trustees to select an investment among several securities makes it impossible to ascertain the amount of the loss (if any) which has arisen to the trust from the omission to invest, except, perhaps, in the possible case (which has not occurred here) of a particular security having been offered to the trustees, in conformity with the terms of the trust.

Nowadays, however, in view of *Nestlé v National Westminster Bank*,[171] reproduced below, the trustees would be charged with the loss of profit that would have been made, taking account of the average performance of the investments within the specified range.

### v. Negligent Failure to Review and Diversify Trust Investments

Trustees must take reasonable steps to keep the trust investments under review and to diversify these as appropriate. However, as Dillon LJ said in the *Nestlé* case,[172] **10–147**

> what the prudent man should do at any time depends on the economic and financial conditions of that time—not on what judges of the past, however eminent, have held to be the prudent course in the conditions if 50 or 100 years before.

Thus, he and the other members of the Court of Appeal who decided the case further indicated[173] that if a negligent investment policy (one that no prudent trustee could have pursued) causes loss, the trustee

---

164 Followed in *Re Massingberd* (1890) 63 L.T. 296.
165 *Re Jones* (1883) 49 L.T. 91. For lost capital appreciation see *Midland Bank Trustee Ltd v Federated Pension Services* [1995] Jersey L.R. 352.
166 Trustee Act 2000 ss.3 and 16–24.
167 *Byrchall v Bradford* (1822) 6 Madd. 235.
168 *Pride v Fooks* (1840) 2 Beav. 430 at 432.
169 *Shepherd v Mouls* (1845) 4 Hare 500; *Robinson v Robinson* (1851) 1 De G.M. & G. 247.
170 *Shepherd* at 504.
171 [1994] 1 All E.R. 118; excerpted at 10–149ff.
172 [1994] 1 All E.R. 118 at 126.
173 *Nestlé* at 126–127 (criticising *Robinson v Robinson* (1851) 1 De. G.M. & G. 247).

can be required to make good to the trust fair compensation for the capital growth there would have been if a proper investment policy had been followed, i.e. compensation for loss of profit taking account, it seems, of the average performance of authorised investments during the period. It would seem to follow that if trustees invest in unauthorised investments (as contrasted with negligent investment in authorised investments) they could be similarly accountable for the profit that would have been made if they had properly invested in authorised investments.

10–148 In the *Nestlé* case itself, the Court of Appeal refused to hold the defendant trustee liable despite its failure to keep the trust investments under review over a long period of time. Their Lordships' reasons appear in the extract below. Their decision may be contrasted with that in *Re Mulligan*,[174] a New Zealand case where in order to favour the life tenant, the trustees did not diversify by investing in equities and the court robustly ordered them to pay the difference between the current value of the fund and the value which it would have reached had the trustees performed their duty.

*Nestlé v National Westminster Bank Plc*

Court of Appeal [1993] 1 W.L.R. 1260

10–149 STAUGHTON L.J. (with whom DILLON and LEGGATT L.JJ. agreed): When Mr William Nestlé died in 1922, the value of his trust fund (after payment of debts, legacies and estate duty) was about £50,000. In November 1986, when the plaintiff, his granddaughter Miss Georgina Nestlé, became absolutely entitled after the death of the last life tenant, it was worth £269,203. That, it might be thought, was a substantial improvement. But during the same period the cost of living had multiplied by a factor of 20, so that it would have required £1m to provide equivalent wealth: see the BZW equity-gilt study of 1988. The same source shows that an equity price index rose by 5203 per cent in that period. An equivalent appreciation in the value of the trust fund would have left it worth £2.6m in 1986. It is true that a small portion of the fund was advanced to life tenants, that some capital was used to supplement income for an annuity, and that there were no doubt transaction costs; against that, a sum of about £5,000 was added to the fund in 1959 when Mr Nestlé's house and contents were sold. Nevertheless, it is apparent that the investments retained or made by the trustees fell woefully short of maintaining the real value of the fund, let alone matching the average increase in price of ordinary shares.

10–150 Of course it is not a breach of trust to invest the trust fund in such a manner that its real value is not maintained. At times that will be impossible, and at others it will require extraordinary skill or luck. The highest that even the plaintiff puts her claim is that, if the equity portion in the fund as it stood in 1922 (74 per cent) had been invested so as to achieve no more than the index, the fund as a whole would have been worth over £1.8m in 1986. . . .

10–151 In the experts' reports and during the course of the trial it appeared that there were four main strands to the plaintiff's case. (1) The trustees misunderstood the investment clause in the will. (2) The trustees failed to conduct a regular and periodic review of the investments. (3) Throughout the trust period, but in particular in the later stages when there were life tenants domiciled abroad, they retained or bought too high a proportion of fixed interest securities and too few ordinary shares. (4) To the extent that the trustees did invest in ordinary shares, they concentrated too heavily on shares in banking and insurance companies, to the exclusion of other sectors.

**Misunderstanding, and Failure to Review**

10–152 In my judgment the first two charges were proved. It was admitted that at times the trustees misunderstood the investment clause; but the evidence showed that they continually misunderstood it, and there is nothing to show that they ever understood it correctly. To a novice in these matters it seems that they might deserve to be forgiven, since only among much other detail are to be found the words "stocks shares bonds debentures or securities of any railway or other company." But there is authority which shows plainly that the word "company" in such a clause is not limited by its context. Trustees are not allowed to make mistakes in law; they should take legal advice, and if they are still left in doubt they can apply to the court for a ruling. Either course would have revealed their mistake in this case.

[174] [1998] 1 N.Z.L.R. 481.

I also consider that, for a substantial period, the trustees failed to conduct regular periodic reviews of the investments. From 1922 to 1959 there was only one change of an investment, other than changes which were forced on the trustees by rights issues or because a security reached its redemption date. . . . 10–153

However, the misunderstanding of the investment clause and the failure to conduct periodic reviews do not by themselves, whether separately or together, afford the plaintiff a remedy. They were symptoms of incompetence or idleness—not on the part of National Westminster Bank but of their predecessors; they were not, without more, breaches of trust. The plaintiff must show that, through one or other or both of those causes, the trustees made decisions which they should not have made or failed to make decisions which they should have made. If that were proved, and if at first sight loss resulted, it would be appropriate to order an inquiry as to the loss suffered by the trust fund. 10–154

It may be difficult to discharge that burden, and particularly to show that decisions were not taken when they should have been. But that does not absolve a plaintiff from discharging it, and I cannot find that it was discharged in this case. . . . 10–155

**The Balance of the Fund between Equities and Gilts**

In my judgment they should, in the investment climate prevailing from 1960 onwards, have followed Professor Briston's policy, subject only to one important consideration—the overseas domicile of life tenants. If all the beneficiaries had been subject to United Kingdom tax, they should have regarded the 76.8 per cent of the fund that was in ordinary shares in 1959 (or even the 82.6 per cent in 1960) as devoted to equity investment, and only the balance as available for fixed interest securities. No doubt there were times during the period from 1960 to 1986 when it would not have been a breach of trust, and may even have been wise, to depart temporarily from that policy. But in the main I am convinced that it is the policy which they should have followed. With hindsight, one can see that the BZW Equity Index rose from 789.9 to 6353.2 in that period; the gilt index fell from 74.6 to 48.4. But my conclusion is based on the evidence of Professor Briston and Mr Harris, not on hindsight. 10–156

That, however, assumes that all the beneficiaries were subject to United Kingdom tax, which they were not. George Nestlé lived in Tanganyika from 1933 to 1963, when he moved to Malta and lived there until he died in 1972. Elsie, his widow, continued to live there until 1980, when she returned to England. She died in 1982. John Nestlé went to live in Cyprus in 1969, and died there in 1986. The fiscal effects of residence/ordinary residence/domicile overseas were, as I understand it, twofold: first, the life tenant would not be liable for United Kingdom income tax on investments outside the United Kingdom, or (more significantly) on the income from gilt-edged securities which were tax exempt; secondly, neither estate duty nor capital transfer tax would be payable on the death of a life tenant in respect of such securities. 10–157

The obligation of a trustee is to administer the trust fund impartially, or fairly (I can see no significant difference), having regard to the different interests of beneficiaries. Wilberforce J. said in *Re Pauling's Settlement Trusts (No.2)*:[175] 10–158

> "The new trustees would be under the normal duty of preserving an equitable balance, and if at any time it was shown they were inclining one way or the other, it would not be a difficult matter to bring them to account."

At times it will not be easy to decide what is an equitable balance. A life tenant may be anxious to receive the highest possible income, whilst the remainderman will wish the real value of the trust fund to be preserved. If the life tenant is living in penury and the remainderman already has ample wealth, common sense suggests that a trustee should be able to take that into account, not necessarily by seeking the highest possible income at the expense of capital but by inclining in that direction. However, before adopting that course a trustee should, I think, require some verification of the facts. In this case the trustees did not, so far as I am aware, have any reliable information as to the relative wealth of the life tenants and the plaintiff. They did send an official to interview Mr John Nestlé in Cyprus on one occasion; but the information which they obtained was conflicting and (as it turned out) incomplete. 10–159

Similarly I would not regard it as a breach of trust for the trustees to pay some regard to the relationship between Mr George Nestlé and the plaintiff. He was merely her uncle, and she would have received nothing from his share of the fund if he had fathered a child who survived him. The trustees would be entitled, in my view, to incline towards income during his life tenancy and that of his widow, on that ground. 10–160

---

[175] [1963] Ch. 576 at 586.

Again common sense suggests to me that such a course might be appropriate, and I do not think that it would be a breach of the duty to act fairly, or impartially.

10–161 The dominant consideration for the trustees, however, was that George's fund from 1960, and John's from 1969, would not be subject to United Kingdom income tax in so far as it was invested in exempt gilts. That was a factor which the trustees were entitled—and I would say bound—to take into account. A beneficiary who has been left a life interest in a trust fund has an arguable case for saying that he should not be compelled to bear tax on the income if he is not lawfully obliged to do so.

10–162 It was no more than a factor for the trustees to bear in mind, and would rarely justify more than a modest degree of preference for income paid gross over capital growth.

10–163 A trustee should also bear in mind, as these trustees did, that estate duty or capital transfer tax is likely to be reduced in such a case if part of the fund is invested in tax-exempt gilts. That may provide a compensating benefit for the remainderman. Of course it is by no means certain that the benefit will materialise; the life tenant may return to this country, as happened in the case of Mrs Elsie Nestlé. It has been said that nothing in this world is certain except death and taxes. But even the tax benefit was imponderable, since it could not be forecast what rate of tax would be applicable on the death of a life tenant.

10–164 It is said that the trustees should have anticipated that Elsie would return to the United Kingdom, or at least have made inquiries as to her intentions. I can see some force in the second part of that argument. It would have been prudent to ask her to let them know if she planned to come back to this country. But this was never put to the bank's witnesses. And I cannot find that any loss to the trust fund resulted from failure to request information from Elsie. From time to time during her life tenancy there were indications that she might return, but it was only at a late stage that this attained any degree of probability; and I doubt whether even then it would have been right for the trustees to switch investments, thus reducing her income and foregoing any prospect of a saving in capital transfer tax.

10–165 I do not consider it necessary to examine separately the balance of the two different funds from 1961 to 1986. From the point of view of the plaintiff, what mattered was the balance of the fund as a whole. The proportion in ordinary shares varied between 59.55 per cent. and 35.9 per cent. On occasion the lower figure may be attributable not to a change in investments but to a fall in the value of equities, for example in 1974 when there was a catastrophic fall. But there can be no doubt that there were other occasions when money was switched from ordinary shares to gilt-edged securities.

10–166 The policy of the trustees during this period was to achieve a 50/50 split between equities and fixed-interest. This was not to be an initial division of the kind favoured by Professor Briston, which would have resulted in a much higher proportion of equities by 1986; it was to be a division that was rebalanced from time to time, as envisaged by Professor Brealey. Whilst I much prefer Professor Briston's method in general for trust funds during this period, I consider that the circumstances of this trust, and in particular the overseas life tenants, justified the policy which the trustees adopted. They did not fail to act fairly or impartially by adopting it.

10–167 But it is said that the trustees failed to implement their own policy: the proportion of ordinary shares fell on one occasion to 35.9 per cent, and in six years it was below 40 per cent. In my judgment the trustees were not obliged to rebalance the fund annually, still less at more frequent intervals. It would have been questionable to switch immediately into equities when they fell through the floor in 1974, merely because the ordinary shares then held were only 36.37 per cent. of the fund. There was evidence that it is not a wise policy for trustees to be changing investments continually; and whilst I would not regard that as a justification for sheer inertia, I accept that an ordinary fund manager who has no special expertise should not busy himself with constant changes. The equity content started as 59.55 per cent. in 1961 and ended as 51.31 per cent. in 1986. Over those 26 years the average, according to my arithmetic, was 44.56 per cent. I would not regard that as revealing a serious departure from the trustees' policy, or a failure to act fairly and impartially. But I should add that, if I had found a breach of trust in this respect, I would have been reluctant to accept that compensation should be measured by the difference between the actual performance of the fund and the very least that a prudent trustee might have achieved. There is said to be 19th century authority to that effect; but I would be inclined to prefer a comparison with what a prudent trustee was likely to have achieved —in other words, the average performance of ordinary shares during the period.

**Diversification**

10–168 The complaint here is that there was undue emphasis on the shares of banks and insurance companies during the period from 1922 to 1960. Indeed the equities in the annuity fund when it was set up in 1922 were entirely of that description.

> However, there was evidence from the experts on both sides that bank and insurance shares were regarded as safest in the earlier period of this trust, "a low risk portfolio." I am inclined to agree with Professor Briston that there should have been diversification in the 1950s, rather than from 1960 onwards. But I cannot accept that failure to diversify in that decade was a course which no prudent trustee would have followed. . . **10–169**
>
> I would dismiss the appeal. The judge took the view that "the bank had acted conscientiously, fairly and carefully throughout the administration of [the] trust." I cannot join in that accolade. But it is not shown that there was loss arising from a breach of trust for which the trustees ought to compensate the trust fund. **10–170**

### vi. Trust Funds in Trade

If a trustee in breach of trust lends funds to a third party who knows they are trust funds but not that the loan is a breach of trust and employs the trust funds in trade, the beneficiaries cannot claim from the third party a share of the profits. For example, suppose that a trustee in breach of trust lends £1,000 of trust moneys to X, who employs the fund in her trade. The agreement between the trustee and X provides that X is to pay interest at the rate of 15 per cent. By employing this fund of £1,000 in her trade, X makes a profit during the first year of £300. The beneficiaries cannot claim from X a share of that profit; all that they can require is that she replace, with interest, the fund which she borrowed. What is the position if X knew, not merely that the funds were trust funds, but also that the loan was itself a breach of trust? In this latter case, it would seem that X is a constructive trustee, that she may not "traffic in his trust", and must therefore account for her profit.[176] Of course, if the trust instrument authorises a loan of trust funds to a third party, and such a loan is made, the beneficiaries have no right to claim profits.[177] **10–171**

On the other hand, if it is the trustee herself who in breach of trust employs trust funds in her own trade, the beneficiaries may, instead of taking interest, require her to account for the profit. Thus, if in breach of trust she employs £1,000 of trust moneys in her own trade and thereby makes a profit during the first year of £200, the beneficiaries (on calling upon her to replace the fund of £1,000), may, instead of taking interest on that sum, claim the profit of £200.[178] Even if the trust funds so employed by the trustee in her own trade were mixed up with her private moneys, so that the fund used by her was a mixed one, the beneficiaries may still claim a proportionate share of the profits.[179] But it is either the one or the other, either interest or profit. They cannot, even if they find it advantageous to do so, claim interest for part of the time and profit for the other part.[180] These matters are discussed further in Chapter 13.[181] **10–172**

## 3. Impounding the Trustee's Beneficial Interest and the Rule in *Re Dacre*[182]

If a beneficiary is also trustee, but is in default to the estate in her character of trustee, she is not entitled to receive any further part of her beneficial interest until her default is made good. Her beneficial **10–173**

---

[176] *Stroud v Gwyer* (1860) 25 Beav. 130; *Vyse v Foster* (1872) 8 Ch. App. 309 at 334; *Belmont Finance Co Ltd v Williams Furniture Ltd* [1979] Ch. 250; *Beach Petroleum NL v Johnson* (1993) 43 F.C.R. 1; *Robins v Incentive Dynamics Pty Ltd (In Liquidation)* (2003) 45 A.C.S.R. 244.

[177] *Parker v Bloxam* (1855) 20 Beav. 295 at 302–304; *Evans v London Co-operative Society Ltd, The Times*, 6 July 1976.

[178] *Jones v Foxall* (1852) 15 Beav. 388; *Williams v Powell* (1852) 15 Beav. 461; *Townsend v Townsend* (1859) 1 Giff. 201; *Re Davis* [1902] 2 Ch. 314.

[179] *Docker v Somes* (1834) 2 My. & K. 655; *Edinburgh TC v Lord Advocate* (1879) 4 App. Cas. 823. Indeed, if the trust funds were the sine qua non of the purchase of a valuable asset later sold at a profit it is arguable that the trust should take the whole profit for to allow the trustee a proportion for herself would be to allow her to profit from her position.

[180] *Heathcote v Hume* (1819) 1 Jac. & W. 122; *Vyse v Foster* (1872) 8 Ch. App. 309 at 334; *Tang Man Sit v Capacious Investments Ltd* [1996] A.C. 514.

[181] See paras 13–084ff.

[182] [1916] 1 Ch. 344. See too *Jacubs v Rylance* (1874) L.R. 17 Eq. 341; *Re Brown* (1886) 32 Ch.D. 597; *Selangor United Rubber Estates Ltd v Cradock (No.4)* [1969] 1 W.L.R. 1773 at 1776–1779.

interest may also be applied in satisfaction of her liability. Take X who is a trustee, for herself for life, remainder to Y. X commits a breach of trust, and has not yet satisfied her liability. Until she does so, she cannot receive any further part of her beneficial interest, and that interest may be applied in satisfaction of her liability. The rule holds good where X's beneficial interest is derivative as well as where it is original. For example, X holds on trust for several beneficiaries, of which she is not herself one. She is in default to the estate in her character of trustee. One of the beneficiaries dies, and then X becomes entitled to that beneficiary's share as intestate successor or as legatee or devisee. X is now derivatively a beneficiary, and the rule applies as stated above.

**10–174** What is the position of an assignee from the trustee-beneficiary X? The assignee is in the same position as her assignor, i.e. she takes subject to the equity available against the trustee-beneficiary.[183] She takes subject to that equity even if the trustee-beneficiary's default to the estate was subsequent to the assignment.[184]

**10–175** It can, in fact, be most unsafe to take an assignment of the beneficial interest of a trustee-beneficiary, especially if that interest is reversionary. But it was held in *Re Towndrow*[185] that the rule does not apply to a case in which the trustee-beneficiary's liability relates to one trust (of a specific legacy) and her beneficial interest is derived from another trust (of the residuary estate), even though she is trustee of both trusts and both trusts are created by the same will. The rule in *Re Dacre* therefore applies only where the default relates to, and the beneficial interest is derived from, the same trust. Consistently with this, where money is paid to a defendant on the agreed basis that she will hold it on trust for the payor in a segregated trust bank account, and in breach of duty she pays it into her personal bank account, the payor cannot use the rule in *Re Dacre* to impound the intended trustee's own interest in the segregated trust account because the payor's money has never formed part of the fund against which he claims.[186]

## 4. Defences

### A. Power of the Court to Relieve Trustees from Personal Liability

#### Trustee Act 1925 s.61

**10–176** If it appears to the court that a trustee, whether appointed by the court or otherwise, is or may be personally liable for any breach of trust, whether the transaction alleged to be a breach of trust occurred before or after the commencement of this Act, but has acted honestly and reasonably, and ought fairly to be excused for the breach of trust and for omitting to obtain the directions of the court in the matter in which he committed such a breach, then the court may relieve him either wholly or partly from personal liability for the same.

**10–177** This section[187] enables the court to excuse not just breaches of trust in the management of trust property but also payments to the wrong persons.[188] The question of fairness should be considered

183 *Irby v Irby (No.3)* (1858) 25 Beav. 632.
184 *Doering v Doering* (1889) 42 Ch.D. 203; *Re Knapman* (1881) 18 Ch.D. 300 at 307.
185 [1911] 1 Ch. 662.
186 *Moriarty v Various Customers of BA Peters Plc* [2011] W.T.L.R. 1661.
187 Re-enacting the Judicial Trustees Act 1896 s.3. See generally Lord Maugham, "Excusable Breaches of Trust" (1898) 14 L.Q.R. 159; L. Sheridan, "Excusable Breaches of Trust" (1955) 19 Conv. (N.S.) 420; C. Stebbings, *The Private Trustee in Victorian England* (Cambridge University Press, 2002), Ch.6; J. Lowry and R. Edwards, "Excuses" in P. Birks and A. Pretto (eds), *Breach of Trust* (2002).
188 *Re Alsop* [1914] 1 Ch. 1; *Ward-Smith v Jebb* (1964) 108 Sol. Jo. 919; *Re Wightwick* [1950] 1 Ch. 260; *Re Evans* [1999] 2 All E.R. 777.

separately from the question whether the trustee acted honestly and reasonably: is it fair for the trustee to be excused when the inevitable result is to deny compensation to the beneficiaries? The burden is on the trustee[189] to satisfy the threefold obligation[190] of proving that she acted honestly and reasonably and ought fairly to be excused. Appellate courts are generally reluctant to interfere with a lower court's exercise of discretion,[191] but *Santander UK Plc v R.A. Legal Solicitors*,[192] excerpted below, shows that they will do so if the lower court's order rested on an error of law.

In the *Santander* case, Briggs LJ rejected Andrew Smith J's finding at first instance that an analogy could be drawn between s.61 and the equivalent relieving provision in the companies legislation under which directors can be said to have acted "reasonably" although they have breached their duty of care to the company.[193] Briggs LJ also held that if a defendant trustee's negligence has increased the risk of loss caused by a fraud perpetrated by a third party then it should not be excused on the basis that the fraud would have been carried through even if the trustee had acted with reasonable care. These findings closed down one possible route to rescuing solicitors from liability to pay the orthodox measure of substitutive compensation in the conveyancing cases exemplified by *A.I.B. Group (UK) Plc v Mark Redler & Co (a firm)*,[194] discussed above.[195] **10–178**

The courts are reluctant to grant relief to a paid trustee but may do so in special circumstances.[196] The taking of legal advice will be a significant consideration if such advice is followed but a breach of trust occurs because the advice was erroneous. Relevant considerations will include the standing of the legal adviser and the value of the property affected by the advice,[197] whether the adviser was given full and accurate information by the trustee,[198] and whether the trustee is herself a solicitor (in which case she cannot shelter unthinkingly behind counsel and still has a duty to consider the matter for herself).[199] If the adviser was negligent then the trustee should sue her to recover the loss for the trust and it seems hardly likely that the court would excuse the trustee if she failed to sue.[200] One must distinguish between trustees obtaining advice on behalf of the trust beneficiaries and trustees obtaining advice for their own personal protection and benefit. In the former case any cause of action arising from negligent advice will be a trust asset so that, if not barred by the limitation period, the beneficiaries could sue for themselves on joining the trustees as co-defendants with the adviser if the trustees refused to sue; in the latter case the beneficiaries generally have no rights against the adviser, being able only to sue the trustees for any breach of trust.[201] **10–179**

---

189 *Re Stuart* [1897] 2 Ch. 583; *Re Turner* [1897] 1 Ch. 536.

190 *Marsden v Regan* [1954] 1 W.L.R. 423 at 434–435, per Evershed MR See too *Mitchell v Halliwell* [2005] EWHC 937 (Ch) at [49] (no relief for honest trustee who unreasonably failed to ensure that beneficiaries took independent advice).

191 *Marsden v Regan* [1954] 1 W.L.R. 423.

192 [2014] P.N.L.R. 20; excerpted at paras 10–180ff.

193 *Santander UK Plc v R.A. Legal Solicitors* [2013] P.N.L.R. 24 at [65]–[70].

194 [2014] 3 W.L.R. 1367.

195 See paras 10–071ff. Other cases of the same kind include *Lloyds TSB Bank Plc v Markandan & Uddin (a firm)* [2012] P.N.L.R. 20; *Nationwide Building Society v Davisons Solicitors* [2013] P.N.L.R. 12; *Ikbal v Sterling Law* [2014] P.N.L.R. 9.

196 *National Trustees Co of Australasia v General Finance Co* [1905] A.C. 373; *Re Windsor Steam Coal Co* [1929] 1 Ch. 151; *Hawkesley v May* [1956] 1 Q.B. 304; *Re Pauling's Settlement Trusts (No.1)* [1964] Ch. 303 (partial relief); *Re Rosenthal* [1972] 1 W.L.R. 1273.

197 *National Trustees Co of Australasia*, above; *Re Allsop* [1914] 1 Ch. 1 at 13; *Marsden v Regan* [1954] 1 All E.R. 475 at 482; *Wong v Burt* (2004) 7 I.T.E.L.R. 263 at [49]–[58]; *Re Equilift Ltd* [2010] B.P.I.R. 116 at [15].

198 *Cherney v Neuman* [2011] EWHC 2156 (Ch) at [311].

199 ibid., at [319].

200 *National Trustees Co of Australasia*, above.

201 *Wills v Cooke* (1979) 76 L.S.G. 706; *Parker-Tweedale v Dunbar Bank Plc* [1990] 2 All E.R. 577 at 583. But for exceptions to this rule, see *Hayim v Citibank NA* [1987] A.C 730 at 747–748; *Bradstock Trustee Services Ltd v Nabarro Nathanson* [1995] 1 W.L.R. 1405; *HR v JAPT* [1997] P.L.R. 99.

### *Santander UK Plc v R.A. Legal Solicitors*

### Court of Appeal [2014] P.N.L.R. 20

**10–180** The claimant bank agreed to lend £150,000 to a borrower for the purpose of buying property. The defendant firm of solicitors undertook the conveyancing for the bank and the borrower, and the claimant transferred the money to the defendant to be held on trust and released to the vendor only when the documents of title had been obtained and a charge in favour of the bank created. The defendants dealt with a second firm of solicitors who fraudulently presented themselves as acting for the vendor. However, the vendor had never agreed to sell the property. On the day before completion, the defendant released the bank's money in the belief that they were completing the sale. However, completion never took place, and the bank never obtained a charge over the property. The money was not recovered from the fraudsters and so the bank sued the defendant solicitors for breach of trust on the basis that it had acted without authority when it had released the funds without completion having taking place.

**10–181** Andrew Smith J. held that the defendants had acted in breach of trust, but had done so in the genuine belief that completion was taking place. He excused the defendants from liability under the Trustee Act 1925 s.61, reasoning that the bank's loss had been caused by a third party's fraud for which the defendants could not fairly be treated as responsible. The bank successfully appealed from his findings in connection with s.61.

**10–182** BRIGGS L.J. (with whom ETHERTON C. and PROUDMAN J. agreed): . . . Section 61 of the Trustee Act 1925 has become the principal mechanism by which the law tempers the rigour of a trustee's otherwise strict (i.e. not fault based) liability where a fraudulent intervention in a conveyancing transaction of which the purchaser's solicitor is entirely unaware causes an unauthorised disposal of the lender's advance in breach of trust. It is precisely because of the strictness of the solicitor's trust liability that lenders which are the victims of such fraud prefer to base their claims for recovery upon breach of trust rather than breach of contract or negligence, because both of those causes of action generally require the lender to prove that the solicitor has been guilty of a breach of a duty of care. The formulation now in s.61 dates back at least to the nineteenth century (see s.3 of the Judicial Trustees Act 1896) and applies to all kinds of trustees, lay and professional, in the following terms:

> "If it appears to the court that a trustee. . . is or may be personally liable for a breach of trust. . ., but has acted honestly and reasonably and ought fairly to be excused for the breach of trust. . ., then the court may relieve him either wholly or partly from personal liability for the same."

**10–183** Invocation of s.61 involves at least two main stages. First, the trustee must show (the onus being on him) that he has acted both honestly and reasonably. In the context of mortgage fraud, institutional lenders have tended to focus upon the second of those requirements, and to dispute it in individual cases by citing a litany of examples, large and small, of aspects of the handling of the transaction where the solicitor trustee departed from standard or best practice. The present case is no exception, and Abbey's criticisms included matters happening well before and well after the transfer and loss of its advance, with apparent disregard of the question whether those alleged departures from best practice had anything at all to do with its loss.

**10–184** In the context of mortgage fraud, this court has interpreted s.61 as requiring the trustee to prove that he acted reasonably only in relation to those aspects of his conduct which are connected with the beneficiary lender's loss. This is best expressed by Sir Andrew Morritt C. in the *Davisons* case:[202]

> "The section only requires Mr Wilkes (the trustee) to have acted reasonably. That does not, in my view, predicate that he has necessarily complied with best practice in all respects. The relevant action must at least be connected with the loss for which relief is sought and the requisite standard is that of reasonableness not of perfection."

**10–185** There was considerable debate on this appeal as to precisely what type of "connection" this judicial interpretation of s.61 requires. Mr Pooles submitted that the relevant conduct had to be causative of the loss. Mr Grant submitted that this imposed too narrow a range of relevant conduct, and that the concept of connection should be liberally applied on a case by case basis, rather than by reference to a rigid formula.

**10–186** There are, I think, competing policy issues which affect this question. On the one hand, the court

---

[202] *Davisons Solicitors v Nationwide Building Society* [2013] P.N.L.R. 12 at [48].

should be slow to gloss the general words of a statute, all the more so where it confers a broad discretion. On the other hand, mortgage fraud of this kind occurs in a business context in which those advising the lender and the solicitors, and their respective insurers, need to have reasonable clarity as to the application of s.61, so as to avoid every case having to be taken all the way to trial, with a full investigation of all potentially relevant circumstances, so as to obtain a particular trial judge's discretionary decision.

It is in my view clear that a strict causation test casts the net too narrowly for the purpose of identifying relevant conduct. In most mortgage fraud cases, the effective, primary or predominant cause of the loss is the third party's fraud rather than the conduct of the solicitor trustee. **10–187**

Furthermore, it is also too restrictive to apply a "but for" test which disregards conduct, however unreasonable, on the basis that even if the solicitor had acted reasonably in that respect, the fraud, and therefore the loss, would still have occurred. The current best practice for conveyancing solicitors has evolved over many years, in the light of developing experience, for the purpose (among others) of providing reasonable, albeit not cast-iron, protection from fraud, both to lenders and purchasers. In my judgment it would not be appropriate to exclude as irrelevant conduct which consisted of a departure from best or reasonable practice which increased the risk of loss caused by fraud, even if the court concludes that the fraudster would nonetheless have achieved his goal if the solicitor had acted reasonably. **10–188**

In this respect the *Markandan* case provides a useful example.[203] There, the fraudster was an imposter who pretended to be operating a branch office of a well-known firm of solicitors. The purchaser's solicitors failed to check whether that branch office existed: see per Rimer L.J. at [60]. Plainly, that omission increased the risk that the fraudster would succeed in his plan. **10–189**

On the other hand, it would in my view extend the net too wide if it accommodated every aspect and detail of the solicitor trustee's conduct which occurred, or played any part in, the process which began with the transfer of the loan money by the lender to the solicitor trustee and ended with its theft by the fraudster. As would appear, the criticisms of RA Legal's conduct in the present case appear to have been pleaded on that broad assumption. **10–190**

Between those extremes, it seems to me that some element of causative connection will usually have to be shown, and that conduct (even if unreasonable) which is completely irrelevant or immaterial to the loss will usually fall outside the court's purview under s.61. This is, again, well illustrated by a careful comparison between the *Markandan* and *Davisons* cases. In the former, the Court of Appeal refused relief under s.61 because of two aspects of the solicitor trustee's conduct. The first, which I have already described, plainly increased the risk of the already-planned fraud succeeding. The second was a failure by the trustee solicitor to have regard to an earlier breach of undertaking by the fraudster when parting with the money for a second time. Again, the relevance or materiality of that conduct to the loss is clear. By contrast, although departures from best practice were identified both by the trial judge and by the Court of Appeal in the *Davisons* case, they had no causative significance at all. At [50], the Chancellor concluded that even if Davisons had in all respects acted in accordance with best practice, the impostor would have complied with the requisitions, supplied written undertakings, and still disappeared with the balance of the purchase money. He concluded: **10–191**

> "the lapse from best practice, if any, did not cause the loss to Nationwide."

It may be said that this part of the Chancellor's analysis was concerned with the second question, namely whether the solicitor trustee ought fairly to be excused. Nonetheless the presence in the first case and absence in the second case of some causative element between the conduct complained of and the lender's loss cannot sensibly be ignored.

I would, finally, caution against an over-mechanistic application of the requirement to show the necessary connection between the conduct complained of and the lender's loss. There may be highly unreasonable conduct which lies at the fringe of materiality in terms of causation, and only slightly unreasonable conduct which goes to the heart of a causation analysis. It would be wrong in my view to allow this purely mechanistic application of a causation-based test for the identification of relevant conduct to exclude the former from any consideration under s.61. **10–192**

An important issue in the present case relates to the standard to be applied to conduct connected with the loss. I have referred to the former Chancellor's summary in the Davisons case, at [48], as that of **10–193**

---

[203] *Lloyds TSB plc v Markandan & Uddin (a firm)* [2012] P.N.L.R. 20.

reasonableness not of perfection. It is well-established that the standard is likely to be higher for a paid than for an unpaid trustee: see *Lewin on Trusts* (18th edn.) at paras 39–145.

10–194 In the present case the judge sought to derive assistance from the jurisprudence about the similarly-worded provisions of s.727(1) of the Companies Act 1985 (now s.1157(1) of the Companies Act 2006), which provides that:

> "If in any proceedings for negligence, default, breach of duty or breach of trust against an officer of a company or a person employed by a company as auditor (whether he is or is not an officer of the company) it appears to the court hearing the case that that officer or person is or may be liable in respect of the negligence, default, breach of duty or breach of trust, but that he has acted honestly and reasonably, and that having regard to all the circumstances of the case (including those connected with his appointment) he ought fairly to be excused for the negligence, default, breach of duty or breach of trust, that court may relieve him, either wholly or partly, from his liability on such terms as it thinks fit."

He referred to *Barings plc v Coopers & Lybrand*,[204] and also to *Maelor-Jones v Heywood-Smith*,[205] as suggesting that something approaching "pervasive and compelling" negligence must be shown before a trustee is cut off from relief under s.61.

10–195 The difficulty with equating s.61 with s.727(1), at least for the purpose of interpreting s.61, is that s.727(1) appears to contemplate that a company officer or auditor may have acted honestly and reasonably, even though negligent, whereas s.61 contemplates no such thing in relation to trustees. It would in my judgment be wrong, by any process akin to reverse engineering, to interpret s.61 by reference to the historically more recent and undoubtedly more difficult provisions now to be found in s.727 of the Companies Act 1985. Generally, negligence requires a finding of unreasonable conduct, in the sense that the defendant must be found to have failed to apply reasonable care and skill to the task in hand. In the *Re D'Jan of London* case, Hoffman L.J. said of s.727 that:[206]

> "It may seem odd that a person found to have been guilty of negligence, which involves failing to take reasonable care, can ever satisfy a court that he acted reasonably. Nevertheless, the section clearly contemplates that he may do so."

No such oddity appears in s.61, and in my view the judge was wrong to equate the two relieving provisions. I consider that the test of reasonableness rather than perfection identified in the *Davisons* case is amply sufficient for comparable cases under s.61, and calls for no further elaboration.

10–196 The second main stage of the s.61 analysis, usually described as discretionary, consists of deciding whether the trustee ought fairly to be excused for the breach of trust. This requires that regard be had to the effect of the grant of relief not only upon the trustee, but also upon the beneficiaries.[207] Furthermore, s.61 makes it clear that even if the trustee ought fairly to be excused, the court still retains the discretionary power to grant relief from liability, in whole or in part, or to refuse it. In the context of relief sought by solicitor trustees from liability for breach of trust in connection with mortgage fraud, much may depend at this discretionary stage upon the consequences for the beneficiary. An institutional lender may well be insured (or effectively self-insured) for the consequences of third party fraud. But an innocent purchaser may have contributed his life's savings to the purchase and have no recourse at all other than against his insured solicitor, where for example the fraudster is a pure interloper, rather than a dishonest solicitor in respect of whose fraud the losers may have recourse against the Solicitors' Compensation Fund.

10–197 Relief under s.61 is often described as an exercise of mercy by the court. In my judgment the requirement to balance fairness to the trustee with a proper appreciation of the consequences of the exercise of the discretion for the beneficiaries means that this old-fashioned description of the nature of the s.61 jurisdiction should be abandoned. In this context mercy lies not in the free gift of the court. It comes at a price.

10–198 [His Lordship reviewed the facts of the case and continued:] In the wholly exceptional circumstance that the fraudster was a solicitor, rather than a mere imposter, I am prepared to assume that the fraud

---

204 [2003] P.N.L.R. 34.

205 (1989) 54 S.A.S.R. 285.

206 *Re D'Jan of London Ltd* [1993] B.C.C. 646.

207 See *Marsden v Regan* [1954] 1 W.L.R. 423 at 434, per Evershed M.R. and *Bartlett v Barclays Trust Co. (No.1)* [1980] Ch. 515 at 538, per Brightman J.

> would probably have been successfully achieved even if RA Legal had acted reasonably . . . [However, a] conclusion that, but for those aspects where RA Legal's conduct fell seriously and unreasonably short of best practice, the fraud would probably have succeeded by no means leads to the result that those parts of RA Legal's conduct are unconnected with the loss. They all represent departures from a sophisticated regime, worked out over many years, whereby risks of loss to lenders and lay clients are minimised, even if not wholly eradicated. Where solicitors fail, in serious respects, to play their part in that structure, and at the same time are swindled into transferring and then releasing trust money to a fraudster without authority, they cannot expect to persuade the court that it is fair to excuse them from liability, upon the basis that they have demonstrated that they have in all respects connected with that loss, acted reasonably.
>
> . . . In the present case I have come to the clear conclusion that the particular failures which I have described, beginning with the inadequate making of Requisitions on Title, transferring the completion money without the adoption of the Completion Code by Sovereign, and then failing to deal with the absence of a prior mortgage discharge on the pretended completion, were indeed unreasonable, and sufficiently connected with Abbey's loss. In any event, those failings of RA Legal formed part of a larger picture of the shoddy performance of a conveyancing transaction from start to finish, which leaves me in no doubt that it would not be fair to excuse the firm from liability, in whole or in part. **10–199**
>
> The discretion is of course conferred upon the judge, and falls to be exercised by this court only if the judge has made an error of law, failed to take (and take only) the appropriate matters into account, or otherwise reached an irrational decision. I consider that the judge erred in law in adopting an over-lenient view about the requirement to show reasonable conduct, attributable to an incorrect attempt to construe s.61 by reference to the similar, but by no means identical, provisions in the Companies Act. His conclusion that the failure to obtain from Sovereign its commitment to the Completion Code in advance of the transfer of the completion money was inconsequential was, in my view, an error about a matter of legal analysis. The result is that his exercise of discretion cannot stand. Since RA Legal have not shown that they acted reasonably in all respects connected with Abbey's loss, the discretion does not, strictly, arise at all. But even if it had done, and fell to be undertaken afresh by this court, I would have not have regarded it as fair to grant RA Legal any relief from liability for breach of trust, for the reasons given in the previous paragraph. I would therefore allow the appeal. **10–200**

## *B. Exemption Clauses*

It should first be noted that the jurisdiction of the court as to pure matters of law cannot be ousted by provisions in the trust instrument giving the trustees power to determine all questions arising in the execution of the trusts under the instrument.[208] However, the decision of trustees or of a third party can be binding and conclusive on matters of fact, assuming that the specified factual circumstances are conceptually certain,[209] while the decision of someone with expert knowledge in the relevant factual area can even conclusively determine an incidental question of construction.[210] **10–201**

Nor can a settlor oust the jurisdiction of the court by including a clause in the trust instrument that prevents the beneficiaries from applying to the court for the ascertainment and protection of their rights or for directions about the construction and exercise of the trustees' powers.[211] Such a clause **10–202**

208 *Re Wynn* [1952] Ch. 271.

209 *Re Coxen* [1948] Ch. 747; *Re Jones* [1953] Ch. 125; *Re Wright's Will Trusts* [1981] Law.S. Gaz 841.

210 *The Glazier* (1996) 1 Ll. Rep. 370; *Re Tuck's Settlement Trusts* [1978] Ch. 49; *Dundee General Hospitals Board v Walker* [1952] 1 All E.R. 896.

211 *Adams v Adams* (1882) 1 Ch. 369; *Permanent Trustee Co v Dougall* (1934) 34 S.R. (N.S.W.) 83 at 86–87; *AN v Barclays Private Bank & Trust (Cayman) Ltd* [2007] W.T.L.R. 565 at 597. But cf., *In the Matter of an Application for Information about a Trust* [2013] CA (Bda) 8 Civ, where the Supreme Court of Bermuda held that an information control clause in a trust instrument enabling the trust protector to veto the disclosure of trust information to beneficiaries was not invalid on its face, given: (1) that it did not purport to exclude the court's supervisory jurisdiction over the trust generally; and (2) that other mechanisms were in place to ensure proper administration of the trust, viz the trustees were required to have the accounts independently audited; the protector was empowered to obtain financial information from the trustees; and the protector was required to have regard to the interests of the beneficiaries when exercising her supervisory powers.

would effectively render the beneficiaries' rights unenforceable with the result that it could not be said that a trust existed at all.

10–203 If trustees can prove that the settlor knew of, and approved, a clause in the trust deed exempting the trustees from liability for a breach of trust upon a fair non-restrictive construction of the clause, then the trustees will escape liability for the breach unless it was a dishonest breach of trust. So held the Court of Appeal in *Armitage v Nurse*,[212] reproduced below,[213] in giving effect to a clause protecting the trustee from liability "unless such loss or damage shall be caused by his own actual fraud". "Fraud" was held simply to mean dishonesty which "connotes at the minimum an intention on the part of the trustee to pursue a particular course of action, either knowing that it is contrary to the interests of the beneficiaries or being recklessly indifferent whether it is contrary to their interests or not".[214] Whether a trustee has acted dishonestly is tested against objective standards of conduct and it is irrelevant whether the trustee believes that her conduct is honest, i.e. there is no need to show that she has been "self-consciously dishonest".[215]

10–204 Thus, it is permissible for an exemption clause to exempt a trustee from liability for loss arising from negligence of whatever kind, in contrast to Scots law, which follows other civil law systems in distinguishing gross negligence and ordinary negligence, and which does not permit exemption clauses that protect trustees from liability for gross negligence.[216] Similarly, the Trusts (Guernsey) Law 2007 s.39(7) provides that[217]:

> the terms of a trust may not (a) relieve a trustee of liability for a breach of trust arising from his own fraud, wilful misconduct or gross negligence, or (b) grant him any indemnity against the trust property in respect of any such liability.

In its 2006 Report on exemption clauses, the Law Commission considered introducing a similar measure into English law, but rejected this on the basis that English law does not clearly distinguish between gross and ordinary negligence.[218]

10–205 In its 2003 Consultation Paper on exemption clauses, the Law Commission proposed drawing a distinction between lay and professional trustees, suggesting that lay trustees should generally continue to be able to rely on trustee exemption clauses,[219] but that professional trustees should be unable to rely on an exemption clause where their conduct has been so unreasonable, irresponsible or incompetent that in fairness to the beneficiaries their conduct should not be excused.[220] However, in its 2006 Report on the subject, the Law Commission succumbed to special pleading by professional trustees, weakly concluding that reform would be undesirable because it could lead to increased costs, delays in trust administration, a greater tendency towards defensive trusteeship, and a general loss of flexibility in the operation of trusts.[221] Instead it tamely suggested that a rule of practice should be recognised and enforced by regulatory and professional bodies along the following lines[222]:

---

212 [1998] Ch. 241. See too *Wight v Olswang (No.1)* (1999) 1 I.T.E.L.R. 783; *Wight v Olswang (No.2)* (2000) 2 I.T.E.L.R. 689; *Walker v Stones* [2001] Q.B. 902 at 935, 941; *Bonham v Blake Lapthorn Linell (a firm)* [2007] W.T.L.R. 189 at [177].

213 See paras 10–208ff.

214 *Armitage* at [251].

215 *Barnes v Tomlinson* [2007] W.T.L.R. 377 at [78].

216 *Seton v Dawson* (1841) 4 D 310 at 316–317; *Knox v Mackinnon* (1888) 13 App. Cas. 753 at 765; *Clarke v Clarke's Trustees* 1925 S.C. 693; *Lutea Trustees Ltd v Orbis Trustees* [1998] S.L.T. 471.

217 Considered by the Privy Council in *Spread Trustee Co. Ltd v Hutcheson* [2012] 2 A.C. 194.

218 Law Commission, *Trustee Exemption Clauses* (2006), Law Com. No.301, Cm 6874.

219 Law Commission, *Trustee Exemption Clauses* (TSO, 2003), LCCP No.171, para.4.39.

220 Law Commission, *Trustee Exemption Clauses*, para.4.78.

221 Law Commission, *Trustee Exemption Clauses*, para.5.99.

222 Law Commission, *Trustee Exemption Clauses*, para.6.65.

Any paid trustee who causes a settlor to include a clause in a trust instrument which has the effect of excluding or limiting liability for negligence must before the creation of the trust take such steps as are reasonable to ensure that the settlor is aware of the meaning and effect of the clause.

The basic type of exemption clause exempts trustees from liability for a breach of duty. However, a clause may alternatively be drafted to oust a duty that would otherwise be imposed by law so that there can then be no breach of duty. In *Hayim v Citibank S.A.*,[223] for example, Citibank was appointed executor of the testator's American will on terms that the executor "shall have no responsibility or duty with respect to" a Hong Kong house until the deaths of the testator's very elderly brother and sister who resided in the house. This house was given by a Hong Kong will to another executor on trust for Citibank as executor of the American will. Citibank declined to take steps to have the house sold for the benefit of the beneficiaries under the American will who wanted the house to be sold and the siblings to be evicted from it. Substantial losses flowed from the delayed sale of the house. The Privy Council held the clause was "understandable and explicable". To avoid death duties (payable if the siblings had interests in possession in the house) and to avoid placing them at the mercy of the beneficiaries, the clause enabled Citibank to permit the siblings to remain living in the house without Citibank owing any duties to the beneficiaries (other than to account to them if Citibank used the house for its own purposes). **10–206**

It is also not uncommon to see clauses that oust the trustee's duty to diversify investments, e.g. where 90 per cent of the value of the trust fund is in the controlling shareholding of a company transferred by the settlor to the trustees. The statutory duty of care when investing can also be excluded. Thus, a big lottery winner might settle £2 million on trustees to speculate with it for 21 years as if they were the absolute beneficial owners of it and could afford to lose all of it without it affecting their standard of living in any way. Of course, all the duties of trustees cannot be ousted or the trustees would either be nominee-resulting trustees for the settlor or themselves be absolute beneficial owners. The trustees must be left under a duty to perform the trust honestly and in good faith for the benefit of beneficiaries who have a correlative right to make the trustees account for performance of their duty.[224] **10–207**

*Armitage v Nurse*

Court of Appeal [1998] Ch. 241

MILLETT L.J. (with whom HIRST and HUTCHISON L.JJ. agreed):

**The Permitted Scope of Trustee Exemption Clauses**

It is submitted . . . that a trustee exemption clause which purports to exclude all liability except for actual fraud is void, either for repugnancy or as contrary to public policy. . . . What is pleaded is, at the very lowest, culpable and probably gross negligence. So the question reduces itself to this: can a trustee exemption clause validly exclude liability for gross negligence? **10–208**

The submission that it is contrary to public policy to exclude the liability of a trustee for gross negligence is not supported by any English or Scottish authority. The cases relied on are the English cases of *Wilkins v Hogg*[225] and *Pass v Dundas*;[226] and the Scottish cases of *Knox v Mackinnon*[227] and *Rae v Meek*,[228] *Wyman* **10–209**

[223] [1987] A.C. 730.
[224] *Armitage v Nurse* [1998] Ch. 241 at 253.
[225] (1861) 31 L.J. Ch. 41.
[226] (1880) 43 L.T. 665.
[227] (1888) 13 App. Cas. 753.
[228] (1889) 14 App. Cas. 558.

> *or Ferguson (Pauper) v Paterson*[229] and *Clarke v Clarke's Trustees.*[230] These cases, together with two other Scottish cases, *Seton v Dawson*[231] and *Carruthers v Carruthers,*[232] and cases from the Commonwealth and America, were reviewed by the Jersey Court of Appeal in *Midland Bank Trustee (Jersey) Ltd v Federated Pension Services Ltd*[233] in a masterly judgment delivered by Sir Godfray Le Quesne Q.C.
>
> 10–210 I agree with the conclusion of the Jersey Court of Appeal that all these cases are concerned with the true construction of the particular clauses under consideration or of similar clauses in standard form in the nineteenth century. None of them deals with the much wider form of clause which has become common in the present century, and none of them is authority for the proposition that it is contrary to public policy to exclude liability for gross negligence by an appropriate clause clearly worded to have that effect.
>
> 10–211 At the same time, it must be acknowledged that the view is widely held that these clauses have gone too far, and that trustees who charge for their services and who, as professional men, would not dream of excluding liability for ordinary professional negligence, should not be able to rely on a trustee exemption clause excluding liability for gross negligence. Jersey introduced a law in 1989 which denies effect to a trustee exemption clause which purports to absolve a trustee from liability for his own "fraud, wilful misconduct or gross negligence". . . . If clauses such as cl.15 of the settlement are to be denied effect, then in my opinion this should be done by Parliament.

### *C. An Instigating or Consenting Beneficiary Cannot Sue the Trustee and May Be Liable to Indemnify the Trustee*

10–212 A beneficiary[234] who is of full capacity,[235] and who knowingly concurs in a breach of trust by trustees, cannot afterwards complain of it against them[236] unless they knew or ought to have known that her concurrence was the result of undue influence.[237] The position was summarised by Wilberforce J in *Re Pauling's Settlement Trusts (No.1)*[238]:

> The court has to consider all the circumstances in which the concurrence of the cestui que trust was given with a view to seeing whether it is fair and equitable that, having given his concurrence, he should afterwards turn round and sue the trustees: that, subject to this, it is not necessary that he should know that what he is concurring in is a breach of trust, provided that he fully understands what he is concurring in, and that it is not necessary that he should himself have directly benefited by the breach of trust.

10–213 Wilberforce J's approach was approved by the Court of Appeal in *Holder v Holder,*[239] reproduced below.[240] Consequently if a beneficiary consents to an act which the trustees know to be unauthorised although they refrain from telling her this, she may still sue them. The trustees must put the beneficiaries fully in the picture and must not withhold crucial information.[241] As Cotton LJ said in *Re Garnett*[242]:

---

229 [1900] A.C. 271.
230 1925 S.C. 693.
231 (1841) 4 D. 310.
232 [1896] A.C. 659.
233 [1995] Jersey L.R. 352.
234 In charitable trusts only the Attorney General can consent or acquiesce in a breach of trust: *Re Freeston's Charity* [1978] 1 All E.R. 481 at 490, though the Court of Appeal found it unnecessary to say anything on this point: [1979] 1 All E.R. 51 at 63.
235 *Wilkinson v Parry* (1828) 4 Russ. 272 at 276; *Montford v Cadogan* (1816) 19 Ves. 635. She may not fraudulently misrepresent her age to obtain money and then claim the money again on majority: *Overton v Banister* (1844) Hare 503.
236 *Fletcher v Collis* [1905] 2 Ch. 24. If she instigates or requests the breach then a fortiori she cannot sue.
237 *Re Pauling's Settlement Trusts (No.1)* [1964] Ch. 303 at 338. Trustees must take special care in the case of young adults living with their parents.
238 [1962] 1 W.L.R. 86 at 108.
239 *Holder v Holder* [1968] Ch. 353 at 369. See too *Brudenell-Bruce v Moore* [2014] EWHC 3679 (Ch) at [195]–[197].
240 See paras 10–224ff.
241 *Phipps v Boardman* [1964] 2 All E.R. 187 at 204–205; *Mitchell v Halliwell* [2005] EWHC 937 (Ch) esp. at [41]–[52].
242 (1885) 31 Ch.D. 1 at 16.

> the trustee ought not to be allowed . . . to shield herself from accounting for trust money in her hands simply by putting forward a document which has been signed and sealed without any knowledge of the real facts without any communication of their rights, though the release in its terms would bar the parties from insisting upon them.

If, however, the trustees themselves do not appreciate that what they propose is a breach of trust and the beneficiary fully understands and agrees with the proposal then she cannot sue them if things turn out badly. *Fletcher v Collis*,[243] excerpted below, establishes that these principles apply whether the beneficiary's consent or acquiescence[244] is before or after the breach of trust, and they prevent her from suing for breach of trust, whether or not she benefited from consenting to such breach.

Where the beneficiary instigated, requested or consented to a breach of trust which the trustees then committed and another beneficiary called upon the trustee to make good the breach of trust, the court has always had jurisdiction to order the trustee to be indemnified out of the interest of the beneficiary who, being of full capacity, either instigated, requested or concurred in the breach. A motive of personal benefit on the part of the beneficiary was sufficient to invoke the jurisdiction in cases of instigation[245] or request[246]; but personal benefit actually derived by the beneficiary was necessary in cases of concurrence.[247] In order to succeed in claiming an indemnity, the trustee had to show that the beneficiary knew the facts which constituted the breach of trust although it was not necessary to show that the beneficiary knew that these facts amounted in law to a breach of trust.[248] **10–214**

Section 62 of the Trustee Act 1925[249] enlarges the jurisdiction as follows: **10–215**

> Where a trustee commits a breach of trust at the instigation or request or with the consent in writing[250] of a beneficiary, the court may if it thinks fit make such order as to the court seems just for impounding all or any part of the interest of the beneficiary in the trust estate by way of indemnity to the trustee[251] or persons claiming through him.

However, the factors of motive and actual benefit are likely to continue to influence the court in exercising its discretion.

### *Fletcher v Collis*

### Court of Appeal [1905] 2 Ch. 24

Securities were settled on trust for the husband for life, remainder to the wife for life, remainder to children. At the request of the wife and with the (written) consent of the husband, the trustee in 1885 sold off the **10–216**

---

243 [1905] 2 Ch. 24.

244 Mere delay (subject to Limitation Act 1980) is not enough; there must be conduct and circumstances making it inequitable to assert a claim, e.g. having knowledge of entitlement to sue but doing nothing, so that the trustee does things that would otherwise not have been done: *De Busche v Alt* (1877) 8 Ch.D. 286 at 314; *Nelson v Rye* [1996] 1 W.L.R. 1378; *Pullan v Wilson* [2014] W.T.L.R. 669.

245 *Trafford v Boehm* (1746) 3 Atk. 440 at [442]; *Raby v Ridehalgh* (1855) 7 De G.M. & G. 104.

246 *M'Gachen v Dew* (1851) 15 Beav. 84; *Hanchett v Briscoe* (1856) 22 Beav. 496.

247 *Cocker v Quayle* (1830) 1 Russ. & M. 535 at 538; *Booth v Booth* (1838) 1 Beav. 125 at 130; *Blyth v Fladgate* [1891] 1 Ch. 337 at 363. It makes no difference that the concurring beneficiary became a beneficiary after the date of her concurrence; *Evans v Benyon* (1887) 37 Ch.D. 329 at 344. These factors of motive and actual benefit may still influence the exercise of discretion of the court determining whether all or any part of the beneficial interest should be impounded: *Bolton v Curre* [1895] 1 Ch. 544 at 549; *Re Somerset* [1894] Ch. 231 at 275.

248 *Re Somerset* [1894] 1 Ch. 231. See also *Rehden v Wesley* (1861) 29 Beav. 213 at 215.

249 Replacing the Trustee Act 1893 s.45, itself replacing the Trustee Act 1888 s.6.

250 The requirement of writing only refers to consent and not instigation or request: *Re Somerset* [1894] 1 Ch. 231.

251 An order for indemnity can be made in favour of a former trustee: *Re Pauling's Settlement Trusts (No.2)* [1963] Ch. 576. It would be absurd if the trustee who, ex hypothesi, is in breach of trust had to remain trustee in order to have an impounding order for an indemnity.

whole of the trust fund and handed the proceeds to the wife, who spent them. In June 1891 the husband was adjudicated bankrupt. In August 1891 the present action was commenced by the remaindermen against the trustee to make him replace the loss, but proceedings were stayed on an undertaking by the trustee, on the security of (inter alia) certain policies on his life, to make good the trust fund. By means of payments by the trustee and of the policies which fell in on his death in 1902, the whole of the trust fund was replaced, together with interest from August 1891.

**10–217** The personal representative of the deceased trustee then took out a summons for a declaration that she was entitled, during the life of the husband, to the income of the trust fund replaced by the deceased trustee. It was argued for her that a beneficiary who concurs in a breach of trust cannot afterwards complain of it against his trustee. The capital had in fact been replaced by the trustee at the instance of the remaindermen, but since the husband himself had by virtue of his concurrence no claim against the trustee, the income of the capital so replaced should (during the life of the husband) go to her as personal representative of the trustee who replaced it.

**10–218** For the husband's trustee in bankruptcy, who resisted the claim of the personal representative, it was contended that the authorities showed that mere concurrence by a beneficiary does not preclude him from complaining against his trustee: it must be shown that the beneficiary also derived a personal benefit from the breach of trust, which was not the case here.

**10–219** ROMER L.J. (with whom VAUGHAN WILLIAMS and STIRLING L.JJ. agreed): There was one proposition of law urged by the counsel on behalf of the respondents before us to which I accede. It is this: If a beneficiary claiming under a trust does not instigate or request a breach of trust, is not the active moving party towards it, but merely consents to it, and he obtains no personal benefit from it, then his interest in the trust estate would not be impoundable in order to indemnify the trustee liable to make good loss occasioned by the breach. I think this is what was meant and referred to by Chitty J. in his judgment in *Sawyer v Sawyer*,[252] where he says:

> "It strikes me as a novelty in law, and a proposition not founded on principle, to say that the person who merely consents is bound to do more than what he says he consents to do. It does not mean that he makes himself personally liable, nor does he render any property liable to make it good."

But that proposition of law must be taken to be subject to the following right of the trustee as between himself and the beneficiaries. In the case I have before referred to in respect to the general proposition, the beneficiary who knowingly consented to the breach could not, if of full contracting age and capacity, and in the absence of special circumstances, afterwards be heard to say that the conduct of the trustee in committing the breach of trust was, as against him the particular beneficiary, improper, so as to make the trustee liable to the beneficiary for any damage suffered in respect of that beneficiary's interest in the trust estate by reason of the loss occasioned by the breach, and of course if satisfactorily proved the consent of the beneficiary to the breach need not be in writing.

**10–220** I will illustrate what I have said by a concrete case, not only to make my meaning perfectly plain, but also because the illustration will have a bearing upon the case now before us. Take a simple case of a trust under a settlement, say, of £3,000, for a tenant for life, and after the death of the tenant for life for certain remaindermen. Suppose the trustee commits a breach of trust and sells out £1,000, and pays it over to some third person, so that the cestui que trust does not benefit by it himself, and suppose that the tenant for life, being of full age and sui juris, knows of that act of the trustee and consents to it. What would be the position of the trustee in reference to that breach of trust if he were made liable at the instance of the remaindermen for the loss accruing to the trust estate by the breach of trust, assuming the £1,000 to have been lost? The remaindermen would have the right of saying, so far as their interest in remainder is concerned, the capital must be made good by the trustee; but the tenant for life who consented could not himself have brought an action against the trustee to make him liable for the loss of income suffered by the tenant for life by reason of the breach of trust as to the £1,000. On the other hand, the trustee would not have had a right, as against the cestui que trust, the tenant for life, to have impounded the tenant for life's interest on the remaining £2,000 of the trust fund in order to indemnify himself. Now suppose the remaindermen having brought an action to make good the breach of trust against the trustee, and the tenant for life is a co-plaintiff, a defence is put in by the trustee raising his right as against the tenant for life seeking relief in respect of the loss of income, but admitting the right of the remaindermen: what would the court

[252] (1885) 28 Ch.D. 595 at 598.

in such a case do if the question between the tenant for life and the trustee had to be tried out, and the tenant for life was found to have consented knowingly to the breach of trust? To my mind the right thing for the court to do would have been clear. It might order the £1,000 to be paid into court by the trustee; but, pending the life of the tenant for life, it might also order the income to be paid to the trustee, because the income of the £1,000 would have been out of the pocket of the trustee just as much as the corpus from which it proceeded, and not to have given that relief to the trustee would have been to ignore his right, and to have acceded to the claim of the tenant for life in the action by him that I have indicated. Now suppose that the tenant for life is not a plaintiff, but co-defendant with the trustee, so that the question cannot be tried out at the trial as between the tenant for life and the trustee: what might the court do, if so advised, in that case? It might order the £1,000 to be paid into court by the trustee, and it might reserve the question of the right as between the tenant for life and the trustee to the income to be determined at some later period. It will be found that that illustration is pertinent to the case that is now before us. In such a case when the question as to income arose the trustee would be able to say: "The remaindermen are clearly not entitled to the income on the trust fund I have replaced, if the tenant for life is not entitled to it as against me. I replaced it; it is my money, and I am entitled to it"; and, therefore, when the question came to be tried out ultimately as between the tenant for life and the trustee, if that income was still under the control of the court, the court would again have the right to say to the trustee who replaced the corpus: "The income is yours in the absence of the right of the beneficiary, the tenant for life, to claim as against you to make you liable for that income."

Now that right of a trustee which I have been dealing with, the right to resist the claim by the beneficiary to make good as against him the income, has clearly not been affected either by section 6 of the Trustee Act of 1888, or by section 45 of the Trustee Act of 1893. As I pointed out in *Bolton v Curre*,[253] those sections were intended to and did extend the powers of the court for the benefit of the trustee. They clearly extended the powers of court so far as concerns the case of a married woman restrained from anticipation; but they also extended them in another respect by giving power to the court to impound any part of the interest in the trust property of any beneficiary who consented to a breach of trust, provided that consent was in writing. But clearly there was nothing in those sections which was intended to, and nothing in my opinion which operated so as to, deprive the trustee of the right I previously indicated, namely, the right of saying as against a beneficiary who has consented to a breach of trust that the beneficiary cannot make him, the trustee, personally liable to recoup, to the beneficiary who consented, the loss accruing to that beneficiary by the breach of trust committed with his consent. The beneficiary, if he consented to the breach of trust, could not be heard to make that a ground of complaint or a ground of action as against the trustee. . . . **10–221**

Is not this matter that we have to deal with on this appeal in substance one where a beneficiary who has consented to a breach of trust is now for his own benefit calling upon the trustee to make good the loss accruing to the beneficiary by reason of the breach? I think it is . . . . **10–222**

Held, therefore, by the Court of Appeal that the personal representative of the deceased trustee was entitled, during the life of the husband tenant for life, to the income of the fund replaced by the trustee. **10–223**

*Holder v Holder*

Court of Appeal [1968] Ch. 353

The plaintiff was seeking to set aside a sale made to the third defendant by the first two defendant trustees when the third defendant was technically a trustee. HARMAN L.J. (with whom DANCKWERTS and SACHS L.JJ. agreed on this point) dealt as follows with the defence of the plaintiff's consent or acquiescence. **10–224**

There arises a further defence, namely, that of acquiescence, and this requires some further recital of the facts. **10–225**

Completion of the sale was due for Michaelmas, 1961, but by that time the third defendant was not in a position to find the purchase money. The proving executors served a notice to complete in October, 1961, and, the validity of this notice being questioned, served a further notice in December. In February 1962 the plaintiff's solicitor pressed the defendants to forfeit the third defendant's deposit and this was a right given by the contract of sale and is an affirmation of it. Further, in May, 1962, the plaintiff issued a **10–226**

[253] [1895] 1 Ch. 544 at 549.

writ for a common decree of administration against the proving executors, seeking thus to press them to complete the contract and wind up the estate. The contract was in fact completed in June, 1962, and in the same month £2,000 on account was paid to and accepted by the plaintiff as his share and he thereupon took no further steps with his action. In order to complete, the third defendant borrowed £21,000 from the Agricultural Mortgage Corporation with interest at 7 1/2 per cent. He also borrowed £3,000 from his mother with interest at 6 1/2 per cent, and a like sum from his sister at a similar rate of interest. In November 1962 the third defendant demanded possession of Glebe Farm house from the plaintiff, who at that time changed his solicitors, and it was suggested by the new solicitors in February 1963 that the third defendant was disqualified from bidding at the auction. This was the first time any such suggestion had been made by anyone. The writ was not issued till a year later.

10–227 I have found this question a difficult one. The plaintiff knew all the relevant facts but he did not realise nor was he advised till 1963 that the legal result might be that he could object to his brother's purchase because he continued to be a personal representative. There is no doubt strong authority for the proposition that a man is not bound by acquiescences until he knows his legal rights. In *Cockerell v Cholmeley*[254] Sir John Leach M.R. said this:

> "It has been argued that the defendant, being aware of the facts of the case in the lifetime of Sir Henry Englefield has, by his silence, and by being a party to the application to Parliament, confirmed the title of the plaintiffs. In equity it is considered, as good sense requires it should be, that no man can be held by any act of his to confirm a title, unless he was fully aware at the time, not only of the fact upon which the effect of title depends, but of the consequence in point of law; and there is no proof that the defendant, at the time of the acts referred to, was aware of the law on the subject . . .".

10–228 There, however, the judge was asked to set aside a legal right. In *Wilmott v Barber*[255] Fry J. said this:

> "A man is not to be deprived of his legal rights unless he has acted in such a way as would make it fraudulent for him to set up those rights. What, then, are the elements or requisites necessary to constitute fraud of that description? In the first place the plaintiff must have made a mistake as to his legal rights. Secondly, the plaintiff must have expended some money or must have done some act (not necessarily upon the defendant's land) on the faith of his mistaken belief. Thirdly, the defendant, the possessor of the legal right, must know of the existence of his own right which is inconsistent with the right claimed by the plaintiff. If he does not know of it he is in the same position as the plaintiff, and the doctrine of acquiescence is founded upon conduct with a knowledge of your legal rights."

On the other hand, in *Stafford v Stafford*[256] Knight Bruce L.J. said this:

> "Generally, when the facts are known from which a right arises, the right is presumed to be known . . .".

10–229 Like the judge, I should desire to follow the conclusion of Wilberforce J. who reviewed the authorities in *Re Pauling's Settlement Trusts*;[257] and this passage was mentioned without dissent in the same case in the Court of Appeal:[258]

> "The result of these authorities appears to me to be that the court has to consider all the circumstances in which the concurrence of the cestui que trust was given with a view to seeing whether it is fair and equitable that, having given his concurrence, he should afterwards turn round and sue the trustees: that, subject to this, it is not necessary that he should know that what he is concurring in is a breach of trust, provided that he fully understands what he is concurring in, and that it is not necessary that he should himself have directly benefited by the breach of trust."

There is, therefore, no hard and fast rule that ignorance of a legal right is a bar, but the whole of the circumstances must be looked at to see whether it is just that the complaining beneficiary should succeed against the trustee.[259]

10–230 On the whole I am of the opinion that in the circumstances of this case it would not be right to allow the

254 (1830) 1 Russ. & M. 418 at 425.
255 (1880) 15 Ch.D. 96 at 105.
256 (1857) 1 De G. & J. 193 at 202.
257 [1961] 3 All E.R. 713 at 730.
258 [1964] Ch. 303.
259 Endorsed in *Re Freeston's Charity* [1979] 1 All E.R. 51 at 62. The third proposition of Fry J. in *Wilmott v Barber* (1880) 15

plaintiff to assert his right (assuming he had one) because with full knowledge of the facts he affirmed the sale. He has had £2,000 as a result. He has caused the third defendant to embark on liabilities which he cannot recoup. There can in fact be no restitutio in integrum which is a necessary element in rescission. The plaintiff is asserting an equitable and not a legal remedy. He has by his conduct disentitled himself to it. It is extremely doubtful whether the order if worked out would benefit anyone, I think we should not assent to it, on general equitable principles. **10–231**

## *D. Limitation*

**10–232** Claims for breach of trust are subject to the limitation rules contained in the Limitation Act 1980 s.21. This provides that a statutory limitation period of six years shall apply to all actions for breach of trust other than those in which the trustee was a party or privy to fraud and those where the trustee has trust property in her possession or has previously received it and converted it to her use. In those exceptional situations the statute does not require the beneficiaries to bring their action within any time limit. However, their ability to sue the trustee may still be affected by the equitable doctrine of laches.

### Limitation Act 1980 s.21

**10–233**
(1) No period of limitation prescribed by this Act shall apply to an action by a beneficiary under a trust, being an action:
  (a) in respect of any fraud or fraudulent breach of trust to which the trustee was a party or privy; or
  (b) to recover from the trustee trust property or the proceeds thereof in the possession of the trustee, or previously received by the trustee and converted to his use.

(2) Where a trustee who is also a beneficiary under the trust receives or retains trust property or its proceeds as his share on a distribution of trust property under the trust, his liability in any action brought by virtue of subsection (1)(b) above to recover that property or its proceeds after the expiration of the period of limitation prescribed by this Act for bringing an action to recover trust property shall be limited to the excess over his proper share.
This subsection only applies if the trustee acted honestly and reasonably in making the distribution.

(3) Subject to the preceding provisions of this section an action by a beneficiary to recover trust property or in respect of any breach of trust, not being an action for which a period of limitation is prescribed by any other provision of this Act,[260] shall not be brought after the expiration of six years from the date on which the right of action accrued. For the purposes of this subsection the right of action shall not be treated as having accrued to any beneficiary entitled to a future interest in the trust property until the interest fell into possession.

(4) No beneficiary as against whom there would be a good defence under this Act shall derive any greater or other benefit from a judgment or order obtained by any other beneficiary than he could have obtained if he had brought the action and this Act had been pleaded in defence.

**10–234** The following discussion will first consider the situations where the statutory six-year limitation period does not apply before turning to the doctrine of laches. We shall then discuss the situations where the six-year period does apply before turning finally to some statutory rules whose effect is to postpone the inception of this limitation period in certain situations. The discussion is only concerned

---

Ch.D. 96 at 105 has also been rejected in *Taylor Fashions Ltd v Liverpool Victoria Trustees Co. Ltd* [1981] 1 All E.R. 897 at 915–918 and *Habib Bank Ltd v Habib Bank AG Zurich* [1981] 2 All E.R. 650 at 666, 668.

260 Where personal representatives have become trustees upon completing administration of an estate the relationship between s.21(3) and s.22 is unclear. It would seem that the breadth of s.22 (formerly s.20 of the 1939 Act) makes the 12-year period applicable: *Re Diplock* [1948] Ch. 465 at 511–513; *Ministry of Health v Simpson* [1951] A.C. 251 at 276–277.

with claims for breach of trust against express trustees. Claims against constructive and resulting trustees raise different issues that are not discussed in this book.[261]

### i. Section 21(1) Cases Where No Statutory Limitation Period Applies

**10–235** Section 21(1)(a) provides that no statutory limitation period shall apply to proceedings against a trustee who has acted fraudulently or been "party or privy" to a fraud committed by another.[262] According to *Thorne v Heard*[263] a trustee is not relevantly "party or privy" to another's fraud if she innocently commits a breach of trust by transferring trust funds to a third party who then fraudulently embezzles them.

**10–236** Section 21(1)(b) provides that no statutory limitation period shall apply to proceedings against a trustee who has trust property or its proceeds in her possession, or who has previously received trust property and converted it to her use. In *Re Howlett*[264] it was held by Danckwerts J that "receipt" of trust property includes a notional receipt, a finding that enables the judge to charge a trustee who had occupied trust property for some 20 years with an occupation rent. To fall foul of s.21(1)(b), a trustee's retention or conversion must be some wrongful application in her own favour.[265] However she is given some protection by s.21(2). This covers the situation where, e.g. a trustee distributes one-third of the trust property to herself, honestly and reasonably believing that there are only three beneficiaries (herself and two others); a fourth beneficiary then turns up more than six years later. In these circumstances the trustee will be liable to the fourth beneficiary not for a quarter share of the trust property but only for the one-twelfth difference between the one-third share which she took and the one-quarter share which was properly hers.

**10–237** The rule that trustees in possession of trust property are liable without limit of time (in the absence of laches) is often said to be justified by the reason given by Lord Redesdale in *Hovenden v Lord Annesley*,[266] namely that the trustees can only be possessed of the trust estate for, and on behalf of, the beneficiaries, and so time can never run against the beneficiaries in favour of the trustees. However, doubts are expressed about this rationale by Christian Daly and Charles Mitchell in the following extract.

## C. Daly and C. Mitchell, "*Paragon Finance plc v D.B. Thakerar & Co. (a firm)* (1999)"

in C. Mitchell and P. Mitchell (eds), *Landmark Cases in Equity* (Hart Publishing, 2012), pp.655–656

**10–238** [The rule that delay did not bar claims by a beneficiary against an express trustee, now found in the Limitation Act 1980 s.21(1)] . . . is usually attributed to the judgment of Lord Redesdale in *Hovenden v Lord Annesley*,[267] where he offered the following explanation:[268]

"[I]f a trustee is in possession, and does not execute his trust, the possession of the trustee, is the possession of the cestui que trust; and if the only circumstance is, that he does not

---

261 The leading case is now *Williams v Central Bank of Nigeria* [2014] A.C. 1189, noted J. Lee (2015) 131 L.Q.R. 39.

262 See *North American Land Co v Watkins* [1904] 1 Ch. 242; [1904] 2 Ch. 233; *Vane v Vane* (1872) L.R. 8 Ch. 383; *Armitage v Nurse* [1998] Ch. 241 at 260.

263 [1895] A.C. 495.

264 [1949] Ch. 767.

265 *Re Gurney* [1893] 1 Ch. 590; *Re Page* [1893] 1 Ch. 304; *Re Fountaine* [1909] 2 Ch. 382.

266 (1806) 2 Sch. & Lef. 607 at 633–634; cited in, e.g. *Williams v Central Bank of Nigeria* [2014] A.C. 1189 at [13]–[14].

267 In fact the principle is much—at least 150 years—older: J. Brunyate, *Limitation of Actions in Equity* (Stevens & Sons, 1932) 50.

268 (1806) 2 Sch. & Lef. 607 at 633.

perform his trust, his possession operates nothing as a bar, because his possession is according to his title."

Lord Redesdale's statement of the principle, and, more importantly, his explanation for it . . . has been (almost) universally and uncritically followed.[269] His explanation certainly has a superficial attractiveness in relation to claims to recover trust property from an express trustee. However, its explanatory force does not extend much further, because it is premised on the idea that the trustee is in possession of the trust property. This premise necessarily circumscribes the scope of operation of the principle, which does not obviously extend to a claim based on misapplication of trust property or a claim based on the trustee's negligence. In both of these cases the gravamen of the beneficiary's complaint is that the trustee is not in possession of property that ought to be in his possession.

A different explanation of the *Hovenden* principle might run as follows. There are two types of claim that a beneficiary may make against an express trustee: performance claims and reparation claims . . . The objective of a performance claim is to enforce the performance of the trust according to its terms: to compel performance by the trustee of his primary obligation to apply the trust property in accordance with the trust deed, either in specie or substitutively (by paying a money substitute for the relevant property). By contrast, the objective of a reparation claim is to make good a loss occasioned by the trustee's breach of a primary obligation, such as his duty of care. Performance claims involve the assertion and vindication of pre-existing rights. They do not involve an allegation of breach of trust, or the enforcement of new rights arising from such a breach. Accordingly, it is inappropriate to apply the statutes of limitation by analogy to such claims because it is impossible to identify any breach of duty in respect of which time can run, and it is equally impossible to identify the moment from which it should start to run.[270] **10–239**

This account is confronted by at least four obstacles. First, both Lord Redesdale and Lord Eldon were of the view that the principle stated in *Hovenden*, and the explanation for that principle, was not limited to claims by beneficiaries against express trustees, but also applied to claims by landlords against their tenants.[271] This suggests that the principle was not attracted by the particular duties of an express trustee or the particular nature of a performance claim. Rather, the principle appears to be part of the law of adverse possession, in which case its explanatory force in the context of trusts is particularly limited. It merely operates to disable a person who enters into possession of land in the capacity of an express trustee from asserting a claim to the land adversely to his beneficiary. Its explanatory force extends no further. **10–240**

Secondly, although the matter is not free from doubt, it appears that the *Hovenden* principle applied to reparation claims.[272] Claims of this type involve the assertion of a new right to compensation for losses occasioned by reason of a breach of duty. The application of the principle to claims of this type is difficult to reconcile with the account being considered. **10–241**

Thirdly, the operation of Lord Redesdale's principle cannot be justified by appealing to the fact that the claims to which it was applied were performance claims. Since equity was applying the statutes of limitation by analogy, there is no reason why it should have set its face against barring performance claims because the statutes themselves were applicable to such claims.[273] In fact, equity did apply the statute by analogy to performance claims, including bills for an account by a principal against a fiduciary.[274] **10–242**

Fourthly, claims by beneficiaries against express trustees were subject to the equitable doctrine of laches or acquiescence,[275] and some accounts of this doctrine emphasise the violation of the claimant's **10–243**

269 See *Chalmer v Bradley* (1819) 1 J. & W. 51 at 67–68; *Christ's Hospital v Grainger* (1849) 1 M & G 460 at 465; JGN Darby and FA Bosanquet, *A Practical Treatise on the Statutes of Limitations in England and Ireland* (William Maxwell & Son, 1867) 182–83; W. Ashburner, *Principles of Equity* (Butterworth & Co., 1902) 710–711; J.M. Lightwood, *The Time Limit on Actions* (Butterworth & Co., 1909) 68–69; contrast W. Swadling, 'Limitation' in P. Birks and A. Pretto (eds), *Breach of Trust* (Hart, 2002) 326–27. For a particularly striking application of the principle, see *Lister v Pickford* (1865) 34 Beav. 576.

270 Compare *Christ's Hospital v Grainger* (1849) 1 M & G 460 at 466; *Re Nisbet and Potts' Contract* [1906] 1 Ch. 386 at 401–02. A similar kind of argument appealed to Moore-Bick L.J. in *P. & O. Nedlloyd B.V. v Arab Metals Co. (The UB Tiger) (No.2)* [2007] 1 W.L.R. 2288 at [47].

271 *Hovenden v Lord Annesley* (1806) 2 Sch. & Lef. 607 at 633; *Cholmondeley v Clinton* (1821) 4 Bligh 1 at 40.

272 *Smith v Pococke* (1854) 2 Drew 197; *Bright v Legerton* (1860) 29 Beav. 60; (1861) 2 De G. F. & J. 606; *Brittlebank v Goodwin* (1868) L.R. 5 Eq. 545; *Stone v Stone* (1869) L.R. 5 Ch. 74. See also Ashburner at pp. 710–11.

273 Thus actions to recover debts were subject to a statutory limitation period: 21 James 1 c. 16, ss. 1 and 3.

274 *Lockey v Lockey* (1719) Prec. Ch. 518; *Knox v Gye* (1872) L.R. 5 H.L. 656. [Remainder of footnote omitted.]

275 *Bright v Legerton* (1860) 29 Beav. 60; (1861) 2 De G. F. & J. 606; *Re Cross* (1882) 20 Ch. D. 109; *Rochefoucauld v Boustead* [1897] 1 Ch. 196; *Re Taylor* (1900) 81 L.T. 812.

rights or the breach of the defendant's duty.[276] If these accounts are correct then the applicability of laches and acquiescence to performance claims against trustees is inconsistent with the notion that such claims do not involve any allegation of a breach of duty.

10-244 Neither Lord Redesdale's explanation of the *Hovenden* rule nor the only other plausible account of that rule is satisfactory. Hence we are forced to conclude that the rule is inexplicable.

### ii. Laches

10-245 The Limitation Act 1980 s.36 provides that "nothing in the Act shall affect any equitable jurisdiction to refuse relief on the ground of acquiescence or otherwise". This section therefore preserves the equitable doctrine of "laches". "Laches" is an old Law French term that means "neglect" or "slackfulness", and, in essence, the doctrine bars equitable claims where there has been a substantial lapse of time coupled with the existence of circumstances which make it inequitable to enforce the claim. In the words of Lord Selborne LC, in *Lindsay Petroleum Co v Hurd*, the doctrine is available[277]:

> where it would be practically unjust to give a remedy, either because the party has, by his conduct, done that which might fairly be regarded as equivalent to a waiver of it, or where by his conduct and neglect he has, though perhaps not waiving that remedy, yet put the other party in a situation in which it would not be reasonable to place him if the remedy were afterwards asserted.

According to Lord Walker in *Fisher v Brooker*, detrimental reliance by the defendant is "usually an essential ingredient", but this is not an "immutable requirement".[278]

10-246 The field of operation of the doctrine of laches in the context of actions for breach of trust has been narrowed by the introduction of a statutory limitation period for all cases other than those falling within the Limitation Act 1980 s.21(1). However it remains possible that in these exceptional cases the beneficiary may be barred from suing the trustee by an unreasonably long delay amounting to laches.[279]

### iii. Section 21(3) Cases Where the Statutory Limitation Period Does Apply

10-247 Section 21(3) stipulates a six-year limitation period for actions by a beneficiary "to recover trust property or in respect of any breach of trust", the time running from the date when the breach occurred (and not, e.g. from the date when the beneficiary suffered a loss).[280] The first class of action referred to in subs.(3) can only include actions against third parties, since actions against trustees in possession of trust property are covered by s.21(1)(b), and the second class of action referred to in subs.(3) cannot include actions against fraudulent trustees, since these are covered by s.21(1)(a). Since the sub-section is expressed to apply only to actions by a beneficiary, it does not apply to bar an action by the Attorney General to enforce a charitable trust.[281]

---

276 *Mills v Drewitt* (1855) 20 Beav. 632 at 638; Lightwood *The Time Limit on Actions* (Butterworth & Co, 1909), pp.252–255.

277 (1874) L.R. 5 P.C. 221 at 239–240. See also *Weld v Petre* [1929] 1 Ch. 33 at 51–52; *Holder v Holder* [1968] Ch. 353; *Nelson v Rye* [1986] 2 All E.R. 186 at 200–205, although incorrect on other points: *Paragon Finance Plc v Thakerar & Co* [1999] 1 All E.R. 400 at 415–416; *Companhia de Seguros Imperio v Heath Ltd* [2001] 1 W.L.R. 112; *J.J. Harrison (Properties) Ltd v Harrison* [2002] 1 B.C.L.C. 162.

278 [2009] 1 W.L.R. 1764 at [64]. See too *Patel v Shah* [2005] W.T.L.R. 359 at [32], endorsing *Frawley v Neill* [2000] C.P. Rep. 20: the modern approach is to determine "whether it would be unconscionable in all the circumstances for a party to be permitted to assert his beneficial right".

279 *McDonnell v White* (1865) 11 H.L.C. 271; *Sleeman v Wilson* (1871) L.R. 13 Eq. 36; *Tito v Waddell (No.2)* [1977] Ch. 106 at 248–250; *Re Loftus, deceased* [2007] 1 W.L.R. 591 at [33]–[41].

280 *Vant v Campain* (1893) 9 T.L.R. 254; *Re Somerset* [1894] 1 Ch. 231; *Thorne v Heard* [1895] A.C. 495.

281 *Attorney General v Cocke* [1988] Ch. 414.

Section 21(3) takes in cases, e.g. where a trustee has obtained only an indirect benefit from her breach of trust,[282] where she has disobeyed a direction in the trust deed to realise trust assets,[283] where she has disobeyed an instruction in the trust deed to accumulate income,[284] and where she has misused a power of advancement.[285] **10–248**

The last sentence of s.21(3) protects reversionary interests by enacting that time shall not run against a beneficiary until her interest has fallen into possession.[286] Even before that date a remainderman can sue for breach of trust. In such a case if the prior beneficiary is herself barred the trustees must nevertheless replace the fund at the suit of the remainderman, but during the continuance of the prior beneficiary's interest they will be entitled to the income of the property: for a judgment recovered by one beneficiary is not to improve the position of one who is already barred.[287] **10–249**

Where a beneficiary is merely interested under a discretionary trust until obtaining a life interest in possession, e.g. on attaining 25 years, the Court of Appeal has held that time does not run until the beneficiary obtains the interest in possession on her 25th birthday.[288] According to Millett LJ it makes no difference that at 18 a beneficiary, whether or not her interest is in possession, can see trust accounts, etc. so as to be able to discover a breach of trust. The rationale for s.23(1)[289] **10–250**

> is not that a beneficiary with a future interest has not the means of discovery, but that the beneficiary should not be compelled to litigate (at considerable personal expense) in respect of an injury to an interest which he may never live to enjoy. Similar reasoning would apply to exclude a person who is merely the object of a discretionary trust or power which may never be exercised in his favour.

This might appear to suggest that the liability of trustees of a discretionary trust is open-ended, except for those beneficiaries who have received a distribution (thereby acquiring an absolute interest in possession before the relevant breach of trust with the result that they have six years in which to act). However, in *Johns v Johns*[290] the New Zealand Court of Appeal reviewed Millett LJ's words, and concluded that a discretionary beneficiary would fit the rationale identified by his Lordship only if she had a further interest in the trust fund capable of falling into possession at a future date. Otherwise she "would not fit the clear requirement of a future interest in the trust property".[291] **10–251**

### iv. Section 32(1) Cases Where the Inception of the Statutory Limitation Period is Postponed

In certain cases falling within s.21(3) a beneficiary may be able to bring proceedings in respect of a breach of trust committed more than six years previously because the case also falls within the scope of s.32(1). This sub-section postpones the inception of statutory limitation periods in cases of fraud, deliberate concealment and mistake. **10–252**

---

282 *Re Gurney* [1893] 1 Ch. 590.
283 *Re Swain* [1891] 3 Ch. 233.
284 *How v Earl Winterton* [1896] 2 Ch. 626.
285 *Re Pauling's Settlement Trusts (No.1)* [1962] 1 W.L.R. 86 at 115, approved [1964] Ch. 303 at 353.
286 Consent by a life-tenant to an advance in favour of a remainderman does not amount to a release of the life interest so as to convert the remainderman's interest into an interest in possession: *Re Pauling's Settlement Trusts (No.1)* [1964] Ch. 303.
287 *Re Somerset* [1894] 1 Ch. 231; s.19(3) of the Limitation Act 1939 and s.21(4) of the 1980 Act; *Mara v Browne* [1895] 2 Ch. 69 reversed on another point [1896] 1 Ch. 199.
288 *Armitage v Nurse* [1998] Ch. 241.
289 *Armitage* at 261.
290 [2004] 3 N.Z.L.R. 202.
291 *Johns* at [40].

**Limitation Act 1980 s.32(1)**

10-253 Where in the case of any action for which a period of limitation is prescribed by this Act, either:

(a) the action is based upon the fraud of the defendant or his agent or of any person through whom he claims or his agent, or
(b) any fact relevant to the plaintiff's right of action has been deliberately concealed from him by any such person as aforesaid, or
(c) the action is for relief from the consequences of mistake,

the period of limitation shall not begin to run until the plaintiff has discovered the fraud concealment or mistake, as the case may be, or could with reasonable diligence have discovered it.

10-254 "Deliberate commission of a breach of duty in circumstances in which it is unlikely to be discovered for some time amounts to deliberate concealment of the facts involved in that breach of duty."[292] The House of Lords[293] has held that where after a cause of action has arisen there was a deliberate concealment of facts relevant to the claimant's cause of action, time does not begin to run until the concealment was or should have been discovered. In a separate case, the House of Lords has also held that a defendant does not deliberately commit a breach of duty unless she intends to commit the act which constitutes the breach of duty and understands that the act involves a breach of duty.[294]

10-255 It has been held in several cases[295] that s.32(1)(c) applies only in situations where a mistake has been made and has had certain consequences and the claimant is seeking to be relieved from those consequences, as in, e.g. actions to recover money paid under a mistake, actions to rescind or rectify contracts on the ground of mistake, and actions to reopen accounts settled in consequence of mistakes. It applies, in fact, only where mistake is an essential ingredient of the claimant's cause of action, and the section does not help a claimant to ascertain an amount still due to her after the ordinary period of limitation has expired. The anomalous result is that a person who has by mistake paid too much can take advantage of the section, but a person who has by mistake received too little cannot avail herself of it.[296]

## 5. Liability of Trustees between Themselves

10-256 Contribution claims between trustees formerly lay in equity. They now lie under the Civil Liability (Contribution) Act 1978 between trustees who are liable "in respect of the same damage".[297] Because trustees in this position are jointly and severally liable to the beneficiaries,[298] one trustee may find herself obliged to pay more than her fair share of their common liability to restore the trust fund or otherwise compensate the beneficiaries for loss. In this case, she can

---

292 Limitation Act 1980 s.32(2); *King v Victor Parsons & Co.* [1973] 1 W.L.R. 29 at 33 per Lord Denning MR This reflects the old case law on (b) when it was known as fraudulent concealment in Limitation Act 1939 s.26.

293 *Sheldon v R.H. Outhwaite (Underwriting Agencies) Ltd* [1996] A.C. 102. The meaning of deliberate concealment in s.32(1)(b) and s.32(2) is also reviewed in *Williams v Fanshaw Porter Hazelhurst* [2004] P.N.L.R. 544 and *Newgate Stud Co v Penfold* [2008] 1 B.C.L.C. 46.

294 *Cave v Robinson Jarvis and Rolf* [2003] 1 A.C. 384.

295 The leading case is *Test Claimants in the F.I.I. Group Litigation v H.M.R.C.* [2012] 2 A.C. 337 esp. at [42]–[63] and [177]–[185] where earlier cases are discussed.

296 As in *Phillips-Higgins v Harper* [1954] 1 Q.B. 411.

297 Civil Liability (Contribution) Act 1978 ss.1 and 6. Hence a trustee cannot recover a contribution from a co-trustee who is liable only respect of some other damage, or who is not liable to the beneficiaries at all: cf. *Alexander v Perpetual Trustee (WA) Ltd* (2004) 216 C.L.R. 109.

298 See para.10-004.

recover a contribution from one or more of the others,[299] the amount of which will depend on the court's assessment of the shares in which their common liability to the beneficiaries should be borne.

It seems likely that when apportioning liability between trustees the courts will continue to draw on the principles which were developed in the Chancery jurisdiction prior to the enactment of the 1978 Act. Thus, they will start with the presumption that co-trustees should share equal responsibility towards the beneficiaries,[300] and will then look to see whether there is any reason for departing from this rule. A trustee who has wrongfully misapplied trust funds to her own exclusive use,[301] or who has exclusively benefited as a beneficiary from the breach of trust,[302] must reimburse the others in full. So must a trustee who has acted fraudulently if the others have acted in good faith.[303] **10–257**

The courts' general tendency in the cases pre-dating the 1978 Act was to reject the argument that a trustee who played an active part in the management of trust affairs should be liable for a greater share of trust losses than a passive trustee who did nothing and so failed to prevent the losses from occurring.[304] However, this tough line was moderated to the extent that lay trustees were permitted to shift the burden of paying for trust losses on to professional trustees, upon whose expertise the lay trustees had reasonably relied.[305] It may be that the modern proliferation of trust companies will invest this line of authority with greater significance.[306] **10–258**

Contribution claims also lie between wrongdoing trustees and third parties who have incurred liability for knowing receipt of misdirected trust property and dishonest assistants in a breach of trust.[307] The same general principles of apportionment apply to these claims as to claims between trustees. Hence unequal apportionments should be made where one party has acted in good faith and another in bad faith, and where one party has made a gain and another has not. For example, in *Dubai Aluminium Co Ltd v Salaam*,[308] the House of Lords agreed with Rix J's finding at first instance that two fraudsters who had received all the money extracted from the claimant company by a wrong-doing fiduciary should reimburse the other defendants who had compensated the company for its loss, because "it cannot be just and equitable to require one party to contribute in a way which would leave another party in possession of his spoils."[309] **10–259**

Similar findings were made by the High Court of Australia in *Burke v LFOT Pty Ltd*,[310] and by the Court of Appeal in *Niru Battery Manufacturing Co v Milestone Trading Ltd (No.2)*, where Clarke LJ held that the principle applies both where the recipient still has the money at the time of the contribution **10–260**

---

[299] Complete reimbursement is expressly allowed for by s.2(2) of the 1978 Act.

[300] *Lingard v Bromley* (1812) 1 V. & B. 114: *Jesse v Bennett* (1856) 6 De G.M. & G. 609; *Robinson v Harkin* [1896] 2 Ch. 415 at 426; *Gilchrist v Dean* [1960] V.R. 266 at 270–271.

[301] *Lincoln v Wright* (1841) 4 Beav. 427; *Thompson v Finch* (1856) 22 Beav. 316 at 327; *Bahin v Hughes* (1886) 31 Ch.D. 390 at 395; *Wynne v Tempest* [1897] 1 Ch. 110; *Goodwin v Duggan* (1996) 41 N.S.W.L.R. 158 at 166.

[302] *Chillingworth v Chambers* [1896] 1 Ch. 685.

[303] *Baynard v Woolley* (1855) 20 Beav. 583 at 585–586; *Elwes v Barnard* (1865) 13 L.T. 426; *Bellemore v Watson* (1885) 1 T.L.R. 241 at 242; *Re Smith* [1896] 1 Ch. 71.

[304] *Lingard v Bromley* (1812) 1 V. & B.114 at 117; *Wilson v Moore* (1833) 1 My. & K. 126 at 147; *Bahin v Hughes* (1886) 31 Ch.D. 390 at 396; *Bacon v Camphausen* (1888) 55 L.T. 851 at 852.

[305] *Lockhart v Reilly* (1856) 25 L.J. Ch. 697, affirmed (1857) 27 L.J. Ch. 54: *Thompson v Finch* (1856) 22 Beav. 316; *Wilson v Thomson* (1875) L.R. 20 Eq. 459: *Re Partington* (1887) 57 L.T. 654; *Re Turner* [1897] 1 Ch. 536; *Re Linsley* [1904] 2 Ch. 785; and cf. *Linsley v Kirstiuk* (1986) 28 D.L.R. (4th) 495.

[306] Cf. *Fales v Canada Permanent Trust Co* [1977] 2 S.C.R. 302; *Blair v Canada Trust Co* (1986) 32 D.L.R. (4th) 515.

[307] For general discussion of third party liability for breach of trust, see Ch.11.

[308] [2003] 2 A.C. 366 at [50]–[54] and [162]–[164], followed in *Pulvers (a firm) v Chan* [2008] P.N.L.R. 9 at [401] and *Cherney v Neuman* [2011] EWHC 2156 (Ch) at [324]–[325].

[309] [1999] 1 Lloyd's Rep. 415 at 475, following Ferris J's observations to the same effect in *K v P* [1993] Ch. 140 at 149.

[310] (2002) 209 C.L.R. 282.

proceedings, and where she pays it away other than in good faith.[311] In *Charter Plc v City Index Ltd*,[312] Morritt C was led by this dictum to conclude that there was no prospect of the claimant recovering a contribution and therefore struck out the claim. On appeal, Carnwath LJ disagreed because he thought that a party who receives money for her own benefit and then pays it away should be in a "similar position" to a party who never receives anything.[313] However, this is only true if the party has acted in good faith. If she has not (and in *City Index* the claimant had not), it would surely be inequitable to let her recover a portion of her bad faith expenditure from the defendant.

*Bahin v Hughes*

Court of Appeal (1886) 31 Ch. D. 390

10–261 A testator, Robert Hughes, bequeathed a legacy of £2,000 to his three daughters—Eliza Hughes, Mrs Burden and Mrs Edwards—on trust to invest in specified securities and in real securities in England and Wales. Eliza Hughes, who was the active trustee, and Mr Burden invested the fund on the (unauthorised) security of leasehold properties, an investment discovered by Mr Burden. Mrs Edwards had been informed of the proposal, but her concurrence was not obtained. The security proving insufficient, the tenant for life and remaindermen brought this action against Eliza Hughes, Mr Edwards (whose wife had died) and Mr and Mrs Burden, claiming that the defendants were liable to make good the trust fund.[314] Edwards served a third-party notice on Eliza Hughes claiming to be indemnified by her, on the ground that she had assumed the role of sole trustee, that the investment had been made at her instigation, and that she had represented to Mrs Edwards that the mortgage was a proper and sufficient security.

10–262 Held, by Kay J., that the defendants were jointly and severally liable to replace the £2,000, and that the defendant Edwards had no right of indemnity against Eliza Hughes. Edwards appealed.

10–263 COTTON L.J. (with whom BOWEN and FRY L.JJ. agreed): . . . On going into the authorities, there are very few cases in which one trustee, who has been guilty with a co-trustee of breach of trust and held answerable, has successfully sought indemnity as against his co-trustee. In *Lockhart v Reilly*[315] it appears from the report of the case in the Law Journal that the trustee by whom the loss was sustained had been not only trustee, but had been and was a solicitor, and acting as solicitor for his self and his co-trustee, and it was on his advice that Lockhart had relied in making the investment which gave rise to the action of the cestui que trust. The Lord Chancellor (Lord Cranworth) refers to the fact that he was a solicitor, and makes the remark:

> "The whole thing was trusted to him. He was the solicitor, and, independently of the consideration that one cannot help seeing it was done with a view of favouring his own family, yet if that had not been so, the co-trustee leaves it with the solicitor-trustee, by whose negligence (I use no harsher word) all this evil, in a great degree, has arisen."

Therefore the Lord Chancellor, in giving his decision, relies upon the fact of the trustee being a solicitor. In *Thompson v Finch*[316] a right was conceded to prove against the estate of the deceased trustee for the full loss sustained; but it appears that in this case also he was a solicitor, and that he really took this money to himself, for he mixed it with his own money, and invested it on a mortgage; and therefore it was held that the trustee was entitled to indemnity from the estate of the co-trustee, who was a solicitor. This was affirmed in the Court of Appeal; and the Court of Appeal took so strong a view of the conduct of the solicitor that both of the judges concurred in thinking that he ought to be called on to show cause why he should not be struck off the rolls. Of course, where one trustee has got the money into his own hands, and made

311 [2004] 2 All E.R. (Comm.) 289 at [50].
312 [2007] 1 W.L.R. 26 at [33]–[53].
313 [2008] Ch. 313 at [59].
314 Prior to s.18 of the Married Women's Property Act of 1882 (which did not apply to the present case) a married woman could not act as trustee without the participation of her husband (Mr Edwards); he was necessarily a trustee through her trusteeship, and was responsible for her breaches of trust.
315 (1856) 25 L.J. Ch. 697 at 702.
316 (1856) 25 L.J. Ch. 681.

use of it, he will be liable to his co-trustee to give him an indemnity. Now I think it wrong to lay down any limitation of the circumstances under which one trustee would be held liable to the other for indemnity, both having been held liable to the cestui que trust; but so far as cases have gone at present, relief has only been granted against a trustee who has himself got the benefit of the breach of trust, or between whom and his co-trustees there has existed a relation which will justify the court in treating him solely liable for the breach of trust. . .

Miss Hughes was the active trustee and Mr Edwards did nothing, and in my opinion it would be laying down a wrong rule that where one trustee acts honestly, though erroneously, the other trustee is to be held entitled to indemnity who by doing nothing neglects his duty more than the acting trustee. That Miss Hughes made an improper investment is true, but she acted honestly, and intended to do the best she could, and believed that the property was sufficient security for the money, although she made no inquiries about their being leasehold houses. In my opinion the money was lost just as much by the default of Mr Edwards as by the innocent though erroneous action of his co-trustee, Miss Hughes. All the trustees were in the wrong, and every one is equally liable to indemnify the beneficiaries. 10–264

*Appeal dismissed.* 10–265

*Head v Gould*

Chancery Division [1898] 2 Ch. 250

Miss Head and Mr Gould were appointed new trustees of certain marriage settlements (the beneficial interests being the same under both settlements), and thenceforth Gould acted as solicitor to the trusts. Miss Head was one of the remaindermen under these settlements, the tenant for life being her mother. The new trustees sold a house forming part of the trust, and in breach of trust handed the proceeds of sale to the tenant for life. Part of the trust property consisted also of certain policies on the life of Mrs Head, policies which Mrs Head had mortgaged to the trust by way of security for advances of trust capital which the former trustees had made to her at her urgent request for the purpose of assisting the family. These policies were (in breach of trust) surrendered by the new trustees with the concurrence of Mrs Head. 10–266

Miss Head claimed to be indemnified by her co-trustee, Gould, under circumstances which appear from the judgment: 10–267

KEKEWICH J.: . . . It will be convenient here at once to deal with the claim made by Miss Head against her co-trustee, Gould. By her third party notice she seeks to be indemnified by him against loss by reason of the breaches of trust, on the ground that the loss and misapplication (if any) of the trust funds, or any part thereof, were occasioned entirely by his acts or defaults, and that he assumed to act as solicitor to the trust estate and as the sole trustee thereof, and exercised control of the administration of the trust funds, and that whatever was done by herself in connection with the trust was at his instigation and in reliance upon his advice. 10–268

This is a serious charge, and if it had been proved would have entitled her to the relief claimed according to well-known and well-recognised principles. . . . There is before me no evidence bringing the case within those principles, or showing that the charge which is correctly formulated on them is consistent with the facts. My conclusion from such evidence as there is before the court is distinctly adverse to the claim. I know that, before the appointment of herself and Gould as trustees, Miss Head was an active party to the importunities of her mother which induced the former trustees to commit a breach of trust for their benefit, and that she looked to the change of trustees as a means of, in some way or other, obtaining further advances. I know, further, that she was well acquainted with the position of the trust, and that it was all-important to maintain the policies and to appropriate the rents of the house to that purpose. She now affects to ignore all that has been done since her appointment, and professes not to remember having executed the several instruments which must have been executed by her for the sale of the house and the surrender of the policies, or the receipt of moneys arising therefrom. With regret, and under a painful sense of duty, I am bound to say that I do not credit her testimony. True it is that the defendant, Gould, is a solicitor, and that he was appointed a trustee for that very reason. True no doubt, also, that the legal business was managed by him, and I do not propose to absolve him from any responsibility attaching to him on that ground; but I do not myself think that Byrne J. or any other judge ever intended to hold that a man is bound to indemnify his co-trustee against loss merely because he was a solicitor, when that co-trustee was an 10–269 active participator in the breach of trust complained of, and is not proved to have participated merely in consequence of the advice and control of the solicitor. . . .

10–270 Held, therefore, that the trustee, Miss Head, had no claim of indemnity against her co-trustee.

**Questions**

1. "It is misleading to speak of breach of trust as if it were the equitable counterpart of breach of contract at common law. . . . It is tempting, but wrong, to assume that a trustee is . . . under a primary obligation to perform the trust and a secondary obligation to pay equitable compensation if he does not. . . . The primary remedy of the beneficiary . . . is to have the account taken, to surcharge and falsify the account, and to require the trustee to restore to the trust estate any deficiency which may appear when the account is taken." (Lord Millett, writing in the *Law Quarterly Review* in 1998.) **Discuss.**
2. What should the measure of liability be in the following alternative circumstances where, in breach of trust, Samantha Smith and Roger Robinson, trustees of a family trust:
   (a) transfer the £2 million portfolio of investments and cash to a discretionary portfolio manager and either: (i) two months later before any of the investments have been replaced there is a stock-market collapse, so that the portfolio is worth only £1.5 million; or (ii) four years later, after the original investments have all been replaced, there is a stock-market collapse, so that the portfolio is worth only £1.5 million, having been worth £2.5 million earlier;
   (b) transfer investments worth £200,000 to their children Amanda Smith and Jack Robinson in consideration of their marriage and either: (i) two months later before any of the investments have been sold there is a stock-market collapse, so that the investments are worth only £150,000; or (ii) four years later, after the investments have been sold and used to purchase a £250,000 house (now worth £300,000) there is a stock-market collapse, so that if the investments had been retained they would have depreciated from £250,000 to £150,000.
3. The Mega Trust Co would like you to draft some provisions for its standard forms of trust instrument. In particular, it would like provisions which: (a) exclude as much trustee liability for breach of trust as possible; (b) deny the beneficiaries access to as much trust information as possible; and (c) make clear that the trustee has no duty to supervise the activities of any company in which it owns shares (even a majority shareholding) or to seek representation on the board of directors.

   **Advise the company how far (if at all) it is possible in English law to achieve these objectives.**

# 11

# PERSONAL COMPENSATORY LIABILITY OF THIRD PARTIES INVOLVED IN A BREACH OF TRUST

## 1. Introduction

### A. Overview

Third parties involved in a breach of trust can become personally liable to the beneficiaries in several ways. First, a person who is neither a trustee, nor authorised by the trustees, but who takes it on herself to deal with trust property that has come into her hands as though she were a trustee, is personally liable to account to the beneficiaries for the property, as a trustee *de son tort*. **11–001**

Secondly, a person who acts unconscionably by receiving trust property for her own benefit with knowledge that it was transferred to her in breach of trust, or by receiving such property innocently but later acquiring knowledge of the breach and then dealing with it for her own benefit, is personally liable to account to the beneficiaries for her handling of the property as constructive trustee. It is controversial whether such defendants also owe a personal liability in unjust enrichment to make restitution of the value of the property received. If they do, and if such a liability is strict (i.e. does not require proof of fault), then a recipient of misdirected trust funds is also personally liable to repay the value of the property received, regardless of whether she ever knew of their improper provenance, although in some cases good faith recipients can invoke a defence of change of position. **11–002**

Thirdly, a person who dishonestly assists in a breach of trust arguably incurs a duplicative liability which mirrors the liability of the wrongdoing trustees, with the result that she is personally liable to restore the trust fund, or to pay reparative compensation to the beneficiaries, to the same extent as the trustees whose breach of trust she has assisted. It is controversial whether she is also personally liable to pay the beneficiaries the amount of any profits received by the trustees in which she has not shared herself. But it is clear that she is personally liable to account to the beneficiaries for any profits that she makes for herself in which the trustees have not shared. **11–003**

### B. Personal Liability to Account as a Constructive Trustee

Trustees *de son tort*, knowing recipients, and dishonest assistants are all commonly said to owe a personal liability to account to the beneficiaries as constructive trustees. Some courts and commentators have said that this phrase has no particular meaning when used in this context and **11–004** is merely an empty formula for relief. That is incorrect, for the reasons given by Charles Mitchell and Stephen Watterson in the following extract.

### C. Mitchell and S. Watterson, "Remedies for Knowing Receipt"

in C. Mitchell (ed.), *Constructive and Resulting Trusts* (Hart Publishing, 2010), pp.128–130

**11–005** Over the past twenty years it has become fashionable to say that nothing is added to our understanding of liability for knowing receipt by the language of constructive trusteeship, and indeed that this language obscures the true nature of the liability. This was a recurring theme in the work of Peter Birks,[1] which seems to have exercised a strong influence on the thinking of some members of the senior judiciary. For example, Lord Nicholls has written extra-judicially that:[2]

> "The traditional approach to [knowing recipients and dishonest assistants] involves interposing a deemed ('constructive') trusteeship between the wrongful conduct (dishonest participation) and the remedy (liability in equity). This intermediate step seems otiose and, indeed, confusing."

Similarly, in *Paragon Finance plc v D B Thakerar & Co. (a firm)*, Millett L.J. observed of liability for both dishonest assistance and knowing receipt that:[3]

> "Equity has always given relief against fraud by making any person sufficiently implicated in the fraud accountable in equity. . . Such a person is not in fact a trustee at all, even though he may be liable to account as if he were. He never assumes the position of a trustee, and if he receives the trust property at all it is adversely to the plaintiff by an unlawful transaction which is impugned by the plaintiff. In such a case the expressions 'constructive trust' and 'constructive trustee' are misleading for there is no trust and usually no possibility of a proprietary remedy; 'they are nothing more than a formula for equitable relief'."

**11–006** To the extent that these comments concern liability for dishonest assistance, their Lordships are right to say that a dishonest assistant need not receive property, with the result that his liability cannot depend on his owing duties as trustee in his own right. But even so their Lordships do not tell the whole story, because this form of liability can entail fixing the defendant with a duplicative liability which mirrors that of the trustee whose breach has been assisted. Hence it can meaningfully be said that he is "constructively liable as a trustee" in the sense that he is deemed to be liable to pay over the same sums as the trustee .. . . Leaving that point to one side, and focusing our attention on liability for knowing receipt, their Lordships also miss something fundamental when they dismiss the language of constructive trusteeship when it is applied to knowing recipients.[4]

**11–007** In our view, when the courts say that a knowing recipient is personally liable to account as a constructive trustee, this language accurately conveys the distinctive nature of liability for knowing receipt, which

---

1 Although Birks' understanding of the relationship between knowing receipt and unjust enrichment changed he never shifted from his view that the language of constructive trusteeship was a "mystifying label" that should be discarded: e.g. P. Birks *An Introduction to the Law of Restitution* (Clarendon Press, 1985) 80–82; P. Birks "Persistent Problems in Misdirected Money: A Quintet" [1993] L.M.C.L.Q. 218, 236; P. Birks *Unjust Enrichment* 2nd edn (O.U.P., 2005) 293–5. Like views are expressed in C. Rickett 'The Classification of Trusts' (1999) 18 N.Z.U.L.R. 305, 321–4; A. Burrows *The Law of Restitution* 2nd edn (Sweet & Maxwell, 2005) 196–7; M. Cope *Equitable Obligations: Duties, Defences and Remedies* (Lawbook Co., 2007) 224 – although Cope also states at 224, n 39, that 'the personal liability [of a knowing recipient] is the same as the personal liability of an express trustee', a statement with which we broadly agree.

2 Lord Nicholls 'Knowing Receipt: The Need for a New Landmark' in W.R. Cornish et al (eds) *Restitution: Past, Present, and Future* (Hart, 1998) 231, 243.

3 [1999] 1 All E.R. 400 at 409, quoting *Selangor United Rubber Estates Ltd v Cradock (No.3)* [1968] 1 W.L.R. 1555, 1582. The view that Millett L.J. meant to speak of knowing receipt as well as dishonest assistance in this passage is expressed by Rimer J. in *DEG-Deutsche Investitions- und Entwicklungsgesellschaft mbH v Koshy (No.2)* [2002] 1 B.C.L.C. 478 [288] and in *Sinclair Investment Holdings S.A. v Versailles Trade Finance Ltd (in admin recship)* (2007) 10 I.T.E.L.R. 58 [122]; also by Lawrence Collins J. in *Nabb Brothers Ltd v Lloyds Bank International (Guernsey) Ltd* [2005] EWHC 405 (Ch) [70] and *Pakistan v Zardari* [2006] EWHC 2411 (Comm) [88].

4 They also appear to be motivated by the wish to merge dishonest assistance and knowing receipt into a single equitable wrong of 'dishonest participation in a breach of trust', something that we believe would be a false step.

> many modern accounts of the subject misunderstand or ignore.[5] Many of these accounts are motivated by a proper desire to rationalise equitable principles, but they are misguided to the extent that they attempt to characterise liability for knowing receipt in terms of common law models of liability. This project can only be accomplished at the cost of ignoring what the courts actually do—and explicitly tell us that they do—in knowing receipt cases. Liability for knowing receipt cannot be collapsed into a liability for unjust enrichment, nor a liability for primary equitable wrongdoing which mirrors the common law tort of conversion, nor a liability for secondary equitable wrongdoing which mirrors the common law economic torts. Liability for knowing receipt is a distinctive, primary, custodial liability, which closely resembles the liability of express trustees to account for the trust property with which they are charged.
>
> In short, when the courts say that a knowing recipient is "personally liable to account as a constructive trustee", they mean exactly what they say: because of the circumstances in which knowing recipients acquire title to the misapplied property, Equity fixes them with custodial duties which are the same as some of the duties which are voluntarily assumed by express trustees. In cases where a knowing recipient breaches these duties, the accounting mechanisms through which he can be forced to make things right are the same as those through which trust beneficiaries can take action against express trustees. **11–008**

Proceeding on the basis that the courts do mean something when they say that defendants are personally liable to account as constructive trustees, we next encounter the problem that the courts do not always mean the same thing, as the phrase has a different significance according to whether it is used to describe the liability of a trustee *de son tort*, a knowing recipient or a dishonest assistant. **11–009**

In the case of a trustee *de son tort*, the courts mean that when the defendant acquires trust property and deals with it as though she were an express trustee, she is personally liable to account for what she does with it in the same way as an express trustee of the property is liable to account for her stewardship of the property to the beneficiaries.[6] **11–010**

Similarly, when a knowing recipient acquires trust property she is liable to account for what she does with it to the beneficiaries as though she were an express trustee of the property for them.[7] Consistently with this, the remedies awarded against trustees *de son tort* and knowing recipients who fail to deal with the trust property in accordance with the beneficiaries' rights are essentially the same as those which are awarded against express trustees who fail to act in accordance with the terms of the trust: claims are made through the same proceedings for an account, and liability is quantified by reference to the same principles, as those which have been described in the discussion of express trustee liability in Chapter 10. **11–011**

In the case of dishonest assistants, however, the expression means something different. Liability for dishonest assistance can be incurred by defendants who handle misdirected trust property which might be impressed with a constructive trust for the beneficiaries (e.g. a bank which dishonestly receives misdirected trust funds and pays them over to a third party). However liability can also be incurred by defendants whose assistance does not entail receiving misapplied property[8]—and indeed, can be incurred by defendants who assist in a breach of fiduciary duty that does not itself involve any misapplication of property.[9] It follows that when the courts say that a dishonest assistant is personally liable to account to the beneficiaries as a constructive trustee, they cannot mean that she is herself a **11–012**

---

5 But see S. Gardner *An Introduction to the Law of Trusts* 2nd edn (O.U.P., 2003) 281–2; S. Worthington *Equity* 2nd edn (O.U.P., 2006) 179–189, esp. 180 and 188; Cope (n.1), 342–3. [Remainder of footnote omitted.]

6 e.g. *Jasmine Trustees Ltd v Wells & Hind (a firm)* [2008] Ch. 194 at [42].

7 e.g. *Jesse v Bennett* (1856) 6 De G.M. & G. 609 at 612; *Morgan v Stephens* (1861) 3 Giff. 226 at 237; *Rolfe v Gregory* (1865) 4 De G.J. & S. 576 at 578; *John v Dodwell & Co Ltd* [1918] A.C. 563 at 569.

8 *Royal Brunei Airlines Sdn Bhd v Tan* [1995] 2 A.C. 378 at 382; *Houghton v Fayers* [2000] Lloyd's Rep. Bank. 145 at 149.

9 *Novoship (UK) Ltd v Mikhaylyuk* [2015] 2 W.L.R. 526.

trustee of property for which she must account to them: "there is no real trust and usually no chance of a proprietary remedy" against her.[10]

**11–013** Arguably, what they mean instead is that the dishonest assistant can be treated, by a legal fiction, as though she were the trustee or fiduciary whose breach of duty she has assisted, so as to fix her with the same personal liabilities as are owed by that trustee or fiduciary: her liability derives from and duplicates the liability of that primary wrongdoer.[11] Another way of putting this is to say that dishonest assistants can incur a civil secondary liability, analogous to the criminal secondary liability of those who procure, aid or abet a crime.[12] If this conceptualisation of liability for dishonest assistance is correct, then it suggests that the remedies awarded against defendants may simply duplicate the remedies awarded against the trustees or fiduciaries whose breaches of duty they have assisted. However, dishonest assistants can also incur a direct primary liability in their own right, to disgorge profits which they have made for themselves through their equitable wrongdoing, whether or not the trustees have shared in these profits, and whether or not they correspond to a loss to the trust estate.[13]

## 2. Trusteeship *De Son Tort*

**11–014** In *Mara v Browne*, A.L. Smith LJ held that[14]:

> If one, not being a trustee and not having authority from a trustee, takes upon himself to intermeddle with trust matters or to do acts characteristic of the office of trustee he may thereby make himself what is called in law a trustee of his own wrong, i.e. a trustee *de son tort*, or as it is also termed, a constructive trustee.

**11–015** A trustee *de son tort* does not purport to act for herself, but for the beneficiaries.[15] There is no need to show that she has acted dishonestly to fix her with liability: she may have been honest and well intentioned,[16] and it may be that she mistakenly believed herself to be an express trustee, although she was not, e.g. because she was invalidly appointed.[17] Her conduct is equated to a declaration of herself as a trustee,[18] and so she is expected to familiarise herself with the extent of her duties on

---

10 *Coulthard v Disco Mix Club Ltd* [2000] 1 W.L.R. 707 at 731.

11 *US Surgical Corp. v Hospital Products International Pty Ltd* (1982) 2 N.S.W.L.R. 766 at 817 (not considered on appeal); *Royal Brunei Airlines Sdn Bhd v Tan* [1995] 2 A.C. 378 at 385; *Australian Securities Commission v AS Nominees Ltd* (1995) 62 F.C.R. 504 at 523; *Equiticorp Industries Ltd v R. (No.47)* [1998] 2 N.Z.L.R. 481 at 658; *Bankgesellschaft Berlin A.G. v Makris* Q.B.D. (Comm. Ct) 22 January 1999, per Cresswell J; *Grupo Torras S.A. v Al-Sabah (No.5)* [2001] Lloyd's Rep. Bank. 36 at 61–62.

12 *Ultraframe (U.K.) Ltd v Fielding* [2007] W.T.L.R. 835 at [1506], per Lewison J: "liability as a dishonest assistant, as the law has developed, is a secondary liability akin to the criminal liability of one who aids and abets the commission of a criminal offence."

13 *Novoship (U.K.) Ltd v Mikhaylyuk* [2015] 2 W.L.R. 526.

14 [1896] 1 Ch. 199 at 209. See too *Blyth v Fladgate* [1891] 1 Ch. 337; *Lyell v Kennedy* (1899) 14 App. Cas. 437; *Taylor v Davies* [1920] A.C. 636 at 651; *Selangor United Rubber Ltd v Cradock (No.3)* [1968] 1 W.L.R. 1555 at 1579; *Carl Zeiss Stiftung v Herbert Smith (No.2)* [1969] 2 Ch. 276 at [289]. In *Dubai Aluminium Co.Ltd v Salaam* [2003] 2 A.C. 366 at [138], Lord Millett preferred the term "de facto trustee" to the term "trustee *de son tort*".

15 *Nolan v Nolan* [2004] VSCA 109 at [29].

16 *Lyell v Kennedy* (1889) 14 App. Cas. 437 at 459; *Mara v Browne* [1896] 1 Ch. 199 at 209; *Life Association of Scotland v Siddal* (1861) 3 De G.F. & J. 58; *Baden, Delvaux v Société Générale pour Favoriser le Développement du Commerce et de l'Industrie en France SA* [1993] 1 W.L.R. 509 at 577; *Dubai Aluminium Co Ltd v Salaam* [2003] 2 A.C. 366 at [138].

17 As in, e.g. *Re BB's Representation* (2011) 15 I.T.E.L.R. 51 (Royal Court of Jersey). See too *Williams v Central Bank of Nigeria* [2014] A.C. 1189 at [54] per Lord Sumption, approving the statement in Mowbray et al., *Lewin on Trusts*, 18th edn (Sweet & Maxwell, 2008), para.42–74, that: "If a person by mistake or otherwise assumes the character of trustee when it does not really belong to him, he becomes a trustee de son tort and he may be called to account by the beneficiaries for the money he has received under the colour of the trust."

18 *Life Association of Scotland v Siddal* (1861) 3 De G.F. & J. 58 at 72.

taking office, and thereafter she may be liable for a breach of these duties, as though she were an express trustee.[19] However, this does not mean that she has the same powers that she would have if she were an express trustee, and she cannot validly exercise dispositive discretions conferred on the trustees by the trust instrument.[20]

If trust property comes into the hands of a trustee *de son tort* she will hold it on constructive trust for the beneficiaries, to whom she will owe a duty to account for her stewardship of the property. Thus in *Blyth v Fladgate*[21] where a sole trustee had solicitors invest trust funds in Exchequer Bills and, after his death and before appointment of any new trustees, the bills were sold by the solicitors and the proceeds invested in a loan on mortgage, the solicitors were liable for the loss arising when the security was insufficient. 11–016

## 3. Knowing Receipt

In *El Ajou v Dollar Land Holdings Plc*,[22] Hoffmann LJ stated that for the purposes of a claim for knowing receipt the claimant must show 11–017

> first, a disposal of his assets in breach of fiduciary duty; secondly, the beneficial receipt by the defendant of assets which are traceable as representing the assets of the plaintiff; and thirdly, knowledge on the part of the defendant that the assets he received are traceable to a breach of fiduciary duty.

We shall discuss each requirement in turn before considering the remedies awarded to successful claimants and the question whether a strict liability claim in unjust enrichment also lies in cases where the facts would support a claim in knowing receipt.

### *A. Disposal of Assets in Breach of Fiduciary Duty*

As we discuss in Chapter 9,[23] the term "fiduciary duty" is commonly used by the courts in two different senses. Sometimes they use it to describe a duty to avoid conflicts of interest owed by a person in whom another person reposes trust and confidence; and sometimes they use it to describe a trustee-like "stewardship" duty to adhere to the limits of one's authority when dealing with property for another person's benefit.[24] In *El Ajou*, when Hoffmann LJ spoke of a disposal of the claimant's assets in breach of "fiduciary duty", he had the second of these senses in mind: the issue is not whether the person from whom the defendant received the property breached a duty to avoid a conflict of interest between her own interests and the claimant's interests; rather, it is whether she exceeded the terms of her authority to deal with the property for the claimant's benefit. 11–018

It follows that in cases where the person from whom the defendant received the property was free to deal with it as she chose and owed no duty to account the claimant for her dealings, no question of liability for knowing receipt can arise.[25] Liability can only arise where one party owes a stewardship 11–019

---

[19] *Pearce v Pearce* (1856) 22 Beav. 248 at 252.

[20] *Jasmine Trustees Ltd v Wells & Hind (a firm)* [2008] Ch. 194 at [52]–[57].

[21] [1891] 1 Ch. 337. See too *Goddard v DFC New Zealand Ltd* [1991] 3 N.Z.L.R. 580.

[22] [1994] 2 All E.R. 685 at 700.

[23] See paras 9–008—9–017.

[24] "Stewardship" is not a legal term of art and is used here in a loose sense to describe the control and management of property for another person's benefit. For judicial usage of the word in this sense, see, e.g. *Bairstow v Queens Moat Houses Plc* [2001] 2 B.C.L.C. 531 at [53]; *Ultraframe (UK) Ltd v Fielding* [2005] EWHC 1638 (Ch) at [513]; *AIB Group (UK) plc v Mark Redler & Co* [2014] 3 W.L.R. 1367 at [39].

[25] *Tuthill v Equine FX Ltd* [2013] EWHC 1207 (Comm) at [32]; *Gabriel v Little* (2013) 16 I.T.E.L.R. 567 at [46].

duty to the claimant and acts outside the scope of her authority when transferring the relevant property to the defendant. There are a range of people besides trustees who owe such a duty, including agents,[26] partners,[27] executors and administrators of deceased persons' estates,[28] and company directors[29]—which is why many claims for knowing receipt are concerned not with misapplied trust assets but with misapplied corporate assets.[30] Furthermore, as we discuss below,[31] knowing recipients themselves owe a stewardship duty, and it follows that liability for knowing receipt can be incurred by a defendant who receives improperly distributed funds from someone who is herself a knowing recipient.[32]

### *B. Beneficial Receipt of the Claimant's Property or its Traceable Proceeds*

**11–020** Where a trustee transfers legal title to trust property[33] to a defendant in an unauthorised transaction,[34] and the defendant still has the legal title, the beneficiaries will usually seek an order that it be reconveyed,[35] i.e. a proprietary rather than a personal remedy. There is no rule forbidding them to sue for a personal remedy in knowing receipt if they wish (unless the property is registered land and the transfer is made for valuable consideration, in which case the Land Registration Act 2002 s.29, which avoids the beneficiaries' equitable interests in the property, should also immunise the recipient from personal liability in knowing receipt).[36] Most often, however, claims in knowing receipt are brought in cases where the defendant no longer has legal title to the property, e.g. because she transferred it to a third party, as a proprietary remedy is then no longer an option.[37]

**11–021** Claims in knowing receipt also lie with respect to the traceable proceeds of property taken by the wrongdoing trustee. So, the defendant may have to account both for new property which has been

---

26 *Pearse v Green* (1819) 1 Jac. & W. 135 Ct of KB 140–141; 37 E.R. 327 at 329; *Attorney General v Cocke* [1988] Ch. 414 at 420; *Maloney v Filtons Ltd* [2012] EWHC 1395 (Ch) at [97].

27 *London Financial Association v Kelk* (1884) 26 Ch. D. 107 at 151; *Platt v Butcher* unreported 11 November 2005, County Court (Bristol).

28 *Piety v Stace* (1799) 4 Ves. Jr. 620 at 622; *Freeman v Fairlie* (1817) 3 Mer. 29 at 43–44; *Wroe v Seed* (1863) 4 Giff. 425 at 428–429; Administration of Estates Act 1925 s.21.

29 *Re Exchange Banking Co (Flitcroft's Case)* (1882) 21 Ch. D. 519 at 525 and 535–536; *Re Lands Allotment Co* [1894] 1 Ch. 616 CA at 638; *Selangor United Rubber Estates Ltd v Cradock (No.3)* [1968] 1 W.L.R. 1555 at [1575]; *HMRC v Holland* [2011] Bus. L.R. 111 at [56]; *Sinclair Investments (UK) Ltd v Versailles Trade Finance Ltd (In Administration)* [2011] Bus. L.R. 1126 at [34].

30 *Russell v Wakefield Waterworks Co* (1875) L.R. 20 Eq. 474 at 479; *Belmont Finance Corp Ltd v Williams Furniture Ltd (No.2)* [1980] 1 All E.R. 393; *Agip (Africa) Ltd v Jackson* [1991] Ch. 547; *CMS Dolphin Ltd v Simonet* [2001] 2 B.C.L.C. 704; *Relfo Ltd (In Liquidation) v Varsani* [2015] 1 B.C.L.C. 14.

31 See paras 11–074ff.

32 *Bracken Partners Ltd v Gutteridge* [2004] 1 B.C.L.C. 373 (CA); *Evans v European Bank Ltd* (2004) 7 I.T.E.L.R. 19.

33 The tricky question of what counts as "property" for these purposes is discussed in *Westpac Banking Corp v Bell Group Ltd (In Liquidation) (No.3)* (2012) 270 Fed.L.R. 1 at [2137]ff. At [2156] the court opined that: "There is no justification for confining "trust property" for the purposes of [knowing receipt] to tangible things. Importantly, that expression includes . . . choses in action comprising incorporeal property not reducible into physical possession, such as rights arising under a contract which are enforceable by action."

34 Trustees can validly transfer legal title to the trust property to a third party although the transfer is unauthorised, but if they do so under a contract with the recipient, the question whether there is a claim in knowing receipt then turns on whether the contract was legally binding so that the recipient was entitled to receive it: M. Conaglen and R. Nolan, "Contracts and Knowing Receipt: Principles and Application" (2013) 129 L.Q.R. 359. Similar rules affect recipients of corporate property from directors acting beyond their powers: *Rolled Steel Products (Holdings) Ltd v British Steel Corp* [1986] Ch. 246 at 303; *Criterion Properties Ltd v Stratford UK Properties LLC* [2003] 1 W.L.R. 2108 at [4]; *Grimaldi v Chameleon Mining NL (No.2)* (2012) 200 F.C.R. 296 at [254].

35 *Ultraframe (UK) Ltd v Fielding* [2007] W.T.L.R. 835 at [1486].

36 M. Conaglen and A. Goymour, "Knowing Receipt and Registered Land" in C. Mitchell (ed.), *Constructive and Resulting Trusts* (Hart Publishing, 2010).

37 *Ultraframe* [2007] W.T.L.R. 835 at [1577].

exchanged for the property that was misdirected by the trustee and also for profits generated out of the misdirected trust property or substitute property (e.g. dividends paid on company shares).[38] To identify the property received by the defendant as the traceable substitute of the original trust property, the claimant must satisfy the relevant rules of tracing and following.[39] A recent example is *Relfo Ltd (In Liquidation) v Varsani*,[40] where the Court of Appeal accepted that money credited to a bank account held by the defendant in Singapore represented the traceable proceeds of money debited from the claimant's bank account in England.

The defendant must have received title to the relevant property beneficially for herself: she will not be liable if she receives it ministerially, i.e. in her capacity as agent for a third party to whom she owes a duty to account for the property, and who is himself immediately liable to the beneficiaries from the date of the defendant's receipt.[41] **11–022**

## C. Requirement of Knowledge

Until 2000, the starting point for the courts when investigating the degree of knowledge possessed by a defendant in an action for knowing receipt was *Baden, Delvaux v Société Générale pour Favoriser le Développement du Commerce et de l'Industrie en France SA*.[42] This case concerned liability for assisting in a breach of trust, but Peter Gibson J adopted a five-fold classification of knowledge in the case that was later used in knowing receipt cases as well. He distinguished between: (i) actual knowledge; (ii) wilfully shutting one's eyes to the obvious; (iii) wilfully and recklessly failing to make such inquiries as an honest and reasonable man would make; (iv) knowledge of circumstances which would indicate the facts to an honest and reasonable man; and (v) knowledge of circumstances which would put an honest and reasonable man on inquiry.[43] **11–023**

There was no clear alignment between actual knowledge, *Baden, Delvaux* categories (i)–(iii), and dishonesty, on the one hand, and between constructive knowledge, *Baden, Delvaux* categories (iv)–(v), and negligence, on the other. Hence it is difficult to translate decisions expressed in the language of the *Baden, Delvaux* classification into the language of dishonesty and negligence. Nevertheless, the weight of authority indicated that dishonesty of the sort typically displayed by defendants falling into categories (i)–(iii) was sufficient, but not necessary, for liability,[44] and these cases were probably inconsistent with others which held that carelessness of the kind typically exhibited by defendants falling into categories (iv)–(v) was not enough.[45] **11–024**

---

38 *Grimaldi v Chameleon Mining NL (No.2)* (2012) 287 A.L.R. 22 at [510].

39 See Ch.12 for general discussion.

40 [2015] 1 B.C.L.C. 14, discussed at para.12–042. See too *Agip (Africa) Ltd v Jackson* [1990] Ch. 265 at 289–292; *El Ajou v Dollar Land Holdings Plc* [1994] 2 All E.R. 685 at 700; *Boscawen v Bajwa* [1996] 1 W.L.R. 328 at 334; *Foskett v McKeown* [2001] 1 A.C. 102 at 128; *Trustor AB v Smallbone (No.2)* [2001] 1 W.L.R. 1177 at 1184.

41 *Barnes v Addy* (1874) 9 Ch. App. 244 at 254–255; *Agip (Africa) Ltd v Jackson* [1990] Ch. 265 at 291–292; *Twinsectra Ltd v Yardley* [2002] 2 A.C. 164 at 194; *Evans v European Bank Ltd* (2004) 7 I.T.E.L.R. 19 at [164]–[176]. In these circumstances, the defendant may still be liable for dishonest assistance, depending on her state of mind, as in, e.g. *British North American Elevator Co v Bank British North American* [1919] A.C. 658; *Papamichael v National Westminster Bank Plc* [2003] 1 Lloyd's Rep. 341.

42 [1993] 1 W.L.R. 509 (the case was decided in 1983).

43 *Baden, Delvaux* [1993] 1 W.L.R. 509 at 575–587.

44 *Selangor United Rubber Estates Ltd v Cradock (No.3)* [1968] 1 W.L.R. 1555; *Belmont Finance Corp v Williams Furniture Ltd (No.2)* [1980] 1 All E.R. 399 at 405; *International Sales and Agencies Ltd v Marcus* [1982] 3 All E.R. 551 at 558; *Baden, Delvaux v Société Générale pour Favoriser le Développement du Commerce et de l'Industrie en France SA* [1993] 1 W.L.R. 509 at 582; *Houghton v Fayers* [2000] 1 B.C.L.C. 511.

45 *Re Montagu's Settlement Trusts* [1987] Ch. 264; *Lipkin Gorman v Karpnale Ltd* [1987] 1 W.L.R. 987 at 1005; *Barclays Bank Plc v Quincecare Ltd* [1992] 4 All E.R. 363 at 375; *Eagle Trust Plc v SBC Securities Ltd* [1992] 4 All E.R. 488 at 509; *Cowan de*

11-025 In 1995, in *Royal Brunei Airlines Sdn Bhd v Tan*,[46] the Privy Council held that liability for assisting in a breach of trust should no longer be decided with reference to the *Baden, Delvaux* classification, which had become over-theorised and obscure.[47] In 2000, in *BCCI (Overseas) Ltd v Akindele*,[48] the Court of Appeal said the same thing with respect to knowing receipt. Nourse LJ held that dishonesty will suffice, but is not required, to make a defendant liable where she has received and dealt with misapplied trust property for her own benefit,[49] and that as a general rule a defendant will be liable whenever her "state of knowledge [is] . . . such as to make it unconscionable for [her] to retain the benefit of the receipt."[50]

*Bank of Credit and Commerce International (Overseas) Ltd v Akindele*

Court of Appeal [2001] Ch. 437

11-026 The defendant, Chief Akindele, entered a contract with two companies, ICIC (Overseas) Ltd and BCCI (Overseas) Ltd, for the purchase of shares in their holding company, BCCI Holdings (Luxembourg) SA. The contract provided that the defendant would pay US$10 million to BCCI (Overseas) Ltd in exchange for 250,000 shares in the holding company, and on terms that after two years BCCI (Overseas) Ltd would arrange for their sale at a price that would give the defendant a 15 per cent annual return on his investment. The defendant paid the money, and by a further agreement, the shares were later sold and the defendant was paid US$16.679 million. Following the insolvent liquidation of ICIC (Overseas) Ltd and BCCI (Overseas) Ltd, it emerged that these arrangements had been procured as part of a fraudulent scheme by officers of the BCCI group, acting in breach of their fiduciary duty to their employers, the point of which had been to give the false impression that certain dummy loans had been performing normally. The liquidators of the two companies claimed that the defendant was liable to account to them for US$6.679m as a constructive trustee on the basis that he had knowingly assisted the breaches of fiduciary duty or had received the US$16.679 million with knowledge of these breaches. At first instance Carnwath J. dismissed the action on the ground that dishonesty by the defendant was the essential foundation of the claimants' case whether under the head of knowing assistance or of knowing receipt and that this had not been established by the claimants. The liquidators appealed.

11-027 NOURSE L.J. (with whom WARD L.J. and SEDLEY L.J. agreed) stated the facts and then continued:

**The Claimants' Case in this Court**

11-028 The judge[51] identified the two main issues arising on the pleadings as being, first, was the defendant liable for dishonestly assisting or participating in breaches of trust by Mr Naqvi, Mr Hafeez and Mr Kazmi (knowing assistance) and, secondly, was the defendant liable for receiving the divestiture payment with knowledge of the breaches of trust (knowing receipt). In this court the claimants' case has been maintained under both heads. In regard to knowing assistance, while accepting the judge's findings of primary fact, Mr Sheldon submitted that he was wrong not to infer from them that the defendant had acted dishonestly. I cannot accept that submission. Having seen and heard the defendant give evidence and found him to be a credible witness on most points, and after a conscientious consideration of the evidence as a whole, the judge was entitled to find that he had acted honestly. It cannot be said either that there was no evidence to support that finding or that it was against the weight of the evidence as a whole. The defendant not having acted dishonestly, the case in knowing assistance is bound to fail. If the claim is to succeed at all, it can only be in knowing receipt.

---

*Groot Properties Ltd v Eagle Trust Plc* [1991] B.C.L.C. 1045 at 1110; *Polly Peck International Plc v Nadir (No.2)* [1992] 4 All E.R. 769 at 777; *Jonathan v Tilley* (1988) 12 Tru. L.I. 36.

46 [1995] 2 A.C. 378.

47 See paras 11-099—11-100.

48 [2001] Ch. 437.

49 *Bank of Credit and Commerce International (Overseas) Ltd v Akindele* [2001] Ch. 437 at 440.

50 *Bank of Credit and Commerce International (Overseas) Ltd v Akindele* [2001] Ch. 437 at 455.

51 [1999] B.C.C. 669 at 675–676.

## Knowing Receipt

The essential requirements of knowing receipt were stated by Hoffmann L.J. in *El Ajou v Dollar Land Holdings Plc*:[52] 11–029

> "For this purpose the plaintiff must show, first, a disposal of his assets in breach of fiduciary duty; secondly, the beneficial receipt by the defendant of assets which are traceable as representing the assets of the plaintiff; and thirdly, knowledge on the part of the defendant that the assets he received are traceable to a breach of fiduciary duty."

In the present case the first two requirements were satisfied in relation to the defendant's receipt of the US$16.679m paid to him pursuant to the divestiture agreement. But the satisfaction of the third requirement, knowledge on the part of the defendant that the sum received by him was traceable to a breach or breaches of fiduciary duty by Mr Naqvi, Mr Hafeez and Mr Kazmi, is problematical. 11–030

So far as the law is concerned, the comprehensive arguments of Mr Sheldon and Mr Moss have demonstrated that there are two questions which, though closely related, are distinct: first, what, in this context, is meant by knowledge; second, is it necessary for the recipient to act dishonestly? Because the answer to it is the simpler, the convenient course is to deal with the second of those questions first. 11–031

## Knowing Receipt—Dishonesty

As appears from the penultimate sentence of his judgment, Carnwath J. proceeded on an assumption that dishonesty in one form or another was the essential foundation of the claimants' case, whether in knowing assistance or knowing receipt. That was no doubt caused by the acceptance before him (though not at any higher level) by Mr Sheldon, recorded at p.677f, that the thrust of the recent authorities at first instance was that the recipient's state of knowledge must fall into one of the first three categories listed by Peter Gibson J. in *Baden, Delvaux v Société Générale pour Favoriser le Développement du Commerce et de l'Industrie en France SA*,[53] on which basis, said Mr Justice Carnwath, it was doubtful whether the test differed materially in practice from that for knowing assistance. However, the assumption on which the judge proceeded, derived as I believe from an omission to distinguish between the questions of knowledge and dishonesty, was incorrect in law. While a knowing recipient will often be found to have acted dishonestly, it has never been a prerequisite of the liability that he should. 11–032

An authoritative decision on this question, the complexity of whose subject transactions has sometimes caused it to be overlooked in this particular context, is *Belmont Finance Corporation v Williams Furniture Ltd (No.2)*,[54] where the plaintiff ("Belmont") was the wholly-owned subsidiary of the second defendant ("City"), which in turn was the wholly-owned subsidiary of the first defendant ("Williams"). The chairman of all three companies and the sole effective force in the management of their affairs was Mr John James. Reduced to its essentials, what had happened there was that the shareholders of a fourth company ("Maximum") had agreed to sell its shares to Belmont for £500,000 and to buy the share capital of Belmont from City for £489,000, a transaction which, as carried out, constituted a contravention of section 54 of the Companies Act 1948 (prohibition of provision of financial assistance by a company for the purchase of its own shares) and was thus a misapplication of Belmont's funds. 11–033

Belmont having subsequently become insolvent, its receiver obtained an independent valuation of the shares in Maximum as at the date of the transaction which suggested that, instead of being worth £500,000, they were only worth some £60,000. The receiver brought an action in Belmont's name principally against Williams, City and the shareholders of Maximum, claiming that they were liable to Belmont, first, for damages for conspiracy and, secondly, as constructive trustees on the grounds of both knowing assistance and knowing receipt. At the trial, Foster J. found that Mr James genuinely believed that to buy the capital of Maximum for £500,000 was a good commercial proposition for Belmont. He held that there had been no contravention of section 54 and dismissed the action. 11–034

On Belmont's successful appeal to this court Buckley L.J. is recorded[55] as having pointed out that 11–035

---

52 [1994] 2 All E.R. 685 at 700.

53 [1993] 1 W.L.R. 509 at 575–576.

54 [1980] 1 All E.R. 393.

55 At 403.

Mr James had genuinely believed that the transaction was a good commercial proposition for Belmont without having any good grounds for that belief. He continued:

> "After careful consideration I do not feel that we should be justified in disturbing the judge's finding that Mr James genuinely believed that the agreement was a good commercial proposition for Belmont. It was a belief which, on his view of the commercial aspects of the case, Mr James could have sincerely held."

**11-036** Having observed that Mr James, as a director of both Williams and City knew perfectly well what the objects of the transaction were, that other officers of City had the same knowledge and that their knowledge must be "imputed" to the respective companies,[56] and having referred[57] to the judgment of Lord Selborne L.C. in *Barnes v Addy*,[58] Buckley L.J. dealt with the claim in constructive trust:[59]

> "In the present case, the payment of the £500,000 by Belmont to [the shareholders of Maximum], being an unlawful contravention of section 54, was a misapplication of Belmont's money and was in breach of the duties of the directors of Belmont. £489,000 of the £500,000 so misapplied found their way into the hands of City with City's knowledge of the whole circumstances of the transaction. It must follow, in my opinion, that City is accountable to Belmont as a constructive trustee of the £489,000 under the first of Lord Selborne L.C.'s two heads. There remains the question whether City is chargeable as a constructive trustee under Lord Selborne's second head on the ground that Belmont's directors were guilty of dishonesty in buying the shares of Maximum and that City with knowledge of the facts assisted them in that dishonest design. As I understand Lord Selborne L.C.'s second head, a stranger to a trust notwithstanding that he may not have received any of the trust fund which has been misapplied will be treated as accountable as a constructive trustee if he has knowingly participated in a dishonest design on the part of the trustee to misapply the fund; he must himself have been in some way a party to the dishonesty of the trustees. It follows from what I have already held that the directors of Belmont were guilty of misfeasance but not that they acted dishonestly."

**11-037** Goff L.J. also held that City was liable in knowing receipt.[60] Waller L.J. did not add anything of his own on the question of constructive trust. Accordingly, though the claim in knowing assistance failed because the directors of Belmont did not act dishonestly, the claim in knowing receipt succeeded. I will return to that decision when dealing with the question of knowledge.

**11-038** *Belmont Finance Corporation v Williams Furniture Ltd (No.2)* is clear authority for the proposition that dishonesty is not a necessary ingredient of liability in knowing receipt. There have been other, more recent, judicial pronouncements to the same effect. Thus in *Polly Peck International Plc v Nadir (No.2)*,[61] Scott L.J. said that liability in a knowing receipt case did not require that the misapplication of the trust funds should be fraudulent. While in theory it is possible for a misapplication not to be fraudulent and the recipient to be dishonest, in practice such a combination must be rare. Similarly, in *Agip (Africa) Ltd v Jackson*,[62] Millett J. said that in knowing receipt it was immaterial whether the breach of trust was fraudulent or not. The point was made most clearly by Vinelott J. in *Eagle Trust Plc v SBC Securities Ltd*:[63]

> "What the decision in *Belmont (No. 2)* shows is that in a 'knowing receipt' case it is only necessary to show that the defendant knew that the moneys paid to him were trust moneys and of circumstances which made the payment a misapplication of them. Unlike a 'knowing assistance' case it is not necessary, and never has been necessary, to show that the defendant was in any sense a participator in a fraud."

---

56 At 404.
57 At 405.
58 (1874) L.R. 9 Ch. App. 244 at 251.
59 At 405.
60 At 410–412.
61 [1992] 4 All E.R. 769 at 777.
62 [1990] Ch. 265 at 292.
63 [1993] 1 W.L.R. 484 at 497.

**Knowing Receipt—The Authorities on Knowledge**

With the proliferation in the last 20 years or so of cases in which the misapplied assets of companies have come into the hands of third parties, there has been a sustained judicial and extra-judicial debate as to the knowledge on the part of the recipient which is required in order to found liability in knowing receipt. Expressed in its simplest terms, the question is whether the recipient must have actual knowledge (or the equivalent) that the assets received are traceable to a breach of trust or whether constructive knowledge is enough. The instinctive approach of most equity judges, especially in this court, has been to assume that constructive knowledge is enough. But there is now a series of decisions of eminent first instance judges who, after considering the question in greater depth, have come to the contrary conclusion, at all events when commercial transactions are in point. In the Commonwealth, on the other hand, the preponderance of authority has been in favour of the view that constructive knowledge is enough. **11-039**

In *Karak Rubber Co Ltd v Burden*,[64] Brightman J. referred to a person: **11-040**

> "who is a constructive trustee because (though not nominated as a trustee) he has received trust property with actual or constructive notice that it is trust property transferred in breach of trust . . .".

In *Belmont (No.2)*,[65] Buckley L.J. referred to the principle, established by the decision of this court in *Re Lands Allotment Co*,[66] that the directors of a company are treated as if they were actual trustees of the assets of the company which are in their hands or under their control. He continued: **11-041**

> "So, if the directors of a company in breach of their fiduciary duties misapply the funds of their company so that they come into the hands of some stranger to the trust who receives them with knowledge (actual or constructive) of the breach, he cannot conscientiously retain those funds against the company unless he has some better equity. He becomes a constructive trustee for the company of the misapplied funds."

Goff L.J. said that what Belmont had to show, among other things, was that City received all or part of the £500,000 "knowing or in circumstances in which it ought to know, that it was a breach of trust".[67] He answered that question, saying:[68] **11-042**

> "In my judgment the answer to that question must plainly be Yes for they are fixed with all the knowledge that Mr James had. Now, he had actual knowledge of all the facts which made the agreement illegal and his belief that the agreement was a good commercial proposition for Belmont can be no more a defence to City's liability as constructive trustees than in conspiracy. Apart from this, clearly, in my judgment, Mr James knew or ought to have known all the facts that I have rehearsed, showing that there was in any event a misfeasance apart from illegality."

Similarly, in *Rolled Steel Products (Holdings) Ltd v British Steel Corporation*,[69] Browne-Wilkinson L.J. said: **11-043**

> "A third party who has notice—actual or constructive—that a transaction, although intra vires the company, was entered into in excess or abuse of the powers of the company cannot enforce such transaction against the company and will be accountable as constructive trustee for any money or property of the company received by [him]."

In *Agip (Africa) Ltd v Jackson*,[70] Millett J., in reference to a person who receives for his own benefit trust property transferred to him in breach of trust, said: **11-044**

> "He is liable as a constructive trustee if he received it with notice, actual or constructive, that it was trust property and that the transfer to him was a breach of trust. . .".

---

64 [1972] 1 W.L.R. 602 at 632.
65 At 405.
66 [1894] 1 Ch. 616.
67 At 410.
68 At 412.
69 [1986] Ch. 246 at 306.
70 At 291.

11–045 In *Houghton v Fayers*,[71] I myself said that it was enough for the claimant company to establish that the second defendant "knew or ought to have known that the money had been paid to him in breach of [the first defendant's] fiduciary duty to [the claimant]".

11–046 Collectively, those observations might be thought to provide strong support for the view that constructive knowledge is enough. But it must at once be said that in each of the three cases in this court (including, despite some apparent uncertainty in the judgment of Goff L.J.,[72] *Belmont (No.2)*) actual knowledge was found and, further, that the decisions in *Karak* and *Agip* were based on knowing assistance, not knowing receipt. Thus in none of the five cases was it necessary for the question to be examined in any depth and there appears to be no case in which such an examination has been conducted in this court. The groundwork has been done in other cases at first instance. I will refer to those of them in which the question has been considered in depth.

11–047 The seminal judgment, characteristically penetrative in its treatment of authority and, in the best sense, argumentative, is that of Megarry V.C. in *Re Montagu's Settlement Trusts*.[73] It was he who first plumbed the distinction between notice and knowledge. It was he who, building on a passage in the judgment of this court in *Re Diplock*,[74] first emphasised the fundamental difference between the questions which arise in respect of the doctrine of purchaser without notice on the one hand and the doctrine of constructive trusts on the other. Reading from his earlier judgment in the same case, he said:[75]

> "The former is concerned with the question whether a person takes property subject to or free from some equity. The latter is concerned with whether or not a person is to have imposed upon him the personal burdens and obligations of trusteeship. I do not see why one of the touchstones for determining the burdens on property should be the same as that for deciding whether to impose a personal obligation on a [person]. The cold calculus of constructive and imputed notice does not seem to me to be an appropriate instrument for deciding whether a [person's] conscience is sufficiently affected for it to be right to bind him by the obligations of a constructive trustee."

11–048 He added that there is more to being made a trustee than merely taking property subject to an equity.

11–049 The practical importance of that distinction had been explained by the Vice-Chancellor in his earlier judgment. The question in that case was whether the widow and executrix of the will of the 10th Duke of Manchester was liable to account to the 11th Duke in respect of certain settled chattels or the proceeds of sale thereof. Having found that the 10th Duke had had no knowledge that the chattels received by him were still subject to any trust and that he believed that they had been lawfully and properly released to him by the trustees, Megarry V.C. continued[76]:

> "If liability as a constructive trustee depended on his knowledge, then he was not liable as a constructive trustee, and his estate is not liable for any chattels that have been disposed of, as distinct from any traceable proceeds of them. Even if he was not a constructive trustee and was a mere volunteer, his estate is liable to yield up any chattels that remain, or the traceable proceeds of any that have gone. . . . But unless he was a constructive trustee, there appears to be no liability if the chattels have gone and there are no traceable proceeds."

11–050 Megarry V.C. summarised his conclusions in eight subparagraphs.[77] I read the first three:

> "(1) The equitable doctrine of tracing and the imposition of a constructive trust by reason of the knowing receipt of trust property are governed by different rules and must be kept distinct. Tracing is primarily a means of determining the rights of property, whereas the imposition of a constructive trust creates personal obligations that go beyond mere property rights. (2) In considering whether a constructive trust has arisen in a case of the knowing receipt of trust property, the basic question is whether the conscience of the recipient is sufficiently affected to justify the imposition of such a trust. (3) Whether a constructive trust arises in such a case primarily depends on the knowledge of the

71 [2000] 1 B.C.L.C. 511 at 516.
72 At 412.
73 [1987] Ch. 264.
74 [1948] Ch. 465 at 478–479.
75 At 278.
76 At 272.
77 At 285.

recipient, and not on notice to him; and for clarity it is desirable to use the word 'knowledge' and avoid the word 'notice' in such cases."

The effect of the Vice-Chancellor's decision, broadly stated, was that, in order to establish liability in knowing receipt, the recipient must have actual knowledge (or the equivalent) that the assets received are traceable to a breach of trust and that constructive knowledge is not enough. 11–051

In *Eagle Trust Plc v SBC Securities Ltd*,[78] Vinelott J. did not think it would be right to found a decision that the statement of claim in that case disclosed no cause of action solely on the authority of *Re Montagu's Settlement Trusts*. However, on the ground that he (unlike Megarry V.C.) was dealing with a commercial transaction, he arrived at the same conclusion and held that in such a transaction constructive knowledge is not enough. He cited[79] a well known passage in the judgment of Lindley L.J. in *Manchester Trust v Furness*,[80] the latter part of which reads thus: 11–052

"In dealing with estates in land title is everything, and it can be leisurely investigated; in commercial transactions possession is everything, and there is no time to investigate title; and if we were to extend the doctrine of constructive notice to commercial transactions we should be doing infinite mischief and paralyzing the trade of the country."

The decision of Vinelott J. was followed by Knox J. in *Cowan de Groot Properties Ltd v Eagle Trust Plc*[81] (another case of a commercial transaction) and the decisions of both of them by Arden J. at the trial of the action in *Eagle Trust Plc v SBC Securities Ltd*.[82] 11–053

We were also referred to three decisions in New Zealand and one in Canada. In each of *Westpac Banking Corp v Savin*,[83] *Equiticorp Industries Group Ltd v Hawkins*,[84] and *Lankshear v ANZ Banking Group (New Zealand) Ltd*,[85] the preferred view was that constructive knowledge was enough, although in the last-named case the point went by concession. All of them were cases of commercial transactions. In *Westpac Banking Corp v Savin*, a decision of the Court of Appeal, Richardson J., having expressed a provisional preference for the view that constructive knowledge was enough, said:[86] 11–054

"Clearly Courts would not readily import a duty to enquire in the case of commercial transactions where they must be conscious of the seriously inhibiting effects of a wide application of the doctrine. Nevertheless there must be cases where there is no justification on the known facts for allowing a commercial man who has received funds paid to him in breach of trust to plead the shelter of the exigencies of commercial life."

In *Citadel General Assurance Co.v Lloyds Bank Canada*,[87] another case of a commercial transaction, the Supreme Court of Canada held, as a matter of decision, that constructive knowledge was enough. 11–055

**The *Baden* Case**

It will have been observed that up to this stage I have made no more than a passing reference to the five-fold categorisation of knowledge accepted by Peter Gibson J. in the *Baden* case:[88] (i) actual knowledge; (ii) wilfully shutting one's eyes to the obvious; (iii) wilfully and recklessly failing to make such enquiries as an honest and reasonable man would make; (iv) knowledge of circumstances which would indicate the facts to an honest and reasonable man; (v) knowledge of circumstances which will put an honest and reasonable man on inquiry. Reference to the categorisation has been made in most of the knowing receipt cases to which I have referred from *Re Montagu's Settlement Trusts* onwards. In many of them it has been influential 11–056

78 At 503.
79 At 504.
80 [1895] 2 Q.B. 539 at 545.
81 [1992] 4 All E.R. 700.
82 See [1996] 1 B.C.L.C. 121.
83 [1985] 2 N.Z.L.R. 41.
84 [1991] 3 N.Z.L.R. 700.
85 [1993] 1 N.Z.L.R. 481.
86 At 53.
87 (1997) 152 D.L.R. (4th) 411.
88 [1993] 1 W.L.R. 509, 575–576.

in the decision. In general, the first three categories have been taken to constitute actual knowledge (or its equivalent) and the last two constructive knowledge.

11-057 Two important points must be made about the *Baden* categorisation. First, it appears to have been propounded by counsel for the plaintiffs, accepted by counsel for the defendant and then put to the judge on an agreed basis. Secondly, though both counsel accepted that all five categories of knowledge were relevant and neither sought to submit that there was any distinction for that purpose between knowing receipt and knowing assistance (a view with which the judge expressed his agreement[89]), the claim in constructive trust was based squarely on knowing assistance and not on knowing receipt.[90] In the circumstances, whatever may have been agreed between counsel, it is natural to assume that the categorisation was not formulated with knowing receipt primarily in mind. This, I think, may be confirmed by the references to "an honest and reasonable man" in categories (iv) and (v). Moreover, in *Agip* Millett J. warned against over refinement or a too ready assumption that categories (iv) and (v) are necessarily cases of constructive knowledge only.[91]

**Knowing Receipt—The Recipient's State of Knowledge**

11-058 In *Royal Brunei Airlines Sdn Bhd v Tan*,[92] which is now the leading authority on knowing assistance, Lord Nicholls of Birkenhead, in delivering the judgment of the Privy Council, said that "knowingly" was better avoided as a defining ingredient of the liability, and that in that context the *Baden* categorisation was best forgotten.[93] Although my own view is that the categorisation is often helpful in identifying different states of knowledge which may or may not result in a finding of dishonesty for the purposes of knowing assistance, I have grave doubts about its utility in cases of knowing receipt. Quite apart from its origins in a context of knowing assistance and the reservations of Millett and Knox JJ., any categorisation is of little value unless the purpose it is to serve is adequately defined, whether it be fivefold, as in *Baden*, or twofold, as in the classical division between actual and constructive knowledge, a division which has itself become blurred in recent authorities.

11-059 What then, in the context of knowing receipt, is the purpose to be served by a categorisation of knowledge? It can only be to enable the court to determine whether, in the words of Buckley L.J. in *Belmont (No.2)*, the recipient can "conscientiously retain [the] funds against the company" or, in the words of Megarry V.C. in *Re Montagu's Settlement Trusts*, "[the recipient's] conscience is sufficiently affected for it to be right to bind him by the obligations of a constructive trustee". But if that is the purpose, there is no need for categorisation. All that is necessary is that the recipient's state of knowledge should be such as to make it unconscionable for him to retain the benefit of the receipt.

11-060 For these reasons I have come to the view that, just as there is now a single test of dishonesty for knowing assistance, so ought there to be a single test of knowledge for knowing receipt. The recipient's state of knowledge must be such as to make it unconscionable for him to retain the benefit of the receipt. A test in that form, though it cannot, any more than any other, avoid difficulties of application, ought to avoid those of definition and allocation to which the previous categorisations have led. Moreover, it should better enable the courts to give common-sense decisions in the commercial context in which claims in knowing receipt are now frequently made, paying equal regard to the wisdom of Lindley L.J. on the one hand and of Richardson J. on the other.

**Knowing Receipt—A Footnote**

11-061 We were referred in argument to "Knowing Receipt: The Need for a New Landmark", an essay by Lord Nicholls;[94] a work of insight and scholarship taking forward the writings of academic authors, in particular those of Professors Birks, Burrows and Gareth Jones. It is impossible to do justice to such a work within the compass of a judgment such as this. Most pertinent for present purposes is the suggestion made by Lord Nicholls,[95] in reference to the decision of the House of Lords in *Lipkin Gorman v Karpnale Ltd*:[96]

---

89 At 582.
90 See 572.
91 [1990] Ch. 265 at 293, reservations which were shared by Knox J. in *Cowan de Groot* [1992] 4 All E.R. 700 at 761.
92 [1995] 2 A.C. 378.
93 At 392.
94 In Cornish, Nolan, O'Sullivan and Virgo (eds) *Restitution Past, Present and Future* (1998).
95 At p.238.
96 [1991] 2 A.C. 548.

"In this respect equity should now follow the law. Restitutionary liability, applicable regardless of fault but subject to a defence of change of position, would be a better-tailored response to the underlying mischief of misapplied property than personal liability which is exclusively fault-based. Personal liability would flow from having received the property of another, from having been unjustly enriched at the expense of another. It would be triggered by the mere fact of receipt, thus recognising the endurance of property rights. But fairness would be ensured by the need to identify a gain, and by making change of position available as a default in suitable cases when, for instance, the recipient had changed his position in reliance on the receipt."

Lord Nicholls goes on to examine the *Re Diplock*[97] principle, suggesting that it could be reshaped by being extended to all trusts but in a form modified to take proper account of the decision in *Lipkin Gorman v Karpnale Ltd*.[98] 11–062

No argument before us was based on the suggestions made in Lord Nicholls' essay. Indeed, at this level of decision, it would have been a fruitless exercise. We must continue to do our best with the accepted formulation of the liability in knowing receipt, seeking to simplify and improve it where we may. While in general it may be possible to sympathise with a tendency to subsume a further part of our law of restitution under the principles of unjust enrichment, I beg leave to doubt whether strict liability coupled with a change of position defence would be preferable to fault-based liability in many commercial transactions, for example where, as here, the receipt is of a company's funds which have been misapplied by its directors. Without having heard argument it is unwise to be dogmatic, but in such a case it would appear to be commercially unworkable and contrary to the spirit of the rule in *Royal British Bank v Turquand*[99] that, simply on proof of an internal misapplication of the company's funds, the burden should shift to the recipient to defend the receipt either by a change of position or perhaps in some other way. Moreover, if the circumstances of the receipt are such as to make it unconscionable for the recipient to retain the benefit of it, there is an obvious difficulty in saying that it is equitable for a change of position to afford him a defence. 11–063

**Knowing Receipt—The Facts of the Present Case**

I return to the facts of the present case, in order to determine whether the defendant is liable in knowing receipt to repay (together with interest) US$6.679m of the sum received by him pursuant to the divestiture agreement, being the excess over the US$10m he paid to ICIC Overseas pursuant to the 1985 agreement. (By a decision whose forensic good sense dispensed with an analysis of its juristic foundation the claimants abandoned a claim for the full US$16.679m.) The answer to that question depends on whether the judge's findings, though made in the course of an inquiry as to the defendant's honesty, are equally supportive of a conclusion that his state of knowledge was not such as to make it unconscionable for him to retain the benefit of the receipt. 11–064

I start with the defendant's state of knowledge at the date of the 1985 agreement. As to that, the judge found that there was no evidence that anyone outside BCCI had reason to doubt the integrity of its management at that time. More specifically, it is clear that the judge was of the view that the defendant had no knowledge of the underlying frauds within the BCCI group either in general or in relation to the 1985 agreement. He found that the defendant saw it simply as an arm's-length business transaction. Moreover, he was not prepared to draw the conclusion that the high rate of interest and the artificial nature of the agreement were sufficient to put an honest person in the defendant's position on notice that some fraud or breach of trust was being perpetrated. He said that the defendant would have had no reason to question the form of the transaction. 11–065

Those findings, expressed in language equally appropriate to an inquiry as to constructive notice, appear to me to be consistent only with the view that the defendant's state of knowledge at the date of the 1985 agreement was not such as to make it unconscionable for him to enter into it. However, that point, though of great importance, is not in itself decisive. We have also to consider the defendant's state of knowledge at the date of the divestiture agreement, by which time, as the judge said, he did have suspicions as to the conduct of BCCI's affairs. 11–066

In order to understand the judge's reference, it is necessary to go back to what he said[100]: 11–067

[97] [1948] Ch. 465.
[98] At p.241.
[99] (1856) 6 E. & B. 327.
[100] At p.675.

"Towards the end of 1988 the defendant decided to end his relationship with BCCI, and in particular to terminate the share agreement. A number of factors led to this decision. In late 1987 there had been rumours in the Nigerian press of irregularities involving BCCI. He had received warnings from senior business figures in Nigeria. One was Dr Onaolapo Soleye, a former Nigerian Minister of Finance, who has provided a witness statement. He says that he informed the defendant of 'unorthodox and irregular banking practices around the world', and warned him of the effect a scandal relating to BCCI could have on his business image and that of BCCI Nigeria. The defendant also became aware later in 1988 that various BCCI officials had been arrested by US Customs in Tampa in connection with money laundering offences. He considered selling his shares in BCCI Nigeria, but was dissuaded from doing so by Dr Soleye and others, because of the tribal imbalance it would create within the bank. At this time the defendant was seeking to realise £20m of his own money, and to raise a further £40m, to finance a property investment venture in the UK. The major banks involved including NM Rothschild in London and BNP, objected to him raising part of the finance from BCCI."

**11–068** So in late 1987, more than two years after the 1985 agreement was entered into, there were press rumours of irregularities involving BCCI and warnings to the defendant from senior business figures in Nigeria of unorthodox and irregular banking practices around the world. Later in 1988 the defendant became aware that various BCCI officials had been arrested in connection with money laundering offences. He also knew that the major banks involved in financing his property investment venture in the United Kingdom objected to his raising part of the finance from BCCI.

**11–069** There having been no evidence that the defendant was aware of the internal arrangements within BCCI which led to the payment to him of the US$16.679m pursuant to the divestiture agreement, did the additional knowledge which he acquired between July 1985 and December 1988 make it unconscionable for him to retain the benefit of the receipt? In my judgment it did not. The additional knowledge went to the general reputation of the BCCI group from late 1987 onwards. It was not a sufficient reason for questioning the propriety of a particular transaction entered into more than two years earlier, at a time when no one outside BCCI had reason to doubt the integrity of its management and in a form which the defendant had no reason to question. The judge said that the defendant was entitled to take steps to protect his own interest, and that there was nothing dishonest in his seeking to enforce the 1985 agreement. Nor was there anything unconscionable in his seeking to do so. Equally, had I thought that that was still the appropriate test, I would have held that the defendant did not have actual or constructive knowledge that his receipt of the US$6.79m was traceable to a breach or breaches of fiduciary duty by Messrs Naqvi, Hafeez and Kazmi.

**Conclusion**

**11–070** For these reasons, though by a different route in relation to knowing receipt, I have come to the conclusion that Mr Justice Carnwath's decision to dismiss the action was correct. I would affirm it and dismiss the claimants' appeal.

**11–071** Three points should be made here about *Akindele*. First, it may be doubted whether unconscionability is a sufficiently certain concept to bring clarity and predictability to the law in this area.[101] Indeed, it was rejected by Lord Nicholls in *Royal Brunei* as the test for assistance liability for precisely this reason.[102] Nevertheless, there is much to be said for abandoning the over-subtle distinctions of *Baden, Delvaux*,[103] and in practice the courts do not seem to have much trouble with applying Nourse LJ's test. A sceptic might say that this is unsurprising since it makes liability turn on the exercise of a judicial discretion. Be that as it may, *Akindele* has been reaffirmed by the Court of Appeal on several occasions,[104] although

[101] Consider the different readings of *Akindele* in *Papamichael v National Westminster Bank Plc* [2003] 1 Lloyd's Rep. 341 at [246]–[247] and *Criterion Properties Plc v Stratford UK Properties LLC* [2003] 1 W.L.R. 2108 at [20]–[39], not reviewed on appeal [2004] 1 W.L.R. 1846.

[102] [1995] 2 A.C. 378 at 392.

[103] But cf. *Armstrong DLW GmbH v Winnington Networks Ltd* [2013] Ch. 156 at [132] where the judge took the retrograde step of defining unconscionability in terms of the *Baden, Delvaux* degrees of knowledge; this was directly contrary to the terms and spirit of Nourse LJ's judgment in *Akindele*.

[104] *Criterion Properties Plc v Stratford UK Properties LLC* [2003] 1 W.L.R. 2108 at [20]–[39], not reviewed on appeal [2004] 1

there has been no move to relabel this head of liability "unconscionable receipt", as might have been anticipated given the rebranding of "knowing assistance" as "dishonest assistance" which followed the *Royal Brunei* case.[105]

Secondly, in *Credit Agricole Corporation and Investment Bank v Papadimitriou*,[106] Lord Sumption expressed the unorthodox view that: **11–072**

> Whether a person claims to be a bona fide purchaser of assets without notice of a prior interest in them, or disputes a claim to make him accountable as a constructive trustee on the footing of knowing receipt, the question what constitutes notice or knowledge is the same.

This was inconsistent with the passage of Megarry VC's judgment in *Re Montagu's Settlement Trusts*,[107] approved in *Akindele*,[108] where he emphasised the difference between personal liability for knowing receipt and proprietary liability. Defendants who receive legal title to misapplied trust property without notice of the beneficiaries' subsisting equitable interest and in exchange for valuable consideration need not do what every other recipient of misdirected trust property must do, namely reconvey the legal title to the trustees. In these circumstances alone, the defendants' interest in the property takes priority over the beneficiaries' interest. The point of the bona fide purchase defence is thus to resolve a priority dispute between two parties with claims against the same property.[109] Liability for knowing receipt concerns a different question, namely when it is appropriate to make the defendant personally liable to account for the trust assets to the beneficiaries because she has received them knowing that she has no right to do so. Since these are different questions it should not surprise us that the law uses different tests to answer them, and treating them as though they were the same question is to misunderstand them.

Thirdly, the court in *Akindele* seems to have thought that it could not recognise a strict liability claim in unjust enrichment against recipients of misdirected trust funds without departing from the many cases requiring proof of fault for liability in knowing receipt. However no such departure from previous authority would be needed if a court were to recognise that a claim in unjust enrichment against a recipient of misdirected trust funds can lie concurrently with a compensatory claim for knowing receipt. This is discussed further below,[110] after we have examined the nature of the compensatory remedies that are available in actions for knowing receipt. **11–073**

## *D. Remedies*

In the following excerpt, Charles Mitchell and Stephen Watterson argue that a knowing recipient's core duty as constructive trustee of the property she receives is to restore the property immediately. If she breaches this duty by dealing with the property for herself, or by applying it in any other way that is inconsistent with the beneficiaries' rights, then the mechanisms by which they can hold her liable to account are essentially the same as those by which they can hold an express trustee liable to account for unauthorised expenditure.[111] By analogy with the express trustee cases, the knowing recipient can **11–074**

W.L.R. 1846; *Charter Plc v City Index Ltd* [2008] Ch. 313; *Uzinterimpex JSC v Standard Bank Plc* [2008] Bus. L.R. 1762. See too *Arthur v Attorney General of the Turks and Caicos Islands* [2012] UKPC 30 at [33].

105 Cf. S.B. Thomas "Goodbye Knowing Receipt. Hello Unconscientious Receipt" (2001) 21 O.J.L.S. 239.

106 [2015] UKPC 13 at [33].

107 [1987] Ch. 264 at 272–273.

108 See para.11–047. See also *Sinclair Investments (UK) Ltd v Versailles Trade Finance Ltd (In Administrative Receivership)* [2012] Ch. 453 at [106] per Lord Neuberger MR.

109 The defence of bona fide purchase to an equitable proprietary claim is discussed further at paras 12–117ff.

110 See paras 11–087ff.

111 Discussed in Ch.10.

be ordered to restore the property *in specie* if it is still in her hands. By the same analogy, if she has disposed of the property then she must show that this disposal was authorised, or else the account will be falsified, and an order for substitutive performance made, requiring her to pay the current monetary value of the property, or where the property was money, the capital sum plus interest.

**11-075** This analysis of the law was approved by the Privy Council in *Arthur v Attorney General of the Turks and Caicos Islands*[112] and by the Federal Court of Australia in *Grimaldi v Chameleon Mining NL (No.2)*.[113] It is also consistent with Lloyd LJ's statement in *Independent Trustee Services Ltd v GP Noble Trustees Ltd* that once a recipient of misdirected trust funds becomes aware of their improper provenance she comes "under a duty not to part with the remaining funds (and the traceable proceeds in her hands of any which had already gone) otherwise than by restoring them to or for the benefit of the beneficiaries."[114]

## C. Mitchell and S. Watterson, "Remedies for Knowing Receipt"

in C. Mitchell (ed.), *Constructive and Resulting Trusts* (Hart Publishing, 2010), pp.131–138

**11-076** . . . The duties of a knowing recipient are rarely stated, but one cannot fully understand the nature of his liability to account as a constructive trustee without identifying these duties and the mechanisms by which they are enforced.

### 1. The Core Restorative Duty

*(a) The nature of the duty*

**11-077** A knowing recipient's core duty, and generally his only duty of practical significance, is to restore the misapplied trust property.[115] His duty is to restore the property immediately, rather than to restore it on demand.[116] In this respect his position can be contrasted with that of an express bare trustee, who holds the trust property to the order of the beneficiary while the trust subsists, and whose continuing retention of this property is authorised, and therefore legitimate, until the beneficiary gives contrary instructions. In contrast, a knowing recipient's continuing retention of misapplied trust property is unauthorised and illegitimate, and so he owes an immediate restorative duty which does not depend on any demand for restoration having been made.

**11-078** Although an action to enforce the knowing recipient's restorative duty can be brought by the beneficiaries,[117] it does not follow that performance of the duty necessarily entails transfer or payment to them. On the contrary, the duty is essentially to restore the misapplied property to the trustees, so that that the trust can be reconstituted and duly administered. However, much depends on the basis on which the property was held. If it was held on a bare trust, then, whilst the knowing recipient's duty is essentially a duty to restore the property to the trustees (assuming that the trust is still on foot), he could discharge his duty by restoring it directly to the absolutely entitled beneficiary instead.[118] But if the trust is a more elaborate continuing trust, where there is no single absolutely entitled beneficiary, then he cannot

---

112 [2012] UKPC 30 at [37].

113 (2012) 200 F.C.R. 296 at [559].

114 [2013] Ch. 91 at [81].

115 Cf *Re Holmes* [2005] 1 W.L.R. 857 at [22]; *Darkingjung Pty Ltd v Darkingjung Local Aboriginal Land Council* [2006] NSWSC 1217 at [47].

116 Notwithstanding Colman J.'s dictum to the contrary in *Allied Carpets Group plc v Nethercott* [2001] B.C.C. 81 at 89–90.

117 The trustees can also bring an action for knowing receipt in a representative capacity, as discussed in *Morlea Professional Services Pty Ltd v Richard Walter Pty Ltd* (1999) 34 A.C.S.R. 371. In rare cases, a knowing recipient may also bring an action in knowing receipt against a knowing recipient from her, pursuant to her duty to get in the property so that the trust fund can be reconstituted: *Bracken Partners Ltd v Gutteridge* [2004] 1 B.C.L.C. 373 (CA); *Evans v European Bank Ltd* (2004) 7 I.T.E.L.R. 19.

118 Cf *Soar v Ashwell* [1893] 2 Q.B. 390 at 395, where Kay L.J. refers to a defendant who has "concurred with the trustee in committing a breach of trust, and has taken possession of the trust property, knowing that it was trust property, and has not duly discharged himself of it by handing it over to the proper trustees or to the persons absolutely entitled to it". And cf *Target Holdings Ltd v Redferns* [1996] A.C. 421 at 435 (express trustees).

perform his duty in this way, and must instead restore the property to the trustees so that the trust can be reconstituted, and the trust fund administered for all of the beneficiaries.

When can a knowing recipient claim to have performed his duty to restore the trust property? Obviously, if he hands over the property *in specie* then he will have done what he was meant to do . . . By analogy with the express trustee cases, he may also perform his duty by paying a money substitute for the property . . . But what if he hands over different property in lieu of the property which he received? This question arose in *Morlea Professional Services Pty Ltd v Richard Walter Pty Ltd*,[119] where a corporate trustee, which had misapplied trust money by making sham loans to another company, accepted from the other company the transfer of a debt equal in value to the sham loans, with 15% interest. According to the Full Court of the Federal Court of Australia, this 'did not effect actual (in the sense of precisely equivalent) restoration to the trusts'; rather its effect 'was to bring a new asset into the trusts by way of substitution for what was misappropriated', namely 'a debt equivalent in sum to the moneys misappropriated, [which] asset was treated by the trustees as being subject to the trusts and was dealt with accordingly'.[120] In the court's view, trustees who act in this way are bound by their actions vis-à-vis the knowing recipient, but the beneficiaries are not. They might disavow the trustees' actions and refuse to accept the new property as a substitute for the misapplied property. If they take this course then the knowing recipient will be unable to say that he has performed his duty, and will remain liable for the current market value of the property which he received.[121] **11–079**

Can the knowing recipient discharge his duty by returning the property to the wrongdoing trustee from whom he received it? In principle, the duty can generally be discharged in this way, consistently with the fact that, at least until he is replaced by another trustee, the wrongdoing trustee has a duty to recover the misapplied trust property . . . More difficult, though, are cases where the knowing recipient knows that the wrongdoing trustee will misapply the property again if it is returned to him, and will not use it to reconstitute the trust fund as he should. It may be that in this case, the knowing recipient's restorative duty would not be discharged if he retransferred the property to the trustee. This is suggested by *Blyth v Fladgate*,[122] where solicitors acting for a set of trustees were held not to have been discharged from their liability to account for trust property which they had paid over at the direction of the trustees for the purposes of an investment which they actually or constructively knew to be improper. Another way of approaching this question, however, might be to say that, whether or not the knowing recipient's restorative duty is discharged, he may in any event incur an independent liability for dishonestly assisting the wrongdoing trustee's further breach of trust. **11–080**

. . . [Might the court] ever excuse the knowing recipient from performance, or relieve him from liability for non-performance, in the same way that it sometimes relieves express trustees under the Trustee Act 1925 s 61? Consider a case where the property is lost or destroyed or stolen before the knowing recipient can return it. If the loss would not have occurred but for a delay by the knowing recipient in performing his duty of immediate restoration, then it can usually be said that he was at fault and should not be excused.[123] However this may not always be the case. Suppose, for example, that he cannot immediately restore the trust property, because he cannot identify or ascertain the whereabouts of the parties to whom restoration should be made – a rare situation, but one which arose in *Evans v European Bank Ltd*.[124] Or again, suppose that the parties to whom restoration should be made mistakenly deny that restoration is required and refuse to take the property back – another rare situation, but analogous to that which arose in *National* **11–081**

---

119 (1999) 34 A.C.S.R. 371. Cf *Lander v Weston* (1853) 3 Drew. 389 at 394 (Kindersley V-C): express trustees who wrongfully sell trust stock cannot obtain a discharge by replacing some other stock in the fund unless the beneficiaries adopt their transactions – 'they are not discharged by substituting something different'.

120 *Ibid* at [75].

121 *Ibid* at [76].

122 [1891] 1 Ch. 337. See too *Morgan v Stephens* (1861) 3 Giff. 226 at 236–237. Neither case concerned liability for knowing receipt, since the defendants did not initially receive the relevant property in breach of duty, but the result would have been the same if they had: *Bank of China v Kwong Wa Po* [2005] HKCFI 422 at [90], where a recipient of moneys stolen from the claimant bank by ex-employees was not discharged when it repaid the moneys, not to the claimant, but to one of these ex-employees and/or the company which was the vehicle for their frauds.

123 An express trustee would no doubt be in the same position, if it was the case that he had come under a duty immediately to transfer a particular asset to a beneficiary. Bailees of chattels are similarly placed once they have come under a duty to deliver the goods: they are then strictly liable for the goods' loss or destruction.

124 (2004) 7 I.T.E.L.R. 19.

*Bank of New Zealand v Waitaki International Processing (NI) Ltd.*[125] In either case, if the knowing recipient takes reasonable steps to preserve the property pending performance of his duty, and yet it is unexpectedly lost or destroyed in the interim, then it would seem unfair to force him to pay a money substitute in lieu of delivering the property once all the relevant facts are known.

*(b) Remedial implications*

11–082 What remedy do the beneficiaries have if a knowing recipient fails to perform his primary restorative duty? By analogy with the express trustee cases, he can clearly be ordered to restore the property *in specie* if it is still in his hands. By the same analogy, if he disposed of the property then he must show that this disposal was authorised, or else the account will be falsified, and an order for substitutive performance made, requiring him to pay the current monetary value of the property, or where the property is money, the capital sum plus interest . . . [The] beneficiaries would not have to allege a breach of duty against an express trustee before they could obtain an order of either kind, and for exactly the same reasons they do not have to allege a breach of duty against the knowing recipient either. In other words, once they have established that he knowingly received the trust property and was therefore placed under a primary restorative duty, the beneficiaries need not show that he breached this duty by failing to return the property, as they are entitled without more to an order for specific or substitutive performance of his primary duty.

11–083 Authority for this is *Green v Weatherill*,[126] where a daughter received money from her father, to be held on trust for him, and transferred part of the money to her sister, who knew that this transfer constituted a breach of trust. The sister was ordered to pay the relevant sum into court, although there was no allegation in the pleadings that she had committed any breach of her duty as a constructive trustee of the money. Maughan J. explained this as follows:[127]

> In the present action [the defendant] is sued as a constructive trustee of the sum so paid to her with full knowledge of the action and of the nature of the claim was being made as to the sum deposited by her sister with Martin's Bank. In my opinion those facts having been established; she must be taken to be a trustee. It is not alleged in the action that she has committed any breach of trust, and counsel for the plaintiff would be entitled on the pleadings as they stand to ask for an account of the sum received by her with notice of the plaintiff's claim. It is not disputed that the sum paid to the defendant . . . is the sum of 135l, and an account against her is therefore unnecessary. This, therefore, is a case where the Court has ascertained to its satisfaction that the sum of 135l is in the hands of the defendant . . . as a constructive trustee, and I can see no reason why the Court should not order payment by the said defendant of that amount into Court.

11–084 Because the main liability of a knowing recipient is to perform his primary duty of restoration in just the same way as an express trustee, it is a distinctive form of liability which cannot be collapsed into other forms of liability which arise in the law of wrongs or the law of unjust enrichment. Several points can be made in this connection. First, because the knowing recipient is liable to perform or render substitutive performance of his restorative duty, and this liability does not depend on an allegation of a breach of duty, it is easy to see why the knowing receipt cases look like plausible candidates for re-characterisation as claims in unjust enrichment. Claims of this sort also generate a 'restitutionary' liability which entails performance of a primary duty to pay the value of benefits received by the defendant, rather than performance of a secondary duty to pay money triggered by breach of a primary duty . . . However, a liability to make restitution of an unjust enrichment is a crucially different liability from a liability to effect restoration of misapplied trust property, and it is important that this distinction should not be obscured by the latent ambiguity in the term 'restitution'. . .

11–085 Secondly, the fact that the beneficiaries can get a remedy against the knowing recipient without asserting that he has breached his duty as constructive trustee has some implications for the defences that he can raise. If claims for knowing receipt were wrong-based, in the sense that they depended on the knowing recipient's breach of duty, then this might suggest that he was entitled to the defence of contributory negligence.[128] One response might be that contributory negligence is not available as a defence to

---

125 [1999] 2 N.Z.L.R. 211.

126 [1929] 2 Ch. 213.

127 Ibid. at 222–3.

128 P. Jaffey 'The Nature of Knowing Receipt' (2001) 15 Tru. L.I. 151, 157–8.

every wrong; that the courts have been prepared to deny the defence to particular types of wrongdoer on policy grounds; and that this defence may be unavailable against claims for breach of fiduciary duty, because admitting the defence might undermine the fiduciary's core duty of undivided loyalty.[129] However, this response assumes a particular answer to a different question, namely whether knowing recipients owe fiduciary duties. . . And there is a different and better reason why contributory negligence cannot be pleaded against claims for actual or substitutive performance of their restorative duty.[130] Because the beneficiaries need not allege a breach of this duty in order to obtain an order for performance, there is no room for argument that they have been a partial cause of their own loss, because it makes no difference whether they have been caused a loss, whether by the knowing recipient's fault or their own. Where the beneficiaries were aware of the transfer to the knowing recipient, however, the knowing recipient might instead be able to escape liability by arguing that the beneficiaries acquiesced in the trustee's breach of duty, with the result that no claim lies against him at all because the case is effectively one of authorised transfer.

Thirdly, the measure of a knowing recipient's liability may be very different from the measure of other liabilities which he might owe on a different footing. Suppose, for example, that a defendant receives and then disposes of property that subsequently increases in value. If he owed a liability in unjust enrichment, then assuming that a change of position defence were disallowed, the measure of his liability would most probably be the value of the property at the time of receipt, and would certainly be no more than the value of the property when he disposed of it . . . However, if he were chargeable with the property as a knowing recipient, then he would be liable as constructive trustee to pay its current monetary value. An example is an American case, *Re Rothko*,[131] where executors of the renowned painter, Mark Rothko, improperly transferred a large number of his paintings to third parties, who subsequently disposed of them. The value of Rothko's works then appreciated hugely, and in proceedings by the beneficiaries of his estate, the New York Court of Appeals held that the third parties were liable for the current market value of the paintings. 11–086

## *E. Liability in Unjust Enrichment for Misdirected Trust Funds?*

### i. Concurrent Claims in Knowing Receipt and Unjust Enrichment

Some legal scholars have argued that recipients of misdirected trust property should owe a strict liability in unjust enrichment for the value of the property received.[132] This argument has been accepted by eminent judges in extra-judicial writings,[133] but in *BCCI (Overseas) Ltd v Akindele*,[134] Nourse LJ considered that a decision of the House of Lords would be needed to recognise such a claim in English law. Presumably he thought that recognising a strict liability claim would be inconsistent with all the knowing receipt cases since *Barnes v Addy*,[135] which require proof of fault. However these cases only 11–087

---

129 See *Pilmer v Duke Group Ltd* (2001) 207 C.L.R. 165 at [86] and [171]-[172], quoting His Honour Justice W.M.C. Gummow 'Compensation for Breach of Fiduciary Duty' in T.G. Youdan (ed.) *Equity, Fiduciaries and Trusts* (Toronto, Carswell, 1989) 57, 86, and His Honour Justice K.R. Handley 'Reduction of Damages Awards' in P.D. Finn (ed.) *Essays on Damages* (Sydney, Lawbook Co, 1992) 113, 127.

130 This is not to rule out the possibility that a defence of contributory negligence might be raised against a knowing recipient where a reparation claim is made against him, for example where he has lost trust property through his negligence. Cf *Permanent Building Society (in liq) v Wheeler* (1994) 12 A.C.L.C. 674, where Ipp J. correctly noted the difference between a trustee's duty to account, and his duty of care, which can bring issues of causation and relative fault into play.

131 43 N.Y. 2d 305; 372 N.E. 2d 291 (1977).

132 e.g. P. Birks, "Receipt" in P. Birks and A. Pretto (eds) *Breach of Trust* (Hart Publishing, 2002), p.213; R. Chambers and J. Penner, "Ignorance" in S. Degeling and J. Edelman (eds), *Restitution in Commercial Law* (Law Book Co, 2008) (identifying "want of authority" rather than "ignorance" as the reason for restitution). Contra, L.D. Smith, "Unjust Enrichment, Property, and the Structure of Trusts" (2000) 116 L.Q.R. 412.

133 Lord Nicholls, "Knowing Receipt: The Need for a New Landmark", in W.R. Cornish et al. (eds) *Restitution: Past, Present and Future* (Hart Publishing, 1998); Lord Walker, "Dishonesty and Unconscionable Conduct in Commercial Life—Some Reflections on Accessory Liability and Knowing Receipt" (2005) 27 Sydney L.R. 187, 202; Lord Millett, "Proprietary Restitution" in S. Degeling and J. Edelman (eds) *Equity in Commercial Law* (Law Book Co, 2005), p.311.

134 [2001] Ch. 437 at 456.

135 (1874) L.R. 9 Ch. App. 244.

make fault a prerequisite for (compensatory) liability to account as a constructive trustee, and they say nothing about (restitutionary) liability in unjust enrichment to repay the value of the benefit received.

**11-088** Three strands of authority could be drawn upon by a claimant arguing for the introduction of a claim in unjust enrichment. First, it was held by the House of Lords in *Ministry of Health v Simpson*[136] that the recipients of funds improperly distributed in the administration of a deceased person's estate are strictly liable to repay the persons properly entitled to the estate, and it could be argued that there is no compelling reason why this situation should be treated differently from the situation where a defendant receives misdirected trust assets.

**11-089** Secondly, it was held by Lord Nicholls in *Criterion Properties Ltd v Stratford UK Properties LLC* that if the directors of a company (A) act for an improper purpose when causing A to transfer the company's assets to B, then[137]

> irrespective of whether B still has the assets in question, A will have a personal claim against B for unjust enrichment, subject always to a defence of change of position. B's personal accountability will not be dependent upon proof of fault or 'unconscionable' conduct on his part. B's accountability, in this regard, will be 'strict'.

This dictum was followed by Sales J in *Relfo Ltd (In Liquidation) v Varsani*[138] to support his finding that the claimant not only had a claim in knowing receipt against the defendant recipient of the traceable proceeds of the claimant's misdirected assets, but also had a claim in unjust enrichment against him. This was upheld by the Court of Appeal.[139]

**11-090** Thirdly, it has been held that where trust assets are misappropriated by a trustee and used to pay off a security charged on property belonging to an innocent third party, the beneficiaries are entitled to be subrogated to the extinguished rights which were formerly possessed by the charge-holder, and to be treated, by a legal fiction, as though these rights were not extinguished, but were instead assigned to the beneficiaries in order that they might enforce them against the innocent third party.[140] The English courts have held that subrogation is a remedy awarded to reverse unjust enrichment,[141] and if beneficiaries are entitled to acquire proprietary rights against innocent third parties via subrogation on the ground of unjust enrichment, then a fortiori they should also be entitled to a direct personal claim in unjust enrichment against innocent third parties who have been enriched at the beneficiaries' expense.

### ii. Other Jurisdictions

**11-091** The question whether the recipients of misdirected trust funds owe a liability in unjust enrichment has been addressed by the courts of several other jurisdictions. In *Farah Constructions Pty Ltd v Say-Dee Pty Ltd*,[142] the High Court of Australia held that they do not, essentially because the court denied that unjust enrichment is an independent source of rights and obligations in Australian law, a view that was out of line with many previous High Court decisions which hold that it is.[143]

---

136 [1951] A.C. 251.

137 [2004] 1 W.L.R. 1846 at [3]–[4].

138 [2012] EWHC 2168 (Ch) at [86].

139 [2015] 1 B.C.L.C. 14.

140 *McCullough v Marsden* (1919) 45 D.L.R. 645 at 646–647; *Primlake Ltd (In Liquidation) v Matthews Assocs* [2007] 1 B.C.L.C. 666 at [340].

141 *Banque Financière de la Cité v Parc (Battersea) Ltd* [1999] A.C. 221 at 228 and 234, followed in *Niru Battery Manufacturing Co v Milestone Trading Ltd (No.2)* [2004] 2 All E.R. (Comm.) 289, at [27]–[28]; *Filby v Mortgage Express (No.2) Ltd* [2004] EWCA Civ 759 at [62].

142 (2007) 230 C.L.R. 89 at [148]–[158].

143 e.g. *Pavey & Matthews Pty Ltd v Paul* (1987) 162 C.L.R. 221 at 227 and 256–257; *David Securities Pty Ltd v Commonwealth*

In *Gold v Rosenberg*[144] and *Citadel General Assurance Co v Lloyds Bank Canada*,[145] the Supreme Court of Canada held that the "essence" of a knowing receipt claim is that the defendant has been unjustly enriched at the claimant's expense. Unfortunately the court's analysis conflates liability to account for trust property and liability in unjust enrichment to repay the value of property received, with the result that the important remedial differences between these two types of liability were obscured.[146] **11–092**

In *Re Esteem Settlement*,[147] the Royal Court of Jersey held that liability for knowing receipt is not itself a liability in unjust enrichment, but that all recipients of misdirected trust property owe a strict liability in unjust enrichment, whether or not they know of the breach of trust, so that a knowing recipient owes concurrent liabilities in knowing receipt and unjust enrichment. If the English courts decide to recognise a claim in unjust enrichment against the recipients of misdirected trust funds, then the Jersey model would be preferable to the Canadian model. **11–093**

### iii. Change of Position Defence

If the English courts do hold that a claim in unjust enrichment lies against the recipients of misapplied trust property, then it seems likely that recipients who are sued on this basis will often attempt to raise a change of position defence. It therefore seems apposite to give a brief account here of the circumstances in which this defence is available. Note that change of position is not a defence to claims in knowing receipt, first, because it is only a defence to claims in unjust enrichment, and, secondly, because the unconscionability of the defendant's behaviour would automatically debar her from relying on the defence, which is only available to those who have acted in good faith. **11–094**

In practice, the defence of change of position is most often relied on by defendants who have Incurred extraordinary expenditure in reliance on their receipt of the benefit: i.e. they have been led to spend their money on something which they would not have bought if they had not received the benefit.[148] However, the defence is available to a wider class of defendants than this, and there is no need to show that the change in a defendant's position came about because she consciously chose to spend the money, although there must be a causal link, at least on a "but-for" basis, between the receipt of the benefit and the change in the defendant's position.[149] So a defendant who is paid £500 in banknotes and then immediately loses them when her bag is stolen can raise the defence although it cannot be said that she changed her position in reliance on her receipt. A defendant who changes her position in anticipation of a benefit which is subsequently paid to her can also raise the defence.[150] However a defendant who changes her position by purchasing an asset which remains in her possession at the time of the claim cannot rely on the defence to the extent that she remains enriched by her possession of the asset.[151] **11–095**

In *Lipkin Gorman v Karpnale Ltd*,[152] Lord Goff held that the defence is not available to those who **11–096**

*Bank of Australia* (1992) 175 C.L.R. 353 at 379 and 392; *ANZ Banking Group v Westpac Banking Corp* (1998) 164 C.L.R. 662 at 673.

144 [1997] 3 S.C.R. 767.

145 [1997] 3 S.C.R. 805.

146 For these differences, see para.11–086.

147 2002 J.L.R. 53 at [148]–[161].

148 As in, e.g. *Philip Collins Ltd v Davis* [2000] 3 All E.R. 808 at 827–830.

149 *Scottish Equitable Plc v Derby* [2001] 3 All E.R. 818 at 827; *Rose v AIB Group (UK) Plc* [2003] 2 B.C.L.C. 374 at [49]; *Cressman v Coys of Kensington (Sales) Ltd* [2004] 1 W.L.R. 2775 at [49].

150 *Dextra Bank & Trust Co Ltd v Bank of Jamaica* [2002] 1 All E.R. (Comm.) 193.

151 *Lipkin Gorman v Karpnale Ltd* [1991] 2 A.C. 548 at 560.

152 *Lipkin Gorman* at 580; *Credit Suisse (Monaco) SA v Attar* [2004] EWHC 374 (Comm) at [98].

act in bad faith nor to wrongdoers. This good faith requirement clearly excludes defendants who have been self-consciously dishonest, but it can also exclude those who have failed "to act in a commercially acceptable way" and those who have engaged in "sharp practice of a kind that falls short of outright dishonesty".[153] On the other hand, "mere negligence on the part of the recipient is not sufficient to deprive him of the defence of change of position".[154]

## 4. Dishonest Assistance

### A. The Primary Breach

11–097 Claims for dishonest assistance lie against defendants who assist in misapplications of property by trustees, whether express, constructive, or resulting,[155] and other stewards of property, e.g. company directors.[156] Claims also lie against defendants who assist in a breach of duty that does not entail the misapplication of property and is instead a breach of the duty owed by a fiduciary to act in the exclusive interests of her principal.[157]

11–098 There was originally no requirement that a defendant should have assisted in a dishonest breach of duty.[158] Then, in an unreserved judgment not discussing the earlier cases, Lord Selborne LC held that assistants in a breach of trust could not be liable unless "they assist with knowledge in a dishonest and fraudulent design on the part of the trustees".[159] In his speech for the Privy Council in *Royal Brunei Airlines Sdn Bhd v Tan*, Lord Nicholls declined to apply this rule, holding that the claimant did not need to show that the breach of trust assisted by the defendant had been a dishonest breach.[160] This finding was affirmed by the House of Lords in *Twinsectra Ltd v Yardley*.[161]

### B. The Defendant's State of Mind

11–099 Turning to the defendant's own state of mind, the cases on this point had got into a sorry state prior to *Royal Brunei*. In the *Baden, Delvaux* case,[162] Peter Gibson J had held that a defendant might be liable for assisting in a breach of trust even if her behaviour fell short of dishonesty,[163] and he had accepted that any of the five types of knowledge he identified there would serve to render a defendant liable as an assistant in a breach of trust.[164] Subsequently a consensus emerged that, contrary to Peter Gibson J's view, a defendant must have been dishonest to incur liability,[165] but a line of cases pre-dating

---

153 *Niru Battery Manufacturing Co v Milestone Trading Ltd (No.1)* [2002] 2 All E.R. (Comm.) 705 at [125], per Moore-Bick J, affirmed [2004] 1 Lloyd's Rep. 344.

154 *Niru* at [125], per Moore-Bick J, relying on *Dextra Bank & Trust Co Ltd v Bank of Jamaica* [2002] 1 All E.R. (Comm.) 193, where at [42]–[45] the Privy Council declined to hold that the relative fault of the claimant and the defendant can affect the availability of the defence.

155 For the latter: *Bank Tejerat v Hong Kong and Shanghai Banking Corp (CI) Ltd* [1995] 1 Lloyd's Rep. 239; *Heinl v Jyske Bank (Gibraltar) Ltd* [1999] Lloyd's Rep. Bank. 511.

156 *Selangor United Rubber Estates Ltd v Cradock (No.3)* [1968] 1 W.L.R. 1555; *Belmont Finance Corp Ltd v Williams Furniture Ltd (No.2)* [1980] 1 All E.R. 393; *Heinl v Jyske Bank (Gibraltar) Ltd* [1999] Lloyd's Rep. Bank. 511.

157 *Novoship (U.K.) Ltd v Mikhaylyuk* [2015] 2 W.L.R. 526.

158 *Fyler v Fyler* (1841) 3 Beav. 550; *Att.-Gen v Corporation of Leicester* (1844) 7 Beav. 176.

159 *Barnes v Addy* (1874) L.R. 9 Ch. App. 244 at 252, confirmed in *Belmont Finance Corp v Williams* [1979] Ch. 250 at 257.

160 [1995] 2 A.C. 378 at 385.

161 [2002] 2 A.C. 164 at 171 and 195. See too *Williams v Central Bank of Nigeria* [2014] A.C. 1189 at [35] and [178].

162 [1993] 1 W.L.R. 509 (the case was decided in 1983).

163 *Baden, Delvaux* at 577. For Peter Gibson J's five-fold classification, see para.11–023.

164 *Baden, Delvaux* at 575–587.

165 e.g. *Agip (Africa) Ltd v Jackson* [1990] 1 Ch. 265 at 292–293, on appeal: [1991] Ch. 547 at 569; *Lipkin Gorman v Karpnale Ltd* [1989] 1 W.L.R. 1340 at 1354–1355.

*Baden, Delvaux*, and holding that a defendant can be liable if she has honestly but negligently failed to investigate the circumstances of an impugned transaction, was never overruled.[166] The body of law founded on the *Baden, Delvaux* classification also suffered from the more general problem that it was over-theorised: as Lord Nicholls put it in *Royal Brunei*, the courts were led into "tortuous convolutions" in their efforts to investigate the "sort" of knowledge possessed by defendants, "when the truth is that 'knowingly' is inapt as a criterion when applied to the gradually darkening spectrum where the differences are of degree and not kind."[167]

In *Royal Brunei*, Lord Nicholls therefore decided to start afresh. He held that knowledge is best avoided as a defining ingredient of liability, and that the *Baden, Delvaux* scale is best forgotten in this context.[168] He rejected the idea that unconscionability should be the touchstone for liability, unless it is made clear "what, *in this context*, unconscionable *means*",[169] and he held that to fix a defendant with liability, it must be shown that she acted dishonestly. He emphasised that the test for dishonesty in this context is not purely subjective, in the sense that individuals are not "free to set their own standards of honesty in particular circumstances",[170] and must be judged by reference to the standards of right-thinking members of society. So, as the courts have put it in subsequent cases, there is no "Robin Hood" defence to an action for dishonest assistance.[171] **11–100**

*Royal Brunei Airlines Sdn Bhd v Tan*

Privy Council [1995] 2 A.C. 378

LORD NICHOLLS (giving the judgment of the court): The proper role of equity in commercial transactions is a topical question. Increasingly plaintiffs have recourse to equity for an effective remedy when the person in default, typically a company, Is insolvent. Plaintiffs seek to obtain relief from others who were involved in the transaction, such as directors of the company, or its bankers, or its legal or other advisers. They seek to fasten fiduciary obligations directly onto the company's officers or agents or advisers, or to have them held personally liable for assisting the company in breaches of trust or fiduciary obligations. **11–101**

This is such a case. An insolvent travel agent company owed money to an airline. The airline seeks a remedy against the travel agent's principal director and shareholder. Its claim is based on the much-quoted dictum of Lord Selborne L.C., sitting in the Court of Appeal in Chancery, in *Barnes v Addy*:[172] **11–102**

> "[The responsibility of a trustee] may no doubt be extended in equity to others who are not properly trustees, if they are found . . . actually participating in any fraudulent conduct of the trustee to the injury of the cestui que trust. But . . . strangers are not to be made constructive trustees merely because they act as the agents of trustees in transactions within their legal powers, transactions, perhaps of which a court of equity may disapprove, unless those agents receive and become chargeable with some part of the trust property, or unless they assist with knowledge in a dishonest and fraudulent design on the part of the trustees."

In the conventional shorthand, the first of these two circumstances in which third parties (non-trustees) may become liable to account in equity is "knowing receipt", as distinct from the second, where liability arises from "knowing assistance". Stated even more shortly, the first limb of Lord Selborne L.C.'s formulation is concerned with the liability of a person as a recipient of trust property or its traceable proceeds. The second limb is concerned with what, for want of a better compendious description, can be called **11–103**

---

166 *Selangor United Rubber Estates Ltd v Cradock (No.3)* [1968] 1 W.L.R. 1555; *Karak Rubber Co Ltd v Burden (No.2)* [1972] 1 W.L.R. 602; *Rowlandson v National Westminister Bank Ltd* [1978] 1 W.L.R. 798.

167 [1995] 2 A.C. 378 at 391.

168 *Royal Brunei* [1995] 2 A.C. 378 at 392.

169 *Royal Brunei* at 392 (original emphasis).

170 *Royal Brunei* at 389.

171 *Grupo Torras SA v Al-Sabah (No.5)* [2001] Lloyd's Rep. Bank. 36 at 60; *Walker v Stones* [2001] Q.B. 902 at 939; *Twinsectra Ltd v Yardley* [2002] 2 A.C. 164 at 172. Cf. *Consul Developments Pty Ltd v DPC Estates Pty Ltd* (1975) 132 C.L.R. 373 at 398.

172 (1874) L.R. 9 Ch. App. 244 at 251–252.

the liability of an accessory to a trustee's breach of trust. Liability as an accessory is not dependent upon receipt of trust property. It arises even though no trust property has reached the hands of the accessory. It is a form of secondary liability in the sense that it only arises where there has been a breach of trust. In the present case the plaintiff airline relies on the accessory limb. The particular point in issue arises from the expression "a dishonest and fraudulent design on the part of the trustees . . .".

11–104 In short, the issue on this appeal is whether the breach of trust which is a prerequisite to accessory liability must itself be a dishonest and fraudulent breach of trust by the trustee.

**The Honest Trustee and the Dishonest Third Party**

11–105 It must be noted at once that there is a difficulty with the approach adopted on this point in the *Belmont* case.[173] Take the simple example of an honest trustee and a dishonest third party. Take a case where a dishonest solicitor persuades a trustee to apply trust property in a way the trustee honestly believes is permissible but which the solicitor knows full well is a clear breach of trust. The solicitor deliberately conceals this from the trustee. In consequence, the beneficiaries suffer a substantial loss. It cannot be right that in such a case the accessory liability principle would be inapplicable because of the innocence of the trustee. In ordinary parlance, the beneficiaries have been defrauded by the solicitor. If there is to be an accessory liability principle at all, whereby in appropriate circumstances beneficiaries may have direct recourse against a third party, the principle must surely be applicable in such a case, just as much as in a case where both the trustee and the third party have been dishonest. Indeed, if anything, the case for liability of the dishonest third party seems stronger where the trustee is innocent, because in such a case the third party alone was dishonest and that was the cause of the subsequent misapplication of the trust property.

11–106 The position would be the same if, instead of procuring the breach, the third party dishonestly assisted in the breach. Change the facts slightly. A trustee is proposing to make a payment out of the trust fund to a particular person. He honestly believes he is authorised to do so by the terms of the trust deed. He asks a solicitor to carry through the transaction. The solicitor well knows that the proposed payment would be a plain breach of trust. He also well knows that the trustee mistakenly believes otherwise. Dishonestly he leaves the trustee under his misapprehension and prepares the necessary documentation. Again, if the accessory principle is not to be artificially constricted, it ought to be applicable in such a case.

11–107 These examples suggest that what matters is the state of mind of the third party sought to be made liable, not the state of mind of the trustee. The trustee will be liable in any event for the breach of trust, even if he acted innocently, unless excused by an exemption clause in the trust instrument or relieved by the court. But his state of mind is essentially irrelevant to the question whether the third party should be made liable to the beneficiaries for the breach of trust. If the liability of the third party is fault-based, what matters is the nature of his fault, not that of the trustee. In this regard dishonesty on the part of the third party would seem to be a sufficient basis for his liability, irrespective of the state of mind of the trustee who is in breach of trust. It is difficult to see why, if the third party dishonestly assisted in a breach, there should be a further prerequisite to his liability, namely that the trustee also must have been acting dishonestly. The alternative view would mean that a dishonest third party is liable if the trustee is dishonest, but if the trustee did not act dishonestly that of itself would excuse a dishonest third party from liability. That would make no sense.

**Earlier Authority**

11–108 The view that the accessory liability principle cannot be restricted to fraudulent breaches of trust is not to be approached with suspicion as a latter-day novelty. Before the accessory principle donned its *Barnes v Addy* strait-jacket, judges seem not to have regarded the principle as confined in this way. In *Fyler v Fyler*,[174] Lord Langdale M.R. expressed the view that, if trustees invested in an unauthorised investment, solicitors who knowingly procured that to be done for their own benefit "ought to be considered as partakers in the breach of trust" even though the trustees intended in good faith that the investment would be beneficial to the life tenant and not prejudicial to the beneficiaries with interests in capital. The same judge, in *Attorney-General v Corporation of Leicester*,[175] stated:

173 [1979] Ch. 250.
174 (1841) 3 Beav. 550 at 568.
175 (1844) 7 Beav. 176 at 179.

"it cannot be disputed that, if the agent of a trustee, whether a corporate body or not, knowing that a breach of trust is being committed, interferes and assists in that breach of trust, he is personally answerable, although he may be employed as the agent of the person who directs him to commit that breach of trust."

In *Eaves v Hickson*[176] trustees, acting in good faith, paid over the fund to William Knibb's adult children on the strength of a forged marriage certificate produced to them by William Knibb. Sir John Romilly M.R. held that William Knibb was liable to replace the fund, to the extent that it was not recovered from his children, and to do so in priority to the liability of the trustees. Far from this being a case of fraud by the trustees, Sir John Romilly M.R.[177] described it as a very hard case on the trustees, who were deceived by a forgery which would have deceived anyone who was not looking out for forgery or fraud.

This point did not arise in *Barnes v Addy*. There the new sole trustee was engaged in a dishonest and fraudulent design. He intended to misapply the trust fund as soon as it reached his hands. The two solicitors were held not liable because there was no evidence that either of them had any knowledge or suspicion of this. **11–109**

What has gone wrong? Their Lordships venture to think that the reason is that, ever since the *Selangor* case[178] highlighted the potential uses of equitable remedies in connection with misapplied company funds, there has been a tendency to cite and interpret and apply Lord Selborne L.C.'s formulation in *Barnes v Addy* as though it were a statute. This has particularly been so with the accessory limb of Lord Selborne L.C.'s apothegm. This approach has been inimical to analysis of the underlying concept. Working within this constraint, the courts have found themselves wrestling with the interpretation of the individual ingredients, especially "knowingly" but also "dishonest and fraudulent design on the part of the trustees", without examining the underlying reason why a third party who has received no trust property is being made liable at all. . . . **11–110**

To resolve this issue it is necessary to take an overall look at the accessory liability principle. A conclusion cannot be reached on the nature of the breach of trust which may trigger accessory liability without at the same time considering the other ingredients including, in particular, the state of mind of the third party. It is not necessary, however, to look even more widely and consider the essential ingredients of recipient liability. The issue on this appeal concerns only the accessory liability principle. Different considerations apply to the two heads of liability. Recipient liability is restitution-based; accessory liability is not. . . . **11–111**

**Fault-Based Liability**

Given, then, that in some circumstances a third party may be liable directly to a beneficiary, but given also that the liability is not so strict that there would be liability even when the third party was wholly unaware of the existence of the trust, the next step is to seek to identify the touchstone of liability. By common accord dishonesty fulfils this role. Whether, in addition, negligence will suffice is an issue on which there has been a well-known difference of judicial opinion. The *Selangor* decision in 1968 was the first modern decision on this point. Ungoed-Thomas J. held that the touchstone was whether the third party had knowledge of circumstances which would indicate to "an honest, reasonable man" that the breach in question was being committed or would put him on inquiry.[179] Brightman J. reached the same conclusion in *Karak Rubber Co.Ltd v Burden (No.2)*.[180] So did Peter Gibson J. in 1983 in *Baden v Société Générale pour Favoriser le Développement du Commerce et de l'Industrie en France SA*.[181] In that case the judge accepted a five-point scale of knowledge which had been formulated by counsel. **11–112**

Meanwhile doubts had been expressed about this test by Buckley and Goff L.JJ. in the *Belmont* case.[182] Similar doubts were expressed in Australia by Jacobs P. in *DPC Estates Pty Ltd v Grey and Consul Development Pty Ltd*.[183] When that decision reached the High Court of Australia, the doubts were echoed by Barwick C.J., Gibbs and Stephen JJ.[184] **11–113**

---

176 (1861) 30 Beav. 136.
177 At 141.
178 [1968] 1 W.L.R. 1555.
179 [1968] 1 W.L.R. 1555 at 1590.
180 [1972] 1 W.L.R. 602.
181 [1993] 1 W.L.R. 509.
182 [1979] Ch. 250 at 267 at 275.
183 [1974] 1 N.S.W.L.R. 443 at 459.
184 See *Consul Development Pty Ltd v DP Estates Pty Ltd* (1975) 132 C.L.R. 373 at 376, 398, 412.

11–114 Since then the tide in England has flowed strongly in favour of the test being one of dishonesty: see, for instance, Sir Robert Megarry V.C. in *Re Montagu's Settlement Trusts*[185] and Millett J. in *Agip (Africa) Ltd v Jackson*.[186] In *Eagle Trust Plc v SBC Securities Ltd*,[187] Vinelott J. stated that it could be taken as settled law that want of probity was a prerequisite to liability. This received the imprimatur of the Court of Appeal in *Polly Peck International Plc v Nadir (No.2)*.[188] . . .

**Dishonesty**

11–115 Before considering this issue further it will be helpful to define the terms being used by looking more closely at what dishonesty means in this context. Whatever may be the position in some criminal or other contexts (see, for instance, *R. v Ghos*[189]), in the context of the accessory liability principle acting dishonestly, or with a lack of probity, which is synonymous, means simply not acting as an honest person would in the circumstances. This is an objective standard. At first sight this may seem surprising. Honesty has a connotation of subjectivity as distinct from the objectivity of negligence. Honesty, Indeed, does have a strong subjective element in that it is a description of a type of conduct assessed in the light of what a person actually knew at the time, as distinct a from what a reasonable person would have known or appreciated. Further, honesty and its counterpart dishonesty are mostly concerned with advertent conduct, not inadvertent conduct. Carelessness is not dishonesty. Thus for the most part dishonesty is to be equated with conscious impropriety. However, these subjective characteristics of honesty do not mean that individuals are free to set their own standards of honesty in particular circumstances. The standard of what constitutes honest conduct is not subjective. Honesty is not an optional scale, with higher or lower values according to the moral standards of each individual. If a person knowingly appropriates another's property, he will not escape a finding of dishonesty simply because he sees nothing wrong in such behaviour.

11–116 In most situations there is little difficulty in identifying how an honest person would behave. Honest people do not intentionally deceive others to their detriment. Honest people do not knowingly take others' property. Unless there is a very good and compelling reason, an honest person does not participate in a transaction if he knows it involves a misapplication of trust assets to the detriment of the beneficiaries. Nor does an honest person in such a case deliberately close his eyes and ears, or deliberately not ask questions, lest he learn something he would rather not know, and then proceed regardless. However, in the situations now under consideration the position is not always so straightforward. This can best be illustrated by considering one particular area: the taking of risks.

**Taking Risks**

11–117 All investment involves risk. Imprudence is not dishonesty, although imprudence may be carried recklessly to lengths which call into question the honesty of the person making the decision. This is especially so if the transaction serves another purpose in which that person has an interest of his own.

11–118 This type of risk is to be sharply distinguished from the case where a trustee, with or without the benefit of advice, is aware that a particular investment or application of trust property is outside his powers, but nevertheless he decides to proceed in the belief or hope that this will be beneficial to the beneficiaries or, at least, not prejudicial to them. He takes a risk that a clearly unauthorised transaction will not cause loss. A risk of this nature is for the account of those who take it. If the risk materialises and causes loss, those who knowingly took the risk will be accountable accordingly. This is the type of risk being addressed by Peter Gibson J. in the *Baden* case,[190] when he accepted that fraud includes taking "a risk to the prejudice of another's rights, which risk is known to be one which there is no right to take."

11–119 This situation, in turn, is to be distinguished from the case where there is genuine doubt about whether a transaction is authorised or not. This may be because the trust instrument is worded obscurely, or because there are competing claims, as in *Carl Zeiss Stiftung v Herbert Smith & Co (No.2)*,[191] or for other reasons. The difficulty here is that frequently the situation is neither clearly white nor clearly black. The dividing

---

185 [1987] Ch. 264 at 285.
186 [1990] Ch. 265 at 293.
187 [1993] 1 W.L.R. 484 at 495.
188 [1992] 4 All E.R. 769 at 777, per Scott L.J.
189 [1982] Q.B. 1053.
190 [1993] 1 W.L.R. 509 at 574.
191 [1969] 2 Ch. 276.

edge between what is within the trustee's powers and what is not is often not clear-cut. Instead there is a gradually darkening spectrum which can be described with labels such as clearly authorised, probably authorised, possibly authorised, wholly unclear, probably unauthorised and, finally, clearly unauthorised.

The difficulty here is that the differences are of degree rather than of kind. So far as the trustee himself is concerned the legal analysis is straightforward. Honesty or lack of honesty is not the test for his liability. He is obliged to comply with the terms of the trust. His liability is strict. If he departs from the trust terms he is liable unless excused by a provision in the trust instrument or relieved by the court. The analysis of the position of the accessory, such as the solicitor who carries through the transaction for him, does not lead to such a simple, clear-cut answer in every case. He is required to act honestly; but what is required of an honest person in these circumstances? An honest person knows there is doubt. What does honesty require him to do? 11–120

The only answer to these questions lies in keeping in mind that honesty is an objective standard. The individual is expected to attain the standard which would be observed by an honest person placed in those circumstances. It is impossible to be more specific. Knox J. captured the flavour of this, in a case with a commercial setting, when he referred to a person who is "guilty of commercially unacceptable conduct in the particular context involved".[192] Acting in reckless disregard of others' rights or possible rights can be a tell-tale sign of dishonesty. An honest person would have regard to the circumstances known to him, including the nature and importance of the proposed transaction, the nature and importance of his role, the ordinary course of business, the degree of doubt, the practicability of the trustee or the third party proceeding otherwise and the seriousness of the adverse consequences to the beneficiaries. The circumstances will dictate which one or more of the possible courses should be taken by an honest person. He might, for instance, flatly decline to become involved. He might ask further questions. He might seek advice, or insist on further advice being obtained. He might advise the trustee of the risks but then proceed with his role in the transaction. He might do many things. Ultimately, in most cases, an honest person should have little difficulty in knowing whether a proposed transaction, or his participation in it, would offend the normally accepted standards of honest conduct. 11–121

Likewise, when called upon to decide whether a person was acting honestly, a court will look at all the circumstances known to the third party at the time. The court will also have regard to personal attributes of the third party, such as his experience and intelligence, and the reason why he acted as he did. 11–122

Before leaving cases where there is real doubt, one further point should be noted. To inquire, in such cases, whether a person dishonestly assisted in what is later held to be a breach of trust is to ask a meaningful question, which is capable of being given a meaningful answer. This is not always so if the question is posed in terms of "knowingly" assisted. Framing the question in the latter form all too often leads one into tortuous convolutions about the "sort" of knowledge required, when the truth is that "knowingly" is inapt as a criterion when applied to the gradually darkening spectrum where the differences are of degree and not kind. 11–123

**Negligence**

It is against this background that the question of negligence is to be addressed. This question, it should be remembered, is directed at whether an honest third party who receives no trust property should be liable if he procures or assists in a breach of trust of which he would have become aware had he exercised reasonable diligence. Should he be liable to the beneficiaries for the loss they suffer from the breach of trust? 11–124

The majority of persons falling into this category will be the hosts of people who act for trustees in various ways: as advisers, consultants, bankers and agents of many kinds. This category also includes officers and employees of companies in respect of the application of company funds. All these people will be accountable to the trustees for their conduct. For the most part they will owe to the trustees a duty to exercise reasonable skill and care. When that is so, the rights flowing from that duty form part of the trust property. As such they can be enforced by the beneficiaries in a suitable case if the trustees are unable or unwilling to do so. That being so, it is difficult to identify a compelling reason why, in addition to the duty of skill and care vis-à-vis the trustees which the third parties have accepted, or which the law has imposed upon them, third parties should also owe a duty of care directly to the beneficiaries. They have undertaken work for the trustees. They must carry out that work properly. If they fail to do so, they will be liable to 11–125

[192] *Cowan de Groot Properties Ltd v Eagle Trust Plc* [1992] 4 All E.R. 700 at 761.

make good the loss suffered by the trustees in consequence. This will include, where appropriate, the loss suffered by the trustees, being exposed to claims for breach of trust.

11–126 Outside this category of persons who owe duties of skill and care to the trustees, there are others who will deal with trustees. If they have not accepted, and the law has not imposed upon them, any such duties in favour of the trustees, it is difficult to discern a good reason why they should nevertheless owe such duties to the beneficiaries.

11–127 There remains to be considered the position where third parties are acting for, or dealing with, dishonest trustees. In such cases the trustees would have no claims against the third party. The trustees would suffer no loss by reason of the third party's failure to discover what was going on. The question is whether in this type of situation the third party owes a duty of care to the beneficiaries to, in effect, check that a trustee is not misbehaving. The third party must act honestly. The question is whether that is enough.

11–128 In agreement with the preponderant view, their Lordships consider that dishonesty is an essential ingredient here. There may be cases where, in the light of the particular facts, a third party will owe a duty of care to the beneficiaries. As a general proposition, however, beneficiaries cannot reasonably expect that all the world dealing with their trustees should owe them a duty to take care lest the trustees are behaving dishonestly. . . .

**The Accessory Liability Principle**

11–129 Drawing the threads together, their Lordships' overall conclusion is that dishonesty is a necessary ingredient of accessory liability. It is also a sufficient ingredient. A liability in equity to make good resulting loss attaches to a person who dishonestly procures or assists in a breach of trust or fiduciary obligation. It is not necessary that, in addition, the trustee or fiduciary was acting dishonestly, although this will usually be so where the third party who is assisting him is acting dishonestly. "Knowingly" is better avoided as a defining ingredient of the principle and in the context of this principle the *Baden* scale of knowledge is best forgotten.

**Conclusion**

11–130 From this statement of the principle it follows that this appeal succeeds. The money paid to BLT on the sale of tickets for the airline was held by BLT upon trust for the airline. This trust, on its face, conferred no power on BLT to use the money in the conduct of its business. The trust gave no authority to BLT to relieve its cash flow problems by utilising for this purpose the rolling 30-day credit afforded by the airline. Thus BLT committed a breach of trust by using the money instead of simply deducting its commission and holding the money intact until it paid the airline. The defendant accepted that he knowingly assisted in that breach of trust. In other words, he caused or permitted his company to apply the money in a way he knew was not authorised by the trust of which the company was trustee. Set out in these bald terms, the defendant's conduct was dishonest. By the same token, and for good measure, BLT also acted dishonestly. The defendant was the company, and his state of mind is to be imputed to the company.

11–131 The Court of Appeal held that it was not established that BLT was guilty of fraud or dishonesty in relation to the amounts it held for the airline. Their Lordships understand that by this the Court of Appeal meant that it was not established that the defendant intended to defraud the airline. The defendant hoped, maybe expected, to be able to pay the airline, but the money was lost in the ordinary course of a poorly-run business with heavy overhead expenses. These facts are beside the point. The defendant had no right to employ the money in the business at all. That was the breach of trust. The company's inability to pay the airline was the consequence of that breach of trust.

11–132 Did Lord Nicholls mean to lay down a test of self-conscious dishonesty analogous to the test laid down in criminal law by Lord Lane CJ in *R v Ghosh*[193]; i.e. must a defendant have done something that right-thinking people would regard as dishonest, and also have been aware that they would view his actions in this light? There are strong pointers in Lord Nicholls' speech that he did not mean to say this, particularly his statement that[194]:

---

[193] [1982] Q.B. 1053.
[194] [1995] 2 A.C. 378 at 389.

> Whatever may be the position in some criminal or other contexts (see, for instance, *R. v Ghosh*), in the context of the accessory liability principle acting dishonestly, or with a lack of probity, which is synonymous, means simply not acting as an honest person would in the circumstances. This is an objective standard.

Notwithstanding this, the House of Lords subsequently held in *Twinsectra Ltd v Yardley* that self-conscious dishonesty was required. Lord Hutton stated that "dishonesty requires knowledge by the defendant that what he was doing would be regarded as dishonest by honest people".[195] Likewise, Lord Hoffmann held that there must be "a dishonest state of mind, that is to say, consciousness that one is transgressing ordinary standards of honest behaviour."[196] Applying this test to the facts of the case, the majority concluded that a solicitor who had enabled a client to commit a breach of trust by releasing trust money to the client absolutely had not acted dishonestly, although he knew that the client had been meant to take the money as trustee and not as absolute owner. **11–133**

The majority speeches in *Twinsectra* depended on a very strained reading of Lord Nicholls' words in *Royal Brunei*. However the point was then revisited by the Privy Council, in *Barlow Clowes International Ltd v Eurotrust International Ltd*.[197] There a fraudster laundered money stolen from the claimant company through bank accounts held in the names of various Isle of Man companies administered by Eurotrust, another Isle of Man company which provided offshore financial services. One of the Eurotrust directors was found by the trial judge to have strongly suspected that the money passing through his hands had been stolen, but to have consciously decided not to make inquiries lest he discover the truth. The judge also held that he might have seen nothing wrong with this behaviour, because he had had an **11–134**

> exaggerated notion of dutiful service to clients, which produced a warped moral approach that it was not improper to treat carrying out clients' instructions as being all important.[198]

On appeal from the finding that the director was liable for dishonest assistance, counsel argued that on these facts he could not have been relevantly dishonest because he had not known that his actions were dishonest by ordinary standards, as required by *Twinsectra*. Lord Hoffmann rejected this. Conceding that there had been "an element of ambiguity" in Lord Hutton's remarks in *Twinsectra*, he held that neither he nor Lord Hutton had said that a defendant must have considered what normally acceptable standards of honest conduct might be: they had merely said that a defendant must have known about the aspects of the relevant transaction which made his participation transgress those standards.[199] Applying this test to the facts of *Eurotrust*, the defendant was liable. **11–135**

In subsequent cases, the courts have taken Lord Hoffmann at his word and have followed *Eurotrust* rather than *Twinsectra*, although the former is a decision of the Privy Council and the latter a decision of the House of Lords.[200] So it may now be said that the mental element for dishonest assistance is not self-conscious dishonesty of the kind described by Lord Lane CJ in *Ghosh* but objective dishonesty of the kind described by Lord Nicholls in *Royal Brunei* and Lord Hoffmann in *Eurotrust*. **11–136**

---

195 [2002] 2 A.C. 164 at [36].
196 [2002] 2 A.C. 164 at [20].
197 [2006] 1 W.L.R. 1476.
198 [2004] W.T.L.R. 1365 at [133].
199 [2006] 1 W.L.R. 1476 at [15]–[16].
200 e.g. *Abouh-Rahmah v Abacha* [2007] Bus. L.R. 220 at [43]; *Central Bank of Ecuador v Conticorp SA* [2015] UKPC 11 at [9].

## C. Dishonesty and Knowledge

11–137 Although he held that knowledge is not the defining ingredient of liability in *Royal Brunei*, Lord Nicholls acknowledged that the honesty of a defendant's conduct can only be assessed in the light of what she knew when she acted; and in *Eurotrust* Lord Hoffmann said that a dishonest state of mind

> may consist in knowledge that the transaction is one in which [the defendant] cannot honestly participate (for example, a misappropriation of other people's money), or it may consist in suspicion combined with a conscious decision not to make inquiries which might result in knowledge.[201]

11–138 Obviously, the facts which a defendant must have known before she can be said to have acted dishonestly vary from case to case, but it seems that at the very least the defendant must have known that the primary wrongdoer "is not entitled to do what he is doing."[202] The defendant need not have known all the details of the primary wrongdoer's whole design, according to Lewison J in *Ultraframe (UK) Ltd v Fielding*, although by analogy with criminal accessory liability, she must have known in broad terms what the design was, and her liability should not extend to unforeseen and uncontemplated actions by the primary wrongdoer which lay outside the scope of the joint enterprise in which she participated.[203]

11–139 Is a defendant relevantly dishonest if she thinks that she is participating in some wrongful transaction other than the breach of trust in which she has actually participated? The cases are divided,[204] but in principle defendants should not be allowed to say that they did not think they were helping to steal from the claimant because they thought they were helping to steal from someone else. As Fox LJ held in *Agip (Africa) Ltd v Jackson*,[205] "persons who [need] to demonstrate that they [have] acted honestly [cannot] shelter behind transactions or objects which [are] themselves disreputable."

## D. Acts of Assistance

11–140 The word "assistance" might appear to suggest that a defendant must have played some subsidiary part in a design orchestrated by the trustee or fiduciary whose breach of duty the defendant facilitates. Certainly that is the fact-pattern of many cases. However, there are also cases where accessory liability has been incurred by defendants who have instigated the primary breach of duty. An obvious example is *Royal Brunei Airlines Sdn Bhd v Tan*,[206] where the defendant caused the company of which he was the majority shareholder and director to misdirect funds that it held on trust for the claimant. Liability has also been incurred in cases where the defendant has bribed a fiduciary to breach her duty to act exclusively in the interests of her principal.[207]

---

201 [2006] 1 W.L.R. 1476 at [10]. On blind eye knowledge see also Tipping J's remarks in *Westpac New Zealand Ltd v Map & Associates Ltd* [2011] NZSC 89 at [67].

202 *Ultraframe (UK) Ltd v Fielding* [2007] W.T.L.R. 835 at [1504], per Lewison J.

203 *Ultraframe* at [1506].

204 Yes: *Agip (Africa) Ltd v Jackson* [1990] 1 Ch. 265 at 295, affirmed [1991] Ch. 547 at 569; *Ultraframe (UK) Ltd v Fielding* [2007] W.T.L.R. 835 at [1500]; *Otkritie International Investment Management Ltd v Urumov* [2014] EWHC 191 (Comm) at [77]. No: *Brink's Ltd v Abu-Saleh* [1999] C.L.C. 133; *Grupo Torras SA v Al-Sabah (No.5)* [1999] C.L.C. 1469 at 1665–1666, affirmed [2001] Lloyd's Rep Bank 36 at 59.

205 [1991] Ch. 547 at 569.

206 [1995] 2 A.C. 378.

207 e.g. *Fyffes Group Ltd v Templeman* [2000] 2 Lloyd's 643; *Novoship (UK) Ltd v Mikhaylyuk* [2015] 2 W.L.R. 526.

## E. Causation

Generally speaking, the law of civil wrongs, like the criminal law, is "moulded on the philosophy of autonomy",[208] with the result that it does not generally regard loss flowing from the actions of a primary wrongdoer as having been caused by the actions of a participant who has induced or assisted in the commission of the wrong.[209] However, liability for dishonest assistance is an exception to this general rule: a defendant is liable for loss flowing from the primary wrong even if there is no direct causal link between her actions and the loss. Thus, in *Grupo Torras SA v Al-Sabah (No.5)* Mance LJ held that[210]: **11–141**

> The starting point . . . is that the requirement of dishonest assistance relates not to any loss or damage which may be suffered, but to the breach of trust or fiduciary duty. The relevant enquiry is . . . what loss or damage resulted from the breach of trust or fiduciary duty which has been dishonestly assisted.

This was affirmed on appeal,[211] and then reaffirmed by a differently constituted Court of Appeal, in *Casio Computer Ltd v Sayo*, where Tuckey LJ stated that[212]:

> *Grupo Torras* . . . establishes that in a claim for dishonest assistance it is not necessary to show a precise causal link between the assistance and the loss . . . [and that loss] caused by the breach of fiduciary duty is recoverable from the accessory.

Of course, where a defendant's actions have made no difference at all to the implementation of a breach of trust or fiduciary duty, "there is no causative effect and therefore no assistance . . . [so that] the requirements of conscience [do not] require any remedy."[213] Hence a claimant must at least show that the defendant's actions have made the fiduciary's breach of duty easier than it would otherwise have been. But the causation requirement for dishonest assistance is no stronger than this, and it is no answer to a claim, for example, that the claimant's loss would have occurred anyway, because the wrongdoing fiduciary would have committed the breach even if the defendant had not assisted her. Thus a defendant can be liable for actions or omissions which precede the breach,[214] although she cannot be liable if her actions or omissions only occurred after the breach was fully implemented.[215] However, where the breach has entailed the misapplication of funds, the courts are likely to hold that it was not fully implemented until the funds were hidden away where the beneficiaries could not find them, with the consequence that those who assist in money-laundering activities after trust funds have been removed from a trust account can be fixed with liability for dishonest assistance.[216] **11–142**

## E. Remedies

Different remedies can be awarded against dishonest assistants in different situations. Arguably, some are made on the basis that the dishonest assistant is fixed with a civil secondary liability which **11–143**

---

208 G. Williams, "Complicity, Purpose and the Draft Code" [1990] Crim. L.R. 4, 6.
209 H.L.A. Hart and A.M. Honoré, *Causation in the Law*, 2nd edn (Oxford University Press, 1985), p.385.
210 [1999] C.L.C. 1469 at 1667.
211 [2001] Lloyd's Rep Bank 36 at 61.
212 [2001] I.L.Pr. 43 at [16].
213 *Brown v Bennett* [1999] 1 B.C.L.C. 649 at 659, per Morritt LJ.
214 R.P. Austin, "Constructive Trusts" in P.D. Finn (ed.), *Essays in Equity* (Law Book Co, 1985), pp.196, 236–237, discussing *Adams v Bank of New South Wales* [1984] 1 N.S.W.L.R. 285. See too *Aequitas Ltd v Sparad No.100 Ltd* (2001) 19 A.C.L.C. 1006.
215 *Brown v Bennett* [1998] 2 B.C.L.C. 97 at 105.
216 *Heinl v Jyske Bank (Gibraltar) Ltd* [1999] Lloyd's Rep. Bank. 511 at 523, approving *Agip (Africa) Ltd v Jackson* [1990] Ch. 265 at 293. See too *Casio Computer Co Ltd v Sayo* [2001] I.L.Pr. 43 at [22].

derives from and duplicates the liability of the trustee, so that once the amount of the trustee's liability is determined, the dishonest assistant is made jointly and severally liable with the trustee for the same amount.[217] If the wrongdoing trustee is liable to pay money as a form of substitutive performance of her obligation to account for trust property,[218] then the dishonest assistant is jointly and severally liable for the same amount.[219] Similarly, the dishonest assistant can also be ordered to pay the same measure of compensation as the trustee would have had to pay if the beneficiaries had sued her for reparation.[220] Again, there are a series of Canadian cases,[221] and several English decisions,[222] which hold that where the trustee has incurred a liability to disgorge unauthorised profits,[223] the dishonest assistant will be jointly and severally liable for the same amount—although in *Ultraframe (UK) Ltd v Fielding*,[224] Lewison J declined to make a finding to this effect because he thought it would amount to a punitive measure, and the High Court of Australia has also held that a primary wrongdoer and an assistant are not jointly liable for one another's profits, although they may be severally liable to disgorge their own profits.[225]

**11–144** English law also holds that a dishonest assistant must disgorge profits she has made for herself out of her wrongdoing. The Court of Appeal's statement to this effect in *Novoship (UK) Ltd v Mikhaylyuk*[226] is reproduced below. Note, however, that the court refused to order an account of profits on the facts of the case as it considered that the defendants' profits were not relevantly caused by their wrongdoing. Note, too, that the availability of this remedy requires us to think that for some purposes, at least, dishonest assistance can be a form of wrongdoing for which a primary liability is incurred by the defendant.

*Novoship (UK) Ltd v Mikhaylyuk*

Court of Appeal [2015] 2 W.L.R. 526

**11–145** The claimant corporate group alleged that a director, Mikhaylyuk, committed breaches of fiduciary duty when he took bribes to arrange charters of the group's vessels to Henriot Finance Ltd, a company controlled by Nikitin, who made US$150m profits from the charters. Christopher Clarke J. found that Nikitin and Henriot had dishonestly assisted Mikhaylyuk's breaches of fiduciary duty and ordered them to disgorge their profits on the charters. They appealed from this order. The Court of Appeal held that an account of

[217] S.B. Elliott and C. Mitchell, "Remedies for Dishonest Assistance" (2004) 67 M.L.R. 16. Contra P. Ridge, "Justifying the Remedies for Dishonest Assistance" (2008) 124 L.Q.R. 445. Further discussion: M.S. Clapton, "Gain-Based Remedies for Knowing Assistance: Ensuring Assistants Do Not Profit From Their Wrongs" (2008) 45 Alberta L.R. 989; C. Mitchell and S. Watterson, "Remedies for Knowing Receipt" in C. Mitchell (ed.) *Constructive and Resulting Trusts* (2010), pp.150–154.

[218] See paras 10–20ff.

[219] See, e.g. *Macdonald v Hauer* (1976) 72 D.L.R. (3d) 110 at 129; *Re Bell's Indenture* [1980] 1 W.L.R. 1217 at 1231–1233; *Commercial Union Life Assurance Co of Canada v John Ingle Insurance Group Inc* (2002) 22 C.C.L.I. 221, affirmed (2002) 217 D.L.R. (4th) 178; *NCR Australia Pty Ltd v Credit Connection Pty Ltd (In Liquidation)* [2004] N.S.W.S.C. 1 at [150].

[220] See paras 10–102ff. Awards of this sort were made against dishonest assistants in, e.g. *Colour Control Centre Pty Ltd v Ty* N.S.W.S.C. (Eq. Div.) 24 July 1995; *Equiticorp Industries Group Ltd v R. (No.47)* [1998] 2 N.Z.L.R. 481 at 658; *Fyffes Group Ltd v Templeman* [2000] 2 Lloyd's Rep. 643.

[221] Running from *Canada Safeway Ltd v Thompson* [1951] 3 D.L.R. 295 through to *Glenko Enterprises Ltd v Keller* [2001] 1 W.W.R. 229 at 257–258.

[222] *Ostrich Farming Corp Ltd v Wallstreet LLC* Ch. D., Lawtel Report 8 October 1998; *Comax Secure Business Services Ltd v Wilson* Q.B.D. 21 June 2001; *CMS Dolphin Ltd v Simonet* [2001] 2 B.C.L.C. 704, followed in *Quarter Master UK Ltd v Pyke* [2005] 1 B.C.L.C. 245.

[223] See paras 13–066ff.

[224] [2007] W.T.L.R. 835 at [1589]–[1601].

[225] *Michael Wilson & Partners Limited v Nicholls* (2011) 244 C.L.R. 427 at [106].

[226] [2015] 2 W.L.R. 526. See too *Consul Development Pty Ltd v DPC Estates Pty Ltd* (1972) 132 C.L.R. 373 at 397, followed in *US Surgical Corp v Hospital Products International Pty Ltd* (1982) 2 N.S.W.L.R. 766 at [817]; *Crown Dilmun v Sutton* [2004] 1 B.C.L.C. 468 at [204]; *Ultraframe (UK) Ltd v Fielding* [2007] W.T.L.R. 835 at [1595]; *Airbus Operations Ltd v Withey* [2014] EWHC 1126 (QB) at [506].

profits is available against a defendant who has dishonestly assisted a breach of fiduciary duty that did not involve a misapplication of property. However, this remedy should only be awarded where there is a causal link between the dishonest assistance and the profit for which the defendant must account. The benefit derived by Nikitin and Henriot from their dishonest assistance was merely the use of the vessels at the market rate and although they had made a profit on the deal as a result of an unexpected change in the market there had been no sufficiently direct causal link between their wrongdoing and their profits. Hence the judge had erred in ordering them to account for these profits.

LONGMORE, MOORE-BICK AND LEWISON L.JJ.: . . . The question arising on this part of the appeal is whether Mr Nikitin is liable to account for the profits that he (or his companies) made from the Henriot charters. The judge held that he was so liable, because he had dishonestly assisted in a breach of fiduciary duty by Mr Mikhaylyuk either in (a) negotiating the terms of the fixtures with him or (b) concluding charters resulting from those negotiations, in either case at a time when Mr Mikhaylyuk had not disclosed to his principals that he had been bribed by Mr Ruperti and that part of the bribe had been diverted to Mr Nikitin. **11–146**

This raises the following potential issues: (i) is the remedy of an account of profits available against a dishonest assistant as opposed to a fiduciary; (ii) if so, is there a requirement for some causal connection between the dishonest assistance and the profit for which the assistant is asked to account; (iii) if so, what is the nature of that causal connection; (iv) if there is a requirement for a causal connection was it satisfied on the facts of this case; (v) if it is, would it be right, on the facts of this case, to order an account of profits? **11–147**

**Remedies against third parties**

[The claimant] claims an account of Mr Nikitin's profits from the Henriot charters. This is a personal claim only: Mr Brindle accepted that there is no proprietary claim. Mr Berry in turn accepted that a fiduciary would be compelled to account for an unauthorised profit made and falling within the scope of his fiduciary duty. However, he submitted that (a) an account of profits could never be ordered against a third party who had not voluntarily assumed fiduciary obligations to the claimant; alternatively (b) that an account of profits could not be ordered against a third party whose liability arose only because of his dishonest assistance in a breach of fiduciary duty; alternatively (c) an account of profits could not be ordered against a third party unless there had been some misapplication of trust property. These arguments were not deployed below, and so the judge did not deal with them. **11–148**

Where a person is not himself a fiduciary, he may become mixed up in a breach by another of a fiduciary duty. He may be liable in one of two ways: (i) as a knowing recipient of trust property or its traceable proceeds or (ii) as a dishonest accessory to the fiduciary's breach of duty. **11–149**

The former is now known by the shorthand "knowing receipt" and the second by the shorthand "dishonest assistance". Although for the purpose of legal analysis it is convenient to distinguish between the two types of secondary liability, a person may be liable under both heads, depending on the facts of a particular case. Mr Berry correctly points out that neither a knowing recipient nor a dishonest assistant has ever promised either expressly or inferentially to subordinate his own interests to those of the beneficiary. Neither is a fiduciary. In some areas of the law this does lead to a different legal treatment of a dishonest assistant on the one hand, and a fiduciary on the other. This is now settled at the highest level in the case of limitation of actions. Whereas a trustee is not entitled to raise a defence of limitation against a beneficiary alleging a fraudulent breach of trust or seeking to recover trust property, a knowing recipient or a dishonest assistant is entitled to rely on the Limitation Act 1980. This is the result of the decision of the Supreme Court in *Williams v Central Bank of Nigeria*.[227] Mr Berry drew attention in particular to the observations of Lord Neuberger of Abbotsbury P.S.C.:[228] **11–150**

> "So far as raising a limitation defence is concerned, this conclusion places dishonest assisters and knowing recipients (i) in the same position as those who are liable in common law for improper or dishonest conduct, and (ii) in a better position than defaulting trustees. The first result seems appropriate: as Millett L.J. said in the *Paragon* case,[229] 'There is no case for distinguishing between an action for fraud at common law and its counterpart in equity'. As for the second result, it is plainly justifiable,

[227] [2014] A.C. 1189.
[228] At [118].
[229] [1999] 1 All E.R. 400 at 414.

as defaulting trustees have pre-existing fiduciary duties to claimants which dishonest assisters and knowing recipients do not."

11–151 Building on this distinction Mr Berry pointed out that in the case of a common law action based on fraud the response of the courts is to require the fraudster to compensate the victim for loss that he has suffered. The common law does not strip the fraudster of his gain.[230] As Longmore L.J. put it in *Devenish Nutrition Ltd v Sanofi-Aventis SA*:[231]

"Neither the law of restitution nor the law of damages is in the business of transferring monetary gains from one undeserving recipient to another undeserving recipient even if the former has acted illegally while the latter has not."

11–152 However, we note that Longmore L.J. excluded "fiduciary claims" from his reluctance to encourage a restitutionary system of damages.[232] Moreover in the *Williams* case itself Lord Sumption J.S.C. made it clear that equity's intervention in the case of a knowing recipient or dishonest assistant was "purely remedial";[233] and he was careful to distinguish between the question of limitation and the question of remedy. Nor did he rule out the possibility that a knowing recipient might be liable to account for profits.[234] At the heart of the issue, therefore, is the question whether a dishonest assistant should be treated differently from a true fiduciary; and, if so, to what extent.

11–153 There is now a body of modern case law at first instance which recognises that the court has the power to order an account of profits against a dishonest assistant, even where no corresponding loss has been suffered by the beneficiary. They include: *Fyffes Group Ltd v Templeman*;[235] *Ultraframe (UK) Ltd v Fielding*;[236] *Tajik Aluminium Plant v Ermatov (No. 3)*;[237] *OJSC Oil Co Yugraneft v Abramovich*;[238] *Fiona Trust & Holding Corpn v Privalov*;[239] and *Otkritie International Investment Management Ltd v Urumov*.[240] The proposition for which these cases stand is unequivocally supported by *Underhill & Hayton, Law of Trusts and Trustees*.[241] Ranged against this body of case law are the obiter doubts expressed by Rimer J. in *Sinclair Investment Holdings SA v Versailles Trade Finance Ltd*.[242]

11–154 Mr Berry correctly submitted that none of these cases are binding on this court; and further submitted that, apart from the *Sinclair* case, they are wrong. . .

11–155 [Their Lordships rejected this submission and agreed with the statement in *Snell's Equity*[243] that] both a liability to make good loss and a liability to account for profits "follow from the premise that the defendant is held liable to account as if he were truly a trustee to the claimant".

11–156 In our judgment this position is supported both by policy and authority. The policy was articulated by Gibbs J. in *Consul Development Pty Ltd v DPC Estates Pty Ltd*.[244] He said:

"If the maintenance of a very high standard of conduct on the part of fiduciaries is the purpose of the rule it would seem equally necessary to deter other persons from knowingly assisting those in a fiduciary position to violate their duty. If, on the other hand, the rule is to be explained simply because it would be contrary to equitable principles to allow a person to retain a benefit that he had gained from a breach of his fiduciary duty, it would appear equally inequitable that one who knowingly took part in the breach should retain a benefit that resulted therefrom. I therefore conclude, on principle, that a person who knowingly participates in a breach of fiduciary duty is liable

---

230 *Halifax Building Society v Thomas* [1996] Ch. 217 at 227 per Peter Gibson L.J. and 229 per Glidewell L.J.
231 [2009] Ch. 390 at [147].
232 At [149].
233 [2014] A.C. 1189 at [10].
234 See the *Williams* case, at [31].
235 [2000] 2 Lloyd's Rep. 643 (Toulson J.).
236 [2006] F.S.R. 293 at [1589]–[1594] (Lewison J.).
237 [2006] EWHC 7 (Ch) at [23] (Blackburne J.).
238 [2008] EWHC 2613 (Comm) at [377] and [392] (Christopher Clarke J.).
239 [2010] EWHC 3199 (Comm) at [66] (Andrew Smith J.).
240 [2014] EWHC 191 (Comm) at [79] (Eder J.).
241 18th ed (2010), para. 98.3.
242 [2007] 2 All E.R. (Comm.) 993 at [129]–[134].
243 32nd ed (2010), para. 30–079.
244 (1975) 132 C.L.R. 373 at 397.

to account to the person to whom the duty was owed for any benefit he has received as a result of such participation."

If the phrase "knowingly took part in" is replaced by "dishonestly assisted in" we cannot see that it undermines the policy as formulated. It is true that in Australia the concept of "knowing participation" does not correspond precisely to our concepts of knowing receipt and dishonest assistance. However, so far as accounting for profits are concerned, even in Australian law a knowing participant is not generally required to account for profits that he did not make.[245] **11–157**

[Their Lordships quoted passages from *Docker v Somes*,[246] *Rolfe v Gregory*[247] and *Barnes v Addy*,[248] which supported their conclusion, then contined:] . . . *Royal Brunei Airlines Sdn Bhd v Tan*[249] altered the conditions that must be satisfied before liability arises, but did not, in our judgment, alter the nature of the liability. The nature of the liability, as it seems to us, is that the knowing recipient or dishonest assistant has, in principle, the responsibility of an express trustee. That responsibility would include, in an appropriate case, a liability to account for profits. We can see the principle at work in *Cook v Deeks*,[250] a decision of the Privy Council. Messrs Deeks and Hinds were the directors of the Toronto Construction Company. They negotiated a lucrative construction contract with the Canadian Pacific Railway. During the course of the negotiations, they decided to enter into the contract personally, on their own behalves. However, they incorporated a new company, the Dominion Construction Company to carry out the work. It was that company that made the profit under the contract. The Privy Council held that Messrs Deeks and Hinds were guilty of a breach of duty in the course they took to secure the contract, and must be regarded as holding it for the benefit of the Toronto Construction Company. The Board added:[251] **11–158**

"Their Lordships have throughout referred to the claim as one against the defendants GS Deeks, GM Deeks, and TR Hinds. But it was not, and it could not be, disputed that the Dominion Construction Company acquired the rights of these defendants with full knowledge of all the facts, and the account must be directed in form as an account in favour of the Toronto Company against all the other defendants."

The reference to "all the other defendants" is a reference both to the directors and to the Dominion Construction Company. Thus the Dominion Construction Company was ordered to account for the profit that it had made. The Dominion Construction Company was not a fiduciary. This, then, is a case in which an account of profits was ordered against a non-fiduciary who became mixed up in a breach of fiduciary duty. . . **11–159**

[Counsel has also argued that] that the misapplication of trust property is a necessary condition for the availability of an account of profits. This is put in two ways. First, since the Henriot charters were time charters they were no more than contracts for services with no disposition of trust property. We would be surprised if equity were to take a radically different view according to whether a charter were a time charter or a demise charter (or if the dishonest assistant took a licence of land rather than a lease), so we approach this way of putting the point with some scepticism. The second way in which the point is put is that although Mr Mikhaylyuk was a fiduciary, he had no power of disposition over his principal's property (unlike a trustee in whom trust property is vested, or a company director, who has power to dispose of the company's property). *Lewin on Trusts*[252] says that in such a case it is an open question whether a misapplication of trust property is a necessary precondition to an order for an account of profits. **11–160**

[Their Lordships considered *Satnam Investments Ltd v Dunlop Heywood & Co Ltd*[253], *Brown v Bennett*[254] and *Goose v Wilson Sandford & Co*[255] before turning to Peter Smith J.'s decision in *JD Wetherspoon plc v Van* **11–161**

245 *Grimaldi v Chameleon Mining NL (No.2)* (2012) 287 A.L.R. 22 at [536].
246 (1834) 2 My. & K. 655 at 665.
247 (1865) 4 De G.J. & S. 576 at 578 and 579.
248 (1874) L.R. 9 Ch. App. 244 at 251–252.
249 [1995] 2 A.C. 378.
250 [1916] 1 A.C. 554.
251 At 565.
252 18th ed. (2008 and 2012 supplement), para. 40-16.
253 [1999] 3 All E.R. 652.
254 [1999] 1 B.C.L.C. 649.
255 [2001] Lloyd's Rep P.N. 189.

*de Berg & Co Ltd*[256] that] . . . misuse of trust property was not a prerequisite to a liability to account for profits for dishonest assistance in a breach of fiduciary duty. He reasoned thus:

> "In my view in a case for accessory liability there is no requirement for there to be trust property. Such a requirement wrongly associates accessory liability with trust concepts. That has led to difficulties which were addressed by Lord Millett in Paragon Finance. Accessory liability does not involve a trust. It involves providing dishonest assistance to somebody else who is in a fiduciary capacity [and] has committed a breach of his fiduciary duties. The consequences of those breaches (as this case shows) might have different consequences. One might be that the fiduciary has received a bribe. Another is that the fiduciary has made a profit in breach of his fiduciary duty. Another possibility is that assets are available . . . which it can be shown were acquired in breach of the fiduciary duty. Third party recipients are also potential candidates. Finally the breach of fiduciary duty might only sound in damages. In all of those cases I can see no logic or grave difficulty where the fiduciary is involved who has committed a breach of his fiduciary duty that an accessory who acts dishonestly in relation to those breaches should not be liable. It must not be forgotten that in most cases the breach can only occur as a result of the activities of the [assister]."

**11–162** In the *Fiona Trust* case[257] Andrew Smith J. said that he agreed with Peter Smith J. and adopted his reasons. So do we. But in addition as we have said it would be a triumph of form over substance if a dishonest assistant escaped liability by entering into a time charter but not if he entered into a demise charter, or took a licence of land rather than a lease . . . Because dishonesty can take many different forms (as well as having many different consequences) we do not agree that it makes all the difference that the dishonesty consists of receiving as opposed to paying a bribe. As we have said, the only question is whether liability as a dishonest assistant in a breach of fiduciary duty has been established. If it has, then an account of profits is one possible remedy.

**11–163** We therefore conclude that the remedy of an account of profits is available against one who dishonestly assists a fiduciary to breach his fiduciary obligations, even if that breach does not involve a misapplication of trust property.

**Causation**

**11–164** In the decision in the *Ultraframe* case[258] Lewison J. said that a dishonest assistant is liable to account "for any profit that he makes from his dishonest assistance or from the underlying breach of trust". However, he was not considering the precise nature of the test of causation which was not in issue. We have already referred to the observations of Gibbs J. in holding that questions of policy support the availability of the remedy of an account of profits against a dishonest assistant. Gibbs J. concluded in the *Consul* case that a dishonest assistant is "liable to account to the person to whom the duty was owed for any benefit he has received as a result of such participation."[259]

**11–165** This also suggests that a causation test is appropriate. We note also that Gibbs J. referred to a benefit received as a result of the participation (rather than a benefit received as a result of the breach of fiduciary duty). *Snell* suggests that the test should be that of "a sufficiently direct causal connection between the defendant's assistance and the alleged profit accruing to him".[260]

**11–166** A fiduciary's liability to account for a secret profit does not depend on any notion of causation. It is sufficient that the profit falls within the scope of his duty of loyalty to the beneficiary. Arden L.J. made this point in the *Murad* case:[261]

> "If there is a fiduciary duty of loyalty and if the conduct complained of falls within the scope of that fiduciary duty as indicated by Lord Wilberforce in *New Zealand Netherlands Society 'Oranje' Inc v Kuys*[262] then I see no justification for any further requirement that the profit shall have been obtained

---

256 [2009] EWHC 639 (Ch) at [518].
257 *Fiona Trust & Holding Corp. v Privalov* [2010] EWHC 3199 (Comm) at [61].
258 [2007] W.T.L.R. 835 at [1594].
259 132 C.L.R. 373 at 397 (emphasis added).
260 At para. 30–081.
261 [2005] W.T.L.R. 1573 at [57], by reference to the judgment of Morritt L.J. in *United Pan-Europe Communications NV v Deutsche Bank AG* [2000] 2 B.C.L.C. 461 at [47].
262 [1973] 1 W.L.R. 1126.

> by the fiduciary 'by virtue of his position'. Such a condition suggests an element of causation which neither principle nor the authorities require. Likewise it is not in doubt that the object of the equitable remedies of an account or the imposition of a constructive trust is to ensure that the defaulting fiduciary does not retain the profit; it is not to compensate the beneficiary for any loss. Accordingly comparison with the remedy in damages is unhelpful."

Jonathan Parker L.J. made the same point in the *Murad* case.[263] Mr Brindle argued that our conclusion on the question of causation should not run contrary to the decision of this court in the *Murad* case, and in particular what Arden and Jonathan Parker L.JJ. said about the decision of Toulson J. in *Fyffes Group Ltd v Templeman*.[264] Although he did not say that we were bound by the decision in the Murad case (which concerned a fiduciary rather than a dishonest assistant) he did say that we should give full effect to it. **11–167**

It is, therefore, necessary to go back to the *Fyffes* case, and then to see what this court said about it in the *Murad* case. In the *Fyffes* case the claimant employed Mr Templeman as its chartering manager. He negotiated a service agreement with Seatrade under which Seatrade was to provide shipping services to Fyffes. However, unknown to Fyffes Seatrade had agreed to bribe Mr Templeman by paying him a percentage of the freight earned. That was dishonest assistance by Seatrade in Mr Templeman's breach of fiduciary duty to Fyffes. The question was whether Fyffes could require Seatrade to account for the profit that it had made in providing the shipping services under the service agreement. Toulson J. said that there were "cogent grounds, in principle and in practical justice, for following the approach of Gibbs J." in the *Consul* case. He therefore held that "the briber of an agent *may* be required to account to the principal for benefits obtained from the corruption of the agent."[265] But he decided on the facts that he should not order an account. First, he said that Seatrade would have entered into a service agreement with Fyffes, even if Mr Templeman had not been dishonest. Second, he said that the ordinary profit that Seatrade made under the service agreement was not "caused by the bribery of Mr Templeman". Third, he did not see the equity of ordering Seatrade to account to Fyffes for the whole of its profit, because that would amount to the unjust enrichment of Fyffes. As we read this decision the first two reasons for refusing to order an account related to the question of causation; and the third to the overall equity of the result. **11–168**

In the *Murad* case Arden L.J. said:[266] **11–169**

> "Reliance has been placed . . . on the *Fyffes* case where Toulson J. declined to make an order for an account of profits in favour of the principal of a bribed agent as against the briber because the transaction with the defrauded principal was one into which the defrauded principal would have entered in any event. Toulson J. held that those profits were attributable to the provision of services under the agreement, not the payment of the bribe. On the face of it, this holding is precluded by the *Regal* case.[267] However, while it is not entirely clear, it may be that this should be treated as a case where the wrongdoer was held to be entitled to an allowance for his services despite his fraudulent conduct."

The *Regal* case to which Arden L.J. referred was a case about true fiduciaries. The principle that it established was described by Lord Russell of Killowen thus:[268] **11–170**

> "The rule of equity which insists on those, who *by use of a fiduciary position* make a profit, being liable to account for that profit, in no way depends on fraud, or absence of bona fides; or on such questions or considerations as whether the profit would or should otherwise have gone to the plaintiff, or whether the profiteer was under a duty to obtain the source of the profit for the plaintiff, or whether he took a risk or acted as he did for the benefit of the plaintiff, or whether the plaintiff has in fact been damaged or benefited by his action. The liability arises from the mere fact of a profit having, *in the stated circumstances*, been made."

Toulson J. was not, however, dealing with the case of a fiduciary; but with a dishonest assistant. So the *Regal* case does not in terms preclude his decision. In the decision in the *Murad* case Jonathan Parker L.J. said:[269] **11–171**

---

263 At [112].
264 [2000] 2 Lloyd's Rep. 643.
265 Our emphasis.
266 [2005] W.T.L.R. 1573 at [69].
267 *Regal (Hastings) Ltd v Gulliver* [1967] 2 A.C. 134.
268 At 144–145 (emphasis added).
269 [2005] W.T.L.R. 1573 at [120].

"Like Arden L.J . . . I have difficulty in reconciling Toulson J.'s reasoning in the above passage with the authorities to which I have referred, and I note that it appears from the report of the case that none of those authorities was cited to Toulson J. apart from *Target v Redferns* (a case concerning equitable compensation for breach of trust). Had the judge been addressing a claim for equitable compensation for breach of trust, his reasoning would in my judgment have been entirely in accordance with authority . . . but in the context of the 'no conflict' rule, the authorities, as I read them, preclude such an approach."

**11–172** It is fair to say that, although these passages do not in terms disapprove or overrule the *Fyffes* case, they proceed on the assumption that precisely the same principles as regards causation apply in the case of a dishonest assistant as apply in the case of a true (but defaulting) fiduciary. But whether that assumption is correct was not before the court and neither Arden L.J. nor Jonathan Parker L.J. explicitly considered the question. Moreover in the decision in the *Satnam* case[270] this court held that the principle in the *Regal* case and *Phipps v Boardman*[271] did not apply to one who was alleged to be no more than a knowing recipient of trust property. As Nourse L.J. put it: "In the absence of a fiduciary duty the principle of those cases cannot apply." The *Satnam* case was not referred to in the *Murad* case. We do not consider that the decision in *Murad* will bear the weight that Mr Brindle seeks to place on it. . .

**11–173** It is important to appreciate the special position in which a fiduciary finds himself. The essence of the relationship between a fiduciary and beneficiary is that the latter has placed his trust in the former. The core duty of the fiduciary is single minded loyalty to his beneficiary. Thus the breach of duty does not consist in the making of a profit by the fiduciary, but in the keeping of it for himself. That is not a breach of a personal obligation; it is an abuse of the trust and confidence placed in him by his principal who put him in a position to make the profit because he trusted him not to serve his own interests. Equity's response to the breach of this trust is not to give redress for the breach in the form of equitable compensation but to enforce the duty.[272] It is this attitude of equity which explains why a true trustee cannot raise a limitation defence against his beneficiary.[273]

**11–174** We agree with Mr Berry that in the case of one who is not a fiduciary this approach is inappropriate, for the dishonest assistant has no pre-existing duty whose scope can be determined and enforced. It seems to us therefore that the scope of the wrongdoer's liability must be determined by reference to some other principle. In the case of a claim against a fiduciary for equitable compensation (as opposed to an account of profits) in respect of a breach of duty a court of equity will apply a "but for" test of causation, thus precluding recovery for loss that would have occurred even if the breach of duty had not taken place, although the common law rules of causation and remoteness do not apply in such a case . . .

**11–175** In our case Mr Nikitin was not a fiduciary either as regards NOUK or the shipowning companies. He is not sued for a breach of fiduciary duty. He is sued because he has committed an equitable wrong. Where a claim based on equitable wrongdoing is made against one who is not a fiduciary, we consider that, as in the case of a fiduciary sued for breach of an equitable (but non-fiduciary) obligation, there is no reason why the common law rules of causation, remoteness and measure of damages should not be applied by analogy. We recognise that these rules do not apply to the case of a fiduciary sued for breach of a fiduciary duty; but that is because the two cases are different. Arden L.J. made this clear in the decision in the *Murad* case.[274] We note also that In the *Satnam* case some three pages of the court's judgment[275] were devoted to considering the question of causation.

**11–176** The common law does not usually apply a simple "but for" test of causation. The common law distinguishes between a breach which is the effective cause of a loss and one which is merely the occasion for the loss. How to distinguish between the two is a question of the application of common sense.[276] Common sense, as we have seen, also plays its part in determining the extent of equitable compensation.

**11–177** The question of causation has a bearing on the fashioning of the account. Even in the case of a fiduciary the cases stress the importance of identifying as precisely as possible the extent of the benefit or profit attributable to the breach of fiduciary duty.

---

270 [1999] 3 All E.R. 652 at 671.

271 [1967] 2 A.C. 46.

272 See Millett, "Bribes and Secret Commissions Again" [2012] C.L.J. 583.

273 See the *Williams* case [2014] A.C. 1189 at [13].

274 [2005] W.T.L.R. 1573 at [74].

275 [1999] 3 All E.R. 652 at 665–668.

276 *Galoo Ltd v Bright Graham Murray* [1994] 1 W.L.R. 1360.

The judge dealt with the question of causation at a number of points in his judgment.[277] [First] he posed the question whether as regards causation the dishonest assistant was in the same position as a fiduciary.[278] He referred to the well-established proposition that, in the case of a fiduciary, it is no defence to say that the profit would have been earned anyway even if there had been no breach of fiduciary duty; and said, "It seems to me that the same should apply to the assister in respect of whom the need for deterrence is similar."[279] 11–178

However, in the following paragraph, he said:[280] 11–179

> "In the present case, a sufficiently direct casual connection between the assistance and the profit is to be found given that the profit from the deployment of the vessels the subject of the Henriot Finance charters could not have been earned unless those charters had been entered into, and is, thus, a profit which results from Henriot Finance entering into those charters—which, itself, constitutes the dishonest assistance given to Mr Mikhaylyuk's breach of fiduciary duty."

Thus he said that the same test should apply to the dishonest assistant as applies to a fiduciary;[281] and [later] he said first that there was a "sufficiently direct causal connection"[282] but then in the same paragraph he appears to us to apply a simple "but for" test of causation. But he then went on to say:[283] 11–180

> "It is no defence to say that the charters were at commercial rates and not disadvantageous to the owners; or that, if there had been no breach of fiduciary duty, they would have been made anyway and at the same rates or that Henriot Finance would have made the same profit anyway by the charter of other vessels."

We agree with Mr Berry that that paragraph appears to disavow even a "but for" test of causation. 11–181

For the reasons we have given we do not agree with the judge that the same considerations that apply to a fiduciary apply to a dishonest assistant who has no fiduciary duties. We agree with the judge that if Mr Nikitin (or his companies) had not entered into the Henriot charters, the profits would not have been made. In other words, "but for" entry into the charters the profits would not have been made. But in our judgment the simple "but for" test is not the appropriate test. In our judgment what Mr Nikitin acquired as a result of his dishonest assistance (and also as a result of Mr Mikhaylyuk's breach of fiduciary duty) was the use of the vessels at the market rate. That was merely the occasion for him to make a profit. The real or effective cause of the profits was the unexpected change in the market. As the judge recognised,[284] Mr Nikitin made the profits "because he judged the market well". 11–182

We would therefore hold that there was an insufficient direct causal connection between entry into the Henriot charters and the resulting profits. We must stress, however, that had Mr Nikitin been a true fiduciary, and had entry into the Henriot charters been a breach of fiduciary duty, then the causation test we have adopted would not have applied. 11–183

[Their Lordships also held that it would be disproportionate to order an account of profits in relation to the particular form and extent of wrongdoing committed by the defendants.] 11–184

## Questions

1. What do the courts mean when they say that trustees *de son tort*, knowing recipients and dishonest assistants variously owe a "personal liability to account" to the beneficiaries, and how does this affect the measure of compensation that each may have to pay following a breach of trust?

---

277 [2012] EWHC 3586 (Comm).
278 At [513].
279 At [518].
280 At [519].
281 At [518].
282 At [519].
283 At [520].
284 At [525].

2. In *Barnes v Addy* (1874) L.R. 9 Ch. App. 244 at 252, Lord Selborne LC thought that "if persons dealing honestly as agents are at liberty to rely on the legal power of the trustees, [and] are not to have the character of trustees constructively thrust upon them, then the transactions of mankind can safely be carried through; and I apprehend those who create trusts do expressly intend, in the absence of fraud and dishonesty, to exonerate such agents of all classes from the responsibilities which are expressly incumbent by reason of the fiduciary relation upon the trustees." In light of these comments do you think that fault should be a prerequisite for third party liability for breach of trust; and if so, what degree of fault?
3. "The majority of the House of Lords in *Twinsectra* misinterpreted Lord Nicholls' discussion of the fault requirement for accessory liability in *Royal Brunei*. In *Eurotrust* Lord Hoffmann could not admit this if he wanted to get things back on the right track while sitting in the Privy Council." **Discuss.**
4. A stockbroker is directed by trustees to sell an authorised investment and to apply the proceeds to the purchase of an unauthorised investment. He knowingly does so because he bona fide believes this to be in the beneficiaries' best financial interests. Most surprisingly the unauthorised investment halves in value within a year. Can the beneficiaries sue the stockbroker if the trustees are now insolvent; and if so, what might be the measure of his liability?
5. An accountant agrees to falsify her client's records, and certify them as accurate, in what she believes to be a conspiracy to evade the payment of VAT. In fact her client has misappropriated trust funds and the beneficiaries now wish to know whether they can sue the accountant. Would it make any difference if the client would have stolen the money anyway?

# 12

# PROPRIETARY CLAIMS FOLLOWING A BREACH OF TRUST

## 1. Introduction

### A. The Key Features of Proprietary Claims

According to circumstances, several different proprietary claims can lie where trustees act outside the scope of their authority, e.g. by making an unauthorised investment, or misappropriating trust property for themselves, or misdirecting trust property to third party recipients who are not beneficiaries. Where the property has survived in its original form and is held either by a trustee or a third party recipient, the beneficiaries may be entitled to assert a subsisting equitable proprietary interest in the property.[1] Where the property has been exchanged for new property the beneficiaries may be able to assert a new equitable proprietary interest in the substitute property; they may also be entitled to an equitable lien over the substitute property to secure performance of the defendant's personal obligation to pay the value of the missing property, in appropriate cases by invoking the equitable doctrine of subrogation. 12–001

These claims differ in that the first and second are claims to an interest under a trust, while the third is a claim to a security interest, in property held by the defendant. However, all three claims bring the advantage of priority in the defendant's insolvency. If a defendant has never owned an asset free from a claimant's equitable interest, this interest will be unaffected by her insolvency because the asset can never have formed part of her estate. If the claimant has an equitable lien over a defendant's property, this will give him priority over the defendant's unsecured creditors, and possibly over her other secured creditors as well, depending on the relevant priority rules. 12–002

If a claimant has an equitable interest under a trust in property that appreciates in value, the increase will accrue to the claimant. If a claimant has an equitable lien over a defendant's property to secure the repayment of a particular sum, and the property depreciates in value, the claimant can still enforce the whole amount of the lien against the property, and if necessary recover any outstanding amount by a personal action. As Keene LJ said in *Serious Fraud Office v Lexi Holdings Plc (in administration)*,[2] an equitable lien is "a cumulative remedy in aid of an equitable *in personam* claim, not an alternative remedy". 12–003

[1] In the case of misdirected funds, claims in unjust enrichment can also be made by the trustees against the recipient, relying on their own mistake or lack of authority to transfer the funds: *Montrose Investment Ltd v Orion Nominees Ltd* (2004) 7 I.T.E.L.R. 255 at [24]–[25]; *Pulvers (a firm) v Chan* [2008] P.N.L.R. 9 at [380].

[2] [2009] Q.B. 376 at [40].

12-004 Pending the hearing of a proprietary claim a claimant is entitled almost as of right to an interim freezing injunction preserving the claimed assets until the outcome of the trial.[3]

## *B. Following, Tracing and Claiming*

12-005 If a trustee has legal title to trust property which she takes for herself and keeps in its original form, it is usually a simple matter for the beneficiaries to identify the property that forms the subject-matter of their proprietary claim. But more complicated situations can arise. If a trustee transfers legal title to trust property to a third party, the beneficiaries must "follow" the title from the trustee to the third party as an evidential preliminary to asserting an equitable proprietary claim against the third party, i.e. they must prove that title to property now held by the third party was previously held for the beneficiaries by the trustee. Again, if either a trustee or a third party recipient exchanges title to trust property for title to different property, the beneficiaries must "trace" from the old to the new title, i.e. they must demonstrate that the new title was exchanged for the old, before they can assert an equitable proprietary claim to the substitute property. As we shall see, the rules of tracing vary according to whether a "clean" or "mixed substitution" has taken place, the former occurring where the new asset is acquired solely with misapplied trust property, the latter occurring where the new asset is acquired with a mixture of misapplied trust property and the defendant's own property.[4]

12-006 In *Foskett v McKeown*, Lord Millett explained the relationship between following, tracing and claiming in these terms[5]:

> [Following and tracing] are both exercises in locating assets which are or may be taken to represent an asset belonging to the plaintiffs and to which they assert ownership . . . Following is the process of following the same asset as it moves from hand to hand. Tracing is the process of identifying a new asset as the substitute for the old. Where one asset is exchanged for another, a claimant can elect whether to follow the original asset into the hands of the new owner or to trace its value into the new asset in the hands of the same owner. . . . Tracing is also distinct from claiming. It identifies the traceable proceeds of the claimant's property. It enables the claimant to substitute the traceable proceeds for the original asset as the subject matter of his claim. But it does not affect or establish his claim. That will depend on a number of factors including the nature of his interest in the original asset . . . [and] his claim may also be exposed to potential defences as a result of intervening transactions.

12-007 Thus, it can been said that "the rules of following and tracing . . . [are] evidential in nature", and are distinct from "rules which determine substantive rights": "the former are concerned with identifying property in other hands or in another form; the latter with the rights that a claimant can assert against the property in its present form".[6] For the purposes of this chapter the relevance of the rules of following and tracing (which are discussed in section 2) is that these are often necessary precursors to proprietary claims by beneficiaries whose property has been misapplied by a trustee (which are discussed in section 3). However it should be borne in mind that the rules of following and tracing may also come into play in other cases, for example where beneficiaries bring an action in knowing receipt or

---

3 As in, e.g. *Independent Trustee Services Ltd v GP Noble Trustees Ltd* [2009] EWHC 161 (Ch); *UCB Home Loans Corp Ltd v Grace* [2011] EWHC 851 (Ch). If part of the proprietary claim is weak the court has discretion to grant the requested injunction only over part of the claimed assets: *Polly Peck International Plc v Nadir (No.2)* [1992] 4 All E.R. 769. On freezing injunctions generally, see paras 18–074ff.

4 *Foskett v McKeown* [2001] 1 A.C. 102 at 130.

5 ibid., at 127–128.

6 *Glencore International AG v Metro Trading International Ltd* [2001] 1 Lloyd's Rep. 284 at [180], per Moore-Bick J. See too *Boscawen v Bajwa* [1996] 1 W.L.R. 328 at 334; *Waxman v Waxman* (2004) 7 I.T.E.L.R. 162 at [582].

dishonest assistance for the purposes of which it must be proved that property received or handled by the defendant was misdirected trust property or its traceable proceeds[7]; or again, where a constructive trust is impressed on the profits of a breach of fiduciary duty the principal may need to use the tracing rules to claim property that is the traceable proceeds of the profits originally received by the fiduciary.[8]

In the passage which has been quoted above, Lord Millett speaks of a claimant "tracing the value" of an asset into a substitute asset, terminology which derives from Lionel Smith's book on the law of tracing.[9] This language signifies that the purpose of the tracing exercise is to identify the value inhering in one property right as representing the value inhering in another property right. As Tatiana Cutts has argued, however, this idea is problematic for a number of reasons.[10] If a defendant exchanges legal title to a painting worth £20,000 for legal title to a car worth £40,000, the rules of tracing hold that title to the car is the traceable substitute of title to the painting. From the point of view of a claimant who was the equitable beneficial owner of the painting, the fact that the car is worth more than the painting gives her a practical reason for wishing to assert an equitable proprietary interest in the car. But if we understand "value" simply to mean "market value", i.e. the measure of what a right is worth, then it is meaningless to say that the £20,000 value of the painting "has become" or "is now represented by" the £40,000 value of the car. On this understanding of "value", it has no abstract existence that makes it possible to track its movement from one right to another in the same way that the movement of legal rights can be tracked from one person to another. 12–008

It may be that Smith (and through his adoption of Smith's terminology, Lord Millett) uses the term "value" in a different sense, to connote the potential for exchange inherent in an assignable right. For example, he may mean that if a trustee holds title to a painting on trust and exchanges this for title to a car, the trustee has exploited the exchange potential inherent in one right to acquire another. The continuity provided by the tracing process is then sourced in the fact that it is a single actor—the trustee—who uses one right to acquire another. However, as Cutts has also demonstrated, this idea does not work for bank transfers, through which claimants are allowed to trace. Suppose that a trustee holds a bank account on trust and that she arranges a fund transfer of £10,000 to a recipient's bank account by asking her bank to debit the trust account and request a second bank to credit the recipient's account with an equivalent sum (the banks' reciprocal rights and obligations being mediated through the bank settlement system). Here, there is no "exchange" by a single actor and hence no continuity.[11] 12–009

For these reasons we agree with Cutts that talk of "tracing value" is misguided and distracting, and that it is preferable to speak of "tracing" solely in terms of evidential rules that enable claimants to show that one property right is the traceable substitute of another for the purposes of making claims including proprietary claims to the substitute property. As the Jersey Court of Appeal said in *Federal Republic of Brazil v Durant International Corp*[12]: 12–010

> The starting point is to recognise the true nature of the exercise with which the court is engaged when it is asked to trace a plaintiff's property . . . the court is being asked to identify an asset which represents the plaintiff's property, in other words an asset which is not in reality the plaintiff's original property but one which the law is prepared to treat as a 'substitute' for that original. That being the true nature of the

7 For discussion of which see Ch.11.

8 As in, e.g. *Attorney General for Hong Kong v Reid* [1994] 1 A.C. 324. See paras 13–126ff.

9 L.D. Smith, *The Law of Tracing* (Oxford University Press, 1997), p.119.

10 T. Cutts, '"There Is No Law of Tracing and This Is Why It Matters" Obligations VII Hong Kong 2014.

11 At p.144, Smith tries to explain bank transfers through the idea of "tracing in transit". The idea is that if X has a dog which she gives to Y on the understanding that Y will then give a cat to Z, we can say that X has effectively substituted the dog for the cat herself, with the result that the cat is the traceable product of the dog which can be followed into Z's hands. But bank transfers do not entail the transfer of any identifiable asset from one person to another.

12 2013 J.L.R. 273 at [48]–[49].

> process, . . . the court is liable to be making an evaluative judgment . . . [and] is accordingly making a policy choice as to whether the law is prepared to recognise one asset as representing, or as a substitute for, another on the particular facts of the case in hand.

## 2. Following and Tracing

### A. Following

12–011 Following legal title to misdirected trust property into the hands of a third party recipient often presents no great evidential difficulty, but problems can arise when the recipient mixes the property with other property in such a way that it loses its discrete identity.[13] Different rules are used to resolve these problems, according to whether the property has been incorporated into a fungible mixture, i.e. a mixture composed of mutually interchangeable units, each of which can readily be separated from the others without causing damage.[14]

#### i. Fungible Mixtures

12–012 Suppose that trust assets are mixed with other assets in such a way that no one can tell who has contributed what to the mixture, but it remains possible to divide the mixture into identical parts: suppose, for example, that trust crude oil is mixed with other crude oil,[15] or trust shares with other shares.[16] Where the whole mixture is still intact, the beneficiaries' contribution must still be somewhere in the mixture although it has lost its discrete identity, and so the rule in this case is that the beneficiaries can identify any proportionate part of the mixture as their property.[17]

12–013 However, if part of the mixture is consumed or transferred to a third party, the evidential problem becomes more acute. In this case no one can know whether the beneficiaries' contribution subsists in the remainder. Two rules are used to resolve this problem. In the absence of wrongdoing, the remainder is apportioned rateably between contributors to the mixture: e.g. if 10,000 barrels of trust oil are mixed with 50,000 barrels of oil belonging to others, and 30,000 barrels are consumed, one-sixth of the 30,000 barrels remaining (i.e. 5,000 barrels) are deemed to be trust oil.[18] However, where the mixing is done wrongfully, as in the case where a trustee fails to segregate trust assets from her own assets, a different rule applies, namely that evidential uncertainty created by wrongdoing is resolved against the wrongdoer.[19] This does not mean that the wrongdoer is debarred from following her own contribu-

---

13 See generally P. Birks, "Mixtures of Goods" in N. Palmer and E. McKendrick (eds), *Interests in Goods*, 2nd edn (Informa, 1993); P. Matthews, "The Limits of Common Law Tracing" in P. Birks (ed.), *Laundering and Tracing* (Oxford University Press, 1995), pp.42–46; Smith, *The Law of Tracing* (1997), Ch.2; R.J.W. Hickey, "Dazed and Confused: Accidental Mixtures of Goods and the Theory of Acquisition of Title" (2003) 66 M.L.R. 368.

14 *Rysaffe Trustee Co (CI) Ltd v IRC* [2002] S.T.C. 872 at [32]; *Glencore International AG v Alpina Insurance Co Ltd (No.2)* [2004] 1 All E.R. (Comm.) 858 at [16]. See too J. Austin, *Lectures on Jurisprudence*, 4th edn (J. Murray, 1879), p.807; R. Goode, "Are Intangible Assets Fungible?" in P. Birks and A. Pretto (eds), *Themes in Comparative Law* (Oxford University Press, 2002).

15 *Indian Oil Corp. v Greenstone Shipping SA* [1988] Q.B. 345; *Glencore International AG v Metro Trading International Ltd* [2001] 1 Lloyd's Rep. 284.

16 *Brady v Stapleton* (1952) 88 C.L.R. 322.

17 *Lupton v White* (1808) 15 Ves. Jun. 432 at 441; *Indian Oil Corp v Greenstone Shipping SA* [1988] Q.B. 345 at 369–371; *Foskett v McKeown* [2001] 1 A.C. 102 at 143; *Glencore International AG v Metro Trading International Ltd* [2001] 1 Lloyd's Rep. 284 at [185].

18 *Spence v Union Marine Insurance Co* (1868) L.R. 3 C.P. 427.

19 This is a rule of general application in the law of evidence: *Armory v Delamirie* (1722) 1 Str. 505; *Infabrics Ltd v Jaytex Ltd* [1985] F.S.R. 75.

tion into the mixture, but it does mean that losses from the mixture are deemed to have come out of her portion first.[20] So, for example, if a trustee mixes 100 tons of trust gravel with 100 tons of her own gravel, and 80 tons of gravel are then stolen out of the mixture, the trustee can identify 20 tons of the remaining gravel as her own, but she must allow the beneficiaries to identify the remainder as theirs.

### ii. Non-Fungible Mixtures

The process of following legal title to property inevitably comes to an end if the property is destroyed. The law provides that it also comes to an end because the property is deemed to have been destroyed, in three situations: 12–014

- where the asset is physically attached to another, "dominant", asset so that it would cause serious damage, or be disproportionately expensive, to separate the two: here the asset is said to "accede" to the dominant asset[21];
- where the asset is physically attached to land in such a way that it would cause serious damage, or be disproportionately expensive, to separate the two: here the asset is said to become a "fixture" on the land[22]; and
- where the asset is combined with other items to create a wholly new product, under the doctrine of "specification".[23]

At least in the case of specification, however, these rules are modified where the mixing is performed by a wrongdoer. Here, despite the creation of the new thing, the owner of the assets which are wrongfully used to create the new asset can follow her assets into the new asset. So, in *Jones v De Marchant*,[24] a man wrongfully took 18 beaver skins belonging to his wife and used them, together with four skins of his own, to have a fur coat made up which he gave to his mistress. The wife was allowed to recover the coat, a result which can only be explained on the basis that she was permitted to follow her property into the new asset. 12–015

## *B. Tracing*

The rules on tracing resemble the rules on following, to the extent that they also provide that gains and losses to a mixture must be shared rateably between innocent contributors to the mixture. They also provide that evidential uncertainty created by wrongdoing must be resolved against the wrongdoer. 12–016

---

20 *Harris v Truman* (1881) 7 Q.B.D. 340 at 358, affirmed (1882) 9 Q.B.D. 264; *Indian Oil Corp v Greenstone Shipping SA* [1988] Q.B. 345 at 370–371; *Foskett v McKeown* [2001] 1 A.C. 102 at 132; *Glencore International AG v Metro Trading International Ltd* [2001] 1 Lloyd's Rep. 284 at [159] and [182].

21 *Hendy Lennox (Industrial Engines) Ltd v Grahame Puttick Ltd* [1984] 1 W.L.R. 485; *McKeown v Cavalier Yachts Pty Ltd* (1988) 13 N.S.W.L.R. 303 at 311. Which of two assets accedes to the other depends on which is the "dominant" entity, a point which is decided rather impressionistically by reference to overall physical significance rather than monetary value. The doctrine of "accession" derives from the Roman doctrine of *accessio*.

22 *Hobson v Gorringe* [1897] 1 Ch. 182; *Reynolds v Ashby & Son* [1904] A.C. 466; *Melluish (Inspector of Taxes) v BMI (No.3) Ltd* [1996] A.C. 454; *Elitestone Ltd v Morris* [1997] 1 W.L.R. 687; *Chelsea Yacht & Boat Co Ltd v Pope* [2000] 1 W.L.R. 1941; *Savoye v Spicers Ltd* [2015] Bus. L.R. 242 at [26]–[35]. See too H.N. Bennett, "Attachment of Chattels to Land" in Palmer and McKendrick (eds), *Interests in Goods*, 2nd edn (1993).

23 *International Banking Corp v Ferguson, Shaw & Sons* 1910 S.C. 182; *Borden (UK) Ltd v Scottish Timber Products Ltd* [1981] Ch. 25. The doctrine derives from the Roman doctrine of *specificatio*.

24 (1916) 28 D.L.R. 561, endorsed in *Foskett v McKeown* [2001] 1 A.C. 102 at 132–133. See too *Spence v Union Marine Insurance Co Ltd* (1868) L.R. 3 C.P. 427 at [437]–[438]; *Sandeman & Sons v Tyzack and Branfoot Steamship Co Ltd* [1923] A.C. 680 at 694–695. An attempt to extend the principle to mixtures of ideas leading to the creation of a patentable product failed in *IDA Ltd v University of Southampton* [2006] R.P.C. 21 at [40]–[42].

### i. Where a Trustee Mixes Trust Money with Her Own Money

12–017 Suppose that a trustee mixes £10,000 of her own money with £10,000 of trust money in such a way that the funds lose their separate identities. Suppose further that she takes £10,000 out of the mixture and dissipates it. It is impossible to say whose money has been lost and whose money remains. Where the mixing has taken place in a bank account the courts could conceivably have solved this evidential problem by using the "first in, first out" rule in *Clayton's* case,[25] which is discussed below.[26] In *Re Hallett's Estate*,[27] however, the Court of Appeal held that the "first in, first out" rule does not apply in this situation, and instead the court resolved the evidential uncertainty by deeming the trustee to have done the right thing by keeping the beneficiaries' money intact and spending his own money. In Jessel MR's words[28]:

> where a man does an act which may be rightfully performed . . . he is not allowed to say against the person entitled to the property or the right that he has done it wrongfully.

12–018 Suppose, again, that a trustee mixes £10,000 of her own money with £10,000 of trust money in such a way that the funds lose their separate identities. But now suppose that she takes £10,000 out of the mixture and uses it to buy a painting, and that she dissipates the remaining £10,000. In this situation, too, Equity resolves the evidential uncertainty against the trustee by deeming her to have used the beneficiaries' money to buy the painting. This is the rule in *Re Oatway*, where Joyce J said that the trustee[29]

> cannot maintain that the investment which remains represents his money alone and what has been spent and can no longer be traced or recovered was money belonging to the trust.

Joyce J also held that if the mixing takes place in a bank account, the "first in, first out" rule does not apply in this situation either.[30]

12–019 A third situation might arise, which requires us to ask whether beneficiaries can "cherry-pick" between the rule in *Re Hallett's Estate* and the rule in *Re Oatway*? Suppose that a trustee mixes £10,000 of her own money with £10,000 of trust money in such a way that the funds lose their separate identities, that she takes £10,000 out of the mixture and uses it to buy a painting that triples in value, but that £10,000 is left. Is the governing authority *Re Hallett's Estate*, deeming the trustee to have kept the beneficiaries' £10,000 intact, or is it *Re Oatway*, deeming the painting to have been bought with trust money?

12–020 This question was considered in *Shalson v Russo*,[31] where Rimer J said this[32]:

> Normally, it is presumed that if a trustee uses money from a fund in which he has mixed trust money with his own, he uses his own money first: *Re Hallett's Estate*. But [counsel] submits that this is not an inflexible

---

25 (1816) 1 Mer. 529.
26 See paras 12–025ff.
27 (1880) 13 Ch. D. 696.
28 ibid., at [727]. See too *Halley v Law Society* [2002] EWHC 139 (Ch) at [160]. For discussion, see G. Virgo, "*Re Hallett's Estate* (1879–80)" in C. Mitchell and P. Mitchell (eds), *Landmark Cases in Equity* (Hart Publishing, 2012).
29 [1903] 2 Ch. 356 at 360. See too *Grey v Haig* (1855) 20 Beav. 214 at 226.
30 ibid., at 360–361: "The order of priority in which the various withdrawals and investments may have been respectively made is wholly immaterial."
31 [2005] Ch. 281.
32 ibid., at [144].

> rule and that if the trustee can be shown to have made an early application of the mixed fund into an investment, the beneficiary is entitled to claim that for himself. He says, and I agree, that this is supported by *Re Oatway*. The justice of this is that, if the beneficiary is not entitled to do this, the wrongdoing trustee may be left with all the cherries and the victim with nothing.

The same question then arose in a second case, *Turner v Jacob*, where it appears that *Shalson* was not cited to the judge, Patten J. He interpreted *Re Oatway* to stand for the rather different proposition that[33] **12–021**

> where the trustee maintains in the account an amount equal to the remaining trust fund, the beneficiary's right to trace is limited to that fund. It is not open to the beneficiary to assert a lien against an investment made using monies out of the mixed account unless the sum expended is of such a size that it must have included trust monies or the balance remaining in the account after the investment is then expended so as to become untraceable.

The authorities are therefore inconsistent. We believe Patten J's statement of the decision in *Re Oatway* to be closer than Rimer J's statement to what the case actually decided. However we prefer Rimer J's view of the merits. If the principle that underlies the law in this area is that presumptions should be made against trustees who wrongfully create evidential uncertainty by mixing trust property with their own property, we believe that this principle should extend to giving beneficiaries the right to choose whichever presumption produces the best result for them. **12–022**

Because the rules in *Re Hallett's Estate* and *Re Oatway* are designed to resolve evidential uncertainty they do not apply in a situation that is not evidentially uncertain. Suppose that a trustee mixes £50,000 of her own money and £50,000 of trust money and places the mixture in an empty bank account. Suppose that she withdraws £80,000, dissipates it, and then adds another £30,000 of her own money, with the result that there is now £50,000 in the account. Here, the beneficiaries cannot invoke the rule in *Re Hallett's Estate* to identify more than £20,000 in the account as their property because it is not evidentially uncertain that at least £30,000 of the remaining funds came from the trustee's own resources. This rule, established in *James Roscoe (Bolton) Ltd v Winder*,[34] is known as "the lowest intermediate balance rule": "absent any payment in of money with the intention of making good earlier depredations, tracing cannot occur through a mixed account for any larger sum than is the lowest balance in the account between the time the beneficiary's money goes in, and the time the remedy is sought."[35] **12–023**

### ii. Where a Trustee Mixes Trust Funds Together

If trust funds are mixed together and the beneficiaries are equally innocent victims of the trustee's wrongdoing, the beneficiaries will generally have equally strong claims to a rateable share of gains, **12–024**

---

33 [2008] W.T.L.R. 307 at [102].

34 [1915] 1 Ch. 62, endorsed in *Re Goldcorp Exchange Ltd* [1995] 1 A.C. 74 at 107–108, also in *Bishopsgate Investment Management Ltd v Homan* [1995] Ch. 211 at 219, 220. See too *Re Graphicshppe Ltd* (2005) 78 O.R. (3d) 401; *Boughner v Greyhawk Equity Partners Ltd* [2013] ONCA 26.

35 *Re French Caledonia Travel Service Pty Ltd* (2003) 59 N.S.W.L.R. 361 at [175], per Campbell J. For application of the principle where goods are successively withdrawn and deposited in a mixed bulk, see *Glencore International AG v Metro Trading International Ltd* [2001] 1 Lloyd's Rep. 284 at [201]–[202], revisited in *Glencore International AG v Alpina Insurance Co Ltd (No.2)* [2004] 1 All E.R. (Comm.) 858 at [14]–[20]. For a case falling within the scope of Campbell J's proviso, see *Westdeutsche Landesbank Girozentrale v Islington LBC* [1994] 4 All E.R. 890 at 939 (not considered on appeal).

and equally weak claims to avoid taking a rateable share of losses, to the mixed fund.[36] Hence, gains and losses are generally shared between the beneficiaries pro rata: this is the rule in *Re Diplock*.[37]

12–025 Until recently, there was thought to be an exception to this rule, deriving from *Clayton's* case.[38] This case concerned a dispute centring on the appropriation of payments as between a bank and its customer,[39] but it later came to be understood as an authority for the rule that if a trustee places money belonging to two different sets of beneficiaries into the same unbroken running account,[40] any withdrawals that she makes from the account are deemed to be made in the same order as the payments in, on a "first in, first out" basis.[41] Thus, for example, if she puts £10,000 from Trust A into her bank account, then puts in £10,000 from Trust B, and then withdraws £10,000 and loses it (or uses it to buy an asset which triples in value), the loss (or gain) will be attributed solely to the beneficiaries of Trust A.

12–026 As between the beneficiaries of Trust A and Trust B this is an arbitrary and unfair result, and for this reason the "first in, first out" rule has been discarded in many Commonwealth jurisdictions, in favour of the *Re Diplock* pro rata approach.[42] In *Barlow Clowes International Ltd v Vaughan*,[43] the Court of Appeal reaffirmed the general application of *Clayton's* case in English law, except where its application would be impracticable or would result in injustice between the parties. But more recent English cases suggest that the rule will now be applied only very rarely, if at all, for the courts are now swift to find that the rule is an impracticable or unjust method of resolving disputes between the victims of shared misfortune, particularly in cases of large-scale fraud.[44]

12–027 *Barlow Clowes* concerned the liquidation of an investment company whose fraudulent managers had stolen most of the company's assets, leaving thousands of investors out of pocket. The question arose as to how the surviving assets should be distributed between the investors. The court held that the rule in *Clayton's* case should not be used to resolve this question because the investors had all intended that their money should be pooled in a single fund for investment purposes, so that it would conform with their original intentions if they all shared rateably in what remained in the pool.

---

[36] But it seems that if a trustee mixes two trust funds in one account and then purports to withdraw a sum for the beneficiary of one trust but actually uses it for her own purposes then that sum should be allocated to that particular trust: *Re Stillman and Wilson* (1950) 15 A.B.C. 68; *Re Registered Securities Ltd* [1991] 1 N.Z.L.R. 545. Quaere whether these cases can be reconciled with the principal that a wrongdoing trustee's intentions are generally irrelevant (see paras 12–045—12–046)?

[37] [1948] Ch. 465 at 533, 534 and 539. See also *Edinburgh Corp v Lord Advocate* (1879) 4 App. Cas. 823.

[38] (1816) 1 Mer. 529. For the history of the case see Smith, *The Law of Tracing* (1997), pp.183–194; *Re French Caledonia Travel Service Pty Ltd* (2003) 59 N.S.W.L.R. 361 at [20]–[172].

[39] This aspect of the rule established by the case has a continued practical significance for the relationship between banks and their customers, as discussed in P. Hood, "*Clayton's* Case and Connected Matters" [2013] J.R. 501.

[40] e.g. a bank account or a solicitor's trust account. The rule does not apply where there are distinct and separate debts: *The Mecca* [1897] A.C. 286; *Re Sherry* (1884) 25 Ch. D. 692 at 702. Nor does the rule apply to entries on the same day: it is the end-of-day balance which counts: *The Mecca* at 291.

[41] *Pennell v Deffell* (1853) 4 De G.M. & G. 372; *Hancock v Smith* (1889) 41 Ch. D. 456 at [461]; *Re Stenning* [1895] 2 Ch. 433; *Re Diplock* [1948] Ch. 465 at 553–554.

[42] *Re Ontario Securities Commission* (1985) 30 D.L.R. (4th) 1, affirmed (1998) 52 D.L.R. (4th) 767; *Re Registered Securities Commission* [1991] 1 N.Z.L.R. 545; *Keefe v Law Society of New South Wales* (1998) 44 N.S.W.L.R. 451; *ASIC v Enterprise Solutions 2000 Pty Ltd* [2001] Q.S.C. 82; *Re Esteem Settlement* 2002 J.L.R. 53; *Re French Caledonia Travel Service Pty Ltd* (2003) 59 N.S.W.L.R. 361; *Re International Investment Unit Trust* [2005] 1 N.Z.L.R. 270.

[43] [1992] 4 All E.R. 22.

[44] *El Ajou v Dollar Land Holdings Plc (No.2)* [1995] 2 All E.R. 213 at 222; *Russell-Cooke Trust Co v Prentis* [2003] 2 All E.R. 478 at 495; *Commerzbank Aktiengesellschaft v IMB Morgan Plc* [2005] Lloyd's Rep. 298 at [43]–[49]; *Re Ahmed & Co* (2006) 8 I.T.E.L.R. 779 at [131]–[138]; *Charity Commission v Framjee* [2015] 1 W.L.R. 16 at [49]. In *El Ajou (No.2)*, at 223–224, Robert Walker J held that where A and B's money is mixed in an account and *Clayton's* case deems A's money (and not B's) to have been paid to D, B can still trace into the money received by D and claim against her if A makes no claim and is unlikely to do so. This finding was followed in *Campden Hill Ltd v Chakrani* [2005] EWHC 911 (Ch) at [76]–[77].

However, Woolf and Leggatt LJJ[45] also indicated that a "rolling charge" solution might be fairer than rateable sharing so that claimants should share losses and gains to the fund in proportion to their interest in the fund immediately prior to each withdrawal.

This would work as follows. Suppose that a trustee pays £2,000 from Trust A and then £4,000 from Trust B into an empty current bank account. She then withdraws £3,000 and loses it. She then pays in £3,000 from Trust C before withdrawing another £3,000 to buy shares whose value increases tenfold. She then withdraws the remaining £3,000 and loses it. Applying the "rolling charge" rule, the first loss must be borne by A and B in the ratio 1:2, and C need not bear this loss at all. Immediately after the first withdrawal the remaining £3,000 would be attributed to A and B in the ratio 1:2, and after the next deposit, the £6,000 in the account would be attributable to A, B, and C in the ratio 1:2:3. Hence, the shares should be attributed to them in the same proportion, leaving A with shares worth £5,000, B with shares worth £10,000 and C with shares worth £15,000. In contrast, the pro rata rule would attribute all gains and losses in proportion to the total contributions made by each Trust, giving a ratio of 2:4:3, leaving A with shares worth £6,667, B with shares worth £13,333, and C with shares worth £10,000. The "first in, first out" rule, meanwhile, would produce the result that all of A's money is lost, that £1,000 of B's money is lost, that all of the shares belong to B, and that all of C's money is lost. 12-028

In *Shalson v Russo*,[46] Rimer J suggested that the rolling charge rule should always be used to resolve cases of this kind, because the pro rata rule ignores evidence of what has actually happened to the claimants' money: thus, in the example, we know that no part of Trust C's £3,000 can have gone into the trustee's first withdrawal, suggesting that Trust C should not have to share this loss with Trust A and Trust B. Rimer J's position can be supported by reference to *Roscoe v Winder*,[47] but in a case involving thousands of investors and millions of deposits and withdrawals, the expense and practical difficulties of assembling the raw data needed to apply the rolling charge rule may be prohibitive, leaving the courts with a choice between the rough justice of the pro rata rule, and the even rougher justice of "first in, first out". In *Charity Commission v Framjee*,[48] a case where similar evidential problems arose, Henderson J applied the pro rata rule. 12-029

### iii. Where Recipients of Trust Money Mix It with Their Own Money

Where a trustee misdirects trust property to a bona fide purchaser for value without notice of the beneficiaries' equitable interest, they may be able to follow the property into her hands and trace through any mixtures and substitutions that she later carries out into new property. However it will be pointless for them to undertake this exercise as she will have a defence to any proprietary claim that they might bring.[49] 12-030

Where a trustee misdirects trust property to a recipient who is not a bona fide purchaser, the beneficiaries may well wish to follow the property into the recipient's hands and then trace through her subsequent mixtures and substitutions into new property against which they can claim. The tracing rules that apply in this case will vary according to whether the recipient has acted in good faith. 12-031

If she is a bona fide volunteer, the rules governing the situation will be the same as those which govern the case where money belonging to the innocent beneficiaries of separate trust funds is mixed 12-032

45 *Barlow Clowes* at 35, 44.
46 [2005] Ch. 281 at [150].
47 [1915] 1 Ch. 62, discussed in para.12-023.
48 [2015] 1 W.L.R. 16.
49 For discussion of the bona fide purchase defence, see paras 12-117ff.

together by the trustee.[50] Gains and losses will be shared rateably, possibly subject to the rule in *Clayton's* case[51] if the court sees fit to apply it.[52]

12-033 If the recipient takes the property with knowledge of the breach of trust, then whether or not she gives value in exchange for the property, she cannot innocently mix it with her own property. She will owe the beneficiaries a duty as constructive trustee to account to them for the trust property.[53] Hence if she mixes it with her own property she will be counted as a wrongdoer,[54] and the case will be governed by the same rules as those which govern the case where an express trustee wrongfully mixes trust funds with her own money: evidential uncertainties will be resolved against the trustee.[55]

### iv. Payment of Debts

12-034 Like the process of following property rights from hand to hand, the process of tracing through mixtures and substitutions must come to an end when the trust property or its traceable proceeds are dissipated or destroyed. So, if a trustee (or third party recipient) uses trust funds to buy a meal which she consumes, or a house which burns down, then her purchases leave no traceable residue (assuming that the house is uninsured): nothing is left in her hands to which the beneficiaries might assert a proprietary claim. As the Court of Appeal stated in *Re Diplock*[56]:

> The equitable remedies [available to beneficiaries making proprietary claims] presuppose the continued existence of the [trust] money either as a separate fund or as part of a mixed fund or as latent in property acquired by means of such a fund. If such continued existence is not established equity is . . . helpless.

12-035 The rule that the tracing process comes to an end when property is dissipated generally applies in the case where a defendant uses trust money to pay off a debt. The most common example of this in practice arises where money is paid into an overdrawn bank account, a situation discussed by the New Zealand Court of Appeal in *Rea v Russell*.[57]

*Rea v Russell*

New Zealand Court of Appeal [2012] NZCA 536 at [42]–[45]

12-036 O'REGAN P. AND FRENCH AND ASHER JJ.: When money is paid into a bank account, the money as such does not remain identifiable. It becomes legally and beneficially the property of the bank and not the account holder. An asset is substituted for the money that is paid into the bank, that asset being the debt of the bank back to the account holder. To put it the other way, the account holder no longer has the money, but has a chose in action against the bank. The money is not traced in and out of the account as there is no traceable money in the account. Rather, a single debt (the chose in action) can be identified that

---

50 *Re Diplock* [1948] Ch. 465 at 524 and 539.

51 *Re Diplock* [1948] Ch. 465 at 554.

52 See paras 12-026—12-029. If the recipient pays the trust money into an interest-bearing account designated as a trust account as soon as she learns of the trust claim, this will be regarded as effectively unmixing the fund so that the trust claim will then relate only to the money in the designated account: *Re Diplock* [1948] Ch. 465 at 551–552, dealing with the claim against the National Institute for the Deaf, reversed on an amended statement of the facts: ibid., at 559.

53 See paras 11-074ff.

54 *Boscawen v Bajwa* [1996] 1 W.L.R. 328 at 336–338; *Banton v CIBC Trust Corp* (2001) 197 D.L.R. (4th) 212.

55 See paras 12-017—12-023.

56 [1948] Ch. 465 at 521.

57 See too *Northern Counties of England Fire Insurance Co v Whipp* (1884) 26 Ch.D. 482 at 495–496; *Thomson v Clydesdale Bank Ltd* [1893] A.C. 282; *Bishopsgate Investment Management Ltd v Homan* [1995] Ch. 211. Where a defendant has several accounts with a bank, the asset into which a deposit can be traced is the net balance due from the bank on *all* of the accounts, and not only the account to which the deposit is credited: *Cooper v PRG Powerhouse Ltd* [2008] 2 All E.R. (Comm.) 964 at [32].

is of an amount equal to the final credit of the account holder.[58] The new asset, the chose in action, can be traced in place of the old property.

In the case of a payment into an overdrawn account, there is no new asset created, as there is no debt of the bank to the account holder that is created, and the account holder gains no chose in action against the bank. Instead, the account holder's debt to the bank is in whole or in part repaid. The monies paid by the account holder can no longer be identified and there is no property or replacement asset that can be restored. This position was recognised in New Zealand by this Court in *Re Registered Securities Ltd* where Somers J. stated:[59] 12-037

> ". . . as a matter of logic it seems evident that where a claimant's money is paid into an overdrawn account there is no fund or property to which resort can be had. Nor does the position seem different when the account is further overdrawn and the additional sum is expended on some identifiable property. In such a case it is not possible to show that the claimant's money contributed to the new purchase."

The Court relied on the English decision of *Re Tilley's W.T.*,[60] and the Australian decision of *Re Goode*.[61] In the latter case it was held that where a bank account was always in debit, money paid into that account was dissipated and could not be traced. The Court also referred to *Re Diplock*[62] where tracing was refused in the case of funds mistakenly paid to charities and the monies applied by the charities to pay off a debt. The Privy Council also relied on *Re Diplock* in *Re Goldcorp Exchange Ltd (In rec)*[63] where it was observed that monies said to be impressed by a trust and paid into an overdrawn account thereupon cease to exist.[64] 12-038

Thus, it is not possible to trace into an overdrawn account as the money wrongfully paid is not represented by property . . . 12-039

There are two exceptions to the principle that tracing comes to an end when trust money is used to pay off a debt. First, if the debt was secured by a charge over the defendant's property, Equity can treat the debt and the charge, by a legal fiction, as though they have not been extinguished by the payment, enabling the beneficiaries to be treated as though they can trace into the creditor's subsisting chose in action against the defendant.[65] 12-040

Secondly, and more controversially, if a defendant borrows money and uses it to buy an asset, and later uses trust money to repay her creditor, the beneficiaries can arguably trace "backwards" through the loan transaction into the asset and identify the asset as the traceable proceeds of the trust money.[66] The English authorities which directly consider this point are not particularly strong,[67] but "backwards tracing" was implicitly approved by the Court of Appeal in *Relfo Ltd (In Liquidation) v Varsani*.[68] 12-041

---

58 *Foskett v McKeown* [2001] 1 A.C. 102 at 128.

59 [1991] 1 N.Z.L.R. 545 at 554.

60 [1967] 1 Ch. 1179 at 1193.

61 (1974) 4 A.L.R. 579 at 593.

62 [1948] 1 Ch. 465 at 548–550.

63 [1994] 3 N.Z.L.R. 385 at 405. See also the detailed analysis in *Shalson v Russo* [2005] Ch. 281 at 138–140.

64 The same observation was made in *Fortex Group Ltd v MacIntosh* [1990] 3 N.Z.L.R. 171 at 181.

65 *Boscawen v Bajwa* [1996] 1 W.L.R. 328 at 340, rejecting *Re Diplock* [1948] Ch. 465 at 549–550; *Primlake Ltd (In Liquidation) v Matthews Assocs* [2007] 1 B.C.L.C. 666 at 340. As discussed at para.12–102, the point of this is that the beneficiaries can then acquire the fictionally subsisting security via subrogation and enforce it for their own benefit.

66 L.D. Smith, "Tracing into the Payment of a Debt" [1995] C.L.J. 290, esp. 292–295, expanded in Smith, *The Law of Tracing* (1997), pp.146–152.

67 "Backwards tracing" has the support of Dillon LJ in *Bishopsgate Investment Management Ltd v Homan* [1995] Ch. 211 at 216–217 (but was disapproved in the same case by Leggatt LJ at 221 and 222). It was also adopted by Hobhouse J in *Westdeutsche Landesbank Girozentrale v Islington LBC* [1994] 4 All E.R. 890 at 939–940 (approved by CA without comment); by Scott VC in *Foskett v McKeown* [1998] Ch. 265 at 283–284 (not considered on appeal to HL); by Rimer J in *Shalson v Russo* [2005] Ch. 281 at [144] (obiter); and (in effect) by David Richards QC, sitting as a deputy High Court judge in *Law Society v Haider* [2003] EWHC 2486 (Ch) at [40]–[41]. For the view that these cases do not amount to support for "backwards tracing" in English law, see M. Conaglen, "Difficulties with Tracing Backwards" (2011) 127 L.Q.R. 432.

68 [2015] 1 B.C.L.C. 14.

12-042 In *Relfo*, the defendant's bank account in Singapore was credited with some USD 880,000, which was held to be the traceable product of £500,000 transferred out of the claimant company's bank account by a director acting beyond the scope of his authority. Among other claims brought by the company it sued the defendant for knowing receipt. For the purposes of this claim the company had to trace from the chose in action constituted by the company's bank account into the chose in action constituted by the defendant's bank account. There was direct evidence, first, that the director had improperly caused the company to transfer £500,000 from its account to the Latvian account of a second company, Mirren, and, secondly, that earlier on the same day, a corresponding USD amount (minus 1.3 per cent) had been transferred from the Lithuanian account of a third company, Intertrade, to the defendant's Singapore account. There was no direct evidence of any intermediate transactions that "joined up" these two funds transfers. Nevertheless the Court of Appeal upheld Sales J's finding at first instance that he could infer from the surrounding circumstances of the two transfers that such intermediate transactions had taken place as part of a money-laundering operation orchestrated by the director's shady Ukrainian contacts in exchange for a 1.3 per cent "handling fee".[69]

12-043 The relevance of the Court of Appeal's decision for the "backwards tracing" point has been explained by Stephen Watterson[70]:

> [The court's] conclusion, that the Intertrade payment represented the traceable proceeds of Relfo's funds . . . raised a problem of chronology. The Intertrade payment was made before the sums credited to Mirren's account, from Relfo, were paid from that account. The Court of Appeal did not think this precluded a tracing connection. Without taking any general position on the possibility of 'backwards tracing', the Court effectively assumed that, if B pays C, before B is paid by A, a qualifying tracing connection can exist between the two payments (B-C, A-B), at least if (1) B paid C pursuant to a prior arrangement with A, under which A would reimburse B from the misappropriated funds, and (2) A subsequently used those funds to reimburse B in this way . . .

12-044 Similar issues also arose in *Federal Republic of Brazil v Durant International Corp* where the Jersey Court of Appeal endorsed the principle that[71]:

> at least in cases where . . . the account in question remains in credit throughout the relevant period, there is no question of possible insolvency and prejudice to unsecured creditors, and there is no suggestion of any intervention by a *bona fide* purchaser for value . . . [tracing is possible where] there is sufficient evidence to establish a clear link between credits and debits to an account, irrespective (within a reasonable timeframe) of the order in which they occur or the state of the balance on the account.

### v. The Role of Intention

12-045 Backwards tracing was an issue in *Foskett v McKeown* in the Court of Appeal, where Scott VC expressed the view that beneficiaries should be allowed to trace "backwards" through the payment of a debt with trust money into an asset purchased with the borrowed money only if they could prove that it was the trustee's intention at the time of borrowing the money to repay the lender with trust money.[72]

---

69 cf. *Federal Republic of Brazil v Durant International Corp* 2013 J.L.R. 273 at [42]–[43], where the Jersey CA rejected the defendant's contention that "direct evidence of every movement of funds" is needed to establish tracing links as an over-formalistic reading of Buckley LJ's dictum in *Borden (UK) Ltd v Scottish Timber Products Ltd* [1981] Ch. 25 at 46, that claimants must identify their money "at every stage of its journey through life". The same point is also made in *Toksoz v Westpac Banking Corp* [2014] NSWCA 199 at [8]–[9].

70 S. Watterson, "Recovering Misapplied Corporate Assets from Remoter Recipients" (2014) 73 C.L.J. 496, pp.497–498.

71 2013 J.L.R. 273 at [61], approving at 2012 J.L.R. 356 at [219].

72 [1998] Ch. 265 at 283–284.

No doubt he was concerned that beneficiaries might otherwise be able to "backwards trace" into every asset bought by a trustee with money withdrawn from an overdrawn account into which the trustee later pays trust money. However, the tracing rules are not generally concerned with a defendant's intentions, but with establishing that one property right was actually exchanged for another, or with deeming it to have been exchanged for another in cases where the defendant cannot prove that it was not.[73] As Ungoed-Thomas J stated in *Re Tilley's Will Trusts*[74]

> if, having regard to all the circumstances of the case objectively considered, it appears that the trustee has in fact, whatever his intention, laid out trust moneys in or towards a purchase, then the beneficiaries are entitled to the property purchased and any profits which it produces to the extent to which it has been paid for out of the trust money.

The law's focus on transactional links may seem to produce some unpalatable results. Suppose that a trustee misdirects £5 of trust money to an innocent donee, X, who uses it to buy a winning lottery ticket that pays out £1 million. X can prove that she could have used her own resources to buy the ticket, and that she would have done so if she had known the improper provenance of the trust money. Nonetheless, the beneficiaries can say that the £1 million are the traceable proceeds of the trust money. Again, suppose that a trustee steals £5,000 of trust money and uses it to pay her rent, and then uses another £5,000 of her own to buy a diamond. The beneficiaries cannot trace into the ring even if they can prove that the trustee could not have afforded to pay the rent and buy the jewel out of her own resources. In our view, however, the answer to problems of the former sort does not lie in reformulating the tracing rules by requiring beneficiaries to prove causal rather than transactional links between misapplied trust property and substitute assets,[75] but in revisiting the rules of claiming the fruits of misdirected trust property.[76] So far as the problems of the latter sort are concerned, we are not convinced that the beneficiaries should have anything more than a personal claim against the trustee. **12–046**

### vi. The Swollen Assets Theory

*Space Investments Ltd v Canadian Imperial Bank of Commerce Trust Co*[77] concerned a bank trustee that was empowered by the trust instrument to lend trust money to itself. The bank lawfully exercised this power, and then went into liquidation. The beneficiaries could not trace their money into any particular surviving asset and so the Privy Council held that their claims ranked as unsecured debts. In obiter dicta, however, Lord Templeman contrasted the facts of the case with the situation where a bank trustee unlawfully takes trust money and the beneficiaries cannot trace their money into any particular surviving asset. Here, in his Lordship's view, "equity allows the beneficiaries to trace the trust money to all the assets of the bank and to recover the trust money by the exercise of an equitable charge over all the assets of the bank."[78] **12–047**

---

73 Similarly, the rules of following are concerned with identifying the current whereabouts of particular assets, and with deeming them to be in particular locations when no-one can say where they have actually gone. See further Smith, *The Law of Tracing* (1997) pp. 69–70, 82–85 and 136–139.

74 [1967] Ch. 1179 at 1193.

75 As urged in D.A. Oesterle, "Deficiencies of the Restitutionary Right to Trace" (1983) 68 Cornell L.R. 172; C. Rotherham, "The Metaphysics of Tracing: Substituted Title and Property Rhetoric" [1996] Osgoode Hall L.J. 321; S. Evans, "Rethinking Tracing and the Law of Restitution" (1999) 115 L.Q.R. 469.

76 See further paras 12–057ff.

77 [1986] 3 All E.R. 75.

78 *Space Investments* [1986] 3 All E.R. 75 at 76–77, overlooking *Re Hallett & Co* [1894] 2 Q.B. 237 at 245.

12–048 To support this statement he cited Jessel MR's comment in *Re Hallett's Estate*,[79] that "if a man mixes trust funds with his own, the whole will be treated as trust property". However, this was to misread Jessel MR's judgment, which was concerned with the case where a trustee mixes £X of trust money with £Y of his own money in a particular account and then dissipates part of the mixture. Jessel MR said nothing to support Lord Templeman's assertion that in such a case the whole of the trustee's assets constitutes one colossal fund which should be regarded as having been mixed with the trust money, so that if the money in the account is dissipated the beneficiaries can simply switch their attention to some other asset in the trustee's hands. Moreover, Lord Templeman's analysis is inconsistent with the *Roscoe v Winder* principle discussed earlier,[80] that presumptions are made against wrongdoing trustees only where there is evidential uncertainty. In a case where it is certain that a trustee has dissipated trust money out of a particular bank account, this principle prevents the beneficiaries from arguing that some other asset in the trustee's hands should be deemed to represent the traceable proceeds of their property. Essentially for this reason, Lord Templeman's dicta were repudiated by the Court of Appeal in *Serious Fraud Office v Lexi Holdings Plc (in administration)*.[81]

12–049 *Sinclair Investments (UK) Ltd v Versailles Trade Finance Ltd (in admin rec'ship)*[82] concerned a fraud whereby money belonging to a company (TPL) was misdirected into a complex set of transactions referred to as "cross-firing arrangements", the point of which was to create the false impression that a second company (VTFL) had a larger turnover than was actually the case. The question arose whether the complexity and obscurity of these cross-firing arrangements made it impossible to trace through them into surviving assets because the money had effectively disappeared into a "black hole" or "maelstrom". Lord Neuberger MR held that[83]

> [tracing does not come to an end] simply because the defaulting fiduciary, while still holding much of the money, has acted particularly dishonestly or cunningly by creating a maelstrom. Where he has mixed the funds held on trust with his own funds, the onus should be on the fiduciary to establish that part, and what part, of the mixed fund is his property.

Hence he upheld Lewison J's finding at first instance, that

> once it is shown that money held on trust for TPL was paid into a 'maelstrom' account, [VTFL bears] the burden of showing that money in that account is not that of TPL.[84]

This was consistent with Jessel MR's dictum in *Re Hallett's* but care should be taken not to misread Lord Neuberger MR as adopting Lord Templeman's discredited "swollen assets" theory.

## 3. Claiming

12–050 In this section we consider the different proprietary claims that can be made against trust property or its traceable proceeds, assuming that all necessary following and tracing processes have been

[79] (1880) 13 Ch. D. 696 at 719.

[80] See para.12–023.

[81] [2009] Q.B. 376 at [49]–[50]. Lord Templeman's dicta were restrictively distinguished in *Re Goldcorp Exchange Ltd* [1995] 1 A.C. 74 and *Bishopsgate Investment Management Ltd v Homan* [1995] Ch. 211; see also *Ultraframe (UK) Ltd v Fielding* [2007] W.T.L.R. 835 at [1470]–[1475]; *Re BA Peters Plc (in admin.)* [2009] B.P.I.R. 248; *Re Lehman Bros (International) Europe (in admin.)* [2009] EWHC 3228 (Ch) at [190]ff.

[82] [2012] Ch. 453.

[83] ibid., at [138].

[84] ibid., at [141].

successfully completed. We then examine the possible reasons why the law gives the beneficiaries' such proprietary rights in different situations. Finally, we discuss the most important defence[85] which can be raised against an equitable proprietary claim following an unauthorised transfer of trust property to a third party recipient,[86] that the defendant was a bona fide purchaser for value without notice of the beneficiaries' equitable interest in the property.

## *A. Different Types of Proprietary Claim*

### i. Where a Trustee Misappropriates Trust Property for Herself

If a trustee misappropriates trust assets for herself and retains them in their original form, the beneficiaries can require her to reconstitute the trust estate, where necessary by conveying legal title to the assets to new trustees who have been appointed in the meantime.[87] If a trustee misappropriates trust property and uses it exclusively to acquire different property for her own benefit (a "clean substitution"), the beneficiaries can elect either to claim the new property *in specie*, or to take an equitable lien over the new property to secure their personal claim against the trustee to reconstitute the trust fund.[88] If a trustee misappropriates trust property and mixes it with her own property before buying a new asset out of the mixture (a "mixed substitution"), the beneficiaries can elect either to claim a proportionate ownership interest in the new asset, or to enforce an equitable lien over the property to secure their personal claim against the trustee.[89] In all of these cases the beneficiaries' claim is a claim that the trustee should specifically or substitutively perform her duty to deliver up trust property in which they have a subsisting equitable interest.[90] It might also be said that the property represents the profits of a breach of fiduciary duty which the trustee holds on constructive trust for the beneficiaries,[91] but there is no need for them to plead their case in this way.[92] **12–051**

If a trustee misappropriates money from two different trust sources and uses it to buy a new asset, then, according to Scott VC in *Foskett v McKeown*,[93] **12–052**

---

85 In certain contexts (such as the acquisition by the third party of registered title to land) there are other defences that may be available (see, e.g. Land Registration Act 2002 s.29, which in fact replaces the bona fide purchaser defence in relation to dealings with land covered by the Land Registration Act 2002).

86 Where the trustee transfers trust property to the third party in an authorised exercise of her powers, the third party will be protected from a proprietary claim by the beneficiaries through operation of overreaching: see para.12–109.

87 Before the Judicature Acts it would have been necessary for the beneficiaries to bring full execution proceedings, although these would usually have been aborted once relief had been granted in respect of the particular misapplication: see, e.g. *Re Medland* (1889) 41 Ch. D. 476 at 482. Today there is almost never a call for full judicial execution of a trust, but the same principles are applied, the overriding object being to enforce the performance of the trust according to its terms.

88 *Re Hallett's Estate* (1880) 13 Ch. D. 696 at 709; *Foskett v McKeown* [1998] Ch. 265 at 277; [2001] 1 A.C. 102 at 130.

89 *Scott v Scott* (1962) 109 C.L.R. 649; *Re Tilley's Will Trusts* [1967] Ch. 1178 (where the point was conceded); *British Columbia Teachers' Credit Union v Betterley* (1975) 61 D.L.R. (3d) 755; *Foskett v McKeown* [1998] Ch. 265 at 277; [2001] 1 A.C. 102 at 130–131.

90 See Ch.10.

91 *Re EVTR Ltd* (1987) 3 B.C.C. 389 at 393 per Dillon LJ: "It is a long established principle of equity that, if a person who is a trustee receives money or property because of, or in respect of, trust property, he will hold what he receives as a constructive trustee on the trusts of the original trust property." For this proposition the judge cited *Keech v Sandford* (1726) Sel. Cas. Temp. King 61; see also *Aberdeen Town Council v Aberdeen University* (1877) 2 App. Cas. 544.

92 In other words the trustee breaches two duties when she takes trust property for herself. Confusingly, both duties are often described as "fiduciary duties": see paras 9–005—9–017. One is a "stewardship" duty to hold the trust property for the beneficiaries and deal with it only in an authorised way: this is the duty with which are concerned here; the other is a duty to act in the beneficiaries' exclusive interest: this is the duty with which we are concerned in Ch.13, and breach of this duty can lead to the imposition of a constructive trust on the trustee's profits, as discussed at paras 13–126ff.

93 [1998] Ch. 265 at 278. See too Lord Millett's comments on appeal: [2001] 1 A.C. 102 at 132.

> neither set of beneficiaries can claim a first charge over the asset to recover its money. The equities as between the two sets of beneficiaries will be equal. Neither will be entitled to priority as against the other. It follows that they must share proportionately in the asset, bearing pro rata any shortfall and enjoying pro rata any increase in value.

**12-053** If beneficiaries are entitled to an equitable ownership interest in property which generates income, they can claim the income as well: so, for example, if they are entitled to a beneficial interest in a house which has been let for rent, they are also entitled to a beneficial interest in the rental income.[94] If a trustee uses trust funds to buy a house in the trustee's name, with the help of a mortgage loan that the trustee personally covenants to repay, the courts do not treat the trustee as having personally contributed the mortgage money when calculating the quantum of the beneficiaries' claim. So, for example, if the trustee uses £25,000 of trust money to buy a house with the help of a £75,000 purchase loan secured by a mortgage on the property, and the house increases in value, the beneficiaries can claim the whole house, subject to a counter-claim for any mortgage payments actually made by the trustee: but for the £25,000 of trust funds the trustee would not have been able to provide the necessary security for the mortgage loan and so the fruits of the transaction should go to the beneficiaries.[95]

**12-054** An equitable lien is "essentially a positive right to obtain . . . an order for sale of the subject property or for actual payment from the subject fund", and it

> may, in general, be enforced in the same way as any other equitable charge, namely, by sale in pursuance of court order or, where the lien is over a fund, by an order for payment thereout.[96]

Since a beneficial interest in property will "rise or fall in value with the property"[97] it will be to the beneficiaries' advantage to elect for an equitable lien in cases where the property has decreased in value, and pursue a personal claim against the defendant for the difference.

**12-055** An equitable lien can also be a potent remedy in a case where the beneficiaries can trace into a number of different assets and funds. Suppose that a trustee has several bank accounts and mixes £100,000 of trust money with her own money in her No.1 account, then transfers money from the No.1 account to her No.2 and No.3 accounts, and then buys a painting with money from the No.1 account, a car with money from the No.2 account, and a flat with money from the No.3 account. In this case,

> as against the wrongdoer and [her] successors in title, the beneficiary is entitled to locate his contribution in any part of the mixture [i.e. in any of the three accounts, the painting, the car, and the flat] and to subordinate their claims to share in the mixture till his own contribution has been satisfied.[98]

**12-056** If the trustee reinstates the trust by returning the trust property then the beneficiaries will have no claim against her. However, if a trustee uses trust money to buy assets which increase in value it is not enough for her to repay the value of the trust money originally taken: she must account to the beneficiaries for the increase in value as well.[99]

---

94 *Banton v CIBC Corp* (1999) 182 D.L.R. (4th) 486 at 504–505; *Greenwood v Lee* [2003] O.P.L.R. 1.

95 *Paul Davies Pty Ltd v Davies* [1983] N.S.W.L.R. 440; *Re Marriage of Wagstaff* (1990) 99 F.L.R. 390.

96 *Hewett v Court* (1983) 149 C.L.R. 638 at 664, per Deane J.

97 *Australian Postal Corp v Lutak* (1991) 21 N.S.W.L.R. 584 at 590, per Bryson J.

98 *Foskett v McKeown* [2001] 1 A.C. 102 at 132, per Lord Millett. See too *El Ajou v Dollar Land Holdings Plc* [1993] 3 All E.R. 713 at 735–736; on appeal: [1994] 2 All E.R. 685 at 701; *Re Goldcorp Exchange Ltd* [1994] 2 All E.R. 806 at 831.

99 *Scott v Scott* (1962) 109 C.L.R. 649; *Re Hughes* [1970] I.R. 237.

### ii. Where Trust Property is Misdirected to a Third Party

Where trust property is misdirected to a third party recipient, then, again, the beneficiaries can assert an equitable interest in the property or its traceable proceeds unless the recipient is a bona fide purchaser for value without notice of the beneficiaries' interest,[100] or other defences apply (e.g. laches or acquiescence). Even if the recipient has acted in good faith, she must "yield up any [trust property that remains], or the traceable proceeds of any that [has been exchanged for a new asset]".[101] This proprietary liability is not dependent on proof of fault and although it has been said that the recipient holds the property on a constructive trust for the beneficiaries,[102] their proprietary claim must be distinguished from the personal claim in knowing receipt which they can also bring against her, to make her personally accountable for the property as a constructive trustee, in cases where she has received the property with a sufficient degree of knowledge to make her receipt unconscionable or has acquired such a degree of knowledge whilst still holding the property or its traceable proceeds.[103] This point is brought out in the following extract from Lloyd LJ's judgment in *Independent Trustee Services Ltd v GP Noble Trustees Ltd*.[104] **12–057**

*Independent Trustee Services Ltd v GP Noble Trustees Ltd*

Court of Appeal [2013] Ch. 91 at [77]–[80]

LLOYD L.J.: . . . in the case of an innocent volunteer recipient of money which is the product of a breach of trust, the legal title is in the recipient but the equitable title remains in the beneficiaries of the relevant trust throughout. Conventionally, in a situation where the legal title to an asset is held by A but the beneficial ownership is in B, A is regarded as holding the asset on trust for B. To say that, however, is only the beginning of the analysis because it does not tell you what duties A owes to B in respect of the asset. The fact that A is not liable to account to B for the asset if A has parted with it (without receiving traceable proceeds) at a time when he had no knowledge of B's interest shows that this is not a case of a trustee who is subject to strict liability. **12–058**

This situation is inherently unstable in two respects. For so long as A has no notice of B's interest, B's interest is fragile because A may dispose of the property in a way which leaves no traceable product. On the other hand A's immunity from claims in respect of his dealings with the assets is also at risk because it can be brought to an end (for the future) if notice is given to him of B's interest. **12–059**

In *Westdeutsche Landesbank Girozentrale v Islington LBC*[105] Lord Browne-Wilkinson said that innocent receipt by A of property in which B has a beneficial interest, A being unaware of that interest, "does not by itself make [A] a trustee despite the severance of the legal and equitable titles". He said this on the premise,[106] that if A held on trust despite his ignorance and therefore innocence, he would be personally liable, regardless of fault, for any subsequent payment of the money to any third party even though at the time of the payment he was still innocent of B's interest. He recognised[107] that whether A is regarded as a trustee may be no more than a semantic question, so long as it is accepted that A's accountability does not extend to property which left A's hands before he had notice of B's interest. . . **12–060**

Despite what Lord Browne-Wilkinson said, it seems to me that it is appropriate to speak of A holding on trust for B in this situation, provided that one is not misled into thinking that to call the relationship one of trustee and beneficiary tells you, of itself, what the duties and liabilities of the trustee are. Since the trust **12–061**

---

100 *Foskett v McKeown* [2001] 1 A.C. 102 at 127 and 130. For discussion of the bona fide purchase defence, see paras 12–117ff.

101 *Re Montagu's Settlement Trusts* [1987] Ch. 264 at 272, per Megarry VC.

102 *Independent Trustee Services Ltd v GP Noble Trustees Ltd* [2013] Ch. 91 at [80].

103 As to which see paras 11–004—11–011 and 11–074—11–086.

104 See also *Agip (Africa) Ltd v Jackson* [1990] 1 Ch. 265 at 290; *Allan v Rea Brothers Trustees Ltd* [2002] P.L.R. 169 at [55]; *Waxman v Waxman* (2004) 7 I.T.E.L.R. 162 at [583]; *Nabb Brothers Ltd v Lloyds Bank International (Guernsey) Ltd* [2005] I.L.Pr. 37 at [72].

105 [1996] AC 669 at 707.

106 Stated at 703.

107 At 707.

arises from the asset having been extracted, in breach of trust, from a fund held on express trusts, it seems correct to characterise the trust as a constructive trust, rather than a resulting trust. . .

12-062 [Since] an innocent volunteer recipient of trust assets transferred in breach of trust, before he has notice of the trust interest, . . . cannot be made accountable for relevant assets disposed of at a time when he had no notice of the adverse interest, even though the beneficial interest of the beneficiaries continued to exist, the volunteer is (for the time being) able to mix the trust assets with his own, with impunity, and to dispose of them freely, despite the beneficiaries' continuing beneficial interest. So in that situation the volunteer, even if regarded as holding the property on trust, is not constrained by any imposed duty as regards his free powers of dealing with the assets, until he has notice of the inconsistent interest of the beneficiaries. Of course, if he gives a relevant asset away, the beneficiaries may be able to follow it into the hands of the later recipient, and if he disposes of it for value, then he may receive another asset which would represent the trust property in his hands, and the beneficiaries may then be able to assert a claim to that asset by way of tracing. Once he has notice of the beneficiaries' adverse interest, he is no longer free to deal with the assets as he pleases. At that stage there is no conceptual difficulty or oddity in calling him a (constructive) trustee, at least as from that time. . .

**12-063** If the recipient of misdirected trust property mixes it with her own property, the beneficiaries can claim the traceable proceeds of their property,[108] the identity of the residue being determined by rules that vary according to whether or not the recipient has acted in good faith, as discussed above.[109] As previously noted,[110] these rules permit beneficiaries to trace into assets bought by an innocent recipient even though she can prove that she could have bought the asset with her own money, and that she would have done so, had she known that the money which she actually used to buy the asset belonged to the beneficiaries. In the event that the asset increases in value, then it follows from the foregoing discussion that the beneficiaries can capture the whole of the increase by asserting an equitable ownership claim to the asset.

**12-064** This outcome may not offend us in a case where the defendant is a wrongdoing trustee, or a donee from a wrongdoing trustee, as in *Foskett v McKeown*,[111] which is reproduced below. But where the defendant has acted in good faith, it is "an affront to our notions of justice" that she should be liable in this way, as Lord Millett has observed in extra-judicial writing.[112] Suppose that an innocent recipient uses £5 of misapplied trust funds to buy a lottery ticket which pays out £5 million and that she would have used her own £5 for the purpose, had she known of the trust money's tainted source. In our view, the most to which the beneficiaries should be entitled in this case is an equitable lien over the winnings to secure repayment of the £5.[113]

**12-065** The facts of *Foskett v McKeown*[114] were close to this, but they differed in an important respect. A trustee misappropriated trust funds that he used to pay some of the premiums on a life insurance policy. The policy contained an investment element and part of the premiums were used to build up an investment fund inside the policy while another part bought the right to the payment of a death benefit to nominated beneficiaries on the death of the policyholder. The policy also contained a clause which provided that in the event that annual premiums were not paid the policy would not immediately lapse, and instead money would be taken out of the investment fund to keep up the policyholder's right to the payment of the death benefit (until the fund was exhausted).

---

108 *Re Diplock* [1948] Ch. 465 at 524, 539.

109 See paras 12-030—12-033.

110 See para.12-046.

111 [2001] 1 A.C. 102; excerpted at paras 12-068ff.

112 "Proprietary Restitution" in S. Degeling and J. Edelman (eds), *Equity in Commercial Law* (Law Book Co, 2005).

113 An outcome which is supported by *Re Tilley's Will Trusts* [1967] Ch. 1179, as discussed in D.J. Hayton, "Equity's Identification Rules" in Birks (ed.) *Laundering and Tracing* (1995), pp.10-12.

114 [2001] 1 A.C. 102.

The trustee died and the trust beneficiaries claimed a proportionate share of the £1 million death benefit on the ground that this represented the traceable proceeds of trust property. The trustee's children and mother who were the nominated beneficiaries under the policy argued that the trust beneficiaries should be restricted to a lien for the amount of the stolen money. The nominated beneficiaries said that if they had been given a choice whether the right to the death benefit should be paid for with the stolen money, or with money taken out of the investment fund, they would have chosen the latter course. Hence it would now be unfair to make them surrender more than the value of the premiums paid with trust money. This argument appealed to a minority of the House of Lords,[115] but it was rejected by the majority, Lord Millett stating that on the facts as they happened, the trustee had made the opposite choice, and that for the purposes of the case the nominated beneficiaries were in no better a moral position than that which had been occupied by the trustee from whom their rights to the death benefit had derived.[116] **12–066**

We reproduce an extract from Lord Millett's judgment here, as it contains an important discussion of the rules of tracing and the source of beneficiaries' proprietary rights in the traceable proceeds of misdirected trust property. **12–067**

*Foskett v McKeown*

House of Lords [2001] 1 A.C. 102

The claimants paid money to Murphy on trust for themselves, intending that the money should be used to buy land for investment purposes in Portugal. Murphy had previously bought a life insurance policy on his own life, on trust for his children (who would receive 90 per cent of the policy proceeds in the event of his death) and his mother (who would receive 10 per cent). Murphy paid the first two annual premiums with his own money; the source of the money which he used to pay the third premium was disputed; and in breach of trust he used the claimants' money to pay the fourth and fifth premiums. Murphy then committed suicide and the insurer paid £1 million to the surviving trustees of the policy settlement. The claimants sued the trustees, arguing that they had an equitable proprietary interest in at least 40 per cent of the insurance proceeds because at least 40 per cent of the premiums had been paid with stolen trust money. A majority of the House of Lords allowed the claim, and refused to restrict the claimants to a lien over the proceeds for the amount of money paid towards the premiums. **12–068**

LORD MILLETT (with whom LORD BROWNE-WILKINSON and LORD HOFFMANN agreed, and with whom LORD STEYN and LORD HOPE disagreed on the question of remedy): My Lords, this is a textbook example of tracing through mixed substitutions. At the beginning of the story the purchasers were beneficially entitled under an express trust to a sum standing in the name of Mr Murphy in a bank account. From there the money moved into and out of various bank accounts where in breach of trust it was inextricably mixed by Mr Murphy with his own money. After each transaction was completed the purchasers' money formed an indistinguishable part of the balance standing to Mr Murphy's credit in his bank account. The amount of that balance represented a debt due from the bank to Mr Murphy, that is to say a chose in action. At the penultimate stage the purchasers' money was represented by an indistinguishable part of a different chose in action, viz. the debt prospectively and contingently due from an insurance company to its policyholders, being the trustees of a settlement made by Mr Murphy for the benefit of his children. At the present and final stage it forms an indistinguishable part of the balance standing to the credit of the respondent trustees in their bank account. **12–069**

**Tracing and Following**

The process of ascertaining what happened to the purchasers' money involves both tracing and following. These are both exercises in locating assets which are or may be taken to represent an asset belonging to the purchasers and to which they assert ownership. The processes of following and tracing are, however, **12–070**

115 ibid., at 112–13 per Lord Steyn.

116 ibid., at 130: "The trustee cannot be permitted to keep any profit resulting from his misappropriation for himself, and his donees cannot obtain a better title than their donor."

distinct. Following is the process of following the same asset as it moves from hand to hand. Tracing is the process of identifying a new asset as the substitute for the old. Where one asset is exchanged for another, a claimant can elect whether to follow the original asset into the hands of the new owner or to trace its value into the new asset in the hands of the same owner. In practice his choice is often dictated by the circumstances. In the present case the purchasers do not seek to follow the money any further once it reached the bank or insurance company, since its identity was lost in the hands of the recipient (which in any case obtained an unassailable title as a bona fide purchaser for value without notice of the purchasers' beneficial interest). Instead the purchasers have chosen at each stage to trace the money into its proceeds, viz. the debt presently due from the bank to the account holder or the debt prospectively and contingently due from the insurance company to the policy holders.

12-071 Having completed this exercise, the purchasers claim a continuing beneficial interest in the insurance money. Since this represents the product of Mr Murphy's own money as well as theirs, which Mr Murphy mingled indistinguishably in a single chose in action, they claim a beneficial interest in a proportionate part of the money only. The transmission of a claimant's property rights from one asset to its traceable proceeds is part of our law of property, not of the law of unjust enrichment. There is no "unjust factor" to justify restitution (unless "want of title" be one, which makes the point). The claimant succeeds if at all by virtue of his own title, not to reverse unjust enrichment. Property rights are determined by fixed rules and settled principles. They are not discretionary. They do not depend upon ideas of what is "fair, just and reasonable". Such concepts, which in reality mask decisions of legal policy, have no place in the law of property.

12-072 A beneficiary of a trust is entitled to a continuing beneficial interest not merely in the trust property but in its traceable proceeds also, and his interest binds every one who takes the property or its traceable proceeds except a bona fide purchaser for value without notice. In the present case the purchasers' beneficial interest plainly bound Mr Murphy, a trustee who wrongfully mixed the trust money with his own and whose every dealing with the money (including the payment of the premiums) was in breach of trust. It similarly binds his successors, the trustees of the children's settlement, who claim no beneficial interest of their own, and Mr Murphy's children, who are volunteers. They gave no value for what they received and derive their interest from Mr Murphy by way of gift.

**Tracing**

12-073 We speak of money at the bank, and of money passing into and out of a bank account. But of course the account holder has no money at the bank. Money paid into a bank account belongs legally and beneficially to the bank and not to the account holder. The bank gives value for it, and it is accordingly not usually possible to make the money itself the subject of an adverse claim. Instead a claimant normally sues the account holder rather than the bank and lays claim to the proceeds of the money in his hands. These consist of the debt or part of the debt due to him from the bank. We speak of tracing money into and out of the account, but there is no money in the account. There is merely a single debt of an amount equal to the final balance standing to the credit of the account holder. No money passes from paying bank to receiving bank or through the clearing system (where the money flows may be in the opposite direction). There is simply a series of debits and credits which are causally and transactionally linked. We also speak of tracing one asset into another, but this too is inaccurate. The original asset still exists in the hands of the new owner, or it may have become untraceable. The claimant claims the new asset because it was acquired in whole or in part with the original asset. What he traces, therefore, is not the physical asset itself but the value inherent in it.

12-074 Tracing is thus neither a claim nor a remedy. It is merely the process by which a claimant demonstrates what has happened to his property, identifies its proceeds and the persons who have handled or received them, and justifies his claim that the proceeds can properly be regarded as representing his property. Tracing is also distinct from claiming. It identifies the traceable proceeds of the claimant's property. It enables the claimant to substitute the traceable proceeds for the original asset as the subject matter of his claim. But it does not affect or establish his claim. That will depend on a number of factors including the nature of his interest in the original asset. He will normally be able to maintain the same claim to the substituted asset as he could have maintained to the original asset. If he held only a security interest in the original asset, he cannot claim more than a security interest in its proceeds. But his claim may also be exposed to potential defences as a result of intervening transactions. Even if the purchasers could demonstrate what the bank had done with their money, for example, and could thus identify its traceable proceeds in the hands of the bank, any claim by them to assert ownership of those proceeds would be defeated by the bona fide purchaser defence. The successful completion of a tracing exercise may be preliminary to a personal claim[117] or a proprietary one, to the enforcement of a legal right,[118] or an equitable one.

Given its nature, there is nothing inherently legal or equitable about the tracing exercise. There is thus no sense in maintaining different rules for tracing at law and in equity. One set of tracing rules is enough. The existence of two has never formed part of the law in the United States.[119] There is certainly no logical justification for allowing any distinction between them to produce capricious results in cases of mixed substitutions by insisting on the existence of a fiduciary relationship as a precondition for applying equity's tracing rules. The existence of such a relationship may be relevant to the nature of the claim which the plaintiff can maintain, whether personal or proprietary, but that is a different matter. I agree with the passages which my noble and learned friend Lord Steyn has cited from Professor Birks' essay "The Necessity of a Unitary Law of Tracing",[120] and with Dr Lionel Smith's exposition in his comprehensive monograph *The Law of Tracing*.[121] 12–075

This is not, however, the occasion to explore these matters further, for the present is a straightforward case of a trustee who wrongfully misappropriated trust money, mixed it with his own, and used it to pay for an asset for the benefit of his children. Even on the traditional approach, the equitable tracing rules are available to the purchasers. There are only two complicating factors. The first is that the wrongdoer used their money to pay premiums on an equity linked policy of life assurance on his own life. The nature of the policy should make no difference in principle, though it may complicate the accounting. The second is that he had previously settled the policy for the benefit of his children. This should also make no difference. The claimant's rights cannot depend on whether the wrongdoer gave the policy to his children during his lifetime or left the proceeds to them by his will; or if during his lifetime whether he did so before or after he had recourse to the claimant's money to pay the premiums. The order of events does not affect the fact that the children are not contributors but volunteers who have received the gift of an asset paid for in part with misappropriated trust moneys. 12–076

**The Cause of Action**

As I have already pointed out, the purchasers seek to vindicate their property rights, not to reverse unjust enrichment. The correct classification of the purchasers' cause of action may appear to be academic, but it has important consequences. The two causes of action have different requirements and may attract different defences. 12–077

A plaintiff who brings an action in unjust enrichment must show that the defendant has been enriched at the plaintiff's expense, for he cannot have been unjustly enriched if he has not been enriched at all. But the plaintiff is not concerned to show that the defendant is in receipt of property belonging beneficially to the plaintiff or its traceable proceeds. The fact that the beneficial ownership of the property has passed to the defendant provides no defence; indeed, it is usually the very fact which founds the claim. Conversely, a plaintiff who brings an action like the present must show that the defendant is in receipt of property which belongs beneficially to him or its traceable proceeds, but he need not show that the defendant has been enriched by its receipt. He may, for example, have paid full value for the property, but he is still required to disgorge it if he received it with notice of the plaintiff's interest. 12–078

Furthermore, a claim in unjust enrichment is subject to a change of position defence, which usually operates by reducing or extinguishing the element of enrichment. An action like the present is subject to the bona fide purchaser for value defence, which operates to clear the defendant's title. 12–079

**The Tracing Rules**

The insurance policy in the present case is a very sophisticated financial instrument. Tracing into the rights conferred by such an instrument raises a number of important issues. It is therefore desirable to set out the basic principles before turning to deal with the particular problems to which policies of life assurance give rise. 12–080

The simplest case is where a trustee wrongfully misappropriates trust property and uses it exclusively to 12–081

---

117 As in *El Ajou v Dollar Land Holdings Plc* [1993] 3 All E.R. 717.

118 As in *Trustees of the Property of FC Jones & Sons (a firm) v Jones* [1997] Ch. 159.

119 See Scott, *The Law of Trusts* (4th edn, 1989), 605–609.

120 In R. Cranston (ed.), *Making Commercial Law: Essays in Honour of Roy Goode* (1997).

121 L.D. Smith *The Law of Tracing* (1997). See particularly pp.120–130, 277–279 and 342–347.

acquire other property for his own benefit. In such a case the beneficiary is entitled at his option either to assert his beneficial ownership of the proceeds or to bring a personal claim against the trustee for breach of trust and enforce an equitable lien or charge on the proceeds to secure restoration of the trust fund. He will normally exercise the option in the way most advantageous to himself. If the traceable proceeds have increased in value and are worth more than the original asset, he will assert his beneficial ownership and obtain the profit for himself. There is nothing unfair in this. The trustee cannot be permitted to keep any profit resulting from his misappropriation for himself, and his donees cannot obtain a better title than their donor. If the traceable proceeds are worth less than the original asset, it does not usually matter how the beneficiary exercises his option. He will take the whole of the proceeds on either basis. This is why it is not possible to identify the basis on which the claim succeeded in some of the cases.

**12–082** Both remedies are proprietary and depend on successfully tracing the trust property into its proceeds. A beneficiary's claim against a trustee for breach of trust is a personal claim. It does not entitle him to priority over the trustee's general creditors unless he can trace the trust property into its product and establish a proprietary interest in the proceeds. If the beneficiary is unable to trace the trust property into its proceeds, he still has a personal claim against the trustee, but his claim will be unsecured. The beneficiary's proprietary claims to the trust property or its traceable proceeds can be maintained against the wrongdoer and anyone who derives title from him except a bona fide purchaser for value without notice of the breach of trust. The same rules apply even where there have been numerous successive transactions, so long as the tracing exercise is successful and no bona fide purchaser for value without notice has intervened.

**12–083** A more complicated case is where there is a mixed substitution. This occurs where the trust money represents only part of the cost of acquiring the new asset. As James Barr Ames pointed out in "Following Misappropriated Property into its Product",[122] consistency requires that, if a trustee buys property partly with his own money and partly with trust money, the beneficiary should have the option of taking a proportionate part of the new property or a lien upon it, as may be most for his advantage. In principle it should not matter (and it has never previously been suggested that it does) whether the trustee mixes the trust money with his own and buys the new asset with the mixed fund or makes separate payments of the purchase price (whether simultaneously or sequentially) out of the different funds. In every case the value formerly inherent in the trust property has become located within the value inherent in the new asset.

**12–084** The rule, and its rationale, were stated by Samuel Williston in "The Right to Follow Trust Property when Confused with Other Property"[123]:

> "If the trust fund is traceable as having furnished in part the money with which a certain investment was made, and the proportion it formed of the whole money so invested is known or ascertainable, the cestui que trust should be allowed to regard the acts of the trustee as done for his benefit, in the same way that he would be allowed to if all the money so invested had been his; that is, he should be entitled in equity to an undivided share of the property which the trust money contributed to purchase—such a proportion of the whole as the trust money bore to the whole money invested. The reason in one case as in the other is that the trustee cannot be allowed to make a profit from the use of the trust money, and if the property which he wrongfully purchased were held subject only to a lien for the amount invested, any appreciation in value would go to the trustee."

If this correctly states the underlying basis of the rule (as I believe it does), then it is impossible to distinguish between the case where mixing precedes the investment and the case where it arises on and in consequence of the investment. It is also impossible to distinguish between the case where the investment is retained by the trustee and the case where it is given away to a gratuitous donee. The donee cannot obtain a better title than his donor, and a donor who is a trustee cannot be allowed to profit from his trust.

**12–085** In *Re Hallett's Estate*,[124] Jessel M.R. acknowledged that where an asset was acquired exclusively with trust money, the beneficiary could either assert equitable ownership of the asset or enforce a lien or charge over it to recover the trust money. But he appeared to suggest that in the case of a mixed substitution the beneficiary is confined to a lien. Any authority that this dictum might otherwise have is weakened by the fact that Jessel M.R. gave no reason for the existence of any such rule, and none is readily apparent. The dictum was plainly obiter, for the fund was deficient and the plaintiff was only claiming a lien. It has usually

---

122 (1906) 19 Harvard L.R. 511.

123 (1888) 2 Harvard L.R. 28, 29.

124 (1880) 13 Ch.D. 696 at 709.

been cited only to be explained away.[125] It was rejected by the High Court of Australia in *Scott v Scott*.[126] It has not been adopted in the United States.[127] In *Primeau v Granfield* Learned Hand J. expressed himself in forthright terms: "On principle there can be no excuse for such a rule."[128]

In my view the time has come to state unequivocally that English law has no such rule. It conflicts with the rule that a trustee must not benefit from his trust. I agree with Burrows that the beneficiary's right to elect to have a proportionate share of a mixed substitution necessarily follows once one accepts, as English law does, (i) that a claimant can trace in equity into a mixed fund and (ii) that he can trace unmixed money into its proceeds and assert ownership of the proceeds. **12–086**

Accordingly, I would state the basic rule as follows. Where a trustee wrongfully uses trust money to provide part of the cost of acquiring an asset, the beneficiary is entitled at his option either to claim a proportionate share of the asset or to enforce a lien upon it to secure his personal claim against the trustee for the amount of the misapplied money. It does not matter whether the trustee mixed the trust money with his own in a single fund before using it to acquire the asset, or made separate payments (whether simultaneously or sequentially) out of the differently owned funds to acquire a single asset. **12–087**

Two observations are necessary at this point. First, there is a mixed substitution (with the results already described) whenever the claimant's property has contributed in part only towards the acquisition of the new asset. It is not necessary for the claimant to show in addition that his property has contributed to any increase in the value of the new asset. This is because, as I have already pointed out, this branch of the law is concerned with vindicating rights of property and not with reversing unjust enrichment. Secondly, the beneficiary's right to claim a lien is available only against a wrongdoer and those deriving title under him otherwise than for value. It is not available against competing contributors who are innocent of any wrongdoing. The tracing rules are not the result of any presumption or principle peculiar to equity. They correspond to the common law rules for following into physical mixtures (though the consequences may not be identical). Common to both is the principle that the interests of the wrongdoer who was responsible for the mixing and those who derive title under him otherwise than for value are subordinated to those of innocent contributors. As against the wrongdoer and his successors, the beneficiary is entitled to locate his contribution in any part of the mixture and to subordinate their claims to share in the mixture until his own contribution has been satisfied. This has the effect of giving the beneficiary a lien for his contribution if the mixture is deficient. **12–088**

Innocent contributors, however, must be treated equally inter se. Where the beneficiary's claim is in competition with the claims of other innocent contributors, there is no basis upon which any of the claims can be subordinated to any of the others. Where the fund is deficient, the beneficiary is not entitled to enforce a lien for his contributions; all must share rateably in the fund. **12–089**

The primary rule in regard to a mixed fund, therefore, is that gains and losses are borne by the contributors rateably. The beneficiary's right to elect instead to enforce a lien to obtain repayment is an exception to the primary rule, exercisable where the fund is deficient and the claim is made against the wrongdoer and those claiming through him. It is not necessary to consider whether there are any circumstances in which the beneficiary is confined to a lien in cases where the fund is more than sufficient to repay the contributions of all parties. It is sufficient to say that he is not so confined in a case like the present. It is not enough that those defending the claim are innocent of any wrongdoing if they are not themselves contributors but, like the trustees and Mr Murphy's children in the present case, are volunteers who derive title under the wrongdoer otherwise than for value. On ordinary principles such persons are in no better position than the wrongdoer, and are liable to suffer the same subordination of their interests to those of the claimant as the wrongdoer would have been. They certainly cannot do better than the claimant by confining him to a lien and keeping any profit for themselves. **12–090**

Similar principles apply to following into physical mixtures.[129] There are relatively few cases which deal with the position of the innocent recipient from the wrongdoer, but *Jones v De Marchant*[130] may be cited **12–091**

---

125 See e.g. *Re Tilley's Will Trusts* [1967] Ch. 1179 at 1186, per Ungoed-Thomas J.; A. Burrows, *The Law of Restitution* (1993), p.368.

126 (1963) 109 C.L.R. 649 at 661–662, cited by Morritt L.J. below: [1998] Ch. 265 at 300–301.

127 See the American Law Institute, *Restatement of the Law, Trusts 2d* (1959) at p.202(h).

128 (1911) 184 F. 480 at 482.

129 See *Lupton v White* (1808) 15 Ves. Jun. 432; and *Sandeman & Sons v Tyzack and Branfoot Steamship Co Ltd* [1913] A.C. 680 at 695, where Lord Moulton said: "If the mixing has arisen from the fault of 'B', 'A' can claim the goods."

130 (1916) 28 D.L.R. 561.

as an example. A husband wrongfully took 18 beaver skins belonging to his wife and used them, together with four skins of his own, to have a fur coat made up which he then gave to his mistress. Unsurprisingly the wife was held entitled to recover the coat. The mistress knew nothing of the true ownership of the skins, but her innocence was held to be immaterial. She was a gratuitous donee and could stand in no better position than the husband. The coat was a new asset manufactured from the skins and not merely the product of intermingling them. The problem could not be solved by a sale of the coat in order to reduce the disputed property to a divisible fund, since (as we shall see) the realisation of an asset does not affect its ownership. It would hardly have been appropriate to require the two ladies to share the coat between them. Accordingly it was an all or nothing case in which the ownership of the coat must be assigned to one or other of the parties. The determinative factor was that the mixing was the act of the wrongdoer through whom the mistress acquired the coat otherwise than for value.

**12-092** The rule in equity is to the same effect, as Page Wood V.C. observed in *Frith v Cartland*[131]:

> ". . . if a man mixes trust funds with his own, the whole will be treated as the trust property, except so far as he may be able to distinguish what is his own."

This does not, in my opinion, exclude a pro rata division where this is appropriate, as in the case of money and other fungibles like grain, oil or wine. But it is to be observed that a pro rata division is the best that the wrongdoer and his donees can hope for. If a pro rata division is excluded, the beneficiary takes the whole; there is no question of confining him to a lien. *Jones v De Marchant* is a useful illustration of the principles shared by the common law and equity alike that an innocent recipient who receives misappropriated property by way of gift obtains no better title than his donor, and that if a proportionate sharing is inappropriate the wrongdoer and those who derive title under him take nothing.

**Insurance Policies**

**12-093** In the case of an ordinary whole-life policy the insurance company undertakes to pay a stated sum on the death of the assured in return for fixed annual premiums payable throughout his life. Such a policy is an entire contract, not a contract for a year with a right of renewal. It is not a series of single premium policies for one year term assurance. It is not like an indemnity policy where each premium buys cover for a year after which the policyholder must renew or the cover expires. The fact that the policy will lapse if the premiums are not paid makes no difference. The amounts of the annual premiums and of the sum assured are fixed in advance at the outset and assume the payment of annual premiums throughout the term of the policy. The relationship between them is based on the life expectancy of the assured and the rates of interest available on long term government securities at the inception of the policy.

**12-094** In the present case the benefits specified in the policy are expressed to be payable "in consideration of the payment of the first Premium already made and of the further Premiums payable". The premiums are stated to be "£10220.00 payable at annual intervals from 06 Nov 1986 throughout the lifetime of the life assured". It is beyond argument that the death benefit of £1m paid on Mr Murphy's death was paid in consideration for all the premiums which had been paid before that date, including those paid with the purchasers' money, and not just some of them. Part of that sum, therefore, represented the traceable proceeds of the purchasers' money.

**12-095** It is, however, of critical importance in the present case to appreciate that the purchasers do not trace the premiums directly into the insurance money. They trace them first into the policy and thence into the proceeds of the policy. It is essential not to elide the two steps. In this context, of course, the word "policy" does not mean the contract of insurance. You do not trace the payment of a premium into the insurance contract any more than you trace a payment into a bank account into the banking contract. The word "policy" is here used to describe the bundle of rights to which the policyholder is entitled in return for the premiums. These rights, which may be very complex, together constitute a chose in action, viz. the right to payment of a debt payable on a future event and contingent upon the continued payment of further premiums until the happening of the event. That chose in action represents the traceable proceeds of the premiums; its current value fluctuates from time to time. When the policy matures, the insurance money represents the traceable proceeds of the policy and hence indirectly of the premiums.

**12-096** It follows that, if a claimant can show that premiums were paid with his money, he can claim a

[131] (1865) 2 H. & M. 417 at 420.

> proportionate share of the policy. His interest arises by reason of and immediately upon the payment of the premiums, and the extent of his share is ascertainable at once. He does not have to wait until the policy matures in order to claim his property. His share in the policy and its proceeds may increase or decrease as further premiums are paid; but it is not affected by the realisation of the policy. His share remains the same whether the policy is sold or surrendered or held until maturity; these are merely different methods of realising the policy. They may affect the amount of the proceeds received on realisation but they cannot affect the extent of his share in the proceeds. In principle the purchasers are entitled to the insurance money which was paid on Mr Murphy's death in the same shares and proportions as they were entitled in the policy immediately before his death.
>
> Since the manner in which an asset is realised does not affect its ownership, and since it cannot matter whether the claimant discovers what has happened before or after it is realised, the question of ownership can be answered by ascertaining the shares in which it is owned immediately before it is realised. Where A misappropriates B's money and uses it to buy a winning ticket in the lottery, B is entitled to the winnings. Since A is a wrongdoer, it is irrelevant that he could have used his own money if in fact he used B's. This may seem to give B an undeserved windfall, but the result is not unjust. Had B discovered the fraud before the draw, he could have decided whether to keep the ticket or demand his money back. He alone has the right to decide whether to gamble with his own money. If A keeps him in ignorance until after the draw, he suffers the consequence. He cannot deprive B of his right to choose what to do with his own money; but he can give him an informed choice. **12–097**
>
> The application of these principles ought not to depend on the nature of the chose in action. They should apply to a policy of life assurance as they apply to a bank account or a lottery ticket . . . . **12–098**

### iii. Where a Trustee Makes an Unauthorised Investment

When an express trust is declared, "the trust fund" is generally defined in the trust deed in terms such as "property transferred to the trustees to hold on the terms of this trust and all the property from time to time representing the same",[132] but the latter clause can simply be regarded as spelling out what is inevitably involved in the settlor creating a trust. The reason is that the trustees will be given powers of disposition, sale and investment,[133] and for these to be effective, the trustees must be able to transfer their legal title to trust assets clear of the beneficiaries' equitable interest. Hence the doctrine of overreaching provides that whenever the trustees exercise a power to sell or dispose of trust assets in an authorised fashion, the recipient takes clear legal title, and in the case of sale, the trust will instantly attach instead to the proceeds of sale.[134] Again, if the trustees use trust money to buy a new asset in a valid exercise of their powers of investment, the same thing happens: the beneficiaries' equitable interest in the money is overreached, the vendor gets clear legal title to the money, and the trust attaches to the new asset. **12–099**

Now consider the case where trustees act in an unauthorised way when they sell trust assets or use trust money to buy new assets. In *Wright v Morgan*, Viscount Dunedin held that where[135] **12–100**

> a trustee has made an improper investment, the law is well settled. The *cestuis que trustent* as a whole have a right, if they choose, to adopt the investment and to hold it as trust property. But if there is not unanimity then it is not trust property, but the trustee who has made it must keep the investment himself. He is debtor to the trust for the money which has been applied in its purchase.

132 See, e.g. para.1.5 of the Discretionary Trust Precedent set out at para.1–102.

133 See, e.g. paras 1.1 and 1.3 of the Schedule to the Discretionary Trust Precedent set out at para.1–110.

134 *State Bank of India v Sood* [1997] Ch. 276. See too C. Harpum, "Overreaching, Trustees' Powers, and the Reform of the 1925 Property Legislation" [1990] C.L.J. 277; D. Fox, "Overreaching" in P. Birks and A. Pretto (eds) *Breach of Trust* (Hart Publishing, 2002); R.C. Nolan "Property in a Fund" (2004) 120 L.Q.R. 108, 111–117; R.C. Nolan, "Understanding the Limits of Equitable Property" (2006) 1 J. of Eq. 18, 24–28.

135 [1926] A.C. 788 at 798, citing *Parker v McKenna* (1874) L.R. 10 Ch. 96. See too *Re Patten* (1883) 52 L.J. (Ch.) 787; *Power v Banks* [1901] 2 Ch. 487 at 496; *Re Jenkins and HE Randall and Co's Contract* [1903] 2 Ch. 362.

These rules would be worked out in proceedings for an account either by affirming the purchase in a case where the beneficiaries all consent to that outcome, or else, in a case where they do not, by falsifying the account to delete the unauthorised expenditure from the record and requiring the trustees to reconstitute the trust fund by paying over the amount of the outgoing from their own pockets.[136]

12-101 In a case where the trustee uses trust money to make an unauthorised investment which triples in value, and the beneficiaries cannot all consent to take the investment because some are minors or unborn, can the trustee keep it for herself and repay the amount of the purchase money plus interest? Presumably she cannot. In this case, the adult beneficiaries could apply (at the trustee's expense) to the court under the Trustee Act 1925 s.57 for an order authorising the purchase; alternatively, they could move to replace the trustee, and the new trustee could then demand the investment on the beneficiaries' behalf.[137]

### iv. Where Trust Funds are Used to Pay Off a Mortgage

12-102 Suppose that a trustee misappropriates trust money and uses it to pay off a debt secured by a mortgage on her house, or suppose that a trustee misdirects trust money to a third party who does the same thing. Here, the courts can allow the beneficiaries, by means of a legal fiction, to trace their money into the discharged mortgage, and to be treated as though the mortgage has been "kept alive" and transferred to them as security for the repayment of their money.[138] This remedy is termed "subrogation", which literally means "substitution": the beneficiaries are treated, by a fiction, as though they were substituted into the position previously occupied by the original mortgagee. In *Banque Financière de la Cité v Parc (Battersea) Ltd*,[139] Lord Hoffmann emphasised that the language of "revival" and "transfer" used by the courts in these cases is metaphorical. The law does not actually transfer the original mortgage from the creditor to the beneficiaries. Instead, it imposes a new equitable lien on the defendant's property, the content and priority status of which resemble those of the extinguished mortgage, but are not necessarily identical with them.

## *B. Sources of Proprietary Rights*

12-103 It is easier to describe the different types of proprietary claim which the beneficiaries can bring following a breach of trust than it is to explain why the beneficiaries are entitled to bring such claims. In the following discussion we will start by considering proprietary claims to trust property that subsists in its original form either in the hands of the trustee or in the hands of a third party recipient. We will then examine proprietary claims to the traceable proceeds of trust property.

### i. Rights in the Trust Property

12-104 When a trust is set up, the settlor either declares herself to be trustee of property which she owns, or transfers title to property to others to hold on trust. In either case, the reason why the beneficiaries then acquire an equitable beneficial interest in the trust property is that the settlor intended this to

---

136 *Re Biss, (Deceased)* [1903] 2 Ch. 40. For discussion of the accounting process, see paras 10–122ff.

137 *Young v Murphy* [1996] 1 V.R. 279.

138 *McCullough v Marsden* (1919) 45 D.L.R. 645; *Boscawen v Bajwa* [1996] 1 W.L.R. 328; *Primlake Ltd (In Liquidation) v Matthews Assocs* [2007] 1 B.C.L.C. 666 at [340].

139 [1999] 1 A.C. 221 at 236. See too *Cheltenham & Gloucester Plc v Appleyard* [2004] EWCA Civ 291 at [49]; *Filby v Mortgage Express Ltd (No.2)* [2004] EWCA Civ 759 at [63]; *Day v Tiuta International Ltd* [2014] EWCA Civ 1246 at [43].

happen and exercised her power as owner of the property to bring the trust into existence. It follows that the new rights created for the beneficiaries when the trust is set up are sourced in consent: the settlor consents to the creation of these new rights which she gifts to the beneficiaries.

The trustees' consent is also required for the arrangement to work: a trust will not fail for want of a trustee, but no one is legally compelled to become trustee of an express trust against their wishes.[140] Once the trustees' consent is given, however, they are not allowed to change their minds, and if necessary equity will enforce their agreement to hold the trust property for the beneficiaries by ordering them to perform their duties *in specie*. Suppose, for example, that a trustee improperly takes physical possession of a painting, legal title to which she holds on trust for the beneficiaries. In this case, nothing happens to interrupt the beneficiaries' continuing equitable rights to the painting, and they can enforce these rights (and oblige the trustee to perform her continuing duties) by obtaining a declaration of their equitable beneficial interest and an order for conveyance of the legal title to new trustees if necessary. **12–105**

Suppose, alternatively, that a trustee holds legal title to a painting on trust for the beneficiaries and that in breach of trust she transfers title (along with physical possession) to a third party recipient who is not a bona fide purchaser for value without notice. In this case, again, the beneficiaries can obtain a declaration of their equitable beneficial interest and an order for reconveyance against the recipient. These rights are sourced in the settlor's intention to create them and give them to the beneficiaries. **12–106**

## ii. Rights in Traceable Substitutes

Now consider the case where a trustee uses trust property to acquire substitute property in an unauthorised transaction. If she acquires the substitute property from a bona fide purchaser for value without notice of the beneficiaries' equitable interest in the trust property then they will lose their equitable rights in the trust property because the bona fide purchaser will have a defence to any proprietary claim that they may bring against her.[141] However, the cases hold that the beneficiaries have an equitable interest in the substitute property. **12–107**

In *Foskett v McKeown*,[142] the majority of the House of Lords said that the reason for this is that the beneficiaries have a subsisting equitable interest in the substitute property. This is a difficult idea. The beneficiaries' right to the substitute property cannot be the same right as the right which they previously had to the trust property. The reason is that a property right is a right to specific property which cannot be detached from the property to which it relates and reattached to some new property.[143] For example, an ownership right in land relates to the land, and so it cannot be the same right as the right to the sale proceeds of the land, even if one right is exchanged for the other. **12–108**

In *Foskett*, their Lordships ignored this, and focussed on the beneficiaries' interests as interests in the trust fund established by the settlor. Lord Browne-Wilkinson held that[144]: **12–109**

> The only trusts at issue are the express trusts of the purchasers' trust deed. Under those express trusts the purchasers were entitled to equitable proprietary interests in the original moneys [which they paid over to

---

140 See paras 8–006—8–007.
141 See paras 12–117ff.
142 [2001] 1 A.C. 102.
143 P. Birks, "Tracing, Property, and Unjust Enrichment" (2002) 54 C.L.P. 231, 244–245; R. Chambers, "Tracing and Unjust Enrichment" in J.W. Neyers et al. (eds), *Understanding Unjust Enrichment* (Hart Publishing, 2004), pp.273–274. See too A. Burrows, "Proprietary Restitution: Unmasking Unjust Enrichment" (2001) 117 L.Q.R. 412.
144 [2001] 1 A.C. 102 at 110. Cf. *Taylor v Plumer* (1815) 3 M. & S. 562 at 575.

> the trustee]. Like any other equitable proprietary interest, those equitable proprietary interests under the purchasers' trust deed which originally existed in the moneys paid to [the trustee] now exist in any other property which, in law, now represents the original trust assets. . . . If, as a result of tracing, it can be said that certain of the policy moneys are what now represent part of the assets subject to the trusts of the purchasers trust deed, then as a matter of English property law the purchasers have an absolute interest in such moneys.

**12–110** Similarly, Lord Millett held that the beneficiaries have "a continuing beneficial interest not merely in the trust property but in its traceable proceeds also",[145] and in reply to criticism that this reasoning entails the adoption of a fiction, he has written extra-judicially that "'the fiction of persistence' is not a fiction [because the] beneficiaries' interests in the new investment are exactly the same as their interest in the old."[146] However, this cannot be true: the new property is not the old property, and prior to the acquisition of the new property with trust property, no one owed any obligation to the beneficiaries in respect of the new property. It follows that the beneficiaries' right in the new property after it has been acquired must be a new right whose existence calls for explanation.

**12–111** To the extent that they recognised this, the majority of the House of Lords in *Foskett* explained the beneficiaries' new right in the traceable proceeds of trust property as a right which arose in order to "vindicate their property rights" in the original trust property.[147] However, the mere fact of the beneficiaries' equitable ownership of the original trust property is not enough in itself to explain their acquisition of a new proprietary right in a traceable substitute.[148] In Peter Birks' terms, it is not an "event" to which the new right can respond.[149]

**12–112** To explain this further, and to identify the reason why the beneficiaries have proprietary rights to substitute property acquired through unauthorised transactions entered by trustees and third parties, we should start by recalling what happens when a trustee sells trust property using her power of sale to enter an authorised transaction with a buyer, or uses trust money to buy an authorised investment using her powers of investment to enter an authorised transaction with a seller.[150] In such cases, the beneficiaries' interest in the trust property is overreached, and they acquire a new interest in the substitute property, by a process which the beneficiaries cannot afterwards call into question. The source of the beneficiaries' new rights in the substitute property is ultimately the settlor's intention that they should have rights in the original trust property and any new property acquired in exchange for the original property, along with the trustee's intention that the beneficiaries should acquire rights in substitute property when she acquires these through an authorised exercise of her powers under the trust deed, to be held by her on the same terms as those on which she held the original trust property.[151]

---

145 *Foskett* at 127.

146 Lord Millett, "Proprietary Restitution" in Degeling and Edelman (eds), *Equity in Commercial Law* (2005), pp.315–316, adding that "wrongfully substituted assets are [not] held on a constructive trust . . . [but] continue to be held on the same trusts throughout. If the claimant was the beneficiary under an express trust, the substituted assets are held on the same express trusts." In his essay in the same volume, "Old and New in the Law of Tracing", Charles Rickett says essentially the same thing when he writes at pp.135–138 and 140–144 that equitable property rights possess the attribute of "transmissibility", arguing that if this were not so then every time a trustee effects an authorised substitution of trust property for a new asset, the new asset would be held on a new trust, and the disposal of the original asset would have to comply with the formality rules which govern the disposition of subsisting equitable interests.

147 [2001] 1 A.C. 102 at 129, per Lord Millett. See too Lord Browne-Wilkinson's comments at 110 and Lord Hoffmann's comments at 115.

148 As suggested in R. Grantham and C. Rickett, "Property Rights: A Legally Significant Event" [2003] C.L.J. 417; Lord Millett, "Proprietary Restitution" in Degeling and Edelman (eds), *Equity in Commercial Law* (2005); G. Virgo *The Principles of the Law of Restitution*, 2nd edn (Oxford University Press, 2006), pp.570–574.

149 See, e.g. P. Birks, "Tracing, Property, and Unjust Enrichment" (2002) 54 C.L.P. 231, 245.

150 See para.12–099.

151 See too Chambers, "Tracing and Unjust Enrichment" in Neyers et al. (eds), *Understanding Unjust Enrichment* (2004), pp.263, 267.

The same analysis can also be used to explain the case where trustees purport to acquire new property for the beneficiaries, but act beyond the scope of their powers. As noted above,[152] the beneficiaries can retrospectively adopt the unauthorised transaction, which looks like an ad hoc variation of the trust, retrospectively giving the beneficiaries rights whose source, again, is the settlor's intention, agreed to by the trustee, to create such rights in their favour. **12–113**

What of the case where a trustee misappropriates trust property and uses it to acquire new property for herself? Here one can also say that when the trustee first takes office she agrees with the settlor that she will hold whatever traceable proceeds of trust funds come into her hands for the beneficiaries, and that the beneficiaries' equitable proprietary right to these therefore responds to the trustee's intention that the beneficiaries should have them. Obviously it is tempting to say of this situation that the trustee does not actually intend the beneficiaries to acquire an interest in the new property, as she actually intends to take them for herself. However, it is not the trustee's current intention, but her original intention at the time of taking office, which is the source of the beneficiaries' proprietary right. Equity will not allow the trustee to go back on her word, and will, in effect, specifically enforce her promise to act for the beneficiaries. **12–114**

Finally, we come to the case where the traceable proceeds of misdirected trust assets are in the hands of third party recipients. Here, the recipients have not previously agreed to hold the new assets for the beneficiaries, and the beneficiaries' right to them could therefore be explained either on the basis that the recipient commits a wrong (analogous to conversion at common law) when she interferes with the beneficiaries' rights in the original trust property, or else that she is unjustly enriched at the beneficiaries' expense when trust assets are used to acquire new assets for the benefit of the recipient.[153] **12–115**

In *Foskett*, Lord Millett denied that beneficiaries can claim the traceable proceeds of trust property in the hands of third parties on the ground of unjust enrichment.[154] However, his Lordship's reasons for saying this do not stand up to scrutiny. They depend on the premise that the law of property and the law of unjust enrichment cannot both be in issue in a single claim. This entails a categorical error, since property and unjust enrichment are not categories that can be opposed: the first is a type of right, the second is a source of rights.[155] Moreover, his Lordship purports to analyse claims to traceable proceeds in the hands of third parties in the same way that he analyses claims to traceable proceeds in the hands of trustees. Yet for the reasons we have explained, the two types of claim are different, since the trustees have previously agreed to hold the proceeds for the beneficiaries while the third parties have not. **12–116**

## *C. The Bona Fide Purchase Defence*

The law generally holds that no one can pass a better title to property to another person than the title she possesses. Exceptionally, however, a bona fide purchaser for value of legal title to property can take free of any prior equitable interest in the property, provided that she had no notice of this equitable interest. This rule was largely settled during the Chancellorship of Lord Nottingham, in the late seventeenth century.[156] **12–117**

---

152 See para.12–100.

153 P. Birks, "Property and Unjust Enrichment: Categorical Truths" [1997] N.Z.L.R. 623, 661; A. Burrows, *The Law of Restitution*, 2nd edn (Oxford University Press, 2002), pp.64–66 and 208–209.

154 [2001] 1 A.C. 102 at 127.

155 P. Birks, *Unjust Enrichment*, 2nd edn (Oxford University Press, 2005), pp.32–38.

156 See, generally, "Introduction" in D.E.C. Yale (ed) *Lord Nottingham's Chancery Caes* (Vol.II) (Selden Society, 1961), Vol.79.

**12–118** The burden of proof lies on the defendant to establish the provision of value, good faith, and lack of notice.[157] According to Lord Wilberforce, the question whether the purchaser has acted in good faith is separate from the question whether she had notice,[158] but there are no clear examples of these two questions operating independently in the case law. Defendants must show not only that they had no actual notice but also that they had no constructive notice of the equitable interest.[159] The doctrine of constructive notice has been explained by Lord Browne-Wilkinson as follows[160]

> if the party asserting that he takes free of the earlier rights of another knows of certain facts which put him on inquiry as to the possible existence of the rights of that other and he fails to make such inquiry or take such other steps as are reasonable to verify whether such earlier right does or does not exist, he will have constructive notice of the earlier right and take subject to it.

**12–119** Defendants must also show that they have given value,[161] but no enquiry is normally made into the adequacy of the consideration provided.[162] For the purposes of the defence the relevant value must have passed under a valid contract between the defendant and the party from whom she received the relevant property. A mere factual exchange will not suffice. So, in *Banque Belge pour l'Etranger v Hambrouck*[163] the Court of Appeal held that the defence was not available to a woman who had received misappropriated money in exchange for cohabiting with her lover as this constituted an immoral consideration that was not recognised by law. The same point arose in a different form in *Independent Trustee Services Ltd v G.P. Noble Trustees Ltd* where money was paid under a consent order that was later set aside, with the result that the consent order then fell to be treated as though it had never had any legal effect.

*Independent Trustee Services Ltd v G.P. Noble Trustees Ltd*

Court of Appeal [2013] Ch. 91

**12–120** The defendant's former husband was the trustee of various pension schemes from which he misappropriated money. He paid the defendant some of this money under a consent order which embodied the terms of an agreement by which they had compromised her claim for ancillary relief. She had no notice of his breach of trust and since the payment was made in satisfaction of his liability under the consent order, she acquired legal title to the money as a bona fide purchaser for value without notice. She then discovered that he had not made full disclosure of his assets and won an order that the consent order should be set aside and that her ancillary relief application should be reheard. At this point, however, the claimant trustee company, which had been appointed as the trustee of the pension schemes by the Pensions Regulator, brought an action to recover the money, arguing that the effect of setting aside the consent order was that she had taken back the consideration which she had provided by agreeing to that order

---

157 *Pilcher v Rawlins* (1873) L.R. 7 Ch. App. 259 at 268–269. *Attorney General v Biphosphated Guano Co.* (1879) 11 Ch. D. 327; *Re Nisbet and Potts' Contract* [1906] 1 Ch. 386 at 404, 409 and 410; *G.L. Baker v Medway Supplies Ltd* [1958] 1 W.L.R. 1217 at 1220; *Barclays Bank Plc v Boulter* [1998] 1 W.L.R. 1 at 8.

158 *Midland Bank Ltd v Green* [1981] A.C. 513 at 528.

159 *Pilcher v Rawlins* (1872) L.R. 7 Ch. App. 259; *Cave v Cave* (1880) 15 Ch. D. 639; *Northern Counties of England Fire Insurance Co v Whipp* (1884) 26 Ch. D. 482 at 495–496; *Earl of Sheffield v London Joint Stock Bank Ltd* (1888) 13 App. Cas. 333; *Thomson v Clydesdale Bank Ltd* [1893] A.C. 282; *Carl Zeiss Stiftung v Herbert Smith & Co (No.2)* [1969] 2 Ch. 276; *Kingsnorth Finance Co Ltd v Tizard* [1986] 1 W.L.R. 783. Note that the doctrine of notice now has only a very limited role to play in registered conveyancing.

160 *Barclays Bank Plc v O'Brien* [1994] 1 A.C. 180 at 195–196. See too *Macmillan Inc v Bishopsgate Investment Trust Plc (No.3)* [1995] 1 W.L.R. 978 at 1014; *Sinclair Investments (UK) Ltd v Versailles Trade Finance Ltd (in admin rec'ship)* [2012] Ch. 453 at [97]–[112].

161 The rule does not protect volunteers: *Mansell v Mansell* (1732) 2 P. Wms 678; *Re Strachan* (1876) 4 Ch. D. 123; *Banque Belge pour l'Etranger v Hambrouck* [1921] 1 K.B. 321; *Wu Koon Tai v Wu Yau Loi* [1997] A.C. 179 at 184 and 189–190.

162 *Basset v Nosworthy* (1673) Rep. temp. Finch 102; *Midland Bank Ltd v Green* [1981] A.C. 513.

163 [1921] 1 K.B. 321 at 326 and 329.

and, therefore, she had retrospectively ceased to be a bona fide purchaser for value of the money, and should therefore be treated as though she had held the money subject to the beneficial title of the pension schemes throughout. This claim was rejected at first instance but allowed by the Court of Appeal.

LLOYD L.J. (with whom PATTEN and TOMLINSON L.JJ. agreed): . . . [The question whether] the prior equitable interests of the beneficiaries under the original trust can be asserted against the recipient . . . depends on whether the respondent can successfully deploy the defence that she is a bona fide purchaser for value without notice. It is clear that this is a defence for her, the onus being on her to raise it and to establish it; it is not up to the claimant to prove that she does not have that status. This is not a case in which anything is likely to turn on evidential points, but it seems to me that it is important to keep it in mind that this is how the point works. **12–121**

So, the question is whether she can establish that defence when the value that she gave at the time of receipt of the legal title to the money was given under a transaction . . . which was voidable and has since then been avoided. It may or may not matter at whose instance it was avoided, but in the present instance it was at her initiative. **12–122**

The question whether the recipient of the legal title had notice is to be determined at the time of acquisition of that title, at the latest. The cases in which an earlier date may be relevant do not matter for present purposes and I will ignore that possibility. I am not aware of any circumstances in which the question whether the recipient had notice could be affected by anything that happened later. That is because it is a question of fact. **12–123**

Mr Twigger's argument was that whether the purchaser gave value ought to be tested as at the same date. He pointed out that it is settled that a purchaser for value without notice can give an effectively valid and clear title by a subsequent transfer, even if the transferee under that disposition does have notice of the beneficiaries' title.[164] . . . The policy behind this principle is that otherwise the title of the purchaser, having acquired for value without notice, would be capable of being blighted by the later assertion of the breach of trust . . . Consistently with this, Mr Twigger relied on a number of statements in the cases to the effect that, once the property is in the hands of a purchaser for value without notice the equitable title of the beneficiaries is extinguished.[165] . . . The point is expressed rather graphically by Dr Lionel Smith, as follows:[166] **12–124**

> "The effect of the defence is to allow the defendant to hold its legal proprietary rights unencumbered by the pre-existing equitable proprietary rights. In other terms, when the defence operates, the pre-existing equitable proprietary rights are stripped away and lost in the transaction by which the defendant acquires its legal proprietary rights."

. . . Undoubtedly the giving of value would normally be determined, one way or the other, as at the moment of acquisition of the legal title. That is because, normally, once value has been given it is not taken away or given back. Transactions by which value passes are not normally set aside at a later stage. However, there are circumstances in which a transaction can be set aside, either to recognise that it was void from the start, or if it is voidable for some reason and an aggrieved party with the necessary standing chooses to avoid it. What we have to address on this appeal is the effect of the avoidance of a relevant transaction, where the earlier subsistence of the transaction was what enabled a recipient to show that value was given for the receipt . . . I am not aware of any case or text in which this point has been considered . . . **12–125**

In the present case, the situation is a little more complex than that of a contract or other dealing between two parties. There had been an agreement between Mr and Mrs Morris, but the making of the consent order was not (as it would have been in some other areas of the court's jurisdiction) purely contractual. It depended on the court's willingness to exercise its statutory jurisdiction under the Matrimonial Causes Act 1973 . . . Nevertheless, it seems to me that the analogy with a contract or other consensual disposition, set aside as being voidable for misrepresentation or on some other ground, is of some value in determining the effect of the setting aside of the consent order. **12–126**

In principle it seems to me that there is much to be said for the proposition that, where a defendant **12–127**

---

164 See *Wilkes v Spooner* [1911] 2 K.B. 473.

165 See *Re Diplock* [1948] Ch. 465 at 539, interpreting Lord Parker of Waddington's speech in *Sinclair v Brougham* [1914] A.C. 398, and *Foskett v McKeown* [2001] 1 A.C. 102 at 129 where Lord Millett said that a proprietary claim "is subject to the bona fide purchaser for value defence, which operates to clear the defendant's title."

166 *The Law of Tracing* (1997), p. 386.

relies on the defence of having been a bona fide purchaser for value without notice at the time of receipt, and for that purpose has to show that value was given under a transaction, but by the time that the point is raised the relevant transaction has been set aside, then it is no longer open to the defendant to deploy that defence successfully or, at any rate, that the fact that the transaction has been set aside, and the circumstances in which it was, are relevant to the enquiry as to whether value was given for the transfer of the legal title. Otherwise, the question whether the defence can be made good would have to be determined on a false basis, ignoring not only the factor vitiating the original transaction but also the fact that the transaction has been set aside on the ground of that factor, and the parties to that transaction restored, so far as they can be, to their original positions, as if the transaction had never taken place.

**12–128** Mr Twigger submitted that this is not so, and that if the defence was open to the defendant immediately after the time of receipt, then subsequent changes, including the setting aside of the relevant transaction, make no difference. He argued that this should be so as a matter of policy in the interests of certainty. He postulated that, if later events could be relevant to the issue of value, someone who had for years had a valid title could suddenly find that his title had disappeared. By analogy he argued that authorities concerned with what counts as value in the context of a purchase of land all focus on the substance of the transaction by which title passed. That is no doubt correct. However, the special case which we have to consider is also one in which what is in issue is the transaction under which title was acquired, but in the unusual situation in which that transaction has later been set aside.

**12–129** . . . Mr Twigger pointed out that in any case of a voidable transaction liable to be rescinded, and even in case of a disposal in breach of trust, the transfer of the property does have some effect unless and until it is challenged. In a case such as the present there would be no likelihood that, once a new trustee was in place, the assets dealt with in breach of trust would not be pursued, as best they could be, into the hands of those who had dealt with them or received them. That would not always be the case, even in a case of breach of trust. A dealing with trust assets might be in breach of trust but nevertheless profitable, as in the case of a successful though unauthorised investment, and the beneficiaries might choose to ratify the trustee's improper dealing and claim the benefit of the assets acquired, which would be inconsistent with following the money used for their acquisition. (Of course such following would only be possible, at all, if the seller had notice of the breach of trust.)

**12–130** Support for Mr Twigger's argument in this respect might be found in the judgment of Potter L.J. in the Court of Appeal in *Twinsectra Ltd v Yardley*,[167] and in particular the proposition that, until rescission, in the case of a transaction which is voidable for misrepresentation, the original owner has no proprietary interest in the subject matter of the dealing, but has only a "mere equity" consisting of his right to set aside the transaction . . . [However, the] significant distinction between cases such as those under consideration in *Twinsectra Ltd v Yardley* . . . and the present case is that in those cases the transferor under the voidable transaction had the whole legal and beneficial title to start with . . . It seems to me that it is wrong, for present purposes, to draw an analogy from that type of case, where the victim of the misrepresentation has a "mere equity" of rescission, to the case of breach of trust. In the latter case the beneficiaries have more than a mere equity; they still own their beneficial interests in the trust property unaffected by the disposition made without authority under the trust. A trustee does not own the beneficial interest in the property and cannot pass it to a transferee unless he does so by an act authorised under the trust which overreaches the interest of the trust beneficiaries.

**12–131** . . . In a different area of the law, a person in possession of land, even though unlawfully as against the true owner, has the right to exclude others and can pass the benefit of his period of possession to an assignee, with a view to establishing a title by adverse possession. In the same way, a person who holds under a title acquired in breach of trust, even if not a bona fide purchaser for value without notice, has, in a sense, a kind of a title which can be passed to others and which could, in practice, remain undisturbed by any claim by a party entitled to complain of the breach of trust, even if the title has not passed through someone who has the benefit of the status of bona fide purchaser for value without notice.

**12–132** Nevertheless, it seems to me that the possibility of that occurring in practice does not falsify the proposition that a transferee of the legal title to property under a disposition made in breach of trust, or a successor in title to such a person, does not have the beneficial title to the property, which remains held on the original trusts, unless either the transferee, or a successor in title, was a bona fide purchaser for value without notice. The trustee acting in breach of trust can transfer the legal title, but cannot vest

[167] [1999] Lloyd's Rep. Bank. 438 at 461–2.

the beneficial interest in the property in a bona fide purchaser for value without notice, since he does not own that title and is not acting in a way which enables him, under the trust, to overreach the beneficiaries' equitable interest. Despite that inability, the availability of the bona fide purchaser defence means that a transaction in favour of a bona fide purchaser for value without notice is as effective as it would be if he could vest the beneficial title in the purchaser. Thereafter the purchaser can deal with the asset free from any prior claim of the beneficiaries. That, however, does not provide the answer to the question arising in the circumstances of the present case.

The limit of the exceptional circumstances posed by the present case is that, if the transaction under which value was given at the time of the acquisition of title has subsequently been set aside, and if the adverse claim by the third party (here the trustee on behalf of the original beneficiaries) is made after that has happened, then (if the claimant is right) the question whether value has been given is to be addressed with the benefit of knowing that the transaction has been set aside. **12–133**

In any given case, much may depend on the details of what has happened by way of the rescission or setting aside of the transaction. I will turn to the details of the present case in due course. But for the moment I address Mr Twigger's submission which was that, whatever the details may be, the rescission or setting aside is irrelevant to the claim by the beneficiaries against the third party, here Mrs Morris. Because she has once had the status of bona fide purchaser for value without notice, he contended that she is thereafter immune from a claim against her, whatever may have happened thereafter. **12–134**

It is not the present case, but his proposition would presumably apply even if the conduct which led to the transaction being set aside was that of the recipient of the legal title. Any misrepresentation or other conduct of the recipient which led to the transaction being set aside at the instance of the party who had transferred the legal title would, in itself, be entirely separate and distinct from the circumstances which gave the beneficiaries a right to pursue the assets into the hands of their recipients. In theory (I accept that it may not be at all likely to arise often in practice) an ancillary relief order might be set aside because the recipient had not complied with the duty of full disclosure, for example if a wife had not disclosed funds received from a large lottery win or an inheritance. If an order made in those circumstances were set aside at the instance of the husband, and if it had in the meantime been satisfied by a payment arranged by the husband but using money which he had obtained or procured in breach of trust, it is hard to see why the value given by the wife in those circumstances should be regarded as concluding the issue of recovery by the beneficiaries of the trust for once and for all. The wife would not have committed any wrong as against the beneficiaries, but her entitlement to use the bona fide purchaser for value without notice defence would be difficult to maintain if the value had been given under a transaction whose benefit she herself had obtained by misrepresentation and non-disclosure, and which had been set aside on that ground. **12–135**

. . . In relation to the argument that to allow the setting aside of the transaction to be taken into account might render titles precarious even after a long time, it is, of course, possible that a breach of trust might come to light only after some considerable time, so that the rights of the aggrieved beneficiaries might be asserted only after a good deal of time had elapsed. That might, therefore, lead to a transferee's title being challenged after some years. However, if the transferee was innocent, in the sense of having no notice of the breach of trust at the time of acquiring the legal title, intervening dealings with the property before the time when notice was given would not give rise to any claim against the transferee, except to any traceable proceeds of the disposition, and any person who had in the meantime acquired legal title to any part of the property for value without notice would himself be safe in his possession because he himself would have the defence. In relation to any innocent transferee, the procedures for following and tracing would be applied in a different and less stringent manner as compared to those which would operate if the transferee is not innocent, where there would be less reason to be sensitive in relation to that process. **12–136**

As it seems to me, if the defence of bona fide purchaser for value without notice depends, as regards value, on a transaction which has been set aside by the time the defence falls to be raised, the fact of the setting aside should be capable of being relevant to whether the defence can be made out. I do not accept Mr Twigger's argument that this involves imposing a trust on the recipient in circumstances in which that cannot properly be done, for the reasons given above. Nor is he correct to speak of the equitable title to the beneficiaries in the original trust being revived or revested. Rather, that title has continued to subsist in the meantime and it is no longer capable of being defeated by the bona fide purchaser defence, any more than it would be if the property were again in the hands of the person guilty of the original breach of trust. Neither in principle nor in practice can I see any sound reason for the court being required to shut its eyes to the fact that, by the time the point arises, the transaction on which the recipient of the property depends to show that he or she is a bona fide purchaser for value without notice has been set aside, at the instance of **12–137** whichever party, on grounds such as misrepresentation, non-disclosure or any other such vitiating factor, so that it is to be treated, as far as possible, as if it had never happened, or at any rate had never had any legal effect. . .

**Questions**

1. Is the following approach sensible for a claimant beneficiary where her trustees have misdirected trust funds?
   (a) Go for a proprietary claim to trust assets or their traceable proceeds, if possible.
   (b) Go for personal liability: (i) of the trustees for breach of trust; (ii) of any third party who has dishonestly assisted in a breach of trust and is therefore personally liable to the same extent as the trustee or fiduciary whose breach she has assisted; (iii) of any third party who has beneficially received the trust property but has disposed of it after her conscience was affected that she had improperly received the property; or (iv) of any third party who has beneficially received the trust property and who has disposed of it, on the basis that her knowledge or ignorance of its improper provenance is irrelevant because she is strictly liable to repay the value received in unjust enrichment unless she can establish a change of position defence.
2. Theo is the sole trustee of a trust for Baz. Theo enters a contract to buy a vintage car under which he pays the car dealer £40,000 and promises to pay him the £20,000 balance of the purchase price in one year's time. A year later, Theo decides not to make this payment out of his personal resources and instead transfers £20,000 to the car dealer's bank account from the Baz Trust Account, which he maintains at Caring Bank Plc. The car has now doubled in value. At the same time Theo transfers another £5,000 out of the trust account into his personal account with the bank, bringing the balance in that account from £5,000 up to £10,000. He then takes £5,000 out of his current account and uses it to buy shares which have now doubled in value. Finally he transfers another £5,000 out of the trust account into his girlfriend Gigi's personal account. Innocently believing the money to be a legitimate birthday gift, Gigi spends it all. Theo makes all three transfers from the trust account with the help of the bank manager Roxy, whom he tells untruthfully that the purpose of the transfers is to evade tax. Roxy is happy to assist him as she believes that paying tax is morally wrong because the Government spends some of it on nuclear weapons. **Advise Baz.**

# 13

# REMEDIES FOR BREACH OF FIDUCIARY DUTY

## 1. Introduction

### A. Preliminary Points

To set the scene, some points which have been made in Chapter 9 should be repeated here. First, the expression "fiduciary duty" has been used by the courts in different senses.[1] They have used it to describe duties that are typically owed by trustees, such as the duty to adhere to the limits of one's authority when handling property for another person's benefit. They have also used it to describe the duty owed by a person, commonly termed a "fiduciary", to act in the exclusive interest of a principal. This chapter concerns breaches of fiduciary duty in the latter sense. **13–001**

Secondly, this duty is manifested in the rule that the fiduciary cannot validly act in her own interests when there is a conflict between her personal interests and the interests of her principal. The courts have taken a stern line against fiduciaries when defining the situations in which a conflict of interest exists.[2] **13–002**

Thirdly, the "no conflicts" rule was not originally conceptualised by the courts as a rule that imposed a primary duty on the fiduciary to avoid conflicts of interest, breach of which would trigger a secondary duty to pay compensation for loss caused by the breach. It was conceptualised differently, as a rule which disabled the fiduciary from validly contracting with her principal and thus rendered any such contract voidable, meaning that it would be legally enforceable unless it was rescinded by the principal.[3] **13–003**

On this conception of the "no conflicts" rule, no question could arise of the fiduciary incurring a compensatory liability for breach of duty, but in the late twentieth century compensatory awards for breach of fiduciary duty began to be made on a large scale, forcing a reappraisal of the nature of the rule. This conceptual reappraisal is not yet complete and the law is currently in an state of transition between the two ideas of fiduciary "disability" and fiduciary "duty". One consequence has been that the courts currently operate two distinct and mutually incompatible theories of why gain-based remedies are available for breach of fiduciary duty[4]: one holds that fiduciaries are disabled from taking unauthorised profits for themselves, while the other holds that their breach of a primary duty to avoid conflicts of interest triggers a secondary liability to disgorge their profits. This contradiction makes the law hard to understand and apply, and it must be hoped that the courts will soon resolve it. **13–004**

---

1 See paras 9–008—9–017.
2 See paras 9–027—9–064.
3 See paras 9–073—9–077.
4 See, e.g. *DEG-Deutsche Investitions und Entwicklungsgesellschaft mbH v Koshy* [2004] 1 B.C.L.C. 131 at [104]–[109].

### *B. Overview of the Chapter*

13-005 In Chapter 9 we noted that trustees owe fiduciary duties to their beneficiaries, and that fiduciary duties are also owed by other parties to their principals.[5] In section 2 below, we review the circumstances in which fiduciary duties are imposed. In sections 3–7 we then discuss five remedies for breach of fiduciary duty, considering when they are awarded and how they work: rescission of a contract between a principal and a fiduciary, or between a principal and a third party, accompanied in appropriate cases by consequential orders for the return of property transferred under the contract; "pecuniary rescission", meaning the award of a money sum representing the value of property transferred under a voidable contract that can no longer be restored *in specie*; equitable compensation for other types of loss sustained by the principal; an account of the profits made by the fiduciary through her breach of duty and a consequential order that she pay the amount of such profits to the principal; and a constructive trust imposed on such profits. In section 8 we finally discuss whether the rules governing the operation of these remedies are apt to achieve the goals which the courts pursue when making awards for breach of fiduciary duty, and whether these goals are themselves appropriate and well-conceived.

13-006 In a case in the Supreme Court of Canada, *3464920 Canada Inc v Strother*, McLachlin CJ observed that[6]:

> [there is an ongoing] discussion throughout the Commonwealth as to the role causation, and other limiting factors used at common law should play in devising appropriate remedies for breach of . . . fiduciary duties . . . Underlying this debate is the tension between the need to deter fiduciaries from abusing their trust on the one hand, and the goal of achieving a remedy that is fair to all those affected, on the other.

The following account of remedies for breach of fiduciary duty should be read with these words in mind: do the rules governing the award and assessment of remedies against defaulting fiduciaries operate too harshly, too leniently, or are they just right?

## 2. When Are Fiduciary Duties Imposed?

### *A. Fiduciary Relationships*

13-007 As Joshua Getzler has explained,[7] the idea that fiduciary duties should be imposed on parties in certain types of relationship is sourced in late medieval and early modern legal rules that constrained co-owners from dealing with the shared property without due consideration of one another's interests, prevented the exploitation of wards by their guardians, required bailees and agents to prioritise their principals' interests when dealing with third parties on their principals' behalf, and regulated the activities of office holders. The courts of Chancery drew on these bodies of doctrine when developing the rule that trustees owe fiduciary duties to their beneficiaries, a rule which has formed part of English trust law since at least the early eighteenth century.[8] During the nineteenth and twentieth centuries, the courts then drew on the example of the trustee-beneficiary

---

5 See paras 9-018–9-019.

6 [2007] 2 S.C.R. 177 at [156].

7 J. Getzler, "Rumford Market and the Genesis of Fiduciary Obligations" in A. Burrows and Lord Rodger of Earlsferry (eds), *Mapping the Law: Essays in Memory of Peter Birks* (Oxford University Press, 2006), pp.590–597.

8 *Keech v Sandford* (1726) Sel. Cas. Ch. 61, though trustees were not regularly described as "fiduciaries" in this sense until the nineteenth century: e.g. *Woodhouse v Meredith* (1820) 1 J. & W. 204 at 213 (arguendo); *Hoghton v Hoghton* (1852) 15 Beav. 278 at 287–288. (arguendo); *New Sombrero Phosphate Co v Erlanger* (1877) 5 Ch.D. 73 at 118; *Boswell v Coaks (No. 1)* (1886) 11 App. Cas. 232 at 245; *Bray v Ford* [1896] A.C. 44 at 51–52.

relationship in turn to hold that fiduciary duties should also be owed by other parties in analogous relationships.[9]

Certain features of the trustee-beneficiary relationship have been thought particularly relevant to the question whether an analogy can be drawn between this relationship and others. Trustees assume office voluntarily and thereby acquire powers whose exercise affects the beneficiaries' property rights and legal relations with third parties. Beneficiaries have a reasonable expectation that the trustees will not abuse their powers and position in a way that detrimentally affects them. Other relationships possess similar features and have consequently been held to be fiduciary relationships as a matter of law. Examples are the relationships between the executor or administrator and the beneficiary of a deceased person's estate,[10] between a solicitor and a client,[11] between a principal and an agent,[12] between partners,[13] between a company promoter and the company,[14] and between a company director and the company.[15] **13–008**

These fiduciary relationships are status-based: they arise as a matter of law as a result of the parties' relationship. There are additionally fact-based fiduciary relationships where fiduciary duties are imposed on an ad hoc basis according to the factual circumstances of a case. To give some examples: an army sergeant owed a fiduciary duty to the Crown which he breached when he took bribes to escort smugglers' lorries through police checks with the aid of his military uniform[16]; a solicitor who took it on himself to negotiate on behalf of trustees and beneficiaries for the purchase of company shares owed them a fiduciary duty as a "self-appointed agent" which he breached when he bought some of the shares for himself[17]; and a financier owed a fiduciary duty to an applicant for a loan that he breached when the applicant supplied him with confidential information that he communicated to a third party who used it to conclude a deal to the profit of the third party and the financier.[18] **13–009**

Various cases concerning joint ventures also show that although these are business arrangements, the parties to which are often arm's-length contracting parties who owe one another no fiduciary duties, situations can arise where one joint-venturer is reasonably entitled to expect that the other will act in their joint interest to the exclusion of her own several interest, with the result that a fiduciary duty is owed.[19] Other cases show that although the employment relationship is not generally a **13–010**

---

9 e.g. *Re West of England & South Wales District Bank, Ex p. Dale & Co* (1879) 11 Ch.D. 772 at 778 per Fry J: "a fiduciary relationship . . . is one in respect of which if a wrong arise, the same remedy exists against the wrong-doer on behalf of the principal as would exist against a trustee on behalf of the cestui que trust."

10 *Re Diplock* [1948] Ch. 465; *Commissioner of Stamp Duties (Queensland) v Livingston* [1965] A.C. 694 at 707.

11 *Nocton v Lord Ashburton* [1914] A.C. 932; *McMaster v Byrne* [1952] 1 All E.R. 1362; *Clark Boyce v Mouat* [1994] 1 A.C. 428; *Hilton v Barker Booth & Eastwood (a firm)* [2005] 1 W.L.R. 567. See too S. Degeling and M. Legg, "Fiduciary Obligations of Lawyers in Australian Class Actions: Conflicts between Duties" (2014) 37 U.N.S.W.L.J. 914.

12 *Lowther v Lowther* (1806) 13 Ves. 95 at [103]; *Parker v McKenna* (1874) 10 Ch. App. 96 at 124–125; *Boston Deep Sea Fishing Co v Ansell* (1888) 39 Ch. D. 389; *Hurstanger Ltd v Wilson* [2008] Bus. L.R. 216; *FHR European Ventures LLP v Cedar Capital Partners LLC* [2015] A.C. 250.

13 *Bentley v Craven* (1853) 18 Beav. 75; *Thompson's Trustee v Heaton* [1974] 1 All E.R. 1239; *John Taylors (a firm) v Masons* [2005] W.T.L.R. 1519.

14 *Lydney Iron Ore Co v Bird* (1886) 33 Ch. D. 85 at 94; *Gluckstein v Barnes* [1900] A.C. 240.

15 *Re West of England & South Wales District Bank, Ex p. Dale & Co* (1879) 11 Ch. D. 772; *Furs Ltd v Tomkies* (1936) 54 C.L.R. 583; *Regal (Hastings) Ltd v Gulliver* [1967] 2 A.C. 134; Companies Act 2006 s.175.

16 *Reading v Attorney General* [1949] 2 K.B. 232.

17 *Boardman v Phipps* [1967] 2 A.C. 46, discussed at para.9–063. Cf. *English v Dedham Vale Properties Ltd* [1978] 1 W.L.R. 93.

18 *United Pan Europe Communications NV v Deutsche Bank AG* [2000] 2 B.C.L.C. 461.

19 *Lac Minerals Ltd v International Corona Resources Ltd* (1989) 61 D.L.R. (4th) 14; *Hospital Products Ltd v US Surgical Corp* (1984) 156 C.L.R. 41; *Noranda Australia Ltd v Lachlan Resources* (1988) 14 N.W.S.L.R. 1; *John v James* [1991] F.S.R. 397 at 433; *Elliott v Wheeldon* [1993] B.C.L.C. 53 at 57; *Murad v Al-Saraj* [2005] W.T.L.R. 1573; *Chirnside v Fay* [2007] 1 N.Z.L.R. 433; *Ross River Ltd v Waveley Commercial Ltd* [2014] 1 B.C.L.C. 545.

fiduciary relationship either, some employees can owe fiduciary duties to their employers while the employment relationship subsists.[20]

13–011 Such decisions are all very context-specific and although the courts have often described the circumstances in which fiduciary duties are imposed, their comments do not amount—and are not usually meant to amount—to finely grained tests that can predictably discriminate between cases where duties are imposed and cases where they are not. For example,[21] in *Reading v Attorney General*, Asquith LJ said that a fiduciary relationship exists[22]

> (a) whenever the plaintiff entrusts to the defendant property . . . and relies on the defendant to deal with such property for the benefit of the plaintiff or for purposes authorized by him, and not otherwise . . . and (b) whenever the plaintiff entrusts to the defendant a job to be performed . . . and relies on the defendant to procure for the plaintiff the best terms available.

In *Attorney-General v Blake*, Lord Woolf MR said that[23]:

> [The most important] category of fiduciary relationship . . . is the relationship of trust and confidence, which arises whenever one party undertakes to act in the interests of another or places himself in a position where he is obliged to act in the interests of another.

In *Arklow Investments Ltd v Maclean*, Henry J said that[24]:

> The [fiduciary] concept captures a situation where one person is in a relationship with another which gives rise to a legitimate expectation, which equity will recognise, that the fiduciary will not utilise his or her position in such a way which is adverse to the interests of his principal.

And in *Grimaldi v Chameleon Mining NL (No.2)*, Finn J said that "there is no generally agreed and unexceptionable definition of who is a fiduciary", but that the following description sufficed for the purposes of the case[25]

> a person will be in a fiduciary relationship with another when and insofar as that person has undertaken to perform such a function for, or has assumed such a responsibility to, another as would thereby reasonably entitle that other to expect that he or she will act in that other's interest to the exclusion of his or her own or a third party's interest.

13–012 These are apt descriptions of the status-based and fact-based fiduciary relationships which have been identified above. But a legal test needs to explain the cases which fall outside its scope as well as those which fall within it, and on that measure these dicta do less well, since there are relationships which possess the features that are said to be relevant and which are not fiduciary under English law. An example is the doctor-patient relationship,[26] where there are power and assumption

---

20 *Attorney General v Blake* [1998] Ch. 439; *Nottingham University v Fishel* [2000] I.C.R. 1462; *Neary v Dean of Westminster* [1999] I.R.L.R. 288; *Generics (UK) Ltd v Yeda Research and Development Co Ltd* [2013] Bus. L.R. 777. See too A. Frazer, "The Employee's Contractual Duty of Fidelity" (2015) 131 L.Q.R. 53; R. Flannigan, "Employee Fiduciary Accountability" [2015] J.B.L. 189.

21 See also *Hospital Products Ltd v United States Surgical Corp* (1984) 156 C.L.R. 41 at 96–97; *Frame v Smith* [1987] 2 S.C.R. 99 at [136], adopted in *International Corona Resources Ltd v LAC Minerals Ltd* [1989] 2 S.C.R. 574; *Hodgkinson v Simms* [1994] 3 S.C.R. 377 at [29]–[37]; *Perez v Galambos* [2009] 3 S.C.R. 247 at [67]–[68].

22 [1949] 2 K.B. 232 at 236.

23 [1998] Ch. 439 at 454.

24 [2000] 1 W.L.R. 594 at 598.

25 (2012) 200 F.C.R. 296 at [177].

26 *Sidaway v Board of Governors of the Bethlem Royal Hospital* [1985] A.C. 871 at 884: "there is no comparison to be made

of responsibility on one side and on the other side, vulnerability to abuse of that power and a reasonable expectation that the power will not be abused.

Again, it often happens that one commercial party has significant power to affect the financial interests of another commercial party, but the courts rarely find that such relationships are fiduciary, and will only do so when there is strong evidence that one has agreed to act in the interests of the other. Thus in *JP Morgan Chase Bank v Springwell Navigation Corporation*, Gloster J held that[27] **13–013**

> the mere fact that one party to a commercial relationship 'trusts' the other does not predicate a fiduciary relationship. The word 'trust', like the word 'advice', has a variety of meanings. In a broad sense, trust is an important element in many commercial dealings . . . Springwell no doubt 'trusted' Chase to conduct itself in a commercially appropriate manner. But I do not consider that Springwell had any legitimate expectation that, in its commercial dealings with Springwell, Chase would subordinate its interests to those of Springwell.

On the same theme, in *Frame v Smith*, Wilson J said that[28]: **13–014**

> Because of the requirement of vulnerability of the beneficiary at the hands of the fiduciary, fiduciary obligations are seldom present in dealings of experienced businessmen of similar bargaining strength acting at arm's length . . . The law takes the position that such individuals are perfectly capable of agreeing as to the scope of discretion or power to be exercised, i.e., any 'vulnerability' could have been prevented through the more prudent exercise of their bargaining power and the remedies for the wrongful exercise or abuse of that discretion or power . . . are adequate in such a case.

These comments reflect the courts' general attitude that they should not introduce uncertainty into commercial dealings by the "over-ready use of equitable concepts such as fiduciary obligations",[29] and that arm's-length commercial parties should be entitled (and even encouraged) to act in their own self-interest, negotiate the best possible deal for themselves, and take whatever profit-making opportunities come their way. As Sales J said in *Vercoe v Rutland Fund Management Ltd*,[30] **13–015**

> a degree of self-seeking and ruthless behaviour [in commercial dealings] is expected and accepted . . . In a fiduciary relationship, by contrast, self-seeking behaviour is required to be reined in on the grounds that special obligations of trust have been assumed by the fiduciary to the other party.

## *B. Scope of Fiduciary Duties*

Once the court has decided that two parties are in a fiduciary relationship, "that relationship must be examined to see . . . what is the scope and ambit of the duties" that should be imposed on the fiduciary.[31] As Lord Browne-Wilkinson has observed, it is not the case that "all fiduciaries owe the **13–016**

between the relationship of doctor and patient with that of solicitor and client, trustee and cestui qui trust or the other relationships treated in equity as of a fiduciary character." The High Court of Australia takes the same view: *Breen v Williams* (1996) 186 C.L.R. 71; but the Supreme Court of Canada does not: *McInerny v Macdonald* [1992] 2 S.C.R. 138; cf. *Norberg v Wynrib* [1992] 2 S.C.R. 226 at 272.

27 [2008] EWHC 1186 (Comm) at [574], followed in *Barclays Bank plc v Svizera Holdings BV* [2014] EWHC 1020 (Comm) at [8] and *Bailey v Barclays Bank Plc* [2014] EWHC 2882 (QB) at [88].

28 [1987] 2 S.C.R. 99 at 137–138, followed in *International Corona Resources Ltd v LAC Minerals Ltd* [1989] 2 S.C.R. 574 at [149].

29 *Cobbe v Yeoman's Row Management Ltd* [2008] 1 W.L.R. 1752 at [81] per Lord Walker.

30 [2010] EWHC 424 (Ch) at [343].

31 *Boardman v Phipps* [1967] 2 A.C. 46 at 127 per Lord Upjohn. See too *University of Nottingham v Fishel* [2000] I.C.R. 1462 at 1490–1493; *Ross River Ltd v Waveley Commercial Ltd* [2014] 1 B.C.L.C. 545 at [12].

same duties in all circumstances",[32] and as Lord Wilberforce has said, a person "may be in a fiduciary position quoad a part of his activities but not quoad other parts; each transaction, or group of transactions, must be looked at."[33] The courts must therefore determine "the subject matter over which the fiduciary obligations extend",[34] by asking what function or responsibility the fiduciary has assumed, and in Finn J's words[35]

> [this] may be narrow and circumscribed, as is often the case with specific agencies; it may be broad and general, as is characteristically the case with the functions of company directors; its scope may have been antecedently defined or determined; it may have been ordained by past practice; it may be left to the fiduciary's discretion to determine; and it may evolve over time as is commonly the case with partnerships.

**13–017** In the following extract, Sarah Worthington argues that the courts should take a more nuanced approach to the scope of the fiduciary duty owed by directors under English law, as the current rules are operating unfairly in "corporate opportunity" cases.

## S. Worthington, "Fiduciary Duties and Proprietary Remedies: Addressing the Failure of Equitable Formulae"

(2013) 72 C.L.J. 720, 746–747

**13–018** [A] line of cases [has been] focused on determining whether an opportunity is a "corporate opportunity" (i.e. an opportunity which, given the specific ambit of the director's fiduciary duty, might legitimately be pursued for the benefit of the company),[36] or, similarly, a "partnership opportunity".[37] There is good reason to suppose that modern courts are drawing this line in the wrong place,[38] and that deeper thought about the precise import of the general rule against conflicts of duty and interest would see wider adoption of the approach taken in the partnership case of *Aas v Benham*.[39] It must surely be true that even fiduciaries have a private sphere of operation,[40] despite some assertions to the contrary,[41] and that not every successful profit-making endeavour can be captured by the principal.[42]

**13–019** For example, most modern companies have unrestricted objects. This cannot mean that directors have a duty to present to the company for its approval every personal investment they propose to make, or

---

32 *Henderson v Merrett Syndicates Ltd* [1995] 2 A.C. 145 at 206. See too *Re Coomber* [1911] 1 Ch. 723 at 728–729.

33 *New Zealand Netherlands Society "Oranje" Inc v Kuys* [1973] 1 W.L.R. 1126 at [1130]. See too *United Pan-Europe Communications NV v Deutsche Bank AG* [2000] 2 B.C.L.C. 461 at [47]; *Saltri III Ltd v MD Mezzanine SA SICAR (t/a Mezzanine Facility Agent)* [2013] 1 All E.R. (Comm) 661 at [123].

34 *Birtchnell v Equity Trustees Executors & Agency Co Ltd* (1929) 42 C.L.R. 384 at 408 per Dixon J. See also *Chan v Zacharia* (1983) 154 C.L.R. 178 at 195; *Hospital Products Ltd v United States Surgical Corp* (1984) 156 C.L.R. 41 at 102; *Streeter v Western Areas Exploration Pty Ltd (No.2)* (2011) 278 A.L.R. 291 at [70].

35 *Grimaldi v Chameleon Mining NL (No.2)* (2012) 200 F.C.R. 296 at [179].

36 Earlier cases on the equitable rule vary in their approach, some taking a narrow view of which opportunities are caught (*Balston Ltd v Headline Filters Ltd* [1990] F.S.R. 385 at 412; *Industrial Development Consultants Ltd v Cooley* [1972] 1 W.L.R. 443), and some a wider view (*Bhullar v Bhullar* [2003] EWCA Civ 424; *O'Donnell v Shanahan* [2009] EWCA Civ 751).

37 *Aas v Benham* [1891] 2 Ch. 244.

38 See the discussion in L. Sealy and S. Worthington, *Sealy & Worthington's Cases and Materials in Company Law*, 10th edn (Oxford 2013), 372ff. The explanation is perhaps simple: the courts' focus has been on establishing the existence of a fiduciary breach, rather than identifying its precise genesis.

39 [1891] 2 Ch. 244.

40 See Lindley L.J. in *Aas v Benham* [1891] 2 Ch. 244 at 256, giving the example of a partner using his increased scientific knowledge, gleaned from working with the partnership, to publish a book on the subject, being a book which did not in any way compete with the partnership business: this profit would not be recoverable by the other partners.

41 *O'Donnell v Shanahan* [2009] EWCA Civ 751 at [69] (Rimer L.J.), suggesting, in the context of directors as fiduciaries, that a director was always a director; he did not have "off-duty" time. Similarly, see *Bhullar v Bhullar* [2003] EWCA Civ 424 at [41]: a fiduciary has "one capacity and one capacity only".

42 Hence the suggestion here of a strict and limiting "scope" or "line of business" test.

> otherwise run the risk that the company will be able to claim the gain as a disloyal profit made in breach of the conflict rule on the basis that every opportunity is a potential corporate opportunity. Yet, taken at face value, that is just the proposition advanced in *Bhullar v Bhullar*,[43] where the court held that the director had one capacity only, and that was as a fiduciary. In that case, the directors had purchased on their own account a block of land adjacent to one already owned by the company. The court held that this had been acquired in breach of their fiduciary obligations, and was therefore held on constructive trust for the company. Since the company was in the business of buying property for investment, that conclusion might not seem unreasonable. On those bald facts, the acquisition was certainly one within the scope of the fiduciary endeavour . . . This would be true whether or not the company had the funds to make the investment, or would, if given the choice, have decided to do so. All those matters are for the principal to determine, not for the fiduciary to presume. But in this particular case the company was a family-owned company, and on the breakdown of the family relationship the other side of the family had insisted that no further property investments be made. That was taken by the court as going merely to the issue of the principal's choice, in the way just noted. But on another reading, the assertion goes instead to the issue of scope. If, as a result of the bar on future investment, the company is no longer a company interested in property investment (notwithstanding that its corporate capacity was not so limited), then the defendant fiduciaries' acquisition would not involve a conflict; indeed, it would not be disloyal in any way. The court, however, refused to accept that scope could be limiting in this way.

## C. The Significance of Contract

One way in which a fiduciary can successfully argue that there are limits on the scope of her fiduciary duty is by invoking the terms of a contract with her principal. Where two parties have a contract which sets out their respective rights and duties in a way that limits the extent to which one is obliged to act in the interests of the other, or indeed excludes any such obligation, this will displace any fiduciary duty that would otherwise arise. On this topic, Mason J made the following comments in *Hospital Products Ltd v United States Surgical Corp*[44]: 13–020

> That contractual and fiduciary relationships may co-exist between the same parties has never been doubted. Indeed, the existence of a basic contractual relationship has in many situations provided a foundation for the erection of a fiduciary relationship. In these situations it is the contractual foundation which is all important because it is the contract that regulates the basic rights and liabilities of the parties. The fiduciary relationship, if it is to exist at all, must accommodate itself to the terms of the contract so that it is consistent with, and conforms to, them. The fiduciary relationship cannot be superimposed upon the contract in such a way as to alter the operation which the contract was intended to have according to its true construction.

Similarly, in *Henderson v Merrett Syndicates Ltd*, Lord Browne-Wilkinson said[45] 13–021

> the extent and nature of the fiduciary duties owed in any particular case fall to be determined by reference to any underlying contractual relationship between the parties. Thus, in the case of an agent employed under a contract, the scope of his fiduciary duties is determined by the terms of the underlying contract. Although an agent is, in the absence of contractual provision, in breach of his fiduciary duties if he acts for another who is in competition with his principal, if the contract under which he is acting authorises him so to do, the normal fiduciary duties are modified accordingly: see *Kelly v Cooper*.[46] The existence of a contract does not exclude the co-existence of concurrent fiduciary duties (indeed, the contract may well be their source); but the contract can and does modify the extent and nature of the general duty that would otherwise arise.

43 [2003] EWCA Civ 424.
44 (1984) 156 C.L.R. 41 at 97.
45 [1995] 2 A.C. 145 at 206. See too *Hilton v Barker Booth & Eastwood* [2005] 1 W.L.R. 567 at [30].
46 [1993] A.C. 205.

**13-022** *Kelly v Cooper* was a Privy Council decision from Bermuda. The defendant estate agents were instructed by the claimant to sell his house on a commission basis. The claimant's neighbour also instructed the defendants to sell his house. A purchaser offered to buy the neighbour's house and his offer was accepted. The purchaser then offered to buy the claimant's house. The defendants failed to tell the claimant that the purchaser had agreed to buy the neighbour's house and as a result the claimant agreed to sell his house for a lower price than he could have negotiated if he had known that the purchaser planned to amalgamate the two properties. The court held that the defendant's failure to disclose the information did not entail a breach of fiduciary duty. The reason was that a term was implied into the contract between the claimant and the defendants that in the ordinary course of business the defendants could act for many sellers, and treat information that they obtained from each seller as confidential. Hence the fiduciary duty they would otherwise have owed to the claimant, not to act for another principal with conflicting interests, was displaced by the parties' contract.

**13-023** A fiduciary can also escape liability where she owed a fiduciary duty but her principal consented to her acting in a way that would otherwise have entailed a breach of duty. It has been said that a fiduciary owes a positive duty to disclose conflicts of interest to her principal,[47] but the better view is that disclosure and consent merely "provide a mechanism by which the fiduciary can avoid liability" if she wishes to act despite a conflict of interests.[48] A principal cannot validly consent to a breach of duty unless she is sui juris and her consent must not have been procured by the fiduciary taking improper advantage of the parties' relationship.[49] The principal's consent must furthermore be an informed consent: the fiduciary must make "full and frank disclosure of all material facts".[50] The burden of proving that these conditions obtained lies on the fiduciary.[51]

## *D. Termination of Fiduciary Relationships*

**13-024** The courts do not recognise "the concept of a fiduciary obligation which continues notwithstanding the determination of the particular relationship which gives rise to it".[52] Fiduciary duties come to an end with the ending of the relationship which led to their imposition.[53] However, a fiduciary cannot escape liability for breach of fiduciary duty by resigning her post and then taking an opportunity for herself that previously came to her in her fiduciary capacity.[54]

---

47 *Item Software (UK) Ltd v Fassihi* [2005] 2 B.C.L.C. 91 at [41]–[44] and [63]–[65]; cf. Companies Act 2006, s.177.

48 M. Conaglen, "Fiduciaries" in J. McGhee (ed.), *Snell's Equity*, 32nd edn (Sweet & Maxwell, 2010), p.190. See too M. Harding, "Two Fiduciary Fallacies" (2007) 2 J. Eq. 1.

49 *Gibson v Jeyes* (1801) 6 Ves. 266; *Coles v Trecothick* (1804) 9 Ves. 234; *Morse v Royal* (1806) 12 Ves. 355; cf. *Fox v Mackreth* (1788) 2 Bro. C.C. 400.

50 *New Zealand Netherlands Society "Oranje" Inc v Kuys* [1973] 1 W.L.R. 1126 at 1132. See too *Dunne v English* (1874) L.R. 18 Eq. 524 at 533; *Boardman v Phipps* [1967] 2 A.C. 46 at 109; *Newgate Stud Co v Penfold* [2008] 1 B.C.L.C. 46 at [227]; *Sharma v Sharma* [2014] B.C.C. 73 at [43]; *FHR European Ventures LLP v Cedar Capital Partners LLC* [2015] A.C. 250 at [5].

51 *Hurstanger Ltd v Wilson* [2007] 1 W.L.R. 2351 at [35]. The principal must have been made aware of the facts, but it is not necessary that he understood their legal characterisation, i.e. that they would constitute a breach of fiduciary duty: *Sharma v Sharma* [2014] B.C.C. 73 at [47], approving *Knight v Frost* [1999] B.C.C. 819 at 828.

52 *Attorney General v Blake* [1998] Ch. 439 at 453 per Lord Woolf MR, adding that: "Equity does not demand a duty of undivided loyalty from a former employee to his former employer".

53 *Walsh v Shanahan* [2013] EWCA Civ 411 at [34].

54 *Industrial Development Consultants Ltd v Cooley* [1972] 1 W.L.R. 443; *Canadian Aero Services Ltd v O'Malley* (1973) 40 D.L.R. (3d) 371; *Abbey Glen Pty Co v Stumborg* (1978) 85 D.L.R. (3d) 35; *CMS Dolphin Ltd v Simonet* [2001] 2 B.C.L.C. 704. Contrast *Queensland Mines Ltd v Hudson* (1978) 18 A.L.R. 1; *Island Export Finance Ltd v Umunna* [1986] B.C.L.C. 460; *Framlington Group Plc v Anderson* [1995] 1 B.C.L.C. 475; *CMS Dolphin Ltd v Simonet* [2001] 2 B.C.L.C. 704; *Foster Bryant Surveying Ltd v Bryant* [2007] Bus. L.R. 1565.

## 3. Rescission of Contracts

Where a fiduciary has been bribed by a third party to procure a principal's entry into a contract with the third party, the principal can rescind the contract.[55] Even in the absence of bribery, the principal can rescind a contract with a third party where the fiduciary acted for the third party in relation to the transaction without the principal's consent and with the third party's knowledge of the fiduciary's double employment.[56] **13–025**

A principal can also rescind a contract she has entered with her fiduciary under the self-dealing and fair dealing rules. The operation of these rules in the context of trusts law was described by Megarry VC in *Tito v Waddell (No.2)* as follows[57]: **13–026**

> The self-dealing rule is . . . that if a trustee sells the trust property to himself, the sale is voidable by any beneficiary *ex debito justitiae*, however fair the transaction. The fair-dealing rule is . . . that if a trustee purchases the beneficial interest of any of his beneficiaries, the transaction is not voidable *ex debito justitiae*, but can be set aside by the beneficiary unless the trustee can show that he has taken no advantage of his position and has made full disclosure to the beneficiary, and that the transaction is fair and honest.

In *Re Thompson's Settlement*,[58] Vinelott J held that the self-dealing rule also prevents a fiduciary from validly concurring in a transaction relating to her principal's property which requires the principal's concurrence where the fiduciary "has an interest in or owes a fiduciary duty to another in relation to the same transaction". **13–027**

In *Tito*, Megarry VC said that the self-dealing rule and the fair dealing rule are "two rules: the consequences are different, and the property and the transactions which invoke the rules are different."[59] However, the better view is that the rules are not separate, but applications of the same principle to differing sets of facts, namely the principle that "no one who has a duty to perform shall place himself in a situation to have his interests conflicting with that duty".[60] The rules are often said to be different because the substantive fairness of a transaction is relevant in cases covered by the "fair dealing rule", but irrelevant in cases covered by the "self-dealing rule". However this difference is more apparent than real, because the relevance of the fairness of the transaction in "fair dealing" cases is that it provides evidence as to whether the fiduciary has made full disclosure of all the material facts to the principal with whom she has dealt, and whose consent she needs before she can act in a way that might cause a conflict between the principal's interests and her own.[61] **13–028**

Where a trustee purports to buy trust property of which she is the sole legal owner, the purported sale will infringe the rule that a person cannot sell (or lease) the property to herself.[62] Usually, however, there is more than one trustee, and in that situation where the trustees collectively sell trust property to an individual trustee the sale is not caught by the two-party rule in contract and property **13–029**

---

55 *Panama and South Pacific Telegraph Co v India Rubber, Gutta Percha, and Telegraph Works Co* (1875) L.R. 10 Ch. App. 515 at 526; *Grant v Gold Exploration & Development Syndicate Ltd* [1900] 1 Q.B. 233 at 248–249; *Armagas Ltd v Mundogas S.A. (The Ocean Frost)* [1986] A.C. 717 at 742–743; *Logicrose Ltd v Southend United FC (No.2)* [1988] 1 W.L.R. 1256; *UBS AG (London Branch) v Kommunale Wasserwerke Leipzig GmbH* [2014] EWHC 3615 (Comm) at [701].

56 *Transvaal Lands Co v New Belgium (Transvaal) Land & Development Co* [1914] 2 Ch. 488 at [505]; *Logicrose Ltd v Southend United Football Club Ltd (No.2)* [1988] 1 W.L.R. 1256 at 1260–1261; *UBS AG (London Branch) v Kommunale Wasserwerke Leipzig GmbH* [2014] EWHC 3615 (Comm) at [623].

57 [1977] Ch. 106 at 241.

58 [1986] Ch. 99 at 115. See too *Brudenell-Bruce v Moore* [2012] W.T.L.R. 931.

59 [1977] Ch. 106 at 241.

60 *Broughton v Broughton* (1855) 5 De G.M. & G. 160 at 164, quoted in *Movitex Ltd v Bulfield* [1988] B.C.LC 104 at 117.

61 M. Conaglen, "A Re-Appraisal of the Fiduciary Self-Dealing and Fair Dealing Rules" [2006] C.L.J. 366.

62 *Rye v Rye* [1962] A.C. 496; *Ingram v IRC* [2000] 1 A.C. 293.

law,[63] and the self-dealing rule will apply. The latter rule also prevents a trustee from selling trust property to a company of which she is the main shareholder,[64] managing director or other principal officer,[65] or to a partnership of which she is a member.[66] However, sale of property to a trustee's spouse is not absolutely prohibited by the self-dealing rule; rather, by virtue of the fair dealing rule, the trustee must show that the transaction is in the best interests of the beneficiaries.[67] These principles are illustrated by *Wright v Morgan*.

*Wright v Morgan*

Privy Council [1926] A.C. 788

13–030 The owner of two estates in New Zealand provided by his will that they should be offered at certain valuations to his son Harry Herbert, who was one of the trustees under the will. After the testator's death, Harry Herbert sold his rights under the will, including his right to purchase the land, to his brother Douglas, who was also a trustee. The trustees later sold the properties to Douglas, in the case of one estate after he had ceased to be a trustee, although he had arranged the sale before retiring from the trust. Proceedings were successfully brought by one of the beneficiaries to have the sales to Douglas set aside, and for an account of his profits.

13–031 VISCOUNT DUNEDIN (giving the judgment of the court): The leading question . . . is whether the option to purchase given by the will to Harry Herbert was assignable and assigned to Douglas to the effect of making him entitled to purchase the trust estate, he himself being a trustee. Technically speaking, he was not a trustee at the time of the purchase of Windermere, but their Lordships have no hesitation in holding with the Court of Appeal that although he had actually resigned, the whole scheme had been arranged by him prior to his resignation, and that in law he must be treated as being a trustee at the time of the will.

13–032 Speaking generally, any vested interest is assignable unless there is something in the nature of the interest, or something in the words of the settlement which creates the interest which contradicts the nature of assignability. Their Lordships do not doubt that Harry Herbert's option might have been assigned to a third person. There is nothing in the nature of the interest itself which points to non-assignability, nor are there any words in the will which would seem to forbid assignation. When, however, it is found that the assignation is in favour of the person who is himself a trustee, quite another question arises. The appellant argued that this right to purchase was property in the person of Harry Herbert, who was a cestui que trust, and that it is well settled that a trustee may purchase the interest of a cestui que trust. In one sense of the word "property" it is true that this option was the property of Harry Herbert, but the quality of the property was not like the property of land or of a chattel. It was only a right to enter into a contract. If the option had been exercised by Harry Herbert himself, and the property bought, then Harry Herbert might have transferred to a trustee just as well as to any one else. The object of the sale would, in that case, have been no longer trust property. So also if the option had been transferred to a stranger, the resulting contract which would have been its sequel would have been between the trustees and, to use a colloquial expression, an outsider. But as it was, the option transferred to Douglas only gave Douglas a right to ask from the trustees a contract of sale, and that contract of sale was *ex rei necessitate*, a contract between the trustees and himself as a trustee, and that is what the law will not allow. It would be profitless to quote the many cases which have arisen to illustrate the doctrine. They may all be referred to the same root idea, that equity will not allow a

---

63 Law of Property Act 1925 s.72. This is overlooked by J. Edelman, "The Fiduciary 'Self-Dealing' Rule" in J. Glister and P. Ridge (eds), *Fault Lines in Equity* (Hart Publishing, 2012), where he argues, incorrectly, that the self-dealing rule does not apply to trustees. Further see B.H. McPherson, "Self-dealing Trustees" in A.J. Oakley (ed.), *Trends in Contemporary Trust Law* (Oxford University Press, 1996).

64 *Silkstone & Haigh Moor Coal Co v Edey* [1900] 1 Ch. 167; *Farrars v Farrars Ltd* (1888) 40 Ch. D. 395. A mortgagee can exercise her power of sale in favour of a company in which he is interested only if she shows she acted in good faith and took all reasonable steps to obtain the best price reasonably obtainable: *Tse Kwong Lam v Wong Chit Sen* [1983] 1 W.L.R. 1349; cf. *Bank of Scotland v Neath Port Talbot CBC* [2008] B.C.C. 376.

65 *Re Thompson's Settlement* [1986] Ch. 99 at 114–115; cf. *Eberhardt v Christiana Window Glass Co* (1911) 9 Del. Ch. 284 (US).

66 *Colgate's Executor v Colgate* (1873) 23 N.J. Eq. 372 (US).

67 *Newgate Stud Co v Penfold* [2008] 1 B.C.L.C. 46 at [233]ff., following *Burrell v Burrell's Trustees* 1915 S.C. 33. See too *Ferraby v Hobson* (1847) 2 Ph. 255 at 261; *Re Douglas* [1928] 29 S.R. (N.S.W.) 48; *Re King's Will Trusts* (1959) 173 E.G. 627; *Tito v Waddell (No.2)* [1977] Ch. 106 at 240.

> person, who is in a position of trust, to carry out a transaction where there is a conflict between his duty and his interest. Accordingly, the real test to be applied to the circumstances is, assuming that Harry Herbert's option was validly assigned, so far as power to assign was concerned, to Douglas, did a conflict of duty and interest arise which would prevent Douglas from entering into a binding contract with the trustees? It was argued that no such conflict would arise, because by the terms of the will, which was the wish of the testator, the whole conditions of sale are regulated; valuers are to be appointed, and their decision to be accepted as to the price to be payable. There was no possibility of the higgling of the market between vendor and purchaser. Nevertheless, a conflict of duty and interest may arise, although there is no direct association between the two parties as vendor and purchaser. Probably no better illustration could be found than in the old case of the *York Buildings Co v Mackenzie*[68] in the House of Lords. It was a Scotch case, but the Scotch law is the same as the English in the matter, and was especially so stated to be in the subsequent case of *Aberdeen Ry Co v Blaikie Brothers*.[69] In the former case the person who had bought, and whose purchase was set aside after eleven years of possession, was what is called the common agent. The case occurred in an old form of process for the realization of the landed estates of a debtor called a ranking and sale. The common agent was appointed by the Court to look after and carry into effect the sale. He arranged the date of the sale, fixed the upset price, and answered questions to inquirers, but the actual sale was not conducted by him. It was by public auction, and termed a judicial sale. The common agent Mackenzie bought at the judicial sale. It was not averred that the price was inadequate, but, although it was after eleven years, the House of Lords, reversing the judgment of the Court of Session, held that his position of common agent was a position of trust, and that his duty and interest so conflicted as to make it impossible that he should be a purchaser of the property at the sale. Now, applying the principles of that case to the present, their Lordships hold that the position of Douglas as a trustee and as the assignee of the option to purchase was one which would involve a conflict of duty and interest. It was of moment when the sale should take place, because the option could only be exercised when the trustees had decided that now was the moment to sell. The best moment for the trust was the moment when prices generally were high. The best moment for a purchaser was when prices generally were low, and such prices would be naturally reflected in the value fixed by the valuers. So also as to the terms of payment, the best term for the trust was cash down; the best term for the purchaser was some easier arrangement. Their Lordships do not think it necessary to go into the actual terms of payment here, although it is perhaps startling to find that the whole transaction was carried out by the payment in cash of quite an infinitesimal sum. The criterion, however, is not what was done, but what might be done. Their Lordships, therefore, come to the conclusion that this case falls within the general rule, and that the sale being, as carried out, a sale of trust property to a trustee, cannot be allowed to stand, as in a question with infant beneficiaries who cannot be affected as the daughter might have been affected, by the lapse of time since the transaction was effected to her knowledge but not to theirs.

Where a fiduciary contracts with her principal in breach of the foregoing rules, the principal has a number of remedies open to him. He can rescind the contract with the result that it is "treated in law as never having come into existence."[70] As discussed in Chapter 18,[71] rescission of a contract under which legal title to property is transferred also has proprietary consequences: a trust is retrospectively imposed on the property and the principal can insist that the legal title is reconveyed back to him. Where this has become impossible owing to the intervention of third party rights, i.e. because the fiduciary has resold the property to a bona fide purchaser, the principal can instead claim the proceeds of the resale.[72] **13–033**

## 4. Pecuniary Rescission

In the latter case, the principal can alternatively claim a money sum representing the current market value of the property. The term "pecuniary rescission" has been used to describe awards of this **13–034**

68 (1795) 3 Pat. 378.
69 (1854) 1 Macq. 461.
70 *Johnson v Agnew* [1980] A.C. 367 at 393.
71 See paras 18–249—18–252.
72 *Ladywell Mining Co v Brookes* (1887) 35 Ch. D. 400 at 418.

type.[73] They are compensatory awards,[74] but their purpose is not to compensate the principal for every kind of loss caused by the fiduciary's breach of duty, including consequential loss. It is rather to make the fiduciary pay the money value of the property that she would have been obliged to reconvey to the principal, had she not put this beyond her power by selling it to a bona fide purchaser. In other words, the fiduciary is ordered to pay the money as a form of substitute performance of her duty to return the property *in specie*. In this respect awards of "pecuniary rescission" resemble substitutive performance awards made against trustees who have misapplied trust property.[75] An example is provided by *McKenzie v McDonald*,[76] which was decided at an early stage of his career by Sir Owen Dixon, who later became Chief Justice of the High Court of Australia.

*McKenzie v McDonald*

Supreme Court of Victoria [1927] V.L.R. 134

13-035 The plaintiff agreed to exchange her farm for a shop belonging to the defendant estate agent. In breach of fiduciary duty, the defendant advised her that the farm was worth £2300 and the shop £2000, and paid her the £300 difference in cash. In fact the farm was worth £2445 and the shop was worth £1550. By the time this came to light, rescission was barred because the defendant had sold the farm (at a profit) to a third party. Dixon A.-J. ordered that the defendant should either pay the claimant £595, which was the difference between the true value of the properties less the £300 paid, or, at the defendant's election, that he should take back the shop on paying the claimant £2000, and also pay her £145, which was the difference between the farm's represented and true values.

13-036 DIXON A.-J.: . . . The plaintiff impeaches the transaction of exchange on the ground that a confidential relationship had been established between herself and the defendant "*in hac rae*" which placed him under a duty of full disclosure and fair dealing when he assumed the position of a contractor with her.

13-037 . . . Did the defendant occupy such a position of confidence towards the plaintiff as to bring him within the equitable requirements of full disclosure and fair and open dealing? In my opinion he did. He assumed the function of advising and assisting a woman in a difficult situation in the acquisition of a residence by means of the disposal or pledging of her property. He was necessarily furnished with an intimate knowledge of her financial position, her obligations, and family needs. He proceeded to advise her on the wisdom and practicability of raising money by mortgage, and acted for her in an effort to do so. He undertook the sale of her farm, and acquired such information as he could in relation to it, and offered his counsel as to its condition and the price she had asked and in effect should ask. In this circumstance he was, in my opinion, an agent who came within "the rule of the Court; which, however, does not prevent an agent from purchasing from his principal, but only requires that he shall deal with him at arm's length, and after a full disclosure of all that he knows with respect to the property."[77] This is part of "that great rule of the Court, that he who bargains in matter of advantage with a person placing confidence in him is bound to show that a reasonable use has been made of that confidence; a rule applying to trustees, attorneys, or anyone else."[78] "A principle . . . resting upon grounds connected with the clearest principles of equity and the general security of contracts, viz. that an agent to sell shall not convert himself into a purchaser unless he can make it perfectly clear that he furnished his employer with all the knowledge which he himself possessed."[79]

13-038 No attempt has been made by the defendant to show that he made a reasonable use of the confidence

---

73 This term seems to have been invented by Peter Birks: P. Birks, "Unjust Factors and Wrongs: Pecuniary Rescission for Undue Influence" [1997] R.L.R. 72.

74 *McKenzie v McDonald* [1927] V.L.R. 134 at 146–147; *Bristol & West Building Soc v Mothew* [1998] Ch. 1 at 17; *Mahoney v Purnell* [1996] 3 All E.R. 61 at 86–91.

75 As to which, see paras 10–020ff.

76 See too *Re Leeds and Hanley Theatres of Varieties Ltd* [1902] Ch. 809; *Coleman v Myers* [1977] 2 N.Z.L.R. 225 at 359–362 and 379; *Mahoney v Purnell* [1996] 3 All E.R. 61; *Li Sau Ying v Bank of China (Hong Kong) Ltd* [2004] HKCFA 78, as analysed in L. Ho, "Establishing Undue Influence and Seeking Equitable Compensation" [2005] Singapore J. L. Studies 438 at [445].

77 *Murphy v O'Shea* (1845) 2 Jones & Lat. 422 at 425 per Sir E. Sugden L.C.

78 *Gibson v Jeyes* (1801) 6 Ves. Jun. 266 at 278 per Lord Eldon.

79 *Lowther v Lord Lowther* (1806) 13 Ves. Jun. 95 at 103 per Lord Erskine.

placed in him, or that he furnished the plaintiff with all the knowledge which he himself possessed. On the contrary, the evidence affirmatively proves, I think, that set out to make a bargain with her as advantageous to himself as possible, and to that end suppressed the opinion he had obtained from Lockhart, whom he knew to be well informed, that the land could be sold at 4l. 10s. per acre, and that the tenant might be expected to buy at that price, took no steps to find a purchaser, and wrote a misleading an untruthful report which he intended to dishearten his client and make her eager to accept the means of meeting her obligation to Mrs Nairn, which he had it in mind to propose. When he came to make that proposal I think he misstated his motives and intentions, under-estimated somewhat the value of the farm, grossly over-estimated the value of the shop, and adopted a form of expression, in dealing with the income she would receive, likely to mislead her.

In these circumstances, the plaintiff was entitled to have the agreement of exchange of the 25th September set aside. **13–039**

This agreement has, however, been fully carried into execution, and Mrs Nairn has been procured to vary her contract, a new mortgage has been given over the farm, and Littlewood has apparently obtained an equitable interest therein. **13–040**

The fact that the agreement has been superseded by assurance of the interests to which it related would not have made the remedy of rescission inappropriate for a breach of fiduciary duty, which, until recently, received in all Courts of Equity the plain appellation of fraud. **13–041**

But, although no point was made of it by the defendant, the position of the third parties concerned and the creation of the encumbrances upon the farm make it peculiarly difficult to adopt that remedy. Doubtless it is not necessary to restore the parties precisely to their former position if, by the exercise of the powers of the Court, a substantial restitution can be achieved. See *Robinson v Abbott*[80] [where] the views expressed by Holroyd J. seem to be fully borne out by the observations made by members of the House of Lords in *Nocton v Lord Ashburton*[81]—a case which shows that the jurisdiction to remedy breaches of fiduciary duty extends to decreeing compensation to the person whose confidence has been abused. **13–042**

In this case the defendant obtained, by his abuse of the plaintiff's confidence, a farm, in my opinion worth 2445l., for a shop, in my opinion worth 1550l., together with 300l., and, as the encumbrances were duly allowed for, the defendant was on this footing better off, and the plaintiff worse off, by 595l. The defendant, however, sold the farm for 4l. 10s. per acre, not 4l. 5s., the value I have assigned to it. It may be said that he is accountable to the plaintiff for this sum, and no doubt if he were being called upon to account to, as distinct from indemnifying, the plaintiff, this would be so. **13–043**

The sale at 4l. 10s. was effected upon long terms, with a special provision relating to the deposit, and it does not afford an absolute criterion for ascertaining the defendant's liability. I therefore treat the defendant as having obtained on the farm, upon the exchange, 5s. per acre more than the value assigned to the farm in the agreement of exchange, and as by his own dealings he has rendered it difficult to restore the farm to the plaintiff, he must recoup this difference to her. On the other hand, there is no difficulty in restoring to him the shop for which he obtained an allowance of 450l. more, in my opinion, than its value. The cases of *Ballantyne v Raphael*[82] and *Curwen v Yan Yean Land Co Ltd*[83] were dealt with in *Robinson v Abbott*[84] in a manner which seems to show that if the defendant desires to take the shop in specie there is no reason why he should not be permitted to do so. I therefore propose to decree him to pay 595l. to the plaintiff by way of compensation, but to order further that if within 21 days he notifies the plaintiff of his election so to do he shall take over the shop at a value of 2000l., of which 450l. is contained in the sum stated for compensation. **13–044**

Dixon AJ took the date for assessing the value of the defendant's compensatory liability to be the date when he received title to the farm, a proposition for which other cases can also be cited.[85] However, if it is right to characterise awards of "pecuniary rescission" as a monetised substitute for **13–045**

---

80 (1893) 20 V.L.R. 346 at 365–8.

81 [1914] A.C. 932.

82 (1889) 15 V.L.R. 538.

83 (1891) 17 V.L.R. 64.

84 (1893) 20 V.L.R. 346 at 367–8.

85 *Kupchak v Dayson Holdings Co Ltd* (1965) 53 D.L.R. (2d) 482 at [14]; *Mahoney v Purnell* [1996] 3 All E.R. 61; *Hartigan v International Society for Krishna Consciousness Inc* [2002] NSWSC 810 at [104].

performance of the fiduciary's duty to return property received under a contract with her principal, the fiduciary's liability should be the property's current market value,[86] as held by other authorities.[87]

## 5. Equitable Compensation

### A. Introduction

**13–046** The source of the modern rule entitling a principal to recover equitable compensation for loss caused by a breach of fiduciary duty is widely taken[88] to be *Nocton v Lord Ashburton*.[89] The claimant released a security over land belonging to a third party at the request of the defendant, who was the claimant's solicitor, and who had a second security over the land, the priority status of which was thereby advanced. The third party defaulted on his debt to the claimant, who successfully sued the defendant for the amount of his loss. Viscount Haldane LC held this result to follow from the fact that the defendant had breached his fiduciary duty.

**13–047** Viscount Haldane justified this finding by invoking the "pecuniary rescission" doctrine discussed in the previous section, stating that[90]:

> When, as in the case before us, a solicitor has had financial transactions with his client . . . a Court of Equity has always assumed jurisdiction to scrutinize his action . . . and in proper cases to order the solicitor to replace property improperly acquired from the client, or to make compensation if he had lost it by acting in breach of a duty which arose out of his confidential relationship to the man who had trusted him.

**13–048** However, *Nocton* was not a case in which property passed between the parties under a contract which the principal later sought to rescind, and so the court's finding that the defendant was liable to compensate the claimant marked a new departure for the law. In effect, the court recognised a different type of remedy, assessed by reference to different principles, which might conceivably be developed by analogy with the rules governing the assessment of tort damages at common law. In the extra-judicial words of Justice Gummow[91]:

> [The issues raised by 'pecuniary rescission' cases] . . . do not arise where no property has passed between principal and fiduciary or vice versa and loss has been sustained by other means, for example, advice given in breach of duty. In such cases, and *Nocton v Lord Ashburton* may be considered one of them, greater assistance may be found in the common law principles regulating claims in tort or, perhaps, contract. In *Nocton v Lord Ashburton* the Court of Appeal had found deceit and awarded damages. While the House of Lords reversed that finding and Lord Haldane[92] said that the measure of damages in equity might not always be the same as in an action in deceit, he also said 'in this case the question is of form only'. Lord Dunedin said the equitable remedy would 'practically come to much the same'.[93]

---

[86] As argued in D. O'Sullivan, S. Elliott and R. Zakrzewski, *The Law of Rescission* (Oxford University Press, 2008) paras 15.25–15.26.

[87] *McCarthy v Kenny* [1939] 3 D.L.R. 556; *Koutsonicolis v Principe (No.2)* (1987) 48 S.A.S.R. 328.

[88] e.g. *Breen v Williams* (1996) 186 C.L.R. 71 at 135–136; *Swindle v Harrison* [1997] 4 All E.R. 705 at 731–732; *Canson Enterprises Ltd v Boughton & Co* [1991] 3 S.C.R. 534 at 570; *Maguire v Makaronis* (1997) 188 C.L.R. 449 at 468–469.

[89] [1914] A.C. 942.

[90] [1914] A.C. 942 at 956–957.

[91] The Hon Mr Justice Gummow, "Compensation for Breach of Fiduciary Duty" in T.G. Youdan (ed.), *Equity, Fiduciaries and Trusts* (Carswell, 1989), p.74. See also V. Vann, *Equitable Compensation in Australia: Principles and Problems* (Saarbrücken, 2009), pp.71–75; *AB Jr v MB* Cayman Islands Grand Court, 18 December 2012 at 444–484.

[92] [1914] A.C. 942 at 958.

[93] Ibid. at 965.

The Commonwealth courts were not quick to follow the lead established by *Nocton*, and it was not until the last decades of the twentieth century that they began to make awards of equitable compensation for breach of fiduciary duty on a regular basis. Consequently, various questions about the assessment of such awards still await an answer. A significant barrier to the resolution of these issues has been the widespread misapprehension that "equitable compensation" is a remedy that operates in the same way in every case where a defendant has breached an equitable duty. This has led some courts to draw the incorrect conclusion that equitable compensation awards for breach of fiduciary duty should be assessed in the same way as substitutive performance claims against trustees who have misapplied trust property.[94] It has also led them to form the mistaken belief that causation and remoteness are "common law concepts" that have no bearing on compensatory awards for breach of fiduciary duty. This is discussed in the following excerpt from an article by Charles Mitchell. **13-049**

## C. Mitchell, "Equitable Compensation for Breach of Fiduciary Duty"

(2013) 66 C.L.P. 307, 19–20

[In] McLachlin J.'s minority concurring judgment in *Canson Enterprises Ltd v Boughton*[95] . . . she said that by analogy with "restitution" awards (by which she meant orders that a defaulting trustee should reconstitute the trust fund), the award of equitable compensation for breach of fiduciary duty also seeks "to restore to the plaintiff what has been lost as a result of the breach". However, she added that "the losses made good are only those which, on a common sense view of causation, were caused by the breach". Steven Elliott and James Edelman comment that this reasoning runs:[96] **13-050**

> "reparative and substitutive thinking together. In effect McLachlin J. wished to distinguish equitable compensation from common law damages on the basis that it is substitutive rather than reparative, but she was unable to make the analogy with restitution of trust property work because she could not convincingly describe the object of the substitution. Her Ladyship inevitably ended with a reparative model confusingly clothed in substitutive language."

The same criticism can be made of many Australian cases in which the courts have purported to analyse reparation claims for breach of fiduciary duty as though they were substitutive compensation claims to reconstitute a trust fund.[97] Typically they cite Street J.'s dicta in *Re Dawson*[98] about the reconstitution of trust funds, along with McLachlin J.'s judgment in *Canson* and Lord Browne-Wilkinson's speech in *Target Holdings Ltd v Redferns*,[99] as authority for the following propositions: because claims for equitable compensation for breach of fiduciary duty resemble claims to reconstitute a trust fund, the relevant question "is not whether the loss was caused by or flowed from the breach" and so "principles governing remoteness of damages" are irrelevant;[100] hence, also, "there is no translation into this field of discourse of the doctrine of novus actus interveniens";[101] but on the other hand, the court must still decide whether the fiduciary's breach of duty and the principal's loss were connected, using a "common sense" approach to causation **13-051**

---

94 For which see paras 10–020ff.

95 [1991] 3 S.C.R. 534 at 555.

96 S.B. Elliott and J. Edelman, "Money Remedies against Trustees" (2004) 18 Tru. L.I. 116, pp.122–3. See too L. Smith, "The Measurement of Compensation Claims against Trustees and Fiduciaries" in E. Bant and M. Harding (eds), *Exploring Private Law* (2010) pp. 372–73.

97 e.g. *Hill v Rose* [1990] V.R. 129; *Gemstone Corp of Australia Ltd v Grasso* (1994) 13 A.C.S.R. 695 at 714; *O'Halloran v RT Thomas & Family Pty Ltd* (1998) 45 N.S.W.L.R. 262 at 272–73; *Aequitas v Sparad No. 100 Ltd* (2001) 19 A.C.L.C. 1006 at [442]; *WA Fork Truck Distributors Pty Ltd v Jones* [2003] WASC 102 at [104]–[105]; *GM & AM Pearce & Co Pty Ltd v Australian Tallow Producers* [2005] VSCA 113 at [65]; *V-Flow Pty Ltd v Holyoake Industries (Vic) Pty Ltd* [2013] FCAFC 16 at [56]. For critical comment, see V. Vann, *Equitable Compensation in Australia: Principles and Problems* (2009) chap 3, esp. pp. 106–07.

98 [1966] 2 N.S.W.R. 211.

99 *Target Holdings Ltd v Redferns* [1996] 1 A.C. 421.

100 *Hill* at 144.

101 *Maguire v Makaronis* (1997) 188 C.L.R. 449 at 470.

with the full benefit of hindsight. These propositions are inconsistent because they are not founded on a single idea of the fiduciary's liability. They are also incoherent: it makes no sense to say, as Ipp J. has felt constrained to say, that:[102]

> "I am required by the rules of equity, in assessing compensation, to leave aside questions of causation (save that compensation will only be awarded for losses caused by the breach of fiduciary duties)."

13–052 The Australian courts have tried to paper over the cracks in their theory by appealing to a grand but vague idea that equity does things differently from the common law, and that "common law concepts" of causation and remoteness are irrelevant to claims for equitable compensation.[103] Lionel Smith has observed that this reasoning will not do, either, not because it asserts that equity and the common law can do things differently, but because it ignores the differences between distinct types of equitable claim.[104] . . . The courts of every Commonwealth jurisdiction would do much better to recognize that the rules governing claims to reconstitute trust funds do not apply to claims for equitable compensation for breach of fiduciary duty.

13–053 For these reasons, we share Justice Gummow's view, quoted above, that when asking what causation and remoteness rules govern equitable compensation claims for breach of fiduciary duty, analogies can more usefully be drawn with damages claims in tort than with equitable claims to reconstitute trust funds—a view which has also been expressed by Hodgson JA in the New South Wales Court of Appeal.[105]

## *B. Causation*

13–054 English law provides that a principal must prove that there was a breach of fiduciary duty, that he suffered damage, and that the damage was caused by the breach. This emerges from *Swindle v Harrison*, where Mummery LJ held that "there is no equitable by-pass of the need to establish causation".[106] Harrison borrowed £180,000 from a loan company to buy a hotel. The loan was secured by a charge on her house. When the time came for completion, she was £75,000 short and so she took a bridging loan from her solicitor, Swindle, believing that she could borrow this sum from a brewery later on. The bridging loan was secured by a charge on the hotel. Swindle failed to tell her that his firm was making a profit on this arrangement. Nor did he tell her that a loan from the brewery was unlikely to be forthcoming, as turned out to be the case. Harrison's business failed and she defaulted on her debts. The loan company took her house, and Swindle sought possession of the hotel. She counterclaimed, arguing among other things that Swindle's breach of duty had caused her to lose the value of the equity that she had formerly had in her house. The Court of Appeal accepted that he had breached his fiduciary duty, but even so the counter-claim failed. The judges gave different reasons for this, but each stressed that Harrison would have gone ahead with the purchase even if Swindle had committed no breach of duty, as she would have forfeited her deposit if she had not completed the hotel purchase, and she could not have borrowed the money elsewhere.

13–055 Does it suffice for a principal to show that his fiduciary's breach of duty was a material cause of his loss, or can the fiduciary escape liability if she can show that the principal would have entered the

---

[102] *Biala Pty Ltd v Mallina Holdings Ltd* (1993) 13 W.A.R. 11 at 77–78.

[103] *Canson* at 556; *Hill* at 144; *O'Halloran* at 273; *Harrison v Schipp* [2001] NSWCA 13 at [123]; *Re Purcom No 34 Pty Ltd (in liq) (No. 2)* [2010] FCA 624 at [23]; *Secure Parking (WA) Pty Ltd v Wilson* [2012] WASCA 230 at [76]; *Michael Wilson & Partners Ltd* [2012] NSWCA 383 at [171].

[104] Smith at p. 369. His criticism is aimed at McLachlin J.'s judgment in *Canson*, but it applies with equal force to the other cases cited in the previous footnote.

[105] *Cassis v Kalfus (No. 2)* [2004] N.S.W.C.A 315 at [99].

[106] [1997] 4 All E.R. 705 at 733.

impugned transaction anyway? In *Brickenden v London Loan & Savings Co*,[107] the Privy Council took the former view. The claimant finance company lent money to a couple named Biggs. The defendant solicitor acted for the claimant in the transaction. He failed to disclose that Biggs owed him debts, which Biggs was able to repay with the loan money received from the claimant. The Biggses defaulted and the court ordered the defendant to compensate the claimant for the full amount of the loan. Lord Thankerton held that[108]:

> When a party, holding a fiduciary relationship, commits a breach of his duty by non-disclosure of material facts, which his constituent is entitled to know in connection with the transaction, he cannot be heard to maintain that disclosure would not have altered the decision to proceed with the transaction, because the constituent's action would be solely determined by some other factor, such as the valuation by another party of the property proposed to be mortgaged. Once the court has determined that the non-disclosed facts were material, speculation as to what course the constituent, on disclosure, would have taken is not relevant.

As we discuss in section 6, a similar rule prevents fiduciaries from avoiding liability to disgorge gains by arguing that they would have made the gains even if they had performed their fiduciary duty.[109] But as Justice Heydon has extra-judicially observed, "it is one thing to strip a fiduciary of profit without much inquiry . . . [and] another to hold him accountable for all loss without inquiry into relative causes."[110] Later courts have interpreted Lord Thankerton's words narrowly, to mean that they may not speculate as to the course a principal would otherwise have taken, but that a fiduciary can escape liability if she can prove that principal would have acted no differently. This was the result of *Swindle*, and of other more recent cases.[111] **13–056**

Where a principal would not have entered an impugned transaction, but for the breach of duty, a further question arises, as to what the principal would have done instead. The evidence may show that the principal would have maintained the status quo ante (i.e. would not have entered *any* transaction), and in such cases the principal can recover all the losses caused by the fiduciary's breach of duty (subject to any applicable remoteness cap).[112] In *Hodgkinson v Simms*, La Forest J went further and stated that this should be presumed in every case,[113] but Sirko Harder has rightly pointed out that this will not do as a default rule. This is because it does not always follow from the fact that a principal would not have entered the impugned transaction that he would not have entered any transaction.[114] Sometimes the facts will not support this conclusion, and where the evidence shows that the principal would have entered into an alternative transaction, this should be taken into account when assessing compensation. **13–057**

For example, in *Stevens v Premium Real Estate Ltd*[115] the defendant estate agent failed to inform **13–058**

---

107 [1934] 3 D.L.R. 465.

108 ibid., at 469.

109 See paras 13–105ff.

110 J.D. Heydon, "Causal Relationships Between a Fiduciary's Default and the Principal's Loss' (1994) 110 L.Q.R. 328, 332.

111 *Hodgkinson v Simms* [1994] 3 S.C.R. 377 at [76]; *Rama v Millar* [1996] 1 N.Z.L.R. 257 at 261; *Gilbert v Shanahan* [1998] 3 N.Z.L.R. 528; *Beach Petroleum NL v Abbott Tout Russell Kennedy* (1999) 48 N.S.W.L.R. 1 at [444]–[449]; *Nationwide Building Society v Balmer Radmore (a firm)* [1999] P.N.L.R. 606 at 671–672; *Longstaff v Birtles* [2002] 1 W.L.R. 470 at [36]; *DEG-Deutsche Investitions und Entwicklungsgesellschaft mbH v Koshy* [2004] 1 B.C.L.C. 131 at [147] and [159]; *Bank of Ireland v Jaffery* [2012] EWHC 1377 (Ch) at [354]–[360]; *Nicholls v Michael Wilson & Partners Ltd* [2012] NSWCA 383 at [179]–[181]. See too J. Glister, "Equitable Compensation" in Glister and Ridge (eds), *Fault Lines in Equity* (2012), pp.162–167.

112 See, e.g. *Morkot v Watson & Brown Solicitors* [2015] P.N.L.R. 9 at [64]ff.

113 [1994] 3 S.C.R. 377 at 440–441.

114 S. Harder, "Equitable Compensation for a Fiduciary's Non-Disclosure and Hypothetical Courses of Events" (2011) 5 J. Eq. 22. See too S.M. Waddams, "Fiduciary Duties and Equitable Compensation" (1996) 27 Can. Bus. L.J. 466, 468.

115 [2009] 2 N.Z.L.R. 284.

her clients, the claimants, that a prospective buyer of their house often bought residential properties and resold them at a profit. The defendant had worked for the buyer in the past and hoped to be instructed by him on any resale that might eventuate. The claimants sold their house to the buyer for NZD 2.575 million. He made some minor improvements and resold the property a few months later for NZD 3.555 million. The market value of the house at the time of the first sale had been NZD 3.25 million, but there was evidence that the claimants would have been willing to sell for NZD 2.8 million. In the minority, Elias CJ would have awarded the claimants NZD 225,000, which was the difference between the price paid and the price they would have been willing to accept. But the majority of the New Zealand Supreme Court awarded NZD 675,000, which was the difference between the price paid and the market price. Their reason was that the defendant had not proved that the claimants would have sold their house for less than its market value. The onus lay on the defendant to prove (rather than merely speculate as to) what the claimants would have done, and they did not agree with Elias CJ that the claimants had discharged this burden.

## *C. Remoteness and Intervening Cause*

**13–059** For reasons which have been explained,[116] many Australian courts have denied that awards of equitable compensation for breach of fiduciary duty are contained by a remoteness rule. In *Cassis v Kalfus (No.2)*,[117] however, Hodgson JA held that a principal could not recover for some of the losses caused by a fiduciary's breach of duty because they "should be regarded as too remote, because not foreseeable, or because so substantially caused by other factors that they are not reasonably attributed to [the fiduciary's] breach of duty." In his identification of foreseeability as a relevant test, the judge went further towards helping defendant fiduciaries than any other judge has been prepared to go, and it is arguable that directness is a more appropriate test of remoteness in this context; i.e. that the best analogy is with the remoteness rules that contain tortious liability for deceit[118] rather than those that contain liability for negligence.[119] If that is correct, then the courts should hold that loss is not too remote to be recoverable regardless of whether it is the exact kind of damage that one would expect, provided that it is caused by the fiduciary's breach of duty and is not due to the operation of independent causes which have no connection with the breach.[120]

**13–060** This approach is consistent with the result in *Canson Enterprises Ltd v Boughton & Co.*[121] The defendant solicitor acted for the claimant company in the purchase of land for development. He failed to disclose that there had been an intermediate sale of the property that had realised a profit of CAD 115,000 for the intermediate purchaser. The claimant would not have gone ahead with the deal if it had been aware of this fact. Following acquisition of the land the claimant employed engineers and contractors to construct a building on the property, work which was done negligently. The claimant won damages from them but failed to enforce its judgment. So it sued the solicitor, arguing that the losses flowing from the negligent construction work had been caused by his breach of fiduciary duty. The Supreme Court of Canada denied recovery, in effect because the contractors' negligence had been an intervening act that was a more proximate cause of the claimant's loss than the solicitor's breach of duty.[122]

---

116 See paras 13–049–13–053.

117 [2004] NSWCA 315 at [101].

118 *Smith New Court Securities Ltd v Citibank NA* [1997] A.C. 254.

119 *Overseas Tankship (UK) Ltd v Morts Dock & Engineering Co Ltd (The Wagon Mound) (No 1)* [1961] A.C. 388.

120 *Re Polemis* [1921] 3 K.B. 560 at 577.

121 [1991] 3 S.C.R. 534. See too *Hodgkinson v Simms* [1994] 3 S.C.R. 377 at [93].

122 Cf. *Corr v IBC Vehicles Ltd* [2008] 1 A.C. 884 at [15] per Lord Bingham: "It is not fair to hold a tortfeasor liable, however gross

## D. Contributory Fault

In *Day v Mead*,[123] the claimant invested money in a company that went into receivership the following year. He did so on the advice of the defendant solicitor, who was a director of the company and had other conflicts of interest. The trial judge awarded compensation for breach of fiduciary duty, but reduced the sum payable on the basis that the claimant had acted imprudently in failing to obtain independent and competent financial advice before making such a large investment. This was upheld by the New Zealand Court of Appeal, where Cooke P said that[124]: 13–061

> Whether or not there are reported cases in which compensation for breach of a fiduciary obligation has been assessed on the footing that the plaintiff should accept some share of the responsibility, there appears to be no solid reason for denying jurisdiction to follow that obviously just course . . . Of course, before reducing an award on the ground that the claimant has been partly the author of his or her own loss, the court will have to give much weight to the well established principle that, largely for exemplary purposes, high standards are expected of fiduciaries. A strong case is needed to relieve the fiduciary of complete responsibility.

This has also been accepted in Canada, where the courts have held that recovery may be reduced where the principal has "failed to take some reasonable step that might have reduced or eliminated the loss"[125] and that "losses that are the result of the plaintiffs' unreasonable actions may be barred".[126] 13–062

In contrast, the Australian courts have held that the compensation payable by a defaulting fiduciary should never be reduced on the ground that the principal contributed to his loss in a blameworthy way. In *Pilmer v Duke Group Ltd (In Liquidation)*,[127] the majority considered that this idea suffered from "severe conceptual difficulties". These were essentially the same as those which had previously been identified by Justice Gummow in extra-judicial writing[128]: 13–063

> While negligence is concerned with the taking of reasonable care, a fiduciary traditionally has more expected of him. His duty is one of undivided and unremitting loyalty. The fiduciary acts in a 'representative' capacity in the exercise of his responsibility. One must fear that introduction of concepts of contributory negligence into that setting inevitably will work a subversion of fundamental principle.

The English courts have taken an intermediate position. The leading case is *Nationwide Building Society v Balmer Radmore (a firm)*.[129] The claimant building society suffered losses on around 400 residential mortgage loans when the borrowers defaulted and the properties were repossessed and sold at a loss. The defendant solicitors had breached their fiduciary duty to the claimant when they had failed to disclose features of the purchase transactions of which they were aware and knowledge of which would have affected the claimant's lending decisions: e.g. the fact that a property had been 13–064

---

his breach of duty may be, for damage caused to the claimant not by the tortfeasor's breach of duty but by some independent, supervening cause . . . for which the tortfeasor is not responsible."

123 [1987] 2 N.Z.L.R. 443.

124 ibid. at 450–51.

125 *Lemberg v Perris* (2010) 76 C.C.L.T. (3d) 276 at [88].

126 *Wardrope v Smith* [2013] ONSC 330 at [167]. In neither case did the court hold that a reduction for contributory negligence was appropriate on the facts.

127 (2001) 207 C.L.R. 165 at [85]–[86].

128 The Hon Mr Justice Gummow, "Compensation for Breach of Fiduciary Duty" in Youdan (ed.), *Equity, Fiduciaries and Trusts* (1989), p.86, cited with approval in *Pilmer* at [171]. See too the Hon Mr Justice Handley, "Reduction of Damages Awards" in P.D. Finn (ed.), *Essays on Damages* (Law Book Co, 1992), p.127; M. Conaglen *Fiduciary Loyalty* (Hart Publishing, 2010), pp.172–176.

129 [1999] P.N.L.R. 606.

substantially overvalued by the surveyors, or that a very recent (or even simultaneous) sale of the property to the borrower's vendor had taken place at a price significantly lower than the price agreed between the vendor and the borrower. The question arose whether the defendant's liability should be reduced to reflect the claimant's contributory negligence, and Blackburne J held that it should not.[130] He distinguished *Day* on the basis that the defendant there had acted in good faith, whereas the defendant firm in the present case had acted with conscious disloyalty, and he held that in these circumstances the defence should not be allowed.

**13–065** Later English cases have assumed that *Balmer Radmore* disables fiduciaries from pleading a principal's contributory negligence in every case, regardless of the character of the fiduciary's breach,[131] but that is not what the case decided, and it must still be regarded as an open question whether English law allows contributory negligence to be pleaded by a defaulting fiduciary who has acted in good faith.

## 6. Accounts of Profits and Consequential Orders to Pay the Amount of a Profit to the Principal

### *A. Terminology*

**13–066** "A claim for equitable compensation for losses sustained by a claimant is in principle a quite different remedy from a claim for an account of profits made by a defaulting fiduciary."[132] The reason is that the "amount recoverable in an action claiming an account of profits is dependent upon the profit made by the fiduciary, not the loss suffered by the beneficiary."[133] It follows that

> an account of profits [is often] a more advantageous remedy than equitable compensation, since the actual profits obtained by the [fiduciary are] higher than [the loss] suffered by the [principal].[134]

**13–067** We start with this point because in *Sinclair Investments (UK) Ltd v Versailles Trade Finance Ltd (in administration)*[135] and again in *FHR European Ventures LLP v Cedar Capital Partners LLC*,[136] Lord Neuberger described an order that a fiduciary pay the value of gains made in breach of fiduciary duty as an award of "equitable compensation" in a sum corresponding to the value of the fiduciary's gains. This was unfortunate. No good can come of describing a gain-based liability as though it were a liability to compensate for loss. We must hope that the courts do not use this language in future cases.

**13–068** The reasoning which led Lord Neuberger to adopt his "equitable compensation" terminology rested on the mistaken premise that all personal claims in equity are the same. In *Sinclair*, he noted that trustees are accountable to their beneficiaries for trust property and owe them a personal compensatory liability to reconstitute the trust fund if they dissipate the property in an unauthorised transaction[137]; that fiduciaries owe a personal duty to account to their principals for gains received in breach of their

---

130 ibid., at 676–677.

131 *Day v Cook* [2002] 1 B.C.L.C. 1 at [47]; *Leeds & Holbeck Building Society v Arthur & Cole (a firm)* [2002] P.N.L.R. 4 at [3]; *De Beer v Kanaar & Co (No.2)* [2002] EWHC 688 (Ch) at [92].

132 *Barnsley v Noble* [2014] EWHC 2657 (Ch) at [300] per Nugee J.

133 *Target Holdings Ltd v Redferns* [1996] A.C. 421 at 440 per Lord Browne-Wilkinson. See too *United Pan-Europe Communications NV v Deutsche Bank AG* [2000] 2 B.C.L.C. 461 at [47] per Morritt LJ.

134 *CMS Dolphin Ltd v Simonet* [2001] 2 B.C.L.C. 704 at [97] per Lawrence Collins J.

135 [2012] Ch. 453.

136 [2015] A.C. 250 at [1].

137 [2012] Ch. 453 at [40]–[41], citing *Target Holdings Ltd v Redferns* [1996] A.C. 421 at 434, and *Foskett v McKeown* [2001] 1 A.C. 102 at 130. See Ch.10.

fiduciary duty[138]; and that knowing recipients of misapplied trust funds and dishonest assistants in a breach of trust are personally "accountable in equity" to compensate the beneficiaries.[139] These observations led him to the conclusion that "the traditional way in which a non-proprietary claim is assessed in equity is through the medium of an equitable account, which in turn leads to equitable compensation"[140]—including claims against fiduciaries for an account of profits.

This reasoning contains a non sequitur. It does not follow from the fact that accounting mechanisms are used to quantify the loss-based compensatory liabilities of trustees, knowing recipients and dishonest assistants that the function of accounting mechanisms used to identify gains made by defaulting fiduciaries must be to quantify a compensatory liability. As we have noted in Chapter 10,[141] there are different types of accounting order and they support different types of claim: accounts in common form and accounts on the footing of wilful default support loss-based claims, and accounts of profits support gain-based claims. **13–069**

A second terminological problem that hinders understanding of the law in this area concerns the expression "account of profits". As in the passages quoted at the start of this section, the courts often use this term to describe a two-part order that can be made where a principal has established that his fiduciary made an improper gain[142]: first, the court directs that an inquiry should be undertaken into the relevant transactions (usually by a Chancery Master or district judge) to ascertain exactly what profit the fiduciary has made; and secondly, the court orders the fiduciary to pay the amount of this profit to the principal once it has been identified. Strictly speaking, however, an order for an "account of profits" is merely the first of these orders, i.e. an order that the amount of the fiduciary's profit should be established by investigating what has happened. Different orders for consequential or declaratory relief can then follow: that the fiduciary pay the principal the amount of the profit or that she hold the profit on constructive trust. This is what Lord Neuberger meant when he said in *FHR* that the expression "equitable accounting can encompass both proprietary and non-proprietary claims".[143] **13–070**

## *B. Personal and Proprietary Remedies*

Where a fiduciary has made a gain through her breach of fiduciary duty, as Lord Reed said in *AIB Group (UK) Plc v Mark Redler & Co*, the principal has "a personal claim to payment of the amount brought out by an account of profits".[144] The principal might also be entitled to a declaration that the fiduciary holds the profit on constructive trust for him. The latter remedy cannot be awarded unless the fiduciary's profit or its traceable proceeds survives in an identifiable form in the fiduciary's hands; otherwise there will be no property to which the constructive trust can attach. In *Sinclair*, the Court of Appeal also held that the principal can only claim a proprietary interest in gains deriving from property or opportunities directly attributable to the principal. However, the Supreme Court has now held in *FHR* that a constructive trust is imposed on bribe money received by a fiduciary, leaving the status of *Sinclair* unclear. This is discussed below in section 7. **13–071**

138 ibid., at [42], citing *Chan v Zacharia* (1984) 154 C.L.R. 178 at 199.
139 ibid., at [43], citing *Paragon Finance plc v DB Thakerar & Co* [1999] 1 All E.R. 400 at 408–409 and *Dubai Aluminium Co Ltd v Salaam* [2003] 2 A.C. 366 at [142]. See Ch.11.
140 ibid., at [45].
141 See paras 10–130—10–133.
142 The court will not order an account of profits if the principal has failed to explain in her pleadings what gain she alleges the fiduciary to have made: *City of London Group Plc v Lothbury Financial Services Ltd* [2012] EWHC 3148 (Ch) at [89]–[91].
143 [2015] A.C. 250 at [36].
144 [2014] 3 W.L.R. 1367 at [120].

**13–072** It follows that both personal and proprietary remedies are potentially available in a wide range of cases where the fiduciary has made a profit. These include cases where the fiduciary takes property belonging to her principal and exploits it to generate secondary gains for herself[145]; cases where she exploits a profit earning opportunity that she should have taken for her principal to make gains for herself[146]; and cases where she takes a bribe from a third party to prioritise the third-party's interests over the interests of her principal.[147] The courts can award both remedies on an alternative (although not a cumulative) basis: i.e. they cannot order a fiduciary both to deliver up property to the principal and to pay over its value, but they can allow the principal choose between the two. As Lord Templeman said in *Attorney General for Hong Kong v Reid*, "there is no reason why equity should not provide two remedies, so long as they do not result in double recovery",[148] and as Lord Neuberger said in *FHR*, "the principal can elect between the two remedies".[149]

**13–073** One consideration guiding the principal's choice will be the solvency of the fiduciary: if she is wealthy enough to pay the value of her profit the principal may be content to rely on his personal claim, as in *Regal Hastings Ltd v Gulliver*,[150] which was pleaded only as a personal claim, and *Boardman v Phipps*, where counsel and judges focussed their attention on the defendants' personal liability, although at first instance Wilberforce J made a declaration of constructive trust concurrently with an order that the defendants should repay the value of their profits and both orders were upheld on appeal.[151] Where the fiduciary is insolvent, however, the principal will prefer a proprietary remedy as this will enable him to take property out of the fiduciary's estate without having to share it with her other creditors.

**13–074** A second consideration relates to secondary gains accruing in the fiduciary's hands. Suppose, for example, that a fiduciary breaches her fiduciary duty by taking a bribe from a third party, and that she uses the money to purchase property. If the property decreases in value then the principal will prefer to enforce the fiduciary's personal obligation to pay the initial amount of the bribe, and in *Reid* Lord Templeman held not only that the principal can bring a personal claim with that end in mind,[152] but also that the principal can first make a proprietary claim against the property and then make a personal claim against the fiduciary for the balance.[153] In effect, therefore, Lord Templeman held that the principal has an equitable lien over the property to secure performance of the fiduciary's obligation to pay the amount of the bribe.

**13–075** What happens, though, if the property increases in value? In *Reid*, Lord Templeman held that in this case the principal can say that the bribe money was held for him on constructive trust from the moment of receipt, with the result that the property, as the traceable proceeds of the bribe money, is also held for him on constructive trust.[154] Suppose, though, that the property were not impressed with a constructive trust. Could the principal then make the different argument that the fiduciary owes him

---

145 e.g. *Aberdeen Town Council v Aberdeen University* (1877) 2 App. Cas. 544. Where the fiduciary is a trustee, an alternative route to recovery for the beneficiaries would be to adopt the transaction with retrospective effect as having been undertaken on their behalf, with the result that the fiduciary's secondary gains fall to be treated in the same way as the other trust property: see para.12–114.

146 e.g. *Boardman v Phipps* [1967] 2 A.C. 46; *Bhullar v Bhullar* [2003] 2 B.C.L.C. 241.

147 e.g. *FHR European Ventures LLP v Cedar Capital Partners LLC* [2015] A.C. 250.

148 [1994] 1 A.C. 324 at 331.

149 [2015] A.C. 250 at [7].

150 [1967] 2 A.C. 134.

151 [1964] 2 All E.R. 187 at 208; [1965] Ch. 992 at 1006, 1021; [1967] 2 A.C. 46 at 99, 112. The House of Lords' decision is excerpted at paras paras 9–031—9–062.

152 [1994] 1 A.C. 324 at 331–332.

153 ibid., at 336: the fiduciary "remains liable for the amount of the bribe if, in the event, the value of the property then recovered by the injured person proved to be less than that amount".

154 ibid., at 331–332.

a personal obligation to account for her "profits" and that these include secondary gains made out of property received by the fiduciary and used to buy other property that has increased in value?

In *Reid* Lord Templeman did not consider this question, but it was addressed by Lord Neuberger MR in *Sinclair*. In that case the claimant sought a declaration that gains made by the defendant fiduciary were impressed with a constructive trust, and the Court of Appeal refused to make such a declaration because the relevant gains had not been derived from property belonging to the principal, nor had they been obtained by misappropriating an opportunity that should have been taken for the principal. This aspect of the decision in *Sinclair* has been superseded by the Supreme Court's finding in *FHR* that constructive trusts are imposed in a wider set of circumstances than this.[155] For the purposes of the present discussion, however, we should notice the part of Lord Neuberger's judgment in *Sinclair* where he discussed the content of the defaulting fiduciary's personal liability. Here is what he said[156]: 13–076

> [P]revious decisions of this court establish that a claimant cannot claim proprietary ownership of an asset purchased by the defaulting fiduciary with funds which, although they could not have been obtained if he had not enjoyed his fiduciary status, were not beneficially owned by the claimant or derived from opportunities beneficially owned by the claimant. However, those cases also establish that in such a case a claimant does have a personal claim in equity to the funds. There is no case which appears to support the notion that such a personal claim entitles the claimant to claim the value of the asset (if it is greater than the amount of the funds together with interest), and there are judicial indications which tend to militate against that notion. 13–077
>
> [Counsel suggested] . . . that, essentially as a matter of equitable policy, a fiduciary should not be allowed to profit from his breach of duties, even to the extent of retaining any profit from such an asset after compensating a claimant in full. If that is indeed correct . . . then it seems to me that this should be dealt with by extending, or adjusting, the rules relating to equitable compensation rather than those relating to proprietary interests. Such a course, as I see it, would do less violence to the law as consistently laid down (where it has been specifically addressed) in a number of domestic cases of high authority, whereas it would involve little interference with established authority relating to equitable compensation. In addition, the law relating to proprietary interests, being within the law of property, is inherently rather less flexible than the law relating to equitable compensation. Furthermore, extending the law relating to equitable compensation in such a case would interfere far less with the legitimate interests of other creditors than extending the law relating to proprietary interests. 13–078

For reasons we have explained, this passage is couched in the confusing language of personal liability to pay "equitable compensation" assessed by reference to the value of the fiduciary's gain. But the gist of Lord Neuberger's remarks is that although cases prior to *Sinclair* did not recognise the possibility that a fiduciary might owe a personal liability to disgorge the value of secondary gains, it would be possible to "extend" or "adjust" the law to impose such liability, although this was not something that the claimant in *Sinclair* had asked the court to do. 13–079

Lord Neuberger added that it "may even be that tracing can be invoked to support such a personal claim" although he found it "a little hard to see how that could work".[157] However, when he later revisited this point in *FHR*, he expressed the more negative view that[158] 13–080

> if the principal has a proprietary claim to the bribe or commission, he can trace and follow it in equity, whereas (unless we develop the law of equitable tracing beyond its current boundaries) a principal with a right only to equitable compensation would have no such equitable right to trace or follow.

155 See paras paras 13–182—13–187.
156 [2012] Ch. 453 at [89]–[90].
157 ibid., at [91].
158 [2015] A.C. 250 at [1]. See too his comments at [44].

13–081 It seems, then, that in cases where the fiduciary receives a bribe from a third party and a constructive trust is imposed on the bribe money, the courts will make an additional order that the fiduciary owes a personal obligation to pay the principal the value of secondary gains stemming from the money. But there seems to be no case in which the court has ordered the fiduciary to pay the principal the value of such secondary gains on a stand-alone basis, i.e. where there is no constructive trust of the property.

13–082 It is unclear from Lord Neuberger's analysis of the case law in *Sinclair* and *FHR* whether he believed the reason for this to be that no principal has ever asked for such an order or, instead, that the law does not allow orders of this kind. There is a suggestion in *Sinclair* that Lord Neuberger may have believed such orders to be inappropriate because they would leave the principal more than fully compensated for his loss, contrary to his notion that the fiduciary's obligation is an obligation to pay "equitable compensation".[159] If that idea formed part of his Lordship's reasoning then it should be rejected since the fiduciary's liability is a liability to disgorge her gain and not a liability to compensate the principal for his loss. There are also dicta in *Sinclair* and *FHR* that such a claim would be impossible where the principal needs to use the rules of tracing to establish what property was acquired with the bribe money—the reason being that the tracing rules can only be used to support claims by litigants who initially had a proprietary interest in the property they seek to trace.[160]

13–083 It is unclear to us, however, why a principal should need to use the tracing rules in cases of this kind. When an account of profits is taken with a view to quantifying a fiduciary's personal gain-based liability to her principal, a broad-ranging enquiry is made into all the factual circumstances of a case, and all causally related gains and losses fall within its scope. Where the fiduciary misappropriates a profit-making opportunity and exploits it, for example by running a business in competition with her principal's business, the law does not concern itself with tracing through particular transactions to ascertain what was received in exchange for particular property: it simply looks at receipts and expenses with a view to identifying a bottom-line profit figure. On Lord Neuberger's analysis, however, a different approach must be taken where the fiduciary receives property from a third party in breach of duty, and the principal's personal claim to secondary gains deriving from this property will founder because the rules of tracing cannot be used to support it. We doubt if this is correct.

## C. How Accounts of Profits Work

13–084 As the name suggests, the purpose of an account of profits is to identify the net profits made by the fiduciary, as opposed to her gross receipts.[161] Broadly speaking, the fiduciary "should be accountable for the profits properly attributable to the breach of fiduciary duty, taking into account the expenses connected with those profits and a reasonable allowance for overheads (but not necessarily salary for the wrongdoer)."[162] The exercise of matching receipts against costs is largely a mathematical exercise, but there is a margin of discretion to the extent that a doubtful expense may be allowed to an honest fiduciary but disallowed to a dishonest one.[163] Note, too, that at least in cases where a constructive trust has been imposed on property held by the fiduciary, and the value of this property rises and falls between the date of the fiduciary's receipt and the date of judgment, she may be personally liable to

159 [2012] Ch. 453 at [46]–[47], although he says that this may not be an insuperable difficulty because equitable compensation is "a more flexible concept than common law damages". For critical comment, see paras 13–067—13–069.

160 [2012] Ch. 453 at [91]; [2015] A.C. 250 at [1] and [44].

161 *Regal Hastings Ltd v Gulliver* [1967] 2 A.C. 134 at 154 per Lord Wright, followed in *Patel v Brent L.B.C.* [2004] W.T.L.R. at [29].

162 *CMS Dolphin Ltd v Simonet* [2001] 2 B.C.L.C. 704 at [97] per Lawrence Collins J. See too *Nottingham University v Fishel* [2000] I.C.R. 1462 at 1498–1499.

163 *Colburn v Simms* (1843) 2 Hare 543 at 560.

pay her principal the highest intermediate value, on the basis that she has a continuing duty to realise the property at the most advantageous moment and account for the proceeds to the principal.[164]

In *Ultraframe (UK) Ltd v Fielding*, Lewison J said that the following principles govern the framing of an account of profits[165]: **13–085**

> (i) The fundamental rule is that a fiduciary must not make an unauthorised profit out of his fiduciary position;
> (ii) The fashioning of an account should not be allowed to operate as the unjust enrichment the claimant;
> (iii) The profits for which an account is ordered must bear a reasonable relationship to the breach of duty proved;
> (iv) It is important to establish exactly what has been acquired;
> (v) Subject to that, the fashioning of the account depends on the facts. In some cases it will be appropriate to order an account limited in time; or to order an account of all the profits of a business subject to all just allowances for the fiduciary's skill, labour and assumption of business risk. In some cases it may be appropriate to order the making of a payment representing the capital value of the advantage in question, either in place of or in addition to an account of profits.

To this, Lewison J later added in *Fanmailuk.com v Cooper*[166] that the court might also regard the entire capital value of a business as representing the profit flowing from a breach of duty, and make an order requiring the fiduciary to disgorge that amount.

In *Grimaldi v Chameleon Mining NL (No.2)*,[167] Finn J emphasised the same points.[168] In the following extract from his judgment he also discusses cases where the fiduciary used her principal's money to fund her own business, and where the courts were willing to apportion the profits of the business between the principal and the fiduciary according to their respective contributions—money, in the case of the principal; time, skill and effort, in the case of the fiduciary. These cases support the point made previously,[169] that when taking an account of profits for the purpose of quantifying a fiduciary's personal gain-based liability the court is concerned with setting expenses against receipts and is not concerned with tracing property into substitute property, especially (but not only) in cases where the principal's property became "mixed up with the consequences and liabilities" of the fiduciary's business.[170] **13–086**

*Grimaldi v Chameleon Mining NL (No.2)*

Full Court of the Federal Court of Australia (2012) 200 F.C.R. 296 at [515]–[531]

In many contexts the identification of the breach and of the benefit or profit resulting from it will be straightforward and uncontroversial, as where a trustee improperly purchases a house with a mixed fund of his own and trust moneys. In such a case, where a proportionate interest in the property itself is not sought, then, apart from his liability to account for the moneys misused, the fiduciary will be liable in the usual case for the same proportion of any profit from the purchase as the trust moneys bore to the total purchase price.[171] This will be because the sole source of profit will generally be the capital outlaid.[172] . . . **13–087**

---

164 *Nant-y-glo and Blaina Ironworks Co v Grave* (1878) 12 Ch. D. 738, affirmed in *Target Holdings Ltd v Redferns* [1996] 1 A.C. 421 at 440.
165 [2005] EWHC 1638 (Ch) at [1588].
166 [2011] EWHC 902 (Ch).
167 (2012) 200 F.C.R. 296.
168 Ibid. at [513]–[514].
169 See para.13–083.
170 *Flockton v Bunning* (1872) L.R. 8 Ch. App. 323n at 326n. Cf. *Primeau v Granfield* 184 F. 480 (1911) at 487 per Learned Hand J: "the law has never gone into such metaphysics".
171 *Scott v Scott* (1963) 109 C.L.R. 649.
172 For examples in other fiduciary contexts where the calculation is simple, see *McKenzie v McDonald* [1927] V.L.R. 134 (profit made on a purchase and resale) and *Attorney-General v Edmunds* (1868) L.R. 6 Eq. 381.

13-088 The courts have long recognised that benefits or the profits derived by a misbehaving fiduciary may be attributable to multiple sources only one of which was the breach of fiduciary duty or trust; personal skill, expertise and exertion, goodwill or the financial contributions of the fiduciary and of third parties may have played their part as well in generating profits. In such circumstances, the assessment of the actual profit or benefit derived may involve a difficult, complex and costly exercise of attribution. If such an exercise is to be undertaken—and at best it can only result in some reasonable approximation of the profit for which the fiduciary must account[173]—the remedy invoked will be by way of an account of profits. What requires emphasis is that the profits inquiry in cases involving, variously, the establishment of a competing business by utilising the resources of the fiduciary's former employer,[174] using "trust" moneys in the fiduciary's own business,[175] reviving a trust business for the fiduciary's own benefit,[176] or misappropriating an opportunity,[177] raise their own particular concerns. They are not resolved by the application of a common "general rule".[178]

13-089 . . . [Finn J turned to consider "that category of case where profits are sought to be recovered from trust moneys improperly introduced into a trade or business either at its inception or afterwards":] The leading authority is *Docker v Somes*[179] which established that, if trust moneys were improperly employed in a trustee's own trade or business, the beneficiaries were entitled to insist upon having a proportionate share of the profits instead of, as previously, interest only on the amount of the trust moneys so employed. Though of some length Lord Brougham's reasoning is revealing. He began with what was the then orthodoxy:[180]

> "Wherever a trustee, or one standing in the relation of a trustee, violates his duty, and deals with the trust estate for his own behoof, the rule is that he shall account to the cestui que trust for all the gain which he has made. Thus, if trust money is laid out in buying and selling land, and a profit made by the transaction, that shall go not to the trustee who has so applied the money, but to the cestui que trust whose money has been thus applied. In like manner (and cases of this kind are more numerous), where a trustee or executor has used the fund committed to his care in stock speculations, though the loss, if any, must fall upon himself, yet for every farthing of profit he may make he shall be accountable to the trust estate. So, if he lay out the trust money in a commercial adventure, as in buying or fitting out a vessel for a voyage, or put it in the trade of another person, from which he is to derive a certain stipulated profit, although I will not say that this has been decided, I hold it to be quite clear that he must account for the profits received by the adventure or from the concern. In all these cases it is easy to tell what the gains are; the fund is kept distinct from the trustee's other monies, and whatever he gets he must account for and pay over. It is so much fruit, so much increase on the estate or chattel of another, and must follow the ownership of the property and go to the proprietor. . ."

13-090 His Lordship went on to explain why the then orthodoxy was that profits could not be claimed where money had been mixed:[181]

> "The reason which has induced Judges to be satisfied with allowing interest only I take to have been this: they could not easily sever the profits attributable to the trust money from those belonging to the whole capital stock; and the process became still more difficult, where a great proportion of the gains proceeded from skill or labour employed upon the capital."

13-091 Confronted by counsel with an example which was designed to deter him permitting apportionment ("from taking the course which all principle points out"), Lord Brougham made the important comment:[182]

> "[Counsel] feigned the instance of an apothecary buying drugs with £100 of trust money, and earning £1000 a year by selling them to his patients; and so he might have taken the case of trust money laid out in purchasing a piece of steel or skein of silk, and these being worked up into goods of the finest

173 *My Kinda Town Ltd v Soll* [1982] F.S.R. 147 at 159.
174 *Timber Engineering Co Pty Ltd v Anderson* [1980] 2 N.S.W.L.R. 488.
175 *Willett v Blanford* (1841) 1 Hare 253.
176 *Re Jarvis* [1958] 1 W.L.R. 815.
177 *Green & Clara Pty Ltd v Bestobell Industries Pty Ltd (No. 2)* [1984] W.A.R. 32.
178 cf. *Re Jarvis* at 820.
179 (1834) 2 My. & K. 655.
180 Ibid. at 664–5.
181 Ibid. at 665.
182 Ibid. at 667–8.

fabric, Birmingham trinkets or Brussels lace, where the work exceeds by 10,000 times the material in value. But such instances, in truth, prove nothing; for they are cases not of profits upon stock, but of skilful labour very highly paid; and no reasonable person would ever dream of charging a trustee, whose skill thus bestowed had so enormously augmented the value of the capital, as if he had only obtained from it a profit."

Apportionment was permissible. The profits "which might be supposed to come from the money misapplied [could be severed] from the rest of the capital embarked".[183] Nonetheless an escape route was left:[184] 13–092

"Should in any case a serious difficulty arise in tracing and apportioning the profits, this may be a reason for preferring a fixed rate of interest in that case."

A significant body of nineteenth century case law built on *Docker v Somes*.[185] Many of the cases involved the shares of deceased partners being improperly left in the new partnership.[186] 13–093

The subsequent case law did not attempt to trace the precise application of the moneys misused. It had been "mixed up with the consequences and liabilities" of the business.[187] That was sufficient. Nor was it the case, where the trustee/fiduciary started a business on his own account using a mixed fund, or used trust moneys in an existing business, that the profits should necessarily be apportioned according to the respective contributions of his own and trust moneys to the business' capital. 13–094

As was affirmed in *Vyse v Foster* . . . by James L.J.:[188] 13–095

". . . there was no rule for apportioning the profits according to the respective amounts of the capital, but that the division would be affected by considerations of the source of the profit, the nature of the business, and the other circumstances of the case. It is obvious that it must be so, for it would be easy to suggest a number of instances in which the profit of a business has no ascertainable reference to the capital – e.g. solicitors, factors, brokers . . . Indeed, in almost every case where the business consists of buying and selling, the difference between prosperity and ruin mainly depends on the skill, industry, and care of the dealers."

The need to apportion commonly requires the court to direct inquiries concerning the sources of profit in the particular business concerned and then to determine the profits which are attributable to those sources[189]; a like need to apportion can arise, we note in passing, where intellectual property is misused in another business.[190] 13–096

Contemporary Australian authority conforms to the above: where a portion of the profits made is "not the product or consequence of the plaintiff's property but the product of the fiduciary's skill, efforts, property and resources", it would be inequitable to order an account of the "entire profits".[191] However, it is for the fiduciary to establish that inequity.[192] 13–097

The courts have on occasion sought, understandably, to short-circuit the apportionment inquiries by resort to the device of awarding "just allowances" to the fiduciary. This can take the form of dividing between the fiduciary and the principal all the profits made in the proportions that the fiduciary's own and the trust's money bore to the total capital, but only after making an allowance to the fiduciary for his or her own skill and exertion.[193] The same just allowances device has been employed where the capital or business used when generating the profit represented, or was constituted by, the trust property 13–098

---

183 Ibid. at 666.

184 Ibid. at 673.

185 See, e.g. *Wedderburn v Wedderburn* (1838) 4 My. & Cr. 41; *MacDonald v Richardson* (1858) 1 Giff 81.

186 See *Lindley & Banks on Partnership* (19th edn, 2010) paras 26–40—26–41. See also *Lewin on Trusts* (18th edn, 2008) para.20–33.

187 *Flockton v Bunning* (1872) L.R. 8 Ch. App. 323n at 326n; see also *Primeau v Granfield* 184 F. 480 (1911) – a tracing/accounting case.

188 Ibid. at 331. See also *Willett v Blanford* (1842) 1 Hare 253.

189 See *Manley v Sartori* [1927] 1 Ch. 157; *Page v Rattiffe* (1896) 75 L.T. 371.

190 See, e.g. *Colbeam Ltd v Stock Affiliates Pty Ltd* (1968) 122 C.L.R. 25 at 42; see also Ricketson, *The Law of Intellectual Property: Copyright, Designs and Confidential Information* para. [2.75].

191 *Warman v Dwyer* (1995) 182 C.L.R. 544 at 561.

192 Ibid.

193 See Yates v Finn (1880) 13 Ch. D. 839; Lord Provost of Edinburgh v Lord Advocate (1879) 4 App. Cas. 823 at 838–9.

misused;[194] or, for that matter, in exceptional circumstances where, without misusing trust property at all, but in consequence of a breach of fiduciary duty, the fiduciary has made profits by deploying his or her own knowledge, skill and experience.[195] In cases of the latter two varieties, the courts have shown quite some reticence in granting just allowances, as of course.

13–099 As was said in *Warman v Dwyer*:[196]

> "Whether it is appropriate to allow an errant fiduciary a proportion of profits or to make an allowance in respect of skill, expertise and other expenses is a matter of judgment which will depend on the facts of the given case. However, as a general rule, in conformity with the principle that a fiduciary must not profit from a breach of fiduciary duty, a court will not apportion profits in the absence of an antecedent arrangement for profit-sharing but will make allowance for skill, expertise and other expenses."

13–100 Allowances are not granted as of right and it is here that a court will exercise its powers to do what is "practically just". Considerations such as whether the fiduciary has acted honestly or dishonestly; how and for what has the fiduciary been remunerated; would the denial of an allowance leave the principal unjustly enriched; what risk has been borne by the principal; etc, come into play.[197]

**13–101** Two points should be made respecting cases where the fiduciary has contributed time, skill and effort to the generating of profits. First, there is a difference between an order that these profits should be apportioned between the parties (as in, e.g. *Docker v Somes*[198]) and an order that all of the profits should be allocated to the principal, subject to the making of an equitable allowance to the fiduciary for the value of her work (as in, e.g. *Boardman v Phipps*[199]). It lies in the court's discretion to make one order or the other—or neither—depending on the facts of the case.

**13–102** This leads to the second point, which is that the courts have said that they can order an allowance on the basis that "it would be inequitable . . . for the [principal] to step in and take the profit without paying for the skill and labour which has produced it"[200]; but in *Guinness Plc v Saunders*,[201] Lord Goff conversely held that the exercise of the courts' discretion to order an allowance should be restricted to cases where an award would not have the effect of encouraging fiduciaries to put themselves in a position of conflict. It can be assumed that the courts will be guided by the same considerations when deciding whether to apportion profits. It can be hard to predict how the courts will balance one consideration against the other,[202] although it is safe to assume that they will be less likely to favour a dishonest fiduciary than an honest one.[203]

---

194 See *Boardman v Phipps* [1967] 2 A.C. 46 at 104; *Timber Engineering Co Pty Ltd v Anderson* [1980] 2 N.S.W.L.R. 488 at [13]–[27]; *Paul A. Davies (Aust) Pty Ltd v Davies* [1983] 1 N.S.W.L.R. 440 at 448 and 451; *Re Jarvis* [1958] 1 W.L.R. 815 at 820.

195 cf. *O'Sullivan v Management Agency and Music Ltd* [1985] Q.B. 428.

196 (1995) 182 C.L.R. 544 at 562.

197 See generally *Harris v Digital Pulse Pty Ltd* (2003) 56 N.S.W.L.R. 298 at 311–336; and see Ford and Lee, *Principles of the Law of Trusts*, vol. 2, para. [17.2650].

198 (1834) 2 My. & K. 655.

199 [1967] 2 A.C. 46.

200 *Phipps v Boardman* [1964] 1 W.L.R. 993 at 1018 per Wilberforce J; affirmed [1967] 2 A.C. 46 at 104 and 112. See too *O'Sullivan v Management Agency and Music Ltd* [1985] Q.B. 42; *Badfinger Music Ltd v Evans* [2001] W.T.L.R. 1.

201 *Guinness Plc v Saunders* [1990] 2 A.C. 663 at 701, followed in, e.g. *Quarter Master UK Ltd (In Liquidation) v Pyke* [2005] 1 B.C.L.C. 245 at [76]–[77] and *Cobbetts LLP v Hodge* [2010] 1 B.C.L.C. 30 at [118]; though cf. *Nottingham University v Fishel* [2000] I.C.R. 1462 at 1499–1500, and see too *Imageview Management Ltd v Jack* [2009] Bus. L.R. 1034 at [54]–[60].

202 Compare the views taken by Elias CJ and by Tipping and Blanchard JJ in *Chirnside v Fay* [2007] 1 N.Z.L.R. 433.

203 Cf. *Phipps v Boardman* [1965] Ch. 992 at 1021.

## D. Causation

Consistently with Lewison J's comment in *Ultraframe* that profits claimed by a principal must "bear a reasonable relationship" to the breach of duty committed by the fiduciary, Arden LJ accepted in *Murad v Al-Saraj*[204] that some rule is needed to distinguish between the gains which a fiduciary derives from her breach and the gains which she derives from other sources, for "no fiduciary is liable for all the profits [she] ever made from any source".[205] The question arises, however, what this rule should be? In *United Pan-Europe Communications NV v Deutsche Bank AG*,[206] Morritt LJ said that the best approach is to ask whether the gains made by the fiduciary fall within the scope of her duty.[207] He took this to be a different question from the question whether the fiduciary's receipt of a gain was caused by her breach of duty, which he believed to be an irrelevant issue. His comments to this effect were followed by Arden LJ in *Murad*[208] and by the Court of Appeal in *Novoship (UK) Ltd v Mikhaylyuk*,[209] where it was said that "a fiduciary's liability to account for a secret profit does not depend on any notion of causation." **13–103**

It may be that these dicta reflect an understanding of the rules governing gain-based liability for breach of fiduciary duty that considers the fiduciary to be disabled from taking gains for herself, and does not consider her to owe a positive duty to avoid conflicts of interest, breach of which triggers a gain-based liability.[210] However, Arden LJ appears to have thought in *Murad* that the same rules of attribution would apply whichever way the fiduciary's liability is analysed,[211] and if one takes the latter view of the fiduciary's duty (as the courts clearly do in the equitable compensation cases considered in section 5), then it is unhelpful to collapse the question whether there was a fiduciary duty in the first place (which requires one to consider what function or responsibility the fiduciary undertook) into the question whether this duty was breached with the result that the fiduciary made a gain that she should now be ordered to disgorge (which requires one to consider how and why particular gains came into her hands). For these reasons we prefer the view that a principal must establish a causal link between the gain and the breach of duty before the fiduciary should have to pay the value of the gain to the principal (or hold it on constructive trust for him).[212] **13–104**

Obviously this still leaves us with the question of what test should be used to decide whether a fiduciary's gain has been caused by a breach of duty. The answer is a simple one. The breach must have been one cause of the gain. It need not have been the only cause, nor need it have been the predominant cause, for "in this sort of case the court 'does not allow an examination into the relative importance of contributory causes'".[213] The court "lays the burden on the defaulting fiduciary to show that the profit is not one for which [she] should account",[214] and she cannot escape liability by proving that she would have made the gain even if she had not breached his duty because "the question **13–105**

[204] [2005] W.T.L.R. 1573, excerpted below at paras 13–107ff.
[205] ibid., at [62]. cf. *3464920 Canada Inc v Strother* (2005) 7 I.T.E.L.R. 748 at [47].
[206] [2000] 2 B.C.L.C. 461 at [47].
[207] See para.13–016.
[208] [2005] W.T.L.R. 1573 at [57].
[209] [2015] 2 W.L.R. 526 at [96].
[210] See paras 9–073—9–077 and 13–003—13–004.
[211] [2005] W.T.L.R. 1573 at [49]: "for the purposes simply of the question on this appeal, I do not think it matters which way the [fiduciary's] liability is analysed."
[212] Cf. *Maguire v Makaronis* (1997) 188 C.L.R. 449 at 468: there is "a need to specify criteria for a sufficient connection (or 'causation') between breach of duty and the profit derived." See too *Swain v Law Society* [1982] 1 W.L.R. 17 at 37; *Estate Realties Ltd v Wignall* [1992] 2 N.Z.L.R. 615 at 631; *Button v Phelps* [2006] EWHC 53 (Ch) at [66].
[213] *Fexuto Pty Ltd v Bosnjak Holdings Pty Ltd (No.2)* (1998) 29 A.C.S.R. 290 at 297.
[214] *Murad v Al-Saraj* [2005] W.T.L.R. 1573 at [77], per Arden LJ.

whether or not the benefit would have been obtained but for the breach of trust has always been treated as irrelevant".[215] In Lord Radcliffe's words[216]:

> If a trustee has placed himself in a position in which his interest conflicts with his duty and has not discharged himself from responsibility to account for the profits that his interest has secured for him, it is neither here nor there to speculate whether, if he had done his duty, he would not have been left in possession of the same amount of profit.

**13–106** In effect, therefore, the fiduciary must prove that her breach of duty had no causative effect at all, by showing that she acquired the gain exclusively as a result of activities legitimately undertaken in her own interest. In *Murad v Al-Saraj*, excerpted below, the defendant fiduciary failed to do this, with the result that liability was imposed.

*Murad v Al-Saraj*

Court of Appeal [2005] W.T.L.R. 1573

**13–107** The claimants agreed to participate in a property development deal with the defendant who owed them a fiduciary duty. The claimants put up £1 million in cash in the belief that he would also contribute cash towards the purchase price, but in fact he never paid any cash to the vendor who instead released him from a legally unenforceable liability arising out of their prior personal dealings. Had the claimants been aware of this fact, they would have gone ahead with the deal but rather than agreeing to a half and half capital profit split on resale of the hotel, they would have insisted on a higher profit share for themselves. After the hotel was sold, the facts came to light, and the claimants asserted that the defendant was liable to account for the whole of his share of the profits to them, as the proceeds of his breach of fiduciary duty, and that he held these profits on constructive trust for them. The defendant claimed to keep that portion of the profits which the claimants would have let him take even if he had made full disclosure. This was rejected by a majority of the court.

**13–108** ARDEN L.J. (with whom JONATHAN PARKER L.J. agreed; CLARKE L.J. gave a dissenting judgment): . . . The judge gave a remedy of account because there was a fiduciary relationship. For wrongs in the context of such a relationship, an order for an account of profits is a conventional remedy. The Murads considered that that remedy would be more beneficial to them because, if they were awarded damages at common law, they would simply be entitled to recover the difference between the profit share to which they agreed and that which they would have negotiated if the true position had been disclosed to them. The reference to deceit is, however, a reminder that the judge's finding was that Mr Al-Saraj's failure to disclose the set off arrangement to the Murads was both deliberate and fraudulent, a point to which I shall have to return.

**13–109** A distinguishing feature of this case is that, because the claim was brought both in tort and for breach of fiduciary duty, the judge carefully made all the findings which might be relevant if his conclusion on fiduciary duty was reversed on appeal. He accordingly made a finding as to what the Murads would have done if they had been given the information withheld from them. As I have explained, he held that the Murads would still have entered into a joint venture with Mr Al-Saraj but they would have agreed with him that he should have a reduced profit share. The appellants seize on that finding as relevant also to the question of liability to account as a fiduciary. The finding is highly compressed, and it is not clear, on the facts as found by the judge, exactly why the Murads would have agreed to give Mr Al-Saraj a profit share in the changed circumstances. I consider it most likely that what the judge had in mind was that the Murads would have agreed to give Mr Al-Saraj a profit share in return for a cash injection (other than by way of loan). In other words, what the judge found was that the Murads would have given him a profit share in return for an investment not as a reward for the service of introducing the Murads to the Park Hotel

---

[215] *Brickenden v London Loan & Savings Co* [1934] 3 D.L.R. 465 at 469; *Industrial Development Consultants Ltd v Cooley* [1972] 1 W.L.R. 443 at 453; *Beach Petroleum NL v Kennedy* (1999) 48 N.S.W.L.R. 1 at [440]; *Gwembe Valley Development Co Ltd (in rec.) v Koshy (No.3)* [2004] 1 B.C.L.C. 131 at [145]–[146].

[216] *Gray v New Augarita Porcupine Mines Ltd* [1952] 3 D.L.R. 1 at 15. See too *Manley v Santori* [1927] 1 Ch. 157.

venture. If the position had been the latter, the more obvious course for Mr Al-Saraj would have been to attempt to convince the judge on the taking of the account that he ought to be allowed a profit share as an introductory fee.

. . . [Counsel for Al-Saraj argued that] the account ordered by the judge would . . . result in unjust enrichment of the Murads. It is (he submits) wrong in principle that the Murads should receive the benefit of any profits which, if there had been full disclosure, they would have been content for Mr Al-Saraj to have. They all along anticipated being co-venturers with him and so expected him to have a share of the profits from the acquisition of Parkside Hotel. Increases in profits not attributable to his wrongful conduct should be excluded from the profits for which he has to account . . . To test [this] argument . . . it is necessary to go back to first principle. It has long been the law that equitable remedies for the wrongful conduct of a fiduciary differ from those available at common law . . . Equity recognises that there are legal wrongs for which damages are not the appropriate remedy. In some situations therefore, as in this case, a court of equity instead awards an account of profits. As with an award of interest . . . the purpose of the account is to strip a defaulting fiduciary of his profit. . . **13–110**

[The] liability of a fiduciary to account does not depend on whether the person to whom the fiduciary duty was owed could himself have made the profit . . . [This] is established by numerous authorities. It is sufficient for me to cite the well-known passage from the speech of Lord Russell of Killowen in the *Regal* case:[217] **13–111**

> "The rule of equity which insists on those, who by use of a fiduciary position make a profit, being liable to account for that profit, in no way depends on fraud, or absence of bona fides; or upon such questions or considerations as whether the profit would or should otherwise have gone to the plaintiff, or whether the profiteer was under a duty to obtain the source of the profit for the plaintiff, or whether he took a risk or acted as he did for the benefit of the plaintiff, or whether the plaintiff has in fact been damaged or benefited by his action. The liability arises from the mere fact of a profit having, in the stated circumstances, been made."

. . . The fact that the fiduciary can show that that party would not have made a loss is, on the authority of the *Regal* case, an irrelevant consideration so far as an account of profits is concerned. Likewise, it follows in my judgment from the *Regal* case that it is no defence for a fiduciary to say that he would have made the profit even if there had been no breach of fiduciary duty. **13–112**

In the present case, the conduct of Mr Al-Saraj was held to be fraudulent. This was not the position of the directors in the *Regal* case. The principle, however, established by the *Regal* case applies even where the fiduciary acts in the mistaken belief that he is acting in accordance with his fiduciary duty. As Lord Russell made clear in the passage cited above, liability does not depend on fraud or lack of good faith. The existence of a fraudulent intent will, however, be relevant to the question of the allowances to be made on the taking of the account. . . **13–113**

I accept that any rule that makes a wrongdoer liable for all the consequences of his wrongful conduct or for actions which did not cause the injured party any loss needs to be justified by some special policy. But . . . in the field of fiduciaries there are policy reasons which have for a long time been accepted by the courts. **13–114**

For policy reasons, the courts decline to investigate hypothetical situations as to what would have happened if the fiduciary had performed his duty. In *Regal* case Lord Wright made the following point, to which I shall have to return below:[218] **13–115**

> "Nor can the court adequately investigate the matter in most cases. The facts are generally difficult to ascertain or are solely in the knowledge of the person being charged. They are matters of surmise; they are hypothetical because the inquiry is as to what would have been the position if that party had not acted as he did, or what he might have done if there had not been the temptation to seek his own advantage, if, in short, interest had not conflicted with duty."

Again, for policy reasons, on the taking of an account, the court lays the burden on the defaulting fiduciary to show that the profit is not one for which he should account.[219] This shifting of the onus of proof is **13–116**

[217] *Regal Hastings Ltd v Gulliver* [1967] 2 A.C. 134 at 144–5.
[218] Ibid. at 154.
[219] See, for example, *Manley v Sartori* [1927] Ch 157.

consistent with the deterrent nature of the fiduciary's liability. The liability of the fiduciary becomes the default rule.

13–117 . . . I have already set out Lord Wright's observations in the *Regal* case about the difficulties of investigating the conduct of a defaulting trustee. Under the rule of equity applied in that case . . . cases can be found where the fiduciary or trustee acted in all good faith believing that he was acting in the interests of his beneficiary but yet has been made to account for the profits obtained as a result of the breach of trust without limitation. Now, in a case like the *Regal* case, if the rule of equity under which the defendants were held liable to account for secret profits were not inflexible, the crucial issue of fact would be: what the company would have done if the opportunity to subscribe for shares in its subsidiary had been offered to it? In the passage just cited, as I have said, Lord Wright makes the point that it is very difficult to investigate that issue. However, while that may have been so in the past in the days of Lord Eldon and Lord King, that would not be the case today. The court has very extensive powers under the Civil Procedure Rules for instance to require information to be given as to a party's case. If the witness cannot attend the hearing, it may be possible for his evidence to be given by way of a witness statement or it may be possible for him to give evidence by video-link. The reasons for the rule of equity are many and complex . . . There have been calls for its re-examination . . . It may be that the time has come when the court should revisit the operation of the inflexible rule of equity in harsh circumstances, as where the trustee has acted in perfect good faith and without any deception or concealment, and in the belief that he was acting in the best interests of the beneficiary. I need only say this: it would not be in the least impossible for a court in a future case, to determine as a question of fact whether the beneficiary would not have wanted to exploit the profit himself, or would have wanted the trustee to have acted other than in the way that the trustee in fact did act. Moreover, it would not be impossible for a modern court to conclude as a matter of policy that, without losing the deterrent effect of the rule, the harshness of it should be tempered in some circumstances. In addition, in such cases, the courts can provide a significant measure of protection for the beneficiaries by imposing on the defaulting trustee the affirmative burden of showing that those circumstances prevailed. Certainly the Canadian courts have modified the effect of equity's inflexible rule[220] though I express no view as to the circumstances in which there should be any relaxation of the rule in this jurisdiction. That sort of question must be left to another court.

13–118 In short, it may be appropriate for a higher court one day to revisit the rule on secret profits and to make it less inflexible in appropriate circumstances, where the unqualified operation of the rule operates particularly harshly and where the result is not compatible with the desire of modern courts to ensure that remedies are proportionate to the justice of the case where this does not conflict with some other overriding policy objective of the rule in question.

13–119 However that is not this case. Mr Al-Saraj was found to have made a fraudulent misrepresentation to the Murads who had placed their trust in him. I do not consider that, even if we were free to revisit the *Regal* case, this would be an appropriate case in which to do so. The appropriate remedy is that he should disgorge all the profits, whether of a revenue or capital nature, that he made from inducing the Murads by his fraudulent representations from entering into the Parkside Hotel venture, subject to any allowances permitted by the court on the taking of the account.

13–120 The imposition of liability to account for secret profits and the placing of the burden of proof on the defaulting trustee are not, however, quite the end of the matter. The kind of account ordered in this case is an account of profits, that is a procedure to ensure the restitution of profits which ought to have been made for the beneficiary and not a procedure for the forfeiture of profits to which the defaulting trustee was always entitled for his own account. That is [counsel for Al-Saraj's] case and I agree with him on this point. Even when the fiduciary is not fraudulent, the profit obtained from the breach of trust has to be defined. It may indeed be derivative, as where a trustee misappropriates trust property and then sells it and make a profit out of something else. But equity does not take the view that simply because a profit was made as part of the same transaction the fiduciary must account for it. I can give an example of that. In *Giddings v Giddings*,[221] a tenant for life renewed a lease belonging to the trust. The renewed lease, however, included land which had not been within the original lease. Sir John Copley M.R. dealt with the point briefly. He held that the remaindermen were only entitled to the benefit of the lease so far as it related to the land

---

220 See *Peso Silver Mines Ltd v Cropper* (1966) 58 D.L.R. (2d) 1; see also the decision of the Privy Council on appeal from Australia in *Queensland Mines Ltd v Hudson* (1978) 52 A.J.L.R. 399.

221 (1826) 3 Russ. 241.

originally leased to the tenant for life. Another example is *Docker v Somes*,[222] where Lord Brougham expressed the view that in some circumstances a trustee who had applied considerable skill and labour to trust property which he had misapplied would be awarded a share of the product of his skill and labour:

> "Mr. Solicitor General might have taken the case of trust money laid out in purchasing a piece of steel or skein of silk, and these being worked up into goods of the finest fabric, Birmingham trinkets or Brussels lace, where the work exceeds by 10,000 times the material in value. But such instances, in truth, prove nothing; for they are cases not of profits upon stock, but of skilful labour very highly paid; and no reasonable person would ever dream of charging a trustee, whose skill thus bestowed had so enormously augmented the value of the capital, as if he had only obtained from it a profit; although the refinements of the civil law would certainly bear us out, even in charging all gains accruing upon those goods as in the nature of accretions belonging to the true owners of the chattels."

In the present case, any recognisable contribution made by Mr. Al-Saraj was to the business of the joint venture. As the *Warman* case[223] shows, there can be particular difficulty applying the above principles where the trustee mixes trust property with his own business. The profit which belongs to the trust has to be disentangled from that which belongs to the defaulting trustee because it is a profit of his business. I have explained above how these difficulties were resolved in the Warman case by limiting the account to two years' profits. The problem in the *Warman* case has also faced courts within our own jurisdiction. In *Vyse v Foster*,[224] one of the partners in a business died but his capital remained in the business and was thus used by the surviving partners. One of the residuary legatees of the deceased partner sought an account of the share of the profits of the business to which she was entitled. The matter came before James and Mellish L.JJ. (Mellish L.J. did not deliver a separate judgment). This court was prepared in principle to ascertain the share of the profits of the business but when it came down to working out how this was to be done this court decided that the appropriate remedy would be to order repayment of the capital with interest. In his judgment, James L.J. held that the share of profits to which the plaintiff was entitled could not simply be ascertained by working out the proportion of the capital to which she was entitled: 13–121

> "But it was pointed out by Vice-Chancellor Wigram, in the case of *Willett v Blanford*,[225] and his judgment was afterwards repeated and approved of by the Lords Justices, that there was no rule for apportioning the profits according to the respective amounts of the capital, but that the division would be affected by considerations of the source of the profit, the nature of the business, and the other circumstances of the case. It is obvious that it must be so, for it would be easy to suggest a number of instances in which the profit of a business has no ascertainable reference to the capital—e.g., solicitors, factors, brokers, or, as was the case before the Lords Justices, bankers. Indeed, in almost every case where the business consists of buying and selling, the difference between prosperity and ruin mainly depends on the skill, industry, and care of the dealers; no doubt also greatly on their credit and reputation, and the possession of ready money to take advantage of favourable opportunities and to enable them to bide their time in unfavourable states of the market, and also greatly on established goodwill and connection of the house."

In the end, as I have said, James L.J. held that it would be too difficult to work out the share of profits to which the legatee was entitled and instead this court awarded her interest on her share of the residue to compensate her for the fact that her capital had been employed in the partnership business.

Does this line of authority help Mr Al-Saraj in this case? I think not. The hypothetical share, which the Murads would have given him if he had disclosed the set off arrangement, is not relevant to this argument because it was never actually agreed or put up as his contribution. Mr Al-Saraj under this approach would have to say that the £500,000 which he actually put up by way of set off should be treated as his investment in the joint venture. But that was the very sum that he lied to the Murads about. It was not a cash sum as they had been led to believe and accordingly I do not consider that he can say that he is entitled to an order which treats the £500,000 as his contribution to the profits made by the venture. . . 13–122

222 (1834) 2 My. & K. 655 at 688.
223 *Warman v Dwyer* (1995) 182 C.L.R. 544.
224 (1872) 9 Ch. App. 309.
225 (1842) 1 Hare 253.

13–123 *Warman v Dwyer*,[226] mentioned by Arden LJ in her judgment, was a decision of the High Court of Australia. Warman was the distribution agent for an Italian company that manufactured gearboxes. In breach of fiduciary duty, Warman's employee, Dwyer, formed a joint venture with the Italian manufacturer in competition with his employer, and made substantial profits. The question arose whether Dwyer and his associated companies should account for all of these profits, and the court held not, ordering them instead to account only for the profits made in the first two years of business. The court made the following comments[227]:

> In the case of a business it may well be inappropriate and inequitable to compel the errant fiduciary to account for the whole of the profit of his conduct of the business or his exploitation of the principal's goodwill over an indefinite period of time. In such a case, it may be appropriate to allow the fiduciary a proportion of the profits, depending upon the particular circumstances. That may well be the case when it appears that a significant proportion of an increase in profits has been generated by the skill, efforts, property and resources of the fiduciary, the capital which he has introduced and the risks he has undertaken, so long as they are not risks to which the principal's property has been exposed. Then it may be said that the relevant proportion of the increased profits is not the product or consequence of the plaintiff's property but the product of the fiduciary's skill, efforts, property and resources.

13–124 In his dissenting judgment in *Murad*,[228] Clarke LJ interpreted *Warman* to mean that a "but-for" causation test can sometimes be used to determine the scope of a fiduciary's liability to account. His Lordship considered that proof of this lay in the attention paid by the court to the trial judge's finding that Warman's business relationship with the Italian manufacturer would only have continued for about another year even if Dwyer had not breached his duty. However, a different view of the case is possible, namely that the court effectively held that the profits made by Dwyer and his companies after the first two years were too remote a consequence of his breach of duty to justify ordering them to account for these later profits. On this view, the significance of the trial judge's finding about the counterfactual was that it gave the court one means of assessing the point in time at which the defendant's gains could fairly be attributed to his own efforts rather than his breach of duty.[229]

13–125 Note, finally, that where a fiduciary is paid by a principal to do work that she is suborned by a third party to undertake in a way that enures to the third party's benefit, the fiduciary forfeits her entitlement to remuneration by her principal and must repay this if she has already received it.[230] However there can be "breaches of duty which do not go to the whole contract, and which would not prevent the agent from recovering [her] remuneration".[231]

## 7. Constructive Trusts

13–126 The law governing the imposition of a constructive trust on the profits of a breach of fiduciary duty derives from *Keech v Sandford*,[232] which is reproduced in Chapter 9.[233] The defendant trustee held a

---

226 (1995) 182 C.L.R. 544.
227 ibid., at 561.
228 [2005] W.T.L.R. 1573 at [154].
229 *3464920 Canada Inc v Strother* (2005) 7 I.T.E.L.R. 748 at [60], per Newbury JA, observing that the time-limited order made in *Warman* reflected "the dilution of the causal link" between the defendant's breach and the gains accruing in his hands. However, this presupposes a sliding scale of causative potency which is hard to conceptualise, and which is difficult to reconcile with the all-or-nothing nature of the standard causation test.
230 *Andrews v Ramsay & Co* [1903] 2 K.B. 635 at 636–638, followed in *Imageview Management Ltd v Jack* [2009] Bus. L.R. 1034.
231 *Keppel v Wheeler* [1927] 1 K.B. 577 at 592 per Atkin LJ; see too *Bank of Ireland v Jaffery* [2012] EWHC 1377 (Ch) at [373].
232 (1726) Sel. Cas. T. King 61.
233 See paras 9–028—9–030.

lease of the profits of a market on trust for an infant beneficiary. He unsuccessfully sought to renew the lease on the infant's behalf and then took the renewal for himself. Lord King LC decreed that he held the renewed lease on trust for the infant.

This rule applies whether the trustee obtains a renewal by virtue of a provision in the lease to that effect or whether she obtains it by virtue of the advantage which her position as sitting tenant gives her.[234] The principle applies not only to trustees and tenants for life,[235] but also to mortgagees,[236] directors[237] and partners.[238] But unlike trustees and tenants for life the latter group of persons are not irrebuttably precluded from taking the renewal of a lease for themselves. In *Re Biss*,[239] a lease formed part of the personalty of an intestate, and after the lessor had refused to renew to the administratrix, one of her sons (helping her run the deceased's business at the premises) obtained a renewal for himself. It was held, however, to be unimpeachable, since the son could show affirmatively that he acted bona fide and did not take advantage of the other persons interested. Romer LJ said,[240] **13–127**

> where the person renewing the lease does not clearly occupy a fiduciary position he is only held to be a constructive trustee of the renewed lease if, in respect of the old lease, he occupied some special position and owed, by virtue of that position, a duty towards the other persons interested.

Constructive trusts have also been awarded in other cases where a fiduciary has misappropriated a profit-making opportunity which came to her in her fiduciary capacity. As we have noted above,[241] Wilberforce J made a declaration in *Boardman v Phipps* that the defendants held shares on constructive trust which they had acquired in breach of their fiduciary duties, and this order was affirmed by the appellate courts. Similar declarations of trust have been made in many other "opportunity cases",[242] and indeed it has been said that "any property acquired, or profit made" by a fiduciary through a breach of fiduciary duty is held on constructive trust for her principal.[243] Moreover, in the words of Mason J[244]: **13–128**

> Neither principle nor authority provide any support for the proposition that relief by way of constructive trust is available only in the case where a profit or benefit obtained by the fiduciary was one which it was an incident of his duty to obtain for the person to whom he owed the fiduciary duty. Once it is established that the fiduciary is liable to account for a profit or benefit which he has obtained there can be no objection to his being held to account as a constructive trustee of that profit or benefit. It can make no difference that it was not his duty to obtain the profit or benefit for the person to whom the duty was owed. What is important is that the advantage has accrued to him in breach of his fiduciary duty or by his misuse of his fiduciary

---

234 *Re Knowles' Will Trusts* [1948] 1 All E.R. 866.

235 *James v Dean* (1808) 15 Ves. Jun. 236; *Lloyd-Jones v Clark-Lloyd* [1919] 1 Ch. 424; Settled Land Act 1925, ss.16 and 107.

236 *Rushworth's Case* (1676) Freem.Ch. 13; *Leigh v Burnett* (1885) 29 Ch. D. 231.

237 *GE Smith Ltd v Smith* [1952] N.Z.L.R. 470; *Crittenden & Cowler Co v Cowler* 72 N.Y. 701 (1901).

238 *Featherstonhaugh v Fenwick* (1810) 17 Ves. 298; cf. *Piddock v Burt* [1894] 1 Ch. 343; *John Taylors (a firm) v Masons (a firm)* [2001] EWCA Civ 2106; *Lindsley v Woodfall* [2004] 2 B.C.L.C. 131.

239 [1903] 2 Ch. 40.

240 ibid., at 61.

241 See para.13–073. The House of Lords' decision is excerpted at paras 9–031—9–062.

242 e.g. *Carter v Palmer* (1842) 8 Cl. & Fin. 657; *Bowes v City of Toronto* (1858) 11 Moo. P.C. 463; *Bagnall v Carlton* (1877) 6 Ch. D. 371; *Cook v Deeks* [1916] 1 A.C. 554; *Furs Ltd v Tomkies* (1936) 54 C.L.R. 583 at 592; *Industrial Development Consultants Ltd v Cooley* [1972] 1 W.L.R. 443; *Bhullar v Bhullar* [2003] 2 B.C.L.C. 241.

243 *Keith Henry & Company Pty Ltd v Stuart Walker & Company Pty Ltd* (1958) 100 C.L.R. 342 at 350, per Dixon CJ, McTiernan and Fullagar JJ. See too *Chan v Zacharia* (1983) 154 C.L.R. 178 at 199. English dicta to like effect are set out in Lord Neuberger's judgment in *FHR European Ventures LLP v Cedar Capital Partners LLC* [2015] A.C. 250 at [19]–[20], reproduced below at paras 13–149—13–150.

244 *Hospital Products Ltd v US Surgical Corp* (1984) 156 C.L.R. 41 at 107–108, followed in *Grimaldi v Chameleon Mining NL (No. 2)* (2012) 200 F.C.R. 296 at [575].

position. The consequence is that he must account for it and in equity the appropriate remedy is by means of a constructive trust.

13–129 Notwithstanding these authorities, the English courts were formerly divided over the question whether proprietary relief is available in cases where a fiduciary has received a secret commission or bribe from a third party. One line of cases, the best known of which is *Lister & Co v Stubbs*,[245] held that the fiduciary merely owed a personal liability to account for and pay over the amount of the bribe to her principal, while another, stemming from the Privy Council's decision in *Attorney General for Hong Kong v Reid*,[246] held that the money was additionally held by the fiduciary on a constructive trust. In *FHR European Ventures LLP v Cedar Capital Partners LLC*, this controversy was definitively resolved when a seven-member Supreme Court held that a constructive trust would be imposed on money paid to a fiduciary as a bribe or secret commission. This brought English law into line with the law of various Commonwealth jurisdictions which have the same rule.[247]

*FHR European Ventures LLP v Cedar Capital Partners LLC*

Supreme Court [2015] A.C. 250

13–130 The facts are given in the judgment of the court, which was delivered by LORD NEUBERGER. The other members of the court were LORD MANCE, LORD SUMPTION, LORD CARNWATH, LORD TOULSON, LORD HODGE and LORD COLLINS.

13–131 This is the judgment of the court on the issue of whether a bribe or secret commission received by an agent is held by the agent on trust for his principal, or whether the principal merely has a claim for equitable compensation in a sum equal to the value of the bribe or commission. The answer to this rather technical sounding question, which has produced inconsistent judicial decisions over the past 200 years, as well as a great deal of more recent academic controversy, is important in practical terms. If the bribe or commission is held on trust, the principal has a proprietary claim to it, whereas if the principal merely has a claim for equitable compensation, the claim is not proprietary. The distinction is significant for two main reasons. First, if the agent becomes insolvent, a proprietary claim would effectively give the principal priority over the agent's unsecured creditors, whereas the principal would rank pari passu, ie equally, with other unsecured creditors if he only has a claim for compensation. Secondly, if the principal has a proprietary claim to the bribe or commission, he can trace and follow it in equity, whereas (unless we develop the law of equitable tracing beyond its current boundaries) a principal with a right only to equitable compensation would have no such equitable right to trace or follow.

**The facts**

13–132 On 22 December 2004, FHR European Ventures LLP purchased the issued share capital of Monte Carlo Grand Hotel SAM (which owned a long leasehold interest in the Monte Carlo Grand Hotel) from Monte Carlo Grand Hotel Ltd ("the vendor") for €211·5m. The purchase was a joint venture between the claimants in these proceedings, for whom FHR was the vehicle. Cedar Capital Partners LLC provided consultancy services to the hotel industry, and it had acted as the claimants' agent in negotiating the purchase. It is common ground that Cedar accordingly owed fiduciary duties to the claimants in that connection. Cedar had also entered into an agreement with the vendor ("the exclusive brokerage agreement") dated 24 September 2004, which provided for the payment to Cedar of a €10m fee following a successful

[245] (1890) 45 Ch.D. 1. See too *Metropolitan Bank v Heiron* (1880) 5 Ex.D. 319; *Powell v Thomas & Evan Jones & Co* [1905] 1 K.B. 11; *Attorney General's Ref. (No. 1 of 1985)* [1986] Q.B. 491 at 504–505; *Sinclair Investments (UK) Ltd v Versailles Trade Finance Ltd* [2012] Ch. 453.

[246] [1994] 1 A.C. 324, followed in *Fyffes Group Ltd v Templeman* [2000] 2 Lloyd's Rep 643; *Daraydan Holdings Ltd v Solland International Ltd* [2005] Ch. 119.

[247] Australia: *Grimaldi v Chameleon Mining NL (No.2)* (2012) 200 F.C.R. 296; Canada: *Insurance Corporation of British Columbia v Lo* (2006) 278 D.L.R. (4th) 148; Singapore: *Sumitomo Bank Ltd v Thahir* [1993] 1 S.L.R. 735; New Zealand: *Attorney General for Hong Kong v Reid* [1994] 1 A.C. 324.

conclusion of the sale and purchase of the issued share capital of Monte Carlo Grand Hotel SAM. The vendor paid Cedar €10m on or about 7 January 2005.

On 23 November 2009 the claimants began these proceedings for recovery of the sum of €10m from Cedar (and others). The trial took place before Simon J., and the main issue was whether, as it contended, Cedar had made proper disclosure to the claimants of the exclusive brokerage agreement. Simon J. gave a judgment[248] in which he found against Cedar on that issue. There was then a further hearing to determine what order should be made in the light of that judgment, following which Simon J. gave a further judgment.[249] In that judgment he concluded that he should (i) make a declaration of liability for breach of fiduciary duty on the part of Cedar for having failed to obtain the claimants' fully informed consent in respect of the €10m, and (ii) order Cedar to pay such sum to the claimants, but (iii) refuse to grant the claimants a proprietary remedy in respect of the moneys. 13–133

The claimants appealed to the Court of Appeal against conclusion (iii), and it allowed the appeal[250] for reasons given in a judgment given by Lewison L.J., with supporting judgments from Pill L.J. and Sir Terence Etherton C. Accordingly, the Court of Appeal made an order which included a declaration that Cedar received the €10m fee on constructive trust for the claimants absolutely. Cedar now appeals to the Supreme Court on that issue. There is and was no challenge by Cedar to the judge's conclusions (i) and (ii), so the only point on this appeal is whether, as the Court of Appeal held, the claimants are entitled to the proprietary remedy in respect of the €10m received by Cedar from the vendor. 13–134

**Prefatory comments**

The following three principles are not in doubt, and they are taken from the classic summary of the law in the judgment of Millett L.J. in *Bristol and West Building Society v Mothew*.[251] First, an agent owes a fiduciary duty to his principal because he is "someone who has undertaken to act for or on behalf of [his principal] in a particular matter in circumstances which give rise to a relationship of trust and confidence". Secondly, as a result, an agent "must not make a profit out of his trust" and "must not place himself in a position in which his duty and his interest may conflict"—and, as Lord Upjohn pointed out in *Phipps v Boardman*,[252] the former proposition is "part of the [latter] wider rule". Thirdly, "a fiduciary who acts for two principals with potentially conflicting interests without the informed consent of both is in breach of the obligation of undivided loyalty; he puts himself in a position where his duty to one principal may conflict with his duty to the other". Because of the importance which equity attaches to fiduciary duties, such "informed consent" is only effective if it is given after "full disclosure", to quote Jessel M.R. in *Dunne v English*.[253] 13–135

Another well established principle, which applies where an agent receives a benefit in breach of his fiduciary duty, is that the agent is obliged to account to the principal for such a benefit, and to pay, in effect, a sum equal to the profit by way of equitable compensation. The law on this topic was clearly stated in *Regal (Hastings) Ltd v Gulliver*, by Lord Russell of Killowen, where he said:[254] 13–136

> "The rule of equity which insists on those, who by use of a fiduciary position make a profit, being liable to account for that profit, in no way depends on fraud, or absence of bona fides; or on such questions or considerations as whether the profit would or should otherwise have gone to the plaintiff, or whether the profiteer was under a duty to obtain the source of the profit for the plaintiff, or whether he took a risk or acted as he did for the benefit of the plaintiff, or whether the plaintiff has in fact been damaged or benefited by his action. The liability arises from the mere fact of a profit having, in the stated circumstances, been made."

The principal's right to seek an account undoubtedly gives him a right to equitable compensation in respect of the bribe or secret commission, which is the quantum of that bribe or commission (subject to any permissible deduction in favour of the agent—e.g. for expenses incurred). That is because where an agent acquires a benefit in breach of his fiduciary duty, the relief accorded by equity is, again to quote 13–137

---

248 [2012] 2 B.C.L.C. 39.
249 [2011] EWHC 2999 (Ch).
250 [2014] Ch. 1.
251 [1998] Ch. 1 at 18.
252 [1967] 2 AC 46 at 123.
253 (1874) L.R. 18 Eq. 524 at 533.
254 (Note) [1967] 2 A.C. 134 at 144–145.

Millett L.J. in the *Mothew* case,[255] "primarily restitutionary or restorative rather than compensatory". The agent's duty to account for the bribe or secret commission represents a personal remedy for the principal against the agent. However, the centrally relevant point for present purposes is that, at least in some cases where an agent acquires a benefit which came to his notice as a result of his fiduciary position, or pursuant to an opportunity which results from his fiduciary position, the equitable rule ("the rule") is that he is to be treated as having acquired the benefit on behalf of his principal, so that it is beneficially owned by the principal. In such cases, the principal has a proprietary remedy in addition to his personal remedy against the agent, and the principal can elect between the two remedies.

13–138 Where the facts of a particular case are within the ambit of the rule, it is strictly applied. The strict application of the rule can be traced back to the well known decision in *Keech v Sandford*,[256] where a trustee held a lease of a market on trust for an infant, and, having failed to negotiate a new lease on behalf of the infant because the landlord was dissatisfied with the proposed security for the rent, the trustee negotiated a new lease for himself. Lord King L.C. concluded, at p 62, that, "though I do not say there is a fraud in this case" and though it "may seem hard", the infant was entitled to an assignment of the new lease and an account of the profits made in the meantime—a conclusion which could only be justified on the basis that the new lease had been beneficially acquired for the infant beneficiary.

13–139 Since then, the rule has been applied in a great many cases. The question on this appeal is not so much concerned with the application of the rule, as with its limits or boundaries. Specifically, what is in dispute is the extent to which the rule applies where the benefit is a bribe or secret commission obtained by an agent in breach of his fiduciary duty to his principal.

13–140 On the one hand, Mr Collings Q.C. contends for the appellant, Cedar, that the rule should not apply to a bribe or secret commission paid to an agent, because it is not a benefit which can properly be said to be the property of the principal. This has the support of Professor Sir Roy Goode, who has suggested that no proprietary interest arises where an agent obtains a benefit in breach of his duty unless the benefit either (i) flows from an asset which was (a) beneficially owned by the principal, or (b) intended for the principal, or (ii) was derived from an activity of the agent which, if he chose to undertake it, he was under an equitable duty to undertake for the principal. Sir Roy suggested that "to treat [a principal] as having a restitutionary proprietary right to money or property not derived from any asset of [the principal] results in an involuntary grant by [the agent] to [the principal] from [the agent's] pre-existing estate".[257] Professor Sarah Worthington has advanced a slightly different test. She suggests (summarising at the risk of oversimplifying) that proprietary claims arise where benefits are (i) derived from the principal's property, or (ii) derived from opportunities in the scope of the agent's endeavours on behalf of the principal, but not (iii) benefits derived from opportunities outside the scope of those endeavours.[258]

13–141 On the other hand, it is suggested by Mr Pymont Q.C. on behalf of the respondent claimants in this appeal, that the rule does apply to bribes or secret commissions received by an agent, because, in any case where an agent receives a benefit, which is, or results from, a breach of the fiduciary duty owed to his principal, the agent holds the benefit on trust for the principal. This view has been supported by Lord Millett writing extra-judicially. In "Bribes and Secret Commissions",[259] he suggested that, on grounds of practicality, policy and principle, a principal should be beneficially entitled to a bribe or secret commission received by his agent.[260] He bases his conclusion on the proposition that equity will not permit the agent to rely on his own breach of fiduciary duty to justify retaining the benefit on the ground that it was a bribe or secret commission, and will assume that he acted in accordance with his duty, so that the benefit must be the principal's. This approach is also supported by Lionel Smith,[261] whose view, in short, is that the basic rule should be that an agent who obtains a benefit in breach of his fiduciary duty to his principal holds that benefit on trust for his principal.

13–142 The decision as to which view is correct must be based on legal principle, decided cases, policy

---

[255] At 18.

[256] (1726) Sel. Cas. Ch. 61.

[257] "Proprietary Restitutionary Claims" in W.R. Cornish et al (eds), *Restitution: Past, Present and Future* (1998) p. 69 and see more recently (2011) 127 L.Q.R. 493.

[258] "Fiduciary Duties and Proprietary Remedies: Addressing the Failure of Equitable Formulae" [2013] C.L.J. 720.

[259] [1993] R.L.R. 7.

[260] And see more recently [2012] C.L.J. 583.

[261] "Constructive Trusts and the No-Profit Rule" [2013] C.L.J. 260.

considerations, and practicalities. We start by summarising the effect of many of the cases which touch on the issue; we then turn to the policy and practical arguments, and finally we express our conclusion.

**The decided cases**

There is a number of 19th century cases not involving bribes or secret commissions, where an agent or other fiduciary makes an unauthorised profit by taking advantage of an opportunity which came to his attention as a result of his agency and judges have reached the conclusion that the rule applied. Examples include *Carter v Palmer*,[262] where a barrister who purchased his client's bills at a discount was held by Lord Cottenham to have acquired them for his client. The Privy Council in *Bowes v City of Toronto*[263] concluded that the mayor of a city who bought discounted debentures issued by the city was in the same position as an agent vis-à-vis the city, and was to be treated as holding the debentures on trust for the city. *Bagnall v Carlton*[264] involved complex facts, but, pared to a minimum, agents for a prospective company who made secret profits out of a contract made by the company were held to be "trustees for the company" of those profits: per James, Baggallay and Cotton L.JJ. 13–143

In the Privy Council case *Cook v Deeks*,[265] a company formed by the directors of a construction company was held to have entered into a contract on behalf of the construction company as the directors only knew of the contractual opportunity by virtue of their directorships. In *Phipps v Boardman*,[266] where agents of certain trustees purchased shares, in circumstances where they only had that opportunity because they were agents, Wilberforce J. held that the shares were held beneficially for the trust. More recently, in *Bhullar v Bhullar*,[267] the Court of Appeal reached the same conclusion on similar facts to those in *Cook* (save that the asset acquired was a property rather than a contract). Jonathan Parker L.J. said this:[268] 13–144

> "[W]here a fiduciary has exploited a commercial opportunity for his own benefit, the relevant question, in my judgment, is not whether the party to whom the duty is owed (the company, in the instant case) had some kind of beneficial interest in the opportunity: in my judgment that would be too formalistic and restrictive an approach. Rather, the question is simply whether the fiduciary's exploitation of the opportunity is such as to attract the application of the rule."

Turning now to cases concerned with bribes and secret commissions, the effect of the reasoning of Lord Lyndhurst L.C. in *Fawcett v Whitehouse*[269] was that an agent, who was negotiating on behalf of a prospective lessee and who accepted a "loan" from the lessor, held the loan on trust for his principal, the lessee. In *Barker v Harrison*,[270] a vendor's agent had secretly negotiated a sub-sale of part of the property from the purchaser at an advantageous price, and Knight Bruce V.-C. held that that asset was held on trust for the vendor. In *Re Western of Canada Oil, Lands and Works Co (Carling, Hespeler, and Walsh's Cases)*,[271] the Court of Appeal (James and Mellish L.JJ., Bramwell B. and Brett J.) held that shares transferred by a person to individuals to induce them to become directors of a company and to agree that the company would buy land from the person, were held by the individuals on trust for the company. In *Re Morvah Consols Tin Mining Co (McKay's Case)*,[272] the Court of Appeal (Mellish and James L.JJ. and Brett J.) decided that where a company bought a mine, shares in the vendor which were promised to the company's secretary were held by him for the company beneficially. The Court of Appeal (Jessel M.R., James L.J. and Baggallay J.A.) in *Re Caerphilly Colliery Co (Pearson's Case)*[273] concluded that a company director, who received shares from the promoters and then acted for the company in its purchase of a colliery from the promoters, held the shares on trust for the company. In *Eden v Ridsdale Railway Lamp and Lighting Co Ltd*,[274] a company was 13–145

262 (1842) 8 Cl. & Fin. 657.
263 (1858) 11 Moo. P.C. 463.
264 (1877) 6 Ch. D. 371.
265 [1916] 1 A.C. 554.
266 [1964] 1 W.L.R. 993 (affirmed [1965] Ch. 992, and [1967] 2 A.C. 46).
267 [2003] 2 B.C.L.C. 241.
268 Ibid. at [28].
269 (1829) 1 Russ. & M. 132.
270 (1846) 2 Coll. 546.
271 (1875) 1 Ch. D. 115.
272 (1875) 2 Ch. D. 1.
273 (1877) 5 Ch. D. 336.
274 (1889) 23 Q.B.D. 368.

held by the Court of Appeal (Lord Esher M.R., Lindley and Lopes L.JJ.) to be entitled as against a director to shares which he had secretly received from a person with whom the company was negotiating. There are a number of other 19th century decisions to this effect, but it is unnecessary to cite them.

**13–146** Inducements and other benefits offered to directors and trustees have been treated similarly. In *Sugden v Crossland*,[275] Stuart V.-C. held that a sum of money paid to a trustee to persuade him to retire in favour of the payee was to be "treated as a part of the trust fund". Similarly, in *Nant-y-glo and Blaina Ironworks Co v Grave*,[276] shares in a company given by a promoter to the defendant to induce him to become a director were held by Bacon V.-C. to belong to the company. In *Williams v Barton*,[277] Russell J. decided that a trustee, who recommended that his co-trustees use stockbrokers who gave him a commission, held the commission on trust for the trust.

**13–147** The common law courts were meanwhile taking the same view. In *Morison v Thompson*,[278] Cockburn C.J., with whom Blackburn and Archibald JJ. agreed, held that a purchaser's agent who had secretly agreed to accept a commission from the vendor of a ship, held the commission for the benefit of his principal, the purchaser, in common law just as he would have done in equity.[279] In *Whaley Bridge Calico Printing Co v Green*,[280] Bowen J. (albeit relying on equity at least in part) held that a contract between the vendor and a director of the purchaser, for a secret commission to be paid out of the purchase money, was to be treated as having been entered into for the benefit of the purchaser without proof of fraud.

**13–148** It is fair to say that in the majority of the cases identified in the previous five paragraphs it does not appear to have been in dispute that, if the recipient of the benefit had received it in breach of his fiduciary duty to the plaintiff, then he held it on trust for the plaintiff. In other words, it appears to have been tacitly accepted that the rule applied, so that the plaintiff was entitled not merely to an equitable account in respect of the benefit, but to the beneficial ownership of the benefit.

**13–149** However, many of those cases contain observations which specifically support the contention that the rule applies to all benefits which are received by an agent in breach of his fiduciary duty. In *Sugden*,[281] Stuart V.-C. said that "it is a well-settled principle that, if a trustee make a profit of his trusteeship, it shall enure to the benefit of his cestui que trusts". And in *McKay's Case*,[282] Mellish L.J. said that it was "quite clear that, according to the principles of a Court of Equity, all the benefit which the agent of the purchaser receives under such circumstances from the vendor must be treated as received for the benefit of the purchaser". In *Carling's Case*,[283] James L.J. said the arrangement amounted to a "a simple bribe or present to the directors, constituting a breach of trust on their part" and that "the company would be entitled to get back from their unfaithful trustees what the unfaithful trustees had acquired by reason of their breach of trust". In *Pearson's Case*[284] Jessel M.R. said that the director as agent could not "retain that present as against the actual purchasers" and "must be deemed to have obtained [the benefit] under circumstances which made him liable, at the option of the cestuis que trust, to account either for the value . . . or . . . for the thing itself . . ." In *Eden*[285] Lord Esher M.R. said that if an agent "puts himself in a position which the law does not allow [him] to assume . . . he commits a wrong against his principal", and "if that which the agent has received is money he must hand it over to his principal, if it is not money, but something else, [the] principal may insist on having it". Lindley and Lopes L.JJ. each said that they were "of the same opinion" as Lord Esher, and Lindley L.J. observed, that it would be "contrary to all principles of law and equity to allow the plaintiff to retain the gift".[286]

**13–150** It is also worth noting that in *Morison*,[287] Cockburn C.J. quoted with approval from two contemporary

---

[275] (1856) 3 Sm. & G. 192.
[276] (1878) 12 Ch. D. 738.
[277] [1927] 2 Ch. 9.
[278] (1874) L.R. 9 Q.B.D. 480.
[279] Ibid. at 484, where Cockburn C.J. referred to the earlier decision of Lord Ellenborough to the same effect in *Diplock v Blackburn* (1811) 3 Camp. 43.
[280] (1879) 5 Q.B.D. 109.
[281] (1856) 3 Sm. & G. 192 at 194.
[282] (1875) 2 Ch. D. 1 at 5.
[283] (1875) 1 Ch. D. 115 at 124.
[284] (1877) 5 Ch. D. 336 at 340–341.
[285] (1889) 23 Q.B.D. 368 at 371.
[286] Ibid. at 372.
[287] (1874) L.R. 9 Q.B. 480 at 485–486.

textbooks. First, he cited *Story on Agency*,[288] where it was said that it could be "laid down as a general principle, that, in all cases when a person is . . . an agent for other persons, all profits and advantages made by him in the business, beyond his ordinary compensation, are to be for the benefit of his employers." Secondly, he referred to *Paley on Principal and Agent*,[289] which stated that "not only interest, but every other sort of profit or advantage, clandestinely derived by an agent from dealing or speculating with his principal's effects, is the property of the latter, and must be accounted for".

The cases summarised above and the observations set out above are all consistent with the notion that the rule should apply to bribes or secret commissions paid to an agent, so that the agent holds them on trust for his principal, rather than simply having an equitable duty to account to his principal. It is true that in many of those cases there was apparently no argument as to whether the benefit obtained by the fiduciary was actually held on trust for the principal. However, in some of the cases there was a dispute on the nature of the relief; in any event, the fact that it was assumed time and again by eminent barristers and judges must carry great weight. 13–151

However, there is one decision of the House of Lords which appears to go the other way, and several decisions of the Court of Appeal which do go the other way, in that they hold that, while a principal has a claim for equitable compensation in respect of a bribe or secret commission received by his agent, he has no proprietary interest in it. 13–152

The House of Lords decision is *Tyrrell v Bank of London*.[290] The facts of the case are somewhat complex and the reasoning of the opinions of Lord Westbury L.C., Lord Cranworth and Lord Chelmsford is not always entirely easy to follow. The decision has been carefully and interestingly analysed by Professor Watts.[291] In very brief terms, a solicitor retained to act for a company in the course of formation secretly arranged to benefit from his prospective client's anticipated acquisition of a building called the "Hall of Commerce" by obtaining from the owner a 50% beneficial interest in a parcel of land consisting of the Hall and some adjoining land. After the client had purchased the Hall from the owner, it discovered that the solicitor had secretly profited from the transaction and sued him. Romilly M.R. held[292] that the solicitor had held on trust for the client both (i) his interest in (and therefore his subsequent share of the proceeds of sale of) the Hall, and (ii) with "very considerable hesitation", his interest in the adjoining land.[293] On appeal, the House of Lords held that, while Romilly M.R. was right about (i), he was wrong about (ii): although the client had an equitable claim for the value of the solicitor's interest in the adjoining land, it had no proprietary interest in that land. 13–153

Lord Westbury L.C. made it clear[294] that the fact that the client had not been formed by the time that the solicitor acquired his interest in the land did not prevent the claim succeeding as the client had been "conceived, and was in the process of formation". He also made it clear[295] that, in respect of the profit which the solicitor made from his share of the Hall (which he described as "the subject matter of the transaction", and, later,[296] "that particular property included in the [client's] contract"), the solicitor "must be converted into a trustee for the [client]". However, he was clear that no such trust could arise in relation to the adjoining land, which was outside "the limit of the agency", and so "there [was] no privity, nor any obligation", although the solicitor "must account for the value of that property".[297] Lord Cranworth agreed, making it clear that the financial consequences for the solicitor were no different from those that followed from Romilly M.R.'s order, although he had "thought that possibly we might arrive at the conclusion that the decree was, not only in substance, but also in form, perfectly correct".[298] Lord Chelmsford agreed, and discussed bribes,[299] holding that the principal had no right to a bribe received by his agent. 13–154

Although there have been suggestions that, with the exception of Lord Chelmsford's obiter dicta 13–155

288 (1839) para. 211.
289 (1833) p. 51.
290 (1862) 10 H.L. Cas. 26.
291 "*Tyrrell v Bank of London*—An Inside Look at an Inside Job" (2013) 129 L.Q.R. 527.
292 (1859) 27 Beav. 273.
293 Especially at 300.
294 (1862) 10 H.L. Cas. 26 at 39–40.
295 Ibid. at 44.
296 Ibid. at 45.
297 Ibid. at 46.
298 Ibid. at 49.
299 Ibid. at 59–60.

about bribes, the decision of the House of Lords in *Tyrrell* was not inconsistent with the respondents' case on this appeal, it appears clear that it was. If, as the House held, the solicitor was liable to account to the client for the profit which he had made on the adjoining land, that can only have been because it was a benefit which he had received in breach of his fiduciary duty; and, once that is established, then, on the respondents' case, the Rule would apply, and that profit would be held on trust for the client (or, more accurately, his share of the adjoining land would be held on trust), as in *Fawcett*, *Sugden*, *Carter*, *Bowes* and *Barker*, all of which had been decided before *Tyrrell*, and of which only *Fawcett* was cited to the House.

**13–156** We turn to the Court of Appeal authorities which are inconsistent with the notion that the rule applies to bribes or secret commissions. In *Metropolitan Bank v Heiron*,[300] the Court of Appeal held that a claim brought by a company against a director was time-barred: the claim was to recover a bribe paid by a third party to induce the director to influence the company to negotiate a favourable settlement with the third party. It was unsuccessfully argued by the bank that its claim was proprietary. Brett L.J. said[301] "[n]either at law nor in equity could this sum . . . be treated as the money of the company", but he apparently considered that, once the company had obtained judgment for the money there could be a trust. Cotton L.J. expressed the same view. James L.J. simply thought that there was an equitable debt and applied the Limitation Acts by analogy. This approach was followed in *Lister & Co v Stubbs*,[302] where an agent of a company had accepted a bribe from one of its clients, and an interlocutory injunction was refused on the ground that the relationship between the company and its agent was that of creditor and debtor not beneficiary and trustee. Cotton L.J. said[303] that "the money which [the agent] has received . . . cannot . . . be treated as being the money of the [company]". Lindley L.J. agreed and said[304] that the notion that there was a trust "startled" him, not least because it would give the company the right to the money in the event of the agent's bankruptcy. Bowen L.J. agreed.

**13–157** *Lister* was cited with approval by Lindley L.J. in *Re North Australian Territory Co (Archer's Case)*,[305] and it was followed in relation to a bribe paid to an agent by Henn Collins M.R. (with whom Stirling and Mathew L.JJ. agreed) in *Powell & Thomas v Evan Jones & Co*,[306] where the principal was held entitled to an account for the bribe, but not to a declaration that the bribe was held on trust. The same view was taken in the Court of Appeal in *Attorney General's Reference (No 1 of 1985)*,[307] where Lord Lane C.J. quoted from the judgments of Cotton and Lindley L.JJ. in what he described as "a powerful Court of Appeal in *Lister*", and followed the reasoning. In *Regal (Hastings) Ltd v Gulliver*,[308] the decision in *Lister* was referred to by Lord Wright,[309] as supporting the notion that "the relationship in such a case is that of debtor and creditor, not trustee and cestui que trust". However, that was an obiter observation, and it gets no support from the other members of the committee.

**13–158** More recently, in 1993, in *Attorney General for Hong Kong v Reid*,[310] the Privy Council concluded that bribes received by a corrupt government legal officer were held on trust for his principal, and so they could be traced into properties which he had acquired in New Zealand. In his judgment on behalf of the Board, Lord Templeman disapproved the reasoning in *Heiron*, and the reasoning and outcome in *Lister*, and he thought his conclusion inconsistent with only one of the opinions, that of Lord Chelmsford, in *Tyrrell*. In *Daraydan Holdings Ltd v Solland International Ltd*,[311] Lawrence Collins J. indicated that he would follow *Reid* rather than *Lister*, as did Toulson J. In *Fyffes Group Ltd v Templeman*.[312] But in *Sinclair Investments (UK) Ltd v Versailles Trade Finance Ltd*,[313] in a judgment given by Lord Neuberger of Abbotsbury MR,

---

300 (1880) 5 Ex. D. 319.
301 Ibid. at 324.
302 (1890) 45 Ch. D. 1.
303 Ibid. at 12.
304 Ibid. at 15.
305 [1892] 1 Ch. 322 at 338.
306 [1905] 1 K.B. 11 at 22.
307 [1986] Q.B. 491 at 504–505.
308 [1967] 2 AC 134.
309 Ibid. at 156.
310 [1994] 1 A.C. 324.
311 [2005] Ch. 119 at [75] ff.
312 [2000] 2 Lloyd's Rep. 643 at 668–672.
313 [2012] Ch. 453.

the Court of Appeal decided that it should follow *Heiron* and *Lister*, and indeed *Tyrrell*, for a number of reasons,[314] although it accepted that this court might follow the approach in *Reid*. In this case, Simon J. considered that he was bound by *Sinclair*, whereas the Court of Appeal concluded that they could and should distinguish it.

**Legal principle and academic articles**

As mentioned above, the issue raised on this appeal has stimulated a great deal of academic debate. The contents of the many articles on this issue provide an impressive demonstration of penetrating and stimulating legal analysis. One can find among those articles a powerful case for various different outcomes, based on analysing judicial decisions and reasoning, equitable and restitutionary principles, and practical and commercial realities. It is neither possible nor appropriate to do those articles justice individually in this judgment, but the court has referred to them for the purpose of extracting the principle on which the rule is said to be based.[315] **13–159**

The respondents' formulation of the rule, namely that it applies to all benefits received by an agent in breach of his fiduciary duty to his principal, is explained on the basis that an agent ought to account in specie to his principal for any benefit he has obtained from his agency in breach of his fiduciary duty, as the benefit should be treated as the property of the principal, as supported by many judicial dicta including those [quoted] above and can be seen to be reflected in Jonathan Parker L.J.'s observations above. More subtly, it is justified on the basis that equity does not permit an agent to rely on his own wrong to justify retaining the benefit: in effect, he must accept that, as he received the benefit as a result of his agency, he acquired it for his principal. Support for that approach may be found in Mellish L.J.'s judgment in *McKay's Case*,[316] and Bowen J.'s judgment in *Whaley Bridge*.[317] **13–160**

The appellant's formulation of the rule, namely that it has a more limited reach, and does not apply to bribes and secret commissions, has various different formulations and justifications. Thus, it is said that, given that it is a proprietary principle, the rule should not apply to benefits which were not derived from assets which are or should be the property of the principal, a view supported by the reasoning of Lord Westbury L.C. in *Tyrrell*.[318] It has also been suggested that the rule should not apply to benefits which could not have been intended for the principal and were, rightly or wrongly, the property of the agent, which seems to have been the basis of Cotton L.J.'s judgment in *Heiron*[319] and *Lister*.[320] In *Sinclair*[321] it was suggested that the effect of the authorities was that the rule should not apply to a benefit which the agent had obtained by taking advantage of an opportunity which arose as a result of the agency, unless the opportunity "was properly that of the [principal]". Professor Worthington's subsequent formulation, referred to above, is very similar but subtly different (and probably more satisfactory). **13–161**

Each of [these] formulations . . . have their supporters and detractors. In the end, it is not possible to identify any plainly right or plainly wrong answer to the issue of the extent of the rule, as a matter of pure legal authority. There can clearly be different views as to what requirements have to be satisfied before a proprietary interest is created. More broadly, it is fair to say that the concept of equitable proprietary rights is in some respects somewhat paradoxical. Equity, unlike the common law, classically acts in personam;[322] yet equity is far more ready to accord proprietary claims than common law. Further, two general rules which law students learn early on are that common law legal rights prevail over equitable rights, and that **13–162**

---

314 Set out at [77] ff.

315 Those articles include D. Hayton, "The Extent of Equitable Remedies: Privy Council versus the Court of Appeal" [2012] Co. Law 161; W. Swadling, "Constructive Trusts and Breach of Fiduciary Duty" (2012) 18 Trusts and Trustees 985; G. Virgo, "Profits Obtained in Breach of Fiduciary Duty: Personal or Proprietary Claim?" [2011] C.L.J. 502; J. Edelman "Two Fundamental Questions for the Law of Trusts" (2013) 129 L.Q.R. 66; and others listed by Sir Terence Etherton, "The Legitimacy of Proprietary Relief" (2014) 2 Birkbeck Law Review 59, p. 60. At p. 62 Sir Terence refers to "this relentless and seemingly endless debate", which, in the Court of Appeal in this case, Pill L.J. described as revealing "passions of a force uncommon in the legal world": [2014] Ch. 1 at [61].

316 (1875) 2 Ch. D. 1 at 6.

317 (1879) 5 Q.B.D. 109 at 113.

318 (1862) 10 H.L. Cas. 26.

319 (1880) 5 Ex. D. 319 at 325.

320 (1890) 45 Ch. D. 1 at 12.

321 [2012] Ch. 453 at [88].

322 See e.g. *Maitland on Equity* 2nd ed (1936), p. 322.

where there are competing equitable rights the first in time prevails; yet, given that equity is far more ready to recognise proprietary rights than common law, the effect of having an equitable right is often to give priority over common law claims—sometimes even those which may have preceded the equitable right. Given that equity developed at least in part to mitigate the rigours of the common law, this is perhaps scarcely surprising. However, it underlines the point that it would be unrealistic to expect complete consistency from the cases over the past 300 years. It is therefore appropriate to turn to the arguments based on principle and practicality, and then to address the issue, in the light of those arguments as well as the judicial decisions discussed above.

**Arguments based on principle and practicality**

13–163 The position adopted by the respondents, namely that the rule applies to all unauthorised benefits which an agent receives, is consistent with the fundamental principles of the law of agency. The agent owes a duty of undivided loyalty to the principal, unless the latter has given his informed consent to some less demanding standard of duty. The principal is thus entitled to the entire benefit of the agent's acts in the course of his agency. This principle is wholly unaffected by the fact that the agent may have exceeded his authority. The principal is entitled to the benefit of the agent's unauthorised acts in the course of his agency, in just the same way as, at law, an employer is vicariously liable to bear the burden of an employee's unauthorised breaches of duty in the course of his employment. The agent's duty is accordingly to deliver up to his principal the benefit which he has obtained, and not simply to pay compensation for having obtained it in excess of his authority. The only way that legal effect can be given to an obligation to deliver up specific property to the principal is by treating the principal as specifically entitled to it.

13–164 On the other hand, there is some force in the notion advanced by the appellant that the rule should not apply to a bribe or secret commission paid to an agent, as such a benefit is different in quality from a secret profit he makes on a transaction on which he is acting for his principal, or a profit he makes from an otherwise proper transaction which he enters into as a result of some knowledge or opportunity he has as a result of his agency. Both types of secret profit can be said to be benefits which the agent should have obtained for the principal, whereas the same cannot be said about a bribe or secret commission which the agent receives from a third party.

13–165 The respondents' formulation of the rule has the merit of simplicity: any benefit acquired by an agent as a result of his agency and in breach of his fiduciary duty is held on trust for the principal. On the other hand, the appellant's position is more likely to result in uncertainty. Thus, there is more than one way in which one can identify the possible exceptions to the normal rule, which results in a bribe or commission being excluded from the rule: see the differences between Professor Goode and Professor Worthington described above, and the other variations there described. Clarity and simplicity are highly desirable qualities in the law. Subtle distinctions are sometimes inevitable, but in the present case, as mentioned above, there is no plainly right answer, and, accordingly, in the absence of any other good reason, it would seem right to opt for the simple answer.

13–166 A further advantage of the respondents' position is that it aligns the circumstances in which an agent is obliged to account for any benefit received in breach of his fiduciary duty and those in which his principal can claim the beneficial ownership of the benefit. Jessel M.R. in *Pearson's Case*[323] referred in a passage cited above to the agent in such a case having "to account either for the value . . . or . . . for the thing itself . . ." The expression equitable accounting can encompass both proprietary and non-proprietary claims. However, if equity considers that in all cases where an agent acquires a benefit in breach of his fiduciary duty to his principal, he must account for that benefit to his principal, it could be said to be somewhat inconsistent for equity also to hold that only in some such cases could the principal claim the benefit as his own property. The observation of Lord Russell in *Regal (Hastings)*, and those of Jonathan Parker L.J. in *Bhullar* quoted above would seem to apply equally to the question of whether a principal should have a proprietary interest in a bribe or secret commission as to the question of whether he should be entitled to an account in respect thereof.

13–167 The notion that the rule should not apply to a bribe or secret commission received by an agent because it could not have been received by, or on behalf of, the principal seems unattractive. The whole reason that the agent should not have accepted the bribe or commission is that it puts him in conflict with his duty to his principal. Further, in terms of elementary economics, there must be a strong possibility that the bribe

[323] (1877) 5 Ch. D. 336 at 341.

has disadvantaged the principal. Take the facts of this case: if the vendor was prepared to sell for €211·5m, on the basis that it was paying a secret commission of €10m, it must be quite likely that, in the absence of such commission, the vendor would have been prepared to sell for less than €211·5m, possibly €201·5m. While Simon J. was not prepared to make such an assumption without further evidence, it accords with common sense that it should often, even normally, be correct; indeed, in some cases, it has been assumed by judges that the price payable for the transaction in which the agent was acting was influenced pro rata to account for the bribe.[324]

The artificiality and difficulties to which the appellant's case can give rise may be well illustrated by reference to the facts in *Eden* and in *Whaley Bridge*. In *Eden*, the promoter gave 200 shares to a director of the company when there were outstanding issues between the promoter and the company. The Court of Appeal held that the director held the shares on trust for the company. As Finn J. said in *Grimaldi v Chameleon Mining NL (No 2)*,[325] the effect of that decision, if *Heiron* and *Lister* were rightly decided, would appear to be that where a bribe is paid to an agent, the principal has a proprietary interest in the bribe if it consists of shares but not if it consists of money, which would be a serious anomaly. **13–168**

In *Whaley Bridge*, a director of a company who negotiated a purchase by the company for £20,000 of a property was promised but did not receive £3,000 out of the £20,000 from the vendor. The outcome according to Bowen J. was that the vendor was liable to the company for the £3,000, because the company was entitled to treat the contract between the vendor and the director as made by the director on behalf of the company. Bowen J. held that it "could not be successfully denied" that if the £3,000 had been paid to the director he would have held it on trust for the company. Mr Collings suggested that the decision was correct because, unlike in this case, the director and vendor had agreed that the £3,000 would come out of the £20,000 paid by the company. Not only is there no trace of such reasoning in Bowen J.'s judgment, but it would be artificial, impractical and absurd if the issue whether a principal had a proprietary interest in a bribe to his agent depended on the mechanism agreed between the briber and the agent for payment of the bribe. **13–169**

The notion that an agent should not hold a bribe or commission on trust because he could not have acquired it on behalf of his principal is somewhat inconsistent with the long-standing decision in *Keech*, the decision in *Phipps* approved by the House of Lords, and the Privy Council decision in *Bowes*. In each of those three cases, a person acquired property as a result of his fiduciary or quasi-fiduciary position, in circumstances in which the principal could not have acquired it: yet the court held that the property concerned was held on trust for the beneficiary. In *Keech*, the beneficiary could not acquire the new lease because the landlord was not prepared to let to him, and because he was an infant; in *Boardman*, the trust could not acquire the shares because they were not authorised investments; in *Bowes*, the city corporation would scarcely have been interested in buying the loan notes which it had just issued to raise money. **13–170**

The respondents are also able to point to a paradox if the appellant is right and a principal has no proprietary right to his agent's bribe or secret commission. If the principal has a proprietary right, then he is better off, and the agent is worse off, than if the principal merely has a claim for equitable compensation. It would be curious, as Mr Collings frankly conceded, if a principal whose agent wrongly receives a bribe or secret commission is worse off than a principal whose agent obtains a benefit in far less opprobrious circumstances, eg the benefit obtained by the trustees' agents in *Boardman*. Yet that is the effect if the rule does not apply to bribes or secret commissions. **13–171**

Wider policy considerations also support the respondents' case that bribes and secret commissions received by an agent should be treated as the property of his principal, rather than merely giving rise to a claim for equitable compensation. As Lord Templeman said giving the decision of the Privy Council in *Attorney General for Hong Kong v Reid*,[326] "bribery is an evil practice which threatens the foundations of any civilised society". Secret commissions are also objectionable as they inevitably tend to undermine trust in the commercial world. That has always been true, but concern about bribery and corruption generally has never been greater than it is now: see for instance, internationally, the OECD Convention on Combating Bribery of Foreign Public Officials in International Business Transactions 1999 and the United Nations Convention against Corruption 2003, and, nationally, the Bribery Acts 2010 and 2012. Accordingly, one **13–172**

324 See e.g. *Fawcett v Whitehouse* (1829) 1 Russ. & M. 132 at 136.
325 (2012) 287 A.L.R. 22 at [570].
326 [1994] 1 A.C. 324 at 330.

would expect the law to be particularly stringent in relation to a claim against an agent who has received a bribe or secret commission.

13–173 On the other hand, a point frequently emphasised by those who seek to justify restricting the ambit of the rule is that the wide application for which the respondents contend will tend to prejudice the agent's unsecured creditors, as it will serve to reduce the estate of the agent if he becomes insolvent. This was seen as a good reason in *Sinclair*[327] for not following *Reid*. While the point has considerable force in some contexts, it appears to us to have limited force in the context of a bribe or secret commission. In the first place, the proceeds of a bribe or secret commission consists of property which should not be in the agent's estate at all, as Lawrence Collins J. pointed out in *Daraydan*[328] (although it is fair to add that insolvent estates not infrequently include assets which would not be there if the insolvent had honoured his obligations). Secondly, as discussed above, at any rate in many cases, the bribe or commission will very often have reduced the benefit from the relevant transaction which the principal will have obtained, and therefore can fairly be said to be his property.

13–174 None the less, the appellant's argument based on potential prejudice to the agent's unsecured creditors has some force, but it is, as we see it, balanced by the fact that it appears to be just that a principal whose agent has obtained a bribe or secret commission should be able to trace the proceeds of the bribe or commission into other assets and to follow them into the hands of knowing recipients (as in *Reid*). Yet, as Mr Collings rightly accepts, tracing or following in equity would not be possible, at least as the law is currently understood, unless the person seeking to trace or follow can claim a proprietary interest. Common law tracing is, of course, possible without a proprietary interest, but it is much more limited than equitable tracing. Lindley L.J. in *Lister*[329] appears to have found it offensive that a principal should be entitled to trace a bribe, but he did not explain why, and we prefer the reaction of Lord Templeman in *Reid*, namely that a principal ought to have the right to trace and to follow a bribe or secret commission.

13–175 Finally, on this aspect, it appears that other common law jurisdictions have adopted the view that the rule applies to all benefits which are obtained by a fiduciary in breach of his duties. In the High Court of Australia, Deane J. said in *Chan v Zacharia* that any benefit obtained:[330]

> "in circumstances where a conflict . . . existed . . . or . . . by reason of his fiduciary position or of opportunity or knowledge resulting from it . . . is held by the fiduciary as constructive trustee."

More recently, the Full Federal Court of Australia has decided not to follow *Sinclair*: see *Grimaldi*, where the decision in *Reid* was preferred.[331] Although the Australian courts recognise the remedial constructive trust, that was only one of the reasons for not following *Sinclair*. As Finn J. who gave the judgment of the court said[332] (after describing *Heiron* and *Lister* as imposing "an anomalous limitation . . . on the reach of *Keech v Sandford*"[333]), "Australian law" in this connection "matches that of New Zealand . . ., Singapore, United States jurisdictions . . . and Canada". As overseas countries secede from the jurisdiction of the Privy Council, it is inevitable that inconsistencies in the common law will develop between different jurisdictions. However, it seems to us highly desirable for all those jurisdictions to learn from each other, and at least to lean in favour of harmonising the development of the common law round the world.

**Conclusions**

13–176 The considerations of practicality and principle discussed above appear to support the respondents' case, namely that a bribe or secret commission accepted by an agent is held on trust for his principal. The position is perhaps rather less clear when one examines the decided cases, whose effect we have summarised above. However, to put it at its lowest, the authorities do not preclude us adopting the respondents' case in that they do not represent a clear and consistent line of authority to the contrary effect. Indeed, we consider that, taken as a whole, the authorities favour the respondents' case.

13–177 First, if one concentrates on the issue of bribes or secret commissions paid to an agent or other fiduciary,

327 [2012] Ch. 453 at [83].
328 [2005] Ch. 119 at [78].
329 (1890) 45 Ch.D. 1 at 15.
330 (1984) 154 C.L.R. 178 at 199.
331 (2012) 287 A.L.R. 22 at [569]–[584].
332 Ibid. at [582].
333 Ibid. at [569].

the cases, with the exception of *Tyrrell*, were consistently in favour of such payments being held on trust for the principal or other beneficiary until the decision in *Heiron* which was then followed in *Lister*. Those two decisions are problematical for a number of reasons. First, relevant authority was not cited. None of the earlier cases referred to above were put before the court in *Heiron* (where the argument seems to have been on a very different basis) or in *Lister*. Secondly, all the judges in those two cases had given earlier judgments which were inconsistent with their reasoning in the later ones. Brett L.J. (who sat in *Heiron*) had been party to the decision in *McKay's* and *Carling's Cases*; Cotton L.J. (who sat in *Heiron* and *Lister*) had been party to *Bagnall* (which was arguably indistinguishable), James L.J. (who sat in *Heiron*) was party to *Pearson's* and *McKay's Cases*, as well as *Bagnall*; Lindley L.J. (who sat in *Lister*) had been party to *Eden*; and Bowen L.J. (who sat in *Lister*) had decided *Whaley Bridge*. Thirdly, the notion, adopted by Cotton and Brett L.JJ. that a trust might arise once the court had given judgment for the equitable claim seems to be based on some sort of remedial constructive trust which is a concept not referred to in earlier cases, and which has authoritatively been said not to be part of English law.[334] Fourthly, the decisions in *Heiron* and *Lister* are difficult to reconcile with many cases not concerned with bribes or secret commissions paid to agents, such as those set out above. If the reasoning in *Heiron* and *Lister* is correct, then either those other cases were wrongly decided or the law is close to incoherent in this area.

As for the domestic cases subsequent to *Lister*, they are all explicable on the basis that it was either conceded or decided that the reasoning in the Court of Appeal in *Lister* was binding. Further, even after *Lister*, cases were being decided in which it seems to have been accepted or decided by Chancery judges that where an agent or other fiduciary had a duty to account for a benefit obtained in breach of his fiduciary duty, the principal was entitled to a proprietary interest in the benefit—examples include Wilberforce J. in *Phipps*, Lord Templeman in *Reid*, and Lawrence Collins J. in *Daraydan Holdings Ltd*. **13–178**

Were it not for the decision in *Tyrrell*, we consider that it would be plainly appropriate for this court to conclude that the courts took a wrong turn in *Heiron* and *Lister*, and to restate the law as being as the respondents contend. Although the fact that the House of Lords decided *Tyrrell* in the way they did gives us pause for thought, we consider that it would be right to uphold the respondents' argument and disapprove the decision in *Tyrrell*. In the first place, *Tyrrell* is inconsistent with a wealth of cases decided before and after it was decided. Secondly, although *Fawcett* was cited in argument, it was not considered in any of the three opinions in *Tyrrell*; indeed, no previous decision was referred to in the opinions, and, although the opinions were expressed with a confidence familiar to those who read 19th century judgments, they contained no reasoning, merely assertion. Thirdly, the decision in *Tyrrell* may be explicable by reference to the fact that the solicitor was not actually acting for the client at the time when he acquired his interest in the adjoining land—hence the reference in Lord Westbury L.C.'s opinion to "the limit of the agency" and the absence of "privity [or] obligation". In other words, it may be that their Lordships thought that the principal should not have a proprietary interest in circumstances where the benefit received by the agent was obtained before the agency began and did not relate to the property the subject of the agency. **13–179**

Quite apart from these three points, we consider that, the many decisions and the practical and policy considerations which favour the wider application of the rule and are discussed above justify our disapproving *Tyrrell*. In our judgment, therefore, the decision in *Tyrrell* should not stand in the way of the conclusion that the law took a wrong turn in *Heiron* and *Lister*, and that those decisions, and any subsequent decisions (*Powell & Thomas, Attorney General's Reference (No. 1 of 1985)* and *Sinclair*), at least in so far as they relied on or followed *Heiron* and *Lister*, should be treated as overruled. **13–180**

In this case, the Court of Appeal rightly regarded themselves as bound by *Sinclair*, but they managed to distinguish it. Accordingly, the appeal is dismissed. **13–181**

In *FHR*, the Supreme Court clearly held that a constructive trust is imposed on bribe money and secret commissions paid to a fiduciary to act against her principal's interests. To the extent that previous decisions held otherwise, they were overruled. But what did their Lordships make of the respondents' argument that *all* benefits received by a fiduciary in breach of her fiduciary duty are held on constructive trust? This rule would align the circumstances in which a constructive trust is imposed with the circumstances in which a fiduciary owes a personal liability to account for and pay over the value of gains made in breach of fiduciary duty. However, it was not necessary for the court to adopt **13–182**

334 *Westdeutsche Landesbank Girozentrale v Islington L.B.C.* [1996] A.C. 669 at 714–6 per Lord Browne-Wilkinson.

this rule to decide the appeal and it is not clear from Lord Neuberger's judgment that they did in fact ground their decision on it.

13–183 As Matthew Conaglen has noted, this leaves us with some unanswered questions[335]:

> For example, will benefits obtained indirectly from a breach of fiduciary duty, as in *Sinclair v Versailles*, be caught by the principle in *FHR*? In *Sinclair*, the fiduciary profited by selling shares which he did not hold, or deal with, in a fiduciary capacity, but where the fiduciary's misapplication of other funds (in a Ponzi scheme) allowed him to inflate the value of his shareholding. If the fiduciary must account for such profit, as the Court of Appeal indicated in *Sinclair*, *FHR* suggests that the principal will have a proprietary right to that profit (assuming it, or its traceable product, can be located). . .
>
> 13–184 Relatedly, if the fiduciary takes a loan from his principal in a way that involves a breach of fiduciary duty, will the principal have a proprietary claim in respect of any profits which the fiduciary generates from employment of the loan monies? Traditionally, a breach of fiduciary duty renders a transaction voidable, rather than void, which means that the principal can rescind the loan transaction, but has no proprietary interest (beyond the mere equity to rescind) in the loan monies (even assuming they can be identified or traced) until the transaction is rescinded.[336] It is unclear to what degree the decision in FHR might alter this position. Presumably, the results will be similar if the right to rescind is recognised as binding on unsecured creditors in the event of the fiduciary's insolvency.[337]

13–185 The argument has sometimes been made that because a fiduciary is disabled from validly taking gains for herself when she receives them in circumstances where her personal interests and her principal's interests are in conflict, it follows inexorably that she must hold these gains on trust for the principal.[338] It may be that this was in Lord Templeman's mind when he held in *Reid* that[339]:

> As soon as the bribe was received it should have been paid or transferred instanter to the person who suffered from the breach of duty. Equity considers as done that which ought to have been done. As soon as the bribe was received, whether in cash or in kind, the false fiduciary held the bribe on a constructive trust for the person injured.

There are also traces of such thinking in Lord Neuberger's judgment in *FHR*.

13–186 Obviously this argument is predicated on the "disability" view of the rules governing fiduciary behaviour, and as we have said, that model is now coming under pressure from the "duty" model on which claims for equitable compensation are premised.[340] Laying that point to one side, however, and assuming the correctness of the "disability" model, the argument is still problematic for the different reason that it is conclusory, i.e. it affirms what it seeks to prove.[341]

13–187 Nor is it possible to prove the point by generalising out of the case where a trustee misappropriates trust property for herself and uses it to make secondary gains which she holds on trust for the beneficiaries. There the trustee promises on taking office that she will hold the trust property and its traceable proceeds for the beneficiaries, and the law prevents her from going back on this promise and allows the beneficiaries to adopt the transaction and take the gains.[342] Other cases where fiduciaries make gains in breach of their fiduciary duty cannot convincingly be rationalised in this way. Most

---

335 M. Conaglen, "Proprietary Remedies for Breach of Fiduciary Duty" (2014) 73 C.L.J. 490, 492.

336 e.g. *Daly v Sydney Stock Exchange Ltd* (1986) 160 C.L.R. 371 at 387–88.

337 Although that issue is itself difficult: P. Watts, "Constructive Trusts and Insolvency" (2009) 3 J.Eq. 250.

338 D.J. Hayton, "Proprietary Liability for Secret Profits" (2011) 127 L.Q.R. 487; Lord Millett, "Bribes and Secret Commissions Again" (2012) 71 C.L.J. 583, 585 and 591–92.

339 [1994] 1 A.C. 324 at 331.

340 See paras 13–003—13–004.

341 J.E. Penner, "The Difficult Doctrinal Basis for the Fiduciary's Proprietary Liability to Account for Bribes" (2012) 18 T. & T. 1000.

342 See para.12–114.

obviously a principal and a fiduciary do not agree when the fiduciary takes office that she will hold all bribes received to act against the principal's interests on trust for the principal. Hence, in Lord Neuberger's words, "a bribe paid to a fiduciary could not possibly be said to be an asset which the fiduciary was under a duty to take for the beneficiary".[343] But such reasoning can also appear strained in opportunity cases, as McLachlin CJ noted in *3464920 Canada Inc v Strother*[344]:

> Where a fiduciary uses the plaintiff's asset to make a profit for himself, the logic of the remedy of account is clear; presumptively the profits the trustee earned would have been earned for the plaintiff, but for the breach. The plaintiff is simply claiming what is rightfully his. The link between the breach and the remedy of account is arguably less clear where the breach involves using information or an opportunity which the plaintiff would not have enjoyed in any event.

## 8. Assessment

The law governing the award of remedies for breach of fiduciary duty is on the move. Personal claims for equitable compensation have now been widely recognised, and the courts have struggled to understand the differences and similarities between these and other types of personal equitable claim, including compensatory claims against trustees to reconstitute trust funds where these have been depleted by unauthorised disposals of trust property, compensatory claims against third parties implicated in a breach of trust, compensatory claims against trustees and other fiduciaries for breach of their duty of care, and claims against fiduciaries to disgorge their profits. In many cases the courts have failed to distinguish clearly between all of these different claims and have sought to analyse them as though they were a single claim governed by a single set of principles. On occasion this has unfortunately led to poor decision-making founded on incoherent reasoning. **13–188**

A second theme of this chapter has been the "feedback" effect of developments in the law of remedies for breach of fiduciary duty for the courts' understanding of this duty. In particular, the conceptual structure of claims for equitable compensation is predicated on an idea of fiduciary "duty" that equates it with a duty to perform a contractual obligation or duty of care in negligence, in the sense that the fiduciary is placed under a primary obligation, failure to perform which triggers a secondary obligation to compensate the principal for loss. It is possible to conceive the gain-based liability of fiduciaries in the same way, but this is not the way in which the Chancery courts have traditionally thought of a fiduciary's liability to account for profits, and gain-based claims against fiduciaries continue to be decided by resort to concepts and language that are inconsistent with the cases on compensatory liability. This has created a tension that will have to be resolved, and we suspect that in the long run the pull of common law concepts will prove too strong for the courts to resist when deciding gain-based as well as loss-based claims against fiduciaries. **13–189**

That is not to say that one common law claim or another is necessarily the most appropriate analogue in the event that the courts choose to answer questions relating to the assessment of compensatory or disgorgement claims against fiduciaries by looking across to the assessment of common law claims. Before they engage in this kind of analogising exercise, it is important for the courts to be clear why they are picking one comparator rather than another. Can a claim for breach of fiduciary duty most aptly be compared with a claim for breach of contract, or negligence, or deceit? The courts cannot answer this question without first identifying the goals which they seek to achieve, first, by imposing fiduciary duties, secondly by making particular remedies available when these duties are **13–190**

343 *Sinclair Investments (UK) Ltd v Versailles Trade Finance Ltd* [2012] Ch. 453 at [80].
344 [2007] 2 S.C.R. 177 at [155].

breached, and thirdly, by selecting the rules which govern the assessment of these remedies where that is appropriate.

13–191 As we have discussed in this chapter and in Chapter 9, the courts' approach to these questions has traditionally been a strict one. They have given two reasons for this: first, that fiduciaries must be given "an incentive . . . to resist the temptation to misconduct themselves"[345]; and secondly, that principals would often face insuperable evidential difficulties, were they required to prove various matters such as bad faith on the fiduciary's part or that she has done everything she could have done on the principal's behalf.[346]

13–192 It can be questioned whether deterrence is a convincing rationale for the strict treatment meted out to fiduciaries. In Lionel Smith's view,[347] deterrence reasoning comprises an undesirable incursion of public law into the private law sphere: it disrupts the internal rationality of private law because it looks outside the relationship between the claimant and defendant, and the conduct giving rise to the litigation. More pragmatically, he has also observed that "a rule that only takes away the defendant's gain is not much of a deterrent" by comparison with a penalty[348]—which the English courts have always said they will not impose on defaulting fiduciaries.[349] Taking a different tack, John Langbein has pointed to the harmful *over-deterrent* effect of a rule which can strip fiduciaries of unauthorised gains made through transactions which are prudently entered in their principals' best interests.[350] The rule has bad effects for principals because it deters fiduciaries from seeking out and developing opportunities in a way that would benefit the principals as well as the fiduciaries. By stifling entrepreneurship it is also bad for society.[351]

13–193 Langbein has also questioned the continued validity of the second, evidence-based rationale, observing that the strict rules governing fiduciary liability were developed 200 years ago when shortcomings in the fact-finding processes of the Chancery courts set a premium on rules that avoided fact-finding. The fusion of the Chancery and common law courts, and successive reforms of civil procedure, have left the courts far better equipped in this respect, and at the same time[352]

> improvements in the standards, practices and technology of trust recordkeeping, as well as enhanced duties of disclosure . . . have largely defused the old concern that a trustee operating under a potential conflict could easily conceal wrongdoing.

---

345 *Murad v Al-Saraj* [2005] W.T.L.R. 1573 at [74] per Arden LJ. The reports contain many similar dicta, e.g. *Docker v Somes* (1834) 2 My. & K. 655 at 665; *Bray v Ford* [1896] A.C. 44 at 51; *Guinness Plc v Saunders* [1990] 2 A.C. 663 at [701]; *Lindsley v Woodfull* [2004] 2 B.C.L.C. 131 at [30].

346 This was a frequent refrain of Lord Eldon's: e.g. *Ex p. Lacey* (1802) 6 Ves. Jun. 625 at 627; *Ex p. James* (1803) 8 Ves. Jun. 337 at 345. Lord Wright expressed similar concerns in *Regal (Hastings) Ltd v Gulliver* [1967] 2 A.C. 134 at 154.

347 L. Smith, "The Motive, Not the Deed", in J. Getzler (ed.), *Rationalizing Property, Equity and Trusts* (Oxford University Press, 2003), pp.60–61.

348 Smith, "The Motive, Not the Deed", in *Rationalizing Property, Equity and Trusts* (2003), p.60. But cf. R. Cooter and B.J. Freedman, "The Fiduciary Relationship: Its Economic Character and Legal Consequences" (1991) 66 N.Y.U. Law Review 1045, 1048–1056, arguing that the rules requiring disgorgement of fiduciary gains have a greater deterrent effect than Smith admits because they require disgorgement even in cases where the fiduciary has not acted disloyally.

349 e.g. *Re Brogden* (1886) 38 Ch. D. 546 at 557. Saying that a rule has a weak deterrent effect is different from saying that it has *no* deterrent effect: M. Conaglen, "The Nature and Function of Fiduciary Loyalty" (2005) 121 L.Q.R. 452, 464.

350 J.H. Langbein, "Questioning the Trust Law Duty of Loyalty: Sole Interest or Best Interest?" (2005) 114 Yale L.J. 929. See too J.H. Langbein, "Mandatory Rules in the Law of Trusts" (2004) 98 Northwestern University Law Review 1105. But cf. M.B. Leslie, "In Defense of the No Further Inquiry Rule: A Response to Professor John Langbein" (2005) 47 William and Mary Law Review 541; and note T. Frankel, *Fiduciary Law* (Oxford University Press, 2011), pp.149–152.

351 J. Lowry and R. Edmunds, "The No Conflict–No Profit Rules and the Corporate Fiduciary: Challenging the Orthodoxy of Absolutism" [2000] J.B.L. 122, arguing that the answer is to assimilate the American corporate opportunities doctrine into English law. This is doubted in D. Kershaw, "Lost in Translation: Corporate Opportunities in Comparative Perspective" (2005) 25 O.J.L.S. 603.

352 Langbein (2005), above, p.932.

Obviously the courts are not blind to such concerns, and they have counseled against the inflexible and over-enthusiastic application of the deterrent principle which may "convert equity into an instrument of hardship and injustice in individual cases".[353] They have sometimes sought to moderate the law's harshness by making allowances to honest fiduciaries who have contributed time, skill and effort towards making the gains for which they are liable to account. In *Murad v Al-Saraj* the Court of Appeal suggested in obiter dicta that the time may have come for the English courts to "revisit the operation of the inflexible rule of equity in harsh circumstances",[354] and to take a more nuanced approach where the fiduciary has acted in good faith, but this suggestion has not yet been taken up. **13–194**

It seems inevitable that different courts will have different ideas of where to draw the line between inappropriately punitive and appropriately stern treatment of disloyal fiduciaries. They may also reasonably disagree over questions of systemic design, such as whether there should be a single set of assessment rules that applies to every defaulting fiduciary, or whether variations should be built in to the rules, enabling the different treatment of fiduciaries according to whether they have acted in good or bad faith. When these issues arise in future cases, we must hope that the courts decide them in a principled and transparent way, clearly stating their reasons. We must also hope that they do not water down the rules affecting the assessment of remedy in cases where they regret having imposed a fiduciary duty on a particular defendant. In such cases they would do better not to impose the duty at all, and to maintain a rigorous set of quantification rules for application to defendants who deserve them.[355] **13–195**

A final point arises in connection with the imposition of constructive trusts on the gains made by defaulting fiduciaries. One effect of imposing such a trust may be to strip the fiduciary of secondary gains that otherwise she would be able to keep, if (which is uncertain) English law is not currently able to grant principals a personal remedy which produces this effect. A court that wished to pursue a vigorous deterrent policy against breaching fiduciaries might therefore feel that constructive trusts should be awarded in all cases. It should not be overlooked, however, that this will also have the effect of giving the principal priority over the fiduciary's other creditors in the event of her insolvency, and whether that is a desirable outcome is a question that turns on a different set of considerations from those which are focused on the relationship between the fiduciary and her principal. **13–196**

**Questions**

1. Patrick bought some land for £500,000. He employed a local solicitor, Larry, to do the conveyancing work. Larry's knowledge of local land prices led him to believe, correctly, that the market value of the property was only £400,000. However he said nothing about this to Patrick, as he believed that Patrick must have been negligently advised by Queenie, the estate agent acting for Patrick in the transaction. Larry did not wish to draw this to Patrick's attention because Queenie is his sister-in-law. In fact, Queenie knew that the land was only worth £400,000, but advised Patrick to pay £500,000 because the vendor had agreed to pay her a commission of two per cent on the sale price. Patrick was unaware of this and believed that the only remuneration Queenie would receive for her work was the two per cent commission on the sale price that he himself had agreed to pay her.

---

353 *Chan v Zacharia* (1983) 154 C.L.R. 178 at 205.

354 [2005] W.T.L.R. 1573 at [82], per Arden LJ. For concurring dicta, see [121] per Jonathan Parker LJ and [156]–[158] per Clarke LJ. The same point was previously made in *Holder v Holder* [1968] Ch. 353 at 398.

355 As observed in *Maguire v Makaronis* (1997) 188 C.L.R. 449 474. See too I.L. Rotman, *Fiduciary Law* (Carswell, 2005), p.696.

The sale went ahead, and as agreed, Patrick paid Queenie £10,000 for her work. Patrick then employed a firm of builders to put up a house on the property. This work was done negligently, but Patrick cannot recover the £50,000 cost of necessary repairs from the builders because they have become insolvent. Patrick has also learnt that the land was worth £100,000 less than he paid for it, and that Queenie received a secret commission from the vendor on the sale. He says that he would not have bought the land at all if either Larry or Queenie had told him its true market value. He also says that he would not have instructed Queenie to act for him if he had known of her arrangement with the vendor.

**Advise Patrick.**

2. When awarding remedies for breach of fiduciary duty, the courts must weigh up "the need the need to deter fiduciaries from abusing their trust on the one hand, and the goal of achieving a remedy that is fair to all those affected, on the other": *3464920 Canada Inc v Strother* [2007] 2 S.C.R. 177 at [156] per McLachlin CJ.

**Have the courts struck the right balance between principals and fiduciaries when deciding the issues considered in this chapter?**

3. Is the imposition of a constructive trust on the profits of a breach of fiduciary duty fair to the fiduciary's creditors?

# PART VI

# TRUSTS IMPOSED BY LAW

# 14

# RESULTING TRUSTS

## 1. Introduction

### A. Trusts Imposed by Law

As explained in Chapter 1, it is possible to categorise trusts according to the reason for which a particular trust arises.[1] An express trust arises where a party (the settlor) has successfully exercised her power to set up a trust, either by declaring that she holds property on trust, or by transferring property to trustees to hold on trust. All other trusts are imposed by law. If we put statutory trusts to one side, there are only two types of trust imposed by law: resulting trusts and constructive trusts.[2] We examine resulting trusts in this chapter, and we will examine constructive trusts in Chapter 15. 14–001

When examining trusts imposed by law, we have to confront the question of justification. Once it is accepted that a holder of property has, in general, a power to set up a trust of that property,[3] the existence of an express trust can be justified simply by pointing to the settlor's successful exercise of that power. In contrast, if the law imposes a trust, we need to ask two questions: first, why is it that the defendant has come under a duty to the claimant; and secondly, even if the imposition of that duty can be justified, why has a trust been imposed? As we saw in Chapter 1, the existence of a trust has significant consequences, not only for the beneficiary and the trustee, but also for third parties, such as creditors of the trustee. 14–002

A good example of the consequences of finding a trust is provided by *Chase Manhattan Bank NA v Israel-British Bank (London) Ltd*.[4] The claimant bank had been instructed to pay (just over) USD 2 million to the defendant. By mistake, it made that payment twice. Goulding J found that the second payment was held by the defendant on trust for the claimant. The trust was clearly not an express trust, as neither party had attempted to exercise any power to set up a trust. The existence of the trust had important consequences for the creditors of the defendant, which was insolvent. It meant that those creditors had no access to the second USD 2 million payment: as that right was subject to a trust, the claimant's right to it was protected in the defendant's insolvency. 14–003

When considering such a case, we have to ask the two questions set out above: why did the defendant come under a duty to the claimant; and why was a trust imposed? As to the first, it may be said 14–004

---

1 For a useful discussion of different possible approaches to classifying trusts, see N. McBride, "On the Classification of Trusts" in P. Birks and F. Rose (eds), *Restitution and Equity, Volume 1: Resulting Trusts and Equitable Compensation* (Informa, 2000).

2 See paras 1–046—1–052.

3 As we noted at para.1–056. of course, "property" here refers to any right held by a party, as it is possible for a settlor (S) to set up a trust of even a purely personal right against another (as occurs where the trust property is a bank account, i.e. S's personal right against S's bank).

4 [1981] Ch. 105.

that, as a recipient of a mistaken payment, the defendant would be unjustly enriched at the claimant's expense if it were not under a duty to make restitution of the value of the payment to the claimant.[5] As to the second, the question is why the defendant, rather than simply owing a personal obligation to make restitution to the claimant, held the second USD 2 million on trust for the claimant. Different explanations have been suggested for the trust[6]; it has also been argued that there is no need for a trust, and that the court should simply have found that the claimant had nothing more than a personal right to repayment of the USD 2 million, with the result that it had no special protection in the defendant's insolvency.[7] This shows that when considering trusts imposed by law, we must be alert to the question of justification.[8]

**14–005** When considering the justification of resulting and constructive trusts, we also need to be alert to the fact that some trusts commonly referred to as "resulting" or "constructive" may, on closer inspection, turn out to have been misclassified. That will be the case if a trust can be shown to have arisen as a result of an actual or presumed exercise by a party of a power to set up a trust.[9] The terms resulting and constructive should be applied only to trusts that arise by operation of law, i.e. for some reason other than a settlor's successful exercise of her power to set up a trust. Whilst it is important to be aware of this argument, it is clear, nonetheless, that many trusts currently classified as resulting or as constructive *cannot* be explained as express trusts: the trust recognised in the *Chase Manhattan* case, for example, is clearly not an express trust.[10]

**14–006** It is also important to note that, even if a trust is indeed imposed by law, this does not mean that the parties' intentions can have *no* role to play in its justification.[11] The distinction between express trusts and those imposed by law depends on the fact that in the former case, a party has successfully exercised her power to set up a trust. This does not preclude a party's intention to set up a trust as being one of the factors that may lead to the imposition of a resulting or constructive trust. For example, if the formality rule imposed by s.53(1)(b) of the Law of Property Act 1925[12] (1925 Act) prevents the

---

5 See, e.g. *Barclays Bank Ltd v WJ Simms Son & Cooke (Southern) Ltd* [1980] Q.B. 677 at 695; *Kleinwort Benson Ltd v Lincoln CC* [1999] 2 A.C. 349.

6 See, e.g. *Westdeutsche Landesbank Girozentrale v Islington LBC* [1996] A.C. 669 at 715 per Lord Browne-Wilkinson: "Although the mere receipt of the moneys, in ignorance of the mistake, gives rise to no trust, the retention of the moneys after the recipient bank learned of the mistake may well have given rise to a constructive trust". This view focuses on the defendant's knowledge of the claimant's mistake: see too B. McFarlane, "Trusts and Knowledge: Lessons from Australia" in J. Glister and P. Ridge (eds), *Fault Lines in Equity* (Hart Publishing, 2012). For a different explanation, regarding the trust as a resulting trust, and arising independently of any knowledge by the defendant of the claimant's mistake, see, e.g. R. Chambers, *Resulting Trusts* (Oxford University Press, 1997), pp.125–135.

7 This argument has been made, e.g., in W. Swadling, "A New Role for Resulting Trusts" (1996) 16 L.S. 110.

8 See, e.g. *Westdeutsche Landesbank Girozentrale v Islington LBC* [1996] A.C. 669 at [684] where Lord Goff, in rejecting the claim of a resulting trust of money paid by the claimant to the defendant under an ultra vires contract, asked "why should the plaintiff bank be given the additional benefits which flow from a proprietary claim, for example the benefit of achieving priority in the event of the defendant's insolvency? After all, it has entered into a commercial transaction, and so taken the risk of the defendant's insolvency, just like the defendant's other creditors who have contracted with it, not to mention other creditors to whom the defendant may be liable to pay damages in tort." For further consideration of this question, see A. Burrows, "Proprietary Restitution: Unmasking Unjust Enrichment" (2001) 117 L.Q.R. 412.

9 See, e.g. W. Swadling, "Explaining Resulting Trusts" (2008) 124 L.Q.R. 72, making that argument in relation to so-called presumed resulting trusts; and W. Swadling, "The Nature of the Trust in *Rochefoucauld v Boustead*" in C. Mitchell (ed.), *Constructive and Resulting Trusts* (Hart Publishing, 2010), making that argument in relation to the type of trust (often said to be constructive) in *Rochefoucauld*: see para.15–033.

10 As seen from the two different views set out at n.6 there is also disagreement as to whether the trust in that case is best seen as constructive or as resulting.

11 As noted by P. Birks, *An Introduction to the Law of Restitution*, rev edn (Clarendon Press, 1989), p.65, there is "a fine but important distinction between intent conceived as creative of rights, as in an express trust or contract, and intent conceived as a fact which, along with others, calls for the creation of rights by operation of law." See too R. Chambers, "Constructive Trusts in Canada" (1999) 37 Alberta Law Review 173 (reproduced in (2001) 15 Tru. L.I. 214 and (2002) 16 Tru. L.I. 2).

12 See paras 3–026ff.

claimant from proving a declaration of trust of land, it may still be possible for the claimant, relying in part on a party's intention to create a trust, to show that the circumstances warrant the court in imposing a resulting or constructive trust.[13] Such trusts are expressly excluded from the scope of the formality rule by s.53(2) of the 1925 Act: as they arise by operation of law, there is no need for the claimant to prove a declaration of trust. Similarly, if a party attempts to set up a trust of property that she does not yet have, this attempt to set up an express trust will fail, for want of subject matter[14]; if, however, she later acquires that property, it may be that she will immediately hold it subject to a constructive trust imposed by law.[15] Such a trust does not arise purely from her earlier attempt to set up a trust, but may, for example, arise in order to give effect to her binding promise to hold on trust, for which consideration was given by the claimant.[16]

A final point is that resulting and constructive trusts play an important role in the operation of express trusts, and in protecting beneficiaries of such express trusts.[17] For example, as explained in Chapter 1, a key feature of a beneficiary's right under a trust is that it is capable of binding a third party who acquires the trust property, if the trustees had no power under the terms of the trust to make the transfer to the third party. In such a case, it is clear that the third party is not, in general, subject to all the terms of the original trust.[18] As a result, although the point is controversial, it can be argued that the third party is bound not by the original express trust, but rather by a new trust, imposed by law. Indeed, in *Independent Trustee Services Ltd v GP Noble Trustees Ltd*, Lloyd LJ described the trust binding the third party as constructive, stating that "[s]ince the trust arises from the asset having been extracted, in breach of trust, from a fund held on express trusts, it seems correct to characterise the trust as a constructive trust, rather than a resulting trust."[19] We will explore this point further in Chapter 15. Similarly, we also saw in Chapter 1 that another key feature of a beneficiary's right under a trust is that it allows the beneficiary to assert a claim in relation to new property acquired by the trustees through an unauthorised use of the original trust property. In such a case, as the terms of the original trust did not allow for the acquisition of such property, it is possible to argue (although again the point is controversial) that the trust of the new property is imposed by law.[20] **14–007**

### *B. The Consequences of a Trust Imposed by Law and the Role of Conscience*

If a court recognises that a resulting or constructive trust has arisen in favour of a claimant, then as the beneficiary of the trust she acquires an equitable interest in the trust property. This means that, if property subject to the resulting or constructive trust can still be identified at the time of the defendant's insolvency, the claimant, as in *Chase Manhattan*, will be protected from the risks of that insolvency. It also means that if the defendant transfers the property subject to the trust to a third party, the claimant may be able to assert a right against that third party; and that, if the defendant uses the property subject to the resulting or constructive trust to acquire new property, the claimant **14–008**

---

13 See, e.g. the analysis of Russell LJ in *Hodgson v Marks* [1971] Ch. 892.
14 See para.2–082.
15 See paras 2–082—2–084.
16 See, e.g. *Pullan v Koe* [1913] 1 Ch. 9, extracted at paras 2–073—2–077.
17 See B. McFarlane, "The Centrality of Constructive and Resulting Trusts" in C. Mitchell (ed.), *Constructive and Resulting Trusts* (2010), pp.195–199.
18 As explained by, e.g. R. Nolan, "Equitable Property" (2006) 122 L.Q.R. 232. See further paras 17–011—17–014.
19 [2013] Ch. 91 at [80].
20 For an argument to this effect see, e.g. R. Chambers, "Tracing and Unjust Enrichment" in J. Neyers et al. (eds), *Understanding Unjust Enrichment* (Hart Publishing, 2004). See further paras 15–207—15–210.

will also be able to assert an equitable interest in that new property.[21] In other words, the resulting or constructive trust gives valuable proprietary protection to the claimant.[22]

**14-009** In an express trust, the proprietary protection given to the beneficiary coincides with personal rights that the beneficiary has against the trustees. The trustees are, for example, under a personal duty to account to the beneficiaries for the trust property,[23] and also owe fiduciary duties to the beneficiary.[24] In *Westdeutsche Landesbank Girozentrale v Islington LBC*,[25] Lord Browne-Wilkinson stated that it would be inappropriate to fix a party with such duties unless his conscience were affected with knowledge of the circumstances said to give rise to the trust in favour of the claimant. In that case, money had been paid by the claimant to the defendant under a contract which turned out to be void, as beyond the powers of the defendant local authority. The claimant argued that, as in the *Chase Manhattan* case, the money was held by the defendant on a trust imposed by law. One of the reasons given by both Lord Browne-Wilkinson[26] and Lord Goff[27] for refusing to find a resulting or constructive trust was that, by the time that the defendant was aware that its contract with the claimant was ultra vires, it no longer had either the money paid under the contract or its traceable proceeds. This reasoning was based in part on the assumption that, if a trust had arisen at the moment when the money was received, the defendant would have been under a personal duty to account for the money from that point, and such a result would be unfair if, at that point, the defendant had had no reason to believe that there were any limits on the use it could make of the money. It can similarly be argued that if the defendant is, e.g. an infant when she receives property, it would be harsh to impose any immediate personal duties to account for that property.[28]

**14-010** The reasoning of the House of Lords in *Westdeutsche* has an important consequence: it means that a resulting or constructive trust should not arise unless and until the trustee's conscience is affected by knowledge of the relevant circumstances.[29] For example, Lord Browne-Wilkinson justified the result in *Chase Manhattan* by noting that the defendant had been made aware of the claimant's mistake at a point when it still held the mistaken payment, and by stating that the trust in favour of the claimant arose only at that time, and not when the defendant first received the payment.[30] The need for the defendant's conscience to be affected by knowledge of the circumstances giving rise to the claimed resulting or constructive trust places a significant limit on the circumstances in which such trusts can arise.

**14-011** The conscience-based limit on constructive trusts proposed in *Westdeutsche* has not won universal acceptance. As we will see in Chapter 15,[31] Lloyd LJ, in *Independent Trustee Services Ltd v GP Noble Trustees Ltd*,[32] whilst accepting that a donee of trust property can be under no personal liability if she has no knowledge of the initial trust, also stated that a constructive trust arose as soon as the donee acquired the trust property.[33] On this view, a resulting or constructive trust can exist even at a time

---

21 In *Attorney General of Hong Kong v Reid* [1994] 1 A.C. 324, for example, a constructive trust arising as a result of the defendant's acceptance of a bribe allowed the claimant to assert an equitable interest in other property acquired with the bribe and in the hands of a third party who had not paid for it.
22 See, e.g. *Westdeutsche Landesbank Girozentrale v Islington LBC* [1996] A.C. 669 at 705.
23 See paras 9-005—9-017.
24 See paras 9-018ff.
25 [1996] A.C. 669 at 705-706.
26 [1996] A.C. 669 at 705-706.
27 [1996] A.C. 669 at 689-690.
28 As in *Re Vinogradoff* [1935] W.N. 68.
29 [1996] A.C. 669 at 706-707, recognising that an equitable proprietary interest can burden a defendant's legal estate before his conscience is affected, but refusing to use the term "trust" to describe this interest.
30 [1996] A.C. 669 at 714-715.
31 See para.15-203. See too paras 12-057—12-063.
32 [2013] Ch. 91 at [80].
33 See too the criticism of Lord Browne-Wilkinson's analysis by Rimer J in *Shalson v Russo* [2005] Ch. 281 at [111].

when the trustee cannot be personally liable for disposing of the trust assets: the proprietary aspect of a trust can be separated from its personal aspects, as is seen from the fact that a beneficiary can enforce her "proprietary rights against a recipient of trust property or its traceable proceeds, even if the recipient had no knowledge of the breach of trust, provided that the recipient did not give value for the property."[34] Certainly, various authorities appear to contradict the view that trusts cannot be imposed by law unless and until the trustee's conscience is affected,[35] although in *Westdeutsche* Lord Browne-Wilkinson explained those cases as ones in which

> by the time action was brought, [the trustee] or his successors in title have been become aware of the facts which gave rise to a resulting trust: his conscience was affected as from the time of such discovery and thereafter he held on a resulting trust under which the property was recovered from him.[36]

It may be, however, that there is less to this disagreement than meets the eye. First, in a case such as *Chase Manhattan*, even if Lord Browne-Wilkinson's view is correct and a trust does not arise at the moment when the defendant receives the mistakenly paid money, it seems that the claimant at that point nonetheless has more than a merely personal right against the defendant. That is because the claimant has the *potential* to acquire an equitable interest under a trust: such an interest will arise if the claimant informs the defendant of the mistake (or, indeed, if the defendant discovers the mistake by some other means). The claimant's right at this point can therefore be compared to the right of a party who, for example, has the equitable power to set aside a transfer of property made as a result of an innocent misrepresentation by the recipient of the property. Such a right, sometimes called a "mere equity", has proprietary effect in the sense that it is capable of being transferred,[37] is protected in the recipient's insolvency, is capable of binding third parties later receiving the property from the recipient,[38] and can support a claim in relation to traceable proceeds of that original property.[39] It thus shares the key proprietary attributes of an equitable interest under a trust, set out at para.14–008. **14–012**

Secondly, even when the party subject to the resulting or constructive trust has knowledge of the facts on which the trust is based, so that the claimant has a full-blown equitable interest, and the benefit of the defendant's liability to account, this does not mean that the beneficiary enjoys all the same personal rights as those which are generally enjoyed by the beneficiaries of an express trust: **14–013**

> It is a mistake to suppose that in every situation in which a constructive trust arises the legal owner is necessarily subject to all the fiduciary obligations and disabilities of an express trustee.[40]

---

34 *Ultraframe (UK) Ltd v Fielding* [2007] W.T.L.R. 835 at [1518]. For discussion of the personal liability to account as a constructive trustee that is owed by knowing recipients see paras 11–017ff.

35 *Birch v Blagrave* (1755) Amb. 264; *Childers v Childers* (1857) 1 De G. & J. 482; *Re Vinogradoff* [1935] W.N. 68; *Re Diplock* [1948] Ch. 465; *Re Muller* [1953] N.Z.L.R. 879.

36 [1996] A.C. 669 at 705–706.

37 See, e.g. *Stump v Gaby* (1852) 2 De M. & G. 623.

38 See, e.g. *Blacklocks v JB Developments (Godalming) Ltd* [1982] Ch. 183. See now Land Registration Act 2002 s.116(b). Although note, outside the context of registered land, a mere equity, unlike a full-blown equitable interest, does not bind a later bona fide purchaser for value without notice of an *equitable* interest in the same property: see *Phillips v Phillips* (1861) 4 De G.F. & J. 208.

39 See, e.g. *El Ajou v Dollar Land Holdings* [1993] 3 All E.R. 717 at 734.

40 *Lonrho Plc v Fayed (No.2)* [1992] 1 W.L.R. 1 at 12 per Millett J. See too Chambers, *Resulting Trusts* (1997) pp.194–200; L.D. Smith, "Constructive Fiduciaries?" in P. Birks (ed.), *Privacy and Loyalty* (Clarendon Press, 1997), pp.263–267; Lord Millett, "Restitution and Constructive Trusts" (1998) 114 L.Q.R. 399, 404–405; C. Mitchell and S. Watterson, "Remedies for Knowing Receipt" in Mitchell (ed.), *Constructive and Resulting Trusts* (2010), pp.142–144. On the question whether a resulting or constructive trustee enjoys the same right of indemnity as an express trustee, see *Nolan v Collie* (2003) 7 V.R. 287 at [32]–[34]; *Re Loftus, (Deceased)* [2005] 1 W.L.R. 1890 at [202], not considered on appeal [2007] 1 W.L.R. 591.

## C. Defining Resulting Trusts

14-014 There is a well-established group of trusts known as resulting trusts. In *Westdeutsche Landesbank Girozentrale v Islington LBC*, Lord Browne-Wilkinson defined them by reference to the circumstances in which they arise.

*Westdeutsche Landesbank Girozentrale v Islington LBC*

House of Lords [1996] A.C. 669 at 705–706

14-015 LORD BROWNE-WILKINSON: Under existing law a resulting trust arises in two sets of circumstances:

(A) Where A makes a voluntary payment to B or pays (wholly or in part) for the purchase of property which is vested either in B alone or in the joint names of A and B, there is a presumption that A did not intend to make a gift to B: the money or property is held on trust for A (if he is the sole provider of the money) or in the case of a joint purchase by A and B in shares proportionate to their contributions. It is important to stress that this is only a presumption, which presumption is easily rebutted either by the counter-presumption of advancement or by direct evidence of A's intention to make an outright transfer.[41]

(B) Where A transfers property to B on express trusts, but the trusts declared do not exhaust the whole beneficial interest.[42]

14-016 In this chapter, resulting trusts arising in the first set of circumstances identified by Lord Browne-Wilkinson will be called "Type (A)" resulting trusts, and those arising in the second set of circumstances will be called "Type (B)" resulting trusts. Whilst it is clear that a trust may arise in each of those two cases, important questions remain. First, why does a trust arise in those two sets of circumstances? Is the reason for which the trust arises the same in each case? Secondly, can the principle or principles underlying those cases operate more broadly, and so allow for the recognition of a trust in other circumstances?

## D. Terminology

14-017 Why are trusts arising in the two sets of circumstances set out by Lord Browne-Wilkinson in *Westdeutsche* called "resulting trusts"? There are two reasons. First, in each case, the party who ends up as the beneficiary of the resulting trust (A in Lord Browne-Wilkinson's examples) starts off with some property. In the Type (A) case, the beneficiary was, initially, the unencumbered holder of either the eventual trust property, or of money used to purchase that eventual trust property. In the Type (B) case, the beneficiary of the eventual trust was, initially, the unencumbered holder of the eventual trust property. The word "resulting" derives from the Latin *resalire*, meaning "to jump back" and it can be said that the resulting trust gives "back" an interest to the beneficiary, but only in the very loose sense that the beneficiary initially had an interest in either the trust property or property used to acquire the trust property.[43]

14-018 It should be stressed that this notion of giving "back" is a very loose one, as of course the beneficiary of the resulting trust ends up with an equitable interest, whereas, in each of the Type (A) and Type (B) cases, she is likely to have started out with a full legal interest. For example, in a case where A makes a voluntary payment for B, which is then held by B on resulting trust for A, the final position is that A

---

41 *Underhill & Hayton*, pp.317ff.; *Vandervell v IRC* [1967] 2 A.C. 291 at 312 ff.; *Re Vandervell's Trusts (No.2)* [1974] Ch. 269 at pp.288ff.

42 ibid. and *Barclays Bank Ltd v Quistclose Investments Ltd* [1970] A.C. 567.

43 The difficulties inherent in the view that the beneficiary of a resulting trust "retains" an equitable interest are discussed below at para.14-166. For an in-depth discussion of the notion of "retention" in this context, see J. Mee, "'Automatic Resulting Trusts': Retention, Restitution, or Reposing Trust?" in Mitchell (ed.), *Constructive and Resulting Trusts* (2010).

has only an equitable interest in the payment whereas, at the start of the story, she had a full legal interest. It is therefore clear that the right A acquires under a resulting trust may be a new right that she never previously held.

The second reason for the use of the term "resulting trust" is to distinguish such trusts from other types of trust. First, the use of the term assumes that such trusts are not express trusts, and therefore assumes that the trusts arising in the circumstances identified by Lord Browne-Wilkinson do not arise simply as a result of a party having successfully exercised her power to set up a trust. Certainly, even though "jumping back" may be involved, the trust arising where a settlor S successfully sets up a trust by transferring property to a trustee T to hold on trust for S is not conventionally referred to as a "resulting trust". However, as we have said already,[44] this does not mean, that the intentions of the parties necessarily have no role to play in resulting trusts. Indeed, in *Westdeutsche* itself, having described the two types of resulting trust, Lord Browne-Wilkinson went on to say that[45]: **14–019**

> Both types of resulting trust are traditionally regarded as examples of trusts giving effect to the common intention of the parties. A resulting trust is not imposed by law against the intentions of the trustee (as is a constructive trust) but gives effect to his presumed intention.

That analysis is somewhat controversial, and it will be examined in more detail below.[46] But it does at least make it clear that, even if resulting trusts are imposed by law, we will have to consider the role played by the intentions of the parties.

On the approach taken here to questions of terminology, the field of non-express trusts is therefore divided into resulting trusts and constructive trusts, and in line with Lord Browne-Wilkinson's analysis, resulting trusts are sub-divided into two categories according to the circumstances which give rise to them. Constructive trusts, in contrast, are imposed in a wider range of situations, and more explanations have been advanced for their imposition: e.g. to perfect the defendant's intention to transfer beneficial ownership to the claimant; to compensate the claimant for the loss that she detrimentally incurs in reliance on the defendant's assurances; to strip the defendant of the profits of her wrongdoing; or to reverse the defendant's unjust enrichment at the claimant's expense. These explanations are all reviewed in the next chapter.[47] **14–020**

## 2. Type (A) Resulting Trusts

### *A. Overview*

Lord Millett has written extra-judicially that[48]: **14–021**

> Resulting trusts arise in three situations: voluntary payment or transfer; purchase in the name of another; and incomplete disposal of the beneficial interest. The first two have been described as 'apparent gifts'; the last as 'failing trusts'.

The "apparent gift" cases constitute the first type of resulting trust identified by Lord Browne-Wilkinson in *Westdeutsche* and will be referred to here as "Type (A) resulting trusts". These trusts are also often referred to as "presumed resulting trusts".

---

44 See para.4–006.

45 [1996] A.C. 669 at 708.

46 See paras 14-088—14-091 and 14-161—14-164.

47 See e.g. paras 15-213.

48 Lord Millett, "Pension Schemes and the Law of Trusts" (2000) 14 Tru L.I. 66, 73.

14-022 In *Vandervell v IRC*,[49] Lord Upjohn attempted a brief statement of the relevant principles:

> Where A transfers, or directs a trustee for him to transfer, the legal estate in property to B otherwise than for valuable consideration it is a question of the intention of A in making the transfer whether B was to take beneficially or on trust and, if the latter, on what trusts. If, as a matter of construction of the document transferring the legal estate, it is possible to discern A's intentions, that is an end of the matter and no extraneous evidence is admissible to correct and qualify his intentions so ascertained . . . But if, as in this case (a common form share transfer), the document is silent, then there is said to arise a resulting trust in favour of A. But this is only a presumption and is easily rebutted. All the relevant facts and circumstances can be considered in order to ascertain A's intentions with a view to rebutting this presumption.

14-023 In a later instalment of the Vandervell saga, *Re Vandervell's Trusts (No.2)*,[50] Megarry J glossed this statement by noting that "Lord Upjohn is obviously assuming that A is not the husband or father of B, and does not stand *in loco parentis* to him, so that no question of presumption of advancement arises." In cases of this kind, as we discuss below,[51] the presumption is not that a trust was intended, but that A intended a simple gift, and so intended B to hold the transferred right absolutely, free of any trust. Megarry J also referred to Type (A) resulting trusts as "presumed resulting trusts", noting that "the matter is one intention, with the rebuttable intention of a resulting trust applying if the intention is not made manifest."[52]

14-024 An example of a Type (A) resulting trust is provided by the Supreme Court's decision in *Prest v Petrodel Resources Ltd*.[53] In a wife's claim for ancillary relief, it was found that certain property held by companies controlled by her husband were held by those companies on resulting trust for him. This meant that although there was no justification for "piercing the corporate veil" and regarding the company's property as being held by the husband, his beneficial interest in particular properties held by the company on resulting trust for him meant that the court, in exercising its jurisdiction to order ancillary relief, could make an order that the company should convey those properties to the wife.

14-025 For example, in relation to three flats acquired by a company (PRL) for a nominal consideration of £1, Lord Sumption stated that

> [s]ince no explanation has been forthcoming for the gratuitous transfer of [such] properties to PRL, there is nothing to rebut the ordinary presumption of equity that PRL was not intended to acquire a beneficial interest in them. The only question is who did hold the beneficial interest.[54]

As one of the flats had been transferred directly to the company by the husband, "[t]here is therefore an ordinary resulting trust back to the husband".[55] A second flat had been transferred to the company by the husband's brother, but had been paid for by the husband, and

> there is no evidence to rebut the ordinary inference that the husband was the beneficial owner of the property at the time of the transfer to PRL, and that the company held it on a resulting trust for him.[56]

14-026 Each of those two examples from *Prest* represents one of the sub-groups of the Type (A) resulting trust: particular factual situations in which such a trust *may* arise. The first is where A makes

---

49 [1967] 2 A.C. 291 at 312.
50 [1974] Ch. 269 at 289.
51 See paras 14-043–14-048.
52 [1974] Ch. 269 at [289].
53 [2013] 2 A.C. 415.
54 [2013] 2 A.C. 415 at [49].
55 [2013] 2 A.C. 415 at [49].
56 [2013] 2 A.C. 415 at [49].

a gratuitous transfer of property to B: it extends to cases in which A makes a gratuitous transfer of that right into the joint names of A and B. The second is where B acquires property, but all or part of the money for its acquisition is provided by A; it similarly extends to cases in which the right is jointly acquired by A and B. In such cases, if a resulting trust arises as a result of A's provision of part only of the purchase price, the extent of A's beneficial interest will be proportionate to A's contribution.

### *B. Presumptions*

#### i. Presumption of Resulting Trust: General Position

If A makes a gratuitous transfer of property to B, or if A provides all or part of the purchase price of a property acquired by B, a Type (A) resulting trust *may* arise. It must be remembered, though, that in such cases the presumption of a resulting trust may be displaced. Indeed, as Lord Browne-Wilkinson noted in *Westdeutsche*, the presumption may be "easily rebutted" by direct evidence of A's intention to make an outright transfer to B.[57] This reflects a more general point about the nature of presumptions, colourfully made by an American judge: "presumptions may be looked on as the bats of the law, flitting in the twilight, but disappearing in the sunshine of actual facts."[58] **14–027**

One such actual fact dispelling a presumption of resulting trust occurs where A simply makes a gift to B, i.e. transfers a property right to B with a donative intent. The finding of a gift is not, however, the only means by which the presumption can be rebutted.[59] In *Westdeutsche* itself, for example, the claimant bank, when making payments to the defendant local authority in the mistaken belief that it had a contractual duty to do so, clearly did not intend to make gift. Nonetheless, as Lord Browne-Wilkinson explained, **14–028**

> any presumption of resulting trust is rebutted since it is demonstrated that the bank paid, and the local authority received, the upfront payment with the intention that the moneys so paid should become the absolute property of the local authority. . .the presumption of resulting trust is rebutted by evidence of any intention inconsistent with such a trust, not only by evidence of an intention to make a gift.[60]

#### ii. Presumption of Resulting Trust: Voluntary Conveyances of Land

**Law of Property Act 1925 s.60**

(1) A conveyance of freehold land to any person without words of limitation, or any equivalent expression, shall pass to the grantee the fee simple or other the whole interest which the grantor had power to convey in such land, unless a contrary intention appears in the conveyance. . . **14–029**

(3) In a voluntary conveyance a resulting trust for the grantor shall not be implied merely by reason that the property is not expressed to be conveyed for the use or benefit of the grantee.

---

57 [1996] A.C. 669 at 708.

58 *Mackowick v Kansas City St J. & CB Rwy* 196 Mo. 550 at 571, 94 S.W. 256 at 262 (1906) per Lamm J.

59 See too *Prest v Petrodel Resources Ltd* [2013] 2 A.C. 415 at [50], where Lord Sumption noted that the presumption of resulting trust would have been rebutted if there had been evidence that money had been provided to PRL by the husband by way of loan or capital subscription.

60 [1996] AC 669 at 708, citing with approval the analysis of this point by W Swadling, "A New Role for Resulting Trusts" (1996) 16 LS 110 at 133.

14-030 Considering this section in *Lohia v Lohia*, HHJ Nicholas Strauss QC, at first instance, stated that[61]:

> on a plain reading of s 60, the presumption [of resulting trust] has been abolished [in relation to a voluntary conveyance of land]. It seems to me that s 60(1) establishes a general rule that a conveyance should be construed according to the words it uses, so that it is possible to tell from it who holds the legal and beneficial estate in the land. Consistently with this, s 60(3) provides in effect that a voluntary conveyance means what it says; it is not necessary to use additional words to make it effective. It is likely that by 1925 the suspicion with which gifts of land were formerly viewed, which was at least one of the underlying reasons for the presumption, would no longer have been regarded as material, and the purpose of s 60(3) was accordingly to do away with the presumption of a resulting trust in the cases of voluntary conveyance and to make it necessary for the person seeking to establish a resulting trust to prove it.

14-031 It was also found on the facts of *Lohia* that A had in any case intended to make a gift to B, so that, even if a presumption of resulting trust had arisen, it would have been rebutted. On appeal, the Court of Appeal agreed with that finding of fact, and so did not take on what Sir Christopher Slade referred to there as "the knotty question [of] whether the presumption of resulting trust on the voluntary conveyance of land survives the enactment of s.60(3)".[62] Mummery LJ similarly said that a court would be "bold" to decide that question "without having heard very extensive argument."[63] It is also worth noting that, when finding that various legal estates in land were held on Type (A) resulting trusts in *Prest v Petrodel Resources Ltd*,[64] the Supreme Court did not refer to s.60(3), and so, whilst the analysis of HHJ Nicholas Strauss QC drew on powerful academic support,[65] it would be unwise to regard his judgment in *Lohia* as having finally determined the question of whether there is still a presumption of resulting trust in a case where A makes a gratuitous transfer of a legal estate in land to B. Indeed, as John Mee has convincingly argued, it is impossible to have a full understanding of the purpose of s.60(3) without first undertaking a detailed historical examination of the position before 1926, and of the "complex relationship between resulting uses and resulting trusts."[66]

14-032 Perhaps the most important practical point is that when A conveys a legal estate in land to B and receives nothing directly in return, a court will simply focus on the available evidence in order to determine if, as was found to be the case in *Lohia*, A intended to make an outright transfer to B (for example by way of gift) or if, as was found to be the case in *Prest*, A intended that the estate would be held on trust for A. Given Lord Browne-Wilkinson's statement that the presumption of resulting trust can be "easily rebutted",[67] it may, therefore, be said that the position in relation to a voluntary conveyance of land is not so different from the case where A buys land that is put into B's name, or where A makes a voluntary conveyance of other property to B.

14-033 There is a practical difficulty, however. As we will discuss,[68] there is a particular, technical reason why the existence or non-existence of a presumption of resulting trust can be crucial, viz. that a rule

---

61 (2000) 3 I.T.E.L.R. 117 at 129.

62 [2001] EWCA Civ 1691 at [34].

63 [2001] EWCA Civ 1691 at [24].

64 [2013] 2 A.C. 415: see, e.g. at [52] per Lord Sumption.

65 See, e.g. Chambers, *Resulting Trusts* (1997), pp.18–19.

66 J. Mee, "Resulting Trusts and Voluntary Conveyances of Land" [2012] Conv. 307, 308. See too J. Mee, "Resulting Trusts and Voluntary Conveyances of Land: 1674–1925" (2011) 32 J.L.H. 215. Mee's position is that, prior to 1926, the doctrine of resulting trusts itself (rather than merely the presumption of a resulting trust) did not apply in relation to land, as only a doctrine of resulting uses was applied. As s.60(3) then abolishes the doctrine of resulting uses in the context of land, there is no longer any resulting use or trust doctrine that can avail A, and so A must instead turn to other doctrines, such as that in *Rochefoucauld v Boustead* [1897] 1 Ch. 196 (see paras 15–030—15–045) to claim that B holds land on trust for A. It would seem, for example, that the *Rochefoucauld* doctrine is applicable to the facts of *Hodgson v Marks* [1971] Ch. 892.

67 [1996] A.C. 669 at 708.

68 See paras 14–049ff.

forbidding reliance on evidence of an achieved improper purpose may prevent A from proving directly that a trust was intended, but does not prevent A simply relying on the presumption. As we will also see when considering the scope of the presumption of advancement[69] it is very unfortunate that this evidential rule, which has been the subject of much criticism, gives such undue prominence to the existence or non-existence of a presumption. It means, for example, that if s.60(3), as suggested at first instance in *Lohia*, operates to remove any presumption of resulting trust on a voluntary conveyance of land, A may be prevented from claiming a beneficial interest where to do so would entail bringing evidence of an achieved improper purpose. Yet if the same purpose had instead involved A buying land and putting it in B's name, or A transferring property other than land gratuitously to B, A could instead have simply relied on the presumption of resulting trust.

It may be argued that, whether or not it is justifiable as a matter of statutory interpretation, the view of s.60(3) adopted at first instance in *Lohia*, with its special treatment of voluntary conveyances of land, can be justified as a matter of policy.[70] First, there are many reasons why A might buy property in B's name without intending an outright transfer that do not obtain in the case of a transfer of property from A to B: e.g. overlooking the need to protect A's position in the course of a complex transaction involving vendors and mortgagees.[71] Secondly, special formality rules apply to conveyances of land and not to transfers of personal property, increasing the likelihood that a transferor has thought carefully about whether she really wants another person to have the benefit of her legal estate in land and so reducing the need for a rule that she should be presumed not to have intended this. **14–034**

Alternatively, the *Lohia* interpretation of s.60(3) could be seen as useful if it were to become part of a wider judicial move to reject the presumption of resulting trust, whether or not land is involved. In *Lohia*, for example, HHJ Nicholas Strauss QC noted that, by 1925, there was no longer any reason for equity to think it unlikely that A would have intended an outright gratuitous transfer of land to B. It can similarly be argued that there is no longer any reason to presume, in any context, that the fact of A's gratuitous transfer of property to B means that A intended to create a trust.[72] This would give consistency with voluntary conveyances of land and would also prevent the presumption having a potentially decisive effect in cases involving achieved improper purposes. Certainly, the apparent weakness of the presumption, coupled with its apparent dispensability in relation to voluntary conveyances of land, prompts the thought that in all Type (A) cases a resulting trust should arise only if A can provide evidence of an intention, known to B, that B was to hold on trust for A.[73] **14–035**

### iii. Presumption of Resulting Trust: Family Homes

Until recently, it was clear that a Type (A) resulting trust might arise in a case where A and B buy a shared family home together but do not make an express written declaration of trust as to their shares.[74] Whether the home was conveyed into the joint names of A and B, or into the names of only one of them, in the absence of clear evidence as to their intentions, and in the absence of any operative presumption of advancement,[75] it would be presumed that a trust was intended under which each **14–036**

---

[69] See paras 14–043—14–048.
[70] R. Chambers (2001) 15 Tru. L.I. 26, 29.
[71] Cf. *Brown v Brown* (1993) 31 N.S.W.L.R. 582.
[72] J. Mee, "Resulting Trusts and Voluntary Conveyances of Land" [2012] Conv 307, 325: "The presumption of resulting trust in this context is an anachronism which should not be tolerated in the modern law."
[73] See para.14–049. for further discussion of this point.
[74] An express written declaration of trust signed by the parties is conclusive in the absence of fraud or mistake (*Goodman v Gallant* [1986] Fam. 106) or undue influence (*Humphreys v Humphreys* [2005] 1 F.C.R. 712).
[75] See paras 14–043—14–048.

party's share would be proportionate to their contributions to the purchase price.[76] So, for example, in the case of a house costing £100,000, if A paid £40,000 and B paid £60,000, A would be entitled to 40 per cent and B to 60 per cent; and the position was the same if A did not pay £40,000 but obtained a £40,000 discount off the market price, as a sitting tenant of the house.[77]

**14–037** However, the relevance of resulting trusts to such cases has diminished as a result of the recognition of the common intention constructive trust of the family home, a concept discussed in Chapter 15.[78] Rather than being used to support a claim under a resulting trust, A's contribution to the purchase price can instead be used as evidence supporting an inference of a common intention to share beneficial ownership of the home; the extent of A's share is then determined by that common intention, and in ascertaining the parties' common intention as to A's share, a court can look beyond the relative size of the contributions to the purchase price, and take account of other factors, looking at the parties' whole course of dealing in relation to the property. In *Midland Bank Plc v Cooke*,[79] for example, A's financial contribution amounted to less than seven per cent of the purchase price, but it allowed for the inference of a common intention, and the court then found that the parties, a married couple, had intended to hold equal beneficial shares of the property.

**14–038** The approach taken in cases such as *Midland Bank v Cooke* illustrates the weakness of the presumption of resulting trust: the courts' preference is to ascertain the parties' intentions as to their beneficial shares (even if this involves a process of inference, divination, or even imputation) rather than to apply the stark mathematics of the resulting trust. Indeed, in *Jones v Kernott*, the Supreme Court confirmed that the effect of the House of Lords' decision in *Stack v Dowden* was to prevent the presumption of resulting trust from operating in cases where a home is bought "in joint names for joint occupation by a married or unmarried couple, where both are responsible for any mortgage".[80] This leaves open the possibility that a Type (A) resulting trust may still be relevant in other domestic cases, for example where the shared home is bought in the name of B alone, or where it is bought by parents and children,[81] or siblings, rather than a couple.

**14–039** In *Stack v Dowden*,[82] however, the majority of the court seemed to have in mind a wider prohibition on resulting trusts, with Baroness Hale stating, for example, that the courts should generally avoid using resulting trust reasoning as a means of establishing equitable interests in shared homes,[83] because it is too focused on one type of contribution to the parties' relationship, viz. financial contributions, to the exclusion of other types, e.g. home-making, child-care, etc., with the result that it delivers outcomes that are unfair and discriminatory against women who support their partners by staying at home while their partners go out to work. Indeed, speaking for the Privy Council in *Abbott v Abbott*, a case in which legal title to the home was in the name of B alone, Baroness Hale reiterated this

---

76 *Pettit v Pettit* [1970] A.C. 777 at 814. It has been unclear whether acquisition costs, e.g. legal fees and stamp duty, count as part of the purchase price. *Huntingford v Hobbs* [1993] 1 F.L.R. 736 suggests that they do, but in *Curley v Parkes* [2004] EWCA Civ 1515 at [22], Peter Gibson LJ held otherwise. At [23] he also held that removal costs do not form part of the purchase price either.

77 *Abbey National BS v Cann* (1989) 59 P. & C.R 381; *Springette v Defoe* [1992] 2 F.L.R. 388; *Mckenzie v Mckenzie* [2003] EWHC 601 (Ch) at [81]; *R (on the application of Kelly) v Hammersmith & Fulham LBC* [2004] EWHC 435 (Admin). See too *Laskar v Laskar* [2008] 1 W.L.R. 2695 at [22]–[26].

78 See paras 15–046ff.

79 [1995] 2 F.L.R. 915.

80 [2012] 1 A.C. 776 at [25].

81 As in, e.g. *City of London Building Society v Flegg* [1988] A.C. 54.

82 [2007] 2 A.C. 432.

83 *Stack* at [60], with the agreement of Lord Hoffmann at [1], Lord Hope at [3], and Lord Walker at [31]. See too *Fowler v Barron* [2008] 2 F.L.R. 831 at [30] and [52].

point, stating that: "It is now clear that the constructive trust is generally the more appropriate tool of analysis in most matrimonial cases."[84]

The more limited wording used in *Jones v Kernott* to formulate the bar on resulting trusts may perhaps be seen as a concession to Lord Neuberger's speech in *Stack v Dowden*, where he took a very different approach, albeit one that led, on the facts of the case, to the same outcome. He considered that resulting trusts should not be completely abandoned in the domestic context (not least because defining the scope of such a context is a very difficult exercise),[85] as he believed that they might still have a role to play.[86] In *Laskar v Laskar*,[87] a case in which he subsequently sat as a judge of the Court of Appeal, Lord Neuberger specifically rejected the argument that the only way to establish an equitable interest in a family home is by way of a constructive trust. A mother and daughter had bought a house together as an investment, without intending to live in it. The court used a traditional resulting trust analysis under which the parties' shares were allocated in proportion to their contributions to the purchase price, and Lord Neuberger said that "it would not be right to apply the reasoning in *Stack v Dowden* to such a case as this, where the parties primarily purchased the property as an investment for rental income and capital appreciation, even where their relationship is a familial one."[88] It seems, therefore, that there are still some family home cases in which resulting trust reasoning should be used to determine the parties' equitable interests. 14–040

It follows that at least in a *Laskar*-type "investment" case, the resulting trust may still be used to govern the allocation of equitable interests in a home.[89] It may well be the case, however, that it is possible to exaggerate the differences between the underlying basis of a Type (A) resulting trust on the one hand and the common intention constructive trust on the other. In *Westdeutsche*, after all, Lord Browne-Wilkinson described the former as "traditionally regarded as examples of trusts giving effect to the common intention of the parties."[90] At a general level, it may be said that in each case the court wishes to uncover the intention of the parties, and in some cases a purely mathematical approach to the quantification of beneficial interests would clearly be at odds with such intentions. 14–041

In *Gallarotti v Sebastianelli*,[91] for example, A and B were friends and each contributed to the purchase of a flat in which they were to live. The property was put in the sole name of B. It was expressly agreed that each would have a 50 per cent interest in the flat, but that agreement was dependent on A making larger contributions than B to the mortgage, as the sum initially provided by A was smaller than that provided by B. A did not in the end make those larger contributions. This agreement was not put in writing and so no declaration of trust could be proved. Arden LJ stated that[92]: 14–042

> In the case of a constructive trust, the court looks at the conduct of the parties throughout their relationship. It is not restricted, as it would be in the case of a resulting trust, to examining the contributions made to the acquisition. The common intention constructive trust is thus more flexible. It is also more appropriate where the parties have incurred expenditure on the strength of their personal relationship and without expectation of having to account, or to call for an account, of every item as they would have to do in the case of a true legal partnership.

---

84 [2008] 1 F.L.R. 1451 at [4].
85 See too N. Hopkins, "The Relevance of Context in Property Law: A Case for Judicial Restraint?" (2011) L.S. 175.
86 [2007] 2 A.C. 432 at [110]ff.
87 [2008] 1 W.L.R. 2695.
88 *Laskar* at [17].
89 See, e.g. *R v Muzafar and Qurban* (unreported 10 June 2014, Leeds County Court): purchase by father of a property put in the names of two of his sons and used as a home for his daughter.
90 [1996] A.C. 669 at 708.
91 [2012] 2 F.L.R. 1231.
92 *Gallarotti* at [5].

Despite these differences, the result reached by applying the constructive trust analysis was that A was found to have a 25 per cent share: this almost exactly matched the extent of his contributions to the purchase price and mortgage. As in *Stack v Dowden* itself, an approach based on the parties' common intention led, effectively, to the same result as a standard resulting trust analysis. This should be no surprise given the importance of intentions to a Type (A) resulting trust.[93]

### iv. Presumption of Advancement

**14–043** In *Westdeutsche*, Lord Browne-Wilkinson stated that in a Type (A) resulting trust the presumption of resulting trust can be rebutted "either by the counter-presumption of advancement or by direct evidence of A's intention to make an outright transfer."[94] The presumption of advancement is said to arise in specific factual circumstances where courts have assumed that the more likely default position is that A, rather than intending that B, the gratuitous transferee, is to hold on trust for A, instead intends to make a gift to B. The specific circumstances in which this presumption of advancement applies have, traditionally, been very confined. They consist of cases where A is the father of B, or stands in loco parentis to B,[95] or is the husband of B, or the fiancé of B.[96] The presumption of advancement does not arise where A is merely cohabiting with B,[97] nor where A is the wife of B.[98] The English cases are divided on the question whether the presumption arises as between a mother and her children,[99] but authorities from elsewhere in the Commonwealth say that it does.[100]

**14–044** These distinctions derive from cases which date back several hundred years, and some have ceased to reflect contemporary socio-economic reality and ideas of gender equality. Specifically, there is no longer a good reason to think that fathers but not mothers have a duty to support their children[101] or

---

93 It should also be noted that, even where standard resulting trust reasoning is used, so that the parties' shares are fixed at the time of acquisition of the property, and later contributions to the mortgage payments beyond those initially agreed cannot be used to increase A's share, equitable accounting principles can be applied when the proceeds of sale of the property are divided between A and B and A's greater mortgage payments can be taken into account at that stage: see, e.g. *Bernard v Josephs* [1982] Ch. 391; *Re Pavlou* [1993] 1 W.L.R. 1046; *Re Byford* [2004] 1 F.L.R. 56; *Stack v Dowden* [2007] 2 A.C. 432 at [117], per Lord Neuberger.

94 [1996] A.C. 669 at 708.

95 *Hepworth v Hepworth* (1870) L.R. 11 Eq. 10; *Shephard v Cartwright* [1955] A.C. 431; *Re Cameron The Times*, 2 April 1999; *Lavelle v Lavelle* [2004] 2 F.C.R. 418 at [14]. For a presumption of advancement to arise on the basis that a transferor is in loco parentis to a transferee, it must be shown that he assumed the duty of a father to make provision for a child: *Bennett v Bennett* (1876) 10 Ch.D. 414 at 477, followed in *Sansom v Gardner* [2009] EWHC 3369 (QB) (where this was not established on the facts).

96 *Tinker v Tinker* [1970] P. 136; *Silver v Silver* [1958] 1 W.L.R. 259; *Moate v Moate* [1948] 2 All E.R. 486 (intended husband: marriage afterwards solemnised); Law Reform (Miscellaneous Provisions) Act 1970 s.2(1); *Mossop v Mossop* [1988] 2 All E.R. 202.

97 *Chapman v Jaume* [2012] 2 F.L.R. 830 at [24]; *Stack v Dowden* [2007] 2 A.C. 432 at [112]; *Calverley v Green* (1984) 56 A.L.R. 483.

98 *Re Curtis* (1885) 52 L.T. 244; *Mercier v Mercier* [1903] 2 Ch. 98; *Abrahams v Trustee of Property of Abrahams* [2000] W.T.L.R. 593.

99 Yes, at least where she is a widowed mother: *Garrett v Wilkinson* (1848) 2 De G. & Sm. 244 at 246; *Sayre v Hughes* (1886) L.R. 5 Eq. 376; *Re Grimes* [1937] I.R. 470. No: *Re De Visme* (1863) 2 De G.J. & S. 17; *Bennet v Bennet* (1879) 10 Ch.D. 474; *Sekhon v Alissa* [1989] 2 F.L.R. 94.

100 *Re Brownlie* [1990] 3 N.Z.L.R. 243; *Brown v Brown* (1993) 31 N.S.W.L.R. 582 at 591; *Re Dreger Estate* (1994) 97 Manitoba R. (2d) 39; *Nelson v Nelson* (1995) 184 C.L.R. 538; *Pecore v Pecore* [2007] 1 S.C.R. 795 at [32]–[33].

101 The duty to support was regularly relied on in older cases as the rationale for the presumption of advancement, so that, for example, the presumption would not apply if the child were "fully advanced in the father's lifetime" so that the duty to support had already been fully discharged: see *Grey v Grey* (1677) 2 Swans 594 at 600–601; 36 E.R. 742 at 744 per Lord Nottingham. The absence of such a duty on a mother to a child was given in *Bennet v Bennet* (1879) 10 Ch. D. 474 as a reason not to apply the presumption of advancement in such cases. For consideration of this, and other possible rationales for the presumption of advancement, see J. Glister, "The Presumption of Advancement" in Mitchell (ed.), *Constructive and Resulting Trusts* (2010).

the financial wherewithal to advance their children in life, nor to think that husbands but not wives have the duty and means to benefit their spouses.

The outdated nature of the presumption of advancement has not escaped the attention of Parliament, which has enacted legislation to abolish it, although this has not been brought into force and the passing of time, and the swing of the political pendulum, makes it appear ever less likely that it will do so. **14–045**

### Equality Act 2010 s.199

(1) The presumption of advancement (by which, for example, a husband is presumed to be making a gift to his wife if he transfers property to her, or purchases property in her name) is abolished. **14–046**
(2) The abolition by subsection (1) of the presumption of advancement does not have effect in relation to—
 (a) anything done before the commencement of this section, or
 (b) anything done pursuant to any obligation incurred before the commencement of this section.

Even if this section is not brought into force, it would be no surprise if the courts were to redress the present inequality of treatment by doing away with presumptions of advancement between spouses altogether, since the strength of the presumption between husband and wife is now said to be very weak.[102] Moreover, the gender bias inherent in the rules affecting spouses probably contravenes art.5 of the Seventh Protocol to the European Convention of Human Rights, which asserts the equality of spousal rights and responsibilities.[103] Similarly, Lord Neuberger in *Laskar v Laskar* considered the possibility that the presumption of advancement might apply as between a mother and a daughter, but noted that: "it was said as long ago as 1970 to be a relatively weak presumption which can be rebutted on comparatively slight evidence."[104] Any such presumption would be "even weaker where, as here, the child was over 18 years of age and managed her own affairs at the time of the transaction."[105] So, even if the presumption were said to apply, it would have been rebutted on the facts of the case, where property was jointly purchased by mother and daughter as "an investment for rental income and capital appreciation",[106] and so a resulting trust arose to reflect the contribution to the purchase price made by the mother. **14–047**

The legislative solution offered by s.199 is more radical, as it abolishes all presumptions of advancement, including that between a father (and possibly a mother) and a child. It should be remembered, however, that, in such circumstances, the particular relationship between A and B will clearly be an important factor to be taken into account by a court in determining whether or not a gratuitous transfer by A was intended to take effect as a trust for A. For example, it has been said that although the question whether the presumption arises between mother and child is uncertain, this is "of little **14–048**

---

102 *Pettitt v Pettitt* [1970] A.C. 777 at 793; *McGrath v Wallis* [1995] 2 F.L.R. 114 at 155; *Ali v Khan* (2002) 5 I.T.E.L.R. 232 at [30]. In *Bhura v Bhura* [2015] 1 F.L.R. 153, the presumption of advancement between spouses was said to be "on its death-bed" given the passing of s.199 of the Equality Act 2010.

103 Written Answer, *Hansard*, HL Vol.588, col.197 (21 April 1998). Note however that the UK has not yet ratified the Seventh Protocol.

104 [2008] 1 W.L.R. 2695 (CA) at [20], citing Lord Upjohn in *Pettitt v Pettitt* [1970] A.C. 777 at 814.

105 Note too that in *Pecore v Pecore* [2007] 1 S.C.R. 795 and *Madsen Estate v Saylor* [2007] 1 S.C.R. 838, the Supreme Court of Canada has held that the presumption of advancement should no longer apply to transfers by parents to their adult children. See, e.g. *Pecore* at [36] per Rothstein J: "[I]t is common nowadays for ageing parents to transfer their assets into joint account with their adult children in order to have that child assist them in managing their financial affairs. There should therefore be a rebuttable presumption that the adult child is holding the property in trust for the ageing parent to facilitate the free and efficient management of that parent's affairs."

106 [2008] 1 W.L.R. 2695 at [17].

practical importance, since very slight intention is sufficient to establish advancement, there being very little additional motive required beyond the mother/child relationship to induce a mother to make a gift to her child."[107] The question of the scope of the presumption of advancement remains relevant only as a result of the unfortunate approach currently taken to illegality: much can still turn "upon the precise family relationship" between the parties, "so that, for example, distinctions between a wife or partner, a child or brother become central", when the courts are asked to determine "the enforceability of a transaction between two parties implicated in illegal purpose".[108] To this we shall now turn.

## v. The Presumptions and Improper Purposes

14–049 The analysis so far has suggested that very little practical purpose is served by either the presumption of resulting trust or the presumption of advancement: in any case where a Type (A) resulting trust might arise, a court simply needs to establish whether or not A could objectively have been understood to have intended B to hold the right acquired on trust for A. The presumptions will therefore be useful only in the rare case where there is no relevant evidence as to A's intentions. The presumptions have, however, come to be very important in cases where the evidence on which A would have to rely to establish such an intention involves reference to an achieved improper purpose. This position, it is submitted, is unfortunate, but the analysis on which it depends, put forward by a majority of the House of Lords in *Tinsley v Milligan*,[109] has recently been confirmed by the Supreme Court.[110]

### *Tinsley v Milligan*

### House of Lords [1994] 1 A.C. 340

14–050 Stella Tinsley and Kathleen Milligan, a cohabiting couple, jointly purchased a house which they registered only in Tinsley's name to enable Milligan (with the knowledge and assent of Tinsley) to make false social security benefit claims for the benefit of both of them. Their relationship ended after four years, when Tinsley moved out. She claimed possession of the house as legal owner, and Milligan counterclaimed for an order for sale and a declaration that the house was held by Tinsley on trust for the two of them in equal shares. Milligan confessed her fraud to the Department of Social Security (the DSS) with whom she made her peace, and thereafter was paid benefit on a lawful basis. Tinsley was prosecuted, convicted, and fined, and had to make some repayment to the Department. The question for the House of Lords was as to the effect of the carrying out of this illegal transaction on Milligan's claim to an interest under a trust.

14–051 LORD BROWNE-WILKINSON (with whom LORD JAUNCEY and LORD LOWRY agreed, but with whom LORD KEITH and LORD GOFF disagreed): My Lords, I agree with the speech of my noble and learned friend, Lord Goff of Chieveley, that the consequences of being a party to an illegal transaction cannot depend, as the majority in the Court of Appeal held, on such an imponderable factor as the extent to which the public conscience would be affronted by recognising rights created by illegal transactions. However, I have the misfortune to disagree with him as to the correct principle to be applied in a case where equitable property rights are acquired as a result of an illegal transaction.

14–052 Neither at law nor in equity will the court enforce an illegal contract which has been partially, but not fully, performed. However, it does not follow that all acts done under a partially performed contract are of no effect. In particular it is now clearly established that at law (as opposed to in equity), property in goods or land can pass under, or pursuant to, such a contract. If so, the rights of the owner of the legal title thereby acquired will be enforced, provided that the plaintiff can establish such title without pleading or leading evidence of the illegality. It is said that the property lies where it falls, even though legal title

[107] *Crown Prosecution Service v Malik* [2003] EWHC 660 (Admin) at [27] per Richards J.
[108] *Collier v Collier* (2002) 6 I.T.E.L.R. 270, at [97], per Mance LJ.
[109] [1994] 1 A.C. 340.
[110] See the extract below from *Les Laboratoires Servier v Apotex Inc* [2015] A.C. 430.

to the property was acquired as a result of the property passing under the illegal contract itself. I will first consider the modern authorities laying down the circumstances under which a legal proprietary interest acquired under an illegal transaction will be enforced by the courts. I will then consider whether the courts adopt a different attitude to equitable proprietary interests so acquired. . . .

From these authorities the following propositions emerge: (1) property in chattels and land can pass under a contract which is illegal and therefore would have been unenforceable as a contract; (2) a plaintiff can at law enforce property rights so acquired provided that he does not need to rely on the illegal contract for any purpose other than providing the basis of his claim to a property right; (3) it is irrelevant that the illegality of the underlying agreement was either pleaded or emerged in evidence: if the plaintiff has acquired legal title under the illegal contract that is enough. **14–053**

I have stressed the common law rules as to the impact of illegality on the acquisition and enforcement of property rights because it is the appellant's contention that different principles apply in equity. In particular it is said that equity will not aid Miss Milligan to assert, establish or enforce an equitable, as opposed to a legal, proprietary interest since she was a party to the fraud on the DSS. The house was put in the name of Miss Tinsley alone (instead of joint names) to facilitate the fraud. Therefore, it is said, Miss Milligan does not come to equity with clean hands: consequently, equity will not aid her. **14–054**

Most authorities to which we were referred deal with enforcing proprietary rights under a trust: I will deal with them in due course. But before turning to them, I must point out that if Miss Tinsley's argument is correct, the results would be far reaching and, I suggest, very surprising. There are many proprietary rights, apart from trusts, which are only enforceable in equity. For example, an agreement for a lease under which the tenant has entered is normally said to be as good as a lease, since under such an agreement equity treats the lease as having been granted and the "lessee" as having a proprietary interest enforceable against the whole world except the bona fide purchaser for value without notice. . . . **14–055**

In my judgment to draw such distinctions between property rights enforceable at law and those which require the intervention of equity would be surprising. More than 100 years has elapsed since the administration of law and equity became fused. The reality of the matter is that, in 1993, English law has one single law of property made up of legal and equitable interests. Although for historical reasons legal estates and equitable estates have differing incidents, the person owning either type of estate has a right of property, a right in rem not merely a right in personam. If the law is that a party is entitled to enforce a property right acquired under an illegal transaction, in my judgment the same rule ought to apply to any property right so acquired, whether such right is legal or equitable. **14–056**

In the present case, Miss Milligan claims under a resulting or implied trust. The court below have found, and it is not now disputed, that apart from the question of illegality Miss Milligan would have been entitled in equity to a half share in the house in accordance with the principles exemplified in *Gissing v Gissing*;[111] *Grant v Edwards*;[112] and *Lloyds Bank plc v Rosset*.[113] The creation of such an equitable interest does not depend upon a contractual obligation but on a common intention acted upon by the parties to their detriment. It is a development of the old law of resulting trust under which, where two parties have provided the purchase money to buy a property which is conveyed into the name of one of them alone, the latter is presumed to hold the property on a resulting trust for both parties in shares proportionate to their contributions to the purchase price. In arguments, no distinction was drawn between strict resulting trusts and a *Gissing v Gissing* type of trust. **14–057**

A presumption of resulting trust also arises in equity when A transfers personalty or money to B.[114] Before 1925, there was also a presumption of resulting trust when land was voluntarily transferred by A to B: it is arguable, however, that the position has been altered by the 1925 property legislation.[115] The presumption of a resulting trust is, in my view, crucial in considering the authorities. On that presumption (and on the contrary presumption of advancement) hinges the answer to the crucial question "does a plaintiff claiming under a resulting trust have to rely on the underlying illegality?" Where the presumption of resulting trust applies, the plaintiff does not have to rely on the illegality. If he proves that the property is vested **14–058**

---

111 [1971] A.C. 886.

112 [1986] Ch. 638.

113 [1991] 1 A.C. 107.

114 See *Snell's Equity*, 29th edn (1990), pp.183–184; *Standing v Bowring* (1885) 31 Ch.D. 282 at 287, per Cotton L.J.; and *Dewar v Dewar* [1975] 1 W.L.R. 1532 at 1537.

115 See *Snell's Equity*, p.182.

in the defendant alone but that the plaintiff provided part of the purchase money, or voluntarily transferred the property to the defendant, the plaintiff establishes his claim under a resulting trust unless either the contrary presumption of advancement displaces the presumption of resulting trust or the defendant leads evidence to rebut the presumption of resulting trust. Therefore, in cases where the presumption of advancement does not apply, a plaintiff can establish his equitable interest in the property without relying in any way on the underlying illegal transaction. In this case Miss Milligan as defendant simply pleaded the common intention that the property should belong to both of them and that she contributed to the purchase price: she claimed that in consequence the property belonged to them equally. To the same effect was her evidence in chief. Therefore Miss Milligan was not forced to rely on the illegality to prove her equitable interest. Only in the reply and the course of Miss Milligan's cross-examination did such illegality emerge: it was Miss Tinsley who had to rely on that illegality.

**14–059** Although the presumption of advancement does not directly arise for consideration in this case, it is important when considering the decided cases to understand its operation. On a transfer from a man to his wife, children or others to whom he stands in loco parentis, equity presumes an intention to make a gift. Therefore in such a case, unlike the case where the presumption of resulting trust applies, in order to establish any claim the plaintiff has himself to lead evidence sufficient to rebut the presumption of gift and in so doing will normally have to plead, and give evidence of, the underlying illegal purpose.

**14–060** Against this background, I turn to consider the authorities dealing with the position in equity where A transferred property to B for an illegal purpose. The earlier authorities, primarily Lord Eldon, support the appellant's proposition that equity will not aid a plaintiff who has transferred property to another for an illegal purpose. . . .

**14–061** [His Lordship reviewed various authorities, and then continued:] During the 19th century, there was originally a difference of view as to whether a transaction entered into for an illegal purpose would be enforced at law or in equity if the party had repented of his illegal purpose before it had been put into operation, i.e. the doctrine of locus poenitentiae. It was eventually recognised both at law and in equity that if the plaintiff had repented before the illegal purpose was carried through, he could recover his property.[116] The principle of locus poenitentiae is in my judgment irreconcilable with any rule that where property is transferred for an illegal purpose no equitable proprietary right exists. The equitable right, if any, must arise at the time at which the property was voluntarily transferred to the third party or purchased in the name of the third party. The existence of the equitable interest cannot depend upon events occurring after that date. Therefore if, under the principle of locus poenitentiae, the courts recognise that an equitable interest did arise out of the underlying transaction, the same must be true where the illegal purpose was carried through. The carrying out of the illegal purpose cannot, by itself, destroy the pre-existing equitable interest. The doctrine of locus poenitentiae therefore demonstrates that the effect of illegality is not to prevent a proprietary interest in equity from arising or to produce a forfeiture of such right: the effect is to render the equitable interest unenforceable in certain circumstances. The effect of illegality is not substantive but procedural. The question therefore is, "In what circumstances will equity refuse to enforce equitable rights which undoubtedly exist."

**14–062** It is against this background that one has to assess the more recent law. Although in the cases decided during the last 100 years there are frequent references to Lord Eldon's wide principle, with one exception . . . none of the English decisions are decided by simply applying that principle. They are all cases where the unsuccessful party was held to be precluded from leading evidence of an illegal situation in order to rebut the presumption of advancement. Lord Eldon's rule would have provided a complete answer whether the transfer was made to a wife or child (where the presumption of advancement would apply) or to a stranger. Yet with one exception none of the cases in this century has been decided on that simple basis.

**14–063** The majority of cases have been those in which the presumption of advancement applied: in those authorities the rule has been stated as being that a plaintiff cannot rely on evidence of his own illegality to rebut the presumption applicable in such cases that the plaintiff intended to make a gift of the property to the transferee. Thus in *Gascoigne v Gascoigne*;[117] *McEvoy v Belfast Banking Co Ltd*;[118] *Re Emery's Investments*

[116] See *Taylor v Bowers* (1876) 1 Q.B.D. 291; *Symes v Hughes* (1870) L.R. 9 Eq. 475.
[117] [1918] 1 K.B. 223.
[118] [1934] N.I. 67.

*Trusts*;[119] *Chettiar v Chettiar*;[120] and *Tinker v Tinker*,[121] the crucial point was said to be the inability of the plaintiff to lead evidence rebutting the presumption of advancement. In each case the plaintiff was claiming to recover property voluntarily transferred to, or purchased in the name of, a wife or child, for an illegal purpose. Although reference was made to Lord Eldon's principle, none of those cases was decided on the simple ground (if it were good law) that equity would not in any circumstances enforce a resulting trust in such circumstances. On the contrary in each case the rule was stated to be that the plaintiff could not recover because he had to rely on the illegality to rebut the presumption of advancement.

In my judgment, the explanation for this departure from Lord Eldon's absolute rule is that the fusion of law and equity has led the courts to adopt a single rule (applicable both at law and in equity) as to the circumstances in which the court will enforce property interests acquired in pursuance of an illegal transaction, viz., the *Bowmakers* rule.[122] A party to an illegality can recover by virtue of a legal or equitable property interest if, but only if, he can establish his title without relying on his own illegality. In cases where the presumption of advancement applies, the plaintiff is faced with the presumption of gift and therefore cannot claim under a resulting trust unless and until he has rebutted that presumption of gift: for those purposes the plaintiff does have to rely on the underlying illegality and therefore fails. **14–064**

The position is well illustrated by two decisions in the Privy Council [*Singh v Ali*[123] and *Chettiar v Chettiar*[124]]. . . . In my judgment these two cases show that the Privy Council was applying exactly the same principle in both cases although in one case the plaintiff's claim rested on a legal title and in the other on an equitable title. The claim based on the equitable title did not fail simply because the plaintiff was a party to the illegal transaction; it only failed because the plaintiff was bound to disclose and rely upon his own illegal purpose in order to rebut the presumption of advancement. The Privy Council was plainly treating the principle applicable both at law and in equity as being that a man can recover property provided that he is not forced to rely on his own illegality. **14–065**

I therefore reach the conclusion that, although there is no case overruling the wide principle stated by Lord Eldon, as the law has developed the equitable principle has become elided into the common law rule. In my judgment the time has come to decide clearly that the rule is the same whether a plaintiff founds himself on a legal or equitable title: he is entitled to recover if he is not forced to plead or rely on the illegality, even if it emerges that the title on which he relied was acquired in the course of carrying through an illegal transaction. **14–066**

As applied in the present case, that principle would operate as follows. Miss Milligan established a resulting trust by showing that she had contributed to the purchase price of the house and that there was common understanding between her and Miss Tinsley that they owned the house equally. She had no need to allege or prove why the house was conveyed into the name of Miss Tinsley alone, since that fact was irrelevant to her claim: it was enough to show that the house was in fact vested in Miss Tinsley alone. The illegality only emerged at all because Miss Tinsley sought to raise it. Having proved these facts, Miss Milligan had raised a presumption of resulting trust. There was no evidence to rebut that presumption. Therefore Miss Milligan should succeed. This is exactly the process of reasoning adopted by the Ontario Court of Appeal in *Gorog v Kiss*[125] which in my judgment was rightly decided. **14–067**

### *Les Laboratoires Servier v Apotex Inc*

### Supreme Court [2015] A.C. 430

The facts of the case did not raise any issues as to trusts. The effect of illegality on a claim was however a key issue. Dissatisfaction had been expressed with the test adopted by the majority in *Tinsley v Milligan*, and the Supreme Court considered whether that relatively rigid test should be replaced with a more flexible approach. Lord Sumption however affirmed Lord Browne-Wilkinson's approach in *Tinsley*. **14–068**

LORD SUMPTION (with whom LORD NEUBERGER and LORD CLARKE agreed): English law has a **14–069**

---

119 [1959] Ch. 410.
120 [1962] A.C. 294.
121 [1970] P. 136 at 141, 142.
122 [1945] K.B. 65.
123 [1960] A.C. 167.
124 [1962] A.C. 294.
125 (1977) 78 D.L.R. (3d) 690.

long-standing repugnance for claims which are founded on the claimant's own illegal or immoral acts. The law on this point was already well established when Lord Mansfield C.J. articulated it in his celebrated statement of principle in *Holman v Johnson:*[126]

> "No court will lend its aid to a man who founds his cause of action on an immoral or an illegal act. If, from the plaintiff's own stating or otherwise, the cause of action appears to arise ex turpi causa, or [from] the transgression of a positive law of this country, there the court says that he has no right to be assisted. It is on that ground the court goes; not for the sake of the defendant, but because they will not lend their aid to such a plaintiff. So if the plaintiff and defendant were to change sides, and the defendant was to bring his action against the plaintiff, the latter would then have the advantage of it; for where both are equally in fault, potior est conditio defendentis."

. . . Lord Mansfield C.J.'s formulation begs many questions. But as these citations show, two features of this area of law have been characteristic of it from the outset. First, it is a rule of law and not a mere discretionary power. Secondly, it is based on public policy, and not on the perceived balance of merits between the parties to any particular dispute.

**14–070** The question what is involved in "founding on an immoral or illegal act" has given rise to a large body of inconsistent authority which rarely rises to the level of general principle. The main reason for the disordered state of the case law is the distaste of the courts for the consequences of applying their own rules, consequences which Lord Mansfield C.J. had pointed out two centuries ago. The only rational way of addressing this problem, if these consequences are regarded as intolerable, is to transform the rule into a mere power whose actual exercise would depend on the perceived equities of each case. . .This development had been foreshadowed by some earlier decisions of the Court of Appeal. But it was decisively rejected by the House of Lords in *Tinsley v Milligan* . . .In the House of Lords, the Committee was divided on the correct test as well as on the correct result. But it was unanimous in rejecting the public conscience test, on the ground that it was unprincipled. The leading speech on this point was that of Lord Goff of Chieveley [who] acknowledged that:[127]

> "The real criticism of the present rules is not that they are unprincipled, but rather that they are indiscriminate in their effect, and are capable therefore of producing injustice."

**14–071** Indeed, in the case before him, he regarded the claimant's misconduct as "relatively minor" and pointed out that she had already made amends for it by repaying the sums dishonestly obtained in social security benefits. However, he considered that the illegality defence was governed by "established rules of law".[128] Endorsing the view of Ralph Gibson L.J. in the passage from which I have cited above, he rejected,[129] the public conscience test as contrary to 200 years of authority, because it required the court to:

> "weigh, or balance, the adverse consequences of respectively granting or refusing relief. This is little different, if at all, from stating that the court has a discretion whether to grant or refuse relief. It is very difficult to reconcile such a test with the principle of policy stated by Lord Mansfield C.J. in *Holman v Johnson* . . .or with the established principles to which I have referred."

Its adoption, he said:[130]

> "would constitute a revolution in this branch of the law, under which what is in effect a discretion would become vested in the court to deal with the matter by the process of a balancing operation, in place of a system of rules, ultimately derived from the principle of public policy enunciated by Lord Mansfield C.J. in *Holman v Johnson.*"

As he pointed out,[131] short of treating the application of the rule as discretionary, it is difficult to make a principled distinction between degrees of iniquity.

---

126 (1775) 1 Cowp. 341 at 343.
127 [1994] 1 A.C. 340 at 364.
128 *Tinsley* at 364.
129 *Tinsley* at 358.
130 *Tinsley* at 363.
131 *Tinsley* at 362.

Lord Browne-Wilkinson, agreed with Lord Goff on this point, observing that:[132] 14–072

"the consequences of being a party to an illegal transaction cannot depend, as the majority in the Court of Appeal held, on such an imponderable factor as the extent to which the public conscience would be affronted by recognising rights created by illegal transactions."

The other members of the Committee all agreed with the speeches of Lord Goff and Lord Browne-Wilkinson on this point.

The House was divided on the question what should be substituted for the public conscience test. Lord Keith of Kinkel and Lord Goff favoured a rule which would bar any claim tainted by a sufficiently close factual connection with the illegal purpose, and would have dismissed the claim to an equitable interest in the house on that ground. Lord Browne-Wilkinson, with whom Lord Jauncey of Tullichettle and Lord Lowry agreed, preferred the "reliance test" derived from the decision of the Court of Appeal in *Bowmakers Ltd v Barnet Instruments Ltd*[133] and of the Privy Council in *Palaniappa Chettiar v Arunasalam Chettiar*.[134] The effect of this test was that the claim was barred only if the claimant needed to rely on (ie to assert, whether by way of pleading or evidence) facts which disclosed the illegality.[135] Both are intended to exclude those consequences of an illegal act which are merely collateral to the claim. Neither makes the application of the illegality defence dependent on a value judgment about the significance of the illegality or the consequences for the parties of barring the claim. For present purposes, it is enough to point out that neither test is discretionary in nature. Neither of them is based on achieving proportionality between the claimant's misconduct and his loss, a concept derived from public law which is not easily transposed into the law of obligations. On the contrary, Lord Goff recognised, as Lord Mansfield C.J. had before him, that the practical operation of the law in this field will often produce disproportionately harsh consequences. 14–073

The Court of Appeal was bound by *Tinsley v Milligan*, and we have not been invited to depart from it on this appeal. It was, however, suggested and accepted by Etherton L.J., that a wider view of the law was open to the courts in the light of Lord Hoffmann's observation in *Gray v Thames Trains Ltd* that[136]: 14–074

"the maxim ex turpi causa expresses not so much a principle as a policy. Furthermore, that policy is not based on a single justification but on a group of reasons, which vary in different situations."

I do not think that this dictum will bear the weight that has been placed on it. A court will commonly examine the policy rationale of a rule of law in order to discover what the rule is. This is what Lord Hoffmann was doing in the passage cited, which introduces an extended discussion of the "various rules" which the courts had evolved to deal with the dilemma that the denial of relief to one party would confer an unjustified benefit on the other. These rules did not seek to deal with the dilemma by leaving the court to make a value judgment about the seriousness of the illegality and the impact on the parties of allowing the defence. As Lord Hoffmann explained them, they dealt with it by defining as a matter of law when the illegality defence applied and when it did not. In Lord Hoffmann's view two rules were relevant where the illegality defence was raised in answer to a claim for compensation. There was a "narrower rule" that you cannot recover damage which is the consequence of a sentence imposed on you for a criminal act; and a wider rule that you cannot recover compensation for loss which you have suffered in consequence of your own criminal act. The former test operated automatically, once it was ascertained that the loss claimed was a penalty imposed by a criminal court or the necessary consequence of the sentence, such as loss of earnings during a period of imprisonment. The latter test was simply a question of causation. Neither the narrower nor the wider rule depended on the court's assessment of the significance of the illegality, the proportionality of its application or the merits of the particular case. Nor does anything else in the speeches justify a test which would include such an assessment. 14–075

*Tinsley v Milligan* has had its critics. The Law Commission in successive reports on the illegality defence made little secret of its preference for [a more flexible approach]. The Commission initially proposed the introduction of a statutory scheme adopting a discretionary approach to the application of the illegality defence, on the ground that the House of Lords' decision in *Tinsley v Milligan* had ruled out the development of judge-made law in that direction. They later withdrew that proposal, because recent decisions of 14–076

---

132 *Tinsley* at 369.
133 [1945] K.B. 65.
134 [1962] A.C. 294.
135 See Lord Browne-Wilkinson [1994] 1 A.C. 340 at 370 and 375–6; cf. Lord Jauncey, at 366.
136 [2009] A.C. 1339 at [30].

judges at first instance and in the Court of Appeal suggested to them that the effect of that decision was being eroded by lower courts.[137] In the latter report, the Commission observed that the public conscience test, although rejected in *Tinsley v Milligan*, was nevertheless:[138]

> "useful in suggesting that the present rules should be regarded as no more than guidance that help the court to focus its attention on particular features of the case before it. What lies behind these 'rules' is a set of policies. This is why the courts are sometimes required to 'bend' the rules (if possible) to give better effect to the underlying policies as they apply to the facts of the case before them."

**14–077** I confess that I find this difficult to justify as an approach to authority or the proper development of the law. It is directly inconsistent with the decision of the House of Lords in *Tinsley v Milligan* and the whole of the reasoning which underlies it. It makes the law uncertain, by inviting the courts to depart from existing rules of law in circumstances where it is difficult for them to acknowledge openly what they are doing or to substitute a coherent alternative structure. The present position was to my mind accurately stated by Lord Walker of Gestingthorpe when commenting on the Commission's original proposals in *Stone & Rolls Ltd v Moore Stephens*:[139]

> ". . . These proposals, if enacted by Parliament, would introduce more flexibility into this area of the law (although without reintroducing a general 'public conscience' discretion) . . .The present state of the law is as laid down by the majority of the House in *Tinsley v Milligan*. Any legislative change is likely to widen the test, not to narrow it."

**14–078** The current position where there is a Type (A) case can therefore be summed up as follows. If the presumption of advancement applies (e.g. where A transfers property to his wife or son) the onus is on A, if he wishes to claim a resulting trust, to produce evidence rebutting the presumption. If this requires A to rely on facts which disclose an achieved illegal purpose, the approach adopted in *Tinsley*, and approved in *Les Laboratoires Servier*, will prevent A from relying on such evidence, and A will be unable to enforce any trust.[140] But if the presumption of resulting trust applies, as in *Tinsley* itself, A can establish a trust by means of this presumption, without needing to bring any evidence of an illegal purpose. In such cases, then, the presumptions may prove decisive.

**14–079** In *Les Laboratoires Servier*, Lord Sumption, echoing Lord Goff's comments in *Tinsley*, noted that the approach taken to illegality can produce "draconian consequences. . .if it is applied too widely."[141] It should be noted that, even if the transfer from A to B was motivated by an illegal purpose, A will be prevented from bringing evidence of that purpose only if the illegal purpose was in fact achieved.[142] In *Tribe v Tribe*,[143] for example, A transferred shares to B, one of his children, as A was worried that he would have to sell those shares to meet possible claims against him. The illegal purpose of thus hiding assets from A's creditors had not, in fact been "wholly or partly carried into effect",[144] as those

---

137 See *The Illegality Defence: A Consultative Report* (L.C.C.P. No.189, 2009) at paras 3.104–3.105, 3.123–3.124.

138 At para.3.140.

139 [2009] A.C. 1391 at [130]–[131].

140 See, e.g. *Gascoigne v Gascoigne* [1918] 1 K.B. 223 (where there were existing creditors and where tax was paid on the basis that the bungalow belonged to the wife); *Re Emery's Investment Trusts* [1959] Ch. 410 (where it seems that American withholding tax was evaded).

141 [2015] A.C. 230 at [22].

142 The discussion here is premised on the validity of the transfer of legal title from A to B. It should be noted however that some statutes invalidate such transfers if undertaken with a view to defeating creditors: e.g. Insolvency Act 1986 ss.339–342 (transactions at an undervalue) and 423–425 (transactions defrauding creditors) allow for such transactions to be set aside in certain circumstances. Similarly, under s.37 of the Matrimonial Causes Act 1973, there is a jurisdiction to set aside dispositions made by A with the intention of defeating a spouse's claim to financial relief, and under the Inheritance (Provision for Family and Dependants) Act 1975, the court has power to make orders in relation to dispositions made by A, the deceased, other than for full valuable consideration and with the intention of defeating applications for financial provision.

143 [1996] Ch. 107.

144 [1996] Ch. 107 at 134, per Millett L.J. See too *Symes v Hughes* (1875) L.R. 9 Eq. 475; *Petherpermal Chetty v Muniandi Servai*

claims never materialised. As a result, A was permitted to rebut the presumption of advancement by bringing evidence that he intended B to hold the shares on trust for him.

Notwithstanding the vote of confidence recently given by the Supreme Court in *Les Laboratoires Servier* the current law appears to be seriously defective, both in terms of outcomes and process. Indeed, in *Bilta (UK) Ltd v Nazir (No.2)*,[145] the Supreme Court, sitting in a panel of seven, returned to the general topic of illegality. Lord Sumption again considered the law to have been correctly stated in *Tinsley*, but Lord Toulson and Lord Hodge instead preferred the approach of the majority of the Court of Appeal in *Tinsley*, according to which the court asks directly if it would be contrary to sound policy to admit a particular claim, and therefore has some flexibility in applying the illegality defence. Indeed, Lord Toulson and Lord Hodge considered that such an approach was supported by the decision of the Supreme Court in *Hounga v Allen*,[146] and that Lord Sumption, in his analysis in *Les Laboratoires Servier* had not given appropriate weight to that decision. Lord Neuberger did not take a position on that question, and stated that the issue would have to be reconsidered on another occasion, for the following reasons.[147] 14–080

*Bilta (UK) Ltd v Nazir (No.2)*

Supreme Court [2015] 2 W.L.R. 1168 at [15]—[17]

LORD NEUBERGER (with whom LORD CLARKE and LORD CARNWATH agreed): In my view, while the proper approach to the defence of illegality needs to be addressed by this court (certainly with a panel of seven and conceivably with a panel of nine Justices) as soon as appropriately possible, this is not the case in which it should be decided. We have had no real argument on the topic: this case is concerned with attribution, and that is the issue on which the arguments have correctly focussed. Further, in this case, as in the two recent Supreme Court decisions in the *Les Laboratoires* and *Hounga* cases, the outcome is the same irrespective of the correct approach to the illegality defence. 14–081

It would, in my view, be unwise to seek to decide such a difficult and controversial question in a case where it is not determinative of the outcome and where there has been little argument on the topic. In *Les Laboratoires*, the majority did opine on the proper approach not because it was necessary to decide the appeal, but because they considered that the Court of Appeal (who had reached the same actual decision) had adopted an approach which was inconsistent with *Tinsley*. Similarly in *Hounga*, as Lord Sumption has shown,[148] it may well not have been necessary to consider the proper approach to the illegality defence, but it none the less remains the fact that it was the subject of argument, and that Lord Wilson did express a view on the point, and two of the four other members of the court agreed with his judgment. 14–082

*Les Laboratoires* provides a basis for saying that the approach in *Tinsley* has recently been reaffirmed by this court and that it would be inappropriate for this court to visit the point again. However, it was not argued in *Les Laboratoires* that *Tinsley* was wrongly decided, and, as Lord Toulson pointed out in his judgment, the majority decision was reached without addressing the reasoning in *Hounga*. Lord Sumption is right to say that, unless and until this court refuses to follow *Tinsley*, it is at the very least difficult to say that the law is as flexible as Lords Toulson and Hodge suggest in their judgment, but (i) in the light of what the majority said in *Hounga*,[149] there is room for argument that this court has refused to follow *Tinsley*, and (ii) 14–083

---

(1908) 24 T.L.R. 462; *Perpetual Executors Association of Australia Ltd v Wright* (1917) 23 C.L.R. 185; *Martin v Martin* (1959) 110 C.L.R. 297; *Chettiar v Chettiar* [1962] A.C. 294 at 302; *Sekhon v Alissa* [1989] 2 F.L.R. 94; *Collier v Collier* (2002) 6 I.T.E.L.R. 270, esp. [103]–[107]. And for a case where the party wishing to invoke the doctrine had gone too far down the road, see *Q v Q* [2009] 1 F.L.R. 935 at [126]–[130].

145 [2015] 2 W.L.R. 1168.

146 [2014] 1 W.L.R. 2889.

147 See too Lord Mance at [34], stating that "This is not, in my view, the occasion on which to embark on any re-examination either of the House of Lords' decision in *Tinsley v Milligan* or of the Supreme Court's recent decisions in *Hounga v Allen* and *Les Laboratoires Servier v Apotex*. . .I agree however that these cases and their inter-relationship merit further examination by this court whenever the opportunity arises."

148 [2015] 2 W.L.R. 1168 at [99].

149 [2014] 1 W.L.R. 2889 at [42]–[43].

> in the light of the Law Commission report, *The Illegality Defence* (Law Com No 320, 2010), the subsequent decisions of the Court of Appeal, and decisions of other common law courts, it appears to me to be appropriate for this court to address this difficult and controversial issue—but only after having heard and read full argument on the topic.

**14-084** It is therefore clear that the law in this area is not in a happy state. The debate unfortunately makes the Supreme Court seem like a dysfunctional family, the members of which are compelled, on meeting up, to join again in a divisive and interminable argument. If a suitable case were to be fully enough argued in front of a large enough panel, what should the Supreme Court decide?

**14-085** The current position, as to outcomes, seems to be that, in a case such as *Tinsley*, as the presumption of resulting trust applies, A can claim the benefit of such a trust even after successfully practising a deceit based on A's having no interest in the relevant property.[150] In a case such as *Tribe*, even where the presumption of advancement operates, A can claim the benefit of such a trust if, by chance rather than as the result of any repentance of the illegal purpose, A has not in fact needed to put her planned deceit into practice. As to process, perhaps more importantly, the current approach means that great weight is placed on the location and operation of the presumptions even though, as we have seen, their general relevance is much reduced, and there is a strong argument that the law would manage better without them. As has been pointed out by the High Court of Australia,[151] the English Court of Appeal,[152] and the English Law Commission,[153] it is highly unsatisfactory to make a transferor's ability to recover property transferred for an illegal purpose turn on the essentially irrelevant question of whether or not he and the transferee are in a special relationship giving rise to a presumption of advancement. Matters are worsened by the fact that there is uncertainty as to which presumption applies to transfers from wife to husband and mother to child.

**14-086** It would certainly be unfortunate if the presumptions were retained solely in order to operate the current approach as to illegality. It can therefore be argued, contrary to the approach of Lord Sumption in *Les Laboratoires Servier*, that matters would be greatly improved if the law were amended in line with the Law Commission's recommendation, published in 1999, that there should be a structured statutory discretion to decide the effects of illegality on resulting trusts. Factors to be taken into account would be[154]:

> (a) the seriousness of the illegality; (b) the knowledge and intent of the illegal trust beneficiary; (c) whether invalidity would tend to deter the illegality; (d) whether invalidity would further the purpose of the rule which renders the trust 'illegal'; and (e) whether invalidity would be a proportionate response to the claimant's participation in the illegality.

No legislation was enacted in response to this recommendation, and in 2010, the Law Commission published another report[155] in which it noted that the courts had begun to develop a structured discretion to deal with illegality cases at common law,[156] and concluded that there is no need for general

---

150 This inconsistency is something which, it seems, Millett LJ was keen to avoid in *Tribe v Tribe* [1996] Ch. 107 at 129: "The transferor's own conduct would be inconsistent with the retention of any beneficial interest in the property" because "the only way in which a man can protect his property from his creditors is by divesting himself of all beneficial interest in it."

151 *Nelson v Nelson* (1995) 184 C.L.R. 538.

152 *Tribe v Tribe* [1996] Ch. 107 at 118; *Silverwood v Silverwood* (1997) 74 P. & C.R. 453 at 458–459; *Lowson v Coombes* [1999] Ch. 373 at 385; *Collier v Collier* (2002) 6 I.T.E.L.R. 270, at [105]–[106]. See too *Q v Q* [2009] 1 F.L.R. 935 at [138].

153 Law Commission, *Illegal Transactions: The Effect of Illegality on Contracts and Trusts* (Law Commission, 1999) Law Com. No.154, paras 3.19–3.24.

154 Law Commission, *Illegal Transactions: The Effect of Illegality on Contracts and Trusts*, para.8.63.

155 Law Commission, *The Illegality Defence* (TSO, 2010), Law Com. No.320, HC Paper No.412, (2010 Report).

156 *Stone & Rolls Ltd (In Liquidation) v Moore Stephens (a firm)* [2009] 1 A.C. 1391; *Gray v Thames Trains Ltd* [2009] 1 A.C. 1339.

legislation in this area. However, it still considered that more targeted legislation is needed to abolish the *Tinsley* reliance principle and give the courts a discretion to determine the effect of illegality on trusts; that conclusion is surely strengthened by the approach taken in *Les Laboratoires Servier*.[157]

## C. Justifying the Type (A) Resulting Trust

Three suggestions have been made as to the principle underlying Type (A) resulting trusts. 14–087

### i. A Response to A's Intention to Create a Trust

The first of these, which has the clearest support from the case-law, is that such trusts are based on A's intention (as objectively interpreted) that B should hold the property acquired on trust for A. In *Vandervell v IRC*, for example, Lord Upjohn identified the crucial question as being whether A intended B to "take beneficially or on trust".[158] 14–088

Academic support for this view as accurately representing the current basis of Type (A) resulting trusts has been provided by John Mee, who has noted that[159]: 14–089

> Although in most cases the courts do not spell out the nature of the presumption of resulting trust, this seems quite natural. The label 'presumption of resulting trust' is fairly self-explanatory . . . since it is a 'presumption that it was a trust and not a gift.'

It is also useful to look at cases where a presumption of advancement has been rebutted, as in such cases A must prove directly the fact presumed in other cases. In *Sidmouth v Sidmouth*, for example, in considering whether the presumption of advancement was rebutted as between a father and a son, Lord Langdale MR asked if there was "anything to manifest an intention to make the son a trustee for the father".[160]

This analysis of the nature of the Type (A) resulting trust has attracted some criticism. First, there is a practical concern that, in particular cases where a resulting trust has been recognised, A did not in fact have the intention that B should hold on trust for A.[161] In *Re Vinogradoff*,[162] for example, A transferred shares into the joint name of herself and her four-year old niece; a resulting trust arose although it may seem unlikely that A wished to make her niece a trustee. As John Mee has noted, however,[163] three points can be made in response: first, the result in *Re Vinogradoff* has itself been criticised[164]; secondly, A's plan in making the transfer was most likely to have been that she would have the benefit of the income from the shares during her lifetime, and B would then become solely entitled to the shares on A's death, so that, consistently with A's intentions, the right outcome should have been a resulting trust for A's lifetime only[165] (and not an absolute resulting trust as was found in the case); and thirdly, if A's plan was merely that B should be a passive nominee, there is in fact 14–090

[157] The interpretation given to *Stone & Rolls Ltd (In Liquidation) v Moore Stephens (a firm)* [2009] 1 A.C. 1391 by Lord Sumption in *Les Laboratoires Servier* is quite different from that adopted by the Law Commission in its 2010 Report.

[158] [1967] 2 A.C. 291 at 312. See too Briggs LJ, writing extra-judicially: "Resulting Trusts after *Prest*" (2014) 181 *ACTAPS Newsletter* 4, 6: "I suggest that the only underlying principle of law is that a resulting trust will be inferred or implied (where not imposed in express terms) where to do so would give effect to the common intention or understanding of the parties."

[159] J. Mee, "Presumed Resulting Trusts, Intention and Declaration" [2014] C.L.J. 86, 100.

[160] (1840) 2 Beav. 447, 454, quoting *Fowkes v Pascoe* (1875) L.R. 10 Ch. App. 343 at 352.

[161] This concern has been expressed by Chambers, *Resulting Trusts* (1997), pp.25–26.

[162] [1935] W.N. 68.

[163] Mee, "Presumed Resulting Trusts, Intention and Declaration" [2014] C.L.J. 86, 99.

[164] See, e.g. J. Penner *The Law of Trusts*, 8th edn (Oxford University Press, 2012), p.119, referring to the result in *Re Vinogradoff* as "atrocious".

[165] As was found in *Fowkes v Pascoe* (1875) L.R. 10 Ch. App. 343.

nothing unlikely about A having intended that B would, during A's life at least, hold on a bare trust for A.

14–091 The second criticism of the "intention to create a trust" analysis is a conceptual one. William Swadling has argued that A's intention alone cannot suffice to generate a trust, because her intention must be *expressed* through the specific means of a declaration of trust.[166] In response, however, it can be said that, in a Type (A) case, we are not dealing with a mere intention: there is also the fact of a transfer from A to B, and the court is attempting to establish the nature of that transfer. It does not seem unreasonable to look to the objective intention of A in attempting to answer the vital question of whether B takes the transferred property absolutely, or instead holds it on trust for A.[167]

### ii. A Response to A's Declaration of a Trust

14–092 Swadling has argued that where a Type (A) resulting trust arises as a result of a presumption, the fact presumed is not that A objectively intended B to hold on trust for A; it is rather that A declared such a trust. An important consequence of this view is that the underlying principle on which such trusts arise is therefore the same as that applied in express trusts: the trust arises because A successfully exercised her power to set up a trust. It follows that Type (A) resulting trusts can be justified on the same grounds as express trusts. As Swadling notes, however, the question remains whether, in the modern world, we should continue to presume such a declaration of trust simply because, for example, A has made a gratuitous transfer to B.

14–093 The principal difficulty with this view is that there is very little support in the case-law for the idea that, in a presumed resulting trust, the court is presuming that A did in fact declare a trust in A's favour.[168] Swadling relies on the analysis of Lord Nottingham in *Cook v Fountain*,[169] but as Mike McNair has shown in a thorough historical analysis of that decision, Lord Nottingham's analysis was quite unusual and may well have been skewed by a political desire to favour one of the parties. In any case, it is clear that the trust recognised in the case itself was not a resulting one, did not arise on a gratuitous conveyance, and was found as a result of circumstantial evidence rather than through the operation of a presumption. It is true that, in *Westdeutsche*, Lord Browne-Wilkinson expressly adopted an important point made by Swadling: the presumption of a resulting trust may be rebutted not only by evidence of intention to make a gift to B, but "by evidence of any intention inconsistent with such a trust".[170] This is, however, consistent with the first view of resulting trusts, as responses to A's intention to create a trust, as well as with the view that such trusts are responses to a declaration of trust by A.

14–094 The link drawn, on Swadling's view, between Type (A) resulting trusts and express trusts may also be a weakness. If such resulting trusts are simply presumed express trusts, and so are not truly imposed by law, the structure of the formality provisions governing trusts of land may be difficult to justify.[171] Whilst s.53(1)(b) of the 1925 Act prevents A from proving an oral declaration of trust of land, resulting trusts are expressly excluded from the scope of the formality rule by s.53(2) of the 1925 Act. This is simple to explain if such trusts arise by operation of law, rather than by means of a declaration,

---

166 W. Swadling, "Explaining Resulting Trusts" (2008) 124 L.Q.R. 72, 80.

167 For further defence of the "intention to create a trust" argument from Swadling's objection, see Mee, "Presumed Resulting Trusts, Intention and Declaration" [2014] C.L.J. 86 at 106–109.

168 As noted by Mee, "Presumed Resulting Trusts, Intention and Declaration" [2014] C.L.J. 86, 90–94.

169 (1733) 3 Swans. 585. See M. McNair, "*Coke v Fountaine* (1676)" in Mitchell & Mitchell (eds) *Landmark Cases in Equity* (2012).

170 [1996] A.C. 669 at 708.

171 This point is made by R. Chambers, "Is There a Presumption of Resulting Trust?" in Mitchell (ed.), *Constructive and Resulting Trusts* (2010), p.267, p.280. But cf. Mee, "Presumed Resulting Trusts, Intention and Declaration" [2014] C.L.J. 86, 105–06, who sees less force in this objection.

but it is harder to justify if at least some resulting trusts rest on a presumption that an express trust has been declared.

### iii. A Response to B's Unjust Enrichment at A's Expense

A third view of the reasons why Type (A) resulting trusts arise has been developed by Robert Chambers,[172] building on the work of Peter Birks,[173] and has been given some support, both judicially and extra-judicially, by Lord Millett.[174] On this view, each of Type (A) and Type (B) resulting trusts are imposed in order to reverse the unjust enrichment of the transferee at the transferor's expense.[175] Claims in unjust enrichment arise under English law when a defendant is enriched at the expense of a claimant in circumstances which make her enrichment unjust,[176] the question whether her enrichment is relevantly unjust being governed by "the binding authority of previous decisions", so that the courts do not have "a discretionary power to order repayment whenever it seems in the circumstance of the particular case just and equitable to do so".[177] **14–095**

On this view, resulting trusts are imposed not in response to A's actual or presumed intention to create a trust, or in response to a presumed declaration of trust by A, but rather in response to the fact that A (actually or presumably) did not intend to make a gift to B.[178] Intention can thus be said to play a negative, rather than a positive role. **14–096**

In contrast to the two views discussed so far, this view identifies a common underlying basis for each of Type (A) and Type (B) resulting trusts. It would also allow for such trusts to arise in further situations, in which it can also be said that B has been unjustly enriched by her receipt of property acquired at A's expense. As the question of unjust enrichment focuses on the intention of A alone, and does not require that A actually or presumably had a positive intention to create a trust, it may also seem to provide a readier explanation of cases such as *Re Vinogradoff*,[179] in which it may seem unlikely that A intended B to hold on trust. **14–097**

The principal difficulty with the unjust enrichment analysis is that it was rejected by the House of Lords in *Westdeutsche,* as can be seen in the extract set out below.[180] Lord Browne-Wilkinson's analysis ascribes a more positive role to the intention of A, which is consistent with **14–098**

---

172 See, e.g. Chambers, *Resulting Trusts* (1997), R. Chambers, "Resulting Trusts in Canada" (2000) 38 Alberta L.R. 378, reprinted (2002) 16 Tru. L.I. 104 and 138; R. Chambers, "Resulting Trusts" in A. Burrows and Lord Rodger (eds), *Mapping the Law: Essays in Memory of Peter Birks* (Oxford University Press, 2006); R. Chambers "Is There a Presumption of Resulting Trust?" in Mitchell (ed.), *Constructive and Resulting Trusts* (2010), p.267.

173 P. Birks, "Restitution and Resulting Trusts" in S. Goldstein (ed.), *Equity and Contemporary Legal Developments* (Hebrew University of Jerusalem, 1992), p.361.

174 See his judgments in *Air Jamaica v Charlton* [1999] 1 W.L.R. 1399 and in *Twinsectra v Yardley* [2002] 2 A.C. 164. Note too Lord Millett, "Restitution and Constructive Trusts" (1998) 114 L.Q.R. 399, 416; Lord Millett, "The Law of Restitution: Taking Stock" (1999) 14 Amicus Curiae 1, 7–8.

175 P. Birks, "Restitution and Resulting Trusts" in Goldstein (ed.), *Equity and Contemporary Legal Developments* (1992), p.361; Chambers, *Resulting Trusts* (1997); R. Chambers, "Resulting Trusts in Canada" (2000) 38 Alberta L.R. 378, reprinted (2002) 16 Tru. L.I. 104 and 138; R. Chambers, "Resulting Trusts" in A. Burrows and Lord Rodger (eds), *Mapping the Law: Essays in Memory of Peter Birks* (2006).

176 *Banque Financière de la Cité v Parc (Battersea) Ltd* [1999] 1 A.C. 221 at 227 and 234; *Sempra Metals Ltd v IRC* [2008] 1 A.C. 561 at [23].

177 *Kleinwort Benson Ltd v Birmingham CC* [1996] 4 All E.R. 733 at 737. See too *Sempra Metals Ltd v IRC* [2008] 1 A.C. 561 at [46]; *Test Claimants in the FII Group Litigation v HMRC* [2012] 2 A.C. 337 at [162]. For an excellent introductory account of the circumstances which render a defendant's enrichment unjust, see A. Burrows *The Law of Restitution*, 3rd edn (Oxford University Press, 2010), Chs 3–13.

178 Chambers, *Resulting Trusts* (1997), pp.19–27; P. Birks, *Unjust Enrichment* (Oxford University Press, 2003), pp.136–137.

179 [1935] W.N. 68; discussed at para.14–090. See too *Lench v Lench* (1805) 10 Ves. Jun. 511; *Childers v Childers* (1857) 1 De G. & J. 482.

180 See paras 14–174ff.

the view that a Type (A) resulting trust depends on A's having an actual or presumed intention to create a trust. His Lordship also stated that "a resulting trust arises in order to give effect to the intention of the parties".[181] It is less clear why B's intention should be relevant, but the point perhaps is that B's conscience can be said to be bound only if it was possible for B to have understood A's intention as being an intention to create a trust.[182] In either case, the focus of unjust enrichment analysis is misplaced, as it looks only to the question of A's absence of an intention to benefit B.

**14-099** From the perspective of principle, rather than of authority, the main objection to the unjust enrichment theory is that it proves too much. Pushed to its logical limits, it suggests that a resulting trust should arise whenever A transfers property to B, and her intention to benefit B is vitiated by mistake or undue influence, or is conditional on the happening of a future event which subsequently fails to materialise. That view was rejected in *Westdeutsche*: even though A's intention to make the transfer to B was vitiated by the mistaken belief that there was a valid contract between the parties, no resulting trust arose, as it was clear that A had never intended B to hold on trust for A. Indeed, in principle, it seems very doubtful that claimants in all these various situations of unjust enrichment should be given equitable proprietary rights and thus priority over the defendant's unsecured creditors, rather than a personal restitutionary remedy.[183]

**14-100** One way of dealing with this point, is to distinguish, as Chambers does, between cases where the basis for A's payment fails at some time after receipt of the benefit, and cases where it fails immediately, and to confine resulting trusts to the latter class of case, in which there is no moment when B has held the relevant asset free of any claim.[184] Another way of dealing with it might be to argue that unjust enrichment may give rise to a trust, but only if B's conscience is affected by B's awareness of the circumstances vitiating the transfer from A to B.[185]

**14-101** Certainly, the basic question of justification may be more difficult to answer on an unjust enrichment analysis than under either of the previous two analyses, as we have to explain not only why B is under a duty to A, but also why this duty takes the form of a trust. Even if it is accepted that A should have more than a merely personal right against B, it could still be argued that there is no need for an immediate trust. For example, a case in which A transfers property to B following an innocent misrepresentation by B can be seen as another example of unjust enrichment. In such cases, the standard response is that A acquires an equitable power to rescind the transaction: unless and until that power is exercised, A thus has a "mere equity". It might then seem strange to argue that an immediate trust should arise in the case where A makes a mistaken, gratuitous transfer to B.[186] Indeed, it may be that, whatever the outcome of the wider debate as to the circumstances in which unjust enrichment may

---

[181] "Constructive Trusts and Unjust Enrichment" (1996) 10 Tru L.I. 98, 99, echoed in *Tinsley v Milligan* [1994] 1 A.C. 340 at 371; *Westdeutsche Landesbank Girozentrale v Islington LBC* [1996] A.C. 669 at 708.

[182] See paras 14-004–14-013.

[183] Lord Millett, "Restitution and Constructive Trusts" (1998) 114 L.Q.R. 399, 416; Lord Millett, "The Law of Restitution: Taking Stock" (1999) 14 Amicus Curiae 1, 7–8.

[184] Chambers, *Resulting Trusts* (1997), pp.110 and 155–170. See too Birks, *Unjust Enrichment* (2003), pp.162–178; P. Birks, "Retrieving Tied Money" in W. Swadling (ed.), *The Quistclose Trust: Critical Essays* (Hart Publishing, 2004), pp.130–138. For possible examples of such immediate failure of basis, see, e.g. *Nesté Oy v Lloyds Bank Plc* [1983] 2 Lloyd's Rep.658, where to the knowledge of the payee no performance at all could have taken place under the contract for which the payment formed the consideration. See too *Re Ames' Settlement* [1946] Ch. 217; *Criterion Properties Plc v Stratford* [2004] 1 W.L.R. 1846 at [4]; *Re Farepak Food & Gifts Ltd* [2007] 2 B.C.L.C. 1, further proceedings [2010] 1 B.C.L.C. 444. It might also be possible to see *Sinclair v Brougham* [1914] A.C. 398 as such a case.

[185] See, e.g. B. McFarlane, *The Structure of Property Law* (Hart Publishing, 2008) pp.299–322.

[186] See further B. Häcker, "Proprietary Restitution After Impaired Consent Transfers: A Generalised Power Model" [2009] CL.J. 324.

give rise to a form of equitable property right,[187] Type (A) resulting trusts can be more easily explained on the classically accepted basis of A's intention to create a trust.[188]

## 3. Type (B) Resulting Trusts

### *A. Overview*

Lord Millett has written extra-judicially that[189]: 14–102

> Resulting trusts arise in three situations: voluntary payment or transfer; purchase in the name of another; and incomplete disposal of the beneficial interest. The first two have been described as 'apparent gifts'; the last as 'failing trusts'.

The "failing trusts" cases constitute the second type of resulting trust identified by Lord Browne-Wilkinson in *Westdeutsche*, and they arise, in his Lordship's words: "Where A transfers property to B on express trusts, but the trusts declared do not exhaust the whole beneficial interest."[190] These trusts have also often been referred to as "automatic resulting trusts",[191] although, as we will see,[192] Lord Browne-Wilkinson's speech in *Westdeutsche* warns of the dangers of the term "automatic", and so they will be referred to here as "Type (B) resulting trusts".

A simple example occurs in a case such as *Re Shaw*,[193] where George Bernard Shaw, in his will, 14–103
directed trustees to hold funds on trust for the purpose of undertaking research into the possibility of a 40-letter alphabet. As this purpose was found not to be charitable, his attempt to set up a purpose trust failed. It was clear, however, that the trustees were not intended to be free to use the funds for their own benefit. As a result, the funds were held on resulting trust for Shaw's estate.

An Important example, albeit arising on more complicated facts, is *Vandervell v IRC*,[194] the facts of 14–104
which have been explained in Chapter 3.[195] Shares were held on trust for Vandervell, and he directed that they be transferred to the Royal College of Surgeons, subject to an option to purchase the shares for a fixed sum. That option to purchase was granted to the Vandervell trustee company. It seemed clear that the trustee company was not intended to have the benefit of the option, but rather that it was intended to hold it on trust. It was not clear however who were the beneficiaries of the trust of the option. A majority of the House of Lords held that the option was held on resulting trust for Vandervell. In Lord Upjohn's view, it was simply a matter of "what is the proper inference to draw from the facts", with the most plausible interpretation being that, as no trusts had been declared of the option, the company should hold them on trust for Vandervell, subject to any trust that he might later declare.[196]

Such Type (B) resulting trusts therefore arise where property is transferred by an intending settlor 14–105

---

187 For useful but contrasting contributions to that wider debate, see, e.g. A. Burrows, "Proprietary Restitution: Unmasking Unjust Enrichment" (2001) 117 L.Q.R. 412; J. Penner, "Value, Property and Unjust Enrichment: Trusts of Traceable Proceeds" in R. Chambers et al. (eds), *Philosophical Foundations of the Law of Unjust Enrichment* (Oxford University Press, 2009).

188 See Mee, "Presumed Resulting Trusts, Intention and Declaration" [2014] CL.J. 86.

189 Lord Millett, "Pension Schemes and the Law of Trusts" (2000) 14 Tru L.I. 66, 73.

190 [1996] A.C. 669 at 706.

191 See, e.g. *Re Vandervell's Trusts (No.2)* [1974] Ch. 269 at 274 per Megarry J: such trusts arise "where the transfer to B [from A] is made on trusts which leave some or all of the beneficial interest undisposed of. Here B automatically holds on a resulting trust for A to the extent that the beneficial interest has not been carried to him or others."

192 See para.14–111.

193 [1957] 1 W.L.R. 729. See para.5–003.

194 [1967] 2 A.C. 291.

195 See paras 3–065—3–069.

196 [1967] 2 A.C. 291 at 315–317.

to trustees[197] on express trusts which fail, whether for failure of marriage consideration, uncertainty, lapse, disclaimer, perpetuity, illegality, non-compliance with requisite statutory formalities, or for any other reason.[198] They also arise if settlors fail to dispose exhaustively of the whole beneficial interest under their express trusts[199]: this would occur, for example, if a settlor transfers property to trustees to hold on trust for a life tenant, and does not specify any remainder interest. Where express trusts of funds subscribed by many settlors do not exhaust the funds there is a resulting trust in favour of the settlors rateably in proportion to the amounts subscribed by them.[200] Note, however, that in the case of charitable trusts that fail, the funds are often applied cy-près, a doctrine that we consider in Chapter 6.[201]

## *B. Finding a Type (B) Resulting Trust*

### i. General Principles

**14–106** Where an intending settlor A has transferred a property to B on trust, the crucial question is whether the trust is complete and therefore succeeds in "disposing of" or "exhausting" the entire beneficial interest. In some cases, as in *Re Shaw*, it is the operation of a legal rule that invalidates the planned trust and creates the potential space filled by the resulting trust. In other cases, the operation of a legal rule prevents such a gap occurring: there is no resulting trust, for example, if the doctrine of acceleration applies to prevent there being a temporary failure to exhaust the beneficial interest under a trust.[202] Thus, if A by will leaves property to B to hold on trust C for life and after C's death to D absolutely, and C disclaims her interest, D's interest is accelerated so as to take effect immediately, thereby ousting any possible resulting trust of the income until C's death. For the doctrine to apply the remainderman must have a vested interest and there must be no contrary intention manifested in the trust document.[203]

**14–107** Likewise, there is no resulting trust where the rule in *Hancock v Watson*[204] applies. This rule states that

> if you find an absolute gift to a legatee in the first instance, and trusts are engrafted or imposed on that absolute interest which fail, either from lapse or invalidity or any other reason, then the absolute gift takes effect so far as the trusts have failed to the exclusion of the residuary legatee or next-of-kin as the case may be.[205]

---

197 If a settlor declares herself trustee of a trust which fails, she will become absolute beneficial owner of the property once more. A resulting trust is not needed to accomplish this, and in fact would be impossible, as a person cannot be a trustee solely for her own benefit: *Westdeutsche Landesbank Girozentrale v Islington LBC* [1996] A.C. 669 at 703, per Lord Browne-Wilkinson.

198 *Hodgson v Marks* [1971] Ch. 892 at 933, per Russell LJ; *Re Ames's Settlement* [1946] Ch. 217 though see now ss.16 and 24 of the Matrimonial Causes Act 1973. If the settlor were a testator then the property would result to his estate: if the property were specifically devised or bequeathed it would fall into residue; if the property were comprised in the residuary gift then it would pass to the next-of-kin under the intestacy rules set out in the Administration of Estates Act 1925 as amended. On the impact of illegality, see paras 14–049ff.

199 *Re West* [1900] 1 Ch. 84; *Re Gillingham Bus Disaster Fund* [1958] Ch. 300.

200 See too *Re British Red Cross Balkan Fund* [1914] 2 Ch. 419 (where in the absence of the Attorney General a resulting trust was erroneously admitted); *Re Welsh Hospital Fund* [1921] 1 Ch. 655 at 662; *Re Hobourn Aero Components Ltd's Air Raid Disaster Fund* [1946] Ch. 194; *Air Jamaica Ltd v Charlton* [1999] 1 W.L.R. 1399 (for which, see paras 14–151—14–159.

201 See paras 6–298ff.

202 *Re Flower's Settlement Trusts* [1957] 1 W.L.R. 401.

203 *Re Scott* [1975] 2 All E.R. 1033.

204 [1902] A.C. 14. See too *Lassence v Tierney* (1849) 1 Mac. & G. 551.

205 *Hancock* [1902] A.C. 14 at 22 per Lord Davey.

The rule is equally applicable to inter vivos settlements.[206]

In many cases, the question of whether the trust is complete depends on a careful and fact-specific analysis of A's intentions. As we saw in Chapter 5,[207] for example, there may be a fine line between a case such as *Re Abbott*,[208] (where it was found that there was room for a resulting trust, as A had intended funds held on trust to be used for their benefit of the beneficiaries only whilst at least one of them survived) and a case such as *Re Osoba*,[209]in which there was no room for a resulting trust as A was regarded as having set up a trust for the benefit of three beneficiaries absolutely as joint tenants, so that the whole beneficial interest was disposed of by the terms of the initial transfer. **14–108**

Following *Barclays Bank Ltd v Quistclose Investments Ltd*,[210] it was thought that a resulting trust conforming to the pattern described here would also arise following the failure of a purpose trust to apply money lent for a specific purpose. However, *Quistclose* and subsequent authorities were reinterpreted in *Twinsectra Ltd v Yardley*[211] in such a way as to render thls analysis otiose, as Lord Millett stated that there was no initial purpose trust in those cases, but rather an immediate trust for the lender, subject to a power to apply the money to the purpose.[212] One view, however, that immediate trust can be seen as a Type (B) resulting trust, if it responds to the failure of the lender's intention to create a purpose trust.[213] **14–109**

There is no resulting trust for A on the failure of an express trust if B, the trustee, is expressly intended to take the property beneficially for herself, subject to a charge for some purpose. Thus, in *Re Foord*,[214] where a testator left his estate to his sister "absolutely . . . on trust" to pay his widow an annuity and the estate exceeded the annuity the slster was held beneficially entitled to the balance. **14–110**

There is an important question as to whether a Type (B) resulting trust can arise in a case where A has clearly indicated that she does *not* wish or intend such a trust to arise. In *Westdeutsche*, Lord Browne-Wilkinson disapproved of the term "automatic" as a description of such trusts, as he thought that: **14–111**

> If [A] has expressly, or by necessary implication, abandoned any beneficial interest in the trust property, there is in my view no resulting trust: the undisposed-of equitable interest vests in the Crown as bona vacantia: see *Re West Sussex Constabulary's Widows, Children and Benevolent (1930) Fund Trusts*.[215]

This "bona vacantia" solution means that B still holds on trust, but on trust for the Crown rather than A, with the Crown stepping in to avoid there being ownerless goods (the literal meaning of "bona vacantia"). We will consider the conceptual significance of this possibility below,[216] but it is first useful to note some specific contexts in which bona vacantia has been discussed, and to consider the *West Sussex* case relied on by Lord Browne-Wilkinson.

---

[206] *Attorney General v Lloyd's Bank* [1935] A.C. 382; *Re Burton's Settlement Trusts* [1955] Ch. 348; *Watson v Holland* [1985] 1 All E.R. 290.
[207] See paras 5–011—5–014.
[208] [1900] 2 Ch. 326.
[209] [1979] 2 All E.R. 393.
[210] [1970] A.C. 567. See too *Re ETVR* [1987] B.C.L.C. 646.
[211] [2002] A.C. 164.
[212] See paras 5–035ff.
[213] See *Twinsectra Ltd v Yardley* [2002] 2 A.C. 164 at [69] and [92].
[214] [1922] 2 Ch. 519. See too *Cook v Hutchinson* (1836) 1 Keen 42. But contrast the resulting trust in *Re West* [1900] 1 Ch. 84.
[215] [1996] A.C. 669 at 708.
[216] See paras 14–160—14–170.

## ii. Dissolution of Unincorporated Associations

**14–112** When an unincorporated association is dissolved it is necessary to ascertain whether its property falls to be distributed on a resulting trust to persons providing such property[217]; or on a contractual basis to the members of the association; or as bona vacantia to the Crown.

**14–113** The rules of an unincorporated association usually vest the assets of the association in trustees on trust for the members. However, this trust bears no relation to the members' claims to the surplus assets when the association is dissolved. So far as these are concerned, the old view[218] that they arise under resulting trusts has been totally discredited. It is now well established that the interests and rights of persons who are members of any type of unincorporated association are governed exclusively by contract.[219] Hence, if the rules of the association by which the members are contractually bound inter se provide for a particular method of distribution when the association is dissolved, this method will be used,[220] subject to the rights of third parties to share in the surplus assets.

**14–114** Third party rights to share in the fund will arise either by the duly authorised procedure in the association's constitution for creating contracts or express trusts, or by declarations of trust made by a donor at the time of transferring property to the association. However, to avoid invalidating a donor's declaration of trust for infringing the beneficiary principle or perpetuity rules, the courts tend to interpret such gifts not as declarations of trust, but as out-and-out gifts to the members as an accretion to the funds which are the subject-matter of the contract by which the members are all bound, inter se, with the result that such gifts will fall to be dealt with in just the same way as the funds which the members themselves have subscribed to the association's funds.[221]

**14–115** The present position is set out in *Re Bucks Constabulary Fund Friendly Society (No.2)*,[222] reproduced below. This decision should be preferred to *Re West Sussex Constabulary's Benevolent Fund*,[223] parts of which are also reproduced here, because it pays proper attention to the primacy of the members' contracts in determining beneficial entitlements to the assets of the association, as stipulated in *Re Recher's Will Trusts*.[224] Finally, however, we also reproduce part of Lewison J's judgment in *Hanchett-Stamford v Attorney General*,[225] where he considers the situation where an association becomes moribund because all the members but one have died, and refuses to follow Walton J's dictum in *Re Bucks (No.2)*, that in such a case the assets should be treated as bona vacantia and pass to the Crown.

---

217 As was the case, for example, in *Re St Andrew's (Cheam) Lawn Tennis Club Trust* [2012] 1 W.L.R. 3487. Although note there that, seemingly in order to reach a practically workable solution, Arnold J identified a specific party as having provided the property even though other, smaller contributions were made to its acquisition. For discussion see, e.g. T. Boncey & F. Ng (2014) 20 Trusts & Trustees 287.

218 *Re Printers and Transferrers Amalgamated Trades Protection Society* [1899] 2 Ch. 184; *Re Lead Co's Workmen's Fund Society* [1904] 2 Ch. 196.

219 *Tierney v Tough* [1914] 1 I.R. 142; *Re St. Andrew's Allotment Association* [1969] 1 W.L.R. 229; *Re William Denby Ltd's Sick Fund* [1971] 1 W.L.R. 973; *Re West Sussex Constabulary's Benevolent Fund Trusts* [1971] Ch. 1; *Re Sick & Funeral Society of St John's Sunday School* [1973] Ch. 51 (per capita basis but child members only to have a half share); *Re GKN Nuts and Bolts Ltd Sports and Social Club* [1982] 1 W.L.R. 774; *Re Bucks Constabulary Fund Friendly Society (No.2)* [1979] 1 All E.R. 623; *Boyle v Collins* [2004] 2 B.C.L.C. 471 at [26]–[27], per Lewison J, considering *Abbatt v Treasury Solicitor* [1969] 1 W.L.R. 561.

220 Otherwise, distribution will be on the basis of equality.

221 *Re Recher's Will Trusts* [1972] Ch. 526; *Re Lipinski's Will Trusts* [1976] Ch. 235. See generally paras 5–075ff.

222 [1979] 1 All E.R. 623.

223 [1971] Ch. 1.

224 [1972] Ch. 526 at 538–539. See paras 5–083—5–092.

225 [2009] Ch. 173.

*Re West Sussex Constabulary's Widows, Childrenand Benevolent (1930) Fund Trusts*

Chancery Division [1971] Ch. 1

In 1930 members of the West Sussex Constabulary established a fund to provide for their widows and orphans. In 1968 the West Sussex Constabulary was amalgamated with other forces, and the question arose how the assets of the fund should be dealt with. These came from (1) contributions of past and present members; (2) entertainments, raffles, sweepstakes; (3) collecting boxes; (4) donations and legacies. Goff J. held that (4) were held on resulting trusts for the donors while (1), (2), and (3) were bona vacantia. These holdings are now of doubtful value in view of *Re Bucks (No.2)*, but the following dicta are still good law. **14–116**

GOFF J.: I must now turn to the moneys raised from outside sources. Counsel for the Treasury Solicitor made an overriding general submission that there cannot be a resulting trust of any of the outside moneys because in the circumstances it is impossible to identify the trust property; no doubt something could be achieved by complicated accounting, but this, he submitted, would not be identification but notional reconstruction. I cannot accept that argument. In my judgment, in a case like the present, equity will cut the Gordian knot by simply dividing the ultimate surplus in proportion to the sources from which it has arisen. . . . There may be cases of tolerable simplicity where the court will be more refined, but in general, where a fund has been raised from mixed sources, interest has been earned over the years and income—and possibly capital—expenditure has been made indiscriminately out of the fund as an entirety, and then the venture comes to an end prematurely or otherwise, the court will not find itself baffled but will cut the Gordian knot as I have said. **14–117**

Then counsel divided the outside moneys into three categories, first, the proceeds of entertainments, raffles and sweepstakes; secondly, the proceeds of collecting-boxes; and, thirdly, donations, including legacies if any, and he took particular objections to each. **14–118**

I agree that there cannot be any resulting trust with respect to the first category. I am not certain whether Harman J. in *Re Gillingham Bus Disaster Fund*[226] meant to decide otherwise. In stating the facts he referred to "street collections and so forth".[227] In the further argument[228] there is mention of whist drives and concerts but the judge himself did not speak of anything other than gifts. If, however, he did, I must respectfully decline to follow his judgment in that regard, for whatever may be the true position with regard to collecting-boxes, it appears to me to be impossible to apply the doctrine of resulting trust to the proceeds of entertainments and sweepstakes and such-like money-raising operations for two reasons: first, the relationship is one of contract and not of trust, the purchaser of a ticket may have the motive of aiding the cause or he may not; he may purchase a ticket merely because he wishes to attend the particular entertainment or to try for the prize, but whichever it be, he pays his money as the price of what is offered and what he receives; secondly, there is in such cases no direct contribution to the fund at all; it is only the profit, if any, which is ultimately received and there may even be none. **14–119**

In any event, the first category cannot be any more susceptible to the doctrine than the second to which I now turn. Here one starts with the well-known dictum of P.O. Lawrence J. in *Re Welsh Hospital (Netley) Fund* where he said[229]: **14–120**

> "So far as regards the contributors to entertainments, street collections etc., I have no hesitation in holding that they must be taken to have parted with their money out-and-out. It is inconceivable that any person paying for a concert ticket or placing a coin in a collecting-box presented to him in the street should have intended that any part of the money so contributed should be returned to him when the immediate object for which the concert was given or the collection made had come to an end. To draw such an inference would be absurd on the face of it."

This was adopted by Upjohn J., in *Re Hillier's Trusts*[230] where the point was actually decided.

. . . In *Re Ulverston and District New Hospital Building Trusts*[231] Jenkins L.J. threw out a suggestion that there might be a distinction in the case of a person who could prove that he put a specified sum in a **14–121**

226 [1958] Ch. 300.
227 Ibid. at 304.
228 Ibid. at 309.
229 [1921] 1 Ch. 655 at 660.
230 [1954] 1 W.L.R. 9.
231 [1956] Ch. 622 at 633.

collecting-box, and, in the *Gillingham* case[232] Harman J. after noting this, decided that there was a resulting trust with respect to the proceeds of collections.

14–122 . . . [For] for my part I cannot reconcile the decision of Upjohn J. in *Re Hillier's Trusts* with that of Harman J. in the *Gillingham* case. As I see it, therefore, I have to choose between them. On the one hand it may be said that Harman J. had the advantage, which Upjohn J. had not, of considering the suggestion made by Jenkins L.J. On the other hand that suggestion with all respect, seems to me somewhat fanciful and unreal. I agree that all who put their money into collecting-boxes should be taken to have the same intention, but why should they not all be regarded as intending to part with their money out and out absolutely in all circumstances? I observe that P.O. Lawrence J. in *Re Welsh Hospital*[233] used very strong words. He said any other view was inconceivable and absurd on the face of it. That commends itself to my humble judgment, and I therefore prefer and follow the judgment of Upjohn J. in *Re Hillier's Trusts*.

### *Re Bucks Constabulary Fund Friendly Society (No.2)*

### Chancery Division [1979] 1 W.L.R. 936

14–123 The Bucks Constabulary Fund Friendly Society was established to provide for the relief of widows and orphans of deceased members of the Bucks Constabulary. It was an unincorporated association registered under the Friendly Societies Act 1896 but it had no rules providing for the distribution of its assets in the event of it being wound up. When it was wound up the question arose whether the surplus assets were bona vacantia passing to the Crown or whether they should be distributed among the members equally per capita or on some other basis.

14–124 WALTON J.: There are basically two claimants to the fund, the Solicitor for the Affairs of Her Majesty's Treasury, who claims the assets as ownerless property, bona vacantia, and the members of the friendly society at the date of its dissolution on 14th October 1969.

14–125 Before considering the relevant legislation . . . and the decided cases, it is I think desirable to view the question of the property of unincorporated associations in the round. If a number of persons associate together, for whatever purpose, if that purpose is one which involves the acquisition of cash or property of any magnitude, then, for practical purposes, some one or more persons have to act in the capacity of treasurers or holders of the property. In any sophisticated association there will accordingly be one or more trustees in whom the property which is acquired by the association will be vested. These trustees will of course not hold such property on their own behalf. Usually there will be a committee of some description which will run the affairs of the association; though of course in a small association the committee may well comprise all the members; and the normal course of events will be that the trustee, if there is a formal trustee, will declare that he holds the property of the association in his hands on trust to deal with it as directed by the committee. If the trust deed is a shade more sophisticated it may add that the trustee holds the assets on trust for the members in accordance with the rules of the association. Now in all such cases it appears to me quite clear that, unless under the rules governing the association the property thereof has been wholly devoted to charity, or unless and to the extent to which the other trusts have validly been declared of such property, the persons, and the only persons, interested therein are the members. Save by way of a valid declaration or trust in their favour, there is no scope for any other person acquiring any rights in the property of the association, although of course it may well be that third parties may obtain contractual or proprietary rights, such as a mortgage, over those assets as the result of a valid contract with the trustees or members of the committee as representing the association.

14–126 I can see no reason for thinking that this analysis is any different whether the purpose for which the members of the association associate are a social club, a sporting club, to establish a widows' and orphans' fund, to obtain a separate Parliament for Cornwall, or to further the advance of alchemy. It matters not. All the assets of the association are held in trust for its members (of course subject to the contractual claims of anybody having a valid contract with the association) save and expect to the extent to which valid trusts have otherwise been declared of its property. I would adopt the analysis made by Brightman J. in *Re Recher's Will Trusts*.[234] . . .

232 [1958] Ch. 300.
233 [1921] Ch. 655 at 661.
234 [1972] Ch. 526 at 538–539.

All this doubtless seems quite elementary, but it appears to me to have been lost sight of to some extent in some of the decisions which I shall hereafter have to consider in detail in relation to the destination on dissolution of the funds of unincorporated associations. **14–127**

Now in the present case I am dealing with a society which was registered under the Friendly Societies Act 1896. This does not have any effect at all on the unincorporated nature of the society, or (as I have in substance already indicated) on the way in which its property is held. But the latter point is in fact made very explicit by the provisions of s.49(1) of the 1896 Act which reads as follows: **14–128**

> "All property belonging to a registered society, whether acquired before or after the society is registered, shall vest in the trustees for the time being of the society, for the use and benefit of the society and the members thereof, and of all persons claiming through the members according to the rules of the society."

There can be doubt, therefore, that in the present case the whole of the property of the society is vested in the trustees for the use and benefit of the society and the members thereof and of all persons claiming through the members according to the rules of the society. I do not think I need go through the rules in detail. They are precisely what one would expect in the case of an association whose main purpose in life was to enable members to make provision for widows and orphans. Members paid a contribution in exchange for which in the event of their deaths their widows and children would receive various benefits. There is a minimal benefit for which provision is made in the case of a member suffering very severe illness indeed, but, as counsel for the Treasury Solicitor was able to demonstrate from an analysis of the accounts, virtually the entire expenditure of the association was, as indeed one would expect, on the provision of widows' and orphans' benefits. But, of course, there is no trust whatsoever declared in their favour. I am not called on, I think, to decide whether they are, within the meaning of s.49(1), persons claiming through the members according to the rules of the society, or whether they are simply the beneficiaries of stipulations by the members for the benefit of third parties. All parties are agreed that accrued rights of such persons must be given full effect. There is indeed no rule which says what is to happen to surplus assets of the society on a dissolution. But in view of s.49(1) there is no need. The assets must continue to be held, the society having been dissolved, and the widows and orphans being out of the way, simply for the use and benefit of the members of the society, albeit they will all now be former members. **14–129**

This indeed appears so obvious that in a work of great authority on all matters connected with friendly societies, *Baden Fuller*, the learned author says this[235]: **14–130**

> "If the rules provide for the termination of the society they usually also provide for the distribution of the funds in that event, but if on the termination of a society no provision has been made by the rules for the distribution of its funds, such funds are divisible among the existing members at the time of the termination or dissolution in proportion to the amount contributed by each member for entrance fees and subscriptions, but irrespective of fines or payments made to members in accordance with the rules."

In my judgment this accurately represents the law, at any rate so far as the beneficiaries of the trust on dissolution are concerned, although not necessarily so far as the quantum of their respective interests is concerned; a matter which still remains to be argued. The effective point is that the claims of the Treasury Solicitor to the funds as bona vacantia are unsustainable in the present case. I say "in the present case" because there are undoubtedly cases where the assets of an unincorporated association do become bona vacantia. To quote *Baden Fuller* again:[236] **14–131**

> "A society may sometimes become defunct or moribund by its members either all dying or becoming so reduced in numbers that it is impossible either to continue the society or to dissolve it by instrument; in such cases the surplus funds, after all existing claims (if any) under the rules have been satisfied or provided for, are not divisible among the surviving members . . . or the last survivor . . . or the representative of the last survivor . . . nor is there any resulting trust in favour of the personal representatives of the members of the society . . . not even in favour of honorary members in respect of donations by them . . . but a society which, though moribund, had at a testator's death one member and three annuitant beneficiaries, was held to be existing so as to prevent the lapse of a legacy

[235] *The Law of Friendly Societies* (4th edn, 1926), p.186.
[236] ibid., pp.186–187.

bequeathed to it by the testator. . . . In these circumstances two cases seem to occur: if the purposes of the society are charitable, the surplus will be applicable cy-près . . . but if the society is not a charity, the surplus belongs to the Crown as bona vacantia."

14–132 Before I turn to a consideration of the authorities, it is I think pertinent to observe that all unincorporated societies rest in contract to this extent, that there is an implied contract between all of the members inter se governed by the rules of the society. In default of any rule to the contrary, and it will seldom if ever be that there is such a rule, when a member ceases to be a member of the association he ipso facto ceases to have any interest in its funds. Once again, so far as friendly societies are concerned, this is made very clear by s.49(1), that it is the members, the present members, who, alone, have any right in the assets. As membership always ceases on death, past members or the estates of deceased members therefore have no interest in the assets. Further, unless expressly so provided by the rules, unincorporated societies are not really tontine societies, intended to provide benefits for the longest liver of the members. Therefore, although it is difficult to say in any given case precisely when a society becomes moribund, it is quite clear that if a society is reduced to a single member neither he, still less his personal representatives on his behalf, can say he is or was the society and therefore entitled solely to its fund. It may be that it will be sufficient for the society's continued existence if there are two members, but if there is only one the society as such must cease to exist. There is no association, since one can hardly associate with oneself or enjoy one's own society. And so indeed the assets have become ownerless.

14–133 [The judge referred to various cases and went on:] Finally . . . there comes a case which gives me great concern, *Re West Sussex Constabulary's Widows, Children and Benevolent (1930) Fund Trusts*.[237] The case is indeed easily distinguishable from the present case in that what was there under consideration was a simple unincorporated association and not a friendly society, so that the provisions of s.49(1) of the 1896 Act do not apply. Otherwise the facts in that case present remarkable parallels to the facts in the present case. Goff J. decided that the surplus funds had become bona vacantia. . . .

14–134 It will be observed that the first reason given by the judge for his decision is that he could not accept the principle of the members' clubs as applicable. This is a very interesting reason, because it is flatly contrary to the successful argument of Mr Ingle Joyce who appeared for the Attorney-General in the case Goff J. purported to follow, *Cunnack v Edwards*. His argument was as follows:[238]

> "This society was nothing more than a club, in which the members had no transmissible interest: *Re St James' Club*.[239] Whatever the members, or even the surviving member, might have done while alive, when they died their interest in the assets of the club died with them";

and in the Court of Appeal[240] he used the arguments he had used below. If all that Goff J. meant was that the purposes of the fund before him were totally different from those of a members' club then of course one must agree, but if he meant to imply that there was some totally different principle of law applicable one must ask why that should be. His second reason is that in all the cases where the surviving members had taken, the organisation existed for the benefit of the members for the time being exclusively. This may be so, so far as actual decisions go, but what is the principle? Why are the members not in control, complete control, save as to any existing contractual rights, of the assets belonging to their organisation? One could understand the position being different if valid trusts had been declared of the assets in favour of third parties, for example charities, but that this was emphatically not the case was demonstrated by the fact that Goff J. recognised that the members could have altered the rules prior to dissolution and put the assets into their own pockets. If there was no obstacle to their doing this, it shows in my judgment quite clearly that the money was theirs all the time. Finally he purports to follow *Cunnack v Edwards* and it will be seen from the analysis which I have already made of that case that it was extremely special in its facts, resting on a curious provision of the 1829 Act which is no longer applicable. As I have already indicated, in the light of s.49(1) of the 1896 Act the case before Goff J.[241] is readily distinguishable, but I regret that, quite apart from that, I am wholly unable to square it with the relevant principles of law applicable.

14–135 The conclusion therefore is that, as on dissolution there were members of the society here in question

---

237 [1971] Ch. 1.
238 [1895] 1 Ch. 489 at 494.
239 (1852) 2 De G. M. & G. 383 at 387.
240 [1896] 2 Ch. 679.
241 [1971 Ch. 1.

in existence, its assets are held on trust for such members to the total exclusion of any claim on behalf of the Crown. The remaining question under this head which falls now to be argued is, of course, whether they are simply held per capita, or, as suggested in some of the cases, in proportion to the contributions made by each. . . .

I think that there is no doubt that, as a result of modern cases springing basically from the decision of O'Connor M.R. in *Tierney v Tough*,[242] judicial opinion has been hardening and is now firmly set along the lines that the interests and rights of persons who are members of any type of unincorporated association are governed exclusively by contract, that is to say the rights between themselves and their rights to any surplus assets. I say that to make it perfectly clear that I have not overlooked the fact that the assets of the society are usually vested in trustees on trust for the members. But that is quite a separate and distinct trust bearing no relation to the claims of the members inter se on the surplus funds so held on trust for their benefit. 14–136

That being the case, prima facie there can be no doubt at all but that the distribution is on the basis of equality, because, as between a number of people contractually interested in a fund, there is no other method of distribution if no other method is provided by the terms of the contract, and it is not for one moment suggested here that there is any other method of distribution provided by the contract. We are, of course, dealing here with a friendly society, but that really makes no difference to the principle. The Friendly Societies Acts do not incorporate the friendly society in any way and the only effect that it has is, as I pointed out in my previous judgment in this case, that there is a section which makes it crystal clear in the Friendly Societies Act 1896 that the assets are indeed held on trust for the members. 14–137

. . .An ingenious argument has been put up by counsel for the third and fifth defendants, who are ad idem on this particular point, which runs very simply as follows: the members of the society are entitled in equity to the surplus funds which are distributable among them, therefore they are to be distributed among them according to equitable principles and those principles should, like all equitable principles, be moulded to fit the circumstances of the case, and in one case it would therefore be equitable to distribute in equal shares, in another case it might be equitable to distribute in proportion to the subscriptions that they have paid, and I suppose that in another case it might be equitable to distribute according to the length of their respective feet, following a very well known equitable precedent. Well, I completely deny the basic premise. The members are not entitled in equity to the fund: they are entitled at law. It is a matter, so far as the members are concerned, of pure contract, and, being a matter of pure contract, it is, in my judgment, as far as distribution is concerned, completely divorced from all questions of equitable doctrines. It is a matter of simple entitlement, and that entitlement, in my judgment, at this time of day must be, and can only be, in equal shares. 14–138

### *Hanchett-Stamford v Attorney-General*

### Chancery Division [2009] Ch. 173

In 1914 the Performing and Captive Animals Defence League was founded as an unincorporated association. Its purposes included bringing about a ban on performing animals. In 1949, following the decision in *National Anti-Vivisection Society v IRC*,[243] the Inland Revenue decided that the league did not have charitable status since its principal object was to change the law. Mr and Mrs Hanchett-Stamford joined the league as life members in the mid-1960s, and after her husband's death in 2006, Mrs Hanchett-Stamford was left as the sole surviving member. She decided to wind up the league and to transfer its assets to an active animal charity. Hence she sought a declaration that the work and objects of the league were charitable under the Charities Act 2006 s.2(2)(k) and an order appointing herself and her solicitor as trustees of the fund. Lewison J. refused the relief sought, holding that the league's purposes were not exclusively charitable because one of its objects was seeking a change in the law to ban performing animals. However he also held that on her husband's death the league had ceased to exist and its rules had ceased to bind Mrs Hanchett-Stamford, who was therefore entitled to its assets absolutely as its sole surviving member 14–139

LEWISON J. (after reviewing *Re Bucks (No.2)* continued): . . . There is, I think, no difficulty in accepting Walton J.'s ultimate conclusion. Nor is there any difficulty in accepting that the member's rights are 14–140

[242] [1914] I.R. 142.
[243] [1948] A.C. 31.

contractual rather than equitable. Nor is there any difficulty in accepting that on a member's death he ceases to have any interest in the assets of the unincorporated association. Accretion on death is inherent in the beneficial interest in any asset being held by joint tenants in equity; and is no doubt reinforced by contractual restrictions such as the rules of an association. It, therefore, follows that the estate of a deceased member can have no claim to the assets. In *Neville Estates Ltd v Madden*[244] Cross J. applied the same principle to cessation of membership through resignation. This must be a facet of the contractual relations between members. Walton J. also said that if there is only one member of an unincorporated association, it must cease to exist. That, too, must I think be right both for the reasons that Walton J. gave; and also because if the members' rights are based in contract, a contract must cease to bind once there is no other party who can enforce it.

**14–141** However, what I find more difficult to accept is that a member who has a beneficial interest in an asset, albeit subject to contractual restrictions, can have that beneficial interest divested from him on the death of another member. It leads to the conclusion that if there are two members of an association which has assets of, say £2m, they can by agreement divide those assets between them and pocket £1m each, but if one of them dies before they have divided the assets, the whole pot goes to the Crown as bona vacantia. Since Walton J. was not dealing with a case in which there was only one surviving member, his observations were obiter. Nor did he explain his reasoning on this question beyond the extract from his judgment that I have quoted.

**14–142** I must, I think, look a little more carefully at the authorities that are said to have this effect. In *Cunnack v Edwards*[245] a society was established to raise a fund, by the subscriptions, fines and forfeitures of its members, to provide annuities for the widows of its deceased members. There was also a category of honorary members. In 1848 Mr Edwards became an ordinary member and remained a member until his death in 1878, when he died a widower. He was the last surviving ordinary member. It appeared that all the other members had predeceased him, except Sir Vyvyan, an honorary member, and it was believed the only honorary member of the society. On joining the society he had signed a declaration that his object in joining the society was not that any widow of his should claim any benefit from it (to which he relinquished his right), but merely for the encouragement of the society. Sir Vyvyan died in 1879. The last annuitant had also died. Thus at the date when the matter came before the court there were no surviving members of the society and all the widows' pensions had been paid. The question was: what was to happen to the surplus funds. The two original claimants were the personal representatives of Mr Edwards and the Crown. The personal representatives of Sir Vyvyan made no claim. The Crown argued that the surplus was either held on charitable trusts and ought to be applied cy-près; or that the surplus was bona vacantia. Chitty J. held that the fund was not a charitable fund, and stood over the question of bona vacantia, giving leave to add as a party a representative of deceased members of the society generally. The argument for the Crown was:[246]

> "This society was nothing more than a club, in which the members had no transmissible interest . . . Whatever the members, or even the surviving member, might have done while alive, when they died their interest in the assets of the club died with them. The earlier deceased members have had all the benefit they bargained for when they joined—their widows have received their annuities. When Edwards was alive he and Sir R. Vyvyan might have dissolved the society in the statutory way and voted themselves the funds; but they did not do so. As a fact, Sir R. Vyvyan was the surviving member, and his representatives disclaim all beneficial interest; still he had just as much right to this fund as Edwards."

**14–143** Thus the argument for the Crown turned on the fact that at the date of the proceedings there were no surviving members, but it did not exclude the possibility that if there had been a surviving member that surviving member could have claimed the assets. Chitty J. dealt with the claim of the personal representatives of Mr Edwards as follows:[247]

> "The claim of the representative of the last surviving member may be disposed of in a few words. The society was not a tontine society, and there is no ground for saying that the fund belonged in equity to

244 [1962] Ch. 832.
245 [1895] 1 Ch. 489 and (on appeal) [1896] 2 Ch. 679.
246 [1895] 1 Ch. 489 at 494–495. (Emphasis added by Lewison J.).
247 At 496.

the last survivor. There is nothing in the rules, or in any principle of equity, applicable to the case on which this claim can be rested. It was said that the last surviving member might have held a meeting under section 26 of the statute of George IV, and voted the funds to himself. To this proposition, extravagant as it is, it is sufficient answer to say that the last survivor never attempted to do anything of the kind."

In the result Chitty J. held that the surplus was held on a resulting trust for its contributors. The case then went to the Court of Appeal. On appeal Mr Edwards's personal representatives abandoned his claim and the contest was between the deceased members generally on the one hand, and the Crown on the other. Counsel for the Crown repeated the same arguments that he had advanced before Chitty J., which included the passage I have emphasised. The Court of Appeal held that when each subscriber paid money to the society his entire beneficial interest in the money was exhausted. Lord Halsbury said:[248] **14–144**

"There never was and there never could be any interest remaining in the contributor other than the right that his wife, if she survived him, should become entitled to a widow's portion thus provided. This was the final and exhaustive destination of all the sums contributed to the common fund. Under these circumstances, I am at a loss to see what room there is for the contention that there is any resulting trust."

A.L. Smith L.J. said:[249] **14–145**

"As the member paid his money to the society, so he divested himself of all interest in this money for ever, with this one reservation, that if the member left a widow she was to be provided for during her widowhood. Except as to this he abandoned and gave up the money for ever."

Accordingly, the case turned on the circumstances in which the money was paid to the society. Thus the entirety of the bargain was that the money was to be used to pay widows' pensions, and not to return any part of the money to the contributor. On the facts, there were no surviving members of the association when the case came to court, so that the question before me did not arise; and the successful argument for the Crown admitted of the possibility that a single surviving member could during his lifetime claim the assets of the friendly society. In addition, as Walton J. pointed out in *Re Bucks Constabulary (No.2)*, the case concerned a friendly society and the legislation then in force required the rules to state all the uses applicable to the assets of the society, and they stated none in favour of members. I do not consider that this case is authority for the proposition that the sole surviving member of an unincorporated association, while still alive, cannot lay claim to its assets. Moreover although it was no doubt true, as Chitty J. held and as Walton J. emphasised, that the society was not a tontine society in the sense that it was not its intention to provide benefits for the ultimate survivor, any case in which property is held on a joint tenancy in equity produces a tontine effect, even if that is not its purpose. **14–146**

[He reviewed *Tierney v Tough*[250] and *Abbatt v Treasury Solicitor*,[251] then continued:] The thread that runs through all these cases is that the property of an unincorporated association is the property of its members, but that they are contractually precluded from severing their share except in accordance with the rules of the association; and that, on its dissolution, those who are members at the time are entitled to the assets free from any such contractual restrictions. It is true that this is not a joint tenancy according to the classical model; but since any collective ownership of property must be a species of joint tenancy or tenancy in common, this kind of collective ownership must, in my judgment, be a subspecies of joint tenancy, albeit taking effect subject to any contractual restrictions applicable as between members. In some cases (such as *Cunnack v Edwards*) those contractual restrictions may be such as to exclude any possibility of a future claim. In others they may not. The cases are united in saying that on a dissolution the members of a dissolved association have a beneficial interest in its assets, and Lord Denning M.R. goes as far as to say that it is a "beneficial equitable joint tenancy". I cannot see why the legal principle should be any different if the reason for the dissolution is the permanent cessation of the association's activities or the fall in its membership to below two. The same principle ought also to hold if the contractual restrictions are abrogated or varied by agreement of the members. I do not find in the authorities considered by Walton J. anything that binds me to hold that where there is one **14–147**

248 [1896] 2 Ch 679 at 681.
249 At 683.
250 [1914] 1 I.R. 142.
251 [1969] 1 W.L.R. 561.

identifiable and living member of an unincorporated association that has ceased to exist, the assets formerly held by or for that association pass to the Crown as bona vacantia. In addition, article 1 of the First Protocol of the European Convention for the Protection of Human Rights and Fundamental Freedoms guarantees the peaceful enjoyment of possessions. It says: "No one shall be deprived of his possessions except in the public interest and subject to the conditions provided for by law . . .".

14–148 On the face of it for one of two members of an unincorporated association to be deprived of his share in the assets of the association by reason of the death of the other of them, and without any compensation, appears to be a breach of this article. It is also difficult to see what public interest is served by the appropriation by the state of that member's share in the association's assets. This, in my judgment, provides another reason why the conclusion that a sole surviving member of an unincorporated association, while still alive, cannot claim its assets is unacceptable.

14–149 I therefore respectfully decline to follow Walton J.'s obiter dictum that a sole surviving member of an unincorporated association cannot claim the assets of the association, and that they vest in the Crown as bona vacantia. I might add that the Attorney General suggested in argument, without arguing in favour of one outcome, that there were three possible outcomes: first, that the last surviving member is entitled to the assets; secondly, that the assets are held jointly between the last surviving member and the estate of the member whose death caused the dissolution; thirdly, that the assets were ownerless or bona vacantia. For the reasons I have given, I conclude the first outcome is correct and I reject the second and third.

### iii. Pension Scheme Surpluses

14–150 A number of important cases in this area concern surpluses within a pension scheme. In *Davis v Richard & Wallington Ltd*,[252] for example, the funds of the scheme were held on trust but the trust deed was silent as to the destination of any surplus, and there was no way to amend the deed to deal with the surplus.[253] Scott J held that the surplus derived primarily from over-funding arising from the contributions of the employer (which was obliged to make up any deficiencies if the employees' contributions proved inadequate), and that the portion of the surplus which derived from the employer's contributions should be held on resulting trust for the employer. However, as regards the surplus derived from the employees' contributions he held that this should pass to the Crown as bona vacantia because the circumstances of the case pointed "firmly and clearly to the conclusion that a resulting trust in favour of the employees should be excluded". Why? Because equity should not impute to the employees an intention that would lead to an unworkable result, the value of benefits being different for each employee.[254] Nor should equity impose a resulting trust if this would lead to employees receiving more than the legislature intended when stipulating the statutory limits under exempt approved schemes. However, these reasons for refusing to impose a resulting trust for the employees were regarded as unconvincing by Lord Millett in *Air Jamaica Ltd v Charlton*.[255]

*Air Jamaica Ltd v Charlton*

Privy Council [1999] 1 W.L.R. 1399

14–151 Air Jamaica Ltd was privatised and its employee pensions plan was discontinued, leaving a surplus of $400 million. The pensions plan was established by a trust deed, one clause of which (clause 13.3) provided that "any balance of the Fund shall be applied to provide additional benefits for Members and after their death for their widows or their designated beneficiaries in such equitable and non-discriminatory manner

---

252 [1990] 1 W.L.R. 1511.

253 See now Pensions Act 1995 ss.68, 69.

254 But if the proportionate return under a resulting trust were effectively impossible to calculate and administer, why not have a per capita distribution to cut the Gordian knot, in line with Goff J's recommendation in *Re West Sussex Constabulary's Fund Trusts* [1970] 1 All E.R. 544 at 548?

255 [1999] 1 W.L.R. 1399.

as the Trustees may determine". The surplus would have been distributed in line with this clause if it had been valid, but the Privy Council advised that it was void for perpetuity. Clause 4 of the trust deed stated: "No moneys which at any time have been contributed by the Company under the terms hereof shall in any circumstances be repayable to the Company". The company purported to amend the trust deed, by removing clause 4 and replacing clause 13.3 with a clause providing that the surplus would be held on trust for the company. The Privy Council advised that clause 4 invalidated these amendments, but that it did not prevent a resulting trust from arising in favour of the company, and of the contributing members, in respect of the surplus funds.

LORD MILLETT (speaking for the court, which also consisted of LORD STEYN, LORD HOPE, SIR CHRISTOPHER SLADE and SIR ANDREW LEGGATT): Prima facie the surplus is held on a resulting trust for those who provided it. This sometimes creates a problem of some perplexity. In the present case, however, it does not. Contributions were payable by the members with matching contributions by the company. In the absence of any evidence that this is not what happened in practice, the surplus must be treated as provided as to one half by the company and as to one half by the members. **14–152**

The Attorney General contended that neither the company nor the members can take any part in the surplus, which has reverted to the Crown as bona vacantia. He argued that cl.4 of the trust deed precludes any claim by the company, while the members cannot claim any part of the surplus because they have received all that they are entitled to. There is authority for both propositions. Their Lordships consider that they can be supported neither in principle nor as a matter of construction. **14–153**

In *Re ABC Television Ltd Pension Scheme*[256] Foster J. held that a clause similar to cl.4 of the present trust deed "negatives the possibility of implying a resulting trust". This is wrong in principle. Like a constructive trust, a resulting trust arises by operation of law, though unlike a constructive trust it gives effect to intention. But it arises whether or not the transferor intended to retain a beneficial interest—he almost always does not—since it responds to the absence of any intention on his part to pass a beneficial interest to the recipient. It may arise even where the transferor positively wished to part with the beneficial interest, as in *Vandervell v IRC*.[257] In that case the retention of a beneficial interest by the transferor destroyed the effectiveness of a tax avoidance scheme which the transferor was seeking to implement. The House of Lords affirmed the principle that a resulting trust is not defeated by evidence that the transferor intended to part with the beneficial interest if he has not in fact succeeded in doing so. As Plowman J. had said in the same case at first instance:[258] **14–154**

> "As I see it, a man does not cease to own property simply by saying 'I don't want it'. If he tries to give it away the question must always be, has he succeeded in doing so or not?"

Lord Upjohn expressly approved this.[259]

Consequently their Lordships think that clauses of this kind in a pension scheme should generally be construed as forbidding the repayment of contributions under the terms of the scheme, and not as a pre-emptive but misguided attempt to rebut a resulting trust which would arise dehors the scheme. The purpose of such clauses is to preclude any amendment that would allow repayment to the company. Their Lordships thus construe cl.4 of the trust deed as invalidating the 1994 amendments, but not as preventing the company from retaining a beneficial interest by way of a resulting trust in so much of the surplus as is attributable to its contributions. **14–155**

The members' contributions stand on a similar footing. In *Davis v Richards & Wallington Industries Ltd*[260] Scott J. held that the fact that a party has received all that he bargained for is not necessarily a decisive argument against a resulting trust, but that in the circumstances of the case before him a resulting trust in favour of the employees was excluded. The circumstances that impressed him were twofold. He considered that it was impossible to arrive at a workable scheme for apportioning the employees' surplus among the different classes of employees and he declined[261] to "impute to them an intention that would lead to an unworkable result". He also considered that he was precluded by statute from "imputing to the employ- **14–156**

256 May 22, 1973, unreported.
257 [1967] 1 All E.R. 1.
258 [1966] Ch. 261 at 275.
259 [1967] 1 All E.R. 1 at 9.
260 [1991] 2 All E.R. 563.
261 At 1544.

> ees an intention" that they should receive by means of a resulting trust sums in excess of the maximum permitted by the relevant tax legislation.
>
> 14–157 These formulations also adopt the approach to intention that their Lordships have already considered to be erroneous. Their Lordships would observe that, even in the ordinary case of an actuarial surplus, it is not obvious that, when employees are promised certain benefits under a scheme to which they have contributed more than was necessary to fund them, they should not expect to obtain a return of their excess contributions. In the present case, however, the surplus does not arise from over-funding but from the failure of some of the trusts. It is impossible to say that the members "have received all that they bargained for". One of the benefits they bargained for was that the trustees should be obliged to pay them additional benefits in the event of the scheme's discontinuance. It was the invalidity of this trust that gave rise to the surplus. Their Lordships consider that it would be more accurate to say that the members claim such part of the surplus as is attributable to their contributions because they have not received all that they bargained for.
>
> 14–158 Pension schemes in Jamaica, as in England, need the approval of the Inland Revenue if they are to secure the fiscal advantages that are made available. The tax legislation in both countries places a limit on the amount which can be paid to the individual employee. Allowing the employees to enjoy any part of the surplus by way of resulting trust would probably exceed those limits. This fact is not, however, in their Lordships' view a proper ground on which to reject the operation of a resulting trust in favour of the employees. The Inland Revenue had an opportunity to examine the pension plan and to withhold approval on the ground that some of its provisions were void for perpetuity. They failed to do so. There is no call to distort principle in order to meet their requirements. The resulting trust arises by operation of the general law, dehors the pension scheme and the scope of the relevant tax legislation.
>
> 14–159 Scott J. was impressed by the difficulty of arriving at a workable scheme for apportioning the surplus funds among the members and the executors of deceased members. This was because he thought it necessary to value the benefits that each member had received in order to ascertain his share in the surplus. On the separate settlement with mutual insurance analysis which their Lordships have adopted in the present case, however, no such process is required. The members' share of the surplus should be divided pro rata among the members and the estates of deceased members in proportion to the contributions made by each member without regard to the benefits each has received and irrespective of the dates on which the contributions were made.

## *C. Justifying the Type (B) Resulting Trust*

**14–160** William Swadling has argued that the Type (B) resulting trust simply "defies legal analysis" and that no convincing justification can be provided for it.[262] On this view, there is no good reason why A should receive the protection of an equitable interest in a case where a transfer made to B on trust does not dispose of the beneficial interest in the property. Before any such conclusion can be reached, we need to examine three suggestions as to the principle underlying the trust.

### i. A Response to A's Intention to Create a Trust

**14–161** In *Westdeutsche Landesbank Girozentrale v Islington LBC*,[263] Lord Browne-Wilkinson stated that each of Type (A) and Type (B) resulting trusts[264]

> are traditionally regarded as examples of trusts giving effect to the common intention of the parties. A resulting trust is not imposed by law against the intentions of the trustee (as is a constructive trust) but gives effect to his presumed intention.

262 Swadling, "Explaining Resulting Trusts" (2008) 124 L.Q.R. 72, 102.
263 [1996] A.C. 669 at 705–706.
264 [1996] A.C. 669 at 708.

We have already considered this explanation of Type (A) resulting trusts.[265] There would seem to be an immediate difficulty, however, in extending it to Type (B) resulting trusts. On one view at least, such trusts may arise even in a case where A does not intend to have any beneficial interest: that is why such trusts have often been described as "automatic". Megarry J used that term in *Re Vandervell's Trusts (No.2)*,[266] when attempting to understand how, in *Vandervell v IRC*,[267] a resulting trust arose in favour of Mr Vandervell even when, for reasons of tax planning, he would presumably have been very keen to avoid such a result.

There may be three ways to respond to this criticism of Lord Browne-Wilkinson's view. First, as was noted by Lord Upjohn in *Vandervell* itself, the finding of a resulting trust in a case of a failed express trust gives A the possibility of making a further attempt to dispose of a beneficial interest and, as Mee has argued: **14–162**

> It seems plausible to suggest that such a rule would reflect the legal response which settlors *as an abstract class* would be likely to prefer in the scenario under discussion (even if some settlors might, in individual sets of circumstances, prefer a rule that the trustee would take beneficially).[268]

Indeed, Lord Upjohn's view of the facts of *Vandervell* was that the proper inference to be drawn was that A intended that B should hold the option of trust for A, subject to any trust that A might later declare.[269] The fact that tax consequences arose from A's failure to declare such trusts does not in itself render that view of the facts implausible.

The second response, developed by Lord Browne-Wilkinson in *Westdeutsche*,[270] is to argue that, if A does indeed, on the facts, make clear that he does not wish there to be any resulting trust, then B will hold on trust for the Crown rather than for A. Whilst his Lordship relied on the decision in *Re West Sussex Constabulary's Widows, Children and Benevolent (1930) Fund Trusts*[271] to support that view, we have seen that this case is controversial, and was rejected by Lord Millett in *Air Jamaica v Charlton*, where he regarded the decision in *Vandervell v IRC* as showing that "a resulting trust is not defeated by evidence that [A] intended to part with the beneficial interest if he has not in fact succeeded in doing so."[272] Nonetheless, in *Vandervell v IRC*, it was recognised that it is certainly open to A to intend that B (even if B is a trustee company) should take beneficially, and by so doing to dispose effectively of the beneficial interest, so to that extent A can ensure that no resulting trust arises. Indeed, Lord Millett himself, writing extra-judicially, has supported the view that if no resulting trust arises on the failure of an express trust, the trustees simply hold the property for their own benefit and thus free from any trust.[273] **14–163**

The third response is to accept the importance of intention, but to modify Lord Browne-Wilkinson's view by drawing a distinction between Type (A) and Type (B) resulting trusts. In the former case, it can be argued that the trust arises as a response to A's objectively apparent intention that B hold on trust for A. In the latter case, the relevant intention of A may simply be that B should hold as trustee; **14–164**

---

265 See paras 14–088—14–091.
266 [1974] Ch. 269 at 294.
267 [1967] 2 A.C. 219.
268 J. Mee, "'Automatic' Resulting Trusts: Retention, Restitution or Reposing Trust?" in Mitchell (ed.), *Constructive and Resulting Trusts* (2010).
269 [1967] 2 A.C. 291 at 315–317.
270 [1996] A.C. 669 at 708.
271 [1971] Ch. 1.
272 [1999] 1 W.L.R. 1399 at 1412.
273 "Pension Schemes and the Law of Trusts" (2000) 14 Tru. L.I. 66, 74; a similar analysis can be applied to *Burgess v Wheate* (1759) 1 Wm. Bl. 123.

there is no need to show that A intended B, in the circumstances which have occurred, to hold *for A*. After all, Type (B) resulting trusts arise in the case of failed trusts and A's actual intention was that the failed trust should succeed. The resulting trust can be seen as a practical, next best solution, which at least allows A another chance to create a trust:[274] as Maitland put it, from A's perspective, "I have made [B] a trustee for somebody, and a trustee he must be—if for no one else then for me or my representatives."[275]

### ii. A Result of A's Retention of a Beneficial Interest

**14–165** This view is associated with the idea that Type (B) resulting trusts are automatic. As applied to the standard case in which A, the unsuccessful settlor of the trust, begins with unencumbered property, it depends on the idea that, before attempting to set up any trust, A has both a legal and a distinct beneficial interest in the right. When A transfers the right to B to hold on trust, B acquires the legal interest but, to the extent that it remains undisposed of, A must, as a matter of logic, retain the beneficial interest: "What a man fails effectually to dispose of remains automatically vested in him."[276]

**14–166** This view finds much support in the case-law,[277] but its fatal weakness was exposed by Lord Browne-Wilkinson in *Westdeutsche*.[278] Its premise is flawed as, if A holds an unencumbered property right, this does not mean that she has any pre-existing and distinct equitable interest which may be retained. Equity has no reason to intervene where A simply owns property, and, in the absence of grounds for equitable intervention, there can be no distinct equitable interest. In Lord Browne-Wilkinson's words[279]:

> A person solely entitled to the full beneficial ownership of money or property, both at law and in equity, does not enjoy an equitable interest in that property. The legal title carries with it all rights. Unless and until there is a separation of legal and equitable estates, there is no separate equitable title. Therefore to talk about [A] 'retaining' its equitable interest is meaningless. The only question is whether the circumstances under which the money was paid were such as, in equity, to impose a trust on [B]. If so, an equitable interest arose for the first time under that trust.

**14–167** Given this obvious difficulty with the retention theory, it is reasonable to ask why it has such prominence in the case-law. As John Mee has pointed out,[280] there are aspects of the right acquired by the beneficiary of a resulting trust which match those of the unencumbered right initially held by that party. If, for example, A initially has a freehold of land, and ends up as the beneficiary of a Type (B) resulting trust of that land, A has, both at the start and end of the story, a liberty against B to use the land, and a power to set up a trust of the land. This cannot disguise the fact, however, that the right acquired by A under the resulting trust is a new one.

---

274 See Mee, "'Automatic' Resulting Trusts: Retention, Restitution or Reposing Trust?" in Mitchell (ed.), *Constructive and Resulting Trusts* (2010), pp.208–209: "the key feature in the relevant situation is the fact that the settlor has transferred property to another person, reposing trust in that person to hold the property according to the settlor's instructions".

275 F.W. Maitland, *Equity – A Course of Lectures*, 2nd edn (Cambridge University Press, 1936), p.77.

276 *Re Vandervell (No.2)* [1974] Ch. 269 at 289 per Megarry J.

277 See too *Vandervell v IRC* [1967] 2 A.C. 291 at 313 per Lord Upjohn "if the beneficial interest was in A and he fails to give it away effectively to another or others or on charitable trusts it must remain in him" and at 329 per Lord Wilberforce "the equitable, or beneficial interest, cannot remain in the air: the consequence in law must be that it remains in the settlor."

278 [1996] A.C. 669 at 706. See too Swadling, "Explaining Resulting Trusts" (2008) 124 L.Q.R. 72, 99–100.

279 [1996] A.C. 669 at 706.

280 Mee, "'Automatic' Resulting Trusts: Retention, Restitution or Reposing Trust?" in Mitchell (ed.), *Constructive and Resulting Trusts* (2010).

### iii. A Response to B's Unjust Enrichment at A's Expense

As we saw above,[281] it has been argued, notably by Chambers, that each of a Type (A) and Type (B) resulting trust can be seen as imposed to reverse B's unjust enrichment at A's expense. This analysis may seem particularly compelling when applied to the latter type of resulting trust: if A has transferred a right to B on the basis that B should hold it on a particular trust, and that planned trust has failed, it would seem clear that B would be unjustly enriched at A's expense were B to hold the right free from any trust. 14–168

Support for this analysis can be derived from Lord Millett's formulation in *Air Jamaica v Charlton*[282]: 14–169

> Like a constructive trust, a resulting trust arises by operation of law, though unlike a constructive trust it gives effect to intention. But it arises whether or not the transferor intended to retain a beneficial interest—he almost always does not—since it responds to the absence of any intention on his part to pass a beneficial interest to the recipient. It may arise even where the transferor positively wished to part with the beneficial interest, as in *Vandervell v IRC*.[283]

Many of the points made about this explanation of Type (A) trusts are also relevant here, most notably the key one that, in *Westdeutsche*, the House of Lords rejected the view that resulting trusts are a response to B's unjust enrichment at A's expense. As a matter of principle, Swadling has also argued that "if our only desire is to strip out [B's] enrichment, a response in the nature of a personal claim for the value received serves that purpose perfectly well", so that a trust is not necessary.[284] Mee has further argued that the unjust enrichment model proposed by Chambers blurs the distinction between cases in which A has no intention to give any rights to B (as where B steals A's property and uses it to acquire a right, and A then argues that B holds that right on trust for A) and those in which A does intend that B should take as trustee. In the latter case, in which a Type (B) resulting trust may arise, an absence of intention to benefit B can mean only that A had "a positive intention to create a trust, not merely an absence of intention to benefit (B)."[285] Intention then plays a more positive role in the creation of the Type (B) resulting trust than would be allowed by the unjust enrichment model. 14–170

## 4. Other Types of Resulting Trust?

In *Westdeutsche*, Lord Browne-Wilkinson identified two sets of circumstances in which a resulting trust may arise. We have now considered each of those types of resulting trust. We can now consider the question that we previously raised,[286] of whether the principle or principles underlying those cases can operate more broadly, so as to allow for the recognition of other forms of resulting trust. 14–171

The answer to that question, of course, depends on identifying the principle or principles underlying the Type (A) and Type (B) resulting trusts. In the preceding sections, we looked at three competing explanations of the former type of trust and at three competing explanations of the latter type of trust. We noted that, if each type of resulting trust is based on the need to prevent A's unjust enrichment at B's expense, then that underlying principle is capable of applying more broadly and could lead to the recognition of other circumstances in which resulting trusts arise. That was precisely the question 14–172

---

281 See paras 14–095—14–101.
282 [1999] 1 W.L.R. 1399 at 1412.
283 [1967] 2 AC 291.
284 Swadling, "Explaining Resulting Trusts" (2008) 124 L.Q.R. 72, 101.
285 Mee, "'Automatic' Resulting Trusts: Retention, Restitution or Reposing Trust?" in Mitchell (ed.), *Constructive and Resulting Trusts* (2010), p.227.
286 See para.14–016.

at stake in *Westdeutsche* itself, as the claimant bank attempted to argue that a trust had arisen when the defendant local authority received payments made by the bank under a void contract with the local authority. However, the House of Lords rejected the unjust enrichment analysis and found that no trust had arisen.

**14–173** It is therefore appropriate to end the chapter with an extract from Lord Browne-Wilkinson's speech in *Westdeutsche*. One important point to bear in mind is that, whilst confining resulting trusts to the two classic types of case, his Lordship identified other situations (such as the "stolen bag of coins" example discussed in the extract below) in which a trust may be imposed by law, but labelled such a trust as constructive rather than resulting.[287] It is clear, then, that even if resulting trusts are limited to the situations in which Type (A) and Type (B) resulting trusts may arise, this is not true of all trusts imposed by law. We will examine constructive trusts in the next chapter.

*Westdeutsche Landesbank Girozentrale v Islington LBC*

House of Lords [1996] A.C. 669

**14–174** The appellant bank sued the respondent council to recover £1,145,525 paid under an interest rate swap agreement that was void because beyond the powers of the council. The Court of Appeal upheld the judge's decision that the bank was entitled to recover the money on the ground that the council had been unjustly enriched at the bank's expense, with compound interest. The council appealed against the award of compound interest, arguing that the court could only have had jurisdiction to make such an interest award if the money had been held on trust for the bank, and arguing too that no trust had arisen in the bank's favour. The House of Lords unanimously held that although the bank had a personal claim to recover the money in a common law action for money had and received, it had no proprietary equitable claim; by a 3:2 majority, it followed that only simple interest was payable (Lords Goff and Woolf dissenting on the basis that compound interest should be awarded by way of an equitable remedy in aid of the common law, so that the bank could have restitution of the user value of its money[288]).

**14–175** LORD BROWNE-WILKINSON (with whom LORD SLYNN and LORD LLOYD agreed, but with whom LORD GOFF and LORD WOOLF disagreed, reviewed the courts' jurisdiction to make awards of compound interest, and then continued):

**Was there a Trust? The Argument for the Bank in Outline**

**14–176** The bank submitted that, since the contract was void, title did not pass at the date of payment either at law or in equity. The legal title of the bank was extinguished as soon as the money was paid into the mixed account, whereupon the legal title became vested in the local authority. But, it was argued, this did not affect the equitable interest, which remained vested in the bank (the retention of title point). It was submitted that whenever the legal interest in property is vested in one person and the equitable interest in another, the owner of the legal interest holds it on trust for the owner of the equitable title: "the separation of the legal from the equitable interest necessarily imports a trust." For this latter proposition (the separation of title point) the bank, of course, relies on *Sinclair v Brougham*[289] and *Chase Manhattan Bank NA v Israel-British Bank (London) Ltd.*[290]

**14–177** The generality of these submissions was narrowed by submitting that the trust which arose in this case was a resulting trust "not of an active character" (see *Sinclair v Brougham*,[291] per Viscount Haldane L.C.). This submission was reinforced, after completion of the oral argument, by sending to your Lordships

---

[287] In contrast, on the view of Chambers, the trust arising in a case where B simply takes A's right and uses it to acquire a new right is best described as a resulting trust, not a constructive trust: see Chambers, *Resulting Trusts* (1997), pp.116–118. A similar view was taken by Millett J in *El Ajou v Dollar Land Holdings* [1993] 3 All E.R. 717 at 734, but it is clearly inconsistent with Lord Browne-Wilkinson's analysis in *Westdeutsche* [1996] A.C. 669 at 716.

[288] See now *Sempra Metals Ltd v IRC* [2008] A.C. 561, which holds that claims in unjust enrichment do lie to recover the user value of money as compound interest.

[289] [1914] A.C. 398.

[290] [1981] Ch. 105.

[291] [1914] A.C. 398 at 421.

Professor Peter Birks' paper "Restitution and Resulting Trusts".[292] Unfortunately your Lordships have not had the advantage of any submissions from the local authority on this paper, but an article by William Swadling "A New Role for Resulting Trusts?"[293] puts forward counter-arguments which I have found persuasive. . . .

**The Breadth of the Submission**

Although the actual question in issue on the appeal is a narrow one, on the arguments presented it is necessary to consider fundamental principles of trust law. Does the recipient of money under a contract subsequently found to be void for mistake or as being ultra vires hold the moneys received on trust even where he had no knowledge at any relevant time that the contract was void? If he does hold on trust, such trust must arise at the date of receipt or, at the latest, at the date the legal title of the payer is extinguished by mixing moneys in a bank account: in the present case it does not matter at which of those dates the legal title was extinguished. If there is a trust two consequences follow: (a) the recipient will be personally liable, regardless of fault, for any subsequent payment away of the moneys to third parties even though, at the date of such payment, the "trustee" was still ignorant of the existence of any trust;[294] (b) as from the date of the establishment of the trust (i.e. receipt or mixing of the moneys by the "trustee") the original payer will have an equitable proprietary interest in the moneys so long as they are traceable into whomsoever's hands they come other than a purchaser for value of the legal interest without notice. Therefore, although in the present case the only question directly in issue is the personal liability of the local authority as a trustee, it is not possible to hold the local authority liable without imposing a trust which, in other cases, will create property rights affecting third parties because moneys received under a void contract are "trust property". 14–178

**The Practical Consequences of the Bank's Argument**

Before considering the legal merits of the submission, it is important to appreciate the practical consequences which ensue if the bank's arguments are correct. Those who suggest that a resulting trust should arise in these circumstances accept that the creation of an equitable proprietary interest under the trust can have unfortunate, and adverse, effects if the original recipient of the moneys becomes insolvent: the moneys, if traceable in the hands of the recipient, are trust moneys and not available for the creditors of the recipient. However, the creation of an equitable proprietary interest in moneys received under a void contract is capable of having adverse effects quite apart from insolvency. The proprietary interest under the unknown trust will, quite apart from insolvency, be enforceable against any recipient of the property other than the purchaser for value of a legal interest without notice. 14–179

Take the following example. T (the transferor) has entered into a commercial contract with R1 (the first recipient). Both parties believe the contract to be valid but it is in fact void. Pursuant to that contract: (i) T pays £1m to R1 who pays it into a mixed bank account; (ii) T transfers 100 shares in X company to R1, who is registered as a shareholder. Thereafter R1 deals with the money and shares as follows: (iii) R1 pays £50,000 out of the mixed account to R2 otherwise than for value; R2 then becomes insolvent, having trade creditors who have paid for goods not delivered at the time of the insolvency. (iv) R1 charges the shares in X company to R3 by way of equitable security for a loan from R3. 14–180

If the bank's arguments are correct, R1 holds the £1m on trust for T once the money has become mixed in R1's bank account. Similarly R1 becomes the legal owner of the shares in X company as from the date of his registration as a shareholder but holds such shares on a resulting trust for T. T therefore has an equitable proprietary interest in the moneys in the mixed account and in the shares. 14–181

T's equitable interest will enjoy absolute priority as against the creditors in the insolvency of R2 (who was not a purchaser for value) provided that the £50,000 can be traced in the assets of R2 at the date of its insolvency. Moreover, if the separation of title argument is correct, since the equitable interest is in T and the legal interest is vested in R2, R2 also holds as trustee for T. In tracing the £50,000 in the bank account of R2, R2 as trustee will be treated as having drawn out "his own" moneys first, thereby benefiting T at the expense of the secured and unsecured creditors of R2. Therefore in practice one may well reach the position where the moneys in the bank account of R2 in reality reflect the price paid by creditors for goods not delivered by R2: yet, under the tracing rules, those moneys are to be treated as belonging in equity to T. 14–182

---

292 Published in S. Goldstein (ed.), *Equity and Contemporary Legal Developments* (1992).
293 (1996) 16 L.S. 110.
294 A. Burrows, "Swaps and the Friction between Common Law and Equity" [1995] R.L.R. 15.

14–183 So far as the shares in the X company are concerned, T can trace his equitable interest into the shares and will take in priority to R3, whose equitable charge to secure his loan even though granted for value will pro tanto be defeated.

14–184 All this will have occurred when no one was aware, or could have been aware, of the supposed trust because no one knew that the contract was void.

14–185 I can see no moral or legal justification for giving such priority to the right of T to obtain restitution over third parties who have themselves not been enriched, in any real sense, at T's expense and indeed have had no dealings with T. T paid over his money and transferred the shares under a supposed valid contract. If the contract had been valid, he would have had purely personal rights against R1. Why should he be better off because the contract is void?

14–186 My Lords, wise judges have often warned against the wholesale importation into commercial law of equitable principles inconsistent with the certainty and speed which are essential requirements for the orderly conduct of business affairs.[295] If the bank's arguments are correct, a businessman who has entered into transactions relating to or dependent upon property rights could find that assets which apparently belong to one person in fact belong to another; that there are "off balance sheet" liabilities of which he cannot be aware; that these property rights and liabilities arise from circumstances unknown not only to himself but also to anyone else who has been involved in the transactions. A new area of unmanageable risk will be introduced into commercial dealings. If the due application of equitable principles forced a conclusion leading to these results, your Lordships would be presented with a formidable task in reconciling legal principle with commercial common sense. But in my judgment no such conflict occurs. The resulting trust for which the bank contends is inconsistent not only with the law as it stands but with any principled development of it.

**The Relevant Principles of Trust Law**

14–187 (i) Equity operates on the conscience of the owner of the legal interest. In the case of a trust, the conscience of the legal owner requires him to carry out the purposes for which the property was vested in him (express or implied trust) or which the law imposes on him by reason of his unconscionable conduct (constructive trust).

14–188 (ii) Since the equitable jurisdiction to enforce trusts depends upon the conscience of the holder of the legal interest being affected, he cannot be a trustee of the property if and so long as he is ignorant of the facts alleged to affect his conscience, i.e. until he is aware that he is intended to hold the property for the benefit of others in the case of an express or implied trust, or, in the case of a constructive trust, of the factors which are alleged to affect his conscience.

14–189 (iii) In order to establish a trust there must be identifiable trust property. The only apparent exception to this rule is a constructive trust imposed on a person who dishonestly assists in a breach of trust who may come under fiduciary duties even if he does not receive identifiable trust property.[296]

14–190 (iv) Once a trust is established, as from the date of its establishment the beneficiary has, in equity, a proprietary interest in the trust property, which proprietary interest will be enforceable in equity against any subsequent holder of the property (whether the original property or substituted property into which it can be traced) other than a purchaser for value of the legal interest without notice.

14–191 These propositions are fundamental to the law of trusts and I would have thought uncontroversial. However, proposition (ii) may call for some expansion. There are cases where property has been put into the name of X without X's knowledge but in circumstances where no gift to X was intended. It has been held that such property is recoverable under a resulting trust.[297] These cases are explicable on the ground that, by the time action was brought, X or his successors in title have become aware of the facts which gave

[295] *Barnes v Addy* (1874) L.R. 9 Ch. App. 244 at 251, 255, and *Scandinavian Trading Tanker Co AB v Flota Petrolera Ecuatoriana* [1983] 2 A.C. 694 at 703–704.

[296] [Authors' note: Lord Browne-Wilkinson refers here to the personal liability of a dishonest assistant to account in equity "as a constructive trustee"; dishonest assistants often do not handle misapplied trust property, and in such cases therefore cannot hold it on constructive trust for anyone as Lord Millett makes clear in *Dubai Aluminium Co Ltd v Salaam* [2003] 2 A.C. 366 at [141]–[142]. See paras 11–012—11–013.

[297] *Birch v Blagrave* (1755) Amb. 264; *Childers v Childers* (1857) 1 De G. & J. 482; *Re Vinogradoff* [1935] W.N. 68; *Re Muller* [1953] N.Z.L.R. 879.

rise to a resulting trust; his conscience was affected as from the time of such discovery and thereafter he held on a resulting trust under which the property was recovered from him. There is, so far as I am aware, no authority which decides that X was a trustee, and therefore accountable for his deeds, at any time before he was aware of the circumstances which gave rise to a resulting trust.

Those basic principles are inconsistent with the case being advanced by the bank. The latest time at which there was any possibility of identifying the "trust property" was the date on which the moneys in the mixed bank account of the local authority ceased to be traceable when the local authority's account went into overdraft in June 1987. At that date, the local authority had no knowledge of the invalidity of the contract but regarded the moneys as its own to spend as it thought fit. There was therefore never a time at which both (a) there was defined trust property and (b) the conscience of the local authority in relation to such defined trust property was affected. The basic requirements of a trust were never satisfied. . . . 14–192

**The Retention of Title Point**

It is said that, since the bank only intended to part with its beneficial ownership of the moneys in performance of a valid contract, neither the legal nor the equitable title passed to the local authority at the date of payment. The legal title vested in the local authority by operation of law when the moneys became mixed in the bank account but, it is said, the bank "retained" its equitable title. 14–193

I think this argument is fallacious. A person solely entitled to the full beneficial ownership of money or property, both at law and in equity, does not enjoy an equitable interest in that property. The legal title carries with it all rights. Unless and until there is a separation of the legal and equitable estates, there is no separate equitable title. Therefore to talk about the bank "retaining" its equitable interest is meaningless. The only question is whether the circumstances under which the money was paid were such as, in equity, to impose a trust on the local authority. If so, an equitable interest arose for the first time under that trust. 14–194

This proposition is supported by *Re Cook*,[298] *Vandervell v IRC*,[299] per Lord Upjohn and Lord Donovan, *Commissioner of Stamp Duties v Livingston*,[300] and Underhill and Hayton's Law of Trusts and Trustees.[301] 14–195

**The Separation of Title Point**

The bank's submission, at its widest, is that if the legal title is in A but the equitable interest in B, A holds as trustee for B. 14–196

Again I think this argument is fallacious. There are many cases where B enjoys rights which, in equity, are enforceable against the legal owner, A, without A being a trustee, for example an equitable right to redeem a mortgage, equitable easements, restrictive covenants, the right to rectification and an insurer's right by subrogation to receive damages subsequently recovered by the assured.[302] Even in cases where the whole beneficial interest is vested in B and the bare legal interest is in A, A is not necessarily a trustee, for example where title to land is acquired by estoppel as against the legal owner; a mortgagee who has fully discharged his indebtedness enforces his right to recover the mortgaged property in a redemption action, not an action for breach of trust. 14–197

The bank contended that where, under a pre-existing trust, B is entitled to an equitable interest in trust property, if the trust property comes into the hands of a third party, X (not being a purchaser for value of the legal interest without notice), B is entitled to enforce his equitable interest against the property in the hands of X because X is a trustee for B. In my view the third party, X, is not necessarily a trustee for B: B's equitable right is enforceable against the property in just the same way as any other specifically enforceable equitable right can be enforced against a third party. Even if the third party, X, is not aware that what he has received is trust property B is entitled to assert his title in that property. If X has the necessary degree of knowledge, X may himself become a constructive trustee for B on the basis of knowing receipt. But unless he has the requisite degree of knowledge he is not personally liable to account as trustee: *Re Diplock*[303] and *Re Montagu's Settlement Trusts*.[304] Therefore, innocent receipt of property by X subject to an existing 14–198

---

298 [1948] Ch. 212.
299 [1967] 2 A.C. 291 at 311 and 317.
300 [1965] A.C. 694 at 712.
301 15th edn, 1995, p.866.
302 *Lord Napier and Ettrick v Hunter* [1993] A.C. 713.
303 [1948] Ch. 465 at 478.
304 [1987] Ch. 264.

equitable interest does not by itself make X a trustee despite the severance of the legal and equitable titles. *Underhill and Hayton Law of Trusts and Trustees*,[305] while accepting that X is under no personal liability to account unless and until he becomes aware of B's rights, does describe X as being a constructive trustee. This may only be a question of semantics: on either footing, in the present case the local authority could not have become accountable for profits until it knew that the contract was void.

**Resulting Trust**

14–199 This is not a case where the bank had any equitable interest which predated receipt by the local authority of the upfront payment. Therefore, in order to show that the local authority became a trustee, the bank must demonstrate circumstances which raised a trust for the first time either at the date on which the local authority received the money or at the date on which payment into the mixed account was made. Counsel for the bank specifically disavowed any claim based on a constructive trust. This was plainly right because the local authority had no relevant knowledge sufficient to raise a constructive trust at any time before the moneys, upon the bank account going into overdraft, became untraceable. Once there ceased to be an identifiable trust fund, the local authority could not become a trustee: *Re Goldcorp Exchange Ltd*.[306] Therefore, as the argument for the bank recognised, the only possible trust which could be established was a resulting trust arising from the circumstances in which the local authority received the upfront payment.

14–200 [His Lordship explained the circumstances under which resulting trusts arise, as set out at para 14–014, and continued:] Applying these conventional principles of resulting trust to the present case, the bank's claim must fail. There was no transfer of money to the local authority on express trusts: therefore a resulting trust of type (B) above could not arise. As to type (A) above, any presumption of resulting trust is rebutted since it is demonstrated that the bank paid, and the local authority received, the upfront payment with the intention that the moneys so paid should become the absolute property of the local authority. It is true that the parties were under a misapprehension that the payment was made in pursuance of a valid contract. But that does not alter the actual intentions of the parties at the date the payment was made or the moneys were mixed in the bank account. As the article by William Swadling demonstrates,[307] the presumption of resulting trust is rebutted by evidence of any intention inconsistent with such a trust, not only by evidence of an intention to make a gift.

14–201 Professor Birks,[308] while accepting that the principles I have stated represent "a very conservative form" of definition of a resulting trust, argues from restitutionary principles that the definition should be extended so as to cover a perceived gap in the law of "subtractive unjust enrichment"[309] so as to give a plaintiff a proprietary remedy when he has transferred value under a mistake or under a contract the consideration for which wholly fails. He suggests that a resulting trust should arise wherever the money is paid under a mistake (because such mistake vitiates the actual intention) or when money is paid on a condition which is not subsequently satisfied.

14–202 As one would expect, the argument is tightly reasoned but I am not persuaded. The search for a perceived need to strengthen the remedies of a plaintiff claiming in restitution involves, to my mind, a distortion of trust principles. First, the argument elides rights in property (which is the only proper subject matter of a trust) into rights in "the value transferred".[310] A trust can only arise where there is defined trust property: it is therefore not consistent with trust principles to say that a person is a trustee of property which cannot be defined. Second, Professor Birks' approach appears to assume (e.g. in the case of a transfer of value made under a contract the consideration for which subsequently fails) that the recipient will be deemed to have been a trustee from the date of his original receipt of money, i.e. the trust arises at a time when the "trustee" does not, and cannot, know that there is going to be a total failure of consideration. This result is incompatible with the basic premise on which all trust law is built, viz. that the conscience of the trustee is affected. Unless and until the trustee is aware of the factors which give rise to the supposed trust, there is nothing which can affect his conscience. Thus neither in the case of a subsequent failure of consideration nor in the case of a payment under a contract subsequently found to be void for mistake or

[305] 15th edn, pp.369–370.
[306] [1995] 1 A.C. 74.
[307] "A New Role for Resulting Trusts?" (1996) 16 L.S. 110, 133.
[308] "Restitution and Resulting Trusts" in S. Goldstein (ed.), *Equity and Contemporary Legal Developments* (1992), p.360.
[309] ibid. at p.368.
[310] ibid. at p.361.

failure of condition will there be circumstances, at the date of receipt, which can impinge on the conscience of the recipient, thereby making him a trustee. Thirdly, Professor Birks has to impose on his wider view an arbitrary and admittedly unprincipled modification so as to ensure that a resulting trust does not arise when there has only been a failure to perform a contract, as opposed to total failure of consideration.[311] Such arbitrary exclusion is designed to preserve the rights of creditors in the insolvency of the recipient. The fact that it is necessary to exclude artificially one type of case which would logically fall within the wider concept casts doubt on the validity of the concept.

If adopted, Professor Birks' wider concepts would give rise to all the practical consequences and injustices to which I have referred. I do not think it right to make an unprincipled alteration to the law of property (i.e. the law of trusts) so as to produce in the law of unjust enrichment the injustices to third parties which I have mentioned and the consequential commercial uncertainty which any extension of proprietary interests in personal property is bound to produce. **14–203**

**The Authorities**

Three cases were principally relied upon in direct support of the proposition that a resulting trust arises where a payment is made under a void contract. **14–204**

*(A) Sinclair v Brougham*[312]

The case concerned the distribution of the assets of the Birkbeck Permanent Benefit Building Society, an unincorporated body which was insolvent. The society had for many years been carrying on business as a bank which, it was held, was ultra vires its objects. The bank had accepted deposits in the course of its ultra vires banking business and it was held that the debts owed to such depositors were themselves void as being ultra vires. In addition to the banking depositors, there were ordinary trade creditors. The society had two classes of members, the A shareholders who were entitled to repayment of their investment on maturity and the B shareholders whose shares were permanent. By agreement, the claims of the ordinary trade creditors and of the A shareholders had been settled. Therefore the only claimants to the assets of the society before the court were the ultra vires depositors and the B shareholders, the latter of which could take no greater interest than the society itself. **14–205**

The issues for decision arose on a summons taken out by the liquidator for directions as to how he should distribute the assets in the liquidation. In the judgments, it is not always clear whether this House was laying down general propositions of law or merely giving directions as to the proper mode in which the assets in that liquidation should be distributed. The depositors claimed, first, in quasi-contract for money had and received. They claimed secondly, as the result of an argument suggested for the first time in the course of argument in the House of Lords,[313] to trace their deposits into the assets of the society. **14–206**

**Money Had and Received**

The House of Lords was unanimous in rejecting the claim by the ultra vires depositors to recover in quasi-contract on the basis of moneys had and received. In their view, the claim in quasi-contract was based on an implied contract. To imply a contract to repay would be to imply a contract to exactly the same effect as the express ultra vires contract of loan. Any such implied contract would itself be void as being ultra vires. **14–207**

Subsequent developments in the law of restitution demonstrate that this reasoning is no longer sound. The common law restitutionary claim is based not on implied contract but on unjust enrichment: in the circumstances the law imposes an obligation to repay rather than implying an entirely fictitious agreement to repay.[314] In my judgment, your Lordships should now unequivocally and finally reject the concept that the claim for moneys had and received is based on an implied contract. I would overrule *Sinclair v Brougham* on this point. **14–208**

It follows that in *Sinclair v Brougham* the depositors should have had a personal claim to recover the moneys at law based on a total failure of consideration. The failure of consideration was not partial: the **14–209**

---

311 ibid. at pp. 356–359 and 362.

312 [1914] A.C. 398.

313 ibid. at 404.

314 *Fibrosa Spolka Akcyjna v Fairbairn Lawson Combe Barbour Ltd* [1943] A.C. 32 at 63–64, per Lord Wright; *Pavey & Matthews Pty Ltd v Paul* (1987) 69 A.L.R. 577 at 579, 583, 603; *Lipkin Gorman (a firm) v Karpnale Ltd* [1991] 2 A.C. 548 at 578; *Woolwich Building Society v IRC (No.2)* [1993] A.C. 70.

depositors had paid over their money in consideration of a promise to repay. That promise was ultra vires and void; therefore the consideration for the payment of the money wholly failed. So in the present swaps case (though the point is not one under appeal) I think the Court of Appeal were right to hold that the swap moneys were paid on a consideration that wholly failed. The essence of the swap agreement is that, over the whole term of the agreement, each party thinks he will come out best: the consideration for one party making a payment is an obligation on the other party to make counter-payments over the whole term of the agreement.

14–210 If in *Sinclair v Brougham* the depositors had been held entitled to recover at law, their personal claim would have ranked pari passu with other ordinary unsecured creditors, in priority to the members of the society who could take nothing in the liquidation until all creditors had been paid.

**The Claim in Rem**

14–211 The House of Lords held that, the ordinary trade creditors having been paid in full by agreement, the assets remaining were to be divided between the ultra vires depositors and the members of the society pro rata according to their respective payments to the society. . . .

14–212 As has been pointed out frequently over the 80 years since it was decided, *Sinclair v Brougham* is a bewildering authority: no single ratio decidendi can be detected; all the reasoning is open to serious objection; it was only intended to deal with cases where there were no trade creditors in competition and the reasoning is incapable of application where there are such creditors. In my view the decision as to rights in rem in *Sinclair v Brougham* should also be overruled. Although the case is one where property rights are involved, such overruling should not in practice disturb long-settled titles. However, your Lordships should not be taken to be casting any doubt on the principles of tracing as established in *Re Diplock*.

14–213 If *Sinclair v Brougham*, in both its aspects, is overruled the law can be established in accordance with principle and commercial common sense: a claimant for restitution of moneys paid under an ultra vires, and therefore void, contract has a personal action at law to recover the moneys paid as on a total failure of consideration; he will not have an equitable proprietary claim which gives him either rights against third parties or priority in an insolvency; nor will he have a personal claim in equity, since the recipient is not a trustee.

14–214 *(B) Chase Manhattan Bank NA v Israel-British Bank (London) Ltd*[315]

In that case Chase Manhattan, a New York bank, had by mistake paid the same sum twice to the credit of the defendant, a London bank. Shortly thereafter, the defendant bank went into insolvent liquidation. The question was whether Chase Manhattan had a claim in rem against the assets of the defendant bank to recover the second payment.

14–215 Goulding J. was asked to assume that the moneys paid under a mistake were capable of being traced in the assets of the recipient bank: he was only concerned with the question whether there was a proprietary base on which the tracing remedy could be founded.[316] He held that, where money was paid under a mistake, the receipt of such money without more constituted the recipient a trustee: he said that the payer "retains an equitable property in it and the conscience of [the recipient] is subjected to a fiduciary duty to respect his proprietary right".[317]

14–216 It will be apparent from what I have already said that I cannot agree with this reasoning. First, it is based on a concept of retaining an equitable property in money where, prior to the payment to the recipient bank, there was no existing equitable interest. Further, I cannot understand how the recipient's "conscience" can be affected at a time when he is not aware of any mistake. Finally, the judge found that the law of England and that of New York were in substance the same. I find this a surprising conclusion since the New York law of constructive trusts has for a long time been influenced by the concept of a remedial constructive trust, whereas hitherto English law has for the most part only recognised an institutional constructive trust.[318] In the present context, that distinction is of fundamental importance. Under an institutional constructive trust, the trust arises by operation of law as from the date of the circumstances which give rise to it: the function of the court is merely to declare that such trust has arisen in the past. The consequences that

[315] [1981] Ch. 105.
[316] ibid. at 116.
[317] ibid. at 119.
[318] *Metall und Rohstoff AG v Donaldson Lufkin & Jenrette Inc* [1990] 1 Q.B. 391 at 478–480.

flow from such trust having arisen (including the possibly unfair consequences to third parties who in the interim have received the trust property) are also determined by rules of law, not under a discretion. A remedial constructive trust, as I understand it, is different. It is a judicial remedy giving rise to an enforceable equitable obligation: the extent to which it operates retrospectively to the prejudice of third parties lies in the discretion of the court. Thus for the law of New York to hold that there is a remedial constructive trust where a payment has been made under a void contract gives rise to different consequences from holding that an institutional constructive trust arises in English law.

However, although I do not accept the reasoning of Goulding J., Chase Manhattan may well have been rightly decided. The defendant bank knew of the mistake made by the paying bank within two days of the receipt of the moneys.[319] The judge treated this fact as irrelevant,[320] but in my judgment it may well provide a proper foundation for the decision. Although the mere receipt of the moneys, in ignorance of the mistake, gives rise to no trust, the retention of the moneys after the recipient bank learned of the mistake may well have given rise to a constructive trust.[321] **14–217**

[His Lordship considered *Re Ames' Settlement*,[322] and then continued:] **14–218**

**The Stolen Bag of Coins**

The argument for a resulting trust was said to be supported by the case of a thief who steals a bag of coins. At law those coins remain traceable only so long as they are kept separate: as soon as they are mixed with other coins or paid into a mixed bank account they cease to be traceable at law. Can it really be the case, it is asked, that in such circumstances the thief cannot be required to disgorge the property which, in equity, represents the stolen coins? Moneys can only be traced in equity if there has been at some stage a breach of fiduciary duty, i.e. if either before the theft there was an equitable proprietary interest (e.g. the coins were stolen trust moneys) or such interest arises under a resulting trust at the time of the theft or the mixing of the moneys. Therefore, it is said, a resulting trust must arise either at the time of the theft or when the moneys are subsequently mixed. Unless this is the law, there will be no right to recover the assets representing the stolen moneys once the moneys have become mixed. **14–219**

I agree that the stolen moneys are traceable in equity. But the proprietary interest which equity is enforcing in such circumstances arises under a constructive, not a resulting, trust. Although it is difficult to find clear authority for the proposition, when property is obtained by fraud equity imposes a constructive trust on the fraudulent recipient: the property is recoverable and traceable in equity. Thus, an infant who has obtained property by fraud is bound in equity to restore it.[323] **14–220**

**Restitution and Equitable Rights**

Those concerned with developing the law of restitution are anxious to ensure that, in certain circumstances, the plaintiff should have the right to recover property which he has unjustly lost. For that purpose they have sought to develop the law of resulting trusts so as to give the plaintiff a proprietary interest. For the reasons that I have given in my view such development is not based on sound principle and in the name of unjust enrichment is capable of producing most unjust results. The law of resulting trusts would confer on the plaintiff a right to recover property from, or at the expense of, those who have not been unjustly enriched at his expense at all, for example the lender whose debt is secured by a floating charge and all other third parties who have purchased an equitable interest only, albeit in all innocence and for value. **14–221**

Although the resulting trust is an unsuitable basis for developing proprietary restitutionary remedies, the remedial constructive trust, if introduced into English law, may provide a more satisfactory road forward. The court by way of remedy might impose a constructive trust on a defendant who knowingly retains property of which the plaintiff has been unjustly deprived. Since the remedy can be tailored to the circumstances of the particular case, innocent third parties would not be prejudiced and restitutionary **14–222**

---

319 [1981] Ch. 105 at 115.

320 ibid. at 114.

321 *Snell's Equity* (29th edn, 1991), p.193, Pettit *Equity and the Law of Trusts* (7th edn, 1993) p.168; *Metall und Rohstoff AG v Donaldson Lufkin & Jenrette Inc* [1990] 1 Q.B. 391 at 473–474.

322 [1946] Ch. 217.

323 *Stocks v Wilson* [1913] 2 K.B. 235 at 244; *R. Leslie Ltd v Sheill* [1914] 3 K.B. 607. Moneys stolen from a bank account can be traced in equity: *Bankers Trust Co v Shapira* [1980] 1 W.L.R. 1274 at 1282. See also *McCormick v Grogan* (1869) L.R. 4 H.L. 82 at 97.

defences, such as change of position, are capable of being given effect. However, whether English law should follow the United States and Canada by adopting the remedial constructive trust will have to be decided in some future case when the point is directly in issue.

**Questions**

1. Six years before her death Miss Spry opened a current account with Barclays Bank in the joint names of herself and her 25-year-old nephew, Neal Smug. Both of them called on the manager when they came to open the joint account. Miss Spry told the manager that as she was getting frail her nephew would look after her banking affairs for her. She also said that if she died before her nephew then he could keep any credit balance in the account on her death. It was arranged that the bank would honour cheques drawn on the account either by Miss Spry or by Neal. Although Miss Spry kept the cheque book in her desk, all the cheques were signed by Neal. As envisaged by the parties, only Miss Spry paid money into the account. At her death a credit balance of £2,000 remained. Who is entitled to this money if Miss Spry left her estate to the RSPCA in her will?
2. Fearing that his wife might divorce him at some time, and that a new business venture might prove financially damaging, Harold transferred legal title to his cottage to Simon, who agreed that when matters had resolved themselves so that it was safe to do so he would reconvey the cottage to Harold. The conveyance purported to be for £200,000, but in fact, as agreed, Simon paid nothing. Advise Harold who now seeks to recover the cottage. Does it matter: (a) if Simon is Harold's 15 year-old son; or (b) if only six months have elapsed and Harold's wife is still living with him and he is sufficiently secure financially to pay his debts as they fall due?
3. "The courts should be given a statutory discretion to determine the effects of illegality in resulting trust cases." **Discuss.**
4. "A resulting trust is a default mechanism to locate the beneficial ownership of property and not a proprietary remedy for unjust enrichment." **Discuss.**
5. The members of the Ravers Anonymous Club, an unincorporated association whose purposes are not charitable, have dissolved the association one week after having received £10,000 from Sir Lancelot Hellfire for the purposes of the Club, and one month after having received £1,000 from various raffles and sweepstakes, along with £150 from collections taken at a public meeting held to publicise the Club. In accordance with the Club rules the members received ten days' written notice of the meeting called to dissolve the association. What should happen to the above sums?

# 15

# CONSTRUCTIVE TRUSTS

## 1. Introduction

### A. Trusts Imposed by Law

As explained in Chapter 1, we can categorise trusts according to the reason for which a particular trust arises.[1] An express trust arises when a party (the settlor) successfully exercises her power to set up a trust, either by declaring that she holds property on trust, or by transferring property to trustees to hold on trust. All other trusts are imposed by law. If we put statutory trusts to one side, there are only two types of trust imposed by law: resulting trusts and constructive trusts.[2] We examined resulting trusts in Chapter 14; we examine constructive trusts in this chapter. 15–001

As we have said already,[3] when examining trusts imposed by law, one must confront the question of justification. If the law imposes a trust, one must ask two questions: first, why has the defendant been placed under a duty to the claimant; and secondly, even if the imposition of that duty can be justified, why has a trust been imposed? As we saw in Chapter 1, the existence of a trust has significant consequences, not only for the beneficiary and the trustee, but also for third parties, such as creditors of the trustee. 15–002

The practical importance of constructive trusts can be illustrated by reference to the facts of *Attorney General for Hong Kong v Reid*.[4] The Privy Council advised that when the defendant fiduciary received a bribe to act in a way that was contrary to the interests of the claimant principal, he did not merely incur a personal obligation to pay the value of the money to the principal, but also held the money on constructive trust for the principal. The significance of this in the factual circumstances of *Reid* was threefold. First, it meant that the principal could trace from the bribe money into assets, such as land, acquired by the fiduciary with that money. Secondly, the principal could assert a proprietary claim to such assets, which protected the principal in the fiduciary's insolvency, and also gave it the benefit of any increase in the value of the assets. Thirdly, the principal could assert a proprietary claim to such assets in the hands of third parties,[5] as those third parties, it seems,[6] were not bona fide purchasers for value of a legal estate without notice. 15–003

It is therefore clear that when a constructive trust is imposed on property held by a defendant, 15–004

---

1 For a useful discussion of different possible approaches to classifying trusts, see N. McBride, "On the Classification of Trusts" in P. Birks and F. Rose (eds), *Restitution and Equity, Volume 1: Resulting Trusts and Equitable Compensation* (Informa, 2000).

2 See paras 1–046—1–052.

3 See para.14–002.

4 [1994] 1 A.C. 324; approved in *FHR European Ventures LLP v Cedar Capital Partners LLC* [2015] A.C. 250.

5 Respectively the wife and the solicitor of the agent.

6 [1994] 1 A.C. 324 at 330.

the beneficiaries acquire the same proprietary rights in the trust assets as they would under an express trust.[7] Until trial the beneficiaries can preserve the position by obtaining (virtually[8] as of right) an interim injunction restraining dealings with "their" property. Moreover, if a constructive trust is imposed on property and the defendant's conscience is affected with knowledge of the circumstances which led to the imposition of the constructive trust, she will be personally liable to account to the beneficiaries for her dealings with the property in her capacity as trustee.[9]

**15-005** The question of justification is, therefore, an urgent one. In a case such as *Reid*, we cannot justify the advantages gained by the claimant principal by pointing to any party's successful exercise of a power to set up a trust. The third party paying the bribe or secret commission did not intend that it should be held on trust for the principal, nor did the defendant fiduciary when he received the bribe. Yet those other creditors of the fiduciary who had only personal claims against him deserve a convincing explanation as to why the claimant principal was given the important advantages of an equitable beneficial interest under the constructive trust.

## *B. The Nature of Constructive Trusts*

**15-006** Under English law, constructive trusts arise as a result of legal rules which state that they arise in certain circumstances. These rules do not give the courts a discretion to impose constructive trusts—or to refuse to do so—according to their assessment of the equities of a case: the courts' role is purely declaratory. In contrast, some other Commonwealth jurisdictions, e.g. Canada[10] and Australia,[11] distinguish "substantive" or "institutional" constructive trusts from "remedial" constructive trusts, and recognise that the courts have the power to impose the latter type of constructive trust as well as the former. Different judges and scholars attach different meanings to the terms "institutional" and "remedial constructive trust",[12] but most use them to distinguish constructive trusts which arise through the operation of legal rules from constructive trusts which arise following the exercise of a

---

7 W. Swadling, "The Fiction of the Constructive Trust" (2011) 64 C.L.P. 399, 406–412 takes the contrary view, arguing that constructive trusts are not genuine trusts, and simply involve either a court order that the defendant pay money to the claimant, or a court order that the defendant transfer property to the claimant. As exemplified by the consequences of the trust in *Attorney General for Hong Kong v Reid* [1994] 1 A.C. 324, however, that does not seem to be the current way in which such trusts operate.

8 *Polly Peck International Plc v Nadir (No.2)* [1992] 4 All E.R. 769 at 784.

9 *Independent Trustee Services Ltd v GP Noble Trustees Ltd* [2013] Ch. 91 at [77]–[81] (referring to the constructive trust imposed on misdirected trust property in the hands of a knowing recipient). See paras 11-075 and 12-057—12-062. The courts also use the language of personal liability to account as a constructive trustee when describing the liability of dishonest assistants in a breach of trust, but in this case they mean something different. This is discussed at paras 11-012—11-013.

10 *Sorochan v Sorochan* [1986] 2 S.C.R. 38; *Lac Minerals Ltd v International Corona Resources Ltd* [1989] 2 S.C.R. 574; *Soulos v Korkontzilas* [1997] 2 S.C.R. 217; *Kerr v Baranow* [2011] 1 S.C.R. 269; *Sun Indalex Finance, LLC v United Steelworkers* [2013] 1 S.C.R. 271 at [228].

11 *Muschinski v Dodds* (1985) 160 C.L.R. 583; *Bathurst CC v PWC Properties Pty Ltd* (1998) 195 C.L.R. 566; *Giumelli v Giumelli* (1999) 196 C.L.R. 101; *John Alexander's Clubs Pty Ltd v White City Tennis Club Ltd* (2010) 241 C.L.R. 1 at [128]–[129]; *Grimaldi v Chameleon Mining NL (No.2)* (2012) 200 F.C.R. 296 at [504]–[511].

12 For an excellent survey of different usages of the term, see M. Bryan, "Constructive Trusts: Understanding Remedialism" in J. Glister and P. Ridge (eds), *Fault Lines in Equity* (Hart Publishing, 2012). Some judges have used the term "remedial constructive trust" to refer to the personal liability of strangers who dishonestly participate in a breach of trust (see n.9, above): e.g. *Clarke v Marlborough Fine Art (London) Ltd* [2002] 1 W.L.R. 1731 at [66]; *Kilcarne Holdings Ltd v Targetfollow (Birmingham) Ltd* [2005] 2 P. & C.R. 8 at [261]. This usage seems to have been prompted by *Paragon Finance plc v DB Thakerar & Co (a firm)* [1999] 1 All E.R. 400 at 408–409, where Millett LJ distinguished constructive trusts of property from the personal liability of dishonest participants in a breach of trust. However it is best avoided, lest this personal liability become confused with the "discretionary proprietary remedy" to which Millett LJ also refers at 415.

judicial discretion,[13] either retrospectively or prospectively from the date of the court order.[14] It is controversial whether the courts should have a discretion to vary property rights in this way,[15] but whatever the rights and wrongs of this question, it is clear that English law does not currently recognise "remedial" constructive trusts of this kind.

For example, in *Westdeutsche Landesbank Girozentrale v Islington LBC*, Lord Browne-Wilkinson described the distinction between an institutional and a remedial constructive trust as follows[16]: **15–007**

> Under an institutional constructive trust, the trust arises by operation of law as from the date of the circumstances which give rise to it: the function of the court is merely to declare that such trust has arisen in the past. The consequences that flow from such trust having arisen (including the possibly unfair consequences to the third parties who in the interim have received trust property) are also determined by rules of law, not under a discretion. A remedial constructive trust . . . is different. It is a judicial remedy giving rise to an enforceable equitable obligation: the extent to which it operates retrospectively to the prejudice of third parties lies in the discretion of the court.

As later confirmed by Etherton LJ,[17] **15–008**

> the current general view is that English law does not at present recognise a remedial constructive trust of the kind described by Lord Browne-Wilkinson with its critical features of judicial discretion and retrospectivity . . . In that respect, our law differs from that in some other jurisdictions, most notably the U.S. and Canada.

## *C. The Diversity of Constructive Trusts*

Constructive trusts have been imposed in a wide variety of circumstances. This makes it hard to understand why they are imposed, and how (if at all) they differ from resulting trusts. It also makes it very difficult, if not impossible, to find any general underlying justification that explains each and every constructive trust. To proceed, then, we need to break down the circumstances in which constructive trusts have been imposed into discrete categories, and to consider the possible justifications for each such type of constructive trust. At the end of the chapter we will see if any general themes emerge. **15–009**

We have already discussed several situations in which constructive trusts are imposed, namely: (a) cases concerning incomplete transfers and the rule in *Re Rose*[18]; (b) cases concerning secret and **15–010**

---

13 Cf. *Grimaldi v Chameleon Mining NL (No.2)* (2012) 200 F.C.R. 296 at [504] per Finn J: "We emphasise the remedial use of the constructive trust so as to exclude from consideration those classes of case where, on the proof of particular facts in a given context (e.g. the death of one party to an agreement for mutual wills: *Birmingham v Renfrew* (1937) 57 C.L.R. 666; or the entitlement under contract to an expectancy after the consideration for it is executed: cf. *Tailby v Official Receiver* (1888) 13 App. Cas. 523) the circumstances are 'construed' as giving rise to a constructive trust."

14 See, e.g. *Fortex Group Ltd v Macintosh* [1998] 3 N.Z.L.R. 171 at 172–173, endorsed in *Regal Casting Ltd v Lightbody* [2009] 2 N.Z.L.R. 433 at [162]–[163].

15 D. Wright, *The Remedial Constructive Trust* (1998), reviewed by P. Birks (1999) 115 L.Q.R. 681; P. Birks, "Rights, Wrongs, and Remedies" (2000) 20 O.J.L.S. 1; T. Etherton, "Constructive Trusts: A New Model for Equity and Unjust Enrichment" [2008] C.L.J. 265.

16 [1996] A.C. 669 at 714–715.

17 *Crossco Unlimited (No.4) v Jolan Ltd* [2012] 2 All E.R. 754 at [84]. See also *Re Goldcorp Exchange Ltd* [1995] 1 A.C. 74 at 104; *Sinclair Investments (UK) Ltd v Versailles Trade Finance Ltd* [2012] Ch. 453 at [37]; *FHR European Ventures LLP v Cedar Capital Partners LLC* [2015] A.C. 250 at [47]. In *Thorner v Major* [2009] 1 W.L.R. 776 at [20]–[21], Lord Scott would have preferred to base his finding for the claimant on the grounds of a remedial constructive trust, but none of the other members of the court took that view. Writing extra-judicially, the Chancellor, Sir Terence Etherton, has expressed support for the imposition of remedial constructive trusts in cases about shared homes: T. Etherton, "Constructive Trusts: A New Model for Equity and Unjust Enrichment" [2008] C.L.J. 265.

18 Named for *Re Rose, Midland Bank Executor & Trustee Co Ltd v Rose* [1952] Ch. 499. See too *Mascall v Mascall* (1984) 49 P. & C.R. 119; *Corin v Patton* (1990) 169 C.L.R. 450; *Pennington v Waine* [2002] 1 W.L.R. 2075. See paras 2–022ff 2–0097ff.

half-secret trusts[19]; (c) cases concerning mutual wills[20]; (d) cases concerning a failure to comply with formality rules in relation to trusts of land[21]; and (e) cases concerning the profits of a breach of fiduciary duty.[22] In this chapter we shall look at some further situations, under the following headings: (f) specifically enforceable contracts of sale; (g) assignments for value of future property; (h) receipt of property subject to an undertaking; (i) shared homes; (j) the *Pallant v Morgan* equity; (k) proceeds of breach of confidence; (l) unlawful killing; and (m) the protection of pre-existing property rights.

## 2. Specifically Enforceable Contracts of Sale

### A. Nature of the Trust

**15–011** If two parties enter a specifically enforceable contract to sell land or other property, then the vendor will hold the property on constructive trust for the purchaser until the contract is completed by conveyance of the property.[23] This form of constructive trust is very well-established: in *Lysaght v Edwards*, for example, Jessel MR found such a trust and said that the point had been settled "for more than two centuries".[24]

**15–012** There are, nonetheless, some uncertainties as to the nature and operation of the purchaser's interest in such a case. For example, as Mason J observed in *Chang v Registrar of Titles*[25]

> there has been controversy as to the time when the trust relationship arises and as to the character of that relationship. Lord Eldon considered that a trust arose on execution of the contract.[26] Plumer M.R. thought that until it is known whether the agreement will be performed the vendor 'is not even in the situation of constructive trustee; he is only a constructive trustee *sub modo*, and providing nothing happens to prevent it. It may turn out that the title is not good, or the purchaser may be unable to pay.'[27] Lord Hatherley said that the vendor becomes a trustee for the purchaser when the contract is completed, as by payment of the purchase money.[28] Jessel M.R. held that a trust *sub modo* arises on the execution of the contract but that the constructive trust comes into existence when title is made out by the vendor or is accepted by the purchaser.[29]

**15–013** In *Scott v Southern Pacific Mortgages Ltd*,[30] the Supreme Court had to consider the nature of the constructive trust in slightly unusual circumstances. The case concerned a sale and leaseback transaction. The vendor, a home owner in financial difficulties, sold her home to the purchasing firm, at a discount to its market value, in return for the firm promising that she could remain in occupation of the home for as long as she wished during her life. The firm financed its acquisition of the home by means of a loan from the lender, secured by a legal charge over the home. The difficulty was that the firm had not told the lender that it had promised to allow the vendor to remain in occupation; in fact, the terms of the mortgage loan expressly prevented such an arrangement. When the firm ran into financial

---

19 e.g. *Ottaway v Norman* [1972] Ch. 698; *Blackwell v Blackwell* [1929] A.C. 318. For discussion, see paras 3–131ff.

20 See paras 3–167ff.

21 See paras 3–032ff.

22 See paras 13–126ff.

23 *Holroyd v Marshall* (1862) 10 H.L.C. 191 at 209; *Dougan v Ley* (1946) 71 C.L.R. 152; *Oughtred v IRC* [1960] A.C. 206; *Neville v Wilson* [1997] Ch. 44.

24 (1876) 2 Ch. D. 499 at 506.

25 (1976) 137 C.L.R. 177 at 184. See too *Martin Commercial Fueling Inc v Virtanen* (1997) 154 D.L.R. (4th) 290, esp. at [8]–[10].

26 *Paine v Meller* (1801) 6 Ves. Jun. 349; *Broome v Monck* [1803–1813] All E.R. Rep. 631 (1805).

27 *Wall v Bright* (1820) 1 Jac. & W 494.

28 *Shaw v Foster* (1872) L.R. 5 H.L. 321.

29 *Lysaght v Edwards* (1876) 2 Ch.D. 499, accepted in *Rayner v Preston* (1881) 18 Ch.D. 1.

30 [2015] A.C. 385.

problems, the lender wished to enforce its charge by selling the home. The vendor claimed that she had an equitable interest in the land that was capable of binding the lender, as it had arisen before the lender's charge. To make out that argument, she claimed that, on exchange of contracts with the purchasing firm, the firm had acquired an equitable interest under a constructive trust. That equitable interest could then itself be subject to an equitable proprietary right of the vendor arising, for example, through proprietary estoppel as a result of the purchaser's promise to allow her to remain in occupation. One of the questions for the Supreme Court, therefore, was whether the equitable interest of a purchaser of land, arising on exchange of contracts, is such that it can itself be the subject matter of an equitable interest held by another party.

The Supreme Court unanimously held that, until the point when the purchasing firm acquired its legal estate in the land, any rights arising in favour of the vendor as a result of a promise by the firm were purely personal rights, and so could not bind a third party such as the lender. Lord Collins (with whom Lord Sumption agreed) stated that, although a purchaser in such a case has a right that can bind third parties (as where the vendor makes a second sale of the land to a third party), "it does not follow that the purchaser has proprietary rights for all purposes."[31] It was held instead that, as a general rule, **15–014**

> where the proprietary right is claimed to be derived from the rights of a person who does not have the legal estate, then the right needs to be 'fed' by the acquisition of the legal estate before it can be asserted otherwise than personally.[32]

Lady Hale, despite feeling some unease as to its practical consequences, reached the same conclusion.[33]

It may well be, however, that the analysis of the Supreme Court depends principally on the nature of the right acquired by a purchaser where its acquisition of the land is financed by a mortgage, rather than on the nature of the rights acquired by a purchaser on exchange of contracts. As Lady Hale put it: "If all the purchaser ever acquires is an equity of redemption, he cannot create an interest which is inconsistent with the terms of his mortgage."[34] In other words, given that it had already been established that there is no moment in time when such a purchaser holds a legal estate free from the charge held by the lender,[35] it would then be inconsistent with the protection afforded to the lender if an equitable interest, capable of binding the lender, could arise in the period before the sale was formally completed and the charge granted to the lender. Note that it had previously been accepted that if a purchaser, after exchange of contracts but before acquiring legal title, enters into a sub-sale, the sub-purchaser acquires an equitable interest (presumably under a sub-trust) and is therefore protected if the purchaser goes into insolvency[36]: to that extent, at least, the purchaser acquires an equitable interest that may itself be the subject matter of another party's equitable interest. **15–015**

The court's analysis in *Scott* nonetheless confirms Lord Walker's point in *Jerome v Kelly*[37] that "[it would] be wrong to treat an uncompleted contract for the sale of land as equivalent to an immediate, irrevocable declaration of trust." Lord Walker's approach has been elaborated by Peter Turner,[38] who argues that the vendor-purchaser constructive trust in fact consists of a number of distinct **15–016**

---

31 ibid., at [65].
32 ibid., at [71].
33 ibid., at [122].
34 ibid., at [122].
35 *Abbey National Building Society v Cann* [1991] 1 A.C. 56.
36 See, e.g. *Berkley v Poulett* (1977) E.G.L.R. 86.
37 [2004] 1 W.L.R. 1409 at [32].
38 P. Turner, "Understanding the Constructive Trust between Vendor and Purchaser" (2012) 128 L.Q.R. 582.

equitable rights, not all of which arise immediately, but that it is nonetheless reasonable to say that a "trust in some sense exists at every stage between the formation and discharge by performance of a specifically enforceable contract of sale." It is thus possible to agree with the view that a trust arises as soon as the contract for the sale of unique property is entered into, whilst also agreeing that the rights of the parties change over time, so that the purchaser acquires a fuller form of equitable ownership only once the purchase price is paid.[39]

**15–017** At the time of formation of the contract, for example, the vendor has the right to protect her own interest prior to completion.[40] She can keep the rents and profits until the date fixed for completion,[41] and retain possession of the property until the contract is completed by payment of the purchase price.[42] If she parts with possession to the purchaser before actual completion, or even conveys the land, then she may fall back on her equitable lien over the property to ensure that she is paid.[43] It is nonetheless possible to regard the purchaser as having an interest under a constructive trust from the time of formation of the contract because she is given potential protection against a third party receiving the property from the vendor and, as Turner argues[44]:

> A uniquely equitable feature of all trusts of property is that they keep the property available for the performance of an obligation. The property is kept alive through a general rule that, subject to defences, a person who acquires an interest in property takes subject to the interest anyone else may have acquired under a trust.

**15–018** If the vendor sells the property to a third party who has a defence to the purchaser's interest under the trust, the purchaser can trace into the sale proceeds received by the vendor, and assert a proprietary claim to these proceeds, subject to accounting to the vendor for the price agreed between the vendor and purchaser.[45] This will be useful if the contractual claim against the vendor for damages is not worthwhile, e.g. if the vendor is bankrupt or has generated a surplus through her dealings with the third party.[46]

### *B. Scope of the Trust*

**15–019** Whilst contracts for the sale of land constitute the core case of this form of constructive trust, it can clearly also apply in other situations where a party is under a contractual duty to transfer unique property. For example, we saw in Chapter 3[47] that in *Neville v Wilson*,[48] adopting views expressed by Lord Radcliffe in the House of Lords in *Oughtred v IRC*,[49] the Court of Appeal found that a constructive trust arose on the making of a contract to transfer a beneficial interest in shares in a private company. Indeed, it seems that the same principle can apply even if the enforceable duty to make a transfer is non-contractual: in *Mountney v Treharne*,[50] for example, a court had made an order, in ancillary relief proceedings following a divorce, that the husband had to transfer his interest in the matrimonial

---

39 *Miliangos v George Frank (Textiles) Ltd* [1976] A.C. 443 at 467.
40 *Shaw v Foster* (1872) L.R. 5 H.L. 321 at 328; *Re Watford Corporation's Contract* [1943] Ch. 82 at 85.
41 *Cuddon v Tite* (1858) 1 Giff. 395.
42 *Gedge v Montrose* (1858) 26 Beav. 45; *Phillips v Silvester* (1872) L.R. 8 Ch. 173.
43 *Nives v Nives* (1880) 15 Ch. D. 649; *Re Birmingham* [1959] Ch. 523; *London & Cheshire Insurance Co Ltd v Laplagrene* [1971] Ch. 499.
44 Turner, "Understanding the Constructive Trust between Vendor and Purchaser" (2012) 128 L.Q.R. 582, 597.
45 *Bunny Industries Ltd v FSW Enterprises Pty Ltd* [1982] Qd. R. 712.
46 *Lake v Bayliss* [1974] 1 W.L.R. 1073.
47 See paras 3–105ff.
48 [1997] Ch. 144.
49 [1960] A.C. 206 at 227. See too the views of Upjohn J at first instance in that case: [1958] Ch. 383 at 390.
50 [2003] Ch. 135.

home to his wife. It was held that, as a result of that order, a trust arose and so an immediate equitable interest arose in favour of the wife, which was critical given that the husband had subsequently been made bankrupt.

It also seems that the underlying principle is not confined to constructive trusts, but can give rise to other forms of equitable interest. In *Walsh v Lonsdale*,[51] for example, it was held that where A is under a specifically enforceable contractual duty to grant a lease to B, B immediately acquires an equitable lease; in *Holroyd v Marshall*,[52] an immediate equitable security interest arose as a result of the borrower's contractual promise to transfer title to mill machinery to trustees, so that the title could be held as security for a debt owed by the transferor. However, a trust is appropriate where the duty is to make an outright transfer, rather than to grant a lease or to make a transfer by way of security. **15–020**

There is some debate as to the proper role, if any, of the availability of specific performance. For example, in *Tailby v Official Receiver*,[53] Lord Macnaghten stated, in the context of an agreement to give a security interest over receivables, that there was no requirement that the contract be capable of specific performance. Simon Gardner has also argued that, in the context of equitable leases, the supposed requirement of specific performance has no sound historical basis. Peter Turner, in contrast, has supported the orthodox requirement, noting however that, at the time of the formation of the contract at least, it is the *potential* for specific performance, arising from the uniqueness of the property to be transferred, that is of importance.[54] **15–021**

## C. Justifying the Trust

The vendor–purchaser constructive trust has been the subject of some fierce academic criticism. William Swadling, for example, has argued that it is a "fiction" which "cannot be justified", as the simple fact that a defendant may be ordered by a court to transfer property to the claimant is not, in itself, sufficient to justify giving the claimant all the advantages of a beneficial interest under a trust.[55] Certainly, Swadling is correct to doubt the usefulness of the formula often used to justify this form of constructive trust: that "equity looks upon as done that which ought to be done". The difficulty with the formula, taken literally, is that where, for example, A is under a duty to grant B a lease, or to transfer a right to B, it seems odd that equity should pretend that this duty has already been performed. In any case, the outcome of the vendor-purchaser constructive trust, at least when it initially arises, is not that the purchaser is already regarded in equity as an owner: as previously noted,[56] the vendor retains certain valuable rights in relation to the property until the purchase price is paid. **15–022**

The maxim may be of some assistance, however, if it is applied only "within the parameters of what are clearly understood boundaries"[57] and is not interpreted literally. It reflects an underlying principle that if A holds particular property and is under a duty to transfer that property to B, or to give B a right in relation to it, then B can acquire an immediate equitable interest in relation to the property. As Peter **15–023**

---

51 (1882) 21 Ch. D. 9.
52 (1862) 10 H.L. Cas. 191.
53 (1888) 13 App. Cas. 523.
54 Turner, "Understanding the Constructive Trust between Vendor and Purchaser" (2012) 128 L.Q.R. 582, 589–592.
55 W. Swadling, "The Vendor-Purchaser Constructive Trust" in S. Degeling and J. Edelman (eds), *Equity in Commercial Law* (Sweet & Maxwell, 2005), pp.475–476, 487–488; Swadling, "The Fiction of the Constructive Trust" (2011) 64 C.L.P. 399, 408.
56 See para.15–017.
57 *HR Trustees Ltd v Wembley plc (In Liquidation)* [2011] EWHC 2974 (Ch) at [59].

Turner[58] and Lionel Smith[59] have noted, it is characteristic of equity to give B the benefit of protection against third parties where a duty of A relates to specific property held by A. In Turner's view, the vendor–purchaser constructive trust is justified as a means of protecting the purchaser's interest in due performance of the contract, responding in particular to the need to prevent the purchaser failing to obtain the property promised under the contract: "Equity's policy is that contracts to convey unique property need greater stability against third parties than contracts to convey non-unique property."[60]

15–024 The emphasis on uniqueness ties in with a requirement that the contract be, potentially at least, specifically enforceable. A different view, building on that requirement, is that whenever B has the power to acquire property held by A, B necessarily has an equitable interest in that property, and so it is no surprise that a constructive trust arises when A is under a specifically enforceable duty to convey specific property to B.[61] A further view, which again builds on a conception of the nature of the trust, is that the fact of A's holding a specific right, and being under a duty to B in relation to that right, is itself sufficient to give B an equitable interest, as such interests, by definition, arise when B has a right in relation to another right.[62]

## 3. Assignments for Value of Future Property

### *A. Nature of the Trust*

15–025 As Swinfen Eady LJ stated in *Re Lind*[63]:

> An assignment for value of future property actually binds the property itself directly it is acquired—automatically on the happening of the event, and without any future act on the part of the assignor—and does not merely rest in, and amount to, a right in contract, giving rise to an action. The assignor, having received the consideration, becomes in equity on the happening of the event, trustee for the assignee of the property devolving upon or acquired by him, and which she had previously sold and been paid for.

### *B. Scope of the Trust*

15–026 The constructive trust arising in such a case is clearly related to that in *Pullan v Koe*,[64] which we examined in Chapter 2,[65] and to the underlying principle applied in cases of specifically enforceable contracts to transfer property. In *Pullan*, it was held that, as a result of a prior, binding promise to settle any property later acquired by the wife of the value of £100 or more, a sum of £285 later received by the wife was *immediately* held by her on a trust enforceable in favour of all those within the marriage consideration. The trust in such a case is constructive, rather than express, as it does not require any exercise of a power to set up a trust: such a power cannot be exercised in relation to property not yet held by the purported settlor; and, once the property is received, the trust arises immediately, without the need for any declaration of trust.[66] The point of the principle stated in *Re Lind* is that an ineffective

---

[58] P. Turner, "Understanding the Constructive Trust between Vendor and Purchaser" (2012) 128 L.Q.R. 582, 597–598.
[59] L. Smith, "Fusion and Tradition" in Degeling and Edelman (eds), *Equity in Commercial Law* (2005).
[60] Turner, "Understanding the Constructive Trust between Vendor and Purchaser" (2012) 128 L.Q.R. 582, 603.
[61] See R. Chambers, "The Importance of Specific Performance" in Degeling and Edelman (eds), *Equity in Commercial Law* (2005).
[62] See, e.g. B. McFarlane and R. Stevens, "The Nature of Equitable Property" (2010) 4 J.Eq. 1, 16–17. See further paras 17–056ff.
[63] [1915] 2 Ch. 354 at 360.
[64] [1913] 1 Ch. 9. See too *Re Gillott's Settlement* [1934] Ch. 97 at 157–159.
[65] See paras 2–073ff.
[66] See too *Barclays Bank Plc v Willowbank International Ltd* [1987] B.C.L.C. 717; *Associated Alloys Pty Ltd v ACN 001 452 106 Pty Ltd* (2000) 202 C.L.R. 588.

attempt at an immediate assignment, if made for value, will be regarded in effect as a promise to make such an assignment when possible, and so will have the same effect as in *Pullan*.[67]

It is important to note that this principle applies only where the attempted assignment was for value provided for or on behalf of the claimant. In the absence of such value, there is no reason to impose any duty on the party who attempted to make the assignment, who is simply regarded as having failed in an attempt to make a gift. This is, therefore, one of the contexts in which the maxim that "equity will not assist a volunteer" has some relevance. **15–027**

The principle is also limited to cases where the promise to assign, or the attempted assignment related to specific, identifiable property. It therefore cannot apply in a case such as *Re Goldcorp Exchange Ltd*,[68] where the defendant has simply promised to transfer a particular quantity of unascertained goods to the claimant. The very reason that prevents property passing at common law in such a case,[69] the lack of identifiable property to which the vendor's duty may attach, also prevents a trust, as a trust must have identifiable subject matter.[70] **15–028**

### C. Justifying the Trust

As the principle underlying this trust seems to be identical to that applying in the case of specifically enforceable contracts to transfer property, it stands or falls, as far as justification is concerned, with that principle. The only significant difference is that, in the case of a failed assignment for value, it is also necessary to justify why the defendant, who is unlikely to have made an express contractual promise to assign in the future, should be under such a duty to make the assignment as soon as the property is received. It does not seem unreasonable, however, to imply a promise to make such an assignment, if the intention was that some specific, identifiable property should be transferred. **15–029**

## 4. Receipt of Property Subject to an Undertaking

### A. Nature of the Trust

In Chapter 3, when looking at the formal requirements applying in relation to trusts of land, we considered the Court of Appeal's decision in *Rochefoucauld v Boustead*.[71] It was held there that, even though no written evidence of a declaration of trust could be produced, the defendant had acquired title to land from the claimant's mortgagee on trust for the claimant. In *Bannister v Bannister*,[72] the Court of Appeal regarded the trust thus arising as a constructive trust, and found that such a trust also arose where A transferred her interest in two cottages to B, pursuant to an oral agreement that B would allow A to remain living rent-free in one of those cottages for the rest of her life. Giving the Court of Appeal's judgment, Scott LJ stated that[73]: **15–030**

> It is, we think, clearly a mistake to suppose that the equitable principle on which a constructive trust is raised against a person who insists on the absolute character of a conveyance to himself for the purpose of defeating a beneficial interest, which, according to the true bargain, was to belong to another, is confined to

---

67 [1915] 2 Ch. 345 at 360. See too *Re Burton's Settlements* [1955] Ch. 82 at 103–104 and *Parker v Taswell* (1858) 2 De G. & J. 559.
68 [1995] 1 A.C. 74.
69 See Sale of Goods Act 1979 s.16.
70 See para.4–070.
71 [1897] 1 Ch. 196; discussed at paras 3–032—3–049.
72 [1948] 2 All E.R. 133.
73 ibid., at 136.

> cases where the conveyance itself was fraudulently obtained . . . Nor is it, in our opinion, necessary that the bargain on which the absolute conveyance is made should include any express stipulation that the grantee is in so many words to hold as trustee. It is enough that the bargain should have included a stipulation under which some sufficiently defined beneficial interest in the property was to be taken by another.

**15-031** In each of *Rochefoucauld* and *Bannister*, it can be said that a trust arises where the defendant has acquired property following a promise made to another to hold that property, in some way, on trust for that other. The nature of this trust is a matter of some controversy. As we noted in Chapter 3, there are important practical reasons for wishing to know whether the trust is express or constructive.[74]

**15-032** On one view, the trust is an express one. Certainly, in *Rochefoucauld* itself, the Court of Appeal classified the trust as express when establishing what limitation period should govern the beneficiary's claim.[75] This point may not be decisive, however, for to treat a trust as an express one "within the meaning" of a limitation statute does not mean that it necessarily arose as a result of a party's successful exercise of a power to set up a trust and was thus not imposed by law. For example, in a case where the defendant did indeed agree to hold on trust, there may be good reasons for treating that defendant as an express trustee, and thus preventing her from taking advantage of a limitation period, even if the agreement (because for example of a failure to comply with formal requirements) cannot, in itself, establish a provable trust.[76]

**15-033** William Swadling has also argued in favour of the express trust view as a matter of principle.[77] Perhaps the strongest point is as to the effect of an oral declaration of a trust over land. As Swadling notes, the relevant formality rule in *Rochefoucauld*, the Statute of Frauds 1677 s.7, did not render such an oral declaration void, or even unenforceable; it was rather "a rule describing how, if it came to litigation, an allegation that a declaration of trust respecting land must be proved".[78] The same is true of the successor to s.7, the Law of Property Act 1925 s.53(1)(b), which specifies how a declaration of trust respecting any land or any interest therein must be manifested and proved. This means that an express trust of land can arise by oral declaration: the obstacle imposed by the statute is as to proof of that trust. In *Rochefoucauld*, the Court of Appeal was willing to allow proof of that express trust, as any attempt by the trustee to rely on the statutory formality rule would have been regarded as a "fraud",[79] and so the trust proved was necessarily express.

**15-034** The alternative view is that the type of trust recognised in *Rochefoucauld* and in *Bannister* is a constructive trust. Certainly, *Bannister* is not the only case in which the constructive trust label has been applied by the courts to that type of trust.[80] This view of the trust also has substantial academic support.[81] Perhaps the strongest point in favour of this view is that it permits direct reliance on the

---

74 See paras 3-045–3-050.

75 [1897] 1 Ch. 196 at 207–208. See too Swadling, "The Nature of the Trust in *Rochefoucauld v Boustead*" in C. Mitchell (ed.), *Constructive and Resulting Trusts* (Hart Publishing, 2010), pp.100–103.

76 On this point, note the analysis of Millett LJ in *Paragon Finance v Thakerar* [1999] 1 All E.R. 400, 408–409, distinguishing between different types of constructive trust when considering the relevant limitation rules. It is conceivable that a similar approach could be adopted when considering, for example, the application of conflicts of laws rules, so that a constructive trust arising in a case where the defendant had agreed to hold on trust would be treated in the same way as an express trust.

77 See, e.g. Swadling, "The Nature of the Trust in *Rochefoucauld v Boustead*" in Mitchell (ed.), *Constructive and Resulting Trusts* (2010).

78 Swadling, "The Nature of the Trust in *Rochefoucauld v Boustead*" in Mitchell (ed.), *Constructive and Resulting Trusts* (2010), p.104.

79 [1897] 1 Ch. 196 at 205–206.

80 See too *Paragon Finance Plc v DB Thakerar & Co* [1999] 1 All E.R. 400 at 409 per Millett LJ; *Gissing v Gissing* [1971] A.C. 886 at 905 per Lord Diplock; *de Bruyne v de Bruyne* [2010] EWCA Civ 519 at [51] per Patten LJ.

81 See, e.g. W. Ames, "Constructive Trusts Based on the Breach of an Express Oral Trust of Land" (1906–7) 29 Harvard L.R. 549; T. Youdan, "Formalities for Trusts of Land and the Doctrine in *Rochefoucauld v Boustead*" [1984] C.L.J. 306; B.

statutory exception to the formality rules provided for constructive trusts by s.53(2) of the Law of Property Act 1925.[82] This means that a court does not have to deal with the difficult questions of when, precisely, it is fraudulent for a party to rely on the statutory formality rule[83] and why, precisely, it is constitutionally permissible for a court to read in a fraud-based exception which is not set out in the statute itself.[84] In addition, in a thorough analysis of the facts of *Rochefoucauld*, Ying Khai Liew has argued that, in that case "none of the parties could possibly have acted as settlor",[85] as there was no declaration by any party who had a power to declare a trust. First, the relevant land was not initially held by the beneficiary (the Comtesse) of the eventual trust, as title to it was held by mortgagees, who then sold the land to the eventual trustee (Boustead) using their power of sale as mortgagees. Secondly, there is no evidence that those mortgagees set up a trust in favour of the Comtesse when transferring the land to Boustead, or that they would have had any interest in doing so. Thirdly, Boustead himself could not have declared a trust as he had immediately remortgaged the land to the mortgagees who sold it to him. Liew argues that, as the court in *Rochefoucauld* focussed instead on the agreement between the Comtesse and Boustead, which occurred before any receipt of land by the latter, that agreement was part of the grounds justifying the imposition of a constructive trust.[86]

There is always a hurdle to be cleared if arguing that a trust is imposed by law, rather than as a result of a party's successful exercise of a power to set up a trust. It must be shown that there is a good reason for the law not only to impose a duty on the defendant, but also to do so by means of a trust, which gives the claimant an equitable proprietary right. We will consider below if such a justification can be found for the trust arising in cases such as *Rochefoucald* and *Bannister*, if indeed it is constructive.[87] **15–035**

## *B. Scope of the Trust*

### i. General Position

On either of the express trust or constructive trust analyses of the trust in *Rochefoucald* and *Bannister*, there is an important question to be answered as to the precise requirements of the trust. On the former view, the question is as to the definition of fraud: when will the principle that a "statute cannot be used as an instrument of fraud" allow oral proof of the declaration of trust? On the latter view, the question is as to the precise ground on which a trust is imposed by law. **15–036**

A requirement for this type of trust, it seems, is that there has been a promise by the recipient of the property to hold it on trust, so that any "fraud" involves reneging on that promise. The recipient must have "undertaken a new obligation, not otherwise existing" to the beneficiary[88]; no trust arises, **15–037**

McFarlane, "Constructive Trusts Arising on Receipt of Property *Sub Conditione*" (2004) 120 L.Q.R. 667; N. Hopkins, "Conscience, Discretion and the Creation of Property Rights" (2006) 26 L.S. 475; S. Gardner, "Reliance-Based Constructive Trusts" in Mitchell (ed.), *Constructive and Resulting Trusts* (2010); Y.K. Liew "*Rochefoucauld v Boustead* (1897)" in C. Mitchell and P. Mitchell (eds), *Landmark Cases in Equity* (Hart Publishing, 2012).

82 Section 8 of the Statute of Frauds 1677 played the same role, providing an exception for a trust arising by "the implication or construction of law".

83 Swadling himself admits that "there is no authoritative statement" of what amounts to fraud for the purposes of the doctrine: A. Burrows (ed.), *English Private Law*, 3rd edn (Oxford University Press, 2013), para.4.208.

84 Those problems are discussed by N. Hopkins, *The Informal Acquisition of Rights in Land* (Sweet & Maxwell, 2000), pp.31–32 and P. Critchley, "Instruments of Fraud, Testamentary Dispositions, and the Doctrine of Secret Trusts" (1999) 115 L.Q.R. 631, pp.653–654.

85 Y.K. Liew, "*Rochefoucauld v Boustead* (1897)" in Mitchell and Mitchell (eds), *Landmark Cases in Equity* (2012), p.426.

86 Liew, ibid., p.432.

87 See paras 15–044—15–045.

88 *Lloyd v Dugdale* [2002] 2 P. & C.R. 13 at [52] per Sir Christopher Slade.

for example, if the purchaser only acquires land subject to any rights that might already exist in relation to it.[89] As noted by Lord Diplock in *Gissing v Gissing*,[90] however, it would be surprising if an oral promise alone sufficed, where the trust property is land; something else[91] is required to permit the trust to be proved or to arise without writing.

**15-038** One suggestion is that the additional factor is provided by the prospect of detriment being suffered, usually by the claimant, as a result of action undertaken in reliance on the defendant's promise.[92] In *Bannister*, for example, it can be said that, as the vendor's decision to sell the cottages to the purchaser was influenced by the purchaser's promise to allow the vendor continued rights in one of those cottages, the vendor would be left to suffer a detriment if the purchaser were free to renege on the promise.

**15-039** An alternative view is that the "something else" is provided by the prospect of the recipient acquiring an unfair advantage as a result of the promise[93]; if the promise relates to the very property acquired by the recipient, and if the promise also gave the recipient an advantage in relation to the acquisition of that property, the promise is then enforced. On this view, the key point in *Bannister* is that it would have been unconscionable for the purchaser to be free to use his legal rights in the land as he wished, given that those rights were acquired, in part, because of a promise to use those rights in a particular way.

**15-040** It is important to note that, whatever view is taken as to the basis of the type of trust in *Rochefoucauld* and *Bannister*, and even if they are seen as express trusts, there are clearly strong links between this type of trust and those we have seen in other areas of the law. For example, when considering secret trusts in Chapter 3,[94] we saw that there is a debate as to whether the trusts are properly seen as express or constructive, and also as to the precise grounds on which they arise, and whether the focus should be the risk of unjust detriment to the testator, or the risk of unjust gain to the secret trustee. On most views of the nature of secret trusts, it therefore seems possible to regard them as falling within the same principle as the trusts arising in *Rochefoucauld* and *Bannister*.

**15-041** If one adopts a constructive trust view of the *Rochefoucauld* and *Bannister* type of trust, however, it may be possible to find further cases which fall within the same underlying principle. For example, in *Neale v Willis*,[95] a husband received £50 from his mother-in-law, to enable him to buy a house: the money was provided subject to his express promise that the house would be conveyed into the joint names of himself and his wife. He had the house conveyed into his sole name, but the Court of Appeal, relying on *Bannister*, held that the husband's promise to his mother-in-law should be enforced "by holding that the husband holds the property on constructive trust for himself and his wife."[96] In that case, the mother-in-law was never in a position to create an express trust of the land, and the husband did not agree to hold on trust at a time when he held the land itself, making an express trust analysis

---

89 See *Ashburn Anstalt v Arnold* [1989] Ch. 1 at 26 per Fox LJ: "We do not think it desirable that constructive trusts of land should be imposed in reliance on inferences from slender materials." In *Chaudhary v Yavuz* [2013] Ch. 249, the fact that the recipient acquired property sold subject to incumbrances "discoverable by inspection of the property before the contract" did not give rise to a trust, as it did not mean that the purchaser had made a promise to give effect to any such right.

90 [1971] A.C. 886 at 905.

91 See P. Critchley, "Instruments of Fraud, Testamentary Dispositions, and the Doctrine of Secret Trusts" (1999) 115 L.Q.R. 631 at 646–653.

92 See, e.g. S. Gardner, "Reliance-Based Constructive Trusts" in Mitchell (ed.), *Constructive and Resulting Trusts* (2010).

93 See, e.g. B. McFarlane, "Constructive Trusts Arising on Receipt of Property *Sub Conditione*" (2004) 120 L.Q.R. 667. See too *de Bruyne v de Bruyne* [2010] EWCA Civ 519 at [51] per Patten LJ.

94 See paras 3-131ff.

95 (1968) 19 P. & C.R. 836.

96 ibid., 839.

more difficult.[97] Similarly, in the next section, we will consider the *Pallant v Morgan* constructive trust, which arises as a result of an agreement made between the parties prior to the acquisition of any property: on one view, it might fall under the same general principle as the *Rochefoucauld* and *Bannister* trusts.

### ii. Fictional Trusts?

In *Binions v Evans*, Lord Denning MR relied on *Bannister* to find a constructive trust where the purchasers of land had promised, when acquiring that land, to allow a widow currently in occupation of a cottage on the land to continue living in the cottage for life, or for as long as she wished. The effect of the trust was thus to allow the widow to continue enjoying the right in the property which she had had before the sale of the land; in Lord Denning's view, that was a licence. Similarly, in *Ashburn Anstalt v Arnold*,[98] the Court of Appeal considered if a constructive trust arose to protect a licensee in a case where land was sold by the licensor subject to that licence: no such trust arose as, on the facts, the purchaser had made no promise to undertake a new duty to the licensee.[99] 15–042

The difficulty in these cases is that it has been clearly determined by the House of Lords that a licence to occupy land, even if protected by a contract, gives the licensor only a personal right against the licensee.[100] It seems very strange, therefore, that a trust, presumably giving the beneficiary an equitable interest in land, should arise where the purchaser has simply promised to allow an existing licence to continue.[101] On the express trust view of *Rochefoucauld* and *Bannister*, the cases provide no assistance in a case where the purchaser, rather than agreeing to hold on trust, made some other promise. On the constructive trust view of those cases, it is possible in a case such as *Binions v Evans* to draw on the principle underlying *Rochefoucauld* and *Bannister*, but the operation of that principle should *not* lead to the imposition of a trust.[102] The point is that, on the constructive trust view, there may be a general principle about the need to enforce promises subject to which property has been received, with that principle leading to a trust only if the promisor said that she would hold on trust, and leading instead to a different right over the property (such as a licence) where the promisor instead said that she would give the claimant such a right. On either view, however, it seems reasonably clear that, despite its continued usage,[103] the language of trusts is misleading if the right that the recipient has promised to confer does not amount to a beneficial interest under a trust. 15–043

## *C. Justifying the Trust*

As we have said, trusts are always easier to justify if they can be seen as express. However, the express trust view of the type of trust in *Rochefoucauld* and *Bannister* does require one to accept that the concept that "a statute cannot be used as an instrument of fraud" is sufficiently precise to be sensibly applied, and can be justifiably applied, even if it is not expressly contained in the statute imposing a 15–044

---

[97] It could be argued that the mother-in-law created a trust of the money advanced, but the extent of the wife's interest under the trust arising in *Neale v Willis* was determined by the content of the husband's promise, not by tracing from the money into a proportionate share of the house.

[98] [1989] Ch. 1.

[99] See too *Lloyd v Dugdale* [2002] 2 P. & C.R. 13 at [52] per Sir Christopher Slade and *Chaudhary v Yavuz* [2013] Ch. 249.

[100] See *King v David Allan* [1916] 2 A.C. 54, *National Provincial Bank v Ainsworth* [1965] A.C. 1175.

[101] As pointed out by, e.g. W. Swadling in Burrows (ed.), *English Private Law* (2013), para.4.126; S. Bright, "The Third Party's Conscience and Land Law" [2000] Conv. 398, 402.

[102] See, e.g. B. McFarlane, "Constructive Trusts Arising on Receipt of Property *Sub Conditione*" (2004) 120 L.Q.R. 667, 678–682.

[103] See, e.g. *Chaudhary v Yavuz* [2013] Ch. 249.

formality rule.[104] The constructive trust view avoids the second of those problems, and can also avoid the first if the grounds on which the law imposes a trust are identified and defined. It seems clear that a promise made by the recipient of property to hold it on trust forms a central part of those grounds, and also that a promise alone cannot justify a trust, especially as the promise may not give rise to any contractual right in the claimant. As noted above,[105] the two principal views are, first, that the promise can be enforced to prevent a party suffering a detriment as a result of action undertaken on the basis of the promise and, secondly, that the promise can be enforced to prevent the recipient from enjoying property free from an obligation undertaken in relation to that property, where the promise to undertake it gave the recipient an advantage in relation to the acquisition of the property.

**15-045** A difficulty with the first view is that it has been used to explain cases in which the prospective detriment is not suffered by the claimant: this is the case, for example, in *Neale v Willis*, and in secret trust cases where the risk of detriment is to the party (the mother-in-law, or the testator) initially providing the property, and not to the party benefitting from the intended trust of the property. A difficulty with the second view is that the principle does not fall easily into any recognised legal category[106]: it is, for example, based on a promise, but the promise need not be made to the claimant, and so it is clearly not based on the existence of a contract between the claimant and the recipient; and, whilst the prospect of an unjust benefit is emphasised, the response is to enforce the promise, and is not limited to removing that benefit from the recipient. It has also been pointed out that, at an abstract level, the second view overlaps with a possible justification for express trusts arising where S transfers property to T to hold on trust for B. This may, however, give some support to the second view: given the historical development of such express trusts, we should not be surprised to see equity continuing to intervene in a case where the defendant's receipt of property is coloured by a prior promise to hold that property for the benefit of another.[107]

## 5. Shared Homes: The Common Intention Trust

### A. Nature of the Trust

**15-046** Since the decision of the House of Lords in *Gissing v Gissing*,[108] a particular type of constructive trust has been used by the courts to resolve disputes relating to the beneficial entitlement of parties who have lived together in a marital or quasi-marital relationship. In the cases where the parties are married, or in a civil partnership, and their relationship ends in divorce or dissolution, there is no need to ascertain the parties' pre-existing beneficial interests, as the court has a statutory discretion to vary those rights and in doing so can take account of a wide range of factors related to the parties' relationship. In cases where the parties determined their beneficial interests by means of a written declaration of trust, either before or after acquiring the property, that declaration will generally be decisive,[109] and the rights of the parties will arise under an express trust, which can be proved by the written declaration.

---

104 See the discussion at para.3-165.

105 See paras 15-038—15-039.

106 A point made by Swadling, "The Nature of the Trust in *Rochefoucauld v Boustead*" in Mitchell (ed.), *Constructive and Resulting Trusts* (2010), pp.106-107.

107 See B. McFarlane, "The Centrality of Constructive and Resulting Trusts" in Mitchell (ed.), *Constructive and Resulting Trusts* (2010), pp.199-201. See too *de Bruyne v de Bruyne* [2010] EWCA Civ 519 at [51] per Patten LJ, referring to a principle giving rise to a constructive trust where the defendant's unconscionable conduct is "in the form of a denial or refusal to carry out the agreement to hold the property for the benefit of the third party which was the only basis upon which the property was transferred."

108 [1971] A.C. 886.

109 See, e.g. *Goodman v Gallant* [1986] Fam. 106; *Pankhania v Chandegra* [2013] 3 F.C.R. 16. Whilst decisive as to the parties'

Nonetheless, the "common intention constructive trust" is of great practical importance: first, because no statutory discretion exists for couples who are neither married nor in a civil partnership; secondly, because where third parties are involved, it will be necessary to establish what beneficial interests the spouses or civil partners had at the point when the third party acquired its rights over the relevant property. If, for example, a husband who is the sole legal owner of the marital home grants a charge over that property to a bank without obtaining the valid consent of the wife, the wife may be able to show that, at the time when the charge was granted, she had a pre-existing beneficial interest under a common intention constructive trust which is capable of binding the bank. Thirdly, in practice, it seems that parties often fail to set out their rights by means of a written declaration of trust,[110] even where the default legal entitlements are unlikely to reflect the parties' intentions, or their respective contributions to the costs of acquiring the property. **15–047**

Where the claimant has directly contributed to the costs of acquisition of the property, by providing some or all of a deposit, or some or all of the mortgage payments, one might have thought that her beneficial interest would be determined by means of a resulting trust. As we noted in Chapter 14,[111] however, the common intention constructive trust has displaced the resulting trust in many domestic cases,[112] and certainly where a home is bought "in joint names for joint occupation by a married or unmarried couple, where both are responsible for any mortgage".[113] The common intention constructive trust differs from the resulting trust in some important respects: unlike a resulting trust, it can arise even if the claimant has not provided any part of the purchase price or mortgage payments, and the size of the claimant's share depends on the parties' intentions, rather than on the percentage contribution made to the costs of acquisition. These features of the common intention constructive trust are fundamental to its existence, since its recognition in *Gissing v Gissing*,[114] and its later development, can be seen in part as a response to the limited utility of the resulting trust, which cannot recognise contributions made by the claimant other than the provision of money towards acquisition of the home.[115] **15–048**

Given the role of intention in the common intention constructive trust, it has been suggested that the trust is in fact best seen as an express trust. The same argument can be made as in relation to the *Rochefoucauld v Boustead* trust: it is express as it depends on an oral declaration, proof of which is permitted, even in the absence of writing, in order to ensure that the statutory formality requirement imposed by s.53(1)(b) of the Law of Property Act 1925 is not used by the defendant as an instrument of fraud.[116] However, this argument is harder to sustain in relation to common intention constructive **15–049**

---

initial interests in the property, it is of course possible that those interests might change as a result of the parties' subsequent conduct if, for example, there is a later contrary agreement, or a proprietary estoppel arises: see *Stack v Dowden* [2007] 2 A.C. 432 at [49] per Baroness Hale.

110 Although conveyancers acting for a couple acquiring land have frequently been encouraged by the courts to ensure that the parties do thus set out their rights: see, e.g. *Carlton v Goodman* [2002] 2 F.L.R. 259 at [44] per Ward LJ. In *Stack v Dowden* [2007] 2 A.C. 432 at [52] Baroness Hale noted that, in a case where the legal title is conveyed to a couple, the Land Registry Form TR1 "provides a box for the transferees to declare whether they are to hold the property on trust for themselves as joint tenants, or on trust for themselves as tenants in common in equal shares, or on some other trusts which are inserted on the form. If this is invariably complied with, the problem confronting us here will eventually disappear. Unfortunately, however, the transfer will be valid whether or not this part of the form is completed."

111 See paras 14–036—14–042.

112 See, e.g. *Midland Bank Plc v Cooke* [1995] 2 F.L.R. 915, discussed at para.14–037.

113 *Jones v Kernott* [2012] 1 A.C. 776 at [25] per Lord Walker and Baroness Hale.

114 [1971] A.C. 886.

115 As noted by Baroness Hale in *Stack v Dowden* [2007] 2 A.C. 432 at [59]–[60].

116 See, e.g. *Allen v Snyder* [1977] 2 N.S.W.L.R. 685 at 693 per Glass JA: "The trust is enforced, because it is unconscionable of the legal owner to rely on the statute to defeat the beneficial interest. It could justifiably be called an express trust, as it was in *Rochefoucauld v Boustead*."

trusts, as such trusts have arisen even in cases where the parties have not discussed their beneficial interests, and it would be impossible on the facts to find any declaration of trust, even an oral one.[117]

15-050 The speeches of Lord Diplock in *Gissing v Gissing*[118] and Lord Bridge in *Lloyds Bank Plc v Rosset*[119] confirm that the common intention constructive trust has two key requirements: first, an agreement, arrangement or understanding that the claimant is to have a beneficial share of the property; and secondly, action by the claimant in reliance on that agreement, arrangement or understanding. We will see, however, that the way in which those requirements are applied suggests that the courts may have some doubts as to their suitability.

15-051 There is, in particular, a question of the circumstances in which a court may *infer* or even *impute* a common intention to the parties. The distinction between imputing and inferring a common intention is an important one. As Lord Neuberger noted in *Stack v Dowden*[120]:

> An imputed intention is one which is attributed to the parties, even though no such actual intention can be deduced from their actions and statements, and even though they had no such intention. Imputing involves concluding what the parties would have intended, whereas inference involves concluding what they did intend.

As we will see, in that case, Lord Neuberger disagreed with the other members of the panel by finding that imputation has no role to play in the common intention constructive trust; nonetheless, his statement as to the difference between inference and imputation is helpful and has been widely accepted as a definition of the two concepts.[121]

15-052 The common intention constructive trust may be relevant both when legal title to the property is in the sole name of the defendant, and also when legal title is in the joint names of the claimant and defendant. In the first class of case, in the absence of any trust, the claimant will have no beneficial interest in the property, and so the claimant's purpose in establishing a common intention constructive trust is to show that she does in fact have some share of the beneficial ownership of the property. In the second class of case, in the absence of any express, resulting, or common intention constructive trust, the claimant and the defendant will hold their joint legal title on trust for each other as joint tenants in equity. It seems that this default trust is imposed by statute in cases of co-ownership of land. If that equitable joint tenancy is severed, each party will then have a 50 per cent share of the beneficial ownership of the property. In such a case, then, the purpose of the claimant in establishing a common intention constructive trust is not to show that she has some beneficial interest: it is rather to show that she has an interest greater than the 50 per cent share she would receive by severing the beneficial joint tenancy which arises in the absence of such a trust.

15-053 Whereas the key decisions in the development of the common intention constructive trust dealt with the first class of cases,[122] it happens that the two most recent decisions of our top court have dealt with the latter class of case. This raises the question of whether separate principles govern each class of case: an issue considered by Lord Walker and Baroness Hale in the later of those two recent decisions, *Jones v Kernott*.[123] As can be seen from the extract below, their joint judgment also considers

---

117 See, e.g. *Midland Bank plc v Cooke* [1995] 2 F.L.R. 915: when asked in cross-examination if he and his wife had ever discussed their rights in the home, Mr Cooke replied: "No. We were just happy, I suppose, you know." As noted by Lord Hodson in *Pettitt v Pettitt* [1970] A.C. 777 at 810: "The concept of a normal married couple spending the long winter evenings hammering out agreements about their possessions appears grotesque."

118 [1971] A.C. 886 at 904–905.

119 [1991] 1 A.C. 107.

120 [2007] 2 A.C. 432 at [126].

121 See, e.g. *Jones v Kernott* [2012] 1 A.C. 776 at [26], [73] and [79].

122 See, e.g. *Gissing v Gissing* [1971] 1 A.C. 886; *Lloyds Bank Plc v Rosset* [1991] 1 A.C. 107.

123 [2012] 1 A.C. 776.

the first of those two decisions, *Stack v Dowden*[124] and includes a discussion of the circumstances in which a common intention may be inferred or imputed.[125]

*Jones v Kernott*

Supreme Court [2012] 1 A.C. 776

Mr Kernott and Ms Jones bought a house in their joint names. Their relationship ended after ten years and Kernott moved out. Jones continued to live in the original home, assuming sole responsibility for payment of the mortgage and other outgoings, including repairs and improvements. In 1995, the parties cashed in a jointly owned life insurance policy and divided the proceeds equally. Kernott used his share to pay for the deposit on a house. In 2006, Kernott first sought to realise the financial value of his share of the original home. Jones claimed a declaration that, although legal title to the home was held by the parties jointly, she was the sole beneficial owner. In 2008, Kernott purported to sever the parties' beneficial joint tenancy. The majority of the Court of Appeal (Wall and Rimer L.JJ., with Jacob L.J. dissenting) found that there was no basis on which the parties' shares could be varied from the 50-50 split each would have received had the beneficial joint tenancy been severed immediately after their separation. The Supreme Court unanimously allowed Jones's appeal and re-instated the order of the first instance judge, which had also been confirmed in the High Court, that the parties held the joint legal title on a common intention constructive trust, under which Jones had a 90% share of the beneficial interest in the home. **15–054**

In a joint judgment with which Lord Collins agreed, Lord Walker and Baroness Hale found clear evidence that the parties' intentions as to ownership of the property had changed over time. They inferred that when, in 1995, the life insurance policy was cashed in and Kernott bought a new home, he did so on the basis that he would not be expected to contribute further to the mortgage on the original family home, so that "the logical inference is that they intended that his interest in [the family home] should crystallise then" with Jones taking the benefit of any increase in the value of the home from that point. On that view, the parties had an actual intention, established by inference from the evidence, not only that the parties beneficial entitlements should differ from their legal rights as joint tenants, but also as to the size of each party's beneficial interest. **15–055**

Lord Wilson and Lord Kerr reached the same result, but, in each case, their reasoning differed from that of the majority. Each found that there was insufficient evidence to infer that the parties had actually formed an intention as to the size of their beneficial interests, but that an intention to hold in proportions of (roughly) 90% and 10% could instead be *imputed* to the parties to meet the demands of fairness. Lord Kerr would have preferred, if possible, to avoid the language of imputation, and to have reached that outcome simply as a matter of fairness, without any reference to the parties' intentions. **15–056**

LORD WALKER AND BARONESS HALE: This appeal gives the Supreme Court the opportunity to revisit the decision of the House of Lords in *Stack v Dowden*.[126] That case, like this, was concerned with the determination of the beneficial interests in a house acquired in joint names by an unmarried couple who intended it to be their family home.. . . **15–057**

Mr Stack and Ms Dowden lived together for 19 years, from 1983 to 2002. They did not marry but they had four children born between 1986 and 1991. Ms Dowden was a well-qualified electrical engineer, and throughout the time when they lived together she worked full-time (except for periods of maternity leave) for the London Electricity Board and its successor. Mr Stack was a self-employed builder and decorator until 1987, after which he was employed by Hammersmith and Fulham London Borough Council. **15–058**

They started living together in 1983 in a house acquired in Ms Dowden's sole name at the price of £30,000. The deposit of £8,000 was paid out of a building society account in Ms Dowden's sole name; there was a conflict of evidence as to whether Mr Stack had made any contributions to the account. The balance of £22,000 was raised on a mortgage for which Ms Dowden alone was responsible. She made the mortgage payments and paid other household outgoings. Mr Stack kept his finances separate (he had most of his post, including his bank statements, sent to his father's address). They carried out extensive repairs and improvements to the house. The judge found that Mr Stack was responsible for most of this work but could not put a figure on its contribution to the sale value of the house. **15–059**

124 [2007] 2 A.C. 432.
125 [2012] 1 A.C. 776.
126 [2007] 2 AC 432.

15-060 They moved house in 1993. Ms Dowden received over £66,000 from the sale of their first home. Their new home was bought for £190,000. Nearly £129,000 came from Ms Dowden's building society account and the balance from a bank loan secured on the house and on two endowment policies, one in joint names and one in Ms Dowden's sole name. The house was transferred into their joint names with no express declaration of trust, but a standard-form provision that the survivor could give a good receipt.

15-061 Mr Stack paid the mortgage interest and the premiums on the joint policy, to a total amount of nearly £34,000. The principal of the mortgage loan was repaid by a series of lump sum payments, to which Mr Stack contributed £27,000 and Ms Dowden over £38,000. The utility bills were in Ms Dowden's name and she paid all or most of them. There were some improvements to the property, but not on a large scale. The parties continued to maintain separate bank accounts and each made a number of separate investments.

15-062 In short, there was a substantial disparity between their respective financial contributions to the purchase. The trial judge held that the proceeds of sale should be divided in equal shares. Although Ms Dowden had been the bigger earner, "they have both put their all into doing the best for themselves and their family as they could". The Court of Appeal allowed Ms Dowden's appeal and divided the proceeds 65% to 35% as she had asked. The House of Lords (Lord Hoffmann, Lord Hope of Craighead, Lord Walker of Gestingthorpe, Baroness Hale of Richmond and Lord Neuberger of Abbotsbury) unanimously upheld that order, although Lord Neuberger did so for different reasons from the majority.

15-063 The curious feature of the decided cases up until then had been that, once an intention to share ownership had been established, the courts had tended to adopt a more flexible and "holistic" approach to the quantification of the parties' shares in cases of sole legal ownership than they had in cases of joint legal ownership. In the former, they had adopted a concept of the "common intention" constructive trust which depends upon the shared intentions of the parties. In the latter, they had tended to analyse the matter in terms of a resulting trust, which depends upon the law's presumption as to the intention of the party who makes a financial contribution to the purchase. This point was made by Lady Hale in *Stack v Dowden*:[127] see also Peter Gibson L.J. in *Drake v Whipp*.[128]

15-064 The leading opinion in the House of Lords was that of Lady Hale. Lord Hoffmann, Lord Hope and Lord Walker all agreed with it, though Lord Hope and Lord Walker added some observations of their own. Lord Hope discussed Scots law, drawing attention to the importance in Scotland of the law of unjust enrichment. Lord Walker contributed what he referred to as an "extended footnote", with a detailed commentary on Lord Diplock's speech in *Gissing v Gissing*.

15-065 The conclusions in Lady Hale's opinion were directed to the case of a house transferred into the joint names of a married or unmarried couple, where both are responsible for any mortgage, and where there is no express declaration of their beneficial interests. In such cases, she held that there is a presumption that the beneficial interests coincide with the legal estate. Specifically, "in the domestic consumer context, a conveyance into joint names indicates both legal and beneficial joint tenancy, unless and until the contrary is proved".[129]

15-066 Secondly, the mere fact that the parties had contributed to the acquisition of the home in unequal shares would not normally be sufficient to rebut the presumption of joint tenancy arising from the conveyance:

> "It cannot be the case that all the hundreds of thousands, if not millions, of transfers into joint names . . . are vulnerable to challenge in the courts simply because it is likely that the owners contributed unequally to their purchase".[130]

15-067 Thirdly, the task of seeking to show that the parties intended their beneficial interests to be different from their legal interests was not to be "lightly embarked upon. In family disputes, strong feelings are aroused when couples split up. These often lead the parties, honestly but mistakenly, to reinterpret the past in self-exculpatory or vengeful terms. They also lead people to spend far more on the legal battle than is warranted by the sums actually at stake. A full examination of the facts is likely to involve disproportionate costs. In joint names cases it is also unlikely to lead to a different result, unless the facts are very unusual".[131]

15-068 Fourthly, however, if the task is embarked upon, it is to ascertain the parties' common intentions as to

---

127 At [64]–[65].
128 [1996] 1 F.L.R. 826 at 827, cited in *Stack* at [29].
129 Lady Hale at [58]; Lord Walker at [33].
130 Lady Hale at [68].
131 Lady Hale at [68]; Lord Walker at [33].

what their shares in the property would be, in the light of their whole course of conduct in relation to it.[132] It is the way in which this point was made which seems to have caused the most difficulty in the lower courts. The difficulty is well illustrated in Lord Wilson J.S.C.'s judgment . . . which read the judgment in a way which we would not read it. It matters not which reading is correct. It does matter that any confusion is resolved.

It was also accepted that the parties' common intentions might change over time, producing what Lord Hoffmann referred to in the course of argument as an "'ambulatory' constructive trust".[133] An example[134] was where one party had financed or constructed an extension or major improvement to the property, so that what they had now was different from what they had first acquired. But of course there are other examples. The principal question in this case is whether this is one. **15–069**

At its simplest the principle in *Stack v Dowden* is that a "common intention" trust, for the cohabitants' home to belong to them jointly in equity as well as on the proprietorship register, is the default option in joint names cases. The trust can be classified as a constructive trust, but it is not at odds with the parties' legal ownership. Beneficial ownership mirrors legal ownership. What it is at odds with is the presumption of a resulting trust. **15–070**

**A single regime?**

In an interesting article by Simon Gardner and Katharine Davidson,[135] the authors express the hope that the Supreme Court will "make clear that constructive trusts of family homes are governed by a single regime, dispelling any impression that different rules apply to 'joint names' and 'single name' cases". At a high level of generality, there is of course a single regime: the law of trusts (this is the second of Mustill L.J.'s propositions in *Grant v Edwards*[136]). To the extent that we recognise that a "common intention" trust is of central importance to "joint names" as well as "single names" cases, we are going some way to meet that hope. Nevertheless it is important to point out that the starting point for analysis is different in the two situations. That is so even though it may be necessary to enquire into the varied circumstances and reasons why a house or flat has been acquired in a single name or in joint names (they range, for instance, from *Lowson v Coombes*,[137] where the property was in the woman's sole name because the man was apprehensive of claims by his separated wife, to *Adekunle v Ritchie*,[138] where an enfranchised freehold was in joint names because the elderly tenant could not obtain a mortgage on her own). **15–071**

The starting point is different because the claimant whose name is not on the proprietorship register has the burden of establishing some sort of implied trust, normally what is now termed a "common intention" constructive trust. The claimant whose name is on the register starts (in the absence of an express declaration of trust in different terms, and subject to what is said below about resulting trusts) with the presumption (or assumption) of a beneficial joint tenancy. **15–072**

The official Land Registry application form (TR1) for registration of a transfer was replaced on 1 April 1998 by a new form with a box enabling joint transferees to clarify the beneficial ownership of the property. That should help to avoid uncertainty but in practice it does not always do so (this is explained in detail in a case note).[139] "Anything to declare? Express declaration of trust on Land Registry form TR1: the doubts raised in *Stack v Dowden*" [2007] Conv. 364). We understand that the Land Registry does not propose to implement the recommendations for change made by an expert working party which it convened in response to *Stack v Dowden*.[140] **15–073**

The presumption of a beneficial joint tenancy is not based on a mantra as to "equity following the law" (though many non-lawyers would find it hard to understand the notion that equity might do anything else). There are two much more substantial reasons (which overlap) why a challenge to the presumption of beneficial joint tenancy is not to be lightly embarked on. The first is implicit in the nature of the enterprise. **15–074**

[132] Lady Hale at [60].
[133] Lady Hale at [62].
[134] *Stack* at [70].
[135] "The Future of *Stack v Dowden*" (2011) 127 L.Q.R. 13, 15.
[136] [1986] Ch 638, 651.
[137] [1999] Ch. 373.
[138] [2007] W.T.L.R. 1505.
[139] "Anything to Declare? Express Declaration of Trust on Land Registry Form TR1: the Doubts Raised in *Stack v Dowden*" [2007] Conv. 364.
[140] E. Cooke, "In the Wake of *Stack v Dowden*: The Tale of TR1" [2011] Fam. Law 1152.

If a couple in an intimate relationship (whether married or unmarried) decide to buy a house or flat in which to live together, almost always with the help of a mortgage for which they are jointly and severally liable, that is on the face of things a strong indication of emotional and economic commitment to a joint enterprise. That is so even if the parties, for whatever reason, fail to make that clear by any overt declaration or agreement.. . .

15-075 The notion that in a trusting personal relationship the parties do not hold each other to account financially is underpinned by the practical difficulty, in many cases, of taking any such account, perhaps after 20 years or more of the ups and downs of living together as an unmarried couple. That is the second reason for caution before going to law in order to displace the presumption of beneficial joint tenancy.[141] Lady Hale pointed this out in *Stack v Dowden*[142] at para 68, as did Lord Walker at para 33: "In the ordinary domestic case where there are joint legal owners there will be a heavy burden in establishing to the court's satisfaction that an intention to keep a sort of balance-sheet of contributions actually existed, or should be inferred, or imputed to the parties. The presumption will be that equity follows the law. In such cases the court should not readily embark on the sort of detailed examination of the parties' relationship and finances that was attempted (with limited success) in this case."

**The competing presumption: a resulting trust?**

15-076 In the context of the acquisition of a family home, the presumption of a resulting trust made a great deal more sense when social and economic conditions were different and when it was tempered by the presumption of advancement. The breadwinner husband who provided the money to buy a house in his wife's name, or in their joint names, was presumed to be making her a gift of it, or of a joint interest in it. That simple assumption—which was itself an exercise in imputing an intention which the parties may never have had—was thought unrealistic in the modern world by three of their Lordships in *Pettitt v Pettitt*.[143] It was also discriminatory as between men and women and married and unmarried couples. That problem might have been solved had equity been able to extend the presumption of advancement to unmarried couples and remove the sex discrimination. Instead, the tool which equity has chosen to develop law is the "common intention" constructive trust. Abandoning the presumption of advancement while retaining the presumption of resulting trust would place an even greater emphasis upon who paid for what, an emphasis which most commentators now agree to have been too narrow: hence the general welcome given to the "more promising vehicle" of the constructive trust.[144] The presumption of advancement is to receive its quietus when section 199 of the Equality Act 2010 is brought into force.[145]

15-077 The time has come to make it clear, in line with *Stack v Dowden* (see also *Abbott v Abbott*),[146] that in the case of the purchase of a house or flat in joint names for joint occupation by a married or unmarried couple, where both are responsible for any mortgage, there is no presumption of a resulting trust arising from their having contributed to the deposit (or indeed the rest of the purchase) in unequal shares. The presumption is that the parties intended a joint tenancy both in law and in equity. But that presumption can of course be rebutted by evidence of a contrary intention, which may more readily be shown where the parties did not share their financial resources.

**Inference or imputation?**

15-078 In *Stack v Dowden* Lord Neuberger observed[147]:

> "While an intention may be inferred as well as express, it may not, at least in my opinion, be imputed. That appears to me to be consistent both with normal principles and with the majority view of this House in *Pettitt v Pettitt* , as accepted by all but Lord Reid in *Gissing v Gissing*[148] and reiterated by the

141 Lady Hale in *Stack v Dowden* at [68], Lord Walker at [33].
142 At [68].
143 [1970] A.C. 177.
144 see S.Gardner and K. Davidson, "The Future of Stack v Dowden" (2011) 127 L.Q.R. 13, 16.
145 [For discussion of the role of resulting trusts and the nature of the presumption of advancement, see paras 14–043—14–048.
146 [2008] 1 F.L.R. 1551.
147 At [125]–[126].
148 [1971] A.C. 886 at 897, 898, 900, 901, and 904.

Court of Appeal in *Grant v Edwards*.[149] The distinction between inference and imputation may appear a fine one (and in *Gissing v Gissing* Lord Pearson, who, on a fair reading I think rejected imputation, seems to have equated it with inference),[150] but it is important.

"An inferred intention is one which is objectively deduced to be the subjective actual intention of the parties, in the light of their actions and statements. An imputed intention is one which is attributed to the parties, even though no such actual intention can be deduced from their actions and statements, and even though they had no such intention. Imputation involves concluding what the parties would have intended, whereas inference involves concluding what they did intend."

Rimer L.J. made some similar observations in the Court of Appeal in this case.[151] . . .

The decision in *Stack v Dowden* produced a division of the net proceeds of sale of the house in shares roughly corresponding to the parties' financial contributions over the years. The majority reached that conclusion by inferring a common intention.[152] Only Lord Neuberger reached the same result by applying the classic resulting trust doctrine (which involved, it is to be noted, imputing an intention to the parties). 15-079

In deference to the comments of Lord Neuberger and Rimer L.J., we accept that the search is primarily to ascertain the parties' actual shared intentions, whether expressed or to be inferred from their conduct. However, there are at least two exceptions. The first, which is not this case, is where the classic resulting trust presumption applies. Indeed, this would be rare in a domestic context, but might perhaps arise where domestic partners were also business partners.[153] The second, which for reasons which will appear later is in our view also not this case but will arise much more frequently, is where it is clear that the beneficial interests are to be shared, but it is impossible to divine a common intention as to the proportions in which they are to be shared. In those two situations, the court is driven to impute an intention to the parties which they may never have had. 15-080

Lord Diplock, in *Gissing v Gissing*,[154] pointed out that, once the court was satisfied that it was the parties' common intention that the beneficial interest was to be shared in some proportion or other, the court might have to give effect to that common intention by determining what in all the circumstances was a fair share. And it is that thought which is picked up in the subsequent cases, culminating in the judgment of Chadwick L.J in *Oxley v Hiscock*[155] in particular the passage which was given qualified approval in *Stack v Dowden*: "the answer is that each is entitled to that share which the court considers fair having regard to the whole course of dealing between them in relation to the property."[156] 15-081

Chadwick L.J. was not there saying that fairness was the criterion for determining whether or not the property should be shared, but he was saying that the court might have to impute an intention to the parties as to the proportions in which the property would be shared. In deducing what the parties, as reasonable people, would have thought at the relevant time, regard would obviously be had to their whole course of dealing in relation to the property. 15-082

However, while the conceptual difference between inferring and imputing is clear, the difference in practice may not be so great. In this area, as in many others, the scope for inference is wide. The law recognizes that a legitimate inference may not correspond to an individual's subjective state of mind.. . . 15-083

In several parts of the British Commonwealth federal or provincial legislation has given the court a limited jurisdiction to vary or adjust proprietary rights in the home when an unmarried couple split up. Most require a minimum period of two years' cohabitation (or less if there are children) before the jurisdiction is exercisable. In England the Law Commission has made recommendations on similar lines, *Cohabitation: The Financial Consequences of Relationship Breakdown*,[157] but there are no plans to implement them in the near future. 15-084

In the meantime there will continue to be many difficult cases in which the court has to reach a 15-085

---

149 [1986] Ch. 638 at 651–653.
150 [1971] A.C. 886 at 902.
151 [2010] 1 W.L.R. 2401 at [76]–[77].
152 See Lady Hale's opinion at [92], following her detailed analysis of the facts starting at [86].
153 See *Stack v Dowden* at [32].
154 [1971] A.C. 886 at 909.
155 [2005] Fam 211 at [65], [66] and [69].
156 Ibid. at [69].
157 Law Com. No. 307, 2007.

conclusion on sparse and conflicting evidence. It is the court's duty to reach a decision on even the most difficult case. . .[the facts of the case were then examined.]

**Discussion**

15-086 It is always salutary to be confronted with the ambiguities which later emerge in what seemed at the time to be comparatively clear language. The primary search must always be for what the parties actually intended, to be deduced objectively from their words and their actions. If that can be discovered, then, as Mr Nicholas Strauss Q.C. pointed out in the High Court, it is not open to a court to impose a solution upon them in contradiction to those intentions, merely because the court considers it fair to do so.

15-087 In a case such as this, where the parties already share the beneficial interest, and the question is what their interests are and whether their interests have changed, the court will try to deduce what their actual intentions were at the relevant time. It cannot impose a solution upon them which is contrary to what the evidence shows that they actually intended. But if it cannot deduce exactly what shares were intended, it may have no alternative but to ask what their intentions as reasonable and just people would have been had they thought about it at the time. This is a fallback position which some courts may not welcome, but the court has a duty to come to a conclusion on the dispute put before it.

15-088 In this case, there is no need to impute an intention that the parties' beneficial interests would change, because the judge made a finding that the intentions of the parties did in fact change. At the outset, their intention was to provide a home for themselves and their progeny. But thereafter their intentions did change significantly. He did not go into detail, but the inferences are not difficult to draw. They separated in October 1993. No doubt in many such cases, there is a period of uncertainty about where the parties will live and what they will do about the home which they used to share. This home was put on the market in late 1995 but failed to sell. Around that time a new plan was formed. The life insurance policy was cashed in and Mr Kernott was able to buy a new home for himself. He would not have been able to do this had he still had to contribute towards the mortgage, endowment policy and other outgoings on 39 Badger Hall Avenue [the original family home and thus the contested property]. The logical inference is that they intended that his interest in Badger Hall Avenue should crystallise then. Just as he would have the sole benefit of any capital gain in his own home, Ms Jones would have the sole benefit of any capital gain in Badger Hall Avenue. In so far as the judge did not in so many words infer that this was their intention, it is clearly the intention which reasonable people would have had had they thought about it at the time. But in our view it is an intention which he both could and should have inferred from their conduct.

15-089 A rough calculation on this basis produces a result so close to that which the judge produced that it would be wrong for an appellate court to interfere. If we take the value of the property as £60,000 in late 1993 (or £70,000 in late 1995) and the value in 2008 as £245,000, and share the £60,000 (or £70,000) equally between the parties, but leave the balance to Ms Jones, that gives him £30,000 (£35,000) and her £215,000 (£210,000), roughly 12% (15%) and 88% (86%) respectively. This calculation ignores the mortgage, which may be the correct approach, as in 2008 the mortgage debt was almost fully covered by the endowment policy which was always meant to discharge it. Introducing the mortgage liability in 1993 (or 1995) into the calculation would be to Mr Kernott's disadvantage, because at that stage the endowment policy would not have been sufficient to discharge the debt, so the equity would have been less.

**Further accounting**

15-090 On this approach, there is no scope for further accounting between the parties (which was obviously contemplated as a future possibility by Rimer L.J. on his approach). Had their beneficial interests in the property remained the same, there would have been the possibility of cross-claims: Mr Kernott against Ms Jones for an occupation rent, and Ms Jones against Mr Kernott for his half share in the mortgage interest and endowment premiums which she had paid. It is quite likely, however, that the court would hold that there was no liability to pay an occupation rent, at least while the home was needed for the couple's children, whereas the liability to contribute towards the mortgage and endowment policy would accumulate at compound interest over the years since he ceased to contribute. This exercise has not been done. In a case such as this it would involve a quite disproportionate effort, both to discover the requisite figures (even supposing that they could be discovered) and to make the requisite calculations, let alone to determine what the ground rules should be. The parties' legal advisers are to be commended for the proportionate approach which they have taken to the preparation of this case.

**Conclusion**

In summary, therefore, the following are the principles applicable in a case such as this, where a family home is bought in the joint names of a cohabiting couple who are both responsible for any mortgage, but without any express declaration of their beneficial interests. 15-091

(1) The starting point is that equity follows the law and they are joint tenants both in law and in equity.
(2) That presumption can be displaced by showing (a) that the parties had a different common intention at the time when they acquired the home, or (b) that they later formed the common intention that their respective shares would change.
(3) Their common intention is to be deduced objectively from their conduct: "the relevant intention of each party is the intention which was reasonably understood by the other party to be manifested by that party's words and conduct notwithstanding that he did not consciously formulate that intention in his own mind or even acted with some different intention which he did not communicate to the other party".[158] Examples of the sort of evidence which might be relevant to drawing such inferences are given in *Stack v Dowden*.[159]
(4) In those cases where it is clear either (a) that the parties did not intend joint tenancy at the outset, or (b) had changed their original intention, but it is not possible to ascertain by direct evidence or by inference what their actual intention was as to the shares in which they would own the property, "the answer is that each is entitled to that share which the court considers fair having regard to the whole course of dealing between them in relation to the property".[160] In our judgment, the whole course of dealing in relation to the property" should be given a broad meaning, enabling a similar range of factors to be taken into account as may be relevant to ascertaining the parties' actual intentions.
(5) Each case will turn on its own facts. Financial contributions are relevant but there are many other factors which may enable the court to decide what shares were either intended (as in case (3)) or fair (as in case (4)).

This case is not concerned with a family home which is put into the name of one party only. The starting point is different. The first issue is whether it was intended that the other party have any beneficial interest in the property at all. If he does, the second issue is what that interest is. There is no presumption of joint beneficial ownership. But their common intention has once again to be deduced objectively from their conduct. If the evidence shows a common intention to share beneficial ownership but does not show what shares were intended, the court will have to proceed as at (4) and (5) above. 15-092

LORD COLLINS: I agree that the appeal should be allowed for the reasons given in the joint judgment of Lord Walker of Gestingthorpe and Baroness Hale of Richmond JJ.S.C. 15-093

It is not surprising that the decision in *Stack v Dowden* gave rise to difficulties. It was a decision which was responding to the increasing number of cohabiting couples with joint interests in their homes, and to the fact that couples (whether married or unmarried) rarely make agreements about their respective shares in their homes, and to the enormous inflation in property prices which has made the division of ownership by reference to initial financial contributions artificial and potentially productive of injustice. 15-094

The absence of legislative intervention (which continues despite the Law Commission Report on *Cohabitation: The Financial Consequences of Relationship Breakdown*[161]) made it necessary for the judiciary to respond by adapting old principles to new situations. That has not been an easy task. It is illustrated by the fact that in both *Stack v Dowden* and in this case the results at the highest appellate level have been unanimous but the reasoning has not.. . . 15-095

I agree, therefore, that authority justifies the conceptual approach of Lord Walker and Baroness Hale JJ.S.C. that, in joint names cases, the common intention to displace the presumption of equality can, in the absence of express agreement, be inferred (rather than imputed[162]) from their conduct, and where, in such 15-096

---

158 Lord Diplock in *Gissing v Gissing* [1971] A.C. 886 at 906.
159 [2007] 2 A.C. 432 at [69]. [See the extract at para.15-120.]
160 *Oxley v Hiscock* [2005] Fam. 211 at [69].
161 Law Com. No. 307, 2007.
162 See para.[31] of the joint judgment [extracted at para.15-080.]

a case, it is not possible to ascertain or infer what share was intended, each will be entitled to a fair share in the light of the whole course of dealing between them in relation to the property.

15-097 That said, it is my view that in the present context the difference between inference and imputation will hardly ever matter,[163] and that what is one person's inference will be another person's imputation. A similar point has arisen in many other contexts, for example, the difference between implied terms which depend on the parties' actual intention, terms based on a rule of law, and implied terms based on an intention imputed to the parties from their actual circumstance.

15-098 LORD KERR: I agree that this appeal should be allowed. There are differences of some significance in the reasoning that underlies the joint judgment of Lord Walker of Gestingthorpe and Baroness Hale of Richmond JJ.S.C. and that contained in Lord Wilson J.S.C.'s judgment. I agree with Lord Collins of Mapesbury that these are both terminological and conceptual. I am less inclined to agree, however, that the divergence in reasoning is unlikely to make a difference in practice. While it may well be that the outcome in many cases will be the same, whether one infers an intention or imputes it, that does not mean that the process by which the result is arrived at is more or less the same. Indeed, it seems to me that a markedly and obviously different mode of analysis will generally be required.. . .

15-099 It is hardly controversial to suggest that the parties' intention should be given effect to where it can be ascertained and that, although discussions between them will always be the most reliable basis on which to draw an inference as to that intention, these are not the only circumstances in which that exercise will be possible. There is a natural inclination to prefer inferring an intention to imputing one. If the parties' intention can be inferred, the court is not imposing a solution. It is, instead, deciding what the parties must be taken to have intended and where that is possible it is obviously preferable to the court's enforcing a resolution. But the conscientious quest to discover the parties' actual intention should cease when it becomes clear either that this is simply not deducible from the evidence or that no common intention exists. It would be unfortunate if the concept of inferring were to be strained so as to avoid the less immediately attractive option of imputation. In summary, therefore, I believe that the court should anxiously examine the circumstances in order, where possible, to ascertain the parties' intention but it should not be reluctant to recognise, when it is appropriate to do so, that inference of an intention is not possible and that imputation of an intention is the only course to follow.

15-100 In this context, it is important to understand what is meant by "imputing an intention". There are reasons to question the appropriateness of the notion of imputation in this area but, if it is correct to use this as a concept, I strongly favour the way in which it was described by Lord Neuberger in *Stack v Dowden*,[164] where he said that an imputed intention was one which was attributed to the parties, even though no such actual intention could be deduced from their actions and statements, and even though they had no such intention. This exposition draws the necessary strong demarcation line between attributing an intention to the parties and inferring what their intention was in fact.

15-101 The reason that I question the aptness of the notion of imputing an intention is that, in the final analysis, the exercise is wholly unrelated to ascertainment of the parties' views. It involves the court deciding what is fair in light of the whole course of dealing with the property. That decision has nothing to do with what the parties intended, or what might be supposed would have been their intention had they addressed that question. In many ways, it would be preferable to have a stark choice between deciding whether it is possible to deduce what their intention was and, where it is not, deciding what is fair, without elliptical references to what their intention might have—or should have—been. But imputing intention has entered the lexicon of this area of law and it is probably impossible to discard it now.

15-102 While the dichotomy between inferring and imputing an intention remains, however, it seems to me that it is necessary that there be a well marked dividing line between the two. As soon as it is clear that inferring an intention is not possible, the focus of the court's attention should be squarely on what is fair and, as I have said, that is an obviously different examination than is involved in deciding what the parties actually intended.

**Is there sufficient evidence in the present case from which the parties' intentions can be inferred?**

15-103 Lord Walker and Baroness Hale JJ.S.C. have concluded that the failure of the parties to sell their home in Badger Hall Avenue in late 1995, leading as it did to the cashing in of the life insurance policy, meant that

[163] As Lord Walker and Baroness Hale JJSC recognise at [34] [extracted at para.15-083.]

[164] At [126]. [See para.15-051.]

Mr Kernott intended that his interest in the Badger Hall Avenue property should crystallise then. That may indeed have been his intention but, for my part, I would find it difficult to infer that it actually was what he then intended. As the deputy High Court judge, Nicholas Strauss Q.C. put it in his judgment,[165] the bare facts of his departure from the family home and acquisition of another property are a slender foundation on which to conclude that he had entirely abandoned whatever stake he had in the previously shared property.

On the other hand, I would have no difficulty in concluding, as did Mr Strauss Q.C. and as would Lord Wilson J.S.C., that it was eminently fair that the property should be divided between the parties in the shares decreed by Judge Dedman. Like Lord Wilson J.S.C., therefore, I would prefer to allow this appeal on the basis that it is impossible to infer that the parties intended that their shares in the property be apportioned as the judge considered they should be but that such an intention should be imputed to them. **15–104**

LORD WILSON: In the light of the continued failure of Parliament to confer upon the courts limited redistributive powers in relation to the property of each party upon the breakdown of a non-marital relationship, I warmly applaud the development of the law of equity, spear-headed by Baroness Hale of Richmond and Lord Walker of Gestingthorpe in their speeches in *Stack v Dowden*, and reiterated in their judgment in the present appeal, that the common intention which impresses a constructive trust upon the legal ownership of the family home can be imputed to the parties to the relationship. . . **15–105**

In *Oxley v Hiscock*,[166] Chadwick L.J. pointed out that assertions that the family home was held under a constructive trust raised two questions. The home had been held in Mr Hiscock's sole name so, for Chadwick L.J., the first question was whether Mrs Oxley could establish that they had nevertheless had a common intention that she should have some beneficial share in it. In the present case, however, the home is held in the joint names of the parties so, for us, the first question is whether Ms Jones can establish that they nevertheless had (albeit not necessarily at the outset) a common intention that the beneficial shares of herself and Mr Kernott should be in some proportions other than joint and equal. The second question, which arises in the event only of an affirmative answer to the first, is to determine the proportions in which the beneficial shares are held. **15–106**

In relation to the second question Chadwick L.J. concluded[167] that, where there was no evidence of any discussion between the parties as to the proportions in which their beneficial shares in the family home were to be held, each was "entitled to that share which the court considers fair having regard to the whole course of dealing between them in relation to the property"; and he had made clear[168] that such an entitlement arose because "what the court is doing, in cases of this nature, is to supply or impute a common intention as to the parties' respective shares (in circumstances in which there was, in fact, no common intention) on the basis of that which . . . is shown to be fair . . .". . . **15–107**

The analysis by Chadwick L.J. of the proper approach to the second question was correct. In [passages of their judgment[169]] Lord Walker and Baroness Hale JJ.S.C. reiterate that, although its preference is always to collect from the evidence an expressed or inferred intention, common to the parties, about the proportions in which their shares are to be held, equity will, if collection of it proves impossible, impute to them the requisite intention. Before us is a case in which Judge Dedman, the trial judge, found—and, was entitled on the evidence to find—that the common intention required by the first question could be inferred. Thus the case does not require us to consider whether modern equity allows the intention required by the first question also to be imputed if it is not otherwise identifiable. That question will merit careful thought. **15–108**

In her ground-breaking speech in *Stack v Dowden*[170] Lady Hale quoted with emphasis, the words of Chadwick L.J. in *Oxley v Hiscock*,[171] which I have quoted above. Then she quoted a passage from a Discussion Paper published by the Law Commission in July 2002 and entitled Sharing Homes about the proper approach to identifying the proportions which "were intended". Finally she added four sentences to each of which, in quoting them as follows, I take the liberty of attributing a number: **15–109**

---

165 [2010] 1 W.L.R. 2401 at [48].
166 [2005] Fam 211 at [68] and [69].
167 In his summary: [2005] Fam 211 at [69].
168 [2005] Fam 211 at [66].
169 [i.e. paras [31] and [51(4)]; extracted at paras 15–080—15–091.
170 [2007] 2 A.C. 432 at [61].
171 [2005] Fam 211 at [69].

"[1] That may be the preferable way of expressing what is essentially the same thought, for two reasons. [2] First, it emphasises that the search is still for the result which reflects what the parties must, in the light of their conduct, be taken to have intended. [3] Second, therefore, it does not enable the court to abandon that search in favour of the result which the court itself considers fair. [4] For the court to impose its own view of what is fair upon the situation in which the parties find themselves would be to return to the days before *Pettit v Pettitt* without even the fig leaf of section 17 of the [Married Women's Property Act 1882]."

**15–110** I leave on one side Lady Hale's first sentence although, whereas Chadwick L.J. was identifying the criterion for imputing the common intention, the context of the passage in the Discussion Paper suggests that the Law Commission was postulating a criterion for inferring it. On any view Lady Hale's second sentence is helpful; and, by her reference to what the parties must, in the light of their conduct, be taken to have intended (as opposed to what they did intend), Lady Hale made clear that, by then, she was addressing the power to resort to imputation. Lady Hale's fourth sentence has been neatly explained—by Mr Nicholas Strauss Q.C., deputy judge of the Chancery Division, who determined the first appeal in these proceedings[172]—as being that, in the event that the evidence were to suggest that, whether by expression or by inference, the parties intended that the beneficial interests in the home should be held in certain proportions, equity would not "impose" different proportions upon them; and Lord Walker and Baroness Hale JJ.S.C. endorse Mr Strauss Q.C.'s explanation.[173]

**15–111** The problem has lain in Lady Hale's third sentence. Where equity is driven to impute the common intention, how can it do so other than by search for the result which the court itself considers fair? The sentence was not obiter dictum so rightly, under our system, judges below the level of this court have been unable to ignore it. Even in these proceedings judges in the courts below have wrestled with it. Mr Strauss Q.C. observed,[174] that it was difficult to see how—at that final stage of the inquiry—the process could work without the court's supply of what it considered to be fair. In his judgment on the second appeal Rimer L.J. went so far as to suggest[175] that Lady Hale's third sentence must have meant that, contrary to appearances, she had not intended to recognise a power to impute a common intention at all.

**15–112** I respectfully disagree with Lady Hale's third sentence.

**15–113** Lord Walker and Baroness Hale JJ.S.C. observe[176] that in practice the difference between inferring and imputing a common intention to the parties may not be great. I consider that, as a generalisation, their observation goes too far—at least if the court is to take (as in my view it should) an ordinarily rigorous approach to the task of inference. Indeed in the present case they conclude[177] that, in relation to Chadwick L.J.'s second question the proper inference from the evidence, which, if he did not draw, the trial judge should have drawn, was that the parties came to intend that the proportions of the beneficial interests in the home should be held on a basis which in effect equates to 90% to Ms Jones and to 10% to Mr Kernott (being the proportions in favour of which the judge ruled). As it happens, reflective perhaps of the more rigorous approach to the task of inference which I prefer, I regard it, as did Mr Strauss Q.C. in his judgment,[178] as more realistic, in the light of the evidence before the judge, to conclude that inference is impossible but to proceed to impute to the parties the intention that it should be held on a basis which equates to those proportions. At all events I readily concur in the result which Lord Walker and Baroness Hale JJ.S.C. propose.

---

172 [2010] 1 W.L.R. 2401 at [30].
173 [At [46]; extracted at para.15–086.]
174 [2010] 1 W.L.R. 2401 at [31].
175 [2010] 1 W.L.R. 2401 at [77].
176 [At [34]; extracted at para.15–083.]
177 [At [48] and [49]; extracted at paras 15–088—15–089.]
178 [2010] 1 W.L.R. 2401 at [48] and [49].

## B. Scope of the Trust

### i. Common Intention that the Beneficial Entitlements Will Differ from the Position at Common Law

The common intention constructive trust requires a bilateral understanding between the parties that the claimant's beneficial entitlement will differ from her rights at law. Where the defendant is the sole legal owner, this requires a common intention that the claimant should have *some* beneficial interest in the property. Where the claimant and defendant are joint legal owners, this requires a common intention that each should have a distinct (and therefore usually unequal)[179] beneficial interest in the property. **15–114**

The parties' intentions are to be judged objectively in the usual way. In Lord Diplock's words[180] **15–115**

> the relevant intention of each party is the intention which was reasonably understood by the other party to be manifested by that party's words or conduct notwithstanding that he did not consciously formulate that intention in his own mind or even acted with some different intention which he did not communicate to the other party.

It does not suffice that each party happened separately to form the same intention, because an express common intention means one that is communicated between the parties: it is the external manifestation of intention by one party to the other that is crucial, regardless of uncommunicated private intentions.[181]

In *Lloyds Bank Plc v Rosset*, Lord Bridge drew an important distinction between cases in which there is evidence capable of establishing an express agreement between the parties and cases where there is no such evidence, but where there is evidence of conduct from which the court can infer the existence of an agreement. For a court to hold that the parties formed an express common intention, evidence of discussions is required, "however imperfectly remembered and however imprecise their terms may have been".[182] For example, if the defendant gives the claimant an excuse (such as the age of the claimant, or the need to protect assets from the claimant's former spouse) as to why legal title to the property should be vested in the defendant's name alone, this may be interpreted as evidence from which the court can objectively determine that the parties commonly intended the beneficial ownership to be shared, as otherwise there would have been no need for such an excuse.[183] It should be noted, however, that there is a clear distinction between an intention to share the current use and possession of property and an intention that the claimant should have a share of ownership of the **15–116**

---

179 Strictly speaking, an intention that the parties should each have a 50% beneficial interest suffices, as in such a case the intention is that the parties will be tenants in common in equity, whereas they are necessarily joint tenants at law: see s.1(6) Law of Property Act 1925.

180 Lord Diplock in *Gissing v Gissing* [1971] A.C. 886 at 906. See too *Austin v Keele* (1987) 61 A.L.J.R. 605 at 610, per Lord Oliver.

181 *Springette v Defoe* (1992) 24 H.L.R. 552; *Mollo v Mollo* [2000] W.T.L.R. 227 at 242–243; *Lightfoot v Lightfoot-Brown* [2005] 2 P. & C.R. 22.

182 *Lloyds Bank Plc v Rosset* [1991] 1 A.C. 107 at 132 per Lord Bridge.

183 See *Eves v Eves* [1975] 1 W.L.R. 1338; *Grant v Edwards* [1986] Ch. 638. The reasoning in these excuse cases has been described as "fallacious" on the basis that "if I give an excuse for rejecting an invitation to what I expect to be a dull party, it does not mean that I thereby agree to come: on the contrary, it means that I do not agree to come, but for one reason or another find it hard to say so outright" (S. Gardner, "Rethinking Family Property" (1993) 109 L.Q.R. 263, 265). But the reasoning in the cases is correct if the provision of the excuse, by suggesting that a technicality is the only reason why the claimant was not included on the legal title, leads the claimant reasonably to believe that she in fact had a share of the property. Cf. *Williamson v Sheikh* [2008] EWCA Civ 990 (declaration of express trust drafted but not executed because the legal owner told his partner that she could trust him to do the right thing if they separated).

property, and vague statements made in a casual context will not, by themselves, establish an express agreement that the claimant should have a beneficial share.[184]

15–117 If there is no evidence of relevant express discussions between the parties, however reasonable it might have been for the parties to discuss the matter and reach an arrangement on beneficial ownership, then the common intention can only be established by inferences from the conduct of the parties. The judgment of Lord Walker and Lady Hale in *Jones v Kernott*, along with that of Lord Collins, makes it clear that it is *not* permissible for a court to impute a common intention that the parties' equitable rights are to differ from their legal entitlements.[185] At this stage of the inquiry, only an actual intention will suffice. In *Geary v Rankine*,[186] for example, Lewison LJ stated that:

> Whether the beneficial interests are to be shared at all is still a question of a party's actual shared intentions. An imputed intention only arises where the court is satisfied that the parties' actual common intention, express or inferred, was that the beneficial interest would be shared, but cannot make a finding about the proportions in which they were meant to be shared.

This is true in a case where the property is in the parties' joint names just as in a case where it is in the sole name of one of the parties: the *existence* of the common intention constructive trust must be based on an actual common intention, either expressed by the parties or inferred on the evidence.

15–118 The question then is as to when a court will be willing to make an inference of such a common intention. In answering that question, it is useful to distinguish between those cases in which the legal title is in the joint names of the claimant and the defendant, and those in which it is in the sole name of the defendant.

### (1) Inferring a Common Intention Where the Legal Title is in the Joint Names of Claimant and Defendant

15–119 As was made clear by Lord Walker and Lady Hale in their statement of principle in *Jones v Kernott*, the "starting point is that equity follows the law and that [the parties] are joint tenants both in law and in equity." In *Stack v Dowden*, Lord Walker and Lady Hale each suggested that there is a "considerable burden" on a claimant wishing to establish an inference that the parties had a common intention that they should have different beneficial interests, as such an inference could be supported only in "very unusual" cases.[187] At least where property is bought "in joint names for joint occupation by a married or unmarried couple, where both are responsible for the mortgage",[188] the fact that the parties made, overall, unequal financial contributions will not, by itself, justify a departure from the starting point of a beneficial joint tenancy. In the particular context of such cohabitation, it can easily be accepted that the parties' intentions are more likely to be informed by an ethos of equality and sharing rather than one of pure "balance-sheet" accounting.[189]

15–120 Whilst the starting point of a beneficial joint tenancy is hard to displace in such cases, the court

---

184 See, e.g. *Lissimore v Downing* [2003] 2 F.L.R. 308 and *James v Thomas* [2008] 1 F.L.R. 1598.

185 In contrast, Lord Wilson's judgment at [78] emphasises the importance of imputation (extracted at para.15–105).

186 [2012] 2 F.L.R. 1509 at [19]. See too *Thompson v Hurst* [2015] 1 F.L.R. 238 at [22] per Etherton LJ: "In the case of a single legal owner, such as the present, where there is no express declaration of trust, the claimant has first to establish some sort of implied trust, normally what is now termed a common intention constructive trust. . .The claimant must show that it was intended that he or she was to have a beneficial interest at all. That can only be achieved by evidence of the parties' actual intentions, express or inferred, objectively ascertained."

187 [2007] 2 A.C. 432 at [15] and [68].

188 See *Jones v Kernott* [2012] 1 A.C. 776 at [25].

189 See *Stack v Dowden* [2007] 2 A.C. 432 at [68]; *Jones v Kernott* [2012] 1 A.C. 776 at [22].

can take account of a broad range of factors in determining if a contrary common intention can be inferred. In *Stack v Dowden*, Lady Hale stated that[190]:

> In law, 'context is everything' and the domestic context is very different from the commercial world. Each case will turn on its own facts. Many more factors than financial contributions may be relevant to divining the parties' true intentions. These include: any advice or discussions at the time of the transfer which cast light upon their intentions then; the reasons why the home was acquired in their joint names; the reasons why (if it be the case) the survivor was authorised to give a receipt for the capital moneys;[191] the purpose for which the home was acquired; the nature of the parties' relationship; whether they had children for whom they both had responsibility to provide a home; how the purchase was financed, both initially and subsequently; how the parties arranged their finances, whether separately or together or a bit of both; how they discharged the outgoings on the property and their other household expenses. When a couple are joint owners of the home and jointly liable for the mortgage, the inferences to be drawn from who pays for what may be very different from the inferences to be drawn when only one is owner of the home. The arithmetical calculation of how much was paid by each is also likely to be less important. It will be easier to draw the inference that they intended that each should contribute as much to the household as they reasonably could and that they would share the eventual benefit or burden equally. The parties' individual characters and personalities may also be a factor in deciding where their true intentions lay. In the cohabitation context, mercenary considerations may be more to the fore than they would be in marriage, but it should not be assumed that they always take pride of place over natural love and affection. At the end of the day, having taken all this into account, cases in which the joint legal owners are to be taken to have intended that their beneficial interests should be different from their legal interests will be very unusual.
>
> This is not, of course, an exhaustive list. There may also be reason to conclude that, whatever the parties' intentions at the outset, these have now changed. An example might be where one party has financed (or constructed himself) an extension or substantial improvement to the property, so that what they have now is significantly different from what they had then. 15–121

It is also worth noting that, notwithstanding the court's emphasis on the "very unusual" circumstances required to support an inference of a common intention that the parties would have unequal beneficial shares, such an inference was made in both *Stack v Dowden* and *Jones v Kernott*. It also seems clear that the disparity in the parties' financial contributions to the costs of acquiring the property was crucial to that inference, and to the calculation of the individual beneficial shares arising under the common intention constructive trust. This demonstrates a point noted in Chapter 14[192]: whilst there is a clear conceptual difference between common intention constructive trust and resulting trust reasoning, it is possible to exaggerate the difference in the outcomes they produce.[193] 15–122

### (2) Inferring a Common Intention Where the Legal Title is in the Sole Name of the Defendant

In *Lloyds Bank Plc v Rosset*, where legal title to the property was in the sole name of Mr Rosset, Lord Bridge stated that[194] 15–123

---

190 [2007] 2 A.C. 432 at [69].

191 [This point is mentioned as, prior to 1995, the form of transfer prescribed by the Land Registry in the case of a conveyance to two or more parties required the transferees to state if the survivor was able to give such a receipt. It was determined prior to *Stack v Dowden* that a positive answer to this question did not amount to an express declaration of a beneficial joint tenancy (see, e.g. *Huntingford v Hobbs* [1993] 1 F.L.R. 736), but it was stated in *Stack* that it was nonetheless a potentially relevant factor against a finding that the parties intended to hold as tenants in common in equity.]

192 See para.14–042.

193 In *Stack v Dowden* [2007] 2 A.C. 432, for example, Lord Neuberger reached the same result as the other members of the panel, but by using resulting trust reasoning rather than finding a common intention constructive trust: see [122].

194 [1991] 1 A.C. 107 at 133.

> direct contributions to the purchase price by the partner who is not the legal owner, whether initially or by payment of mortgage instalments, will readily justify the inference necessary to the creation of a constructive trust. But, as I read the authorities, it is at least extremely doubtful that anything less will do.

On this view, the wide list of factors identified by Lady Hale in *Stack v Dowden*,[195] set out in the previous extract, is not applicable in a case where the claimant is not on the legal title and needs to resort to a common intention constructive trust in order to show that she has any beneficial interest in the property.

**15–124** The limit identified by Lord Bridge had the advantage of making it clear to the parties and their advisers what evidence was required in cases where there had been no express discussions as to beneficial ownership of the home.[196] As a matter of principle, however, it is very hard to justify such a limit on the evidence that can be used to support an inference of common intention. Whilst the making of a direct financial contribution may well provide support for such an inference, there is no reason to think that, in the absence of such a contribution by the claimant, the parties cannot possibly have intended that the parties' beneficial interests in the property should differ from their rights at law.

**15–125** In *Stack v Dowden*, Lord Walker stated that[197]:

> Lord Bridge's extreme doubt 'whether anything less will do' was certainly consistent with many first-instance and Court of Appeal decisions, but I respectfully doubt whether it took full account of the views (conflicting though they were) expressed in *Gissing v Gissing*.[198] It has attracted some trenchant criticism from scholars as potentially productive of injustice.[199] . . . Whether or not Lord Bridge's observation was justified in 1990, in my opinion the law has moved on, and your Lordships should move it a little more in the same direction, while bearing in mind that the Law Commission may soon come forward with proposals which, if enacted by Parliament, may recast the law in this area.[200]

**15–126** Baroness Hale referred with approval to Lord Walker's view in her own speech in *Stack*, stating that[201]:

> The law has indeed moved on in response to changing social and economic conditions. The search is to ascertain the parties' shared intentions, actual, inferred or imputed, with respect to the property in the light of their whole course of conduct in relation to it.

**15–127** It might therefore seem that the *Rosset* limit on the evidence that may be used to infer a common intention that the parties' beneficial interests should differ from their entitlements at law has been rejected. Care must be taken, however, in working out the effect of *Stack v Dowden* on the means by which a common intention can be established. As noted above,[202] it is now clear from the statement of the relevant principles given by Lord Walker and Lady Hale in *Jones v Kernott* that the court cannot impute the common intention necessary to *establish* a common intention constructive trust: that the parties' beneficial interests should differ from their legal rights (if any). The question is therefore whether the wide list of factors identified by Lady Hale in *Stack*[203] are relevant to the inference of common intention in a case where the legal title is in the name of the defendant alone.

---

195 [2007] 2 A.C. 432.

196 Although it can be argued that the advantages of certainty in this context are exaggerated: see L. Fox O'Mahony, "Property Outsiders and the Hidden Politics of Doctrinalism" (2015) 67 C.L.P. 409, 430–431.

197 [2007] 2 A.C. 432 at [26].

198 [1971] A.C. 886, especially Lord Reid at 896–7 and Lord Diplock at 909.

199 See K. Gray and S.F. Gray, *Elements of Land Law* (4th edn, 2004) paras 10.132–10.137. [See now the 5th edn, 2008 at paras 7.3.62–7.3.66.]

200 [Those Law Commission proposals will be considered at para.15–152.]

201 [2007] 2 A.C. 432 at [60].

202 See para.15–117.

203 [2007] 2 A.C. 432.

In *Abbott v Abbott*, a sole name case, Lady Hale relied on *Stack*, noting that "the law has indeed moved on" since *Rosset*, and that "[t]he parties' whole course of conduct in relation to the property must be taken into account in determining their shared intentions as to ownership." Three factors, however, limit the weight of that decision. First, it was a Privy Council case and so does not have the binding weight in English law of a decision of the House of Lords or the Supreme Court; secondly, it was made after *Stack* and before the principles of that case were "revisited"[204] in *Jones v Kernott*; thirdly, the defendant had in any case conceded that the claimant had some beneficial interest, and so the question on the facts was as to how to quantify that interest, not whether it could be established. **15–128**

Indeed, after conducting a thorough survey of the authorities in sole name cases since *Jones v Kernott*, Brian Sloan has found very little evidence that the courts are reaching decisions inconsistent with the limits on inference imposed in *Rosset*, and has suggested that a further Supreme Court decision is required if those limits are to be rejected.[205] There is, after all, a tension at the heart of *Stack* and *Jones*. On the one hand, there is a clear desire to tackle common intention constructive trusts generally, in sole name and joint name cases, and to show that the law has "moved on" since *Rosset*. On the other hand, there is the insistence that, in joint names cases at least, there is a heavy burden to displace in seeking to establish an inference that the parties' entitlements in equity differ from their rights at law, and the fact that the outcome in each case corresponded very closely to the extent of the parties' direct financial contributions to the costs of acquisition of the property. This contributes to the lack of clarity in the relevant principles which, as Sloan notes, makes it very difficult for lower courts confidently to develop the law. **15–129**

### ii. Detrimental Reliance

In a case where the required common intention is established by means of express discussions between the parties, it is clear that this expressed intention, if it has not taken the form of a written declaration of trust, cannot, by itself, establish a trust.[206] In *Gissing v Gissing*, Lord Diplock's assumption was that the parties' common intention would be that the claimant had to act in some specific way to facilitate the acquisition of the property, by: **15–130**

> contributing to the purchase price or to the deposit or the mortgage instalments when it is purchased upon mortgage or to make some other material sacrifice by way of contribution to or economy in the general family expenditure.[207]

Since then, however, the courts have rejected the idea that the common intention must be that the claimant would acquire an interest in the property in exchange for some quid pro quo. It will suffice if the claimant has "acted to his or her detriment or significantly altered his or her position in reliance on the agreement".[208]

The action in reliance need not consist of making a direct financial contribution to the costs of **15–131**

---

[204] [2012] 1 A.C. 776.

[205] B. Sloan, "Keeping Up with the *Jones* Case: Establishing Constructive Trusts in 'Sole Legal Owner' Scenarios" (2015) L.S. 226. Sloan notes that the only decision arguably inconsistent with the *Rosset* approach is *Aspden v Elvy* [2012] 2 F.L.R. 807, where a common intention to share beneficial ownership of a barn, formerly owned by Mr Aspden but transferred by him to Ms Elvy, was found on the basis of "substantial contributions", both financial and physical, made by Aspden to work done in converting the barn. The limits in *Rosset* would not be greatly extended, however, by allowing inferences from financial contributions to significant improvements to property.

[206] See, e.g. *Gissing v Gissing* [1971] A.C. 886 at 805; *Grant v Edwards* [1986] Ch. 638 at 647 and 652.

[207] [1971] A.C. 886 at 905.

[208] Lord Bridge in *Lloyds Bank Plc v Rosset* [1991] 1 A.C. 107 at 132.

acquisition of the property. In *Eves v Eves*,[209] for example, the claimant's reliance was established by her having painted the house, broken up a patio with a sledgehammer, disposed of rubble, and built a new garden shed. As a matter of principle, it would seem that the reliance requirement can be established by conduct with no direct relation to the property in question, such as giving up a job or accommodation elsewhere as a result of the common intention that the claimant had or would acquire a beneficial interest in the shared home. That is certainly the case in relation to proprietary estoppel. Whilst that doctrine is distinct from the common intention constructive trust,[210] as it shares a requirement of detrimental reliance, decisions interpreting that requirement must also be of relevance to the common intention constructive trust.[211] The particular context in which the trust arises, however, may mean that the courts have to adopt a broad approach to the factual question of reliance,[212] lest it be too easy for a claim to be defeated by the allegation that the claimant's conduct was motivated not by a belief as to her beneficial entitlement in the property, but rather by her love and affection for the defendant, or for any children.[213]

**15–132** In a case where the required common intention is instead inferred from the parties' conduct in relation to the property, detrimental reliance is far less prominent. Indeed, the concept was mentioned in neither *Stack v Dowden*[214] nor *Jones v Kernott*.[215] This is easily explained by the fact that, in such cases, the very actions of the claimant which support the inference of common intention, such as direct financial contributions to the costs of acquisition of the property, also provide evidence of reliance on that intention. Conversely, in a case where the conduct of the parties does not support such an inference, this is likely to be because that conduct can be explained as motivated not by any belief that the claimant had or would acquire a beneficial interest different from his or her legal entitlement (if any), but rather by other factors.[216]

### iii. Quantifying the Interest under the Trust

**15–133** The basic rule, applying in all cases, is that the size of the claimant's beneficial interest under the common intention constructive trust will be determined solely by that common intention.[217] It may well be the case that, whilst there is an express or inferred common intention that the claimant's beneficial interests should differ from her legal right (if any), it is not possible to find any express

---

[209] [1975] 1 W.L.R. 1338. See too *Lalani v Crump Holdings Ltd* Ch. D. 18 June 2004, at [47]: the acts alleged to give rise to detriment need not be "dealings with the property by way of contributions or by way of improvements [and other] conduct, contributions or sacrifices may suffice".

[210] See paras 15–140—15–144.

[211] See, e.g. *Grant v Edwards* [1986] 1 Ch. 638 at 657 per Browne-Wilkinson VC.

[212] See, e.g. the approach adopted by Browne-Wilkinson VC in *Grant v Edwards* [1986] 1 Ch. 638 (looking at all acts done by the claimant as part of the couple's life together) which is broader than each of the approaches adopted in the same case by Nourse LJ (looking at conduct on which the claimant could not reasonably have been expected to embark but for having a beneficial interest) and Mustill LJ (preferring the quid pro quo approach which is now inconsistent with Lord Bridge's analysis in *Lloyds Bank Plc v Rosset* [1991] 1 A.C. 107 at 132). For discussion see, e.g. A. Lawson, "The Things We Do For Love: Detrimental Reliance in the Family Home" (1996) 16 L.S. 218.

[213] The same concern is shown in proprietary estoppel cases, even where there is no romantic relationship between the claimant and the defendant: see, e.g. *Campbell v Griffin* [2001] W.T.L.R. 981 at [27] per Robert Walker LJ. Notwithstanding the view of Lord Denning MR in *Greasley v Cooke* [1980] 1 W.L.R. 1307, however, it may be going too far to say that a "presumption of reliance" operates, so that the defendant has to disprove reliance. Rather, as is usually the case, the claimant should prove each part of his claim: see, e.g. *Steria Ltd v Hutchison* [2007] I.C.R. 445 at [129] per Neuberger LJ and *Sidhu v van Dyke* (2015) 251 C.L.R. 505. See further B. McFarlane, *The Law of Proprietary Estoppel* (Oxford University Press, 2014), paras 3.98–3.283.

[214] [2007] 2 A.C. 432.

[215] [2012] 1 A.C. 776.

[216] See, e.g. *James v Thomas* [2008] 1 F.L.R. 1598 at [36] per Chadwick LJ.

[217] See, e.g. *Clough v Killey* (1996) 72 P. & C.R. D22 per Peter Gibson LJ: "it is only common sense that where the parties form a common intention as to the specific shares they are to take, those shares prima facie are the shares to which the court will give effect."; *Oxley v Hiscock* [2005] Fam. 211 at [69] per Chadwick LJ.

or inferred intention as to the *size* of that beneficial interest. In such a case, it is clear from *Stack v Dowden* and *Jones v Kernott* that the court may *impute* the missing intention.

In *Midland Bank Plc v Cooke*,[218] for example, the claimant's direct financial contribution to the purchase price of the property, registered in the sole name of her husband, amounted to less than 7 per cent of the costs of acquisition. Even under the limits imposed by *Rosset*,[219] it nonetheless allowed for the inference of a common intention that she should have a beneficial interest in the property. It was clear from the parties' evidence that they had not discussed, or even thought about, the size of any such share. Looking at the nature of their relationship, and their sharing of household expenses, the Court of Appeal found that the claimant had a 50 per cent share in equity. Waite LJ stated starkly that[220] **15–134**

> positive evidence that the parties neither discussed nor intended any agreement as to the proportions of their beneficial interest does not preclude the court, on general equitable principles, from inferring one.

Despite the reference to "inferring", the decision must have involved an imputation. As noted by Lord Neuberger in *Stack*, when disagreeing with the view of the other members of the panel that it was permissible, such imputation involves imposing on the parties an intention as to the size on the claimant's share when no such intention actually existed.

In *Jones v Kernott*, Lord Walker and Baroness Hale, with whom Lord Collins agreed, affirmed that imputation of intention as to the size of the claimant's beneficial interest is permissible.[221] They nonetheless responded to Lord Neuberger's concern as expressed in *Stack* in two ways. First, they took a broad view of the process of inference, and thus argued that the line between inference and imputation is a fine one. Secondly, they affirmed that the process of imputation involves finding "the share which the court considers fair having regard to the whole course of dealing in relation to the property",[222] rather than the imposition of a result which the court deems fair on more general grounds, perhaps based on the parties' relationship and needs, but unconnected to their dealings in relation to the property itself. As Tomlinson LJ noted in *Graham-York v York*, even when imputation is permitted[223] **15–135**

> the court is not concerned with some form of redistributive justice. Thus it is irrelevant that it may be thought a 'fair' outcome for a woman who has endured years of abusive conduct by her partner to be allotted a substantial interest in his property on his death. The plight of [the claimant] attracts sympathy, but it does not enable the court to redistribute property interests in a manner which right-minded people might think amount to appropriate compensation. [The claimant] is 'entitled' to the share which the court considers fair having regard to the whole course of dealing between them *in relation to the property*. It is these last words, which I have emphasised, which supply the confines of the enquiry as to fairness.

Two points in particular arise from *Jones v Kernott*. First, on what basis will a common intention as to the size of the claimant's interest be inferred? The issue is important: inference is, unlike imputation, permitted in relation to the initial question of whether a common intention constructive trust can be established. Lord Walker and Baroness Hale, with whom Lord Collins agreed, found that an agreement as to a 90:10 split could be inferred because the parties must have intended, when their **15–136**

---

218 [1995] 2 F.L.R. 915.
219 Discussed at paras 15–123—15–124.
220 [1995] 2 F.L.R. 915 at 920.
221 [2012] 1 A.C. 776 at [31] and [51] (extracted at paras 15–080—15–091).
222 [2012] 1 A.C. 776 at [51] (extracted at para.15–091), quoting from the judgment of Chadwick LJ in *Oxley v Hiscock* [2005] Fam 211 at [69].
223 [2015] EWCA Civ 72 at [22].

insurance policy was cashed in and Mr Kernott bought a new home, that "his interest in [the property] should crystallise then." This meant that Mr Kernott was denied any benefit from the significant appreciation in the value of the house after that point. In the absence of clear evidence, it may be doubted that Mr Kernott would have made such an agreement. Lord Kerr, along with Lord Wilson, and also Wall and Rimer LJJ in the Court of Appeal, found that no such inference could be made:

> the bare facts of [Mr Kernott's] departure from the family home and acquisition of another property are a slender foundation on which to conclude that he had entirely abandoned whatever stake he had in the previously shared property.[224]

**15–137** Secondly, what does it mean to impute a common intention? The logic of Lord Kerr's objection[225] to the idea of imputation seems impeccable: why retain the language of intention at all, if the court is simply deciding what would be fair in light of the parties' whole course of dealing with the property? To pretend, through the idea of imputation, that the outcome has anything to do with the parties' intentions is a fiction. This raises an important wider point as to the role of intention within this type of constructive trust, which we will now consider as part of our examination of the justification of the common intention constructive trust.

## *C. Justifying the Trust*

### i. Comparison with Related Doctrines

**15–138** The common intention constructive trust has been described by the Canadian Supreme Court as "doctrinally unsound".[226] It suffers from the basic problem that it is premised on the parties' objectively established common intentions as to beneficial ownership when, in fact, such intentions rarely exist.[227] As a result, the cases consist of a "judicial quest for the fugitive or phantom common intention."[228] Indeed, the English courts' acceptance that it is permissible to *impute* such an intention, albeit only as to the size of the parties' beneficial shares, shows the truth of the point made by Lord Kerr in *Jones v Kernott*[229]: the notion of the parties' intention is used as a fiction in an attempt to provide some justification for the imposition of a trust.

**15–139** A further difficulty is caused by the pedigree of the common intention constructive trust. As John Mee has noted,[230] a number of distinct and competing principles have influenced its identification and development. On the one hand, Lord Diplock's discussion of the trust in *Gissing v Gissing* proceeds from a discussion of so-called presumed resulting trusts, and this influence can be seen from the fact that, where a common intention constructive trust is based on an inference as to the parties' intentions, the courts have traditionally focussed, particularly in cases where the legal title is in the sole name of the defendant, on the question of whether the claimant has made any direct financial contribution to the costs of acquiring the property. Nonetheless, in contrast to the position under a resulting trust, the size of any interest arising under the common intention constructive trust is not determined solely by the extent of any such financial contributions, but is rather said to depend on

---

224 [2012] 1 A.C. 776 at [76] (extracted at para.15–103).
225 [2012] 1 A.C. 776 at [74] (extracted at para.15–101).
226 *Kerr v Baranow* [2011] 1 S.C.R. 269 at [25] per Cromwell J.
227 A point noted by, e.g. S. Gardner, "Rethinking Family Property" (1993) 109 L.Q.R. 263.
228 *Pettkus v Becker* (1980) 2 S.C.R. 834 at 843 per Dickson J.
229 [2012] 1 A.C. 776 at [74] (extracted at para.15–101).
230 See J. Mee, "*Pettitt v Pettitt* (1970) and *Gissing v Gissing* (1971)" in Mitchell and Mitchell (eds), *Landmark Cases in Equity* (2012) and, more generally, J. Mee, *The Property Rights of Cohabitees* (Hart Publishing, 1999).

the parties' actual or imputed intentions, even if that approach may lead in some cases to the same outcome as a resulting trust.

One attempt to justify the common intention constructive trust consists in seeing it as an application of the same principle underlying the promise-based strand of proprietary estoppel: the claimant's rights under the trust arise because it would be unconscionable for the defendant to leave her to suffer a detriment as a result of her reasonable reliance on a seriously intended promise, made by the defendant, that she had or would have an interest in the defendant's land.[231] Certainly, some of the language employed by Lord Diplock in *Gissing v Gissing*[232] is very close to that used in proprietary estoppel, where *any* conduct of the claimant is relevant if it is undertaken in reliance on a promise of a beneficial interest and gives rise to the prospect of detriment if the defendant were free to renege on the promise. **15–140**

The analogy with proprietary estoppel, however, is far from straightforward and differing views have been expressed on it; even, as can be seen in the following extract, by the same judge. **15–141**

*Stack v Dowden*

House of Lords [2007] 2 A.C. 432 at [37]

LORD WALKER: I add a brief comment as to proprietary estoppel. In his judgment in *Oxley v Hiscock*,[233] Chadwick L.J. considered the conceptual basis of the developing law in this area, and briefly discussed proprietary estoppel, a suggestion first put forward by Sir Nicholas Browne-Wilkinson V.-C. in *Grant v Edwards*.[234] I have myself given some encouragement to this approach (see *Yaxley v Gotts*[235]), but I have to say that I am now rather less enthusiastic about the notion that proprietary estoppel and "common interest" constructive trusts can or should be completely assimilated. Proprietary estoppel typically consists of asserting an equitable claim against the conscience of the "true" owner. The claim is a "mere equity". It is to be satisfied by the minimum award necessary to do justice,[236] which may sometimes lead to no more than a monetary award. A "common intention" constructive trust, by contrast, is identifying the true beneficial owner or owners, and the size of their beneficial interests. **15–142**

Lord Walker's caution is well-placed. First, the breadth of the factors that a court may take into account in inferring a common intention that the claimant's beneficial entitlement should differ from her legal rights (if any), at least where legal title is in the joint names of claimant and defendant, means that such an intention may be inferred in cases where it is unlikely that a court would find the express or implied promise required for proprietary estoppel claim. Secondly, as noted by Lord Walker, the effect of a successful proprietary estoppel claim differs from the finding of a common intention constructive trust. In the latter case, the parties' common intention, whether actual or imputed, determines the content of the claimant's right in the property,[237] whereas in the former case, there is no guarantee that the defendant's promise will be enforced,[238] since the court will carefully consider the nature of the claimant's reliance and the extent of any detriment potentially arising from it.[239] **15–143**

---

231 For an excellent historical survey of the relationship between proprietary estoppel and common intention constructive trusts, see P. Matthews, "The Words Which Are Not There: A Partial History of the Constructive Trust" in Mitchell (ed.), *Constructive and Resulting Trusts* (2010), pp.24–60.

232 [1971] A.C. 886 at 905.

233 [2005] Fam 211 at [70]–[71].

234 [1986] Ch. 638 at 656.

235 [2000] Ch. 162 at 177.

236 *Crabb v Arun D.C.* [1976] Ch. 179 at 198.

237 See para.15–133.

238 See, e.g. *Jennings v Rice* [2003] 1 P. & C.R. 8; *Ottey v Grundy* [2003] W.T.L.R. 1253. Note too the analysis of Hoffmann LJ in *Walton v Walton* (C.A., 15 April 1994).

239 See, e.g. *Powell v Benney* [2007] EWCA Civ 1283; *Henry v Henry* [2010] 1 All E.R. 988. Note too *Southwell v Blackburn* [2014]

15–144 Moreover, as noted by Lord Walker, a proprietary estoppel claim can be said to give rise to a "mere equity". The point seems to be that it does not impose an immediate duty on the defendant to perform her promise: rather, a court looks back over the parties' conduct and asks if it would *now* be unconscionable for the defendant to be wholly free to renege on her promise.[240] In contrast, at least in a case where the parties' common intention precedes, or arises at the same time as, the acquisition of the property in sole or joint names, the common intention constructive trust arises as soon as the property is acquired, even if it may be of an "ambulatory" nature, so that the extent of the parties' shares may change over time, as the common intention of the parties changes.[241] In fact, the better analogy in such a case may be with the constructive trust arising under *Rochefoucauld v Boustead*[242] or under the *Pallant v Morgan* equity.[243] Again, however, the difficulty is that each of those types of constructive trust, like the promise-based strand of proprietary estoppel, requires clear evidence of a specific promise by the defendant and does not permit the broad process of inference recognised in *Jones v Kernott*.

15–145 It should finally be noted that English law is not alone in struggling to provide a doctrinally coherent means by which the beneficial interests of cohabitants may be determined. Other jurisdictions have adopted different approaches to resolve that question, but none of those approaches is free from doctrinal difficulties.[244]

15–146 The approach in Canada, for example, has been that constructive trusts arising in relation to family homes respond to unjust enrichment.[245] In their wish to do justice between the parties, the courts have made awards designed to fulfil the claimant's expectations rather than to reverse a transfer of value to the defendant, thereby riding roughshod over the requirement that a claimant in unjust enrichment must prove that the defendant's enrichment has been acquired at her expense, and taking a very loose approach to the identification of benefit, and to the question whether the claimant should be entitled to a personal or a proprietary remedy.[246]

---

EWCA Civ 1347: A and B had cohabited, and B's claim to a beneficial share of the property under a common intention constructive trust was rejected at first instance. B's proprietary estoppel claim, however, succeeded and, as confirmed by the Court of Appeal, A was ordered to pay a sum of money (£28,5000) to B.

240 See the analysis of Hoffmann LJ in *Walton v Walton* (CA, 15 April 1994). In a case concerning a third party, the court will instead have to establish the rights held by the claimant at the time when the third party acquired its rights, by asking if *at that time*, it would have been unconscionable for the defendant to be wholly free to renege on her promise. This is consistent with the fact that an "equity" arising by proprietary estoppel can have effect from the moment of the facts giving rise to it, and does not operate only prospectively from the time of a court order: see s.116(a) Land Registration Act 2002.

241 See *Stack v Dowden* [2007] 2 A.C. 432 at [62] and [138], *Jones v Kernott* [2012] 1 A.C. 776 at [15]. Note that Etherton C, writing extra-judicially, has suggested that the common intention constructive trust is in fact a form of remedial constructive trust: T. Etherton, "Constructive Trusts: A New Model for Equity and Unjust Enrichment" [2008] C.L.J. 265. On this view, contrary to Lord Walker's analysis in *Stack* at [37] (extracted at para.15–142), the trust would arise with prospective effect only, and so would differ from a right arising through proprietary estoppel which, as discussed at n.240 has effect before that time.

242 See paras 15–030—15–045.

243 See paras 15–153—15–182.

244 See Mee, *The Property Rights of Cohabitees* (1999).

245 *Deglman v Guaranty Trust Co* [1954] S.C.R. 725; *Pettkus v Becker* [1980] 2 S.C.R. 834; *Sorochan v Sorochan* [1986] 2 S.C.R 38; *Peter v Beblow* [1993] 1 S.C.R. 980; *Kerr v Baranow* [2011] 1 S.C.R. 269.

246 For critical comment, see Mee, *The Property Rights of Cohabitees* (1999), esp. pp. 219–222 and 224; M. McInnes, "Reflections on the Canadian Law of Unjust Enrichment: Lessons From Abroad" (1999) 78 Can. Bar. Rev 416; J. McCamus, "Restitution on Dissolution of Marital or Other Intimate Relationships: Constructive Trust or *Quantum Meruit*?" in J. W. Neyers et al. (eds), *Understanding Unjust Enrichment* (Hart Publishing, 2004), esp. pp.372–375; M. McInnes, "Cohabitation, Trusts and Unjust Enrichment in the Supreme Court of Canada" (2011) 127 L.Q.R. 339.

## ii. Wider Questions of Policy

It was suggested above[247] that, whilst the common intention constructive trust has clearly been influenced by other doctrines, it is impossible to justify as an application of any one of those principles. This is perhaps unsurprising, as it seems clear that from *Gissing v Gissing* onwards, the common intention constructive trust has been fashioned as a response to the specific and very difficult problem of affording sufficient protection to cohabitants, particularly on the termination of their relationship. This point is made in the following extract: it is from a case where the Court of Appeal considered an argument that the type of constructive trust arising under the *Pallant v Morgan* equity (which we discuss in section 6), was an example of a common intention constructive trust. 15–147

*Crossco No 4 Unlimited v Jolan Ltd*

Court of Appeal [2012] 2 All ER 754 at [85]

ETHERTON L.J.: I do not accept [counsel's] argument that the [*Pallant v Morgan* type] constructive trust is properly analysed as an example of a common intention constructive trust. [The] line of cases on the common intention constructive trust can be seen clearly in retrospect as a specific jurisprudential response to the problem of a presumption of resulting trust and the absence of legislation for resolving disputes over property ownership where a married or unmarried couple have purchased property for their joint occupation as a family home.[248] The jurisprudence in that distinctive area is driven by policy considerations and the special facts that normally apply in the dealings between those living in an intimate relationship. They include the fact that such parties do not normally take legal advice about, or expect to reduce to a formal or indeed any written agreement, their mutual property rights and interests in the family home. Further, those rights and interests must be seen in the context of an enduring but often-changing relationship of inter-dependency, mutual co-operation, compromise and joint contributions. Those special features are why, as the jurisprudence has now clearly established, the usual presumption of a resulting trust does not apply in such a situation, and the parties' respective property rights in the family home are to be ascertained by having regard to their intentions as disclosed by what they have said and done over the entire course of their ownership or, where it is clear that the beneficial interests are to be shared but it is impossible to divine a common intention as to the proportions in which they are to be shared, by imputing to them the intentions which they would have had as reasonable and just people if they had thought about it . . . Since the parties' actual, inferred or imputed intentions might change over time, the common intention constructive trust has been described as an "ambulatory" trust. 15–148

Those special features, in terms of policy, facts and law, do not apply in a commercial context. 15–149

As we will see below,[249] the other members of the Court of Appeal in *Crossco* felt bound by earlier Court of Appeal authority to hold that the *Pallant v Morgan* type of constructive trust was an example of a common intention constructive trust. Nonetheless, each of Arden and McFarlane LJJ expressed some support for Etherton LJ's analysis of the development of the common intention constructive trust in shared homes cases.[250] It would certainly be surprising, for example, if the broad approach to inferring a common intention, and the permissibility of imputing a common intention in some situations, was also adopted by the courts in a commercial context. 15–150

From a policy perspective, however, there are still pressing difficulties in justifying the common intention constructive trust. For example, it may still be difficult, even after *Stack v Dowden* and *Jones v Kernott*, for a long-term cohabitant to show that he or she has a beneficial interest where the property is registered in the sole name of the defendant, there is no evidence of an expressed agreement between 15–151

---

247 At paras 15–138—15–141.
248 See *Stack v Dowden* [2007] 2 A.C. 432 at [40] to [46]; *Jones v Kernott* [2012] 1 A.C. 776 at [25], [56], [57], [61] and [78].
249 At paras 15–176—15–179.
250 [2012] 2 All E.R. 754 at [121] and [129].

the parties as to the claimant's having a beneficial share, and the claimant has made no direct financial contribution to the costs of acquiring the property. Yet many would argue that, in such a case, the nature of the claimant and defendant's relationship, and the broader contributions made by the former to the parties' lives together may mean that the claimant should not be left empty-handed if the relationship ends for reasons other than the death of the defendant.[251]

**15–152** Of course, had the parties been married or in a civil partnership, much of the pressure would be taken off the law of constructive trusts, as the parties would then have been subject to a broad statutory jurisdiction allowing for the variation of their property rights, with consideration given to a broad range of factors, such as the nature of their relationship and their future needs.[252] Indeed, in an eminently sensible set of proposals, the Law Commission recommended that a similar (but not identical) statutory scheme should be put in place for cohabitants who are unmarried and not in a civil partnership, allowing for financial relief to be available to claimants.[253] Such a scheme, if enacted, would not be a panacea, as of course there would still be cases (such as those involving third parties) where it is necessary for a court to establish the parties' individual beneficial entitlements (if any) at a past point in time. Parliament's failure to implement such a scheme, however, raises a difficult dilemma: should the courts continue to develop the common intention constructive trust, stretching it so as to fill the gap left by an absence of statutory intervention? Or should the courts acknowledge that, in relation to a politically sensitive area of the law, they should not distort existing legal principles in order to achieve similar outcomes to those that Parliament has chosen not to impose through legislation?[254]

## 6. The *Pallant v Morgan* Equity

### *A. Nature of the Trust*

**15–153** In *Pallant v Morgan*,[255] land was sold at auction. Pallant's agent was authorised to bid up to £2,000 for lot 16; Morgan's agent could go up to £3,000. Not wanting to bid against each other and push the prices up, the agents agreed, in the auction room, that, if Morgan acquired both lots 15 and 16, he would sell on to Pallant part of lot 15 and part of lot 16. Pallant's agent therefore pulled out of the bidding for lot 16, which Morgan succeeded in buying for less than £2,000. Morgan also acquired lot 15. The parties then failed to agree on the details of how to divide the land, and so Morgan kept it all for himself. Harman J held that, whilst the agents had authority to bind their principals to an agreement, the auction room agreement was too uncertain to be specifically enforceable. Nevertheless,

---

[251] *Burns v Burns* [1984] Ch. 317 is often cited as an example of an unjust outcome: the parties' relationship ended after nearly 20 years, during which time the claimant had cared for the couple's children and had contributed to household expenses. The family home was registered in the sole name of the defendant, there had been no express discussions as to beneficial ownership, and the claimant had made no direct financial contribution to the purchase price or mortgage payments. No constructive trust arose and at 332 and 345, Fox and May LJJ, and whilst recognising the harshness of the claimant being left without a remedy, stated that any reform had to come from Parliament. For a nuanced examination of the decision, see J. Mee, "*Burns v Burns*: The Villain of the Piece?" in S. Gilmore et al., (eds), *Landmark Cases in Family Law* (Hart Publishing, 2011).

[252] Similarly, if the relationship had ended by the death of the defendant, and no adequate financial provision had been made for the claimant, some financial protection would be available to the claimant under the Inheritance (Provision for Family and Dependants) Act 1975.

[253] Law Commission, *Cohabitation: The Financial Consequences of Relationship Breakdown* (TSO, 2007), Law Com. No.307, Cm.7182.

[254] Indeed, protecting a claimant by means of a common intention constructive trust, and thus giving her a beneficial interest capable of binding third parties, would give her a more significant right than the right to financial relief proposed by the Law Commission.

[255] [1953] Ch. 43.

he held that Morgan should hold plot 16 on trust for himself and Pallant jointly because his bid had been made on the basis of an agreement for division and it would be "tantamount to sanctioning fraud" to allow him to retain all of plot 16 for himself.[256] Pallant however had no rights in relation to plot 15.

The "*Pallant v Morgan* equity", like a specifically enforceable contract for sale,[257] can give rise to a trust. The principle was later summarised by Megarry J[258]: **15–154**

> If A and B agree that A will acquire some specific property for the joint benefit of A and B on terms yet to be agreed and B in reliance on A's agreement is thereby induced to refrain from attempting to acquire the property equity ought not to permit A when he acquires the property to insist on retaining the whole benefit for himself to the exclusion of B.

It seems clear that a trust arising as a result of the *Pallant v Morgan* equity is properly seen as a constructive rather than an express trust. The agreement between the parties pre-dates the defendant's acquisition of the property, and the trust arises even if the defendant, having acquired the property, does not attempt to exercise her power to create a trust. The trust also differs from the form of constructive trust arising as a result of a specifically enforceable contract: as made clear in *Pallant* itself, there is no requirement that the parties' agreement be sufficiently certain to be contractually enforceable. The trust can also be based on an oral agreement in relation to land and it is clear that, as a result of the formality rule imposed by s.2 of the Law of Property (Miscellaneous Provisions) Act 1989, such an oral agreement is not contractually binding. **15–155**

## *B. Scope of the Trust*

The *Palllant v Morgan* equity was given a wide interpretation in *Banner Homes Group Plc v Luff Developments Ltd (No.2)*,[259] where Chadwick LJ held that, whilst it is often triggered in cases where the claimant has suffered detriment, a constructive trust can also be imposed where the claimant has suffered no detriment, but the defendant has gained an advantage as a result of the parties' arrangement. **15–156**

> *Banner Homes Group plc v Luff Developments Ltd*
>
> Court of Appeal [2000] Ch. 372
>
> Banner Homes sought a declaration that Luff Developments held half of the shares in its wholly-owned subsidiary, Stowhelm Ltd, on trust for Banner Homes. The subsidiary had been set up in order to purchase land. Banner Homes had also been interested in buying that land, but had entered into negotiations with Luff Developments for a joint venture in which they would set up a company to acquire and develop the land. It did not appeal against a finding that there had been no contractual agreement for such a joint venture, but it claimed nonetheless that a constructive trust arose as a result of that agreement. The first instance judge found that each side had an implied power to withdraw from the agreement and so rejected the claim. The Court of Appeal allowed Banner Homes' appeal. Chadwick LJ gave an important summary of the requirements of the *Pallant v Morgan* equity. **15–157**

---

256 [1953] Ch. 43 at 48.

257 See paras 15–011—15–024.

258 *Holiday Inns of America Inc v Broadhead* Ch. D. 19 December 1969 (where Megarry J considered interlocutory relief; for later proceedings see (1974) 232 E.G. 951, 1087); the words reproduced in the text are quoted in *Banner Homes Group plc v Luff Developments Ltd (No.2)* [2000] Ch. 372 at 391.

259 [2000] Ch. 372 at 396–399, followed in *Cox v Jones* [2004] 2 F.L.R. 1010 at [46]. In both cases, the claimant suffered detriment on the facts.

15–158 CHADWICK L.J.: It is important . . . to identify the features which will give rise to a *Pallant v Morgan* equity and to define its scope; while keeping in mind that it is undesirable to attempt anything in the nature of an exhaustive classification. As Millett J. pointed out in *Lonrho plc v Fayed (No. 2)*,[260] in a reference to the work of distinguished Australian commentators, equity must retain its 'inherent flexibility and capacity to adjust to new situations by reference to mainsprings of the equitable jurisdiction.' Equity must never be deterred by the absence of a precise analogy, provided that the principle invoked is sound. Mindful of this caution, it is, nevertheless, possible to advance the following propositions.

15–159 (1) A *Pallant v Morgan* equity may arise where the arrangement or understanding on which it is based precedes the acquisition of the relevant property by one party to that arrangement. It is the pre-acquisition arrangement which colours the subsequent acquisition by the defendant and leads to his being treated as a trustee if he seeks to act inconsistently with it. Where the arrangement or understanding is reached in relation to property already owned by one of the parties, he may (if the arrangement is of sufficient certainty to be enforced specifically) thereby constitute himself trustee on the basis that 'equity looks on that as done which ought to be done;' or an equity may arise under the principles developed in the proprietary estoppel cases. As I have sought to point out, the concepts of constructive trust and proprietary estoppel have much in common in this area.. . .

15–160 (2) It is unnecessary that the arrangement or understanding should be contractually enforceable. Indeed, if there is an agreement which is enforceable as a contract, there is unlikely to be any need to invoke the *Pallant v Morgan* equity; equity can act through the remedy of specific performance and will recognise the existence of a corresponding trust. On its facts *Chattock v Muller*,[261] is, perhaps, best regarded as a specific performance case. In particular, it is no bar to a *Pallant v Morgan* equity that the pre-acquisition arrangement is too uncertain to be enforced as a contract—see *Pallant v Morgan* itself, and *Time Products Ltd. v. Combined English Stores Group Ltd*,[262] —nor that it is plainly not intended to have contractual effect—see *Island Holdings Ltd v Birchington Engineering Co Ltd*.[263]

15–161 (3) It is necessary that the pre-acquisition arrangement or understanding should contemplate that one party ("the acquiring party") will take steps to acquire the relevant property; and that, if he does so, the other party ("the non-acquiring party") will obtain some interest in that property. Further, it is necessary that (whatever private reservations the acquiring party may have) he has not informed the non-acquiring party before the acquisition (or, perhaps more accurately, before it is too late for the parties to be restored to a position of no advantage/no detriment) that he no longer intends to honour the arrangement or understanding.

15–162 (4) It is necessary that, in reliance on the arrangement or understanding, the non-acquiring party should do (or omit to do) something which confers an advantage on the acquiring party in relation to the acquisition of the property; or is detrimental to the ability of the non-acquiring party to acquire the property on equal terms. It is the existence of the advantage to the one, or detriment to the other, gained or suffered as a consequence of the arrangement or understanding, which leads to the conclusion that it would be inequitable or unconscionable to allow the acquiring party to retain the property for himself, in a manner inconsistent with the arrangement or understanding which enabled him to acquire it. *Pallant v Morgan* itself provides an illustration of this principle. There was nothing inequitable in allowing the defendant to retain for himself the lot (lot 15) in respect to which the plaintiff's agent had no instructions to bid. In many cases the advantage/detriment will be found in the agreement of the non-acquiring party to keep out of the market. That will usually be both to the advantage of the acquiring party—in that he can bid without competition from the non-acquiring party—and to the detriment of the non-acquiring party—in that he loses the opportunity to acquire the property for himself. But there may be advantage to the one without corresponding detriment to the other. Again, *Pallant v Morgan* provides an illustration. The plaintiff's agreement (through his agent) to keep out of the bidding gave an advantage to the defendant—in that he was able to obtain the property for a lower price than would otherwise have been possible; but the failure of the plaintiff's agent to bid did not, in fact, cause detriment to the plaintiff—because, on the facts, the agent's instructions would not have permitted him to outbid the defendant. Nevertheless, the equity was invoked.

---

260 [1992] 1 WLR 1, 9.
261 (1878) 8 Ch. D. 177.
262 2 December 1974 (unrep).
263 7 July 1981 (unrep).

(5) That leads, I think, to the further conclusions: (i) that although, in many cases, the advantage/detriment will be found in the agreement of the non-acquiring party to keep out of the market, that is not a necessary feature; and (ii) that although there will usually be advantage to the one and correlative disadvantage to the other, the existence of both advantage and detriment is not essential—either will do. What is essential is that the circumstances make it inequitable for the acquiring party to retain the property for himself in a manner inconsistent with the arrangement or understanding on which the non-acquiring party has acted. Those circumstances may arise where the non-acquiring party was never "in the market" for the whole of the property to be acquired; but (on the faith of an arrangement or understanding that he shall have a part of that property) provides support in relation to the acquisition of the whole which is of advantage to the acquiring party. They may arise where the assistance provided to the acquiring party (in pursuance of the arrangement or understanding) involves no detriment to the non-acquiring party; or where the non-acquiring party acts to his detriment (in pursuance of the arrangement or understanding) without the acquiring party obtaining any advantage therefrom.. . . 15–163

The *Pallant v Morgan* equity does not seek to give effect to the parties' bargain, still less to make for them some bargain which they have not themselves made, as the cases to which I have referred make clear. The equity is invoked where the defendant has acquired property in circumstances where it would be inequitable to allow him to treat it as his own; and where, because it would be inequitable to allow him to treat the property as his own, it is necessary to impose on him the obligations of a trustee in relation to it. It is invoked because there is no bargain which is capable of being enforced; if there were an enforceable bargain there would have been no need for equity to intervene in the way that it has done in the cases to which I have referred. 15–164

I am satisfied, also, that the judge was wrong to reject the constructive trust claim on the grounds that Banner had failed to show that it had acted to its detriment in reliance on the arrangement agreed on 15 July 1995. There was evidence, to which I have referred, that the existence of the arrangement led Banner to regard the site as "out of play"; that is to say, the existence of the arrangement made it unnecessary, and inappropriate, for Banner to consider the site as a potential acquisition for its own commercial portfolio. But, as the judge himself recognised, one of the reasons why Luff wanted Banner kept 'on board'—and so did not disclose its own doubts as to the future of the joint venture—was that, "if dropped, Banner might emerge as a rival for the site." In other words, Luff saw it as an advantage that Banner's belief that the site was out of play should be maintained. Luff wanted to keep Banner out of the market. In those circumstances, it does not lie easily in Luff's mouth to say that Banner suffered no detriment. But whether or not Banner suffered detriment from the fact that it never regarded itself as free to consider the site as a potential acquisition of its own does not seem to me conclusive. Luff obtained the advantage which it sought. Further, Luff obtained the advantage of knowing that it had Banner's support, as a potential joint venturer whose commitment was not in doubt, in an acquisition on which it had not been willing to embark on its own. 15–165

As I have sought to show, the *Pallant v Morgan* equity is invoked where it would be inequitable to allow the defendant to treat the property acquired in furtherance of the arrangement or understanding as his own. It may be just as inequitable to allow the defendant to treat the property as his own when it has been acquired by the use of some advantage which he has obtained under the arrangement or understanding as it is to allow him to treat the property as his own when the plaintiff has suffered some detriment under the arrangement or understanding. That, as it seems to me, is this case. 15–166

It is important to note that, whilst the *Pallant v Morgan* equity does not depend on there being a legally binding agreement between the parties, nor, it seems, on the claimant having believed that there was such an agreement in place,[264] no claim will arise if the parties have positively agreed not to be bound unless and until formal contracts have been exchanged.[265] The same points are true in relation to a proprietary estoppel claim[266]; the difference is that such a claim necessarily depends 15–167

---

264 See, e.g. *Holiday Inns v Broadhead* (1974) 232 E.G. 951 at 1087, as analysed by Lord Scott in *Cobbe v Yeoman's Row Management Ltd v Cobbe* [2008] 1 W.L.R. 1752 at [24].

265 See *London & Regional Investments Ltd v TBI Plc* [2002] EWCA Civ 355 at [47]–[50] per Mummery LJ.

266 See, e.g. *Sutcliffe v Lloyd* [2007] 2 E.G.L.R. 13 at [38] per Wilson LJ; *Cobbe v Yeoman's Row Management Ltd v Cobbe* [2008] 1 W.L.R. 1752.

on the prospect of the claimant's suffering a detriment whereas, as *Banner Homes* makes clear, the *Pallant v Morgan* equity can instead apply where there is the prospect of the defendant's acquiring an unjust advantage.

## C. Justifying the Trust

**15–168** A number of different explanations have been proposed for the *Pallant v Morgan* equity, and thus for constructive trusts arising on that basis. These explanations share a desire to link such trusts to other types of constructive trust. For example, one academic suggestion[267] is that a *Pallant v Morgan* constructive trust is just one example of a trust arising in response to the prospect of a party's suffering a detriment as a result of an undertaking by the defendant to hold on trust: on this view, the same principle also underlies trusts arising in response to proprietary estoppel and mutual wills, secret trusts, and the *Rochefoucauld v Boustead* trust. The difficulty with this view, as applied to *Pallant v Morgan*, is that, detriment does not in fact seem to be a requirement of the *Pallant v Morgan* equity (as Chadwick LJ pointed out in *Banner Homes*). A second academic suggestion,[268] building on this point, sees a trust based on that equity instead as just one example of a trust arising to prevent the defendant holding property free from a promised right of the claimant, where the defendant's promise gave the defendant an advantage in relation to the acquisition of the property. On that view, the same principle also underlies secret trusts and the *Rochefoucauld v Boustead* trust.

**15–169** Two further views, each of which has attracted some judicial support, also seek to align trusts arising on the basis of *Pallant v Morgan* with other types of constructive trust. The view adopted by Chadwick LJ in *Banner Homes* was that such a trust is an example of the common intention constructive trust.[269] As seen in the next extract, a majority of the Court of Appeal in *Crossco No 4 Unlimited v Jolan Ltd* felt bound to adopt that view. In the same case, Etherton LJ proposed instead that a trust arising on the basis of *Pallant v Morgan* is an example of a trust arising in response to a breach of fiduciary duty (such as that which was subsequently recognised in *FHR European Ventures LLP v Cedar Capital Partners LLC*[270]).

*Crossco No 4 Unlimited v Jolan Ltd*

Court of Appeal [2012] 2 All E.R. 754

**15–170** The dispute in the case arose in the context of the division of a family business, following the death of one of its two founding brothers. The general scheme of division was that the remaining brother would take over the trading side and the widow the property side. One of the trading operations was an amusement arcade run from the ground floor of a building. Under the terms of the formal division, the freehold of the building went to the widow, and the lease of the ground floor to the brother. There had been informal discussions about how to deal with the lease, but no final agreement had been reached by the time of the formal division. The widow's side sought to exercise a break clause in the lease, as it wished to redevelop the building. The brother's side objected that thus evicting the arcade business was contrary to an informal oral agreement made between the parties. The Court of Appeal unanimously rejected that argument, as it was found that there had been no such agreement, even an informal one, as to the nature and duration of

---

267 See S. Gardner, "Reliance-Based Constructive Trusts" in Mitchell (ed.), *Constructive and Resulting Trusts* (2010).

268 See B. McFarlane, "Constructive Trusts Arising on a Receipt of Property *Sub Conditione*" (2004) 120 L.Q.R. 667. See too *de Bruyne v de Bruyne* [2010] EWCA Civ 519 at [51] per Patten LJ, referring to a principle giving rise to a constructive trust where the defendant's unconscionable conduct is "in the form of a denial or refusal to carry out the agreement to hold the property for the benefit of the third party which was the only basis upon which the property was transferred."

269 For which, see paras 15–046ff.

270 [2015] A.C. 250. See paras 13–129ff.

any rights that the brother's side was to have in the ground floor. In determining the case, the judges also expressed views on the basis of the *Pallant v Morgan* equity.

ETHERTON L.J.: I do not accept [counsel's] argument that the *Banner Homes* constructive trust is properly analysed as an example of a common intention constructive trust. [There then follows the analysis of the nature and special features of the common intention constructive trust which has been extracted above.[271]] . . . Those special features, in terms of policy, facts and law, do not apply in a commercial context. They did not apply in *Banner Homes*. They did not apply in any of the cases to which Chadwick L.J. referred as examples of the application of the *Pallant v Morgan* equity. In attempting to find some underlying coherence in the cases, Chadwick L.J. drew on the principles of the common intention constructive trust as applied in *Gissing v Gissing* and *Rosset*, and on judicial statements endorsing a close relationship between the common intention constructive trust and proprietary estoppel to be found in *Yaxley* and *Grant v Edwards*. 15–171

The passage of time and developments in the law have, in my judgment, shown the connection between the common intention constructive trust and the *Pallant v Morgan* equity as explained and applied in *Banner Homes* to be untenable. In a commercial context, it is to be expected that the parties will normally take legal advice about their respective rights and interests and will normally reduce their agreements to writing and will not expect to be bound until a contract has been made.[272] They do not expect their rights to be determined in an "ambulatory" manner by retrospective examination of their conduct and words over the entire period of their relationship. They do not expect the court to determine their respective property rights and interests by the imputation of intentions which they did not have but which the court considers they would have had if they had acted justly and reasonably and thought about the point. 15–172

It is not necessary to resort to the common intention constructive trust to provide an explanation for the cases in which the *Pallant v Morgan* equity was, or is said to have been, applied. They can all be explained, and, in my judgment, ought to be explained in wholly conventional terms by the existence and breach of fiduciary duty. In *Chattock v Muller* Sir Richard Malins V.-C. held that the defendant had attended the auction as the plaintiff's agent. Similarly, in *Pallant v Morgan* Harman J. held that the defendant's agent bid for lot 16 on behalf of both parties. *Holiday Inns*, *Time Products* and *Island Holdings* were joint venture cases, in which it is to be inferred that the particular nature of the relationship between the joint venturers was such as to give rise to fiduciary duties. In the absence of agency or partnership, it would require particular and special features for such fiduciary duties to arise between commercial co-venturers. It is clear, however, that in special circumstances they can arise .. . . In my judgment, the result in *Banner Homes* can only properly be explained on that basis .. . . 15–173

It is not possible to do full justice in the context of this judgment to the alternative explanations put forward by McFarlane[273] and Gardner[274] for the *Pallant v Morgan* equity and *Banner Homes*. Their merit is that they are put forward as principled explanations for a range of constructive trusts, including, for example, (in addition to the *Pallant v Morgan* equity and *Banner Homes*) secret trusts, trusts arising under the doctrine of *Rochefoucauld v Boustead* and, in Gardner's case, those associated with mutual wills and proprietary estoppel. Neither [counsel] argued in favour of them. It is sufficient for the purpose of this judgment to say that: (1) they provide explanations of a range of constructive trusts at a high level of abstraction; but (2) the cases in which the *Pallant v Morgan* equity has been applied can be explained in a wholly conventional way as examples of breach of an existing fiduciary duty, and (3) it is a sound policy that they should be so explained and confined. It is sound policy because, by contrast with the common intention constructive trust, such a policy recognises the need for certainty in commercial transactions, and it reflects the usual practice and desirability for business transactions to be effected by binding written contracts, often after the receipt of legal advice. 15–174

If the cases in which the *Pallant v Morgan* equity has been applied are interpreted as I suggest, then they can be seen as cases in which the court is, pursuant to the constructive trust, depriving the defendant of the advantage obtained in breach of trust. The irrelevance of lack of complete agreement, whether documented or not, is then easily explained, as is the latitude with which the court devises the best way to deprive the defendant of the unconscionable advantage: compare *Holiday Inns* (where the plaintiff's 15–175

[271] See paras 15–148—15–149.

[272] See, e.g. Lord Walker in *Cobbe* [2008] 1 W.L.R. 1752 at [68] and [81].

[273] B. McFarlane, "Constructive Trusts Arising on a Receipt of Property *Sub Conditione*" (2004) 120 L.Q.R. 667.

[274] S. Gardner, "Reliance-Based Constructive Trusts" in C. Mitchell (ed.), *Constructive and Resulting Trusts* (2010).

expectation was to receive a lease, but it was granted a beneficial interest) and *Yaxley* (in which the plaintiff was granted a 99-year lease rent free).

15–176 ARDEN L.J.: . . .[T]he reasoning in *Banner Homes* . . . makes it clear that the ratio of that case is firmly based on a common intention constructive trust. By common intention constructive trust, I mean a constructive trust of the kind enunciated in *Gissing*. The analysis of *Banner Homes* which I have set out at the start of this paragraph was accepted by Lord Scott in *Cobbe*. The speech of Lord Walker in *Stack v Dowden* and the joint judgment of Lady Hale and Lord Walker in *Jones v Kernott* may mean that common intention constructive trusts may be limited in the future to family cases, but I do not consider that that position is so clear as to make it possible at this stage for this court to hold that *Banner Homes* cannot stand with decisions of the House of Lords and Supreme Court, and to treat the ratio of *Banner Homes* as not binding on it.

15–177 *Banner Homes* is invoked, in practice, in circumstances where parties have been in commercial negotiations over the acquisition of some property but the negotiations have for some reason failed so that there is no legally enforceable agreement. The advantage of the re-interpretation of the case law proposed by Etherton L.J. would be that it would restrict the number of situations in which *Banner Homes* can be used. That would be consistent with developments in the law of proprietary estoppel. The House of Lords made it clear that where parties have been dealing on the basis that their negotiations are "subject to contract", proprietary estoppel will not ordinarily be available: see *Cobbe*. The result is not unconscionable because the disappointed party will always have known that that was the position .... For the law in general to provide scope for claims in respect of unsuccessful negotiations that do not result in legally enforceable contracts would, in my judgment, be likely to inhibit the efficient pursuit of commercial negotiations, which is a necessary part of proper entrepreneurial activity.

15–178 MCFARLANE L.J.: In order to arrive at his conclusion, Etherton L.J. has considered the development of the law in subsequent decisions, which include determinations by the UK Supreme Court and the House of Lords. The approach in those subsequent cases leads my lord to the conclusion that, by implication, the *Banner Homes* decision must now be seen to be based upon fiduciary duty. My lady, Arden L.J., sees advantage in the interpretation put forward by my lord. I for my part also understand the path that Etherton L.J. has threaded through the decisions and particularly see the attraction of his conclusion at that the line of cases from *Gissing* to *Jones v Kernott* relating to domestic arrangements are driven by different policy considerations and may have features which are distinct from those arising from strictly commercial circumstances.

15–179 Whilst Etherton L.J. may well be correct to interpret the oblique consequences of subsequent decisions as developing a construction of *Banner Homes* which is based on fiduciary duty, that approach was not expressly described by Chadwick L.J. in the case itself, and has not been, or at least was not, the interpretation afforded to the decision at the time. Absent an express declaration from the Supreme Court, and despite being attracted to the analysis of Etherton L.J., I consider that the solid jurisprudential ground must remain as Arden L.J. has described and I therefore agree with her that it is not open to this court to reinterpret the ratio of *Banner Homes* a decade after its genesis.

15–180 It is somewhat surprising that the majority in *Crossco* subscribed to the view that Chadwick LJ's analysis of the *Pallant v Morgan* equity continued to have binding effect, notwithstanding the developments in the common intention constructive trust in *Stack v Dowden* and *Jones v Kernott*. There is much to be said for the view of Etherton LJ that the common intention constructive trust should not be extended beyond the context in which it has developed. Certainly, as we saw above,[275] there are real difficulties in providing a convincing justification of that type of trust, and so, if we wish to justify the *Pallant v Morgan* equity, it will be better to look elsewhere.

15–181 Etherton LJ's suggestion that the *Pallant v Morgan* equity responds to a breach of fiduciary duty is an interesting one, and certainly accords with a desire to limit the applicability of the equity, at least in relation to pre-contractual negotiations. It is well-recognised that, in a simple case of an agent and a principal, the agent has a duty to act exclusively in the principal's interest, but it may be hard to find such a fiduciary duty in a joint venture case, where business rivals agree to co-operate, but in a specific

275 See paras 15–138ff.

and limited way.[276] It can be argued that, in a case such as *Pallant v Morgan* or *Banner Homes*, the relevant duty of the defendant is simply a duty to honour the terms of a promise,[277] and that it would be confusing to regard such a duty as fiduciary.

There is of course a wider issue as to the extent to which equitable concepts should operate in the commercial context.[278] As shown by the promise-based strand of proprietary estoppel, however, the absence of a binding contract does not necessarily prevent a claim arising on the basis of a promise made by the defendant. Indeed, it may be that a promise-based analysis of *Pallant v Morgan*, similar to that of Ben McFarlane or Simon Gardner, is consistent with the view of Etherton LJ, in as far as the defendant's promise is crucial in establishing that, in relation to the acquisition of particular property, and to an extent determined by the content of the defendant's promise,[279] the defendant must act for the benefit of the claimant.[280] **15–182**

## 7. Proceeds of Breach of Confidence

### *A. The Nature of the Trust*

The equitable doctrine of breach of confidence, which now also extends to the protection of private information, **15–183**

> depends on the broad principle of equity that he who has received information in confidence shall not take unfair advantage of it. He must not make use of it to the prejudice of him who gave it without obtaining his consent.[281]

The same principles have been extended to cases where there is a reasonable expectation of privacy in relation to the information. The information must have the necessary quality of confidentiality or privacy, must have been imparted or acquired in circumstances where there is a reasonable expectation that the information is confidential or private,[282] and there must have been an unauthorised use of the information, at a time when the defendant knew, or had sufficient notice, that the information was confidential or private.[283] No claim will arise if the maintenance of confidence is not in the public interest[284] or if the duty of confidentiality was at an end at the relevant time because the information was in the public domain and so available to all on reasonable inquiry.[285] The doctrine of breach of

---

276 See para.13–010.

277 In *Vercoe v Rutland Fund Management Ltd* [2010] EWHC 424 at [358], for example, Sales J stated that in a case such as *Pallant v Morgan*, "where property has been acquired by one person as a result of an explicit agreement with another that, in return for him not seeking to acquire the property himself, it will be held after acquisition for the benefit of both of them. . .a constructive trust may be imposed to give effect to the agreement."

278 See paras 13–013—13–015.

279 cf. J. Edelman, "When Do Fiduciary Duties Arise?" (2010) 126 L.Q.R. 302, who argues that the incidence and content of fiduciary duties is determined by the parties' consent.

280 Compare the general argument used by Lionel Smith to justify constructive trusts arising in cases of breach of fiduciary duty: see L. Smith, "Constructive Trusts and the No-Profit Rule" [2013] C.L.J. 260.

281 *Seager v Copydex Ltd* [1967] 1 W.L.R. 923 at 931.

282 See, e.g. *Attorney-General v Guardian Newspapers (No.2)* [1990] 1 A.C. 109 at 281, per Lord Goff.

283 *Coco v Clark (Engineers) Ltd* [1969] R.P.C. 41 at [47], endorsed by the C.A. in *Murray v Yorkshire Fund Managers* [1998] 2 All E.R. 1015 at 1020; *Attorney General v Jonathan Cape* [1975] 3 All E.R. 484 at [494]; *Fraser v Thames Television* [1983] 2 All E.R. 101 at 116.

284 *Initial Services Ltd v Putterill* [1968] 1 Q.B. 396 at 405; *Lion Laboratories Ltd v Evans* [1984] 2 All E.R. 417; *Francome v Mirror Group Newspapers* [1984] 2 All E.R 408.

285 *Peter Pan Manufacturing Co v Corsets Silhouette Ltd* [1964] 1 W.L.R. 96; *British Syphon Co v Homewood* [1956] 1 W.L.R. 1190; *Attorney General v Guardian Newspapers (No.2)* [1990] 1 A.C. 109. *Attorney General v Blake* [1998] Ch. 439.

confidence will not be applied in such a way as to interfere unjustifiably with the defendant's right to freedom of expression, protected by art.10 of the European Convention on Human Rights.[286]

**15–184** The equitable right of confidence can be protected by the grant of an injunction to prevent disclosure, but if it is too late and the confidence has been disclosed then the confider may be entitled to an award of monetary compensation,[287] or to an account of the defendant's profits[288]—although the trend of recent case law suggests where there is no fiduciary relationship between the parties, the court will usually restrict the claimant to the compensatory award.[289] Where the defendant acquires specific property by means of a breach of confidence, the claimant may wish to argue that the defendant must not only account for those profits, but in fact holds the property itself on trust for the claimant. If such a trust is imposed, it will clearly be constructive. It is far from clear, however, that such a trust can arise in English law.

## *B. The Scope of the Trust*

**15–185** There is some overseas Commonwealth authority suggesting that a constructive trust may sometimes be imposed on profits acquired through a breach of confidence or privacy. For example, in *LAC Minerals Ltd v International Corona Resources Ltd*,[290] the Supreme Court of Canada held that LAC was constructive trustee of land that it had bought for itself, because it had been told in confidence by a potential joint-venturer that the land could well contain gold deposits.

**15–186** Dicta to the same effect can also be found in some English cases. In *Attorney General v Guardian Newspapers Ltd (No.2)*, Lord Goff considered obiter that if a confidant disclosed information in a book so that it lost its quality of confidentiality, and then sought to profit further from his wrongdoing by selling the film rights to the book "the copyright in the book, including the film rights, are held by him on constructive trust for the confider".[291] In *Ocular Sciences Ltd v Aspect Vision Care Ltd*,[292] Laddie J considered that the approach taken by the court in *LAC Minerals* "makes eminent sense" and, whilst refusing to find a constructive trust on the facts of the case, stated that "the imposition of a constructive trust is part of the equitable armoury of the court."[293] Similarly, in *United Pan-Europe Communications NV v Deutsche Bank AG*[294] the Court of Appeal stated that in principle a constructive trust could be awarded in response to a breach of confidence.

**15–187** It seems, however, that there is no English case in which a constructive trust has actually been imposed in response to a breach of confidence, and it is important to note that, where the breach

---

[286] See, e.g. *Campbell v MGN Ltd* [2004] 2 A.C. 457 at [29], per Lord Nicholls.

[287] See, e.g. *Saltman Engineering Co Ltd v Campbell Engineering Co Ltd* (1948) 65 R.P.C. 203 at 219; *Seager v Copydex Ltd* [1967] 1 W.L.R. 923 at 932; and *Seager v Copydex (No.2)* [1969] 1 W.L.R. 809; *Indata Equipment Supplies Ltd v ACL Ltd* [1998] F.S.R. 248 at 259–262, 263 and 264; *Campbell v MGN Ltd* [2002] E.M.L.R. 617 at [75], affirmed [2004] 2 A.C. 457; *Douglas v Hello! Ltd (No.3)* [2006] Q.B. 125 at [120], [243]–[250] and [259]; *OBG Ltd v Allan* [2008] 1 A.C. 1 at [276].

[288] *Peter Pan Manufacturing Corp v Corsets Silhouette Ltd* [1964] 1 W.L.R. 96 at 106; *Attorney General v Observer Ltd* [1990] 1 A.C. 109 at 255–256, 262 and 288; *OBG Ltd v Allan* [2008] 1 A.C. 1 at [276]; *Vestergaard Frandsen A/S v BestNet Europe Ltd* [2010] F.S.R. 2 at [93].

[289] *CF Partners (UK) LLP v Barclays Bank Plc* [2014] EWHC 3049 (Ch) at [1168]–[1181], considering *Experience Hendrix LLC v PPX Enterprises Inc* [2003] 1 All E.R. (Comm.) 830; *Vercoe v Rutland Fund Management Ltd* [2010] EWHC 424; and *Walsh v Shanahan* [2013] EWCA Civ 411.

[290] (1989) 61 D.L.R. (4th) 15. See too *Minera Aquiline Argentina SA v IMA Exploration Inc* (2007) 10 W.W.R. 648. Cf. *Australian Broadcasting Corporation v Lenah Game Meats Pty Ltd* (2001) 208 C.L.R. 199 at [311].

[291] *Attorney General v Guardian Newspapers (No.2)* [1990] 1 A.C. 109 at 288.

[292] [1997] R.P.C. 289 at 404.

[293] [1997] R.P.C. 289 at 416.

[294] [2000] 2 B.C.L.C. 461.

of confidence also involves a breach of fiduciary duty, any trust arising may more easily be seen as responding to the breach of fiduciary duty.

### C. Justifying the Trust

Given the paucity of English authority supporting the imposition of a constructive trust in response to a breach of confidence, the question here is whether the recognition of such a trust *would* be justified. In a breach of confidence case which does not also feature a breach of fiduciary duty, the claimant would face some significant obstacles in seeking to establish a constructive trust.[295] First, it would be necessary to show that a remedy responding to the defendant's gain is required, as several recent cases have indicated that claimants do not have a right in every case simply to elect to receive an account of profits rather than a compensatory award.[296] Sales J said that the central question is whether "the claimant's interest in performance of the obligation in question . . . makes it just and equitable that the defendant should retain no benefit from his breach of that obligation."[297] It certainly seems that a remedy related to the gain of the defendant will not be awarded if the breach of confidence was not deliberate.[298] **15–188**

Secondly, even once that hurdle is cleared, the further question arises whether the defendant should have only a personal duty to account for the profits, or whether she should also hold those profits on trust, an additional response to her wrongdoing that requires additional justification. **15–189**

Thirdly, the reference by Laddie J in *Ocular Sciences* to the "imposition" of a constructive trust as part of the court's "equitable armoury" may suggest that a remedial constructive trust was contemplated; as noted above,[299] such trusts are not generally recognised in English law. **15–190**

## 8. Unlawful Killing

### A. The Nature of the Trust

There is a clear public policy in preventing one who has unlawfully killed another from enjoying the benefit of property that they would otherwise have gained as a result of that death: this has been recognised in legislation as the "forfeiture rule".[300] This rule applies, for example, where a murderer stands to gain under the will of her victim, or, where the victim left no will, under the usual intestacy rules. It also applies where one joint tenant kills another, and so would otherwise benefit from the operation of the doctrine of survivorship. **15–191**

There are different ways of giving effect to the rule. The most direct is simply to find that the property has not in fact passed as it would have done had the death been lawful.[301] In such a case, no constructive trust is required. Another means, where property has already been acquired by the killer, is to impose a constructive trust of the property for the benefit of others, who are entitled following **15–192**

---

295 For further discussion see, e.g. M. Conaglen, "Thinking about Proprietary Remedies for Breach of Confidence" [2008] I.P.Q. 82; N. Witzleb, "Justifying Gain-Based Remedies for Invasions of Privacy" (2009) 29 O.J.L.S. 325.

296 See the cases cited at n.289.

297 *Vercoe v Rutland Fund Management Ltd* [2010] EWHC 424 at [339]. See [340]–[345] for discussion of the principles to be considered in determining if an account of profits is available.

298 See, e.g. *Seager v Copydex (No.1)* [1967] 1 W.L.R. 923 at 932 per Lord Denning MR; *Vercoe v Rutland Fund Management Ltd* [2010] EWHC 424 at [336].

299 See para.15–008.

300 Forfeiture Act 1982, s.1. See too Law Commission, *The Forfeiture Rule and the Law of Succession* (2005) Law Com. No.295, Cm.6625.

301 *Re Crippen* [1911] P. 108. See too *Re Sigsworth* [1935] Ch. 89.

the forfeiture of the killer's interest.[302] Where the killer would otherwise have acquired rights under a will or an intestacy, those entitled should be identified by asking what would have happened to the victim's property if the killer had died immediately before the victim.[303] Such a trust is clearly imposed by law, as it does not arise in response to any party choosing to set up a trust.

## *B. The Scope of the Trust*

**15–193** Murder[304] and manslaughter[305] including manslaughter by reason of diminished responsibility[306] invoke the forfeiture rule, as does incitement to murder,[307] but it does not apply to a killer who is found not guilty by reason of insanity.[308] The Forfeiture Act 1982 now enables the court to modify the effect of the forfeiture rule where the killer has not been convicted of murder, and the justice of the case requires it, if the killer brings proceedings within three months of conviction.[309]

**15–194** Where property is held by two joint tenants, and one murders the other, it has been held that survivorship still operates to mean that the murderer is solely entitled at law, but that a constructive trust arises, under which a half share of the beneficial interest is held by the next of kin of the victim.[310] A different approach, reaching a very similar result, would be to apply the forfeiture rule to mean that that the killer and the next of kin each holds a half share of the property as tenants in common.[311] On one variant of the constructive trust approach, where property is held by three or more joint tenants, the policy of preventing the gain of the killer may be achieved by effecting a partial severance, so that the killer has a proportionate share as tenant in common with the remaining joint tenant(s), who hold the remaining share as joint tenants, with the doctrine of survivorship applying as between them to mean that nothing passes to the estate of the victim.[312] Where a remainderman murders the life tenant, it has been argued that the victim should be deemed to live her actuarial life-span (except for a death-bed mercy killing), so that for the period of this notional life-span the victim's interest should be held on constructive trust for her estate; thereafter, devolution should occur normally.[313]

## *C. Justifying the Trust*

**15–195** There is little controversy as to the underlying policy behind the forfeiture rule and so, where a constructive trust is required to give effect to it, such a trust can be justified simply by pointing to the that policy. It might be observed that there are of course other means of confiscating property from

---

302 *Schobelt v Barber* (1966) 60 D.L.R. (2nd) 519; *Re Pechar* [1969] N.Z.L.R. 574; *Rasmanis v Jurewitsch* [1970] N.S.W.L.R. 650; *Beresford v Royal Insurance Co Ltd* [1938] A.C. 586 at 600. See further G. Jones, "Stripping a Criminal of the Profits of Crime" (2000) 1 Theoretical Inquiries in Law 59.

303 This is the position as from 1 February 2012 and is applied by Estates of Deceased Persons (Forfeiture Rule and Law of Succession) Act 2011. It means, for example, that if a daughter unlawfully kills her parents, who have left no will, her share under the intestacy rules should pass to the daughter's children, the deceased's grandchildren. The result in *Re Jones (Deceased)* [1998] 1 F.L.R. 246 would therefore be different if the same facts arose today.

304 See, e.g. *Beresford v Royal Insurance Co Ltd* [1938] A.C. 586 at 600.

305 *Davitt v Titcumb* [1990] Ch. 110.

306 *Re Giles* [1972] Ch. 544.

307 *Evans v Evans* [1989] 1 F.L.R. 351.

308 *Re Giles* [1972] Ch. 544; *Re Pitts* [1931] 1 Ch. 546; *Re Plaister* (1934) S.R. (N.S.W.) 547; *Permanent Trustee Co v Gillett* (2004) 6 I.T.E.L.R. 1063 at [36]ff.

309 See, e.g. *Re K* [1985] Ch. 85; *Dunbar v Plant* [1998] Ch. 412; *Dalton v Latham* [2003] W.T.L.R. 687.

310 *Schobelt v Barber* (1966) 60 D.L.R. (2nd) 519; *Re Pechar* [1969] N.Z.L.R. 574.

311 See, e.g. *Re K* [1985] Ch. 85 at 99.

312 *Rasmanis v Jurewitsch* [1970] N.S.W.L.R. 650.

313 T. Youdan "Acquisition of Property by Killing" (1973) 89 L.Q.R. 235 at 250–251.

criminals, and so, if the aim of the rule is simply to prevent the unlawful killer making a gain, it could be achieved by those means. The constructive trust, however, also ensures that the benefit of the property in question goes not to the State, but rather to an appropriate party, and so can also preserve the policy behind the underlying rules as to the destination of property on the death of the victim.

## 9. The Protection of Pre-existing Property Rights

### *A. The Nature of the Trusts*

In this section, we will examine four different types of constructive trust which have, at the least, a common effect: each can operate to provide some protection to a pre-existing property right of the claimant. By treating them together, we do not mean to assume that they are identical; rather, we simply wish to note that some common issues arise when considering them. **15–196**

One such issue is whether the trusts are best seen as constructive trusts or as resulting trusts. The first type of trust can protect the claimant's pre-existing property right where the claimant, by mistake, transfers the property to the defendant. In *Chase Manhattan Bank v Israel-British Bank (London) Ltd*,[314] for example, as we saw in Chapter 14,[315] Goulding J held that money paid in the mistaken belief that it was owed by the payor to the recipient was held on trust for the payor by the recipient.[316] We also saw that in *Westdeutsche Landesbank Girozentrale v Islington LBC*[317] Lord Browne-Wilkinson held that Goulding J had erred in assuming that the trust was based on a retention of an equitable property right by the payor and so would arise, in any case where such a mistake was made, as soon as the payor received the money. His Lordship stated that although **15–197**

> the mere receipt of the moneys, in ignorance of the mistake, gives rise to no trust, the retention of the moneys after the recipient bank learned of the mistake may well have given rise to a constructive trust.[318]

As he also noted, such a constructive trust may also protect the claimant where the claimant's transfer of the property right is procured by the fraud of the defendant. He thought it "difficult to find clear authority for the proposition", but stated nevertheless that "when property is obtained by fraud equity imposes a constructive trust on the fraudulent recipient: the property is recoverable and traceable in equity."[319]

The second type of trust can protect the claimant's pre-existing property right where the property is stolen. The link between this type of trust and that arising in a case of a transfer procured by fraud is clear in Lord Browne-Wilkinson's analysis in *Westdeutsche*, where the effects of fraud and theft are equated, and it is stated that if stolen money is used to set up a bank account, the account will be **15–198**

---

314 [1981] Ch. 105.

315 See para.14–003.

316 *Chase Manhattan* remains good law in England, although its status has been diminished by Lord Browne-Wilkinson's gloss on the case in *Westdeutsche Landesbank Girozentrale v Islington LBC* [1996] A.C. 669, and by sceptical judicial reactions to this gloss in *Barclays Bank Plc v Box* [1998] Lloyd's Rep. Bank. 185 at 200–201; *Papamichael v National Westminster Bank Plc* [2003] 1 Lloyd's Rep. 341 at [232]–[242]; *Shalson v Russo* [2005] Ch. 281 at [108]–[127]; *Fitzalan-Howard v Hibbert* [2010] P.N.L.R. 11 at [49]; *Maqsood v Mahmood* [2012] EWCA Civ 251 at [35]–[38]; *Wuhan Guoyu Logistics Group Co Ltd v Emporiki Bank of Greece SA* [2014] 1 All E.R. (Comm.) 870 at [19].

317 [1996] A.C. 669.

318 ibid., at 715, referring to *Metall und Rohstoff AG v Donaldson Lufkin & Jenrette Inc* [1990] 1 Q.B. 391 at 473–474.

319 [1996] A.C. 669 at 716, referring to *Stocks v Wilson* [1913] 2 K.B. 235 at 244; *R. Leslie Ltd v Sheill* [1915] 3 K.B. 607; *Bankers Trust Co v Shapira* [1980] 1 W.L.R. 1274 at 1282; *McCormick v Grogan* (1869) L.R. 4 H.L. 82 at 97. Note that in *Shalson v Russo* [2005] Ch. 281 at [111], Rimer J doubted the strength of those authorities, as well as the proposition that property obtained by fraud is automatically held on trust for the person defrauded: see further para.14–011.

held by the thief on trust for the victim of the theft.[320] It is, however, sensible to distinguish cases of fraud from cases of theft: a transfer procured by fraud will, generally, suffice to transfer the claimant's property right to the defendant (although the claimant will have a right, recognised at common law as well as in equity, to rescind the transaction). In contrast, where the claimant's property is stolen, there is no transfer of that property right to the thief. At that point, then, there appears to be no need for the claimant to rely on a trust, as the claimant still has her initial property right.[321] It is only when the thief uses the property to acquire a new right (for example by paying stolen money into a bank account) that a trust may be necessary. This is because the new right will be held by the thief: a bank account, for example, is a contractual right against the bank, and the bank makes its contract with the thief as the account-holder. At that point, the claimant may then wish to show that the thief holds that new right on trust for the claimant.

**15-199** There is a question, in relation to each of these two types of trust, as to whether the trust is best seen as constructive or resulting. In *Westdeutsche*, Lord Browne-Wilkinson clearly said that each such trust is constructive, as it does not fall within either of the two traditional classes of resulting trust, and is inconsistent with their basis because "[a] resulting trust is not imposed by law against the intentions of the trustee (as is a constructive trust) but gives effect to his presumed intention."[322] Others have argued, however, that, the trust, like those two traditional classes of resulting trust, are based on the need to prevent an unjust enrichment of the defendant, and so should be seen as resulting trusts.[323]

**15-200** The question of terminology is not an important one. As far as the actual operation of the claimant's rights under the trust are concerned, it makes no difference whether the trust is labelled as constructive or resulting. The key point, on either view, is that the trusts is not an express one and so, for example, it falls outside the formality requirements imposed in cases where a party attempts to exercise a power to set up a trust.[324] The important question is rather as to the justification for the trusts: do they depend on the need to prevent unjust enrichment, or do they arise on some other basis? We will consider this question below.[325]

**15-201** The third and fourth types of trust are principally important in protecting the pre-existing equitable interest of a beneficiary of a trust. The third arises where either the trustee (T) or the third party (C) uses the initial trust assets, without authority from B or under the terms of the trust, to acquire new assets. As we saw in Chapter 12,[326] it is possible for B then to assert a proprietary claim, under a trust, in relation to those new assets. There is, again, a question as to the nature of such a trust.

**15-202** Indeed, where the initial trust is an express one, arguments can be made that the trust should be seen as express, constructive, or resulting. Certainly, the analysis of the House of Lords in *Foskett v McKeown*[327] may support an express trust view, as in that case B's right in relation to the new assets

---

320 [1996] A.C. 669 at 715–716. See too *Black & Black v S. Freedman & Co* (1910) 12 C.L.R. 105. Note too *Banque Belge pour l'Etranger v Hambrouck* [1921] 1 K.B. 321; *Agip (Africa) Ltd v Jackson* [1991] Ch. 547.

321 For a full consideration of this issue, see R. Chambers "Trust and Theft" in E. Bant and M. Harding (eds), *Exploring Private Law* (Cambridge University Press, 2010). Chambers points out that it is conceptually possible for a trust to arise where the thief takes possession of a physical thing, as the thief thereby acquires a relative common law title (see, e.g. *Costello v Chief Constable of Derbyshire* [2001] 1 W.L.R. 1437) which could, in theory, be held on trust for the claimant; in practice, however, there is no need for such a trust to arise to protect the claimant, who retains her initial property right.

322 [1996] A.C. 669 at 708.

323 See, e.g. R. Chambers, *Resulting Trusts* (Oxford University Press, 1997), pp.125–132 (dealing with cases of mistake and fraud) and pp.116–118 (dealing with cases of theft). In the case of fraud, Millett J in *El Ajou v Dollar Land Holdings* [1993] 3 All E.R. 717 at 734 used the terminology of resulting trusts.

324 See, e.g. Law of Property Act 1925 s.53(2), discussed set out at para.3–026.

325 See paras 15–206—15–212.

326 See paras 12–107ff.

327 [2001] 1 A.C. 102: see paras 12–108—12–116.

was said to be based on B's subsisting equitable interest in the initial assets. In Chapter 12, however, we noted that there are some important problems with such a view: an inherent feature of any property right, whether legal or equitable, is that it must relate to a specific asset, and so it is very difficult to say that, because B's initial right is an equitable interest in the initial trust assets it *must* turn into a new equitable interest in the new assets. Again, the resulting trust analysis of the third type of trust depends on the view that it arises in response to the need to prevent the unjust enrichment of T or C, at B's expense.[328]

The fourth type of trust arises where the beneficiary (B) is able to assert a proprietary claim against a third party (C) who acquired the trust property as a result of an unauthorised disposition made by the trustee (T) and cannot rely on the bona fide purchaser defence, or any other defence, against B. We examined such claims in Chapter 12.[329] We noted there that, in *Independent Trustee Services Ltd v GP Noble Trustees Ltd*, Lloyd LJ described that proprietary claim of B as based on a trust and explained that[330]: **15–203**

> Since the trust arises from the asset having been extracted, in breach of trust, from a fund held on express trusts, it seems correct to characterise the trust as a constructive trust, rather than a resulting trust.

It is important to note that, on Lloyd LJ's analysis, if C receives the trust property as a gift from T, and without any knowledge of the trust, this constructive trust exists even before C has acquired such knowledge. On that view, which differs from that of Lord Browne-Wilkinson in *Westdeutsche*,[331] a trust can be said to exist even before C owes any duty to B not to use the trust property for C's own benefit. The difference between the views of Lloyd LJ and Lord Browne-Wilkinson is not large, however, as even on the latter's view, B has, in the period before C acquires knowledge of the initial trust, at least a *power* to impose a trust on C by informing C of the initial trust.[332]

## *B. The Scope of the Trusts*

Constructive trusts have been recognised not only where property has been transferred by mistake, or in cases of fraud or theft, but also where the transfer was procured by the undue influence of the recipient,[333] and where the transferor's ability to make decisions has otherwise been comprised by his relationship with the recipient.[334] Such "vitiation of intention" cases have even extended to cases where property has been transferred under a contract on the basis that the payor will receive counter-performance, and such counter-performance is not received; but, it was crucial in those cases that the recipient knew, when it received the payment, that there was no prospect of its providing the contractual counter-performance.[335] **15–204**

---

328 See, e.g. R. Chambers, "Tracing and Unjust Enrichment" in J. W. Neyers et al. (eds), *Understanding Unjust Enrichment* (Hart Publishing, 2004); Birks, "Property and Unjust Enrichment: Categorical Truths" [1997] N.Z.L.R. 623, 661; A. Burrows, *The Law of Restitution*, 2nd edn (Oxford University Press, 2002), pp.64–66 and 208–209.
329 See paras 12–057ff.
330 [2013] Ch. 91 at [80].
331 As acknowledged by Lloyd LJ in the *Independent Trustee Services* case: [2013] Ch. 91 at [80].
332 paras 14–012—14–013.
333 *Janz v McIntosh* (1999) 182 Sask. R. 197.
334 *Louth v Diprose* (1992) 175 C.L.R. 621; *McCulloch v Fern* [2001] NSWSC 406; *Smith v Smith* [2004] N.S.W.S.C. 663. On the Australian law governing unconscionable transactions and the law of unjust enrichment, see M. Bryan "Unjust Enrichment and Unconscionability in Australia: A False Dichotomy?" in Neyers et al., (eds), *Understanding Unjust Enrichment* (2004).
335 *Neste Oy v Lloyd's Bank Plc* [1983] 2 Lloyds Rep. 658; *Re Farepak Food and Gifts Ltd* [2007] 2 B.C.L.C. 1; subsequent proceedings [2010] 1 B.C.L.C. 444.

15-205 It should be noted, however, that not all cases of vitiated intent give rise to an immediate trust. As we have noted elsewhere,[336] in a case where the transferor's intention to make a contract is vitiated as a result of an innocent misrepresentation made by the recipient under that contract, the transferor instead acquires an equitable power to rescind the transaction. Whilst the exercise of that power may give rise to a trust, the transferor before then has only a "mere equity". Similarly, where the transferor's unilateral mistake suffices to allow a gift to be set aside, the transferor is seen as having an equitable power to rescind the gift.

## C. *Justifying the Trusts*

15-206 A number of possible explanations have been suggested as to the basis on which each of the four types of trust considered here arises. The final type of trust is intimately connected with the ability of a beneficiary's right under a trust to bind a third party, and thus with the proprietary status of such a right. Questions as to the justification of such a trust therefore depend on what underlying view one takes of the very nature of a beneficiary's rights under a trust. We will consider the debate as to that question in Chapter 17.

### i. Unjust Enrichment?

15-207 We have seen that, on one view, the first three of the trusts considered in this section responds to the need to prevent the defendant's being unjustly enriched at the claimant's expense. This claim has been made as part of a broader argument about the role of unjust enrichment in the recognition of equitable property rights, and has been accompanied by the view that the trusts in question are best seen as resulting trusts.[337] Nonetheless, even if the trusts are regarded as constructive in nature, it may still be possible to regard them as responses to unjust enrichment. Indeed, even if, as held in *Westdeutsche*, the two classic cases of "presumed" and "automatic" resulting trust depend on the positive intention of the transferor, rather than on unjust enrichment, this does not necessarily mean that unjust enrichment has no role to play in understanding trusts imposed by law.[338]

15-208 As we saw in Chapter 14,[339] there are some general difficulties with the unjust enrichment analysis, both as a matter of authority and of principle. The essential difficulty is in establishing when an unjust enrichment should give rise to a trust, rather than to a personal claim. In *Westdeutsche*, for example, the payor's intention to make the transfer was vitiated by the mistaken belief that there was a valid contract between the parties, and so it seems clear that the recipient was unjustly enriched at the expense of the payor, yet no trust arose. Lord Browne-Wilkinson insisted instead that a trust could arise if the recipient's conscience is affected by knowledge of the circumstances making his or her enrichment unjust, at a time when he or she still holds the property received from the claimant, or its traceable proceeds. Unjust enrichment is also present in cases where a contract is voidable as a result of an innocent misrepresentation, or where a gift can be rescinded for unilateral mistake, but in each of those cases, a trust can only arise if the claimant elects to set aside the transaction.[340] In *Shalson v*

---

[336] See paras 14-012, 14-101, and 18-244–18-252.

[337] See, e.g. Chambers, *Resulting Trusts* (1997), Ch.5. For the view that a trust responding to unjust enrichment is necessarily resulting, see the suggestion of Millett J in *El Ajou v Dollar Land Holdings Plc* [1993] 3 All E.R. 717 at 734. Note too *Evans v European Bank Ltd* (2004) 7 I.T.E.L.R. 19 at [112], per Spigelman CJ; Millett, "Tracing the Proceeds of Fraud" (1991) 107 L.Q.R. 71, 81.

[338] See paras 15-119—15-200.

[339] See paras 14-095—14-101 and 14-168—14-170.

[340] Prior to such rescission, the claimant has a "mere equity": see further paras 14-012 and 14-101.

*Russo*,[341] for example, Rimer J doubted that property received under a fraudulently induced contract is immediately held on trust by the recipient, even before any rescission of the contract.

It may nonetheless be possible to defend the unjust enrichment analysis of these trusts, and much of the current law, if one adopts Lord Browne-Wilkinson's requirement that no trust can arise unless and until the defendant is aware of the facts alleged to affect her conscience.[342] On this view, the presence or absence of this knowledge of the defendant determines if unjust enrichment gives rise to a trust or merely a personal claim. So, where the claimed subject matter of the trust is held by a thief or fraudster herself, a constructive trust arises, as the defendant was necessarily aware of the facts alleged to affect her conscience: the claimant's prior entitlement and the fact that the defendant's acquisition of the property occurred without the authority of the claimant. If, in contrast, the claim is based on the unilateral mistake of the claimant, or a non-fraudulent misrepresentation by the recipient, then a trust can arise only if the defendant later acquires knowledge of the mistake, or of the falsity of the representation, and still holds the property or its traceable proceeds at that point. **15–209**

Where the transfer occurs under a fraudulently induced contract, two analyses are possible.[343] On one view, there is no immediate trust,[344] as, unless and until the contract is rescinded, it provides a legal basis for the recipient's holding of the property and so means that the recipient is not unjustly enriched. On another view, there is an immediate trust, but the transferor will lose her interest under that trust if she affirms the contract, otherwise loses the right to rescind it. It is certainly worth noting that the right held by the transferor in such a case, even prior to rescission, behaves like a beneficial interest in as much as it is capable of binding third parties, and, unlike a "mere equity", can bind a bona fide purchaser for value of a subsequent equitable interest.[345] **15–210**

### ii. Wrongs?

Another possible explanation for at least some of the four types of trust considered in this section looks to the wrongful conduct of the defendant. Certainly, in a case of fraud or theft, it can be said that the defendant acquired particular property by breaching a duty owed to the claimant. A wrongs-based analysis, however, is of no assistance in a case, such as *Chase Manhattan Bank v Israel-British Bank (London) Ltd*,[346] in which the claimant simply makes a unilateral mistake when transferring property to the defendant. It should also be noted that there is clearly no general principle that a constructive trust arises in the claimant's favour whenever a defendant acquires property by committing a wrong against the claimant. For example, damages based on the defendant's gain rather than the claimant's loss are only very rarely awarded in response to a tort or a breach of contract,[347] and it would be a step still further to say that the defendant should also hold any profits gained through a wrong on trust for the claimant. Moreover, Lord Browne-Wilkinson's requirement that the defendant should be aware of the facts alleged to affect her conscience does not mean that the defendant can always be regarded as a wrongdoer: the defendant commits no wrong by having innocently received **15–211**

---

341 [2005] Ch. 281 at [111].

342 *Westdeutsche Landesbank Girozentrale v Islington LBC* [1996] A.C. 669 at 705.

343 For extended discussion, see B. Häcker, *Consequences of Impaired Consent Transfers*, (Hart Publishing, 2009), pp.125–159; E. Bant, "Reconsidering the Role of Election in Rescission" (2012) 32 O.J.L.S. 467. Note too the discussion at paras 14–008–14–013.

344 See *Shalson v Russo* [2005] Ch. 281 at [111]. See too B. Häcker, "Proprietary Restitution After Impaired Consent Transfers: A Generalised Power Model" [2009] C.L.J. 324.

345 See, e.g. *Car & Universal Finance v Caldwell* [1965] 1 Q.B. 525.

346 [1981] Ch. 105.

347 In *Attorney General v Blake* [2001] 1 A.C. 268, for example, the House of Lords, in awarding such damages, was at pains to emphasise the exceptional nature of the award: see, e.g. per Lord Nicholls at 284–285.

property mistakenly transferred by the claimant; the point is rather that it may be unconscionable for the defendant to retain the benefit of that property if she still holds the property or its traceable proceeds when she acquires knowledge of the claimant's mistake.

### iii. Enforcing a Subsisting Property Right?

**15–212** We have noted above[348] that, when considering the third type of the four trusts considered here, the House of Lords in *Foskett v McKeown*[349] regarded it as giving effect to a beneficiary's subsisting equitable property right. We also noted that there some important problems with such a view. Similarly, we have also seen that,[350] in *Westdeutsche Landesbank Girozentrale v Islington LBC*[351] Lord Browne-Wilkinson held that Goulding J had erred in assuming that the trust arising in the case of a mistaken payment was based on a retention of an equitable property right by the payor. The point is that, whilst each of the four types of trust considered in this section has the *effect* of giving some protection to an initial property right of the claimant, that does not mean that each can be justified purely by referring to the existence of such a right: some other event may have to occur before the trust arises. The fourth type of constructive trust considered here, arising where C receives trust property through an unauthorised disposition by T, might seem to be a straightforward case of the assertion of a pre-existing equitable interest. Even in that case, however, we have noted[352] a disagreement between Lloyd LJ[353] and Lord Browne-Wilkinson[354] as to whether a further fact (C's knowledge of the initial trust) is required before a trust can arise.

## 10. Explaining Constructive Trusts: General Themes?

### A. The Diversity of Constructive Trusts

**15–213** This chapter has demonstrated the truth of the point made at its start: constructive trusts arise in a very diverse set of circumstances. This means that, in seeking to explain or justify why such trusts arise, it is best to break down the inquiry by looking at specific types of constructive trust.

**15–214** It is certainly hard to formulate a workable *positive* thesis as to why all constructive trusts arise. For example, it has often been said that unconscionability is at the heart of the constructive trust[355] or, similarly, that such trusts arises where "the defendant has acquired property in circumstances where it would be inequitable to allow him to treat it as his own."[356] The difficulty here is that broad concepts such as unconscionability or inequity, by themselves, can only state a conclusion: they cannot provide reasons for which that conclusion was reached.[357] They may also confuse the question of why the defendant is under a duty to the claimant with the crucial question of why that duty gives rise to a trust, rather than to a merely personal claim. More specifically, it has been suggested, principally in

---

348 See paras 12–107ff.
349 [2001] 1 A.C. 102.
350 See para.15–197.
351 [1996] A.C. 669.
352 See para.15–203.
353 In *Independent Trustee Services Ltd v GP Noble Trustees Ltd* [2013] Ch. 9 at [80].
354 In *Westdeutsche Landesbank Girozentrale v Islington LBC* [1996] A.C. 669 at 705.
355 See, e.g. the famous statement of Judge Cardozo in *Beatty v Guggenheim Exploration Co* (1919) 225 N.Y. 380 at 386: "a constructive trust is the formula through which the conscience of equity finds expression."
356 *Banner Homes Group plc v Luff Developments Ltd* [2000] Ch. 372 at 400 per Chadwick LJ; also *Gissing v Gissing* [1971] A.C. 886 at 905 per Lord Diplock; *Paragon Finance Plc v DB Thakerar & Co* [1999] 1 All E.R. 400 at 408–409 per Millett LJ.
357 See, e.g. Smith, "Fusion and Tradition" in Degeling and Edelman (eds), *Equity in Commercial Law* (2005).

jurisdictions other than England, that constructive trusts are based on unjust enrichment. As noted in this Chapter,[358] that concept may have a role to play in relation to some constructive trusts, but it clearly cannot explain those trusts where the content of the claimant's rights depends not on the extent of the benefit acquired by the defendant, but on the content of the promise made by the defendant, or on the extent of any detrimental reliance by the claimant or another party.

It is similarly difficult to support a *negative* thesis as to the basis of all constructive trusts. For example, it has sometimes been said that constructive trusts, in contrast to express or resulting trusts, are *not* concerned with the intention of the parties, but are instead imposed "against the intentions of the trustee".[359] Nevertheless it can be argued that in all of the cases discussed in sections 2–6, above, as well as the cases on *Re Rose*, mutual wills, and secret trusts, discussed elsewhere in the book, constructive trusts were imposed in order to give effect to an intention that the claimant should acquire an interest in property, whether outright or under a trust.[360] **15–215**

Of course, if a party has successfully exercised her power to set up a trust, and there are no formality requirements preventing proof of that trust, there is no need for a constructive trust. We have seen cases, however, in which an intention to create a trust was present, but it was not possible for the claimant to prove that an express trust was created.[361] In such cases, it seems, a constructive trust may still arise; but not *simply* as a result of the initial intention to create a trust. There must be some other factor which justifies the imposition of a constructive trust: as we have seen, it has been variously suggested that such a factor may be constituted by fraud,[362] detrimental reliance,[363] or the acquisition of an advantage by the defendant in relation to the receipt of property.[364] **15–216**

## *B. A Common Thread?*

It seems that asking why constructive trusts arise is rather like asking why a court awards damages. A damages award can be made on many different grounds: as a result of a contract; a non-contractual promise which is nonetheless binding; a proprietary estoppel; a wrong, such as a tort or a breach of contract; unjust enrichment; public policy, etc. The same is true of a constructive trust. The common thread in such trusts is to do with the *content* of the claimant's right, not the basis on which it was acquired. If a constructive trust arises, the claimant has a beneficial interest in property, with all the advantages flowing from that.[365] So a general theme, relevant to all constructive trusts, is to ask why the claimant acquires such an interest, rather than a mere personal claim against the defendant. **15–217**

One way of approaching this question is to look at the precise content of the defendant's duty, and to distinguish between cases where that duty does, or does not, relate to specific property held by the **15–218**

---

358 See paras 15-207—15-210.

359 *Westdeutsche Landesbank Girozentrale v Islington LBC* [1996] A.C. 669 at 708 per Lord Browne-Wilkinson. See too *Rathwell v Rathwell* [1978] 2 S.C.R. 436 at 454 per Dickson J; *Air Jamaica Ltd v Charlton* [1999] 1 W.L.R. 1399 at 1512 per Lord Millett.

360 In the terminology of G. Elias, *Explaining Constructive Trusts* (Clarendon Press, 1990), such constructive trusts are "perfectionary" as they give effect to a party's intention. See too R. Chambers, "Constructive Trusts in Canada" (1999) 37 Alberta L.R. 173, reprinted in (2001) 15 Tru L.I. 215 and (2002) 16 Tru. L.I. 2; *Bathurst CC v PWC Properties Pty Ltd* (1998) 195 C.L.R. 566 at [39]; *Paragon Finance plc v DB Thakerar & Co* [1999] 1 All E.R. 400 at 408–409.

361 See paras 15–030—15–045.

362 See, e.g. N. Hopkins, "Conscience, Discretion and the Creation of Property Rights" (2006) 26 L.S. 475; Swadling, "The Nature of the Trust in *Rochefoucauld v Boustead*" in Mitchell (ed.), *Constructive and Resulting Trusts* (2010) (although of course on Swadling's view the trust is an express one, with fraud operating so as to prevent the defendant relying on s.53(1)(b) of the Law of Property Act 1925 to object to the oral proof of the express trust).

363 See, e.g. S. Gardner, "Reliance-Based Constructive Trusts" in Mitchell (ed.), *Constructive and Resulting Trusts* (2010).

364 See, e.g. B. McFarlane, "Constructive Trusts Arising on Receipt of Property *Sub Conditione*" (2004) 120 L.Q.R. 667

365 For which see para.15–003.

defendant. For example, it is clear that, if the duty does not relate to specific property, no constructive trust can arise. In *Re Goldcorp's Exchange Ltd*,[366] for example, the defendant had made a contractual promise to transfer ownership of gold bullion to the claimant. No legal title to property passed under the contract, however, because the promise did not relate to any specific or ascertained gold. For the same reason, no constructive trust of any bullion arose, even though the defendant had behaved badly in leading the claimant to believe that it would hold specific gold at the claimant's instructions. The problem for the claimant was that the defendant's contractual duty was simply to provide that quantity of gold, and so the duty did not relate to any specific property held by the defendant. In contrast, in the type of constructive trust arising in a specifically enforceable contract to transfer property,[367] the defendant's duty clearly does relate to specific property.

**15–219** Indeed, in the cases reviewed in this chapter where a constructive trust does arise, it is generally clear that the defendant's duty does relate to specific property held by the defendant. In many cases, this is because the defendant's duty is based on a promise, and that promise related to specific property that the defendant held at the time, or now holds. The more difficult cases, then, are where no such promise has been made. This is why cases involving unjust enrichment, or wrongful conduct (such as the receipt of a bribe) are more controversial. In those cases, however, it may be that Lord Browne-Wilkinson's analysis in *Westdeutsche*,[368] albeit criticised in some quarters,[369] provides some assistance. The idea is that a trust involves the trustee's being under a duty not to use property for her own benefit (unless and to the extent permitted by the terms of the trust). For such a duty to arise, the defendant must be aware of the facts giving rise to the duty; if not, it would be unfair to say that the defendant somehow behaves wrongfully by using that property as her own. On that view, for example, the trust in the *Chase Manhattan* case was justified only from the point where the recipient bank discovered the mistake of the claimant,[370] but it is clear that a fiduciary who knowingly accepts a bribe holds it on trust from the moment when it is received.[371] The most difficult question,[372] which may be crucial for the future development of constructive trusts, is whether Lord Browne-Wilkinson's analysis is purely negative, so that no constructive trust can arise in the absence of such knowledge, or whether it can be used to support a positive formula, under which such a trust arises if: (i) the grounds on which the defendant's duty arises demand that the duty is one not to use specific property held by the defendant for the defendant's own benefit[373]; *and* (ii) the defendant is aware of the facts constituting the grounds on which that duty arises.

---

366 [1995] 1 A.C. 74. See para.14–070.

367 See paras 15–011ff.

368 [1996] A.C. 669 at [705].

369 See, e.g. W. Swadling, "Property and Conscience" (1998) 12 Tru. L.I. 228; *Meagher, Gummow & Lehane's Equity: Doctrines and Remedies*, 5th edn (LexisNexis, 2015), paras 14–010.

370 See the analysis of Lord Browne-Wilkinson in *Westdeutsche Landesbank Girozentrale v Islington LBC* [1996] A.C. 669 at 714–715.

371 As was held by the Supreme Court in *FHR European Ventures LLP v Cedar Capital Partners LLC* [2015] A.C. 250.

372 For consideration of this question, see, e.g. B. McFarlane, "Trusts and Knowledge: Lessons from Australia" in Glister and Ridge (eds), *Fault Lines in Equity* (2012).

373 There may of course be cases in which the grounds on which the duty arises are not inconsistent with the defendant using the property to her own benefit, to some extent: so the *Pallant v Morgan* equity can arise where the defendant's promise was that the parties would divide up the benefit of particular property (as in the case itself: [1953] Ch. 43), and a common intention constructive trust can arise where the common intention was that each party should have a share of the beneficial interest. A trust may still arise in such cases as the promise or common intention controls the extent to which the defendant can use the property for her own benefit.

**Questions**

1. "A specifically enforceable contract for the sale of land certainly gives the purchaser some equitable property rights, but it would be a mistake to say that those rights amount to a beneficial interest under a trust." **Do you agree?**
2. "The decisions in *Stack v Dowden* and *Jones v Kernott* have made the law less clear, without making it significantly more fair." **Do you agree?**
3. "[The circumstances] which give rise to a common intention constructive trust and the circumstances where a proprietary estoppel arises [are similar, but] the remedies available to the court may differ between the two kinds of case. If the court finds that . . . a proprietary estoppel arises, the court has a [wide] power to craft and impose whatever remedy it considers to be equitable in the circumstances. That remedy may take the form of declaring that the claimant shall become the beneficial owner of the property or of a share in it (thus having the same effect as a finding that there is a constructive trust), but it may take other forms." (Park J in *Lalani v Crump Holdings Ltd* (2007).) **Discuss.**
4. To what extent, if at all, do the trusts recognised in *Rochefoucauld v Boustead* and *Pallant v Morgan* have a common basis?

# PART VII

# TRUSTS AND THE CONFLICT OF LAWS

# 16

# TRUSTS AND THE CONFLICT OF LAWS

## 1. Introduction

### A. Background

The conflict of laws is that part of English private law which deals with issues concerning elements connected with other legal systems.[1] In particular, conflict of laws rules provide answers to two key questions about any given dispute. First, can the substantive dispute be heard in an English court? This is the question of *jurisdiction*. Secondly, if so, what system of law should apply to each point in issue? This is the question of *choice of law*. The presence of the second question allows for the important possibility that, even if the substantive dispute is to be heard in England, the issues arising may be determined entirely by the law of other legal systems. If, for example, the English court has to determine the law of Scotland or of New York, it will approach this as a determination of a question of fact, and, if each side takes opposing views of the content of the foreign law, each side will provide experts to testify on that content, and the English court will then decide on the correctness of the parties' submissions as to the content of the relevant foreign law. **16–001**

Those two key questions, of course, may be of relevance to the law of trusts. The facts of *Webb v Webb* provide a simple example.[2] A father provided the purchase money for a flat in Antibes in France and his son was registered as the owner. The father later claimed that the son held the property on resulting trust for the father. The son's initial objection was that the English courts did not have jurisdiction to hear the dispute: he argued that, as it pertained to land in France, the dispute had to be heard in the French courts. It was held, both by the English court and by the European Court of Justice, that the English court did in fact have jurisdiction to determine the dispute. **16–002**

The rules governing the conflict of laws extend beyond the questions of jurisdiction and of choice of law. For example, even if an English court can hear a case, and so technically has jurisdiction, there is also the question of whether it *should* hear the case. There are exceptional circumstances in which an English court will stay or strike out the proceedings on the ground of forum non conveniens, because the defendant shows that there is another forum to whose jurisdiction she is amenable, in which justice can be done at substantially less inconvenience and expense, and where the claimant will not be deprived of a legitimate personal or juridical advantage which would be available to her under the English jurisdiction.[3] Further, the question sometimes arises whether the English court will recognise **16–003**

1 Note of course that Scotland and Northern Ireland are examples of such other systems.
2 [1994] Q.B. 696: see paras 16–017–16–028.
3 See, e.g. *Spiliada Maritime Corp v Cansulex Ltd* [1987] A.C. 460 and *Chellaram v Chellaram (No.2)* [2002] 3 All E.R. 17 and

or enforce a foreign judgment purporting to determine an issue that relates to the action before the court. In the absence of special legislation for the reciprocal recognition and enforcement of foreign judgments, the successful claimant in foreign proceedings will need to bring English proceedings for summary judgment based on the res judicata established between the parties by the foreign court, assuming it had jurisdiction according to English law and there was no fraud or absence of natural or substantial justice.[4]

## B. Significance

**16-004** Detailed matters relating to the conflict of laws are best left to major works on the subject.[5] We will consider here, in outline, the basic rules on jurisdiction developed by the English common law, as well as the rules now applying under the EU Regulation on Jurisdiction and the Recognition and Enforcement of Judgments in Civil and Commercial Matters,[6] referred to here as the Recast Brussels Regulation, which replaces the Brussels I Regulation[7] and applies to legal proceedings instituted on or after 10 January 2015. We will also consider, again in outline, the choice of law rules applied by the Recognition of Trusts Act 1987, which gives effect in English law to The Hague Convention on the Law Applicable to Trusts and on their Recognition.

**16-005** There are three main reasons for considering, in outline, the application of conflict of laws rules to trusts. First, in practice, trusts may well have strong international elements. For example, a settlor of British nationality domiciled[8] in California may create a trust of assets, half of which are in Bermuda and half in Ontario, and appoint four trustees, one habitually resident in Bermuda, one habitually resident in Ontario and two old friends habitually resident in England. One-third of the beneficiaries may be habitually resident in California, one-third in England, and one-third in Jersey. The trust instrument may specify Californian law as governing the validity of the trust, and Bermudian law as governing administration of trust assets there, and Ontario law as governing administration of the assets there. It may also confer express powers on the trustees to change the law governing the validity of the trust and to change the place of administration and the law governing administration. An alleged breach of trust may lead the beneficiaries to bring an action against the trustees before the Chancery Division of the English High Court.

**16-006** Secondly, the application of conflict of laws rules may raise important questions about the very nature and classification of trusts. As we will see, general equitable principles play a significant role, especially the maxim "equity acts in personam".[9] Other maxims that may be applicable are, for example, "equity will do nothing in vain" and "equity will not require persons to do acts illegal by the

---

compare the position under the Brussels I Regulation (Regulation (EC) 44/2001 of 22 December 2000 on jurisdiction and the recognition and enforcement of judgments in civil and commercial matters [2001] OJ L012) arts 23 and 27 and now under the Recast Brussels Regulation (Regulation (EC) 1215/2012 of the European Parliament and of the Council of 12 December 2012 on jurisdiction and the recognition and enforcement of judgments in civil and commercial matters [2015] OJ L351) arts 29, 31 and 33–34.

4 *Reid v Reid* [2000] C.C.J. 8; *Adams v Cape Industries Plc* [1990] Ch. 433.

5 The leading general work is *Dicey, Morris and Collins: The Conflict of Laws*, 15th edn (Sweet & Maxwell, 2013). There is also a very useful treatment by Jonathan Harris in *Underhill and Hayton: Law of Trusts and Trustees*, 18th edn (LexisNexis, 2010), Ch. 24. An excellent and more detailed discussion of many of the issues touched on in this chapter is provided by D. J. Hayton, "'Trusts' in Private International Law" (2014) 366 Recueil des Cours 17.

6 Regulation (EU) 1215/2012.

7 Regulation (EC) 44/2001.

8 Domicile is a technical concept: it does not mean habitual residence. No one can be without a domicile since it is this that connects her with some legal system for many conflict of laws purposes. See further Civil Jurisdiction and Judgments Act 1982 ss.41–46.

9 See, e.g. *Webb v Webb* [1994] Q.B. 696.

law of the place where the acts are to be performed", e.g. where foreign exchange laws or cultural heritage laws prevent trustees from getting money or archaeological artefacts out of the country for the beneficiaries.[10]

A third point, linked to this second point, is that the conflict of laws rules mean that an English court may have to apply foreign law as to trusts, or trust-like concepts. The Hague Trusts Convention contains rules as to when a particular arrangement should be recognised as a trust, and, as a result of the Recognition of Trusts Act 1987, those rules are now part of English law. As we have seen,[11] the Convention's definition of a trust is necessarily broader than that of English law—it includes, for example, private purpose trusts—and, as a result, an English court may have to recognise and apply an arrangement which would not count as a trust under English law but is valid under a foreign law chosen by the party setting up that arrangement. **16-007**

## 2. Jurisdiction

### A. At Common Law

The Recast Brussels Regulation is now of primary importance in questions of jurisdiction. It applies in civil and commercial matters, although some exceptions are made and it does not apply, for example, to "rights in property arising out of a matrimonial relationship or out of a relationship deemed by the law applicable to such relationship to have comparable effects to marriage", nor to "bankruptcy", nor to "wills and succession, including maintenance obligations arising by reason of death".[12] In some cases, then, the common law position remains relevant. **16-008**

The basic common law position[13] is that jurisdiction to hear a claim against a defendant could be founded on the service of proceedings on the defendant when present in England, even if the defendant was in the jurisdiction only temporarily.[14] However there were exceptions to this principle. For example, in disputes raising questions of title to foreign land, English courts refused to accept jurisdiction, on the basis that the jurisdiction in which the land was situated was the appropriate forum.[15] In *Penn v Lord Baltimore*,[16] that rule was held not to apply where the claim was that foreign land was held on trust for the claimant, and the English court was found to have jurisdiction to determine the claim, arising from a contract to settle a boundary dispute originally between the proprietor of the colony of Maryland (Lord Baltimore) and William Penn, the proprietor of the colony of Pennsylvania.[17] Jurisdiction was founded on the fact that the defendant was resident in England, and the rule as to disputes concerning title to foreign land did not apply as: "The conscience of the party was bound by this agreement; and being within the jurisdiction of this court, which acts in personam, the court may properly decree it as an agreement". **16-009**

The approach in *Penn v Lord Baltimore* was later explained as resting on the fact that, even if a decree of specific performance necessarily meant that a constructive trust of the foreign land arose, the court issuing such a decree **16-010**

10 *Re Lord Cable* [1976] 3 All E.R. 417. See too arts 15, 16 and 18 of the Hague Convention, extracted at paras 16–045—16–047.
11 See para.1–039.
12 Article 1 of the Recast Brussels Regulation, Regulation (EU) 1215/2012.
13 Subject now to limits introduced by international conventions and also by the Civil Jurisdiction and Judgments Act 1982.
14 See, e.g. *Maharanee of Baroda v Wildenstein* [1972] 2 Q.B. 283.
15 *British South Africa Co v Compania de Mocambique* [1893] A.C. 602. For discussion of current exceptions to the rule, including the important inroads made by s.30 of the Civil Jurisdiction and Judgments Act 1982, see *Dicey, Morris and Collins: The Conflict of Laws* (2013), Rule 131.
16 (1750) 1 Ves. Sen. 444.
17 For consideration of the historical background to the case, and of previous litigation between the parties, see P. Mitchell, "*Penn v Lord Baltimore* (1870)" in C. Mitchell and P. Mitchell (eds), *Landmark Cases in Equity* (Hart Publishing, 2012).

> did not affect or profess to affect by its decree the property itself; it acted only in personam and compelled the vendor to do whatever was necessary to be done, either in this country or abroad, to transfer the property to the purchaser.[18]

It is possible that the approach may lead to awkward practical questions if the courts of the foreign jurisdiction are unwilling to recognise the judgment of the English court[19]: given that the practical consequences of finding a trust may be similar to deciding a question of title to the foreign land, the approach has also been said to be "open to the strong objection that the court is doing indirectly what it dare not do directly."[20] As we will now see, however, a similar approach has been taken to the interpretation of the rule now set out in art.24(1) of the Recast Brussels Regulation. Further, as we will see below,[21] such an approach is also consistent with the view that a beneficial interest of a trust is conceptually different from a right to ownership of property as, on that view, the finding of a trust does not amount to a finding as to title to foreign land: the defendant's title to the land is not denied by the claimant, who rather claims that the title is held by the defendant on trust.

**16–011** In cases where the intended defendant is not in England, the court may give permission for service of proceedings outside the jurisdiction. There is a list of grounds on which such permission may be given,[22] although even in such cases permission will not be given unless England is the proper place to bring the claim.[23] Those grounds include, for example[24]: a claim where "the whole subject matter of the claim" relates to property located within in England[25]; a claim made in respect of a trust "which is created by operation of a statute, or by a written instrument, or created orally and evidenced in writing" and which is either governed by English law, or provides that jurisdiction in respect of such a claim shall be conferred on the English courts[26]; and a claim "made for a remedy against the defendant as constructive trustee where the defendant's alleged liability arises out of acts committed within the jurisdiction".[27]

### *B. The Recast Brussels Regulation*

**16–012** The *general* jurisdictional rule, set out in art.4 of the Recast Regulation, is that "persons domiciled in a Member State shall, whatever their nationality, be sued in the courts of that Member State." Such a person may however be sued in a different Member State if a *special* jurisdiction exists. One example, set out by art.7(6), is in the case of a "dispute brought against a settlor, trustee or beneficiary of a trust created by the operation of a statute, or by a written instrument, or created orally and evidenced in writing".[28] In such a case, the defendant may be sued in "the courts of the Member State in which the trust is domiciled".[29]

---

18 *IRC v G. Angus & Co* (1889) 23 Q.B.D. 579 at [596] per Lindley LJ.

19 See *Dicey, Morris and Collins: The Conflict of Laws* (2013), para.23–051.

20 *British South Africa Co v Compania de Mocambique* [1892] 2 Q.B. 358 at 404–405.

21 See paras 17–056ff.

22 See PD 6B, supplementing Section IV of CPR Pa 6.

23 CPR r.6.37(3).

24 For other grounds potentially relevant in relation to trusts, see, PD 6B, 3.1, grounds (13), (14) and (16).

25 PD 6B, 3.1, ground (11).

26 PD 6B, 3.1, grounds (12) and (12A).

27 PD 6B, 3.1, ground (15).

28 It seems clear that the party must be sued *in her capacity as* settlor, trustee or beneficiary. Note that no reference is made to other parties (such as a protector, enforcer, or a party with a power to appoint or remove trustees) and in *Gomez v Gomez-Monche Vives* [2009] Ch. 245, the C.A. held that the predecessor of art.7(6) did not apply to a party, termed under the trust deed an "appointor", who had a fiduciary power to direct who should receive trust funds. A narrow reading was given of the provision as it departs from the general jurisdictional rule that the defendant should be sued in the place of her domicile. For criticism of this aspect of the decision, see D. Hayton, "Jurisdiction over Trust Disputes under Art 5(6) of Brussels I" (2008) 14 T. & T. 384.

29 For a very helpful discussion of the application of the Recast Brussels Regulation to matters concerning trusts, see D. Hayton, "'Trusts' in Private International Law" (2014) 366 Recueil des Cours 17, 40–57.

The purpose of this rule is to allow litigation to take place in a jurisdiction that recognises the trust concept, if a trust has been set up in that jurisdiction, even if the defendant is domiciled in a different Member State. The wording of the section ensures, however, that it does not apply to constructive trusts.[30] **16–013**

A trust, of course, is not a legal person, but is treated as domiciled in the UK or a part of it if the system of law with which the trust has its closest and most real connection is the law of a part of the UK.[31] In *Gomez v Gomez-Monche Vives*,[32] for example, it was claimed that the defendant had received more than she was entitled to under a trust, and the Court of Appeal recognised that as she was sued as a beneficiary of a trust, and, as English law had been chosen to govern the trust, the trust was domiciled in England, and so a special jurisdiction arose meaning that the defendant could be sued in England rather than in Spain. **16–014**

The Recast Brussels Regulation also allows for effect to be given to exclusive jurisdiction agreements. Article 25(3) states that: **16–015**

> The court or courts of a Member State on which a trust instrument has conferred jurisdiction shall have exclusive jurisdiction in any proceedings brought against a settlor, trustee, or beneficiary, if relations between those persons or their rights or obligations under the trust are involved.

Such clauses are subject to certain restrictions: in particular, they cannot exclude the jurisdiction of a court which is given *exclusive* jurisdiction by art.24.

Article 24(1) of the Recast Brussels Regulation, which is identical to art.16(1) of the Brussels I Regulation, states that **16–016**

> in proceedings which have as their object rights *in rem* in immovable property or tenancies of immovable property, the courts of the Member State in which the property is situated [will have exclusive jurisdiction].[33]

Such exclusive jurisdiction rules are relatively rare under the Regulation, as they depart from the default position under art.4 that:

> persons domiciled in a Member State shall, whatever their nationality, be sued in the courts of that Member State.

The basic effect of art.24(1), of course, is the same as that existing at common law: in disputes over title to foreign land, the jurisdiction in which the land is situated is the only the appropriate forum.

In *Webb v Webb*, the question arose as to whether the rule now encapsulated in art.24(1) applied to a claim that land in France was held on trust. Judge Paul Baker QC held that it did not. On appeal, the Court of Appeal referred the question of interpretation of the rule to the European Court of Justice, which is the court with power to give a definitive interpretation of the rule.[34] Extracts from each stage of the proceedings, including part of the advice given to the ECJ by the Advocate General, are set out **16–017**

---

30 See *Chellaram v Chellaram (No.2)* [2002] 3 All E.R. 17 at [138].

31 Civil Jurisdiction and Judgments Act 1982, s.45.

32 [2009] Ch. 245.

33 There is an exception for "tenancies of immovable property concluded for temporary private use for a maximum period of six consecutive months" as then the courts of the Member State in which the defendant is domiciled will also have jurisdiction, if the tenant is a natural person and domiciled in the same Member State as the landlord.

34 At the time, the rule was contained in a Convention (the Brussels Convention) rather than an EU Regulation, but under the Convention, the ECJ was given the power to interpret its terms.

below. The references in the case are to art.16(1) of the Brussels I Regulation, which is identical to art.24(1) of the Recast Brussels Regulation.

*Webb v Webb*

Chancery Division and European Court of Justice [1994] Q.B. 696

16–018 JUDGE PAUL BAKER Q.C.: The plaintiff in the present case does not rely upon any contract for sale. He relies on a fiduciary relationship between him and his son. The son, he says, is his trustee. That is one of the foundations of equitable jurisdiction, and here again the main method of enforcement is an order in personam against the defendant. He can be required to execute the trust by transfers or rendering accounts. The relief claimed does not include any form of vesting order, or an order directing the rectification of some register of title, or even a declaration that the plaintiff is the legal owner of the property. What he claims is a declaration that the defendant holds the property and its contents on an express or resulting trust for him and an order to execute such deeds and documents as shall be required to vest the legal ownership in the plaintiff.

16–019 The orders sought in this case do not seek to disturb the title of the defendant otherwise than by his own act. Accordingly, in my judgment the proceedings do not have as their object rights in rem. They have as their object the establishment of the defendant's accountability as a trustee for the plaintiff."

16–020 ADVOCATE GENERAL DAMON: [W]e have both the Commission and the defendant—the Commission expressly and the defendant more implicitly—laying stress on the *purpose* of the claim and submitting that the action is one in rem, with the father claiming to be the owner, which at the hearing led counsel for the defendant to sum up the plaintiff's claim, not without humour, in these words: "What is the plaintiff's claim? My Lords, the plaintiff's claim is to own the flat!"

16–021 The question is not an easy one and I have pondered on the correct approach to take, for the claim of ownership undeniably underlies the claim for the recognition of such a trust.

16–022 However, the approach which looks at the actual *aim* pursued by the plaintiff in the main proceedings is not supported by the relevant provision, by prevailing academic opinion or by the case law of the court. The jurisdiction *ratione materiae* of a court must necessarily be assessed in the light of the *subject matter* of the claim, as defined in the originating application, without looking at purpose. . ..

16–023 [I]n the case in point, can the action brought by the plaintiff in the main proceedings be regarded as an action laying claim to the immovable property situated in France on the basis of an equitable interest if the subject matter of the dispute relates to the possible existence of a trust between himself and his son, or, alternatively, to the question of the parties' intention when the property was purchased? Is this not rather a *preliminary question*, which, whilst indeed having decisive consequences as regards ownership, is intrinsically based at this stage on a purely personal relationship?

16–024 . . . The dividing line therefore appears to lie between actions whose principal subject matter is a dispute over ownership between persons who do not claim *inter se* any fiduciary relationship and actions concerning a breach of fiduciary duty which, if found to have been committed, will have effects in rem. In such a case, the personal nature of the relations is, in my view, the overriding factor.

16–025 JUDGMENT OF THE EUROPEAN COURT OF JUSTICE: . . . The son and the Commission, who consider that the test for applying article 16(1) is the plaintiff's ultimate purpose and that by his action the father is ultimately seeking to secure ownership of the flat, contend that the main proceedings are covered by article 16(1). That argument cannot be accepted. . ..

16–026 The aim of the proceedings before the national court is to obtain a declaration that the son holds the flat for the exclusive benefit of the father and that in that capacity he is under a duty to execute the documents necessary to convey ownership of the flat to the father. The father does not claim that he already enjoys rights directly relating to the property which are enforceable against the whole world, but seeks only to assert rights as against the son. Consequently, his action is not an action in rem within the meaning of article 16(1) of the Convention but an action in personam. . ..

16–027 As the father and the United Kingdom rightly point out, the immovable nature of the property held in trust and its location are irrelevant to the issues to be determined in the main proceedings which would have been the same if the dispute had concerned a flat situated in the United Kingdom or a yacht.

16–028 The answer to be given to the question submitted to the court must therefore be that an action for a declaration that a person holds immovable property as trustee and for an order requiring that person to execute such documents as should be required to vest the legal ownership in the plaintiff does not constitute an action in rem within the meaning of article 16(1) of the Convention.

## 3. Choice of Applicable Law

### A. Characterisation

A distinction needs to be made between the testator's will or the settlor's trust document, which may be considered as the "rocket-launcher" on the one hand, and the trust itself—the "rocket"—on the other hand.[35] The law that governs whether or not the property of the testator or settlor has been effectively vested under a valid will or other instrument in personal representatives or trustees, free or not from third-party rights (e.g. under forced heirship regimes,[36] matrimonial property regimes[37] or bankruptcy or defrauding creditor[38] laws) may well be different from the law that governs the trust provisions once the intended trust property has wholly or partly survived the application of the law, or laws, relating to the preliminary issues. It if is for the *lex fori* (the law of the jurisdiction whose court is hearing the case) to characterise the issues which arise in a particular dispute.[39] **16–029**

Once the court of the forum has held that, under the applicable law, the owner of assets has effectively vested them in a person as trustee (including settlor-trustee), it seems it should be the applicable (or proper) law governing the trust that determines what interests have then arisen in favour of intended beneficiaries. **16–030**

When a particular law governs a trust, it governs the "internal" aspects of the trust. As far as the trustees' "external" relations with third parties are concerned, e.g. in contracting with them or transferring property to them, one has to apply the conflict of laws rules applicable to contracts or to the transfer of property. Thus, a trustee of a trust governed by the law of Jersey may rely when contracting in Jersey on art.32(1)(a) of the Trusts (Jersey) Law 1984 (as amended): "if the other party knows that the trustee is acting as trustee, any claim by the other party shall be against the trustee as trustee and shall extend only to the trust property." In contrast, if the trustee contracts in England under English law (not expressly choosing Jersey law to govern the contract) she will be personally liable since any person contracting under English law is personally liable except to the extent she expressly restricts liability. **16–031**

### B. The Hague Convention

The determination of the law applicable to a trust is now governed by the Recognition of Trusts Act 1987, which gave effect in English law to the Hague Convention on the Law Applicable to Trusts and on their Recognition.[40] The motivation for the Convention, and the conference that led to it, **16–032**

---

35 *Re Lord Cable* [1976] 3 All E.R. 417 at 431; *Attorney General v Campbell* (1872) L.R. 5 H.L. 524. See too art.4 of the Hague Convention.

36 For example, under French law a deceased's children have rights to part of her estate so that if she has three children she may only freely dispose of, say, one-quarter of her estate: *Re Annesley* [1926] Ch. 692; *Re Adams* [1967] I.R. 424.

37 See, e.g. *Rybolovlev v Rybolovleva* (2012) 15 I.T.E.L.R. 554, a Swiss Federal Court decision considering the Convention and Swiss matrimonial property rules.

38 See, e.g. Insolvency Act 1986 ss.339–342, 423–425.

39 *Macmillan Inc v Bishopsgate Investment Trust (No.3)* [1996] 1 All E.R. 585; *RZB v Five Star LLC* [2001] 3 All E.R. 257. For discussion of the difficult issues which may arise in relation to forced heirship claims, see *European Succession Laws*, edited by D.J. Hayton, 2nd edn (Jordans, 2002), esp. paras 1–67 to 1–69.

40 The Convention was signed on 1 July 1985 and came into force (when ratified by sufficient countries) on 1 January 1992. There are currently 12 contracting states to the Convention: the UK (including Isle of Man, Jersey, Guernsey, Gibraltar, Bermuda, Hong Kong, British Virgin Islands, Turks and Caicos, and Montserrat—but not the Cayman Islands), Italy, Australia, Canada (for Alberta, New Brunswick, British Columbia, Newfoundland, Prince Edward Island, Manitoba, Saskatchewan), Malta, the Netherlands, Luxembourg, Liechtenstein, San Marino, Switzerland, and Monaco. China is also a Contracting State, but for the Special Administrative Region of Hong Kong only.

was supplied chiefly by civil law countries, which wanted to have some means of dealing with trust issues that might arise in litigation in their jurisdictions. It is important to note, therefore, that the Convention does not merely deal with arrangements that fall within English law's definition of a trust. For example, art.2 of the Convention includes within its definition of a trust a private purpose trust, as we have noted in Chapter 5.[41]

**16–033** The Hague Convention does not introduce the trust into the internal private law of states that do not have the concept of the trust; nor does it oblige such states, when recognising a trust, to allow the rights of the beneficiaries to bind a third party who has acquired the trust property.[42] Rather, it simply makes foreign states recognise trusts of property as a matter of private international law, although, for recognition to mean something, the internal private law needs to recognise that the trust fund is separate from the owner's private patrimony, so as to be immune from claims of the owner's creditors, heirs and spouse.[43] Article 11 thus states that the recognition of an arrangement as a trust "shall imply, as a minimum, that the trust property constitutes a separate fund" and that the "personal creditors of the trustee shall have no recourse against the trust assets."

**16–034** Although civil law states do not have equitable proprietary interests, virtually all have some concept of a ring-fenced fund as a separate pool of assets, distinct from its owner's private patrimony.[44] The Convention builds on this by making it clear that the trust assets constitute a separate fiduciary fund and are not available to the trustee's personal creditors or heirs.[45] It must similarly be the case that if a trustee acting in breach of trust acquires assets with trust money, such assets from the date of their acquisition are also to be recognised, under the Convention, as trust assets.[46]

**16–035** It should be noted that there are some differences between the scheme of the Recognition of Trusts Act 1987 and of the Hague Convention on which it is based.[47] For example, whilst the Convention is confined, under art.3, to "trusts created voluntarily and evidenced in writing",[48] the 1987 Act extends to any other trusts of property arising (e.g. orally or by statute) under the law of any part of the UK or by virtue of a judicial decision in the UK or elsewhere.[49]

### *C. Settlor's Choice of Law or Close Connection with Trust*

**16–036** Article 4 of The Hague Convention excludes from its scope "preliminary issues relating to the validity of wills or of other acts by virtue of which assets are transferred to the trustee", reflecting the

---

41 See para.5–106. Article 2 of the Convention is set out at para.1–039.

42 Under English conflict of laws, the proprietary effect of such a transfer would be governed by the *lex situs* (the law of the place where the property was situated at the time of the transfer): see, e.g. *Winkworth v Christie Manson* [1980] 1 Ch. 496.

43 As noted by D.J. Hayton, "The Netherlands Implementation of the Hague Trusts Convention" (1996) 5 J. Int. P. 127, the Dutch legislation initially implementing the Convention included such provision.

44 For example, property subject to a matrimonial property regime; to a commercial partnership regime; or a deceased's estate vested in her heir; or a *fondo patrimoniale* for an Italian's children's upbringing.

45 See art.2, para.2(a) and the second sentence of art.11.

46 Even if, as discussed at para.14–202. such assets are on one view of English law held on a constructive trust, the recognition of the trust flows naturally from the requirements of art.11, even though constructive trusts are not covered by the Convention (see Arts 2 and 3).

47 See too n.61 and n.63: Art.13 and Art.16, para.(2) of the Convention do not form part of the 1987 Act.

48 The French text is *"et dont la preuve est apportée par écrit"* which appears to need dilution to reflect "evidenced" in writing and so covers trusts which are first established in respect of a nominal sum, with substantial assets being added subsequently and with written evidence subsequently arising, whether produced by the settlor or the trustees, e.g. in their accounts.

49 Recognition of Trusts Act 1987. The application of choice of law rules to constructive trusts is discussed by J. Harris "Constructive Trusts and Private International Law: Determining the Applicable Law" (2012) 18 T. & T. 965. No comparable extension has been made in Australia: see *Hiralal v Hiralal* [2013] N.S.W.S.C. 984 at [188] confirming that the Convention did not apply to constructive trusts.

distinction drawn above between the "rocket" comprised by the trust itself, on the one hand, and the "rocket-launcher", on the other.[50]

Articles 6 and 7, taken together, then provide that a trust is governed by the law expressly or impliedly chosen by the settlor, or in the absence of such choice, by the law with which the trust is most closely connected. 16–037

### Hague Convention on the Law Applicable to Trusts and on their Recognition, arts 6 and 7

6. A trust shall be governed by the law chosen by the settlor. The choice must be express or be implied in the terms of the instrument creating or the writing evidencing the trust, interpreted, if necessary, in the light of circumstances of the case. 16–038

Where the law chosen under the previous paragraph does not provide for trusts or the category of trust involved, the choice shall not be effective and the law specified in Art.7 shall apply.

7. Where no applicable law has been chosen, a trust shall be governed by the law with which it is most closely connected. 16–039

In ascertaining the law with which a trust is most closely connected reference shall be made in particular to—

(a) the place of administration of the trust designated by the settlor;
(b) the situs of the assets of the trust;
(c) the place of residence or business of the trustee;
(d) the objects of the trust and the places where they are to be fulfilled.

As was the case under the common law, the weight of various factors taken into account under art.7 will vary according to context. For example, in a testamentary trust the domicile of the testator at her death traditionally had much significance,[51] and is likely still to be important under art.7. In the case of an inter vivos trust the domicile or habitual residence of the settlor at the time she created the trust has some significance as well as the place of execution of the trust instrument. As for the trustee's place of residence or business, it must be remembered that trustees (other than professional corporate trustees) are often chosen for their personal qualities irrespective of where they live or work.[52] Thus, if the testator or settlor expressly designates where the trust is to be administered this will be a more significant factor. The fact that the greater balance of objective factors leads to some applicable law that would not uphold the trust should not lead the court to treat this of itself as a factor that with others points the way to an applicable law that would uphold the trust.[53] 16–040

It seems that, under the Convention[54] as under the common law,[55] there will be a presumption in 16–041

---

[50] See para.16–029. For discussion of the scope of art.4, see *Dervan and MD Events Ltd v Concept Fiduciaries Ltd* (30 November 2012, Royal Court of Guernsey), noted in St. John A. Robilliard, "Recent Guernsey Trust Cases" (2013) 19 T & T 1028 at 1031 and Le Tissier, "Whose Law is it Anyway?" (2013) PCB 62. See too *Clark and Whitehouse, Ntrs* [2012] C.S.O.H. 55, finding that, under art.4, the law chosen by the settlor does not govern the question of whether the steps necessary for the creation of the trust were valid, and so does not determine, for example, whether the settlor had the power to alienate the property intended to be held on trust.

[51] *Re Lord Cable* [1976] 3 All E.R. 417 at 431. Older cases tended to assume that the law of the testator's domicile because it governed the validity of the will also governed trust dispositions in that will, but this does not necessarily follow: *Chellaram v Chellaram (No.2)* [2002] 3 All E.R. 17.

[52] As in *Chellaram v Chellaram (No.2)* [2002] 3 All E.R. 17 where the judge held the trust to be governed by Indian law despite the majority of the trustees being resident in England.

[53] *Re CIS 213/2004* [2008] W.T.L.R. 189; *Berezovsky v Abramovich* [2010] EWHC 647 (Comm) at [183].

[54] See art.8: "The law specified by Article 6 or 7 shall govern the validity of the trust, its construction, its effects, and the administration of the trust."

[55] *Chellaram v Chellaram (No.1)* [1985] Ch. 409.

favour of one applicable law governing all aspects of the trust. It should be noted, however, that it is perfectly possible for a settlor to state that some aspects of the trust are to be governed by one law, whilst other aspects are to be governed by a different law.[56] If a settlor chooses one law to govern the validity of the trust, and another to govern its administration, it would be wise also to specify which matters are to fall within administration since there is little case law guidance on what amounts to matters of administration as opposed to matters of validity.[57]

**16–042** A settlor might also go further and expressly empower her trustees to change the law governing the validity of the trust and to change the law governing the administration of the trust, with or without changing the principal place of administration of the trust.[58] If the trust instrument authorises the trustees to retire in favour of foreign trustees and to transfer the assets to such foreign trustees it seems likely that this power to change the place of administration impliedly carries with it the power to change the law governing administration to the law with which those foreign trustees are familiar, so far as this will be the law of a state that has its own internal law of trusts. For the law governing validity to be changed as well, the authority to transfer assets to foreign trustees will need to state that this is so,[59] so that such assets shall thereafter be exclusively governed by such foreign law so far as not contravening mandatory rules (such as the rule against perpetuities) of the original "mother" law.[60]

## *D. Limitations upon Free Choice of Law*

**16–043** The clear policy of the Convention, as manifested in art.6, is that the settlor has the power to choose the law governing the trust. This means, for example, that an Italian settlor might transfer property situated in Italy to Italian trustees, to hold on trust for Italian beneficiaries, choosing English law to govern the trust, thereby avoiding the inconvenience that Italian domestic law does not have a concept of the trust. It would seem that an Italian court would have to recognise such an arrangement as a trust.[61] Similarly, if an English court had jurisdiction in a dispute concerning an off-shore private purpose trust, governed by, for example, Cayman law, and such trust met the requirements of Cayman law and the definition of a trust in art.2 of the Convention,[62] it would seem that an English court must recognise and enforce that trust, even though it would be invalid as a matter of English law.

**16–044** The Convention includes, however, some restrictions on the freedom of the settlor to achieve particular results by her choice of governing law:

---

56 For split laws in a contractual context see, e.g. *Forsikrings Vesta v Butcher* [1986] 2 All E.R. 488 at 504–505. See too the Contracts (Applicable Law) Act 1990 implementing the 1980 Rome Convention, especially arts 3 and 4.

57 Some guidance may be found in *Pearson v IRC* [1981] A.C. 753 and *Chellaram v Chellaram (No.1)* [1985] Ch. 409 at 432.

58 *Chellaram v Chellaram (No.2)* [2002] 3 All E.R. 17 at [146] and [160]–[161].

59 *Chellaram v Chellaram (No.2)* [2002] 3 All E.R. 17.

60 As Lord Walker remarked in *West v Trennery* [2005] 1 All E.R. 827 at [41]: the second settlement serves "as a vehicle to receive and continue the act of bounty effected by the first settlement, with the rule against perpetuities acting as a sort of umbilical cord between the two settlements".

61 See art.11 of the Hague Convention. The example is not chosen at random: for discussion of such a *"trust interno"*, and its recognition by Italian courts, see M. Lupoi, (2012) Columbia Journal of European Law Online 4. In such a case, a court could draw on the discretion not to recognise the trust given by art.13 of the Hague Convention: it is important to note that, given the uncertainty arising from that discretion, art.13 was not included in the Recognition of Trusts Act 1987, and so is *not* part of English law.

62 As noted at para.5–106, that definition is broad enough to include a private purpose trust.

### Hague Convention on the Law Applicable to Trusts and on their Recognition, arts 15, 16 and 18

15. The Convention does not prevent the application of provisions of the law designated by the conflicts rules of the forum, in so far as those provisions cannot be derogated from by voluntary act, relating in particular to the following matters— 16–045

(a) the protection of minors and incapable parties;
(b) the personal and proprietary effects of marriage;
(c) succession rights, testate and intestate, especially the indefeasible shares of spouses and relatives;
(d) the transfer of title to property and security interests in property;
(e) the protection of creditors in matters of insolvency;
(f) the protection, in other respects, of third parties acting in good faith.

If recognition of a trust is prevented by application of the preceding paragraph, the court shall try to give effect to the objects of the trust by other means.

16. The Convention does not prevent the application of those provisions of the law of the forum which must be applied even to international situations, irrespective of rules of conflict of laws. . .[63] 16–046

18. The provisions of the Convention may be disregarded when their application would be manifestly incompatible with public policy (*ordre public*). 16–047

Article 15 ensures the application of the internal mandatory rules of a state whose law is applicable according to the conflicts rules of the forum, irrespective of the law applicable to the trust. Mandatory succession rules have special significance, especially if a settlor's trust assets are found in the civil law forum of a forced heir who seeks such assets. Choice of law rules may lead to the *lex successionis, lex situs* or *lex fori* being invoked so as wholly or partly to undo the effects of a trust. Whereas art.15 refers to matters that may be related to trusts, art.16 allows for a court to apply any of its own mandatory rules of international application that apply directly to trusts.[64] 16–048

Article 18 may be relevant, for example, if the off-shore private purpose trust was governed by a law which contained no perpetuity period, and was a trust of English land: it is very likely that an English court would refuse to recognise such a trust and would instead give effect to the English policy rules as to the administration of land within the jurisdiction. A more difficult question arises if the subject matter of the trust is instead property held outside England: opinions differ as to whether the rules of English law refusing enforceability to private purpose trusts can be seen as part of *ordre public*,[65] although it should be noted that the concept of *ordre public* is generally taken to be quite limited. Much would depend on the specific nature of the private purpose.[66] Certainly, if the trusts were private non-charitable purpose trusts of movables in the Isle of Man, Jersey, Bermuda or Cayman valid under special legislation with an expressly designated enforcer, the English court should not invalidate them, nor should it if trustees of such trusts purchase English assets as investments or even if such assets are transferred to the trustees to become original settled assets.[67] After all, if the main aim of 16–049

63 Article 16, para. 2, states that "If another State has a sufficiently close connection with a case then, in exceptional circumstances, effect may also be given to rules of that State which have the same character as in the preceding paragraph". Article 16, para. 3 gives a Contracting State the power to decide that it will not apply para. 2. The U.K. used that power, and so Article 16 para. 2 is not part of the 1987 Act: it was rejected for reasons similar to those applying to Article 13: see n.61.

64 See J. Harris, *The Hague Trusts Convention* (Hart Publishing, 2002), p.381.

65 For differing views on this point, in the context of the Cayman Special Trusts (Alternative Regime) legislation, contrast A. Duckworth, "STAR Wars: Smiting the Bull" (1999) Tru. L.I. 158 and P. Matthews, "STAR: Big Bang or Red Dwarf?" (1998) 12 Tru. L.I. 98.

66 If, for example, it was merely to develop the income yield and capital growth of the trust fund, it could be argued that in default of any disposal of the beneficial interest there should be a resulting trust for the settlor.

67 See D.J. Hayton, "Developing the Obligation Characteristic of the Trust" (2001) 117 L.Q.R. 96.

the Hague Convention is to allow for the recognition of trusts in civil law jurisdictions which have no concept of the trust *at all*, it would perhaps be a little rich for an English court to refuse to give effect to an arrangement simply because it does not accord with the English conception of the trust.[68]

**Questions**

1. Cameron desires to create a trust to further the purposes of the Conservative Party for as long as it exists and for it to be enforceable by the Leader from time-to-time of the Conservative Party. He wants to settle either English company shares worth £15 million or £15 million and will be happy if the trustees buy London premises for the Party in due course, whether holding title directly or through an underlying company owned by the trust. He knows that under arts 12 and 15 of the Trusts (Jersey) Law 1984 (as amended in 1996 and 2006) a non-charitable purpose trust for ever will be valid. Advise him, considering whether a small initial settlement might be set up with Jersey trustees of Jersey assets of a trust governed by Jersey law and to which assets could later be added; or whether to create the trust by transferring the whole trust fund to trustees in England of a trust governed by Jersey law.

2. Wanda, who was living with Martin, inherited £200,000. They sold his flat for £300,000 and bought a flat with their joint £500,000. She was in Australia looking after her terminally ill mother at the time for completion of the purchase and so Martin became sole registered proprietor. Wanda's mother died 10 months later, by which time Martin had become infatuated with Flo. He sold the flat to a person who had been interested in buying the flat when Martin bought it. He used the £500,000 proceeds of sale to buy in his name a villa in Italy where he lived with Flo. Wanda has just discovered this, a year after the purchase of the villa in Italy.

   **Advise Wanda. Would your advice differ if the Martin–Flo relationship had broken down and Martin had obtained a job in London and was now living in his mother's house?**

3. Hubert and his Dutch wife lived in England until he died after 40 years of marriage, leaving his estate (including the marital home) to her as executrix and trustee on trust for herself for life remainder to their two children. She sold the marital home and moved to the Netherlands and used the trust fund to buy a house there. She opened a trust account with a Dutch bank, separate from her private account but a week before she died she sold shares owned as trustee and paid the €100,000 proceeds into her private account. Dutch creditors seek to make the house and the €100,000 available to satisfy their claims.

   **Advise the two children.**

4. Taken together, do arts 15, 16 and 18 undermine one of the main aims of the Hague Convention: the recognition of trusts in states that do not have a trust as part of their own domestic law? **Discuss.**

---

[68] See Duckworth, "STAR Wars: Smiting the Bull" (1999) Tru. L.I. 158, 162 and Harris, *The Hague Trusts Convention* (2002), p.396.

# PART VIII

# THE NATURE OF A TRUST

# 17

# THE NATURE OF A TRUST: PROPERTY OR OBLIGATION?

## 1. The Debate

We noted in Chapter 1 that there is a debate about the true nature of the rights of B, a beneficiary of a trust.[1] In this long-running controversy, the key disagreement is as to the nature of a trust itself. On one view, which we will refer to here as the "proprietary view", the creation of a trust gives B a property right, arising in equity, in the trust property. A number of important rules and principles of trusts law are then explained as recognising and giving effect to B's equitable property right in the trust property. On another view, which we will refer to here as the "obligational view", the creation of a trust imposes particular duties on T, and the rights acquired by B are defined by the content of those duties. On this view, a different explanation needs to be found for those rules and principles of trusts law that might otherwise be seen as based on the proprietary nature of B's rights.[2] 17–001

It would be a mistake to say that, in analysing the nature of a trust, only two views are possible: whilst each of the proprietary and obligational views can be taken as marking one end of a spectrum, that spectrum is broad enough to include a large number of different views. It is nonetheless necessary, in coming to any conclusion as to the nature of a trust, to consider and evaluate each of the proprietary view and the obligational views. 17–002

We are considering this debate here, rather than at the start of the book, as it turns on which of the competing views offers the most coherent and satisfying explanation of the key rules and principles of trusts law, and so it can be assessed only after having looked at the detail of those rules and principles. 17–003

Throughout this book, we have seen a number of very important features of B's rights under a trust that differentiate B's position from that of a party with a purely personal right. We can, for example, compare B's position, where T holds property on trust for B, with that of C, where D has a simple duty to pay C £100. First, B is protected in the event of T's insolvency; C is not protected in the event of D's insolvency. Secondly, if T makes an unauthorised transfer of the trust property to a third party, and that third party cannot establish the defence of bona fide purchase for value,[3] B will be able to make a proprietary claim against that third party; if D were to make a gift of £100 to a third party, rather than paying that £100 to C, C has no claim against that third party. Thirdly, if T acquires new assets through an authorised or unauthorised use of the trust property, B can claim that those new assets are 17–004

1 See para.1–097.
2 Of course, in many cases, an express trust will involve two or more trustees, and two or more beneficiaries. For ease of exposition, however, we will refer in this chapter to T and to B.
3 See paras 12–057ff.

held subject to the terms of the initial trust in B's favour; if D takes £100 and, rather than giving it to C, instead uses it to gamble and turns it into £1,000, C has no claim to that £1,000.

**17-005** It is therefore indisputable that there is a difference between the nature of B's rights, arising under a trust, and the right of C, in the case of a pure debt. B and C each benefits from the existence of an obligation: T is under a duty to B, and D is under a duty to C. The crucial difference is that T's duty to B relates to specific property; D's duty to C does not. That explains the first and second of the three key differences between B's position and C's position that were noted in the preceding paragraph; on the view of the House of Lords in *Foskett v McKeown* it also explains the third.[4] For this reason, the difference between B's position and C's position is consistently described by the courts[5] and the legislature[6] in the same way as it has been consistently described in this book[7]: as turning on the fact that B has an equitable or beneficial interest in the trust property or, synonymously, an equitable or beneficial property right; or, in relation to some trusts at least, equitable or beneficial ownership of the trust property.[8]

**17-006** It might therefore seem that the debate between the proprietary view and the obligational view of the trust is over before we have even begun. Yet the obligational view has attracted many eminent supporters over the centuries,[9] and lies behind a number of more recent analyses of the nature of the trust.[10] It is vital to note that such proponents of the obligational view do not claim that the right of B under a trust is no different to the right of C to be paid a debt of £100; nor do they seek to deny any of the three fundamental features of a right under a trust noted above. The debate is not as to what the basic rules and principles of the law of trusts should be; it is rather as to the best way to explain those rules and principles. On the obligational view, focussing on the particular nature of T's duties to B is the key to understanding the trust, and to explaining why B's rights differ from those of C; on the proprietary view, the door is instead opened by focussing on B's direct link to the trust property.

**17-007** It should not be thought that this debate is either illusory or unimportant. We will see later in this chapter that there is some substantial common ground between commentators currently engaged in the debate[11]; but the differences in their positions, and between the proprietary view and the obligational view, are nonetheless real. Nor should it be thought that, because the debate interests academics, it is of only academic interest. It is true that, just as those favouring an obligational view do not deny the fundamental point that B has a right that is protected in T's insolvency and which may bind certain third parties, those adopting a proprietary view equally do not claim that B's right is identical in its effect to the full title enjoyed by O, a party who simply owns property outright. It is accepted on all sides, for example, that B will have no claim against C if C is a bona fide purchaser for value of the trust property without notice of the trust.[12] In contrast, as we saw in Chapter 1,[13] if O's property is

---

4 [2001] 1 A.C. 102 (extracted at paras 12-068—12-098). As noted at paras 12-108—12-116, however, that analysis can be questioned.

5 See, e.g. *Westdeutsche Landesbank Girozentrale v Islington LBC* [1996] A.C. 669 (extracted at paras 14-174ff); *Foskett v McKeown* [2001] 1 A.C. 102 (extracted at paras 12-068—12-098); *Independent Trustee Services Ltd v GP Noble Trustees Ltd* [2013] Ch. 91 (extracted at paras 12-058—12-062 and 12-120—12-137.

6 See, e.g. Law of Property Act 1925, s.53(1)(c), discussed at paras 3-050ff.

7 See, e.g. para.4-070.

8 See, e.g. *Shell UK Ltd v Total UK Ltd* [2011] Q.B. 86 (extracted at paras 17-094—17-105), referring to the case where B has rights under a fixed trust, rather than under a discretionary trust.

9 See paras 17-047—17-054.

10 See, e.g. L. Smith, "Unravelling Proprietary Restitution" (2004) 40 Can. Bus. L.J. 317; B. McFarlane & R. Stevens, "The Nature of Equitable Property" (2010) 4 J. Eq. 1; T. Cutts, "The Nature of 'Equitable Property': a Functional Analysis" (2012) 6 J. Eq. 44; J. Edelman, "Two Fundamental Questions for the Law of Trusts" (2013) 129 L.Q.R. 66.

11 See paras 17-038—17-045.

12 See para.12-057.

13 See para.1-019.

stolen and then sold by the thief to C, who buys in good faith and with no notice of O's initial property right, O will be able to assert that property right against C.[14]

17–008 It is nonetheless clear that the accepted, key features of the trust cannot, by themselves, provide the answers to every practical question that may arise as to the operation of B's rights. As we will see in later in this chapter,[15] there are a number of practical points which will be determined differently according to whether a court expressly or impliedly favours the proprietary view or the obligational view.

## 2. The Proprietary View

17–009 Whilst we have noted that the language used by the courts is not a decisive test, the proprietary view is, of course, consistent with, and derives support from, that language. It provides a straightforward explanation for two of the three key features of the trust discussed above.[16] For example, in a careful analysis of the nature of B's rights against C, an innocent donee to whom T makes an unauthorised disposition of trust property, Lloyd LJ in *Independent Trustee Services Ltd v GP Noble Trustees Ltd*[17] explained that

> in the case of an innocent volunteer recipient of money which is the product of a breach of trust, the legal title is in the recipient but equitable title remains in the beneficiaries of the relevant trust throughout.

In *Foskett v McKeown*,[18] when analysing the third of the three features discussed above, Lord Browne-Wilkinson invoked the "hard-nosed property rights" of B in explaining why B could bring a claim in relation to the traceable proceeds of trust property against innocent donees who had received, and retained, such proceeds.

17–010 There is also, of course, some strong academic support for the proprietary view.[19] Brian Simpson, for example, in analysing the history of the trust, stated that: "the Chancellors modelled the incidents of equitable ownership upon the common law."[20] Before exploring the view further, however, we need to define it.

### A. Defining the Proprietary View

17–011 The proprietary view does not entail the clearly incorrect proposition that *all* the rights of B under a trust are proprietary, and that none of those rights are based simply on the content of duties owed by T to B. In other words, the proprietary view does not seek to explain all rules and principles of the law of trusts as resting on B's holding of an equitable property right. For example, one of the key features of B's rights under a trust is that B may be able to assert a claim against C, a third party who acquires the trust property as a result of an unauthorised transfer by T.[21] On the proprietary view, this can be explained by seeing B as having an equitable interest in the trust property, rather than only a right correlating to T's duty to B: a key feature of property rights, as opposed to personal rights, is that they are

---

14 See, e.g. *Farquarhson Bros and Co v King and Co* [1902] A.C. 325. Where the property consists of goods, O's claim against C will arise in the tort of conversion.

15 See the discussion at paras 17–093ff of *Shell UK Ltd v Total UK Ltd* [2011] Q.B. 86.

16 See para.17–004.

17 [2013] Ch. 91 at [77]–[80] (extracted at paras 12–058—12–062).

18 [2001] 1 A.C. 102 (extracted at paras 12–068—12–098).

19 See, e.g. A.W. Scott, "The Nature of the Rights of the 'Cestui Que Trust'" (1917) 17 Col. L. Rev. 269.

20 A.W.B. Simpson, *An Introduction to the History of the Land Law* (Oxford University Press, 1961), p.194.

21 See paras 1–050 and 12–057ff.

capable of binding third parties. As Richard Nolan has explained,[22] however, it is clear that B's position against C is not entirely the same as B's initial position against T. For example, under the terms of an initial express trust, T may have agreed to particular positive duties to manage and invest the trust property. C, merely by acquiring the trust property, will not be under those same positive duties to B. As Nolan explains in the following extract, even on the proprietary view, it is therefore necessary to distinguish the core, negative duty of T—the duty not to use the trust property for T's own benefit, unless specifically authorised to do by the terms of the trust—from the additional positive duties that T may have agreed to assume under the terms of the initial trust. This is because only the former are capable of binding C, a third party who simply receives the trust property and has not agreed, nor can be regarded as having agreed,[23] to act as a trustee.

## R. Nolan, "Equitable Property"

(2006) 122 L.Q.R. 232, 233, 261–262, 255–256

17–012 . . . In short, a beneficiary's core proprietary rights under a trust consist in the beneficiary's primary, negative right to exclude non-beneficiaries from the enjoyment of trust assets. Infringement of this primary right will generate secondary rights by which a beneficiary may also prevent (or at least restrict) access to assets by non-beneficiaries.[24] By contrast, a beneficiary's positive claims to access benefits from trust assets, which will exist in conjunction with his negative, exclusionary rights, may or may not themselves be regarded as proprietary by reason of their utility rather than their enforceability. . ..

17–013 The constant, negative, exclusionary aspect of an equitable property right under a trust may be conjoined with one of many possible fractions of positive benefit which a settlor can instruct trustees to carve out of the trust assets and deflect to a beneficiary: fixed interests or discretionary interests; interests in possession or remainder and so on. Whether the resulting bundle of rights itself satisfies and particular definition (usually statutory) of "property" or "proprietary interest" will depend on the definition used, which will necessarily vary, depending in turn on the purpose for which the definition is established. . ..

17–014 Any positive claims to take benefit from assets by virtue of a trust are not the concern of third parties, unless they have for reasons beyond mere receipt of assets made themselves amenable to such claims. It is in this way, by limiting the extent of the claims which can be made against third parties, by limiting the proprietary claims founded on an equitable interest under a trust, that the Chancery courts have reconciled the perceived need to restrict the number of proprietary claims which may affect third parties with the huge flexibility that the law of trusts affords to intending settlers who want to apportion and allocate the various benefits from assets amongst several different people.

17–015 It is also possible for participants in the debate to adopt the proprietary view, and thus be in agreement, but at the same time to hold different views as to the separate question of what counts as a property right. This is why, in the extract above, Nolan leaves open the question of whether a right held by B and correlating to T's positive duty to use the trust property in a particular way for B's benefit, even if it will not be capable of binding C where C merely receives the trust property, counts as "proprietary".[25]

---

[22] R. Nolan, "Equitable Property" (2006) 122 L.Q.R. 232.

[23] If C, because of C's conduct after acquiring the trust property, is regarded as a "trustee *de son tort*", then C will be subject to the positive duties imposed by the initial trust: see paras 11–014–11–016.

[24] For the distinction between "primary rights" (those rights which arise from facts or events, rather than from an infringement of some other right) and "secondary rights" (those rights which arise from infringement of some other right), see J Austin, *Lectures on Jurisprudence* (1885) Lecture XLV, esp at pp 762 et seq. The distinction, as used here, is essentially between the extra-curial behaviour legitimated by a property right and its judicial vindication following infringement. It is not about the difference between property rights and restitutionary rights, as to which see P Birks, *Introduction to the Law of Restitution* (1985) at pp 50–52.

[25] R. Nolan, "Equitable Property" (2006) 122 L.Q.R. 232, 261–262 (extracted at para.17–013).

This does not mean, however, that no settled definition can be given of the proprietary view. For example, for the purposes of his analysis, Nolan adopts a meaning of "proprietary" which identifies what is often regarded as a necessary feature of any right that is proprietary. On that meaning[26]: **17–016**

> an asset is termed 'property' or 'proprietary' when the component parts of that interest include a primary right to exclude any one of a very large and indefinite class of people from access to some enjoyment of the asset, whether or not those people have in fact consented to such exclusion, and secondary claims to vindicate that primary right.

Certainly, whilst general debates as to the nature of property do of course continue, there is a significant body of support[27] for the idea that a proprietary right necessarily involves a "right to exclude" or, more precisely, that it imposes a prima facie duty of non-interference on the rest of the world. In this chapter, therefore, we will adopt that notion of property when defining and evaluating the proprietary view of the trust. **17–017**

It is important to bear in mind, however, that, whilst we have thus adopted a stable meaning of what it means for a right to be proprietary, others engaged in the debate may have adopted, expressly or impliedly, a different meaning. For example, the term "property" is often applied, not least by economists, to any valuable asset; it is sometimes also used to refer to any assert the value of which can be realised by trading, for example by means of transferring the asset to another person.[28] Neither of those usages of the term is relevant to the debate we are considering here between the proprietary and obligational views of the trust.[29] This is because it is perfectly consistent with the obligational view to accept that B's right under a trust is valuable, and that its value can be realised by trading. **17–018**

For example, consider a classic example of an obligation which gives rise to a purely personal right, and confers no property on the party whose right correlates to the obligation: D's duty to pay C a debt of £100. C's right is clearly different to a right under a trust: if D were to make a gift of £100 to X, rather than paying C, C can have no claim against X; nor is C protected in D's insolvency. The vital difference, of course, between C's right and a right under a trust is that D's duty to pay C £100 does not relate to any specific property held by D, as D can use any money to pay C. So, in the terms in which our debate is framed, only the obligational view is consistent with the nature of a pure debt. Yet C's right to sue D for £100 is a valuable asset held by C, and C can realise its value by trading, for example by making an equitable or statutory assignment of the debt to X. It follows that the mere facts that B, the beneficiary of a trust, has a valuable right, and can realise the value of that right, often by transferring it,[30] cannot be conclusive in the debate between the proprietary and obligational views of the trust. **17–019**

---

[26] R. Nolan, "Equitable Property" (2006) 122 L.Q.R. 232, 235.

[27] See, e.g. K. Gray, "Property in Thin Air" [1991] C.L.J. 252; T. Merrill "Property and the Right to Exclude" (1998) 77 Nebraska L.R. 730; S. Douglas & B. McFarlane, "Defining Property Rights" in J. Penner & H. Smith (eds) *Philosophical Foundations of Property Law* (Oxford University Press, 2013).

[28] See, e.g. *OBG Ltd v Allan* [2008] A.C. 1 at [309] per Lady Hale (dissenting). Lady Hale's argument there was that, because a chose in action is "property" in the sense of being an asset, separate to its holder, which can be transferred, it should be protected by means of a strict duty of non-interference prima facie binding on the rest of the world. It is submitted, however, that the view of the majority in that case is to be preferred, as the question of transferability differs from that of exclusion. There are, for example, some rights which do impose a strict general duty of non-interference but which cannot be effectively transferred (e.g. a non-assignable lease).

[29] That is not to say, of course, that such meanings of property are never relevant. For example, the term "property" as used in the Insolvency Act 1986 is given a broad meaning by s.436 of that Act (see, e.g. *Bristol Airport plc v Powdrill* [1990] Ch. 744) as its aim is to vest the realisable assets of the insolvent party in, e.g. the trustee in bankruptcy who can then realise the value in those assets to meet the debts of the insolvent party.

[30] See paras 3–050ff for discussion of the methods by which B can realise the value of a right under a trust. It is of course possible for S, when setting up a trust, to ensure that B cannot transfer B's right; even in such a case, however, it may still

## B. The Diversity of Trusts

**17-020** As we saw in Chapter 1,[31] there is a great diversity to the law of trusts, both across jurisdictions and within English law, and so care must be taken in making general statements that purport to apply to all forms of trust. A good example is provided by the difference between a fixed trust and a discretionary trust.[32] In *Baker v Archer-Shee*,[33] for example, B was the life tenant under a trust of shares, i.e. T held shares subject to a duty to use those shares for the benefit of B during B's life, and then to use the shares for the benefit of others on B's death. T thus had a duty to pay dividends declared on the shares to B, although T was allowed to deduct expenses before making those payments. The shares, and T, were based in New York. To apply legislation determining B's tax liability,[34] it was necessary to ask if B could be regarded as owning the dividends as soon as they were paid to T, so that the dividends were chargeable to income tax immediately, whether or not the dividends were later remitted to B in the UK. A majority of the House of Lords held that, by virtue of her rights under the trust, B could be regarded, in effect, as the real owner of income produced by the trust property as soon as that income was produced, and could be assessed for income tax accordingly. Lord Wrenbury stated that B was "entitled in equity specifically during her life to the dividends upon the stocks".[35] The decision thus provides support for the proprietary view.

**17-021** In *Gartside v IRC*,[36] by way of contrast, the House of Lords considered the application of tax legislation in a case where B was the beneficiary of a discretionary trust rather than a fixed trust. The question under that legislation (which governed estate duty rather than income tax) was whether B, before receiving any distribution from T under the discretionary trust, had an "interest in possession" or even an "interest" in the trust property.[37] The House of Lords, allowing B's appeal from the decision of the Court of Appeal, held that, as the trust was a discretionary trust, B's right did not count as such an interest. Lord Wilberforce explained this in the following words.

> **17-022** No doubt in a certain sense a beneficiary under a discretionary trust has an "interest": the nature of it may, sufficiently for the purpose, be spelt out by saying that he has a right to be considered as a potential recipient of benefit by the trustees and a right to have his interest protected by a court of equity. Certainly that is so, and when it is said that he has a right to have the trustees exercise their discretion "fairly" or "reasonably" or "properly" that indicates clearly enough that some objective consideration (not stated explicitly in declaring the discretionary trust, but latent in it) must be applied by the trustees and that the right is more than a mere spes.[38] But that does not mean that he has an interest which is capable of being taxed by reference to its extent in the trust fund's income: it may be a right, with some degree of concreteness or solidity, one which attracts the protection of a court of equity, yet it may still lack the necessary quality of definable extent which must exist before it can be taxed. . ..
>
> **17-023** The Master of the Rolls and Salmon L.J. in the Court of Appeal were persuaded by an argument which was suggested [by the Revenue] to meet this difficulty. The beneficiary's right, it was claimed, is analogous to that of a competitor in a beauty competition; she has a right to be considered for the prize: if she is excluded, she can be awarded damages which a jury can assess. The analogy was inevitably left at some distance because it could hardly be suggested that a charge for estate duty could be assessed by any similar

---

be possible for B to realise the value of her right by declaring, in exchange for payment from C, a sub-trust in C's favour (compare, e.g. *Don King v Warren* [2000] Ch. 291 and see para.1-057).

31 See paras 1-037—1-052.

32 See, e.g. paras 1-041—1-045 and 4-055.

33 [1927] A,C, 844.

34 Income Tax Act 1918 Sch.D, Case 4.

35 [1927] A.C. 844, 866.

36 [1968] A.C. 553.

37 Finance Act 1940, s.43.

38 [i.e. more than a mere hope.]

> procedure: and it is clear enough that it fails at the critical point, namely, of establishing that a person with a chance of success has an interest in more than the broadest popular sense, *in the fund*.

As we will consider further below,[39] the mere fact that B's right under a particular type of trust is not regarded as an "interest" or even as "property", as that term is used by a specific statute, does not mean that such a trust must necessarily be regarded as consistent only with the obligational view rather than the proprietary view. This point is made by Nolan, who notes that[40] 17–024

> where a tax is levied by reference to the benefits of holding 'property', or by reference to receipts from 'property', then the notion of 'property' is generally, and entirely understandably, taken to involve positive claims of access to some benefit of definable extent, unless the meaning of the word is deliberately extended.

So, the decision in *Gartside v IRC* does not mean that the right of B under a discretionary trust lies outside the definition of property which we have adopted, which looks not to the positive rights of B to a specific benefit, but rather to the rights of B to exclude others from access to the trust property. Indeed, under a discretionary trust as under any trust, B has a right which is capable of binding C, a third party who acquires the trust property through an unauthorised disposition by T; and B is also protected should T go into insolvency. As Nolan notes,[41] therefore, the decision in *Gartside v IRC* does not, by itself, make it impossible to regard a beneficiary of a discretionary trust as having rights that are "proprietary" in the "general, negative, exclusionary sense".

## 3. The Nature of the Debate

Before moving on to consider the obligational view, it is worth pausing to consider the nature of the debate between the proprietary and obligational views. The debate is certainly a long-standing one. The 1917 edition of the Columbia Law Review, for example, contains both an article by Austin Scott (who was to become the leading American commentator on the law of trusts, as well as one of the authors of the seminal *Restatement of Restitution*[42]) championing the proprietary view[43] and a response by Harlan Stone (who was to become Chief Justice of the US) defending the then-prevailing obligational view.[44] Nearly a century on, the debate continues, albeit with less eminent participants.[45] Three points arise from considering the duration of the debate. 17–025

### A. The Absence of a Conclusive Test

No single judicial decision or legislative act can serve as the silver bullet that will determine the duel between the proprietary view and the obligational view of the trust. As we will see in this chapter, there have been a number of decisions in which a court has specifically been faced with questions such as whether B has property in, or ownership of, the trust property, and whether a claim made by B to 17–026

---

39 See para.17–027.

40 R. Nolan, "Equitable Property" (2006) 122 L.Q.R. 232, 256 (footnotes omitted).

41 R. Nolan, "Equitable Property" (2006) 122 L.Q.R. 232, 257 (footnote omitted).

42 W.A. Seavey & A.W. Scott, *Restatement of the Law: Restitution* (American Law Institute, 1937).

43 A.W. Scott, "The Nature of the Rights of the 'Cestui Que Trust'" (1917) 17 Col. L. Rev. 269.

44 H. Stone, "The Nature of the Rights of the 'Cetui Que Trust'" (1917) 17 Col. L. Rev. 467.

45 For recent, and contrasting contributions see, e.g. B. McFarlane & R. Stevens, "The Nature of Equitable Property" (2010) 4 J. Eq. 1; J. Penner, "The (True) Nature of a Beneficiary's Equitable Proprietary Interest under a Trust" (2014) 27 Can. J.L. & Juris 473.

enforce her rights under the trust is a claim in rem (i.e. in relation to a thing) rather than in personam (i.e. against a person). The decisions are not always consistent. For example, in *Baker v Archer-Shee*,[46] the House of Lords, as noted above,[47] held that, in a fixed trust, B could be regarded, in effect, as the real owner of income produced by the trust property as soon as that income was produced, before it was passed to B by T, and could be assessed for income tax accordingly. In contrast, as we saw in Chapter 16,[48] in *Webb v Webb*,[49] each of Judge Paul Baker QC in the High Court and the European Court of Justice held that B's claim that T held land on a resulting trust for B, and should therefore transfer that land to B, was a claim that T was simply under a particular duty to B, and so was not made in proceedings which had as their object a right in rem. The former decision, of course, supports the proprietary view, the latter the obligational view; neither settles the debate.

**17–027** There are several reasons why such individual decisions cannot conclusively determine the issue. First, the question faced by the court in each of *Baker v Archer-Shee* and *Webb v Webb* arose in a specific statutory context, and the meaning given to a particular term necessarily depends on the context in which it is used.[50] A court in an individual case never decides if, in the abstract, B's rights are best seen as proprietary or as simply correlating to T's duties. This does not mean, of course, that such decisions are irrelevant when considering the merits of each of the proprietary and obligational views. It does however reduce the impact of any specific decision, as it is very often possible to explain away a court's implicit preference for the proprietary view or the obligational view as depending on the practical consequences of adopting that view on the facts of the instant case.

**17–028** In relation to *Baker v Archer-Shee*, for example, it could be argued that the majority's view of the nature of B's entitlement was informed by a desire to prevent parties from using the terms of a trust as a simple way to limit B's income tax liability.[51] Conversely, it could be said that the minority's view was informed by a wish to interpret taxation legislation, where ambiguous, to the benefit of the taxpayer. *Webb v Webb*, meanwhile, could be explained on the basis that the decisions in the case produced the desirable consequence that litigation between a claimant and a defendant both based in England, and concerning the possible effect of their discussions in England, could continue in England. Moreover, the rule at issue,[52] on which the defendant unsuccessfully relied, is that proceedings which have as their object a right in rem in immovable property can be brought *only* in the jurisdiction where that property is situated. Such exclusive jurisdiction provisions are narrowly interpreted, as they form an exception to the general rule that a defendant should be sued in the courts of her domicile.[53] Against this background, it was no surprise that the claim to enforce a right under a trust was seen as based on the obligation of T to B, and not on a proprietary right of B.

**17–029** Secondly, the maxim that "equity acts in *personam*", whilst it has sometimes been relied on by courts in considering, for example, how conflict of laws rules should be applied to particular equita-

---

46 [1927] A.C. 844.

47 See para.17–020.

48 See paras 16–017—16–028.

49 [1994] Q.B. 696.

50 The warning of W. Cook, the Wittgenstein of the conflicts of laws, is apt. In "Substance and Procedure in the Conflict of Laws" (1933) 42 Yale L.J. 333 he stated at 337 that: "[T]he tendency to assume that a word which appears in one or more legal rules, and so in connection with more than one purpose, has and should have precisely the same scope in all of them, runs through all legal discussions. It has the tenacity of original sin and must constantly be guarded against."

51 For example, Lord Wrenbury stated ([1972] A.C. 844, 866) that if tax were not assessed on the basis that B in effect owned the trust property, then "it results that a person residing here (whether a British subject or not) can by creating a foreign trust of stocks and shares and accumulating or spending the income abroad escape taxation upon that income."

52 See now Recast Brussels Regulation, Regulation (EU) No 1215/2012 of the European Parliament and of the Council of 12 December 2012 on jurisdiction and the recognition and enforcement of judgments in civil and commercial matters [2012] OJ L351, art.24.

53 Recast Brussels Regulation, art.42.

ble claims,[54] does not provide conclusive evidence for the obligational view of the trust. The maxim derives from a historical difference between common law and equity that related not to the nature of a claimant's rights, but rather to the means by which a judgment in favour of the claimant could be executed.[55] At common law, there was the possibility of execution in rem: against assets of the defendant. In equity, by contrast, there was no procedural means of ordering such execution, as the Chancellor did not have local officers who could enforce such an order. Execution therefore had to be against the person of the defendant: if she refused to comply with an order of a court of Equity, she could be imprisoned. This is the original meaning of the maxim that "equity acts in *personam*" and it tells us nothing about the nature of the right on which the successful claim was based.

Similarly, the proprietary view is not necessarily inconsistent with the fact that B's right under a trust can be defeated by C, to whom T makes an unauthorised transfer of the trust property, if C is a bona fide purchaser for value without notice of the trust. The point is that, even if O is an outright owner of property, it may be possible for C to have a defence against O's pre-existing property right. If O's pre-existing legal property right is in money used as currency, for example, then, exceptionally, a bona fide purchaser defence does apply: if X steals a £10 note from O and spends it in C's shop, then C, assuming she had no notice of the theft, is immune from any claim by O.[56] Where O's property right is in goods, and X, who has an inferior title to O, sells those goods to C, there is no general bona fide purchase defence available to C, but there are a number of specific situations in which C will have a defence to O's pre-existing legal property right.[57] If, therefore, the existence of such a defence is inconsistent with a right's being proprietary, then there are no property rights in English law.[58] **17–030**

Thirdly, to think that the debate between the proprietary view and the obligational view could be settled by a single case or legislative provision (other than a somewhat unlikely statute directed specifically to ending the debate) is to misunderstand the nature of the debate. Its participants are attempting to put forward a broad general principle which they regard as best fitting and justifying the wide set of rules and principles that go into establishing the nature of a trust and the entitlements of B. Particular decisions can of course have an important role in shaping those rules and principles, and any theory of the trust must be based on the general patterns produced by those individual decisions, but the law of trusts is sufficiently diverse[59] and complex that the impact of any single decision will be limited. **17–031**

## *B. The Nature of Judge-Made Law*

Each of the proprietary view and the obligational view attempts to make the best sense of the rules and principles, developed initially by courts of Equity, that define the nature and operation of the trust. Yet it is clear that, in formulating those rules, the courts were not (and are not) guided by a monolithic notion of "property" or of "obligation", but rather, ultimately, by a desire to ensure that the result in any particular case conforms with the need to prevent particular forms of unconscionable conduct, so that a defendant is not permitted to act in a way which would "shock the conscience of the court".[60] **17–032**

---

54 See, e.g. *Ewing v Orr Ewing (No.1)* (1883) 9 App. Cas. 34, 40 per Lord Selborne LC.

55 See, e.g. *Snell's Equity*, edited by J. McGhee, 33rd edn (Sweet & Maxwell, 2015), para.5–018, on which the account in this paragraph is based.

56 See, e.g. *Miller v Race* (1758) 1 Burr. 452; *Wookey v Pole* (1820) 4 A. & B. 1.

57 See Sale of Goods Act 1979 ss.21–26.

58 Even a registered legal title to land may be defeated in certain circumstances: see, e.g. Land Registration Act 2002 Schs 4 and 6.

59 See paras 1–040—1–052.

60 The phrase used by, for example, Lord Walker in *Cobbe v Yeoman's Row Management Ltd* [2008] 1 W.L.R. 1752 at [92] (in the context of proprietary estoppel), and Peter Millett QC, sitting as a deputy High Court judge, in *Alec Lobb (Garages) Ltd v Total Oil Great Britain Ltd* [1983] 1 W.L.R. 87, 95 (in the context of unconscionable bargains).

This makes it difficult to super-impose either the proprietary view or the obligational view onto the judge-made rules and principles which derive from a series of discrete equitable interventions. This point is made, for example, in a leading work on equity[61]:

> The difficulty in relating the equitable system of proprietary interests to the very close concern of equity with the conduct of the parties to each suit and with the moulding of remedies to fit the result desired will continue for so long as equity is administered as a distinct body of principles and remedies. What must be avoided is the erection of an inflexible system of characterisation by which development will be distorted.

17–033 As noted by the authors of that work,[62] this concern as to the difficulty of applying concepts of property and obligation to the trust is present in the following extract.

*Livingston v Commissioner of Stamp Duties (Queensland)*

High Court of Australia (1960) 107 C.L.R. 411

17–034 Mrs Coulson was to receive, under the terms of her husband's will, one-third of the residue of his estate. Mrs Coulson died, without leaving a will, before administration of the estate had been completed, and so no specific assets had been transferred to her under the will. The appellant claimed that the respondent taxpayer was liable to pay tax, either as the administrator of Mrs Coulson or as one of her next of kin, as a result of Queensland legislation which applied to "every devolution by law of any beneficial interest in property", where that property was situated in Queensland. Her husband's will was being administered in New South Wales, but some of his assets were situated in Queensland. One of the arguments made by the respondent taxpayer was that Mrs Coulson's right, as the beneficiary of an unadministered estate, did not count as a "beneficial interest" in any specific assets of the deceased husband situated in Queensland, but was rather a right to ensure that the estate was properly administered. A majority of the High Court of Australia (including Kitto J.) found in favour of the respondent taxpayer, and its order was approved on a further appeal to the Privy Council.[63]

17–035 KITTO J.: Mrs Coulson's rights as one of the residuary legatees under Livingston's will may be described in two ways, each of them correct. They may be described by saying that she was entitled to have the administration of the estate completed, and one-third of the residue, when ultimately ascertained, paid or transferred to her. They may also be described by saying that she was entitled at her death to have every individual asset which at that time was comprised in the estate dealt with in a due course of administration. Both descriptions recognise that she was entitled to have a process carried out; but while the one emphasizes the purpose of the process and its ultimate benefit to her, the other directs primary attention to the property presently available for the carrying out of the process. Which description is to be used on a given occasion is a question of appropriateness to the purpose in hand; but it is important always to remember that there is only the one set of rights that is being referred to. I venture to think that for the purpose of solving a concrete legal problem with respect to such a set of rights, more hindrance than help is likely to come from an attempt to classify them according to Austinian[64] terminology as rights in personam or rights in rem. More than forty years ago those distinguished jurists Prof AW Scott and Prof Harlan F Stone (as he then was)[65] learnedly disputed as to whether the rights of a *cestui que trust*[66] were *in rem* or *in personam*. . .but it may be doubted whether much illumination was provided for a case like the present. . .I incline to the view of Mr RW Turner, who wrote in his book *The Equity of Redemption*:[67] 'It is a moot question whether the whole discussion raised by these arbitrary classifications borrowed from Roman law and distorted to fit in with new facts is not a mere academical tourney with no real bearing

---

61 *Meagher, Gummow and Lehane's Equity: Doctrines and Remedies*, edited by J.D. Heydon et al., 5th edn (LexisNexis Australia, 2015), para.4.155.

62 See *Meagher, Gummow and Lehane's Equity: Doctrines and Remedies*, edited by Heydon et al. (2015), para. 4.160.

63 *Commissioner of Stamp Duties (Queensland) v Livingstone* [1965] AC 694 (PC) (extracted at paras 17–041—17–044).

64 [See, e.g. R Campbell (ed) J Austin *Lectures on Jurisprudence or the Philosophy of Positive Law* (Linn & Co, 1874), at [408].]

65 [See the articles cited at para.17–025.]

66 [An old-fashioned term for a beneficiary.].

67 R. Turner, *The Equity of Redemption* (1931) p. 152.

> upon the practice of the law, and, being faulty in hypothesis and unsatisfactory in result, would be better abandoned altogether."

It is important to note that the *Livingston* case did not specifically concern the rights of a beneficiary under a trust: during the period when an estate is being administered, a potential beneficiary under the will does not yet have any entitlement to specific property, as, once the debts of the deceased and the expenses of the administration have been met, there may be no assets left to satisfy the legacies made by the deceased. Kitto J's analysis, however, can also be applied to the debate as to the nature of a trust. It is certainly true that we should not expect specific practical questions, for example as to the application of tax legislation,[68] or as to conflict of laws rules,[69] to be easily solved by asking whether a taxpayer's rights conform to a particular academic concept of a proprietary right. Nonetheless, it may still be of some importance to consider whether the rights of a particular party, such as a beneficiary of a trust, are best seen as *in rem* (the proprietary view) or as *in personam* (the obligational view). **17–036**

One reason for this is that in attempting to answer that question, it is necessary to consider the complex of B's rights under a trust as a whole: this is in itself a valuable process as it would be odd if different practical questions related to B's entitlements were answered in isolation from each other. Another reason is that in seeking to understand how the law of trusts relates to other parts of private law, it is surely helpful to employ one of the principal tools used to structure and distinguish particular elements of private law: the divide between property and obligation. Indeed, as we will now see, the debate as to the nature of B's rights under a trust, which has of course continued unabated by the doubts of Kitto J, has led to some progress in our understanding of the trust. **17–037**

### C. Signs of Progress

When considering the debate as to the nature of the trust, longevity should not be equated with sterility. The debate has borne some dividends, and it can be suggested that there is at least now some consensus as to how B's rights under a trust should *not* be understood. **17–038**

We have seen, for example, that in *Westdeutsche Landesbank Girozentrale v Islington LBC*,[70] the House of Lords rejected the view that S, a party who simply owns property, has both a legal title and a distinct equitable title to that property. In Lord Browne-Wilkinson's words: **17–039**

> A person solely entitled to the full beneficial ownership of money or property, both at law and in equity, does not enjoy an equitable interest in that property. The legal title carries with it all rights. Unless and until there is a separation of legal and equitable estates, there is no separate equitable title.

The rejection of this view can also be seen in the advice provided by Viscount Radcliffe when the dispute between the Queensland tax authorities and Mrs Coulson's administrator reached the Privy Council. It had been argued there that: (i) the executors holding the property of Mrs Coulson's deceased husband had title to that property, but were not permitted to use it for their own benefit, and so did not have equitable title to that property; (ii) the equitable title to the property therefore had to be located somewhere; and therefore (iii) that equitable title was vested in the beneficiaries under the **17–040**

---

68 See too *Baker v Archer-Shee*, discussed at para.17–020.

69 See, e.g. *Webb v Webb* discussed at para.17–028.

70 [1996] A.C. 669 at 705–706.

will, such as Mrs Coulson; and (iv) her equitable title then devolved on her death to her administrator, who was therefore liable to pay tax. As can be seen in the following extract, Viscount Radcliffe, on behalf of a very strong panel,[71] exposed the error in that argument.

*Commissioner of Stamp Duties (Queensland) v Livingston*

Privy Council [1965] A.C. 694 at 712–713

17–041 The facts of the case are set out at 17–034.

17–042 VISCOUNT RADCLIFFE: A second line of criticism has occasionally been expressed to the effect that it is incredible that Lord Herschell should have intended by his proposition to deny to a residuary legatee all beneficial interest in the assets of an unadministered estate. Where, it is asked, is the beneficial interest in those assets [i.e. the assets of the deceased husband] during the period of administration? It is not, ex hypothesi, in the executor: where else can it be but in the residuary legatee? This dilemma is founded on a fallacy, for it assumes mistakenly that for all purposes and at every moment of time the law requires the separate existence of two different kinds of estate or interest in property, the legal and the equitable. There is no need to make this assumption. When the whole right of property is in a person, as it is in an executor, there is no need to distinguish between the legal and equitable interest in that property, any more than there is for the property of a full beneficial owner. What matters is that the court will control the executor in the use of his rights over assets that come to him in that capacity; but it will do it by the enforcement of remedies which do not involve the admission or recognition of equitable rights of property in those assets. Equity in fact calls into existence and protects equitable rights and interests in property only where their recognition has been found to be required in order to give effect to its doctrines.

17–043 Criticisms of this kind arise from the fact that the terminology of our legal system has not produced a sufficient variety of words to represent the various meanings which can be conveyed by the words "interest" or "property". Thus propositions are advanced or rebutted by the employment of terms that have not in themselves a common basis of definition. For instance, there are two passages quoted by the Chief Justice in his dissenting judgment in this case which illustrates the confusion.[72] There is the remark of Jordan CJ in *McCaughey v Commissioner of Stamp Duties*[73]: "The idea that beneficiaries in an unadministered or partially administered estate have no beneficial interest in the items which go to make up the estate is repugnant to elementary and fundamental principles of equity". If by "beneficial interest in the items" it is intended to suggest that such beneficiaries have any property right at all in any of those items, the proposition cannot be accepted as either elementary or fundamental. It is, as has been shown, contrary to the principles of equity. But, on the other hand, if the meaning is only that such beneficiaries are not without legal remedy during the course of the administration to secure that the assets are properly dealt with and the rights that they hope will accrue to them in the future are safeguarded, the proposition is no doubt correct. They can be said, therefore, to have an interest in respect of the assets, or even a beneficial interest in the assets, so long as it is understood in what sense the word "interest" is used in such a context. . ..

17–044 Nor can the solution of the difficulty be advanced by referring to those cases in Equity Courts in which a creditor or a pecuniary or residuary legatee has been allowed to follow and recover assets which have been improperly abstracted from an estate. The basis of such proceedings is that they are taken on behalf of the estate and, if they are successful, they can only result in the lost property being restored to the estate for use in the due course of administration. Thus, while they asset the beneficiary's right of remedy, they assert the estate's right of property, not the property right of creditor or legatee; indeed, the usual situation in which such an action has to be launched is that in which the executor himself, the proper guardian of the estate, is in default, and thus his rights have to be put in motion by some other person on behalf of the estate.

---

[71] Its other members were Lord Reid, Lord Evershed, Lord Pearce and Lord Upjohn.

[72] [The judgment of Dixon C.J. in *Livingston v Chief Commissioner of Stamp Duties* (1962) 107 C.L.R. 411, the decision appealed to the Privy Council.]

[73] (1945) 46 SRNSW 192, 204.

It has therefore been accepted in more recent contributions to the debate,[74] and not only by those favouring the obligational view,[75] that the proprietary view, if it is to be justified, cannot be based on the idea that, as T is not permitted to use the property for her own benefit, B *must* have the beneficial interest in the trust property. Whilst the *Livingston* case concerned not a trust, but rather an unadministered estate, it demonstrates an important point. It is possible for a party (in *Livingston*, the executors of the deceased husband's estate) to hold property subject to particular duties, whilst the parties who benefit from, and can enforce those duties (such as Mrs Coulson) are *not* regarded as having any beneficial ownership of that property. Moreover, this does not mean that those parties who benefit from performance of the duties, such as Mrs Coulson, have a purely personal right against the current executors: as recognised by Viscount Radcliffe, such a party may still be able to "follow and recover" property acquired by a third party from the executors in an unauthorised transaction. A link can be drawn to the analysis of the rights of a beneficiary of a discretionary trust in *Gartside v IRC*[76]: even if B in such a case does not have ownership of any specific property, she still has more than a merely personal right against the current trustees. 17–045

## 4. The Obligational View

### A. Development of the Obligational View

As noted at the start of this chapter,[77] the obligational view states that, in seeking to understand the nature of the trust, it is necessary to focus on the particular nature of T's duties to B, rather than on any direct link between B and the trust property. As the following extract demonstrates, the obligational view of the trust has a distinguished pedigree. This is worth noting as, whilst the proprietary view has been the prevailing one in modern times, Austin Scott, when advocating that view in 1917,[78] was disagreeing with a large number of past commentators. 17–046

#### J. Edelman, "Two Fundamental Questions for the Law of Trusts"

(2013) 129 L.Q.R. 66, 72–74

On one view. . .the interest of the beneficiary under a trust. . .is an interest or encumbrance upon the rights held by the trustee. Although this approach to the interest of a beneficiary may be inconsistent with modern nomenclature which equates common law and equity by common labels of "ownership" or "property right", it is a distinction with a distinguished lineage. Five examples can be given spanning two centuries. 17–047

First, in 1791, in Sanders' classic essay, which became *Sanders on Uses and Trusts*,[79] he explained that at common law the beneficiary under a trust had "neither *jus in re* nor *jus in rem*. The *jus in re* meant an estate, the *jus in rem* a demand."[80] Sanders then proceeded to enumerate the differences between the rights of the beneficiary and the rights of the legal owner.[81] 17–048

---

74 See, e.g. L. Smith, "Unravelling Proprietary Restitution" (2004) 40 Can. Bus. L.J. 317; B. McFarlane & R. Stevens, "The Nature of Equitable Property" (2010) 4 J. Eq. 1.

75 See, e.g. J. Penner, "The (True) Nature of a Beneficiary's Equitable Proprietary Interest under a Trust" (2014) 27 Can. J.L. & Juris 473, 486–489.

76 [1968] A.C. 553.

77 See para.17–006.

78 A.W. Scott, "The Nature of the Rights of the 'Cestui Que Trust'" (1917) 17 Col. L. Rev. 269.

79 F W Sanders, *An Essay on Uses and Trusts* (2nd edn, 1799). The final edition was the 5th by G W Sanders and J Warner in 1844.

80 Sanders, *An Essay on the Nature and Laws of Uses and Trusts* (1791) p. 107.

81 Sanders, *An Essay on the Nature and Laws of Uses and Trusts* (1791) p. 108–111.

17-049 Secondly, in 1882, the definition of a trust in Dr Whitley Stokes' carefully drafted Indian Trusts Act 1882 s. 3, described the trustee's duties and the beneficiary's interest as "annexed" to the trustee's ownership of the trust property:

> "A 'trust' is an obligation annexed to the ownership of property, and arising out of confidence reposed in and accepted by the owner, or declared and accepted by him, for the benefit of another, or of another and the owner."

17-050 Thirdly, in 1899 the influential article by Walter Hart followed the same approach.[82] In this article, the many and varied definitions of a trust were considered. Hart explained that Sir Arthur Underhill's definition of a trust was "undoubtedly the best definition yet given".[83] That definition was:

> "an equitable obligation, either expressly undertaken or constructively imposed by the Court, whereby the obligor (who is called a trustee) is bound to deal with property over which he has control (which is called the trust property), for the benefit of persons (who are called the beneficiaries or *cestuis que trust*) of whom he may or may not himself be one."

The only doctrinal objection raised by Hart was that the enforceability of trusts only in courts of equity was merely a matter of history.[84] The objection was not entirely accurate. Historically there were instances where common law courts expressly took notice of a trust.[85]

17-051 Fourthly, from 1935, the *United States Restatement of the Law of Trusts § 2*, focussed on the nature of the express trust as concerned with the duties of the trustee in relation to the rights held by the trustee: "subjecting the person by whom the property is held to equitable duties to deal with the property for the benefit of another person."[86]

17-052 Fifthly, in the first edition of the leading Australian text on trusts in 1958,[87] Jacobs focussed upon the trustee's duties in relation to the trust rights he or she holds, describing the trust as existing when the:

> "holder of a legal or equitable interest in certain property is bound by an equitable obligation to hold his interest in that property not for his own exclusive benefit but for the benefit. . .of another person or persons. . .."

However, years later, as a Justice of the High Court of Australia, Jacobs J. saw "no difficulty" in describing a trust as involving a beneficiary as "the beneficial owner of the estate of which the vendor is the legal owner".[88]

17-053 Each of these definitions focussed attention on the beneficiary's power or right as one which relates to the rights of the trustee or, conversely, the particular liability or obligation of the trustee in relation to the trust rights which are held. Perhaps the best, and clearest, description of this conception of the trust which emphasises that the beneficiary's rights or powers are not directly in relation to the trust assets was given by F W Maitland, in his lectures at Cambridge, first published in 1910:[89]

> "Equity did not say that the cestui que trust was the owner of the land, it said that the trustee was the owner of the land, but added that he was bound to hold the land for the benefit of the cestui que trust. There was no conflict here. Had there been a conflict here the. . .Judicature Act. . .would have abolished the whole law of trusts. Common law says that A is the owner, equity says that B is the owner, but equity is to prevail, therefore B is the owner and A has no right or duty of any sort or kind in or about the land. Of course the Judicature Act has not acted in this way; it has left the law of trusts

---

82 W Hart, "What is a Trust?" (1899) 15 LQR 294.
83 W Hart, "What is a Trust?" (1899) 15 LQR 294 at 298.
84 W Hart, "What is a Trust?" (1899) 15 LQR 294 at 298.
85 *Winch v Keeley* (1787) 1 Term Rep 619, 623; *Jonathan Scott v Robert Surman Salem Oewn* (1742) Willes 400, 402; *Boddington v Castelli* (1853) 1 El & Bl 879; discussion in *Duckworth v Water Corporation* [2012] WASC 30 at [66]-[70].
86 *American Law Institute, Restatement of the Law of Trusts* (1935). The reporter was Austin Scott. The definition was reproduced in the Second Restatement in 1957, and the Third Restatement in 2003, although "equitable duties" is replaced by "duties".
87 K Jacobs, *The Law of Trusts in New South Wales* (1958) p. 7.
88 *Chang v Registrar of Titles* (1976) 137 CLR 177, 190.
89 F Maitland, *Equity: also The Forms of Action at Common Law* (1910) pp.17–18.

just where it stood, because it found no conflict, no variance even, between the rules of the common law and the rules of equity."

This approach to understanding a beneficiary's interest as requiring as a necessary condition a particular encumbrance upon the rights that the trustee holds, rather than being an interest in the trust assets themselves, has gained significant academic support in recent years.[90] One commentator, Professor McFarlane, has suggested that the rights of the beneficiary should be described as "persistent rights"[91] to differentiate them very clearly from common law property rights and to elucidate that the rights of the beneficiary are not merely personal rights. As McFarlane has explained, the special nature of a beneficiary's rights is that they are not merely personal rights, but nor are they rights to the assets itself. The nature of the beneficiary's powers and rights, he argues, is that they are in relation to the trustee's rights, whatever the trustee's rights might be. This is why the beneficiary's rights under a trust are of the same nature whether the trust asset is a right to an intangible (a debt, shares) or a right to a tangible thing (land, chattels). It is also why, as Hart observed, the best descriptions of a beneficiary's rights have focussed on those rights being "annexed" to the trust property, or upon the nature of the obligation of the trustee to deal with the *trustee's* rights to the trust property.[92] **17–054**

The danger in using the label "proprietary" to describe a beneficiary's rights under a trust may be manifest unless lawyers recognise that the word "property" is like the word "love". It is often used in a number of different senses. It is essential not to forget that when we speak of "proprietary right" or "ownership" in equity we are using those terms in a very different sense from the sense in which they are used at common law. **17–055**

## B. The "New" Obligational View

Some of the earlier obligational accounts of the trust seem to have regarded B's rights as essentially only personal rights against T.[93] The difficulty with such views, of course, lies in explaining any of the three key features of B's rights set out above[94]: in particular, the ability of B to make a claim against C, a third party acquiring the trust property in an unauthorised disposition by T. More recent proponents of the obligational view have therefore differentiated the rights of B from simply personal rights, such as the right to a debt, by focussing on the requirement that, for a trust to exist, T's duty to B must relate to the trust property: that is, to the specific rights held by T on trust for B. This emphasis has formed the basis of what has been called the "new obligational" view,[95] according to which the rights of B are best seen *neither* as proprietary rights in the trust property nor as personal rights against T. **17–056**

---

90 A Burrows, *The Law of Restitution* (3rd edn, 2010); R Chambers, "Constructive Trusts in Canada" (1999) Alberta Law Rev 173; L Smith, "Unravelling Proprietary Restitution" [2004] Canadian Business Law Journal 317; B McFarlane & R Stevens, "The Nature of Equitable Property" (2010) 4 J Eq 1.

91 B McFarlane, *The Structure of Property Law* (2008) at p. 364.

92 W Hart, "What is a Trust?" (1899) 15 LQR 294 at 302.

93 See, e.g. F.W. Maitland, *Lectures on Equity* (1929), Chs 9–11; H. Stone, "The Nature of the Rights of the 'Cestui Que Trust'" (1917) 17 Col. L. Rev. 467, esp. 477–480.

94 See para.17–004.

95 The term used (in an article rejecting that view) by J.Penner, "The (True) Nature of a Beneficiary's Equitable Proprietary Interest under a Trust" (2014) 27 Can. J.L. & Juris 473.

## B. McFarlane & R. Stevens, "The Nature of Equitable Property"

(2010) 4 J. Eq. 1, 3–6

### THE NEW ANALYSIS

#### A. Equitable property rights and rights against a thing

17–057 The chief characteristic of a property right in relation to a thing is that it allows B to exclude others from making use of that thing. It has been argued that equitable property rights possess this characteristic.[96] The most obvious problem with that argument is that B may have an equitable property right in relation to an intangible asset. For example, A can hold a personal right against Z, such as a bank account, on trust for B. In such a case, there is no independent physical thing against which B has a right. After all, there is no thing against which A has a right: A merely has a right to receive payment from Z. If I have title to land or a car I can exclude others from making use of it, it is not meaningful to speak of excluding another from making use of a debt owed to me.

17–058 One possible reason for the view that an equitable property involves the creation of a right to a thing is that the common law permits several people to hold rights in relation to a single thing at the same time. In relation to land, for example, a lessee, his landlord, and a neighbour with an easement over the property all have rights in relation to the land that are *prima facie* exigible against all others. In relation to goods, relativity of title means that many persons may have a right in relation to the thing exigible against all others save such person or persons with a better title to the thing. However, the right to an intangible asset, such as a bank account, is incapable of division in this way. The one and only right is the contractual right against the bank, and this is vested in the person who has contracted with the bank by opening the account. The possibility of an equitable property right in relation to a bank account therefore demonstrates that equitable property rights cannot be understood as depending on the divisibility of an initial common law property right.

17–059 Indeed, even where an equitable property right relates to a physical thing, it does not give its holder a right to that thing. For example, let us say A has title to a car and declares that he holds his right to the car on trust for B. If X then steals that car, or carelessly damages it, B has no direct claim against X. X is not liable to B for conversion[97] or for negligently causing damage.[98] This is not simply a matter of B's equitable right being invisible to the common law court: B has no claim, either at law or in equity, against X. B therefore does not have a right against the car: he does not have a right to exclude *all* non-beneficiaries from the enjoyment of the trust assets.[99]

17–060 As A has title to the car, X's interference with that thing means that A can bring a claim against X. As A holds his title on trust for B, A is under a duty to use that right, and its products, for B's benefit. So, if A refuses to bring a claim against X, B can apply to court to force A to do so. B can use an expedited procedure to combine such an application with A's claim against X.[100] However, that procedural concession does not hide the key fact that two separate claims must be made: B has no direct claim against X as X has infringed no right of B.[101] It has been suggested that B can be seen as having an "indirect" right *in rem*:[102] that is, B has a right prima facie binding on anyone interfering with the car, but that right is indirect as it

---

96 See for example R Nolan, 'Equitable Property' (2006) 122 LQR 232 at 233.

97 See, e.g. *MCC Proceeds v Shearson Lehmann* [1998] 4 All ER 675; A Tettenborn, 'Trust Property and Conversion: An Equitable Confusion' [1996] CLJ 36. If B happens to have possession of the car at the time of X's intervention, he will be able to bring a claim in conversion against X: see *Healey v Healey* [1915] 1 KB 938. That claim, however, is based on the property right B acquires as a result of his possession (see, e.g. *Armory v Delamirie* (1722) 5 Strar 505), not on his position as beneficiary.

98 See, e.g. *Leigh and Sillivan Ltd v Aliakmon Shipping Co Ltd (The Aliakmon)* [1986] AC 785 at 812 *per* Lord Brandon.

99 See too *The Lord Compton's Case* (1587) 3 Leo 197: where feoffees to uses are disseised, and then release to the disseisor, the cestui que use has no claim against the disseisor, even if the disseisor has notice of the use.

100 That expedited procedure is commonly referred to as the *Vandepitte* procedure (see e.g. *Barbados Trust Company Ltd v Bank of Zambia* [2007] EWCA Civ 148 at [30] and [35] *per* Waller LJ) and is named for the case: *Vandepitte v Preferred Accident Insurance Corporation of New York* [1933] AC 70.

101 See *Barbados Trust Company Ltd v Bank of Zambia* [2007] EWCA Civ 148 *per* Waller LJ.

102 See J Penner, '*The Structure of Property Law (Book Review)*' [2009] RLR 250 at 254.

must be asserted through A. That suggestion must be rejected, as any "indirect" claim depends not on X's interference with the car itself, but rather on X's interference with A's right. For example, if A consents to X's interference with the car then X's interference, by itself, gives B no direct or indirect claim against X.[103]

### B. Equitable property rights and rights against a person

Attempts have been made to argue that an equitable property right, such as a right under a trust, is no more than a personal right.[104] These attempts generally start from the insight that an equitable property right cannot plausibly be seen as a right against a thing.[105] The acceptance of the traditional, exhaustive dichotomy between rights against a thing and rights against a person then leads to the conclusion that an equitable property right must be in the latter category. However, such attempts fail to account for the key conceptual and practical difference between an equitable property right and a personal right. **17–061**

This difference can be seen by returning to the position where A has title to a car and declares that he holds his right to the car on trust for B. If A then makes a gift of the car to C, B will be able to bring a claim directly against C. Attempts have been made to argue that this is consistent with B's right under the trust being no more than a personal right against A. These attempts depend on showing that B's claim against C is based on a *new* direct right that B acquires against C because of C's unconscientious conduct in accepting the gift from A.[106] **17–062**

However, B can bring a claim directly against C even if C, when acquiring his right from A, had no actual knowledge or constructive notice of the trust. It therefore seems very difficult to argue that B's ability to bring a direct claim against C rests on B's having acquired a new right against C. Rather, it is B's *pre-existing* right under the trust that binds C. The ability of an equitable property right to bind a third party such as C also explains a key feature of such rights: their protection if A becomes bankrupt. On that event, A's rights pass to his trustee in bankruptcy. Like C in our example, that trustee in bankruptcy will be bound by any pre-existing equitable property right of B. **17–063**

### C. Equitable property rights and rights against a right

The key to understanding equitable property rights lies in explaining why such a right is capable of binding a third party, such as C in the example above, who acquires a right from A; yet is not capable of binding a third party, such as X in the prior example, who steals or carelessly damages a thing to which B's right relates. The crucial difference between the position of C and of X is that the former, unlike the latter, has acquired a right that *derives from the right which A holds on trust for B*. If A gives his car to C, or C acquires the car in his capacity as A's trustee in bankruptcy, C acquires A's right to the car. As that right was held by A on trust for B, B's right is prima facie binding on C. It is only prima facie binding, as C may have a defence to B's right: for example, C may be able to show that he is a bona fide purchaser i.e. that he acquired A's right for value and had no actual knowledge or constructive notice of B's right. However, in our example, C cannot rely on that defence as he has not acquired A's right for value. In contrast, where X steals or carelessly damages A's car, X does not acquire a right that depends on A's ownership of the car. If X takes possession of the car he will acquire a right against the car, but that right does not derive from A: it is original, coming from X's own conduct in taking possession. As a result, B cannot assert his right under the trust against X.[107] **17–064**

---

103 It will be possible for B to assert a right directly against X if it can be shown that X has dishonestly assisted in a breach of trust by A. The right that B has that others do not dishonestly assist A's breach of trust is, observably, not the same right that B has against A and is analogous to the right that a promisee has against third parties to a contract, see further B McFarlane, 'Equity, Obligations and Third Parties' [2008] Sing J LS 308.

104 See, e.g. F Maitland *Lectures on Equity* (1929) chs. 9–11; H Stone, 'The Nature of the Rights of the Cestui Que Trust' (1917) 17 Col L Rev 467.

105 For example Stone, *ibid* at 470; L Smith, 'Unravelling Proprietary Restitution' [2004] Canadian Business Law Journal 317.

106 See e.g. F Maitland, *Lectures on Equity* (1929), ch.9 at pp.117–121; Stone, *ibid* at 474ff. Smith, *ibid* suggests that, originally at least, B's new right against C was based on C's unjust enrichment at B's expense.

107 The distinction between the positions of C, a party acquiring a right that depends on A's right, and of X, a party who does not, also explains the effect on B of a forfeiture or escheat of an estate held by A on trust for B. Where A's estate is forfeited, A's right is acquired by the superior landlord who is *prima facie* bound by B's right against A's estate: see Stone 'The Nature of the Rights of the Cestui Que Trust' (1917) 17 Col L Rev 467 at 481. When A's estate is subject to an escheat, A's right is instead lost and B cannot assert his right against the superior lord, who can prevent B from enjoying the land without relying on any right acquired from A: see Maitland, *Lectures on Equity* (1929), lecture 9 at p.120.

17–065 This analysis explains why it is vital to talk of A holding a *right* on trust for B (eg A's ownership of a car) rather than of A holding a *thing* on trust for B (eg the car itself).[108] It also explains why an equitable property right can exist in relation to a personal right.[109] If A has a personal right against Z, such as a bank account, B can have a right against A's right against Z. So, if C acquires A's personal right, for example because A makes a statutory assignment of the right to C, or because C is A's trustee in bankruptcy, B's right against A's right will be prima facie binding on C.

17–066 The analysis in the extract above can be related to the meaning of "property" adopted in this chapter, which follows that adopted by Richard Nolan for the purpose of his analysis in the extract set out above.[110] On that definition, the proprietary view regards B as having a right to exclude others from the trust assets; if B has no such general right of exclusion, B's right cannot be regarded as truly proprietary. This explains why McFarlane and Stevens consider the case where the trust property consists of a physical thing and a stranger, X, then interferes with that thing: if B has a right to exclude others, it might be expected that, in such a case, it would be possible for B to bring a claim directly against X. As noted by McFarlane and Stevens, the orthodox position in such a case, however, is that B has no such direct claim,[111] but must rather rely on, or compel, T to sue X, with any damages acquired by T then being held on trust for B.

17–067 The indirectness of B's protection against X is particularly important if T permits X to interfere physically with the trust property: in such a case, it seems that B's only claim is a personal claim against T. Yet one would think that if B's right were truly proprietary, B would necessarily have a claim against a party who has physically interfered, without B's authority, in the trust property. This question is not of purely academic interest: indeed, it was central to a Court of Appeal decision, *Shell UK Ltd v Total UK Ltd*,[112] made after publication of McFarlane and Stevens' article. As we will see later in this chapter,[113] however, that decision does not provide any decisive support either for or against the new obligational view of the trust; indeed, its reasoning has been widely criticised, by commentators who adopt a proprietary view as well as by those who subscribe to the obligational view.

17–068 The model proposed by McFarlane and Stevens is consistent with the differences which have been explained already,[114] between the rights of B under a trust and the rights of O, an outright owner of property. In particular, it explains why it is possible for B to have an "equitable property right" in relation to a purely personal right of T, such as a bank account. It is, therefore, consistent with the fact that a very broad range of rights (including even a non-assignable right held by T against X) are capable of forming the subject-matter of a trust.[115] It also explains why B has no claim against C where C acquired trust property in an unauthorised disposition from T as an innocent donee and later disposed of the trust property herself, so that she no longer has either that property or its traceable proceeds.[116] Again, in such a case, C can be seen to have interfered with the trust property, and has perhaps been enriched as a result, yet B has no claim. On the obligational view of the trust, this can be explained: first, any enrichment of C as a result of acquiring the trust property was at the expense of T, who had ownership of that property, not of B, who had no true proprietary right in that property; secondly, there was no

108 See W Swadling in A Burrows (ed), *English Private Law* (2nd edn, 2007) at 4.140–4.153.
109 See, e.g. R Chambers, *An Introduction to Property Law in Australia* (2nd edn, 2008) at [13–90].
110 See paras 17–016–17–017.
111 In addition to the cases cited in the extract above (see nn.97–99), see, e.g. Restatement (Third) of Trusts §§ 107–108 (2003) (for the position in the US).
112 [2011] Q.B. 186.
113 See paras 17–106—17–111.
114 See para.17–007.
115 See para.1–057.
116 If C had acquired such knowledge, a claim in knowing receipt could be made against her: see paras 11–017ff.

point in time when C can be said to have been under a duty to B in relation to the trust property, as no such duty can be imposed on C when C is unaware of the initial trust in B's favour and thus innocent.

The "right against a right" model is also consistent with a particular feature of equity that we encountered in Chapter 1. Rules and principles relating to trusts can be seen as depending on equity's role as a supplemental to the common law. Whilst the common law may establish the allocation of property rights or personal rights by, for example, deciding if T is an owner of a car, or if T has a contractual right against X, equity can then come in and impose a duty on T in relation to such rights, such as a duty to use that right for the benefit of B. **17–069**

As argued by McFarlane and Stevens later in their article,[117] the obligational model provides a relatively simple means of explaining the incidence of constructive and resulting trusts. On the proprietary view, such trusts may be somewhat difficult to explain[118]: as no-one has exercised a power to give B a proprietary right, why should the courts intervene to recognise a right that will interfere with the defendant's ownership of the property? On the obligational view, however, the key feature of the trust is that T holds a right subject to a duty to B to use that right for the benefit of B, and not to use it for T's own benefit (unless and to the extent that T is also a beneficiary of the trust). This means that, if the *content* of T's duty matches that description, a trust exists, irrespective of the grounds on which that duty arose.[119] So in a case such as *Attorney General for Hong Kong v Reid*,[120] for example, the crucial question is simply as to whether the agent who receives a bribe is under an immediate duty to the principal to give the bribe *itself* to the principal, or is instead under a duty to pay the *value* of the bribe to the principal. In the former case, on the obligational view, a trust necessarily arises: there is then no further question of policy as to whether the principal's right should count as proprietary. **17–070**

The challenge for any obligational view of the trust, of course, is to explain the three key features of the trust identified at the start of this chapter,[121] as it is those features which most commonly lead judges and commentators to describe B's rights as proprietary. The model proposed by McFarlane and Stevens builds on an insight of Robert Chambers[122]: the subject matter of a trust, strictly speaking, is always a right or rights held by T. So, even though we would naturally speak of a trust of land, for example, in such a case it is in fact a specific estate in land (e.g. a legal freehold) that is held by T on trust for B. On the obligational model of the trust, it is the nature of T's duty to B, as a duty relating to a specific right or rights of T, that justifies B's protection in insolvency; it also justifies B's ability to make a claim against C where T makes an unauthorised disposition of trust property to C. **17–071**

Of course, if one's definition of property is such that *any* right protected in insolvency or capable of binding certain third parties counts as proprietary, then B's right under a trust is necessarily a property right.[123] Yet such a right nonetheless varies in significant ways from the right of O, an absolute owner of physical property, and the new obligational view of the trust attempts to explain those differences. **17–072**

---

117 B. McFarlane & R. Stevens, "The Nature of Equitable Property" (2010) 4 J. Eq. 1, 15–22.

118 As noted at para.1–052.

119 See too B. McFarlane, "The Centrality of Constructive and Resulting Trusts" in C. Mitchell (ed.), *Constructive and Resulting Trusts* (Hart Publishing, 2010).

120 [1994] 1 A.C. 324; approved in *FHR European Ventures LLP v Cedar Capital Partners LLC* [2015] A.C. 250. See paras 13–126ff.

121 See para.17–004.

122 First apparent in R. Chambers, *An Introduction to Property Law in Australia* (Law Book Co, 2001), p.115; see now R. Chambers, *An Introduction to Property Law in Australia*, 3rd edn (Thomson Reuters Australia, 2013), para.13.90. See para.1–058.

123 See para.17–004.

## C. Objections to the "New" Obligational View

**17-073** There has of course been criticism of both the general obligational view of the trust and of the new obligational view. It is impossible to cover all the points made in this debate,[124] but we will focus here on some of the most prominent.

### i. The *Saunders v Vautier* Power

**17-074** The *Saunders v Vautier* principle,[125] discussed in detail in Chapter 7,[126] allows all of the beneficiaries of a trust, acting together, to call for the trust property to be transferred to them by T: if that power is exercised by the beneficiaries, they then have the trust property itself, and the trust comes to an end.[127] As in *Saunders v Vautier* itself, the exercise of this power can trump an outstanding duty of T, such as a duty not to pay out capital to a beneficiary with a current entitlement. It might therefore seem that this principle, which allows B direct access to the trust property itself, is consistent only with a proprietary view of the trust.

**17-075** It is, however, possible to recognise a collective power in all the beneficiaries of a trust to acquire the trust property in the future without admitting that each specific beneficiary has a current, individual, proprietary right. Certainly, if we are regarding the right to exclude others as the key indicator of a property right, the potential to acquire the trust property in the future, after a transfer by T, does not by itself make B's right proprietary.[128] As noted, for example, by the authors of a leading Australian work[129] "a power to become the owner of trust assets in future is different from being the owner, legal or equitable, of the trust assets at present." Moreover, the *Saunders v Vautier* principle applies to all trusts, but, if it is to be the test of proprietary status, it would seem strange to regard the right of, for example, an object of a discretionary trust as equivalent to that of a solely entitled beneficiary under a fixed trust.

### ii. A "Trust Shall Not Fail for Want of a Trustee"

**17-076** In Chapter 1,[130] we noted that trusteeship can be regarded as an office, and that the position of T is thus different from that of a contracting party such as, for example, D, a debtor who simply owes a creditor, C, £100. For example, if T is not properly performing her duties as trustee, a court can remove and replace her; a court cannot do the same to D. We also noted in Chapter 1[131] that the notion of an office also lies behind the maxim, discussed in Chapter 2,[132] that "a trust shall not fail for want

---

124 For further grounds of disagreement with the obligational view, see, e.g. S. Gardner, "'Persistent Rights' Appraised" in N. Hopkins (ed) *Modern Studies in Property Law: Vol.7* (Hart Publishing, 2013).

125 (1841) 4 Beav. 115.

126 See paras 7-004—7-029. See too paras 5-031—5-032.

127 As noted at para.1-037, the *Saunders v Vautier* power is not recognised in all legal systems that have a concept of a trust, and so the argument based on that power, whilst applicable to the analysis of the trust in English law, would not be determinative of the nature of the trust in, for example, jurisdictions of the US. See further P. Matthews, "The Comparative Importance of the Rule in *Saunders v Vautier*" (2006) 122 L.Q.R. 266 (extracted at paras 7-015—7-029).

128 Indeed, T. Cutts, "The Nature of 'Equitable Property': A Functional Analysis" (2012) 6 J. Eq. 44, 45 uses the *Saunders v Vautier* power as the basis of an obligational account of the trust, under which "the settlor confers upon the beneficiary an unconditional power to impose on the trustee a duty to transfer to the former the rights to the trust res."

129 *Meagher, Gummow and Lehane's Equity: Doctrines and Remedies*, edited by J.D. Heydon et al, 5th edn (LexisNexis, 2015), para.4.105.

130 See paras 1-086—1-090.

131 See para.1-086.

132 See para.2-004.

of a trustee". That maxim might suggest that the relationship between T and B, and the obligations imposed on T, are not central to a trust; rather, it is the existence of B's proprietary right, held of any particular trustee, that motivates the courts' protection of B.[133]

The notion of trusteeship as an office, and the consequences which flow from it, are, as identified in Chapter 1, important parts of the operation of a trust. They are not, however, inconsistent with an obligational view of the trust.[134] On that view, indeed, the obligation owed by T is a *special* one, which differs in its nature and effects from a purely contractual duty such as a duty to pay a debt: the notion of trusteeship as an office can help to explain more precisely the special nature of T's duty. The key point, made in the following extract, is that the trust involves a form of *depersonalised* duty. **17–077**

### B. McFarlane "The Trust and its Civilian Analogues"

in L. Smith (ed.), The Worlds of the Trust (Cambridge University Press, 2013), pp.522–523

[Some civilian commentators] have objected to the notion that a right can be separated from its holder: on this view, a right against a right cannot be distinguished from a right against a person. The concept of a persistent right, as developed by equity, precisely allows this separation. This can be seen not only in. . .the ability of the beneficiary to assert his right against particular strangers to the initial trust relationship. . .but also in the phenomenon. . .of the trust as office. This latter phenomenon allows, for example, for the replacement of a trustee, and so for a trust to continue despite the death or removal of an initial trustee. This depersonalisation of the trust obligation is permitted by the trust's focus on the duties of a trustee *in his capacity as* holder of a particular right. After all, the defining feature of a trustee is that he both holds a right and has a duty not to use that right for his own benefit. The personality, or creditworthiness, of the trustee is not critical to the performance of that core duty: its negative nature thus permits its extension to strangers to the trust, provided that such a stranger also holds the right initially held on trust, or a product of that right. This may finally account for the fact that the right of a beneficiary occupies an awkward position between property and obligation. The trust requires a relationship between beneficiary and trustee—unlike the ancient use, the trust does not permit a beneficiary to have a direct, unmediated relationship with an asset. Yet the *particular identity* of the trustee is not critical to the relationship, as the relationship is defined by the holding of a right subject to a negative duty. On the view that a beneficiary of a trust has a right against a right (the "persistent rights" theory), the trustee is necessary; but only because the object of a trust must be a right, and all rights must be held by someone. **17–078**

The notion of trusteeship as an office may also be apparent in the power of a court to supervise the administration of a trust. The obligational view also gains some support from the approach of the Privy Council in *Schmidt v Rosewood Trust Ltd*,[135] when dealing with requests, made by an object of a power held by trustees, for disclosure by the trustees of information relating to the trust. It was stated that, even in a case where a court orders disclosure of trust documents to a beneficiary of a fixed trust, that decision is based not on recognising any proprietary right of B to such documents, but is rather made as an exercise of the court's general jurisdiction "to supervise (and where appropriate intervene in) the administration of trusts".[136] On this view, at least some of the protection given to B under a trust can be seen as based not on any proprietary entitlement of B, but rather on the particular means of enforcement and protection given to the duty owed by T to B; a duty which, owing to its content, is a special type of duty. **17–079**

133 See, e.g. P.S. Davies & G. Virgo (eds) *Equity & Trusts: Text, Cases and Materials* (Oxford University Press, 2013), p.60.

134 The discussion here in some ways demonstrates the point made at para.17–026 that any single aspect of a trust's operation is unlikely to be decisive when assessing the obligational and proprietary views.

135 [2003] 2 A.C. 709. See paras 9–089—9–093.

136 [2003] 2 A.C. 709 at [66] (extracted at para.9–092).

### iii. James Penner's Analysis

17-080 A broader challenge to the new obligational view of the trust, not limited to any specific point as to the operation of a trust, has been made by James Penner.

#### J. Penner, "The (True) Nature of a Beneficiary's Equitable Proprietary Interest under a Trust"

(2014) 27 Can J. L. & Juris. 473 at 473–476, 487, 495

17-081 The purpose of this paper is to present and defend what I see as the conceptual sense of the "orthodox" understanding of the trust under which the trust beneficiaries are regarded as the "beneficial owners" of the property held on trust for them. As I understand it, the "right against a right" view is aimed primarily at this characterisation of the trust beneficiary's interest. . ..Again, as I understand it, the source of the problem posed by "beneficial ownership" for Smith,[137] McFarlane and Stevens lies in its suggestion that the beneficiary under a trust has a direct right to the trust assets, obscuring the interposition of the trustee. In other words, what Smith, McFarlane and Stevens wish to claim is that any sort of "derivative" interest in an asset such as the beneficiary's interest in a trust asset, derivative because the beneficiary realises his interest in the trust assets via his claims against the title-holder of that asset (the trustee) cannot amount to any form of "ownership" in any real sense. I believe this claim to be false, and that is what I attempt to show here. Moreover, I aim to show that the notion of "beneficial ownership", once properly explained, is actually essential for understanding the nature of the trust and the rules of trust law. . .

17-082 . . . Smith, McFarlane and Stevens have identified the wrong "right" of the trustee to, in, or against which the trust beneficiary has a right. It is not the right of the trustee to exclude third parties from the trust assets, but rather the trustee's *powers of title*, for example the power to realise the value of the assets through contractual exchanges but primarily, of course, the power to transfer the trust assets to the beneficiary when required under the terms of the trust.[138] If that is right, then we shall see that the beneficiary's interest in the trust assets can perfectly reasonably be regarded as beneficial ownership, and indeed, that it would be wrong to characterise the beneficiary's interest as anything else. . ..

17-083 The "truth" if I may so immodestly put it, is that ownership never really was, and certainly is not now, about rights to possession. We have always had the right to immediate, exclusive possession of our bodies, but we do not own them. What ownership is about is title, which comprises the powers to transfer, confer rights in, or otherwise dispose of (within the confines of the *numerus clausus*) the right to possess tangibles or the right (through legal action or equitable suit) to realise the value of intangibles. And since beneficiaries have the right that the trustee exercise his powers of title not for his own benefit but only according to the terms of the trust, it not only makes perfect sense to say that the beneficiaries are the beneficial owners of the title to trust assets, it is essential. Otherwise, as I will go on to show, the beneficiaries' interest is misconceived as a mere "encumbrance" on the trustee's title. . .

17-084 . . . I would argue that one of the advantages of my account, focussing as it does on the interest that a beneficiary has *in the powers of title* held by the trustee, not in any possessory interest in the trust assets themselves, clarifies the case of legatees, discretionary objects and so on, and that the usage "beneficial interest" has an essential role to play here. Because the objects of a trust, as I have argued, never have any possessory interests in the trust assets just in virtue of their being objects of a trust (though under the terms of a trust they may, as explained above, have the right to make the trustee put them in possession of tangible trust assets), it is not essential to a trust, or to the conception of a beneficial interest under a trust, that any object has any immediate, vested interests in the trust assets. As explained above, all beneficial interests under trusts (excepting, again, the case where the terms of the trust require the objects to be

---

137 [The reference here is to L Smith, "Trusts and Patrimony" (2008–9) 28 E.T. & P.J. 332.

138 Cf Tatiana Cutts, "The Nature of 'Equitable Property': A Functional Analysis", (2012) 6 *Journal of Equity* 44, 57 et seq, who argues that a beneficiary's interest under a trust consists of a power to require the trustee to exercise his powers of title to transfer the trust asset to the beneficiary; by contrast, the proposal here is that the beneficiary's interest is a right, correlative with the trustee's duty to exercise his powers of title to carry out the administrative and dispositive provisions of the trust.

> put in possession of tangible trust assets), are essentially future interests in the sense that they require the trustee to exercise his power of transfer to transfer the legal title to trust assets to the objects (title to money representing income, or the title to the trust assets themselves in the case of a capital distribution, either on the dissolution of the trust or by way of power of appointment). There is no problem of finding a "beneficial interest" here that correlates with the trustee's absence of a beneficial interest, so long as it is understood that there can be interests which *exhaust* the beneficial interest in the trust assets, though such interests are future or contingent interests. The essential point to notice here is that the trustee can hold trust assets not to his own benefit yet at the same time so that the benefit will enure only to the benefit of others on a future, contingent basis. Those future and contingent interests absorb all the benefit the assets have. Thus it is a mistake to confine the notion of beneficial interest to *presently* vested or indefeasible interests; indeed, not so confining the notion is *entailed* by understanding the beneficiary's interest as an interest in the trustee's powers of title, for an interest in the exercise of a power is, in the requisite sense, always a future interest.

Penner also argues that B should be regarded as having a beneficial interest because[139]: **17–085**

> Equity regards a beneficial owner of property as having the power to create a trust. Only someone with a beneficial interest in property can do that—it is not equivalent to having legal title, which is why a beneficiary under a trust can create a sub-trust but why a trustee of a trust, with the legal title but no beneficial interest, has no power to declare any trust whatsoever of the trust assets he legally owns.

Four points can be made in response to Penner's analysis. First, whilst it purports to be a rejection of the new obligational view, under which B is seen as having a right against T's rights, it could just as well be seen as a development of that view. This is because it clarifies the nature of those rights which T holds subject to a duty to B and which T must use only according to the terms of the trust. It is perfectly consistent with, and indeed is a valuable contribution to, the model proposed by McFarlane and Stevens[140] to say that T's duty to B attaches not only to any rights T may have against strangers interfering with the trust property, but also to any powers of title which T has by virtue of holding the trust property. **17–086**

Secondly, Penner regards his analysis as an improvement as it directs attention away from the issue, examined by McFarlane and Stevens,[141] of the rights that B may have if a stranger, X, physically interferes with trust property. He notes, correctly, that[142]: **17–087**

> modern wealth management trusts. . .hold intangibles such as shares, bonds, and bank balances, that is, financial instruments which are rights *in personam* and which, accordingly can give the trustee no rights to possession at all since they cannot be physically possessed.

Yet as Edelman has noted, the fact that the subject-matter of a trust may be a purely personal right provides[143]:

> perhaps the greatest conceptual obstacle for the conception of a beneficiary as an owner of the trust asset. If a trustee (T) holds a debt on trust for a beneficiary (B) what does it mean to say that B has a property right in the debt itself?. . .a third party who "interferes" with a debt which is held on trust will not be liable to the

---

139 J. Penner, "The (True) Nature of a Beneficiary's Equitable Proprietary Interest under a Trust" (2014) 27 Can. J.L. & Juris 473, 493.

140 B. McFarlane & R. Stevens, "The Nature of Equitable Property" (2010) 4 J. Eq. 1 (extracted in part at paras 17–057—17–065).

141 McFarlane & Stevens, "The Nature of Equitable Property" (2010) 4 J. Eq. 1, 3–4 (extracted at paras 17–057—17–060).

142 J. Penner, "The (True) Nature of a Beneficiary's Equitable Proprietary Interest under a Trust" (2014) 27 Can. J.L. & Juris 473, 482–483.

143 J. Edelman, "Two Fundamental Questions for the Law of Trusts" (2013) 129 L.Q.R. 66, 71.

beneficiary unless the third party's involvement amount to knowing assistance in a breach of trust nor liable to the trustee unless the third party intentionally induces a breach of contract.

**17-088** Contrary to Penner's suggestion, the reason why a proponent of the obligational view might consider a case in which X physically interferes with trust property is not because of any assumption that the "paradigm case of a trust is one in which the trustee holds the legal title to tangible assets and retains the assets for the trustee's own possession."[144] It is rather because of a desire to test the proprietary view in a context where it might seem to be most apt: where the terms of the trust give B an absolute entitlement to physical property. Such a case, albeit rare, also provides a convenient test for proprietary status, given the working definition of property adopted in this context by at least one supporter of a proprietary view of the trust.[145] On that view, the key feature of a proprietary right is that it confers a right of exclusion on B, so that others are under a strict general duty not to interfere with the trust property. Yet, in such a case, the orthodox view, accepted by Penner,[146] is that B has no direct claim against X if X physically interferes with the trust property.

**17-089** Thirdly, it seems clear that Penner is relying on a meaning of "beneficial interest" or "equitable ownership" which is broader than the test for proprietary status adopted here, and so does not necessarily involve B's having a direct, general right to exclude others from the trust property. To that extent, then, there is no inconsistency between Penner's view and the new obligational view it opposes. It may well be that Penner's definition focusses instead on B's having a right to the benefit of T's powers of title in the trust property. The question, though, is as to the sense in which such a right to benefit is proprietary. The usual test would be to consider whether B has an abstract right to the benefit, good not only against T but also, prima facie at least, against the rest of the world. It seems that B does not: after all, B has no claim against an innocent donee who benefits from the receipt of trust property but who disposes of that property and its proceeds before learning of the trust in B's favour.[147]

**17-090** Finally, Penner also suggests that a key feature of beneficial ownership is the "power to create a trust".[148] It is difficult to see, however, why the location of a power to set up a particular type of right should be decisive when considering the nature of such a right. It is also the case that T may be given a power under a trust to settle the trust property into new trusts[149] (such trusts cannot of course benefit T) but it seems strange to say that such a T has any beneficial interest in the trust property. Further, the basic position is that anyone who holds a right can exercise a power to create a trust of that right[150]: that is why, for example, B can set up a sub-trust. The subject matter of the sub-trust, of course, is B's right under the initial trust; it is not the trust property. That is why, if a sub-trust is created, even a passive one, the sub-beneficiary does not get a direct claim to the trust property: as discussed in Chapter 4, B does not simply "drop out of the picture".[151] So, whilst B does have the power to create

144 J. Penner, "The (True) Nature of a Beneficiary's Equitable Proprietary Interest under a Trust" (2014) 27 Can. J.L. & Juris 473, 481.

145 See R. Nolan, "Equitable Property" (2006) 122 L.Q.R. 232, 235 (extracted at para.17-016).

146 See, e.g. J. Penner, "Review of Ben McFarlane, *The Structure of Property Law*" [2009] R.L.R. 250, 254-255, accepting that B has no direct claim against X but arguing that B's right "indirect though it is" may still be a right in rem.

147 See paras 1-023ff.

148 Penner, "The (True) Nature of a Beneficiary's Equitable Proprietary Interest under a Trust" (2014) 27 Can. J.L. & Juris 473, 493.

149 See, e.g. cl.3.1 of the Discretionary Trust Precedent set out at para.1-104.

150 Penner argues (ibid., 491) that an existing trustee has no power to set up another trust of the trust property. Certainly, T may well have no authority to do so under the terms of the initial trust, but that does not necessarily mean that any purported declaration of trust by T would be invalid for all purposes. If, for example, the initial B waived or surrendered rights under the first trust, would there be any obstacle to a claim by the beneficiary of the trust later declared by T?

151 See para.3-082.

a trust, this does not mean that, even on Penner's terminology, B has a beneficial interest in the trust property; it simply means that B has a beneficial interest in B's own right under the initial trust.

## 5. The Significance of the Debate: An Example

The debate between the proprietary and obligational views of the trust is as how best to explain a set of core, accepted features of the trust. It is not primarily a debate as to how the trust *should* operate. Nonetheless, there are some important practical questions as to the law of trusts which may be answered differently according to whether a court, expressly or impliedly, adopts a proprietary or obligational view. **17–091**

In Chapter 5, for example, we saw that a proprietary view of the trust can support English law's refusal to admit private purpose trusts: if all trusts necessarily involve specified individuals (the beneficiaries) with at least a potential collective right to the trust property under the principle in *Saunders v Vautier*, that refusal could be easily explained. Indeed, the specific debate as to whether English law should move from a beneficiary principle to an enforcer principle, considered in Chapter 5,[152] has been influenced by participants' views on the wider debate as to the nature of a trust.[153] This does not mean, however, that English law's current attachment to the beneficiary principle is necessarily inconsistent with the obligational view. On that view, there is a separate question as to whether T's core trust duties must be owed to, and enforced by, someone who benefits from their performance. There may be good reasons for recognising such a limit (to do, for example, with incentives for enforcement and to ensure that the choice to waive enforcement is given to those who would lose out from such waiver) even if one takes an obligational view of the trust. **17–092**

It has been suggested in this chapter[154] that a key question in the debate between the proprietary and obligational views concerns the protection given to B against third parties who interfere with the trust property. Precisely that issue was considered by the Court of Appeal in *Shell UK Ltd v Total UK Ltd*. **17–093**

*Shell (UK) Ltd v Total (UK) Ltd*

Court of Appeal [2011] Q.B. 86

In December 2005, a number of very large explosions and fires occurred at the Buncefield Oil Storage Terminal in Hertfordshire, England. The explosions and fires were due to the carelessness of the defendant. No-one was killed or seriously injured, but a large amount of property was destroyed or damaged. The claimant, Shell UK Ltd, was one of a group of companies who used the oil storage terminal, and its pipelines, to store and distribute oil. As a result of damage to the terminal and pipelines, Shell was unable to distribute oil to its customers for a period and so suffered a large financial loss. It sued the defendant to recover that consequential loss. Shell, however, was not the registered owner of the terminal: instead, the terminal was registered to two trustee companies, who held their rights on trust for a number of companies, including Shell (and also the defendant). The defendant, Total UK Ltd, admitted that it was liable in negligence to the trust company but, relying chiefly on the decision of the House of Lords in *The Aliakmon*[155] argued that it was not liable in the tort of negligence to the beneficiaries of the trust, and therefore could not be made to pay for consequential loss suffered only by a beneficiary, and not by the trustee. **17–094**

[152] See para.5–108.

[153] See, e.g. and compare D. Hayton, "Developing the Obligation Characteristic of the Trust" (2001) 117 L.Q.R. 96 (favouring the enforcer principle and the obligational view); P. Matthews, "From Obligation to Property, and Back Again? The Future of the Non-Charitable Purpose Trust" in D. Hayton (ed.) *Extending the Boundaries of Trusts and Similar Ring-fenced Funds* (Kluwer Law International, 2002) (preferring the beneficiary principle and, to some extent, the proprietary view).

[154] See paras 17–016 and 17–066.

[155] *Leigh & Sillavan Ltd v Aliakmon Shipping Co Ltd (The Aliakmon)* [1986] AC 785.

17-095 WALLER LJ (giving the judgment of the court, to which LONGMORE and RICHARDS LJJ also contributed): Pursuant to two "Participants Agreements" Shell was entitled to the use of the relevant facilities, of which it was a part beneficial owner in common, for the purpose of receipt and delivery of the fuel. But its claims have failed before David Steel J largely because Shell was unable to overcome the rule that there can be no recovery for negligent infliction of mere economic loss. The House of Lords considered this aspect of the law over 20 years ago and reiterated English law's traditional refusal to allow recovery in such circumstances, unless such loss was the foreseeable consequence of physical injury to the claimant or the claimant's property. . .In *Leigh & Sillavan Ltd v Aliakmon Shipping Co Ltd, The Aliakmon* Lord Brandon of Oakbrook, setting out the exclusionary rule said[156]:

> ". . . in order to enable a person to claim in negligence for loss caused to him by reason of loss of or damage to property, he must have had either the legal ownership of or a possessory title to the property concerned at the time when the loss or damage occurred, and it is not enough for him to have only had contractual rights in relation to such property which have been adversely affected by the loss of or damage to it."

17-096 Shell's response to Total's defence is that (i) even if it had no possessory title to the damaged tanks and pipelines it had a (shared) equitable ownership of them and that is enough to give it title to claim for its economic loss. To the extent that it needs to join the legal owners of the pipelines, it has done so because the trustee companies are parties to the action; (ii) it anyway did have a good (shared) possessory title to the pipelines at the time of the damage; (iii) the rule requiring a legal or possessory title before recovering for economic loss has always been subject to exceptions (see the *Hedley Byrne* case)[157] and justice requires a further exception to be made to fit the facts of this case; (iv) the rule should anyway be abandoned, although Shell recognised that that is not an option open to this court; (v) whatever the law of negligence may be, Shell has alternative claims in nuisance and under the rule of *Rylands v Fletcher*,[158] which cover the same ground; beneficial ownership of land has always been sufficient to sustain a claim in nuisance, of which the rule in *Rylands v Fletcher* is an aspect.

17-097 For Shell, Mr Laurence Rabinowitz QC accepted that Lord Brandon in *The Aliakmon* had confined the right to sue for negligent loss of or damage to property to a person who had "the legal ownership of or a possessory title to" the relevant property but he submitted that his Lordship was not intending to rule out the owner in equity at any rate if that equitable owner had (as Shell had) joined the legal owner to the proceedings. . .

17-098 It is fair to say that Lord Brandon's speech in *The Aliakmon* does not resolve the question which divides the parties in this case. . .[But] [w]hat, after all, would be the point of requiring the beneficial owner to join the legal owner in the action if the beneficial owner could then recover only his physical loss, but not his associated economic loss.

17-099 In the absence of any directly applicable authority, it is necessary to look in a little more detail at the exclusionary rule and the rationale for it. The rule is[159]:

> ". . . no duty is owed by a defendant who negligently damages property belonging to a third party, to a claimant who suffers loss because of a dependence upon that property or its owner."

17-100 So on the facts of this case Total, who has admittedly damaged the pipelines owned by [the trustee companies], submits that it owes no duty to Shell who has a contractual right to have its fuel loaded into, carried and discharged from the pipelines. If Shell was a complete stranger to the transaction that would be understandable but Shell is not a complete stranger. It is the (co-) beneficial owner of the pipelines and the contract to use the pipeline is only an incident of its beneficial ownership (albeit a necessary incident, since it is a co-owner of the pipelines with others who also wish to use it). On the face of things, it is legalistic to deny Shell a right to recovery by reference to the exclusionary rule. It is, after all, Shell who is (along with BP, Total and Chevron) the "real" owner, the "legal" owner being little more than a bare trustee of the pipelines.

17-101 It can be seen that the judges [in cases establishing the "exclusionary rule" in relation to carelessly

---

156 [1986] AC 785 at 809.

157 *Hedley Byrne & Co Ltd v Heller & Partners Ltd* [1964] AC 465.

158 (1868) LR 3 HL 330.

159 See *Clerk and Lindsell on Torts* (19th edn, 2006) p 470 (para 8–115).

caused economic loss] were not particularly enamoured of the law that they were laying down but felt it necessary because otherwise many other actions from persons with a mere contractual interest would be well founded and that would mean the law would find itself redressing more than "the proximate and direct consequences of wrongful acts". This argument has come to be known as the "floodgates argument" which was, indeed, also relied on by Lord Brandon in *The Aliakmon* when refusing to carve out a specific exception to the exclusionary rule in favour of c&f (or cif) purchasers of goods at sea. But the floodgates argument does not apply with nearly as much force to the suggestion that the beneficial owner of land (or chattels) should be entitled to sue since it is his position as "owner" not as contractor which has been damnified.

The editors of *Clerk and Lindsell* summarise the position by saying:[160] **17–102**

> "To allow all claims for such economic loss would lead to unacceptable indeterminacy because of the ripple effects caused by contracts and expectations. Proximity requires some special relationship between the defendant and the person suffering relational economic loss, one which goes beyond mere contractual or non-contractual dependence on the damaged property."

Beneficial ownership of the damaged property goes well beyond contractual or non-contractual dependence on the damaged property and does indeed constitute a special relationship of the kind required by the learned editors. It is, in fact, a closer relationship in many ways than that of a bare trustee having no more than the legal title. **17–103**

We would be prepared to hold that a duty of care is owed to a beneficial owner of property (just as much as to a legal owner of property) by a defendant, such as Total, who can reasonably foresee that his negligent actions will damage that property. If, therefore, such property is, in breach of duty, damaged by the defendant, that defendant will be liable not merely for the physical loss of that property but also for the foreseeable consequences of that loss, such as the extra expenditure to which the beneficial owner is put or the loss of profit which he incurs. Provided that the beneficial owner can join the legal owner in the proceedings, it does not matter that the beneficial owner is not himself in possession of the property. **17–104**

We must confess to being somewhat influenced by what Lord Goff of Chieveley called "the impulse to do practical justice".[161] It should not be legally relevant that the co-owners of the relevant pipelines, for reasons that seemed good to them, decided to vest the legal title to the pipelines in their service companies and enjoy the beneficial ownership rather than the formal legal title. Differing views about the wisdom of the exclusionary rule are widely held but however much one may think that, in general, there should be no duty to mere contracting parties who suffer economic loss as a result of damage to a third party's property, it would be a triumph of form over substance to deny a remedy to the beneficial owner of that property when the legal owner is a bare trustee for that beneficial owner. **17–105**

Permission to appeal to the Supreme Court was granted to Total, but the case was settled. As noted by the Court of Appeal,[162] Shell relied on a number of different grounds in claiming compensation for the consequential loss it had suffered as a result of the damage to the oil plant, and it may well have been that a decision in favour of Shell could have been reached on other grounds.[163] The Court of Appeal's reasoning is significant to the present discussion, however, given that we have identified the extent of B's protection against X, a stranger interfering with the trust property, as a potentially critical test of the proprietary status of B's rights under a trust. **17–106**

Unfortunately, however, the reasoning of the Court of Appeal is far from clear and has been subject to much criticism.[164] It is odd, for example, to suggest that to draw a distinction between the position **17–107**

---

[160] *Clerk and Lindsell on Torts* (19th edn, 2006) p 472 (para 8–116).

[161] See *White v Jones* [1995] 1 All ER 691 at 702–703, [1995] 2 AC 207 at 259–260.

[162] See para.17–096.

[163] For example, it may be that, as in, e.g. *Healy v Healy* [1915] 1 K.B. 938, Shell was a beneficiary which also had, in fact, possession of the trust property and gained a common law proprietary right — enforceable, for example, through claims in conversion or negligence, by virtue of that possession.

[164] See, e.g. A. Rushworth & A. Scott, "Total Chaos?" [2010] L.M.C.L.Q. 536; P. Turner, "Consequential Economic Loss and the Trust Beneficiary" [2010] C.L.J. 445; J. Edelman, "Two Fundamental Questions for the Law of Trusts" (2013) 129 L.Q.R. 66, 67–72.

of B and that of O, an absolute owner, is "legalistic"[165]: as we noted above,[166] there are a number of significant differences between the rights of such parties. Of course, the finding in favour of B might seem to support the proprietary view but James Penner, one proponent of that view, has stated that[167]:

> McFarlane, Stevens and I could agree that *Shell UK v Total UK* is wrongly decided. There is no reason why a beneficiary without possession of the trust assets. . .should have a claim for consequential economic loss against a third party in virtue of his damaging those assets.

**17–108** In fact, the result in the case notwithstanding, it can be argued that the reasoning of the Court of Appeal is founded on a rejection of the proprietary view of the trust. This is because the court views B's claim as falling within an exception to the "exclusionary rule" which prevents the recovery of carelessly caused pure economic loss. That analysis assumes, of course, that the rule prima facie applies. This in turn assumes that the defendant, X, did *not* interfere with any property right of B. After all, if such interference had occurred, B's loss would not be pure economic loss: no exclusionary rule applies to the recovery of economic loss flowing from damage to the claimant's property.

**17–109** The mistake in the court's reasoning, it is submitted, lies in its misinterpretation of the exception to the exclusionary rule as formulated by *Clerk and Lindsell*.[168] That exception is based on "proximity" which is stated to require "some special relationship between the defendant and the person suffering relational economic loss". It therefore requires a special relationship between the claimant and the defendant. The court, however, states that the case falls within the exception as B's "[b]eneficial ownership of the damaged property goes well beyond contractual or non-contractual dependence on damaged property and does indeed constitute a special relationship of the kind required".[169] There is an obvious flaw in this reasoning. The existence of a trust means there is a special relationship between the claimant and the *trustee*. But the exception identified by *Clerk and Lindsell* instead requires a special relationship between the claimant and the *defendant*. No such relationship exists between B and X simply as a result of X, a stranger, damaging trust property.

**17–110** It can also be noted that the court laid down a requirement that T must be joined by B if an action is to be brought by B against X. That requirement does preserve a difference between the position of B and of O, as an outright owner of property can clearly sue a party interfering with that property without needing to join any other party. On one view,[170] the joinder requirement is not merely procedural, but reflects the substantive point that the right being enforced against X is in truth T's right as owner of the property, which T enforces on B's behalf because T holds that right subject to a duty to B. The joinder requirement, however, is of no real comfort to X, not least because T can be compelled by B to join the action.[171] Moreover, the court in *Shell UK v Total UK* assumed that B could then recover consequential losses suffered by B, and not by T. That is the crucial practical point for a party in X's position: is X liable not only for consequential loss caused to T, who has the right to the trust property, but also to B, a beneficiary of the trust? There are, it is submitted, sound practical reasons for saying that X should not be so liable. There is no limit, after all, on the possible number of beneficiaries of a trust,

165 [2011] Q.B. 86 [132] (extracted at para.17–100).

166 See para.17–007.

167 Penner, "The (True) Nature of a Beneficiary's Equitable Proprietary Interest under a Trust" (2014) 27 Can. J.L. & Juris 473, 485 fn.36.

168 [2011] Q.B. 86 [135] (extracted at para.17–102).

169 [2011] Q.B. 186 [136] (extracted at paras 17–103).

170 For discussion of the nature of the joinder requirement, see, e.g. *Roberts v Gill & Co* [2011] 1 A.C. 240 at [55]–[72].

171 Indeed, B does not need to compel first but B can bring one action combining both B's claim against T and then T's claim against X: this procedural concession to B derives from *Vandepitte v Preferred Accident Insurance Corp of New York* [1933] A.C. 70.

or the possible losses that each could suffer from X's damage to the trust property. This is precisely why economic loss suffered by parties who have a contract with an owner of property, but no right to that property themselves, is not generally recoverable from a defendant who carelessly causes such loss. If an owner of property cannot impose the risk of such extended liability on third parties by merely entering a contract, why should it be possible for her to do so by setting up a trust?

In considering any academic debate as to different conceptions of the law, it is important to ask why the debate matters: what turns on it in practice? The facts of *Shell UK v Total UK*, and the reasoning adopted by the Court of Appeal, provide a convincing example that it is important to be aware of the differences between the proprietary and obligational views. Not because the outcome will necessarily be dictated by which of those views is expressly or impliedly preferred by the court, but rather because, if the debate is simply overlooked, there is a great risk of confusion. **17–111**

**Questions**

1. Does it matter whether one adopts a proprietary view or an obligational view of the trust?
2. How do the courts distinguish between those aspects of a trustee's duties under a trust which may bind a third party and those which may not?
3. Do the current limits imposed on liability in knowing receipt provide convincing support for the obligational view of the trust?
4. Did the Court of Appeal in *Shell UK Ltd v Total UK Ltd* reach the correct result? If so, did it adopt the best reasoning in support of that result?

# PART IX

# EQUITABLE REMEDIES

# 18

# EQUITABLE REMEDIES

## 1. Equitable and Common Law Remedies

The following equitable remedies are discussed in this chapter: injunctions; specific performance; damages awarded in addition to, or in lieu of, injunctions and specific performance; rescission; and rectification.[1] 18–001

Equitable remedies are those which, historically, were granted by the courts exercising an exclusive equitable jurisdiction prior to the fusion of the courts by the Judicature Acts 1873–1875. It is a controversial issue whether it desirable to fence equitable remedies off and treat them separately from common law remedies, retaining and emphasising the differences which existed between them prior to 1873. 18–002

On one view,[2] this is desirable because equitable remedies possess unique characteristics, most notably that they are discretionary, and are subject to discretionary defences. In this, they are said to differ from common law remedies which may be claimed as of right on proof of a legal wrong (with or without proof of consequent loss, depending on the cause of action). Equitable remedies are also said to possess the distinctive feature that their effect is to force a defendant, through the threat of punishment or otherwise, to comply with her legal obligations in kind.[3] So, for example, a defendant who is made the subject of injunctive relief or a decree of specific performance may not leave her "primary" contractual or tortious obligations unfulfilled, and may not choose instead to fulfil the "secondary" obligation to pay damages which arises on breach of a primary duty of performance, as she can at common law. In equity she must, on pain of punishment, act or refrain from acting in the manner specified in the court order. Indeed, even if she chooses to take the punishment rather than act as she should, the court may simply by-pass her and in an appropriate case empower someone else to do the act instead.[4] On this view of the law, it makes sense to consider equitable remedies alongside one another, because this enables us to gain a better understanding of their common features. 18–003

On another view,[5] it is misleading to distinguish equitable and common law remedies on the ground that the former are discretionary and the latter are not, given that both are granted and 18–004

---

1 Others are declarations; appointment of receivers; cancellation and delivery up of documents; and disclosure (formerly termed discovery), being the process whereby a party to a suit is obliged to divulge the existence of documentation relevant to the issues in the claim.

2 J. Heydon, M. Leeming and P. Turner, *Meagher, Gummow and Lehane's Equity: Doctrines and Remedies*, 5th edn (LexisNexis, 2014), Ch.2.

3 "*In specie*" in Latin, from which root the term "specific performance" derived.

4 For example, it is possible for the court to order that a conveyance or transfer of the defendant's land which she has promised to convey to the claimant be executed by someone other than the defendant if she will not execute it herself.

5 A. Burrows, *Fusing Common Law and Equity: Remedies, Restitution and Reform* (Hochelaga Lecture, 2002), pp.1–26; A. Burrows, "We Do This at Common Law But That in Equity" (2002) 22 O.J.L.S. 1; cf. S. Worthington, *Equity*, 2nd edn (Oxford University Press, 2006), Ch.2.

withheld in line with clearly established rules and principles. Granted that some of these allow the courts a wide discretion when exercising their equitable jurisdiction, the same can also be said of certain common law principles (e.g. the rules limiting the award of compensatory damages, and the rules authorising the award of punitive damages). Moreover, it is untrue that the common law lacks the means to compel the performance of primary obligations, for this is the function of the award of an agreed sum in contract cases.

18-005 It is also said to diminish our understanding of the law to consider equitable and common law remedies separately, because this obscures the full range of the courts' remedial armoury in private law, and disguises the similarities which exist between some equitable and common law remedies, e.g. an account of profits in equity and an award of restitutionary damages at common law. Granted that there are some differences between equitable and common law remedies (e.g. common law damages, in contrast to equitable damages awarded in lieu of an injunction, are not awarded in response to an anticipated wrong),

> nothing would be lost, and some simplicity and rationality would be gained, if one took the small steps necessary to move to a fully-fused system of remedies where it would be unnecessary to use the labels common law and equitable.[6]

On this second view of the law, the discussion which follows in this chapter would serve a better purpose if it appeared alongside a discussion of common law remedies in books on contract, tort, unjust enrichment, and remedies.

## 2. Injunctions

### A. Overview

#### i. Definition and Classification

18-006 An injunction is an order of the court forbidding the initiation or the continuance of some act or state of affairs or commanding that an act be done. An injunction may therefore be prohibitory or mandatory and the distinction, as in the case of positive and negative covenants in regard to land, is one of substance not form[7]: while an order of the court requiring the demolition of a house could be framed as an order not to leave it standing, the order would nonetheless be mandatory. A tell-tale sign is that mandatory injunctions normally require some expenditure on the part of the defendant. In addition, whereas the execution of prohibitory injunctions generally needs no supervision (the defendant simply has to refrain from committing the prohibited act), the execution of a mandatory order may do so, e.g. in the case of an order to demolish a house in a particular manner.

#### ii. Distinguished from Specific Performance

18-007 Positive contractual obligations of certain kinds are normally enforced, in equity, by orders for specific performance rather than mandatory injunctions.[8] What is the point of insisting on this difference? Does it matter whether a claimant obtains a mandatory injunction or a decree of specific

---

6 A. Burrows, *Remedies for Torts and Breach of Contract*, 3rd edn (Oxford University Press, 2004), pp.11–12.
7 *Truckell v Stock* [1957] 1 W.L.R. 161.
8 See Section 3 below.

performance? In terms of enforcement, it cannot matter for both remedies are enforced in the same way: in the case of an individual defendant, by imprisonment,[9] fine or sequestration of assets (or any combination of these) and in the case of a corporation (whose officers may, additionally, be punished in their individual capacities), by fine or sequestration of assets or both.[10]

Nonetheless it does matter which order a claimant must ask for because, as will be seen, the number of grounds on which a decree for specific performance may be refused is greater than the number of grounds on which a final injunction may be refused. And this appears to be for a justifiable reason: by contract an individual may either, by negative stipulation, put herself under disabilities that she does not have under the general law or, by positive stipulation, impose on herself obligations which she does not have under the general law (apart from the contract). In the former case, she is merely restricting her freedom to act, which restriction can be enforced by a prohibitory injunction without imposing burdens on her over and above those which the general law imposes. But in the latter case, where the defendant has agreed to do something which the general law does not require her to do, the court will be astute to enquire into the justice of making her perform her promise in kind. It will want to be certain that, for example, the claimant is ready, willing and able to perform her own contractual obligations, that there is "mutuality" between the parties, and so on. **18–008**

Moreover, it is often said that, unlike the case with mandatory injunctions, no decree of specific performance will lie on an interim basis (i.e. pending trial). If true, it would matter very much whether a claimant's claim were for a mandatory injunction or a decree of specific performance, for in the first case she might obtain interim relief but in the second she could not. The case of *Sky Petroleum Ltd v VIP Petroleum Ltd*,[11] however, tends to blur the distinction and, indeed, suggests that specific performance may lie on an interim basis. There, the claimant applied for an interim prohibitory injunction restraining the defendant from failing to supply it with petrol, which failure was allegedly in breach of contract. Goulding J treated the motion as one for an interim decree of specific performance, looking at the substance rather than the form, and granted it. **18–009**

*Sky Petroleum Ltd v VIP Petroleum Ltd*

Chancery Division [1974] 1 W.L.R. 576

The claimants had contracted to purchase all their petrol, at fixed prices, from the defendants. During a petrol shortage the defendants purported to terminate the contract on the ground of breach of certain credit provisions therein by the claimants. Pending trial of that issue, the claimants sought an injunction to restrain the defendants from withholding supplies. **18–010**

GOULDING J.: What I have to decide is whether any injunction should be granted to protect the plaintiffs in the meantime. There is trade evidence that the plaintiffs have no great prospect of finding any alternative source of supply for the filling stations which constitute their business. The defendants have indicated their willingness to continue to supply the plaintiffs, but only at prices which, according to the plaintiffs' evidence, would not be serious prices from a commercial point of view. There is, in my judgment, so far as I can make out on the evidence before me, a serious danger that unless the court interferes at this stage the plaintiffs will be forced out of business. In those circumstances, unless there is some specific reason which debars me from doing so, I should be disposed to grant an injunction to restore the former position under the contract until the rights and wrongs of the parties can be fully tried out. The most serious hurdle in the way of the plaintiffs is the well known doctrine that the court refuses specific performance of a contract to sell and purchase chattels not specific or ascertained. That is a well-established and salutary **18–011**

---

9 Contempt of Court Act 1981 s.14(1), discussed in *Lomas v Parle* [2004] 1 W.L.R. 1642 and *Re W (A Child) (Abduction: Committal)* [2012] 1 W.L.R. 1036.

10 RSC Orders 45 and 52, as incorporated into the Civil Procedure Rules 1998.

11 [1974] 1 W.L.R. 576. See also *Capita Trust Co (Channel Islands) Ltd v Chatham Maritime J3 Developments Ltd* [2007] L. & T.R. 2; *Ashworth v Royal National Theatre* [2014] 4 All E.R. 238.

> rule, and I am entirely unconvinced by Mr Christie, for the plaintiffs, when he tells me that an injunction in the form sought by him would not be specific enforcement at all. The matter is one of substance and not of form, and it is, in my judgment quite plain that I am, for the time being, specifically enforcing the contract if I grant an injunction. However, the ratio behind the rule is, as I believe, that under the ordinary contract for the sale of non-specific goods, damages are a sufficient remedy. That, to my mind, is lacking in the circumstances of the present case. The evidence suggests, and indeed it is common knowledge that the petroleum market is in an unusual state in which a would-be buyer cannot go out into the market and contract with another seller, possibly at some sacrifice as to price. Here, the defendants appear for practical purposes to be the plaintiffs' sole means of keeping their business going, and I am prepared so far to depart from the general rule as to try to preserve the position under the contract until a later date. I therefore propose to grant an injunction.

### iii. Final and Interim Injunctions

**18-012** All injunctions may be classified as interim (formerly termed "interlocutory") or final (also termed "permanent" and "perpetual"[12]). Interim injunctions are those granted pending the final resolution of an issue between the parties. Final injunctions are those which are finally decisive of an issue between the parties. The courts have developed a special approach to the granting of interim injunctions, which differs from their approach to the granting of final injunctions.[13]

### iv. Quia Timet Injunctions

**18-013** Unlike the common law, which is generally limited to the award of damages to make good injury which has already occurred, equity can act to restrain future wrongs. Indeed, all final prohibitory injunctions achieve as much, in that, although they are normally sought only where a wrong has already been committed, they ensure, so far as any court order can, that the wrong will not be repeated, thus rendering unnecessary a multiplicity of suits. It was only one step from that to hold that a threatened future wrong should be restrained before it had occurred by the issuing of a quia timet injunction. "Quia timet" is Latin for "because she fears": a claimant who fears that a defendant will imminently cause her harm can obtain an order that she should not do so. However, "mere vague apprehension is not sufficient to support an action for a quia timet injunction. There must be an immediate threat to do something".[14]

## *B. Equitable Principles Governing the Grant of Final Injunctions*

### i. Adequacy of Common Law Remedies

**18-014** Equity had no cause to supplement an existing legal remedy which was adequate and it came to be required that before any equitable remedy would be awarded, the available legal remedy should be inadequate—a matter to be determined having regard to the nature of the injury (whether it is assessable in monetary terms), the prospect of its being repeated (when, otherwise, a multiplicity of suits would be necessary) and, to a lesser extent, the ability of a defendant to satisfy an award of damages.

---

12 The terms "permanent" and "perpetual injunction" are often used but are rather misleading as such orders might not, on their terms, be intended to have permanent or perpetual effect. For example, the order granted in the case of a one-year restrictive covenant being enforced against a former employee would endure only for one year.

13 See paras 18-025ff.

14 *Graigola Merthyr Co Ltd v Swansea Corporation* [1929] A.C. 344 at 353 per Lord Buckmaster. See too *Fletcher v Bealey* (1884) 28 Ch. D. 688 at [698]; *Morris v Redland Bricks Ltd* [1970] A.C. 652; *Hooper v Rogers* [1975] Ch. 43; *London Borough of Islington v Elliott* [2012] EWCA Civ 56 at [29]–[40].

Damages are often found to be an inadequate remedy, and injunctions are often awarded, for the torts of trespass to land and nuisance, reflecting the strong protection afforded by the law to a landowner's right to the quiet enjoyment of her property.[15] But injunctions can be awarded to restrain other torts, too,[16] and equitable wrongs,[17] and breaches of contract, of which Sachs LJ observed in *Evans Marshall & Co Ltd v Bertola SA* that[18]: **18–015**

> The courts have repeatedly recognised there can be claims under contracts in which, as here, it is unjust to confine a plaintiff to his damages for their breach. Great difficulty in estimating these damages is one factor that can be and has been taken into account. Another factor is the creation of certain areas of damage which cannot be taken into monetary account in a common law action for breach of contract. Loss of goodwill and trade reputation are examples. Generally, indeed, the grant of injunctions in contract cases stems from such factors.

### ii. Equity Will not Act in Vain

This principle, like the last, is common to specific performance. The idea is that if issuing an injunction would be futile, no injunction will be issued. In Arden LJ's words, "the court must be astute to see that there is a real prospect that something will be gained".[19] In *Wookey v Wookey*,[20] a family case, it was said that no order should be made where there was evidence that it would not be complied with and that nothing would be done about the non-compliance in judicial terms (because the subject of the order would, on account of youth, not be imprisoned and, on account of impecuniosity, not be fined). This is perhaps an extreme application of the principle but it can be defended. **18–016**

More regular applications of the principle are to be found in cases where it would be impossible for the defendant to comply with the order (because, for example, in a case where a mandatory injunction was sought requiring her to tear down a building, she no longer owned the land and had no right to tear down any building upon it). Another illustration is provided by the *Spycatcher* case,[21] where a final injunction was refused against a newspaper preventing it from publishing certain information. The information had been confidential but it had already been published in a book that had become widely available in the UK by the time of the litigation. **18–017**

### iii. Delay and Acquiescence

The requirement that one who seeks equitable relief must do so without delay, even within the statutory limitation period (the doctrine of "laches") is often factually indistinguishable from the doctrine of acquiescence whereby knowing failure to object to a wrong may give rise to an inability to resurrect **18–018**

---

15 See, e.g. *Hodgson v Duce* (1856) 2 Jur. N.S. 1014; *Eardley v Granville* (1876) 3 Ch. D. 826; *Litchfield-Speer v Queen Anne's Gate Syndicate (No.2) Ltd* [1919] 1 Ch. 407; *Anchor Brewhouse Developments Ltd v Berkley House (Docklands Developments) Ltd* (1987) 38 B.L.R. 82; *Harrow LBC v Donohue* [1995] 1 E.G.L.R. 257 (distinguishing acts of mere trespass—where damages might be substituted for an injunction—and dispossession—where a claimant is entitled as a matter of right to the protection of an injunction).

16 As noted in J. Murphy, "Rethinking Injunctions in Tort Law" (2007) 27 O.J.L.S. 509, arguing that the law attaches just as much importance to, and so should be just as willing to award injunctions to protect, other interests besides proprietary interests, e.g. bodily integrity.

17 See, e.g. *Fox v Fox* (1870) L.R. 11 Eq. 142; *Buttle v Saunders* [1950] 2 All E.R. 193.

18 [1973] 1 W.L.R. 349 at 380. See too *Manning v AIG Europe UK Ltd* [2005] 1 B.C.L.C. 1 (breach of subordinated debt agreement); *Sheffield United Football Club Ltd v West Ham United Football Club Plc* [2009] 1 Lloyd's Rep. 167 (breach of arbitration clause).

19 *Dadourian Group International Inc v Simms (Practice Note)* [2006] 1 W.L.R. 2499 at [35].

20 [1991] Fam. 121.

21 *Attorney General v Observer Ltd* [1990] 1 A.C. 109.

an objection to it at a later date. The cases on delay diverge on the question whether mere delay (i.e. unaccompanied by acquiescence) will bar the grant of relief,[22] but the position now seems to be that if detriment is present, this will usually lead the court to conclude that it would be unconscionable for the claimant to seek to enforce her rights, "but, absent detriment, the court would need to find some other factor which made it unconscionable for the party having the benefit of the rights to change her mind."[23] As to acquiescence, the test is whether the claimant represented that she would no longer enforce her rights.[24]

**18–019** An example of how acquiescence may operate to bar not just equitable but any relief is to be found in *Gafford v Graham*.[25] The defendant was in breach of a restrictive covenant which prevented him from converting his bungalow or extending his barn without the claimant's consent. He breached the covenant in 1986 but, as the Court of Appeal said, "the [claimant] made no complaint until his solicitor wrote to the defendant about three years after the acts complained of", despite full knowledge of the breaches. At first instance, the judge had awarded the claimant damages in respect of the conversion and extension. The Court of Appeal, however, held that his acquiescence was a bar not just to equitable relief but to all relief and discharged the order for damages. It held that, in all the circumstances, it would be unconscionable for the claimant to enforce the (legal) rights which he undoubtedly had in 1986. This, notwithstanding that the claimant's action was begun well within the limitation period. The case is an example (closely related to proprietary estoppel) of how equity can operate to extinguish accrued legal rights. Not all cases in which equitable relief is refused, however, are so draconian: normally, a claimant's delay will, if it has any effect, merely serve to deprive her of her (presumably more adequate) equitable remedy. Her legal rights and remedies for breach (i.e. her right to damages) will remain intact in the absence of something like an estoppel.

### iv. Clean Hands

**18–020** A claimant who has behaved improperly may be denied equitable relief, although the "clean hands" principle will not be triggered where the claimant's conduct is morally shabby but legally unimpeachable.[26] There must also be a close connection between the claimant's misconduct and the relief which she seeks. "Equity does not demand that its suitors shall have led blameless lives",[27] and mere general depravity is not enough in itself to deny a claimant relief.[28] The availability of injunctive relief can therefore turn on the factual question whether the claimant's misbehaviour is sufficiently closely connected with the relief sought to justify withholding the remedy. In *Grobelaar v News Group Newspapers Ltd*[29] the House of Lords granted an injunction restraining a newspaper from repeating an unproven allegation that a footballer had thrown football matches, although he was proven to have taken bribes, to have told his co-conspirator that he had thrown matches in exchange for the money, and to have lied about this in court. On the other side of the line is *Royal Bank of Scotland Plc v Highland Financial Partners LP*,[30] where the Court of Appeal declined to grant an anti-suit injunction

---

22 *Fullwood v Fullwood* (1878) 9 Ch. D. 176, per Fry J: no.; *HP Bulmer Ltd & Showerings Ltd v J Bollinger SA* [1977] 2 C.M.L.R. 625, per Goff LJ: only if "inordinate".
23 *Harris v Williams-Wynne* [2006] 2 P. & C.R. 595 at [39], per Chadwick LJ, cf. *Fisher v Brooker* [2009] 1 W.L.R. 1764 at [64].
24 *Allen v Veranne Builders Ltd* [1988] E.G.C.S. 2.
25 [1995] 3 E.G.L.R. 75.
26 *Dering v Earl of Winchelsea* (1787) 1 Cox Eq. Cas. 318; *Loosley v NUT* [1988] I.R.L.R. 157; *Lonhro Plc v Fayed (No.5)* [1993] 1 W.L.R. 1489; *Ministry of Justice v Prison Officers Association* [2008] I.C.R. 702.
27 *Loughran v Loughran* (1934) 292 U.S. 216 at [292], per Brandeis J.
28 *Meyers v Casey* (1913) 17 C.L.R. 90: *Attorney General v Equiticorp Industries Group Ltd* [1996] 1 N.Z.L.R. 528.
29 [2002] 1 W.L.R. 3024.
30 [2013] 1 C.L.C. 596.

restraining the defendants from pursuing proceedings in Texas because the claimant had suppressed facts in the course of the substantive proceedings before the English court and had continued to argue, even after discovery of the true position, that it had not concealed those facts.

A claimant who has herself defaulted on a contract cannot obtain injunctive relief to enforce any of its terms.[31] That is an application, in the field of contract, of the clean hands maxim. It is, however, a different requirement from the similar doctrine that a claimant who comes to equity must do equity, which looks not to whether the claimant's hands are already soiled by wrong-doing, but rather to the future question whether the claimant is prepared to fulfil her outstanding obligations.[32] In applications for specific performance, this translates into a requirement that the claimant demonstrate that she is "ready, willing and able" to perform her side of the bargain. Both requirements are morally defensible in that, by seeking an equitable remedy which lies beyond the legal remedy to which she is entitled, a claimant must appeal to a court of conscience. **18–021**

### v. No Undue Hardship

Interim and mandatory injunctions in particular provide scope for an argument that an injunction ought to be refused as a matter of discretion on the ground of hardship to the defendant. In the former case, this is because, *ex hypothesi*, the claimant has not yet established her right to any relief because there has not yet been a trial.[33] In the latter, the reason is that compliance with a mandatory injunction will often involve the defendant in expenditure which may be out of all proportion to the benefit which the claimant will derive from the grant of an injunction. **18–022**

As we discuss below,[34] the Senior Courts Act 1981 s.50 gives the court a statutory jurisdiction to award damages in lieu of an injunction, in recognition of the fact that the award of injunctions can sometimes be oppressive to defendants (particularly mandatory ones requiring, for example, the demolition of buildings). By giving courts of equity the power to award damages in lieu, Parliament made it easier to justify declining to grant injunctions in such cases. **18–023**

### vi. Public Policy

Although in specific performance cases the notion has long been accepted that public interest considerations might affect the availability of equitable remedies in contract,[35] the matter is more controversial as regards those torts such as trespass and private nuisance which create a perimeter of inviolability around the notion of private ownership of land. In *Lawrence v Fen Tigers Ltd*,[36] however, Lord Neuberger found it "hard to see how there could be any circumstances in which [public interest considerations] arose and could not, as a matter of law, be a relevant factor" although he also thought that "it is very easy to think of circumstances in which [they] might arise but did not begin to justify the court refusing, or, as the case may be, deciding, to award an injunction if it was otherwise minded to do so." **18–024**

---

31 *Measures Bros Ltd v Measures* [1910] 2 Ch. 248.

32 Although Lord Denning MR appears to have confused the doctrines in *Shell (UK) Ltd v Lostock Garage Ltd* [1976] 1 W.L.R. 1187.

33 The position is slightly different where the claimant has won proceedings but the defendant appeals and the claimant seeks an interim injunction pending resolution of the appeal: *Novartis AG v Hospira UK Ltd* [2014] 1 W.L.R. 1264 at [41].

34 See paras 18–189ff.

35 See para.18–136.

36 [2014] A.C. 822 at [124]. On the same topic, see *Miller v Jackson* [1977] Q.B. 966; *Kennaway v Thompson* [1981] Q.B. 88; *Dennis v Ministry of Defence* [2003] 2 E.G.L.R. 121.

## C. Interim Injunctions

### i. General Principles

18–025 Unlike final injunctions, where equitable principles are in play, interim injunctions are granted or refused on grounds which have nothing to do, either historically or logically, with the maxims of equity. The principles on which the court acts, or has acted up to the introduction of the Civil Procedure Rules at least, are designed to achieve justice between the parties under circumstances of ignorance or uncertainty (i.e. when it is not known whether the claimant's claim is well founded). Note, however, that the Civil Procedure Rules and the Human Rights Act 1998 have an effect on the substance of these principles and it will be necessary to qualify what follows.[37]

18–026 In order to circumvent the necessity, at an early stage of an action, of deciding disputed questions of fact or determining points of law with insufficient argument, the House of Lords laid down guidelines for the exercise of judicial discretion whether to grant an interim injunction in *American Cyanamid Co v Ethicon Ltd*,[38] reproduced below. The House had previously held in *JT Stratford & Son Ltd v Lindley*[39] that a claimant had to show a prima facie case that she would succeed at trial in obtaining injunctive relief. The decision in *Cyanamid* is to the effect that a claimant need only show that she has a case that is not frivolous or vexatious and that there is a serious question to be tried. Once that is established, the question whether an injunction should be granted turns on the balance of convenience, a much used shorthand phrase to describe the balancing exercise in which the court engages in order to minimise the risk of doing injustice.

18–027 That balancing exercise is undertaken as follows: once a serious question for trial is raised, unless there is no arguable defence to the claim (in which case an injunction should be granted until trial[40]), the court considers whether damages would be an adequate remedy for loss caused to the claimant by not granting an injunction pending trial. If so, and the defendant can afford to pay, then the balance favours no injunction. If the loss likely to be caused is not remediable in damages (either as a matter of legal principle or practice, i.e. the defendant could not pay them) then the court considers to what extent the claimant would be able to compensate the defendant for any loss caused to her by granting an injunction pending trial, thus making the claimant's relief conditional on the provision of a cross-undertaking in damages. This has the result that if damages would not be an adequate remedy for the claimant (either as a matter of principle or practice) then if the defendant's potential loss is compensable, the balance favours an injunction. Where damages would be inadequate for both parties, however, either as a matter of principle or practice, injustice is best avoided by maintaining the status quo. "Special factors" might properly be taken into account, but only as a last resort can the merits be examined and, even then, only if the strength of one case is disproportionate to the other.

---

37 See paras 18–070—18–072.

38 [1975] A.C. 396.

39 [1965] A.C. 269. *Cyanamid* has been said to be irreconcilable with this decision but as *Cyanamid* was the later case, that is the one the Court of Appeal should follow: *Hubbard v Pitt* [1976] Q.B. 142.

40 Unless, with the defendant's consent, the hearing of the motion is treated as the trial of the action in which case a final injunction will lie.

*American Cyanamid Co v Ethicon Ltd*

House of Lords [1975] A.C. 396

LORD DIPLOCK (with whom VISCOUNT DILHORNE, LORD CROSS, LORD SALMON and LORD EDMUND-DAVIES agreed): . . . In my view the grant of interlocutory injunctions in actions for infringement of patents is governed by the same principles as in other actions. I turn to consider what those principles are. 18–028

My Lords, when an application for an interlocutory injunction to restrain a defendant from doing acts alleged to be in violation of the plaintiff's legal right is made upon contested facts, the decision whether or not to grant an interlocutory injunction has to be taken at a time when *ex hypothesi* the existence of the right or the violation of it, or both, is uncertain and will remain uncertain until final judgment is given in the action. It was to mitigate the risk of injustice to the plaintiff during the period before that uncertainty could be resolved that the practice arose of granting him relief by way of interlocutory injunction; but since the middle of the 19th century this has been made subject to his undertaking to pay damages to the defendant for any loss sustained by reason of the injunction if it should be held at the trial that the plaintiff had not been entitled to restrain the defendant from doing what he was threatening to do. The object of the interlocutory injunction is to protect the plaintiff against injury by violation of his right for which he could not be adequately compensated in damages recoverable in the action if the uncertainty were resolved in his favour at the trial; but the plaintiff's need for such protection must be weighed against the corresponding need of the defendant to be protected against injury resulting from his having been prevented from exercising his own legal rights for which he could not be adequately compensated under the plaintiff's undertaking in damages if the uncertainty were resolved in the defendant's favour at the trial. The court must weigh one need against another and determine where "the balance of convenience" lies. 18–029

In those cases where the legal rights of the parties depend upon facts that are in dispute between them, the evidence available to the court at the hearing of the application for an interlocutory injunction is incomplete. It is given on affidavit and has not been tested by oral cross-examination. The purpose sought to be achieved by giving to the court discretion to grant such injunctions would be stultified if the discretion were clogged by a technical rule forbidding its exercise if upon that incomplete untested evidence the court evaluated the chances of the plaintiff's ultimate success in the action at 50 per cent or less, but permitting its exercise if the court evaluated his chances at more than 50 per cent. 18–030

The notion that it is incumbent upon the court to undertake what is in effect a preliminary trial of the action upon evidential material different from that upon which the actual trial will be conducted, is, I think, of comparatively recent origin, though it can be supported by references in earlier cases to the need to show "a probability that the plaintiffs are entitled to relief"[41] or "a strong prima facie case that the right which he seeks to protect in fact exists".[42] These are to be contrasted with expressions in other cases indicating a much less onerous criterion, such as the need to show that there is "certainly a case to be tried"[43] which corresponds more closely with what judges generally treated as sufficient to justify their considering the balance of convenience upon applications for interlocutory injunctions, at any rate up to the time when I became a member of your Lordships' House. . . . 18–031

*Hubbard v Vosper*[44] was treated by Graham J. and the Court of Appeal in the instant appeal as leaving intact the supposed rule that the court is not entitled to take any account of the balance of convenience unless it has first been satisfied that if the case went to trial upon no other evidence than is before the court at the hearing of the application the plaintiff would be entitled to judgment for a permanent injunction in the same terms as the interlocutory injunction sought. 18–032

Your Lordships should in my view take this opportunity of declaring that there is no such rule. The use of such expressions as "a probability", "a prima facie case", or "a strong prima facie case" in the context of the exercise of a discretionary power to grant an interlocutory injunction leads to confusion as to the object sought to be achieved by this form of temporary relief. The court no doubt must be satisfied that the claim is not frivolous or vexatious; in other words, that there is a serious question to be tried. 18–033

It is no part of the court's function at this stage of the litigation to try to resolve conflicts of evidence on affidavit as to facts on which the claims of either party may ultimately depend nor to decide difficult 18–034

---

41 *Preston v Luck* (1884) 27 Ch.D. 497 at 506, per Cotton L.J.

42 *Smith v Grigg Ltd* [1924] 1 K.B. 655 at 659, per Atkin L.J.

43 *Jones v Pacaya Rubber and Produce Co Ltd* [1911] 1 K.B. 455 at 457, per Buckley L.J.

44 [1972] 2 Q.B. 84.

questions of law which call for detailed argument and mature considerations. These are matters to be dealt with at the trial. One of the reasons for the introduction of the practice of requiring an undertaking as to damages upon the grant of an interlocutory injunction was that "it aided the court in doing that which was its great object, viz. abstaining from expressing any opinion upon the merits of the case until the hearing".[45] So unless the material available to the court at the hearing of the application for an interlocutory injunction fails to disclose that the plaintiff has any real prospect of succeeding in his claim for a permanent injunction at the trial, the court should go on to consider whether the balance of convenience lies in favour of granting or refusing the interlocutory relief that is sought.

**18–035** As to that, the governing principle is that the court should first consider whether, if the plaintiff were to succeed at the trial in establishing his right to a permanent injunction, he would be adequately compensated by an award of damages for the loss he would have sustained as a result of the defendant's continuing to do what was sought to be enjoined between the time of the application and the time of the trial. If damages in the measure recoverable at common law would be adequate remedy and the defendant would be in a financial position to pay them, no interlocutory injunction should normally be granted,—however strong the plaintiff's claim appeared to be at that stage. If, on the other hand, damages would not provide an adequate remedy for the plaintiff in the event of his succeeding at the trial, the court should then consider whether, on the contrary hypothesis that the defendant were to succeed at the trial in establishing his right to do that which was sought to be enjoined, he would be adequately compensated under the plaintiff's undertaking as to damages for the loss he would have sustained by being prevented from doing so between the time of the application and the time of the trial. If damages in the measure recoverable under such an undertaking would be an adequate remedy and the plaintiff would be in a financial position to pay them, there would be no reason upon this ground to refuse an interlocutory injunction.

**18–036** It is where there is doubt as to the adequacy of the respective remedies in damages available to either party or to both, that the question of balance of convenience arises. It would be unwise to attempt even to list all the various matters which may need to be taken into consideration in deciding where the balance lies, let alone to suggest the relative weight to be attached to them. These will vary from case to case.

**18–037** Where other factors appear to be evenly balanced it is a counsel of prudence to take such measures as are calculated to preserve the status quo. If the defendant is enjoined temporarily from doing something that he has not done before, the only effect of the interlocutory injunction in the event of his succeeding at the trial is to postpone the date at which he is able to embark upon a course of action which he has not previously found it necessary to undertake; whereas to interrupt him in the conduct of an established enterprise would cause much greater inconvenience to him since he would have to start again to establish it in the event of his succeeding at the trial.

**18–038** Save in the simplest cases, the decision to grant or to refuse an interlocutory injunction will cause to whichever party is unsuccessful on the application some disadvantages which his ultimate success at the trial may show he ought to have been spared and the disadvantages may be such that the recovery of damages to which he would then be entitled either in the action or under the plaintiff's undertaking would not be sufficient to compensate him fully for all of them. The extent to which the disadvantages to each party would be incapable of being compensated in damages in the event of his succeeding at the trial is always a significant factor in assessing where the balance of convenience lies; and if the extent of the uncompensatable disadvantage to each party would not differ widely, it may not be improper to take into account in tipping the balance the relative strength of each party's case as revealed by the affidavit evidence adduced on the hearing of the application. This, however, should be done only where it is apparent upon the facts disclosed by evidence as to which there is no credible dispute that the strength of one party's case is disproportionate to that of the other party. The court is not justified in embarking upon anything resembling a trial of the action upon conflicting affidavits in order to evaluate the strength of either party's case.

**18–039** I would reiterate that, in addition to those to which I have referred, there may be many other special factors to be taken into consideration in the particular circumstances of individual cases. The instant appeal affords one example of this.

[45] *Walkefield v Duke of Buccleugh* (1865) 12 L.T. 628 at 629.

### ii. Exceptions?

Much judicial ink has been spilled over the relationship of the *Cyanamid* guidelines to instant cases, and in particular, on the question whether apparent exceptions to the *Cyanamid* approach are truly exceptions or merely different ways of striking the balance of convenience in instant cases. There certainly seem to be categories of case (whether "exceptions" or not) where the claimant has to show more than that her case is not frivolous or vexatious, raising merely a serious question to be tried. They include the following. **18–040**

#### (1) Trade Disputes

The Trade Union and Labour Relations (Consolidation) Act 1992 s.221(2) provides that, on an application for an interim injunction, where the defendant claims that she acted in contemplation or furtherance of a trade dispute, the court is to have regard to the likelihood of the defendant's establishing at the trial any of the matters which, under the Act, confer immunity from tortious liability. **18–041**

#### (2) Trial of Action Unlikely or Delayed

In *Cambridge Nutrition Ltd v BBC*,[46] the claimant sought an injunction preventing the defendant from broadcasting a programme (in the making of which they had participated) until after the imminent publication of a government report on the claimant's low calorie diet, the subject matter also of the programme. The programme, however, would have had no impact if broadcast after the publication of the report and, if an injunction were granted to trial, it would effectively prevent the broadcast for good. Clearly, if the *Cyanamid* principles are designed to achieve a fair resolution pending trial, others must be used to achieve such resolution where there is likely to be no trial. The court therefore looked at the merits of the claim and, finding the basis of it to be implausible (an oral agreement not to broadcast until after publication of the report—for which there was remarkably little evidence) declined to grant an injunction. **18–042**

#### (3) No Arguable Defence

This has already been mentioned in the discussion above of *Cyanamid*. **18–043**

#### (4) Injunctions to Restrain the Presentation of Winding-Up Petitions

It has been held since *Cyanamid* that the guidelines do not apply to an interim injunction to restrain the bringing of other proceedings on the ground that these latter would be an abuse of the court's process: the grant of such injunction finally determines the matter.[47] So a claimant would fail unless she demonstrated not merely a serious issue whether the defendant's proceedings would be an abuse but, over and above that, that the defendant was bound to fail in those proceedings. In *Ward v Coulson Sanderson and Ward Ltd*[48] the Court of Appeal followed that reasoning to hold that *Cyanamid* did not apply to injunctions to restrain the presentation of a winding-up petition by a creditor. **18–044**

---

46 [1990] 3 All E.R 523. See also *Cayne v Global Natural Resources Plc* [1984] 1 All E.R. 225.

47 *Bryanston Finance v De Vries (No.2)* [1976] Ch. 63, per Stephenson LJ and Sir John Pennycuick. Buckley LJ concurred in refusing the injunction but purported to follow *Cyanamid*.

48 [1986] P.C.C. 57.

### (5) Mandatory Interlocutory Injunctions

18–045 For the grant of a mandatory injunction on an interlocutory basis there must be a "high degree of assurance" that it will appear at trial that the injunction was rightly granted.[49]

### iii. *Series 5 Software Ltd v Clarke*

18–046 Besides these "exceptions", note should also be taken of Laddie J's decision in *Series 5 Software Ltd v Clark,* which cannot be interpreted as anything other than a first instance rejection of the *Cyanamid* approach, but which has stood the test of time and is often followed nowadays. Taken collectively these authorities all suggest that the precision which *Cyanamid* sought to bring is illusory, first, because apart from a few cases which are resolved by Lord Diplock's preliminary considerations, the courts are required to move on to a vague balancing act, and, secondly, because when it has suited them, the courts have simply declined to apply the guidelines.[50]

*Series 5 Software Ltd v Clarke*

Chancery Division [1996] 1 All E.R. 853

18–047 LADDIE J.: It is, of course, comparatively rare for applications for interlocutory relief to reach the House of Lords. However, 1975 was an exception. In that year two cases, both of which involved an analysis of the courts' power to grant interlocutory injunctions, were heard more or less one after the other. The first was *F Hoffmann-La Roche & Co AG v Secretary of State for Trade and Industry*.[51] . . . In the course of that case their Lordships considered the circumstances in which interlocutory injunctions were granted and the conditions to which their grant could be subject. In particular Lord Diplock said:[52]

> "An interim injunction is a temporary and exceptional remedy which is available before the rights of the parties have been finally determined and, in the case of an ex parte injunction, even before the court had been apprised of the nature of the defendant's case. *To justify the grant of such a remedy the plaintiff must satisfy the court first that there is a strong prima facie case that he will be entitled to a final order restraining the defendant from doing what he is threatening to do*, and secondly that he will suffer irreparable injury which cannot be compensated by a subsequent award of damages in the action if the defendant is not prevented from doing it between the date of the application for the interim injunction and the date of the final order made on trial of the action. Nevertheless, at the time of the application it is not possible for the court to be absolutely certain that the plaintiff will succeed at the trial in establishing his legal right to restrain the defendant from doing what he is threatening to do. If he should fail to do so the defendant may have suffered loss as a result of having been prevented from doing it while the interim injunction was in force; and any loss is likely to be *damnum absque injuria* for which he could not recover damages from the plaintiff at common law. So unless some other means is provided in this event for compensating the defendant for his loss there is a risk that injustice may be done." (Emphasis added.)

18–048 Then, having explained that the imposition of the cross-undertaking is designed to mitigate the risk to the defendant, Lord Diplock proceeded:[53]

> "Beside mitigating the risk of injustice to the defendant the practice of exacting an undertaking as to damages facilitates the conduct of the business of the courts. It relieves the court of the necessity to embark at an interlocutory stage upon an enquiry as to the likelihood of the defendant's being able

---

49 *Shepherd Homes Ltd v Sandham* [1971] Ch. 340; *Locabail International Finance Ltd v Agroexport* [1986] 1 W.L.R. 657; *Nottingham Building Society v Eurodynamics Systems* [1993] F.S.R. 468 at 474.

50 A. Keay "Whither *American Cyanamid*?: Interim Injunctions in the 21st Century" (2004) 23 C.J.Q. 132.

51 [1973] A.C. 295.

52 At 360–361.

53 At 361.

to establish facts to destroy *the strong prima facie case which ex hypothesi will have been made out by the plaintiff*. The procedure on motion is unsuited to inquiries into disputed facts. This is best left to the trial of the action . . ." (Emphasis added.)

This was consistent with the approach which was followed in many, but not all, cases before *American Cyanamid*. The court had to pay regard to the strength or otherwise of the plaintiff's case as revealed by a consideration of all the affidavit evidence. 18–049

Judgment in *Hoffmann-La Roche* was given just before the long vacation on July 3, 1974. 18–050

That brings me to *American Cyanamid*, the hearing for which commenced after the long vacation on November 12, 1974. It can be assumed that the panel read the parties' briefs before that date. The panel consisted of Lord Diplock, Viscount Dilhorne, Lord Cross, Lord Salmon and Lord Edmund-Davies—that is, it included two members of the panel which decided *Hoffmann-La Roche*. If the House of Lords intended to say that it was inappropriate on an application for interlocutory relief, save in rare cases, to take into account the apparent strength of the plaintiff's case, it would mean that Lord Diplock performed a *volte face* on this issue in a matter of four months. In my view it is inconceivable that Lord Diplock and Lord Cross could have forgotten what was said in the *Hoffmann-La Roche* judgment a few months earlier. Therefore, if they were saying the opposite of what was said in *Hoffmann-La Roche*, they must have been aware that they were doing so but chose not to mention that fact or explain it in *American Cyanamid*. That is a proposition I find difficult to accept. It seems to me that it is therefore appropriate to consider whether what Lord Diplock said in *Hoffmann-La Roche* is incompatible with what he said in *American Cyanamid* only a few months later. For this it is necessary to consider the *American Cyanamid* decision with some care. 18–051

The *American Cyanamid* case was concerned with the alleged infringement of the main claim in the plaintiff's patent for absorbable surgical sutures. In response to the allegation of infringement, Ethicon presented a classic squeeze argument beloved of patent lawyers. It said that its sutures did not fall within the monopoly defined by the claim—that is it did not infringe, or, in the alternative, if the claim was construed widely enough to include its product, the patent was invalid on a number of grounds under the Patents Act 1949. 18–052

In the House of Lords, as in the High Court and the Court of Appeal, both parties had addressed the question of whether the plaintiff had demonstrated a strong prima facie case. In the course of his judgment, Lord Diplock said:[54] 18–053

> "Your Lordships should in my view take this opportunity of declaring that there is no such rule. The use of such expressions as 'a probability', 'a prima facie case', or 'a strong prima facie case' in the context of the exercise of a discretionary power to grant an interlocutory injunction leads to confusion as to the object sought to be achieved by this form of temporary relief. The court no doubt must be satisfied that the claim is not frivolous or vexatious; in other words, that there is a serious question to be tried."

The first question to be answered is precisely what was "such rule" the existence of which the House of Lords disapproved. This can be found in the early part of Lord Diplock's judgment. In the High Court, Graham J. had held that the plaintiff had made out a strong prima facie case and went on to say that the balance of convenience favoured the grant of interlocutory relief. The way in which the Court of Appeal dealt with the application was set out in the following passage in Lord Diplock's judgment:[55] 18–054

> "As Russell L.J. put it in the concluding paragraph of his reasons for judgment with which the other members of the court agreed—'. . . if there be no prima facie case on the point essential to entitle the plaintiff to complain of the defendant's proposed activities, that is the end of the claim to interlocutory relief.' 'Prima facie case' may in some contexts be an elusive concept, but the sense in which it was being used by Russell L.J. is apparent from an earlier passage in his judgment. After a detailed analysis of the more conflicting expert testimony he said: 'I am not satisfied on the present evidence that on the proper construction of this specification, addressed as it is to persons skilled in the relevant art or science, the claim extends to sterile surgical sutures produced not only from a homopolymer of glycolide but also from a copolymer of glycolide and up to 15 per cent of lactide. That is to say that I do not consider that a prima facie case of infringement is established.' In effect what the Court of Appeal was doing was trying the issue of infringement on the conflicting affidavit evidence as it stood, without

54 [1975] A.C. 396 at 407.
55 [1975] A.C. 396 at 404–405.

the benefit of oral testimony or cross-examination. They were saying: 'If we had to give judgment in the action now without any further evidence we should hold that Cyanamid had not satisfied the onus of proving that their patent would be infringed by Ethicon's selling sutures made of XLG.' The Court of Appeal accordingly did not find it necessary to go into the questions raised by Ethicon as to the validity of the patent or to consider where the balance of convenience lay."

**18-055** As Lord Diplock put it:[56]

> "[The Court of Appeal] considered that there was *a rule of practice so well established as to constitute a rule of law* that precluded them from granting any interim injunction unless on the evidence adduced by both the parties on the hearing of the application the applicant had satisfied the court that on the balance of probabilities the acts of the other party sought to be enjoined would, if committed, violate the applicant's legal rights." (Emphasis added.)

Lord Diplock then made it clear that it was in order to enable the existence of that rule of law to be considered that leave to appeal had been granted.

**18-056** The result of applying that "rule of law" was that in the Court of Appeal the motion lasted for two working weeks while the parties argued questions of polymer chemistry, infringement and validity. In the House of Lords the defendant tried to do the same thing. The note of argument there shows that sophisticated arguments of patent ambiguity, construction, inutility, false suggestion, insufficiency and unfair basis were advanced. In effect, the Court of Appeal had abandoned any attempt to evaluate the pros and cons of granting an interlocutory injunction and had said that there was a mandatory initial hurdle at which the plaintiff had fallen. The flexibility and absence of strict rules which had been advocated by the Court of Appeal in *Hubbard v Vosper* was ignored. If such a rule of law as envisaged by the Court of Appeal in *American Cyanamid* did exist, it would inevitably force the parties to engage in trying to prove at the interlocutory stage all those issues which were for determination at the trial. In a case as complicated as *American Cyanamid* it was likely to be impossible to show a strong prima facie case of infringement and validity and any attempt to do so would force the parties to expound at length on complicated technical and legal issues. But those were issues which at an interlocutory stage the court could not hope to resolve. It would have followed that if such a rule of law existed, interlocutory injunctions in patent cases, or in any other complicated case, would become a thing of the past no matter how severe was the damage to be suffered by the plaintiff in the interim.

**18-057** When Lord Diplock said that there was no such rule, he was referring to the so-called rule of law which the Court of Appeal had followed. In dismissing this approach, the House of Lords approved of the decision in *Hubbard v Vosper* and in particular that part of the decision in which the Court of Appeal deprecated any attempt to fetter the discretion of the court by laying down any rules which would have the effect of limiting the flexibility of the remedy.[57]

**18-058** Once it had disposed of the inflexible rule as applied by the Court of Appeal in the instant case, the House of Lords went on to consider what principles a court should bear in mind when deciding whether to grant interlocutory relief. First, it said:[58]

> ". . . [the court should] consider whether if the plaintiff were to succeed at the trial in establishing his right to a permanent injunction he would be adequately compensated by an award of damages for the loss he would have sustained as a result of the defendant's continuing to do what was sought to be enjoined between the time of the application and the time of the trial. If damages in the measure recoverable at common law would be adequate remedy and the defendant would be in a financial position to pay them, no interlocutory injunction should *normally* be granted, *however strong the plaintiff's claim appeared to be at that stage*." (Emphasis added.)

It should be noticed from the emphasised words in that passage that this approach was not said to be invariably the correct one and furthermore the words used suggest that where damages for the plaintiff was not an adequate remedy the apparent strength of the plaintiff's claim might well be a relevant consideration.

---

56 [1975] A.C. 396 at 405.
57 See [1975] A.C. 396 at 407.
58 [1975] A.C. 396 at 408.

Having considered the issue of adequacy of damages, Lord Diplock proceeded as follows:[59] 18–059

> "It is where there is doubt as to the adequacy of the respective remedies in damages available to either party or to both, that the question of balance of convenience arises. It would be unwise to attempt even to list all the various matters which may need to be taken into consideration in deciding where the balance lies, let alone to suggest the relative weight to be attached to them. These will vary from case to case."

The reality is that the balance of convenience issue will need to be considered in most cases because evidence relating to the adequacy of damages normally will be contradictory and there will be no possibility of resolving the differences by cross-examination. In the result, normally there will be doubt as to the adequacy of damages. It follows that in most cases it will be the exercise of taking into account all the issues relevant to the balance of convenience which will be the major task of the court faced with an application for interlocutory relief. As Lord Diplock went on to point out:[60] 18–060

> "Save in the simplest cases, the decision to grant or to refuse an interlocutory injunction will cause to whichever party is unsuccessful on the application some disadvantages which his ultimate success at the trial may show he ought to have been spared and the disadvantages may be such that the recovery of damages to which he would then be entitled either in the action or under the plaintiff's undertaking would not be sufficient to compensate him fully for all of them. The extent to which the disadvantages to each party would be incapable of being compensated in damages in the event of his succeeding at the trial is always a significant factor in assessing where the balance of convenience lies . . .".

In many cases before *American Cyanamid* the prospect of success was one of the important factors taken into account in assessing the balance of convenience. The courts would be less willing to subject the plaintiff to the risk of irrecoverable loss which would befall him if an interlocutory injunction was refused in those cases where it thought he was likely to win at the trial than in those cases where it thought he was likely to lose. The assessment of the prospects of success therefore was an important factor in deciding whether the court should exercise its discretion to grant interlocutory relief. It is this consideration which *American Cyanamid* is said to have prohibited in all but the most exceptional case, so it is necessary to consider with some care what was said in the House of Lords on this issue. 18–061

Lord Diplock said:[61] 18–062

> ". . . if the extent of the uncompensatable disadvantage to each party would not differ widely, it may not be improper to take into account in tipping the balance the relative strength of each party's case as revealed by the affidavit evidence adduced on the hearing of the application. . . . The court is not justified in embarking on anything resembling a trial of the action on conflicting affidavits in order to evaluate the strength of either party's case."

It appears to me that there is nothing in this which is inconsistent with the old practice. Although couched in terms "it may not be improper", this means that it is legitimate for the court to look at the relative strength of the parties' case as disclosed by the affidavits. The warning contained in the second of the quoted sentences is to avoid courts at the interlocutory stage engaging in mini-trials, which is what happened, at least in the Court of Appeal, in *American Cyanamid* itself. Interlocutory applications are meant to come on quickly and to be disposed of quickly. 18–063

The supposed problem with *American Cyanamid* centres on the following statement by Lord Diplock:[62] 18–064

> "[Assessing the relative strength of the parties' case], however, should be done only where it is apparent upon the facts disclosed by evidence as to which there is no credible dispute that the strength of one party's case is disproportionate to that of the other party."

If this means that the court cannot take into account its view of the strength of each party's case if there is any dispute on the evidence, as suggested by the use of the words "only" and "no credible dispute", then a new inflexible rule has been introduced to replace that applied by the Court of Appeal. For example, all a

---

59 [1975] A.C. 396 at 408.
60 [1975] A.C. 396 at 408–409.
61 [1975] A.C. 396 at 409.
62 [1975] A.C. 396 at 409.

defendant would have to do is raise a non-demurrable dispute as to relevant facts in his affidavit evidence and then he could invite the court to ignore the apparent strength of the plaintiff's case. This would be inconsistent with the flexible approach suggested in *Hubbard v Vosper*[63] which was cited with approval earlier in *American Cyanamid*.[64] Furthermore, it would be somewhat strange, since *American Cyanamid* directs courts to assess the adequacy of damages and the balance of convenience, yet these too are topics which will almost always be the subject of unresolved conflicts in the affidavit evidence.

**18–065** In my view Lord Diplock did not intend by the last-quoted passage to exclude consideration of the strength of the cases in most applications for interlocutory relief. It appears to me that what is intended is that the court should not attempt to resolve difficult issues of fact or law on an application for interlocutory relief. If, on the other hand, the court is able to come to a view as to the strength of the parties' case on the credible evidence, then it can do so. In fact, as any lawyer who has experience of interlocutory proceedings will know, it is frequently the case that it is easy to determine who is most likely to win the trial on the basis of the affidavit evidence and any exhibited contemporaneous documents. If it is apparent from that material that one party's case is much stronger than the other's then that is a matter the court should not ignore. To suggest otherwise would be to exclude from consideration an important factor and such exclusion would fly in the face of the flexibility advocated earlier in *American Cyanamid*. As Lord Diplock pointed out in *Hoffmann-La Roche*, one of the purposes of the cross-undertaking in damages is to safeguard the defendant if this preliminary view of the strength of the plaintiff's case proves to be wrong.

**18–066** Accordingly, it appears to me that in deciding whether to grant interlocutory relief, the court should bear the following matters in mind.

(1) The grant of an interlocutory injunction is a matter of discretion and depends on all the facts of the case.
(2) There are no fixed rules as to when an injunction should or should not be granted. The relief must be kept flexible.
(3) Because of the practice adopted on the hearing of applications for interlocutory relief, the court should rarely attempt to resolve complex issues of disputed fact or law.
(4) Major factors the court can bear in mind are (a) the extent to which damages are likely to be an adequate remedy for each party and the ability of the other party to pay, (b) the balance of convenience, (c) the maintenance of the status quo, and (d) any clear view the court may reach as to the relative strength of the parties' cases.

**18–067** In coming to this conclusion I am encouraged by the following considerations.

(1) The House of Lords in *American Cyanamid* did not suggest that it was changing the basis upon which most courts had approached the exercise of discretion in this important area.
(2) The only issue which it was expressly addressing was the existence of the inflexible rule of law which had been applied as a mandatory condition by the Court of Appeal.
(3) It would mean that there was no significant inconsistency between the *Hoffmann-La Roche* and *American Cyanamid* decisions.
(4) It would be consistent with the approval given by the House of Lords to the decision in *Hubbardv Vosper* and, implicitly, the decision to the same effect in *Evans Marshall & Co Ltd v Bertola SA*[65] (a decision of Lord Edmund-Davies when in the Court of Appeal).
(5) It would preserve what is one of the great values of interlocutory proceedings, namely an early, though non-binding, view of the merits from a judge. Before *American Cyanamid* a decision at the interlocutory stage would be a major ingredient leading to the parties resolving their differences without the need for a trial. There is nothing inherently unsatisfactory in this. Most clients ask for and receive advice on prospects from their lawyers well before there has been cross-examination. In most cases the lawyers have little difficulty giving such advice. It should also be remembered that in many jurisdictions on the continent trials are conducted without discovery or cross-examination. There is nothing inherently unfair in a court here expressing at least a preliminary view based on written evidence. After all, it is what the courts managed to do for a century and a half.

---

63 [1972] 2 Q.B. 84.
64 [1975] A.C. 396 at 407.
65 [1973] 1 W.L.R. 349.

(6) Allowing parties to come to an earlier view on prospects would assist in reducing the costs of litigation. This is an issue to which much attention is being given at the moment.
(7) It would mean that the approach of the courts in England and Wales to the grant of interlocutory relief would be the same as that followed in Scotland. . . .

### iv. Applications without Notice

In cases where the nature of the interim relief sought requires that the defendant be taken by surprise, or where the relief sought is urgent, in that it must be granted right away, if it is to be granted at all, interim injunctions may be applied for without notice (formerly termed ex parte), i.e. in the absence of the party against whom the order is sought. An order can then be made, normally effective only over a short period, which will be reviewed at a hearing with notice to the other side at the end of that period (or at an earlier time if the defendant applies before the end of the period to have the order discharged). On applications without notice, applicants must fully and frankly disclose all the facts in their knowledge which are relevant to the exercise of the court's discretion, and this extends to disclosing possible defences which the defendant may have. Breach of this duty is a serious matter that will entitle (though not oblige) the court to discharge the injunction without more, and leave the applicant to apply again.[66] **18–068**

### v. Injunctions against Lawful Action

The court's power to grant interim injunctions is not limited to forbidding actions which are inherently unlawful. Freezing orders[67] are made to restrain defendants from actions which are lawful in themselves (e.g. withdrawing money from a bank account); and in harassment cases, the courts have granted interim injunctions forbidding defendants to enter specified "exclusion zones", even though they have the same basic right as any other member of the public to use the public highway running through these zones.[68] **18–069**

### vi. The Effect of the Civil Procedure Rules (CPR)

By virtue of s.2 of the Civil Procedure Act 1997 and the Civil Procedure Rules 1998,[69] all civil claims brought after 25 April 1999 have fallen to be dealt with according to the CPR. Based on a review of civil justice by Lord Woolf, the then Master of the Rolls, these were intended to effect a fundamental change in the administration of civil justice. For present purposes, it is pertinent to note that the principles according to which the courts have, since *Cyanamid*, awarded interim relief, must now be read subject to the "overriding objective" of allowing the court (through, among other things, active "case management") to deal with cases justly. This may include taking steps to ensure that the parties are on an equal footing, saving expense, and dealing with a case in ways which are appropriate to the amount involved, the importance of the case, the complexity of the case and the financial situation of the parties. Some or all of these might well militate in favour of the approach boldly (and, it is **18–070**

---

66 *Lloyd's Bowmaker Ltd v Britannia Arrow Holdings Plc* [1988] 1 W.L.R. 1337 at 1343–1344; *Memory Corporation Plc v Sidhu (No.2)* [2000] 1 W.L.R. 1443 at 1459; *Network Telecom (Europe) Ltd v Telephone Systems International Inc* [2004] 1 All E.R. (Comm.) 418, cf. *Dadourian Group International Inc v Simms* [2009] 1 Lloyd's Rep. 601 at [196]–[210].

67 See paras 18–074ff.

68 See, e.g. *Burris v Azadani* [1995] 1 W.L.R. 1372: *Dailchi Pharmaceuticals UK Ltd v SHAC* [2004] 1 W.L.R. 1503; *Harvey Nichols & Co Ltd v Coalition to Abolish the Fur Trade* [2014] EWHC 4685 (QB).

69 SI 3132/1998.

suggested, sensibly) advocated by Laddie J in *Series 5 Software Ltd v Clark,*[70] which has been set out above.

### vii. The Effect of the Human Rights Act 1998

**18–071** The Human Rights Act 1998 most obviously affects the award of interim injunctions through s.12(3), which imposes a special threshold test which must be satisfied before a court may grant an interim injunction which might affect the exercise of a defendant's right to freedom of expression under art.10 of the European Convention. The section sets a higher threshold for the grant of interim injunctions against the news media than the *Cyanamid* guideline of a "serious question to be tried" or a "real prospect of success" at the trial, as it provides that interim injunctions should not be granted "so as to restrain publication before trial unless the court is satisfied that the applicant is likely to establish that publication should not be allowed." In *Cream Holdings Ltd v Banerjee*[71] the House of Lords held that the word "likely" in s.12(3) will generally mean "more likely than not", although there are some cases where a lesser degree of likelihood may suffice: for example, "where the potential adverse consequences of the disclosure are particularly grave".[72] Applying this test, their Lordships concluded that the applicants were not entitled to an interim injunction preventing the disclosure of confidential information because the matters which the defendant newspaper wished to publish were of serious public interest, suggesting that the applicants' prospects of success at trial were insufficiently strong to justify an interim injunction.

**18–072** In *Greene v Associated Newspapers Ltd,*[73] the question arose whether the *Cream Holdings* test also applies where an applicant seeks an interim injunction restraining the publication of material which is alleged to be defamatory. The Court of Appeal held that it does not, reasoning that defamation cases raise different issues from cases concerned with breach of confidence and breach of privacy[74]: confidentiality and privacy, once lost, are lost forever, unlike reputations which can be rebuilt. Defamation cases therefore continue to be governed by the rule in *Bonnard v Perryman*[75]: if a defendant in a libel action makes a statement verified as true in which she maintains that she can and will justify her alleged libel, then the claimant cannot have an interim injunction to restrain the publication of an allegedly defamatory statement unless it is plain that the plea of justification is bound to fail. However, the defamation rule does not apply, and the *Cream Holdings* test is used, in comparative advertising cases concerned with trade mark infringements.[76] It is also used where publication of information would allegedly create a substantial risk that the course of justice in an ongoing criminal trial will be seriously impeded or prejudiced, contrary to the Contempt of Court Act 1981.[77]

---

70 [1996] 1 All E.R. 853.
71 [2005] 1 A.C. 253, followed in, e.g. *Douglas v Hello! Ltd (No.3)* [2006] Q.B. 135; *Browne v Associated Newspapers Ltd* [2008] Q.B. 103.
72 *Cream Holdings* at [22], per Lord Nicholls.
73 [2005] Q.B. 972.
74 Cf. *Campbell v MGN Ltd* [2004] A.C. 457; *Re S (a child)* [2005] 1 F.L.R. 591.
75 [1891] 2 Ch. 269.
76 *Boehringer Ingelheim Ltd v Vetplus Ltd* [2007] Bus. L.R. 1456, discussed in I. Simon Fhima, "Trade Marks and Free Speech" (2013) 44 I.I.C. 293.
77 *Attorney General v Random House Group Ltd* [2010] E.M.L.R. 9.

## viii. Two Special Types of Interim Injunction

Both *Mareva* (now "freezing") injunctions and *Anton Piller* (now "search") orders are interim orders. As Lord Donaldson MR made plain in *Polly Peck International v Nadir (No.2)*,[78] there is no question of *Cyanamid* applying to *Mareva* injunctions, "which proceed on principles quite different from those applicable to other interlocutory injunctions." The same is true of *Anton Piller* or search orders. Together they have been described by the same judge as the law's "nuclear weapons".[79] 18–073

### (1) Freezing Injunctions

Section 37 of the Senior Courts Act 1981 provides that: 18–074

> (1) The High Court may by order (whether interlocutory or final) grant an injunction or appoint a receiver in all cases in which it appears to the court to be just and convenient to do so . . .
> (3) The power of the High Court under subsection (1) to grant an interlocutory injunction restraining a party to any proceedings from removing from the jurisdiction of the High Court, or otherwise dealing with, assets located within that jurisdiction shall be exercisable in cases where that party is, as well as in cases where he is not, domiciled, resident or present within that jurisdiction.

This provision is now the statutory basis for the order that was first granted in *Nippon Yusen Kaisha v Karageorgis*[80] but which took its former name ("*Mareva* injunction") from the second case of its grant, *Mareva Compania Naveira SA v International Bulkcarriers SA*.[81] The criteria for obtaining a freezing injunction are: (1) a good arguable case[82]; (2) that there is a real risk that any judgment will go unsatisfied by reason of the disposal by the defendant of her assets, unless she is restrained by court order from disposing of them; and (3) it would be just and convenient in all the circumstances of the case to grant the relief sought. 18–075

On (1), it has been said that this amounts to a case "which is more than barely capable of serious argument, but not necessarily one which the judge considers would have a better than 50 per cent chance of success".[83] The requirement in (2) is not that of "nefarious intent" (i.e. that the defendant will dissipate assets so that a judgment will be unsatisfied) but, rather an objective risk that there will be dissipation making it likely that the result of her dissipation will be that the judgment goes unsatisfied.[84] The requirement in (3) is no mere formula: it may be regarded as justifying the approach taken in *Polly Peck International v Nadir (No.2)*[85] with regard to banks whose business, depending on the confidence of their investors, might be destroyed at a stroke: the claimant's cross-undertaking in damages would be of little consolation or utility. 18–076

It is important for third parties to know just what acts are prohibited by the order, since they can commit a contempt of court if they have notice of the terms of an injunction with which they act 18–077

---

78 [1992] 2 Lloyd's Rep. 238 at 249.
79 *Bank Mellat v Nikpour* [1985] F.S.R. 87 at 91–92.
80 [1975] 1 W.L.R. 1093.
81 [1975] 2 Lloyd's Rep. 509.
82 The court is bound therefore to consider the merits of the case.
83 *Ninemia Corporation v Trave Schiffahrtsgesellschaft GmbH (The "Niedersachsen")* [1983] 2 Lloyd's Rep. 600 at 605 per Mustill J.
84 89 In *Derby & Co Ltd v Weldon* [1990] Ch. 48, the Court of Appeal rejected the subjective interpretation of the requirement even in the case of the wide ("draconian", per May LJ) relief granted there. A fortiori, then, in a standard case.
85 [1992] 2 Lloyd's Rep. 238.

inconsistently, as we have seen.[86] In *Customs & Excise Commissioners v Barclays Bank Plc*,[87] however, the House of Lords held that third parties such as banks owe no duty of care, and so cannot be liable for the tort of negligence, if they break the terms of a freezing order, e.g. by allowing withdrawals from a frozen bank account.

**18-078** The injunction is available both before and after judgment and may restrict dealings with all assets of the defendant or merely assets up to a certain value (i.e. the value of the claimant's claim plus costs).[88] However, it gives the claimant no right in rem or security or priority over the defendant's creditors (of which the claimant has not yet shown herself to be one).

**18-079** Prior to the enactment of the Civil Jurisdiction and Judgments Act 1982, there was no power in the High Court to grant a freezing injunction against a defendant who had assets in the jurisdiction but against whom there was no substantive claim subject to the jurisdiction, the claimant asserting no proprietary interest in the assets.[89] The Act, which gives effect to the Convention on Jurisdiction and the Enforcement of Judgments in Civil and Commercial Matters, has been interpreted by the Court of Appeal[90] to provide that such an injunction can be obtained in England before trial or after judgment even though the claimant has no cause of action, in England, against the defendant: so long as a court in another contracting state has jurisdiction, it suffices.

### (2) Search Orders

**18-080** In *Anton Piller KG v Manufacturing Processes Ltd*,[91] the Court of Appeal approved the making of an order, in substance an interim mandatory injunction, requiring the defendants to allow the claimant's solicitors to enter the defendants' premises to inspect documents and remove them to the claimant's solicitors' custody. The jurisdiction to make such orders was subsequently placed on a statutory footing by the Civil Procedure Act 1997 s.7. Failure to comply with the order is a contempt by the defendant and so, even though the order does not entitle the claimant to enter as if she had a search warrant, the defendant has good reason to allow her so to do. The order is made so as to safeguard vital evidence which is needed to prove the claim although it may be granted simply to obtain information necessary to safeguard the claimant's rights, to locate assets against which a judgment might be enforced, and to preserve property which might otherwise be dissipated or destroyed.

**18-081** Because of the truly draconian effect of an order of this sort which, to a greater extent than the freezing injunction, involves serious inroads into civil liberties,[92] it is now accepted that they are to

---

86 See para.18-007. In the particular case of freezing injunctions, note Eveleigh LJ's comments in *Z Ltd v A-Z and AA-LL* [1982] Q.B. 558 at 583, but cf. *Z Bank v D* [1994] 1 Lloyd's Rep. 656.

87 [2007] 1 A.C. 181.

88 On the question whether assets are relevantly "owned" or "controlled" by a defendant when they are vested in a company owned by the defendant, see *Group Seven Ltd v Allied Investment Corp Ltd* [2014] 1 W.L.R. 735 and *Lakatamia Shipping Co Ltd v Su* [2015] 1 W.L.R. 291, both noted by Aitken (2015) 131 L.Q.R. 26.

89 *Siskina (Owners of Cargo Lately Laden on Board) v Distos Compania Naveira SA* [1979] A.C. 210, although in his dissenting speech in *Mercedes-Benz AG v Leiduck* [1996] A.C. 284, Lord Nicholls considered the law should move on to allow "free-standing" freezing injunctions auxiliary to foreign proceedings and in 1999 the Privy Council gave leave for an appeal from the Bahamas to raise the point, but the appeal ultimately was not proceeded with.

90 *Babanaft International Co SA v Bassatne* [1990] Ch. 13. See also *Republic of Haiti v Duvalier* [1990] Q.B. 202; *Baltic Shipping Co v Translink Shipping Ltd* [1995] 1 Lloyd's Rep. 673; *Bank of China v NBM LLC* [2002] 1 W.L.R. 884; *Parbulk II A/S v PT Humpuss Intermoda Transportasi TBK (The Mahakam)* [2012] 2 All E.R. (Comm) 513.

91 [1976] Ch. 55.

92 i.e. the right to be heard before the making of an order against one, the right to be free from arbitrary search and seizure, and the right to privacy in one's own home (orders were commonly made against defendants to be executed at their places of residence).

be granted sparingly.[93] The three essential requirements (according to Ormrod LJ in the *Anton Piller* case[94]) are: (1) an extremely strong prima facie case; (2) the potential or actual damage to the claimant (if an order is not made) must be very serious; and (3) there must be clear evidence that the defendant has in her possession incriminating documents or things and that there is a real possibility that she may destroy such material before any application with notice can be made.[95] Even if all the conditions are met, the court still has to be satisfied that the need for the order outweighs the injustice of making an order against a defendant without her having been heard.[96] This has the effect that an order will not be made against persons of good standing who are likely to obey an order of the court to deliver up.[97]

There is a common law principle enshrined in the Civil Evidence Act 1968 s.14(1), that no person may be obliged in civil proceedings to produce any document or thing which may incriminate her (or her spouse).[98] *Emmanuel v Emmanuel*[99] clarifies, however, that an order may be made if the risk of incrimination extends only to a charge of perjury in the proceedings in the context of which the order is sought. In *C Plc v P*,[100] child pornography was found on a computer that the defendant had handed over pursuant to a search order made in connection with an action for breach of confidence and copyright infringement. The defendant had only permitted the examination of his computer to take place after asserting his privilege against self-incrimination. Nevertheless, the Court of Appeal upheld the trial judge's direction that the computer should be passed to the police, because the privilege against self-incrimination did not apply to material constituting freestanding evidence which was not produced under compulsion. **18–082**

## 3. Specific Performance

### A. Overview

A decree of specific[101] performance is an order of the court compelling the defendant personally to do what she has promised to do. Such orders are only available to enforce positive obligations; negative obligations must be enforced by injunction. Compulsion may take various forms, e.g. empowering a person other than the defendant to execute a conveyance which the latter has promised but refused to execute,[102] or, more generally, committing the defendant to prison on account of her contempt[103] **18–083**

---

93 The frequency with which orders came to be granted (see Oliver LJ's reference to them as "very, very commonly employed" and "almost commonplace" in *Dunlop Holdings Ltd v Staravia Ltd* [1982] Com. L.R. 3) led to the expression of judicial concern in a number of cases about claimants' failures to demonstrate, and judicial failure to insist on demonstration, of the necessity of making an order (e.g. Hoffmann J in *Lock International Plc v Beswick* [1989] 1 W.L.R. 1268) and led to the establishment of a committee under Staughton LJ which made recommendations (largely followed in the model orders which preceded the current model orders contained in CPR) on future practice.

94 [1976] Ch. 55 at 62.

95 The Staughton Committee added a fourth requirement that the harm likely to be caused by the execution of the order to the defendant and her business affairs must not be excessive or out of proportion to the legitimate object of the order.

96 This is no mere formula and is a more important element in the judicial balancing exercise in search order cases than in freezing injunction or other cases of applications without notice. This is for the reason that although interlocutory, once executed the order cannot be "unexecuted". There is often no sense in a defendant's bothering to discharge a search order at a hearing with notice to the other side once it has been executed.

97 e.g. barristers and their clerks: *Randolph M Fields v Watts* (1985) 129 Sol. Jo. 67.

98 Subject to the exceptions contained in the Theft Act 1968 s.31, and the Senior Courts Act 1981 s.72.

99 [1982] 1 W.L.R. 669.

100 [2008] Ch. 1.

101 Referring to the performance in kind (in Latin, *in specie*) of a contractual (or primary) obligation rather than the performance of the secondary obligation to pay damages for loss caused by breach of a primary obligation.

102 Senior Courts Act 1981 s.39.

103 Sequestration of assets until compliance is also available against both individuals and corporations and is the only way of

(i.e. disobedience to the order of the court) until she complies with the court order and purges her contempt.

18-084 In *Johnson v Agnew*,[104] Lord Wilberforce held that if a decree is granted, the contract continues "under control of the court",[105] so that a further court order is needed to dissolve the decree before either party can terminate the contract for breach and ask for damages. He also held that the court can refuse to dissolve the decree "if to do so would be unjust".[106] The advantage of this is that it enables the court to prevent a claimant who has won an order for specific performance from changing her mind and asserting a right to damages after the defendant has detrimentally relied on the original order. However, it also means that whenever an order for specific performance is made, the parties' original rights under the contract are replaced by a set of new equitable rights which replicate the parties' original rights, including the right to terminate the contract for breach, but which are subject to equitable principles that would not have affected the parties' original rights at common law.

18-085 This model of the law is complex, and it is also inconsistent with Lord Wilberforce's own statement that "if an order for specific performance is sought and is made, the contract remains in effect and is not merged in the judgment for specific performance".[107] Hence there is much to be said for the different view that even after an order for specific performance has been made, both parties' common law rights under the contract subsist, including the right to terminate for breach and sue for damages, and that either party can exercise these rights without complying with equitable requirements such as the rule that a claimant must come into court with clean hands.[108]

### *Johnson v Agnew*

### House of Lords [1980] A.C. 367

18-086 The claimants, in arrears of mortgage, contracted to sell their properties to the defendant at a price in excess of the amount owing on mortgage and sufficient to allow them to purchase another property. The defendant failed to complete and an order for specific performance was made. Before it was carried out the claimants' mortgagees enforced their securities so that (a) the claimants could no longer convey the properties and (b) there was insufficient even to pay off the mortgages, let alone purchase another property with the proceeds. The claimants therefore sought an order that the defendant should pay the purchase price, less the moneys received on the mortgagees' sales, and an inquiry as to damages.

18-087 LORD WILBERFORCE (with whom LORD SALMON, LORD FRASER, LORD KEITH and LORD SCARMAN agreed): My Lords, this appeal arises in a vendors' action for specific performance of a contract for the sale of land, the appellant being the purchaser and the vendors respondents. The factual situation is commonplace, indeed routine. An owner of land contracts to sell it to a purchaser; the purchaser fails to complete the contract; the vendor goes to the court and obtains an order that the contract be specifically performed; the purchaser still does not complete; the vendor goes back to the court and asks for the order for specific performance to be dissolved, for the contract to be terminated or "rescinded", and for an order for damages. One would think that the law as to so typical a set of facts would be both simple and clear. It is no credit to our law that it is neither. . . .

18-088 By April 3, 1975, specific performance of the contract for sale had become impossible. The vendors took no action upon the order for specific performance [entered on 26 November 1974] until November

---

proceeding against corporations for contempt, although their directors may, of course, be imprisoned. Fines may also be imposed.

104 [1980] A.C. 367.

105 *Johnson* at 398. See too Megarry VC's comments in *Singh (Sudagar) v Nazeer* [1979] Ch. 474 at 480–481.

106 *Johnson* at 399.

107 *Johnson* at 393, citing *Austins of East Ham Ltd v Macey* [1941] Ch. 338 at 341, where Sir Wilfrid Greene MR stressed that after an order for specific performance has been made "the contract is still there". See too *John Barker & Co Ltd v Littman* [1941] Ch. 405 at 412.

108 M. Hetherington, "Keeping the Plaintiff out of His Contractual Remedies: The Heresies That Survive *Johnson v Agnew*" (1980) 96 L.Q.R. 403; *Meagher, Gummow and Lehane's Equity: Doctrines and Remedies* (2014), para.20–265.

5, 1976, when they issued a notice of motion seeking (a) an order that the purchaser should pay the balance of the purchase price and an inquiry as to damages or (b) alternatively a declaration that they were entitled to treat the contract as repudiated by the purchaser and to forfeit the deposit and an inquiry as to damages.

On February 25, 1977, Megarry V.C. dismissed the motion. He rejected the first claim on the ground that, as specific performance was no longer possible, it would be unjust to order payment of the full purchase price. The second claim was not pressed, on the ground that it was precluded by authority: *Capital and Suburban Properties Ltd v Swycher*.[109] **18–089**

The vendors appealed to the Court of Appeal who again rejected each alternative: they followed the previous decision in *Swycher's* case. However they held that the vendors could recover damages under the Chancery Amendment Act 1858 (Lord Cairns' Act), which enables the court to award damages in addition to or in substitution for specific performance. They accordingly made an order discharging the order for specific performance and an order for an inquiry as to damages. They fixed the date on which damages should be assessed as November 26, 1974, being the date of entry of the order for specific performance. The purchaser is now appealing against this order. **18–090**

In this situation it is possible to state at least some uncontroversial propositions of law. **18–091**

First, in a contract for the sale of land, after time has been made, or has become, of the essence of the contract, if the purchaser fails to complete, the vendor can either treat the purchaser as having repudiated the contract, accept the repudiation, and proceed to claim damages for breach of the contract, both parties being discharged from further performance of the contract; or he may seek from the court an order for specific performance with damages for any loss arising from delay in performance. (Similar remedies are of course available of purchasers against vendors.) This is simply the ordinary law of contract applied to contracts capable of specific performance. **18–092**

Secondly, the vendor may proceed by action for the above remedies (viz., specific performance or damages) in the alternative. At the trial he will however have to elect which remedy to pursue. **18–093**

Thirdly, if the vendor treats the purchaser as having repudiated the contract and accepts the repudiation, he cannot thereafter seek specific performance. This follows from the fact that, the purchaser having repudiated the contract and his repudiation having been accepted, both parties are discharged from further performance. **18–094**

At this point it is important to dissipate a fertile source of confusion and to make clear that although the vendor is sometimes referred to in the above situation as "rescinding" the contract, this so-called "rescission" is quite different from rescission ab initio, such as may arise for example in cases of mistake, fraud or lack of consent. In those cases, the contract is treated in law as never having come into existence. (Cases of a contractual right to rescind may fall under this principle but are not relevant to the present discussion.) In the case of an accepted repudiatory breach the contract has come into existence but has been put an end to or discharged. Whatever contrary indications may be disinterred from old authorities, it is now quite clear, under the general law of contract, that acceptance of a repudiatory breach does not bring about "rescission ab initio". **18–095**

Fourthly, if an order for specific performance is sought and is made, the contract remains in effect and is not merged in the judgment for specific performance. This is clear law, best illustrated by the judgment of Sir Wilfrid Greene M.R. in *Austins of East Ham Ltd v Macey*[110] in a passage which deals both with this point and with that next following. It repays quotation in full. **18–096**

> "The contract is still there. Until it is got rid of, it remains as a blot on the title, and the position of the vendor, where the purchaser has made default, is that he is entitled, not to annul the contract by the aid of the court, but to obtain the normal remedy of a party to a contract which the other party has repudiated. He cannot, in the circumstances, treat it as repudiated except by order of the court and the effect of obtaining such an order is that the contract, which until then existed, is brought to an end. The real position, in my judgment, is that, so far from proceeding to the enforcement of an order for specific performance, the vendor, in such circumstances is choosing a remedy which is alternative to the remedy of proceeding under the order for specific performance. He could attempt to enforce that order and could levy an execution which might prove completely fruitless. Instead of doing that, he

[109] [1976] Ch. 319.
[110] [1941] Ch. 338 at 341.

elects to ask the court to put an end to the contract, and that is an alternative to an order for enforcing specific performance."

18–097 Fifthly, if the order for specific performance is not complied with by the purchaser, the vendor may either apply to the court for enforcement of the order, or may apply to the court to dissolve the order and ask the court to put an end to the contract. This proposition is as stated in *Austins of East Ham Ltd v Macey*[111] and is in my opinion undoubted law, both on principle and authority. It follows, indeed, automatically from the facts that the contract remains in force after the order for specific performance and that the purchaser has committed a breach of it of a repudiatory character which he has not remedied, or as Megarry V.C. puts it, that he is refusing to complete.

18–098 These propositions being, as I think they are, uncontrovertible, there only remains the question whether, if the vendor takes the latter course, i.e., of applying to the court to put an end to the contract, he is entitled to recover damages for breach of the contract. On principle one may ask "Why ever not?" If, as is clear, the vendor is entitled, after, and notwithstanding that an order for specific performance has been made, if the purchaser still does not complete the contract, to ask the court to permit him to accept the purchaser's repudiation and to declare the contract to be terminated, why, if the court accedes to this, should there not follow the ordinary consequences, undoubted under the general law of contract, that on such acceptance and termination the vendor may recover damages for breach of contract?

18–099 I now consider the arguments which are said to support the negative answer.

18–100 The principal authority lies in the case of *Henty v Schröder*,[112] in which Sir George Jessel M.R. is briefly reported as having laid down that a vendor "could not at the same time obtain an order to have the agreement rescinded and claim damages against the defendant for breach of the agreement."

18–101 At first instance, [*Henty*] has been followed usually uncritically . . . [and it was also] endorsed by the Court of Appeal in *Capital and Suburban Properties Ltd v Swycher*,[113] but on a new basis which I shall shortly consider, and in the present case.

18–102 This is however the first time that this House has had to consider the right of an innocent party to a contract for the sale of land to damages on the contract being put an end to by accepted repudiation, and I think that we have the duty to take a fresh look. I should certainly be reluctant to invite your Lordships to endorse a line of authority so weak and unconvincing in principle. Fortunately there is support for a more attractive and logical approach from another bastion of the common law whose courts have adopted a more robust attitude. . . .

18–103 [He then considered *McDonald v Dennys Lascelles Ltd*,[114] *Holland v Wiltshire*,[115] and *Mckenna v Richey*,[116] before continuing:] My Lords, I am happy to follow the latter case. In my opinion *Henty v Schröder* cannot stand against the powerful tide of logical objection and judicial reasoning. It should no longer be regarded as of authority: the cases following it should be overruled. . . .

18–104 The second basis for denying damages in such cases as the present is that which underlines the judgment of the Court of Appeal in *Swycher's* case. This is really a rationalisation of *Henty v Schröder*, the weakness of which case the court well perceived. The main argument there accepted was that by deciding to seek the remedy of specific performance the vendor (or purchaser) has made an election which either is irrevocable or which becomes so when the order for specific performance is made. A second limb of this argument (but in reality a different argument) is that the vendor (or purchaser) has adequate remedies under the order for specific performance so that there is no need, or equitable ground, for allowing him to change his ground and ask for damages.

18–105 In my opinion, the argument based on irrevocable election, strongly pressed by the appellant's counsel in the present appeal, is unsound. Election, though the subject of much learning and refinement, is in the end a doctrine based on simple considerations of common sense and equity. It is easy to see that a party who has chosen to put an end a contract by accepting the other party's repudiation cannot afterwards seek specific performance. This is simply because the contract has gone—what is dead is dead. But it is no more difficult to agree that a party, who has chosen to seek specific

---

[111] And see *Singh (Sudagar) v Nazeer* [1979] Ch. 474 at 480, *per* Megarry V.-C.
[112] (1879) 12 Ch.D. 666 at 667.
[113] [1976] Ch. 319.
[114] (1933) 48 C.L.R. 457.
[115] (1954) 90 C.L.R. 409.
[116] [1950] V.L.R. 360.

performance, may quite well thereafter, if specific performance fails to be realised, say, "Very well, then, the contract should be regarded as terminated." It is quite consistent with a decision provisionally to keep alive, to say, "Well, this is no use—let us now end the contract's life." A vendor who seeks (and gets) specific performance is merely electing for a course which may or may not lead to implementation of the contract—what he elects for is not eternal and unconditional affirmation, but a continuance of the contract under control of the court which control involves the power, in certain events, to terminate it. If he makes an election at all, he does so when he decides not to proceed under the order for specific performance, but to ask the court to terminate the contract: see the judgment of Sir Wilfrid Greene M.R. in *Austins of East Ham Ltd v Macey* quoted above. The fact is that the election argument proves too much. If it were correct it would deny the vendor not just the right to damages, but the right to "rescind" the contract, but there is no doubt that this right exists: what is in question is only the right on "rescission", to claim damages.

In my respectful opinion therefore *Swycher's* case, whether it should be regarded as resting upon *Henty v Schröder*, or upon an independent argument based on election was wrongly decided In so far as it denied a right to contractual damages and should so far be overruled. The vendors should have been entitled, upon discharge of the contract, on grounds of normal and accepted principle, to damages appropriate for a breach of contract. **18–106**

There is one final point, on this part of the case, on which I should make a brief observation. Once the matter has been placed in the hands of a court of equity, or one exercising equity jurisdiction, the subsequent control of the matter will be exercised according to equitable principles. The court would not make an order dissolving the decree of specific performance and terminating the contract (with recovery of damages) if to do so would be unjust, in the circumstances then existing, to the other party, in this case to the purchaser. This is why there was, in the Court of Appeal, rightly, a relevant and substantial argument, repeated in this House, that the non-completion of the contract was due to the default of the vendors: if this had been made good, the court could properly have refused them the relief sought. But the Court of Appeal came to the conclusion that this non-completion, and the ultimate impossibility of completion, was the fault of the purchaser. I agree with their conclusion and their reasons on this point and shall not repeat or add to them. . . **18–107**

## *B. Equitable Principles Governing the Grant of Specific Performance*

Not all positive contractual stipulations or promises will be specifically enforced, and in the rest of this section we shall examine the principles upon which the court's discretion to order specific performance will be exercised. It is nowadays refused only according to reasonably settled principles, the most important of which are: (1) lack of consideration; (2) adequacy of common law remedies; (3) equity will not act in vain; (4) illegality or public policy; (5) lack of mutuality of a sort irremediable by imposition of terms; (6) that the contract is incapable of being enforced in its entirety; (7) that the order could not be enforced without the constant supervision of the court; (8) delay; (9) lack of clean hands; (10) undue hardship; (11) performance would involve the defendant in a breach of contract (or trust); (12) set-off; (13) mistake and misrepresentation; and (14) misdescription of subject-matter. Each of these is considered below. **18–108**

### i. Lack of Consideration

Lack of consideration prevents there being a contract at all so that there is nothing to perform, *in specie* or otherwise.[117] The consideration provided by a deed, although sufficient for the courts to discover a binding contract at law, is insufficient for the courts to hold that this contract is specifically **18–109**

---

[117] A similar consideration requires that, for example, contracts for the sale or disposition of interests in land must comply with s.2 of the Law of Property (Miscellaneous Provisions) Act 1989 before specific performance may be ordered. Likewise contracts void at law for other reasons, e.g. mistake, illegality and uncertainty.

enforceable in equity.[118] Nor will past consideration support a suit in equity.[119] However, there is no equitable test of adequacy of consideration (it follows the law in that respect) and the provision of money or money's worth, however small the sum, will suffice.[120]

### ii. Inadequacy of Damages

18–110 The best way to illustrate how this principle operates in relation to the enforcement of positive contractual stipulations is to examine different types of contract, some that have been held to be specifically enforceable and then some that have been held not to be.

#### (1) Contracts for the Disposition of an Interest in Land

18–111 Each piece of real estate is regarded as unique and, therefore, damages will be an inadequate remedy for a purchaser in the sense that damages will not enable her to buy a replacement in the market, as held in *Adderley v Dixon*.[121] Although damages will, clearly, be an adequate remedy for a vendor (who wants only money), a decree will lie against a purchaser on grounds of mutuality[122]:

> A contract to mortgage property, real or personal, will, normally at least, be specifically enforceable, for a mere claim to damages or repayment is obviously less valuable than a security in the event of the debtor's insolvency.[123]

*Adderley v Dixon*

Court of Chancery (1824) 1 Sim. & St. 607

18–112 The claimants took assignments of certain debts which had been proven in the estates of two bankrupts. This entitled them to whatever dividend might be declared on the debts in the bankruptcy. The claimants then contracted to sell their rights under the assignments for 2 shillings and sixpence in the pound to the defendant. The claimants sought specific performance of the purchaser's obligation to pay the price.

18–113 SIR JOHN LEACH V.C.: Courts of Equity decree the specific performance of contracts not upon any distinction between realty and personalty, but because damages at law may not in the particular case, afford a complete remedy. Thus a Court of Equity decrees performance of a contract for land, not because of the real nature of the land, but because damages at law, which must be calculated upon the general money value of land, may not be a complete remedy to the purchaser, to whom the land may have a peculiar and special value. So a Court of Equity will not, generally, decree performance of a contract for the sale of stock or goods, not because of their personal nature, but because damages at law, calculated upon the market price of the stock or goods, are as complete a remedy to the purchaser as the delivery of the stock or goods contracted for; inasmuch as, with the damages, he may purchase the same quantity of the like stock or goods.

---

118 *Re Pryce* [1917] 1 Ch. 234 at 241, per Eve J Mere covenantees are therefore volunteers in equity and can only enforce the covenant at law: *Cannon v Hartley* [1949] Ch. 213. In marriage settlement cases, however, children of a marriage may obtain specific performance, as they are treated in equity as having provided consideration: *Re Pryce; Re Kay's Settlement* [1939] Ch. 329.

119 *Robertson v St John* (1786) 2 Bro. C.C. 140

120 *Mountford v Scott* [1975] Ch. 258. But cf. *Milroy v Lord* (1862) 4 De G.F. & J. 264 and *Peffer v Rigg* [1977] 1 W.L.R. 285.

121 (1824) 1 Sim. & St. 607. See too *Hall v Warren* (1804) 9 Ves. 605. In *Verrall v Great Yarmouth Borough Council* [1981] 1 Q.B. 202, the Court of Appeal affirmed the grant of specific performance to enforce a contractual licence to occupy premises. As no other premises could be found damages would have been an inadequate remedy (the promisee being unable to hire any premises with any damages awarded).

122 As in, e.g. *Alchemy Estates Ltd v Astor* [2008] 3 E.G.L.R. 143. It follows that the vendor can "thrust the property down the purchaser's throat", per Lindley LJ in *Hope v Walter* [1900] 1 Ch. 257 at 258. But, on mutuality, see below, paras 18–137–18–138.

123 *Swiss Bank Corp v Lloyd's Bank Ltd* [1980] 2 All E.R. 419 at 425, per Buckley LJ.

In *Taylor v Neville*, cited in *Buxton v Lister*,[124] specific performance was decreed of a contract for sale of 800 tons of iron, to be delivered and paid for in a certain number of years and by instalments; and the reason given by Lord Hardwicke is that such sort of contracts differ from those that are immediately to be executed and they do differ in this respect, that the profit upon the contract, being to depend upon future events, cannot be correctly estimated in damages where the calculation must proceed upon conjecture. In such a case, to compel a party to accept damages for the non-performance of his contract, is to compel him to sell the actual profit which may arise from it, at a conjectural price. In *Ball v Coggs*,[125] specific performance was decreed in the House of Lords of a contract to pay the plaintiff a certain annual sum for his life, and also a certain other sum for every hundred weight of brass wire manufactured by the defendant during the life of the plaintiff. The same principle is to be applied to this case. Damages might be no complete remedy, being to be calculated merely by conjecture; and to compel the plaintiff in such a case to take damages would be to compel him to sell the annual provision during his life for which he had contracted at a conjectural price. In *Buxton v Lister* Lord Hardwicke puts the case of a ship carpenter purchasing timber which was peculiarly convenient to him by reason of its vicinity; and also the case of an owner of land covered with timber contracting to sell his timber in order to clear his land; and assumes that as, in both those cases, damages would not, by reason of the special circumstances, be a complete remedy, equity would decree specific performance. 18–114

The present case being a contract for the sale of the uncertain dividends which may become payable from the estates of the two bankrupts, it appears to me that, upon the principle established by the cases of *Ball v Coggs* and *Taylor v Neville*, a Court of Equity will decree specific performance, because damages at law cannot accurately represent the value of the future dividends; and to compel this purchaser to take such damages would be to compel him to sell these dividends at a conjectural price. 18–115

It is true that the present bill is not filed by the purchaser, but by the vendor, who seeks, not the uncertain dividends, but the certain sum to be paid for them. It has, however, been settled, by repeated decision, that the remedy in equity must be mutual; and that, where a bill will lie for the purchaser, it will also lie for the vendor. 18–116

### (2) Chattels of Especial Value

The Court of Chancery had always claimed jurisdiction to order the return of a specific chattel wrongly retained by another[126] (not properly a contractual claim) but, as rationalised by Lord Eldon,[127] its justification for so doing was that such chattels possessed a sentimental value which could not be quantified in money terms.[128] Extending that reasoning in *Sky Petroleum Ltd v VIP Petroleum Ltd*,[129] Goulding J held that the court had jurisdiction to order specific performance of a contract to sell non-specific chattels in a case where the remedy of damages would be inadequate. 18–117

---

124 (1746) 3 Atk. 383 at 384.

125 (1710) 1 Bro. P.C. 140.

126 *Pusey v Pusey* (1684) 1 Vern. 273 (an ancient horn, reputedly a gift of Canute).

127 *Nutbrown v Thornton* (1804) 10 Ves. 160 at 163.

128 *Falcke v Gray* (1859) 4 Dr. 651; *Thorn v Commissioners of Public Works* (1863) 32 Beav. 490 (stones from Old Westminster Bridge); *Phillips v Lamdin* [1949] 2 K.B. 33 (ornate Adam door). Damages would clearly be an inadequate remedy if an award would not enable the promisee to go into the market place and purchase a similar chattel. By definition it could not do so in cases of this sort. Note also that s.52 of the Sale of Goods Act 1979 enables the court, additionally, to decree specific performance of contracts for the sale of "specific or ascertained goods", i.e. identified and agreed upon when the contract is made. Neither under the statutory nor under the equitable jurisdictions (both being discretionary) will specific performance be decreed of contracts for the sale of "ordinary articles of commerce", even though specific or ascertained goods within the Act, as damages would be an adequate remedy: *Cohen v Roche* [1927] 1 K.B. 169 (set of Hepplewhite chairs); *Whiteley Ltd v Hilt* [1918] 2 K.B. 808, at [819]. Inadequacy of damages seems, therefore, to be the touchstone.

129 [1974] 1 W.L.R. 576 (enforcement of obligation to supply petrol during petrol shortage, no alternative source available).

### (3) Shares in a Private Limited Company

18–118 There being no readily available market in such shares, in light of the restriction on the transferability of shares in private companies and of the criminal prohibition in s.755 of the Companies Act 2006,[130] damages will normally be an inadequate remedy.[131]

### (4) Contracts for the Sale of Other Personal Property

18–119 Such contracts are not specifically enforceable so that, for example, contracts for the sale of shares in which there is a ready market, i.e. those of a quoted public company, and, indeed, any other contract[132] for the disposition of personal property, tangible or intangible, will not be specifically enforced unless it can be shown in the instant case that damages would not be an adequate remedy.[133] A contract to leave personal or real property by will is not enforceable directly (which would interfere with freedom of testamentary power) but a legatee who receives it in breach will be ordered to yield it up[134] and, before death of the testator, the promisee can obtain a declaration of right and an injunction restraining any inconsistent disposition.[135]

### (5) Contracts for Personal Services

18–120 By statute,[136] contracts of employment are not specifically enforceable. The equitable approach, which applies to contracts of service not covered by the statute and any contract for personal services, is illustrated by Fry LJ's comment in *De Francesco v Barnum*: "The courts are bound to be jealous lest they should turn contracts of service into contracts of slavery".[137] In *Chappell v Times Newspapers Ltd*, Geoffrey Lane LJ further explained that "if one party has no faith in the honesty or integrity or the loyalty of the other, to force him to serve or to employ that other is a plain recipe for disaster".[138] However there seems to be no hard and fast rule,[139] and in *Geys v Société Générale, London*

---

130 Prohibiting a private company (other than a company limited by guarantee and not having a share capital) from offering its securities to the public directly or indirectly.

131 See, e.g. *Pena v Dale* [2004] 2 B.C.L.C. 508; *Gaetano Ltd v Obertor Ltd* [2009] EWHC 2653 (Ch) at [48].

132 Note, however, that in the case of contracts to assign choses in action there is no need (save for the purpose of perfecting legal title) to obtain specific performance at all, since an assignment for value operates without more as an assignment in equity on the principle that equity considers that done which ought to be done: per Lord Macnaghten in *Tailby v Official Receiver* (1888) App. Cas. 523 at 547–548. The operation of this principle does not depend on the specific enforceability of the contract to assign.

133 Additionally, a contract for the transfer of the goodwill of a business is too uncertain to enforce *in specie: Darbey v Whitaker* (1857) 4 Drew. 134 (unless premises or other business assets are contracted to be transferred with it). This appears to be an example of a contract sufficiently certain at law but not specifically enforceable for lack of certainty, an odd conclusion save that, for specific performance to lie, the court must be able to supervise the exact performance of the contract (per Lord Hardwicke LC in *Buxton v Lister* (1746) 3 Atk. 383 at 386). As imprisonment may result from non-compliance, this requirement is understandable.

134 *Synge v Synge* [1894] 1 Q.B. 466 (on the ground that the legatee is a volunteer and takes subject to the equity).

135 *Schaefer v Schumann* [1972] A.C. 572 (Privy Council).

136 Trade Union and Labour Relations (Consolidation) Act 1992 s.236: "no court shall . . . by way of an order of specific performance . . . compel an employee to do any work or to attend at any place for the doing of any work."

137 (1890) 45 Ch. D. 430.

138 [1975] 1 W.L.R. 482 at 506.

139 In *Giles (CH) & Co Ltd v Morris* [1972] 1 W.L.R. 307, Megarry J denied that there was a rule preventing enforcement: it was, rather, a question of looking at the particular obligations in question. In *Hill v CA Parsons & Co Ltd* [1972] Ch. 305 the Court of Appeal by a majority enforced a contract for personal services in what were described as exceptional circumstances. See also *Lumley v Wagner* (1852) 1 De G.M. & G. 604, where a singer was prevented by injunction from breaching her promise to sing only at the plaintiff's theatre, effectively thereby being forced to sing for the plaintiff. This and other cases were

*Branch*,[140] Lord Wilson noted that it is a "big question whether nowadays the more impersonal, less hierarchical, relationship of many employers with their employees requires review of the usual unavailability of specific performance."

### (6) Contracts to Pay Money

In *South African Territories Ltd v Wallington*,[141] a contract to make a loan was not specifically enforced because damages would be an adequate remedy. In *Beswick v Beswick*,[142] the contract was to pay an annuity to a third party. It was enforced because damages would have been an inadequate remedy in the sense that either: (i) damages awarded to the promisee would have been nominal; (ii) a multiplicity of suits might need to be brought if there were future breaches; or (iii) the worth of an annuity, depending on the longevity of the annuitant, might be too conjectural to quantify.[143] It remains doubtful whether a promisee could obtain specific performance of a promise to pay a lump sum to a third party: if she could, it would require an English court to uphold (i) as a sufficient reason for enforcing a promise *in specie* and, moreover, one which the promisee could not have enforced for her own benefit.[144] 18–121

*Beswick v Beswick*

House of Lords [1968] A.C. 58

Peter Beswick agreed with his nephew to transfer to him his business in consideration of the nephew's (a) employing Peter as a consultant for life and (b) paying thereafter to Peter's widow an annuity at the rate of £5 per week for life. Peter died and the nephew refused to make any payments to the widow but the first. She sued for specific performance in her capacity as administratix of Peter's estate and in her personal capacity. The House unanimously rejected her personal claim as a *ius quaesitum tertio* but allowed her representative claim. 18–122

LORD UPJOHN (with whom LORD PEARCE, LORD REID, LORD HODSON and LORD GUEST concurred): As it is necessary to keep clear and distinct the right of the widow as administratix of her husband and personally, I think it will be convenient to use letters: letter A represents the deceased and A1 the widow, as personal representative. B the widow in her personal capacity and C the appellant. And in other examples I shall give, these letters will serve the same purpose. 18–123

Much is common ground between the parties: (1) B was not a party to the agreement: (2) A did not enter into the agreement as trustee for B in relation to the annuity to be paid to her; (3) A1 stands for all relevant purposes in the shoes of A and is entitled to sue C for breach of his admitted repudiation of the agreement (see paragraph 5 of the defence), but the parties differ fundamentally as to the remedy to which A1 is entitled in such an action. . . . 18–124

Leaving section 56 out of account, there was no real dispute between the parties as to their respective rights (as distinct from remedies) under the agreement (a) B has no rights thereunder. But it was clear from the whole tenor of the agreement that the annuity was to be paid to her for her own beneficial enjoyment, so if C paid it to her she could keep it and did not hold it as a constructive trustee for A1; (b) C would completely perform his obligation under the contract by continuing to pay the annuity to B during 18–125

reviewed in the Court of Appeal by Mance LJ in *Lady Navigation Inc v Lauritzencool AB* [2005] 2 All E.R. (Comm.) 183, where he concluded that there is no general rule that injunctive relief will be withheld if the practical effect would be to compel performance of a contract for personal services.

140 [2013] 1 A.C. 523 at [77].

141 [1898] A.C. 309.

142 [1968] A.C. 58.

143 But query: actuaries and judges in personal injury cases do it routinely.

144 Because in that case, damages clearly would be adequate. Note that it is not to be thought that the question whether such promise be specifically enforceable is an academic one. A defendant is at risk of imprisonment for failure to comply with a decree of specific performance but cannot nowadays (since abolition of debtors' prison) be gaoled for inability to pay a civil debt.

her life. Neither A nor A1 could compel C to pay it to A or A1, but (c) A or A1 and C could, if they pleased, agree to modify, compromise or even discharge further performance of the contract by C, and B would have no right to complain. If authority be wanted for these fundamental propositions, it is to be found in *Re Schebsman*[145] and *Re Stapleton-Bretherton*.[146]

18–126 But when A dies and his rights pass to A1, it is said that the remedy of specific performance is no longer appropriate against C. The argument was first that the estate of A suffered no damage by reason of C's failure to pay B, so A1 is entitled to nominal damages but as she is not otherwise interested in the agreement as such it would be wrong to grant specific performance; for that remedy is available only where damages will be an inadequate remedy. Here nominal damages are adequate. Further, it was argued, to do so would really be to confer upon B a right which she does not have in law or equity to receive the annuity. Then, secondly, it was said that if the remedy of specific performance is granted it might prejudice creditors of A so that the parties ought to be left to their strict rights at law. Thirdly, it is said that there are procedural difficulties in the way of enforcing an order for specific performance in favour of a third party. I will deal with these points, though in reverse order.

18–127 As to procedural difficulties, I fear I do not understand the argument. The point if valid applies to an action for specific performance by A just as much as by A1 yet in the authorities I have quoted no such point was ever taken; in *Drimmie v Davies*[147] indeed the action was by executors. Further, it seems to me that if C fails to obey a four-day order obtained by A1, B could enforce it under the clear and express provisions of RSC Ord.45 r.9 (formerly Ord.42 r.26). Alternatively A1 could move for and obtain the appointment of a receiver of the business upon which the annuity is charged and the receiver would then be directed by the Court to pay the annuity to B out of the profits of the business. Finally, A1 could issue a writ of fi. fa. under Ord.45 r.1, but as A1 would then be enforcing the contract and not modifying or compromising it the court would obviously in executing its order compel her to carry out the contract *in toto* and hand the proceeds of execution to B. This point is entirely without substance.

18–128 Then as to the second point. Let me assume (contrary to the fact) that A died with substantial assets but also many creditors. The legal position is that prima facie the duty of A1 is to carry out her intestate's contracts and compel C to pay B; but the creditors may be pressing and the agreement may be considered onerous; so it may be her duty to try and compromise the agreement with C and save something for the estate even at the expense of B.[148] So be it, but how can C conceivably rely upon this circumstance as a defence by him to an action for specific performance by A1? Of course not; he, C, has no interest in the estate; he cannot plead a possible jus tertii which is no concern of his. It is his duty to fulfil his contract by paying C. A1 alone is concerned with the creditors, beneficiaries or next of kin of A and this point therefore can never be a defence by C if A1 in fact chooses to sue for specific performance rather than to attempt a compromise in the interest of the estate. This point seems to me misconceived. In any event, on the facts of this case there is no suggestion that there are any unpaid creditors and B is sole next of kin, so the point is academic.

18–129 Then, as to the first point. On this question we were referred to the well-known dictum of Lush L.J. in *Lloyd's v Harper*:[149]

> "I consider it to be an established rule of law that where a contract is made with A for the benefit of B, A can sue on the contract for the benefit of B and recover all that B could have recovered if the contract had been made with B himself."

While in the circumstances it is not necessary to express any concluded opinion thereon, if the learned Lord Justice was expressing a view on the purely common law remedy of damages, I have some difficulty in going all the way with him. If A sues for damages for breach of contract by reason of the failure to pay B he must prove his loss; that may be great or nominal according to circumstances.

18–130 I do not see how A can, in conformity with clearly settled principle in assessing damages for breach of contract, rely at common law on B's loss. I agree with the observations of Windeyer J. in . . . *Coulls v Bagot's*

145 [1944] Ch. 83.
146 [1941] Ch. 482.
147 [1899] 1 Ir. R. 176.
148 See *Ahmed Angullia v Estate & Trust Agencies (1927) Ltd* [1938] A.C. 624 at 632, per Lord Romer.
149 (1880) 16 Ch.D. 290 at 321.

*Executor and Trustee Co Ltd*[150] in the High Court of Australia. But I note, however, that in *Lloyd's v Harper*[151] James and Cotton L.JJ. treated A as trustee for B and I doubt whether Lush L.J. thought otherwise.

However, I incline to the view that on the facts of this case damages are nominal for it appears that A died without any assets save and except the agreement which he hoped would keep him and then his widow for their lives. At all events let me assume that damages are nominal. So it is said nominal damages are adequate and the remedy of specific performance ought not to be granted. That is, with all respect, wholly to misunderstand that principle. Equity will grant specific performance when damages are inadequate to meet the justice of the case. 18–131

But in any event quantum of damages seldom affects the right to specific performance. If X contracts with Y to buy Blackacre or a rare chattel for a fancy price because the property or chattel has caught his fancy he is entitled to enforce his bargain and it matters not that he could not prove any damage. 18–132

In this case the court ought to grant a specific performance order all the more because damages are nominal. C has received all the property: justice demands that he pay the price and this can only be done in the circumstances by equitable relief. It is a fallacy to suppose that B is thereby obtaining additional rights: A1 is entitled to compel C to carry out the terms of the agreement. The observations of Holmes L.J. already quoted are very much in point. 18–133

My Lords, in my opinion the Court of Appeal were clearly right to grant a decree of specific performance. . . . 18–134

### iii. Equity Never Acts in Vain

Equity never acts in vain and, therefore, it will not decree performance of the impossible or the futile. Therefore, a vendor of land who has wrongfully conveyed away the property will not be ordered to convey to a purchaser what she no longer has unless the transferee is, for example, a company controlled by the vendor and used as a crude device or sham to avoid specific performance.[152] Likewise, an agreement for a lease which has already expired will not be enforced,[153] nor an agreement for a partnership not being of fixed duration,[154] nor an agreement to purchase property when the claimant has no funds to pay the purchase price.[155] 18–135

### iv. Illegality and Public Policy

A contract which is illegal is void and there is nothing to enforce, specifically or otherwise. A contract which is valid but which, if executed, might achieve some goal contrary to public policy might not be enforced specifically. *Wroth v Tyler*[156] provides a good example of this. In that case, a husband contracted to sell his property. After conclusion of the contract, his wife registered a charge against the property under the Matrimonial Homes Act 1967, which gave her the right (but no more than the right) not to be evicted. The purchasers sought either specific performance or damages in lieu. Specific performance was refused on the ground that if it were ordered, the purchasers would have to take the property subject to the wife's occupation. But they would be able to evict the husband and other members of the family. The splitting up of a family in that way would be an end contrary to public policy and so it was preferable for the purchasers to be awarded damages in lieu. 18–136

---

150 (1967) 40 A.L.J.R. 471.

151 (1880) 16 Ch.D. 290 at 315, 317.

152 *Jones v Lipman* [1962] 1 W.L.R. 832.

153 *Turner v Clowes* (1869) 20 L.T. 214 It might be otherwise if the lessee would derive some benefit by being granted legal rights under the lease: *Walters v Northern Coal Mining Board Co* (1855) 5 De G.M. & G. 629.

154 *Henry v Birch* (1804) 9 Ves. 357: either partner might dissolve it at will.

155 *Wilkie v Redsell* [2003] EWCA Civ 926.

156 [1974] Ch. 30.

## v. Mutuality

18–137 It used to be said that specific performance will not be granted to a promisee who could not herself be the subject of a decree,[157] i.e. all the obligations imposed by the contract upon the claimant promisee must themselves be specifically enforceable. This is the traditional statement of the requirement of mutuality. However, Fry's statement of it, which required mutuality at the time of entering into the contract (rather than it sufficing at the date of the hearing) was rejected in *Price v Strange*.[158] There Goff LJ stated that "want of mutuality raises a question of the court's discretion to be exercised according to everything that has happened up to the decree", so that "the court will grant specific performance if it can be done without injustice or unfairness to the defendant".[159] This might involve some payment to the defendant as in *Price*.[160] Where injustice can be avoided by the imposition of terms on the claimant or an award of damages to the defendant, a decree may be made. Indeed, since the decision in *Price*, there has been a steady academic and judicial retreat from the doctrine of mutuality as a coherent explanation for the outcome of older, decided cases or, indeed, as a sound objection as a matter of moral principle. This is to be welcomed, for it seems at times to have been used as a principle to justify the specific enforcement of certain types of contract (such as those for the disposition of land when, quite plainly, damages would be an adequate remedy for a vendor) and, capriciously, to deny the specific enforceability of others. In other words, it was serving a dual role in the case law. The judicial retreat from it must now be almost complete in light of the High Court's decision in *Rainbow Estates Ltd v Tokenhold Ltd*.[161]

18–138 A word of background explanation about this decision is necessary. A landlord's repairing covenant is enforceable by statute notwithstanding any equitable rule restricting the tenant's remedy "whether based on mutuality or otherwise".[162] This provision was enacted precisely because it was thought that repairing covenants were not specifically enforceable either because, the tenant's covenants not being so enforceable, the landlord's covenants could not be so for want of mutuality, or, alternatively, because of the need for constant supervision. The court in this case, however, decided that neither of these reasons had been the ratio of any decided case and, there being no reason in principle why a tenant's repairing covenant should not be specifically enforced (so long as oppression was avoided and the work required to be done was sufficiently defined), the court in an appropriate case would order specific performance of a tenant's repairing covenant. The qualifications in parentheses would mean, however, that appropriate cases were rare.

---

157 *Flight v Bolland* (1828) 4 Russ. 298 (minor failing to obtain decree because, *qua minor,* suit could not be maintained against him).

158 [1978] 1 Ch. 337.

159 *Price* at 354. At 368–369 Buckley LJ stated: "The court will not compel a defendant to perform his obligations specifically if it cannot at the same time ensure that any unperformed obligations of the plaintiff will be specifically performed unless, perhaps, damages would be an adequate remedy to the defendant for any default on the plaintiff's part." There is some tension between this finding and the HL's decision in *White & Carter (Councils) Ltd v McGregor* [1962] A.C. 413, that the court has no general equitable discretion to prevent the innocent party to a contract from forcing performance on to the other party and claiming payment. For discussion, see *Ministry of Sound (Ireland) Ltd v World Online Ltd* [2003] 2 All E.R. (Comm.) 823 at [67]–[72].

160 *Price* at 357.

161 [1999] Ch. 64. See too *Bolkiah v Brunei Darussalam* [2007] UKPC 63 at [42] where Lord Scott laid particular stress on Buckley LJ's statement in *Price* at 369 that "considerations of mutuality go to discretion, not to jurisdiction".

162 Landlord and Tenant Act 1985 s.17.

## vi. Entire Contracts Only

That the contract sought to be enforced *in specie* should be capable of being enforced in its entirety is an old rule[163] but one which may now be more flexible. In *CH Giles & Co Ltd v Morris*,[164] a case where specific performance was sought of a contract for the sale of shares, one of the terms of which required the vendors to procure the appointment of a particular individual as managing director of the company, Megarry J said 18–139

> the court may refuse to let the disadvantages and difficulties of specifically enforcing the obligation to perform personal services outweigh the suitability of the rest of the contract for specific performance . . .[165]

Where the contract can properly be construed as two distinct contracts, specific performance may be obtained to enforce one of them.[166]

## vii. Need for Constant Supervision

*Ryan v Mutual Tontine Westminster Chambers Association*[167] holds that breach of a contract which would need constant supervision by the court if it were to be performed *in specie* will only sound in damages. In *Posner v Scott-Lewis*,[168] however, Mervyn Davies J at a tenant's request, and on facts difficult to distinguish from *Ryan*, made an order against the landlord for the appointment of a resident porter whom the landlord had covenanted to employ for the purpose of carrying out certain duties at a block of flats: he found that there was a sufficient definition of what had to be done in order to comply with the order of the court. 18–140

*Co-operative Insurance Society Ltd v Argyll Stores (Holdings) Ltd*[169] provided the House of Lords with the opportunity to review and reconcile the authorities clustered around this principle. The owner of Safeway supermarkets was the anchor-tenant in a new shopping mall in Hillsborough. It covenanted to keep the demised premises open for retail trade during normal business hours, but then decided to close all of its loss-making stores of which the demised premises were one. The tenant was content to pay damages for breach but resisted an order for specific performance. The Court of Appeal, by a majority, granted a decree which the House of Lords discharged. 18–141

> *Co-operative Insurance Society Ltd v Argyll Stores (Holdings) Ltd*
>
> House of Lords [1998] A.C. 1
>
> LORD HOFFMANN (with whom LORD BROWNE-WILKINSON, LORD SLYNN, LORD HOPE and LORD CLYDE agreed): . . . In 1955 Lord Goddard C.J. said:[170] 18–142

---

163 *Ogden v Fossick* (1862) 4 De G.F. & J. 426.

164 [1972] 1 W.L.R. 307. See too *Rainbow Estates Ltd v Tokenhold Ltd* [1997] Ch. 64 at 73; *Internet Trading Clubs Ltd v Freeserve (Investments) Ltd* [2001] E.B.L.R. 142 at [30] per Tomkinson J, considering *Odessa Tramways Co v Mendel* (1878) 8 Ch. D. 235.

165 *Giles* at 317–318.

166 e.g. *Lewin v Guest* (1826) 1 Russ. 325 (Separate contracts to purchase two plots; purchaser obliged to take one plot even though vendor could not show title to other). It would be otherwise where, e.g. a vendor knew that from purchaser's point of view the purchases were interdependent: *Poole v Shergold* (1786) 1 Cox Eq. Cas. 273.

167 [1893] 1 Ch. 116 (lessor's covenant to provide resident porter who would always be in attendance at block of flats). See also *Dowty Boulton Paul Ltd v Wolverhampton Corporation* [1971] 2 All E.R. 277 (mandatory injunction refused to enforce covenant to maintain aerodrome for period of over 60 years: same principle applied).

168 [1987] Ch. 25.

169 [1998] A.C. 1.

170 *Att.-Gen. v Colchester Corporation* [1955] 2 Q.B. 207 at 217.

> "No authority has been quoted to show that an injunction will be granted enjoining a person to carry on a business, nor can I think that one ever would be, certainly not where the business is a losing concern."

In this case his prediction has been falsified. The appellant defendants, Argyll Stores (Holdings) Ltd ("Argyll"), decided in May 1995 to close their Safeway supermarket in the Hillsborough Shopping Centre in Sheffield because it was losing money. This was a breach of a covenant in their lease, which contained in clause 4(19) a positive obligation to keep the premises open for retail trade during the usual hours of business. Argyll admitted the breach and, in an action by the landlord. Co-operative Insurance Society Ltd ("CIS") consented to an order for damages to be assessed. But the Court of Appeal,[171] reversing the trial judge, ordered that the covenant be specifically performed. It made a final injunction ordering Argyll to trade on the premises during the remainder of the term (which will expire on 3 August 2014) or until an earlier subletting or assignment. The Court of Appeal suspended its order for three months to allow time for Argyll to complete an assignment which by that time had been agreed. After a short agreed extension, the lease was assigned with the landlord's consent. In fact, therefore, the injunction never took effect. The appeal to your Lordships is substantially about costs. But the issue remains of great importance to landlords and tenants under other commercial leases. . . .

**18–143** The judge refused to order specific performance. He said that there was on the authorities a settled practice that orders which would require a defendant to run a business would not be made. He was not content, however, merely to follow authority. He gave reasons why he thought that specific performance would be inappropriate. Two such reasons were by way of justification for the general practice. An order to carry on a business, as opposed to an order to perform a "single and well-defined act", was difficult to enforce by the sanction of committal. And where a business was being run at a loss, specific relief would be "too far-reaching and beyond the scope of control which the court should seek to impose." The other two related to the particular case. A resumption of business would be expensive (refitting the shop was estimated to cost over £1m) and although Argyll had knowingly acted in breach of covenant, it had done so "in the light of the settled practice of the court to award damages." Finally, while the assessment of damages might be difficult, it was the kind of exercise which the courts had done in the past.

**The Settled Practice**

**18–144** There is no dispute about the existence of the settled practice to which the judge referred. It sufficient for this purpose to refer to *Braddon Towers Ltd v International Stores Ltd* where Slade J. said:[172]

> "Whether or not this may be properly described as a rule of law. I do not doubt that for many years practitioners have advised their clients that it is the settled and invariable practice of this court never to grant mandatory injunctions requiring persons to carry on business."

But the practice has never, so far as I know, been examined by this House and it is open to CIS to say that it rests upon inadequate grounds or that it has been too inflexibly applied.

**18–145** Specific performance is traditionally regarded in English law as an exceptional remedy, as opposed to the common law damages to which a successful plaintiff is entitled as of right. There may have been some element of later rationalisation of an untidier history, but by the 19th century it was orthodox doctrine that the power to decree specific performance was part of the discretionary jurisdiction of the Court of Chancery to do justice in cases in which the remedies available at common law were inadequate. This is the basis of the general principle that specific performance will not be ordered when damages are an adequate remedy. By contrast, in countries with legal systems based on civil law, such as France, Germany and Scotland, the plaintiff is prima facie entitled to specific performance. The cases in which he is confined to a claim for damages are regarded as the exceptions. In practice, however, there is less difference between common law and civilian systems than these general statements might lead one to suppose. The principles upon which English judges exercise the discretion to grant specific performance are reasonably well settled and depend upon a number of considerations, mostly of a practical nature, which are of very general application. I have made no investigation of civilian systems, but a priori I would expect that judges take much the same matters into account in deciding whether specific performance would be inappropriate in a particular case.

---

171 [1996] Ch. 286.

172 [1987] 1 E.G.L.R. 209 at 213.

The practice of not ordering a defendant to carry on a business is not entirely dependent upon damages being an adequate remedy. In *Dowty Boulton Paul Ltd v Wolverhampton Corporation*[173] Sir John Pennycuick V.C. refused to order the corporation to maintain an airfield as a going concern because: "It is very well established that the court will not order specific performance of an obligation to carry on a business."[174] He added: "It is unnecessary in the circumstances to discuss whether damages would be an adequate remedy to the company."[175] Thus the reasons which underlie the established practice may justify a refusal of specific performance even when damages are not an adequate remedy. **18–146**

The most frequent reason given in the cases for declining to order someone to carry on a business is that it would require constant supervision by the court. In *JC Williamson Ltd v Lukey and Mulholland*[176] Dixon J. said flatly: "Specific performance is inapplicable when the continued supervision of the court is necessary in order to ensure the fulfilment of the contract." **18–147**

There has, I think, been some misunderstanding about what is meant by continued superintendence. It may at first sight suggest that the judge (or some other officer of the court) would literally have to supervise the execution of the order. In *CH Giles & Co Ltd v Morris*[177] Megarry J. said that "difficulties of constant superintendence" were a "narrow consideration" because: **18–148**

> "there is normally no question of the court having to send its officers to supervise the performance of the order. . . . Performance . . . is normally secured by the realisation of the person enjoined that he is liable to be punished for contempt if evidence of his disobedience to the order is put before the court . . .".

This is, of course, true but does not really meet the point. The judges who have said that the need for constant supervision was an objection to such orders were no doubt well aware that supervision would in practice take the form of rulings by the court, on applications made by the parties, as to whether there had been a breach of the order. It is the possibility of the court having to give an indefinite series of such rulings in order to ensure the execution of the order which has been regarded as undesirable.

Why should this be so? A principal reason is that, as Megarry J. pointed out in the passage to which I have referred, the only means available to the court to enforce its order is the quasi-criminal procedure of punishment for contempt. This is powerful weapon: so powerful, in fact, as often to be unsuitable as an instrument for adjudicating upon the disputes which may arise over whether a business is being run in accordance with the terms of the court's order. The heavy-handed nature of the enforcement mechanism is a consideration which may go to the exercise of the court's discretion in other cases as well, but its use to compel the running of a business is perhaps the paradigm case of its disadvantages and it is in this context that I shall discuss them. **18–149**

The prospect of committal or even a fine, with the damage to commercial reputation which will be caused by a finding of contempt of court, is likely to have at least two undesirable consequences. First, the defendant, who *ex hypothesi* did not think that it was in his economic interest to run the business at all, now has to make decisions under a sword of Damocles which may descend if the way the business is run does not conform to the terms of the order. This is, as one might say, no way to run a business. In this case the Court of Appeal made light of the point because it assumed that, once the defendant had been ordered to run the business, self-interest and compliance with the order would thereafter go hand in hand. But, as I shall explain, this is not necessarily true. **18–150**

Secondly, the seriousness of a finding of contempt for the defendant means that any application to enforce the order is likely to be a heavy and expensive piece of litigation. The possibility of repeated applications over a period of time means that, in comparison with a once-and-for-all inquiry as to damages, the enforcement of the remedy is likely to be expensive in terms of cost to the parties and the resources of the judicial system. **18–151**

This is a convenient point at which to distinguish between orders which require a defendant to carry on an activity, such as running a business over or more or less extended period of time, and orders which require him to achieve a result. The possibility of repeated applications for rulings on compliance with the **18–152**

[173] [1971] 1 W.L.R. 204.
[174] At 211.
[175] At 212.
[176] (1931) 45 C.L.R. 282 at 297–298.
[177] [1972] 1 W.L.R. 307 at 318.

order which arises in the former case does not exist to anything like the same extent in the latter. Even if the achievement of the result is a complicated matter which will take some time, the court, if called upon to rule, only has to examine the finished work and say whether it complies with the order. This point was made in the context of relief against forfeiture in *Shiloh Spinners Ltd v Harding*.[178] If it is a condition of relief that the tenant should have complied with a repairing covenant, difficulty of supervision need not be an objection. As Lord Wilberforce said:[179]

> "what the court has to do is to satisfy itself, ex post facto, that the covenanted work has been done, and it has ample machinery, through certificates, or by inquiry, to do precisely this."

This distinction between orders to carry on activities and orders to achieve results explains why the courts have in appropriate circumstances ordered specific performance of building contracts and repairing covenants: see *Wolverhampton Corporation v Emmons*[180] (building contract) and *Jeune v Queens Cross Properties Ltd*[181] (repairing covenant). It by no means follows, however, that even obligations to achieve a result will always be enforced by specific performance. There may be other objections, to some of which I now turn.

**18–153** One such objection, which applies to orders to achieve a result and a fortiori to orders to carry on an activity, is imprecision in the terms of the order. If the terms of the court's order, reflecting the terms of the obligation, cannot be precisely drawn, the possibility of wasteful litigation over compliance is increased. So is the oppression caused by the defendant having to do things under threat of proceedings for contempt. The less precise the order, the fewer the signposts to the forensic minefield which he has to traverse. The fact that the terms of a contractual obligation are sufficiently definite to escape being void for uncertainty, or to found a claim for damages, or to permit compliance to be made a condition of relief against forfeiture, does not necessarily mean that they will be sufficiently precise to be capable of being specifically enforced. So in *Wolverhampton Corporation v Emmons*, Romer L.J. said that the first condition for specific enforcement of a building contract was that:[182]

> "the particulars of the work are so far definitely ascertained that the court can sufficiently see what is the exact nature of the work of which it is asked to order the performance."

**18–154** Similarly in *Morris v Redland Bricks Ltd*,[183] Lord Upjohn stated the following general principle for the grant of mandatory injunctions to carry out building works:

> "the court must be careful to see that the defendant knows exactly in fact what he has to do and this means not as a matter of law but as a matter of fact, so that in carrying out an order he can give his contractors the proper instructions."

Precision is of course a question of degree and the courts have shown themselves willing to cope with a certain degree of imprecision in cases of orders requiring the achievement of a result in which the plaintiffs' merits appeared strong; like all the reasons which I have been discussing, it is, taken alone, merely a discretionary matter to be taken into account.[184] It is, however, a very important one.

**18–155** I should at this point draw attention to what seems to me to have been a misreading of certain remarks of Lord Wilberforce in *Shiloh Spinners Ltd v Harding*.[185] He pointed out, as I have said, that to grant relief against forfeiture subject to compliance with a repairing covenant involves the court in no more than the possibility of a retrospective assessment of whether the covenanted work has been done. For this reason, he said:

> "Where it is necessary, and, in my opinion, right, to move away from some 19th century authorities, is to reject as a reason against granting relief, the impossibility for the courts to supervise the doing of work."

---

178 [1973] A.C. 691.
179 At 724.
180 [1901] 1 K.B. 515.
181 [1974] Ch. 97.
182 At 525.
183 [1970] A.C. 652 at 666.
184 See Spry, *Equitable Remedies*, 4th edn (1990), p.112.
185 At p.724.

This is plainly a remark about cases involving the achievement of a result such as doing repairs, and, within that class, about making compliance a condition of relief against forfeiture. But in *Tito v Waddell (No.2)*[186] Sir Robert Megarry V.C. took it to be a generalisation about specific performance and, in particular, a rejection of difficulty of supervision as an objection, even in cases of orders to carry on an activity. Sir Robert Megarry V.C. regarded it as an adoption of his own views (based, as I have said, on incomplete analysis of what was meant by difficulty of supervision) in *CH Giles & Co Ltd v Morris*.[187] In the present case[188] Leggatt L.J. took this claim at face value. In fact, Lord Wilberforce went on to say that impossibility of supervision "is a reality, no doubt, and explains why specific performance cannot be granted of agreements to this effect . . .". Lord Wilberforce was in my view drawing attention to the fact that the collection of reasons which the courts have in mind when they speak of difficulty of supervision apply with much greater force to orders for specific performance, giving rise to the possibility of committal for contempt, than they do to conditions for relief against forfeiture. While the paradigm case to which such objections apply is the order to carry on an activity, they can also apply to an order requiring the achievement of a result.

There is a further objection to an order requiring the defendant to carry on a business, which was emphasised by Millett L.J. in the Court of Appeal. This is that it may cause injustice by allowing the plaintiff to enrich himself at the defendant's expense. The loss which the defendant may suffer through having to comply with the order (for example, by running a business at a loss for an indefinite period) may be far greater than the plaintiff would suffer from the contract being broken. As Professor R.J. Sharpe explains:[189] **18–156**

> "In such circumstances, a specific decree in favour of the plaintiff will put him in a bargaining position vis-à-vis the defendant whereby the measure of what he will receive will be the value to the defendant of being released from performance. If the plaintiff bargains effectively, the amount he will set will exceed the value to him of performance and will approach the cost to the defendant to complete."

This was the reason given by Lord Westbury L.C. in *Isenberg v East India House Estate Co Ltd*[190] for refusing a mandatory injunction to compel the defendant to pull down part of a new building which interfered with the plaintiff's light and exercising instead the Court of Chancery's recently-acquired jurisdiction under Lord Cairns's Act 1858 to order payment of damages: **18–157**

> ". . . I hold it . . . to be the duty of the court in such a case as the present not, by granting a mandatory injunction, to deliver over the defendants to the plaintiff bound hand and foot, in order to be made subject to any extortionate demand that he may by possibility make, but to substitute for such mandatory injunction an inquiry before itself, in order to ascertain the measure of damage that has been actually sustained."

It is true that the defendant has, by his own breach of contract, put himself in such an unfortunate position. But the purpose of the law of contract is not to punish wrongdoing but to satisfy the expectations of the party entitled to performance. A remedy which enables him to secure, in money terms, more than the performance due to him is unjust. From a wider perspective, it cannot be in the public interest for the courts to require someone to carry on business at a loss if there is any plausible alternative by which the other party can be given compensation. It is not only a waste of resources but yokes the parties together in a continuing hostile relationship. The order for specific performance prolongs the battle. If the defendant is ordered to run a business, its conduct becomes the subject of a flow of complaints, solicitors' letters and affidavits. This is wasteful for both parties and the legal system. An award of damages, on the other hand, brings the litigation to an end. The defendant pays damages, the forensic link between them is severed, they go their separate ways and the wounds of conflict can heal. **18–158**

The cumulative effect of these various reasons, none of which would necessarily be sufficient on its own, seems to me to show that the settled practice is based upon sound sense. Of course the grant or refusal of specific performance remains a matter for the judge's discretion. There are no binding rules, but this does not mean that there cannot be settled principles, founded upon practical considerations of the kind which I have discussed, which do not have to be re-examined in every case, but which the courts will apply in all **18–159**

---

186 [1977] Ch. 106 at 322.
187 [1972] 1 W.L.R. 307 at 318.
188 [1996] Ch. 286 at 292–293.
189 In "Specific Relief for Contract Breach", Ch.5 of *Studies in Contract Law* (1980), edited by Reiter and Swan p.129.
190 (1863) 3 De G.J. & S. 263 at 273.

but exceptional circumstances. As Slade J. said, in the passage which I have quoted from *Braddon Towers Ltd v International Stores Ltd*,[191] lawyers have no doubt for many years advised their clients on this basis. In the present case. Leggatt L.J.[192] remarked that there was no evidence that such advice had been given. In my view, if the law or practice on a point is settled, it should be assumed that persons entering into legal transactions will have been advised accordingly. I am sure that Leggatt L.J. would not wish to encourage litigants to adduce evidence of the particular advice which they received. Indeed, I doubt whether such evidence would be admissible.

**The Decision of the Court of Appeal**

18–160 I must now examine the grounds upon which the majority of the Court of Appeal[193] thought it right to reverse the judge. In the first place, they regarded the practice which he followed as outmoded and treated Lord Wilberforce's remarks about relief against forfeiture in *Shiloh Spinners Ltd v Harding*[194] as justifying a rejection of the arguments based on the need for constant supervision. Even Millett L.J., who dissented on other grounds, said that such objections had little force today.[195] I do not agree. As I have already said, I think that Lord Wilberforce's remarks do not support this proposition in relation to specific performance of an obligation to carry on an activity and that the arguments based on difficulty of supervision remain powerful.

18–161 The Court of Appeal said that it was enough if the contract defined the tenant's obligation with sufficient precision to enable him to know what was necessary to comply with the order. Even assuming that this to be right, I do not think that the obligation in clause 4(19) can possibly be regarded as sufficiently precise to be capable of specific performance. It is to "keep the demised premises open for retail trade." It says nothing about the level of trade, the area of the premises within which trade is to be conducted, or even the kind of trade, although no doubt the tenant's choice would be restricted by the need to comply with the negative covenant in clause 4(12)(a) not to use the premises "other than as a retail store for the sale of food groceries provisions and goods normally sold from time to time by a retail grocer food supermarkets and food superstores . . .". This language seems to me to provide ample room for argument over whether the tenant is doing enough to comply with the covenant.

18–162 The Court of Appeal thought that once Argyll had been ordered to comply with the covenant, it was, as Roch L.J. said,[196] "inconceivable that they would not operate the business efficiently." Leggatt L.J. said,[197] that the requirement

> "was quite intelligible to the defendants, while they were carrying on business there. . . . If the premises are to be run as a business, it cannot be in the defendants' interest to run it half-heartedly or inefficiently . . .".

This treats the way the tenant previously conducted business as measuring the extent of his obligation to do so. In my view this is a non sequitur: the obligation depends upon the language of the covenant and not upon what the tenant has previously chosen to do. No doubt it is true that it would not be in the interests of the tenant to run the business inefficiently. But running the business efficiently does not necessarily mean running it in the way it was run before. Argyll had decided that, from its point of view, the most efficient thing to do was to close the business altogether and concentrate its resources on achieving better returns elsewhere. If ordered to keep the business open, it might well decide that the next best strategy was to reduce its costs as far as was consistent with compliance with its obligations, in the expectation that a lower level of return would be more than compensated by higher returns from additional expenditure on more profitable shops. It is in my view wrong for the courts to speculate about whether Argyll might voluntarily carry on business in a way which would relieve the court from having to construe its order. The question of certainty must be decided on the assumption that the court might have to enforce the order according to its terms.

18–163 CIS argued that the court should not be concerned about future difficulties which might arise in

191 [1987] 1 E.G.L.R. 209 at 213.
192 [1996] Ch. 286 at 294.
193 [1996] Ch. 286.
194 [1973] A.C. 691 at 724.
195 At 303.
196 At 298.
197 At 292.

connection with the enforcement of the order. It should simply make the order and see what happened. In practice Argyll would be likely to find a suitable assignee (as it in fact did) or conduct the business so as to keep well clear of any possible enforcement proceedings or otherwise come to terms with CIS. This may well be true, but the likelihood of Argyll having to perform beyond the requirements of its covenant or buy its way out of its obligation to incur losses seems to me to be in principle an objection to such an order rather than to recommend it. I think that it is normally undesirable for judges to make orders in terrorem, carrying a threat of imprisonment, which work only if no one inquires too closely into what they mean.

The likelihood that the order would be effective only for a short time until an assignment is an equivocal argument. It would be burdensome to make Argyll resume business only to stop again after a short while if a short stoppage would not cause any substantial damage to the business of the shopping centre. On the other hand, what would happen if a suitable assignee could not be found? Would Argyll then have to carry on business until 2014? Mr Smith, who appeared for CIS, said that if the order became oppressive (for example, because Argyll were being driven into bankruptcy) or difficult to enforce, they could apply for it to be varied or discharged. But the order would be a final order and there is no case in this jurisdiction in which such an order has been varied or discharged, except when the injuncted activity has been legalised by statute. Even assuming that there was such a jurisdiction if circumstances were radically changed. I find it difficult to see how this could be made to apply. Difficulties of enforcement would not be a change of circumstances. They would have been entirely predictable when the order was made. And so would the fact that Argyll would suffer unquantifiable loss if it was obliged to continue trading. I do not think that such expedients are an answer to the difficulties on which the objections to such orders are based. 18–164

Finally, all three judges in the Court of Appeal took a very poor view of Argyll's conduct. Leggatt L.J. said that they had acted "with gross commercial cynicism";[198] Roch L.J. began his judgment by saying that they had "behaved very badly" and Millett L.J. said that they had no merits.[199] The principles of equity have always had a strong ethical content and nothing which I say is intended to diminish the influence of moral values in their application. I can envisage cases of gross breach of personal faith, or attempts to use the threat of non-performance as blackmail, in which the needs of justice will override all the considerations which support the settled practice. But although any breach of covenant is regrettable, the exercise of the discretion as to whether or not to grant specific performance starts from the fact that the covenant has been broken. Both landlord and tenant in this case are large sophisticated commercial organisations and I have no doubt that both were perfectly aware that the remedy for breach of the covenant was likely to be limited to an award of damages. The interests of both were purely financial: there was no element of personal breach of faith, as in the Victorian cases of railway companies which refused to honour obligations to build stations for landowners whose property they had taken: compare *Greene v West Cheshire Railway Co*.[200] No doubt there was an effect on the businesses of other traders in the Centre, but Argyll had made no promises to them and it is not suggested that CIS warranted to other tenants that Argyll would remain. Their departure, with or without the consent of CIS, was a commercial risk which the tenants were able to deploy in negotiations for the next rent review. On the scale of broken promises, I can think of worse cases, but the language of the Court of Appeal left them with few adjectives to spare. 18–165

It was no doubt discourteous not to have answered Mr Wightman's letter. But to say, as Roch L.J. did,[201] that they had acted "wantonly and quite unreasonably" by removing their fixtures seems to me an exaggeration. There was no question of stealing a march, or attempting to present CIS with a fait accompli, because Argyll had no reason to believe that CIS would have been able to obtain a mandatory injunction whether the fixtures had been removed or not. They had made it perfectly clear that they were closing the shop and given CIS ample time to apply for such an injunction if so advised. 18–166

**Conclusion**

I think that no criticism can be made of the way in which Judge Maddocks exercised his discretion. All the reasons which he gave were proper matters for him to take into account. In my view the Court 18–167

[198] [1996] Ch. 286 at 295.
[199] At 301.
[200] (1871) L.R. 13 Eq. 44.
[201] At 299.

of Appeal should not have interfered and I would allow the appeal and restore the order which he made.

### viii. Delay or Laches

18–168 There being no statutory limit on the time after which a claim for specific performance may be brought[202] equitable considerations govern and may deprive a claimant of the right to performance *in specie* where there is delay either sufficient to be evidence of the plaintiff's abandonment of the contract,[203] or coupled with circumstances which make it unjust to order specific performance.[204]

### ix. Lack of Clean Hands

18–169 If the claimant is guilty of some impropriety connected to the contract[205] she may not be entitled to an equitable remedy. The jurisdiction of the court to consider this matter cannot be ousted by agreement.[206] However, this last point was decided in a case where a clause in a sale agreement, which provided that the consideration was to be paid in cash "free from any equity cross-claim set-off or other deduction whatsoever", was held not to prevent the purchaser from raising an unclean hands defence. This was for the reason that the wording was not apt to exclude such a claim but alternatively for the reason that, even if it had been apt, "it could not have the effect of fettering the discretion of the court. Once the court is asked for the equitable remedy of specific performance, its discretion cannot be fettered".[207] Although defensible on its own, this decision does not sit easily with the long-established practice[208] of parties contracting that a particular obligation, if breached, shall "sound only in damages". This is just as much an attempt to oust the discretionary jurisdiction of the court to award a specific remedy. Perhaps all that can be said about it is that it is not, all other things being equal, an objectionable one.

### x. Undue Hardship

18–170 Specific performance may be refused if undue hardship will be caused to either of the parties or a third party.[209] The decisions in individual cases tend to turn on the facts, but *Wroth v Tyler*[210] is reproduced here by way of illustration. There is Commonwealth authority requiring the hardship to have existed at

---

202 Limitation Act 1980 s.36. Nor do the Limitation Acts apply by analogy: *Talmash v Mugleston* (1826) 4 L.J.O.S. Ch. 200.

203 *Parkin v Thorold* (1852) 16 Beav. 59 at 73. The claimant will still have her legal remedy.

204 *Lindsay Petroleum Co v Hurd* (1874) L.R. 5 P.C. 221. Where the plaintiff took possession and waited 10 years before seeking a decree to have the legal title vested in him, mere delay with no injustice to the defendant was no bar: *Williams v Greatrex* [1957] 1 W.L.R. 31. See too *Ridgeway Motors (Isleworth) Ltd v Michael* Ch. D. 13 June 1996 (claim for SP after 17 years struck out for laches); *Yewbelle Ltd v London Green Developments Ltd* [2007] 1 E.G.L.R. 137 at [92], where Lewison J held that: "In cases where the contract in question concerns land to be exploited for commercial purposes, the period of delay that can lead to the refusal of specific performance may be comparatively short."

205 *Moody v Cox* [1917] 2 Ch. 71 at 87–88; *van Gestel v Cann, The Times*, 7 August 1987 (claim that plaintiff guilty of fraud unconnected with contract of no assistance to defendant).

206 *Quadrant Visual Communications Ltd v Hutchison Telephone (UK) Ltd* [1993] B.C.L.C. 442.

207 [1993] B.C.L.C. 442 at 451.

208 Endorsed by the Court of Appeal in *Co-operative Insurance Society Ltd v Argyll Stores (Holdings) Ltd*, above and not criticised on this point by the House of Lords.

209 *Thomas v Dering* (1837) 1 Keen 729 at 747–748.

210 [1974] Ch. 30. Other situations include: trustee vendors, contractually obliged to discharge personally incumbrances on property, relieved from so doing as purchase price insufficient to cover secured amounts (*Wedgwood v Adams* (1843) 6 Beav. 600); purchaser not obliged to take property which had no right of access, so no possibility of enjoyment (*Denne v Light* (1857) 8 De G.M. & G. 774).

the date of contract,[211] but in England it has been held that specific performance can also be refused on the ground of hardship arising after contract.[212]

*Wroth v Tyler*

Chancery Division [1974] Ch. 30

The defendant contracted to sell his property to the claimants for £6,000. The next day, the defendant's wife registered a charge against the property under the Matrimonial Homes Act 1967 which gave her the right not to be evicted or excluded from the property. She refused to remove the charge and the defendant told the claimants he could not complete. The claimants sought specific performance or damages in lieu. The property was worth £7,500 at the date fixed for completion and £11,500 at the date of the hearing. **18–171**

MEGARRY J.: The issues before me may be summarised as follows. (1) Delay apart, are the plaintiffs entitled to specific performance of the contract with vacant possession? If they are, a form of order is sought that will require the defendant to make an application to the court for an order against his wife terminating her rights of occupation under the Matrimonial Homes Act 1967 in accordance with section 1(2). (2) Delay apart, are the plaintiffs, as an alternative, entitled to specific performance of the contract subject to the rights of occupation of the defendant's wife, with damages or an abatement of the purchase price in respect thereof? If they are, they will be able to make the application to the court under the Act of 1967, by virtue of section 1(2) and section 2(3). (3) If, apart from delay, the plaintiffs would be entitled to an order for specific performance under either of these two heads, is their right to it barred by delay? (4) If the plaintiffs have no right to specific performance, then it is common ground that they are entitled to damages. There is, however, an acute conflict as to the measure of damages. . . . **18–172**

The defendant says that the damages must be assessed as at the date of the breach, in accordance with the normal rule: the plaintiffs says that this is a case where damages must be assessed as at the date of assessment, that is, today, if I assess the damages. . . . Damages assessed as at the date of breach would be £1,500, but as at the date of the hearing would be £5,500. At which figure should damages for the loss of the bargain be assessed? The defendant says that the former figure applies, in accordance with the general rule, but the plaintiffs say that the latter figure applies, for unless it does, they will be unable to acquire an equivalent house at today's prices. . . . **18–173**

I may summarise my conclusions as to the essentials of the right given by the Act to an occupying spouse as follows. The right is in essence a personal and non-assignable statutory right not to be evicted from the matrimonial home in question during marriage or until the court otherwise orders; and this right constitutes a charge on the estate or interest of the owning spouse which requires protection against third parties by registration. For various reasons, the right may be said to be one which readily fits into no category known to conveyancers before 1967; the phrase sui generis seems apt, but of little help. **18–174**

With that in mind, I turn to the first question before me. Delay apart, are the plaintiffs entitled to specific performance of the contract with vacant possession? If they are, the form of order sought will require the defendant to make an application to the court under section 1(2) to terminate his wife's rights of occupation which arose and became a charge on the defendant's estate on January 1, 1968, and were protected by registration on May 28, 1971. . . **18–175**

It seems to me that where a third party has some rights over the property to be sold, there are at least three categories of cases. First, there are those cases where the vendor is entitled as of right to put an end to the rights of the third party, or compel his concurrence or co-operation in the sale. Second, and at the other extreme, there are cases where the vendor has no right to put an end to the third party's rights, or compel his concurrence or co-operation in the sale, and can do no more than to try to persuade him to release his rights or to concur in the sale. **18–176**

A vendor must do his best to obtain any necessary consent to the sale; if he has sold with vacant possession he must, if necessary, take proceedings to obtain possession from any person in possession who has no right to be there or whose right is determinable by the vendor, at all events if the vendor's right to possession is reasonably clear; but I do not think that the vendor will usually be required to embark upon difficult or uncertain litigation in order to secure any requisite consent or obtain vacant possession. Where **18–177**

---

[211] e.g. *Nicholas v Ingram* [1958] N.Z.L.R. 972.

[212] *Patel v Ali* [1984] Ch. 283 at [288] (husband and wife vendors; husband bankrupted, causing delay; wife seriously ill; young children; wife dependent on proximity of relatives so moving difficult).

the outcome of any litigation depends upon disputed facts, difficult questions of law, or the exercise of a discretionary jurisdiction, then I think the court would be slow to make a decree of specific performance against the vendor which would require him to undertake such litigation. In such a case, the vendor cannot know where the litigation will end. If he succeeds at first instance, the defendant may carry him to appeal; if he fails at first instance, the purchaser may say that there ought to be an appeal. No doubt the line between simple and difficult cases will sometimes be hard to draw; and it may be that specific performance will be readily decreed only where it is plain that the requisite consent is obtainable without difficulty. The form of decree appropriate to such cases might specifically require the defendant to undertake such litigation; the court moulds the decree as need be. But it may be that the court will do no more than direct the defendant to procure the requisite consent.[213]

**18–178** In the present case the defendant has endeavoured to persuade his wife to concur in the sale, but has failed. It is true that after the failure of his initial attempt on the Friday night he then instructed his solicitors to withdraw from both the sale and his Norfolk purchase; but he again tried to persuade his wife on the Sunday, and there is some evidence of later attempts. As the evidence stands, I think that the defendant has sufficiently attempted to obtain her consent, short of litigation. The mere fact that he sought to withdraw from the contract before he had made all his attempts does not seem to me to make much difference; if a later attempt had succeeded, he could still have completed at the date fixed for completion.

**18–179** Persuasion having failed, I think that the court should be slow to grant a decree of specific performance that would require an unwilling husband to make an application to the court under section 1(2) of the Act of 1967, particularly as the decision of the court depends upon the application of phrases such as "just and reasonable" under section 1(3). In any case, the court would be reluctant to make an order which requires a husband to take legal proceedings against his wife, especially while they are still living together. Accordingly, although this is a contract of a type which the court is normally ready to enforce by a decree of specific performance, in my judgment it would, in Lord Redesdale L.C.'s phrase, be "highly unreasonable" to make such a decree if there is any other form of order that could do justice; and that I must consider in due course. Let me add that I would certainly not regard proceedings under the Act by the defendant against his wife as being without prospect of success. As the evidence stands (and of course I have not heard the defendant's wife) there is at least a real prospect of success for the defendant. He does not in any way seek to deprive his wife of a home; the difference between them is a difference as to where the matrimonial home is to be. In that, the conduct of the wife towards the plaintiffs and the defendant must play a substantial part.

**18–180** I turn to the second main question, that of Mr Blackburne's alternative claim to specific performance for which he contended if he failed in his main claim to specific performance, and if he also was limited to damages assessed as at the date of the breach. This alternative claim was for specific performance of the contract, but with the plaintiffs taking subject to the charge in favour of the defendant's wife, and receiving damages or an abatement of the purchase money. By virtue of section 2(3) of the Act of 1967, section 1(2) to (5) would apply to the plaintiffs as they apply to the defendant, in that the plaintiffs would be persons deriving title under the defendant, and affected by the charge. If the plaintiffs took subject to the charge in favour of the defendant's wife, the result would be remarkable, for reasons which I have already indicated. The defendant has no rights of occupation under the Act, for his right of occupation stems from his estate in the land, and so section 1(1) of the Act gives him no statutory rights of occupation. The defendant's daughter has no rights of occupation under the Act, for the Act does not purport to confer such rights on anyone except a spouse. The defendant's wife alone has statutory rights of occupation, and on the facts of this case, these are expressed as being no more than "a right not to be evicted or excluded from the dwelling house or any part thereof". It has not been contended that this language is wide enough to empower the wife to authorise others to occupy the house with her, so that on that footing the plaintiffs, after completion, would be unable to evict the wife without an order of the court made under the Act, whereas the defendant and the daughter would have no defence to proceedings to evict them.

**18–181** There seems to be considerable force in the contention that this would be the result. Neither the defendant nor the daughter would have any rights of their own to remain in the house, and what the statute gives the wife is not a positive right of occupation, whether a licence or otherwise, but a mere negative right not to be evicted or excluded. A person who is given a positive right of occupation might be envisaged as

[213] See *Long v Bowring* (1864) 33 Beav. 585; *Seton's Judgments and Orders*, 7th edn (1912), p.2204.

having been given the right to permit others to occupy with him or her: but a mere negative right not to be evicted or excluded cannot so readily be construed in this sense. . . .

If one leaves the position of the children on one side as being debatable, there remains the position of the defendant vis-à-vis the plaintiffs. Even if the wife not only is protected against eviction or exclusion, but also has the right to permit others to occupy the dwelling with her, the defendant has contracted to give vacant possession to the plaintiffs. Could he, then, in breach of his contract, remain in occupation under cover of his wife's statutory right not to be evicted or excluded? Would a decree of specific performance of the contract subject only to his wife's statutory rights in effect be nugatory as to his contractual obligation not himself to remain in occupation but to give vacant possession? The Act seems to me to have created much doubt and uncertainty in this sphere, but there is at least a real possibility that a decree of specific performance subject to the wife's right not to be evicted or excluded would enable the plaintiffs, by taking suitable proceedings, to evict the defendant and perhaps the daughter, and thus split up the family. These circumstances seem to me to make the case one in which the court should be slow to decree specific performance if any reasonable alternative exists. I shall accordingly turn to the question of damages to see whether they would provide the plaintiffs with an adequate remedy. . . . **18–182**

[He then held that the measure of damages perhaps at common law but certainly in lieu of specific performance was to be assessed at the date of judgments and so awarded £5,500 damages.] **18–183**

## xi. Breach of Contract

It is a well-established principle that the court will not grant a decree if compliance with it would involve the defendant in breach of a prior contract (or, indeed, trust).[214] **18–184**

## xii. Set-Off

In *BICC plc v Burndy Corp*,[215] the Court of Appeal accepted by a majority that a right of equitable set-off (where a defendant seeks to defend a claim on the basis that the plaintiff is liable, under a related cross-claim, to her in a sum equal to or greater than the claim made by the claimant) could stand as a complete defence to a claim by a claimant not merely for a debt but also for specific performance. **18–185**

## xiii. Mistake and Misrepresentation

A contract which is not avoidable in equity for mistake or misrepresentation might sound only in damages if, owing to misrepresentation or (even unilateral) mistake, performance *in specie* would involve real hardship for the defendant amounting to injustice.[216] **18–186**

## xiv. Misdescription of Subject-Matter

Although the authorities on this relate to sales of land the principles ought to apply to contracts for the disposition of personalty which are otherwise specifically enforceable. A misdescription in the contract will amount to a breach because the vendor cannot then convey what she has contracted to convey. Quite apart from the common law rules determining the rights of an innocent party, equity **18–187**

---

214 *Harvela Investments Ltd v Royal Trust Co of Canada Ltd* [1985] Ch. 103 at 122.

215 [1985] Ch. 232.

216 *Tamplin v James* (1880) 15 Ch. D. 215 (land correctly described in plans, not consulted by purchaser; purchaser obliged to buy despite unilateral error in thinking adjacent land included. No injustice.), cf. *Denny v Hancock* (1870) 6 Ch. App. 1 (similar error was caused by vendor's unsatisfactory plans: no decree). See also *Riverlate Properties v Paul* [1975] Ch. 133; *Geest Plc v Fyffes Plc* Q.B.D. (Comm.) 23 March 1998.

developed the following rules[217] to deal specifically with this kind of breach when a question arose, assuming the contract was not discharged at law, whether it should be performed *in specie*.

18–188 If the misdescription is substantial so that the purchaser does not get what she wanted, i.e. but for the misdescription she would never have contracted at all, then the vendor cannot enforce either at law or in equity even with abatement of price.[218] If insubstantial, the vendor can enforce though with abatement of price by way of compensation.[219] Whether substantial or not, the purchaser can enforce and take whatever the vendor has and secure an abatement.[220]

## 4. Damages in Addition to or in Lieu of Injunctions and Specific Performance

### *A. The Courts' Jurisdiction*

18–189 Section 50 of the Senior Courts Act 1981 provides:

> Where the Court of Appeal or the High Court has jurisdiction to entertain an application for an injunction or specific performance, it may award damages in addition to, or in substitution for, an injunction or specific performance.

This provision embodies and confers upon the named courts the jurisdiction that was previously conferred upon the Court of Chancery by s.2 of the Chancery Amendment Act 1858 (Lord Cairns' Act) which was later repealed.[221]

18–190 Lord Cairns' Act enabled the Court of Chancery: (i) to award damages (previously only awardable in common law courts) for past unlawful conduct "in addition to" awarding injunctions to restrain future unlawful conduct; and (ii) to award damages "in substitution for" the grant of an injunction to restrain future unlawful conduct.

18–191 Guidance on the court's exercise of the discretion in (ii) was given by A.L. Smith LJ in *Shelfer v City of London Electric Lighting Co*,[222] where he said that as a "working rule" four conditions should generally be met before an award of damages in lieu was made: the injury to the claimant's rights had to be small, capable of being estimated in money, and adequately compensable by a small sum; it must also be oppressive to the defendant to grant the injunction.[223] These criteria were interpreted narrowly and applied rigidly in later cases,[224] and in recent decades a divergence of view also opened up between courts who thought that public interest considerations might justify an award of damages in lieu[225] and courts who thought that this would only be appropriate in "marginal" cases where the

---

[217] Applicable to open contracts. In practice, parties to contracts for the sale of land use Standard Conditions which moderate the position. These, however, are subject to the Unfair Contract Terms Act 1977 and to a judicial reluctance to allow parties to escape their equitable duties, e.g. *Rignall Developments Ltd v Halil* [1988] Ch. 190.

[218] *Flight v Booth* (1834) 1 Bing. N.C. 370; *Walker v Boyle* [1982] 1 W.L.R. 495

[219] *Jacobs v Revell* [1900] 2 Ch. 858; *Bechal v Kitsford Holdings Ltd* [1989] 1 W.L.R. 105.

[220] *Rutherford v Acton-Adams* [1915] A.C. 866 at 870.

[221] J.A. Jolowicz, "Damages in Equity—A Study of Lord Cairns' Act" [1975] C.L.J. 224; P.M. McDermott, *Equitable Damages* (Butterworths, 1994), Ch.3; and for judicial statements that the courts' former jurisdiction under Lord Cairns' Act is now embodied by s.50, see, e.g. *Jaggard v Sawyer* [1995] 1 W.L.R. 269 at 284, per Millett LJ; *Regan v Paul Properties DPF No.1 Ltd* [2007] Ch. 135 at [24], per Mummery LJ.

[222] [1895] 1 Ch. 287 at 322–323.

[223] [1995] 1 W.L.R. 269 at 280–281.

[224] M. Wilde, "Nuisance Law and Damages in Lieu of an Injunction: Challenging the Orthodoxy of the *Shelfer* Criteria" in S.G.A. Pitel, J.W. Neyers and E. Chamberlain (eds), *Tort Law: Challenging Orthodoxy* (Hart Publishing, 2013).

[225] *Wheeler v JJ Saunders Ltd* [1996] Ch. 19; *Marcic v Thames Water Plc* [2002] Q.B. 929 (overturned by the HL on other grounds).

damage to the defendant was "minimal".[226] These matters were all considered by the Supreme Court in *Lawrence v Fen Tigers Ltd*.

*Lawrence v Fen Tigers Ltd*

Supreme Court [2014] A.C. 822

In 2006 the claimants bought a house in the country situated near a motor racing stadium and motocross track. These were operated by the defendants in accordance with planning permissions that placed limits on the frequency and times of stadium and track activities but placed no conditions on the level of noise emitted by these activities. The claimants brought an action in nuisance. The trial judge held as a matter of law that the permissions could not relevantly have changed the character of the area so as to affect his assessment of whether the noise amounted to a nuisance. On the facts it had and so the claimants were entitled to an injunction, although the defendants could ask for this order to be discharged and replaced with an award of damages in lieu. The defendants appealed and the Court of Appeal held that no nuisance had been committed. They held as a matter of law that planning permissions can relevantly change the character of a locality for the purposes of a nuisance claim, and as a matter of fact that the noise of motor sports had become an established part of the character of the locality following the implementation of the planning permissions in respect of the stadium and track. The claimants appealed. **18–192**

The Supreme Court held, inter alia, that the Court of Appeal were wrong to treat the existence of planning permission for the defendants' activities as determinative of the character of the locality and so they should not have overturned the judge's finding that the noise amounted to a nuisance. The claimants were entitled to an injunction, but the defendants could have this replaced with an award of damages in lieu. Their Lordships' views on the circumstances in which this is appropriate that are reproduced below. **18–193**

LORD NEUBERGER: . . . [In] addition to awarding the appellants damages for the nuisance by noise which they had suffered in the past, the judge granted them an injunction limiting the levels of noise which could be emitted from the stadium and the track, and he also gave liberty to apply. He was not invited to award the appellants damages instead of an injunction. On this appeal, however, the respondents contend that, if the judge was right in concluding that their activities at the stadium and the track constituted a nuisance, then this was a case where he ought to have awarded damages instead of an injunction. **18–194**

Where a claimant has established that the defendant's activities constitute a nuisance, prima facie the remedy to which she is entitled (in addition to damages for past nuisance) is an injunction to restrain the defendant from committing such nuisance in the future; of course, the precise form of any injunction will depend very much on the facts of the particular case. However, ever since Lord Cairns' Act (the Chancery Amendment Act 1858), the court has had power to award damages instead of an injunction in any case, including a case of nuisance: see now section 50 of the Senior Courts Act 1981. Where the court decides to refuse the claimant an injunction to restrain a nuisance, and instead awards her damages, such damages are conventionally based on the reduction in the value of the claimant's property as a result of the continuation of the nuisance. Subject to what I say below, this is clearly the appropriate basis for assessing damages, given that nuisance is a property-related tort and what constitutes a nuisance is judged by the standard of the ordinary reasonable person. **18–195**

The question which arises is what, if any, principles govern the exercise of the court's jurisdiction to award damages instead of an injunction. The case which is probably most frequently cited on the question is *Shelfer v City of London Electric Lighting Co*,[227] but there has been a substantial number of cases in which judges have considered the issue, some before, and many others since. For present purposes, it is necessary to consider *Shelfer* and some of the subsequent cases, which were more fully reviewed by Mummery L.J. in *Regan v Paul Properties DPF No 1 Ltd*.[228] **18–196**

In *Shelfer* the Court of Appeal upheld the trial judge's decision to grant an injunction to restrain noise and vibration. Lindley L.J. said:[229] **18–197**

---

[226] *Watson v Croft Promo-Sport* [2009] 3 All E.R. 249 at [51].
[227] [1895] 1 Ch. 287.
[228] [2007] Ch. 135 at [35]–[59].
[229] At 315–316.

"[Ever] since Lord Cairns' Act was passed the Court of Chancery has repudiated the notion that the legislature intended to turn that court into a tribunal for legalising wrongful acts; or in other words, the court has always protested against the notion that it ought to allow a wrong to continue simply because the wrongdoer is able and willing to pay for the injury he may inflict. Neither has the circumstance that the wrongdoer is in some sense a public benefactor (eg, a gas or water company or a sewer authority) ever been considered a sufficient reason for refusing to protect by injunction an individual whose rights are being persistently infringed."

**18–198** A.L. Smith L.J. said, in a frequently cited passage:[230]

"a person by committing a wrongful act (whether it be a public company for public purposes or a private individual) is not thereby entitled to ask the court to sanction his doing so by purchasing his neighbour's rights, by assessing damages in that behalf, leaving his neighbour with the nuisance, or his lights dimmed, as the case may be. In such cases the well known rule is not to accede to the application, but to grant the injunction sought, for the plaintiff's legal right has been invaded, and he is prima facie entitled to an injunction. There are, however, cases in which this rule may be relaxed, and in which damages may be awarded in substitution . . . In my opinion, it may be stated as a good working rule that—(1) If the injury to the plaintiff's legal rights is small, (2) And is one which is capable of being estimated in money, (3) And is one which can be adequately compensated by a small money payment, (4) And the case is one in which it would be oppressive to the defendant to grant an injunction:—then damages in substitution for an injunction may be given."

**18–199** Significant obiter observations were subsequently made on the question in *Colls v Home & Colonial Store Ltd*,[231] where the House of Lords reversed the courts below who had concluded that the defendant had infringed the plaintiff's right to light (and had awarded an injunction). Lord Macnaghten said that he had "some difficulty in following out [the] rule" that "an injunction ought to be granted when substantial damages would be given at law".[232] He added that "if there is really a question as to whether the obstruction is legal or not, and if the defendant has acted fairly and not in an unneighbourly spirit", then he was "disposed to think that the court ought to incline to damages rather than to an injunction".[233] Lord Lindley (as he had by then become), after reviewing some of the previous cases on the topic, including *Shelfer*, described "the result of the foregoing review of the authorities" as "not altogether satisfactory", and adding that "there is the uncertainty as to whether the proper remedy is an injunction or damages", but that "the good sense of judges and juries may be relied on for adequately protecting rights to light on the one hand and freedom from unnecessary burdens on the other".[234]

**18–200** [His Lordship considered *Kine v Jolly*,[235] *Slack v Leeds Industrial Co-operative Society Ltd*,[236] and *Fishenden v Higgs & Hill Ltd*,[237] then continued:] In more recent times, the Court of Appeal seems to have assumed that the approach of Lindley and A.L. Smith L.JJ. in *Shelfer* represents the law, and indeed that the four tests suggested by A.L. Smith L.J. are normally to be applied, so that, unless all four tests are satisfied, there was no jurisdiction to refuse an injunction. That seems to have been the approach of Geoffrey Lane L.J. in *Miller v Jackson*[238] and of Lawton L.J. in *Kennaway v Thompson*.[239]

**18–201** *Jaggard v Sawyer*[240] was a case where the Court of Appeal upheld the trial judge's decision to award damages instead of an injunction restraining the defendant trespassing on the plaintiff's land. In so doing, the judge effectively gave the defendant a right of way to his house over the plaintiff's land, against the plaintiff's will, in return for a capital payment from the defendant to the plaintiff.[241]

---

230 At 322–323.
231 [1904] A.C. 179.
232 At 192.
233 At 193.
234 At 212–3.
235 [1905] 1 Ch 480.
236 [1924] 2 Ch 475.
237 (1935) 153 LT 128.
238 [1977] Q.B. 966.
239 [1981] Q.B. 88.
240 [1995] 1 W.L.R. 269.
241 See 286–287.

Sir Thomas Bingham M.R. (with whom Kennedy L.J. agreed), specifically tested the trial judge's decision to award damages by reference to A.L. Smith L.J.'s four tests, and emphasised that "the test is one of oppression, and the court should not slide into application of a general balance of convenience test".[242] He held that the judge had rightly concluded that the four tests were satisfied. 18–202

Millett L.J. said that "A.L. Smith L.J.'s checklist has stood the test of time", but emphasised that "it is only a working rule and does not purport to be an exhaustive statement of the circumstances in which damages may be awarded instead of an injunction".[243] As he immediately went on to emphasise on the next page, the decision whether or not to award damages instead of an injunction is a discretion. Accordingly, he said, the cases where judges have awarded or refused to award damages can be no more than "illustrations of circumstances in which particular judges have exercised their discretion". He also suggested that "The outcome of any particular case usually turns on the question: would it in all the circumstances be oppressive to the defendant to grant the injunction to which the plaintiff is prima facie entitled?" He then went on to refer to the significance of the defendant's state of mind, including openness, good faith, and understanding. 18–203

Some seven years ago, in *Regan*,[244] the Court of Appeal rejected the trial judge's view that, where the defendant's building interfered with the claimant's right to light, the onus was on the claimant to show that damages were not an adequate remedy. In his judgment, Mummery L.J. then effectively decided that an injunction should be granted on the basis that three of A.L. Smith L.J.'s tests were not satisfied.[245] 18–204

In *Watson v Croft Promosport Ltd*,[246] the Court of Appeal reversed the trial judge's decision to award damages instead of an injunction in a case where the nuisance was very similar in nature and cause to that alleged in this case. Sir Andrew Morritt C. described "the appropriate test" as having been "clearly established by the decision of the Court of Appeal in *Shelfer*", namely "that damages in lieu of an injunction should only be awarded under 'very exceptional circumstances'".[247] He also said that Shelfer "established that the circumstance that the wrongdoer is in some sense a public benefactor is not a sufficient reason for refusing an injunction", although he accepted that "the effect on the public" could properly be taken into account in a case "where the damage to the claimant is minimal".[248] 18–205

It seems to me that there are two problems about the current state of the authorities on this question of the proper approach for a court to adopt on the question whether to award damages instead of an injunction. 18–206

The first is what at best might be described as a tension, and at worst as an inconsistency, between two sets of judicial dicta since *Shelfer*. Observations in *Slack*, *Miller*, *Kennaway*, *Regan*, and *Watson* appear to support the notion that A.L. Smith L.J.'s approach in *Shelfer* is generally to be adopted and that it requires an exceptional case before damages should be awarded in lieu of an injunction, whereas the approach adopted in *Colls*, *Kine*, and *Fishenden* seems to support a more open-minded approach, taking into account the conduct of the parties. In *Jaggard*, the Court of Appeal did not need to address the question, as even on the stricter approach it upheld the trial judge's award of damages in lieu, although Millett L.J. seems to have tried to reconcile the two approaches. 18–207

The second problem is the unsatisfactory way in which it seems that the public interest is to be taken into account when considering the issue whether to grant an injunction or award damages. The notion that it can be relevant where the damages are minimal, but not otherwise, as stated in *Watson*, seems very strange. Either the public interest is capable of being relevant to the issue or it is not. As part of this second problem, there is a question as to the extent to which it is relevant that the activity giving rise to the nuisance has the benefit of a planning permission. 18–208

So far as the first problem is concerned, the approach to be adopted by a judge when being asked to award damages instead of an injunction should, in my view, be much more flexible than that suggested in the recent cases of *Regan* and *Watson*. It seems to me that (i) an almost mechanical application of A.L. Smith L.J.'s four tests, and (ii) an approach which involves damages being awarded only in "very 18–209

---

242 At 282–283.
243 At 287.
244 [2007] Ch. 135.
245 See [70]–[73].
246 [2009] 3 All E.R. 249.
247 At [44].
248 At [51].

exceptional circumstances", are each simply wrong in principle, and give rise to a serious risk of going wrong in practice. (Quite apart from this, exceptionality may be a questionable guide in any event.[249])

18–210 The court's power to award damages in lieu of an injunction involves a classic exercise of discretion, which should not, as a matter of principle, be fettered, particularly in the very constrained way in which the Court of Appeal has suggested in *Regan* and *Watson*. And, as a matter of practical fairness, each case is likely to be so fact-sensitive that any firm guidance is likely to do more harm than good. On this aspect, I would adopt the observation of Millett L.J. in *Jaggard* where he said:[250]

> "Reported cases are merely illustrations of circumstances in which particular judges have exercised their discretion, in some cases by granting an injunction, and in others by awarding damages instead. Since they are all cases on the exercise of a discretion, none of them is a binding authority on how the discretion should be exercised. The most that any of them can demonstrate is that in similar circumstances it would not be wrong to exercise the discretion in the same way. But it does not follow that it would be wrong to exercise it differently."

18–211 Having approved that statement, it is only right to acknowledge that this does not prevent the courts from laying down rules as to what factors can, and cannot, be taken into account by a judge when deciding whether to exercise his discretion to award damages in lieu. Indeed, it is appropriate to give as much guidance as possible so as to ensure that, while the discretion is not fettered, its manner of exercise is as predictable as possible. I would accept that the prima facie position is that an injunction should be granted, so the legal burden is on the defendant to show why it should not. And, subject to one possible point, I would cautiously (in the light of the fact that each case turns on its facts) approve the observations of Lord Macnaghten in *Colls*, where he said:[251]

> "In some cases, of course, an injunction is necessary—if, for instance, the injury cannot fairly be compensated by money—if the defendant has acted in a high-handed manner—if he has endeavoured to steal a march upon the plaintiff or to evade the jurisdiction of the court. In all these cases an injunction is necessary, in order to do justice to the plaintiff and as a warning to others. But if there is really a question as to whether the obstruction is legal or not, and if the defendant has acted fairly and not in an unneighbourly spirit, I am disposed to think that the court ought to incline to damages rather than to an injunction. It is quite true that a man ought not to be compelled to part with his property against his will, or to have the value of his property diminished, without an Act of Parliament. On the other hand, the court ought to be very careful not to allow an action for the protection of ancient lights to be used as a means of extorting money."

18–212 The one possible doubt that I have about this observation relates to the suggestion in the antepenultimate sentence that the court "ought to incline to damages" in the event he describes. If, as I suspect, Lord Macnaghten was simply suggesting that, if there was no prejudice to a claimant other than the bare fact of an interference with her rights, and there was no other ground for granting an injunction, I agree with him. However, it is right to emphasise that, when a judge is called on to decide whether to award damages in lieu of an injunction, I do not think that there should be any inclination either way (subject to the legal burden discussed above): the outcome should depend on all the evidence and arguments. Further, the sentence should not be taken as suggesting that there could not be any other relevant factors: clearly there could be. (It is true that *Colls*, like a number of the cases on the issue of damages in lieu, was concerned with rights of light, but I do not see such cases as involving special rules when it comes to this issue. *Shelfer* itself was not a right to light case; nor were *Jaggard* and *Watson*. However, in many cases involving nuisance by noise, there may be more wide ranging issues and more possible forms of relief than in cases concerned with infringements of a right to light.)

18–213 Where does that leave A.L. Smith L.J.'s four tests? While the application of any such series of tests cannot be mechanical, I would adopt a modified version of the view expressed by Romer L.J. in *Fishenden*.[252] First, the application of the four tests must not be such as "to be a fetter on the exercise of the court's discretion". Secondly, it would, in the absence of additional relevant circumstances pointing the other way, normally

[249] See *Manchester City Council v Pinnock* [2011] 2 A.C. 104 at [51].
[250] [1995] 1 W.L.R. 269 at 288.
[251] [1904] A.C. 179 at 193.
[252] 153 L.T. 128 at 141.

be right to refuse an injunction if those four tests were satisfied. Thirdly, the fact that those tests are not all satisfied does not mean that an injunction should be granted.

As for the second problem, that of public interest, I find it hard to see how there could be any circumstances in which it arose and could not, as a matter of law, be a relevant factor. Of course, it is very easy to think of circumstances in which it might arise but did not begin to justify the court refusing, or, as the case may be, deciding, to award an injunction if it was otherwise minded to do so. But that is not the point. The fact that a defendant's business may have to shut down if an injunction is granted should, it seems to me, obviously be a relevant fact, and it is hard to see why relevance should not extend to the fact that a number of the defendant's employees would lose their livelihood, although in many cases that may well not be sufficient to justify the refusal of an injunction. Equally, I do not see why the court should not be entitled to have regard to the fact that many other neighbours in addition to the claimant are badly affected by the nuisance as a factor in favour of granting an injunction. 18–214

It is also right to mention planning permission in this context. In some cases, the grant of planning permission for a particular activity (whether carried on at the claimant's, or the defendant's, premises) may provide strong support for the contention that the activity is of benefit to the public, which would be relevant to the question of whether or not to grant an injunction. Accordingly, the existence of a planning permission which expressly or inherently authorises carrying on an activity in such a way as to cause a nuisance by noise or the like, can be a factor in favour of refusing an injunction and compensating the claimant in damages. This factor would have real force in cases where it was clear that the planning authority had been reasonably and fairly influenced by the public benefit of the activity, and where the activity cannot be carried out without causing the nuisance complained of. However, even in such cases, the court would have to weigh up all the competing factors. 18–215

In some such cases, the court may well be impressed by a defendant's argument that an injunction would involve a loss to the public or a waste of resources on account of what may be a single claimant, or that the financial implications of an injunction for the defendant would be disproportionate to the damage done to the claimant if she was left to her claim in damages. In many such cases, particularly where an injunction would in practice stop the defendant from pursuing the activities, an injunction may well not be the appropriate remedy. 18–216

Since writing this, I have read with interest Lord Sumption J.S.C.'s suggestions as to how the law on the topic of damages instead of an injunction in nuisance cases might develop. At any rate on the face of it, I can see much merit in the proposals which he proffers. However, it would be inappropriate to go further than I have gone at this stage, in the light of the arguments which were raised on this appeal. There may well be objections, qualifications, and alternatives which could be made in relation to Lord Sumption J.S.C.'s suggested approach, and they should be considered before the law on this topic is developed further. In that connection, I see real force in what Lord Mance J.S.C. says [on this topic]. 18–217

A final point which it is right to mention on this issue is the measure of damages, where a judge decides to award damages instead of an injunction. It seems to me at least arguable that, where a claimant has a prima facie right to an injunction to restrain a nuisance, and the court decides to award damages instead, those damages should not always be limited to the value of the consequent reduction in the value of the claimant's property. While double counting must be avoided, the damages might well, at least where it was appropriate, also include the loss of the claimant's ability to enforce her rights, which may often be assessed by reference to the benefit to the defendant of not suffering an injunction. 18–218

Support for such an approach may be found in the reasoning in *Jaggard*, which suggests that this is a proper approach to damages where an injunction is refused to restrain a trespass, and damages were awarded instead. Bingham M.R. said, when explaining and approving an earlier case where a judge had assessed damages for breach of a restrictive building covenant, which he then applied to the claim in *Jaggard*:[253] 18–219

> "The defendants had committed a breach of covenant, the effects of which continued. The judge was not willing to order the defendants to undo the continuing effects of that breach. He had therefore to assess the damages necessary to compensate the plaintiffs for this continuing invasion of their right. He paid attention to the profits earned by the defendants, as it seems to me, not in order to strip the defendants of their unjust gains, but because of the obvious relationship between the profits earned

[253] [1995] 1 W.L.R. 269 at 281–282.

by the defendants and the sum which the defendants would reasonably have been willing to pay to secure release from the covenant."

18–220 To the same effect, Millett L.J. said in *Jaggard*:[254]

"In my view there is no reason why compensatory damages for future trespasses and continuing breaches of covenant should not reflect the value of the rights which she has lost, or why such damages should not be measured by the amount which she could reasonably have expected to receive for their release."

18–221 However, there are factors which support the contention that damages in a nuisance case should never, or only rarely, be assessed by reference to the benefit to the defendant in no injunction being granted, as pointed out by Lord Carnwath J.S.C. below. For that reason, as well as because we have not heard argument on the issue, it would be inappropriate for us to seek to decide on this appeal whether, and if so in what circumstances, damages could be recoverable on this basis in a nuisance claim.

18–222 There are differences between the various members of the court on this final issue. Most, probably all, of these differences are ones of emphasis and detail rather than of principle, but I none the less accept that we are at risk of introducing a degree of uncertainty into the law. The nature of the issue, whether to award damages in lieu of an injunction, is such that a degree of uncertainty is inevitable, but that does not alter the fact that it should be kept to a reasonable minimum. Given that we are changing the practice of the courts, it is inevitable that, in so far as there can be clearer or more precise principles, they will have to be worked out in the way familiar to the common law, namely on a case by case basis. . .

18–223 LORD SUMPTION: . . . The ordinary principle is that the court does not grant an injunction in a case where there is an adequate legal remedy. In particular, it does not do so where damages would be an adequate remedy. Where an injunction is granted, it is usually because the injury to the claimant is "irreparable", in the sense that money cannot atone for it. However, this principle has never been consistently followed in cases of nuisance. The leading case is *Shelfer v City of London Electric Lighting Co* which created a strong presumption in favour of an injunction, to be displaced only in the four narrowly defined categories identified by A.L. Smith L.J.[255] The exceptions applied only to cases where the injury to the claimant was small and the grant of an injunction would be oppressive. In *Colls v Home and Colonial Stores Ltd* Lord Macnaghten wondered why an injunction should be granted "when substantial damages would be given at law",[256] and there were subsequent attempts to widen the discretion. But the courts have not taken the hint. In *Regan v Paul Properties DPF No 1 Ltd*[257] and *Watson v Croft Promosport Ltd*,[258] the Court of Appeal have reverted to substantially the same position as the Court of Appeal in *Shelfer* more than a century before.

18–224 The courts might have defended the special treatment of nuisance by pointing to the traditional attitude of equity to land as being unique, an approach which is exemplified in its willingness to grant specific performance of contracts for the sale of land. From this, it might have been concluded that paying the claimant enough to buy a comparable property elsewhere where there was no nuisance was not equivalent to letting him use his existing land free of the nuisance. In fact the *Shelfer* principle was based mainly on the court's objection to sanctioning a wrong by allowing the defendant to pay for the right to go on doing it. This seems an unduly moralistic approach to disputes, and if taken at face value would justify the grant of an injunction in all cases, which is plainly not the law. In his dissenting judgment in the Court of Appeal in *Co-operative Insurance Society Ltd v Argyll Stores (Holdings) Ltd*[259] (subsequently upheld in the House of Lords[260]), Millett L.J. said:

"The competing arguments in the present case, and the difference in the views of the members of this court, reflect a controversy which has persisted since the dispute between Sir Edward Coke and Lord Ellesmere L.C. Sir Edward Coke resented the existence of an equitable jurisdiction which deprived the

[254] At 292.
[255] [1895] 1 Ch. 287 at 322–323.
[256] [1904] A.C. 179 at 192.
[257] [2007] Ch. 135.
[258] [2009] 3 All E.R. 249.
[259] [1996] Ch. 286 at 304.
[260] [1998] A.C. 1.

defendant of what he regarded as a fundamental freedom to elect whether to carry out his promise or to pay damages for the breach. Modern economic theory supports Sir Edward Coke; an award of damages reflects normal commercial expectations and ensures a more efficient allocation of scarce economic resources. The defendant will break his contract only if it pays him to do so after taking the payment of damages into account; the plaintiff will be fully compensated in damages; and both parties will be free to allocate their resources elsewhere. Against this there is the repugnance felt by those who share the view of Fuller C.J. in *Union Pacific Railway Co v Chicago, Rock Island and Pacific Railway Co*[261] that it is an intolerable travesty of justice that a party should be allowed to break his contract at pleasure by electing to pay damages for the breach. English law has adopted a pragmatic approach in resolving this dispute . . . The leading principle is usually said to be that equitable relief is not available where damages are an adequate remedy. In my view, it would be more accurate to say that equitable relief will be granted where it is appropriate and not otherwise; and that where damages are an adequate remedy it is inappropriate to grant equitable relief."

In my view, the decision in *Shelfer* is out of date, and it is unfortunate that it has been followed so recently and so slavishly. It was devised for a time in which England was much less crowded, when comparatively few people owned property, when conservation was only beginning to be a public issue, and when there was no general system of statutory development control. The whole jurisprudence in this area will need one day to be reviewed in this court. There is much to be said for the view that damages are ordinarily an adequate remedy for nuisance and that an injunction should not usually be granted in a case where it is likely that conflicting interests are engaged other than the parties' interests. In particular, it may well be that an injunction should as a matter of principle not be granted in a case where a use of land to which objection is taken requires and has received planning permission. However, at this stage, in the absence of argument on these points, I can do no more than identify them as calling for consideration in a case in which they arise. **18–225**

LORD MANCE: . . . With regard to remedy, I am broadly in agreement with Lord Neuberger P.S.C. However, I would adopt the qualifications made by Lord Carnwath J.S.C. I do not think that a grant of planning permission can give rise to any presumption that there should be no injunction, and, while I would, in a case where it was relevant, like to hear argument on this, I am not at present persuaded that cases on the right to light involve the same considerations as those arising, or are therefore necessarily helpful, where the question is the appropriate remedy in respect of a nuisance of the present different nature. **18–226**

I would only add in relation to remedy that the right to enjoy one's home without disturbance is one which I would believe that many, indeed most, people value for reasons largely if not entirely independent of money. With reference to Lord Sumption J.S.C.'s concluding paragraph, I would not therefore presently be persuaded by a view that "damages are ordinarily an adequate remedy for nuisance" and that "an injunction should not usually be granted in a case where it is likely that conflicting interests are engaged other than the parties' interests"—a suggested example of the latter being given as a case where a use of land has received planning permission. I would see this as putting the significance of planning permission and public benefit too high, in the context of the remedy to be afforded for a private nuisance. As already indicated, I agree with Lord Neuberger P.S.C.'s nuanced approach. . . **18–227**

LORD CLARKE: . . . [As] I see it, the most important aspect of this case relates to the correct approach to remedies. In particular I agree with the views of Millett LJ in *Co-operative Insurance Society Ltd v Argyll Stores (Holdings) Ltd*,[262] which was a dissenting judgment but was subsequently upheld by the House of Lords. He concluded that the general principle is or should be that equitable relief will be granted where it is appropriate and not otherwise and that, where damages are an adequate remedy, it is inappropriate to grant equitable relief. Lord Sumption J.S.C. set out Millett L.J.'s views . . . as I read it, with approval. I entirely agree with Lord Sumption . . . that the decision in *Shelfer v City of London Electric Lighting Co* is out of date and that it is unfortunate that it has been followed so recently and so slavishly. Indeed, I would so hold now in this appeal, although (in the absence of submissions) I would not now lay down precise principles which should be followed in the future. They must be developed on a case by case basis and in each case all will depend on the circumstances. I agree with Millett L.J.'s general approach. **18–228**

[261] (1896) 163 U.S. 564 at 600.
[262] [1996] Ch 286 at 305.

18–229 LORD CARNWATH: On the way the case has been argued in the lower courts, the final issue addressed by Lord Neuberger P.S.C. does not strictly arise. As the judge recorded, it was accepted that if a nuisance was established an injunction should follow, the only issue being its terms. The defendants have sought to open the issue in this court for the first time, on the basis that in the lower courts having regard to the authorities such an argument would have been doomed to failure. However, the result is that we have no relevant findings, either as to how the judge would have exercised his discretion if he been able to do so, or as to how he would have assessed future damages, had he decided on that course. In those circumstances, we should approach the issue with caution, conscious that anything we say can be no more than guidance.

18–230 With that caveat, I agree with Lord Neuberger P.S.C. and the rest of the court that the opportunity should be taken to signal a move away from the strict criteria derived from *Shelfer*. This is particularly relevant to cases where an injunction would have serious consequences for third parties, such as employees of the defendant's business, or, in this case, members of the public using or enjoying the stadium. In that respect, in my view, the Court of Appeal in *Watson* was wrong to hold that the judge had no power to make the order he did, and to limit public interest considerations to cases where the damage to the claimant is "minimal".

18–231 As has been seen, Peter Gibson L.J. in *Wheeler* saw more flexible remedial principles as a possible answer to the public interest aspect of cases such as *Gillingham*,[263] rather than creating an exception to the law of nuisance. Commenting on the restrictive view taken by the Court of Appeal in *Watson*, Maria Lee has said:[264]

> "The fact that something should go ahead in the public interest does not tell us where the costs should lie; we need not assume that injured parties should bear the burden associated with broader social benefits . . . The continued strength of private nuisance in a regulatory state probably depends on a more flexible approach to remedies."

I agree.

18–232 . . . While therefore I agree generally with the observations of Lord Neuberger P.S.C. and Lord Sumption J.S.C. on this aspect, I have three particular reservations.

18–233 First, I would not regard the grant of planning permission for a particular use as in itself giving rise to a presumption against the grant of an injunction. As I have said, the circumstances in which permissions may be granted differ so much as to make it unwise to lay down any general propositions. I would accept however that the nature of, and background to, a relevant planning permission may be an important factor in the court's assessment.

18–234 Secondly, I would be cautious of too direct a comparison with cases relating to rights of light, particularly where (as in *Kine v Jolly*[265]) the court was asked to make a mandatory injunction to demolish a house built in good faith.[266] Cases such as the present are not concerned with such drastic alternatives. The judge is not asked to bring the defendant's activity to an end altogether, but to set reasonable limits for its continuation. In so doing he should take into account not only the claimant's environment but also the viability of the defendant's business. In some cases it may be appropriate to combine an injunction with an award of damages (as happened at first instance in *Watson v Croft Promosport Ltd*). I also agree with Lord Mance J.S.C. that special importance should attach to the right to enjoy one's home without disturbance, independently of financial considerations.

18–235 Thirdly, without much fuller argument than we have heard, I would be reluctant to open up the possibility of assessment of damages on the basis of a share of the benefit to the defendants. The issues are complex on any view.[267] *Jaggard v Sawyer*,[268] to which Lord Neuberger P.S.C. refers, gives Court of Appeal support for an award on that basis for trespass or breach of a restrictive covenant, but the same

263 [1993] QB 343.

264 "Tort Law and Regulation: Planning and Nuisance" (2011) 8 JPL 986, 989–990.

265 [1905] 1 Ch. 480

266 See also M. Wilde, "Nuisance Law and Damages in Lieu of an Injunction: Challenging the Orthodoxy of the *Shelfer* Criteria" in S. Pitel and others (eds), *Tort Law: Challenging Orthodoxy* (2013) at p. 372, citing Sargant L.J. in *Slack v Leeds Industrial Co-operative Society* [1924] 2 Ch 475 at 496.

267 For a detailed academic discussion of the recent authorities, see C. Rotherham, "Gain-based Relief in Tort after *Attorney General v Blake*" (2010) 126 L.Q.R. 102.

268 [1995] 1 W.L.R. 269.

approach has not hitherto been extended to interference with rights of light.[269] In cases relating to clearly defined interference with a specific property right, it is not difficult to envisage a hypothetical negotiation to establish an appropriate "price". The same approach cannot in my view be readily transferred to claims for nuisance such as the present relating to interference with the enjoyment of land, where the injury is less specific, and the appropriate price much less easy to assess, particularly in a case where the nuisance affects a large number of people. Further, such an approach seems to represent a radical departure from the normal basis regarded by Parliament as fair and appropriate in relation to injurious affection arising from activities carried out under statutory authority.

## *B. Quantification of Damages in Lieu*

### i. Damages in Lieu of an Injunction

In *Lawrence*, the Supreme Court seems to have accepted the view expressed by the Court of Appeal in *Jaggard v Sawyer*[270] that at least in cases of trespass and breach of restrictive covenant, the best approach to quantifying the damages awarded in lieu of an injunction is to ask what price the parties would have agreed should be paid by the defendant in exchange for the claimant releasing her rights. Lord Carnwath denied that this was a viable approach in nuisance cases, because he considered the inchoate nature of the claimant's injury to make it harder for the courts to assess an appropriate price. Given the intensely artificial nature of the assessment exercise even in trespass cases, however, that is a weak reason for taking a different approach in nuisance cases, and to make matters worse he does not explain what else the courts are meant to do. **18–236**

Damages for a hypothetical loss of bargain are also known as "licence fee damages" and "*Wrotham Park*" damages, after *Wrotham Park Estate Co Ltd v Parkside Homes Ltd*,[271] where Brightman J awarded damages in lieu of an injunction for breach of a restrictive covenant in a sum equal to five per cent of the defendant property developer's anticipated profit, which he calculated to be the price the parties would have agreed should be paid for relaxation of the covenant. The obvious difficulty with such damages is that they depend on the premise that the parties would respectively have been willing to buy and sell a licence for the relaxation of the claimant's right, when the reality of many cases is that the claimant would never have been willing to sell. Nevertheless, that is the approach the courts are expected to take, whether assessing licence fee damages at common law or assessing licence fee damages in lieu of an injunction. As Lord Nicholls makes clear in the following extract from *Attorney General v Blake*, the basic principles are the same in either case, although common law damages are designed to compensate the claimant for losses which have already happened, whereas damages in lieu are designed to compensate the claimant for losses which will happen in the future.[272] **18–237**

*Attorney-General v Blake*

[2001] 1 A.C. 268 at 281

LORD NICHOLLS: ... The common law courts' jurisdiction to award damages was confined to loss or injury flowing from a cause of action which had accrued before the writ was issued. Thus in the case of a continuing wrong, such as maintaining overhanging eaves and gutters, damages were limited to the loss **18–238**

[269] See *Forsyth-Grant v Allen* [2008] Env. L.R. 877.
[270] [1995] 1 W.L.R. 269.
[271] [1974] 1 W.L.R. 798.
[272] See also *Lunn Poly Ltd v Liverpool and Lancashire Properties Ltd* [2006] EWCA Civ 430; *Sinclair v Gavaghan* [2007] EWHC 2256 (Ch); *Enfield LBC v Outdoor Plus Ltd* [2012] EWCA Civ 608; *Eaton Mansions (Westminster) Ltd v Stinger* [2013] EWCA Civ 1308.

suffered up to the commencement of the action.[273] Lord Cairns's Act liberated the courts from this fetter. In future, if the court declined to grant an injunction, which had the effect in practice of sanctioning the indefinite continuance of a wrong, the court could assess damages to include losses likely to follow from the anticipated future continuance of the wrong as well as losses already suffered. The power to give damages in lieu of an injunction imported the power to give an equivalent for what was lost by the refusal of an injunction.[274] It is important to note, however, that although the Act had the effect of enabling the court in this regard to award damages in respect of the future as well as the past, the Act did not alter the measure to be employed in assessing damages.[275] Thus, in the same way as damages at common law for violations of a property right may by measured by reference to the benefits wrongfully obtained by a defendant, so under Lord Cairns's Act damages may include damages measured by reference to the benefits likely to be obtained in future by the defendant. This approach has been adopted on many occasions. Recent examples are *Bracewell v Appleby*[276] and *Jaggard v Sawyer*,[277] both cases concerned with access to a newly-built house over another's land.

18–239 The measure of damages awarded in this type of case is often analysed as damages for loss of a bargaining opportunity or, which comes to the same, the price payable for the compulsory acquisition of a right. This analysis is correct. The court's refusal to grant an injunction means that in practice the defendant is thereby permitted to perpetuate the wrongful state of affairs he has brought about. But this analysis takes the matter now under discussion no further forward. A property right has value to the extent only that the court will enforce it or award damages for its infringement. The question under discussion is whether the court will award substantial damages for an infringement when no financial loss flows from the infringement and, moreover, in a suitable case will assess the damages by reference to the defendant's profit obtained from the infringement. The cases mentioned above show that the courts habitually do that very thing.

### ii. Damages in Lieu of Specific Performance

18–240 On the measure of damages to be awarded in lieu of specific performance, Lord Wilberforce in *Johnson v Agnew*[278] rejected the view that damages could be assessed on different bases under the Act and at common law. Megarry J had said in *Wroth v Tyler*[279] that the purpose of an award was to offer a true substitute for specific performance—which could only be refused at trial. Hence the date of trial, rather than the date of breach, might be the relevant one in assessing compensation. This view is, with respect, clearly right, and is reconcilable with Lord Wilberforce's view. The common law rule does not invariably select the date of breach as the relevant one in determining loss.[280] Furthermore, since it is always reasonable to seek specific performance of a contract for the sale of land[281] any increase in loss caused by denial of the relief at trial (so late in the day) ought, as a matter of justice, to be taken into account because "if to follow [the normal rule] would give rise to injustice, the court has power to fix such other date as may be appropriate in the circumstances."[282]

18–241 Various Commonwealth cases have adopted Megarry J's reasoning in *Wroth* to develop special principles of assessment for equitable damages in cases where common law damages could alternatively

---

273 See *Battishill v Reed* (1856) 18 C.B. 696.
274 See *Leeds Industrial Co-operative Society Ltd v Slack* [1924] A.C. 851 at 859, per Viscount Finlay.
275 See *Johnson v Agnew* [1980] AC 367 at 400, per Lord Wilberforce.
276 [1975] Ch. 408.
277 [1995] 1 W.L.R. 269.
278 [1980] A.C. 367.
279 [1974] Ch. 30.
280 Cf. *Hooper v Oates* [2014] Ch. 287 at [38], per Lloyd LJ: "the breach date is the right date for assessment of damages only where there is an immediately available market for the sale of the relevant asset or, in the converse case, for the purchase of an equivalent asset" — and that is "most unlikely to be the case where the asset in question is land".
281 Except, perhaps, if one knows or ought to know that one's own hands are unclean.
282 Per Lord Wilberforce at 401. Note also Millett LJ's explanation, in *Jaggard* at 290–291, of Lord Wilberforce's view as it affects injunction cases concerned with the prevention of future wrongs.

have been awarded. The most significant is *Semelhago v Paramadevan*.[283] The parties entered a contract for the sale of a house for CAD 205,000 with a closing date at the end of October 1986. The purchaser had CAD 75,000 in cash, and he planned to mortgage his existing house to secure a loan for the remaining CAD 130,000. To this end he negotiated a six-month open mortgage, intending to sell his existing house over the next six months and repay the loan with the proceeds. However the vendor reneged on the deal and transferred title to a third party in December 1986. The purchaser therefore issued a writ for specific performance or damages in lieu, and stayed in his existing house. This was worth CAD 190,000 in the autumn of 1986, but had risen in value to CAD 300,000 by the time of trial. By then the new house which he had planned to buy from the vendor had also risen in value, to CAD 325,000.

At trial the purchaser elected to take damages rather than specific performance, and in-line with *Wroth* the trial judge assessed these at CAD 120,000, representing the difference between the purchase price and the value of the new house at the time of trial. The Ontario Court of Appeal reduced this to CAD 81,000, accepting the vendor's argument that certain items should be deducted, namely the interest which the purchaser had avoided paying on the CAD 130,000 loan which would have been needed to finance the purchase, the interest earned on the CAD 75,000 that he would have used for the down payment, and the legal fees which he would have incurred. The vendor appealed, arguing that a deduction should also be made to reflect the fact that the purchaser's existing house had risen in value, a gain which he would not have made if he had sold it as planned. The Supreme Court of Canada rejected this, Sopinka J stating that[284]: **18–242**

> If the respondent had received a decree of specific performance, he would have had the property contracted for and retained the amount of the rise in value of his own property. Damages are to be substituted for the decree of specific performance. I see no basis for deductions that are not related to the value of the property which was the subject of the contract. To make such deductions would depart from the principle that damages are to be a true equivalent of specific performance.

This result seems to overcompensate by the claimant by overriding the normal rule that a claimant must mitigate her loss between the date of breach and the date of judgment. However, *Semelhago* is a perfectly logical extension of the *Wroth* principle that equitable damages under Lord Cairns' Act are a monetised substitute for specific performance. As Lionel Smith has observed,[285] the purpose of an order for specific performance is not to compensate the claimant for the loss of her performance interest under the contract, but to vindicate her performance right by compelling the defendant to perform his promise. If equitable damages in lieu of specific performance are awarded with the same goal in mind, then the duty to mitigate has no application for the same reasons that it has no application to a claim for specific performance: since neither remedy is designed to compensate the claimant for her loss, complaints that the claimant has been "overcompensated" miss the point. **18–243**

---

[283] [1996] 2 S.C.R. 415. See too *Souster v Epsom Plumbing Contractors Ltd* [1974] 2 N.Z.L.R. 515; *Metropolitan Trust Co of Canada v Pressure Concrete Services Ltd* (1975) 60 D.L.R. (3d) 431; *Kopec v Pyret* (1987) 36 D.L.R. (4th) 1; *Mills v Ruthol Pty Ltd* (2004) 61 N.S.W.L.R. 1. In *Semelhago* at [22] Sopinka J also held that contracts for the sale of land are not routinely specifically enforceable, and that claimants must produce evidence that the property is "unique to the extent that its substitute is not readily available". For critical comment on this aspect of the case, see R. Chambers, "The Importance of Specific Performance" in S. Degeling and J. Edelman (eds), *Equity in Commercial Law* (Sweet & Maxwell, 2005).

[284] *Semelhago* at [19].

[285] L.D. Smith, "Understanding Specific Performance" in N. Cohen and E. McKendrick (eds), *Comparative Remedies for Breach of Contract* (Hart Publishing, 2005). See too C. Webb, "Performance and Compensation: An Analysis of Contract Damages and Contractual Obligation" (2006) 26 O.J.L.S. 41, developing ideas in D. Friedmann, "The Performance Interest in Contract Damages" (1995) 111 L.Q.R. 628.

## 5. Rescission

### A. Rescission of Contracts

18–244 The equitable right to rescind a contract is the right of a contracting party to set the contract aside and be restored to her former position. The contract must be distinguished as a voidable transaction from a transaction that is void ab initio (e.g. a contract void for illegality or a very fundamental mistake). The situation must also be distinguished from the case where a contract with no inherent invalidity is said to be rescinded for the future when the innocent party accepts the wrongdoer's repudiatory breach of contract as terminating the contract, but leaving the innocent party free to sue the wrongdoer for her past breaches of a valid contract.[286]

18–245 Equity can set aside a transaction in circumstances where the common law would not,[287] and by applying the maxim "those who come to equity must do equity" it can grant relief on terms, e.g. so that a contract is set aside so long as the vendor offers the property in question to the purchaser at a proper price.[288] Whether the differences between the equitable and common law versions of rescission should be perpetuated is a controversial topic. Some would argue that the current distinctions between the bars to rescission in law and equity are indefensible, and that it is confusing and unnecessary for the law to operate more than one version of the remedy.[289] Others would argue that it is desirable to maintain a common law right of election as a self-help remedy, available automatically on strong facts, and an equitable remedy that is available at the discretion of the court on weaker facts where a more sensitive balancing of interests is required.[290]

18–246 Rescission has been awarded in cases:

- where a party has been induced to enter a contract by a fraudulent misrepresentation[291];
- where a party has been induced to enter a contract by an innocent misrepresentation,[292] although the court now has a discretion to award damages in lieu of rescission if it would be equitable to do so[293];
- where a party has entered a contract as a result of another's undue influence[294];
- where a poor ignorant person has entered into a disadvantageous transaction without any independent legal advice[295];

---

286 *Johnson v Agnew* [1980] A.C. 367 at 396–398; *Photo Production Ltd v Securicor Transport Ltd* [1980] A.C. 827 at 844.

287 The differences between rescission in equity and at common law are rehearsed in *Alati v Kruger* (1955) 94 C.L.R. 216 at 223–224, endorsed by Dunn LJ in *O'Sullivan v Management Agency & Music Ltd* [1985] Q.B. 428 at 457.

288 *Grist v Bailey* [1967] Ch. 532; *Magee v Pennine Insurance Co Ltd* [1969] 2 Q.B. 507.

289 This outlook informs, e.g. Carnwath LJ's comments in *Halpern v Halpern* [2008] Q.B. 195 at [70]ff.

290 For the latter view, see, e.g. D. O'Sullivan, S. Elliott and R. Zakrzewski, *The Law of Rescission*, 2nd edn (Oxford University Press, 2014), Ch.10.

291 *Banwaitt v Dewji* [2014] EWCA Civ 67; *Hayward v Zurich Insurance Company Plc* [2015] EWCA Civ 327 at [28].

292 *Shalson v Russo* [2005] Ch. 281.

293 Misrepresentation Act 1967 s.2(2). Indeed, s.2(1) allows damages of a tortious measure to be awarded for a negligent misrepresentation: *Royscot Trust Ltd v Rogerson* [1991] 2 Q.B. 297; *Witter Ltd v TBP Industries Ltd* [1996] 2 All E.R. 573.

294 *Barclays Bank Plc v O'Brien* [1994] 1 A.C. 180; *Royal Bank of Scotland Plc v Etridge (No.2)* [2002] 2 A.C. 773.

295 *Cresswell v Potter* [1978] 1 W.L.R. 255; *Crédit Lyonnais Nederland NV v Burch* [1997] 1 All E.R. 144; *Portman BS v Dusangh* [2001] W.T.L.R 117.

- where the other party to a contract of utmost good faith (e.g. an insurance contract) has breached her duty of disclosure[296]; and
- where the other party to a contract has breached a fiduciary duty.[297]

Note, however, that there is no equitable jurisdiction to grant rescission of a contract on the ground of common mistake where the contract is valid at common law.[298] Nor is there an equitable jurisdiction to grant rescission of a contract where one party has made a unilateral mistake as to a fact or state of affairs which is the basis upon which the terms of the contract are agreed, but that assumption does not become a term of the contract.[299]

In *TSB Bank Plc v Camfield*[300] the Court of Appeal held that if a claimant can set aside a transaction for misrepresentation (or undue influence) then it must be set aside entirely rather than partially. So, a claimant who has agreed to mortgage her house for £30,000 can escape liability for the entire sum, although she would have agreed to liability for £15,000 irrespective of the misrepresentation (or undue influence). Note, however, that she must return any benefit she has personally received under the contract before it can be set aside.[301] **18–247**

The Court of Appeal's reasoning in *Camfield* was repudiated, and the opposite result reached, in *Vadasz v Pioneer Concrete SA*[302] where the High Court of Australia held that the court should be concerned to achieve a practically just result when putting the claimant on terms, and should seek to put the claimant in the position which she would have occupied if the misconduct had not occurred. This approach has a strong intuitive appeal, and it was also taken by the New Zealand Court of Appeal in *Scales Trading Co Ltd v Far Eastern Shipping Co Public Ltd*.[303] However, it seems to treat rescission as though it were a compensatory remedy when in fact the point of the remedy is to require the parties to return whatever benefits they may have received under the contract. The *Vadasz* approach also means that a claimant who would have contracted on precisely the same terms irrespective of the defendant's misconduct cannot rescind at all, a proposition that is contradicted by many authorities, including the High Court of Australia's decision a year after *Vadasz* in *Maguire v Makaronis*,[304] where the court was forced to side-step the problem by holding that *Vadasz* does not apply in cases involving fiduciaries. **18–248**

The equitable right to rescind is lost if the party entitled to rescind affirms the transaction[305]; also, if the right is not exercised within a reasonable time.[306] It has traditionally been said that rescission is also barred if the rescinding party cannot make counter-restitution of benefits she has received. However, it can be expected nowadays that the courts will not insist on counter-restitution *in specie* **18–249**

---

296 *Pan Atlantic Insurance Co Ltd v Pine Top Insurance Co Ltd* [1995] 1 A.C. 501; *Manifest Shipping Co Ltd v Uni-Polaris Insurance Co Ltd* [2003] 1 A.C. 469; but note the Consumer Insurance (Disclosure and Representations) Act 2012.

297 See paras 13–025—13–033.

298 *Great Peace Shipping Ltd v Tsavlisis Salvage (International) Ltd* [2003] Q.B. 679, disapproving *Solle v Butcher* [1950] 1 K.B. 671.

299 *Statoil ASA v Louis Dreyfus Energy Services LP* [2008] 2 Lloyd's Rep. 685 at [98]–[105], rejecting *Huyton SA v Distribuidora Internacional De Productos Agricolas SA de CV* [2003] 2 Lloyd's Rep. 780 at [455].

300 [1995] 1 W.L.R. 430.

301 *Camfield* at 432 and 437; *Dunbar Bank Plc v Nadeem* [1998] 3 All E.R. 876 at 883.

302 (1995) 184 C.L.R. 102.

303 [1999] 3 N.Z.L.R. 26.

304 (1996) 188 C.L.R. 449.

305 *Mitchell v Homfray* (1881) 8 Q.B.D. 587; *Leaf v International Galleries Ltd* [1950] 2 K.B. 86; *Peyman v Lanjani* [1985] Ch. 457; *Insurance Corp of the Channel Islands v Royal Hotel Ltd* [1998] Lloyd's Rep. I.R. 151.

306 *Lindsay Petroleum Co v Hurd* (1874) L.R. 5 P.C. 221 at 239–240; *Erlanger v New Sombrero Phosphate Co* (1878) 3 App. Cas. 1218 at 1279–1280 and 1230–1231; *Leaf v International Galleries Ltd* [1950] 2 K.B. 86.

and will be willing to order counter-restitution of the money value of benefits received, meaning that this has effectively ceased to be a bar and is now merely a pre-condition for the court's order.[307] It is also often said by writers that the intervention of third-party rights also constitutes a bar to rescission in equity, but in fact Equity has always managed to protect third-party purchasers without barring rescission,[308] e.g. by letting third parties keep the relevant asset but making the defendant hand over the proceeds of sale or exchange products.[309]

18–250 The latter type of order is possible because the courts have held that equitable rescission of a contract under which legal title to property was transferred leads to the retrospective imposition of a trust on the property with the consequence that the claimant can trace into substitute assets held by the defendant and assert an equitable proprietary claim to them.[310] In the following passage of Potter LJ's judgment in *Twinsectra Ltd v Yardley*, he leaves it unclear whether the trust imposed on the property is a constructive or resulting trust, a question that has not been resolved by more recent English authorities,[311] although the Australian courts have decided that this trust is a ("remedial"[312]) constructive trust.[313]

*Twinsectra Ltd v Yardley*

Court of Appeal [1999] Lloyd's Rep. Bank. 438 at [99]

18–251 POTTER L.J. (with whom SIR IAIN GLIDEWELL and SIR DAVID HIRST agreed) . . .[The] distinction of importance here is that between non-consensual transfers and transfers pursuant to contracts which are voidable for misrepresentation. In the latter case, the transferor may elect whether to avoid or affirm the transaction and, until he elects to avoid it, there is no constructive (resulting) trust; in the former case, the constructive trust arises upon the moment of transfer. The result, so far as third parties are concerned, is that, before rescission, the owner has no proprietary interest in the original property; all he has is the "mere equity" of his right to set aside the voidable contract. That equity binds volunteers and those taking with notice of the equity, but not purchasers for value without notice.[314] Despite dicta of Lord Mustill in *Re Goldcorp Exchange Ltd*[315] (a case in which the purchase monies sought to be traced were unidentifiable), which, if generally applied beyond the context of the facts in that case, would suggest that equitable title does not (or in appropriate circumstances may not) revest on rescission, the general position seems to me that summarised in *Underhill and Hayton*.[316] It is there stated that equity imposes a constructive trust on property where a transferor's legal and equitable title to his property has passed to the transferee according to basic principles of property law but in circumstances (e.g. involving fraud and misrepresentation) where the transferor has an equitable right (i.e. mere equity) to recover the property by having the transfer

---

307 C. Mitchell, P. Mitchell and S. Watterson, *Goff & Jones: The Law of Unjust Enrichment*, 8th edn (Sweet & Maxwell, 2011), Ch. 31, noting *Erlanger v New Sombrero Phosphate Co* (1873) 3 App. Cas. 1218; *Spence v Crawford* [1939] 3 All E.R. 271; *Alati v Kruger* (1955) 94 C.L.R. 216 at 223–224; *O'Sullivan v Management Agency & Music Ltd* [1985] Q.B. 428; *Smith New Court Securities Ltd v Scrimgeour Vickers (Asset Management) Ltd* [1997] A.C. 254 at 262; *Halpern v Halpern (No. 2)* [2008] Q.B. 195.

308 A point well made in O'Sullivan, Elliott and Zakrzewski, *The Law of Rescission* (2014), paras 20.23ff.

309 *Fox v Mackreth* (1788) 2 Bro. C.C. 44; *Lagunas Nitrate Co v Lagunas Syndicate* [1899] 2 Ch. 392 at 434. See also the cases cited in the next fn.

310 *Small v Attwood* (1832) You. 407 at 533–538; *Banque Belge pour l'Etranger v Hambrouck* [1921] 1 K.B. 321 at 332; *Daly v Sydney Stock Exchange Ltd* (1986) 160 C.L.R. 371 at 387–390; *El Ajou v Dollar Land Holdings Plc* [1993] 3 All E.R. 717 at 735; *Shalson v Russo* [2005] Ch. 281 at [120]–[127]. See too S. Worthington "The Proprietary Consequences of Rescission" [2002] 10 R.L.R. 28, 37–38.

311 *Papamichael v National Westminster Bank* [2003] 1 Lloyd's Rep. 341; *London Allied Holdings Ltd v Lee* [2007] EWHC 2061 (Ch) at [276]; *National Crime Agency v Robb* [2015] Lloyd's Rep. F.C. 161 at [43]–[44].

312 See paras 15–006—15–008.

313 *Robins v Incentive Dynamics Pty Ltd (In Liquidation)* (2003) 175 Fed. L.R. 286 at [74]; *Grimaldi v Chameleon Mining NL (No.2)* (2012) 200 F.C.R. 296 at [277].

314 See generally S. Worthington, *Proprietary Interests in Commercial Transactions* (1996) pp. 163–165 and 167.

315 [1995] 1 A.C. 74 at 102–3.

316 15th edn (1995) p.372(f).

set aside, and the court declares that from the outset the transferee has held the property to transferor's order, though nowadays it seems better to regard a restitutionary resulting trust as arising.

The case where a contract is rescinded in equity differs from the case where a contract is rescinded at common law. At common law, the effect of rescission is to revest legal title to property transferred under the contract,[317] except where it has reached the hands of a bona fide purchaser.[318] In equity, unless such property has come into the hands of a bona fide purchaser, the court will declare it to have been held on trust, and provide in its order for the reconveyance of legal title and delivery up of possession, as appropriate.[319] **18–252**

## B. Rescission of Gifts

Rescission is possible where a donor has made a gift of legal title, or a settlor has made a declaration of trust, by reason of another party's misrepresentation or undue influence,[320] or by reason of a unilateral mistake as to present facts. The circumstances in which the court will order rescission of a settlement on the latter ground were reviewed by the Supreme Court in *Pitt v Holt*. **18–253**

*Pitt v Holt*

Supreme Court [2013] 2 A.C. 108

The facts are summarised at paras 9–241ff. **18–254**

LORD WALKER (with whom LORD NEUBERGER, BARONESS HALE, LORD MANCE, LORD CLARKE, LORD SUMPTION and LORD CARNWATH agreed): **18–255**

**Rescission on the ground of mistake**

[His Lordship set out the facts of *Ogilvie v Littleboy*,[321] and noted Lindley L.J.'s statement there, affirmed by the House of Lords in *Ogilvie v Allen*,[322] that:]

> "Gifts cannot be revoked, nor can deeds of gift be set aside, simply because the donors wish that they had not made them and would like to have back the property given. Where there is no fraud, no undue influence, no fiduciary relation between donor and donee, no mistake induced by those who derive any benefit by it, a gift, whether by mere delivery or by deed, is binding on the donor . . . In the absence of all circumstances of suspicion a donor can only obtain back property which he has given away by showing that he was under some mistake of so serious a character as to render it unjust on the part of the donee to retain the property given to him."

[His Lordship also noted that in the Court of Appeal in *Pitt*] . . . Lloyd L.J. reviewed and discussed other 19th century and modern authorities, including the first instance decisions in *Gibbon v Mitchell*[323] and *Re Griffiths, decd*.[324] He questioned the result in the latter case. The framework of his conclusion[325] was that for the exercise of the equitable jurisdiction to set aside a voluntary disposition there must be **18–256**

---

[317] *Load v Green* (1846) 15 M. & W. 216 at 221; *Clough v London and North Western Railway Co* (1871) L.R. 7 Ex. 26 at 32; *Car and Universal Finance Co Ltd v Caldwell* [1965] 1 Q.B. 525.

[318] *White v Garden* (1851) 10 C.B. 919.

[319] As in, e.g. *Transvaal Lands Co v New Belgium (Transvaal) Land & Development Co* [1914] 2 Ch. 488 at 505 (company shares); *Clark v Malpas* (1862) 4 De G.F. & J. 401 (unregistered land); *Norwich Peterborough Building Soc v Steed* [1993] Ch. 116 at 132–133.

[320] *Bridgman v Green* (1755) 2 Ves. Sen. 627; *Re Glubb* [1900] 1 Ch. 354. Discussion in P. Ridge, "Third Party Volunteers and Undue Influence" (2014) 130 L.Q.R. 112.

[321] (1897) 13 T.L.R. 399.

[322] (1899) 15 T.L.R. 294.

[323] [1990] 1 W.L.R. 1304.

[324] [2009] Ch. 162.

[325] At 210 and 211.

(1) a mistake, which is (2) of the relevant type and (3) sufficiently serious to satisfy the *Ogilvie v Littleboy* test. That is a convenient framework against which to consider the authorities, although there is obviously some overlap between the three heads. In general a mistake as to the essential nature of a transaction is likely to be more serious than a mistake as to its consequences.

**What is a mistake?**

18–257 For present purposes a mistake must be distinguished from mere ignorance or inadvertence, and also from what scholars in the field of unjust enrichment refer to as misprediction;[326] the expression may have first received judicial currency in *Dextra Bank and Trust Co Ltd v Bank of Jamaica*.[327] These distinctions are reasonably clear in a general sort of way, but they tend to get blurred when it comes to facts of particular cases. The editors of *Goff & Jones, The Law of Unjust Enrichment*,[328] comment that the distinction between mistake and misprediction can lead to "some uncomfortably fine distinctions", and the same is true of the distinction between mistake and ignorance.

18–258 Forgetfulness, inadvertence or ignorance is not, as such, a mistake, but it can lead to a false belief or assumption which the law will recognise as a mistake . . . The best-known English authority on this point is *Lady Hood of Avalon v Mackinnon*.[329] Under a settlement Lord and Lady Hood had a joint power of appointment, and later Lady Hood as the survivor had a sole power of appointment, in favour of the children and remoter issue of their marriage. They had two daughters. In 1888 half the trust fund had been appointed (subject to the prior life interests of Lord and Lady Hood) to their elder daughter on her marriage, and had been resettled by her. In 1902 and 1904, after Lord Hood's death, Lady Hood appointed a total of £8,600 to her younger daughter. Then, wishing to achieve equality, as she thought, between her daughters, and entirely forgetting the 1888 appointment, she appointed a further £8,600 to her elder daughter (so inevitably producing inequality, unless the appointment were set aside). The elder daughter did not oppose Lady Hood's action for rescission of the last appointment, but the trustees of the resettlement (which contained an after-acquired property covenant) did oppose it. Eve J. granted relief, stating:[330]

> "Having regard to the facts which I have stated, I must assume that Lady Hood, intending only to bring about equality between her daughters, was labouring under a mistake when she thought that equality would be brought about by the execution of the deed appointing £8,600 to her elder daughter. It was obviously a mistake, because the effect of the execution of that deed was to bring about that which Lady Hood never intended and never contemplated."

18–259 In his judgment Eve J. referred at length to the decision of the Court of Appeal in *Barrow v Isaacs & Son*.[331] In that case the Court of Appeal declined to grant relief, on the ground of mistake, from forfeiture of a lease for breach of a covenant against underletting. The solicitors acting for a respectable tenant had overlooked the covenant and the premises had been sublet to a respectable subtenant. Both Lord Esher M.R. and Kay L.J. commented that there was no legal definition of "mistake". Lord Esher M.R. said that the head tenant had had "a mere passive state of mind":[332]

> "I should say that mere forgetfulness is not mistake at all in ordinary language. I cannot find any decision in courts of equity which has ever stated that mere forgetfulness is mistake against which equity would relieve."

But Kay L.J. (with whom Lopes L.J. agreed) seems to have taken the view that there was a mistake which equity had power to relieve, although in the circumstances of the case the court declined to grant relief. The power to relieve would, it seems, have been based on the conscious belief or tacit assumption that the underletting was lawful.

18–260 The fullest academic treatment of this topic is in *Goff & Jones, The Law of Unjust Enrichment*.[333] The editors distinguish between incorrect conscious beliefs, incorrect tacit assumptions, and true cases of mere

326 See Weeliem Seah, "Mispredictions, Mistakes and the Law of Unjust Enrichment" [2007] R.L.R. 93.
327 [2002] 1 All E.R. (Comm.) 193.
328 8th ed (2011), para 9–11.
329 [1909] 1 Ch. 476.
330 At 483–484.
331 [1891] 1 Q.B. 417.
332 At 420–421.
333 8th ed, paras 9–32—9–42.

causative ignorance ("causative" in the sense that but for his ignorance the person in question would not have acted as he did). The deputy judge's first instance decision in *Pitt v Holt*[334] is suggested as an example of mere causative ignorance: "If someone does not apply his mind to a point at all, it is difficult to say that there has been some real mistake about the point". The Court of Appeal adopted a different view of the facts, treating the case[335] as one of an incorrect conscious belief on the part of Mrs Pitt that the SNT had no adverse tax consequences. The editors of *Goff & Jones* are, on balance, in favour of treating mere causative ignorance as sufficient. They comment (in answering a "floodgates" objection):[336]

> "denying relief for mere causative ignorance produces a boundary line which may be difficult to draw in practice, and which is susceptible to judicial manipulation, according to whether it is felt that relief should be afforded—with the court's finding or declining to find incorrect conscious beliefs or tacit assumptions according to the court's perception of the merits of the claim."

It may indeed be difficult to draw the line between mere causative ignorance and a mistaken conscious belief or a mistaken tacit assumption. I would hold that mere ignorance, even if causative, is insufficient, but that the court, in carrying out its task of finding the facts, should not shrink from drawing the inference of conscious belief or tacit assumption when there is evidence to support such an inference. I shall return to the suggestion that this may involve "judicial manipulation."

A misprediction relates to some possible future event, whereas a legally significant mistake normally relates to some past or present matter of fact or law. But here too the distinction may not be clear on the facts of a particular case. The issue which divided the House of Lords in *Kleinwort Benson Ltd v Lincoln City Council*[337] was whether (as Lord Hoffmann put it[338]) the correct view was that, "a person who pays in accordance with what was then a settled view of the law has not made a mistake" and "that his state of mind could be better described as a failure to predict the outcome of some future event (scilicet, a decision of this House) than a mistake about the existing state of the law". There is another interesting discussion of this point in the judgments given in the Court of Appeal in *Brennan v Bolt Burdon*.[339] 18–261

A problem about the boundary between mistake and misprediction arose in *Re Griffiths, decd*,[340] a decision of Lewison J. Like *Sieff v Fox* and some other cases on the *Hastings-Bass* rule, it was a case in which the Revenue was invited to intervene but declined to do so, despite the large sum of inheritance tax at stake. The case was therefore heard without adversarial argument as to the law or the facts. Lloyd L.J. commented[341] that he did not criticise the judge, given the limited argument before him, but that he did question his conclusion. I agree with both limbs of that comment. 18–262

It is important to note the sequence of events in *Re Griffiths*. Mr Griffiths had a valuable holding in Iota, a property company (whose shares did not attract business assets relief). He was aged 73 when, in January 2003, he and his wife took advice about tax planning. They received a lengthy report setting out various options. Most involved making potentially exempt transfers, which progressively reduce inheritance tax on qualifying gifts if the donor survives for three years, and avoid tax entirely if the donor survives for seven years after making the gift. The report recommended that seven-year term insurance cover should be obtained. Mr Griffiths decided to take various steps, the most important of which was a settlement of Iota shares worth over £2.6m. This was effected by a two-stage process which was completed in February 2004. He decided not to obtain term insurance. Unfortunately he was diagnosed with lung cancer in October 2004, and died in April 2005. Had he done nothing, the Iota shares would have formed part of his residuary estate, in which his wife took a life interest, and no inheritance tax would have been payable on his death. 18–263

In those circumstances his executor commenced proceedings asking that the dispositions should be set aside on the ground of mistake:[342] 18–264

---

334 [2010] 1 W.L.R. 1199 at [50].
335 At [216].
336 At para 9–41.
337 [1999] 2 A.C. 349.
338 At 398.
339 [2005] Q.B. 303.
340 [2009] Ch. 162.
341 At 198.
342 [2009] Ch. 162 at [6].

"The relevant mistake on which they rely is that Mr Griffiths mistakenly believed, at the time of the transfers, that there was a real chance that he would survive for seven years whereas in fact at that time his state of health was such that he had no real chance of surviving that long."

The medical evidence (in the form of letters from his general practitioner, from a consultant oncologist and from a consultant rheumatologist) was inconclusive, but the GP expressed the view that it was "extremely unlikely" that the cancer was present in April 2003. On this evidence the judge found that in April 2003 Mr Griffiths had a life expectancy of between seven and nine years. He went on to observe:[343]

"It is unfortunate that in a case involving £1m-worth of tax a proper medical report was not placed before the court and that the claimants are compelled to rely on a single sentence in a letter from [the oncologist]. Although I have hesitated about this finding, I am prepared to find, by a narrow margin that he was suffering from lung cancer on 3 February 2004; and that following the onset of lung cancer at that time his life expectancy did not exceed three years in February 2004. Had the facts been contested, I might not have felt able to make this finding."

**18–265** On the rather uncertain foundation of that finding the judge decided that the assignment of 3 February 2004 should be set aside:[344]

"By that time Mr Griffiths was suffering from lung cancer about which he was unaware. He did therefore make a mistake about his state of health. Had he known in February 2004 that he was suffering from lung cancer he would also have known that his chance of surviving for three years, let alone for seven years, was remote. In those circumstances I am persuaded that he would not have acted as he did by transferring his reversionary interest in the shares to trustees."

The judge did not say whether this was (in the *Goff & Jones* formulation) an incorrect conscious belief or an incorrect tacit assumption. The editors of that work[345] treat it as a tacit assumption but it seems close to the residual category of mere causative ignorance. Had the judge not made his hair's breadth finding about the presence of cancer in February 2004 it would have been a case of misprediction, not essentially different from a failure to predict a fatal road accident. Lloyd L.J. observed[346] that it was strongly arguable that, having declined to follow the financial consultants' recommendation of term insurance, Mr Griffiths was taking the risk of deterioration of his health and failure to survive the statutory period.

**What type of mistake?**

**18–266** Some uncontroversial points can be noted briefly. It does not matter if the mistake is due to carelessness on the part of the person making the voluntary disposition, unless the circumstances are such as to show that he deliberately ran the risk, or must be taken to have run the risk, of being wrong. (There is an illuminating discussion of this point in Lord Hoffmann's speech in *Deutsche Morgan Grenfell Group plc v Inland Revenue Comrs*[347]). Nor need the mistake be known to (still less induced by) the person or persons taking a benefit under the disposition. The fact that a unilateral mistake is sufficient (without the additional ingredient of misrepresentation or fraud) to make a gift voidable has been attributed to gifts being outside the law's special concern for the sanctity of contracts . . .[348] Conversely, the fact that a purely unilateral mistake may be sufficient to found relief is arguably a good reason for the court to apply a more stringent test as to the seriousness of the mistake before granting relief.

**18–267** The Revenue's printed case seeks to play down the distinction between mistake in the law of contract and its role in equitable rescission of voluntary dispositions. It seeks to build boldly on the decision of the Court of Appeal in *Great Peace Shipping Ltd v Tsavliris Salvage (International) Ltd*,[349] which did not follow (and has effectively overruled) *Solle v Butcher*.[350] The argument is that logic requires that a deed which transfers property for no consideration can be set aside only for a mistake of a fundamental nature

343 At [18].
344 At [30].
345 At para 9–36.
346 At 198.
347 [2007] 1 A.C. 558 at [24]–[30].
348 O'Sullivan, Elliott & Zakrzewski, *The Law of Rescission* (2008), para 29.22.
349 [2003] Q.B. 679.
350 [1950] 1 K.B. 671.

that would render a contract void. Mr Jones did not cite any authority for this heterodox submission, and there is high authority (starting with *Ogilvie v Allen*) against it. Equity will grant specific performance of a covenant only if it is supported by valuable consideration . . . But the notion that any voluntary disposition should be accorded the same protection as a commercial bargain, simply because it is made under seal, is insupportable.

Leaving aside for the present the degree of seriousness of the mistake, there is also controversy about its nature (or characteristics), especially as to the distinction between "effect" and "consequences" drawn by Millett J. in *Gibbon v Mitchell*.[351] In that case two funds (May's fund and Henry's fund) were settled in 1946 by Mr Henry Gibbon's parents on the occasion of the marriage of his sister May. The funds were settled on May and Henry respectively for life, on the statutory protective trusts in section 33 of the Trustee Act 1925 (with a modification in the case of Henry's fund), but with power for May to surrender her protected life interest so as to accelerate the interests of her children once they had attained vested interests. For some unknown reason there was no corresponding power in respect of Henry's fund. The consequence was that a purported surrender by Mr Gibbon would cause a forfeiture of his fixed interest and bring into operation a discretionary trust affecting income during the rest of his life. 18–268

In 1987 Mr Gibbon was a prosperous farmer aged 69, with two adult children. He wished to take steps to save inheritance tax and was advised by his accountants and solicitors to surrender his life interest, and at the same time release two powers of appointment, so as to accelerate his children's interests. This advice was expressed in terms of enabling Henry's fund to pass immediately to the two children. His professional advisers failed to recognise, until after the deed of surrender had been executed, that the protective trusts provided a trap. Mr Gibbon applied to the court to have the deed of surrender set aside on the ground of mistake, and also for relief under the Variation of Trusts Act 1958. Millett J. set the surrender aside, and varied the trust by lifting the protective trusts. In his judgment he referred to several of the older authorities, in most of which solicitors had misunderstood or gone beyond their instructions.[352] *Ogilvie v Littleboy* was not cited. Millett J. set out the principle which he drew from them:[353] 18–269

> "In my judgment, these cases show that, wherever there is a voluntary transaction by which one party intends to confer a bounty on another, the deed will be set aside if the court is satisfied that the disponor did not intend the transaction to have the effect which it did. It will be set aside for mistake whether the mistake is a mistake of law or a fact, so long as the mistake is as to the effect of the transaction itself and not merely as to its consequences or the advantages to be gained by entering into it."

It will be observed that this formulation does not include the *Ogilvie v Littleboy* requirement of seriousness, except so far as it might be argued that any mistake as to the effect of a disposition is likely to be relatively serious.

Millett J.'s judgment has been very influential. It is a mark of the high respect in which he is held that an extempore first instance judgment, not (so far as appears from the judgment) based on much adversarial argument, is cited as one of the key authorities in most of the standard works on equity and trusts.[354] But the source from which Millett J.'s statement of principle is derived is far from clear and it has been the subject of some criticism, both from legal scholars and in more recent decisions of the court. 18–270

It is generally agreed that "effect" must mean legal effect (in the sense of the legal character or nature of a transaction). In *Dent v Dent*[355] the deputy judge (David Young Q.C.) understood it as "the purpose or object" of a transaction. Several other first instance judges have commented that the distinction between "effect" and "consequences" is not always clear, including Davis J. in *Anker-Petersen v Christensen*.[356] Lawrence Collins J. went further in *AMP (UK) plc v Barker*,[357] saying of the distinction: 18–271

---

351 [1990] 1 W.L.R. 1304.

352 *Meadows v Meadows* (1853) 16 Beav. 401; *Walker v Armstrong* (1856) 8 De G.M. & G. 531; *Ellis v Ellis* (1909) 26 T.L.R. 166 and *Re Walton's Settlement* [1922] 2 Ch. 509.

353 [1990] Ch. 1304 at 1309.

354 Including *Snell's Equity*, 32nd ed (2010), paras 11–008, 22–052; *Lewin on Trusts*, 18th ed (2008), paras 4–58, 29–231; *Underhill & Hayton's Law of Trusts and Trustees*, 18th ed (2010), paras 15–28—15–34; and Thomas & Hudson, *The Law of Trusts*, 2nd ed (2010), para 20.37.

355 [1996] 1 W.L.R. 683 at 693.

356 [2002] W.T.L.R. 313 at 330.

357 [2001] W.T.L.R. 1237 at [70].

> "If anything, it is simply a formula designed to ensure that the policy involved in equitable relief is effectuated to keep it within reasonable bounds and to ensure that it is not used simply when parties are mistaken about the commercial effects of their transactions or have second thoughts about them."

On that view it comes close to Lindley L.J.'s more general requirement for the mistake to be serious. In *Wolff v Wolff*,[358] Mann J considered that the test was not a limiting factor, and noted that Lawrence Collins J. had referred to commercial consequences, not legal consequences.

**18–272** Lloyd L.J. has now reviewed *Gibbon v Mitchell* twice, first in *Sieff v Fox*[359] and then in *Pitt v Holt*. In *Sieff v Fox*, *Ogilvie v Littleboy* was brought to light after a long period of obscurity (though it is mentioned in Peter Birks's *Introduction to the Law of Restitution*, first published in 1985). Lloyd L.J. noted[360] that a test based on the legal effect of a transaction could not cover the tax consequences of a transaction, but that Lindley L.J.'s more general test in *Ogilvie v Littleboy* might do so. He expressed no final view because of the special circumstances of the case before him.[361]

**18–273** In *Pitt v Holt* Lloyd L.J. went further. He expressed the view[362] that some recent cases about offshore trusts did not accord with English law.[363] He accepted the distinction made by Millett J. in Gibbon v Mitchell but extended it[364] by formulating it as a requirement

> "that, for the equitable jurisdiction to set aside a voluntary disposition for mistake to be invoked, there must be a mistake on the part of the donor either as to the legal effect of the disposition or as to an existing fact which is basic to the transaction."

This extension seems to have been primarily to accommodate cases such as *Lady Hood of Avalon*, where there was "a fundamental error of fact, in relation to a point which lay at the heart of the transaction."[365] He also seems to have had in mind the New Zealand case *University of Canterbury v Attorney General*.[366] The special feature of that case was that the university had to some extent encouraged, or at least failed to correct, the donor's error; it wished to return the gift but the Attorney General, representing the public interest in charity, opposed that course. In addition, the mistake must, Lloyd L.J. said, meet the *Ogilvie v Littleboy* test of sufficient gravity.

**18–274** This approach has been criticised by the editors of *Goff & Jones, The Law of Unjust Enrichment*.[367] I do not agree with all these criticisms of what the editors refer to as the Court of Appeal's "stricter, hybrid approach". But I can see no reason why a mistake of law which is basic to the transaction (but is not a mistake as to the transaction's legal character or nature) should not also be included, even though such cases would probably be rare. If the *Gibbon v Mitchell* test is further widened in that way it is questionable whether it adds anything significant to the *Ogilvie v Littleboy* test. I would provisionally conclude that the true requirement is simply for there to be a causative mistake of sufficient gravity; and, as additional guidance to judges in finding and evaluating the facts of any particular case, that the test will normally be satisfied only when there is a mistake either as to the legal character or nature of a transaction, or as to some matter of fact or law which is basic to the transaction.

**18–275** To confirm the *Gibbon v Mitchell* test as formulated by Millett J. would in my view leave the law in an uncertain state, as the first instance decisions mentioned above tend to demonstrate. It would also be contrary to the general disinclination of equity to insist on rigid classifications expressed in abstract terms. Equity, unlike many continental systems, has not adopted Roman law's classification of mistakes: *error in negotio* (the nature of the intended transaction), *error in corpore* (the subject matter of the transaction), *error in persona* (the identity of the other party to the transaction) and *error in substantia* (the quality of the subject matter). The *Gibbon v Mitchell* test, at any rate if applied narrowly, would cover only the first of

---

358 [2004] S.T.C. 1633 at [23] and [26].
359 [2005] 1 W.L.R. 3811.
360 At [106].
361 At [116].
362 At [208].
363 *Clarkson v Barclays Private Bank and Trust (Isle of Man) Ltd* [2007] W.T.L.R. 1703; *Re Betsam Trust; McBurney v McBurney* [2009] W.T.L.R. 1489; and Re A Trust 2009 J.L.R. 447.
364 At [210].
365 At [206].
366 [1995] 1 N.Z.L.R. 78.
367 8th ed, paras 9–101—9–106.

these categories. But in some situations errors in other categories may be just as basic and just as serious in their consequences.

**The conscience test**

Lindley L.J.'s test in *Ogilvie v Littleboy* requires the gravity of the causative mistake to be assessed in terms of injustice—or, to use equity's cumbersome but familiar term, unconscionableness. Similarly Millett J. said in *Gibbon v Mitchell*:[368] 18–276

> "Equity acts on the conscience. The parties [in] whose interest it would be to oppose the setting aside of the deed are the unborn future children of Mr Gibbon and the objects of discretionary trusts to arise on forfeiture, that is to say his grandchildren, nephews and nieces. They are all volunteers. In my judgment they could not conscionably insist upon their legal rights under the deed once they had become aware of the circumstances in which they had acquired them."

The evaluation of what is or would be unconscionable must be objective. Millett J. identified precisely the class of beneficiaries in whose interest it would be for the forfeiture to stand (apart from tax considerations which made it disadvantageous for the whole family), but he did not do so in order to embark on the impossible task of establishing the state of the consciences of minor and unborn beneficiaries. Nor (apart from a defence of change of position) would the relative prosperity of the donor and the donees be relevant, except so far as it was part of the mistake (as in Lord Scott of Foscote's example in *Deutsche Morgan Grenfell Group plc v Inland Revenue Comrs*:[369] "a gift of £1,000 by A to B where B is believed by A to be impecunious but is in fact a person of substantial wealth . . ."). 18–277

The gravity of the mistake must be assessed by a close examination of the facts, whether or not they are tested by cross-examination, including the circumstances of the mistake and its consequences for the person who made the vitiated disposition. Other findings of fact may also have to be made in relation to change of position or other matters relevant to the exercise of the court's discretion. Justice Paul Finn wrote in a paper, "Equitable Doctrines and Discretion in Remedies":[370] 18–278

> "the courts quite consciously now are propounding what are acceptable standards of conduct to be exhibited in our relationships and dealings with others . . . A clear consequence of this emphasis on standards (and not on rules) is a far more instance-specific evaluation of conduct."

The injustice (or unfairness or unconscionableness) of leaving a mistaken disposition uncorrected must be evaluated objectively, but with an intense focus (in Lord Steyn's well-known phrase in *Re S (A Child)*[371]) on the facts of the particular case. . .

I add a postscript as to the criticism made by the editors of *Goff & Jones, The Law of Unjust Enrichment*, of[372] 18–279

> "a boundary line which may be difficult to draw in practice, and which is susceptible to judicial manipulation, according to whether it is felt that relief should be afforded—with the court's finding or declining to find incorrect conscious beliefs or tacit assumptions according to the court's perception of the merits of the claim."

There is some force in this, although the term "manipulation" is a bit harsh. The fact that a unilateral mistake is sufficient means that the court may have to make findings as to the state of mind, at some time in the past, of a claimant with a lively personal interest in establishing that there was a serious causative mistake. This will often be a difficult task. But as a criticism of the Court of Appeal in *Pitt v Holt* I would reject it. The case was heard on affidavit evidence, without cross-examination, and the Court of Appeal was in as good a position as the deputy judge to draw inferences and make findings of fact.

More generally, the apparent suggestion that the court ought not to form a view about the merits of a claim seems to me to go wide of the mark. In a passage in *Gillett v Holt*[373] since approved by the House 18–280

368 [1990] 1 W.L.R. 1304 at 1310.
369 [2007] 1 A.C. 558 at [87].
370 In W.R. Cornish et al (eds), *Restitution: Past, Present and Future* (1998), p. 260.
371 [2005] 1 A.C. 593 at [17].
372 8th ed, para 9–41.
373 [2001] Ch. 210 at 225.

of Lords[374] I said in discussing proprietary estoppel that although its elements (assurance, reliance and detriment) may have to be considered separately they cannot be treated as watertight compartments:

> "the fundamental principle that equity is concerned to prevent unconscionable conduct permeates all the elements of the doctrine. In the end the court must look at the matter in the round."

In my opinion the same is true of the equitable doctrine of mistake. The court cannot decide the issue of what is unconscionable by an elaborate set of rules. It must consider in the round the existence of a distinct mistake (as compared with total ignorance or disappointed expectations), its degree of centrality to the transaction in question and the seriousness of its consequences, and make an evaluative judgment whether it would be unconscionable, or unjust, to leave the mistake uncorrected. The court may and must form a judgment about the justice of the case. . .

**18–281** [His Lordship considered and rejected the arguments by the Revenue that mistakes about tax should never be relieved, but he said that:] In some cases of artificial tax avoidance the court might think it right to refuse relief, either on the ground that such claimants, acting on supposedly expert advice, must be taken to have accepted the risk that the scheme would prove ineffective, or on the ground that discretionary relief should be refused on grounds of public policy. Since the seminal decision of the House of Lords in *WT Ramsay Ltd v Inland Revenue Comrs*[375] there has been an increasingly strong and general recognition that artificial tax avoidance is a social evil which puts an unfair burden on the shoulders of those who do not adopt such measures. But it is unnecessary to consider that further on these appeals. . .

**18–282** Lord Walker held that unilateral voluntary settlements by deed can be rescinded provided that the settlor made a causative mistake of sufficient gravity to justify the court's intervention. He also held that when deciding whether a settlor's mistake was sufficiently serious for this purpose the courts should draw no special distinction between mistakes as to the legal effect and mistakes as to the wider consequences of the relevant transaction. *Gibbon v Mitchell*[376] had previously held that rescission should be awarded for mistakes of the former but not for mistakes of the latter kind and this rule had been followed in other cases, including the Court of Appeal's judgment in *Pitt v Holt*,[377] where Lloyd LJ held that it required him to withhold relief. Lord Walker's abolition of the effects/consequences rule is welcome. It lacked principled justification and its content was obscure, so that the courts were struggling to apply it consistently. However, Lord Walker's "seriousness" test is sure to generate litigation as it leaves everything to the court's assessment of the facts of cases.

**18–283** Lord Walker did not explain why the rule for the rescission of mistaken settlements should differ from the common law rule governing the restitution of mistaken payments, which requires merely that the transferor must have made a causative mistake tested by application of a "but for" test.[378] One possibility, canvassed in extra-judicial writing by the Chancellor, Sir Terence Etherton,[379] is that rescission can have proprietary consequences (because it can lead to the imposition of a trust on property transferred under the rescinded settlement to beneficiaries[380]) and these require special justification over and above the justification needed for imposing a personal liability on a defendant to repay the value of money received. The plausibility of this rationalisation of Lord Walker's rule is hard

---

374 See especially the speech of Lord Neuberger of Abbotsbury, with which the rest of the House agreed, in *Fisher v Brooker* [2009] 1 W.L.R. 1764 at [63].

375 [1982] A.C. 300.

376 [1990] 1 W.L.R. 1304

377 [2012] Ch. 132 at 217–218.

378 *Barclays Bank Ltd v W & J Simms Son and Cooke (Southern) Ltd* [1980] Q.B. 677; affirmed *Dextra Bank & Trust Co Ltd v Bank of Jamaica* [2002] 1 All E.R. (Comm.) 193 at [28]; *Deutsche Morgan Grenfell Group Plc v IRC* [2007] 1 A.C. 558 at [59]–[60]; *TFL Management Services Ltd v Lloyds TSB Bank plc* [2014] 1 W.L.R. 2006 at [88].

379 Sir T. Etherton, "The Role of Equity in Mistaken Transactions" (2013) 27 Tru. L.I. 159, 170.

380 See paras 18–250—18–252.

to assess because there is no consensus about the principles which govern the award of proprietary remedies for unjust enrichment.[381]

An alternative explanation is that the law places gifts in a different category from other types of transfer, and that the rules governing the reversal of gifts differ from the rules governing the restitution of benefits transferred without donative intent.[382] Again, though, it is unclear that gifts should be treated differently from other non-contractual transfers of benefits. By comparison with civilian systems English law has a very underdeveloped notion of "gift" as a legal category and significant conceptual work needs to be done before an argument along these lines can be seriously mounted.[383] **18–284**

Finally, it seems unlikely that the courts will show much enthusiasm for Lord Walker's suggestion that in "some cases of artificial tax avoidance [they] might think it right to refuse relief . . . on the ground that discretionary relief should be refused on grounds of public policy".[384] Parliament has enacted a general anti-avoidance rule, the effect of which is to render artificial tax avoidance schemes ineffective, but it forms no part of this legislation that a taxpayer who enters a botched scheme that exposes her to a greater tax liability than she would otherwise have incurred should be forbidden to rescind the relevant transactions as a measure designed to punish her for her anti-social conduct. **18–285**

## 6. Rectification

### A. Overview

Outside the testamentary context,[385] rectification is an equitable discretionary order that the terms of a document should be altered, with retrospective effect,[386] so that it accords with what the parties agreed,[387] or, in the case of a voluntary unilateral settlement, with what the settlor intended.[388] For this purpose there is an exception to the "parole evidence rule" permitting oral evidence to be given to establish the relevant mistake with the "convincing proof"[389] that is required. **18–286**

Rectification will not be granted where a bona fide purchaser for value without notice has acquired a proprietary interest under the document.[390] Laches or acquiescence will also bar the claim.[391] In the case of a voluntary unilateral settlement the court may refuse to rectify if a trustee, who took office in ignorance of the settlor's mistake, has a reasonable objection to rectification.[392] **18–287**

---

381 For discussion, see Mitchell, Mitchell and Watterson, *Goff and Jones: The Law of Unjust Enrichment* (2011), Ch.37.

382 Tang Hang Wu, 'Restitution for Mistaken Gifts' (2004) J.C.L. 1, 29–33.

383 B. Häcker, "Mistaken Gifts after *Pitt v Holt*" (2014) 67 C.L.P. 333.

384 [2013] 2 A.C. 108 at 135.

385 The rectification of wills turns on statutory provisions, especially the Administration of Justice Act 1982 s.20, which allows a will to be rectified if the court is satisfied that it fails to carry out the testator's intentions in consequence of a clerical error or a failure to understand her instructions. Discussion in *Marley v Rawlings* [2015] A.C. 129, noted B. Häcker, (2014) 130 L.Q.R. 360.

386 *Lake v Lake* [1989] S.T.C. 865.

387 *Joscelyne v Nissen* [1970] 2 Q.B. 86; *Racal Group Services Ltd v Ashmore* [1994] S.T.C. 416.

388 *Re Butlin's Settlement Trusts* [1976] Ch. 251; *Lake v Lake* [1989] S.T.C. 865.

389 *Joscelyne v Nissen* [1970] 2 Q.B. 86. The content of this rule, and the reasons for it, are well explained by Leggatt J in *Tartsinis v Navona Management Co* [2015] EWHC 57 (Comm) at [84]–[86].

390 *Smith v Jones* [1954] 1 W.L.R. 1089, or nowadays, presumably if an innocent volunteer has changed her position.

391 *Beale v Kyte* [1907] 1 Ch. 564.

392 *Re Butlin's Settlement Trusts* [1976] Ch. 251.

## B. Rectification of Contracts

18–288 "The general rule at common law is that if one party has made a mistake as to the terms of the contract and that mistake is known to the other party, then the contract is not binding. The reasoning is that although the parties appear, objectively, to have agreed terms, it is clear that they are not in agreement."[393] This is a commonly held view of the effect of unilateral mistake on contracts, but a rather different analysis is suggested by cases on "unilateral mistake rectification", which hold that the mistaken party can enforce the contract on the terms which she intended because she can have the contract rectified to conform with these terms, the other party being estopped from resisting rectification by virtue of her unconscionable conduct.[394]

18–289 Outside this situation, rectification of contracts is available only where there was a mistake common to both parties so that the document fails to record what they agreed.[395] Often it is possible to apply rules of construction to rescue parties in this situation, but whether or not that route can be taken, rectification can also be ordered, provided that it can be said with certainty what the parties' contract was, and that it was wrongly expressed in the document. Two approaches to determining the nature of the parties' true agreement are possible[396]: a "subjective approach" which asks whether the parties subjectively had the same understanding of their true agreement (whether or not each communicated what she thought to the other), and an "objective approach" which asks what a reasonable person would understand the parties' shared understanding of their true agreement to have been in light of what they said and did. In obiter dicta in *Chartbrook Ltd v Persimmon Homes Ltd* Lord Hoffmann favoured the "objective" approach.

*Chartbrook Ltd v Persimmon Homes Ltd*

House of Lords [2009] 1 A.C. 1101

18–290 The claimant landowner and defendant developer entered a contract to develop the claimant's land, under which the defendant agreed to obtain planning permission, construct a mixed residential and commercial development, and sell the properties on long leases. The price payable by the defendant included an "Additional Residential Payment" (ARP) which was defined by a term of the contract, the proper interpretation of which was later disputed by the parties. According to the defendant's interpretation, the term required the defendant to pay around £900,000, but according to the claimant the sum due was around £4,500,000. The claim succeeded at first instance and in Court of Appeal, but on appeal the House of Lords found for the defendant, holding that the defendant's interpretation of the term was the right one, that the lower courts had been wrong to exclude evidence of the parties' pre-contractual negotiations, and that even if the claimant's interpretation of the term had been correct, the defendant would have been entitled to rectification. The portion of Lord Hoffmann's speech that concerns this final point is reproduced below.

---

393 *Statoil ASA v Louis Dreyfus Energy Services LP (The Harriette N)* [2009] 1 All E.R. (Comm) 1035 at [87] per Aikens J See too *Hartog v Colin & Shields* [1939] 3 All E.R. 566.

394 *Thomas Bates & Son Ltd v Wyndham's (Lingerie) Ltd* [1981] 1 All E.R. 1077 at 1086; *Commission for New Towns v Cooper (GB) Ltd* [1995] Ch. 259; *Thor Navigation Inc v Ingosstrakh Insurance Co Ltd* [2005] 1 Lloyd's Rep. 547 at [57]–[62] per Gloster J; *Daventry D.C. v Daventry District Housing Ltd* [2012] I W.L.R. 1333 at [184] per Toulson LJ suggesting that the doctrine could apply to dishonourable and unreasonable conduct as well as outright dishonesty.

395 *The Nai Genova* [1984] 1 Lloyd's Rep. 353 at 359, per Slade LJ; *KPMG v Network Rail Infrastructure Ltd* [2007] Bus. L.R. 1336. It is not enough that the parties can be shown to have made a common mistake as to the effect of their transaction: it must be shown that they commonly intended to include or exclude something in their document which was not included or excluded: *Frederick Rose (London) Ltd v William Pimm Jr Co Ltd* [1953] 2 Q.B. 450; *Lloyd v Stanbury* [1971] 1 W.L.R. 535 at 543; *James Hay Pension Trustees Ltd v Hird* [2005] EWHC 1093 (Ch) at [113].

396 L. Bromley, "Rectification in Equity" (1971) 87 L.Q.R. 532; M. Smith, "Rectification of Contracts for Common Mistake, *Joscelyne v Nissen*, and Subjective States of Mind" (2007) 123 L.Q.R. 116; D. McLauchlan, "Refining Rectification" (2014) 130 L.Q.R. 83.

LORD HOFFMANN (with whom LORD HOPE, LORD RODGER, LORD WALKER and BARONESS HALE agreed): The last point is whether, if Chartbrook's interpretation of the agreement had been correct, it should have been rectified to accord with Persimmon's interpretation. The requirements for rectification were succinctly summarized by Peter Gibson L.J. in *Swainland Builders Ltd v Freehold Properties Ltd*:[397] **18–291**

"The party seeking rectification must show that: (1) the parties had a common continuing intention, whether or not amounting to an agreement, in respect of a particular matter in the instrument to be rectified; (2) there was an outward expression of accord; (3) the intention continued at the time of the execution of the instrument sought to be rectified; (4) by mistake, the instrument did not reflect that common intention."

To explain how the claim for rectification arose, I must summarise the relevant pre-contractual exchanges between the parties. They began by discussing a proposal for an outright sale of the land by Chartbrook to Persimmon at a price calculated by reference to such planning permission as Chartbrook might obtain. In early 2001 this structure was abandoned and Persimmon in a letter dated 1 February 2001 proposed the building licence arrangement eventually agreed. The letter included the following passages: **18–292**

". . . we would be prepared to pay you 29.8% of the net sales proceeds generated from the private sale residential element of the scheme and a further 45% of the net sales revenue generated from the disposal of the commercial element of the site. We would pay you this proportion of the income regardless of the development costs incurred by my company and the quantum of accommodation that we ultimately obtain planning permission for. . . . By tying your land value to a percentage of the income, you will also automatically share in any sales uplift that we experience."

This offer of a straightforward sharing of the proceeds was modified in a letter dated 6 February 2001 by the addition of what were described as "guaranteed backstop dates and minimum payments": **18–293**

"Upon receipt of the purchase monies, the revenue will be apportioned to Chartbrook on the basis of 29.8% of the net revenue achieved from the disposal of the private sale residential units and 45% of the net revenue from the disposal of the commercial units. In addition, we are prepared to provide you with guaranteed backstop dates and minimum payments that will be made regardless of the actual performance of the project both in terms of timescales and costs. I set out on the attached schedule our proposals concerning this element of the deal. Based on the current scheme for 80 units, and 9,020 sq ft of commercial floor space, the minimum land value we are prepared to pay to Chartbrook on the disposal of each residential unit is £67,000, together with a further minimum payment of £400,000 on the disposal of the commercial unit. If as a result of improvements in the market, Chartbrook are entitled to more than the minimum payments I suggest an equalisation calculation takes place following the disposal of the last unit. . . . Within the contract, I . . . suggest that a formula is included whereby the land value is calculated using the following inputs: private sale residential accommodation . . . 94.96/sq ft . . . Once the total land value has been calculated, a simple formula can then be applied to divide the land values by the number of units, in order for us to calculate the guaranteed payments that you will receive on the sale of each plot . . .".

On 12 February there was a further modification to make separate provision for the sales of car parking spaces, but the overall offer for land value remained the same. The judge found[398] that Chartbrook accepted this offer in principle and Persimmon's solicitors were instructed to draft an agreement. Their draft was attached to an email dated 1 March 2001 and contained essentially the same formulae for calculating the price as those in the final agreement. The definition of "additional residential payment" was (save for the percentage figure) in precisely the same words as those of the final agreement. **18–294**

Between March and May Chartbrook acquired some additional adjoining land and Persimmon revised its cost estimates. The result was a change in the figures but not in the formulae. In a letter dated 24 May 2001 Persimmon offered a new total land value of £7,191,947. The letter contained a table setting out: **18–295**

". . . the minimum guaranteed land values that you will receive for the respective elements of the scheme, together with the percentage of sales revenue that you will also be entitled to if the project performs better than is currently anticipated."

397 [2002] 2 E.G.L.R. 71 at 74.
398 [2007] 1 All E.R. (Comm.) 1083 at [110].

18-296 The figures in the table were 23.4 per cent for "percentage of sales revenue" and £53,333 for "minimum value per plot". The judge found that this offer was also accepted in principle and the new figures were inserted into the final contract. The words of the definition of ARP in the final draft remained (subject to the change in the percentage figure) exactly the same as in the first draft.

18-297 It is I think clear that a reasonable person who read the February and May letters in the light of the background known to the parties would have taken them to have been intending that Chartbrook should receive an ARP if, but only if, "the project performs better than is currently anticipated".

18-298 Persimmon's case on rectification at the trial was that the letter of 24 May 2001 was an outward expression of the common and continuing intention of the parties and (if Chartbrook was right about its true construction) the definition had been drafted in the mistaken belief that it gave effect to that common intention. On the other hand, the evidence of the two principals of Chartbrook, Mr Vantreen and Mr Reeve, was that they had made no mistake. The definition accorded exactly with what they had thought they were being offered in the letters of February and May 2001. Indeed, they said they would not have done the deal for any less. It was put to them in cross-examination that no rational person could have understood the letters in the sense which they claimed and Mr Vantreen was caused some little difficulty by the fact that, on his copy of the May 2001 letter, he had calculated the amount which (on Persimmon's construction of the definition) the sale price of a 700 sq ft flat would have to exceed before any ARP became payable (£228,000). This calculation would have been irrelevant on his own construction of the definition and he was unable to explain why he had made it. Nevertheless the judge accepted the evidence of Mr Reeve and Mr Vantreen that they had honestly believed that the definition (as they claimed to have understood it) was what had been agreed and they were not been mistaken. The judge therefore held that the mistake was not common to both parties and dismissed the claim for rectification.

18-299 The case was argued at trial on the assumption that rectification required both parties to be mistaken about whether the written agreement reflected what they believed their prior consensus to have been. In the Court of Appeal, Persimmon challenged the finding of fact about what Mr Reeve and Mr Vantreen had believed, but not the underlying proposition of law. The Court of Appeal unanimously dismissed this part of the appeal on the ground that it could not disturb the findings of fact. There are accordingly concurrent findings of fact about the states of mind of Mr Reeve and Mr Vantreen. Your Lordships indicated at the hearing that in accordance with the usual practice, you would not re-examine them.[399]

18-300 In the printed case, however, Persimmon (encouraged by articles in the Law Quarterly Review by Marcus Smith[400] and Professor McLauchlan[401]) asked for leave to challenge, for the first time, the proposition of law. Mr Nugee submitted that the judge and the Court of Appeal had been wrong in their assumption about what a party had to be mistaken about. Rectification required a mistake about whether the written instrument correctly reflected the prior consensus, not whether it accorded with what the party in question believed that consensus to have been. In accordance with the general approach of English law, the terms of the prior consensus were what a reasonable observer would have understood them to be and not what one or even both of the parties believed them to be. In the present case, submitted Mr Nugee, the prior consensus was contained in the May letter, which made it clear that the terms were to be as contended for by Persimmon. If the definition in the final agreement did not have that meaning, it was not in accordance with the prior consensus and if Mr Reeve and Mr Vantreen believed that it was, then they, like the representatives of Persimmon, were mistaken.

18-301 Mr Robert Miles Q.C., for Chartbrook, objected to Persimmon being given leave to advance this argument. He said that if the point had been taken at the trial, the evidence might have taken a different shape. I rather doubt this, but as I understand that the Committee shares my view that Persimmon is entitled to succeed without rectification, the question is academic. Nevertheless, as it has been very well and fully argued, I propose to express an opinion about it.

18-302 Until the decision of the Court of Appeal in *Joscelyne v Nissen*[402] there was a view, based upon dicta in 19th and early 20th century cases, that rectification was available only if there had been a concluded antecedent contract with which the instrument did not conform. In *Lovell & Christmas Ltd v Wall*[403]

[399] See *Smith New Court Securities Ltd v Scrimgeour Vickers (Asset Management) Ltd* [1997] A.C. 254 at 274–275.
[400] "Rectification of Contracts for Common Mistake, *Joscelyne v Nissen* and Subjective States of Mind" (2007) 123 L.Q.R. 116.
[401] "The 'Drastic' Remedy of Rectification for Unilateral Mistake" (2008) 124 L.Q.R. 608.
[402] [1970] 2 Q.B. 86.
[403] (1911) 104 L.T. 85 at 88.

Cozens-Hardy M.R. said that rectification "may be regarded as a branch of the doctrine of specific performance". It presupposed a prior contract and required proof that, by a common mistake, the final completed agreement as executed failed to give proper effect to the prior contract. In *Joscelyne's case* the Court of Appeal declared itself puzzled by the reference to specific performance, but I think it is clear enough that Cozens-Hardy M.R. had in mind a contractual obligation to execute a lease, conveyance, settlement or similar instrument, giving rise to a specifically enforceable obligation to do so. A failure to execute a document giving effect to the terms of the agreement would be a breach of that obligation and the court, in rectifying the instrument, would be specifically performing the agreement. Since the decision in *Joscelyne's case* extended the availability of rectification to cases in which there had been no enforceable prior agreement, specific performance is plainly an inadequate explanation of the doctrine. But for present purposes the significance of cases like *Lovell & Christmas Ltd v Wall* is that the terms of the contract to which the subsequent instrument must conform must be objectively determined in the same way as any other contract. Thus the common mistake must necessarily be as to whether the instrument conformed to those terms and not to what one or other of the parties believed those terms to have been.

Now that it has been established that rectification is also available when there was no binding antecedent agreement but the parties had a common continuing intention in respect of a particular matter in the instrument to be rectified, it would be anomalous if the "common continuing intention" were to be an objective fact if it amounted to an enforceable contract but a subjective belief if it did not. On the contrary, the authorities suggest that in both cases the question is what an objective observer would have thought the intentions of the parties to be. Perhaps the clearest statement is by Denning L.J. in *Frederick E Rose (London) Ltd v William H Pim Jnr & Co Ltd*:[404] **18–303**

> "Rectification is concerned with contracts and documents, not with intentions. In order to get rectification it is necessary to show that the parties were in complete agreement on the terms of their contract, but by an error wrote them down wrongly; and in this regard, in order to ascertain the terms of their contract, you do not look into the inner minds of the parties—into their intentions—any more than you do in the formation of any other contract. You look at their outward acts, that is, at what they said or wrote to one another in coming to their agreement, and then compare it with the document which they have signed. If you can predicate with certainty what their contract was, and that it is, by a common mistake, wrongly expressed in the document, then you rectify the document; but nothing less will suffice."

Likewise in *Etablissements Georges et Paul Levy v Adderley Navigation Co Panama SA* Mustill J said:[405] **18–304**

> "The prior transaction may consist either of a concluded agreement or of a continuing common intention. In the latter event, the intention must have been objectively manifested. It is the words and acts of the parties demonstrating their intention, not the inward thoughts of the parties, which matter."

An example of the application of this objective ascertainment of the terms of the prior transaction is *George Cohen Sons & Co Ltd v Docks and Inland Waterways Executive*[406] in which a landlord negotiating a new lease proposed to the tenant that "the terms and conditions contained in the present lease to be embodied in the new lease where applicable". The tenant accepted this offer, but the new lease as executed made the tenant liable for repairs which under the old lease had been the responsibility of the landlord. In answer to a claim for rectification, the landlord said that the new lease was in accordance with what he had understood to be the effect of his offer. The Court of Appeal said that this was irrelevant. What mattered was the objective meaning of what the landlord had written. Evershed M.R. said:[407] **18–305**

> "If the defendants . . . did misconstrue [the letter] that is unfortunate for them, but at least they cannot be heard to say that their letter was intended to mean anything other than that which the words convey to the reader as a piece of ordinary English."

As against these authorities, there are two cases upon which Mr Miles relied. The first is *Britoil Plc v Hunt Overseas Oil Inc*,[408] in which the Court of Appeal by a majority (Glidewell L.J. and Hobhouse L.J., Hoffmann **18–306**

---

404 [1953] 2 Q.B. 450 at 461.
405 [1980] 2 Lloyd's Rep 67 at 72.
406 (1950) 84 Ll. L. Rep 97.
407 At 107.
408 [1994] C.L.C. 561.

L.J. dissenting) refused to rectify an agreement which was alleged not to be in accordance with what had previously been agreed in summary heads of agreement. Hobhouse L.J., who gave the majority judgment, affirmed the decision of Saville J., who said that the defendants had failed to establish that there was a prior common agreement or intention in terms that the court could ascertain or (which is probably another way of saying the same thing) that the definitive agreement failed to reflect that prior agreement. In other words, the language of the heads of agreement was too uncertain to satisfy the requirement stated by Denning L.J. in *Rose's case*[409] that one should be able to "predicate with certainty what their contract was". Hobhouse L.J. noted[410] that Saville J. "did not base himself upon any consideration of the evidence as to the actual state of mind of the parties" and in my opinion the case lends no support to the view that a party must be mistaken as to whether the document reflects what he subjectively believes the agreement to have been.

**18–307** The other case is the decision of Laddie J. in *Cambridge Antibody Technology Ltd v Abbott Biotechnology Ltd*,[411] in which he rejected a submission that evidence of the subjective state of mind of one of the parties contained in statements which had not been communicated to the other party ("crossed the line") was inadmissible. In my opinion, Laddie J. was quite right not to exclude such evidence, but that is not inconsistent with an objective approach to what the terms of the prior consensus were. Unless itself a binding contract, the prior consensus is, by definition, not contained in a document which the parties have agreed is to be the sole memorial of their agreement. It may be oral or in writing and, even if the latter, subject to later variation. In such a case, if I may quote what I said in *Carmichael v National Power Plc*:[412]

> "The evidence of a party as to what terms he understood to have been agreed is some evidence tending to show that those terms, in an objective sense, were agreed. Of course the tribunal may reject such evidence and conclude that the party misunderstood the effect of what was being said and done."

**18–308** In a case in which the prior consensus was based wholly or in part on oral exchanges or conduct, such evidence may be significant. A party may have had a clear understanding of what was agreed without necessarily being able to remember the precise conversation or action which gave rise to that belief. Evidence of subsequent conduct may also have some evidential value. On the other hand, where the prior consensus is expressed entirely in writing (as in *George Cohen Sons & Co Ltd v Docks and Inland Waterways Executive*) such evidence is likely to carry very little weight. But I do not think that it is inadmissible.

**18–309** In this case there was no suggestion that the prior consensus was based on anything other than the May letter. It is agreed that the terms of that letter were accepted by Chartbrook and no one gave evidence of any subsequent discussions which might have suggested an intention to depart from them. It follows that (on the assumption that the judge was right in his construction of the ARP definition) both parties were mistaken in thinking that it reflected their prior consensus and Persimmon was entitled to rectification.

**18–310** Lord Hoffmann's dicta in *Chartbrook* were followed by the Court of Appeal in *Daventry D.C. v Daventry & District Housing Ltd*.[413] However serious doubts have since been expressed about these principles by senior appellate judges,[414] and it seems unlikely that they will survive a trip to the Supreme Court. Some of the reasons for these doubts are explained by Leggatt J in a passage of his judgment in *Tartsinis v Navona Management Co*.

---

409 [1953] 2 Q.B. 450 at 461.
410 At 571.
411 [2005] F.S.R. 590.
412 [1999] 1 W.L.R. 2042 at 2050–2051.
413 [2012] 1 W.L.R. 1333.
414 Lord Justice Patten, "Does the Law Need to be Rectified? *Chartbrook* Revisited" (Chancery Bar Association Annual Lecture, 29 April 2013), *http://www.chba.org.uk/for-members/library/annual-lectures/does-the-law-need-to-be-rectified-chartbrook-revisited* [Accessed 1 June 2015]; Lord Toulson, "Does Rectification Require Rectifying?" (TECBAR Annual Lecture, 31 October 2013), *https://www.supremecourt.uk/docs/speech-131031.pdf* [Accessed 1 June 2015].

*Tartsinis v Navona Management Co*

Queen's Bench Division (Commercial Court) [2015] EWHC 57 (Comm) at [89]–[98]

LEGGATT J.: . . . The requirement of an outward expression of accord may be said to introduce an element of objectivity into the test for rectification. But it only makes the test objective in the limited sense that objectively manifested intentions are required, and a mere coincidence of uncommunicated subjective intentions is not enough. It does not detract from the principle that rectification for mutual mistake depends upon proving that both parties actually were mistaken about the effect of the instrument. However, in *Chartbrook Ltd v Persimmon Homes Ltd*,[415] the House of Lords, albeit obiter, endorsed a much more strongly objective test. Lord Hoffmann, with whose speech the rest of the House agreed, expressed the opinion[416] that, to establish a case for rectification, it is both necessary and sufficient to show a prior consensus which differs from the objective meaning of the contract and that for this purpose the meaning of the prior consensus is what a reasonable observer would have understood it to be and not what one or even both of the parties understood it to be. On this basis, had he not accepted Persimmon's interpretation of the final contract, Lord Hoffmann would have held that Persimmon was entitled to rectification of the contract so that it reflected the way in which a reasonable observer would have understood earlier letters from Persimmon setting out the terms offered. That was so even though Chartbrook's understanding of what both the letters and the final contract meant was different and, on the assumption made, the contract meant what Chartbrook thought it meant. **18–311**

I am bound to say that, in company with Morgan J. in *Crossco No 4 Unltd v Jolan Ltd*,[417] I have difficulty with this statement of the test of rectification for common mistake. It is one thing to say that a contract should not be rectified just because both parties privately intend it to bear a meaning different from its meaning objectively ascertained. It is quite another thing, however, to say that a contract should be rectified to conform to what a reasonable observer would have understood the parties previously to have agreed, irrespective of the parties' own understanding. **18–312**

In the first place, I find it hard to see any equity in a doctrine which allows a party to obtain rectification of a document to reflect a view of what had been agreed that the party himself did not actually have, just because a reasonable observer would have taken this to be his view. Equally, I find it difficult to see the equity of imposing the view that a hypothetical reasonable observer would have formed of what had been agreed on a party who did not have that understanding of what had been agreed and whose understanding is reflected in the proper interpretation of the final document. **18–313**

In these situations rectification is not serving to avoid the injustice that would otherwise be caused when the objective principle of interpretation leads to a result which fails to reflect the parties' real intention. Instead, the effect is to treat the objective meaning of communications which were not intended to be legally binding as superior to the objective meaning of the document intended to record the parties' final agreement and to allow the former to displace the latter. The looking-glass logic of this approach was exposed by Hobhouse L.J. in *Britoil plc v Hunt Overseas Oil Inc* when he said:[418] **18–314**

> "It is contended that this sentence in this informal document which is not intended to have legal effect is to be treated as a superior statement of the parties' agreement and is to displace the clear language of the considered and carefully drafted definitive agreement.
>
> "It can immediately be seen that this proposition needs to be carefully examined. As a matter of logic it can lead to the result that where there is a succession of documents of increasing formality but without legal effect leading up to a final considered legal document, the ascertainment of the actual agreement between the parties can be thrown back to the successively less formal, less considered and less carefully drafted earlier documents. This cannot be right."

In the *Britoil* case the Court of Appeal—by a majority, with Hoffmann L.J. dissenting—held that rectification for common mistake is available only where it is proved that both parties were in fact mistaken about the effect of the final document. Although the decision in the *Britoil* case was not disapproved, that requirement was not satisfied on the facts assumed in the *Chartbrook* case.

---

415 [2009] 1 A.C. 1101.
416 At [57]–[66].
417 [2011] EWHC 803 (Ch) at [253].
418 [1994] C.L.C. 561 at 573.

18–315 A further objection to the approach adopted in *Chartbrook* is that it allows a party who is mistaken about the effect of a contractual document although the other party is not to obtain rectification of the document without satisfying the requirements which must generally be satisfied before rectification will be granted on the basis of a unilateral mistake. Those requirements are the subject of a distinct body of case law. Broadly speaking, rectification will only be granted in cases of unilateral mistake where the other party knows of the mistake and it is inequitable for him to take advantage of it.[419] The *Chartbrook* approach bypasses these established principles.

18–316 The view of the law endorsed by the House of Lords in *Chartbrook* has since been considered and applied by the Court of Appeal in *Daventry District Council v Daventry & District Housing Ltd*.[420] That was another case where, as was assumed to be the position in *Chartbrook* when discussing rectification, the parties were each mistaken in believing that their final agreement reflected their prior consensus but for different reasons.[421] One party was wrong about the meaning of the pre-contractual documents (objectively understood) but right about the meaning of the legally binding contract (objectively construed). The other party was right about the meaning of the pre-contractual documents but wrong about the meaning of the legal contract. Applying the approach endorsed in *Chartbrook*, the latter party's view prevailed. Toulson L.J. said that the case "highlighted some real difficulties in the present state of the law governing rectification".[422] He pointed out some of those difficulties in cogent terms.[423] Nevertheless, he ultimately concluded that, despite his concern about the correctness of the principle in the *Chartbrook* case, the Court of Appeal ought to follow it. That was because (i) it would be a "bold course" not to follow the opinion of the House of Lords, (ii) the appeal had been argued on the basis that the approach in the Chartbrook case was correct, and (iii) that approach did not on the particular facts lead to an unjust result, although it would have been more satisfactory to reach that result on the basis of unilateral mistake.[424]

18–317 Lord Neuberger M.R. reached the same conclusion as Toulson L.J. and also thought, for similar reasons, that it was right to proceed on the basis of the analysis of rectification in *Chartbrook*, even though he agreed that "the analysis is not without difficulties" and "may have to be reconsidered or at least refined".[425]

18–318 Etherton L.J. dissented in the result but in his judgment gave a summary of the law with which Lord Neuberger M.R. agreed. Etherton L.J. distinguished four different factual situations[426] and concluded that this analysis showed "why it is good policy to favour objective accord or objective change of accord over subjective belief and intention in cases of mutual mistake".[427] I hope I may be forgiven for saying that the analysis seems to me much more compelling if an "objective accord" is taken to refer to a common understanding based on communication between the parties (i.e. what I have called a shared intention) rather than to an intention which an objective observer would have attributed to the parties, irrespective of what the parties themselves understood. Of potential relevance in the present case is the third scenario,[428] namely:

> "where there was objectively a prior accord, but one of the parties then subjectively changed their mind, but objectively did not bring that change of mind to the attention of the other party. It is right that, if the documentation gives effect to the objective prior accord, the formal documentation should not be rectified to reflect the changed but uncommunicated subjective intention; and if the documentation as executed reflects the changed but uncommunicated subjective intention, it should be rectified to give effect to the objective prior accord. To do otherwise would be to force on one of the parties a contract which they never intended to make on the basis of an uncommunicated intention and belief."

18–319 The postulate that "one of the parties then subjectively changed their mind" presupposes that the "prior accord" reflected both parties' subjective intentions; otherwise there would be no scope for one party to

419 See *Chitty on Contracts* (31st Edn) at 5–122—5–129; *Thomas Bates & Son Ltd v Wyndham's (Lingerie) Ltd* [1981] 1 W.L.R. 505.
420 [2012] 1 W.L.R. 1333.
421 See [146] and [154].
422 At [117].
423 At [176]–[177].
424 See [179]–[182] and [185].
425 See [195]–[196].
426 At [85]–[88].
427 At [89].
428 Described at [87].

change their subjective intention. I can well see that where the parties have through communications "crossing the line" established a shared intention which the final document does not reflect, a claim for rectification should not be defeated just because, at some point before the document was executed, the defendant privately changed their mind without telling the claimant. On one view of the facts this was in effect the situation in the *Daventry* case. The disagreement between Etherton L.J. and the majority of the Court of Appeal was essentially over whether the defendant had sufficiently communicated a change of intention by requesting a change in the wording of the draft contract in correspondence between solicitors. On the facts found, the defendant's negotiator caused the change of wording to be made by misleading the defendant's board and solicitors as to what had been agreed, and could not reasonably have believed when the contract was concluded that the change had been brought to the attention of the claimant's negotiator. I cannot help wishing that the majority had felt able to analyse the situation as one of unilateral mistake.

A final point remains to be made here about the relationship between rectification and the construction of contracts in accordance with Lord Hoffmann's approach in *Investors Compensation Scheme v West Bromwich B.S.*[429] This requires the court to go beyond the words of the contract, and if this investigation reveals there to be a "problem" with the drafting, to "interpret" the contract to mean something different from its literal meaning. Given that the courts can resolve a mismatch between the parties' "true" intentions and the literal words of a contract in this way, then the question arises whether any room is left for rectification as a separate doctrine?[430] It is true that the two doctrines differ to the extent that evidence of prior negotiations is excluded from the court's attention when it is engaged in "construction", and admissible when it is engaged in "rectification", but it is difficult to understand and justify this distinction.[431] **18–320**

## *C. Rectification of Unilateral Settlements*

In the case of a unilateral settlement there is no requirement, as in the case of a contract, for an outward expression of accord: what matters is the settlor's subjective intention. Nor does it makes any difference whether there was any outward expression, or objective communication, of her intention. So held Sir Terence Etherton C in *Day v Day*, where he also considered the seriousness of the mistake that must have been made, in the light of Lloyd LJ's findings in the Court of Appeal in *Pitt v Holt*,[432] later affirmed by the Supreme Court,[433] and where Lewison LJ also expressed the view that the rectification of documents effecting voluntary dispositions of property and the rescission of voluntary dispositions for mistake are governed by the same principles. **18–321**

*Day v Day*

Court of Appeal [2014] Ch. 114

Mrs Day made a will appointing her sons Terence, James and Michael as executors, and directing that her house should be sold and the proceeds divided between all six of her children. During her life, she granted a power of attorney to her solicitor, who executed a conveyance of legal title to the house to Mrs Day and her son Terence as beneficial joint tenants. As a result Terence became the sole legal owner of the house by survivorship when Mrs Day died. James and Michael sought rectification of the conveyance, alleging **18–322**

---

[429] [1998] 1 W.L.R. 896.

[430] As noted in A. Burrows, "'Construction' and Rectification" in A. Burrows and E. Peel (eds), *Contract Terms* (Oxford University Press, 2007).

[431] R. Buxton, "Construction and Rectification after *Chartbrook*" (2010) 69 C.L.J. 253. See too *Oceanbulk Shipping & Trading SA v TMT Asia Ltd* [2011] 1 A.C. 662 at [45].

[432] [2012] Ch. 132.

[433] [2013] 2 A.C. 108. On this topic, see also Etherton C's subsequent judgment in *Kennedy v Kennedy* [2015] B.T.C. 2.

that their mother had meant to help Terence take out a loan secured by a mortgage on the house (as had happened), but had not meant to give him a beneficial interest in the property. They claimed that the provisions in the conveyance declaring and giving effect to a beneficial joint tenancy should be replaced with a declaration that Mrs Day and Terence held the beneficial interest in the property on trust for Mrs Day absolutely. The trial judge accepted that Mrs Day had not intended to give Terence a beneficial interest, but refused rectification because she had authorised the solicitor to execute a conveyance on such terms as he saw fit to facilitate the mortgage and he had chosen to effect a beneficial joint tenancy on her behalf. The Court of Appeal overturned this decision.

**18–323** SIR TERENCE ETHERTON C. (with whom ELIAS L.J. agreed), set out the facts and continued: . . . I am not surprised by the recorder's expression of unease, at the end of his judgment and in granting permission to appeal, that he felt bound to dismiss the claim for rectification. The recorder found as a fact that Mrs Day never intended to give, and never thought that she had given, a beneficial interest in the property to the defendant. She always thought that, once the defendant's borrowings had been repaid, the property "would be entirely hers again". The defendant's defence contains the admission that the reason for the transaction was to assist him to raise funds. It made no allegation of a positive intention of Mrs Day, other than is to be found in the terms of the conveyance itself, of any intention to make a gift to him of her beneficial interest in the property. The most the defendant asserted in his defence, by way of a double negative, was that there was "no . . . agreement that he should not acquire a beneficial interest". That was reflected in the double negative elsewhere in the defence by way of a denial "that it was contemplated that the beneficial ownership should not pass to the [defendant]".

**18–324** Furthermore, it is clear that the recorder had a poor view of the defendant's conduct. The recorder considered that it was probable that all the arrangements for the proposed transaction were made by the defendant; and that the defendant always understood perfectly well the meaning and effect of the conveyance, but he deliberately kept quiet about it and indeed encouraged his mother to believe that the property was still hers to dispose of by drafting her last two wills on that footing.

**18–325** It might have been argued, on those findings, that the defendant incorrectly instructed Mr Froud on behalf of Mrs Day and that he was always aware both of Mrs Day's mistake as to the contents and effect of the conveyance and of Mr Froud's mistake in believing that he was carrying out Mrs Day's intentions and instructions. On the hearing of the appeal, however, Mr Michael Norman, the claimants' counsel, expressly disclaimed any such arguments and indeed sought to distance his case from any views expressed by the recorder, or to be inferred from the recorder's express findings, as to improper conduct or motive on the part of the defendant. Mr Norman pointed out that the claimants never made any allegation against the defendant of dishonesty or sharp practice in their statements of case. Their case up to, and including, the trial was one of mutual mistake on the part of both Mrs Day and the defendant as to the provisions and effect of the conveyance.

**18–326** Neither the claimants nor the defendant challenge the conclusions of the recorder that the conveyance was not part of any bargain between Mrs Day and the defendant but was in the nature of a voluntary settlement by her and that, therefore, for the purposes of the doctrine of rectification, the relevant intention was that of Mrs Day and the defendant's intention is irrelevant. The recorder rightly pointed to *Re Butlin's Settlement Trusts* as setting out the relevant legal principles. In that case Brightman J. said:[434]

> "There is, in my judgment, no doubt that the court has power to rectify a settlement notwithstanding that it is a voluntary settlement and not the result of a bargain, such as an ante-nuptial marriage settlement. *Lackersteen v Lackersteen*,[435] a decision of Page-Wood V-C, and *Behrens v Heilbut*,[436] a decision of Harman J., are cases in which voluntary settlements were actually rectified. There are also obiter dicta to the like effect in cases where rectification was in fact refused.[437] Furthermore, rectification is available not only in a case where particular words have been added, omitted or wrongly written as the result of careless copying or the like. It is also available where the words of the document were purposely used but it was mistakenly considered that they bore a different meaning from their correct meaning as a matter of true construction. In such a case, which is the present case, the court will rectify

434 [1976] Ch. 251 at 260–261 and 262.
435 (1860) 30 L.J. Ch. 5.
436 (1956) 222 L.T. Jo. 290.
437 See *Bonhote v Henderson* [1895] 1 Ch. 742; [1895] 2 Ch. 202.

the wording of the document so that it expresses the true intention[438] . . . in the absence of an actual bargain between the settlor and the trustees, (i) a settlor may seek rectification by proving that the settlement does not express his true intention, or the true intention of himself and any party with whom he has bargained, such as a spouse in the case of an ante-nuptial settlement; (ii) it is not essential for him to prove that the settlement fails to express the true intention of the trustees if they have not bargained; but (iii) the court may in its discretion decline to rectify a settlement against a protesting trustee who objects to rectification."

What is relevant in such a case is the subjective intention of the settlor. It is not a legal requirement for rectification of a voluntary settlement that there is any outward expression or objective communication of the settlor's intention equivalent to the need to show an outward expression of accord for rectification of a contract for mutual mistake.[439] In *Chartbrook Ltd v Persimmon Homes Ltd*[440] the House of Lords agreed with Lord Hoffmann's (obiter) explanation of an objective test for rectification for mutual mistake in the case of a contract so as to bring the final document into line with the parties' prior consensus objectively ascertained. Nothing he said there touched upon the requirements for rectification for unilateral mistake in a non-contract case. Although, as I have said, there is no legal requirement of an outward expression or objective communication of the settlor's intention in such a case, it will plainly be difficult as a matter of evidence to discharge the burden of proving that there was a mistake in the absence of an outward expression of intention. 18–327

The argument advanced on behalf of the claimants by Mr Norman is quite simply that, on the finding of the recorder that Mrs Day never intended to give, and never thought she had given, a beneficial interest in the property to the defendant, the claimants are entitled to rectification. The claimants' argument is that both the existence of Mr Froud's power of attorney and the scope of Mr Froud's authority to execute the conveyance are irrelevant. On the facts of the present case, as found by the recorder, I accept that argument. 18–328

It is possible to identify the following stages in the reasoning of the recorder in paras 27 and 28 of his judgment: (1) it is not suggested that Mr Froud's power of attorney should be rectified or set aside or was invalid; (2) therefore she authorised Mr Froud to execute, on her behalf, a conveyance of the property on such terms as he saw fit to facilitate Gateway mortgage; (3) therefore Mr Froud had power validly to execute the conveyance; (4) it is highly improbable that he was acting under any misapprehension as to the terms and effect of the conveyance; (5) there is no evidence that he was acting in any way against the instructions received from Mrs Day. 18–329

It seems to me, with respect to the recorder, that his analysis is flawed. In the first place, the doctrine of rectification is concerned with intention, or rather the mistaken implementation of intention, rather than the power and authority to effect a particular transaction. The intention of the principal and the scope of the agent's authority may, and often will, overlap, but they are not synonymous concepts. In the case of a voluntary settlement, rectification hinges on whether the settlor executed the settlement in the mistaken belief that it implemented his or her intention. Whether or not the settlor's solicitor was authorised to draw up the settlement on any particular terms or, as here, was acting within his actual or apparent authority in executing it on behalf of, and in the name of, the settlor is a different question. The recorder appears to have been of the view that Mr Froud had authority to execute the conveyance on behalf of Mrs Day because he acted pursuant to a general power of attorney and that was a complete answer to any claim Mrs Day might have made in her lifetime for rectification of the conveyance. Mrs Day, however, was the settlor and it is her intention and the implementation of her intention, and not the scope of Mr Froud's authority, which are in issue on the claim for rectification. 18–330

Secondly, on the issue of the scope of authority, the recorder appears to have thought it axiomatic that the general power of attorney, by virtue of its very generality, authorised Mr Froud to execute, on Mrs Day's behalf, a conveyance of the property on such terms as he saw fit to facilitate the Gateway mortgage. If that was the view of the recorder, it is plainly wrong. A solicitor's actual authority is prescribed by any instructions expressly given by the client, whether or not those instructions are then implemented by the solicitor 18–331

---

438 See *Jervis v Howle and Talke Colliery Co Ltd* [1937] Ch 67; *Whiteside v Whiteside* [1950] Ch. 65 at 74; and *Joscelyne v Nissen* [1970] 2 Q.B. 86 at 98.

439 See, for example, the line of pensions cases *AMP (UK) plc v Barker* [2001] Pen. L.R. 77 at [67]–[68], *Gallaher Ltd v Gallaher Pensions Ltd* [2005] Pen. L.R. 103 at [116]–[117] and *Drake Insurance v McDonald* [2005] Pen. L.R. 401 at [34]–[35].

440 [2009] A.C. 1101.

acting pursuant to a general power of attorney. So far as a third party is concerned, a general power of attorney may well clothe the solicitor with apparent authority to effect a transaction and so make the transaction binding on the principal even though the transaction was outside the solicitor's actual authority. In so far, however, as there is any overlap between the principal's intention in carrying out a particular transaction and the scope of the agent's authority to execute that transaction, it is the actual authority of the agent that is relevant and not the agent's apparent or ostensible authority. The actual instructions to the agent may cast light on the actual intention of the principal, which is the relevant factor for rectification. Apparent or ostensible authority of the agent may make the transaction binding on the principal even where it does not coincide with the actual intention of the principal and the express instructions given to the agent, but (subject to the facts of any particular case) there is no obvious reason why such apparent authority should throw any light on the right to rectification.

**18-332** Thirdly, since Mrs Day never formed any intention to confer a beneficial interest in the property on the defendant, the recorder could only reject the claim for rectification if Mrs Day's overriding intention was that the proposed transaction should be carried out in any way that Mr Froud might choose. The recorder, however, never directly addressed that question. He found, on the mere basis of the grant of the general power of attorney, that Mr Froud was authorised to execute the conveyance on such terms as he saw fit to facilitate the Gateway mortgage. Not only was that analysis wrong for the reasons I have given, but it simply did not address the critical question of Mrs Day's actual intention and, in so far as it had any relevance to that issue, the actual instructions given to Mr Froud.

**18-333** In fact, apart from the generality of the power of attorney itself, there was no evidence that the intention of Mrs Day was that Mr Froud could carry out the proposed transaction in any way he chose. The mere statement of such a possible intent shows its inherent improbability. It would mean that it would have been Mrs Day's intention, and within Mr Froud's actual authority, to permit Mr Froud to arrange for the property to be conveyed both legally and beneficially to the defendant alone. I cannot see how such a remarkable conclusion, so obviously against Mrs Day's interests, could be supported by the mere existence of a general power of attorney or, indeed, anything short of the clearest evidence that those were her actual instructions.

**18-334** Leaving aside the general power of attorney, the factual findings of the recorder are all inconsistent with any intention, let alone actual instructions to Mr Froud, to carry out the transaction in any way he might choose. The purpose of the transaction, as admitted in the defence, was to assist the defendant to raise funds. It was not to make a gift to the defendant of a beneficial interest in the property. It was not Mrs Day's actual intention that any beneficial interest should be transferred to the defendant, and no assertion is made in the defence that Mrs Day ever indicated to the defendant that she intended to make any such gift to him. There was no evidence that she ever personally gave any instructions to Mr Froud, and the likelihood is that everything was arranged by the defendant. Bearing in mind all those matters, and the absence of any assertion in the defence that Mrs Day authorised the defendant to instruct Mr Froud to give the defendant a beneficial interest in the property, the only proper inference is that the defendant instructed Mr Froud, on behalf of Mrs Day, to do what was necessary, consistently with Mrs Day's best interests, to allow the property to be used as security to enable the defendant to raise funds. The transfer of a beneficial interest in the property to the defendant went beyond those instructions and Mr Froud's actual authority and was inconsistent with Mrs Day's intention.

**18-335** The recorder's finding that there was no evidence that Mr Froud was acting in any way against instructions received from his principal amounts to no more than a finding that Mr Froud was not expressly forbidden to structure the transaction so as to confer a beneficial interest on the defendant. It forms part of the recorder's reasoning, which I reject for the reasons I have given, that the general power of attorney, by virtue of its generality, is determinative of the claim to rectification because it was authority to Mr Froud to structure the transaction in whatever way he might choose.

**18-336** In any event, I do not consider that the onus was on the claimants to disprove that Mrs Day's intention and instructions to Mr Froud were that Mr Froud had a completely free hand to structure the transaction in whatever way he might choose to enable the defendant to raise funds on the property. The recorder having found that it was not Mrs Day's actual intention to confer any beneficial interest in the property on the defendant, I consider that the evidential burden then passed to the defendant to show that such intention was negated by some different overriding intention on her part. It is quite impossible on the facts for the defendant to do so.

**18-337** Finally, neither side argued that this was a case where the correct remedy, if any, is that the conveyance should be set aside rather than rectified. They were correct to take that line since a transfer of the legal title into joint names was consistent with Mrs Day's intention. Only the provisions of the conveyance declaring that the property was held by Mrs Day and the defendant on trust for sale for themselves as beneficial joint tenants were inconsistent with her intention and any actual authority of Mr Froud. . .

For those reasons I would allow this appeal. 18–338

LEWISON L.J. agreed with ETHERTON C.'s analysis and added the following comments: . . . The equitable jurisdiction to rectify instruments is part of equity's wider power to relieve against the consequences of a mistake. I have found it helpful to approach the judge's findings of fact from this perspective. There are many cases in which equity has exercised this power by setting aside a gift made by mistake. In such cases there is no question of lack of authority. The donor had full power to give away the asset in question, but the existence of his power to give away the asset was no bar to the intervention of equity. As Sir Terence Etherton C. has explained . . . equity intervenes not on the ground of lack of authority but on the ground of a failure of intention. 18–339

The most recent comprehensive discussion of the circumstances in which equity will intervene is the decision of this court in *Pitt v Holt*.[441] There were two issues in that case. The first concerned mistakes made by trustees in the exercise of fiduciary powers. That need not concern us. But the second concerned the circumstances in which equity will intervene in cases of voluntary dispositions made under a mistake. 18–340

Lloyd L.J. gave the leading judgment with which Mummery and Longmore L.JJ. agreed. Most of the cases were cases in which the whole transaction was set aside. But Lloyd L.J. treated cases of rectification of voluntary dispositions as falling within the same principle. Having referred to cases in which a voluntary disposition had been set aside he continued:[442] 18–341

> "Other cases at first instance include *Meadows v Meadows*[443] and *Lister v Hodgson*,[444] in each of which the trusts of the settlement were different from those which had been intended and which the solicitor had been instructed to achieve. In some other cases of this kind the court was able to order that the settlement should take effect as intended, in effect rectifying it.[445]"

It is, in my judgment clear from this passage that rectification and rescission are to be treated in the same way, depending on the facts. This is also consistent with earlier authority. In *Lady Hood of Avalon v Mackinnon*[446] Eve J. said: 18–342

> "I accept Mr Lawrence's argument that whether it is rescission or whether it is rectification is only a question of degree. If the court comes to the conclusion that the plaintiff is entitled to relief, then whether the proper relief be reformation or rescission is really immaterial, because whatever is the proper and necessary relief the court is bound to give it."

In *Pitt v Holt*[447] Lloyd L.J. went on to consider the circumstances in which equity will intervene. He began by referring to what Lindley L.J. had said in *Ogilvie v Littleboy*:[448] 18–343

> "Gifts cannot be revoked, nor can deeds of gift be set aside, simply because the donors wish they had not made them and would like to have back the property given. Where there is no fraud, no undue influence, no fiduciary relation between donor and donee, no mistake induced by those who derive any benefit by it, a gift, whether by mere delivery or by deed, is binding on the donor . . . In the absence of all circumstances of suspicion a donor can only obtain back property which he has given away by showing that he was under some mistake of so serious a character as to render it unjust on the part of the donee to retain the property given to him."

After a full review of the cases Lloyd L.J. began his discussion thus:[449] 18–344

441 [2012] Ch. 132 (currently under appeal to the Supreme Court).
442 At [174].
443 (1853) 16 Beav. 401.
444 (1867) L.R. 4 Eq. 30.
445 See *Walker v Armstrong* (1858) 8 De G.M. & G. 531 (Lords Justices) and *Wollaston v Tribe* (1869) L.R. 9 Eq. 44.
446 [1909] 1 Ch. 476 at 481 (approved in *Pitt v Holt*).
447 [2012] Ch. 132 at [167].
448 (1897) 13 T.L.R. 399 at 400.
449 At [203].

"It seems to me that, as a matter of authority and of principle, the correct test is in part as set out by Lindley L.J. in *Ogilvie v Littleboy*,[450] endorsed by the House of Lords,[451] which I have quoted . . . above. That identifies the critical relevance of the court's view of the effect of the mistake, once identified, upon the conscience of the recipient. Thereby it points to a need to protect the recipient in his possession and enjoyment of the property given. In that respect it sets a very high test as to the gravity of the mistake. However, I do not consider that it can be taken as definitive as to the type of mistake that may be relevant, so as to leave that entirely at large. I would accept that, in general, equity does not define dogmatically the categories of case in which it may intervene. Nevertheless, it seems to me that, with the benefit of the review of the relevant cases over the past 150 years or so, it is possible and right to say in what kinds of case the jurisdiction is available, and in which it is not. I do not aim to set out a hard and fast rule as if in legislation, which permits of no exceptions for unforeseen cases, but in my judgment the authorities do justify setting down certain general rules, as to both inclusion and exclusion."

**18–345** He expressed his ultimate conclusion as follows:[452]

"I would therefore hold that, for the equitable jurisdiction to set aside a voluntary disposition for mistake to be invoked, there must be a mistake on the part of the donor either as to the legal effect of the disposition or as to an existing fact which is basic to the transaction. (I leave aside cases where there is an additional vitiating factor such as some misrepresentation or concealment in relation to the transaction, among which I include *Dutton v Armstrong*.[453]) Moreover the mistake must be of sufficient gravity as to satisfy the *Ogilvie v Littleboy* test, which provides protection to the recipient against too ready an ability of the donor to seek to recall his gift. The fact that the transaction gives rise to unforeseen fiscal liabilities is a consequence, not an effect, for this purpose, and is not sufficient to bring the jurisdiction into play."

**18–346** In our case there was a mistake by Mrs Day as to the legal effect of the transaction. She did not intend to give away a beneficial interest in her house; but that was the effect of the conveyance. The mistake was of sufficient gravity to satisfy the *Ogilvie v Littleboy* test; namely that it is unjust for Terence to retain the benefit of the gift. In determining whether it is unjust for him to retain the benefit of the gift we are entitled, in my judgment, to consider events subsequent to the conveyance and in particular his action in concealing the effect of the conveyance from his mother. That had the effect that Mrs Day did not do anything to correct the mistake during her lifetime (even if only to sever the joint tenancy in equity).

**18–347** I was concerned by the fact that on the judge's findings of fact Mrs Day never communicated her intention to anyone at the time of the transaction. However, I have come to the conclusion that an outward expression of intention is unnecessary in cases of voluntary dispositions. There has been some discussion in cases at first instance whether this is a legal requirement or merely an evidential factor. In *Lansing Linde Ltd v Alber*[454] Rimer J. held that it was a legal requirement. But the tide of authority began to flow in the opposite direction in *AMP (UK) plc v Barker*,[455] which was approved in *Pitt v Holt* (although it has to be said not on this precise point). The cases in which *AMP (UK) plc v Barker* has been followed on this point now include *Gallaher Ltd v Gallaher Pensions Ltd*;[456] *Drake Insurance v McDonald*;[457] *Colorcon Ltd v Huckell*[458] and *Industrial Acoustics Ltd v Crowhurst*.[459] In *Munt v Beasley* Mummery L.J. said:[460]

"I agree with the trend in recent cases to treat the expression 'outward expression of accord' more as an evidential factor rather than a strict legal requirement in all cases of rectification."

**18–348** That was a case of a bilateral transaction (a lease). Whether Mummery L.J.'s view survives in relation to bilateral transactions in the light of the restatement of the test for rectification of bilateral transactions in

---

450 (1897) 13 T.L.R. 399 at 400.
451 (1899) 15 T.L.R. 294.
452 At [210].
453 (1893) 23 Ch. D. 278.
454 [2000] Pen. L.R. 15.
455 [2001] Pen. L.R. 77.
456 [2005] Pen. L.R. 103.
457 [2005] Pen. L.R. 401.
458 [2009] Pen L.R. 201.
459 [2012] Pen. L.R. 371.
460 [2006] EWCA Civ 370 36.

the obiter part of the decision of the House of Lords in *Chartbrook Ltd v Persimmon Homes Ltd*[461] need not detain us here. In *Daventry District Council v Daventry & District Housing Ltd* Etherton L.J. (with whom Lord Neuberger of Abbotsbury M.R. agreed) said:[462]

> "In other words, the requirements of 'an outward expression of accord' and 'common continuing intention' are not separate conditions, but two sides of the same coin, since an uncommunicated inward intention is irrelevant."

That case, too, was concerned with a bilateral transaction. Since Sir Terence Etherton C. has said clearly that an uncommunicated subjective intention is sufficient in the case of a voluntary disposition his statement about bilateral transactions in the *Daventry* case in his previous incarnation cannot be taken as authority to the contrary. Indeed in an incarnation before that he held that to be the case in *Gallaher Ltd v Gallaher Pensions Ltd*.[463] **18–349**

*Industrial Acoustics Co Ltd v Crowhurst*[464] was another voluntary disposition case. Vos J., having considered both *Chartbrook* and *Daventry*, said:[465] **18–350**

> "it seems to me that there will be cases, particularly in a pensions context, where it will be permissible to allow rectification when one can say by implication perfectly clearly that the parties did not intend by the deed they entered into, to effect a particular change, even though they had not stated outwardly to each other (or indeed at all) that they did not intend to effect that change, simply because the change was not in any form discussed."

I am content to endorse that view, at least in a case of a voluntary disposition. Vos J. also (correctly in my judgment) looked at events subsequent to the transaction in order to deduce what, objectively, was the real intention at the time of the disposition. I therefore agree with Sir Terence Etherton C. that in the case of a voluntary disposition it is the subjective intention of the donor or settlor that counts. **18–351**

In my judgment therefore the necessary conditions for equitable relief against the consequences of a mistake are satisfied. The manner in which equity should relieve against the consequences of the mistake on the facts of our case is by way of rectification. **18–352**

I, too, would allow the appeal. **18–353**

Not everyone agrees with Lewison LJ that in the context of voluntary dispositions rectification and rescission should be governed by the same principles. Birke Häcker has argued that this idea is misleading because the kind of mistake that calls for rectification is different from the kind of mistake that is typically addressed through rescission.[466] Rectification of an instrument is appropriate where the settlor (or transferor) believed that she was putting her signature to different terms from those which a proper interpretation of the document yields. The law's concern is that her true intentions should be carried into effect. In contrast, rescission responds to a different kind of mistake, which can be termed a "motivational mistake": the settlor (or transferor) has a piece of incorrect data in her mind which leads her to enter a transaction that she does not "truly" intend to enter. She is not mistaken about the nature of the transaction or its consequences, but she would not have entered it if she had known the relevant facts at the time when she decided to do so. This suggests that rectification and rescission should be seen as complementary remedies aimed at different objectives, and not as alternative remedies aimed at the same objective in different situations. **18–354**

---

461 [2009] AC 1101.
462 [2012] 1 WLR 1333 at [80].
463 [2005] Pen. L.R. 103.
464 [2012] Pen. L.R. 371.
465 At [45].
466 B. Häcker, "Mistaken Gifts after *Pitt v Holt*" (2014) 67 C.L.P. 333, 346, fn.66 and text and 370, fn.180 and text.

### D. Rectification of Pension Schemes

18–355 One question arising out of *Day* is whether the court's findings also apply to the rectification of pension schemes, or whether in the pensions context the court should adopt the objective approach taken by Lord Hoffmann in *Chartbrook*? In many pension cases the parties are not in a bilateral contractual relationship,[467] but on the other hand the members of the scheme are not merely donees and volunteers either. In *Scania (Great Britain) Ltd v Wager*,[468] Sir Andrew Morritt C held that in the pensions context "it is necessary to show that the relevant employer or employers and the trustees shared the same intention, whether or not an outward expression of accord is required, down to the execution of the deed in question".

In *Day*, as we have seen, their Lordships cited several pension cases supporting the view that an outward expression or objective communication of the parties' intentions is unnecessary. Yet in *IBM United Kingdom Pensions Trust Ltd v IBM United Kingdom Holdings Ltd*[469] Warren J held himself to be bound by Lord Hoffmann's objective approach, which he also considered to align with Lawrence Collins J's previous observation in *AMP (UK) Plc v Barker* that[470]

> when one is considering the intentions of a collective body such as a group of trustees or a committee of a board it is their collective intention which is relevant, and it would be a very odd case (and certainly not this one) if that collective intention were not objectively manifested.

**Questions**

1. To what extent do general principles and discretionary factors govern the award of equitable remedies?
2. Given that the general objective of tort damages is to restore the claimant to her ex ante position, why should it matter whether tortious harm is prevented by way of injunction or compensated by way of damages?
3. (a) Should specific performance be confined to a secondary remedy available only after damages have been assessed as "inadequate"?

   (b) When are damages an "*inadequate* remedy"? Do you agree with the decisions on this point in *Sky Petroleum v VIP* and *Beswlck v Beswick*?
4. Is the decision in *Argyll Stores* best explained as being based upon the objection of "constant supervision" or "severe hardship"?
5. When might a court refuse to award specific performance or an injunction in an action for tort or breach of contract and instead award equitable damages in lieu?
6. In *Pitt v Holt*, Lord Walker held that rescission of deeds on the ground of unilateral mistake would not be available to settlors who had executed the deed in a state of "causative ignorance". What

---

467 As Vos J noted in *Industrial Acoustics Co Ltd v Crowhurst* [2012] Pens. L.R. 371 at [41].
468 (2007) 50 P.B.L.R. 12 at [17].
469 [2012] Pens. L.R. 469 at [14]–[27].
470 [2001] Pens. L.R. 77 at [66].

did he mean by this, and are there any reasons for excluding such settlors from a remedy other than a fear of opening the floodgates of litigation?

7. Are the rules governing the rectification of documents different according to whether or not the document is the result of a bargaining process, and if so, are there good reasons for this?

# INDEX

This index has been prepared using Sweet and Maxwell's Legal Taxonomy. Main index entries conform to keywords provided by the Legal Taxonomy except where references to specific documents or non-standard terms (denoted by quotation marks) have been included. These keywords provide a means of identifying similar concepts in other Sweet & Maxwell publications and online services to which keywords from the Legal Taxonomy have been applied. Readers may find some minor differences between terms used in the text and those which appear in the index. Suggestions to *sweetandmaxwell.taxonomy@thomson.com*.